THE OXFORD COMPANION TO

CANADIAN
THEATRE

THE OXFORD COMPANION TO
CANADIAN THEATRE

Edited by
Eugene Benson and L.W. Conolly

TORONTO OXFORD NEW YORK
Oxford University Press
1989

Oxford University Press, 70 Wynford Drive, Don Mills, Ontario, M3C 1J9
Toronto   Oxford   New York   Delhi   Bombay   Calcutta   Madras   Karachi
Petaling Jaya   Singapore   Hong Kong   Tokyo   Nairobi   Dar es Salaam
Cape Town   Melbourne   Auckland
and associated companies in
Berlin   Ibadan

CANADIAN CATALOGUING IN PUBLICATION DATA
Main entry under title:

The Oxford companion to Canadian theatre

ISBN 0-19-540672-9

1. Theatre—Canada—Dictionaries.   1. Benson,
Eugene, 1928–   .   II. Conolly, L. W. (Leonard W.).

PN2301.093 1989   792′.0971   C89-094811-09

Printed in Canada by T.H. Best Printing Company

Introduction

As *The Oxford Companion to Canadian Literature* (1983), edited by William Toye, was the first *Oxford Companion* to be devoted solely to Canadian literature, so this *Companion* is the first to be devoted solely to Canadian drama and theatre. It represents the work of 158 contributors drawn from across Canada, and two from the United States—authorities in their fields who have written 703 entries on a wide range of topics. This *Companion* is witness both to several centuries of theatrical history in Canada and to the spectacular growth in all areas of Canadian theatrical activity that began in the 1960s, when a chain of regional theatres was built across Canada, subsequently to be challenged by much smaller 'alternate' theatres whose avowed goal was the development of a distinctive and indigenous Canadian voice in all aspects of theatre. This voice is now being increasingly heard throughout the world.

Too often books on Canadian history, literature, or art begin with an apology for neglecting either English Canada or French Canada. The anglophone editors of this volume, however, were privileged to secure the participation of many francophone scholars and critics who contributed entries documenting the growth and variety of Quebec, Acadian, and other French-language theatre in Canada. In addition, Canada's rich native and multicultural theatrical mosaic is reflected in entries on AMERINDIAN AND INUIT THEATRE and MULTICULTURAL THEATRE. This *Companion* presents, then, the most comprehensive history and analysis ever accorded theatrical activity in Canada, from its first manifestations in the cultures of our native peoples to the present.

The entries in *The Oxford Companion to Canadian Theatre* can be described as encompassing genres, major subjects, theatres and theatre companies, biography and criticism (of dramatists, actors, directors, designers), and major plays. We call particular attention to the new information and fresh insights in the following representative sample of genre and subject entries:

ACTING
ACTING (Quebec)
ALTERNATE THEATRE
ARCHIVES AND COLLECTIONS

Introduction

BURLESQUE
CABARET
CAFÉ-THÉÂTRE
CENSORSHIP
CHILDREN'S DRAMA AND THEATRE
COLLECTIVE CREATION
CRITICS AND CRITICISM
DIRECTING
DOCUMENTARY DRAMA
FEMINIST THEATRE
GARRISON THEATRE
LITTLE THEATRE AND AMATEUR THEATRE
MOTION PICTURES, CANADIANS IN
MULTICULTURAL THEATRE
POLITICAL AND POPULAR THEATRE
PUPPET THEATRE
RADIO DRAMA
SUMMER STOCK
TELEVISION DRAMA
THÉÂTRE ENGAGÉ
THEATRESPORTS
TOURING STARS AND COMPANIES
VAUDEVILLE

The DRAMA IN ENGLISH and DRAMA IN FRENCH entries—which, combined, run to some 26,000 words—are complemented by lengthy entries on theatrical activities in each of the provinces and in the Northwest Territories and Yukon. Separate entries are given to fifty major plays that are notable for theatrical, literary, or historical reasons. The enormous popularity of plays such as *AURORE L'ENFANT MARTYRE* and *TALKING DIRTY* reveals a great deal about theatrical tastes and values in pre-Second-World-War Quebec and Vancouver in the 1980s respectively, while plays such as *The ECSTASY OF RITA JOE* and *À TOI, POUR TOUJOURS, TA MARIE-LOU* are indisputably classics of Canadian theatre. Considerable attention is paid to Canada's theatrical past through dozens of entries on theatres (location, size, facilities, repertoires) that have long since disappeared, and to many actors, producers, managers, and writers whose names and achievements have been familiar only to a handful of scholars.

The editors spent many sessions conferring with the members of our Advisory Board to determine what to include, whom to include, and in how many words. Our choices will not please everyone, and the omission of some subjects and individuals will be questioned. We are, of course, well aware of some omissions. The large subjects of Dance and Opera were excluded for reasons of space, though we have included the less well-known theatrical forms of burlesque, cabaret, mime, puppetry, and vaudeville. We regret, however, that it was not possible to secure major entries on Design (though many individual designers have entries), Theatrical Copyright, and European Touring Stars and Companies (though British and American are covered). Faced with the realities of space limitations, we also had to make difficult judgements concerning the inclusion or exclusion of individual the-atre artists. It is important to note, however, that the detailed Index in this book (uncommon in an *Oxford Companion*) will help readers locate references to many individuals, plays, theatres, and companies that do not have separate entries. At the end of many entries suggestions for further reading are listed, though it has not been the intention of the editors or contributors to provide exhaustive bibliographical information. Readers are referred to the *Bibliography of Canadian Theatre History: the Beginnings to 1984*, edited by John Ball and Richard Plant, for further guidance, in addition to other bibliographies, cited at the end of numerous entries. We are pleased that the publisher permitted the use of illustrations in this *Companion*; they add a crucial visual dimension to the book—though again, space restrictions necessitated a frus-tratingly high degree of selectivity.

The compilation of the *Companion* was aided by the availability of other reference works and a growing amount of scholarship in the area of Cana-dian drama and theatre. Most entries, however, demanded correspondence and phone calls to check and verify information, and we are grateful to all contributors who responded patiently to our many queries. In some instances the enthusiasm of contributors caused them to submit entries rather longer than could be accommodated; we thank them for accepting so understandingly the necessary cuts. The entries that were chosen for brief treatment allowed only for factual information, but most entries were allot-ted sufficient space for contributors to supplement factual information with critical commentary. From the outset we believed it possible to combine information, interpretation, and evaluation in concisely written entries that can be illuminating and interesting both to the specialist and to the general reader. As editors we have also tried to respect the varied and rich individual voices of our many contributors, while maintaining a necessary sense of common purpose and format. It has been our responsibility to resolve ambi-guities, inconsistencies, and conflicting information among the many entries, though we have avoided intervening in cases of differing opinions and judgements among contributors. Individual entries reflect the critical persuasions of the contributors, though the values and judgements of the editors and their advisers—which we believe to be appropriately eclectic—are broadly embedded in the methodology and criteria that shape the book.

Entries are arranged alphabetically; readers should keep in mind that names, subjects, and play titles that appear in SMALL CAPITALS have entries of their own. Dates in parentheses are publication dates, unless the context indicates otherwise. Entries on individual plays also normally identify the play's publisher. Every attempt has been made to give the date of first publication of Canadian plays (including publication in journals, such as *Canadian Theatre Review*), along with at least the year (often the date and month as well) of first performance and, where known, the theatre or company. Titles of plays have been italicized, whether published or not. Some of the information in this *Companion* is of course already out-of-date, though we have tried to make it current, whenever possible, up to the end of 1988. Diligent though we have been in striving for accuracy, we know that errors will be detected; we hope they will be brought to our attention so that they may be corrected in any subsequent printing of the *Companion*.

We have benefited greatly from the generosity of many people who have assisted us with their advice and guided us with their expertise. Our primary debt is to our Advisory Board—Professors Diane Bessai, Leonard Doucette, Jean Cléo Godin, Richard Plant, Renate Usmiani, as well as William Toye. In addition to coming to the University of Guelph for three annual meetings, they generously provided their erudition over a four-year period. We are also grateful to Harry Lane, Patrick O'Neill, John Ripley, Alan Filewod, Leonard Doucette, Jean Cléo Godin, Richard Plant, David Gardner, and Denis Johnston for reading a large number of entries and offering valuable suggestions. At all stages of our work we have received advice and encouragement from members of the Association for Canadian Theatre History/ Association d'histoire du théâtre au Canada, whose initial interest over ten years ago in a project of this kind laid a solid foundation for the *Companion*. We gratefully recognize also the achievements of La Société d'histoire du théâtre du Québec.

We were particularly fortunate in our staff. Dr Stephen Johnson worked with us, as assistant editor, on a daily basis in 1986 and 1987—his contribution was immense. In 1988 and 1989 (after he had moved to McMaster University) he continued to assist us in every possible way. We also owe a great debt to Jennifer Sumner, our administrative co-ordinator, who joined us in 1987—her expertise in office management, word-processing, and French was invaluable. Renate Benson handled all correspondence with

French-language contributors, and Patricia Sillers translated the entries submitted to us in French with sensitivity and skill. The heavy task of locating suitable illustrations and securing permission to use them was ably executed by Paul Waters when he was a Graduate Service Assistant working on his M.A. in English at Guelph; Mr Waters also provided valuable assistance in compiling the Index. Because of the complexity of our editorial task we had many other graduate students assigned to us by the Departments of English and Drama: we offer our warm thanks to Elaine Baetz, Bruce Barton, Lyndsay Lock, Claire Loughheed, Wendy Philpott, Lisbie Rae, David Sinclair, and Tawnya White-Johnston. Aruna Mehta was our very efficient full-time secretary in 1986, and between 1986 and 1989 we received further generous clerical support from Janice Walker, Gail McGinnis, Olga Griffin, Jill Ostland, Marlene Neal, Sharon Ballantyne, Dorothy Collins, Kate Clendenning, and Marie Walker.

We are grateful also to the many people who provided us with information and statistics: Dan Poland, Operations Manager, the O'Keefe Centre; Gary Thomas, General Manager, the Stratford Festival; Lisa Brant, Archivist, the Stratford Festival, and Dan Ladell, her predecessor; Lise Rochon, Communications Service, the Canada Council; the staff of the Shaw Festival; the Playwrights Union of Canada; Cathy Smalley, Executive Director, the Professional Association of Canadian Theatres; the Alliance of Canadian Cinema, Television and Radio Artists; Canadian Actors' Equity; Shain Jaffe, Great North Artists Management Inc.; B.J. Armstrong, Media Relations Co-ordinator, the Grand Theatre, London; Jane Keyes, Communications Assistant, the Banff Centre School of Fine Arts; Pat Kostuc, Deputy Director, Orpheum Theatre, Vancouver; Ray Wallis, General Manager, New Play Centre, B.C.; Odette Dumas, Publicist, French Theatre, the National Arts Centre, Ottawa; Donna Butt, Artistic Director, Rising Tide Theatre, Newfoundland; Syd Scott, Director, Public Relations, Manitoba Theatre Centre; Bill McLennan, Design-Photography, Museum of Anthropology, University of British Columbia; the staff of the Metropolitan Toronto Library, especially those in its splendid theatre section; Records of Canadian Theatre, University of Guelph; the National Library of Canada; Judith Bresheurs, Yukon Archives; Lisa Picini, Archival Assistant, York University Archives; Shawn Larabe and Jan Bessey, Robarts Research Library, University of Toronto; Dr John Black, Chief Librarian, the University of Guelph, and his staff, particularly Nancy Sadek in Archival and Special Collections, where so many valuable Canadian theatre archives are now deposited. For expert advice on many aspects of computer technology we express our thanks to Stuart Hunter, Associate Professor of English; to Phil Jones, Madge Brochet,

Introduction

and Leon Loo, Computing Services; to Kathleen Scott, Teaching Support Services, University of Guelph; and to Barbara Conolly, Administrator, *Canadian Children's Literature*. In their capacity as Chairs of the Department of English at the University of Guelph, G.D. Killam and Constance M. Rooke encouraged our work and provided office space and ancillary services, and Harry Lane, Acting Chair, Department of Drama, also generously supported our work with facilities and services.

When we commenced planning *The Oxford Companion to Canadian Theatre* in 1984 we were enthusiastically supported by David Murray, Dean of Arts, and William Tossell, then Dean of Research, University of Guelph, who provided the seed money to begin the project. In 1985 the Social Sciences and Humanities Research Council of Canada made us a substantial grant without which this *Companion* could not have been completed. Like so many Canadian scholars we are deeply indebted to the Council. The book has been published with the help of a grant from the Canadian Federation for the Humanities, using funds provided by the Social Sciences and Humanities Research Council of Canada; and the Canada Council helped defray costs incurred in translating entries received in French. We thank these organizations most sincerely.

A special word of gratitude is due to William Toye, Editorial Director of Oxford University Press Canada, who commissioned this book and since 1985 has given us the benefit of his editorial experience along with his particular knowledge of Canadian theatre.

Finally we thank our wives Renate Benson and Barbara Conolly—who have had to tolerate for so long editor-husbands who turned their homes into libraries, disrupted social dinners with theatre shop-talk, and who viewed Christmas, summer holidays, birthdays, and anniversaries as bothersome intrusions on the joys of creating this *Companion*. We have finally returned home after long travel, but we must warn Barbara and Renate that even now we are eyeing the rich literatures of the British Commonwealth, and expect to sally forth soon on an even longer voyage of editorial exploration than the one we have just concluded.

Guelph, Ontario   EUGENE BENSON

August 1989   L.W. CONOLLY

Advisory Board

Diane Bessai   L. E. Doucette   Jean Cléo Godin

Richard Plant   Renate Usmiani   William Toye

Assistant Editor: Stephen Johnson

Administrative Co-ordinator: Jennifer Sumner

French-language Liaison: Renate Benson

Illustrations Co-ordinator: Paul Waters

Contributors

Anne-Marie Alonzo
Université de Montréal

Geraldine Anthony
Mount Saint Vincent University

Brian Arnott

Douglas Arrell
University of Winnipeg

John H. Astington
University of Toronto

David Barnet
University of Alberta

Zina Barnieh

Hélène Beauchamp
Université du Québec à Montréal

Guy Beaulne

John Beckwith
University of Toronto

Anne Bédard
Université Laval

Eugene Benson
University of Guelph

Renate Benson
University of Guelph

Jeniva Berger

Diane Bessai
University of Alberta

Contributors

Mark Blagrave
University of New Brunswick

Sharon Blanchard

André-G. Bourassa
Université du Québec à Montréal

Ronald Bryden
University of Toronto

Carol Budnick
University of Manitoba

Kevin Burns
University of Alberta

Lorraine Camerlain
Jeu

Denis Carrier

Neil Carson
University of Guelph

Jean-François Chassay
Université de Montréal

Joan Coldwell
McMaster University

Paulette Collet
University of Toronto

Odette Condemine
Carleton University

Ray Conlogue
Globe and Mail

L.W. Conolly
University of Guelph

Martine R. Corrivault
Le Soleil

Richard Courtney
Ontario Institute for Studies in Education

Gilbert David

Robertson Davies
University of Toronto

Moira Day
University of Alberta

James DeFelice
University of Alberta

Joyce Doolittle
University of Calgary

L.E. Doucette
University of Toronto

Hervé Dupuïs
Université de Sherbrooke

Murray D. Edwards
University of Victoria

Richard Faubert

Alan Filewod
University of Guelph

Pierre Filion
Université de Montréal

Contributors

Timothy Findley

Howard Fink
Concordia University

Louise H. Forsyth
University of Western Ontario

Marcel Fortin
Collège de Valleyfield, Montreal

Kathleen Fraser
University of Western Ontario

David Gardner

Keith Garebian

Gratien Gélinas

Monique Genuist
University of Saskatchewan

Reid Gilbert
Capilano College

Gilles Girard
Université Laval

Jean Cléo Godin
Université de Montréal

Jeffrey Goffin
University of Calgary

Sherrill Grace
University of British Columbia

Madeleine Greffard
Université du Québec à Montréal

Adrien Gruslin
Jeu

Odette Guimond
Université de Montréal

Francess G. Halpenny
University of Toronto

John E. Hare
University of Ottawa

Ramon Hathorn
University of Guelph

Chantal Hébert
Université Laval

Lorraine Hébert
Jeu

Paul Hébert
Le Théâtre Paul-Hébert

James Hoffman
East Kootenay Community College

Christopher Innes
York University

Sheilagh S. Jameson

Anthony Jenkins
University of Victoria

Chris Johnson
University of Manitoba

Stephen Johnson
McMaster University

Contributors

Denis W. Johnston
University of British Columbia

Patricia Keeney
York University

Don Kerr
University of Saskatchewan

A. Owen Klein
St. Clair College of Applied Arts and
Technology

Richard Paul Knowles
University of Guelph

Georgina Kravetz

Jean Laflamme

Harry Lane
University of Guelph

Gilles Lapointe
Université du Québec à Montréal

Jean-Marc Larrue
Collège de Valleyfield, Montreal

Laurent Lavoie
University College of Cape Breton

Pierre Lavoie
Université de Montréal

Robert G. Lawrence
University of Victoria

Walter Learning
The Charlottetown Festival

Jacques Lebel

Alonzo Le Blanc
Université Laval

Paul Lefebvre

Renée Legris
Université du Québec à Montréal

Normand Leroux
Université de Montréal

Solange Lévesque
Jeu

Ira A. Levine
Ryerson Polytechnical Institute

Rota Herzberg Lister
University of Waterloo

Denyse Lynde
Memorial University of Newfoundland

Pierre Macduff
La Nouvelle Compagnie Théâtrale

Heather McCallum

Larry McDonald
Carleton University

Barbara McEwen
Brock University

Laurent Mailhot
Université de Montréal

Martha Mann
University of Toronto

Contributors

Kenneth W. Meadwell
University of Winnipeg

Ann Messenger
Simon Fraser University

Mary Jane Miller
Brock University

Peter Morris
Queen's University

Edward Mullaly
University of New Brunswick

Elaine F. Nardocchio
McMaster University

Liz Nicholls
Edmonton Journal

Renée Noiseaux-Gurik
Collège Sainte Thérèse

James Noonan
Carleton University

Robert C. Nunn
Brock University

John J. O'Connor
University of Toronto

Patrick B. O'Neill
Mount Saint Vincent University

John Orrell
University of Alberta

Malcolm Page
Simon Fraser University

Brian C. Parkinson
University of Lethbridge

Gordon Peacock
University of Texas

Linda M. Peake
Famous People Players

Richard Perkyns
Saint Mary's University

Richard Plant
Queen's University

Brian Pocknell
McMaster University

Lisbie Rae

Aviva Ravel

Natalie Rewa
Queen's University

John Ripley
McGill University

Jonathan Rittenhouse
Bishop's University

Lucie Robert
Université Laval

Dominique Roy

Mary Rubio
University of Guelph

Judith Rudakoff

D.W. Russell
University of Waterloo

xv

Contributors

Hilary Russell
Historical Research Division,
Environment Canada, Parks

Claude Sabourin
Université du Québec à Montréal

Annette Sainte-Pierre

Denis Salter
McGill University

Michal Schonberg
University of Toronto

Robert Scott
Ryerson Polytechnic Institute

Ben-Z. Shek
University of Toronto

Mary Shortt

Reg Skene
University of Winnipeg

C.J. Skinner
University of Lethbridge

Brian Smith
University of Calgary

Mary Elizabeth Smith
University of New Brunswick

Susan Stone-Blackburn
University of Calgary

Ross Stuart
York University

R.B. Todd
University of British Columbia

Rémi Tourangeau
Université du Québec à Trois-Rivières

William Toye

Gordon Tweedie

Léa V. Usin
University of Ottawa

Renate Usmiani
Mount Saint Vincent University

Michel Vaïs
Jeu

Anton Wagner
York University

Robert Wallace
York University

Jerry Wasserman
University of British Columbia

Doreen Watt
University of Calgary

Herbert Whittaker

Susan M. Williams
McGill University

George Woodcock

Alan Woods
Ohio State University

Illustration Credits

We wish to identify and acknowledge the various sources of the illustrations in this book and to thank the many individuals and public institutions who gave us permission to use them. While every effort has been made to locate and contact copyright holders some errors and omissions may have occurred. Any such oversights are regretted and the editors would appreciate having them brought to their attention.

Thomas Fisher Rare Books Library, University of Toronto, 2, 223; City of Edmonton Archives, 10; Vancouver Public Library, 13; University of British Columbia Museum of Anthropology, 20, 21; Hart House Theatre, University of Toronto, 28 (upper illustration), 256, 304; Young People's Theatre Centre, 28 (lower illustration); photo: J. and L. Caswall Smith, courtesy Metropolitan Toronto Reference Library (MTRL), 31; Arts and Culture Centre, St John's, 32; photo: André Le Coz, courtesy *Jeu*, 35, 227, 491; photo: Basil Zarov, courtesy MTRL, 41, 77, 207; Banff Centre School of Fine Arts, 42; Noble Talent Management Inc., Toronto, 43, 51, 299, 426; photo: François Brunelle, courtesy MTRL, 44 (upper illustration); photo: Jean-Guy Thibodeau, 44 (lower illustration); *Jeu*, 45, 110; Herbert Whittaker, 47, 119, 144; photo: Ed Ellis, courtesy MTRL, 48; photo: Daniel Kieffer, 50, 202, 530, courtesy *Jeu*; MTRL, 52, 79, 135, 158, 179, 188, 213, 270, 296, 312, 318, 325, 332, 360, 377, 419, 430, 463, 475, 477, 525, 561; Blyth Centre for the Arts, 56; New Play Centre and Carousel Theatre, 62; photo: Joel Bernard, courtesy MTRL, 74; photo: Lutz Dille, courtesy MTRL, 75; Annette Saint-Pierre, 87, 327; Confederation Centre of the Arts, Charlottetown, 89; Richard Gustin Photography, courtesy MTRL, 93, 94, 489; photo: Paul Émile Rioux, 97; photo: Ed Ellis, courtesy Citadel Theatre, Edmonton, 102; *Canadian Theatre Review*, no. 10, 103; Robert A. Barnett Collection, Archival and Special Collections, University of Guelph, 107; photo: Bob Brooks, courtesy MTRL, 112; Neptune Theatre Archives, Dalhousie University Archives, 114; photo: Robert C. Ragsdale, courtesy the Stratford Festival, 125, 168; *Literary Garland*, May 1846, courtesy MTRL, 126; Jean Cléo Godin, 128; photo: Cardinal Press Service, courtesy MTRL, 130; photo: John Steele, courtesy Herbert Whittaker, 133; National Archives of Canada, 142, 230, 266, 465; Robert A. Barnett Photography, 147, 337; André-G. Bourassa, 171; photo: André Cornellier, courtesy *Jeu*, 180; New Brunswick Museum, 182, 322, 371; photo: Harvey Studios, courtesy *Canadian Theatre Review*, no. 11, 194; Toby Gordon Ryan Collection, Archival and Special Collections, University of Guelph, 195 (upper photo), 423; Ministry of Culture and Communications, Ontario, 195 (lower photo); photo: McDermid Studio, courtesy Glenbow Museum, Calgary, 196; photo: William Notman and Sons, courtesy National Archives of Canada C-06719, 214; Archival and Special Collections, University of Guelph, 215, 236, 440, 460, 596; Great North Artists Management Inc., Toronto, 216, 586 (lower photo); photo: Andy Tate, courtesy Factory Theatre, Toronto, 226; L'Agence Artistique et Littéraire, 231, 568; Grand Theatre, London, 242; *Canadian Illustrated News*, 29 Aug. 1874, courtesy MTRL, 244; Krieber Photographe, courtesy MTRL, 245; photo: Peter Smith, courtesy the Stratford Festival, 248, 253, 277,

Illustration Credits

401, 504; photo: J. Fleetwood-Morrow, courtesy MTRL, 249; Robert Gurik, 250; photo: Walter Curtin, courtesy National Archives of Canada PA-129866, 251; Diffusion Dimedia Inc., 260; photo: James Hockings, courtesy Grand Theatre, London, 276; photo: Bob Howard, courtesy MTRL, 286; Le Théâtre du Rideau Vert, 295; copyright Yousuf Karsh 1933, 306, 418; photo: André Le Coz, 310, 473, 535; photo: Robert van der Hilst, courtesy *Canadian Theatre Review*, 315; Guy Dubois Photographe, 319, 447; Manitoba Theatre Centre, 329; Vincent Massey, *What's Past is Prologue*, Macmillan Co. (1963), 334; Canadian Mime Theatre, courtesy Joyce Doolittle, 340; photo: Nir Bareket, courtesy MTRL, 341; Black Theatre Canada, 356; courtesy Cameron Porteous and Archival and Special Collections, University of Guelph, 359; photo: Roger Jowett, courtesy MTRL, 364; photo: Lionel Simmons, courtesy Neptune Theatre Archives, Dalhousie University Archives, 369; New Play Centre, Vancouver, 379; Photo Features Ltd., Hull, courtesy MTRL, 381; McLennan Collection, Yukon Archives, 385; Thomas Gibson Collection, Archives, University of Alaska, 386; photo: Lionel Simmons, courtesy Joyce Doolittle, 393; Vancouver Civic Theatres, 405; photo: Andrew Oxenham, courtesy Alan Filewod, 408; photo: Robert A. Barnett, courtesy MTRL, 410; photo: Fred Phipps, courtesy Canadian Broadcasting Corporation, 413; Place des Arts, Montreal, 420; *Globe and Mail* Library, courtesy Herbert Whittaker, 421; Madame R. Prévost, 428; Charlottetown Camera Club Collection, courtesy Public Archives of Prince Edward Island, 429; Manitoba Archives, 431, 589; Franklin T. Graham, *Histrionic Montreal* (1902), 442, 546, 547; Canadian Broadcasting Corporation and National Film, Television and Sound Archives, courtesy National Archives of Canada, 452; James Mavor Moore Papers, courtesy York University Archives, 466; Canadian Theatre Review Publications, 468; Talonbooks, Vancouver, 479; Arnold's Studio, Moncton, courtesy MTRL, 483; photo: David Cooper, courtesy the Shaw Festival, 495; photo: S. Evans, courtesy the Stratford Festival, 505; photo: Douglas Spillane, courtesy the Stratford Festival, 506; Donald Davis, 511; Tavernier Collection, courtesy MTRL, 518, 575; *Macleans Magazine*, 1 Dec. 1962, 521; Theatre Calgary, 527; photo: Michel Brais, 531; photo: André Le Coz, courtesy MTRL, 537; photo: Ian Brown, 542; Provincial Archives, Victoria, B.C., courtesy MTRL, 549; photo: Henri Paul, courtesy *Jeu*, 556; photo: Robert Muckleston, courtesy Herbert Whittaker, 574; photo: David Cooper, 576, 578; Provincial Archives, Victoria, B.C., 577; Maynard Photo, Provincial Archives, Victoria, B.C., courtesy MTRL, 581; York University Archives, 583; Western Canada Pictorial Index, University of Winnipeg, 586 (upper photo); Fred Phillips, 592; photo: Robert C. Ragsdale, 597; photo: Robert C. Ragsdale, courtesy MTRL, 598.

A

Academy of Music (Halifax). Designed by T.R. Jackson of New York, this three-storey brick building at the foot of Spring Garden Road, on Pleasant (later Barrington) Street, opened with a Grand Concert, 9 Jan. 1877. The cost of construction, land, and furnishings was reported to be approximately $100,000. Exterior dimensions were 60' × 155'. Three arched doorways in the stucco façade of the front led into the lower floor, which measured 60' from the stage front to the vestibule at the back, where 425 scarlet-upholstered seats filled the orchestra and parquet. The dress circle held 325 chairs, and benches in the gallery accommodated 500. The full back width of the stage was 58'; the depth from the proscenium to the back wall was 32', plus 4' of apron. The proscenium measured 36' wide × 25' high, and the height to the rigging loft was 55'. Scenery, at opening, included fifteen pairs of flats and fifty-four wings. The stage was lighted with gas, the auditorium with electricity. Extensive interior renovations designed by S.P. Dumaresque in 1916 increased stage lighting by 300 per cent and added a dimming system. Four proscenium boxes, each with twelve blue-upholstered chairs, were installed, and the parquet circle was removed to allow an increase to 534 chairs (upholstered in gold and brown leather) in the orchestra. Greater spacing between chairs reduced dress-circle seating to 270, and the gallery benches were replaced by the old scarlet-covered chairs from the orchestra. The old entrance to the gallery was abolished, floors were tiled in white marble, ladies' and gentlemen's lounges added, and the building was made fireproof.

After the opening concert William NANNARY's production of *Clouds* initiated the first season on 16 Jan. 1877. Nannary's company was in residence for extended seasons through 1879; then came touring companies whose stay rarely exceeded six days, a notable exception being the three-month season of the Valentine Company in 1900. George A. Miln, Albert TAVERNIER, W.S. Harkins, Lewis Morrison, E.A. McDOWELL, Thomas Shea, Arthur Rehan, and Lily Langtry appeared, as did the Boston, Graw, Gilbert, and Wilbur Opera Companies and, from 1903, increasing numbers of movies. Occu-

pancy varied yearly; it was in use for ninety nights in 1884 and 170 in 1900.

A board of directors managed the Academy initially—under H.B. Clarke from 1884, J.D. Medcalfe from 1900, and J.F. O'Connell from 1910. On 10 Apr. 1910 it became the Majestic Theatre, and a policy change announced 'more exclusive attractions in the film field'. The final performance was Victor Herbert's *The Fortune Teller* on 29 June 1929, following which the theatre was closed and demolished to make room for the Famous Players' movie house, the Capitol.

MARY ELIZABETH SMITH

Academy of Music (Montreal). Designed by William Taft and owned by a consortium under Sir Hugh Allan, it was built in 1875 on Victoria St, just north of Sainte-Catherine. It was a brick building with a stone façade, about 130' long by 98' wide, and had a capacity of 2,000, with four boxes, four orchestra sections, and two balconies. After a difficult start and the partial collapse of its roof, Henry Thomas became its manager in 1880, and until 1893 it was Montreal's most prestigious auditorium. It presented many of the great names of the American theatre Joseph Jefferson, Felix Morris, James O'Neill) and of the European stage (Sarah Bernhardt, Coquelin, Mounet-Sully, Henry Irving, Ellen Terry, the Salvinis), as well as famous opera stars (Adelina Patti, Clara Fisher, Emma Albani).

After Thomas died in 1893 the theatre's decline began under the management of his wife and a former employee, Frank Murphy. In 1896 the Academy was declared unsafe by the municipal authorities and Murphy was obliged to move to the MONUMENT NATIONAL. The Allan family then sold the building to David Walker for $60,000. Finally, in 1896, John Sparrow and Joseph Jacobs—who already controlled the Queen's and the THEATRE ROYAL, and were affiliated with the Klaw and Erlanger Syndicate in New York—took control. The Academy then presented VAUDEVILLE, melodrama, and BURLESQUE, while more comfortable and more modern theatres, such as HER MAJESTY'S THEATRE, began to draw the city's elegant audiences.

In 1909-10, through the efforts of Paul

Academy of Music

'Interior View of the New Academy of Music', Montreal, from the Canadian Illustrated News, 4 Dec. 1875

Marcel, the Academy was converted to a French theatre. But despite critical success, it was transformed into a large retail store at the end of the winter of 1910.

JEAN-MARC LARRUE

Academy of Music (Saint John). Designed by Moses Washburn of Boston, it opened on Germain Street on 6 May 1872. Its exterior dimensions were 50' × 180' to 200' (contemporary records of these and other dimensions vary), and the ornate Italianate front topped with a bust of Queen Victoria was 65' high. Solid walnut doors gave access to a parquet (70' × 48') accommodating 546 (or 600) leather-upholstered opera chairs, a dress circle where 402 people could sit on wooden settees, a 100-seat gallery, and six private boxes with white lace curtains and crimson fringe. The interior was decorated with gold leaf and heraldic signs, a bust of Shakespeare, a symbolic lyre, and had a co-ordinated colour scheme of carmine and lavender, with accents of deep blue and Naples yellow, and bronze and gold for the pillars of the dress circle.

The full stage measured 48' × 52' (or 49' × 67'—records again vary), the working area 26' × 49', and the light-blue proscenium arch, displaying masks of comedy and tragedy, was 38' high and 31' wide. There were seventy-two wings, twenty pairs of flats, and many sets, including a working bridge imported from Boston. The act drop depicted Lake Como (from Edward Bulwer-Lytton's *Lady of Lyons*) painted by Orrin

Richards of the Boston Theatre. Scene painting was by Gaspard Meader, scenic artist of the Boston Museum (later scenic artists were Richard Farren and William Gill), and mechanical effects were by A. W. Boyson of Boston. Provision was made for calcium lights and twenty-two stage footlights, a green room, dressing-rooms, orchestra room, properties room, carpenter's room, and janitor's quarters. The theatre was built at a cost of between $50,000 and $60,000 (total indebtedness of $39,000 in 1873 was reduced in 1876 to $13,000).

The opening musical program, directed by L.H. Torrens of Bangor, was followed by a June-July season managed by J.W. LANERGAN. E.A. McDOWELL and William NANNARY subsequently produced many new plays, among them *Charity*, *Geneva Cross*, *Big Bonanza*, *Giroflé-Giroflà*, and *Around the World in 80 Days*. The Academy burned down on 20 June 1877.

MARY ELIZABETH SMITH

Acadian Theatre. Acadian Theatre—the theatre of the French-speaking settlers of the Maritimes—began in 1606 when Marc LESCARBOT presented his *Le THÉÂTRE DE NEPTUNE* at Port Royal. It was a long time, however, before original Acadian plays appeared, since religious institutions and colleges preferred classical, patriotic, religious, and comic plays that taught oratorical skills. *Evangéline*, by Alphonse Turgeon and Flavien Doucet, was presented at Petit Rocher, N.B., on 15 Aug. 1901, and in 1902 Father Alexandre Braud presented his own *Subercase*—a patriotic piece commemorating the last French governor of Acadia—at Collège Sainte-Anne, Pointe-de-l'Église, N.S. In 1930 Father Jean-Baptiste Jégo's *Le Drame du peuple acadien* (1932) was also presented at Collège Sainte-Anne, winning an award from the Académie Française. In north-eastern New Brunswick Father James Branch wrote and produced militant patriotic plays intended to arouse Acadian fervour among the local people: *L'Émigrant acadien* (published in 1929 and staged in 1931 in Lamèque, N.B.); *Vivent nos écoles catholiques; ou, La résistance de Caraquet* and *Jusqu'à mort pour nos écoles*, both published in 1932 and both staged in Paquetville, N.B.

Several plays were produced in 1955 to mark the Bicentennial of the British deportation of Acadians: Brother Gérard's *Pourquoi l'école?* and *Encore vivants malgré tout*; Henri P. LeBlanc's *Une Page d'histoire acadienne, La Survivance en classe*, and *Les Fêtes du Bicentenaire*; and Father Laurent Tremblay's *Un Matin tragique chez les pionniers de la Baie Saint-Marie* and *Fiançailles mouvementées*. In 1956 Laurie Henri founded the first Acadian theatre company, the Troupe Notre-Dame de Grâce, in Moncton, N.B.; it became Le Théâtre Amateur de Moncton (TAM) in 1969 and Le Théâtre Laurie Henri after his death in 1981. With the help of Laval Goupil, Chantal Cadieux, Jacques Bruchesi, and Manuel Pereira, Henri produced a wide range of Acadian plays, often on issues of direct concern to the people of Moncton. Notable productions included *Bonnet rouge* in 1975, adapted from a story collection by Melvin Gallant; Roger Le Blanc's *Kouchibouquoi*, 1976; Germaine Comeau's *Les Pêcheurs déportés*, 1976; and Antonine MAILLET's *Les Crasseux*, 1976, directed by Jean-Claude Marcus. Other Acadian theatres founded in the 1950s were Yvon Le Blanc's P'tit Théâtre de Neptune, and André and Madeleine Hamelin's Théâtre de la Virgule. In 1960 Father Jean-Guy Gagnon created La Cordée de la Rampe company at the Collège Saint-Joseph in Memramcook, where actors Gilles Nadeau, Gerald Turbide, and Gilbert April made their début. This company performed plays by Paul de Néha, Léon Chancerel, Henri Ghéon, and Thornton Wilder, as well as Quebec plays—Marcel DUBÉ's *Zone* (in Moncton, 1963), Auguste Thibault's *Les Moustaches du p'tit Yvon* (in Memramcook, 1961)—and an Acadian work, Pascal Poirier's *L'Arrivée du Père Lefebvre en Acadie* (Memramcook, 1964). In the mid-1960s Father Maurice Le Blanc founded and directed Le Théâtre du Collège de Bathurst (TCB), producing Beaumarchais, Labiche, Lorca, Brecht, and Molière, among others, but also Paul TOUPIN's *Brutus* (in 1967) and a montage of stories, poems, and songs called *À notre Acadie* in 1973. In 1969 Father Jean-Guy Gagnon, with the help of several Acadians from the Moncton area, launched another theatre, Les Feux-Chalins, which presented not only plays but singers and storytellers. The repertoire consisted of foreign plays as well as Quebec and Acadian works. In 1971 they produced *Le Fli*, adapted from *Pantalon-Moustique* by P. Buisonneau and Marc-F. Gélinas; in 1972 Michel TREMBLAY's *À Toi, pour toujours, ta Marie-Lou*; and in 1973 *Qu'est-ce qu'on fait monsieur le maire?*, adapted from Françoise LORANGER's *Médium saignant*. The company's most memorable success was *La SAGOUINE* by Antonine Maillet, starring Viola Léger, and directed by Eugène Gallant in 1971, a production that won distinction not only in Acadia but across Canada and in France. Les Feux-Chalins also produced the first play by Laval Goupil, *Tête d'eau* in 1974.

In 1969 the Univ. of Moncton formed a department of dramatic arts, chaired first by Claire Ifrane, who was succeeded by Jean-Claude Marcus. Besides presenting plays by Slawomir Mrozek, Don Lucian, and José Triana, they created *À notre Acadie* from poems by Ronald Després, and produced Acadian works by Léonard Forest, Raymond LeBlanc, and Guy Arsenault. The department also produced *L'Invasion des Spretzelles* and *Les Jouets rêvent* by Marthe Boisvert in 1975, and *Becquer Bobo* and *Au plus fort la poche* by the poet Herménégilde Chiasson in 1975. Chiasson's other plays—*Histoire en histoire, L'Étoile de Mine de Rien, Les Aventures de Mine de Rien, Renaissance au pluriel, Baisse donc le radio, Cogne Fou, Evangéline mythe ou réalité*, and *Atarel et les Pakmaniens*—were also produced in New Brunswick.

In 1974, in Caraquet, Réjean Poirier founded Les Productions de l'Étoile, which two years later became Le Théâtre Populaire d'Acadie. Audiences were treated to plays by Dario Fo and Michel Tremblay, and *Le Djibou* by Laval Goupil in 1975, the musical *Louis Mailloux* by Calixte Duguay and Jules Boudreau in 1975, and Chiasson's *L'Amer à boire* in 1976. In Maisonnette, Jules Boudreau's company, Les Elouèzes, performed mostly its own plays: *L'Agence Beloeil Inc.* and *La Bringue* (both in 1973), *Louis Mailloux* (in 1975), *Cochu et le soleil* (in 1977), and *La Lambique* (in 1978).

Since the demise of Les Feux-Chalins in 1976 l'Escaouette (founded in 1977 at Moncton) has presented many plays by young Acadian dramatists, most notably Roger Le Blanc's *Le Pêcheur ensorcelé* in 1978. This company tours schools in the Atlantic provinces, and in May 1986 it travelled to Belgium with Garcia Couturier's *Le Gros p'tit gars d'à côté*, directed by Eugène Gallant, first produced in Moncton in 1985.

Several other small groups performed original works: Le Petit Théâtre de Memramcook (1973-), Le Théâtre de la Polyvalente Clément Cormier (1975-), La Gang asteur (1976-8),

3

Acadian Theatre

Le Théâtre amateur d'Acadie (in Robertville, 1976-), Les Cliques et les Claques (in Clare, N.S., 1979-), Les Araignées du Boui-Boui (1974-), and Les Copains du Théâtre (Cheticamp, 1974-). Théâtre-Acadie, incorporated in 1981, began an annual festival of dramatic arts in 1983 for Acadian companies in Moncton, and in 1986 Viola Léger formed her own company, La Compagnie Viola Léger, which offered Colin Higgins's *Harold et Maude* in its first season (1987).

See Zénon Chiasson, 'Le Théâtre en Acadie et les enjeux d'une société minoritaire', in *The Proceedings of the Theatre in Atlantic Canada Symposium* (1988), ed. R. P. Knowles.

LAURENT LAVOIE

Acting (English Canada). As of Aug. 1988 the CBC's computerized Talent Bank contained the names of 14,669 English-language professional actors in Canada, with the ratio of males to females virtually equal. This listing breaks down to 6,283 adult actors, 1,343 children (under 12), and 7,043 extras who play non-speaking parts in crowd scenes. In 1988 the Alliance of Canadian Cinema, Television and Radio Artists (ACTRA) represented 9,679 members in good standing or 'on withdrawal' (including writers and broadcast journalists), while Canadian Actors' Equity counted 3,350 paid-up members, and some 400 suspended or in arrears for dues. (Many actors belong to both unions.) Statistics are not available for amateur actors across Canada, but the number must reach well into the tens of thousands. Toronto is the major English centre, with over eighty actors' agencies and 11,200 resident performers, followed by Montreal (1,120 English), Vancouver (960), Edmonton (164), Ottawa (113), Halifax (99), Calgary (91), Winnipeg (83), Niagara (81), and Stratford (75). Regina, Saskatoon, St John's, Quebec City, Saint John, Sudbury, Thunder Bay, and Charlottetown are next in order, each with fewer than fifty. Of the many Canadian actors living outside of Canada in 1988 the highest concentrations were in Los Angeles (280), New York City (162), Europe in general (107), and London, England (60). Another 56 were scattered throughout the U.S.

During the 1987-8 season, however, only 1,061 speaking roles were available for CBC-TV's various in-house productions. Clearly the competition for work was keen. While salaries for stage productions are graduated according to the seating capacity of the theatre, film rates are determined on a daily basis, with the appropriate unions setting minimum scales in each category. Salaries are negotiable, but leading roles in a Canadian TV series, for example, can range from $3,500 to $12,000 per episode, or up to $35,000 for a co-production with another country (compare Joan Collins's $90,000 per episode for *Dynasty*). However, the majority (63 per cent) of ACTRA members in 1987 earned less than $5,000 for the entire year and Equity members' average annual income was $6,500. At any given moment the unemployment rate among Equity actors is estimated at 70 per cent. While most Canadian actors are adept at working in all media (stage, TV, film, radio, commercials, industrial shows, etc.), and invariably earn some supplemental income from an assortment of part-time jobs, the actor's combined total income as reported in 1986 (*Globe and Mail*, 3 May 1986) averaged $12,537, compared to $20,538 for a film projectionist. The 1986 federal task-force report, *The Status of the Artist*, revealed that 'no single artistic discipline, on average, earned an income above the poverty line.'

The first actors in Canada were the anonymous shamans of the native peoples, participating in performance rituals that paralleled the Dionysian rites of Greece and may have dated back 20,000 to 50,000 years. (See AMERINDIAN AND INUIT THEATRE.) The Amerindians and Inuit of Canada were also the first 'Canadians' to perform in Europe; regrettably, on display as exotic side-show attractions. Beothuks, Hurons, and Inuit were taken by sixteenth-century explorers John Cabot, Jacques Cartier, Martin Frobisher, and others, and enticed to perform native dances before aristocratic gatherings, or to demonstrate hunting and athletic skills. The first known individual actors in Canada were French colonial amateurs in Quebec: Martial Piraubé, the governor's male secretary (who organized and designed a 1640 second birthday tribute to Louis XIV); and the Dérôme sisters, Marie and Elizabeth, townspeople who assisted in Governor Frontenac's 1693 garrison theatre. Madame de La Tour (née Françoise-Marie Jacquelin) (1602-45), the brave defender of her husband's Fort La Tour in Acadia, may have been an actress in France, but she never played in Canada.

Unknown English garrison amateurs appeared as early as 1743 at Fort Anne (today's Annapolis Royal, N.S.) and even, perhaps, as mummers or 'waits' with Humphrey Gilbert's 1583 expedition to Newfoundland. (See GARRISON THEATRE.) The earliest known professional strolling players to visit Canada were a troupe of nine English actors, en route from North Carolina: Messrs (William?) Mills and (Henry?) Giffard, their wives, and five gentlemen named Platt, Horner, Phillips, Farrell (or O'Farrell), and Leggett, who took up residence from 26 Aug. to 28 Oct. 1768 in Halifax.

The first Canadian-born expatriate to make a name for himself in America was William Burke Wood (1779-1861), born in Montreal, who became a revered actor-manager at the Chestnut Street Theatre in Philadelphia. He was followed by a parade of native-born nineteenth and turn-of-the-century actors: Henry J. Finn, William Rufus BLAKE, Graves Simcoe LEE, Arthur McKee RANKIN, Clara MORRIS, May IRWIN, Julia ARTHUR, James K. Hackett, Margaret ANGLIN, Beatrice LILLIE, among others, who after some initial elocutionary training or amateur exposure in Canada, were obliged to make their careers in the U.S. or England. Although there were a dozen or more Canadian-based touring companies before and after 1900, they inevitably drew their complement of players from the central clearing-house of New York City. In the twentieth century, VAUDEVILLE claimed the likes of Rose STAHL and Eva Tanguay, while the decline of mainstream touring redirected other talented Canadians into the movies: Mary Pickford, Mack Sennett, Walter HUSTON, Raymond MASSEY, Walter Pidgeon, Alexander Knox, Fay Wray, Ruby Keeler, Helen Morgan, Ned Sparks, Deanna Durbin, and others. Canada achieved a heady hat-trick in 1929, 1930, and 1931 when three of its actresses in a row won an Academy Award: Mary Pickford (*Coquette*), Norma Shearer (*The Divorcee*), and Marie Dressler (*Min and Bill*). (See MOTION PICTURES.)

At home in Canada the LITTLE THEATRE spawned a new generation of players who, because they were amateur (and otherwise employed), could stay in Canada and sow the seeds for an indigenous theatre. RADIO DRAMA in the 1930s and '40s became the toehold for a burgeoning post-Second World War professional theatre. With the creation of the Canada Council in 1957 and the blossoming of the regional theatre system in the 1960s, the talent drain slowed considerably, and by the 1970s—boosted by the flowering of the ALTERNATE THEATREs—Canada was able to support its own native entertainment industry. Nonetheless, actors such as Hume CRONYN, Christopher PLUMMER, William SHATNER, Geneviève Bujold, Kate REID, Donald SUTHERLAND, Margot Kidder, and, more recently, Kate NELLIGAN, Helen Shaver, Dan Aykroyd, John Candy, Kiefer Sutherland, and Michael J. Fox have continued the traditional talent exodus.

Although actor R.H. THOMSON has said that there is no Canadian star system—except in hockey—this is belied by his own example, and that of William HUTT, Martha HENRY, Gordon PINSENT, and others. Certainly Canadians in leading roles now negotiate billing over the title. In the late 1970s, when unsubsidized DINNER THEATREs like Stage West appeared, or in 1986 when a commercial roadhouse like Toronto's ROYAL ALEXANDRA THEATRE adjusted its policy to include Canadian productions, a limited star system began to come into its own. With it came the end of the too-easy assumption that unless a Canadian actor succeeded abroad he was somehow inferior.

Canadians have assimilated the best of the British heritage (its irony, vocal virtuosity, and technical discipline) and married it to the constant American example (with its love of the physical, emotions on the sleeve, and improvisational skills) to create a versatile hybrid. The audience-performer relationship is at the heart of acting and of star quality. Canadians on the whole are more reserved, less joyously overt about this relationship—often in conscious contrast to Americans—preferring to melt into a role and turn it into a character rather than a star turn: e.g. Raymond Massey as Abe Lincoln, Donald Sutherland in *Casanova*, Nicholas Campbell as Robert Kennedy, or Hume Cronyn in virtually any role. In a sense Canadians are skilled supporting actors even when starring, illuminating the text rather than using it as a vehicle for easy entertainment or personal enhancement. Being quite classically oriented in attitudes to acting, they are probably more British than American in this. The first post-Second World War generation of professional actors tended to speak with transatlantic accents, considered appropriate to Stratford and the early CBC. But a new post-colonial

Acting (English Canada)

Canadian has moved to centre stage, more confident and more individual, no longer dogged by a quiet-spoken, self-deprecating image and mask of shy passivity. Regrettably the Canadian ideal of a bilingual or bicultural actor has not materialized, but something else has taken its place: a multicultural, multi-regional personality that can wear an international hat and speak in its own accent, wherever it stems from.

If style is the marriage of form and content, it follows that Canadians could not speak or act as Canadians until they wrote and thought as Canadians, and that has begun to happen. Alan Filewod has suggested that a distinctive acting style and voice emerged during the 1970s with the staging of COLLECTIVE CREATIONs: 'a genre of performance rather than dramatic literature . . . an actors' theatre . . . that combines intimate realism with a delight in broad gesture, and replaces the traditional British-trained diction with recognizable Canadian accents.' Fuelled in the late 1980s by the U.S. threat to cultural sovereignty, a more positive, scrappy, fun-filled Canadian has appeared, still outdoorsy but feisty and sophisticated as well. Nonetheless, Canada has not yet developed a system or philosophy of acting—no Diderot paradox or Stanislavsky 'method'. There is a love of process and of product, an eclectic range that includes naturalism and performance art. The subject of drama is human behaviour and in Canada, as in the rest of the world, the actor remains the front-line of the theatre, the singer of the song, the mirror of an age, the medium of dramatic expression.

DAVID GARDNER

Acting (Quebec). For those who wish to learn the craft of acting in Quebec, the means are many and diverse. In addition to the five professional acting schools that opened between 1955 and 1970, several universities also offer training which, although not as specialized, provides an interesting alternative to apprentice actors looking for a broad background, as well as an opportunity for graduates of professional theatre schools for further study in playwriting, directing, dramatic theory, criticism, history of drama, and teaching. In addition there is a network of private schools, courses, and workshops, as well as training programs offered by the established theatrical companies.

The growth in actor training is a relatively recent phenomenon linked to the rich flowering of Quebec theatre during the 1960s in which the actor played a major role. If it is possible today to speak of a Quebec style of acting that is distinct from French, American, or English-Canadian acting, it is thanks to the combined efforts of young authors, actors, and directors who, on the fringes of professional theatre, and in the midst of the Quiet Revolution, found a way to release the mannerisms of Quebec speech so long shunned by the professional stage. The volubility of speech and gesture, occasionally excessive, that one sees in a Quebec actor, the generosity and ease of improvisation—the seemingly improvisational delivery of a text—reveals an artistic sensibility that has finally found its voice. This slow, complex evolution in the amateur and semi-professional theatre up to the 1950s eventually came to govern—in the space of fifteen years—the whole of theatrical activity in Quebec. Regardless of repertoire, production, or training, the style of Quebec actors now has recognizable characteristics.

In some respects Quebec acting style is akin to naturalism, while in other respects it seems expressionistic, as if the style were constantly wavering between a psychological interpretation and one that is distanced from the character. In fact this style is a curious combination of traditions and cultures—French and French-Canadian on the one hand, professional and amateur on the other. The Quebec actor's method of portraying a character is influenced by a style used in such popular genres as BURLESQUE and melodrama that was much admired between 1920 and 1940. (The influence of self-taught actors—such as Olivier GUIMOND, Ovila Légaré, Juliette BÉLIVEAU, or Juliette Pétrie—is now recognized in the definition of a style of acting that revives a long tradition of popular storytellers, but it took more than twenty years to discover this.) These methods are plainly evident in improvisational performances as well as in interpretations of the comic repertoire. Today's actors benefit greatly from a generation of actors reacting against the accepted classical training at the Lassalle Conservatory and the NATIONAL THEATRE SCHOOL, influenced by the great reformers of the theatre in France: Jacques Copeau, Louis Jouvet, Charles Dullin, and George Pitoëff—who rushed to join Les COMPAGNONS DE SAINT-LAURENT, Les APPRENTIS-

SORCIERS, L'Egrégore, and Les SALTIM-BANQUES, which advocated greater simplicity of voice, gesture, and staging.

From the moment when—as part of the process of freeing themselves from an imported theatrical culture and the conventional classical training practised at the Lassalle Conservatory—actors learned about improvisation and collective creation, they found a way of speaking, of occupying the stage, and of characterization that finally gave them access to a history, a culture, and a marginalized tradition that had been hidden by the effects of the cultural colonization of Quebec's entire intellectual élite. Between 1970 and 1975 companies such as Les Enfants de Chenier, Le GRAND CIRQUE ORDINAIRE, and Le Théâtre Euh! revolutionized actor training. In their shows actors were the directors, and characters were drawn from a popular oral tradition. With an easy naturalness, they borrowed frank speech, gestures at once exuberant and restrained, and a posture revealing a previously constrained sexuality—rigid in moments of strong emotion and unrestrained and provocative when intoxicated. They also recaptured the language, and through it discovered a voice, a body, and a range of emotions that finally gave them access to characters that fitted them perfectly. Even more important, they acquired their own dynamics of expression, which subsequently allowed them to work out a grammar of acting. This was not unlike the main principles of the Stanislavsky method, but it also put the actor in the foreground, like a master of ceremonies calling upon the spectator's instinct for play. An actor-creator was born, who would lead a whole second generation to demand absolute power over the production and dissemination of its theatre.

Under pressure from organizations such as the Association canadienne du théâtre d'amateurs and the Association québécoise de jeune théâtre, collective-creation groups, springing up throughout the province, took over much of the work in establishing the permanent touring arrangements for Quebec's ALTERNATE THEATRE. COLLECTIVE CREATION became, for the actor, a process of intensive training in combining the functions of author, director, and producer in a theatre of cultural liberation. Around the mid-1970s—having reached a progressive, militant conception of art, and supported by the AQJT in their plan to construct a popular

theatre (i.e., a theatre in the service of the people)—several collectives began using the agit-prop techniques that had been widely practised in Europe in the 1920s, as well as the traditional forms of popular European theatre, such as those that had been updated and interpreted by Vsevolod Meyerhold, Erwin Piscator, Bertolt Brecht, and, in Quebec, by companies such as Le Théâtre Euh! Even though the schools had adjusted their teaching to suit an increasingly assertive Quebec dramaturgy, and a new breed of actors was winning popular favour in the cities and in the outlying regions, they were nonetheless accused of perpetuating a bourgeois system of production and cultural dissemination. Accordingly, a third generation of actors, who wished to train under a progressive program, joined companies whose artistic plan responded to their desire to learn while doing, in an atmosphere of excitement and of front-line intervention in Quebec's political struggle.

A program so specialized—technically, aesthetically, and politically—could not be expected to win unanimous approval, even inside the AQJT. All the children's theatre companies (see CHILDREN'S DRAMA AND THEATRE IN FRENCH), for example, insisted on a clear curriculum for training that returned the actor to his role as interpreter, with the author and director reinstated as the heart of the production team. An actor who specialized in children's theatre benefited from a concrete experience of the audience, which accounted for a style of acting that brought out the phatic dimension of communication, strongly supported by a stage environment that was sensually stimulating. Actors trained in the acting schools do not have such versatility, nor such confident physical and vocal control. While there are a great many qualities that actors trained in the popular theatre have failed to develop, they profit nonetheless from the experience of creation, which enables them to write, direct, and teach. Since the beginning of the 1980s 'progressive' actor training has been the object of serious re-evaluation, since most of the popular-theatre companies that survived the decline in influence of political groups have turned towards the production of theatre for young audiences, the only realistic professional alternative. Their need for proficiency in acting and interpretation confirms the importance of a basic training technique and, therefore, has brought the professional theatre schools back into favour.

Among the most important companies that have their own schools are Omnibus, CARBONE 14, La Veillée, Le NOUVEAU THÉÂTRE EXPÉRIMENTAL DE MONTRÉAL, Le Théâtre Experimental des Femmes, Circus, and Le Théâtre Repère. Each in its own way contributes to liberating the actor by opting for an essentially experimental approach to the actor's work—reinstating the body as a medium of expression, or as a locus of theatricality, or even as a place for articulating a psychoanalytic, indeed mythic, approach to reality. The actor functions as a creator whose psycho-physical contribution fits the theatrical plan conceived and supervised by a director, who is also an instructor. This approach to the actor's work, and to the methods of producing theatre in which the word is only one component, has influenced a new generation of actors attracted by a multi-disciplinary approach to performance.

Even today the most innovative suggestions regarding the training of the actor are articulated on the fringes of the professional theatre training. That said, the recent opening up of the professional schools to methods that restore the emphasis on the expressiveness of the body is a sure sign of a will to rethink their teaching in terms of a theatre capable of resisting the invasion of the mass media, and indeed of subverting the effects of assimilation. More than ever, in a performance society, actors are vested with critical and emancipating duties: possessing, on the one hand, the power to portray an image while creating it, and on the other hand increasingly drawing attention to the making of the role. Thus actors constantly remind the spectator that what is shown on stage is a complete fabrication.

If the term 'Quebec actor' still has a meaning, at a time when internationalism tends to overshadow any nationalist or ethnocentric approach to art, it is in the act of recalling the endless process of liberation and of going back to the beginnings, of recalling the eternal search for identity, for integrity, that can be achieved by individual expressiveness, no matter what theatrical convention is used.

LORRAINE HÉBERT

Aikins, Carroll (1888-1967). Producer, director, and playwright, he utilized European art-theatre principles in helping to estab-lish a Canadian theatre. He did notable work in the early 1920s in the rural Okanagan area of British Columbia, and in the late 1920s at HART HOUSE THEATRE, Toronto. Born into a well-connected family in Stanstead, Que., he attended private school in Winnipeg; after a year at McGill University, and with suspected tuberculosis, he began an extended study tour of Europe, where he became enchanted with the work of Gordon Craig, Jacques Copeau, and Adolphe Appia. He likely witnessed productions of Harley Granville-Barker and Max Reinhardt, and important work of English repertory theatres. In 1919 the Birmingham Repertory Theatre staged his play *The God of Gods*, designed by Barry Jackson. Aikins was also influenced by Americans Lee Simonson and Maurice Browne (of the Chicago Little Theatre), who encouraged him to found a Little Theatre in the Canadian West. In 1919 he made plans to build an art theatre on the property of his 100-acre fruit-ranch near Naramata, B.C. Named the Home Theatre—after the Neighborhood Playhouse (est. 1915) of New York's Lower East Side, from which he was to hire personnel—the building was a combination fruit-storage area on the ground level and theatre above. The theatre (40' by 80') was wooden, with a steeply pitched roof, large dormers, and over the stage a raised fly space with dressing-rooms; it seated 100 on sloping wooden pews, with a stage at floor level backed by a plaster 'sky-dome' and a foyer and scene shop along the sides. Officially opened on 3 Nov. 1920 by Prime Minister Meighen, the theatre, home of the Canadian Players, was dedicated to 'the giving of Canadian plays by Canadian actors'. Students came from across Canada, picked fruit part of the day, then trained under Aikins and other instructors and took part in productions of plays by J.M. Synge, Gilbert Murray, and Anatole France. Only one original Canadian work was presented: *Victory in Defeat*, a pure light-and-sound performance with actors in artistic silhouettes depicting biblical scenes. After two seasons and generally good notices, the venture was ended by a poor fruit market. From 1927 to 1929 Aikins was director of theatre at Hart House, programming in-house and touring productions; his final production, *Antony and Cleopatra*, was called a 'genuine triumph' by the Toronto *Globe*, 4 May 1929.

A thoughtful and sensitive director and

teacher, Aikins could also be, in the words of one former student, 'terribly vague . . . a dreamer'. *The God of Gods* is published in Volume 2 of *Canadian Plays from Hart House Theatre* (1927).

See James Hoffman, 'Carroll Aikins and the Home Theatre', *Theatre History in Canada*, 7 (1986).   JAMES HOFFMAN

Alberta, Theatre in. Theatre in Alberta begins in the 1880s, coinciding with the first wave of colonization that saw Edmonton and Calgary grow from forts and fur-trading posts into the beginnings of today's major cities. There were no formal theatres in the 1880s—when Canadian actor Simcoe LEE presented several evenings of songs and recitations in Edmonton in 1886 he performed in the local schoolhouse. Performances in pioneer days also took place in church or town halls, skating rinks, hotels, and barns. The first professional troupe, led by Caroline Gage, reached Edmonton in 1892, the year after the railway arrived. Although professional companies visited only sporadically in the 1890s, local sheriff W. S. Robertson built the first real theatre in 1892. A frame building on Jasper Ave, Edmonton, with two stores on the main floor and the theatre upstairs, Robertson's Hall served for almost fifteen years as the city's principal theatre and community centre, housing dances, lectures, public meetings, and concerts, as well as local and touring plays.

Although occasional amateur productions had been taking place for several years, the first long-lasting groups date from 1900 when Vernon Barford helped found Edmonton's amateur Garrick Club, which soon separated into two parts. Barford, who was primarily interested in music, established the Edmonton Operatic and Dramatic Society in 1903 to produce operettas. Albert E. Nash, David 'Didie' Robinson, and Eva Protheroe were leading lights in the second group, the Edmonton Amateur Dramatic Club, which won the last Earl Grey competition in Winnipeg in 1911, competing against established LITTLE THEATREs from much larger centres.

In 1896 Colonel and Mrs Jamieson had helped found the Edmonton Amateur Dramatic Company. Responding to positive comment on their professionalism, members of the troupe, under the direction of F. de Journal, adopted the name La Cigale Comedy Company and embarked on a ten-week professional tour of Alberta and British Columbia in the fall of 1896. The performers endured primitive conditions but found an enthusiastic audience for live theatre. Most early professional troupes were equally rough and ready but met with the same positive response. Typical was Harry LINDLEY's Comedy Company, which first reached Edmonton in 1897, performing several plays in repertory and featuring a pirated melodrama called *The Castaways*, with exciting scenic effects.

Major stars from America, England, and Europe began the long journey westward in the first decades of the twentieth century, beginning with Mrs Minnie Maddern Fiske in 1907. She was followed by celebrities such as Sir John Martin-Harvey, Robert Mantell, Ethel Barrymore, Mrs Patrick Campbell, Sarah Bernhardt, and Canada's own Harold Nelson SHAW and the MARKS BROTHERS troupes. (See TOURING STARS AND COMPANIES.) These actors appeared in a variety of Edmonton theatres, including the Thistle Rink Theatre (between curling seasons), the first EMPIRE THEATRE, which opened in 1906, as, more importantly, did the Edmonton Opera House (later the LYCEUM THEATRE), under the management of Alexander Cameron, Edmonton's first theatrical entrepreneur. However, it was not until 1920 that Edmonton got a modern theatre equal to the renowned WALKER THEATRE in Winnipeg: the third Empire Theatre, built by a consortium led by Sir James Lougheed.

The first performances in Calgary took place in the rustic Boynton Hall in 1883. The Calgary Amateur Music and Dramatic Club was founded a year later while there were still fewer than a thousand inhabitants in the area. The finest theatre west of Winnipeg, HULL'S OPERA HOUSE, with approximately 700 seats, opened in 1893, its tall frame structure making it a landmark in early Calgary. Hull's Opera House became home to the amateur Calgary Operatic Society and also hosted many of the early tours until it was superseded by the Grand Theatre, which opened in 1912 with Sir Johnston Forbes-Robertson in Jerome K. Jerome's *The Passing of the Third Floor Back*. The Grand Theatre was home to stock companies, VAUDEVILLE, amateur dramatics, and tours. Under Sir James Lougheed, the Grand became a linchpin of Trans-Canada Theatres Ltd, along with the Empire in Edmonton and the Majes-

Pantages Theatre, Edmonton

tic Theatre in Lethbridge. For many years prairie manager W.B. Sherman operated the Grand as the SHERMAN GRAND THEATRE, mainly for vaudeville. During periods when fewer attractions were on the road, many theatres survived by engaging stock companies for long seasons. One very popular Alberta company was Jeanne Russell's Dominion Stock Company, which was founded around 1908 with its home base at the Dominion Theatre in Edmonton, a theatre managed by Russell's brother-in-law, Lee Brandon.

The first of vaudeville impresario Alexander PANTAGES' theatres in the Prairies opened in Edmonton in 1913 and presented a new bill of acts almost weekly until 1927, when vaudeville was beginning to disappear throughout North America. Stars such as Buster Keaton, Fred Allen, and Stan Laurel appeared in Edmonton's Pantages Theatre. Vaudeville's last stand was to provide a supplement to the new talking-pictures with performances by local semi-professionals such as Fred Doucet, who came to Edmonton in 1915 after gaining theatrical experience in Moose Jaw. Before and after the films, and between reels, he would deliver his trademark monologues, especially his favourite, W.H. Drummond's poem, 'The Habitant', done in a French-Canadian accent.

The last regular professional companies in Alberta for almost thirty years were part of CHAUTAUQUA, a touring educational institution that presented lectures, music, and plays (mostly sentimental dramas and light comedies) throughout the province from 1917 to 1935. Theatre in Alberta did not, however, die with the end of the professional tours, but returned to its amateur roots. Little theatres sprang up in many communities. The Medicine Hat Amateur Dramatic Society, founded in 1914, was followed in the early 1920s by the Medicine Hat Players, which later became known as the Medicine Hat Little Theatre. The Playgoers of Lethbridge began producing in 1924. That same year Margaret Greenham helped found the Banff Literary Dramatic Club, which used the tiny Bretton Hall Theatre. The Coaldale Little Theatre was formed in 1950, in a small mining community near Lethbridge, by Murray Robinson, a local junior-high-school teacher, and his wife Yvonne, who had acquired some theatrical experience in England before coming to Canada as a war bride. The Robinsons insisted on long rehearsal periods, which gave their productions considerable polish and led to success in DOMINION DRAMA FESTIVALs. Elizabeth Sterling HAYNES, a protegée of Roy

MITCHELL, director of HART HOUSE THEA-
TRE in Toronto, helped found the Edmonton
Little Theatre in 1929 and became its first
director; Frank Holroyd was the designer and
Vernon Barford was responsible for music.
The club always suffered the lack of a suitable
theatre, performing in the Normal School
auditorium and then moving to the Empire
Theatre, which proved too costly to rent and
too large for amateurs. The group continued
to move but never found the right home.
Emrys Jones took over as director in 1935
and staged several popular Shakespeare plays.
The Edmonton Little Theatre finally dissolved in 1945 to make way for the Edmonton Community Players, led by playwright
Elsie Park GOWAN and drama teacher Eva O.
Howard, among others. In 1955 Faith Clifton
and her actress daughter Mickie Macdonald
organized a new group, Circle 8. Edmonton's only enduring amateur theatre, however, was Theatre Associates, which Jack
McCreath helped organize in 1959. It turned
a small schoolhouse in Walterdale Flats into
a tiny playhouse, which became home to
some innovative theatre, moving many years
later into a large renovated building in South
Edmonton, where it still performs.

Max Bishop's Paget Players rekindled
interest in amateur theatre in Calgary after
the First World War. Mrs Winnifred Reeve,
an actress, helped launch the Calgary Little
Theatre in 1924. The more successful Green
Room Club was founded in 1929 by E.J.
Thorlakson, with Betty MITCHELL as treasurer. The Green Room Club and the Calgary
Little Theatre competed for talent until 1935
when they amalgamated to form the Theatre
Guild, which opened the Calgary Civic Theatre Playhouse in 1936 under the direction of
Frank Holroyd. It was Workshop 14, however, that became Calgary's best and most
celebrated amateur company, dominating
Dominion Drama Festival competitions for
many years. In 1944 Betty Mitchell, a drama
teacher at Western Canada High School,
agreed to help some of her graduates establish
a company to continue their theatre work
and managed to secure classroom 14 in her
school for their use. In its early years Workshop 14 lived up to its name, emphasizing
ongoing training and high professional standards. Among the group's triumphs were productions of such demanding plays as Ibsen's
Hedda Gabler, R.B. Sheridan's *The Rivals*,
and Christopher Fry's *The Lady's Not for*

Burning. Many Workshop 14 alumni (Conrad
Bain, Chris Wiggins, Ron Hartmann, Jack
McCullagh, and Irene Powlan, for example)
went on to successful careers in television,
theatre, and theatre education. In 1965
Workshop 14 amalgamated with the Musicians and Actors Club to form MAC 14 (see
below), from which emerged THEATRE
CALGARY.

To assist the burgeoning amateur movement throughout the province, little-theatre
representatives E.G. Sterndale Bennett from
Lethbridge, Elizabeth Sterling Haynes from
Edmonton, Norman Davis from Medicine
Hat, and E.J.Thorlakson and Gwillym
Edwards from Calgary met in Aug. 1929 to
form the Alberta Drama League. Starting in
1930, the league organized annual festivals
until these became part of the Dominion
Drama Festival. The Univ. of Alberta's
Department of Extension under E.A. Corbett
then came to the aid of amateur dramatics by
establishing Elizabeth Sterling Haynes, one
of the most influential people in the history
of Alberta theatre, in the post of specialist in
drama. Starting in 1932, Haynes travelled the
province for five years conducting workshops, adjudicating, lecturing, directing,
encouraging, criticizing, and teaching. Her
work was continued by Ronald Elwy Mitchell, Gwen Pharis RINGWOOD, Sydney RISK,
Helen Stuart, and Esther Nelson.

E.A.Corbett and Haynes also opened the
Banff School of Fine Arts (see BANFF
CENTRE) in 1933 to provide training for community-theatre leaders, and in 1943 Donald
Cameron helped to establish the Western
Theatre Conference to emphasize the value
of drama training in schools and universities
and to promote amateur theatre. The first
theatre activity in schools and universities had
been strictly extra-curricular. The student-
run Dramatic Society at the Univ. of Alberta,
for example, was first organized in 1914 and
continued to produce at least one play a year
until the Second World War. But by the time
of the last annual meeting of the Western
Theatre Conference in 1950, both Alberta
and Saskatchewan were ahead of the rest of
Canada in having credit courses in drama in
the school systems and active drama departments in the universities.

Since its establishment in 1955 with one
staff member, the Drama Division of the
provincial government's Alberta Culture
department has played a key role in stimulat-

ing theatre across the province. Walter Kaasa and Jack McCreath, who helped switch the focus of many programs designed for amateurs to meet the needs of the new professional theatres, created the very popular summer school at Drumheller. The Province of Alberta had hoped to facilitate professional theatre by building twin Jubilee Auditoriums in Edmonton and Calgary in 1957, but because of their size they proved completely inadequate for live theatre.

Joseph Shoctor, an Edmonton lawyer, was the driving force behind the formation of the CITADEL THEATRE in Edmonton in 1965, the first professional theatre in the city for over thirty years and, at the time, the only professional theatre between Winnipeg and Vancouver. Artistic directors have included John Hulbert, Robert Glenn (who launched the very successful Citadel School of Performing Arts in 1966), and Sean MULCAHY, who initiated the foundation in 1968 of a school touring group, Citadel on Wheels. John NEVILLE supervised the Citadel's move to its fine new building, which opened in 1976. He was succeeded, in 1978, by Peter Coe, and then—following four seasons directed by Shoctor himself—by Gordon McDougall, who supervised the final phase of the Citadel's expansion—the thrust-stage McLab Theatre—before leaving in 1986. William Fisher was appointed resident director for the 1987-8 season.

The Citadel's competitors have included THEATRE 3 (1970-81), THEATRE NETWORK and NORTHERN LIGHT THEATRE (both founded in 1975), WORKSHOP WEST (founded in 1979), PHOENIX THEATRE (founded in 1981 as successor to Theatre 3), CATALYST THEATRE, and Stage West, a successful commercial DINNER THEATRE operating since 1975.

In Calgary the first step towards professional theatre came in 1965 when the venerable Workshop 14 and the more experimental Musicians and Actors Club amalgamated to form the Mac 14 Club. For two seasons writer/director Kenneth Dyba staged semi-professional productions for the Club at the Allied Arts Centre Theatre, a renovated tractor plant. Christopher NEWTON was hired in 1968 to complete the transformation of Mac 14 into the fully professional Theatre Calgary. In 1971 Newton was succeeded by Clarke Rogers, who resigned in mid-season. Harold Baldridge, a native Albertan living in New York, ran Theatre Calgary from 1972 to

1977. He premièred W.O. MITCHELL's *Back to Beulah* in 1976, begining the theatre's close relationship with Mitchell. Rick McNair, former head of the company's school touring group, Theatre Caravan, enriched Theatre Calgary during his term as artistic director (1978-84) by presenting the work of talented playwrights living in Calgary, particularly that of John MURRELL and Sharon POLLOCK. McNair also supervised the planning for Theatre Calgary's new home, the 750-seat Max Bell Theatre in the Calgary Centre for Performing Arts, which opened in 1985. After McNair's departure Sharon Pollock served briefly as artistic director, before being replaced by Martin KINCH in 1985.

ALBERTA THEATRE PROJECTS, founded in 1972, uses the smaller 465-seat Martha Cohen Theatre in the Centre for Performing Arts. Originally a children's theatre company, ATP has an enviable record of developing and producing the work of such playwrights as John Murrell and Paddy CAMPBELL. Calgary supports a number of smaller companies as well. Lunchbox Theatre, founded by Bartley Bard in 1975, is a thriving LUNCH THEATRE; the Loose Moose company, an experimental theatre run by Keith Johnstone and Mel Tonken, performs in the Pump House Theatre; and the Arete Mime company has toured from its Calgary base since 1976.

If there is one event that symbolizes the thriving Alberta theatre profession it is Edmonton's annual Fringe Festival, which has taken place each August since 1982. Under the direction of Brian Paisley, artistic director of Edmonton's Chinook Theatre (1976-86), the Fringe expanded from forty-five shows in five venues to 160 plays in fourteen venues in 1987, with ticket sales of 120,000 in 1986. Offering the work of Canadian and foreign professionals, of students and amateurs, the Festival embodies the various elements that have helped create the history of theatre in Alberta.

See John Orrell, *Fallen Empires: Lost Theatres of Edmonton 1881-1914* (1981) and E. Ross Stuart, *The History of Prairie Theatre. The Development of Theatre in Alberta, Manitoba and Saskatchewan 1833-1982* (1984).

ROSS STUART

Alberta Theatre Projects. Co-founded as a theatre for young audiences in 1972 in Calgary by Douglas RISKE, artistic director, and

Lucille Wagner, administrative director, it was funded by the federal Local Initiatives Program, with additional support from the Calgary Public and Separate School Boards. The company's first home—the historic Canmore Opera House in Heritage Park—was renovated in 1979 as a fully equipped modern theatre facility inside the log-cabin shell. The long rectangular house seats 165 people facing a small stage that has been ingeniously utilized by designers such as George Dexter, Rick Roberts, Pat Flood, and Phillip SILVER. Directors have included Douglas Riske, Brian Rintoul, Martin Fishman, and Keith TURNBULL.

In its first season (1972-3) ATP produced three original scripts by Paddy CAMPBELL: *The History Show* for young children, *The History Show II* for high schools, and *The Bob Edwards Revue* for families. Avidly committed to regional actors and writers, Riske commissioned numerous new scripts for children and later for adults. The first adult subscription series (1973-4) ran parallel to the children's series. Adult plays were *Fifteen Miles of Broken Glass* (1972) by Tom HENDRY and *Hoarse Muse* (1974) by Paddy Campbell. The children's plays included *Prairie Fire* (unpublished) by Betty Belliveau, *Madwitch* (unpublished) by Paddy Campbell, and *Cyclone Jack* (1972) by Carol BOLT.

Strong Canadian dramas were the foundation for the company's rapid growth. Commissioned productions included Jan Truss's *A Very Small Rebellion* (1978) in 1974, Sharon POLLOCK's *Chautauqua Spelt Energy* (unpublished) in 1979, and three John MURRELL plays: *A Great Noise, a Great Light* (unpublished) in 1976, *WAITING FOR THE PARADE* (1980) in 1977, and a new version of *Memoir* (1978) in 1981. Costs, however, became prohibitive and in 1979 budget cuts and fund-raising were necessary to erase the company's deficit.

Significant changes took place in 1982-3. The 1982 production of Paddy Campbell's *Under the Arch* (unpublished) was ATP's last show for young audiences, and plans for a permanent home in the Calgary Centre for Performing Arts were being formulated. Lucille Wagner resigned to take a position with the Grand Theatre, London, Ont., and the Board of Directors decided to amalgamate the Riske-Wagner jobs into one. Producing director Michael Dobbin was hired for the new post. ATP's new home, the Martha Cohen Theatre, opened in Sept. 1985. Designer Ian McIntosh and architect Joel Barret tried to create the intimate feeling of a Georgian opera house in the 465-seat auditorium. The theatre is technically sophisticated and highly adaptable to end, proscenium, or in-the-round staging—which was utilized in the inaugural production, Claire Luckham's *Trafford Tanzi*.

Now a thriving regional theatre, ATP has been restructured by Michael Dobbin to include a resident ensemble of actors and writers who participate in an annual new play festival. Its current artistic policy is to return more strongly to one of its original mandates of producing new Canadian dramas and to link this to a national network.

The archives of ATP are housed at the Glenbow-Alberta Institute, Calgary.

ZINA BARNIEH

Alhambra Theatre, Vancouver, 1899

Alhambra Theatre. Built of wood with a simplified Moorish exterior reflecting its name, this Vancouver theatre at Pender and Howe Streets was the brainchild of a consortium of four local entrepreneurs (Messrs Sharp, Dyke, Lucas, and Greenwood). It opened on 10 Mar. 1899 with the musical *The Pearl of Pekin*. Seating capacity was 980, including a gallery and proscenium boxes. It was used principally for visiting stock companies, as well as for local amateur performances and occasional political meetings. In 1902 it was renamed the Theatre Royal, and from 1903 to 1905 was known as the People's Theatre. The stock companies that played here were regionally based, and usually consisted of American actors. The Clara Mathes Co., the Watson Co., the Allen Co., the Ed. Redmond Co., and many others provided a mixture of melodrama and comedy, and often combined their plays with VAUDEVILLE acts. The lessee from 1903 to 1905 was Carl Berch, whose own company performed a particularly hackneyed repertoire. In 1906, in consultation with the noted architect Francis Rattenbury, the theatre was extensively renovated (at a cost of $15,000) and seating capacity was increased to 1,200. It reopened in Dec. 1906 as the Orpheum Theatre, one of the Seattle-based Sullivan-Considine vaudeville circuit houses. The theatre has a certain legendary status in Vancouver's theatrical history because it was here in Apr. 1912 that Charles Chaplin appeared with Fred Karno's Company of English Comedians shortly before he began his career in films. The Sullivan-Considine chain retained control until 1913. R.B. TODD

Alianak, Hrant (b. 1950). Born in Khartoum, Sudan, of Armenian parentage, he immigrated to Canada in 1967, and after studies at McGill and York Universities was soon working with Toronto theatre groups as actor and playwright. His plays *Tantrums* (1972) and *The Blues* (1985) were produced by THEATRE PASSE MURAILLE in 1972 and 1976 respectively. His 1978 production of *Lucky Strike* (unpublished) for Toronto's FACTORY THEATRE Lab went on to the Kennedy Centre in Washington, D.C., Café La Mama in New York, and in 1981 to England. *Lucky Strike*, about the last hours of a wounded criminal, exemplifies the dying man's paranoia through the repetition of a single scene introducing, in Alianak's words, 'different tangents'. Alianak now writes, acts, and directs for television and film.

Alianak seeks to bring colour and feeling to the modern stage through image, soundtrack, and cartoon-like gesture. His early 'shorts' are pop-art events. Three actors speaking the names of cowboy pictures and movie stars create a sequence of emotions in *Western* (published in 1973, produced at Theatre Passe Muraille in 1972). In *Mathematics* (published in 1973, produced at Factory Theatre Lab in 1972) everyday objects, thrown onto the stage at precise intervals timed to a monotonous sound-track, comment on the life of an invisible, ordinary, object-ruled cou-

ple. *Christmas* (published in 1974, produced at Theatre Passe Muraille in 1973), the most extensive of these collages, combines music, dance, and silent actors to present the joys and sorrows of Christmas and, amazingly, the interior biography of a tree. The 'found objects' in the later plays are stereotypes and clichés from the American movies Alianak grew up on. Their banality can often be fun, but their predictability also tends to weaken their emotional impact. *The Violinist and the Flower Girl* (1982), produced in a shortened version at Theatre Passe Muraille in 1972, evokes a silent Chaplin movie whose title tells its plot. Unfortunately those stereotypes never add up to a criticism of life—or of the movies. Four gangster plays—*Mousetown* (1982), produced at Factory Theatre Lab in 1974; *Night*, produced at Theatre Passe Muraille in 1975; *Passion and Sin* (1978), produced at TORONTO FREE THEATRE in 1976; and *Lucky Strike*—play and re-play the worn dialogue and empty clichés of a thousand B-movies so that they seem ultimately self-indulgent despite moments of wit, energy, and inspired theatricality.

Return of the Big Five (1975) includes *Brandy, Christmas, Mathematics, Tantrums,* and *Western*. ANTHONY JENKINS

Allan, Andrew (1907-74). Claimed by some as the world's best radio-drama producer, Scottish-born Andrew Edward Fairbairn Allan came to Canada with his parents at seventeen and gained experience as an actor at the Univ. of Toronto, where he also edited the *Varsity*. In 1933 he joined the private Toronto radio station CFRB, where he announced, wrote continuity, and produced occasional drama. In 1938 he went to England, where he worked on radio with, among others, Gracie Fields and George Formby. Returning to Canada in 1939 (surviving the torpedoing of the *Athenia*), he became director of dramatic programs for CBC Vancouver. Here he began to evolve his own particular style and technique, and it was probably in the series 'A Baker's Dozen', written by Fletcher Markle, that he revealed a 'new sound' in radio drama that was to become his hallmark. The success of these broadcasts across Canada led to Allan's being called to Toronto in 1943 to develop the Sunday night 'Stage' series of dramas, which started in 1944 and was broadcast live coast to coast for twelve seasons. Allan's 'new sound'—recognizable Canadian dialects and a gritty realism, with a penchant for sometimes abrasive social comment—permeated the series. He encouraged many Canadian writers and actors, among them Len PETERSON, Lister SINCLAIR, Tommy TWEED, Joseph SCHULL, W.O. MITCHELL, John Drainie, Frank Peddy, Budd Knapp, Ruth Springford, and Jane MALLETT.

Apart from the 'Stage' series Allan is also remembered for his contribution to the CBC 'Wednesday Night' programs, such as the Shakespeare series that employed actors of the calibre of Frances HYLAND, Douglas RAIN, and Christopher PLUMMER.

Allan never lost touch with the stage. He was in constant demand as an adjudicator and was the first artistic director of the SHAW FESTIVAL (1963-5). He died in Toronto on 15 Jan. 1974.

See also RADIO DRAMA IN ENGLISH and Allan's autobiography, A Self-Portrait (1974).
MURRAY D. EDWARDS

Allan, Martha (1895-1942). The daughter of Sir Hugh Montagu Allan (chairman of the Allan Line of steamships), she was born and raised in Montreal and studied drama in Paris before serving as an ambulance driver during the First World War. After the war she studied acting at the Pasadena Playhouse in California. On her return to Montreal she became involved with the Community Players and, from its formation in 1930, the MONTREAL REPERTORY THEATRE, which began in the coach house of her family's estate. The major force in the MRT, Allan produced traditional and experimental work of high quality, wrote the first play to win the Sir Barry Jackson Challenge Trophy at the DOMINION DRAMA FESTIVAL (All on a Summer's Day, produced in 1936), and directed and acted in both English and French, performing leading roles as Candida and Hedda Gabler. She was a strong supporter and active organizer of the Dominion Drama Festival from its inception in 1933, and of the LITTLE THEATRE movement in general. Her death in Victoria, B.C., at the age of forty-seven robbed Canadian theatre of an energetic and effective pioneer. HERBERT WHITTAKER

Allan, Ted (b. 1916). Born Alan Herman in Montreal, Ted Allan wrote twenty-two original scripts and adaptations for CBC radio

between 1950 and 1954. Fourteen of his plays were produced on CBC-TV between 1952 and 1964. Allan's drama about moral corruption in Hollywood, The Money Makers, was premièred by JUPITER THEATRE, Toronto, on 14 Nov. 1952 and starred Lorne GREENE, John Drainie, and Kate REID.

Because of limited stage-production opportunities in Toronto and the CENSORSHIP of his CBC-TV political drama The Legend of the Baskets, Allan moved to London, Eng., in 1954 and remained there until the early 1970s. In 1955 Bernard Braden produced The Money Makers, retitled The Ghost Writers, at the Arts Theatre, London, where it was not a critical success. Allan's murder mystery Double Image (1957), written with Roger MacDougall, was produced by Laurence Olivier at the Savoy Theatre on 14 Nov. 1956 for a seven-month run with Richard Attenborough in the lead. It opened at the CREST THEATRE, Toronto, on 30 Apr. 1958, starring Donald DAVIS, and received mixed reviews. In 1959 it opened at the Michodière Theatre in Paris, running for over four years.

Allan's Legend of Paradiso and The Secret of the World—which depicts the breakdown of a Canadian Communist union leader following Kruschev's 1956 denunciation of Stalin—were produced by Joan Littlewood at the Theatre Royal, Stratford East, in 1959 and 1962. He also wrote the original scenario for Littlewood's 1964 Oh, What a Lovely War! but had to sue to receive proper stage credit. In Nov. 1966 his 'Zen-Buddhist-Hebrew musical', Chu Chem, closed in Philadelphia prior to its scheduled Broadway opening, but was revived—receiving positive notices—at New York's Jewish Repertory Theatre in Dec. 1988. Sean Connery directed Allan's I've Seen You Cut Lemons, a play about mental breakdown and a near-incestuous brother-sister relationship, at the Fortune Theatre, London, where it opened on 5 Dec. 1969. It was revived at FESTIVAL LENNOXVILLE (opening on 3 July 1974) as My Sister's Keeper (1976), receiving unfavourable reviews. However, it served as the basis for John Cassavetes' 1984 film Love Streams. Festival Lennoxville also staged the North American première of The Secret of the World on 13 July 1976.

Much of Allan's writing, such as his screenplay for the film Lies My Father Told Me (1976), has evolved from short stories into radio and television plays, and film scripts. It is characterized by its autobiographical nature, and political commitment. Allan served in the International Brigade with Dr Norman Bethune during the Spanish Civil War and is the co-author (with Sydney Gordon) of *The Scalpel, the Sword: The Story of Doctor Norman Bethune* (1952), which has been translated into nineteen languages. *Bethune: the Making of a Hero*, Allan's film about Bethune (starring Donald SUTHERLAND), was completed in Dec. 1988. His novel, *Love Is a Long Shot*, won the Stephen LEACOCK Award for Humour in 1984. His latest play. *The Third Day Coming*, was produced by John Cassavetes in Los Angeles in 1984.   ANTON WAGNER

Alternate Theatre. It is necessary to distinguish between alternate theatre as a phase of post-colonial consolidation in the arts (or 'la récupération de notre réalité', as it was called in Quebec), linked to international currents of theatrical innovation in the 1960s and 1970s, and a continuing tradition of experimental and popular theatre—sometimes called 'alternative theatre'—that defines itself by its opposition to mainstream theatre, represented by such regional theatres as the MANITOBA THEATRE CENTRE and Halifax's NEPTUNE THEATRE.

Although alternate theatre in English Canada and Quebec followed different courses in response to different historical and cultural conditions, it had much in common. In both cultures alternate theatre led to the growth of new theatre companies, new approaches to performance, and, consequently, new dramatic genres; it also found a major form of expression in the practice of COLLECTIVE CREATION.

In both English Canada and Quebec alternate theatre was a major factor in the growth of an indigenous and professional theatre representing the culmination of several decades of tentative beginnings. The reasons for its success are many, but among them are the increase in nationalist sentiment, both Canadian and Québécois, in the 1960s, and the emergence of an activist generation from the universities, community colleges, and CEGEPs which, absorbing the liberationist ideologies of the 1960s, determined to follow careers in the arts—a choice made possible by the availability of government support through expanded arts-council budgets and government make-work programs.

In one sense, reference to an alternate-the-atre movement is deceptive because it implies a coherence that was not always present, particularly in English Canada. In Quebec its equivalent—the *jeune théâtre* movement—was built on an intellectual tradition and benefited from a more centralized culture; for that reason the history of alternate theatre in Quebec is for the most part the history of the Association québécoise du jeune théâtre, which has met annually for congresses and festivals for over twenty years. In English Canada the vast geographic distances, the absence of a governing ideological consensus (compared to the widespread militant socialism of the *jeune théâtre*), and the relative lack of intellectual discourse have made definition of the term 'alternate theatre' more difficult.

Finally, in both cultures alternate theatre was influenced, especially at the beginning, by major innovations elsewhere, although these influences were admitted more frankly in Quebec than in English Canada. By the late 1960s numerous young artists had returned to Canada from apprenticeships abroad, among them Marc Doré (Théâtre Euh!), Raymond Cloutier (Le GRAND CIRQUE ORDINAIRE) and Paul THOMPSON (THEATRE PASSE MURAILLE) from France; Chris BROOKES (the MUMMERS TROUPE) from the United States; John PALMER and Martin KINCH (founders of TORONTO FREE THEATRE) and Ken KRAMER from Great Britain. Two contributions from foreign artists were especially significant: in 1972 Peter Cheeseman of the Victoria Theatre, England, visited Toronto, and introduced Canadians to his form of localist documentary (see DOCUMENTARY DRAMA) that would take root in the OPEN CIRCLE THEATRE, Toronto, and the GLOBE THEATRE, Regina; and in 1975 Peter Schumann's Bread and Puppet Theatre from the U.S. (which had four years earlier worked with members of Théâtre Euh!) gave workshops at the AQJT festival in Sherbrooke, inspiring several *jeune théâtre* troupes to experiment with giant marionettes (see PUPPET THEATRE) and street theatre. In addition, Sherbrooke's Théâtre du Sang Neuf worked closely with members of the San Francisco Mime Troupe. The *jeune théâtre* troupes frequently proclaimed their affinity with experimental theatres elsewhere, whereas in English Canada alternate theatre tended to downplay such influences. Although in both cultures the new movement was an expression of nationalist ideology, the forms that expression took differed greatly.

1. *English Canada*. Although there had been previous attempts to establish professional theatres in opposition to a dominant aesthetic model (notably, the Theatre of Action in the late 1930s), alternate theatre in English Canada effectively began with the founding of TORONTO WORKSHOP PRODUCTIONS in 1959. Alternate theatre came to define itself in terms of its commitment to Canadian drama when it became apparent that the regional theatre system would offer only token support to indigenous playwriting; but this commitment itself required a gradual evolution.

With the possible exception of TWP, the first generation of alternate theatre defined itself in terms of aesthetics rather than cultural politics, although such brief theatre ventures as John HERBERT's Garret Theatre (1965) and John Palmer's Canadian Place Theatre in Stratford (1969) showed strong commitments to new Canadian plays. But it was not until the early 1970s that the issue of Canadian plays came to characterize alternate theatre; in the late 1960s as much impetus for new indigenous plays came from mainstream theatre as from alternate theatre. At first the thrust of alternate theatre was generational as the 'counter-culture' sought professional opportunities in the theatre. The three most popular productions in Toronto at the turn of the decade reflected this emphasis: at STUDIO LAB THEATRE *Dionysus in '69* ran for over a year, a record nearly matched by the ROYAL ALEXANDRA THEATRE's *Hair* and TWP's *Chicago '70* (about the trial of the Chicago Seven). In 1970 Toronto's Festival of Underground Theatre celebrated the growth of the new theatre culture with troupes from across Canada (including John JULIANI's *SAVAGE GOD* from Vancouver and Jean-Claude GERMAIN's Théâtre du Même Nom from Montreal) and from France and the United States. By this time an active 'Off-Yonge' movement in Toronto centred on Theatre Passe Muraille. TPM's encounter with police CENSORSHIP over its 1969 production of *Futz* reinforced the idea of a radical theatre for a radical generation. Even Passe Muraille's first foray into the documentary form that became its greatest contribution to Canadian drama revealed this orientation: *Doukhobors*, produced in 1971, was not so much an exercise in Canadian history as a statement of anti-establishment freedom.

Alternate theatre changed its course as companies reflected the new wave of nationalism and sought new plays to express it. Lacking suitable Canadian plays, and disposed towards collective action by the ideological fashions of the day, many troupes began creating their own plays, defining their identity and cultural base in local history. Passe Muraille's production of *The FARM SHOW* in 1972 stands as a seminal event in this movement; it signalled the preoccupation of alternate theatre with indigenous material. The new troupes gave aspiring playwrights the chance to develop their craft in co-operation with actors, and these playwrights in turn gave the theatres a new mission. Consequently many of the alternate companies became known principally for their commitment to new drama. Ken GASS's FACTORY THEATRE Lab (1970) billed itself as 'the home of the Canadian playwright' and helped pioneer the system of playwrights' workshops that would become a major feature of alternate theatre. Factory's offshoot, TARRAGON, emphasized more carefully mounted productions of plays selected for their literary values; it was perhaps the first of the alternates to achieve mainstream status in the mid-70s. The general orientation to new plays was related to the growing militancy of Canadian playwrights, who in two conferences in 1971—at Gaspé and Niagara-on-the-Lake—called for a fifty-per-cent quota of Canadian plays in all subsidized theatres. Increasingly the rhetoric of alternate theatre shed its counter-culture vocabulary, replacing it with a defensive nationalism in which analysis of Canada as a cultural colony figured prominently.

Toronto dominated the alternate-theatre movement because of its emergence as the cultural capital of English Canada, its greater population, and the presence of critics like Herbert WHITTAKER and Urjo KAREDA, who did much to encourage the new theatres. But the Toronto experience was paralleled elsewhere. In Vancouver, where it has been estimated that forty troupes surfaced in the decade before 1975, such groups as TAMAHNOUS and Savage God made a national impact; in Alberta, THEATRE NETWORK, ALBERTA THEATRE PROJECTS, THEATRE 3, and NORTHERN LIGHT THEATRE provided the basis of one of Canada's most lively theatre scenes; in Saskatoon, 25TH STREET THEATRE gave the country one of its most popular hits

Alternate Theatre

with *PAPER WHEAT*, a collective revue about the grain co-ops. The most interesting developments occurred outside the large urban areas, in regional centres and rural communities that had little or no tradition of professional theatre. In Newfoundland the Mummers Troupe emerged as Canada's most militant English-language political theatre, and CODCO as its most anarchistic comedy troupe; in Thunder Bay, KAM THEATRE Lab embarked on a program of popular political theatre on local issues (see POLITICAL AND POPULAR THEATRE); in the interior of British Columbia Theatre Energy produced a series of remarkable documentaries on community and feminist issues (see FEMINIST THEATRE), and Caravan Stage toured its populist plays on horse-drawn wagons.

By the mid-1970s the distinction between alternate and mainstream theatre had begun to blur, taking on a financial rather than an ideological definition. A turning-point occurred in 1975 when Bill GLASSCO took a sabbatical from Tarragon; Passe Muraille purchased its new home on Ryerson Ave, Toronto, with the profits from its hit play about sex, *I Love You, Baby Blue*; Gass announced a re-evaluation of Factory's policies; the Mummers Troupe moved into the LSPU (Longshoreman's Protective Union) Hall in St John's; and the increasing nationalism of the theatre profession climaxed with the controversy over the hiring of Robin PHILLIPS at the STRATFORD FESTIVAL. In the years following 1975, as alternate theatre attracted an increasingly middle-class and affluent audience and began to develop a star system of popular actors and playwrights, it generated its own alternative in the form of a flourishing, usually non-Equity, fringe theatre oriented towards experimental performance.

These new companies tend to be young and transitory, many of them formed by recent graduates from the growing number of theatre schools. Few fringe groups have theatres of their own and so concentrate on inexpensive portable shows, often with an emphasis on clowning and *commedia dell'arte*. One of the most productive venues has been Toronto's Theatre Centre, a co-operative resource space formed in 1979 by six performance research troupes (Necessary Angel, Nightwood Theatre, Buddies in Bad Times, Actor's Lab, A.K.A. Performance Interfaces, and Theatre of the Autumn Leaf). Along with Factory Theatre Lab's Brave New Works

series, the Theatre Centre's annual Rhubarb Festival has been one of the most important try-out places for new fringe work in Toronto. In Edmonton an annual Fringe Festival, begun in 1982, now features upwards of 125 shows, some of which—like Ken Brown's solo show *Life After Hockey*, produced in 1985, and Nexus Theatre's *Gimme That Prime Time Religion*, produced in 1983—have won national attention. Similar fringe festivals have been established in Victoria, Vancouver, and Winnipeg.

In English Canada, as in Quebec, the development of the contemporary fringe has been influenced strongly by avant-garde experiments elsewhere, particularly by the work of Robert Wilson and Mabou Mines in New York. This has led to the development of a performance technique that examines the semiotics of performance, creating involved metaphorical structures out of movement patterns and visual images. In this respect Toronto's Nightwood Theatre, a feminist collective, has made a major contribution. Nightwood has also produced a promising playwright in Banuta Rubess, an actress who functioned as writer in the innovative collectives that created *Smoke Damage: A Story of the Witch Hunts* and *This Is For You, Anna*, produced in 1982 and 1983 respectively. With their complex use of documentary fact, polemics, performance metaphors, and non-linear narrative structures, these two plays number among the finest Canadian work of recent years. The other major writer to emerge from the fringe is John KRIZANC, whose major works to date are *TAMARA* and *Prague* (winner of a 1987 Governor General's Award for Drama).

In English Canada, as in Quebec, alternate theatre has experienced a major reorientation since the mid-1970s. In contrast to the first generation of alternate theatre, which sought to develop indigenous theatre by performing for rural and populist audiences, the contemporary fringe is frankly urban in its interests, often demanding considerable sophistication on the part of audiences.

2. *Quebec.* If in English Canada the evolution of alternate theatre was inextricably connected to the legitimization of indigenous drama, in Quebec these two movements were more distinct. The *nouveau théâtre québécois*—the emergence of new playwrights in the wake of the Quiet Revolution that led to the founding of the Centre d'essai des auteurs

dramatiques in 1965—preceded the rise of an alternate theatrical movement oriented in the main towards collective creation. In English Canada very few companies maintained a complete commitment to collective creation; in Quebec most of the dozens of troupes that surfaced in the early 1970s practised collective creation as an ideological principle. So widespread was interest in the form that in the decade 1965-74 there were no fewer than 415 productions of collectively written plays—a figure that by far exceeds any comparable estimate for English Canada. The first collective creations were the product of student companies in the *écoles classiques* in the mid-1960s: their collages of sketches, songs, and poetry reflected the intellectual unrest and nationalism of Quebec youth.

In contrast to the English-Canadian alternate theatre, the *jeune théâtre* movement brought together professional, community, and student companies that frequently changed character according to the availability of funding. The focus of the movement was the Association canadienne du théâtre d'amateurs, founded in 1958 as a Quebec affiliate of the DOMINION DRAMA FESTIVAL. In 1960 ACTA comprised twenty-seven francophone troupes across Canada; during the course of the next decade its membership became increasingly committed to Québécois nationalism and original dramaturgy. In 1968 ACTA redefined itself as an association of non-union troupes and in 1972, recognizing the political transformation that had taken place, changed its name to the Association québécois du jeune théâtre. It continued its annual congresses and festivals but the focus was now on the new professional, or at least semi-professional, troupes.

The companies that made up AQJT fell into three overlapping categories: experimental-performance research troupes like L'ESKABEL and Les Enfants du Paradis (now called CARBONE 14); regionally based politically conscious popular theatres such as Victoriaville's Théâtre Parminou and Rimouski's Les Gens d'en Bas; and militant political troupes like Théâtre Euh! and Théâtre d'la Shop. All owed much to the two major pioneers of the *jeune théâtre*: Jean-Claude GERMAIN's Théâtre du Même Nom (a dig at Montreal's established THÉÂTRE DU NOUVEAU MONDE) and Le Grand Cirque Ordinaire (GCO). Founded in 1969 by the senior class of the French section of the NATIONAL THEATRE SCHOOL,

GCO toured its 'sociopoétique' political clown shows to rural areas. As was the case with TMN and the GCO, most of the *jeune théâtre* troupes were more overtly political than their English-Canadian counterparts. The differences between most *jeune théâtre* troupes and the radicalism of a group like Théâtre Euh! was the latter's affiliation with the Marxist-Leninist party En Lutte.

In the years before 1975 the membership of AQJT grew increasingly militant in its politics, reflecting the intellectual ferment in Quebec in the years leading up to the election of the Parti Québécois in 1976. In 1974 the membership of AQJT elected a radical slate to the association's executive; but instead of radicalizing the movement further, this led to a schism that was resolved only in 1975 when Théâtre Euh! led a walkout of militant troupes. Their reasons for quitting the association were published in AQJT's organ *Jeune Théâtre* as 'Manifeste pour un théâtre au service du peuple'.

Following this split AQJT took a more moderate course. As happened in English Canada, the theatres grew more specialized in their aesthetic and political aims. Companies such as Quebec City's Théâtre de Quartier sought to develop working-class audiences; Théâtre sans détour introduced the 'Theatre of the Oppressed' techniques of Augusto Boal; and the Théâtre expérimental des femmes initiated an annual festival of feminist theatre.

The twenty years of the *jeune théâtre* movement produced as many new theatres in Quebec as there were in all of English Canada, with a corresponding diversity of orientations and specializations. In English Canada the popularity of historical drama and carefully researched documentary theatre indicated a need for empirical evidence to support the idea of a unique Canadian culture; in Quebec, with that evidence inherent in the language and history, the theatre took a more imaginative direction. Hence the widespread popularity of street parades and circus technique, the vigorously physical acting style and, in the experimental theatres, the pronounced emphasis on MIME and scenography.

In English Canada and Quebec alike alternate theatre of the 1970s provided the foundation for the more diverse professional theatre of the 1980s. The impact of the movement can be felt in every aspect of Canadian theatre: in new forms of drama, in new

Alternate Theatre

approaches to design and directing, in new critical perspectives (reflecting a new generation of critics whose attitudes and tastes have been shaped by alternate theatre), and perhaps most importantly in new styles of acting.

Despite these accomplishments a sizeable gap remains between the physical resources and budgets of the theatres committed to new work and Canadian plays and the regional theatres whose policies have changed little since they were first challenged by alternate theatre.

See Jean-Cléo Godin and Laurent Mailhot, *Théâtre québécois II* (1980); Renate Usmiani, *Second Stage: The Alternative Theatre Movement in Canada* (1984); Alan Filewod, *Collective Encounters: Documentary Theatre in English Canada* (1987).   ALAN FILEWOD

Amerindian and Inuit Theatre.

1. *Amerindian Ritual Drama.* The earliest Amerindian ritual dramas were those of the shamans, or spirit-priests (also called magicians, sorcerers, and doctors), who originated in paleolithic times and came to North America with the Indians and Inuit. Their performance tradition can be found among tribal peoples in Siberia, Australia, the Kalahari, and Southeast Asia. In Canada the shamanic ritual drama is of two related kinds: secret initiations and public performances to improve the community's well-being, both of which relate to the trance state and still exist. An initiate in a trance undergoes a

Kwakiutl Hamatsa dance

'death-and-resurrection' ritual to gain power from spirits of various kinds—often a great white bear in the Arctic and sometimes 'the ancestors' among Indians. This power is used in later rituals to help the community overcome tribal crises, to change the weather, cure illness, or solve other problems. In these trance performances the shaman's soul travels to 'the other reality' to gain power. Similar in function to rituals found, for example, in ancient Greece and medieval Europe (performers dancing down church aisles dressed in skins and horns), these shamanistic experiences are illustrated in thousands of North American rock carvings of skeletal humans meeting skeletal birds, fish, animals, and monsters.

The shaman's power is exhibited in a highly theatrical public display. Known as a 'transformer', he assumes the roles of all types of spirits, using masks, dance, different voices, and ventriloquism to act out his encounters and his battles with them. The audience participates as a chorus: singing, chanting, joining in the dialogue with the spirits, and interpreting the shaman's actions. Formally they acted as 'witnesses' (in a Biblical sense) to the shaman's performance and success. These characteristics became models for other Inuit and Indian ritual dramas.

There was once a great variety of ritual drama in Canada, including the Micmacs' marriage and funeral rituals, the prairie Sun Dance, the Ojibways' War Dance, the Crees' Shaking Tent ceremony, and many others that wilted under white domination. The Iroquois False Face 'society' performed curing rituals based on the battle of good spirits against the False Faces—bad spirits who bring disease and destruction. Elements of these rituals, in which actors wearing horrifying masks of the Faces attempt to control evil and eradicate disease, remain.

Most spectacular were the rituals of the Pacific Northwest Coast Indians, which are now being successfully revived. They took a variety of forms. (1) The ubiquitous shamanic displays, which still occur among the Tlingit, although they have been significantly reduced. (2) The 'spirit quest', which grew into the Coast Salish 'spirit dance', a communal ceremony where individuals dance to be possessed by their tutelary spirits; in the past it was performed nightly through the winter, but today it occurs on Saturday nights. (3) The 'potlatch', a drama in which

The Rainbow Creek Dancers, British Columbia

the community 'witnessed' an increase in status for the chief or family member. Under white influence the 'potlatch' became increasingly extravagant 'giving-aways' of all property until the native economy collapsed. (4) The 'spirit play', a complex cycle performed every night throughout the winter, combining many origin myths designed to renew the community spiritually; the most famous contemporary performance is 'Ksan', a reconstruction by the Tshimshian people of Hazleton, B.C., that was presented at the NATIONAL ARTS CENTRE, Ottawa, in 1972. (5) There are also ritual dramas particular to one people. A major example is the 'Xwe-Xwe' performance of the Coast Salish: it is the people's only masked presentation, utilizing a gigantic wooden mask that rests on the shoulders and is held with the teeth. Based on a 'death-and-resurrection' myth about a particular Indian (rather than about a spirit), it is not regularly performed but is danced to celebrate occasions as the Salish determine.

2. *Amerindian Masks*. Indians change face-paint with the seasons in ritual dramatizations of humans as spirits. Masks extend this idea: the actor-dancer becomes the spirit through the power of the mask, while other performers acknowledge that a spirit is present in the mask. The most spectacular masks are those of the Pacific Coast peoples, all of

whom (with the exception of the Coast Salish) have a great many. The oldest are shamanic, representing spirits used by sorcerers. Some are hominoid. Many face and head masks (realistically carved in wood and painted) represent birds, fish, beasts, and monsters—roles in the ritual dramas—and are superbly conceived and designed in relation to highly realistic costumes. Some masks have parts that move in performance; in some cases a mask springs open to reveal a second underneath. Some head masks are enormous: a Raven, for example, with a five-foot beak that opens and clacks.

3. *Amerindian Scenecraft*. Shamans were

Kwakiutl Hamatsa mask

21

Amerindian and Inuit Theatre

masters of theatrical illusion, best exemplified in Mystery Cycles of the Pacific northwest coast, particularly those of the Nootka and southern Kwakiutl tribes. The flickering firelight of the longhouse was controlled for sudden appearances and disappearances, and actual scenes of supposed bloody murder and dismemberment. Magic quartz crystals gave light and birds (puppets) flew around the house. A gigantic face painted on a curtain suddenly became three-dimensional and moved. Screens were devised to part or to sink into the ground for 'revelations' that paralleled European Renaissance scenecraft—except that the Indians operated them by manpower rather than by machinery.

4. *Amerindian Stages*. While most Indians performed rituals in and around the tepee, Indians of British Columbia had large wooden longhouses containing a variety of acting areas. They ranged from arenas for performances like the 'spirit dance' of the Coast Salish to open- or end-stages, sometimes with raised platforms. There remain also intriguing relics such as the last-known wooden platform, which stood outside the Cowichan (Coast Salish) longhouse and was used for 'giving-aways'; it was strikingly similar to both the early wooden stage in the Theatre of Dionysus in Athens and the medieval stage at Valenciennes.

5. *Inuit Theatre*. Inuit (Eskimos) came across the Bering Strait from Siberia into the Arctic at least 5,000 years ago, bringing shamans (called 'angakok', including women) and the ritual drama of their religious ceremonies. At initiation the Inuit shaman was ritually 'killed' by the spirit of a great white bear that devoured his flesh. He acquired the power to see himself as a skeleton and gave each bone its secret name; the spirit then 'spewed him out' and he was 'reborn' as a shaman with spirit power, which he used for the benefit of the community in other highly theatrical displays. Less common in Canada than Alaska, Inuit 'spirit-plays' (ritual dramas) were performed by the whole community in 'societies'. In addition, the three-day Sedna festival each fall celebrated the ritual-myth of the death and resurrection of Sedna, a mermaid-like spirit. These communal dramas included various group mimetic and theatrical performances, such as a ritual battle with a final 'resurrection', harpooning, hunting, and the like. Special igloos, called 'Kaggi' in the Yukon, were built for ritual

dramas; each was circular with a special acting-area and seats arranged according to social status. Contemporary Inuit troupes occasionally tour spirit dances and elements of 'spirit-plays'.   RICHARD COURTNEY

Amos, Janet (b. 1945). Actress, director, and artistic director, she began acting at the age of eight with Dora Mavor MOORE in the NEW PLAY SOCIETY, Toronto. While a student at the Univ. of Toronto, she secured her first professional engagement with THEATRE TORONTO in 1968.

From 1972 to 1976 she worked as an actress with THEATRE PASSE MURAILLE in such collectives as *The FARM SHOW*, *1837*, *The Farmers' Revolt*, and *Them Donnellys*. For the same company (in 1974, 1976, and 1979 respectively), she directed Dennis Lee's *Alligator Pie*, Judy Steed's *Operational Finger Pinkie*, and Janis Rapoport's *Dreamgirls*. In 1979 she became associate director, with James Roy, of Ontario's BLYTH FESTIVAL. As artistic director at Blyth, 1980-4, she concentrated exclusively on new Canadian works by Ted JOHNS, Anne CHISLETT, Peter Colley, and others.

From 1984 to 1988 Amos was artistic director of THEATRE NEW BRUNSWICK, to which she also brought a Canadian emphasis. Her acting at TNB was highly praised, particularly her Maureen in Chislett's *The Tomorrow Box*.   EDWARD MULLALY

Anderson, John Murray (1886-1954). Born in St John's, Nfld, and educated in Edinburgh and Switzerland, he immigrated to New York in 1910. Beginning as a ballroom dancer, he married his partner Genevieve Lyon in 1914. His first success as a producer, *The Greenwich Village Follies*, 1919, pioneered a cadre of Broadway revues remembered for their style and sophistication. He staged thirty-four major musical comedies and revues (twenty-nine on Broadway, five in London) as well as seven circuses for Ringling Brothers, four Aquacades for Billy Rose, eleven pageants, sixty-one movie-house stage shows, and twenty-four elaborate nightclub entertainments. His Broadway productions (he was known as 'Uncle Broadway') included *Knickerbocker* in 1925, *The Ziegfeld Follies* of 1934, 1936, and 1943, and *John Murray Anderson's Almanac* in 1953. In addition to the lyrics for sixty-four songs, he produced three films (*The King of Jazz*, *Lilies of Broadway*, and *Bathing Beauty* starring Esther Williams) and wrote several plays.

See Anderson's memoir *Out Without My Rubbers* (1954).   DAVID GARDNER

Andre, Marion (b. 1920). A native of Poland, where he was active in the Polish underground during the Second World War, Marion Andre Czerniecki immigrated to Canada in 1957. He taught in Montreal schools and at McGill Univ. before being appointed artistic director of the SAIDYE BRONFMAN CENTRE in 1967. In 1972 he moved to Toronto where, after teaching briefly at York Univ., he founded his own theatre company, THEATRE PLUS, and remained artistic director until his retirement in 1985.

Although he is active as a director and playwright, Andre's greatest contribution to Canadian theatre has been as a producer and vigorous advocate of the importance of theatre to the country's social fabric. He cultivated the development of year-round serious theatre in Toronto by producing plays during the summer months of undeniable artistic merit, intellectual force, and socio-political import. Convinced that exposure to outstanding foreign plays would stimulate and enrich Canadian theatre, he brought to audiences in Montreal and Toronto the work (in translation) of many acknowledged masters of contemporary European and American drama, and Theatre Plus became known for its productions of such writers as Jean Anouilh, Friedrich Dürrenmatt, Jean Giraudoux, and Arthur Miller.

Andre views the theatre as a vehicle of moral and political enlightenment and as a forum for grappling with the most significant contemporary issues and ideological conflicts. This orientation has been the motivating force behind all of his theatre work, and has pervaded his own productions at Theatre Plus of such plays as Clifford Odets' *Awake and Sing* in Sept. 1977, Trevor Griffiths' *Occupations* in May 1979, and Michael COOK's *The Gayden Chronicles* in May 1982.

As a director, Andre has tended to select the works of European writers preoccupied, like himself, with the moral and social dislocation of European consciousness prior to and following the Second World War. His productions, frequently praised for their passion and high seriousness, were nonetheless marred by a recurring stridency of tone that detracted from the subtleties of theme and characterization for which these dramatists are widely admired.

In addition to his theatre work, Andre has written short stories, essays, and television and radio scripts. His plays include *The Sand* (produced at York Univ. and published in 1979), *The Invented Lover* (co-written with Martin Bronstein, produced by Theatre Plus in 1980 and published in 1982), and *The Aching Heart of Samuel Kleinerman* (produced at Toronto's Town Hall in the ST LAWRENCE CENTRE in 1984 and published in 1986). The last of these, produced and directed by the author, portrays the ethical dilemma confronting a German-Jewish family whose members are compelled to choose between their own survival and their moral integrity, which can be preserved only by sacrificing their own security to help another family escape the Nazis. The play illustrates Andre's strengths and weaknesses as a writer: on the one hand, his seriousness of theme, sympathy for human suffering, and passionate commitment to humane values; on the other a tendency towards stilted dialogue, one-dimensional characterization, and contrived plots.

Since retiring from Theatre Plus, Andre has continued to work as a freelance director.
                                    IRA A. LEVINE

Angel, Leonard (b. 1945). Born and raised in Montreal, where he studied at McGill Univ. (BA, 1966), he has since lived in Vancouver, studying at the Univ. of British Columbia (Ph.D., 1974) and lecturing in universities in Creative Writing, Philosophy, and Religious Studies. His *How the English Took Quebec and Kept It* won first prize in the B.C. Centennial Playwrights' Competition, 1971. His best play is *The Unveiling* (1982), first produced by the NEW PLAY CENTRE, Vancouver, in 1982, a subdued, carefully observed piece in which the traditional unveiling of a tombstone in a Montreal graveyard leads to unmaskings in a Jewish family. In the one-act *After Antietam* (1978), first produced by the New Play Centre in 1976, a Confederate soldier meets a Southern woman after the Civil War battle. Angel's other plays including *Forthcoming Wedding* (1975), a one-act produced at FACTORY THEATRE Lab in 1972, a sinister drawing room comedy; *Eleanor Marx*, a large-cast biography produced at the Univ. of B.C. in 1983; *Six of One* (1985), a one-act play for a multi-racial cast of dancers, produced at the New Play Centre in 1985; *3,000 Years of Sexual Politics*, dialogues between Menelaus and Helen and between Bernard Shaw and Isadora Duncan, first produced at the Waterfront Theatre, Vancouver, 1986; and *Dancing on the Head of a Pin with a Mouse in My Pocket*, nine vignettes for a disabled cast, performed during Expo 1986.   MALCOLM PAGE

Anglin, Margaret (1876-1958). Born in Ottawa, she was the daughter of Timothy Warren Anglin, Speaker of the House of Commons, and Ellen (McTavish) Anglin, an accomplished amateur actress. While training at the Stanhope-Wheatcroft Dramatic School in New York, she was engaged by Charles Frohman to play Madeline West in Bronson Howard's *Shenandoah* in 1894. North American tours with leading companies (1894-8)—including James O'Neill's—led in 1898 to an all-Canadian tour with her own company in which she charmed audiences with her 'dainty, svelte figure', 'riante, sparkling face', and 'golden' voice as Rosalind in *As You Like It* and other roles. Her bewitching Roxanne to Richard Mansfield's Cyrano de Bergerac in the 1898 North American pre-mière of Rostand's play helped secure an engagement from 1899 to 1903 with Charles Frohman's Empire Theatre in New York, where her finest achievement was the title role in Henry Arthur Jones's *Mrs. Dane's Defence* in 1900. Deep feeling, subtle effects, intelligence, and consistent 'naturalness' defined her acting style, qualities she exploited brilliantly as Ruth Jordan, opposite Henry Miller, in the New York première of William Vaughan Moody's *The Great Divide* on 3 Oct. 1906.

Dissatisfaction with commercial theatre inspired her production of *Antigone* in the Hearst Greek Theatre at the Univ. of California, Berkeley, on 30 June 1910. Eschewing an academic approach, she re-animated only some of the conventions of ancient Greek theatre to recapture its 'spiritual exaltation'. In this and subsequent productions of *Electra*, *Medea*, *Iphigenia in Aulis*, and *Hippolytus* (to 1927), her own performances (according to Montreal critic Samuel MORGAN-POWELL) revealed 'a sombre strength, a vivid, startling, arresting dominance, a sheer beauty of tragic magnetism'. In 1913-14 she became one of the first to produce Shakespeare in the non-representational, symbolic 'new stage-craft' style: critics admired the poeticized *mise-en-scène* but thought her robust acting somewhat ill-suited to Shakespeare's hero-ines. However, in the literate plays of Oscar Wilde and R.B. Sheridan she was imperious, lively, and graceful, drawing generously from her own high-spirited yet well-bred temper-ament. She retired from the stage in 1943 after a North American tour in Lillian Hell-man's *Watch on the Rhine*—which played for a week at Toronto's ROYAL ALEXANDRA THEATRE in Feb. 1943—and a California tour as Mrs Malaprop in Sheridan's *The Rivals*. She acted in RADIO DRAMA and did poetry readings from 1943 to 1950 and made numerous abortive efforts to get back into the theatre as an actress-producer.

Anglin married the American actor How-ard Hull in 1911. In 1952 she moved to Toronto where she died six years later.

See John LeVay, *Margaret Anglin, a Stage Life* (1988).   DENIS SALTER

Anne of Green Gables. A novel by L.M. Montgomery (1874-1942) first published in 1908, it has undergone innumerable reprint-ings and translations and has been adapted for radio, stage, television, and feature-film production, both in Canada and abroad. The success of the novel derives from the natural appeal of Montgomery's winsome red-haired orphan and her inevitable collision with the restrictive Presbyterian society of late nine-teenth-century Prince Edward Island.

A somewhat sentimentalized musical ver-sion of *Anne of Green Gables*, commissioned by the CHARLOTTETOWN FESTIVAL, pre-mièred there on 27 July 1965. Don HARRON adapted the book, Norman Campbell wrote the music, and the lyrics were the collabo-rative effort of Don Harron, Mavor MOORE, Norman Campbell, and Elaine Campbell. Directed and choreographed for many years by Alan Lund, it has become both a mainstay of the Festival and the most popular musical in Canadian theatre history.

A non-musical play based on *Anne of Green Gables*, written by Andrzej Konic, has been extremely popular in Poland, achieving sev-eral thousand performances since its première in 1963. It has played continuously at War-saw's Popular Theatre since 1974 and toured Czechoslovakia in 1980.

The novel was adapted for television in

France (1957), Poland (1958), and England (1972). In 1985 a Canadian adaptation by Joe Wiesenfeld and Kevin Sullivan, produced by Kevin Sullivan, was broadcast in Canada and the U.S. Breaking Canadian TV viewing records and winning numerous awards, it featured notable performances by Megan Follows (Anne), Colleen Dewhurst (Marilla), and Richard Farnsworth (Matthew). Feature films were made of the novel in 1919 and 1940. MARY RUBIO

Apprentis-Sorciers, Les. Founded in 1955 by Jean Bellemare and Jean-Guy SABOURIN, who was artistic director from 1956 to 1966, this amateur company performed in a number of temporary venues before establishing itself in 1957 on Davidson St, Montreal, in a former bakery. In these cramped quarters, with only three rows of seats, the quality of their production of Eugène Ionesco's *The Chairs* (*Les Chaises*), led Gratien GÉLINAS to invite the company to perform at the COMÉDIE-CANADIENNE on 27 Apr. 1958. Also in 1958 the company rented new premises on De Lanaudière, transforming an old printing house into a forty-nine-seat theatre, the Boulangerie, from designs by architect Gérard Pratte and with décor by Fernand Pratte. The company produced plays by Bertolt Brecht, Friedrich Dürenmatt, Maxim Gorky, and Arthur Adamov on the 15' × 18' stage.

Between 1958 and 1962 Les Apprentis-Sorciers expanded their membership, repertoire, and seasons. Their skills reached professional levels, but disagreements about a repertoire that fluctuated between the avant-garde and theatre of social commitment caused eighteen members to break away in 1962 to form Les SALTIMBANQUES, whose focus was on the avant-garde. Les Apprentis-Sorciers quickly regrouped, however, achieving success with Pierre Perrault's *Au Coeur de la rose* and Bertolt Brecht's *Mr. Puntia and His Hired Man Matti* (*Maître Puntia et son valet Matti*).

In the summer of 1965 the group represented Quebec at the Third Amateur Dramatic Festival in Monaco, where they staged a second play by Pierre Perrault, *C'est l'Enterrement de Nicodème, tout le monde est invité*. During 1965-6 the company was inactive, having been evicted from their theatre. They eventually moved to new premises on Papineau St, where they realized the dreams of their chief set designer, Claude Sabourin: a

flexible theatre that could be altered to suit each show. Under the direction of Jean-Pierre Saulnier, their first season there (and their last regular season) included Max Frisch's *Andorra*, Edward Albee's *Zoo Story*, Maxim Gorky's *Petits-bourgeois*, and Quebec playwright Yerri Kemf's *Une Simple Mécanique*. The dynamism and stability of Les Apprentis-Sorciers, however, had diminished, and in 1968 they joined with Les Saltimbanques and Le Mouvement Contemporain to form Le Centre du THÉÂTRE D'AUJOURD'HUI.

Through twelve seasons of challenging contemporary repertoire and innovative staging on meagre resources—the company never charged admission and received only minimal grants—Les Apprentis-Sorciers presented Montreal audiences with a genuine alternative to the prevailing theatrical taste. MADELEINE GREFFARD

Archambault, Joseph-Sergius ('**Palmieri**') (1871-1950). Born in Terrebonne, near Montreal, he was educated at Collège Saint-Laurent and the Université de Montréal, graduating in law in 1897. After several stage appearances at the Collège under the direction of the Rev P. Vanier, he played the role of Palmieri (from which he took his pseudonym) in an amateur production of Adolphe D'Ennery's *Martyre* at the MONUMENT NATIONAL in June 1896. He was subsequently hired by Léon Petitjean for the Variétés company (founded by Petitjean in Nov. 1898), where 'his remarkable diction and his natural gestures' brought him public esteem. From Sept. 1900 to June 1910 Archambault acted with Georges Gauvreau's THÉÂTRE NATIONAL where, along with two other Québécois actors, Jean-Paul Filion and Elzéar Hamel, he became a great success. He took part in outstanding productions of Louis Guyon's *Denis le Patriote* (Sept. 1902), *Jos Montferrand* (Oct. 1903), and *Montcalm* (Nov. 1907). Though more at home with dramatic roles than with comedy, he took part in revues written by Georges Dumestre and Ernest Tremblay for the Théâtre National between 1908 and 1910.

In June 1910 Archambault moved to Quebec City, where for one season he managed the Théâtre Populaire de la Place Jacques-Cartier (see THÉÂTRE DE LA PLACE JACQUES-CARTIER), with Paul Marcel and Henriette Ducange. In 1911 he returned to Montreal, first to Les Nouveautés, and then he followed Julien DAOUST to the THÉÂTRE CANADIEN.

Archambault

In June 1916 he was hired by the Chanteclerc, and became its director in 1918. One year later he retired to Chambly.

A serious, conscientious artist, specializing in dramatic roles, Archambault was one of the most famous French-Canadian actors of his time, although he was never able to compete with the French actors who dominated the local professional groups.

See his memoirs, *Mes Souvenirs de théâtre* (1944).   JEAN-MARC LARRUE

Archibald Cameron of Locheill, ou Un épisode de la Guerre de Sept Ans. Adapted by Joseph-Camille Caisse (1841-1914) and Pierre-Arcade Laporte (1833-1920) from Philippe Aubert de Gaspé's *Les Anciens Canadiens* (the most important novel of nineteenth-century Quebec), this three-act play was first performed at the Collège de l'Assomption, in the town of L'Assomption (where Caisse and Laporte were instructors), on 19 Jan. 1865.

The play opens in the French camp the night before the Battle of the Plains of Abraham. The two protagonists, Jules d'Haberville and Archibald (Arché) Cameron of Locheill, had been college friends in Quebec and lived as brothers before the war began. Under orders from the villain of the piece, Major Montgomery, Arché has burned houses and destroyed crops, including those of the d'Haberville family. For this he is now despised by Jules. After an expository act that is close to the original novel, Act 2 is digressive: Arché, captured by Indians, is rescued from death by another Canadian, Dumais, whose life the young Scot had once saved. Act 2 ends with a *tableau vivant* showing the Battle of the Plains; Act 3 begins a few hours after the battle. Jules has distinguished himself on the French side, Arché on the English, despite an attempt by his nemesis, Montgomery, to have him killed. Jules and Arché meet by chance and, in a poignant scene, the two are reconciled: they will live henceforth in harmony, as will the two cultures they represent.

This play was a favourite on college stages well into the twentieth century. The text was published, with minor changes (by J.G.W. McGown), in 1894, with the title of the original novel. See L.E. Doucette, *Theatre in French Canada, 1606-1867* (1984).

                                    L.E. DOUCETTE

Architecture. Canada has a considerable number of theatre buildings that collectively exhibit a great variety of form, style, and purpose. This variety is related in part to the nature of the country's history and geography and in part to the fact that the design of performing-arts buildings throughout the western world has been in a state of flux for the last hundred years—coincidentally the period in which Canada built virtually all of its theatres. But even though there is no single style of theatre design, past or present, Canada does have in its theatre buildings an architectural legacy of identifiable eras, trends, and influences. Individually these buildings (many of which have separate entries in this book) have their own historical importance; collectively they are a paradigm of Canada's cultural development.

The Frontier Era 'Opera House'. While there are records to indicate professional play production in Saint John, Halifax, Montreal, and other centres in the closing years of the eighteenth century, there is relatively little information about the venues in which these plays were performed. The first formal theatres in Canada were built in the major cities in the early decades of the nineteenth century. (Unfortunately none have survived.) These early theatres were frame-construction buildings, with a simple flat-floored rectangular auditorium and a small proscenium arch that opened into a small stage that had little or no fly loft. The auditorium was sparsely decorated and often contained a balcony. Boxes frequently flanked the proscenium. There was little, if any, public-lobby area. Though modest in both dimensions and appointments, these facilities were often known as 'opera houses', although they served all the performing arts and a multitude of other public-assembly functions. Most communities in Ontario had a facility of this type, such as that in Petrolia (1889), which was brought back into use in 1975 until gutted by fire in 1989.

Early Commercial Theatres. These buildings differed from their 'opera house' predecessors in that they were built in a formal style based on European or American models. The ROYAL ALEXANDRA THEATRE (1907) in Toronto was influenced by buildings designed for the great era of pre-First World War commercial theatre in New York. It has a formal façade and an equally distinguished interior. Its plan also reflects a spatial sophistication and generosity not seen in theatres of the previous era. The Royal Alexandra is also notable for the square rather than rectangular plan of its auditorium and its well-developed facilities for both performers and the public. The NEPTUNE THEATRE in Halifax (built as the Strand in 1915), though considerably smaller than the Royal Alexandra, was designed with the same planning philosophy, except for its façade. The Strand's presence on the street consisted only of its marquee. The auditorium itself is located mid-block in order to make the best use of less-expensive downtown land without sacrificing the benefits of a downtown location.

Movie-Era Theatres. By the beginning of the First World War the movies had begun to establish themselves as the pre-eminent form of mass entertainment and were quickly supplanting live performance. Many of the business interests that controlled film and live shows also owned the venues and the building style favoured by these owners predominated in the period between the wars. In 1913 the Loew's theatre chain opened a major building in downtown Toronto consisting of a 2,149-seat 'continuous run' VAUDEVILLE house called Loew's Yonge Street Theatre on top of which was the 1,410-seat Winter Garden Theatre decorated to simulate a romantic garden setting. (See ELGIN AND WINTER GARDEN THEATRES.) Both auditoriums had a single balcony. These theatres alternated between live entertainment and movies and together represent an evolutionary step from theatre for live performance to the ornate and atmospheric movie palaces to come. Ottawa's Capitol Theatre, which opened in 1920 as Loew's Theatre, also housed vaudeville and touring companies. It was demolished in 1970.

The Post-War 'Multi-Purpose' Auditorium. This North American creation challenged the European tradition of building distinctly different facilities for the performance of opera, symphonic music, chamber music, and plays. Well-intentioned promoters of the multi-purpose auditorium expected that it would serve all these disciplines and serve them equally well, though the needs of opera inevitably proved incompatible with those of, say, chamber music, or even plays. The Jubilee Auditoriums in Edmonton and Calgary—which both seat 2,700 and were built in 1955 to celebrate the fiftieth anniversary of the province of Alberta—are the earliest Canadian examples of the multi-purpose performing-arts facility and are a testament to the belief that a very large seating capacity was the paramount design consideration. Similar facilities—the QUEEN ELIZABETH THEATRE in Vancouver (1959) and the O'KEEFE CENTRE in Toronto (1960), for example—were also constructed. To its credit, this type of facility did have a large stage house, large lobbies, adequate ancillary spaces, and was more fully equipped than any of its predecessors.

Festival and Regional Theatres. The rise of festival and regional theatres, which began with the construction of the permanent STRATFORD FESTIVAL theatre in 1957, marked a new era in Canadian theatre building. This was a time when full-time professional companies built well-designed and well-equipped buildings for their own specific and exclusive purposes. The buildings included generous public spaces, administrative offices, rehearsal rooms, and fabricating shops.

Stratford is the patriarch of Canadian theatre festivals and the Festival Theatre is perhaps Canada's best-known performing-arts building. It is also the most successful open-stage facility. Though built to serve a repertory of Shakespearean plays, the auditorium is designed on the model of a Greek theatre in the fifth century BC, with the addition of a balcony (which the Greeks might have included had they had the technology). The Festival Theatre is most notable for the fact that none of its spectators (2,262 in 1987) is seated more than sixty-five feet from the stage.

The MANITOBA THEATRE CENTRE (founded in 1958) is acknowledged to be Canada's first regional theatre company. In 1970 MTC built an asymmetrical proscenium-style playhouse that reflected the needs of a resident producing company for administrative, shop, and rehearsal space in the same building as the performing space. The SHAW FESTIVAL Theatre (1973) is also a facility whose auditorium reflects a return to a more traditional style.

Educational Theatre Facilities. The majority of Canadian performing-arts facilities are owned by governments or educational institutions. One of the earliest and most notable of these is HART HOUSE THEATRE (1919). The boom period for educational theatre building, however, began in the 1960s and continued through the 1970s as boards of education, community colleges, and universities con-

Architecture

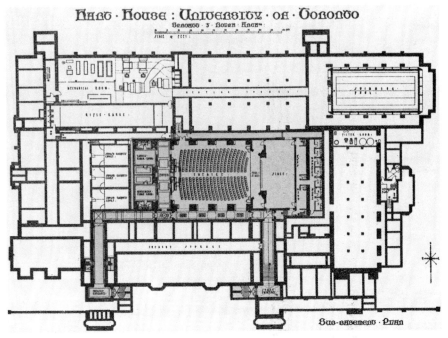

Plan showing the relation of Hart House Theatre to Hart House, University of Toronto

structed a host of poorly designed and poorly equipped facilities that were individually an embarrassment and collectively an opportunity squandered. With some notable exceptions—such as the Frederic Wood Theatre (1964) at the University of British Columbia—these buildings ignored many of the fundamental requirements of theatre design, including adequate seating and sightlines and sufficient stage and ancillary space.

The 'Black Box'. This is a small drama facility whose fashion came and went in about a decade. It had two manifestations: the first was an informal version that adapted any large existing space—most often a warehouse—as a theatre; the second was a purpose-built room of three thousand to four thousand square feet, more or less square in plan, at least two storeys high, with a flat floor, a gallery running around all four walls, and a technical grid over the entire area. Both versions were founded on the belief that drama needed a 'neutral space' that could be shaped into any playing form (arena, thrust, end stage) simply by rearranging the seating. These rooms were comparatively cheap to build and were often constructed as part of a complex of larger spaces, as if admitting a need for intimacy that the accompanying

spaces could not fulfil. Le GRAND THÉÂTRE DE QUÉBEC (1971), the NATIONAL ARTS CENTRE (1969), and Hamilton Place (1973) each included a room of this type as part of the complex. The 'black box' eventually fell somewhat out of favour because its compromises in seating, sightlines, and general ambience seemed to turn audiences away, and because changing the space into different configurations became costly and cumbersome.

Adaptive Re-use. By the early 1970s new play production in Canada was flourishing and theatre companies were being formed in every major city. There was an ensuing and

Young People's Theatre, Toronto

28

immediate need to house these companies, most of which were producing full seasons of plays. Since existing performance spaces were usually already occupied, and since time was short and financial resources small, these companies looked for any kind of building—church, warehouse, industrial building, community hall—that could meet the two essential demands of performing-arts uses: capability of creating free-span space and capability of conforming to public safety and building standards. Many of the theatres that began in re-used buildings, however, soon outgrew these facilities and moved on to purpose-built facilities (for example the CITADEL in Edmonton, the ARTS CLUB in Vancouver), while other facilities (such as TORONTO FREE THEATRE and YOUNG PEOPLE'S THEATRE) have undergone one or more subsequent major renovations.

Restoration of Historic Theatres. It has become evident that theatres in downtown locations are major economic assets. While many such buildings have been lost because of their land value or have been subdivided into small cinemas, a few have been rescued and returned to their original glory. The GRAND OPERA HOUSE, London, which opened in 1901 (after the original 1881 building burned down), was the flagship of a group of theatres built by impresario Ambrose J. SMALL. The theatre had a mid-block location and a typically modest street-front presence, while the auditorium was located in the centre of the block. After the London Little Theatre, which had acquired the building, was replaced by a professional company in 1971, the theatre was renovated and supplemented with space to accommodate offices, shops, rehearsal space, and a studio theatre. Re-opened in 1978, the building won the Governor General's medal for architecture, the only theatre in Canada to have been so honoured. Other recent renovations have included the Elgin and Winter Garden in Toronto, the King's Playhouse in Georgetown, PEI, and the Pantages (formerly the Imperial) in Toronto.

Present Trends. There are two current trends in theatre architecture that augur well for the future. The first is that most major municipalities in Canada are now planning, or have recently built, facilities for the performing arts—examples include the Markham Theatre in Markham, Ont., the Arden Theatre in St Albert, Alta, the Richmond Gateway in Richmond, B.C., the Centre-pointe Theatre in Nepean, Ont., the SUDBURY THEATRE CENTRE, the Northern Arts and Culture Centre in Yellowknife, and the Calgary Centre for the Performing Arts. The second is that they are being built with a better understanding of both the fundamentals and the subtleties of theatre design than at any previous point in Canadian history.

BRIAN ARNOTT

Archives and Collections. Theatrical collections, as well as the theatrical materials to be found in libraries and museums, have long been recognized in most countries as necessary adjuncts to theatrical production. Particularly important are collections of the artistic and administrative records of performance. Canada has sometimes been slow to appreciate and to collect records of its theatrical past. Only in recent years has a substantial amount of this fugitive material been collected and preserved for exhibition and study, and a great deal of the country's theatre history is still undocumented. If this is regrettable, it is also a challenge. The growth of Canadian theatre research and appreciation largely depends on the development of Canadian archival resources. With the expansion of teaching programs in the field, there is an urgent need to locate additional documents in order to promote teaching, research, and publication.

Most items of interest to researchers are to be found in the collections of federal and provincial archives, university libraries, public libraries, historical societies, and museums, although some are also in private hands. The National Archives of Canada in Ottawa, the principal government archives, has a well established program for the acquisition of the papers of Canadians and Canadian organizations prominent in the cultural field. The National Library of Canada has compiled inventories of materials in Canadian library collections, including surveys of theatre, dance, and music resources. In Calgary, the Glenbow- Alberta Institute contains well-organized archives of documents on western Canadian development that includes material on the CHAUTAUQUA movement as well as the papers of such companies as THEATRE CALGARY and ALBERTA THEATRE PROJECTS. Strong collections of nineteenth-century playbills are located in the provincial archives of British Columbia and Quebec, as well as in

Archives and Collections

the New Brunswick Museum. Four institutions in Quebec now take responsibility for acquiring material relating to theatre activity in the province: La Bibliothèque nationale du Québec, Les Archives nationales du Québec, l'Université de Montréal, and l'Université du Québec à Montréal. Unfortunately there has been little or no co-ordination of acquisitions.

Universities are taking more responsibility for collecting theatre archives. The Newfoundland Performing Arts Archive Project, undertaken by Memorial Univ. in 1983, works with the theatre community to collect material on current theatre companies in the province. Dora Mavor MOORE's NEW PLAY SOCIETY collection and the long record of activities at HART HOUSE THEATRE are held at the Univ. of Toronto. Theatre resources at the Univ. of Guelph have been built up to encourage research, and in recent years the Dept. of Drama, in conjunction with the library's Archival and Special Collections, has moved rapidly to acquire the records of a number of theatre companies in Ontario, including the SHAW and BLYTH Festivals, CENTRESTAGE, THEATRE PLUS, OPEN CIRCLE, Black Theatre Canada, PHOENIX THEATRE, FACTORY THEATRE, NDWT, YOUNG PEOPLE'S, TORONTO WORKSHOP PRODUCTIONS, TARRAGON and TORONTO FREE theatres from Toronto, as well as the archives of the Professional Association of Canadian Theatres and the Association for Canadian Theatre History. The Univ. of Western Ontario's Regional History Dept. maintains interesting collections of early programs for the GRAND OPERA HOUSE and other theatres in London. Dalhousie Univ., Halifax, was the first academic institution to take an interest in the records of a theatre company; the NEPTUNE THEATRE records are now maintained in its archives. Papers of distinguished faculty and playwrights have been acquired by a number of Canadian universities: York Univ. has the papers of Mavor MOORE, Herman VOADEN, and Roy MITCHELL; McMaster Univ. has playwright John COULTER's manuscripts; and the Univ. of Calgary has built up manuscript collections of contemporary Canadian playwrights, including Sharon POLLOCK, Michael COOK, Len PETERSON, Joanna GLASS, John MURRELL, Gwen Pharis RINGWOOD, Lois KERR, and George RYGA. The Univ. of Waterloo houses the papers of John HERBERT. Concordia Univ. supports a bibliographic research and publishing resource known as the Concordia RADIO DRAMA project, based on the deposit collection of CBC radio-drama scripts. CBC TELEVISION DRAMA scripts, however, have been deposited with York Univ. This indicates again the need to co-ordinate and rationalize collection building.

The major collection of theatre resources in the country is held by the Arts Dept. of the Metropolitan Toronto Reference Library. Established in 1961, it is particularly strong in materials relating to Canadian theatre history. It includes extensive collections of playbills, posters, newspaper files, photographs, and original stage designs, in addition to scrapbooks, account books, typescripts, plays, and correspondence for theatre companies and individuals active in the nineteenth and twentieth centuries. City archives are frequently excellent sources of local material. Toronto and Vancouver, for example, have collected photographs and architectural drawings of theatre buildings, an invaluable record of life in their respective cities.

The STRATFORD FESTIVAL, the National Ballet of Canada, and the Canadian Opera Company are three major Canadian companies that collect and organize their own records. They have established archives that make available to researchers the great variety of materials generated by the companies. Unfortunately in 1985, as a result of government cutbacks, the NATIONAL ARTS CENTRE, Ottawa, eliminated its archival function, established in 1979.

The study of Canadian theatre is now being treated systematically and professionally. Without archival resources, original research into the development of Canadian society and culture is impossible. The mechanisms and opportunities for gathering important theatrical material exist on the national, provincial, and local levels, but until there are more recognized repositories of theatrical archives and a stable and well-publicized method of co-ordinating acquisitions, the ephemera of theatrical performance, so vital to its reconstruction, will remain undiscovered or be dispersed, lost, or destroyed. Given their recent beginnings and the stringent circumstances under which they have developed, however, archival collections in the field of Canadian theatre give good evidence of continuing perseverance and a well-founded hope of progress.

HEATHER McCALLUM

Army Show, The. Inspired by a CBC radio variety show, the first national tour of the Canadian Army Show opened in Mar. 1943 after six months' preparation. The original Army Show included Johnny Wayne and Frank Shuster (who supplied the material), Peter Mews, Mildred Morey, Roger Doucet, Jimmie Shields, Gordon Blythe, and Lois Maxwell. After touring Canada and giving a special performance in Quebec City for the 1944 Anglo-American War Conference, a new version—again starring Wayne and Shuster, who did their 'Hitler' number—was mounted by Sgt. Major Jimmie Shields to celebrate the second anniversary of the formation of the Canadian Women's Army Corps. In the fall of 1943 the Department of National Defence split the troupe into five units—two musical revues and three variety—to be sent overseas, with material prepared by Wayne and Shuster. A new sixth group put together 'About Faces of 1944'—starring Margaret Cross and featuring Pte. A.E. Tebbs of Toronto as film star Betty Grable—which toured Canada and established a pattern of training performers in Canada before sending them to the war zone.

The first five units arrived in England on 21 Dec. 1943 and joined the Canadian Auxiliary Services Entertainment Unit. They each logged over 6,000 miles entertaining troops throughout England before the allied invasion of Europe. Each troupe travelled in five vehicles, which accommodated the performers, a portable stage, curtains, scenery, lights, and generator. The Army Shows were produced in Great Britain and Europe throughout the war before disbanding in 1947.

PATRICK B. O'NEILL

Arthur, Julia (1869-1950). Born Ida Lewis in Hamilton, Ont., she made her professional début there on 26 Mar. 1885 as Maritana in Daniel Bandmann's touring production of Gilbert À Beckett's and Mark Lemon's *Don Caesar de Bazan*. There followed a gruelling apprenticeship touring North America with Bandmann and other managers in varied parts ranging from hideous old ladies to ingénues. Praised for her dark, sensuous beauty, pleasing voice, and 'natural' effect even in histrionic scenes, Arthur distinguished herself in high comedy—as Lady Windermere, for example, in the first American production of Wilde's play in 1893. At age twenty-five, having played 150 different roles, she joined

Julia Arthur as Imogen in Shakespeare's Cymbeline

Henry Irving's Lyceum Theatre in London, Eng., acting there and touring with the company in North America (1894-7) in minor parts (Lady Anne in Shakespeare's *Richard III* and Rosamund in Tennyson's *Becket*, for example) and as Ellen Terry's understudy. Following Irving's example, she ran her own company in the U.S. (1897-9), presenting a commercial and classical repertoire, including Shakespeare's *As You Like It* and *Romeo and Juliet*, in a 'picturesque' style. Exhaustion forced her to retire in 1899 but she returned to the stage to give benefit performances during the First World War, and later revived her old repertoire along with some newer pieces, although she now seemed old-fashioned. She played Lady Macbeth (to Lionel Barrymore's Macbeth) in a production directed by Arthur Hopkins and designed by Robert Edmond Jones (17 Feb. 1921, New York), where her grand manner, though out of place, was still impressive. As Shaw's Saint Joan (Theatre Guild touring production, 1924-6) she used her powerful, melodic voice along with larger-than-life gestures and attitudes to create an extraordinary degree of spiritual intensity in the best performance of her career. A Victorian idealist, she believed the theatre should provide an inspiring, salutary example; despite her international acclaim, she was also much concerned with the cultural maturation of her native Canada—evidenced by her frequent tours and speeches in Canada. She spent her retirement years in Boston. DENIS SALTER

Artichoke

Arts and Culture Centre, St John's

Artichoke. The first full-length play by Joanna GLASS to be professionally performed, it premièred at Long Wharf Theatre, New Haven, Conn., on 17 Oct. 1975 and in Canada at Toronto's TARRAGON THEATRE on 9 Oct. 1976. It has since been produced in many Canadian and American theatres. The stark patterns of a stringent and restrictive society, familiar in earlier prairie drama (including Glass's own *Canadian Gothic*), become the source of humour in *Artichoke*, in which moral self-righteousness and repressed feeling erupt in unconventional frankness and surprising twists of behaviour.

Margaret Morley (a role created by Canadian actress Colleen Dewhurst) has never forgiven her husband Walter for his sexual misdemeanour with a 'water witch' during the first year of their marriage when the well went dry. Although willing to raise Lily Agnes, the fey child of that encounter who was left on her doorstep nine months later, Margaret instantly banished Walter from the conjugal bed to the smokehouse. Fourteen years later he remains as stubborn about his marital status as she, insisting that since he is the one who did wrong, 'It's up to her to do the forgiving.' A break in the stalemate occurs with the arrival of summer visitor Gibson McFarland, an orphan raised in Margaret's childhood home who is now an academic specializing in the poetry of Alexander Pope. He is seeking sanctuary from the stresses of city life, and Margaret is ripe for belated romantic fulfilment. Enraged to find himself cuckolded, Walter, the virile and land-proud patriarch, resentfully takes refuge with his gossipy neighbours, who provide aphoristic choral comment on the affair. Gibson's view of farm life proves more pastoral than practical and by the end of the summer Margaret is relieved to return to the shared work and life of the farm with Walter. Gib-

son, she decides, is a 'misfit'; a neighbour's more colourful designation is 'artichoke', an inessential vegetable that 'takes forever to get to its heart.'

Freshness of language, a feature of all Glass's plays, is a strong source of comedy in *Artichoke*, ranging from the idiosyncrasies of speech that define the individual characters to the verbal rituals of conflict that expose the evasions of domestic relations. *Artichoke* was first published in 1979 by the Dramatists Play Service.   DIANE BESSAI

Arts and Culture Centre. Housing the administrative offices of Newfoundland's library board, an art gallery, and two theatres, the Centre opened in St John's, Nfld, in 1967 as the $8 million Centennial project of Newfoundland and Labrador. The larger theatre, seating 1,017, opened on 22 May 1967 with a DOMINION DRAMA FESTIVAL production of Newfoundland playwright Tom Cahill's adaptation of Harold Howard's novel *Tomorrow Will Be Sunday*. The proscenium stage is 24' by 50' with an apron that extends an additional 13'. The stage is 40' deep by 100' wide (including wing space). The theatre has subsequently become the home of the Rising Tide Theatre—which offers a subscription season of local and international plays—and the Newfoundland Symphony Orchestra. The Centre's smaller basement theatre offers a variety of less elaborate productions.

Smaller Arts and Culture Centres are located in Grand Falls, Gander, Corner Brook, and Stephenville.   C.J. SKINNER

Arts and Letters Club. A luncheon club founded in Toronto in 1908 to provide a meeting-place for writers, architects, musicians, painters, actors, and others interested in the arts, it met in restaurants until 1910

when it rented space on Court Lane, at the back of what was originally the York County Courthouse on Adelaide St E. Under the leadership of Roy MITCHELL the Arts and Letters Players was formed, a stage was improvised from 150 movable boxes, and plays 'which are otherwise inaccessible to Toronto' were produced in a stylized, expressionistic manner unusual in Toronto's amateur theatre. The first complete play produced was Maurice Maeterlinck's *Interior* in April 1911. In 1920 the Club moved to its present building, at 14 Elm St, which eventually acquired a small proscenium stage. One-act plays after monthly dinners became a tradition, and in the 1920s three full-length plays were produced annually; in the thirties and forties at least one play a year was done, including plays by members John COULTER, Robertson DAVIES, Merrill DENISON, Lister SINCLAIR, and Herman VOADEN. From the Club's annual Spring Revue, which began in 1930, *SPRING THAW* developed. The Revue now takes the form of a cabaret show. Members' interest in performance and theatre continues with original operettas, play-readings, and imported productions of full-length plays.   WILLIAM TOYE

Arts Club, The. Founded in Vancouver in 1958, it began presenting plays in a 125-seat theatre-in-the-round on Seymour St in 1964, directed by Yvonne Firkin and Otto Lowy. For the first eight years the theatre averaged six productions a year, for runs of about three weeks, with largely Equity casts. Shows were mainly comedies and thrillers, such as Muriel Resnik's *Any Wednesday* and Agatha Christie's *The Mousetrap*. Because it owned its building from the start, the Arts was more secure than other new companies.

In 1970 Bill Millerd began directing at the Arts, and two years later became artistic and managing director, expanding operations to a year-round basis, with plays running for about two months, though *Jacques Brel is Alive and Well and Living in Paris*, Bernard SLADE's *Same Time, Next Year*, Noël Coward's *Blithe Spirit* and *Private Lives*, and *Side by Side by Sondheim* ran much longer. During the seventies the Arts came to rival the more heavily subsidized VANCOUVER PLAYHOUSE when Millerd acquired what he called a 'middle audience' that found the Playhouse too formal and was uninterested in experiments. With growing season-ticket sales he intro-

duced more adventurous fare: accessible classics (*A Midsummer Night's Dream*, Tennessee Williams' *Cat on a Hot Tin Roof*) and Canadian work—David FREEMAN's *CREEPS* in 1973, and in subsequent years Freeman's *Battering Ram* and *You're Gonna Be Alright, Jamie Boy*, Michel TREMBLAY's *Bonjour, là, bonjour* and *Broken Pieces* (a translation of *En Pièces détachées*), David FENNARIO's *On the Job*, Rick SALUTIN's *Les Canadiens*, and George F. WALKER's *Gossip*.

When the run-down industrial district of Granville Island was being redeveloped, Millerd secured funding to convert a warehouse into a second Arts Club facility, the 450-seat Granville Island Stage, which opened in Oct. 1979 with *The Incredible Murder of Cardinal Tosca*, by Alden NOWLAN and Walter LEARNING. The Arts' first première followed—Ken MITCHELL's *The Great Cultural Revolution*. The larger theatre made possible large-cast pieces, musicals like John Kander's and Fred Ebb's *Cabaret*, and plays such as Eduardo de Filippo's *Saturday, Sunday, Monday*. Ann Mortifee wrote a musical, *Reflections on a Crooked Walking*, as a Christmas show. Meanwhile, the old Arts Club Theatre continued; Sherman Snukal's first play, *TALKING DIRTY*, ran there for most of its 1,000 performances. In Jan. 1983 Millerd opened the Arts Club Revue Theatre, seating 225, the Arts Club's third, in a warehouse adjoining the Granville Island Theatre. The Fats Waller revue *Ain't Misbehavin'* ran there for twenty months.

Millerd is personally responsible for the Arts' success, for its growth from a small hall to a flourishing three-theatre organization, and for its ability to cover 80 per cent of its annual $3.5 million budget (1987–8) at the box office. He may be faulted sometimes for low standards (he is a better impresario than director) and for excessive loyalty to a small group of local performers. But his flair for picking the right script at the right moment and knowing how long to run it, and for nurturing and exploiting shows like *Talking Dirty* and the collective (written with Peter Eliot Weiss) *Sex Tips for Modern Girls* (produced Mar. 1985) is admirable.

MALCOLM PAGE

At My Heart's Core. Written by Robertson DAVIES in 1950 for the city of Peterborough's centennial celebration, this play brings Canada's pioneers to life in a warm and witty way, depicting Susanna Moodie, Catharine Parr Traill, and Frances Stewart during the 1837 Rebellion led by William Lyon Mackenzie. It combines farce with romantic comedy, and Canadian history with the powerful myth of temptation by the devil. Like *Fortune, My Foe* (1948), Davies' first successful full-length play, *At My Heart's Core* is centrally concerned with Canadian cultural deprivation.

Historical rebellion is the backdrop for the main action: the temptation of three women to revolt against the limitations of their lives. Each is torn between her duty as a settler's wife and the desire of her heart, mind, and spirit for something that cannot be attained while duty is done. The devil-figure, Edmund Cantwell, in conversation with each of the ladies in parallel scenes, brings to light their hidden dissatisfactions and strikes each with discontent. Mrs Stewart could have married Lord Rossmore and shared his aristocratic life in Ireland instead of being in the backwoods of Canada. Mrs Traill could have been a distinguished naturalist instead of spending herself on the work that any settler's wife does. Mrs Moodie might have equalled Maria Edgeworth, whose books she greatly admires, if she could have devoted herself to writing. The devil's role is to bring to the surface the discontent that each woman has felt at her heart's core.

The farcical sub-plot features an Indian servant who protects the household with an iron skillet, and common settlers whose values and perceptions are comically contrasted with those of the gentry. The subjects of art and rebellion tie the two plots together thematically. Happy endings for both plots are ensured when Thomas Stewart returns from York, where he has been helping to quell the Mackenzie Rebellion. Despite the realism of his game leg and a refreshing propensity for high-spirited humour, Judge Stewart is warm, wise, sensible, and understanding, convincingly capable of soothing injuries and resolving conflicts.

At My Heart's Core was first performed by the Peterborough Summer Theatre, directed by Davies. It opened on 28 Aug. 1950 with Davies' wife, Brenda, in the role of Frances Stewart and Kate REID as Catharine Parr Traill. The professional CANADIAN REPERTORY THEATRE production in Ottawa in Jan. 1951—with Brenda Davies, John Primm (Cantwell), and Donald Glen (Stewart)

recreating their roles—won reviewers' praise. Amateur productions followed quickly in Edmonton (Jan.) and London (May). A CBC television production aired on 10 Nov. 1953.

Published in Nov. 1950 by Clarke, Irwin, the play was re-issued in 1966 with Davies' most famous one-act play, also on the subject of Canadian cultural deprivation: *At My Heart's Core and Overlaid*. For this edition the play was slightly revised and an epilogue and notes were added by Davies.

SUSAN STONE-BLACKBURN

À toi, pour toujours, ta Marie-Lou (*Forever Yours, Marie-Lou*). Michel TREMBLAY's play was first produced in French on 29 Apr. 1971 at the THÉÂTRE DE QUAT'SOUS, directed by André BRASSARD; it was published by Leméac the same year. The English translation by Bill GLASSCO and John Van Burek premièred in Nov. 1972 at TARRAGON THEATRE, Toronto; it was published by Talonbooks in 1975.

Tremblay considers this 'string quartet for four voices' his best play; within the cycle of *Les BELLES-SOEURS* it is at once the most sophisticated in dramatic structure and the most vitriolic in its attack on the family ('I want to put a bomb in the family cell'). It works on three levels: as a universal statement on the difficulties of communication between members of a family; as an indictment of socio-economic and clerical pressures that have degraded the family in Quebec; and as a political allegory, the parents representing the past, one daughter (Manon) the status-quo, the other (Carmen) liberation. The main subject of the play, the monstrous family—impotent, frustrated, and unable to communicate—is common in the 'nouveau théâtre québécois' and is a reaction against the Church-imposed idealized family life of earlier literature.

A highly theatrical work, *Forever Yours, Marie-Lou* consists of two interwoven dialogues, one between Léopold and Marie-Lou, the parents, the other between Manon and Carmen. The parents' dialogue occurs just before a fatal 'accident' in which Léopold crashes the car against a cement wall, killing them both; the daughters' dialogue is set ten years after that event. The entire play occurs in one location, the kitchen of the parents' home; however, only the daughters actually occupy this space, centre-stage. The parents, now dead, are given symbolic locales repre-

Pierre Dufresne and Nicole Leblanc in À toi, pour toujours, ta Marie-Lou, *Théâtre populaire du Québec, 1983*

senting their favourite spots: Léopold to one side, in front of a tavern table, Marie-Lou to the other, in front of the television. To underline the absence of communication all four characters remain static, speaking straight at the audience. In the 1977 FESTIVAL LENNOXVILLE production Brassard changed this original setting by placing dummy figures of the parents in the actual kitchen, with the daughters on an upper level, descending whenever they enter the parents' time zone.

The play is composed along musical lines ('it is a purely aural thing for me,' says Tremblay), creating a strong sense of unity and harmony in spite of the harshness of the theme and language. Tremblay conveys the desperate state of the marriage of Léopold and Marie-Lou through heavy irony and a number of repeated key words: 'renvoyer' (vomit), 'péter' (fart), 'cracher' (spit), and 'merde' (shit). Marie-Lou's aversion to both sex and her husband is aptly suggested by such words as 'cochonnerie' (swinishness) and 'écoeurant' (disgusting). Léopold himself is caught in the 'engrenage' (cogwheels) of a monotonous job and fears the onset of madness, which runs in his family. Suicide is his solution. The two daughters react in opposite ways to their parents' death. Manon remains in the house, her life patterned after her mother's prayerful resignation; Carmen

moves out and becomes a sexually liberated singer of cowboy songs on the Main. Both women re-appear in subsequent plays: Carmen as the central martyr figure in *Sainte Carmen de la Main*, Manon as the religious fanatic in *Damnée Manon, Sacrée Sandra*.

RENATE USMIANI

Auditorium, The. Built in Quebec City's fashionable Carré d'Youville in Upper Town, just outside the Porte Saint-Jean, it was designed by the American architect Walter S. Painter. The Renaissance-style amphitheatre, seating 1,500, had an imposing chandelier, a modern fireproof curtain, and a spacious lobby and foyer with inscribed friezes. It was financed by a company headed by S.N. Parent, mayor of Quebec City and later Premier of Quebec, and opened on 31 Aug. 1903 with a two-day gala musical program.

In 1904 manager Ambrose SMALL lured from Montreal's THÉÂTRE NATIONAL as artistic director Paul CAZENEUVE, who opened with a successful *Faust* and Louis Guyon's *Montferrand*. Melodramas such as *Quo Vadis* and *Le Casque de fer* (*The Man in the Iron Mask*, alternating in French and English productions) were also popular at the Auditorium, as was the 1905 visit of Sarah Bernhardt (despite clerical protest). By 1910 variety concerts and VAUDEVILLE supplemented theatrical offerings, and in 1927 the installation of a Casavant organ necessitated physical changes to the building. Two years later it was sold to Famous Players and renamed the Capitol. The Auditorium continued to serve, however, as the centre of cultural activities in Quebec City, attracting international orchestras, ballet troupes, and celebrities such as Mistinguet, Ramon Navarro, and Lily Pons. Eclipsed by the opening of the GRAND THÉÂTRE DE QUÉBEC in 1971, it finally closed its doors in 1982 and now awaits restoration. RAMON HATHORN

Au Retour des oies blanches. Marcel DUBÉ's play premièred on 21 Oct. 1966 at the COMÉDIE-CANADIENNE, Montreal, and was published in 1969. It chronicles, in a series of revelations, the downfall of an upper-class family in Quebec City. The father, Achille—a former high-ranking civil servant in the Union Nationale government—is intent on clearing himself of influence-peddling and fraud, and on preventing

Au Retour des oies blanches

exposure of his having raped Laura, a friend of his daughter Vivi. Vivi confesses that she is enamoured of her 'uncle' Tom—who never appears—and it becomes clear that she had made love to him during a goose-hunt the previous fall. Towards the end of the play the mother, Elizabeth, admits to Vivi that she once had a short affair with Tom, her step-brother-in-law, and that Vivi is his daughter. Upon learning this, Vivi hangs herself. Laura then discloses that Vivi had aborted a child by Tom. In the play's final tableau the mother talks deliriously with her dead daughter, while her self-deluding husband (who had avoided service overseas) dons his officer's uniform. There is a knock on the front door, presumably announcing the return of Tom, and the curtain falls.

Au Retour des oies blanches is Dubé's most classical play, not only because it adheres to the three unities, but because of its borrowings from Sophocles' *Oedipus Rex* and its many other references to the classics. Few critics have seen that it is also an allegory depicting the demise of the Union Nationale party at the moment when it was being returned to its last flickering of power. Dubé shows that the profound effects of the Quiet Revolution were irreversible, and that the hypocrisy, pretentiousness, religiosity, fraudulence, and fear associated with the old order were being unmasked. A central structural device is the interplay between 'paraître' (seeming) and 'être' (being). Dubé skilfully plays on contrasting colours—white, black, and red—both for costumes and objects, to underline this interplay and to prepare for the tragic outcome. He also uses circular and parallel unifying devices, such as the recurrence of events in October (1945, 1965, 1966) linked to Tom and his hunting of wild geese, and the repetition of parts of a recorded song (specially composed). In spite of its melodramatic elements, *Au Retour des oies blanches* is a powerful drama of intense human emotions, expressed in crisp dialogue; effective both visually and aurally, and with a rich sub-text, it holds an important place in Quebec's dramaturgy. An English translation by Jean Remple, *The White Geese*, was published in 1972.   BEN-Z. SHEK

Aurore l'enfant martyre. One of the best-known French-Canadian plays, it is based on a true incident. On 12 Feb. 1920 a ten-year-old girl named Aurore Gagnon died as a result of torture inflicted by her father, Télesphore Gagnon, and her stepmother, Marie-Anne Houde. After two celebrated trials in Apr. 1920, the parents were sentenced—the stepmother to the gallows, and the father to life imprisonment; both sentences were later commuted. Inspired by accounts of the trial, Léon Petitjean (1869?-1923?) and Henri Rollin (a pseudonym for Willie Plante, 1887-1942), members of the Petitjean-Rollin-Nohcor troupe (Nohcor is an anagram of the name Rochon), wrote the first version of *Aurore l'enfant martyre*, a play in two acts first presented at Montreal's Théâtre Alcazar on 17 Jan. 1921. In 1926 or 1927 a second part, 'Le procès de la marâtre', was added to the play.

Described in its publicity as a 'melodrama in four acts' (sometimes in five acts), the first part of *Aurore l'enfant martyre* portrays the torture of Aurore, who dies despite efforts to save her by neighbours and the local priest and doctor. The second part features the trial where they and Aurore's little brother testify about Aurore's ill-treatment. Following emotional pleas by the lawyers, the judge sentences the stepmother to the gallows. Despite the horrifying account of the child's death, early versions of the play included elements of humour and even songs.

An outstanding success from the beginning, *Aurore l'enfant martyre* was performed about 200 times a year from 1921 to 1951 touring Quebec and other French-speaking areas of Canada and New England. The principal directors succeeding Petitjean and Rollin were Alfred Rochon and Louis Préville—who, by agreement with the actress Marcelle Briand-Dairou, held the copyright—and finally, Jean Grimaldi and Marc Forrez. The script, never definitive, evolved following a common popular theatrical tradition whereby actors handed down 'roles' on slips of paper from one generation to another. The only published version (Édition VLB, 1982), was based on a version given to Alonzo Le Blanc by Forrez before his death in 1981.

In 1951 actor Marc Forrez published—under his real name, Émile Asselin—a novel inspired by the play called *La Petite Aurore*. He consequently wrote a script based on the novel for the film *La Petite Aurore l'enfant martyre*, produced in 1951 and released in 1952; it was dubbed into seven or eight languages and gained an international reputation.   ALONZO LE BLANC

Automatic Pilot. Erika RITTER's play, a 1980 CHALMER's Award winner, premièred in a NEW THEATRE production at the Court Theatre, Adelaide Court, Toronto, on 17 Jan. 1980, starring Fiona REID. It subsequently transferred to the TORONTO FREE THEATRE, and has been performed frequently across Canada. It dramatizes the trials of Charlie, a woman of 30, who writes soap operas while working as a stand-up comic at the Canada Goose; the play begins and ends with her routine, with the theatre audience in the role of the night-club audience. When Charlie's husband, Alan, leaves her for a man, she consoles herself with drink and Nick. After Nick ditches her with lunch, roses, and a quotation sounding like Kahlil Gibran, she is pursued by sensitive Gene, Nick's younger brother. When Charlie discovers that Alan is 'marrying' a man and going to Spain, she sinks into self-pity. Gene, though he loves her, leaves, and is last seen discovering himself as a writer.

Automatic Pilot shows a woman unable to come to terms with her freedom. Charlie needs love and a continuing relationship, but cannot let go of Alan even after he makes a new commitment. Gene says the sixties meant commitment and the seventies meant leaving options open, and he belongs to the sixties. When he offers commitment to Charlie, her problem is that she cannot accept it. Ritter suggests that comedy is made out of suffering; Charlie jokes about what is painful to her, her large size and the men in her life. At the end the question remains, can she create comedy only when she is miserable?

Ritter performed at Yuk-Yuk's Komedy Kabaret, Toronto, while writing the play, and used some of the material in a short story, 'You're a Taker' (*Saturday Night*, Dec. 1979). The play was published in 1980 by Playwrights Canada.   MALCOLM PAGE

Awards and Competitions.

Chalmers Canadian Children's Play Award. The Ontario Arts Council through its Floyd S. CHALMERS Fund has presented these awards annually since 1982 to honour outstanding plays written and produced specifically for children between the ages of five and fifteen. Selections are made by a jury of four members, two of whom belong to the Toronto Drama Bench. The winning playwright receives a prize of $3,000. Additional awards totalling $2,000 are available for one or more runners-up. To be eligible, plays must be at least forty minutes in length, produced by a professional company, and performed at least twice during the calendar year in the Metropolitan Toronto area. Past winners have been: Marcel Sabourin (*Pleurer pour rire*, 1982) and Robert Morgan (*How I Wonder What You Are*, 1982); Jim Betts (*Mystery of the Oak Island Treasure*, 1983); Colin Thomas (*One Thousand Cranes*, 1984); Suzanne Lebeau (*Little Victories/Les petits pouvoirs*, 1985) and Duncan McGregor (*Running the Gauntlet*, 1985); Dennis Foon (*Skin*, 1986); Beverley Cooper and Banuta Rubess (*Thin Ice*, 1987); Carol BOLT (*Ice Time*, 1988).

Chalmers Canadian Play Awards. Established in 1972 by the Floyd S. Chalmers Foundation, and administered by the Ontario Arts Council through its Floyd S. Chalmers Fund, they are presented each January for the most outstanding Canadian plays produced professionally during the preceding calendar year in the Metropolitan Toronto area. Their annual value is $8,000: $5,000 to the winner, and $3,000 divided among up to four other finalists in the competition. The winning playwrights are selected by a jury composed of members of the Toronto Drama Bench. Past recipients of the first-place awards have been: David FREEMAN (*CREEPS*, 1972); David FRENCH (*Of the Fields, Lately*, 1973); James REANEY (*The Saint Nicholas Hotel, The Donnellys, Part II*, 1974); John HERBERT (*FORTUNE AND MEN'S EYES*, 1975); W.O. MITCHELL (*Back to Beulah*, 1976) and Larry FINEBERG (*Eve*, 1976); Rick SALUTIN (*Les CANADIENS*, 1977); Roland LEPAGE (*Le Temps d'une vie*, 1978); David FENNARIO (*BALCONVILLE*, 1979); Erika RITTER (*AUTOMATIC PILOT*, 1980); Allan STRATTON (*Rexy!*, 1981) and Charles Tidler (*Straight Ahead/Blind Dancers*, 1981); Anne CHISLETT (*Quiet in the Land*, 1982); Sherman Snukal (*TALKING DIRTY*, 1983); George F. WALKER (*Criminals in Love*, 1984); Michel TREMBLAY (*Albertine, In Five Times*, 1985); John MURRELL (*Farther West*, 1986); Tom Wood (*B-Movie: The Play*, 1987). In 1988 the award was shared by Paul Ledoux and David Young (*Fire*), Ann-Marie MacDonald (*Goodnight Desdemona, Good Morning Juliet*), Michel Tremblay (*The Real World?*), and George F. Walker (*Nothing Sacred*).

Clifford E. Lee National Playwriting Award. This annual award of $3,000 was presented between 1974 and 1981 through funds pro-

37

Awards and Competitions

vided by the Clifford E. Lee Foundation. Administered by the Department of Drama of the Univ. of Alberta, it was designed to honour an original new Canadian play, written in or translated into English, that had not previously been professionally produced. The winner was selected by a jury of three prominent theatre professionals. Winners included Tom GRAINGER, John Murrell, Lezley Havard, Geoffrey Ursell, Gaetan Charlebois, and Paul Gross.

Dora Mavor Moore Awards. Originated in 1979 in the name of Dora Mavor MOORE 'to recognize outstanding achievements in the theatre season of Metropolitan Toronto on an annual basis', they consist of twenty-three prizes in five divisions: Drama and Comedy; Revue and Musical; Innovative/Artistic Excellence; Children's Theatre; and New Dance. The awards are administered by the Toronto Theatre Alliance (founded in 1977) through its charitable wing, the Performing Arts Information Services. The selection procedure for the Drama and Comedy division and the Revue and Musical division operates through nominating committees that select up to five finalists from among all eligible shows. Finalists are placed on a ballot distributed to a voters' list compiled from the membership and staff of Metropolitan Toronto's professional theatre organizations and associations. In the other three divisions the winners are selected by juries. Eligibility criteria vary among the different divisions, but all eligible productions must be fully professional and produced or presented by, or performed in, a theatre that is a member of the Toronto Theatre Association. The awards are presented during a special awards evening held each spring.

Governor General's Literary Awards in Drama. These two awards of $10,000 each are given annually by the Canada Council for the best published plays of the year in English and French. The recipients are selected by separate three-person juries composed of critics, writers, and theatre professionals. Winners for the best play in English since 1981 (when the drama category was established as a separate category of the Governor General's Literary Awards) have been: Sharon POLLOCK (*Blood Relations and Other Plays*, 1981); John GRAY (*BILLY BISHOP GOES TO WAR*, 1982); Anne Chislett (*Quiet in the Land*, 1983); Judith THOMPSON (*White Biting Dog*, 1984); George F. Walker (*Criminals in Love*, 1985);

Sharon Pollock (*Doc*, 1986); John KRIZANC (*Prague*, 1987); and George F. Walker (*Nothing Sacred*, 1988). Recipients for the best drama written in French since 1981 are Marie LABERGE (*C'était avant la guerre à L'Anse à Gilles*, 1981); Réjean DUCHARME (*HA! ha!...*, 1982); Réné Gingras (*Syncope*, 1983); René-Daniel DUBOIS (*Ne blâmez jamais les Bédouins*, 1984); Maryse Pelletier (*Duo pour voix obstinées*, 1985); Anne Legault (*La Visite des sauvages*, 1986); Jeanne-Mance Delisle (*Un Oiseau vivant dans la gueule*, 1987); and Jean Marc Dalpé (*Le Chien*, 1988). The awards are presented at a ceremony held each spring in a different Canadian city.

Jessie Richardson Theatre Awards. These have been presented annually since 1983 by the Vancouver Professional Theatre Alliance for outstanding theatrical achievement in Vancouver. Thirteen awards are given to artists participating in dramatic and musical productions in the following categories: best production, best original musical, best direction, and best performance in leading and supporting roles. Additional awards are presented in choreography and in set, costume, and lighting design. The winning candidates are determined on the basis of ballots distributed to all theatre artists and production personnel who have worked professionally in the Vancouver theatre in the previous year. Every Vancouver theatre is also entitled to cast a vote for each award. They are presented in June at the ARTS CLUB Theatre.

Maggie Bassett Award. It has been presented annually by Theatre Ontario since 1982 to an individual who has made 'a sustained and significant contribution to the development of theatre in Ontario' over an extended period. Anyone involved in professional, educational, or community theatre is eligible. The award is named after Maggie Bassett, a director, actress, and administrator who initiated the Professional Theatre Training Programme and many of the other services of Theatre Ontario. Winners have been: Ken Watts, 1982; Elsie Thomson, 1983; Jean ROBERTS 1984; Herbert WHITTAKER, 1985; Heather McCallum, 1986; Herman VOADEN, 1987; Dennis Sweeting, 1988. The award is presented on World Theatre Day, 27 March.

Nathan Cohen Award. Named after critic Nathan COHEN and presented annually for excellence in theatre criticism, it was established by the Toronto Drama Bench in 1981. Administration of the award has since passed into the hands of the Canadian Theatre Critics Association, which selects the winner on the basis of submitted manuscripts. Eligibility is limited to critics writing professionally for newspapers, periodicals, radio, and television. Winners have been: Martin Knelman, 1982; Boyd Neil, 1983; not awarded in 1984; David Prosser, 1985; David Prosser and Marianne Ackerman, 1986; David Prosser, 1987; Jamie Portman and Marianne Ackerman, 1988.

Pauline McGibbon Award. Named in honour of the former Lieutenant Governor of Ontario, it has been presented anually since 1981 in Toronto. Administered by the Theatre Office of the Ontario Arts Council and adjudicated by a jury of five theatre professionals, the $5,000 cash award (provided by the Province of Ontario) and a medal (contributed by the Ontario Ministry of Citizenship and Culture) are given on a rotating basis to a designer, director, and production professional in the early stages of his or her career who has displayed unique talents and a potential for excellence. Winners have been: Murray LAUFER, 1981; William LANE, 1982; Colleen Blake, 1983; Debra Hanson, 1984; Sky Gilbert, 1985; Fina Khan, 1986; Adam Kolodziej, 1987; Jo Ann McIntyre, 1988.

Sterling Awards. Established in 1987 in honour of Edmonton theatre pioneer Elizabeth Sterling HAYNES, they are patterned on Toronto's Dora awards and Vancouver's Jessies. Winners for the 1987-8 Edmonton season included Frank Moher's *The Third Ascent* (best play), Stephen Heatley (best direction—for *The Third Ascent*), and actors Susan Wright, Larry Yachimec, and Randy Hughson.

Toronto Arts Awards. Established in 1987 to honour achievement in the visual arts, architecture and design, writing, and editing, these awards are sponsored by CBLT-TV, the Toronto Arts Council, *Toronto Life*, and the Toronto Arts Awards Foundation. They are valued at $5,000 in the specialized categories. In 1987 Eric PETERSON won in the performing arts category; in 1988 Judith Thompson in the writing and editing category, Jackie BURROUGHS in the media arts category.

IRA A. LEVINE

Alberta Culture Playwriting Competition. Initiated in 1969, it is open to new plays by Alberta residents, and is administered by the Performing Arts Division of Alberta Culture. Currently there are cash prizes ranging from $150 to $2,500 in six categories: full-length plays, full-length plays by new writers, full-length plays premièred professionally in Alberta, one-act plays, one-act comedies, and plays written by high-school students.

Brenda Donohue Award. Given in memory of actress Brenda DONOHUE, it recognizes a significant and continuing contribution to Toronto's theatre community and carries a cash prize of $1,000. Winners—originally chosen by a committee of trustees, but now chosen by past winners—have been: Jane MALLETT, 1980; Tim Leary, 1981; Mallory Gilbert, 1982; Renee Schouten, 1983; Steven Bush, 1984; Catherine Smalley, 1985; Rudy Webb, 1986; Patricia Hamilton, 1987; The Smile Company, 1988.

Canadian Authors Association Drama Award. Besides similar awards for fiction, non-fiction, and poetry, the CAA gives an annual prize of $5,000 in the category of drama. Entries submitted must have been published or produced in the preceding calendar year. Winners since the award's inception have been: John HIRSCH (*The Dybbuk*, 1976); Rex DEVERELL (*Boiler Room Suite*, 1978); Sheldon ROSEN (*Ned and Jack*, 1980); Ted GALAY (*After Baba's Funeral* and *Sweet and Sour Pickles*, 1981); Allan Stratton (*Rexy!*, 1982); W. O. Mitchell (*Back to Beulah*, 1983); W. D. Valgardson (*Granite Point*, 1984); Ken MITCHELL (*Gone the Burning Sun*, 1985); David French (*Salt-Water Moon*, 1986); John Murrell (*Farther West*, 1987); John Gray (*Rock and Roll*, 1988).

Canadian One-Act Playwriting Competition. Sponsored annually since 1937 by the Ottawa Little Theatre, it is open to unpublished one-act plays by professional and non-professional writers in Canada. The number and nature of prizes have varied: currently, first prize is $1,000 and two gold medals, with second and third prizes of $500 and $300. Past winners include Robertson DAVIES (1946, 1947), Norman Williams (1953, 1954, 1955), Gwen Pharis RINGWOOD (1959), Lennox Brown (1965, 1968, 1969), and Ken Mitchell (1971).

CBC Radio Literary Competition. Since 1979 CBC Radio has held an annual competition for original unpublished radio plays by Canadian writers, along with similar competitions for poetry and short stories. The plays must be from fifteen to thirty minutes long. In 1988 prizes in each category were $3,000,

Awards and Competitions

$2,500, and $2,000, including the rights for one performance on CBC's English radio network.

Molson Prize. The Canada Council awards two Molson prizes annually to recognize distinguished contributions to the arts, humanities, or social sciences in Canada. The prizes were established in 1964 by an endowment provided by the Molson Family Foundation. Their value was originally $15,000 each, and is now $50,000. Winners in the field of theatre include: Jean GASCON, 1965-6; Denise PELLETIER, 1976; John Hirsch, 1977; Jean-Louis ROUX, 1977; Jean DUCEPPE, 1979; Brian MACDONALD, 1983; Marcel DUBÉ, 1984; Mavor MOORE, 1986; Yvette BRIND'AMOUR, 1987; Robertson DAVIES, 1988.

Nova Scotia Drama League Outstanding Theatre Achievement Award. This is given to individuals working in amateur or professional theatre for their outstanding contributions, often over many years, towards making theatre more accessible to the people of Nova Scotia. Recent winners have been Donald Wetmore (1985) and Marguerite MacDougall (1987).

Tyrone Guthrie Awards. These were established in 1953, the first year of the STRATFORD FESTIVAL (under artistic director Tyrone GUTHRIE) to assist company members and staff to pursue specific projects. The number of awards and amount are variable, not normally exceeding $2,000 per award. The Festival also gives an annual Dora Mavor Moore award for an outstanding contribution by a young actor; a Jean A. Chalmers Award, for outstanding work by an apprentice; a Maureen Forrester Award, for a promising young singer, actor, or musician; a Tom Patterson award, for skill and commitment in design; and several others.

Victor C. Polley Award. This is given to a theatre professional in Ontario, in the early stages of a career, who has demonstrated outstanding ability in arts administration or in arts facility management. Named after a former administrator of the ST LAWRENCE CENTRE, and jointly administered by the Centre and by Theatre Ontario, the award consists of a scroll and a cash prize, usually of about $800. Past winners have been: Elaine Calder, 1982-3; Heather Redick, 1984; Christopher Bye, 1985; Victoria Steele, 1986; Tamara Ivanochko, 1987.

DENIS W. JOHNSTON

B

Balconville. David FENNARIO's third published play (Vancouver: Talonbooks, 1980), it was commissioned by Montreal's CENTAUR THEATRE, where it was first produced on 2 Jan. 1979, directed by Guy SPRUNG. Also performed that same year in Toronto and Ottawa and later at the London Old Vic, it was generally acclaimed by the critics, receiving the 1979 CHALMERS Award.

The action takes place in Pointe-Saint-Charles, Montreal, where the author grew up; the situations and characters are reminiscent of those described in his journal, *Without a Parachute* (1972). Balconville is the name one of the characters ironically gives the working-class district where the balconies provide a dubious refuge from the stuffy exiguous apartments. Four of the characters are French Canadians, four are anglophones. The bilingual Bolduc makes only a brief appearance of doubtful dramatic value in the second act. This corrupt politician is a mere tool of exploiters, whose presence is felt throughout the play as loud-speakers blare out Bolduc's empty election promises.

Balconville was billed as the first bilingual play produced in Canada, though at least two-thirds of the dialogue is in English. It is also the only published Fennario play with women characters, who show more gumption than the men. The work has virtually no plot, the second act being almost a repetition of the first, except for the fact that the situation has worsened for most of the char-

The Centaur Theatre production of David Fennario's Balconville, 1979, with (l. to r.) Jean Archambault, Cécile St-Denis, Manon Bourgeois, Robert Parson, Marc Gélinas, Terry Tweed, Peter MacNeill, Lynne Deragon

acters. Paquette has lost his job, Tom's attempt at escaping from his environment has ended in failure, Diane has decided to leave school to become a waitress.

On the balconies where they spend their summers, people are both observers and observed. Privacy is impossible, but paradoxically, because they are so close, they feel desperately lonely. True communication is non-existent; the play is one long quarrel from beginning to end. If there are moments of tenderness, their signs are usually misinterpreted. Prejudice, the language barrier, and the generation gap are obvious obstacles to communication, but the real obstacle is bitterness. For the people of *Balconville* life is a vicious circle from which there is no escape. When they have work, they hate what they are doing; yet when Paquette loses his job, which he used to say 'took his life away', he is crushed. Those who have no work do not look for employment because they know they would find only menial, poor-paying jobs. Irene, the strongest character, realizes that they must help themselves, but she receives little support from those around her. Instead of tackling the bosses and landlords responsible for their plight, they find it easier to take out their frustrations on those closest to them. Unable to face reality, they escape into cheap dreams.

In the final lines of the play the four English-speaking characters ask, 'What are we going to do?', which is echoed by the francophones' question, 'Qu'est-ce qu'on va faire?'. French and English are finally united in a mutual despair. Those final words, however, are addressed to the audience.

PAULETTE COLLET

Banff Centre School of Fine Arts. First known as the Banff School of Drama (1933-6), it began on 7 Aug. 1933 as a three-week school of theatre arts, an outgrowth of the Univ. of Alberta's Department of Extension. The founding director, E.A. (Ned) Corbett, served for three years, adding painting and music to the program, thereby creating the Banff School of Fine Arts (as it was renamed in 1936). Corbett was succeeded by Donald Cameron, who served from 1936 to 1970 and initiated an extraordinary program of growth. In the 1930s and 1940s he added opera, ballet, photography, ceramics, and a variety of other disciplines. He began an ambitious winter program in Advanced Management and played host to conferences of every description. In the summers he added special-interest courses ranging from Conversational French to Geology of the Rocky Mountains. He moved the campus from the

Banff Centre

town centre to its present spectacular wilderness site on Tunnel Mountain.

David Leighton's twelve-year tenure (1970-82) was distinguished by the addition of fine housing and recreation facilities and an increasing emphasis on the training of students at the master-class level. The School became the Banff Centre for Continuing Education in 1978, with Leighton as the first President.

The Banff Centre

When Paul Fleck was appointed President in 1982 many of the once unique programs initiated by his predecessors were being offered by other Canadian institutions. Fleck began a rigorous review of all major programs to prevent the Centre from becoming merely an educational Shangri-la.

Theatre Arts has always been a key program of the Centre; the first head of Theatre was Elizabeth Sterling HAYNES (1933-6). An actress and director, she early attracted theatre luminaries, including Alexander Koiranski, a noted teacher of the Stanislavsky Method. Frederick Koch, founder of the famous Carolina Playmakers, who came in 1937, influenced Gwen Pharis RINGWOOD, then at the beginning of her career as a dramatist. In the late 1940s Cameron brought writers Norman Corwin and E.P. Conkle for several sessions, strengthening what was then one of the few courses in North America on play and media writing. In 1958 Gordon Peacock, Theatre

Head (1958-63), invited the Shakespearean director B. Iden Payne for the School's twenty-fifth anniversary. Payne returned for five further years, his annual Shakespeare production becoming an acclaimed event. In 1975 Laslo Funtek, artistic director of the theatre complex (1962-87), created an ongoing series of master design classes, led by the renowned scenographer Joseph Svoboda. The position was not filled after 1987. In 1985 Bernard Hopkins was appointed Head of Theatre, succeeded in 1988 by Patricia Hamilton.

See D. Cameron, *Campus in the Clouds* (1956); E. A. Corbett, *We have With Us Tonight* (1957); D.and P. Leighton, *Artists, Builders, and Dreamers* (1982).

GORDON PEACOCK

Bannerman, Margaret (1896-1976). A blonde expatriate actress and singer, she was born Margaret le Grand in Toronto and educated at the Mount St Vincent Convent in Halifax. She started acting in Winnipeg but gained fame in England, specially playing genteel society ladies and often replacing stars in extended runs. Her West End début in *Tina* (a musical by Paul A. Rubens and Harry Graham), 2 Nov. 1915, was followed by a long series of drawing-room comedies. As Lady Grayston in Somerset Maugham's *Our Betters* she successfully toured Australia in 1928 and later Canada in 1940. She also sang in variety theatres, pantomimes, and opera before moving permanently in 1937 to the U.S. where she was a favourite both in New York and in regional theatres in Wilmington, Pittsburgh, Houston, and Los Angeles. American roles included the grandmother in *Gigi* in 1952, Mrs St. Maugham in Enid Bagnold's *The Chalk Garden*, 1957, the title-role in Jean Giraudoux's *The Madwoman of Chaillot*, 1958, and Mrs Higgins in the U.S.-Canadian tour of Shaw's *My Fair Lady*, 1959-63. She appeared in several Hollywood films.

DAVID GARDNER

Barbeau, François (b. 1935). Born in the Montreal suburb of Verdun, he studied art and design at Sir George Williams College (now Concordia University) before taking a three-year course in costume-cutting at the Cotnoir-Caponi school. He was subsequently hired by Paul Buissonneau of La Roulotte (a children's theatre operated by the City of Montreal), and in 1958 by the THÉÂTRE DE

QUAT'SOUS as a costume builder and designer. In 1959 he began working as an assistant to designer Robert PRÉVOST at the THÉÂTRE DU RIDEAU VERT and the THÉÂTRE DU NOUVEAU MONDE, while also designing costumes for small Montreal companies such as L'Egrégore. In 1961 he pursued his studies in France, England, and Italy, and on his return to Canada in 1962 became head of costumes for the NATIONAL THEATRE SCHOOL. There

François Barbeau

he had a profound effect on the development of stage design in Quebec, being responsible, from 1971 to 1987, for courses in set decoration. Since 1963 he has been the resident costumer for the Rideau Vert.

Barbeau has become the most important and prolific costume designer for the Quebec stage (over 250 productions so far), combining an outstanding knowledge of the history of clothing and great attention to detail with a brilliant sense of theatricality. Apart from his work for the Rideau Vert, he has designed costumes for the Théâtre du Nouveau Monde, the THÉÂTRE POPULAIRE DU QUÉBEC, the NOUVELLE COMPAGNIE THÉÂTRALE, the Théâtre de Quat'sous, the NATIONAL ARTS CENTRE, the COMPAGNIE JEAN DUCEPPE, and for Les Grands Ballets Canadiens, L'Opéra de Québec, and the cinema. In 1983 he designed costumes for the

Comédie Française production of *Les Estivants* (*Summerfolk*) by Maxim Gorky. In 1979 Barbeau was awarded the Victor-Morin Prize.

PAUL LEFEBVRE

Barbeau, Jean (b. 1945). Born at St-Romuald, Que., he completed classical studies at the Collège de Lévis and attended Université Laval. While studying at Lévis he collaborated on two COLLECTIVE works, *Caïn et Babel* and *La Geôle*, performed by students there in 1966 and 1967 respectively. Disillusioned by the European focus of literary studies at Laval, he devoted his energies to the university's long-established Troupe des Treize, and to two collective creations, *Les Temps tranquilles* and *Le Frame all-dress*, both performed in 1969. But his commitment to collective dramaturgy was weakening—as his unpublished *Et caetera*, performed by the Treize in 1968, indicates.

Leaving Laval in 1969, Barbeau helped found the Théâtre Quotidien de Québec, committed to staging Québécois works, mainly his own. In 1970-1 he had eight new plays performed, five of them by the TQQ: *Le Chemin de Lacroix* (1971); *Goglu* (1971); *Solange* (1974); *Joualez-moi d'amour* (1972); and *Tripez-vous vous* (unpublished). Also in 1970 his *Manon Lastcall* (1972) was broadcast on Radio-Canada and performed at the Conservatoire de Montréal. In 1971, *0-71* was staged at Quebec's THÉÂTRE DU TRIDENT and *Ben-Ur* (1971) by the THÉÂTRE POPULAIRE DU QUÉBEC. *Le Chemin de Lacroix* was performed in English at the Poor Alex (Toronto) in 1972.

Barbeau's works from this first, feverish period depict economically depressed and culturally deprived urban francophones in the acerbically humorous fashion that is Barbeau's trademark. Using a colourful Canadian French distinctly different from the stylized Montreal *joual* of Michel TREMBLAY, he portrays the deep schizophrenia of Quebec's Everyman against the background of the province's controversial Bill 63 (1969). *Joualez-moi d'amour* is his clearest and most concise statement on language: in its one act a 'cultivated' Québécois, Jules, learns from his experience with a Parisian prostitute, Julie, that he can abandon his maternal tongue only at the cost of his virility.

A fallow period of nearly two years ensued during which Barbeau married and moved to Amos (Abitibi), Que., where he now lives.

Jean Barbeau's 0-71, Théâtre du Trident, Quebec City, 1971

Four new plays were performed in 1973: *Le Chant du sink* (1973) by Le Théâtre Populaire du Québec; *Knock-out* by Le THÉÂTRE DU NOUVEAU MONDE; *La Coupe Stainless* (1974) by the Piggery Theatre, North Hatley, Que.; and *Le Théâtre de la maintenance* (1979) by La NOUVELLE COMPAGNIE THÉÂTRALE, the latter representing a new departure, focusing on the unseen face of stage production and questioning the very nature of theatrical experience. As with nearly all of Quebec's politically committed writers, Barbeau's output declined notably in the mid-1970s, especially after the advent of the Parti Québécois government in 1976. *Une Brosse* (produced by Le Théâtre du Trident in 1975) and *Citrouille* (produced by Le Théâtre du Nouveau Monde in the same year), both published in 1975, continue to explore the alienation of Québécois, the latter adding a new dimension—feminism—as it portrays a male chauvinist kidnapped and abused by three women. *Dites-le avec des fleurs* (1976), written in collaboration with Marcel DUBÉ and staged in the summer of 1976 by Le Bateau-Théâtre l'Escale, is a lightweight comedy. *Émile et une nuit* (1979), performed in 1979 by Le THÉÂTRE DU RIDEAU VERT, marks a return to the more serious concerns of Barbeau's most productive period. Since 1980 Barbeau has added six new titles and one adaptation to his *oeuvre*. *Le Jardin de la maison blanche* (1979), performed in 1980 by l'Atelier de la Nouvelle Compagnie Théâtrale, is a dreamlike fantasy directed against North American materialistic values; *Une Marquise de Sade et un lézard nommé King-Kong* (1979), another fantasy, performed by Le Théâtre de la Manufacture in 1980, has had little success; but *La Vénus d'Émilio* (1984), performed in 1980 by La Relève à Michaud, returns to the spirit and style of his earlier works. *Coeur de papa* (1986), performed in 1981 by La Relève à Michaud, at Calixa-Lavallée near Montreal, focuses on more universal problems such as generation conflict. *Le Grand Poucet* (1985), first performed in 1983 at La Salle Fred-Barry, is set, exceptionally, in the Abitibi area and

Jean Barbeau

44

depicts convincingly regional alienation, suggesting the end of the Nationalist Dream. Barbeau's most recent work, *Les Gars* (1984)—first performed in 1983 by La COMPAGNIE JEAN DUCEPPE—returns to an urban setting, underlining the growing isolation of males in modern society.

Admittedly inspired by Tremblay's 1968 ground-breaking *Les BELLES-SOEURS*, Jean Barbeau has defined his own themes and his own idiom. Almost singlehandedly he has managed to shift the often unhealthy focus of Quebec dramaturgy away from Montreal. He remains one of the most productive and most influential playwrights of his generation.

See Elaine F. Nardocchio, *Theatre and Politics in Modern Québec* (1986). L.E. DOUCETTE

Barry, Fred (1887-1964). Born in Montreal of an Irish father and a French-Canadian mother, he attended L'Académie Saint-Jean-Baptiste, where he acquired a taste for theatre. He made his stage début at the age of eleven and soon became an amateur actor for various groups, including Cercle Molière, Cercle Saint-Henri, Cercle National, and Garde Napoléon. About 1911 he was hired by Fernand Dhavrol as a permanent member of the THÉÂTRE NATIONAL, then went to the Chantecler, and in 1914 became a star at the THÉÂTRE CANADIEN.

Dissatisfied with actors' working conditions, Barry helped found two companies, those of Bella Ouellette and Jeanne Demons, which played alternately in Montreal and Quebec. With Albert DUQUESNE he founded the Barry-Duquesne group, which he directed and which played at the National, the Saint-Denis, and the Canadien. In 1930 he became the owner of the Chantecler theatre, renamed the THÉÂTRE STELLA.

Barry also had a successful career in radio, beginning in 1928 at CKAC. In 1934 he appeared in the French film *Maria Chapdelaine*, under the direction of Julien Duvivier, and in 1937 he had top billing in the Barry-Duquesne company tour of France, the first by a Quebec company. He directed the first tour of Gratien GÉLINAS's *Fridolinades* (see *FRIDOLINONS*) in 1938, took part in various revues, and in the creation of *TIT-COQ* in 1948. With his gift for both drama and comedy, Fred Barry was a dominant figure in Quebec theatre. After his death, the Salle Fred-Barry in Montreal (part of the NOU-

Fred Barry as Napoléon in Gaston Arman de Caillavet's and Robert de Flers' Le Roi de Rome

VELLE COMPAGNIE THÉÂTRALE) was named in his honour. ALONZO LE BLANC

Bastien, Jean-Luc (b. 1939). Born in Montreal, he studied acting privately with Suzanne Rivest, Jean Doat, and Francine Riopelle, at the NATIONAL THEATRE SCHOOL, and in France. Beginning his career as an actor in 1964, he was a founding member of Jean-Claude GERMAIN's Les Enfants de Chénier in 1969. Other interests gradually took him away from acting, but in 1970 he began teaching theatre at the Collège Lionel-Groulx (serving as chairman, 1972-5 and 1977-8), and he has also served on the executive of the Association québécoise du jeune théâtre (1970-2) and the Centre d'essai des auteurs dramatiques (1972-5). As an ardent advocate of Quebec playwrights he has also directed a number of new works, including Jean BARBEAU's *Le Théâtre de la maintenance*, Denise BOUCHER's *Les FÉES ONT SOIF*, Jean Daigle's *Coup de sang*, and Normand CHAUR-ETTE's *Fêtes d'automne*.

Since 1970 Bastien has been associated with the NOUVELLE COMPAGNIE THÉÂTRALE—as a judge in competitions for new playwrights; as a workshop leader; as artistic director of the company's Salle Fred-BARRY; and (since 1982) as artistic director of the company itself, where he has extended its reach by encouraging young talented directors to work there and by inviting foreign companies to perform.

See 'Tenir compte de tout le monde' (interview), *Jeu*, 25 (1982).   ADRIEN GRUSLIN

Bastion Theatre Company. Founded by Peter Mannering (artistic director to 1971) in 1963 in Victoria, B.C., as an amateur community theatre company, it achieved professional status in 1971 under Edwin Stephenson, who was succeeded as artistic director by Keith Digby (1982-8) and Barry MacGregor (1988). It is housed in Victoria's McPherson Theatre (capacity 837) and operates a theatre school and a theatre-in-education program (with the Univ. of Victoria). The company has occasionally toured B.C. and has performed at the PLAYHOUSE, Fredericton, and other centres in N.B. (Garson Kanin's *Born Yesterday*, Apr./May 1974), and at the NATIONAL ARTS CENTRE, Ottawa (Feydeau's *A Stitch in Time*, Oct./Nov. 1976). Victoria's conservative audiences have supported Bastion's productions of classics, Broadway standards, and modern plays by established dramatists, of whom Noël Coward and Alan Ayckbourn have been most popular; but one or two Canadian plays have also been produced almost every season. They include Lister SINCLAIR's *The Blood Is Strong* (May 1967); John HIRSCH's *The Box of Smiles* (July 1969); James REANEY's *The Killdeer* (Jan. 1973); Ron Chudley's *After Abraham* (world première, Oct. 1977) and *Comeback* (Nov. 1982); Joanna GLASS's *ARTICHOKE* (Apr. 1979); Erika RITTER's *AUTOMATIC PILOT* (Nov. 1980); David FRENCH's *Jitters* (Apr. 1980); David FREEMAN's *CREEPS* (Oct. 1976); Sharon POLLOCK's *BLOOD RELATIONS* (Nov. 1983); Warren Graves' *The Last Real Summer* (Nov. 1985); John HERBERT's *FORTUNE AND MEN'S EYES* (Nov. 1977); Susanne Finlay's *Monkeyshines* (Jan. 1984); and Allan STRATTON's *Nurse Jane Goes to Hawaii* (the most popular play of the 1981-2 season).

Many local actors have appeared regularly on the Bastion stage: Bill Hosie, Anthony Jenkins, Owen Foran, Margaret Martin, John Krich, Andrew Sabiston, Barbara Poggemiller, and John Gilliland. From across Canada Ann Casson, Douglas RAIN, Pat GALLOWAY, Eric DONKIN, Frances HYLAND, Karen Austin, Lally Cadeau, and Warren Graves, among others, have also appeared.

Burdened by a cumulative deficit of $184,000, Bastion suspended operations in Nov. 1988 pending a consultant's review of its operations.   ROBERT G. LAWRENCE

Bawtree, Michael (b. 1937). Born in Newcastle, Australia, he was educated in England, graduating from Oxford Univ. in 1961. He immigrated to Canada in 1962 and began his career as an author and writer. He became the first resident dramaturge at the STRATFORD FESTIVAL (1964) before moving to Simon Fraser Univ. in 1965 to establish its drama program. His play, *The Last of the Tsars* (1973), was performed at the Stratford Festival in 1966. Bawtree returned to Stratford in 1969, and in 1971 was appointed Literary Manager, the first director of Stratford's Third Stage, and assistant to the Festival's artistic director. His productions at Stratford include Oliver Goldsmith's *She Stoops to Conquer* in 1972 (revived in 1973) and innovative operas at the Third Stage, such as Murray Schafer's *Patria II: Requiems for the Party Girl* and Gabriel CHARPENTIER's *Orpheus* in 1972. In 1975 he helped found COMUS MUSIC THEATRE, and from 1977 to 1983 he was head of The BANFF CENTRE SCHOOL OF FINE ART's summer musical-theatre program. In 1981 Bawtree became artistic director of the Musical Theatre Ensemble, a seven-month training program at Banff for young composers, writers, designers, dancers, and singer-actors.   EUGENE BENSON

Beaulne, Guy (b. 1921). Born in Ottawa into a theatrical family—father Léonard founded his own company and was artistic director of La Société des débats français at the Univ. of Ottawa—he attended Lisgar Collegiate in Ottawa and received his teaching certificate from the Normal School at the Univ. of Ottawa, where he also completed a degree in arts and philosophy in 1943. While a student he was director of student radio

The Caveau company with Prime Minister Mackenzie King and French ambassador Francisque Gay after a performance of Jean-François Regnard's Le Légataire universel, *1948. Guy Beaulne is on the far right.*

broadcasting and drama producer for radio station CKCH in Hull.

From 1944 to 1948 Beaulne was artistic director of La Corporation des diseurs du Caveau in Ottawa, where he founded a theatre workshop, acted, and directed several plays. He also taught elocution and dramatic art in the separate schools in Ottawa as well as at the Normal School. A frequent adjudicator at regional and national drama festivals, he was theatre critic for *Le Droit* (1945-52). On grants from the French government, the Canada Foundation, and l'Institut canadien-français d'Ottawa he studied in Europe from 1948 to 1950—French phonetics at the Sorbonne, and with Denis d'Inès at the Conservatoire national d'art dramatique in Paris. He was the Canadian delegate to the second and third UNESCO Congresses of the International Theatre Institute at Zurich (1949) and Paris (1950). In addition, he was Canadian correspondent for various theatre magazines and for Radio-Canada through Radio-diffusion nationale française.

On his return to Canada in 1950 he became producer of radio drama for Radio-Canada, where he created the series 'Les Nouveautés dramatiques', a theatre workshop for authors, actors, and technicians. From 1956

to 1963 he produced Roger Lemelin's radio and television series 'La Famille Plouffe' for both the French and English radio and television networks, as well as many television plays for Shoestring Theatre at CBMT. Apart from his radio and television work he also acted in Félix LECLERC's *Sonnez les matines* at the THÉÂTRE DU RIDEAU VERT in 1956 and in Shakespeare's *La Mégère apprivoisée* (*The Taming of the Shrew*) at the Chantecler summer theatre in Sainte-Adèle in 1959. Beaulne directed Molière's *The Imaginary Invalid* for the CANADIAN REPERTORY THEATRE in Ottawa (1950), *Tartuffe* and *L'Avare* in English for the MONTREAL REPERTORY THEATRE (1953 and 1954), Marcel DUBÉ's *Chambres à louer* for La Jeune Scène de Montréal (a winner in the Western Quebec Drama Festival in 1955), André Roussin's *L'Amour fou* and *Lorsque l'enfant paraît* for the Théâtre du Rideau Vert and the MOUNTAIN PLAYHOUSE in Montreal (in 1958), and other plays.

An ardent promoter of amateur theatre, particularly the DOMINION DRAMA FESTIVAL, Beaulne founded L'Association canadienne du théâtre d'amateurs (ACTA) in 1958, an organization charged with co-ordinating French-language theatre groups and promoting non-professional theatre, which he directed until 1963. A past president of the Canadian Theatre Centre of the International Theatre Institute, he continued his association with the professional theatre while teaching in dramatic arts and directing at several Quebec institutions. He has written theatre and literary criticism for Canadian and foreign periodicals, lectured widely on the history of the theatre and the development of a national drama, and wrote *Notre théâtre: Conscience d'un peuple* (1967) and the preface to *Théâtre canadien-français*, the fifth volume of *Archives des lettres canadiennes* (1976).

Appointed director of theatre services for Quebec's Ministry of Cultural Affairs in 1963, and later director general of artistic training, Beaulne also held administrative posts with various Canadian theatrical groups before being named director general of Le GRAND THÉÂTRE DE QUÉBEC (1970–6). He received the Centennial Medal in 1967, the Order of Canada in 1975, became a fellow of the Royal Society of Canada in 1976, and was cultural counsellor to Quebec's Délégation générale in Paris from 1976 to 1979. He was director of the CONSERVATOIRE D'ART DRAMATIQUE in Montreal from 1981 to 1987.

As an actor, director, teacher, critic, and administrator Beaulne has received many awards: notably the Robert Speaight award

for his production of Jean-François Regnard's *Légataire universel* at the DDF finals in Ottawa in 1948; the Canadian Radio Award (1952); the Canadian Drama Award in recognition of his exceptional contribution to the development of Canadian theatre (1955); and the Frigon Trophy for the best Canadian television drama producer (1959).

MARCEL FORTIN

Beissel, Henry (b. 1929). Born in Cologne, Germany, he studied philosophy there and in London, Eng., before immigrating to Canada in 1951. After a series of odd jobs, he entered graduate school at the Univ. of Toronto, where he earned an MA in English. He has translated nine plays from five different languages, some of which have been broadcast by CBC Radio. *The Curve* (1976) by the German Tankred Dorst, and *The Emigrants* (1984) by the Polish Slawomir Mrozeck are widely produced, small-cast, all-male black comedies about communication, manipulation, and power.

Tensions between artistic freedom and political repression often figure in Beissel's original plays, such as *Goya* (1978), first produced by Montreal Theatre Lab in 1976, which attempts to capture the disorientation of an aging rebel-genius. Indigenous peoples, emigrants, artists, and outsiders intrigue

Henry Beissel's Inook and the Sun, *Edmonton International Children's Festival, 1982, with (l. to r.) Martin J. Williams, Kent Staines, Steven Hilton, Amanda O'Leary, Dena Simon, Anne McGrath*

Beissel. *Under Coyote's Eye* (1979), first produced at Chicago's The Other Theatre in 1978, dramatizes the ironic story of the last Stone Age Indian, found in 1911 outside a California slaughterhouse. Beissel's best-known play, *Inook and the Sun* (1974), premièred at the STRATFORD FESTIVAL in 1973 as a puppet play for young people in the style of the Japanese Bunraku. It is a spare and powerful quest play inspired by the Inuit peoples, and encourages significant contributions from designers. Felix MIRBT's *Inook* puppets not only enhanced the Stratford production, but influenced the playwright's later works. (See PUPPET THEATRE.) Masks, puppets, and poetry, along with a philosophical turn of mind and facility with language, make Beissel's works intelligent, lyrical, unpredictable. The scope and variety of his published pieces are unusually wide and benefit from collaboration with his wife, poet Arlette Francière, with whom he translated *Waiting for Gauldreault* (1978) by André Simard. While teaching at the Univ. of Alberta, Beissel established and edited *Edge*, a controversial political and literary journal (1963-9) that moved with him to Concordia Univ., Montreal, in 1968. In late 1985 he headed the Book and Periodical Council's task force on censorship. JOYCE DOOLITTLE

Belfry Theatre. Originally the Emmanuel Baptist Church, designed by Thomas Hooper and dedicated in 1893, this vacant heritage building in downtown Victoria, B.C., became in 1974 the Spring Ridge Cultural Centre and home to the One World Revue Co. As a heritage building the church could not be altered structurally, but the interior, with its wrap-around balcony, became a 275-seat theatre with a semi-thrust platform stage, 25' deep and 53' wide. It had no proscenium, wings, or fly-space, and only one dressing-room. The fledgeling One World Revue Company soon expired, but the Spring Ridge Centre was officially registered in Dec. 1975 and its first artistic director, Don Shipley, renamed the building The Belfry and modelled its policy on that of the VANCOUVER EAST CULTURAL CENTRE. Kaleidoscope was the resident professional company in that season, and concerts, films, and local productions played, between performances by visiting companies and BASTION THEATRE's studio production of David FREEMAN's CREEPS. In 1977, however, the Belfry announced its own season of plays. It soon acquiried a reputation for 'strong' plays such as Peter Nichols's *A Day in the Death of Joe Egg*, Stewart Parker's *Spokesong*, and Hugh Leonard's *Da*, productions whose quality owed much to an ingenious use of the awkward stage-space. This impetus continued under the artistic director from 1980 to 1984, James Roy, who emphasized Canadian scripts, productions with nationally renowned actors, and vigorous subscription drives. But by 1984 over-expansion led Roy's successor, Miles Potter, to cut the professional staff and reduce the subscription season. In 1986 Glynis Leyshon assumed the theatre's directorship, continuing the mandate to provide challenging contemporary plays (three out of four Canadian in the 1986-7 season) and instigating workshops for new playscripts. ANTHONY JENKINS

Béliveau, Juliette (1890-1975). Known as 'La p'tite Béliveau' because of her diminutive stature (which allowed her to play children's roles until she was in her forties), this beloved actress excelled in comic parts in BURLESQUE, operetta, and MUSICAL THEATRE. For ten years she was a partner of the famous clown Tizoune (Olivier GUIMOND), and she also partnered Juliette Huot in comic music-hall acts. Gratien GÉLINAS wrote parts for her in his Fridolin revues between 1939 and 1948, and she created the role of Aunt Clara in his *TIT-COQ*. She performed the role more than 500 times on stage before playing it in the film *Tit-Coq*. Gélinas remembers her performance as 'funny, moving, and deeply affecting'. Béliveau (her married name was Larue) acted extensively in film and on radio and was well known for her work in the television series 'Les filles d'Ève' and 'Le Pain du jour'. In Mar. 1966 her service to Quebec theatre was recognized by a multitude of friends assembled in Montreal's Théâtre Saint-Denis.

GRATIEN GÉLINAS

Belles-Soeurs, Les. A 'succès de scandale' at the première performance because of its politically charged use of *joual* and its stark naturalism, Michel TREMBLAY's *Les Belles-Soeurs* has since become recognized as a classic of Québécois theatre in its remarkable fusion of realism, theatricality, and lyricism.

Written in 1965, *Les Belles-Soeurs* was rejected by several groups before receiving a

Belles-Soeurs

Germaine Giroux in Les Belles-Soeurs, *Théâtre du Rideau Vert, Montreal, 1968*

public reading at the Centre d'essai des auteurs dramatiques, Montreal, on 4 Mar. 1968, resulting in production offers from five companies. It premièred at the THÉÂTRE DU RIDEAU VERT on 28 Aug. 1968, directed by André BRASSARD. Audiences were quick to accept the play: it has been performed widely in Canada (the English-language première was at Toronto's ST. LAWRENCE CENTRE, 3 Apr. 1973); in Paris, to glowing reviews (Espace Pierre Cardin, 1973); and in the U.S. It was also shown on CBC-TV (Mar. 1978). A special 15th-anniversary production, directed by Brassard, ran in Ottawa, Montreal, and Quebec; reinterpreted to emphasize the absurdist/comical elements of the play, this production drew mixed reviews. The play was published by Holt, Rinehart and Winston in 1968 and by Leméac in 1972; the English TRANSLATION, by Bill GLASSCO and John Van Burek, by Talonbooks in 1974.

Tremblay has repeatedly referred to himself as 'the poet of the rue Fabre', the street of his childhood in East Montreal. The fifteen female characters of the play serve as symbols of French-Canadian alienation and oppression, as well as realistic representatives of the lives of quiet desperation typical of this working-class neighbourhood. The plot is simple. Germaine Lauzon, a housewife who has won one million gold bond trading stamps, organizes an evening of stamp-licking to fill her booklets. Her neighbours arrive, start their work, and gossip; gradually, unable to bear Germaine's good luck, they purloin more and more of the filled booklets. When Germaine realizes what is happening she is outraged and there follows a wild free-for-all. When the women depart Germaine is left alone and disconsolate until, in an absurdist finale, a rain of new gold bond stamps begins to descend to the strains of 'O Canada'.

The appeal of the play derives from Tremblay's masterful creation of character and his handling of dramatic structure to create a complex, multi-level work. Each of the fifteen women comes vibrantly alive: they include Pierrette, black sheep of the family; Angéline, torn between her sinful love of nightclubs and her loyalty to her devout friend, Rhéauna; Olivine Dubuc, the ill-fated 93-year old who suffers untold indignities at the hands of her daughter-in-law; and Lise, the young girl 'in trouble'. The play's structure reflects both Tremblay's love of Shakespearean soliloquy and Greek chorus, and a method of composition that treats the characters' speeches in the manner of musical scores. Each of the two acts features a major chorus that underlines the theme of the play ('Maudite vie plate' and 'Ode to bingo'). Realistic action is further interrupted when each character at some point delivers a monologue revealing to the audience private truths and feelings; even realistic conversations are structured on musical principles, using leitmotif, variations on a theme, counterpoint, echo effects, and refrain.

RENATE USMIANI

Benson, Susan (b. 1942). Born in Kent, Eng., she studied design for six years before working for the BBC and sewing and painting costumes for the Royal Shakespeare Company. Immigrating to Canada in 1966, she spent three years designing costumes for Vancouver's QUEEN ELIZABETH THEATRE and the Vancouver International Festival. Between 1970 and 1974 she was resident designer at the Krannert Centre for the Performing Arts, Illinois.

Susan Benson

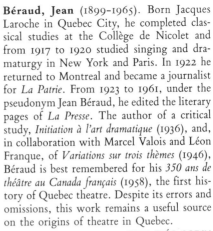

Béraud, Jean (1899-1965). Born Jacques Laroche in Quebec City, he completed classical studies at the Collège de Nicolet and from 1917 to 1920 studied singing and dramaturgy in New York and Paris. In 1922 he returned to Montreal and became a journalist for *La Patrie*. From 1923 to 1961, under the pseudonym Jean Béraud, he edited the literary pages of *La Presse*. The author of a critical study, *Initiation à l'art dramatique* (1936), and, in collaboration with Marcel Valois and Léon Franque, of *Variations sur trois thèmes* (1946), Béraud is best remembered for his *350 ans de théâtre au Canada français* (1958), the first history of Quebec theatre. Despite its errors and omissions, this work remains a useful source on the origins of theatre in Quebec.

JEAN CLÉO GODIN

In 1974, her first year at the STRATFORD FESTIVAL, Benson designed costumes for operas by Eugene Benson and Charles Wilson (*Everyman*) and Gian-Carlo Menotti (*The Medium*) at the Third Stage. In 1975 she designed *Twelfth Night* on the Festival Stage; she also taught that year at the NATIONAL THEATRE SCHOOL. Between 1974 and 1987 she designed costumes for twenty Stratford shows, also co-designing sets for four of them. Her imaginative designs for the 1982 *Mikado* are justly famous—they exemplify her ability to combine delicacy of detail, brilliance of colour, and intelligence of concept.

Benson has also worked at the NATIONAL ARTS CENTRE, the MANITOBA THEATRE CENTRE, Halifax's NEPTUNE THEATRE, THEATRE NEW BRUNSWICK, and Toronto's YOUNG PEOPLE'S THEATRE, among others. Married to designer Michael WHITFIELD, she is also a successful portrait artist and illustrator.

A member of the Royal Canadian Academy of Arts, Benson has won Dora Mavor MOORE Awards for her costume designs for *Twelfth Night* (1980) and *A Funny Thing Happened on the Way to the Forum* (1981), and has represented Canada at the Prague Quadrennial (1979 and 1983). MARTHA MANN

Besnard, Thomas Pope (1806?-1878). Born in Cork, Ireland, this genial amateur was the leading spirit in Canada West's theatricals during his six years' residence there. In 1846, soon after arriving from Ireland, 'T.P.B.', as he was popularly known, was already the most important member of the Toronto Amateur Society, excelling in comic Irish roles. He also introduced various songs into his parts, making a special hit with his own lyrics for 'The City of Toronto', a satirical commentary on current events and prominent citizens. In 1848 Besnard launched his ballad soirée, *An Hour in Ould Ireland*, and for the next two years toured it in Canada West as well as to Montreal and to some American border cities. On 16 Jan. 1849, supported by Toronto and Hamilton amateurs, he presented the first dramatic program at Toronto's new ROYAL LYCEUM THEATRE, of which he became lessee the following December. Though not financially successful, he introduced several talented actors to Toronto, including John and Charlotte NICKINSON. In 1851 he arranged tours throughout the Canadas by the HERON FAMILY and Sir William Don, a popular comedian. It was evident by 1852, however, that Toronto had outgrown amateur management, and after a farewell benefit at the Royal Lyceum in May, Besnard departed for Australia.

MARY SHORTT

Billy Bishop Goes to War. Written by John GRAY (with Eric PETERSON), this musical is based on the life of the Canadian flying ace, Billy Bishop, who shot down seventy-

Billy Bishop Goes to War

Eric Peterson as Billy Bishop in Billy Bishop Goes to War, *Theatre Passe Muraille, Toronto, 1979*

two German planes in the First World War. It premièred at the VANCOUVER EAST CULTURAL CENTRE on 3 Nov. 1978, with Eric Peterson playing the eighteen spoken parts and John Gray as director and narrator/pianist. A sixteen-month Canadian tour was followed by a production at the Arena Theatre, Washington, by on- and off-Broadway productions at the Morosco Theatre and at the Theatre de Lys, in London's West End, at the Edinburgh Festival Mainstage, the Mark Taper Forum in Los Angeles, and the Denver Festival.

The 1980 New York production, presented by Mike Nichols and Lewis Allen, won high praise from critics, and Peterson received the Clarence Derwent award as most promising new actor on Broadway. But the play closed after twelve performances before opening off-Broadway for a long run. A great success at the Edinburgh Festival, it received mixed reviews in London. Musician Ross Douglas and actor Cedric Smith toured a new production in 1980-1, and a CBC-TV version was broadcast on 12 Sept. 1982.

The appeal of *Billy Bishop Goes to War* in its first productions came from the combination of subject (a genuine Canadian hero), composer (a multi-talented musician), and actor (one of Canada's most versatile). The play exposes the futility of war, even while praising the exploits of its hero. Poignant lyrics such as 'Friends Ain't S'posed to Die' and 'In the Sky' are juxtaposed with Peterson's comic impersonations of such characters as Sir Hugh Cecil, Lady St Helen, and King George V, which satirize the colonial mentality—one of Gray's favourite themes—in both Canada and Britain. Gray dedicated the play 'To all those who didn't come back from the war, and to all those who did and wondered why.'

A recording of *Billy Bishop* was released by Tapestry Records in 1979; the text was published by Talonbooks (Vancouver) in 1981, and also appears in *Modern Canadian Plays* (1985), ed. Jerry Wasserman.

JAMES NOONAN

Birney, Earle (b. 1904). Born in Calgary, Alta, he was educated at the Universities of British Columbia, Toronto, California, and London, and taught at the Universities of Utah and Toronto before returning in 1946 to UBC, where he established the world's first Creative Writing Department in 1963. A distinguished Canadian poet, with many collections to his credit, Birney has written several radio plays (he was supervisor of CBC European Foreign Language broadcasts, 1945-

6), including adaptations of poetry and fiction, and three original works: *November Eleven 1948*, a Remembrance Day tribute broadcast that day; *Court-Martial*, co-written with and produced by Mavor MOORE in 1946; and *Trial of a City*, a Joycean historical fantasy that was broadcast in 1952, adapted for the stage as *The Damnation of Vancouver* (produced at UBC in 1957), and published in *Trial of a City and Other Verse* (1952).

ROTA HERZBERG LISTER

Black, Malcolm (b. 1928). Born in Liverpool and trained at the Old Vic School, he immigrated to Canada in 1956. From 1957 to 1959 he was production manager at the CREST THEATRE, Toronto. Since then he has been artistic director at the VANCOUVER PLAYHOUSE (1964-7), THEATRE NEW BRUNSWICK (1978-84), and THEATRE PLUS (1985-9). He was a professor of drama at the Univ. of Washington (1968-70), the City University of New York (1970-4), and York Univ. (1974-8). He has directed more than seventy professional productions across Canada, including works for the BASTION THEATRE, the CITADEL THEATRE, the MANITOBA THEATRE CENTRE, FESTIVAL LENNOXVILLE, and the NATIONAL THEATRE SCHOOL. Among his American directing credits are productions at Philadelphia's Walnut Street Theatre, New Haven's Long Wharf Theatre, The Pasadena Playhouse, and off-Broadway. In musical theatre Black has directed for the St Louis Municipal Opera, the Guelph Spring Festival, Winnipeg's Rainbow Stage, and the Seattle Opera Association.

Black was one of the earliest champions of Canadian drama. At the Vancouver Playhouse he produced plays by west-coast dramatists and commissioned George RYGA to write *The ECSTASY OF RITA JOE*. In 1969, in Seattle, he directed the world première of Beverley SIMONS' *CRABDANCE*. His encouragement of new playwrights continued at Theatre New Brunswick, where he introduced Norm Foster's *Sinners* and *The Melville Boys*, along with other new scripts both on the main stage and in TNB's Young Company. He continued to support new dramatists, including Foster, at Theatre Plus.

Black has written a book about directing, *From First Reading to First Night* (1975). In 1977 he chaired the Canada Council Committee on Theatre Training in Canada.

EDWARD MULLALY

Blackouts, The. This Second World War RCAF musical revue was the first of five revues that originated in Ottawa, played in Canada, and then toured overseas. The others were *Swingtime* (Sept. 1942-5, originally *Joe Boys*); *All Clear* (Sept. 1943-6); *W-Debs* (June 1944-5, an all-female Women's Division production); and *Airscrews*, an all-male concert party. A sixth all-male unit, *The Tarmacs*, was assembled in Oct. 1943 from Canadian airmen in Britain. Although *Blackouts* played the Comedy Theatre in London (1944) and *All Clear* was heard on the BBC, the RCAF shows were primarily small, portable, base shows not designed for civilian audiences. The organizing producer/director was Flight Lieutenant (later Squadron Leader) Robert Coote (1909-82), remembered as Colonel Pickering in the 1964 movie *My Fair Lady*. Canadian entertainers included Jack Bickle, dancer/choreographer; Slim Burgess, comedian; Rex Slocombe, magician; Byng Whitteker, songs/skits; and musicians Wishart Campbell, Neil Chotem, Lloyd Edwards, and Hyman Goodman. Acts consisted of original songs ('Why Am I Always Joe?'; 'He Gave Me His Wings'), production numbers, comedy sketches, acrobatic dances, baton-twirling, magic, and ventriloquism.

DAVID GARDNER

Blais, Marie-Claire (b. 1939). Born and educated in Quebec City, she wrote her first novel, *La Belle Bête* (1959)—translated as *Mad Shadows* (1960)—when she was seventeen, and subsequently gained an international reputation as a novelist. She won the prestigious Prix Médicis in 1966 for *Une Saison dans la vie d'Emmanuel* (1965) and Governor General's Awards for *Les Manuscrits de Pauline Archange* (1968) and *Le Sourd dans la ville* (1979).

Blais has written many plays for radio and television (see RADIO DRAMA and TELEVISION DRAMA) and four stage plays. Her first, *Eléonor*, was produced by Quebec City's L'Estoc company in 1960. *L'Exécution*—produced by the THÉÂTRE DU RIDEAU VERT in Montreal (premièring on 15 Mar. 1968) and directed by Yvette BRIND'AMOUR—is a two-act play set in a boys' school. A cold, charismatic student induces a fellow student to commit a murder, then allows two innocents to be convicted for the crime. The one-act *Marcelle* was one of a group of plays entitled *La Nef des Sorcières*, produced in 1976 by the

THÉÂTRE DU NOUVEAU MONDE, directed by Luce GUILBAULT, which featured a single actress, Pol Pelletier, in a series of monologues. Here Blais intensively but affectionately portrayed the difficulty facing a couple living with a doomed homosexual love. Her most recent play, *Sommeil d'hiver* (1984), uses dramatic symbolism and a feverish style of writing that achieves extraordinary clarity.

Among her many honours, Blais has received the Prix Athanase-David (1982) and the Prix de l'Académie française (1983).

ANNE-MARIE ALONZO

Blake, William Rufus (1802–63). After a brief career as actor-manager of an amateur company, Blake made his professional acting début in Halifax as the Prince of Wales in *Richard III* for Thomas Placide's company of American actors in 1817. He made his New York début at the Chatham Street Theatre in 1824. Married to Placide's daughter, Caroline Waring, in 1826, he managed the opening seasons at Boston's Tremont Theatre in 1827 and the renovated Walnut Street Theatre in Philadelphia before returning to Canada in 1831 to star in Vincent DeCamp's company in Montreal and Quebec. He later managed his own company of American actors at The Theatre, Halifax, for which he produced and probably wrote *FITZALLAN*, the first play by a Canadian-born author produced in Canada. By the late 1830s increasing girth led him to specialize in character roles, though he continued to manage various American theatres, and he ended his career as one of New York's highest paid actors with James Wallack's and Laura Keene's companies. His plays include *Nero*, *The Turned Head*, *Norman Leslie*, and *The Buggs*, a burlesque. Outstanding roles were Jesse Rural in Dion Boucicault's *Old Heads and Young Hearts*, Jeffrey Dale in G.D. Pitt's *The Last Man*, Lord Duberly in George Colman the younger's *The Heir at Law*, and Sir Peter Teazle in Sheridan's *The School for Scandal*.

See Denis Salter, 'William Rufus Blake and the Gentlemanly Art of Comic Acting', *Proceeding of the Theatre in Atlantic Canada Symposium* (1988), ed. Richard Paul Knowles.

PATRICK B. O'NEILL

Blood Relations. Sharon POLLOCK's play about Lizzie Borden, the accused axe murderer of her parents, won the first Governor General's Award for drama in 1981. It pre-

mièred at THEATRE 3, Edmonton, on 12 Mar. 1980, directed by Keith Digby and featuring Janet Daverne as Miss Lizzie with Judith Mabey as the Actress.

Pollock examines the sensational Fall River, Mass., crime through a dramatic re-enactment ten years after Miss Lizzie's acquittal, conducted as a performance game played with her actress friend (a character suggested by the historical Nance O'Neill) who, like the playwright, is fascinated by the ambiguity of the Lizzie Borden myth. Rather than a who-done-it (in contrast to Pollock's earlier version of the play, *My Name is Lisbeth*, first performed in 1976), *Blood Relations* ultimately begs the historical question of whether or not Lizzie was actually guilty. It offers instead what the text calls a 'dream thesis', in which Miss Lizzie, not answering the crucial question directly, 'paints in the background' for her friend's performance of her own younger self during those crucial two days in the summer of 1892. Miss Lizzie plays the part of Bridget, the Bordens' maid. The Actress, although directed in part by Miss Lizzie, has to find her own answers; in the process the audience is also tacitly invited to participate in the investigation. The play begins as a flashback (with the other figures of time past appearing as required). By the second act, however, the Actress is leaving her friend behind in the increasing autonomy of her own interpretation. Indeed, she seems to forget that this is a performance and so, for a time, she becomes a Lizzie Borden who will eventually commit murder.

In the emerging play-within-the-play, the playwright has created a presentational performance of the interpretive process itself. It shows an independent-minded woman deprived of the freedom to live her own life beyond the choices allowed by the oppressive conventions of her time and social class— reluctant marriage or dutiful daughterhood. In her difficult relationship with a beloved father who is abetted by the goadings of an obtuse stepmother, Lizzie's sense of self is under continual threat. Matters come to their first crisis when, in a fit of guilty anger, Mr Borden kills Lizzie's pet birds with an axe; this is because she is rightly resisting his determination to transfer the farm cherished by Lizzie and her sister Emma to his wife's name, thereby ensuring its appropriation by the latter's parasitical brother.

The Actress's interpretation of what follows shows a Lizzie Borden struggling against emotional despair, thereby creating much sympathy for her predicament and horror at the choices left to her. At the end, the Actress herself—and by extension the audience, witnessing her shift from Brechtian detachment to total involvement—is nudged into the unsettling recognition that anyone might be capable of murder. The historical answer to the Borden mystery becomes irrelevant in the face of the disturbing on-stage immediacy of the psychodrama of 1902.

The play was first published in Pollock's *Blood Relations and Other Plays* (1981) and subsequently in *The Penguin Book of Modern Canadian Drama* (1984), ed. Richard Plant and in *Plays by Women 3*, ed. Michelene Wandor (1984). For critical commentary, see Robert Nunn, 'Sharon Pollock's Plays', *Theatre History in Canada* 5 (1984); Diane Bessai, 'Sharon Pollock's Women', *A Mazing Space* (1986), ed. Shirley Neuman and Smaro Kamborelli; and *Canadian Drama and the Critics* (1987), ed. L. W. Conolly.   DIANE BESSAI

Blouin, Paul (b. 1925). Born in Dauphin, Man., he was educated in Saskatchewan, before moving to Montreal where for ten years he studied voice and drama. He sang with the Variétés Lyriques, and acted with the MONTREAL REPERTORY THEATRE, the THÉÂTRE DU NOUVEAU MONDE, the THÉÂTRE DU RIDEAU VERT, and the Théâtre des Noirs where he became interested in directing. In 1954 he joined Radio-Canada, where his direction of the award-winning television serial 'Cap-aux Sorciers' (1955-8) by Guy DUFRESNE established his reputation as a gifted director.

From 1959 to 1986, when he retired from Radio-Canada, Blouin directed fifty-seven plays, twenty-seven written by Quebec dramatists, including Robert Choquette, Marcel DUBÉ, Gratien GÉLINAS, Françoise LORANGER, Pierre Perrault, Robert Rémillard, and Michel TREMBLAY. He also directed works by Garcia Lorca, John Steinbeck, Harold Pinter, Strindberg, Ibsen, Racine, Edward Albee, and Marguerite Duras. His sensitivity to the special qualities of individual actors is legendary—he has directed Gilles PELLETIER, Jacques GODIN, Benoit Girard, Marc Favreau, Dyne Mousseau, Monique Miller, and Janine Sutto, among others—and his skill in cutting established his allusive, economical style.

In 1965 Blouin began directing for theatre

companies, including the Rideau Vert, the NOUVELLE COMPAGNIE THÉÂTRALE, the COMPAGNIE JEAN DUCEPPE, and the Café de la Place, producing Pirandello, Pinter, Anouilh, and Corneille. In 1970 he won the Victor Morin Prize and in 1980 and 1982 the Anik Prize.   RENÉE LEGRIS

Blyth Festival. Dedicated to the development of new Canadian plays, it has become one of the nation's most important theatres, despite its unlikely location, a small rural community in southwestern Ontario. Blyth productions are aimed primarily at local townspeople and farmers, normally not theatregoers, who have provided the Festival with solid support.

James Roy, a native of Blyth and a York Univ. theatre graduate, founded the Blyth Festival in 1975 with the assistance of his wife, playwright Anne CHISLETT, and Keith Roulston, who had come to Blyth in the early 1970s to edit the town newspaper. The founders were aware of the success of THEATRE PASSE MURAILLE's *The FARM SHOW*, which had been created in nearby Clinton in 1972. Similar COLLECTIVEs became part of the Blyth repertoire, especially in the first seasons, and Passe Muraille veterans such as Paul THOMPSON, Janet AMOS, Anne Anglin, David FOX, and Ted JOHNS have contributed to Blyth's success.

Memorial Hall, erected between 1919 and 1921, which had a community hall in the basement and a rundown theatre upstairs, became the home of the Blyth Festival. Helen Gowing and other citizens funded improvements such as a new roof, fire-escapes, and modern electrical wiring. In 1979 the Festival spent over $100,000 on further vital renovations, including air-conditioning. A new wing was added in 1980 to accommodate a box office, dressing rooms, an art gallery, and storage space. In addition, the small balcony, which had originally been declared a fire hazard, was brought up to current safety standards to add 88 seats, making 491 in all.

To open the Blyth Festival, Roy chose Agatha Christie's mystery, *The Mousetrap*; but subsequently Blyth concentrated on new plays, some of them collectives concerned with regional history, others adaptations of works by celebrated regional writers, such as Alice Munro and Harry Boyle. The Festival is best known, however, for two plays: Peter Colley's thriller *I'll Be Back before Midnight*

Blyth Festival

Blyth Memorial Hall

(in the 1979 season), which has been performed throughout Canada, and Anne Chislett's *Quiet in the Land*, produced in 1981. Chislett's *The Tomorrow Box* (1981 season) was so popular it was remounted for a second season in 1983, as was Ted Johns' musical *Country Hearts* (produced 1982-3) and Colleen Curran's comedy *Cake-Walk* (produced 1984-5), which both went on post-season tours. Ted Johns, who has also acted at Blyth, has been one of the Festival's most prolific playwrights, contributing *He Won't Come in From the Barn* (produced in 1981), *The School Show* (produced 1978), and *St Sam and the Nukes* (produced 1980).

Janet Amos, who had acted in *The Farm Show* and at Blyth, became artistic director in 1979. While maintaining its traditional goals, she helped the Festival to improve production standards, expand facilities, and build attendance from outside the community. Her concern about finding new plays led her to secure funding for a workshop program and to begin occasionally to produce Canadian plays that had premièred elsewhere, such as Gratien GÉLINAS's *Bousille and the Just* in 1983 (titled *The Innocent and the Just*). When Amos resigned in 1984 she was replaced by her

assistant Katherine Kaszas, under whom Blyth has set new attendance records, expanded its touring program, raised funds for improved facilities, and seen a growing interest in Blyth plays in theatres across the country.

The archives of the Blyth Festival are housed at the Univ. of Guelph.   ROSS STUART

Blythe, Domini (b. 1947). Born in Cheshire, Eng., she studied at the Central School of Speech and Drama, London (1964-7). A tour of Northern England with the London Arts Theatre in 1967 was followed by minor parts with the Birmingham Repertory Theatre in 1968, the Royal Shakespeare Company in 1969-70, and in Kenneth Tynan's controversial *Oh! Calcutta!* in 1970. Moving to Canada in 1972, she quickly established a reputation as the winsome heroine: Viola, Juliet, Rose Trelawny (in Arthur Wing Pinero's *Trelawny of the 'Wells'*) at the ST. LAWRENCE CENTRE (1972-6), and Judith Anderson (*The Devil's Disciple*) and Cleopatra (*Caesar and Cleopatra*) at the SHAW FESTIVAL (1974-5). She joined the STRATFORD FESTIVAL company in 1976, playing Celia in *As You Like It* (1977-8) and Rosaline in *Love's Labour's Lost* (1979)—and also challenging herself with an elegant but 'emotionally antiseptic' Miss Julie (1977), a moving Lady Macduff (1978), and a tragic Lavinia in Brian Bedford's production of *Titus Andronicus* (1978). In high comedy she played a consummately rendered Marwood to Maggie Smith's Millamant in William Congreve's *The Way of the World* in 1976, along with Sorel Bliss in Noël Coward's *Hay Fever* in 1977, and Gwendolen Fairfax in Oscar Wilde's *The Importance of Being Earnest* in 1979. She returned to the RSC in 1981 in a demanding range of parts—Aspatia in Beaumont and Fletcher's *The Maid's Tragedy*, Queen Elizabeth in *Richard III*, and Helen in C.P. Taylor's *Good*—but returned to Stratford, Ont., in 1983 as Margery in William Wycherley's *The Country Wife*, followed in 1984 by an alluring Elmire to Brian Bedford's Tartuffe and a 'dapper' Portia radiating 'demure feminine charm' to John NEVILLE's Shylock.

DENIS SALTER

Bolt, Carol (b. 1941). A native of Winnipeg, she graduated in 1961 with a BA from the Univ. of British Columbia, where she also studied playwriting. After a year abroad, in Great Britain and Israel, she became a market researcher in Montreal, started a theatre there, and began writing children's plays. Transferred to Toronto in the late 1960s, she met and married actor-playwright David Bolt.

Bolt's first Toronto work, *Daganawida*, a weak play about the French and Indians in Quebec, was produced in 1970 at TORONTO WORKSHOP PRODUCTIONS, directed by George LUSCOMBE. Her association with Luscombe and later Paul THOMPSON of THEATRE PASSE MURAILLE gave her the experience of working in a process of collective collaboration and of making a political or social statement at the same time. This is true of her early works *BUFFALO JUMP* (1972), *Gabe* (1973), and *Red Emma—Queen of the Anarchists* (1974). All three use songs, vignettes, and larger-than-life characters to provide both social commentary and entertainment. *Buffalo Jump*, first produced at Theatre Passe Muraille in 1972 under the direction of Paul Thompson, is a sympathetic picture of the plight of Canada's unemployed in the Depression years and their confrontation with Prime Minister R.B. Bennett. *Gabe*, which premièred at TORONTO FREE THEATRE on 14 Feb. 1973, directed by Robert Handforth, dramatizes the unhappy lives of two young Métis in present-day Batoche. Gabe and Louis, the spiritual heirs of Gabriel Dumont and Louis Riel, show how little was achieved by the heroic struggles of their predecessors. *Red Emma*, which opened at Toronto Free Theatre on 5 Feb. 1974, directed by Martin KINCH, depicts the early life of anarchist Emma Goldman and her role in the attempted assassination of American industrialist Henry Clay Frick in 1892. It was also made into a film for CBC television (1976), directed by Allan King and Martin Kinch. Another successful play that went through the collaborative process and that had a popular run at Theatre Passe Muraille in 1973 was *Pauline*, a collage based on the life and work of the Mohawk poet Pauline Johnson.

Bolt's sympathy with characters who try to reach beyond themselves is reflected in both the style and content of later plays. *Shelter* (1975), first produced at Toronto's Firehall Theatre in Dec. 1974, directed by Eric STEINER, moves away from history to present contemporary women in the world of politics, in this case the comic efforts of a

widow from Elbow, Sask., who runs for and wins her husband's seat in the federal parliament. *One Night Stand* (1977), Bolt's most successful play to date, opened at Toronto's TARRAGON THEATRE in Apr. 1977, again under director Eric Steiner. A taut comic thriller reminiscent of the novel and film *Looking for Mr. Goodbar*, it also played at FESTIVAL LENNOXVILLE in 1978, and was made into a CBC television film by Allan King, with Brent CARVER and Chapelle Jaffe recreating the principal roles they played in the original stage production. (This film version won three Canadian film awards in 1978.) *Escape Entertainment* (1982), a romantic comedy about the film industry in Canada, was first produced at Tarragon Theatre in 1981 directed by Timothy Bond.

A playwright with an instinct for interesting dramatic subjects, Bolt has not always shaped her material well. Several of her plays suggest she needs to take more time to refine her work. Such plays are *Love or Money*, produced at the 1981 BLYTH FESTIVAL, about the legendary Canadian theatre owner Ambrose SMALL; *Norman Bethune: On Board the S.S. Empress of Asia*, produced at the Muskoka Summer Theatre in Gravenhurst, Ont., 1976, for the dedication of Bethune's birthplace; and *Desperados*, a confused play about confused characters in the 1960s, produced in 1977 at Toronto Free Theatre.

Bolt is a successful children's playwright who shows a fine facility for storytelling, engaging songs, mime, and audience participation. She is able to entertain a young audience with serious and specifically Canadian subjects. *Cyclone Jack* (1972) is about Onondaga Olympic runner Tom Longboat; *My Best Friend Is Twelve Feet High* (1972) celebrates joys of togetherness among children; *Tangleflags* (1974) tells how Canadians of different origins compromise to call their town Tangleflags; and *Maurice* (1974) is a musical satire about life under the autocratic Premier Maurice Duplessis of Quebec. *My Best Friend is Twelve Feet High* was produced at the Ontario Youth Theatre in 1972, the others at the YOUNG PEOPLE'S THEATRE, Toronto—*Cyclone Jack* in 1972, *Tangleflags* in 1973, *Maurice* in 1974. Among Bolt's unpublished children's plays are *Blue* and *Finding Bumble*, produced at the Young People's Theatre in 1974 and 1975 respectively. (See CHILDREN'S DRAMA AND THEATRE IN ENGLISH.)

Bolt is also a prolific writer of radio and

television plays. These include *Guy and Jack* for CBC Regina radio in 1970; *Fast Forward* for the CBC 'Stage' series in 1976; *Silent Pictures*, about Canadian-born film star Mary Pickford and the formation of the United Artists studio, for CBC Stereo in 1983; *Tinsel on My Stetson*, a five-part serial on CBC's 'Morningside' in 1984; and *Seeing God*, a drama based on the experimental use of hallucinogenic drugs in the 1950s, produced on the CBC 'Vanishing Point' series in 1985. In 1987 she contributed a five-part serial to CBC's 'Morningside', 'Dancing with Each Other', a comedic look at the DOMINION DRAMA FESTIVAL, and to CBC Stereo's Sextet anthology a play, *Yellow Ribbons*, about a missing twelve-year-old girl. Besides being a regular contributor to the popular children's television program 'Fraggle Rock', Bolt has written the television script *Valerie* for the CBC series 'To See Ourselves' (1971), *Distance* for TV Ontario's 'True North' (1974), and *A Nice Girl Like You* for CBC's 'Collaborators' (1974). (See RADIO DRAMA IN ENGLISH and TELEVISION DRAMA IN ENGLISH.)

Bolt was a founding member of Playwrights Canada. In 1976 she was appointed to the board of directors of the Toronto Arts Council where she serves as co-chair with actress Frances HYLAND of the Theatre Committee.

See *Playwrights in Profile: Carol Bolt* (1976), which includes *Buffalo Jump*, *Gabe*, and *Red Emma*.   JAMES NOONAN

Boules de neige, Les. First produced on 21 May 1903 at the MONUMENT NATIONAL in Montreal, this comedy by Louvigny de Montigny (1876-1955) remains one of the most original and popular plays of the period. Its subject—the effects of gossip on a Quebec community—is developed in three acts: at the Barabé home in Varennes in July; at Dr Beaugy's home in Montreal in October; and at the home of the Harbois family in Montreal in December.

In Act 1 Mr and Mrs Barabé are upset with the Prévairs and with Mrs Prévair's sister Aline Harbois—city people staying at their house. The late-night forays of their visitors lead to neighbourhood gossip and to a misunderstanding—Prévair is alleged to have been seen kissing his sister-in-law, Aline—that scandalizes the Barabés. In Act 2 the Prévairs and Aline, forced by rumours to

return to the city, find that the scandal has 'snowballed' and reached Montreal, causing Aline's fiancé, Dr Beaugy, to break their engagement. The third act, where all the characters meet again at a party, features light-hearted banter, dancing, and most important, party games such as 'gossip' and 'rumour' that encourage tittle-tattle and idle chatter. These frivolous activities conclude with some hope of reconciliation.

Although the play resembles a comedy of manners, some highly dramatic moments emphasize the dangers of gossip, and also the tension arising from the conflict between the freedom of city ways and the social conformity of rural communities. Despite its favourable reception and critical acclaim, the play is marred by discontinuity between speeches that are often verbose, a lack of economy and control in linking scenes, and shallow characterization. Nonetheless, it provides an interesting chronicle of middle-class habits and customs of the time. *Les Boules de neige* was originally published in 1903 by *Le Monde illustré* and subsequently by Librairie Déom frère in 1935. A film version was released in 1953.

Born in Saint-Jerôme, Que., de Montigny wrote other plays—comedies such as *Je vous aime* (1902) and period sketches or folk dramas such as *Le Bouquet de Mélusine* (1928) and *L'Épi rouge et autres scènes du pays* (1953), all of which were produced.

See also the *Dictionnaire des oeuvres littéraires du Québec*, 2 (1980).   RÉMI TOURANGEAU

Brae Manor Theatre. A summer theatre and theatre school founded in 1936 by Filmore Sadler and his wife Marjorie—who had met and married in Boston while studying at the Leland Power School of Theatre—it had close working relations with the MONTREAL REPERTORY THEATRE, whose own school of theatre was also run by the Sadlers. Operating from their home in Knowlton, about 120 kilometres south-east of Montreal, the Sadlers offered weekday classes in acting, voice, movement, and makeup, and the opportunity to act in workshop productions. Students were also involved in preparing a weekly production—directed, designed, and performed by guest artists, with some advanced students also taking roles. Plays were initially presented in a local hotel, but in 1940 the Brae Manor Playhouse, seating about 200, opened adjacent to the Sadlers' home. Guest directors included Herbert WHITTAKER, Malcolm Morley, and Robertson DAVIES, who directed his own *AT MY HEART'S CORE* in 1953, with his wife Brenda in the leading role. Among the actors who appeared at Brae Manor were Amelia HALL, John COLICOS, Christopher PLUMMER, Anna Cameron, Ron Hartmann, and Pierre DAGENAIS. The repertoire was largely light summer fare, but plays by Jean Giraudoux, Bernard Shaw, Christopher Fry, Terence Rattigan, Noël Coward, R.B. Sheridan, and Ferenc Molnár were also produced. Filmore Sadler died in 1954. His wife, after three seasons as sole manager, closed the theatre in 1956.

See also SUMMER STOCK.

HERBERT WHITTAKER

Brassard, André (b.1946). Born in Montreal, he has been fascinated with the theatre since childhood. In 1965, while preparing to audition for the NATIONAL THEATRE SCHOOL, he was asked to direct *The Trojan Women* for Les SALTIMBANQUES, then Montreal's most avant-garde amateur company, and has been directing ever since. Forming his own company, Le Mouvement Contemporain, he attracted a number of talented young performers (Rita Lafontaine, Jean Archambault, Jacques Desnoyers, and others), with whom he produced such authors as Samuel Beckett, Jean Genet, and Fernando Arrabal. The company also staged some early TREMBLAY pieces: *Messe Noire*, 1965, an adaptation of several stories from *Contes pour buveurs attardés*, and *Cinq*, 1966, an early version of *En Pièces détachées*.

The première performance of Tremblay's *Les BELLES-SOEURS*, at the THÉÂTRE DU RIDEAU VERT, 1968, marked the beginning of a new era of professional directing. Brassard and Tremblay worked closely together, with Tremblay providing the scripts, often without stage directions, and Brassard creating the *mise-en-scène*. The system worked well; Tremblay has since described Brassard's contribution as 'as important, if not more important' than his own. The Tremblay/Brassard tandem in turn attracted the best acting talent in Quebec. The group included Rita Lafontaine, Jean Archambault, Hubert Gagnon, and Claude Gai, later joined by Beatrice Picard, Monique Mercure, Michelle Rossignol, Amulette Garneau, Hélène LOISELLE, Denise Proulx, Gilles Renault, Carmen Tremblay, and Denise Filiatraut. In

1969 the NATIONAL ARTS CENTRE opened with an adaptation of *Lysistrata* by Tremblay, directed by Brassard.

Brassard has directed at all major French theatres in Montreal, as well as at leading English-language theatres (the CENTAUR THEATRE, the SAIDYE BRONFMAN CENTRE, the STRATFORD FESTIVAL's Third Stage, and the ST LAWRENCE CENTRE in Toronto, where in 1973 he directed the English-language première of *Les Belles-Soeurs*). He has taught at the National Theatre School, and has produced three films and two television shows. In Dec. 1981 Brassard became director of the French section of the National Arts Centre, intent upon raising standards and encouraging minority (Ontario and Manitoba) francophone theatre. Totally dedicated to his vocation of *metteur-en-scène* ('le mot "religion" n'est pas trop fort'), he prefers fringe to mainstream theatre.

Brassard's approach to directing is entirely subjective and pragmatic: 'I have no preconceived method; I feel a text, and I know it has to be done in such and such a way.' His goal is to activate the audience, transforming their 'voyeurism' from the 'sterile' to the 'fertile'. The most typical element of Brassard's style is the use of a dominant, often overwhelming, stage image: the grotesque statue of the Virgin Mary in Tremblay's *Damnée Manon, Sacrée Sandra* at the THÉÂTRE DE QUAT'SOUS in 1977; the dummy parent figures, stage centre, for the 1977 FESTIVAL LENNOXVILLE production of *À TOI, POUR TOUJOURS, TA MARIE-LOU*; the huge dining-room table in the THÉÂTRE DU NOUVEAU MONDE production of *Bonjour, là, Bonjour*; the giant bust of Nero for the 1982 National Arts Centre production of *Britannicus*. This corresponds with his idea (for Tremblay productions especially) that the physical action of the actors should be kept to a minimum in order to emphasize the interplay of voices. To maximize his actors' energy, he often uses an inclined stage floor, which forces them into a heightened state of awareness.

As Brassard's style has evolved he has moved steadily further away from surface realism. This is well illustrated by his reinterpretations of *Les Belles-Soeurs*: the 1968 version was fully realistic; in 1971, he stylized the production, with an inclined floor and movable furniture wheeled onstage by the actresses; the 15th-anniversary production of 1984 transformed the play into an absurdist

Brassard

comedy, with a symbolic colour scheme for costumes and the kitchen setting de-emphasized through the use of grey tones for the nondescript appliances. His most acclaimed production at the National Arts Centre was an adaptation of Shakespeare's *Pericles* in 1982, in a decentralized space, with locales suggested by miniature models that descended from the flies to hover over the acting area.   RENATE USMIANI

Brind'Amour, Yvette (b. 1918). Born in Montreal, she made her professional début in 1938 with the MONTREAL REPERTORY THEATRE in François Mauriac's *Asmodée*. She subsequently performed on radio and on stage with various other companies, notably L' Arcade and L'ÉQUIPE, where her interpretation of Inès in a 1946 production of Sartre's *Huis-Clos* confirmed her talents as an actress. After studying in 1947 at the René Simon school and the École Charles Dullin in Paris, she founded, in Nov. 1948, the THÉÂTRE DU RIDEAU VERT, where she acquired a reputation both in Canada and abroad as a director and as an actress. Among her most distinguished roles were Inès in *La Reine morte* by Henry de Montherlant in 1956, and Ysé in *Partagé de midi* by Paul Claudel in 1962. Brind'Amour also helped to promote Quebec drama; in 1976, for example, she directed Antonine MAILLET's *Évangeline deusse* and *Gapi* for Rideau Vert. In 1964 she received the medal of the City of Paris and in 1987 she was awarded the Molson Prize for her distinguished contribution to the arts.
                    NORMAND LEROUX

British Columbia, Theatre in. 1. *1850 to the First World War*. As in other Canadian provinces, the beginnings of theatre in B.C. are associated with the military and with traders. The first recorded performances, in 1853, were by sailors of HMS *Trincomalee* in Esquimault harbour, and by employees of the Hudson's Bay Company at Fort Victoria. Nothing is known of their content. Such amateur efforts represented theatrical life in the colonial communities of Vancouver Island throughout the 1850s, and by the end of the decade they had been extended to the garrison at New Westminster on the mainland. A playbill survives for an all-male production of R.B. Sheridan's *The Rivals* at Fort Victoria in 1857. (See GARRISON THEATRE.)

If these early efforts were British in style and content, the beginnings of professional theatre had an American source that was to dominate the province's professional theatrical life in the period before the First World War. In Mar. 1859 the Chapman family, who had spent the previous decade in California, performed in Victoria. They appeared in an Assembly building, but in the following year returned to open the COLONIAL THEATRE, where they performed for three months. Their repertoire took some account of the ethnic origins of their audiences by including *The Warlock of the Glen* in which the Chapmans' daughter performed a highland dance. In the 1860s similar companies visited New Westminster and in one case ventured as far as Hope and Yale. Victoria's most distinguished visitors in that decade were, however, British—Charles and Ellen Kean, who appeared with the Thomas Ward Company in Shakespeare's *Henry VIII* and Dion Boucicault's *Louis XI* in Dec. 1864. The city also had a potentially distinguished theatrical resident during this decade in the young David Belasco, though it is unclear whether he was affected by the nascent theatre around him.

Victoria was the main centre of B.C. theatrical activity until Vancouver was founded in 1886. Vancouver gradually acquired theatres to cater for the increasing number of touring companies that began including B.C. on their circuits in the Pacific Northwest. Visiting troupes included James A. Herne with the Fanny Morgan Phelps Company in 1875; Fanny Janauschek in 1883 and 1885; William A. Brady and his Webster-Brady Dramatic Company in 1888; and Madame Modjeska in 1889 in Shakespeare's *As You Like It* and Friedrich Schiller's *Mary Stuart*. Statistics for the 1870s show at least fifteen visits by legitimate theatre companies, and close to fifty visits by minstrel shows and opera and variety-vaudeville companies. Some legitimate companies did, however, prolong their stay for several months and become almost resident companies.

The discovery of gold in the Cariboo in the 1860s took theatre into the province's interior, where it flourished briefly at the Theatre Royal in Barkerville with the Cariboo Amateur Dramatic Association and with some touring companies entertaining miners. Between 1865 and 1875 there were at least 105 productions of eighty-five plays.

The sign of theatrical stability in burgeoning communities was the construction of a major 'opera house'. In Victoria it was the VICTORIA THEATRE (1885); Herring's Opera House in New Westminster followed in 1887; and there were soon similar buildings in Nanaimo (1890) and Vancouver (the VANCOUVER OPERA HOUSE, 1891). These theatres welcomed the better stock companies as well as individual performers who normally gave one or two high-priced performances. Other theatres were often wooden structures or converted halls. In Vancouver the City Hall provided an auditorium for stock companies in the 1890s. It was there that Harry LINDLEY spiced productions of Dion Boucicault's plays with VAUDEVILLE acts and the distribution of free groceries.

In 1887 Vancouver became the terminus of the Canadian Pacific Railway and by 1891 had a rail link to the U.S. via New Westminster. Vancouver slowly began to overtake Victoria in population and in the extent of its theatrical life, though major touring groups usually visited both cities. By 1912 Vancouver had, in addition to its opera house, three sizeable vaudeville theatres (the Pantages, the ORPHEUM, and the Columbia) and could house stock companies at the Avenue and Empress theatres.

Communities in the interior more often relied on minor touring stock companies and vaudeville troupes that would make their way from the coast to the Okanagan and the Kootenays. The communities of the Kootenays (such as Kaslo, Fort Steele, Rossland, and New Denver) enjoyed a vigorous theatrical life in the first decade of the twentieth century during a short-lived mining boom. British immigrants were also particularly active in such communities in amateur theatricals. The Orchard Players of Kelowna, for example, toured the province in 1912 with productions of Oliver Goldsmith's *She Stoops to Conquer* and Oscar Wilde's *The Importance of Being Earnest*.

There was also activity among other ethnic groups, notably the Chinese, both during Barkerville's heyday and in Vancouver, where the large Chinese community was occasionally entertained by professional companies from San Francisco. (See MULTICULTURAL THEATRE.)

The repertoire of this period initially lagged behind that available in cities such as Toronto and Montreal. By the turn of the century, however, as the number of touring companies increased, Vancouver and Victoria could see the road company of a Broadway play within a year or two of the initial production. The repertoire of resident stock companies also increasingly reflected contemporary drama rather than such late nineteenth-century fare as plays by Boucicault and such perennials as *Uncle Tom's Cabin* and *East Lynne*. Canadian plays were still rarely to be found.

2. *1920-60*. The decade after the First World War was one of transition in the commercial realm. Silent movies were developing, but vaudeville continued to flourish. Touring companies were fewer, and the number of resident stock companies declined. By the onset of the Depression the 'talkies' had arrived and, apart from occasional visitors, theatrical activity depended on indigenous efforts.

The 1920s and early 1930s are particularly remembered for visits by notable British performers and companies: Sir John Martin-Harvey, the Stratford-upon-Avon Company, the Abbey Theatre, Sir Barry Jackson's Birmingham Repertory Theatre, and others. (See TOURING STARS AND COMPANIES.) But Vancouver, at least, still had reputable stock companies: the Allen Company, Charles Royal's company, and the British Guild Players. Local theatrical efforts were also beginning to advance beyond the casual amateurism of earlier decades. At the Univ. of British Columbia Frederic Wood, a native of Victoria who had attended George Pierce Baker's drama classes at Harvard, organized the Players' Club in 1915, and in the following year directed its first performance, Jerome K. Jerome's *Fanny and the Servant Problem*. In 1953 the first Frederic Wood Theatre opened on the UBC campus in two converted huts, and its annual season of productions (now in a new theatre constructed in 1963) have become an integral part of Vancouver theatrical activity. Wood was also involved in the founding of the Vancouver Little Theatre in 1921, as was Dorothy SOMERSET.

In Victoria the Victoria Theatre Guild was founded in 1930 and is still operating (now at the Langham Court Theatre). Similar groups developed in the interior, though none were as elaborate as Carroll AIKINS' brief experiment at Naramata in the early 1920s. By the mid-thirties there were over eighty community theatrical groups in the province. They were encouraged by the frequent tours of the UBC Players' Club, the

British Columbia, Theatre in

establishment of the DOMINION DRAMA FESTIVAL in 1932, and the founding of a provincial drama festival by a teacher of drama in Victoria, Major Llewelyn BULLOCK-WEBSTER, who later became an important force for theatre in the schools.

The Depression years also saw the development of left-wing theatrical groups in both Vancouver and Victoria. Vancouver's Progressive Arts Players (amateurs drawn from the ranks of the unemployed) were active between 1935 and 1938, scoring a notable success in 1936 when their production of Clifford Odets' *Waiting for Lefty* won the award for the best production in English at the 1936 finals of the Dominion Drama Festival.

In the postwar period two attempts were made to establish professional theatrical companies: Sydney RISK's Everyman Theatre (1946-53), and Totem Theatre (1951-4), founded by Thor Arngrim and Stuart Baker. In its early years Risk's company toured extensively in B.C. and other western provinces. Totem was based first in Vancouver before moving to Victoria. Neither company had a stable home and, more important, no reliable source of funding. Yet both were ambitious. Between Nov. 1951 and May 1952, for example, Totem produced twelve plays, and included in an adventurous repertoire Jean-Paul Sartre's *No Exit* and Tennessee Williams' *The Glass Menagerie* and *A Streetcar Named Desire*.

Although graduates of UBC's Players' Club and Dorothy Somerset's Summer School of Theatre (founded in 1939) were well equipped for professional careers, they had little opportunity to develop them in B.C. Peter Mannering, later the founding director of Victoria's BASTION THEATRE Company, moved to the MANITOBA THEATRE CENTRE. Sam Payne became a member of Ottawa's CANADIAN REPERTORY THEATRE, though between 1955 and 1957 he returned to Vancouver to mount summer seasons at the Georgia Auditorium under the banner of Vanguard Productions. After 1958 the Vancouver International Festival also provided seasonal work for local actors for a decade. Its first theatrical production was the première of *The World of the Wonderful Dark* by an alumnus of the Players' Club, Lister SINCLAIR.

3. *1960 to date*. The period from 1960 to the present has seen theatre come of age in B.C., as in other Canadian provinces. By the late 1960s roots had been established that would lead to a remarkable flourishing of activity during the 1970s that the economic recession of the early 1980s did not seriously erode.

Contributing to the success of the theatre movement was the closer integration of theatre into the higher educational system. Dorothy Somerset's efforts at UBC were rewarded by the establishment of a department of theatre in 1958. A similar department at the Univ. of Victoria (1966) added to the capital's limited theatrical life. In 1965 Vancouver City College established Studio 58 under the direction of Anthony Holland.

Interior of the Waterfront Theatre, owned and operated by the New Play Centre and Carousel Theatre, Vancouver

This is a comprehensive theatre-training program that emphasizes performance and mounts several productions each year. More recently these academic efforts have been complemented by the VANCOUVER PLAYHOUSE's training program, and in the area of playwriting by the NEW PLAY CENTRE. Simon Fraser University teacher John JULIANI began his experimental SAVAGE GOD productions in 1966.

There were new theatre buildings in this period. The Frederic Wood Theatre at UBC opened in 1963 at a cost of $600,000, with an adjoining studio named for Dorothy Somerset that provides space for graduate-student productions. The Vancouver Playhouse opened in 1961 beside the QUEEN ELIZABETH THEATRE and, after an unsuccessful experiment with the short-lived Cambie Art

Theatre, began a permanent company in 1963. In Victoria the McPherson Playhouse grew out of the refurbishing of the Pantages vaudeville house (1965), and offered a home to the Bastion Theatre Company. The Vancouver ARTS CLUB, founded in 1960, moved to permanent quarters on Seymour St in Feb. 1964. For the first time in several decades Vancouver and Victoria began to enjoy stable repertory theatre.

The early and mid-1970s saw infusions of public funding that sustained the established companies and allowed new ones to emerge. Locally trained actors were able to form companies that were the true heirs of the province's stock companies of half a century before. Now, however, the actors were Canadians, often developing Canadian material. TAMAHNOUS THEATRE (1971), Touchstone (1976), and CITY STAGE (1972) were the durable leaders in this movement. Other significant companies were Westcoast Actors (1974) and Janus (1977). These new companies usually performed in open spaces such as the converted chapel at the VANCOUVER EAST CULTURAL CENTRE, and more recently the Firehall Theatre, which has brought theatre back to the area of the original townsite where it had its beginnings. In Victoria the Kaleidoscope Company opened in the BELFRY THEATRE in 1975-6.

By the mid-1970s Vancouver in particular had acquired a spectrum of theatrical activity catering for all tastes. The established Playhouse and the Frederic Wood Theatre were able to provide classics and occasionally experimental productions. The Metro Theatre, tucked away at the further reaches of South Granville, was locked into a time-warp of pre-war suburban England with its productions of comedies and thrillers. The Arts Club, entirely self-supporting, maintained a balance between commercial survival and gentle experimentation, and as the early 1980s were to show, had the greatest potential for expansion.

Also of great significance for the future has been the commitment to children's theatre in Vancouver. This began with HOLIDAY THEATRE (1953-69), founded by Joy COGHILL and Myra Benson. Carousel and GREEN THUMB continued it in the 1970s, and the movement since 1978 has been associated with an annual Children's Festival that boasts international participation. Bastion and the Playhouse Company have also organized educational programs. (See CHILDREN'S DRAMA AND THEATRE.)

With all these developments, amateur theatre has lost some of its previous significance. One noteworthy development resulting from post-war immigration has been the performance of plays in modern European languages, often supported by university departments. The French-Canadian community has also made an important contribution through its Troupe Molière, founded in 1946 and directed for many years by Mme Blanche Lambert. The Italian (I Commedianti, founded 1975), the German (the German Theatre, active since 1973), Irish, and Jewish communities have recently been well served by amateur troupes in Vancouver.

The interior of the province has benefited from the touring undertaken by Vancouver-based companies, and by Bastion from Victoria. As in earlier years, it has also relied on its own amateur efforts, and over 200 theatrical groups are now reportedly active. Kamloops has had a professional company since 1974, the Western Canada Theatre Company, founded by Tom KERR and now operating from its own theatre. Summer festivals have also appeared in smaller communities. Since 1976 White Rock has had a largely commercially oriented festival, but in 1984 Nanaimo introduced the more ambitious 'Shakespeare Plus', presenting Canadian plays as well as Shakespeare.

See R.B. Todd, 'The Organization of Professional Theatre in Vancouver, 1886-1914', *B.C. Studies*, 44 (1979-80); Malcolm Page, 'Change in Vancouver Theatre, 1963-80', *Theatre History in Canada*, 2 (1981); Andrew Parkin, 'The New Frontier: Toward an Indigenous Theatre in British Columbia', in *Theatrical Touring and Funding in North America* (1982), ed. L.W. Conolly; Chad Evans, *Frontier Theatre* (1983).   R.B. TODD

Brooker, Bertram Richard (1888-1955). Born in Croydon, Eng., he immigrated to Canada in 1905, first settling in Portage-la-Prairie, Man., then moving in 1921 to Toronto, where he had a successful advertising career and became an important abstract painter, writer, lecturer, and editor. In addition to three books on advertising, Brooker published three novels, one of which, *Think of the Earth* (1936), won the first Governor General's Award for Fiction. He edited *The Yearbook of the Arts in Canada, 1928-1929*

(1929) and *Yearbook of the Arts in Canada* (1936), and wrote poetry—edited by Birk Sproxton in *Sounds Assembling: The Poetry of Bertram Brooker* (1980)—short stories, and plays.

Only two of Brooker's plays, *Within: A Drama of Mind in Revolt* (1985) and *The Dragon: A Parable of Illusion and Disillusion* (1985), have been published; they received successful productions in 1935 and 1936 respectively in Herman VOADEN's Drama Workshop at Toronto's Central High School of Commerce. Both one-act plays are symbolic, expressionistic treatments of mystical ideas, revealing Brooker's interest in theosophy and the theatrical ideas of Edward Gordon Craig. *Within* is an abstract dramatization of forces, such as 'Instinct' and 'Will', warring within the mind. In *The Dragon*, an allegorical treatment of a creation myth, the forces of 'Good' and 'Evil' represent the divisive illusions of this world, but the play ends with their rejection followed by a vision of unity.

See *Canadian Drama*, 11 (1985) for the texts of these two plays. Other plays and play drafts, all unpublished and unproduced, are held by the Univ. of Manitoba.

SHERRILL GRACE

Brookes, Christopher (b. 1943). Born and raised in Newfoundland, he studied drama at Dalhousie Univ., Yale, and the Univ. of Michigan, and worked with Toronto's THEATRE PASSE MURAILLE before returning to Newfoundland where, in 1972, he co-founded the MUMMERS TROUPE. He remained its artistic director for ten years, during which time the company explored traditional and indigenous Newfoundland material and created plays that served as a catalyst for social and economic change.

In May 1980 Brookes took a sabbatical from the Mummers in order to study the growth and development of community theatres. In Oct. 1980 he performed Ron Blair's one-man show, *The Christian Brothers*, at the LSPU Hall in St John's, a building that he had earlier procured for the Resource Foundation for the Arts. In 1983 an award from the International Development Research Centre enabled him to work with theatre companies in Nicaragua; this experience, along with his observations on political theatre in Central America, are detailed in 'Nicaragua Theatre of Politics', *Canadian Forum*,

Jan. 1984, and his book, *Now We Know the Difference: The People of Nicaragua* (1984).

Brookes is now a journalist and broadcaster with the CBC, where his reports, particularly from the Third World and political troublespots, indicate a continuing interest in the type of questions that made the Mummers Troupe such a significant theatre company. His history of the Mummers, *A Public Nuisance*, was published in 1988. C.J. SKINNER

Broue. First produced on 21 Mar. 1979 by Montreal's Théâtre des Voyagements, it was written by Claude Meunier, Jean-Pierre Plante, Francine Ruel, Louis Saia, Michel Côté, Marcel Gauthier, and Marc Messier, and directed by Côté, Gauthier, and Messier, who also played the some twenty roles. In a production by Production 3M Inc it has toured Quebec and North America since 1979.

Broue was revived in Montreal by the COMPAGNIE JEAN DUCEPPE in 1981-2, and an English version, *Brew*, translated by David MacDonald and Michel Frémont-Côté, was produced at Montreal's CENTAUR THEATRE in 1982-3 and then in Toronto. On 22 Jan. 1986 the play's one-thousandth performance was celebrated at Le Théâtre Saint-Denis in Montreal, making it one of the most-performed plays in Canada's theatrical history.

The play's action takes place in a tavern, the last bastion of an unbridled though unconscious *machismo*, at a time when women were still not allowed to enter such establishments. Into the Chez Willie tavern comes a remarkable parade of male characters who reveal themselves in a series of interconnected sketches. Though not a serious investigation of the psychology of the Quebec male, *Broue* examines humorously the habits and moods of typical drinkers in a typical Quebec tavern; intended primarily as entertainment, it presents an unflattering view of the Quebec male. CHANTAL HÉBERT

Broughall, George (1861-1927). Born in Winnipeg, he served as a sergeant with the 90th Battalion of Rifles, 'the little black devils' of the North West Rebellion campaign of 1885. While with the 90th Broughall wrote two plays: *The 90th on Active Service; or, Campaigning in the North West* (1885) and *The Tearful and Tragical Tale of the Tricky Troubadour; or, The Truant Tracked* (1886). *The 90th* was rehearsed at Fort Pitt and produced at Winnipeg's PRINCESS OPERA HOUSE on 29 and 30 July 1885 with a cast of 130 members of the battalion and a chorus of thirty. A musical and burlesque account of the campaign, the play includes songs set to Gilbert and Sullivan airs and many topical references. Heartened by the success of *The 90th*, the battalion produced Broughall's second play on 29 and 30 Sept. 1886, again at the Princess. Whereas *The 90th* shows aspects of collective creation, *Tricky Troubadour*—a burlesque of grand opera—appears to be more the work of a single author and exhibits greater familiarity with contemporary actors and their acting techniques.

KATHLEEN FRASER

Brown, Frederick (1794?-1838). Born in England, he had an undistinguished provincial acting career, in the course of which he married the actress Sophia DeCamp, a younger sister of Mrs Charles Kemble. About 1816 he immigrated to Boston, where he achieved some popularity at the Federal Street Theatre. Early in 1819, and again in 1820, he made his first Montreal appearances at the Mansion House Theatre, where his Othello, Shylock, Romeo, Richard III, Hamlet, and Macbeth were well received. He subsequently played in New York, Baltimore, Philadelphia, Charleston, S.C., and Savannah, and in Aug.-Sept. 1825 he starred again in Montreal, this time at the Royal Circus, as Othello and Rolla in Sheridan's *Pizarro*, among other roles. Shortly afterward he became the first lessee of Montreal's new THEATRE ROYAL, which opened on 21 Nov. 1825 with a company of thirty-two actors and actresses, two musical conductors, fourteen musicians, and five stage technicians. Brown's program for the 1825-6 season was uniformly praised. In all he staged twenty-nine performances of eleven Shakespearean plays, as well as revivals of classics from the non-Shakespearean repertory. Brown also featured a number of British and American touring stars, including Thomas Hamblin, Edmund Kean, Lydia Kelly, and Robert Campbell Maywood.

Brown's attempt to make Montreal theatre competitive with the best in North America was artistically admirable, but financially disastrous. In Oct. 1826 he was obliged to give up the lease. He spent the rest of his life as an itinerant performer in the U.S., except for the seasons of 1829, 1830, and 1831, when he returned to Montreal to play under the man-

agement of his brother-in-law Vincent DeCamp. He died in North Carolina.

The repertory staged by Brown and the quality of his *mise-en-scène* set a standard by which local managers were judged for decades thereafter. JOHN RIPLEY

Buckland, John Wellington (1815-72). English-born Buckland was the first lessee and manager of Montreal's THEATRE ROYAL on Côté St, which opened in 1852. His own qualifications being almost entirely in financial affairs, he relied on theatre professionals to recruit and direct his stock company each summer. To extend the run of an attractive star or play, he occasionally leased the MUSIC HALL in Quebec City. In winter he rented the Theatre Royal to amateurs or touring combinations. His wife, Kate Buckland (neé Horn, 1820-96)—an American actress who was a handsome and popular member of Wallack's and other New York companies in the 1840s and 1850s—frequently played leading roles at the Theatre Royal. A favourite with the military, she lent her charm and expertise to many productions of the Garrison Amateurs. On her husband's death she became proprietor of the Theatre Royal, but retired to private life in 1875. MARY SHORTT

Buffalo Jump. Carol BOLT's play is a dramatization of the plight of Canada's unemployed during the Depression that culminated in the 'On to Ottawa Trek' and the Regina riot of 1935. An earlier version entitled *Next Year Country* (a phrase still used in the play to epitomize the dashed hopes of the unemployed) was produced in 1971 in revue style at the GLOBE THEATRE, Regina, directed by Ken KRAMER. The text of *Buffalo Jump* was developed by Bolt in conjunction with actors at Toronto's THEATRE PASSE MURAILLE and presented there on 18 May 1972, directed by Paul THOMPSON. The title comes from the method used by Plains Indians to kill buffalo—stampeding them over a cliff; the image is used at various points in the play to show how the unemployed face a similar fate. Following documentary evidence in Ronald Liversedge's Marxist-oriented *Recollections of the On to Ottawa Trek* (1961), the play moves chronologically from R.B. Bennett's successful 1930 election campaign to the Regina riot of 1 July 1935; an Afterword notes Bennett's defeat at the polls in October of that same year. The play uses short, fast-moving scenes,

Buffalo Jump

cartoon-like characters played by actors in multiple roles, direct address to the audience, the dispersal of actors among the audience, song, dance, and choral work. Though sometimes confusing because of the abundance of historical material, the play presents a moving case for the men from the Relief Camps and their leader 'Red' Evans, and a condemnation of the federal government's callousness. It is saved from mere propaganda by the entertainment value of its Brechtian-style theatrics. For the 1977 Ottawa production by the GREAT CANADIAN THEATRE COMPANY, directed by Bill Law, Bolt introduced new material and a different ending built around the character of Annie Buller and other Ottawans who supported the trekkers. First published by Playwrights Co-op in 1972, the play is also in *Playwrights in Profile: Carol Bolt* (1976) and *Major Plays of the Canadian Theatre 1934-1984* (1984), edited by Richard Perkyns.

JAMES NOONAN

Bullock-Webster, Llewelyn (1879-1970). Born in Llanbder, Wales, and educated in England, he took his ARCM at the Royal College of Music, London. He worked as juvenile lead in the West End and produced for Sir George Dance before moving about 1900 to British Columbia, where he founded the Prince Rupert Amateur Dramatic Society. After the First World War he was active in Victoria, performing with the Reginald Hincks stock company and founding the annual Yuletide festivities at the Empress Hotel. In 1921 he founded the British Columbia Dramatic School in a second-floor studio theatre seating 70 on Fort Street. Appealing to a broad clientele, he taught public speaking, deportment, and acting. A branch was opened in Vancouver. With the Depression the school closed in 1932 and he became Director of School and Community Drama for the Department of Education, travelling the province to adjudicate, organize workshops and festivals, and dispense his educational pamphlets. He founded the Canadian Drama Awards, first presented in 1935, and was active in the League of Western Writers. He wrote about thirty plays, several of which were published and produced. A very 'English' person, often referred to as 'the Major', he retired to England in 1946.

JAMES HOFFMAN

Burgess, Colin 'Cool' (1840-1905). This Toronto-born 'Prince of Ethiopian Comedians' performed in his teens with other young amateurs in Burgess and Redmond's Ethiopian Star Troupe. In 1862 he joined Duprez and Green's minstrel company in the U.S. and later toured widely with many leading minstrel combinations. For long periods he also worked independently, heading the bill at variety theatres in Chicago, Boston, and Philadelphia. Alone or with a few associates, he toured innumerable small towns in Ontario, Quebec, and the Maritimes, presenting his 'Olio of Oddities' in a succession of one-night stands. In 1877 he headed the first professional company to visit Manitoba, giving ten performances to large audiences in Winnipeg. In 1878 he played for a season in England. Tall and thin, with a long, drooping moustache and a loud, infectious laugh, his mere presence was mirth-provoking. He had great comic talents as a singer and dancer, his specialty being 'Nicodemus Johnson', a song-and-dance act in which he vigorously manipulated grotesque yard-long shoes. As the public's taste changed he ceased to be solely a 'delineator of Negro eccentricities' and developed many white-faced acts.

MARY SHORTT

Burlap Bags. Len PETERSON's best-known radio play was first broadcast on CBC Radio's 'Stage 46' series on 3 Feb. 1946. A television version was produced by Harvey Hart on CBC's 'Quest' series on 3 Jan. 1960, and it was first staged at TORONTO WORKSHOP PRODUCTIONS in the 1959-60 season.

Two tramps—Manitoba and Finley—comment on the rapacity of their fellow boarding-house tenants in scavenging the belongings of Tannahill, who has committed suicide. The play's inner action reconstructs the hallucinatory experiences recorded in Tannahill's diary; he sees the people around him cover their heads with burlap bags to avoid facing the absurdity and madness of life. When he too finally tries to shut out reality, there are no burlap bags left and he is condemned to be free to see.

Peterson has said that *Burlap Bags* (the first play he wrote after his discharge from the Canadian army in 1945) reflects the chaos of the post-war period—Tannahill 'shuffled his way into my madness'. It anticipates by a decade the appearance of European drama of the Absurd as reflected in the plays of Eugène

Ionesco, Samuel Beckett, and Harold Pinter. *Burlap Bags* was published by Playwrights Co-op, Toronto, in 1972.

ROTA HERZBERG LISTER

Burlesque. Traditional burlesque—the ludicrous caricaturing of a familiar dramatic, musical, balletic, or literary work—was introduced to North America in 1839-40 at New York's Olympic Theatre and Niblo's Gardens. The plays of Shakespeare were mocked, for example, with burlesques such as *Hamlet the Dainty*, *Julius Sneezer*, *Julius Seizer*, and *Julius Snoozer*; aristocratic British acting styles were also ridiculed. In Canada the operettas of Gilbert and Sullivan provided material for burlesques such as W.H. FULLER's political satire *H.M.S. Parliament* (1880) and J.W. Bengough's *Bunthorne Abroad; or, the Lass that Loved a Pirate* (1883), a parody of *H.M.S. Pinafore*, *The Pirates of Penzance*, and *Patience* that was first performed in Hamilton in Aug. 1886. George BROUGHALL's *The 90th on Active Service; or, Campaigning in the North West* (1885), a 'musical and dramatic burlesque' on the Riel uprising, was also in the manner of Gilbert and Sullivan, while his *The Tearful and Tragical Tale of the Tricky Troubadour; or, the Truant Tracked* (1886), first performed in Winnipeg in Sept. 1886, parodied grand opera, particularly Verdi's *Il Trovatore*. George SUMMERS was once billed as the 'King of Irish Comedy and Burlesque', and expatriate movie-maker Mack Sennett had his beginnings in Bowery burlesque as the hind end of a horse (c. 1900). Marie Dressler is remembered for her burlesques of *Romeo and Juliet* (she was Romeo) and her early career (1880s-90s) was built around her talents for spoofing opera. (In this field Anna Russell is her spiritual successor.) Literary burlesque survived into the twentieth century in such revue sketches as Beatrice LILLIE's 1942 *Mockbeth* and SPRING THAW's 1951 takeoff on Gratien GÉLINAS's *TIT-COQ*, and still manifests itself in the television parodies by Johnny Wayne and Frank Shuster of classical and Shakespearean works.

A second phase of burlesque is distinguished by its attention to the female form and sexual innuendo, deriving from the tradition of 'breeches' roles for women (the American actress Adah Isaacs Menken was strapped seemingly naked to a horse in the equestrian melodrama *Mazeppa* in 1861). Other opportunities for titillation were the *tableaux vivants* of famous sculptures and paintings, in which the living statuary was seen in various stages of undress. And in 1866 the Amercian musical spectacle *The Black Crook* presented a chorus line of scantily clad French ballet dancers, opening a path for companies such as Lydia Thompson's beefy British Blondes, who toured Canada and the U.S. with burlesques of the classics performed in short togas and flesh-coloured tights. They spawned a wave of all-female minstrel shows, one of which—Mme. Rentz's Female Minstrels (or 'Bare Blondes')—was seen at Ottawa's Music Hall on 10 May 1875; a decade later the Adamless Eden Co. toured Canada. *Tableaux vivants* and motionless *poses plastiques* developed into Spanish Fandangos and the undulations of 'serpentine dancing' (a euphemism for 'bump and grind'), in which large hand-held silks (on sticks) enveloped the backlit dancer. Toronto's Maud Allan (1883-1956), a serious classical dancer, created shock-waves when she introduced her 'Vision of Salomé' at the Palace Theatre in London in Mar. 1908, a role she danced ten years later in Oscar Wilde's play. A host of suggestive imitators quickly followed, including Canada's VAUDEVILLE sensation Eva Tanguay.

At the turn of the century a more sophisticated form of burlesque evolved, consisting of a lively revue-like sequence of vaudeville routines, broad stand-up comedy (off-colour, slapstick, and dialect), interspersed with statuesque chorines strutting their stuff. The 1979 Broadway hit *Sugar Babies* (which played Canada in 1983-4), starring Mickey Rooney and Ann Miller, was a nostalgic recreation of this 1910-to-1930 genre. The raunchier elements of 'burleycue'—epitomized in the-honky tonk saloons of the gold-rush frontier—went underground into midway tents at Canada's fall fairs or at a string of second-class stag theatres. The better-class burlesque roadhouses, almost invariably called the Star (Hamilton, Toronto) or the Gayety (Toronto, Montreal) were part of the Columbia 'wheel' (circuit) in the East (Broadway's first burlesque theatre was the Columbia in 1909), or the Empire chain in the West. In 1913 they merged. The striptease houses, independent at first, eventually came under the banners of the Independent, Progressive, and Mutual circuits. Bill Minsky's burlesque on 42nd Street was New York's most salacious.

Burlesque

By 1930 burlesque greats such as Sophie Tucker, Jimmy Durante, Phil Silvers, and W.C. Fields had begun to move to radio and film, and the third and final phase of burlesque emerged. Burlesque abandoned any pretence of being a family entertainment and resorted to a repetitious parade of striptease artists linked by a smutty master of ceremonies. By 1960, however, protest groups and the popularity of television had killed off burlesque across North America. Striptease resurfaced in the 1960s in taverns in the form of go-go dancers and topless waitresses. The only new wrinkle was the introduction of male striptease in the 1970s and the simulation of sexual encounters in such nude revues as *Oh! Calcutta!*, *Let My People Come* (running in Toronto since 1981), and THEATRE PASSE MURAILLE's erotic *I Love You, Baby Blue*, which played in 1975.   DAVID GARDNER

Burlesque (Quebec). The term burlesque calls to mind a type of show that for a long time, despite its obvious popularity, had a bad reputation in Quebec, as indeed it also had in the United States where it originated. The word 'burlesque' has a variety of meanings, depending on the period and the country in which it is used. VAUDEVILLE and burlesque often overlap, possibly because American burlesque, after making its contribution to the variety show, gradually broke away and evolved towards freer forms that led to the appearance of the 'strip-tease'. Thus vaudeville, which wanted to maintain a certain standard and aspired to greater respectability, took over the variety aspect of burlesque.

The first burlesque shows in Quebec were performed by American touring companies in Montreal at the turn of the twentieth century, notably the Columbia Amusement Company and the B.F. Keith and Edward F. Albee groups. Between 1900 and 1914 several of Montreal's prominent English-speaking theatres—the ORPHEUM, the PRINCESS, and the Bennett—presented the American shows. Lively and high-spirited, they consisted of a series of variety acts—song-and-dance numbers, magic, acrobatics, musical interludes, sketches—and flocks of young women in scanty costumes who later became the celebrated chorus lines and strip-tease acts. Presented without the interventions of a master of ceremonies—such as occurred in music-hall entertainments—the sole link between

the acts was the need to divert the audience.

From 1914 on Quebec comedians became addicted to this form of entertainment, beginning a history of Quebec burlesque that falls into three periods. From 1914 to 1930 Quebec entertainers followed the American formula, performing in English—at the behest of theatre proprietors—until the late 1920s. Emphasizing sight-gags and physical routines—pratfalls, cream-pies in the face, and kicks in the backside—actors known as Swifty, Pizzy-Wizzy, and Pic-Pic won star status at the King Edward, the Midway, and the Starland on Montreal's rue Saint-Laurent, otherwise known as 'the Main'. They were succeeded by Arthur Petrie and Olivier GUIMOND senior (Tizoune), who were the first to present their acts in English and French, and then broke away from the American tradition with French-language shows tailored to local audiences. The chorus line, originally considered a fundamental part of the genre, also disappeared.

1930 to 1950 was the golden age of burlesque, and Montreal's THÉÂTRE NATIONAL, under the leadership of Rose Ouellette (La Poune), became its Mecca. In its peak years the company at the National featured about thirty artists. They produced two shows daily, seven days a week, offering a completely new program each week. Tours arranged by Jean Grimaldi took burlesque throughout the province. The American formula was further modified by the addition of comedy acts running between forty-five and sixty minutes. But perhaps the most important modification was that while the Americans talked frankly about sex, the Quebec artists had to cloak sexual banter and dialogue in the respectability of marriage.

At the beginning of the 1950s, facing competition from other forms of entertainment—CABARET, night-clubs, television, phonograph records—Quebec burlesque went into decline. Revived briefly with the opening of the THÉÂTRE DES VARIÉTÉS in 1967, where Gilles Latulippe attempted to recreate the golden age of the National, it never regained its popularity.

For some artists burlesque had been the sole show-business training ground. A tough and unforgiving genre, it demanded skilled improvisation, teamwork, keen imagination, an extraordinary sense of timing, and a versatile use of the vernacular. Skits and comedy acts challenged authority and conventions, but burlesque's fundamental aim remained to provide entertainment, often generated by jokes that were erotic or scatological. It is regrettable that this down-to-earth form of amusement has fallen into oblivion.

See Bernard Sobel, *A Pictorial History of Burlesque* (1956) and Chantal Hébert, *Le Burlesque au Québec, un divertissement populaire* (1981). CHANTAL HÉBERT

Burroughs, Jackie (b. 1941?). Born in Lancashire, Eng., she was educated at the Univ. of Toronto, where her student roles included a much-praised Saint Joan. After appearing at the Chesterfield Civic Repertory Theatre in England (opposite Donald SUTHERLAND) and studying with Uta Hagen in New York, Burroughs rapidly achieved prominence in Canada in the 1960s with the Straw Hat Players, at the CREST THEATRE, the MANITOBA THEATRE CENTRE, the STRATFORD FESTIVAL, and the Toronto Dance Theatre (with which she has continued to train). Since the late 1960s she has been an important film and television actress, winning many awards, and she also appeared at the 1975 and 1976 Stratford Festivals and the 1979 SHAW FESTIVAL. However, it is in the ALTERNATE THEATRES—such as Theatre Second Floor, TORONTO WORKSHOP PRODUCTIONS, and TORONTO FREE THEATRE—that her most characteristic stage work—provocative and emotionally daring—has been done. Outstanding performances in the 1980s have included the films *The Grey Fox* (1983), *The Wars* (1984) (she won Genie awards for both), and *A Winter Tan* (1987), and demanding stage roles, such as Lomia in Judith THOMPSON's *White Biting Dog* at Toronto's TARRAGON THEATRE in Jan. 1984. HARRY LANE

Bussières, Paul (b. 1943). Born in Quebec City, he studied interior design at Montreal's École des Beaux-Arts from 1958 to 1962, and from 1960 to 1968 designed and acted at the Théâtre de L'Estoc in Quebec City. In 1967 he gave the first introductory course in set and costume design at the CONSERVATOIRE D'ART DRAMATIQUE DU QUÉBEC, where in 1970 he helped to establish a scenography department and became its director.

Bussières has been resident designer at Quebec City's THÉÂTRE DU TRIDENT since its inception in 1970 and has also participated in Trident co-productions with the NATIONAL ARTS CENTRE and the THÉÂTRE DU NOUVEAU MONDE as well as working for the Théâtre du Bois de Coulonge, the Théâtre Lyrique du Québec, the Théâtre du Vieux Québec, and the COMPAGNIE JEAN DUCEPPE, among others. His many design contributions to Quebec theatre—averaging four plays a year for more than twenty-five years—have included works from both the international and the contemporary Quebec repertoires with directors such as Paul HÉBERT, Albert Millaire, Olivier Reichenbach, and Guillermo de Andrea.

A protean aesthetic sense that is both functional and effective enables Bussières to adapt to the particular demands of each play and to establish a close working relationship with the director, always striving to integrate design into the production as a whole. Among his most notable productions are Samuel Beckett's *En Attendant Godot* (*Waiting for Godot*) in 1974 for the Trident; Claude Roussin's and James Rousselle's *Marche, Laura Secord* in 1975 for TNM; Bertolt Brecht's *L'Opéra de Quat'Sous* (*The Threepenny Opera*) in 1977; Arnold Wesker's *La Cuisine* (*The Kitchen*) in 1975; and Molière's *Le Bourgeois Gentilhomme* in 1987. The last three productions were at the Trident. The first professional designer in the Quebec City region as well as the most important and productive, Bussières is also a leading designer in the province of Quebec. GILLES GIRARD

C

Cabaret. An intimate, irreverent, and extremely adaptable entertainment form, usually defined by its presence in a smoky bar, coffee-house, or night-club, it had its origins in Paris in the 1880s, enjoying its European heyday in Germany in the late 1920s and early 1930s, with performers such as Marlene Dietrich and Lotte Lenya (singing the sardonic songs of her husband Kurt Weill and of Bertolt Brecht). Cabaret featured a Master of Ceremonies stringing together a series of monologues (often satiric and sexually suggestive), skits, and song-and-dance numbers ranging from the raunchy to the sentimental. Traditionally, the production requirements were minimal: a stool, piano, and microphone being the essential ingredients. North America extended the character of cabaret by absorbing the light revue into its night-club format, creating a hybrid 'cabaret revue' that can vary in scale from the intimate and the minuscule to the lavish Las Vegas supper-club extravaganzas featuring chorus lines and partial nudity. These middle-class revues, ostensibly satirizing current events while drinks are served, have become first cousins to DINNER THEATRE and are relatively distanced from cabaret's origins.

The first cabaret revues in Canada (as opposed to revues such as Les FRIDOLINONS, *Town Tonics*, and SPRING THAW, which were staged in theatres) were presented at the ARTS AND LETTERS CLUB in Toronto, where male amateurs entertained fellow members and their guests seated at tables. These sporadic, satiric, after-supper entertainments date from 1911, and a continuous annual revue tradition was in place by 1930. During the 1930s the amateurs of the Progressive Arts Clubs and Workers' Theatres, with their left-of-centre orientation, are also reputed to have made frequent use of cabaret as a medium for agit-prop.

Since the Second World War professional cabaret in Canada has favoured the American formula over the European. Intimate cabaret revues like *Up Tempo* brightened Montreal's Café André as early as 1955, and in Toronto the Bohemian Embassy and the 'hippie' coffee-houses along Yorkville St welcomed musicians and comedians alike. In 1961 Old Angelo's restaurant added a post-dinner show called *Well Rehearsed Ad Libs* (starring Dave Broadfoot, Dinah Christie, and Jean Templeton), but a continuous cabaret tradition in Toronto dates from Sylvia Shawn's mounting of one-act plays at Theatre-in-the-Dell in the summer of 1962, soon to be followed there by *The Village Revue* (with Barrie Baldaro) in 1963. Between 1964 and 1986 there was an unbroken parade of revues at the Dell Cabaret, some of which, like *Oh Coward* (starring Tom Kneebone) and *Toronto, Toronto*, ran for over a year. By 1979 one could go to a different cabaret theatre in Toronto every night of the week. Some of these briefly bore historic names such as the Black Cat and the Blue Angel, and another half dozen—Anthony's Villa, Basin Street, Café des Copains, Cabaret East, Café Soho, and Ports of Call—have since disappeared, as has Jiri Schubert's (Pears Ave) Cabaret, a rare attempt to reproduce an authentic European cabaret in Canada. Variations on the cabaret/dinner-theatre format in Toronto include *His Majesty's Feast* (1978-), a sixteenth-century 'eat with your fingers' environmental experience (complete with Henry VIII and a clutch of fools and wenches); and *A Little Night Magic* (1984-), in which comedy and magic are mixed. To give Toronto a taste of Las Vegas, the Royal York Hotel turned its Imperial Room into a supper club featuring headline singers and comedians, and in the summers mounted mini-extravaganza musicals, ice-shows, or revues. Whether in a cabaret setting or in a theatre, the revue was Canada's first manifestation of a truly independent commercial theatre.

As well, cabaret has been almost single-handedly responsible for the creation of a major comedy industry. With the 1959 Chicago example before them, the highly successful Toronto franchise of Second City Cabaret (1973-) opened its own outlets in Edmonton and London, Ont., and utilized its improvisatonal training courses to build a touring 'farm team' company. In 1976 the famed Second City TV (SCTV) series was created, which has rivalled America's *Saturday Night Live* program in developing a generation of Canadian comedians—including

Dan Aykroyd, John Candy, Rick Moranis, and Martin Short—for the Hollywood market. As a launching-pad for young stand-up comics, Mark Breslin's Toronto-based Yuk Yuk's Komedy Kabaret (1975-) has had a similar impact. By 1987 Yuk Yuk's had mushroomed into an international chain of thirteen Canadian and American clubs from coast to coast, a comedy circuit for Breslin's stable of comic talent. Canadians Howie Mandell and Jim Carrey are two of Yuk Yuk's renowned alumni.

Comedy cabarets established since 1979 include: Stages in Halifax; Stitches and The Comedy Nest in Montreal; Hiccups, Andy and Flo's Comedy Tavern, and the Penguin Café in Ottawa; Cheers, Act II, and Rumours in Winnipeg; Punchlines, Stage 33, the Zanzibar, and O'Pressed Hams in Vancouver. Some of the best cabaret in Canada can also be found in the CHARLOTTETOWN FESTIVAL's Cabaret Theatre, and in entertainments behind the scenes of the SHAW and STRATFORD FESTIVALs, where the cast members regularly let off steam. Cabaret concerts by Nancy White and Ann Mortifee since the 1960s have kept the political spark alive in Canada, following in the footsteps of Montreal-born Mort Sahl who worked mainly in the U.S. In legitimate theatre Morris Panych and Ken MacDonald's *Last Call* in Vancouver (1983) was conceived as a post-nuclear cabaret, while Erika RITTER's 1980 comedy *AUTOMATIC PILOT* centred on the life of a stand-up comedienne.

Canada has also adapted the cabaret ambience to several unexpected but appropriate purposes. Mary Ellen Mahoney's Classical Cabaret (1981-), which is seen in southern Ontario, is a concert blend of semi-classical and musical-comedy songs in an informal setting. Nightwood Theatre, Toronto, launched a Five-Minute Feminist Cabaret (1983-), in which twenty or more performers present a five-minute turn. In 1985 native entertainers devised a mask show entitled *Trickster's Cabaret* (Toronto) and the Playwrights Union of Canada sponsored its first annual Playwright's Cabaret in which authors read from their works. DAVID GARDNER

Café-Théâtre. A place for intimate theatre, where the audience is encouraged to drink and occasionally to eat, the modern café-théâtre of Quebec resembles to some extent the cabarets and salons of the nineteenth and the early twentieth centuries, when some groups and associations presented theatre during their meetings held in tearooms or hotels. For example, Monique (Alice Pepin-Benoît) produced a curtain-raiser, *L'Heure est venue*, for members of the Women's Press Club at Montreal's Ritz-Carlton Hotel in 1923. Jules Ferland offered his monologues, sketches, and short plays at the Matou botté cabaret in 1929 and 1930. But the cabaret was primarily a venue dominated by singers, music-hall entertainers, and, later on, strip-tease. In the 1950s and after, night-clubs, notably Le Patriote and La Butte à Mathieu in Montreal, presented plays, monologues, and sketches. As much by the composition of their audience as by the selection of their repertoire, they were similar to what eventually became the café-théâtre.

Strictly speaking, café-théâtre is a phenomenon that belongs to the very recent history of Quebec theatre. It appeared as a fad imported from Europe—along with café-au-lait and the croissant—by young intellectuals, many of them students, who wanted to create a space for themselves in the districts known as 'quartiers latins'. Café-théâtre followed immediately after the introduction of European-style cafés to Quebec—cafés quite different from American bars in that they were only open during the day, and because the drinks consumed there were usually non-alcoholic.

The first—and perhaps still the best known—of the café-théâtres was the Chantauteuil, which opened in Quebec City in the late 1960s under the banner of existentialism. It presented poetry readings, recitals, and short plays. In 1969 the Théâtre Quotidien took up residence there for several years. The author whose name remains linked to the Chantauteuil is Jean BARBEAU, whose *Le Goglu* and *Le Chemin de Lacroix* were presented there. The café-théâtres had their earliest and greatest successes in Quebec City. Le Théâtre du Vieux Québec, the Petit-Champlain, Le Hobbit, Le Zinc, Le Rimbaud, and La Bordée gave the city continuous theatrical programs, despite chronic financial difficulties, and despite government attempts to channel grants towards mainstream theatre. In addition to the principal café-théâtres there were a number of cafés in Quebec City that occasionally presented plays. Le Temporel also achieved some success in the mid-1970s, with its 'lundis'—poetry readings, sketches, or meetings with authors.

There were numerous café-théâtres in metropolitan Montreal, although their importance was not as great. Sometimes they were associated with a regular theatre, acting as its experimental stage. This was the case with the Café de la Place (des Arts), which offered a lunch-time theatre for several years, and the 4-Saoûls Bar. Other café-théâtres—such as L'Espéranto, La Chaconne, Le Molière, Les Fleurs de mal, Le Nelligan, Le Noeud, Le Quartier latin, La Licorne, and L'Ex-tasse—provided a venue for the birth of an alternate theatre of modest technical resources that acted as a counterbalance to the established theatres, which relied chiefly on a foreign repertoire. The playwright René-Daniel DUBOIS, among others, is still associated with café-théâtre. In the greater metropolitan area of Montreal café-théâtre is well established in the suburbs. La Gargouille in Outremont, Le Horla in Saint-Bruno, Le Vieux-fort in La Prairie, Le Rizpainsel in Longueuil, and especially Le Pont-Tournant in Beloeil, have contributed greatly to the decentralization of the theatre scene. Further afield, café-théâtre has been active in Jonquière (Chez L'bedeau), Hull (Le Chateau), and Shawinigan (Le Refuge).

Although constantly at the mercy of financial problems caused by their small size (from thirty to 200 places), the café-théâtres serve a triple function: they assure the survival of workshop theatre by replacing the now rare little theatres, thereby giving young dramatists a chance to make their début; they favour a more relaxed presentation in an intimate atmosphere that allows for close contact with the audience; and they serve neighbourhoods, towns, and regions that are poorly, or badly, served by the established theatre.

LUCIE ROBERT

Cailloux, André (b. 1920). Born in France, he studied at the Swiss Univ. of Fribourg before beginning his stage career as a singer, actor, and magician. After immigrating to Canada he joined Les COMPAGNONS DE SAINT-LAURENT in Montreal as an actor in 1951. He has played nearly 200 roles in a wide-ranging classical repertoire for Les Compagnons, Le THÉÂTRE DU NOUVEAU MONDE, Le THÉÂTRE-CLUB, and Le THÉÂTRE DU RIDEAU VERT, and has also acted in plays by Françoise LORANGER and Antonine MAILLET.

Cailloux's longest association has been with Le Théâtre du Rideau Vert, where in addition to directing he was artistic director of 'Manteau d'Arlequin 5-15', the theatre for young audiences. From 1968 to 1978 he organized highly successful seasons of PUPPET plays and live theatre. In addition to his own work, plays by authors such as Marcel Sabourin, Roland LEPAGE, and Patrick Mainville were produced at Manteau d'Arlequin, while puppeteers Pierre Régimbald and Nicole Lapointe offered the classical tales of Perrault and the Brothers Grimm.

Cailloux has written seven plays for children, of which five have been published: *Frizelis et Gros Guillaume* (1983), *Frizelis et la Fée Doduche* (1973), *L'ile-au-sorcier* (1973), *François et l'oiseau du Brésil* (1977), and *Tombé des étoiles* (1977). They reveal his fondness for magic, fantasy, and imaginative effects—objects appear and disappear, characters are mysteriously transformed. His plays invite audience participation and have an educational aim: for example, pollution control and respect for the past.

Cailloux was also a pioneer in children's television programming as writer, actor, and storyteller. He has published songs, tales, and rhymes for children and founded and still directs 'Le jardin de Grand-Père', where classes are given that help in developing the personalities of children aged three to fifteen.

See also CHILDREN'S DRAMA AND THEATRE IN FRENCH and Hélène Beauchamp, *Le Théâtre pour enfants au Québec: 1950-1980* (1985). HÉLÈNE BEAUCHAMP

Caldwell, Zoë (b. 1933). Born in Hawthorn, Victoria, Australia, she was educated in Melbourne, where she made her professional acting début with the Union Theatre Repertory Company in 1953. In England she acted at the Shakespeare Memorial Theatre, Stratford-on-Avon (1958-61), and at London's Royal Court Theatre before immigrating to Canada in 1961, when she played Rosaline in the STRATFORD FESTIVAL's *Love's Labour's Lost* and Sonja Downfall in Donald Jack's *The Canvas Barricade*. Later that year she appeared at the MANITOBA THEATRE CENTRE as Pegeen Mike in J.M. Synge's *Playboy of the Western World*. Caldwell toured with the CANADIAN PLAYERS in 1963 and starred in the CREST THEATRE's *A Far Country* by Henry Denker in 1964. In 1966 she first appeared at the SHAW FESTIVAL as Orinthia in Shaw's *The Apple Cart* and as Lena Szczepanowska in *Misalliance*. She returned to Stratford in 1967 to play Cleopatra in *Antony and Cleopatra* (opposite Christopher PLUMMER), Lady Anne in *Richard III*, and Mistress Page in *The Merry Wives of Windsor*.

An actress of great emotional power with a distinctive husky voice, she has won Tony awards for her starring roles on Broadway in *The Prime of Miss Jean Brodie* (in 1968) and *Medea* (1982) and for her supporting role as Polly in Tennessee Williams' *Slapstick Tragedy* in 1966. She is married to the noted Canadian-born Broadway producer Robert WHITEHEAD, who directed her in *Medea*.

Caldwell has also directed many plays, including Judith Ross's *An Almost Perfect Person* on Broadway in 1977 and *Richard II* at Stratford in 1979.   EUGENE BENSON

Cameron, Anne (b. 1938). Born Barbara Anne Cameron in Nanaimo, B.C., this playwright has written for several media as Anne Cameron, B.A. Cameron, and Cam Hubert. She is best known for *Dreamspeaker*, produced on CBC television (1977), directed by Claude Jutra and published as a novella (1978), which features a disturbed white boy who runs away and learns wisdom from an old Indian. Other television scripts include *A Matter of Choice* (1978), about rape; *Drying up the Streets* (1979), about drugs; and *The Homecoming* (1979), about Métis rodeo riders. She co-scripted with Ralph Thomas the film about religious cults, *Ticket to Heaven* (1981). Cameron's other works include a feminist Western novel, *The Journey* (1983); two volumes of verse, *Earth Witch* (1984) and *The Annie Poems* (1987); and two books re-telling Indian myths, *Daughters of Copper Woman* (1981) and *Dzelarhons* (1986).

A series of moving poems, in which Indians tell of their heritage and their conflicts with the modern world—collected in the unpublished *Windigo*—received a 'performance' by Indians from Matsqui Prison, B.C., in 1971. The one-act *The Twin Sinks of Allan Sammy* (1970), first produced in 1973 at Tillicum Theatre, Nanaimo, which Cameron founded, portrays an Indian couple who choose to leave the city and return to the reserve. *We're All Here Except Mike Casey's Horse* (1974), workshopped at Vancouver's NEW PLAY CENTRE in 1975, ambitiously portrays seven people in their thirties at a party,

dramatizing their relationships, histories, and quarrels. *Rites of Passage* won the New Play Centre's Womens' Playwriting Competition in 1975 and was first performed there in the same year. Set in a Vancouver Island mining town, it concerns three generations of women who face rites of passage: the eldest faces her husband's approaching death; her daughter's husband walks out; her granddaughter passes through adolescence.

Cameron's feminist commitment to social issues and her faith in the strengths of Indian traditions united in *From the Belly of Old Woman* (broadcast on CBC radio, 1986), in which a battered wife gains determination through her memories of an Indian woman.

See Ann Messenger, 'B.A. Cameron/Cam Hubert: Poet of the Afflicted', *Canadian Drama*, 5 (1979).   MALCOLM PAGE

Campbell, Douglas (b. 1922). Born in Glasgow, Scotland, he began his stage career with London's Old Vic company on a 1941-2 tour in *Medea* with Sybil Thorndike. After extensive touring and repertory work in British theatre and appearances at the Edinburgh Festival (where in 1948 he first worked with Tyrone GUTHRIE), he joined the STRATFORD FESTIVAL Company for its inaugural 1953 season, playing Parolles in *All's Well That Ends Well* and Hastings in *Richard III*. Campbell became a mainstay of the Festival, his most celebrated roles including several Falstaffs (beginning in 1956 in *The Merry Wives of Windsor* and in 1958 in *Henry IV Part I*) and many Shakespearean clowns, from Pompey in *Measure for Measure* in 1954, to Sir Toby Belch in *Twelfth Night* in 1957, and Touchstone in *As You Like It* in 1959. His lead roles at Stratford—Othello in 1959 and Lear in 1985, for example—were less outstanding. Campbell has also directed at Stratford, beginning with Stravinsky's and C. F. Ramuz's *A Soldier's Tale* in 1955 and including several Shakespeare plays: *The Winter's Tale* in 1958, *A Midsummer Night's Dream* in 1960, *Julius Caesar* in 1965, and Lorenz Hart's and Richard Rodgers' *The Boys From Syracuse* (his first musical) in 1986.

In 1954 Campbell co-founded the CANADIAN PLAYERS, acting and directing with them throughout Canada and in the U.S. As associate director of the Guthrie Theatre in Minneapolis he directed Molière's *The Miser* and Arthur Miller's *Death of a Salesman* in

Campbell

Douglas Campbell (l.) and Miles Potter in Rick Salutin's Nathan Cohen: A Review, *Theatre Passe Muraille, Toronto, 1981*

the 1963 opening season; for the 1965 season he was artistic director. He has appeared at many other major U.S. theatres, and has made numerous film and television appearances. He directed Ibsen's *Peer Gynt* for CBC-TV in 1957, and performed the lead in the CBC's 'Great Detective' series.

A bravura actor in the old tradition, with an organ-toned voice, Campbell plays in an open, emotional style that is generally ill-suited to the ironic tone of contemporary playwrights, although he starred in Harold Pinter's *The Homecoming* at Toronto's CEN-TRESTAGE in 1984 and in Ronald Harwood's *The Dresser* for Toronto Arts Productions in 1983. The role of the flamboyant actor Sir, undertaking *King Lear*, was well suited to Campbell's style. RAY CONLOGUE

Campbell, P.L. (Paddy) (b. 1944). Born in England, and raised in Western Canada, she began her early theatrical career in children's theatre, first as an actress in Vancouver (HOLIDAY THEATRE), Edmonton (Playground Players), and Regina (GLOBE THEATRE), then as co-founder and playwright of Calgary's Arts Centre Company. The ten plays she wrote for The Arts Centre Company were influenced by British playwright Brian Way, and written in the audience-participation style he advocated. Of these, *Chinook* (1973), first produced in 1967, is the most widely performed. This imaginative explanation of

how the Chinook wind got its name is a uniquely Canadian voice in participation theatre. Campbell's plays for ALBERTA THEATRE PROJECTS are more ambitious and mature. *Madwitch* (1984), produced in 1973, treats prejudice powerfully. An old native woman is mercilessly mocked by local children. When one child befriends her, adults interpret the encounter as dangerous. Mary is 'put away', but prejudice then shifts against German-born citizens as Canada enters the Second World War. *Under the Arch* (1976), produced in 1975, is 'an irreverent view of Western Canadian History' in a British Music Hall format, with music by William Skolnik, who also collaborated on *Passengers* (performed and published in 1977), a bittersweet fantasy about people stranded in a rural railroad station, and *Hoarse Muse* (performed and published in 1974), a musical comedy about Bob Edwards, maverick editor of the Calgary *Eye Opener*, a pioneer newspaper. Campbell has written historical plays for the Yukon (*The Yukon Play*, produced in 1978) and for Lethbridge (*Who We Were*, produced in 1980), and *Star Gates* (produced in 1986) for young audiences. She has served as vice-chairman of the Guild of Canadian Playwrights (1979–80) and chairman of the Playwrights Union of Canada (1984–5).

JOYCE DOOLITTLE

Canadian Players, The. STRATFORD FESTIVAL co-founder Tom Patterson and actor-director Douglas CAMPBELL formed the Canadian Players in Stratford to take Stratford-quality professional productions to the rest of the country and to provide between-season work for Festival performers. The first tour, which opened in Oct. 1954 in Ottawa, featured Stratford stalwarts Campbell and his first wife Ann Casson, William NEEDLES, William HUTT, and Bruno GERUSSI in a platform production of Bernard Shaw's *Saint Joan*. The tour visited twenty-three centres in southern Ontario in the autumn, moving briefly to northern Ontario, Quebec, and New York State in the New Year. The company's first extensive visit to the U.S. came in the fall of 1955, touring *Saint Joan*, starring Frances HYLAND, in repertory with *Macbeth*; these productions were also given on the company's first tour of western Canada, in the winter of 1956. By the 1956-7 season there was sufficient demand in both Canada and the U.S. to justify sending out two companies, one playing *Hamlet* (with William Hutt) and Ibsen's *Peer Gynt* (with Bruno Gerussi), the other presenting *Othello* (with Tony VAN BRIDGE) and Shaw's *Man and Superman* (with Douglas Campbell). By 1959 one company was playing almost a whole season south of the border.

Companies usually consisted of a stage manager and as few as eight performers, who played many roles with only simple costume changes. Productions were spare but imaginative (e.g. David GARDNER's Eskimo *King Lear* in 1961), using flexible skeletal scenery that could be erected quickly in a theatre, school, or community hall. The repertoire was essentially Shakespeare and Shaw, with occasional variations (e.g. Chekhov's *The Cherry Orchard* in 1959 and Brecht's *The Caucasian Chalk Circle* in 1960). Not until 1964 was a Canadian work included—the historical revue, *All About Us*.

Covering Canada's vast distances proved debilitatingly expensive. The first season (sixteen weeks) lost $40,000 and only the spir-ited fund-raising of Lady Flora Eaton helped pay the bills. Deficits continued to mount despite the efforts of Robin Patterson, who became president in 1955, and general managers Laurel Crosby and (after 1958) Dennis Sweeting. In 1957, when a grant from the Canada Council proved inadequate, the Canadian Players had to retrench to a single company touring only part of the country. That same year the Stratford Festival broke with the Canadian Players by scheduling its own winter tour. The company moved its office to Toronto and within a year was left with only three actors with extensive Stratford experience. The establishment of the MANITOBA THEATRE CENTRE in 1958 and, subsequently, other regional theatres provided Stratford actors with alternate and considerably less arduous winter employment.

These changing circumstances caused the Canadian Players to redefine their purpose. In 1964 the new artistic director Marigold CHARLESWORTH, who had played Juliet for the company in 1958, and administrator Jean

The Canadian Players' King Lear, 1961, with (l. to r.) Herbert Foster as the Fool, Maureen Fitzgerald as Regan, and William Hutt as Lear

ROBERTS made Toronto home base, and in 1965-6 they mounted a nine-month season in the tiny CENTRAL LIBRARY THEATRE. They retained two companies, alternating a half-year in Toronto with a half-year on tour. In July 1966 the Canadian Players and the equally embattled CREST THEATRE merged into the Canadian Crest Players Foundation; however, its relationship with Charlesworth and Roberts ended, and it was not until 1968 that the new organization, under the name THEATRE TORONTO, was able to mount its first season.   ROSS STUART, HARRY LANE

Canadian Repertory Theatre. It grew out of Ottawa's Stage Society, an organization begun in 1948 by Hugh Parker, a native of Ottawa, with Englishman Malcolm Morley as director. When Parker left the Stage Society because of illness, Morley—along with Richard Malcolm and Eric Workman—reorganized the group as the Canadian Repertory Theatre Society in Sept. 1949. It included several actors from the Stage Society—Betty LEIGHTON, Joanna Baker, Floyd Caza, Peter Sturgess, Gertrude Allen, Christopher PLUMMER, and Joyce Spencer. The opening production on 1 Oct. 1949 was the comedy *Quiet Weekend* by Esther McCracken, featuring Morley, Malcolm, and the nineteen-year old Plummer.

During its first thirty-five-week season the company gave six performances a week, including a Saturday matinée, and opened a new play every week. After the first season Morley returned to England and the CRT was reorganized under a new triumvirate of Amelia HALL and Sam Payne as co-directors and Bruce Raymond as business and publicity manager. The plays were performed in the 700-seat auditorium of La Salle Academy, a Catholic boys' school on Guigues St in Ottawa's Lower Town district.

Hall, who stayed with the company until 1954, directed over fifty productions; in her last season she was managing director. Other Canadian actors in the company were William HUTT, William SHATNER, Ted Follows, Eric HOUSE, Anna Cameron, Max Helpmann, Bruce Swerdfager, Richard EASTON, David GARDNER, Lynne Gorman, Ronald Hartmann, Donald DAVIS, and John COLICOS. The CRT produced a great variety of classical and modern drama, but few Canadian plays; Ottawa writer William Doyle's *Days of Grace*, however, was produced in the first season, with Plummer in the lead.

In 1950 the CRT was described as 'the only professional Canadian company . . . doing a weekly winter season of stock.' Though it later resorted to two-week runs for a time, the CRT continued its hectic pace until Mar. 1956, when it had accumulated a deficit of over $4,500; its final production was Ben Travers' *Wild Horses*. By that time several of its actors, including Hall, had moved to the STRATFORD FESTIVAL. Ian Fellows, the last managing director, tried without success to revive it the following year.

The CRT had a loyal following in Ottawa, but never the large audiences needed for financial security. After its demise Ottawa lacked a professional acting company until the inception of the TOWN THEATRE.
                                                    JAMES NOONAN

Canadian Stage Company. Founded in 1988 in Toronto through a merger of TORONTO FREE THEATRE and CENTRESTAGE, it immediately became one of the country's largest arts organizations, with an annual budget in excess of $6 million. Under co-artistic directors Bill GLASSCO and Guy SPRUNG, the company announced a 1988-9 season of fourteen productions on four stages: the Free 'Upstairs' and the Free 'Downstairs' (in the former premises of Toronto Free Theatre on Berkeley St), an open-air stage in High Park, and the Bluma Appel Theatre in the ST. LAWRENCE CENTRE (formerly occupied by CentreStage). The announced mandate of the company is to 'serve the broadest possible audience with bold, relevant plays . . . in productions of superlative standards', with a primary focus on the development and production of Canadian work.
                                                    L. W. CONOLLY

Canadiens, Les. Commissioned by the CENTAUR THEATRE, Montreal, and produced under Guy SPRUNG's direction in 1977, Rick SALUTIN's play simulates the game of ice-hockey, turning sticks into political and cultural weapons, the rink into a battle arena, and the clock countdown into a procession of important dates in Quebec history. When the Forum clock stops at 17:59, for example, we are with Wolfe and Montcalm on the Plains of Abraham. The countdown culminates in 1976, the year of the first Parti Québécois victory in provincial politics. The analogy between ice-hockey and politics

Les Canadiens, *Centaur Theatre, Montreal, 1977, with (l. to r.) Sebastien Dhavernas, Luce Guilbeault, Ray Landry, Raymond Belisle, Michel Rudder, Eric Peterson*

emphasizes national pride and self-assertion, suggesting that although defeated by the English in battle the Québécois were usually winners on ice, and with the 1976 election victory they finally became masters in their own house.

Act 1 builds myth—that of Les Canadiens, 'standard-bearers of the Quebec spirit'. Act 2 is demythologization—the falling away of mere folkloric embellishments of a hockey team, and the sudden realization of contemporary political reality. Where Bertolt Brecht's 'unhappy is the nation that has no heroes' could stand as a motto for Act 1, his 'unhappy is the nation that needs a hero' is the sobering sequel.

Although the play depends on knowledge of both NHL hockey and Quebec history for full appreciation, its analysis of the movement from myth to reality has caught the popular imagination. Crudely textured, semi-documentary in approach, filled with simplistic dialogue and conflicts, the play is a favourite especially with those who find their cultural symbolism in a professional sport. The text was published by Talonbooks in 1977.

KEITH GAREBIAN

Carbone 14. Founded in Montreal in 1975 by Gilles Maheu, this company was first called Les Enfants du Paradis; its goals were to reinstate the importance of MIME, acrobatics, and juggling in the theatrical world. Its first shows borrowed from the various traditions of travelling acrobats, *commedia dell'arte*, and the music hall. In order to attract a new and different audience, the company performed in such unconventional settings as parks, business districts, cafeterias, and nightclubs. It performed onstage for the first time in 1976, at the Conventum, *La Famille Rodriguez*, a well-received COLLECTIVE CREATION focusing on the use of the mask. A second production, *Le Voyage immobile*, presented in 1978 in the Salle Fred-Barry at the Théâtre Denise Pelletier, travelled to New York and Baltimore in 1979, and to Nancy, Amsterdam, and Paris the following year.

In 1981 the group took the name Carbone 14 and moved into L'Espace Libre. They continued to work with improvisations, and in developing their shows they relied on what they called the 'material memory' of the actors—leading to the new name, with its reference to carbon-dating. Their productions—which drew on Brecht, Artaud, the U.S. Bread and Puppet Theatre, Noh theatre, and other sources—brought international recognition. The company took part in several important festivals; at Toronto (1979), Copenhagen (1980 and 1983), Geneva and Cologne (1983), and Liège, Brighton, Granada, Madrid, and Baltimore (1986).

The most notable productions of Carbone 14 include *Pain Blanc; ou L'esthétique de la laideur*, first produced in 1981; and *L'Homme rouge* and *Vies privées*, both produced in 1982, the latter touring Europe and the U.S. In 1987-8 the company toured Australia, Europe, Latin America, and the U.S. before opening a new show, *Le Dortoir*, in Nov. 1988. Carbone 14 has won several awards, including the Montreal Critics Prize for its 1985 adaptation of Peter Weiss's *Marat/Sade* and the 1985 American Theatre Festival Prize for *Le Rail*, based on D.M. Thomas's novel *The White Hotel*.   DOMINIQUE ROY

Cariou, Len (b. 1939). Born in St Boniface, Man., he studied singing as a child in Winnipeg and voice (with Kristin Linkletter) in New York in 1963. His first professional appearance as an actor was at Winnipeg's Rainbow Stage in a 1959 production of *Damn Yankees*. He subsequently performed at the MANITOBA THEATRE CENTRE in a variety of classical and modern works, from Shakespeare's *Taming of the Shrew* to Brecht's *Mother Courage* and Thomas Heggen's and Joshua Logan's *Mister Roberts*. Following four years at the STRATFORD FESTIVAL (1962-5), where he appeared in Edmond Rostand's *Cyrano de Bergerac*, Molière's *Le Bourgeois Gentilhomme*, and William Wycherley's *The Country Wife*, as well as in Shakespeare, Cariou joined the Minnesota Theatre Company, with which he made his New York début in 1968 as Orestes in *The House of Atreus*. He has continued to appear regularly on Broadway as an actor and director, and in 1979 won Tony and Drama Desk awards for his performance in Stephen Sondheim's musical *Sweeney Todd, the Demon Barber of Fleet Street*. His most recent starring role there was as Theodore Roosevelt in the musical *Teddy and Alice* in the winter of 1988. Cariou has also starred at the American Shakespeare Festival at Stratford, Conn., the Mark Taper Forum in Los Angeles, the Kennedy Centre in Washington, D.C., Chicago's Goodman

Memorial Theatre, and the Guthrie Theatre in Minneapolis, where in 1972 he was associate director.

In 1975 Cariou returned to the Manitoba Theatre Centre for one season as artistic director, directing John Steinbeck's *Of Mice and Men* and playing Cyrano in *Cyrano de Bergerac* and Dysart in Peter Shaffer's *Equus*. His 1979 Macbeth at Toronto Arts Productions was a disaster, but in 1981 he was invited back to Stratford by artistic director John HIRSCH, with whom he had worked twenty years earlier in Winnipeg. Cariou was acclaimed as Coriolanus, Petruchio (both in 1981), and Sergius in Shaw's *Arms and the Man*, but was less successful as Prospero in *The Tempest* (both in 1982). At Edmonton's CITADEL THEATRE in 1983-4 he played Lear and directed Arthur Miller's *Death of a Salesman*.

A powerfully built leading man, with a forceful voice and an aggressive stage persona, Cariou has also acted in film (*The Four Seasons*, *A Little Night Music*, and the National Film Board's 1977 pollution-scandal film *One Man*) and on television, including the CBS feature *Who'll Save Our Children?*
          RAY CONLOGUE

Carleton, John (1861-1936). Admitted to the bar in 1883, appointed Queen's Counsel in 1899, and County Court Judge for Carleton, Victoria, and Madawaska, N.B., in 1904, Carleton became Saint John's best-known playwright. He was also a director of the SAINT JOHN OPERA HOUSE. (His brother, William T. Carleton, was a producer with the American theatrical agency, Klaw and Erlanger.) His best-known play, *More Sinned Against than Sinning*, was published in New York in 1883. An Irish three-act melodrama advocating social and political reform, it was first performed by an all-male cast from the Father Mathew Association Dramatic Club, Saint John, with Carleton as Marmaduke Hilton, in a crowded St Malachi's Hall on 17 and 19 Mar. 1884. It was performed again in Saint John's Mechanics' Institute on St Patrick's Day 1885 and 1886, and by 1903 had been seen in cities in the Maritimes, Ontario, Maine, and Montana. A second Irish social drama, *Coom-na-goppel* (1903), in five acts, was published in Boston. *Hildebrand* (1903), a historical drama printed privately in Saint John, was revised as *A Medieval Hun* and published in Boston, 1921. Only a list of *dramatis personae* survives for *In One Night*, a three-act temperance drama presented by the Father Mathew Association in the Mechanics' Institute twice in 1886. No script survives of three other plays: *The Convict's Daughter*, acted on 23 Oct. 1893 at St Patrick's Hall with Carleton in the title role; *Love Was True to Me*, given honourable mention in the *Chicago Ledger* competition and staged as the curtain-raiser at the Saint John Opera House with Sidney Drew on 13 and 14 July 1894; and *The Crimson Wing*, winner of first prize in a 1918 Canadian play competition. Carleton was skilled in the creation of character, stage pictures, and special effects.

MARY ELIZABETH SMITH

Carrier, Roch (b. 1937). Born in Sainte-Justine, Que., he studied at the Collège St Louis d'Edmunston, the Université de Montréal, and the Université de Paris, from which he received a Doctorate in French Literature in 1978. After a short career in journalism in New Brunswick (1958-60) and five years in France, he became a professor of French and Quebec literature at the Collège Militaire de St Jean. Author of over a dozen stories and plays, he has collaborated on several films for the National Film Board of Canada and has served as general secretary of the THÉÂTRE DU NOUVEAU MONDE (1971-4).

Critics have generally favoured Carrier's fiction, particularly his short stories, several of which have been awarded prizes: *Jolis Deuils* won the 1964 Prix Littéraire de la Province de Québec, and *Les Enfants du bonhomme dans la lune* (1979), translated as *The Hockey Sweater and Other Stories* (1979), won the 1980 Prix Littéraire de la Ville de Montréal. The novel *La Guerre, Yes Sir!* (1968), basis for the play, was the runner-up for the same prize in 1968.

To date, Carrier's most popular play has been the stage version of LA GUERRE, YES SIR! (1970), first produced by Montreal's Théâtre du Nouveau Monde in 1970. It is a rollicking fresco of French-Canadian villagers attending the old-fashioned wake of an enlisted native son killed during the Second World War. Full of local colour, the piece also has nationalist significance for it is English-speaking soldiers who bring the body home, stand guard over it, and eventually throw the villagers out when they get too rowdy.

Carrier has adapted two of his other novels

for the stage: *Floralie, où es-tu?* (1969; play published 1974) produced by TNM in 1974, and *Il n'y a pas de pays sans grand-père* (1977), produced in 1978 by La COMPAGNIE JEAN DUCEPPE. Both are set in rural Quebec, although the latter has its bitter old hero hijacking a bus to Montreal to try to free his separatist grandson from prison. The nationalist stance of this play is unusually strident whereas *La Guerre, Yes Sir!* is full of rustic humour and *Floralie* is a poetic dream fantasy with moral overtones.

Albert Millaire in Roch Carrier's La Céleste Bicyclette, *National Arts Centre, 1981*

Carrier's first original play, *La Céleste bicyclette* (1980), received excellent reviews when it was first performed in 1979 at Montreal's Café de la Place. This lyrical fairy tale for adults about a romantic actor who claims to have cycled through the sky was produced in English by Toronto's TARRAGON THEATRE in 1982. His next play was another, less successful, poetic monologue: *Le Cirque noir* (1982) produced in 1982 at Café de la Place.

Apart from *La Guerre, Yes Sir!*, Carrier will probably be best remembered for his delightful short stories, which he has been invited to read all over the world. Most of his works have been translated into English by Sheila Fischman. ELAINE F. NARDOCCHIO

Carver, Brent (b. 1951). Raised and educated in Cranbrook, B.C., he attended the Univ. of British Columbia from 1969 to 1972. His first professional engagement as an actor was in Jacques Brel's *Jacques Brel is Alive and Well and Living in Paris* at the Vancouver ARTS CLUB theatre in 1972. He has played leading musical roles, ranging from the Pirate King in Gilbert and Sullivan's *The Pirates of Penzance* to Jesus in John-Michael Tebelak's and Stephen Schwartz's *Godspell*. In 1973 and 1974 he appeared in the weekly television series 'Inside Canada'. At Theatre London, the CITADEL THEATRE, the STRATFORD FESTIVAL, and elsewhere he has been diversely cast as Ariel in Shakespeare's *The Tempest*; Dubedat in Bernard Shaw's *The Doctor's Dilemma*; Hamlet; and as Horst in Martin Sherman's *Bent* (for which he won the Dora Mavor MOORE award as best actor in the 1981-2 season); and the MC in *Cabaret* at Stratford in 1987. These and other performances have been consistently remarkable for their extraordinary sensitivity and power. Carver has also appeared in major roles in two films: as Rafe in Carol BOLT's *One Night Stand*, which won him an Etrog Award in 1978, and as Robert Ross in Robin PHILLIPS' 1983 film adaptation of Timothy FINDLEY's novel *The Wars*. TIMOTHY FINDLEY

Catalyst Theatre. This innovative theatre for social action began in 1977 when drama students working with David Barnet at the Univ. of Alberta created a documentary play (see DOCUMENTARY DRAMA) about alcoholism called *Drinks Before Dinner*. The Alberta Alcohol and Drug Abuse Commission (AADAC) sponsored a provincial tour of the play and requested a sequel, leading Barnet to found the Catalyst Theatre Society in 1977. In 1979 Barnet hired Jan Selman, a recent MFA graduate from the Univ. of Alberta, as artistic director. Performing commissioned works as well as initiating its own projects, and spared the operational expense of a theatre plant (performances have often taken place in workplaces and schools), the company by 1980 was working on a budget of over $400,000, most of which came from AADAC and other social and activist agencies. In 1985 Selman was succeeded by Ruth Smillie.

Catalyst has explored issues as diverse as drug abuse, sexual abuse, native rights, immigration, and teen suicide. It has produced a series of topical COLLECTIVE CREATIONs, such as the 1982 *Family Portrait* (about teens and parents), as well as single-author plays, notably Frank Moher's *Odd Jobs*, a 1985 co-production with Edmonton's WORKSHOP WEST. *Stand Up For Your Rights*, produced in 1980, about the legal rights of the mentally handicapped, and the 1982 *It's About Time* (about prison conditions) marked the development of an interactive theatre forum comparable to Brazilian director Augusto Boal's well-known 'Theatre of the Oppressed'. Like Boal, Catalyst has used its theatre to enable disadvantaged groups to analyse and cope with their difficulties.

In 1981 Catalyst was one of the principal founders of the Canadian Popular Theatre Alliance, and in 1983 it initiated the national 'Bread & Roses Festival of Popular Theatre' in Edmonton. Some of its work has been seen nationally in the CBC series 'Catalyst Television'. ALAN FILEWOD

Catudal, Michel (b.1940). Born in Saint-Jean d'Iberville, Que., he studied painting at l'École des Beaux Arts from 1957 to 1959 and stagecraft at the NATIONAL THEATRE SCHOOL from 1962 to 1965. During this period he also gained experience in the workshop of the STRATFORD FESTIVAL, where he won a Tyrone GUTHRIE Award. He subsequently became props man for the THÉÂTRE DU NOUVEAU MONDE, several Canadian ballet companies, the MANITOBA THEATRE CENTRE, and for several film productions. After 1968 he designed the sets and occasionally the costumes for La Comédie des Deux Rives (Univ. of Ottawa) and for the Studio at the NATIONAL ARTS CENTRE, under the direction of Jean Herbiet, where he created magnificent costumes and sets at the NAC's studio for *Les Paons* by Michel TREMBLAY, directed by J. Lefebvre; other notable productions were *Monsieur Fugue* by Liliane Atlan and *Oh! Les beaux jours* (*Happy Days*) by Samuel Beckett. Catudal has also created sets for Montreal's Instant Theatre, the London Little Theatre, Le THÉÂTRE D'AUJOURD'HUI, and Le Théâtre International de Montréal (La POUDRIÈRE). In 1974 he designed interesting sets for *La Moscheta de Ruzante* at La NOUVELLE COMPAGNIE THÉÂTRALE and for *Wouf wouf!* by Yves SAUVAGEAU. He has also worked on a COLLECTIVE CREATION, *La Vie à trois étages*, with the THÉÂTRE DE LA MARMAILLE. Among his other sets are Roch CARRIER's *Floralie, where are you?*, produced in 1977 for the National Arts Centre under the direction of Jean GASCON, and Serge Mercier's *Encore un peu*, produced at Le Théâtre Denise Pelletier (NCT) by J.L. BASTIEN in 1980. Since 1970 Catudal has taught at l'Université de Montréal and at Lionel Groulx CEGEP.

RENÉE NOISEAUX-GURIK

Cazeneuve, Paul (1871-1925). Born in Revel, France, he moved to Boston when his father became a professor at Harvard University. After taking courses in diction and acting from visiting Italian actors Tommaso and Alessandro Salvini and from John Lane, he began touring in 1893 with such stars as Edwin Booth, Wilson Barrett, and Madame Modjeska. These North American tours took him to Montreal, and in 1900 Georges Gauvreau, proprietor of the THÉÂTRE NATIONAL, hired him as manager and leading actor.

Cazeneuve set about translating into French American versions of successful European plays (*Les Trois mousquetaires, Le Comte de Monte Cristo,* and *Faust*—twenty-eight successive performances of which were given in 1901), which gave the Théâtre National its first great successes.

In 1904, at the height of his fame, Cazeneuve left Montreal for Quebec where he tried, without success, to establish a permanent French theatre at the AUDITORIUM. He returned to Montreal the following year, and after a brief stint at the THÉÂTRE CANADIEN, in the city's East End, he returned to the National in Feb. 1906, becoming co-owner in the same year.

Partial to dramas and elaborate melodramas, Cazeneuve nonetheless grasped the historical importance of the revue, hitherto relegated to secondary theatres; the revue made its début at the National in 1909. After leaving the National again in 1910, Cazeneuve divided his time between several North American tours and work as a technical adviser for the Fox film studios. He also continued to create French adaptations of European works for Montreal theatres, and English adaptations for American film stars. In 1917 he returned to Montreal as manager of the New Empire, and also managed the National and the Théâtre Canadien in 1918.

The dominant personality of the 'Golden Age' of Montreal theatre and an adapter of some forty plays, Cazeneuve died in Hollywood in poverty and anonymity.

JEAN-MARC LARRUE

Censorship. The first significant case of theatre censorship in Canada arose in 1694 when a proposed production of Molière's *Tartuffe* in Quebec was suppressed by Bishop Saint-Vallier, who accused the lead actor, a young Lieutenant named Jacques de Mareuil, of blasphemy, then excommunicated and imprisoned him. The episode—Canada's first theatrical conflict between church and state—was to affect French Canada up to the twentieth century. Church opposition restricted theatrical activity in Quebec until after the Conquest; and despite the growth of both indigenous and imported theatre in the nineteenth century, the Church still intervened on some occasions. Sarah Bernhardt's first visit to Montreal in 1880, for example, sparked a controversy when Bishop Fabre urged the faithful to refrain from attending her appearance in Eugène Scribe's and Ernest Legouvé's *Adrienne Lecouvreur.* His request that the city council prohibit her Christmas Day program came to naught because existing legislation pertained only to Sunday performances, not to those on weekdays that happened also to be holy days. Fabre's opposition to Bernhardt was reported widely in the American press, particularly in Chicago and St Louis. Bernhardt's visits to Montreal and Quebec City in 1905 also brought clerical condemnation, Archbishop Bruchési publishing two pastoral letters denouncing the stage. (He later attacked Sunday performances and immoral plays.) In 1907 he pressured the management of Montreal's Nouveautés Théâtre to withdraw Henry Bernstein's *La Rafale* (about prostitution and suicide), and to promise to submit future titles to a citizens' committee. Continued clerical attacks on Sunday performances and immoral plays ultimately led to the appointment in July 1913 of Jean-Paul Filion, a well-known actor, as Montreal's first official theatrical censor.

In English Canada clerical strictures against the theatre were less frequent, though by no means uncommon. An article in the Jan. 1770 issue of the *Nova Scotia Chronicle* pronounced that 'a Christian cannot with a safer Conscience enter into the Play-House than into a Brothel', and throughout the nineteenth century Protestant ministers preached anti-theatrical sermons. In 1877, for example, sermons by the Rev. Dr Burns in Halifax and by Canon Baldwin of Montreal's Christ Church Cathedral both deplored the modern theatre. Direct attempts at censoring or suppressing plays occurred occasionally. In 1912 a Methodist minister, John Coburn, led an attempt to censor or suppress a burlesque

Censorship

show, *The Darlings of Paris*, at the Star Theatre in Toronto. A jury acquitted the Star's management, but Coburn's vigilance led to the creation of a Committee of Forty 'to carry on a campaign to clean up the theatres of the city'. And in Dec. 1913 William Banks (a member of the editorial staff of the *Globe*) was appointed Toronto's theatre censor by the Police Commission. A few months later he censored, but did not suppress, American playwright Legrand Howland's *Deborah*, which opened in May 1913 at the PRINCESS THEATRE. Coburn, however, believing the play advocated immorality by sympathetically portraying an unmarried mother, initiated a successful private prosecution against the company. On appeal the convictions were quashed and *Deborah* reopened; the primacy of state over church in matters theatrical was affirmed. The following year a striking example of pre-censorship occurred when the manager of the Princess submitted Shaw's *The Shewing-up of Blanco Posnet* to Banks who, following the example of the English censor, forbade a Toronto production of the play because of its 'blasphemy, profanity and language of the lowest type'. In Sept. 1926 Banks' successor, H.M. Wodson, ordered cuts in the text of Patrick Hastings' *Scotch Mist* for production at the ROYAL ALEXANDRA THEATRE. The cuts were not made, and clerics of various denominations, describing the play as 'an apology for adultery', complained to the Police Commission. The decision, however, was left up to the censor, who publicly reprimanded the management of the theatre; he received apologies and assurances of future compliance. The declining influence of the Methodist Church in theatre censorship is reflected in the church's own ambivalence towards theatregoing. The 1898 edition of *The Doctrine and Discipline of the Methodist Church of Canada* expressly forbade theatre attendance; but by 1914 the rules urged only that 'in the case of those amusements and practices which are of a hurtful or questionable tendency', Methodists 'engage in none injurious to their spiritual life, or incompatible with their allegiance to Jesus Christ the Master.'

Censorship or suppression of plays in Canada for political reasons has been sporadic. An 1839 production in Montreal of Voltaire's *La Mort de César*, on the heels of the 1837 Rebellion, brought accusations of sedition from the editor of the *Gazette*, and protests from T.A. Young, the city's chief of police. The controversy led merely to a curfew of 11:00 p.m. on all public entertainments. In Toronto in 1933, however, city police suppressed *EIGHT MEN SPEAK*—a play about the attempted murder in prison of Tim Buck, the leader of the Communist Party of Canada—after only one performance. Police also banned a performance scheduled for Winnipeg's WALKER THEATRE on 2 May 1934. In Vancouver in 1936 police and city authorities threatened to revoke the license of the Ukrainian Labour Temple for performing Clifford Odets' *Waiting for Lefty*. The production by the Progressive Arts Players nonetheless proceeded and won a place in that year's finals of the DOMINION DRAMA FESTIVAL. The most explicitly political of George RYGA's plays, *Captives of the Faceless Drummer*, with clear analogies to the 1970 FLQ crisis, became the subject of controversy when the VANCOUVER PLAYHOUSE board first deferred then refused to allow its performance, which finally took place at the Vancouver Art Gallery in April 1971.

Since the Second World War police and civic politicians have increasingly assumed the role of guardians of public morality, interfering with many productions. In 1953 Sydney RISK's production of Jack Kirkland's sexually frank *Tobacco Road* at Vancouver's Everyman Theatre was halted when police arrested five actors on stage during a performance. As a result of the ensuing legal wrangles, the Everyman Theatre Company soon folded. More censorship occurred in Vancouver in the 1960s and 1970s. A planned production of the American rock-musical *Hair* (which contains nude scenes) was withdrawn prior to performance by the Vancouver Playhouse in 1969 after the City Licensing Inspector, Milton Harrell, threatened to cancel the theatre's licence. Harrell did cancel the licence of the ARTS CLUB Theatre for performing a sketch (in a play called *Collision Course*) in which a male and a female actor appeared wearing only transparent plastic costumes. Vociferous complaints about Harrell's action, however, persuaded City Council to withdraw his censorship authority. But in Nov. 1970 the Vancouver police morality squad, acting on a complaint, closed Michael McClure's *The Beard* at the Riverqueen Coffee-House, charging management, actors, and a technician with presenting an obscene performance. In May 1971 the accused were convicted and fined; an appeal in November was lost, but in April 1973 the B.C. Court of Appeal dismissed the convictions and ordered a new trial, which was never held. (The Vancouver Playhouse board was exceptionally cautious in the late 1960s and early 1970s. Upset by criticism of William D. Roberts' *The Filthy Piranesi* in 1969, which portrayed a homosexual relationship, and by rumours of marijuana-smoking in the audience during Ryga's *Grass and Wild Strawberries*, the board dismissed the artistic director Joy COGHILL and appointed two of its members to vet all new scripts.)

In Toronto nudity on stage became an issue in the 1970s, the problem having first arisen in 1959 with 'Les Ballets Africains' at the Royal Alexandra; the company's female dancers were ordered to don fishnet brassières. Surprisingly, full nudity in *Hair* was permitted in 1970 in the same theatre on condition (specified by morality officers) that the stage lights be dimmed. The nude review *Oh! Calcutta!*, presented at least 165 times at Toronto's Variety Dinner Theatre in 1983, was also tolerated. Despite Section 170 of the Criminal Code—which allows penalties ranging up to six months in jail and/or a $500 fine for nudity in a public place—nudity in Canadian theatre became commonplace in the 1970s. Section 163 of the Criminal Code—which makes it an offence to present, give, or allow to be presented 'an immoral, indecent or obscene performance'—was, however, used on at least three occasions to close shows in Toronto. In Mar. 1969 criminal charges were laid (at THEATRE PASSE MURAILLE) against the director, three producers, and twelve actors in Rochelle Owens' *Futz*, which included a scene in which a man copulates with a sow. Fines were levied on the director and producers, but an appeal court later quashed the charges. In June 1968 police issued warnings about four-letter words in *Infanticide in the House of Fred Ginger*, though no action was taken. But Section 163 of the Code was invoked in 1973 to prosecute Michael HOLLINGSWORTH's *Clear Light* (at TORONTO FREE THEATRE), for its mixture of infanticide and kinky sex, as well as in 1975 against the collective *I Love You, Baby Blue* (Theatre Passe Muraille) a spoof of the then-current 'blue movies' on cable television. Nudity and crude language in *Baby Blue* initially brought visits from morality-squad officers, who suggested changes in the dia-

logue. Some weeks later, during an election campaign in which pornography was an issue, police arrested the actors. Released on bail, they performed the play illegally while awaiting trial. After only half a day in court, the prosecution withdrew its case. An unusual complaint was laid against the nude review *Let My People Come* at Toronto's Basin St Cabaret in 1981. Anne Stirling Hall, president of the Canadian Association of Burlesque Entertainers, accused actors of hiding behind the 'camouflage of art', doing what some sixty strippers had been arrested for doing in the preceding year. City police laid charges—not for nudity, but for operating an adult-entertainment parlour without a licence. The company was acquitted.

The most celebrated case of theatre censorship in contemporary Quebec was an attempt by civic and church authorities to prevent production and publication of *Les FÉES ONT SOIF* by Denise Boucher. A strong feminist play—attacking, among other things, the cult of the Virgin Mary—*Les Fées ont soif* was selected for the 1978-9 season at Montreal's THÉÂTRE DU NOUVEAU MONDE. In May 1978, TNM submitted its annual request for funds to the Greater Montreal Arts Council. The Council cut TNM's grant by $15,000, citing Boucher's play as the reason. Nevertheless it opened on 18 Nov. and played through Dec. to good houses. In protest against the GMAC's implicit censorship policy, the Association of Theatre Directors, representing some forty-one Quebec theatres, refused to accept Council subsidies; and in June 1978 2,000 people signed a public petition denouncing the attempted censorship. The League of Rights of Man (La Ligue des droits de l'homme), newspaper editorials, and citizens' groups also criticized GMAC's action. Public demonstrations prompted support from the Institut international de théâtre, an affiliate of UNESCO, and a public rebuke of Judge Vadeboncoeur, the controversial chairman of the granting body, by Jean-Paul L'Allier, a former Quebec Minister of Cultural Affairs. Shortly after the opening, however, several Roman Catholic groups asked that the play be stopped and that all texts be removed from circulation. Superior Court Judge Reeves accepted the latter proposal. The ban was lifted in Jan. 1979 by Associate Chief Justice Vallée, whose decision was upheld by the Quebec Court of Appeal in Nov. Finally, in Feb. 1980, the Supreme

Court of Canada refused to hear the charges of blasphemy brought against the play.

See *Canadian Theatre Review*, 13 (1977), a special issue on obscenity and the theatre; J. Laflamme and R. Tourangeau, *L'Église et le théâtre au Québec* (1979); L.W. Conolly, 'The Man in the Green Goggles: Clergymen and Theatre Censorship (Toronto 1912-13)', *Theatre History in Canada*, 1 (1980); L.W. Conolly, 'The Methodist Church and the Theatre in Canada, 1884-1925', *Themes in Drama*, 5 (1983); L. Doucette, *Theatre in French Canada: Laying the Foundations, 1606-1867* (1984).   RAMON HATHORN

Centaur Theatre. Montreal's premier English-language playhouse and one of the country's most successful regional theatres, it was established in 1969 by the Centaur Foundation for the Performing Arts, a non-profit corporation with Dr Herbert C. Auerbach as its president. Maurice PODBREY, a young South African actor-director, then teaching at the NATIONAL THEATRE SCHOOL, was appointed artistic director, a post he continues to occupy.

For its first seasons the company leased a 220-seat auditorium in the Old Stock Exhange at 453 St François-Xavier St in Old Montreal, but in 1974 it bought the entire building and renovated it at a cost of $1.3 million to designs by Montreal architect Victor Prus. Most of the costs were defrayed by government and corporate grants.

The Old Stock Exchange complex, opened in 1975, houses two theatres known as Centaur 1 and Centaur 2. Centaur 1, the remodelled original playhouse, seats 255 in a steeply raked auditorium. Its open- or end-stage has no curtain. The playing area is 36' wide by 22' deep, with a ceiling height of close to 27'. Centaur 2, a traditional proscenium house, seats 440. Its stage is approximately 68' wide by 23' deep, with a proscenium opening 36' wide by 21' high. The stage can accommodate a partial thrust 7' 3" deep.

The Centaur program consists of seven plays presented in an eight-month season from Oct. to June. Although an average of one classic is mounted annually, the repertoire features mainly contemporary international drama. Edward Albee, Edward Bond, Brian Friel, David Mamet, Sam Shepard, Tom Stoppard, and Lanford Wilson are represent-

ative of the dramatists staged. The theatre has also done much to familiarize audiences with the work of South African playwright Athol Fugard, several of whose plays have been produced, including the first performance outside South Africa of *A Lesson from Aloes* in 1980.

While maintaining an international perspective, Centaur is firmly committed to the encouragement of Canadian playwriting. In the theatre's inaugural season (1969-70), Podbrey staged Montreal writer Peter Desbarats's *The Great White Computer*, a play based on a recent riot at Sir George Williams (now Concordia) University. Since then the theatre has staged over forty Canadian plays, some in original productions, others as co-productions with Canadian theatres. Among its major achievements is the discovery and production of the plays of David FENNARIO, whose *On the Job* in 1975, *Nothing to Lose* in 1976, *Toronto* in 1978, *BALCONVILLE* in 1979, and *Moving* in 1983, all premièred at Centaur. Centaur productions of Canadian scripts also include Ronald Garrett's *Autumn at Altenburg* in 1973, Rod Langley's *Bethune* in 1975, Frederick Ward's *Riverlisp* in 1975, Rick SALUTIN's *Les CANADIENS* in 1977, and Beverly Lockwood's *Weeds* in 1979.

Approximately one-third of Centaur's 1985-6 budget of $1.6 million came from ticket sales; most of the rest came from government and corporate sources. The theatre has no capital debt and no operating deficit. Although it is a frankly middle-class anglophone playhouse, Centaur recognizes the predominance of French culture in Quebec and participates in it enthusiastically: francophone artists are employed whenever appropriate; experiments with bilingual plays (such as *Balconville* and *Moving*) have been successfully attempted; translations of French hits (such as the COLLECTIVE CREATION *BROUE* or Michel TREMBLAY's *Albertine, in Five Times*) have been featured; and plays dealing with Quebec's cultural past and present (for example, Rick Salutin's *Les Canadiens* and Rod Langley's *Bethune*) have been commissioned.

JOHN RIPLEY

Central Library Theatre. In 1961 the Toronto Public Library Board, recognizing the increasing theatrical activity in the city, renovated the Central Library's third-floor auditorium, which for thirty years had been used for library meetings and occasional theatrical performances, notably by the Arts Theatre Club. It was conveniently located on St George St near College.

An intimate 209-seat theatre designed by Irving Grossman, it was intended as a rental house for non-commercial groups. A new lighting system, a flexible wingless stage, dressing-room space for eighteen, and permanent seating were installed. The theatre also had a generous foyer and exhibition space and was located near the library's newly opened theatre collection. The Central Library Theatre was officially opened on 19 Jan. 1962 by Gratien GÉLINAS. The first production later that month was *Six Days and a Dream* by John Volinska, produced by the Drao Players, an amateur company.

Principal tenants over the next four years were Jean ROBERTS and Marigold CHARLES-WORTH, who had advised on the renovations and who headed the theatre's first professional company. Roberts and Charlesworth retained the name Red Barn Theatre from their summer seasons at Jackson's Point, Ont., and presented two seasons of classical and contemporary plays in repertory, followed by a very successful six-month run of Harvey Schmidt's and Tom Jones's *The Fantasticks* starring Bruno GERUSSI and, later, Don Francks. In 1965 the CANADIAN PLAYERS, under the same management, rented the theatre for nine months. They offered high-quality productions of Oscar Wilde's *The Importance of Being Earnest*, J.M. Synge's *The Playboy of the Western World*, Tennessee Williams' *The Glass Menagerie*, and T.S. Eliot's *Murder in the Cathedral*. Leading Canadian actors—such as Martha HENRY, Douglas RAIN, and Powys THOMAS—were featured and the productions were designed by artists such as Desmond HEELEY, Brian JACKSON, Mark Negin, and Judy Peyton Ward.

A variety of companies used the theatre during the next fifteen years. With a few notable exceptions they were amateur groups for whom the little theatre offered a reasonable rent and an adaptable playing space. In 1967 a fifteen-week run of John HERBERT's *FORTUNE AND MEN'S EYES* was a critical and box-office success. Among other professional presentations was *Here Lies Sarah Binks*, a musical adapted by Don HARRON from Paul Hiebert's satirical novel, starring Jane MALLETT and Robert CHRISTIE. The Canadian Mime Theatre, the James Joyce Society, the UNIVERSITY ALUMNAE DRAMATIC CLUB, and

the Belmont Theatre, with producers Sylvia and Ben Lennick, also used the space. Early in 1977 the library was closed in preparation for the move to a new building. The property was acquired by the Univ. of Toronto; the newly renovated theatre was renamed the Robert GILL Theatre and made part of the University's Graduate Centre for Study of Drama.   HEATHER McCALLUM

CentreStage. The resident producing company of Toronto's ST. LAWRENCE CENTRE until its 1988 merger with TORONTO FREE THEATRE to form the CANADIAN STAGE COMPANY, it began in 1970 as part of the Toronto Arts Foundation, a non-profit organization headed by Mavor MOORE previously established by the City of Toronto to build and operate the St Lawrence Centre. Under the direction of Leon MAJOR, the company opened the theatre on 26 Feb. 1970 with Jacques LANGUIRAND's multi-media *Man, Inc*. After a financially disappointing first season in which four out of its five productions were Canadian plays, Moore—whose mandate for the Centre had been outspokenly nationalist—resigned. On 1 July 1970 Major became general director of the Centre, with complete responsibility for theatrical, musical, and cultural activities in its two theatres, and for the school-touring Theatre Hour Company inherited from the defunct CREST THEATRE in 1968. For ten years Major supervised a wide range of resident productions as well as co-productions with companies such as the YOUNG PEOPLE'S THEATRE and CENTAUR THEATRE, employing directors such as Keith TURNBULL, Des McANUFF, Martin KINCH, John PALMER, Kurt REIS, and Marigold CHARLESWORTH. Major's repertoire was that of an urban regional theatre, a mixture of period and modern classics and Canadian plays (notably Michael COOK's *Colour the Flesh the Colour of Dust*, produced in the 1973-4 season, and David FENNARIO's *BALCONVILLE*, 1979); he departed from this standard only in avoiding strictly commercial Broadway fare and in producing plays by Bertolt Brecht.

Major's tenure at the Centre—he left in 1980—was plagued with difficulties. The City of Toronto, legally responsible for debts incurred by the resident company, passed a bylaw in 1973 separating the Toronto Arts Foundation from the resident company, which was renamed Toronto Arts Productions. Major was now responsible for fund-raising in addition to other duties, but he effectively lost control of booking for the Centre. Although the resident producer, TAP had only tenant status—with no right, for example, to extend the run of a successful production, or to rent the venue to commercial productions to raise money for its own. In addition, the design of the theatre was widely criticized as cold, stark, with poor sightlines, and extreme separation of actor from audience. Major, his directors, and his resident designer, Murray LAUFER, struggled with the space, succeeding most effectively with the epic productions of Brecht plays, which unfortunately were not popular with Toronto audiences. Although Major certainly had successes—notably Arthur Wing Pinero's *Trelawny of the 'Wells'*, produced in the 1973-4 season—and an aggressive subscription campaign kept audience levels high, competition from the STRATFORD FESTIVAL and Toronto's ALTERNATE THEATRES combined with administrative and design obstacles to sabotage the company's reputation.

Major's successor, Edward GILBERT, was relieved of responsibility for musical and community activities at the Centre. His first season, 1980-1, continued the effort to find a theatrical style to suit the space, and included his own spectacular, histrionic production of *Macbeth* with Len CARIOU; David Hare's nihilistic *Plenty*, directed by Peter Dews, fittingly played in pools of light surrounded by the black emptiness of the immense stage; and the theatre's first musical, Stephen Sondheim's *A Funny Thing Happened on the Way to the Forum*, directed by John HIRSCH, and starring Heath LAMBERTS.

When the theatre closed in 1981 for complete renovations, the 1981-2 season was limited to three plays in guest venues, and three readings in the Town Hall, the Centre's smaller theatre. The 1982-3 season began with two productions at the Bayview Playhouse before the renovations were completed. The company—renamed CentreStage—reopened the transformed venue of the Bluma Appel Theatre on 19 Mar. 1983 with Gilbert's production of Tom Stoppard's *On the Razzle*. The new proscenium stage and elegant interior received good notices; but the production did not, although it was followed by a well-received production of Betty LAMBERT's *Jennie's Story*, directed by Bill GLASSCO. The 1983-4 season, Gilbert's last, included the

highly successful touring production *Brew* (see *BROUE*). After an interim season with Richard OUZOUNIAN as producer—which included productions by Robin PHILLIPS of Noël Coward's *Tonight at 8:30* and John MURRELL's *New World*—Bill Glassco took control in 1985 with a season including a revival of David FRENCH's *Jitters* and Derek GOLDBY's controversial production of Frank Wedekind's *Spring Awakening*. Glassco's 1987-8 season was organized co-operatively with Toronto Free Theatre, prior to a formal merger as the Canadian Stage Company in 1988.

The archives of CentreStage are housed at the Univ. of Guelph.   STEPHEN JOHNSON

Cercle Molière, Le. Founded in St Boniface, Man., by André Castelein de la Lande, Louis-Philippe Gagnon, and Raymond Bernier, this amateur company opened on 23 Apr. 1925 with Edouard Pailleron's *Le Monde où l'on s'ennuie*. Its goal was to be an instrument of francophone education and culture, as well as a means of communicating with anglophones who were interested in French theatre. In 1928 Arthur Boutal became artistic director of the company. Among his many successes were the North American première in 1928 of Alphonse Daudet's *L'Arlésienne* and the award for the best play in French at the 1933 DOMINION DRAMA FESTIVAL for Eugène Brieux's *Blanchette*. Boutal, who died in 1941, was succeeded by his daughter, Pauline, who continued his policy of selecting seasons from the classical and contemporary French repertoire. Despite meagre resources—the company was several times threatened with closure—Cercle Molière productions maintained credible artistic standards, reflected, for example, in the excellent twenty-fifth anniversary production of Molière's *L'Avare* and in the winning of numerous prizes at regional and national drama festivals, often in competition with professional companies. It was not until 1961, however, that French-Canadian drama entered the repertoire, with a production of Marcel DUBÉ's *Chambres à louer*. Roland Mahé, who became artistic director in 1968, continued this policy, producing works by Félix LECLERC, Gratien GÉLINAS, and Michel TREMBLAY; Mahé also brought in actors from Montreal and established a training program for young actors. The first Manitoban play at the Cercle Molière—Roger Auger's *Je*

Jean Sarment's Le Voyage à Biarritz, Le Cercle Molière, *1937, with (l. to r.) Joseph Plante, Gilles Guyot, Arthur Boutal, Louis Gauthier, Suzanne Hubicki, Pauline Boutal, Gaudias Brunet*

m'en vais à Regina—was produced in 1975.

Among the actors who have contributed to the reputation of the Cercle Molière since its founding are Élisa Houde, Henri Bergeron, Léo Rémillard, Armand Laflèche, Robert Trudel, Robert Séguier, Maxime Desaulniers, Denis Bélair, Gilles and Monique Guyot, Paul Léveillé, Francis Fontaine, Jean-Louis Hébert, Irène Mahé, Gilbert Rosset, Jean-Guy Roy, Jeannette Arcand, and Claude Dorge. Despite their commitments to other careers in business, the media, or teaching, these actors enabled the company to survive and to build the theatrical stronghold that now brings credit to French Manitoba.

The oldest French-Canadian amateur theatre in Canada, the Cercle Molière has ambitions to turn professional, although a static audience in a minority population facing an alarming degree of assimilation poses a formidable challenge.

See Annette Saint-Pierre, *Le Rideau se lève au Manitoba* (1980) and *Chapeau bas* (1980).

ANNETTE SAINT-PIERRE

Chalmers, Floyd Sherman (b. 1898). Born in Chicago, this distinguished editor, publisher, and philanthropist was educated in Orillia, Ont., and Toronto. He joined the *Financial Post* in 1919, becoming editor-in-chief in 1925. In 1952 he was appointed president of Maclean-Hunter Ltd. and served as chairman of the board from 1964 to 1969. In 1964 he and his family established the Floyd S. Chalmers Foundation, a major source of private funding for the arts in Canada. In 1972 the Foundation created the prestigious Chalmers Awards for Best Canadian Play and in 1983 the Chalmers Canadian Children's Play Awards. Chalmers was president of the STRATFORD FESTIVAL in 1966-7, Chancellor of York Univ. from 1968 to 1973, and has received many honours, including the Order of Canada.

See his *A Gentleman of the Press* (1969) and *Both Sides of the Street* (1983).

ROTA HERZBERG LISTER

Charbonneau & le Chef. The only published play by John Thomas McDONOUGH, it has become a landmark in Canadian theatre for its treatment of an important event in Canadian history and its appeal to both French- and English-speaking audiences. It is about how a 140-day strike in the Quebec town of Asbestos in 1949 pitted the socially conscious Joseph Charbonneau, Archbishop of Montreal, against the autocratic Premier Maurice Duplessis. By the power, eloquence, and humour of McDonough's dialogue, the large cast of politicians, workers, and churchmen take the play beyond documentary drama, however. Without aiming at historical accuracy in all details, McDonough, a former priest, has written an allegory of social justice that includes the betrayal of Charbonneau by his Church when, in order to satisfy the vengeance of Duplessis, he is forcibly retired to a convent in Victoria, B.C., in 1950.

Originally written in French, *Charbonneau & le Chef* was published first in English in 1968 (Toronto, McClelland and Stewart), and it was produced that year on CBC radio, adapted by Ian Meyer. A 1968 recording in English was released as a CBC-RCA collaboration. The play was published in French—translated and adapted by Paul HÉBERT and Pierre Morency—in 1974 (Montreal, Leméac). The first professional stage presentation of *Charbonneau & le Chef* was in French in Mar. 1971 by the THÉÂTRE DU TRIDENT at the GRAND THÉÂTRE DE QUÉBEC. It was directed by Paul Hébert, who has directed all professional productions of the play in French, including a Quebec revival by the Théâtre du Trident in May 1972, an enormously popular Montreal production in 1973 by the same group in collaboration with La COMPAGNIE JEAN DUCEPPE followed by a successful Quebec tour, a production at the NATIONAL ARTS CENTRE in Sept. 1974, and a sold-out revival in Mar. 1986 at Montreal's PLACE DES ARTS. In these productions the role of le Chef was played by Jean DUCEPPE, and in all but the last Charbonneau was played by Jean-Marie Lemieux. English productions took place at Montreal's SAIDYE BRONFMAN CENTRE in Apr. 1975 and at the Peterborough Summer Theatre that same year; both were reworked versions of the original and neither achieved the stature of the French productions. JAMES NOONAN

Charlesworth. Marigold (b. 1926). Born and educated in England, she acted with the Shakespeare Memorial Theatre Company in Stratford-on-Avon from 1953 to 1954. In 1956 she immigrated to Canada, where with Jean ROBERTS and W.F. Whitehead she founded in 1959 a company at the Red Barn Theatre, Jackson's Point, Ont. She played Ellie Dunn

in Bernard Shaw's *Heartbreak House* at the CREST THEATRE in 1960 and co-directed (with Roberts) the Crest's 1964 *Hamlet*. Between 1962 and 1965 Charlesworth and Roberts presented plays at Toronto's CENTRAL LIBRARY THEATRE. Co-artistic director (again with Roberts) of the CANADIAN PLAYERS (1965-6), she directed Eliot's *Murder in the Cathedral* in 1965, and Wilde's *The Importance of Being Earnest* and Williams' *The Glass Menagerie* in 1966. She was artistic director of Toronto's Theatre Hour Company between 1968 and 1973, and at the NATIONAL ARTS CENTRE her notable productions have included James REANEY's *Colours in the Dark* in 1972 and Timothy FINDLEY's *Can You See Me Yet?* in 1976. At the STRATFORD FESTIVAL she directed *Much Ado About Nothing* in 1977. She freelances now as an actress—noted for her character roles and 'eccentrics', which she believes best suit her talents—and as a director. EUGENE BENSON

Charlottetown Festival, The. Founded in 1965, a year after the opening of CONFEDERATION CENTRE in Charlottetown, PEI, the Festival's first season—under artistic director Mavor MOORE—featured the première of the musical *ANNE OF GREEN GABLES*, John Drainie's *Laugh with Leacock* (with Johnny Wayne and Frank Shuster), and the musical revue *SPRING THAW*. The Festival has adhered to this policy of an all-Canadian repertoire, modifying it in 1968 to one of producing only Canadian musicals, with an emphasis on new work. Prior to this policy non-musical productions included Mavor Moore's *The Ottawa Man* in 1966 and the English-language première of Gratien GÉLINAS's *Yesterday the Children Were Dancing (HIER, LES ENFANTS DANSAIENT)* in 1967. Among early musicals were Moore's adaptation of Stephen LEACOCK stories entitled *Sunshine Town* in 1968; Pierre Berton's original musical *Paradise Hill* in 1967; two variations of Earl BIRNEY's novel *Turvey* (after a major overhauling *The Adventures of Private Turvey*, produced in 1966, was revived as *Private Turvey's War* in 1970); and the revue *The Legend of the Dumbells* in 1977, featuring original DUMBELL sketches by Jack McLaren.

The pastoral musical, as epitomized by *Anne of Green Gables*, is a style frequently associated with the Festival and has provided wholesome summer fare for the tourist family. Second only to *Anne* in popularity (appearing for five seasons and on three tours since its première in 1968) is Moore's adaptation of Elmer Harris's *Johnny Belinda*. (Harris's play, set in Prince Edward Island, has its own distinctive history with a Broadway run of over three hundred performances and a film version that brought Jane Wyman an Academy Award in 1948.) Other musicals with distinct Maritime settings, though less successful in production, include Arthur Samuels' *Ballade*, 1972, Helen Porter's *Joey*, 1973, and Gordon PINSENT's *Rowdyman*, 1976.

Less than half of the Festival's musical premières have been based on original concepts; the majority have been adapted from a wide range of literary or historical sources—the gothic tale of *Jane Eyre* in 1970, the tragic story of *Mary, Queen of Scots*, 1971, the romance of Edward VIII and Wallis Simpson in *Windsor*, 1978, and adaptations of Shakespeare's *Hamlet* (*Kronborg: 1582*, 1974) and *A Midsummer Night's Dream* (*On a Summer's Night*, 1979).

More recently the Festival has acquired a reputation as a producer of musicals that are by and large Broadway derivatives. This trend, first set with Cliff Jones's pop/rock musical *Kronborg*, represented a bold departure for the Festival at the end of its first decade. Since then, however, the Festival's

tourist-oriented programming and its artistic director Alan LUND, whose nineteen-year reign ended with the 1986 season, have been sharply criticized by Canadian artists, the media, and the government and municipal agencies that grant a substantial part of the budget. (It receives funding from the federal government, the Canada Council, the PEI government, the city of Charlottetown, and six other provinces.) Derivative productions such as the 1982 *Skin Deep* and *Singin' and Dancin' Tonight*, and the 1986 *Babies*, and nostalgic tributes such as *By George!* (1976, a salute to Gershwin and the American bicentennial) and *Swing* (1985, a salute to the big-band era) are presented primarily to attract tourist dollars. Charlottetown has become the most showbusiness-oriented of the national summer festivals by putting tourism before art.

Lund's successor as artistic director, Walter LEARNING, opened his first season (1987), however, with the North American première of Alan Bleasdale's controversial musical biography of Elvis Presley, *Are You Lonesome Tonight?*. The Festival's board chairman resigned when Learning declined to censor the show's frank language, the Premier of PEI expressed his distaste in the House of Assembly, and some of the local community

Swing, *Charlottetown Festival, 1985*

protested against its 'unwholesomeness'. Widespread publicity helped create an impressive ninety-two per-cent box office for *Are You Lonesome Tonight?*, but it is still too soon to know if *Learning* is forging significant new directions for the Festival.

See John F. Brown, 'The Charlottetown Festival in Review', *Canadian Drama*, 9 (1983), and 'The Charlottetown Festival: An Update', *Canadian Drama*, 12 (1986).

LINDA M. PEAKE

Charpentier, Gabriel (b. 1925). Born in Richmond, Que., he studied piano and composition in Montreal, Gregorian chant with the Benedictines at Saint-Benoît-du-Lac, Que., and composition and music history in Paris. Among his teachers were Jean Papineau-Couture and Nadia Boulanger. In 1953 he began a thirty-year association with CBC-TV in Montreal as artistic adviser for music-theatre series.

After producing early concert works—*Mass* (1952), *Trois Poèmes de Saint-Jean de la Croix* (1955)—Charpentier began to work in theatre. His incidental-music scores—over fifty by the mid-1980s, including some twenty-five for the THÉÂTRE DU NOUVEAU MONDE and about twenty for the STRATFORD FESTIVAL—have placed him in the forefront of Canadian theatre composers. He has often achieved unusual qualities of integration between music and action—involving singing and rhythmic speech by actors (the *Henry* plays and *Coriolanus* at Stratford, 1979-80 and 1981 respectively) or the appearance of costumed instrumentalists as part of the scene (Molière's *Le Bourgeois gentilhomme* at Stratford in 1964). The ensembles of his scores sometimes require non-standard instruments and effects, including electronics. Besides original scores he has also prepared new versions of works: the Brecht-Weill *Threepenny Opera*, for example.

In 1965 Charpentier collaborated with Jacques LANGUIRAND on the musical play *Klondyke*, and in 1968 his short opera *An English Lesson* premièred at Stratford. Using a whimsical combination of a solo actor, four singers, and a chamber orchestra, the work comments almost surrealistically on Canadian bilingualism. The following year, for the inauguration of the NATIONAL ARTS CENTRE, Charpentier wrote a full-length opera, *Orphée*. His retelling of the Orpheus legend again drew on mixed forces—acting, mime,

singing, dancing, electronics, folk instruments—and entailed audience involvement as well as multi-levelled and circular stage action. For these two operas Charpentier composed both libretto and music.

His largest original project to date is a cycle of ten short operas with the overall title *A Night at the Opera*. Several component works have been separately produced, among them *A Tea Symphony; or, The Perils of Clara*, 1972; *Clara and the Philosophers*, 1976; and *Clarabelle-Clarimage*, 1979. They illustrate the trademarks of his idiom—bilingualism, whimsical humour, and surrealism—as well as his strong sense of ritual.

Charpentier has been a teacher at the NATIONAL THEATRE SCHOOL and at the BANFF CENTRE, and was one of the founders of COMUS MUSIC THEATRE.

JOHN BECKWITH

Chaurette, Normand (b. 1954). This playwright has helped—along with René-Daniel DUBOIS—to give Québécois theatre of the 1980s a new orientation that is devoid of nationalist ideology and that deals with subjects such as creation, madness, and death. *Rêve d'une nuit d'hôpital* (1980), written in 1976 for a Radio-Canada playwriting competition, won the prestigious Paul Gilson Award of the Association radiophonique des programmes de langue française, and was eventually produced on 9 Jan. 1980 by the THÉÂTRE DE QUAT'SOUS. Based on the life of Montreal poet Émile Nelligan—who spent forty years in an asylum—the play is structured in twelve time-frames, like the twelve bells for the Angelus that, symbolically, articulate Nelligan's life. Taking lyricism still further—this time in a tale centred on the frenzy of passion and mysticism that precedes a young girl's suicide—Chaurette's next play, *Fêtes d'automne* (1982), was presented by Montreal's THÉÂTRE DU NOUVEAU MONDE on 19 Mar. 1982. *Provincetown Playhouse, juillet 1919, j'avais 19 ans* (1981), produced on 16 Sept. 1982 at Montreal's Café-Théâtre Nelligan, concerns three homosexual actors who produced a play in 1919 in which a child was actually killed. Two of the actors were executed for the murder, the story of which is told and explained by the third, who escaped conviction by feigning madness. A brilliant play about the cult of the sacrifice of beauty, marked by sensuality, violence, and madness, it is Chaurette's most successful work and has already become a classic of Québécois theatre.

Chaurette's subsequent plays display remarkable powers of invention, but concentrate more on poetic than theatrical effect. *La Société de Métis* (1983), first staged in 1987 at the THÉÂTRE D'AUJOURD'HUI, takes place in a small museum at a seaside resort, where the characters are wall-hangings that come to life during a theatrical presentation. *Fragments d'une lettre d'adieu lus par des géologues* (1986), first produced at the Quat'Sous in Mar. 1988, is a static septet in which the death of an engineer in Cambodia is explained in language that although highly technical does not obscure the humanitarian thrust of the play.   JEAN CLÉO GODIN

Chautauqua. Originating in 1874 as a Methodist summer camp on Lake Chautauqua in New York State, it quickly broadened its curriculum to become a non-denominational educational and entertainment institution. It developed across the United States and penetrated the Canadian West in 1917. The Canadian Chautauquas Company, founded by J.M. Erickson in Calgary, expanded rapidly, its circuits reaching from the west coast across the Prairies into Ontario. At its height it operated nine different circuits during the season, using over thirty large tents and employing approximately fifty young men and eighty or more young women.

Chautauqua staff were mainly university students, and in Canada the superintendent was usually a young woman, a policy introduced by the manager's wife, Nola B. Erickson. Such a 'Chautauqua Girl' was required to prepare the town for the coming event, work with the local committee, supervise the tent boys, present the performers to their audiences, and when the affair concluded (normally after four or six days) persuade the committee to sign a contract for next year's performance.

Lecturers were the backbone of the Chautauqua program, delivering informational, philosophical or inspirational addresses in the oratorical style of the period. During the war the patriotic pro-British feeling of the nation was reflected. Speakers from China, Japan, Greece, and Australia also appeared, while explorers such as Vilhjalmur Stefansson delivered accounts of their experiences. There were scientific lectures that included demonstrations of liquid air and radio. The Chautauqua platform also presented a forum for speakers with a cause, notable among whom were Henry Wise Wood of Alberta expounding his theories concerning the co-operative marketing of grain, and England's Emmeline Pankhurst championing the cause of women.

Musical offerings were an important feature. Programs included opera and concert singers and instrumentalists, Hawaiian groups, Negro singers, Swiss bell ringers and yodellers, Scottish song and dance performances, and popular- and comic-song entertainments.

Theatrical productions emphasized drama, melodrama, and sentimentality. Chautauqua companies strove to present detailed stage settings and scenery—not an easy assignment for a travelling troupe during the twenties and thirties. The most popular plays on Canadian circuits were *Broken Dishes*, *The Patsy*, *Cappy Ricks*, *Peg O' My Heart*, *It Pays to Advertise*, *Smilin' Thru*, *Turn to the Right*, *Daddy Long Legs*, and *New Brooms*.

The most noted figure on the Chautauqua drama circuit was Ralph M. Erwin, an American actor who first performed in Canada in 1924. In 1925 he signed a contract with Erickson to provide a five-person company and produce a play for a six-day circuit. Following this successful start he rose quickly and soon held the position of Dramatic Director. The Ericksons started a School of Theatre in Winnipeg under Erwin's direction, and his companies, named 'The Martin Erwin Players', were prolific and popular—in 1930 five of the dramas on the circuits were Erwin productions.

After 1931 Chautauqua declined, the last circuit operating in 1935. The Depression, radio, movies, and changing values in music, drama, and entertainment were all contributing factors. Although it lasted for only eighteen years in Canada, Chautauqua played a significant role in cultural and social development, particularly in prairie and northern regions. It provided employment and an excellent cultural background to those who worked on the circuits, and the efforts of citizens to bring the performances to their towns fostered community spirit. The programs presented many with their first opportunity to listen to good music, hear lectures, and see live theatre. They answered nostalgic longings for others who had been transplanted from culturally rich environments and eased, somewhat, concern over the cultural deprivation of their children.

See Sheilagh S. Jameson, *Chautauqua in Canada* (1979).   SHEILAGH S. JAMESON

Chilcott, Barbara (b. 1923). Born in New-market, Ont., Barbara Chilcott Davis studied acting with Josephine Barrington in Toronto and at the Central School of Speech and Drama in London, Eng., returning to Canada in 1951 to join her brothers Donald and Murray DAVIS, in their Straw Hat Players. In 1953 the three Davises opened the CREST THEATRE in Toronto, where Barbara established herself as one of the country's leading actresses in roles such as Cleopatra in *Antony and Cleopatra*, Viola in *Twelfth Night*, and Antigone in Jean Anouilh's *Antigone*. In 1957 she went to London, Eng., with the Crest production of J.B. Priestley's *The Glass Cage*, written for Chilcott and her brothers, and in 1963 she founded the Crest Hour Company for school tours. For the STRATFORD FESTIVAL she has played Kate in *The Taming of the Shrew* (1954) and Zenocrate in Christopher Marlowe's *Tamburlaine the Great*, which went to Broadway in 1956. In the 1960s she appeared on British and Canadian television in Arthur Miller's *The Crucible*, Jean Giraudoux's *Tiger at the Gates*, and Ibsen's *Hedda Gabler*, among other plays. When the Crest closed in 1966 Chilcott retired until 1973 when she renewed her acting career in regional theatres and in film. She returned to Stratford in 1981 as Volumnia in *Coriolanus*.

Exotic in appearance, with black hair and bold features, the young Chilcott consciously strove to project strong emotion in her roles. The mature actress, now adept at transcendental meditation, radiates strength and calm. She is married to composer Harry Somers.

SUSAN STONE-BLACKBURN

Children's Drama and Theatre in English. There is a significant tradition of English-Canada drama for children, consisting of publication and amateur performance of largely educational and religious plays by late nineteenth- and early twentieth-century authors such as Ida Emma Baker, Donalda James Dickie, Sister Agnes Mary, Stella Payson, Alexander Stephen, and Dorothy Jane Goulding. Goulding's mother, Dorothy Massey Goulding (a cousin of Vincent and Raymond MASSEY), managed the Toronto Children's Theatre from 1934 for some

twenty-five years—having succeeded Lorna Sheard, who founded it in 1931. Professional theatre for the young in English Canada has grown concurrently with adult theatre—Vancouver's HOLIDAY THEATRE began in 1953, the same year as the STRATFORD FESTIVAL—but in different circumstances. About one quarter of Canada's 200 or more professional theatres aim their work primarily toward young audiences. In contrast to adult companies, however, most have no permanent home; troupes usually of ten or fewer tour extensively with repertoires consisting of two or three one-act plays. When Joy COGHILL and Myra Benson founded Holiday Theatre they set a pattern of family entertainment for weekends and vacations. Later they added school tours, which have since become pervasive in children's theatre—millions of young Canadians see their first live theatre as captive audiences in school gymnasiums. It is a tribute to the ingenuity of the companies that a venue so innately hostile can be so often transformed, for fifty minutes, into another world. However, slipshod, predictable pieces, indifferently performed, continue to undercut the credibility of the genre.

The Companies. Many of the regional theatres established in the 1960s followed the model of the MANITOBA THEATRE CENTRE (1958) and included a Children's Theatre in their mandate. In Alberta the CITADEL THEATRE's Citadel-on-Wheels/Wings (1968) toured to remote northern communities; Regina's GLOBE THEATRE (1966) began as a company performing for children and still gives young audiences high priority. When the VANCOUVER PLAYHOUSE (1962) took over Holiday Theatre, it eventually dropped plays for children in 1977, and THEATRE CALGARY (1968) stopped producing plays for young people in 1986, despite its success with Caravan Theatre and Stagecoach Players. In Ontario, Theatre Hour Company (1962) became affiliated with Toronto Arts Productions (1970) and was renamed CENTRESTAGE Hour. It continues to play selections from classics, old and new, for secondary schools. Toronto's YOUNG PEOPLE'S THEATRE (1966) was founded to produce quality live theatre for young people and their families, and in 1977 became the first Canadian theatre exclusively for the young to own its own building.

More than a dozen companies were formed in the 1970s, a time of economic growth, increased government support, and a surge

Pinocchio, *Globe Theatre, Regina, 1980*

of nationalism. They included: a touring arm of the BASTION THEATRE Company of Victoria (1971); ALBERTA THEATRE PROJECTS, Calgary (1972); the Carousel Players, St Catharines, Ont. (1972); the MERMAID THEATRE, Wolfville, N.S. (1972); PRAIRIE THEATRE EXCHANGE, Winnipeg (1973); Kaleidoscope Theatre for Young People, Victoria (1974); GREEN THUMB THEATRE FOR YOUNG PEOPLE, Vancouver (1975); the Inner Stage, Toronto (1975); the GREAT CANADIAN THEATRE COMPANY, Ottawa (1975); Theatre Direct Canada, Toronto (1976); Theatre on the Move, Islington, Ont. (1976); and Chinook Touring Theatre, Edmonton (1978).

With the recession of the early 1980s, school touring was curtailed. Regional theatres also cut back on works for the young. Some, like Alberta Theatre Projects, now perform for adults only, offering schools selected plays from their regular season at a reduced price. However, a few new companies were formed in the 1980s: Toronto's Jabberwock and Sons Full Theatre Company (1980); the PERSEPHONE Youtheatre of Saskatoon (1982); and Calgary's Quest Theatre (1984).

Repertoire and Writers. There have been several trends in plays for young audiences in its three decades of existence. Early companies performed adaptations of fairy tales; those of Charlotte Chorpenning (U.S.) and Nicholas Stuart Grey (U.K.) were popular choices. Participation plays, written to include spontaneous but guided 'helping' from the audience, were most popular in the 1960s. Englishman Brian Way's technique of teaching drama through improvisation became influential in Canada after his 1959 tour; and plays he wrote for his own British touring company dominated the repertoire of the Globe Theatre in its early years. Other companies—the Citadel, Young People's Theatre, and Wayne Fine's Montreal Youtheatre (1968)—also produced Way's scripts.

Paddy CAMPBELL wrote some of the first Canadian participation plays. Typical are *Chinook* (1973), first performed in 1967, about how the chinook wind got its name, and *Too Many Kings* (1973), first performed in 1969, in which a storyteller's apprentice mistakenly conjures three monarchs, who compete for control of the story. Another is Len PETERSON's *Almighty Voice* (1974), first performed in 1970. It tells the story of the Cree Indian, Almighty Voice, who is forced into hiding after he steals a cow to feed his starving people. Children in the audience are invited to assume roles as Cree or Mounties, and a discussion of issues raised by the play fre-

Children's Drama and Theatre in English

quently follows performances. Many of Rex DEVERELL's plays for the young—written for Regina's Globe, where he is playwright-in-residence—include participation. Among them are *Sarah's Play* (1975), first performed in 1974, about a little girl who finds having one's wishes come true is a mixed blessing, and *Melody Meets the Bag Lady* (1984), first performed in 1982, in which an eccentric vagrant is transformed into a bourgeois matron—only to be changed back again when the children effecting the change regret her loss of individuality. Audience participation, including on-stage participation to aid the performers physically, is encouraged in the children's plays of Calgary's Loose Moose Theatre (1976), whose scripts are often the result of group improvisation, using the techniques of THEATRESPORTS for which they are famous.

Other Canadian authors have written plays for children: James REANEY's *Names and Nicknames* (1973), was first performed in 1963 at the Manitoba Theatre Centre; radio writers Pat Patterson and Dodi Robb contributed musicals like *The Dandy Lion* (1972), first performed in 1965 at the Museum Theatre; and ANNE OF GREEN GABLES (1972), a musical by Norman Campbell, adapted by Donald HARRON from the novel by L.M. Montgomery, has sold out every year at the CHARLOTTETOWN FESTIVAL (where it pre-

mièred) and has toured internationally. But it was only with the 1967 Centennial celebrations—which led to the commissioning of new scripts—and federal 'make-work' schemes like Opportunities for Youth (OFY) and Local Initiative Projects (LIP) in the early 1970s that a large body of new works was written, performed, and published. Eric NICOL's *Beware the Quickly Who* (1973), first performed in 1967, is about a boy's and a nation's identity. It was commissioned—along with Betty LAMBERT's *The Riddle Machine* (1974), a science-fiction fable first performed in 1967—by Holiday Theatre for a cross-country centennial tour. Federal funds encouraged the creation of new plays through the establishment of companies with a distinctive regional bias, such as Alberta Theatre Projects, which 'brought western history to life', and Wolfville's Mermaid Theatre, which used the Micmac legends of Eastern Canada for its first successes. LIP funds also launched Playwrights Co-op (now Playwrights Union of Canada), an important publishing project whose inexpensive editions made children's plays more accessible to directors of children's theatre. Carol BOLT's musical *Cyclone Jack* (1972, first performed in 1972), Paddy Campbell's *Under the Arch* (1976, first performed in 1974), and Dennis Foon's *Raft Baby* (first performed and published in 1978), all reveal the more varied

Rex Deverell's Melody Meets the Bag Lady, *Globe Theatre, Regina, 1982*

theatrical styles available during these years.

With its reliance on schools for tour bookings, theatre for young audiences has often tailored works to fit the aims of the school curriculum. Theatre-in-Education (T.I.E.) is only the most honestly named of many attempts, world-wide, to accommodate both art and education. T.I.E. was begun in England and brought to Canada by Playhouse Holiday in Vancouver, Alberta Theatre Projects, Carousel Theatre in St Catharines, Ont., and Theatre Direct in Toronto, among others. Ideally, members of a T.I.E. company are trained actor/teachers and the performance of a script is only the centerpiece of a package of services that includes both preparation and follow-up. It is an expensive tool, particularly when the company meets with only one or two classes in a school. Indeed, T.I.E. proved to be too costly for most centres and was curtailed by Canadian companies. T.I.E. also spawned the most recent style in theatre for the young—the issue-play. The late twentieth-century trend towards including children in discussions of contemporary problems affecting their lives is reflected in many recent scripts. Some theatre pieces attempt to explore problems through dramatic metaphor. Vancouver's Green Thumb Theatre, under playwright-director Dennis Foon, has been an active contributor to, and advocate of, issue-oriented theatre. Foon has said that the goal of his theatre is 'providing children with tools to cope better with a world that has become increasingly confusing and complex.' Foon's *Skin* (1985), about prejudice, and *Feeling, Yes—Feeling, No* (1982), a project designed to equip children with strategies against sexual assault, are only two of many Green Thumb advocacy plays. Toronto's Theatre Direct is committed to T.I.E. principles and has produced several issue-plays, including *Friends* (1984) by Tom Bentley-Fisher (with Patricia Grant), about day care, and *Getting Wrecked* (1985) by Tom WALMSLEY about drug abuse. *Getting Wrecked* won a Dora Mavor MOORE Award for best play for young people in 1986.

Not all new plays for the young are issue-oriented. Fantasy and adventure still attract playwrights. The 1986 CHALMERS Children's Play Award went to *Running the Gauntlet* (1985), Duncan McGregor's story of the effect of the War of 1812 on children, produced by Carousel Theatre in 1985. Jim Betts has written four plays for Young People's

Theatre that have been popular all over Canada. His *The Mystery of the Oak Island Treasure* (1985), first performed in 1983, won the 1983 Chalmers Children's Play Award and was nominated for a Dora Mavor Moore Award as 'outstanding new play' for young audiences.

Other Theatre Professionals. Directors who devote their careers to theatre for the young were once rare, but are now growing in number. They include Peter Moss (YPT), Dennis Foon (Green Thumb), and Elizabeth Gorrie (Kaleidoscope). Gorrie's lyrical gifts have developed a distinctive style for her company. Working with the barest essentials in set, costuming, and props, and relying on movement, transformations, and imagination, she has created productions of great beauty and power. A designer who influenced the style of his company is Mermaid's Tom Miller, whose giant puppets and masks call for an exaggerated movement and formal voice pattern from the company's actors, many of whom had to be specially trained for the demands of the designs. Influential administrators include Lee Lewis (Mermaid), Lucille Wagner (Alberta Theatre Projects), Colin Gorrie (Kaleidoscope), and Joanne James (Quest Theatre).

Although many theatre workers begin their careers in school touring companies, training for the field is rare. Neither the NATIONAL THEATRE SCHOOL nor the Vancouver Playhouse Theatre School offer special courses in acting, directing, or designing for the young. Drama Departments at the Universities of Calgary, Waterloo, Guelph, and Victoria include undergraduate courses in theatre for young audiences and Calgary and Victoria offer a master's degree in Theatre in Education.

Festivals and Touring. The Vancouver International Children's Festival, established in 1978, has had an important impact on all aspects of theatre for the young in Canada. Each year about a dozen foreign companies and individual performers join twice as many Canadian companies and soloists to present a ten-day event in Vancouver, after which some of these companies travel to other Canadian cities. While most international festivals include some events for young people, the theatre festivals for children across Canada—including, in 1987-8, Vancouver, Edmonton, Calgary, Regina, Winnipeg, Toronto, Ottawa, Montreal, Moncton, and Halifax—

Children's Drama and Theatre in English

are unique in featuring *only* family and young-people's fare. They provide a welcome forum for an exchange of ideas among dedicated workers in the field, who are usually too busy to reflect on issues larger than this week's tour and next year's budget. The stimulation arising from seeing the best of international children's theatre is inevitably reflected in subsequent Canadian plays, and the visits by foreign companies offer useful hints on how better to tailor our plays for tours abroad.

A high quality of production, a growing repertoire, and a body of dedicated career specialists have raised Canadian theatre for the young to a world-class level. Paradoxically, reliance on school bookings, often considered a limitation, has given this genre some advantages over adult companies. More tolerance for difficult, controversial content and innovative staging is shown by schoolteachers who understand today's children and their concerns than by the more conservative adult season ticket subscribers. Children who regularly see school touring productions often become sophisticated theatregoers. But providing an audience for tomorrow is not the goal. Most professionals would agree with Dennis Foon's 1986 statement to *Playboard* magazine: 'We're performing for audiences today. If we do our job right they won't go to the theatre unless theatre changes, because they're going to have a high expectation of what theatre can be.'

See special issues of *Canadian Theatre Review*, 10 (1976) and 41 (1982); a special issues of *Canadian Children's Literature*, 8–9 (1977); Desmond Davis, *Theatre for Young People* (1981); Joyce Doolittle and Zina Barnieh, *A Mirror of Our Dreams: Children and the Theatre in Canada* (1979). Anthologies of plays for children include *A Collection of Canadian Plays*, volume four (1975), edited by Susan Rubes; *Kids Plays* (1980) and *Eight Plays for Young People* (1984), edited by Joyce Doolittle.   JOYCE DOOLITTLE

Children's Drama and Theatre in French. Children's theatre in Quebec first developed within the administrative structures and according to the artistic policies established by adult theatre companies. Although they differed in their artistic aims, Les COMPAGNONS DE SAINT-LAURENT, Le THÉÂTRE CLUB, and Les APPRENTIS-SORCIERS shared a common attitude towards

children's theatre—they produced it only when they had achieved financial stability and occupied a permanent theatre space. Moreover, they chose scripts suited to their mainstage repertoire, usually for their entertainment value—plays by Léon Chancerel for Les Compagnons, improvisations and adaptions of Guignol texts for Les Apprentis-Sorciers. Performances were presented mainly on weekends. The first children's theatre programs were incorporated into the regular seasons of Les Compagnons (from 1949 to 1951), Le Théâtre Club (from 1958 to 1962), and Les Apprentis-Sorciers (from 1961 to 1967). Between 1950 and 1965 audiences grew and the number of performances increased dramatically as children's theatre gradually took its place in the developing Québécois theatre.

During those fifteen years a lack of worthwhile scripts prompted Les Apprentis-Sorciers to promote improvised theatre, and Le Théâtre Club and La Roulotte (Montreal's itinerant summer theatre inaugurated in 1953) to adapt the fairy tales of Charles Perrault and Hans Christian Andersen. Even original scripts were influenced by these adaptations: Luan Asslani's *Les Trois Désirs de Coquelicot* (1973), produced by Le Théâtre Club in 1960, features a young hero whose encounters with elves and fairies teach him a sense of generosity towards others.

The first company to devote itself entirely to young audiences was Le Théâtre pour Enfants de Québec (1965–70). It began as a division of Quebec City's l'Estoc, a small experimental theatre, but soon acquired full autonomy. Under director Pauline Geoffrion it adopted a policy favouring the creation of original plays, commissioning Monique Corriveau, a well-known author of children's novels, to write PUPPET plays. In her five scripts, the recurring characters and the story lines are clearly inspired by existing children's literature and by new television series directed to the young. Geoffrion attracted professional actors to TEQ, providing them with opportunities for extensive regional and provincial touring in plays by Roland LEPAGE, Patrick Mainville, and Pierre Morency. The latter's *Tournebire et le Malin Frigo* (1978), produced in 1969, exemplifies the company's style at that time—it calls for audience participation, shows heroes in courageous adventures against mysterious enemies, and features robots.

When, despite strong management and a

successful artistic policy, TEQ's subsidy was not renewed by the Ministry of Cultural Affairs in 1969, the company folded. Its work, however, was carried on by other theatres. Le THÉÂTRE DU RIDEAU VERT, for example, committed itself to children's plays from 1967 to 1978. Its magnificent opening presentation was Maurice Maeterlinck's *L'Oiseau bleu*; it then offered more than twelve children's productions in four seasons, five of which were new scripts by Roland Lepage and Marcel Sabourin. After 1970, when André CAILLOUX became artistic director of the youth section, puppet shows by Nicole Lapointe and Pierre Régimbald and productions of André Cailloux's scripts were presented each year (on weekends and during schooldays). Magic and the supernatural attracted Cailloux: in his plays objects appear and disappear, characters are repeatedly and mysteriously transformed, and space and time are manipulated with great ease in stories that remain close to the fairy tale. Lapointe and Régimbald adapted the tales of Perrault and the Grimm brothers, using hand and string puppets to create an atmosphere of delight and festivity.

In 1973-4 several events brought together the most active builders of 'le nouveau théâtre pour la jeunesse'. A writers' workshop was organized by Monique Rioux where authors, actors, and children together created new characters and new kinds of story lines. *Cé tellement 'cute' des enfants* (1980) by Marie-Francine Hébert was directly influenced by these workshops. A pioneering play, it shows children using realistic everyday language while playing in back-alleys on a school holiday; in its realism and political commitment the play departs from what was traditionally regarded as being suitable for children—fairy tales, for example. And in 1973 the first in a series of Festival québécois de théâtre pour enfants was held in Longueuil. Many companies still active today were founded about this time: THÉÂTRE DE LA MARMAILLE, 1973; Théâtre de Carton, 1973; Théâtre de l'Oeil, 1973; Théâtre de Quartier, 1975; Théâtre du Carrousel, 1975; Théâtre du Gros Mécano, 1976; Théâtre de l'Avant-Pays, 1976; Théâtre l'Arrière-Scène, 1976; and Théâtre Petit à Petit, 1978. Representing a new children's theatre movement, these companies broke with the past, declaring children's theatre to be more than merely superficial entertainment. They held that it provided the oppor-

tunity for experimentation with socially relevant themes and subjects, and considered young audiences to be their best critics and main source of inspiration.

The scripts of the new movement had a strong social and political character, making children conscious of pollution (*Tohu Bohu*, l'Oeil, 1976), or the need for co-operation (*Le Toutatous*, l'Oeil, 1978). In *Un Jeu d'enfants* (1980), produced at Le Quartier in 1979, children in the audience are invited to enquire about playground space in urban surroundings. Gilles Gauthier's *On n'est pas des enfants d'école* (1984), produced at La Marmaille in 1979, stresses the fact that school is not the only place to learn and that education should encourage sharing and caring. Marcel Sabourin's *Pleurer pour rire* (1984), produced at La

Marcel Sabourin's Pleurer pour rire, *Théâtre de la Marmaille, Montreal, 1981, with (l. to r.) Monique Rioux, Normand Daoust, France Mercille*

Marmaille in 1981, promotes the free expression of emotion and sensuality, as does Théâtre de Carton's 1979 production of *Les Enfants n'ont pas de sexe?* (1981). In *Les Petits Pouvoirs* (1983), produced at Le Carrousel in 1982, Suzanne Lebeau explores the child-parent relationship, especially in daily routines that may foster authoritarianism and tension.

The authors' main contribution in writing those scripts was to move gradually away from a realistic type of linear structure where story begins and ends in a forseeable fashion,

Children's Drama and Theatre in French

and away from familiar, true-to-life, characters. *Un Jeu d'enfants*, for example, presents an immediately recognizable dramatic line. Action is set in a kitchen, in the street, and in the school principal's office; the costumes are identical to clothes worn every day by children like Nicole and François. *Pleurer pour rire*'s characters, on the other hand, are emotions and states of being. Toa, Soa, and Moa live through a story that interweaves past, present, and future, thus making a strong case for children's rights to feelings and free expression of the self. Dressed in fanciful costumes, they prevent more than encourage immediate identification by the audience. Their world is anything but true-to-life. Huge set elements, designed by Daniel Castonguay, that were quite unrealistic in their shape and weird in their autonomous behavior, gave the production an unfamiliar yet universal meaning. The challenge of such plays, for the artists, was to maintain a political analysis of children's reality while creating complex and fanciful theatrical styles.

Until 1975 plays frequently included audience participation. Lebeau's *Ti-Jean voudrait ben s'marier, mais . . .* (1985), produced at Le Carrousel in 1974, blends participation, folklore, and legend. This trend, however, was sometimes criticized on the grounds that such participation involved emotional manipulation. *Une Lune entre deux maisons* (1980), also by Lebeau (produced at Le Carrousel in 1979), tries instead to orient spectators towards sympathy and complicity with the characters. *Une Lune . . .* (which enjoyed international success) was written for three- to six-year-olds, as were *Trois Petits Contes* (1981) by Louise LaHaye (produced at Gyroscope in 1980), which has a drama-workshop structure, and *Coup de fil* by Diane Chevalier, produced at Carton in 1986, which relates the love of Danièle for her five-year-old son and her longing for a love of her own age.

Poetic plays and theatre of the fantastic have not been common in Quebec's theatre for the young. However, François Depatie, who directed his own plays, has written in this area: *Luclac dans l'infini* (THÉÂTRE DU TRIDENT, 1975) about zodiac signs and mathematics, *Le Cadran et le cerf-volant* (Trident, 1974) about time and space, and *En écoutant le coeur des pommes* (NATIONAL ARTS CENTRE, 1976), on memory and the multiple self. Louise Bombardier, surrealistic in her theatrical style, adapted a Tolkien short story

about the artist in the city for *Le Cas rare de Carat* (Gyroscope, 1979), and her *Dis-moi doux* (Bêtes à coeur, 1984) is about words and their emotional sounds.

Puppeteers have made excellent contributions to children's theatre. *Regarde pour voir* (1981), produced at l'Oeil in 1979, a 'how-to' play, shows Lise and Jocelyn learning to make puppets from second-hand material and writing and producing sketches. *Il était une fois en Neuve-France* (l'Avant-Pays, 1976), with the legendary hero Ti-Jean as the main character, and *Une Histoire de marionnettes* (l'Avant-Pays, 1979), on the art of theatre itself, were both written by Diane Bouchard, who also wrote *La Couleur chante un pays* (1981); produced at l'Avant-Pays in 1981, this successful production aimed at the thirteen- to eighteen-year age group introduces its audience to 200 years of Canadian and Quebec paintings.

Set and costume design, music, and lyrics in children's theatre have undergone a qualitative evolution from the timid attempts of 1974 to the very effective productions of the mid-1980s. Michel Robidoux's music for *L'Umiak* (1984), produced at La Marmaille in 1984, was widely acclaimed, as were the designs of Daniel Castonguay, who works mainly with Théâtre de la Marmaille, and Michel DEMERS who is developing an effective modernistic style with Théâtre Petit à Petit and director Claude Poissant.

Adolescent audiences have been catered for by Le Théâtre Club, which has produced classical plays for college students. In 1963 La NOUVELLE COMPAGNIE THÉÂTRALE was founded specifically to produce classics for students: Racine, Marivaux, Goldoni, Shakespeare, and Chekhov, among others. In 1968–9 the NCT included Quebec author Marcel DUBÉ in its season and has since produced contemporary authors alongside Molière, Ruzzante, and Strindberg. In 1971 NCT inaugurated Opération-Théâtre, commissioning authors to write plays about theatre (Jean BARBEAU's *Le Théâtre de la maintenance*) or inviting Quebec companies to present new scripts (Gros Mécano, for example, with Denis Chouinard's *Titre provisoire: Roméo et Juliette*—after Shakespeare—produced in 1984). To foster its well-established relationship with educators, the company also publishes *Les Cahiers de la NCT*, which discusses their plays from historical, sociological, theatrical, and literary points of view.

Some companies and dramatists, realizing that adolescents are interested in social, political, and cultural affairs, have created works directed specifically to these areas. Louis-Dominique Lavigne's *Où est-ce qu'elle est ma gang?* (1984), for example, deals with the gang phenomenom and the search for identity; it was produced at Petit à Petit in 1982. In one collectively authored play, *Sortie de secours* (Petit à Petit, 1984), a youth runs away from difficult situations—no job, no communication, no understanding, no link to a society that discourages individuality and stresses 'normality'. André Simard's *Au pied de la lettre* (Gros Mécano, 1981) dramatizes the consequences of divorce and new surroundings on two young characters. The theme of *Le Sous-sol des anges* by Louis-Dominique Lavigne (Carton, 1984) is suicide. Most recently, Alain Fournier's *Circuit fermé* (l'Atrium, 1986) deals with youth and prostitution. Contemporary Quebec theatre for adolescents speaks clearly to the problems and preoccupations of its audiences.

Theatre for young audiences can be said to present important experiences of life, communication, and artistic practice. While it is universally acknowledged that every young person should have access to these experiences, there is still no clear policy in Quebec on ways to make such access universally available. The establishment of the Maison québécoise du théâtre pour l'enfance et la jeunesse in 1984 represents a significant beginning in this respect.

See Hélène Beauchamp, *Le Théâtre pour enfants au Québec* (1985). Most unpublished scripts are available at Le Centre d'essai des auteurs dramatiques in Montreal.

HÉLÈNE BEAUCHAMP

Chislett, Anne (b. 1942). Born in St John's, Nfld, she was educated at Memorial Univ. and the Univ. of British Columbia and taught English and theatre in Ontario high schools before becoming a full-time playwright in 1980.

In 1975 Chislett and her husband, James G. Roy, founded the BLYTH FESTIVAL, where all her plays have been performed. *A Summer Burning*, adapted from the novel by Harry J. Boyle, was produced and published in 1977, followed by *The Tomorrow Box* (1980) and *Quiet in the Land* (produced 1981, published 1983), which won the CHALMERS Play Award

(1982) and a Governor General's Award (1983). *Another Season's Promise*, produced in 1986, was co-authored by Keith Roulston. *The Tomorrow Box* has been translated into French and Japanese, and performed in Canada and Japan. *Quiet in the Land* played in New York in 1986, after several Canadian productions.

Chislett draws the material for her social-problem plays from the farm communities of southern Ontario. Change is at the heart of the problems, whether in the effect of the feminist ideals of a younger generation on the life of a traditional farm-wife (*The Tomorrow Box*) or in the impact of conscription and religious liberalism on an Old Order Amish community (*Quiet in the Land*).

Women are the focus of attention in *The Tomorrow Box*, where the character of the older farm-wife, Maureen, is strongly developed. At the beginning she is the stereotypical mother-in-law, whose every act and word grate on the nerves of the law student, Alice. When Maureen's husband sells the farm without her knowledge, Alice and her lawyer sister encourage Maureen to take legal action to secure her half-share of the farm's worth and to become a successful independent business woman. Maureen develops into a sympathetic character, in contrast to the men and the 'liberated' younger women who all use treachery to try to control her. The element of deceit involved in the eventual reconciliation of husband and wife makes for an ambiguous, ironic ending.

Quiet in the Land convincingly portrays life in an Amish community during the First World War. The multiple interior and exterior sets, the costumes and the details of religious practices, all carefully follow historical sources. Young Yock's departure for the army and his killing of a man in battle create a crisis for his girlfriend and his father, both firmly committed to Amish pacifism. They are torn apart by their love for him but choose to remain in the old ways, leaving Yock to find his destiny as an outsider.

Another Season's Promise shows a formerly successful farmer fighting banks, big business, and urban indifference as he attempts to preserve both the farm and the ideals that sustained his family for generations. Like the earlier plays, it dramatizes conflict between the old and the new, and explores the moral issues inevitably involved in a changing value-system.

JOAN COLDWELL

99

Choquette, Ernest (1852–1941). Born in Beloeil, Que., he attended the Collège de Saint-Hyacinthe and studied medicine at Université Laval. An outspoken Liberal, he served many years as mayor of Saint-Hilaire and represented Rougemont as a member of the Quebec Legislative Council from 1910 until his death. A member of the Royal Society, he wrote three novels, short stories, two plays, and a collection of personal reminiscences (*Les Carabinades*, 1898).

With the help of critic Charles ab der Halden, Choquette adapted his novel, *Les Ribaud, une idylle de '37* (1898), for the stage. A conventional love story (with, for its time, an unconventional ending in which love triumphs over national duty), it ran for a week at Montreal's THÉÂTRE NATIONAL, starring Paul CAZENEUVE and Jean-Paul Filion. Under a new title—*Madeleine*—it was also performed by the Société Canadienne d'Opérette at the MONUMENT NATIONAL in Jan. 1929. *La Terre* (1916)—a novel advocating French-Canadian commitment to agriculture and avoidance of the materialistic values of the English-Canadian business world—was also adapted for the stage (as *La Bouée*), though less successfully than *Les Ribaud*, and there is no evidence that it was ever produced. It was, however, published with *Madeleine* in 1927.

See *Dictionnaire des oeuvres littéraires du Québec*, vols. 1 and 2 (1978, 1980).

RAMON HATHORN

Christie, Robert (b. 1913). Born and educated in Toronto (BA, Univ. of Toronto, 1934), he distinguished himself in the 1933 DOMINION DRAMA FESTIVAL before joining the John HOLDEN Players in 1934. In 1936 he moved to England, where he appeared in both provincial repertory and the West End and in a season with the Old Vic (193-9). After service in the Canadian Army (1940-5), Christie returned to Canada, working in CBC radio drama and becoming a prominent member of the NEW PLAY SOCIETY. His roles included Aikenhead in Morley Callaghan's *Going Home* in 1950, John A. Macdonald in John COULTER's *RIEL* in 1950, and Bagshaw in Mavor MOORE's *Sunshine Town* in 1955, as well as appearances in *SPRING THAW*. In 1950 he appeared in the English version of Gratien GÉLINAS's *TIT-COQ* in Montreal, and in 1953 he joined the STRATFORD FESTIVAL company for its first four seasons. Christie was notable as Buckingham in *Richard III* (1953) and as Caesar in *Julius Caesar* (1954). He appeared on Broadway in Stratford's production of Christopher Marlowe's *Tamburlaine* in 1956, and in the 1960 Broadway production of Robertson DAVIES' *Love and Libel*. Since then he has appeared in productions as diverse as Stratford's *Satyricon* and THEATRE TORONTO's production of Marlowe's *Edward II* (both in 1969). In 1967 he starred in the CBC-TV series 'Hatch's Mill', and has in recent years devoted his energies to television and to teaching at the Ryerson Polytechnical Institute in Toronto.

HERBERT WHITTAKER

Christmas, Eric (b. 1916). Born in London, Eng., and trained at the Royal Academy of Dramatic Arts, he immigrated to Canada after the Second World War. After an early success as the Principal Dame in the NEW PLAY SOCIETY's production of *Mother Goose* in 1949, Christmas went on to establish himself as an inventive comic actor and to make a signal contribution to Canadian theatre. At the STRATFORD FESTIVAL he created a string of memorable comic portraits, including Costard (1961), Thersites (1963), Bardolph (1965), and Feste (1966). On Broadway he appeared in Noël Coward's *Look After Lulu* in 1959 and in James Costigan's *Little Moon of Alban* in 1960, for his performance in which he won the Clarence Derwent Award. When artistic director Michael LANGHAM left Stratford, Christmas followed him, first to the Guthrie Theatre in Minneapolis and then to California. Since the early 1970s he has been primarily active in the United States, where he has appeared in a number of films, including *The Andromeda Strain* (1971).

NEIL CARSON

Ciceri, Leo (1928–70). Born and raised in Montreal—where he trained with Eleanor STUART, Roeberta Beatty, and dancer Ruth Sorel—he returned from service in the Second World War to study at McGill Univ. (BA, 1948), and acted with the MONTREAL REPERTORY THEATRE and BRAE MANOR THEATRE before entering London's Old Vic School. After graduating in 1950 he went to the Shakespeare Memorial Theatre, Stratford-upon-Avon. In 1952 he played Aumerle in *Richard II* (with Paul Scofield, directed by John Gielgud) at the Lyric Theatre, Hammersmith. He appeared on Broadway as Paris in Jean Giraudoux's *Tiger at the Gates* (starring Michael Redgrave) in 1955, and replaced Christopher PLUMMER, opposite Julie Harris, in Jean Anouilh's *The Lark* in 1956. Ciceri joined Ontario's STRATFORD FESTIVAL in 1960 and in the course of the next ten years established himself as a key member of the company, playing roles that included Lysander in *A Midsummer Night's Dream* (1960), Achilles in *Troilus and Cressida* (1963), Bolingbroke in *Richard II* (1964), Malvolio in *Twelfth Night* (1966), and Mercutio in *Romeo and Juliet* (1968). He played Prospero in *The Tempest* at the MANITOBA THEATRE CENTRE in 1966. Although he undertook non-Shakespearean roles with the TOWN THEATRE, Ottawa, and Toronto's CREST THEATRE (where he scored a singular success as the Pope in Rolf Hochhuth's *The Deputy* in 1984), Ciceri was among the first Canadians whose career is best measured by his Shakespearean characterizations. He died in an automobile accident; the Stratford Festival established a scholarship in his name to the NATIONAL THEATRE SCHOOL.

HERBERT WHITTAKER

Citadel Theatre. The inspiration, and much of the money, for the largest regional theatre in Canada came from Edmonton lawyer, real-estate entrepreneur, and theatre-lover Joe Shoctor. He and four friends purchased an old Salvation Army Citadel in downtown Edmonton for $100,000, and spent a further $150,000 on renovations before opening the 277-seat house on 10 Nov. 1965 with Edward Albee's *Who's Afraid of Virginia Woolf?* directed by Bernard Engel.

The first season—an eight-play assortment of modern classics (including Arthur Miller's *Death of a Salesman* and Tennessee Williams' *The Glass Menagerie*) and lighter Broadway fare—attracted 1,300 subscribers, but controversy over programming (the Albee was contentious) led to the resignation of artistic director John Hulburt midway through the season. He was replaced by another American, Robert Glenn, who presented a blend of U.S. (Neil Simon's *Barefoot in the Park*, Albee's *Tiny Alice*) and European (Bertolt Brecht's *The Threepenny Opera*) productions. Irish-born Seán MULCAHY succeeded Glenn in 1968; his five years were marked by more adventurous programming that included Brendan Behan's *The Quare Fellow*, Seán O'Casey's *The Shadow of a Gunman*, the Citadel's first Shakespeare (*Othello*), Ibsen, and Arthur Schnitzler.

With the appointment of John NEVILLE as artistic director in 1973 the Citadel began to gain a national profile. His Shakespearean productions (beginning with *Much Ado About Nothing* in his first season), his own performances (as Sherlock Holmes, Malvolio, and Alfred Doolittle in Shaw's *Pygmalion*, for example), and the appearances of international stars such as Peggy Ashcroft (who acted with Neville in Samuel Beckett's *Happy Days*) provoked unprecedented activity at the box office. Sixty-five per cent of the 1974-5 offerings—a challenging collection that included Sheridan's *The Rivals*, Jonson's *The Alchemist*, and Michel TREMBLAY's *Forever Yours, Marie-Lou*—were sold on subscriptions before the season started.

Two notable events marked the Neville regime. In 1975 he launched a second stage, Citadel Too, located in a warehouse near the main stage, opening with a double-bill of *The Extermination of Jesus Christ* (from Shaw) and John Larazus's *Babel Rap*. And in Nov. 1976 a new Citadel—a striking red brick and glass building that dominates Edmonton's downtown landscape—opened with Neville's production of *Romeo and Juliet* on the main stage, selling to 99.42 per cent capacity. The $5 million complex, designed by Diamond Myers Wilkin Associated Architects (with theatre consultants Phillip SILVER and the NATIONAL ARTS CENTRE's Andis Celms) includes the 685-seat Shoctor Theatre, a proscenium house; the Rice, a studio space with flexible seating amounting to about 250; and the 240-seat Zeidler Hall, used for children's productions, films, and lectures. By the time Neville left in 1978 to assume artistic directorship of Halifax's NEPTUNE THEATRE, the Citadel had an enviable subscription base of 17,000 season-ticket-holders, accounting for some 77 per cent of audience capacity.

Neville was succeeded by Peter Coe, and everything about his tenure was controversial. The appointment of another foreign director—Coe is an Englishman who came to prominence with a series of West End and Broadway hits in the early 1960s (including chiefly Lionel Bart's *Oliver*)—occasioned objections from Canadian Immigration and Actors' Equity. Though the productions Coe directed at the Citadel, including *Richard III* starring Ron Moody, were almost as provocative as his appointment, he imported inter-

Citadel Theatre

Duddy, *Citadel Theatre, Edmonton, 1984*

national stars—Glynis Johns, Roy Dotrice, Anne Baxter, Paxton WHITEHEAD—and his determination to transfer Citadel productions to New York and abroad (without achieving any notable successes) reflected Shoctor's own orientation. Hugh Leonard's *A Life* went to Broadway briefly and *Mr. Lincoln* (a one-man show starring Dotrice) went to Washington and New York and was filmed for American television. A new Charles Strouse musical, *Flowers for Algernon*, premièred at the Citadel, and had short runs in London and New York.

On Coe's departure in 1981—following a dispute with management over programming—Shoctor himself became artistic director, until the appointment in 1984 of English director Gordon McDougall from the Oxford Playhouse. For the 1983-4 season Shoctor coproduced (with Montreal impresario Sam Gesser) a spectacular and costly fiasco, a million-dollar musical adaptation of Mordecai Richler's celebrated novel *The Apprenticeship of Duddy Kravitz* that was slated for Broadway. Universally panned, it not only failed to reach New York, its Canadian tour was cancelled. McDougall's tenure was marked by a raft of Canadian premières—especially works that, like Peter Whelan's *Clay* and Ariane Mnouchkine's adaptation of *Mephisto*, he had directed at the Oxford Playhouse—but indifferent artistic results, little hospitality to new Canadian plays, and a decline in subscriptions from about 22,000 to about 17,000. The most notorious failure of his regime was *Pieces of Eight*, Jule Styne's musical adaptation of R.L. Stevenson's *Treasure Island*. The highlight of the period was the building of a $9.5 million extension to the Citadel—designed by Sheldon Chandler—which opened with McDougall's production

of J. M. Barrie's *Peter Pan* on 3 Dec. 1984. It includes the Maclab Theatre, a 690-seat house for children's theatre with a thrust stage that is second in North America only to that of the Guthrie in Minneapolis; the Lee Pavilion, a winter garden containing tropical plants and a thirty-foot waterfall; and the Tucker Amphitheatre.

Alberta's decline in economic fortunes has had its effect on the Citadel. All four productions in the 1986-7 season at the Rice Theatre were imports. And the Citadel now negotiates co-productions with other Canadian companies, including a collaboration with Toronto's ROYAL ALEXANDRA THEATRE in the 1986-7 season on David Pownall's adaptation of Jane Austen's *Pride and Prejudice*. Citadel-on-Wheels/Wings, founded in 1968 to tour the province and the North, has been jettisoned in favour of a cheaper in-house programming for young audiences. But one of the ongoing successes has been the International Children's Festival the Citadel has hosted for several years under the directorship of Citadel general manager Wayne Fipke. The 1987 festival assembled twenty-one groups and attracted an audience of 55,000.

Currently led by resident director William Fisher, who succeeded McDougall in 1987, the Citadel Theatre operates five performance spaces on an annual budget of nearly $5 million, of which about half derives from box office, thirty-five per cent from government sources, and fifteen per cent from private fund-raising.   LIZ NICHOLLS

City Stage. Established as a lunch-time theatre by Ray Michal and George Plawski in Vancouver in Feb. 1972 with a Local Initiatives Project grant, City Stage opened in a doughnut store on Howe St with space for only seventy-five people, mostly drawn from the Stock Exchange across the street. Plawski soon left and Michal continued with a policy of two lunchtime performances daily, a new show every two weeks. He produced plays that were both worthwhile and entertaining, such as Jean Anouilh's *Cécile*, Harold Pinter's *The Lover*, David Cregan's *Transcending*, and Joe Orton's *Good and Faithful Servant*. When the original theatre was demolished, City Stage opened a new 150-seat theatre on Thurlow St in 1976, with a new policy of full-length plays for longer runs. The typical play was contemporary, often with a sexual theme: David Williamson's *The Coming of the Stork*, Pinter's *Old Times*, Christopher Hampton's *Treats*, David Mamet's *Sexual Perversity in Chicago*, and North American premières of two plays by Fay Weldon. Joelle Rabu as Piaf had a long run, while Canadian work included two premières of plays by Richard OUZOUNIAN, THEATRE PASSE MURAILLE's *Doukhobors*, and Frank Moher's *Odd Jobs*.

While Michal was successful in finding talented, little-known young actors, and while he saw City Stage as a community theatre for Vancouver's downtown area, he had difficulty in establishing a distinctive presence for City Stage in Vancouver, being overshadowed by the larger and more affluent VANCOUVER PLAYHOUSE and ARTS CLUB. City Stage closed in Oct. 1986 when its rent was raised sixty-five per cent. The theatre was taken over by THEATRESPORTS, who renamed it the Back Alley Theatre.

See Robert Wallace, 'Sharing Space: Ray Michal at City Stage', *Canadian Theatre Review* 39 (1984).   MALCOLM PAGE

Codco. Founded in Toronto in 1973 with financial assistance and encouragement from Paul THOMPSON of THEATRE PASSE MURAILLE, the original company consisted of six Newfoundland actors: Greg Malone, Cathy Jones, Mary Walsh, Dyan Olsen, Tommy Sexton, and Paul Sametz; Andy Jones and Robert Joy joined after the first show, a COLLECTIVE CREATION called *Cod on a Stick*, which ran in Toronto and Newfoundland. The objectives of the company were to provide opportunities for actors to draw on their Newfoundland experiences and at the same time—in a CABARET revue for-

Codco company members (back) Cathy Jones, Tommy Sexton, (front) Mary Walsh, Greg Malone, Andy Jones

mat—to lampoon and satirize the stereotyped perceptions held by many Canadians about Newfoundlanders. The company has never had a permanent theatre space and its scripts have not been published.

Several productions followed *Cod on a Stick*: *Sickness, Death and Beyond the Grave* in 1974; *Das Capital—What Do You Want to See the Harbour For?*, 1975; *Would You Like To Smell My Pocket Crumbs?*, 1975; *Festering Forefathers and Running Sons*, 1975; *Laugh Your Guts Out With Total Strangers*, CBC-TV, 1976; *The Tale Ends*, 1976; *Who Said Anything About Tea?*, 1978; *White Niggers of Bond Street—WNOBS*, 1979; and *Barely Dead and Hardly Missed*, 1981. In addition, Codco has produced a number of short films with the Newfoundland Independent Filmmakers Co-operative.

Although Codco is still active, the original group disbanded in 1979 after having toured Canada and performed in Europe and the U.S., where, in 1975, it was the Canadian representative at the American Bicentennial Festival in Philadelphia.

The Codco scripts have been deposited with the Memorial University of Newfoundland Folklore Archives.   C.J. SKINNER

Coghill, Joy (b. 1926). Born in Findlater, Sask., and taken to Scotland as a child, she returned to Canada as an evacuee during the Second World War. She earned a BA at the Univ. of British Columbia (1949) and an MFA at the Art Institute of Chicago in 1951. From 1951 to 1953 she was co-producer at Vancouver's Everyman Theatre with Sydney RISK, and in 1953 she founded, with Myra

Benson, HOLIDAY THEATRE in Vancouver, becoming artistic director (until 1966) of this pioneering children's theatre. (See CHILDREN'S THEATRE.) Coghill was also active directing, teaching, and acting—she played Puck in Benjamin Britten's opera, *A Midsummer Night's Dream*, at Vancouver's International Festival in 1961. During her two years (1967-9) as artistic director of the VANCOUVER PLAYHOUSE, she presented George RYGA's *The ECSTASY OF RITA JOE* and *Grass and Wild Strawberries*, thus associating the Playhouse with new Canadian work. She also launched the Playhouse's Stage 2, for experimental work, where she directed Betty LAMBERT's *The Visitor*.

From 1970 to 1973 Coghill was head of the English section of the NATIONAL THEATRE SCHOOL, Montreal. During the 1970s and 1980s she acted in cities across the country. Notable performances included Agiluk in Herschel HARDIN's *Esker Mike and His Wife Agiluk* (FACTORY THEATRE Lab tour to England, 1973); the title role in Michel TREMBLAY's *Forever Yours, Marie-Lou* (THEATRE PLUS, Toronto, 1975); Madame Arkadina in Chekhov's *The Seagull* (GLOBE THEATRE, Regina, 1980); Sarah Bernhardt in John MURRELL's *Memoir* (ALBERTA THEATRE PROJECTS, Calgary, 1981); the title role in Eric NICOL's *Ma* (NEW PLAY CENTRE, Vancouver, 1981; CBC-TV, 1982); Mrs Hardcastle in Oliver Goldsmith's *She Stoops to Conquer* (STRATFORD FESTIVAL, 1985); Albertine at 60 in Tremblay's *Albertine in Five Times* (TARRAGON THEATRE, Toronto, and tour, 1985-6); and Edna in Betty LAMBERT's *Jennie's Story* (NATIONAL ARTS CENTRE, Ottawa, 1986). She has also worked extensively for radio and television, and in 1987 she wrote and starred in *Song of this Place*, about Emily Carr, at the VANCOUVER EAST CULTURAL CENTRE.   MALCOLM PAGE

Cohen, Nathan (1923-71). The son of Polish immigrants David and Fanny Kaplansky, whose name had been changed to Cohen by a Halifax immigration official, he was born in Sydney, N.S., and educated at Mount Allison University (1939-42), where he acted and directed with the Mount Allison Players and wrote on politics, theatre, and the arts for the student newspaper *Argosy Weekly*. After graduating, he briefly studied law in Toronto, before returning to Nova Scotia to

edit the *Glace Bay Gazette*, the only labour-owned daily newspaper in Canada.

In 1945 Cohen worked briefly for the National Film Board in Ottawa and then moved to Toronto, joining the Communist Party and working for its paper, the *Canadian Tribune*. He soon broke with the Party and began contributing to the Jewish papers *Vochenblatt*, *New Voice*, and *Canadian Jewish Weekly* on Jewish culture, politics, and the arts. A 1946 review of the NEW PLAY SOCIETY production of Eugene O'Neill's *Ah, Wilderness!* attracted the attention of Mavor MOORE, who recommended him for the new CBC radio program 'Across the Footlights', which began in Oct. 1948 and continued as 'CJBC Views the Shows', which Cohen moderated for nine years. He also published and edited a journal, *The Critic*, from 1950 to 1953, worked as a CBC-TV story editor from 1956 to 1958, and for CBC radio's 'Critically Speaking', which continued until 1967 under the title 'The Arts This Week'. Cohen's national reputation was enhanced by his hosting 'Fighting Words' from Dec. 1952 on radio and 1953 to 1962 on radio and TV, briefly revived by CHCH Hamilton in 1970. Many celebrities, Canadian and international, were put on the intellectual hot seat by Cohen in a witty and forceful manner. From 1957 to 1958 he was the Toronto *Telegram*'s weekly theatre critic and from 1959 to 1965 the Toronto *Star*'s drama critic and Entertainment Editor, and its drama critic until his death.

Cohen's forceful personality, learning, and strongly voiced opinions made him a powerful influence in the development of aesthetic standards for the Canadian theatre as it moved from amateur to professional status. He frequently expressed his strong commitment to the advancement of professionalism in Canada's theatres and the development of an indigenous dramatic literature, but his regular visits to U.S. and European theatres led him to apply perfectionist international standards of critical judgement, thus frequently arousing ill-feeling in the theatrical community. While he often encouraged new ventures, he believed the critic's responsibility was to maintain high principles and standards of evaluation.

Cohen's career was dramatized in Rick SALUTIN's *Nathan Cohen: A Review*, produced by Toronto's THEATRE PASSE MURAILLE in 1981. The Nathan Cohen

Award for excellence in theatre criticism was established in 1981.

See Wayne E. Edmondstone, *Nathan Cohen: The Making of a Critic* (1977).

ROTA HERZBERG LISTER

Colas et Colinette; ou Le Bailli dupé. An operetta by Joseph QUESNEL, it was the first composed in North America and the first dramatic text in French to be composed, performed, and published in Canada.

First performed on 14 Jan. 1790 by Le Théâtre de Société, an amateur troupe the author had helped found, the work was well received. The anonymous reviewer for the *Montreal Gazette/Gazette de Montréal* praised its tight structure, consistency of character portrayal, and above all the impeccably 'moral' resolution of the plot. A modern spectator might be less impressed by its static depiction of character and the predictability of its plot. The setting is quaintly pastoral, in a unidentified village in France, and only the description of costumes and set suggests that the time is roughly contemporary with that of its composition—the late 1780s, according to a note appended to the published text. The plot involves an attempt by an aging village bailiff (unnamed) to win by bribery, ruse, or violence the hand of young Colinette, who loves Colas and hopes to marry him. Colinette's ingenuity, along with the wise integrity of her protector, the village squire Dolmont, are more than a match for the Bailiff, and the two title characters wind up happily with each other. The five characters lack depth or subtlety: the Bailiff is unscrupulous cynicism personified; Dolmont is the very exemplar of a humane seigneur; Colinette is pretty, loyal, and resourceful, while Colas and L'Épine, the only two peasant characters (Colinette has been raised by Dolmont) are simpletons whose rustic speech is a sure and easy source of humour in the play.

Quesnel had hit upon a dramatic form and an innocuous theme most apposite for French Canada at the time. Yet it is a mistake to see this work as a mere anachronistic copy of a continental model. Precisely this type of musically enhanced entertainment was in vogue in France in the 1780s and Quesnel had found a responsive audience for his operetta in Montreal.

When *Colas et Colinette* was revived in Quebec City in 1805, and again in 1807, it proved to have lost none of its appeal. The printer John Neilson decided to publish it, with the author's approval and assistance. But the difficulty of reproducing the musical score proved insurmountable and the work did not appear until 1812, without music and bearing the imprint '1808'. It was included in James Huston's *Répertoire national* (1848), was reprinted in its original form in 1968, and published in English in 1974. *Colas et Colinette* was very successfully recorded for Radio-Canada in 1968, in a sparkling version reconstituted by Godfrey Ridout, and has since been performed in Ottawa, Hamilton, and Milan (Italy).

See L.E. Doucette, *Theatre in French Canada, 1606-1867* (1984). L.E. DOUCETTE

Colicos, John (b. 1928). Born in Toronto and raised in Montreal, he began acting with Joy Thomson's Canadian Art Theatre, trained with Filmore Sadler in Montreal and at the BRAE MANOR THEATRE, and with Eleanor STUART, playing opposite her in Clemence Dane's *Will Shakespeare* for the MONTREAL REPERTORY THEATRE in 1948.

Colicos first acted professionally in radio, working for Rupert Caplan in Montreal, and by 1950 with Andrew ALLAN in Toronto. On stage he played the King in Shaw's *In Good King Charles's Golden Days* for Toronto's UNIVERSITY ALUMNAE DRAMATIC CLUB, winning the best-actor award in the DOMINION DRAMA FESTIVAL finals in 1951. He moved (via summer stock in Bermuda) to London, where he understudied as Lear for an Old Vic European tour of *King Lear*, starring Stephen Murray, whom he replaced in Helsinki in 1952 and then in London. His success in this role took him to Orson Welles's New York production of *King Lear* in 1956 (he played Edmund); to John Houseman's American Shakespeare Festival at Stratford, Conn.; and then to Ontario's STRATFORD FESTIVAL in 1961. His roles there included Berowne in *Love's Labour's Lost* and Aufidius in *Coriolanus* opposite Paul Scofield (both in 1961); Caliban in *The Tempest* and Petruchio in *The Taming of the Shrew* opposite Kate REID (both in 1962); title roles in *Timon of Athens* and Edmund Rostand's *Cyrano de Bergerac* (both in 1963); and a much-praised Lear in 1964. After a period in New York and London, he returned to Canada to play Churchill in Rolf Hochhuth's controversial play, *Soldiers*, which was staged by THEATRE

Colicos

TORONTO at the ROYAL ALEXANDRA THEA-TRE in 1968 before going to New York and London.

Colicos has worked extensively in American and Canadian television and his film credits include Cromwell in *Anne of a Thousand Days* and Nick in *The Postman Always Rings Twice*. In 1982 he played Sir in Ronald Harwood's *The Dresser* at Edmonton's CITADEL THEATRE.   HERBERT WHITTAKER

Collective Creation. This is the process by which a company of actors—using research, improvisation, and co-operative script development—creates an original play. Although a director and playwright, as well as other production personnel, may be involved, the degree of their autonomy is determined by each project. In general, the overall responsibility for content, style, form, and structure rests with all members of the collective, and there is a minimum of hierarchical decision-making.

During its most popular period in Canada—1972 to the early 1980s—theatre companies producing collectives included the MUMMERS TROUPE in Newfoundland, the MULGRAVE ROAD CO-OP in Nova Scotia, THÉÂTRE D'AUJOURD'HUI in Quebec, THEATRE PASSE MURAILLE (TPM) in Toronto, 25TH STREET THEATRE in Saskatchewan, THEATRE NETWORK in Alberta, and Theatre Energy in British Columbia. Although *The FARM SHOW* (TPM, 1972) was the first critically successful collective creation, and the influence of this production and its director Paul THOMPSON have been substantial, the genre developed simultaneously in several parts of Canada.

The antecedents of the collective may be traced indirectly to the documentary and historical plays of Bertolt Brecht and Erwin Piscator; to the integration of popular culture with documentary material by the English directors Joan Littlewood and Peter Cheeseman; to the involvement of the working class in his theatres in Lyon and Villeurbanne by Roger Planchon (with whom Paul Thompson worked); and to the National Film Board's 'Challenge for Change' program, in which communities made films about themselves.

Collective theatre in Canada started as an alternative to established theatre practice. Regional theatres produced very little Canadian work in seasons of primarily British and American plays. Many actors and directors who either declined to work in such productions, or were not considered to have the appropriate skills, wanted a theatre in which they could freely participate, whose focus would be on Canadian themes, and that would have a direct and immediate meaning for themselves and their audience. These theatre workers developed their own plays on subjects that concerned them, and found new audiences, funding, and playing spaces. Receiving little support at first from cultural granting agencies, they used the federal government's unemployment schemes, particularly the Local Initiatives Program. The companies they created were underfunded, highly mobile, usually without permanent venues, and by choice and necessity committed to minimum production budgets. Their collective creations challenged the assumption that theatre was only for and about the dominant economic class. They created a theatre genre in which new groups of people, including farmers (*PAPER WHEAT*, 25th Street Theatre, 1977) and oil workers (*Hard Hats and Stolen Hearts*, Theatre Network, 1977) became both audience and source material. Collective plays also retold Canadian history from contemporary social and political perspectives (*1837: The Farmers' Revolt*, TPM, 1974, and *The Cody Co-op Show*, Mulgrave Road Co-op, 1979); they also explored controversial issues (*They Club Seals, Don't They?*, Mummers, 1978), and adapted literary texts (*The Studhorse Man*, from the novel by Robert Kroetsch, TPM, 1981).

Some collective plays have been loosely described as DOCUMENTARY, in film-maker John Grierson's sense of 'the creative interpretation of actuality'. Paul Thompson has described Theatre Passe Muraille's community-based plays as 'folk drama', and Chris BROOKES, artistic director of the Mummers, has called their issue-based work 'thesis plays'. The themes are usually social and political rather than personal or psychological, although *Maybe There's Something of Me in This* at Theatre Energy in 1981 and *Vertical Dreams* at TAMAHNOUS THEATRE in 1979, are interesting exceptions. Because all members of a collective have equal influence, the typical collective play is an accumulation of characters and ideas without a focus on individual character development. Characters are seen at specific moments in time and in juxtaposition to each other rather than in extended emotional transition. The actors reproduce what they learn about their subjects; although they may fictionalize scenes in order to synthesize or transcend their researched material, they do not invent information.

The collective process starts with the actors' research into historical documents, issues, or living communities, and develops as a shared effort to establish an understanding of the material. Dramatic content evolves in a variety of forms: monologue, group improvisations, collage, mime, song, and dance. Performance techniques emphasize gesture and strong physical metaphor. Scenes are episodic and discontinuous, reflecting the way in which the material was gathered and life was observed. Many more scenes are developed than are finally used, though there is often agreement that one particular scene represents the common experiences of the actors and must be in the final production (e.g. the 'Baling Scene' in *The Farm Show*). Frequently, however, it is not until immediately prior to the opening performance that the collective viewpoint becomes clear and the final structure is determined. Even then the script is rarely written down; the production remains flexible, allowing for dra-

maturgical changes and a degree of spontaneity as the actors recreate the play in each performance.

Part of the dramatic power of a collective creation is the desire of the actors to share their insights with the audience, to depict the characters they have met, and to tell the stories they have been told. Moreover, the eclectic presentational styles and the simple production designs (often utilizing artefacts from the actual environment in which the play is set), give an immediacy and a sense of social event to a collective performance.

The first performance of a community-based collective is invariably before the subject community, a necessary reciprocation that completes the relationship and must happen even if the play is unfinished or under-rehearsed (as with Theatre Network's *Kicker*, 1978, when it played to the people of Inuvik before it began its run in the South). Although there is always risk of censure, these first performances have a history of acceptance and mutual celebration.

Many collective creations have used playwrights (Rick SALUTIN on *1837: The Farmers' Revolt*; Rudy Wiebe on Theatre Passe Muraille's *Far As the Eye Can See*; Gordon

Clare Coulter and David Fox in Far As the Eye Can See, *Tarragon Theatre, 1977 (co-produced with Theatre Passe Muraille)*

Collective Creation

Pengilly on *Hard Hats and Stolen Hearts*; Christopher HEIDE on *The Cody Co-op Show*).

Some published collectives have been successfully remounted, although the collective is essentially a performance, not a literary genre; the written script of a collective creation captures only one moment in the life of the play (usually based on the taping of a single performance) and cannot express the nature of the acting or the dynamic relationship between actors and audience. Collective texts that are rewritten for subsequent production often lose the directness of the original, as was the case with the revised *Paper Wheat* in 1977. Moreover, as collectives became removed from their community base, characters tended to become caricatures: 'remove the fishermen from the audience, remove the need to play the fishermen truthfully,' Chris Brookes has said.

By the beginning of the 1980s the number of collective productions had declined. Still, there was a need for plays about the problems of specific communities, with the objective of animating the communities to take action for social and political change. Hence Popular Theatre (see POLITICAL AND POPULAR THEATRE) started in Canada (CATALYST THEATRE in Edmonton, 1977, and the GREAT CANADIAN THEATRE COMPANY in Ottawa, 1974), synthesizing the cultural base of the collective process with an informed political analysis.

See Diane Bessai, 'Documentary Theatre in Canada: An Investigation into Questions and Backgrounds', *Canadian Drama*, 6 (1980); Renate Usmiani, *Second Stage: The Alternative Theatre Movement in Canada* (1983); and Alan Filewod, *Collective Encounters: Documentary Theatre in English Canada* (1987).   DAVID BARNET

Colonial Theatre. Created out of a recently built concert hall, with 360 seats, the Colonial Theatre was opened in Victoria by George Chapman and his acting family upon their arrival in Feb. 1860 with August Kotzebue's *The Stranger*. The Chapmans—one of several American touring companies to take advantage of the city's burgeoning population (about 3,000 in 1859) and Gold Rush affluence—performed there intermittently during the next five months, with a short tour to New Westminster. The company repeated *The Stranger* and gave *The French Spy* (T.J. Haines), the popular *Black-Eyed Susan* (Douglas Jerrold), *Yankee in a Fix* (Yankee

Addams), *Fazio, or the Italian Wife* (H.H. Milman), and other plays. A one-act farce frequently followed the main piece.

The J.B. Robinson Company, also American, followed (11-29 July 1860), presenting *The Soldier's Bride* (James Hall), *Naval Engagements* (Charles Dance), *The Lady of Lyons* (Edward Bulwer-Lytton), and more. The Potter Troupe played at the Colonial from 8 Oct. to 20 Dec. 1860, giving *The Lady of Lyons* three times, and the following plays at least twice: *The Stranger*, *Ingomar the Barbarian* (Maria Lovell), *Lucretia Borgia* (Victor Hugo), *Romeo and Juliet*, and *Richard III*. In this period, patrons of the Colonial also saw *Othello*, *Hamlet*, *Black-Eyed Susan*, and *The Drunkard* (W.H. Smith). During 1860 the Colonial was the only theatre in Victoria, although the ballroom of the Royal Hotel (sometimes identified as the Royal Theatre or Theatre Royal) was used occasionally for plays.

In 1861 the Robinsons returned to Victoria and opened the Victoria Theatre (3 Jan. 1861), after which the Colonial declined in importance. In Feb. 1861 the Stark-Potter Company performed there briefly, notably in *Othello* and *The Merchant of Venice*. In April the theatre changed its name to the Lyceum. It was occupied very briefly by the Robinsons with *The Barrack Room* (T.H. Bayly), *Black-Eyed Susan*, and *Rule a Wife and Have a Wife* (an adaptation of Francis Beaumont's and John Fletcher's play). The building functioned at intervals as a music hall, ballroom or auditorium until it was destroyed by fire on 3 Nov. 1868.   ROBERT G. LAWRENCE

Comédie-Canadienne, La. From 22 Feb. 1958, when it opened with Jean Anouilh's *L' Alouette*, until 1972, when it became the new home of the THÉÂTRE DU NOUVEAU MONDE, the Comédie-Canadienne was one of the most vigorous and exciting theatres in Montreal. Founded by Gratien GÉLINAS, the theatre occupied a site at the corner of Sainte-Catherine and Saint-Urbain Streets—formerly the home of the Radio Cité and Gaieté theatres. Renovated by architect André Blouin, the theatre contained a 34' × 34' stage, with a backstage depth of 30 feet. Basically a proscenium theatre—with flies, stairs, and trap doors—two 12' forestages could transform it into a thrust stage such as Gélinas had played on at the STRATFORD FESTIVAL. The lighting system and acoustics rivalled those of any theatre in North America. Supported by the private sector (Dow Brewery) and government (the province committed $25,000 a year for four years), Gélinas promised a repertoire of Canadian plays and a policy of accessibility: the curtain rose at the unusually early hour of 7:30 p.m.; tickets were the same price as movie tickets; a club was established whose members could see previews at reduced prices and participate in post-performance discussions with the company; box-offices opened in a dozen towns within a 100-mile radius of Montreal.

Despite these measures, the Comédie-Canadienne suffered financial difficulties. Between 1958 and 1961 it presented eleven original Quebec plays—far more than any other Canadian theatre offered—but was obliged to introduce well-known work from the international repertoire as well. The theatre was rented to other companies—including the THÉÂTRE CLUB and TNM—to increase revenue, and Gélinas also presented popular singers from Quebec and France. A 1969 administrative reorganization created La Fondation de la Comédie-Canadienne, a non-profit organization, but in 1970 the company declared bankruptcy and ceased operations soon afterwards.

Notable among the plays produced by the Comédie-Canadienne were Gélinas's *Bousille et les justes* in 1959 and *HIER, LES ENFANTS DANSAIENT* (1966); Marcel DUBÉ's *Un SIMPLE SOLDAT* (1958), *Florence* (1960), *Les Beaux dimanches* (1965), *AU RETOUR DES OIES BLANCHES* (1966), and *Un matin comme les autres* (1968); Françoise LORANGER's *Double Jeu* (1969) and *Médium saignant* (1970); Félix LECLERC's *Les Temples* (1965); and Guy DUFRESNE's *Le Cri de l'engoulevent* (1960).

MADELEINE GREFFARD

Compagnie Jean Duceppe, La. Founded in Montreal in 1973 by actor Jean DUCEPPE, it won critical acclaim in its first year and also made a profit—without subsidies—largely because of its popular productions of John Thomas McDONOUGH's *CHARBONNEAU & LE CHEF* (revived in 1986) and Arthur Miller's *La Mort d'un commis voyageur* (*Death of a Salesman*) (revived in 1983). After a difficult second year the company eventually averaged nearly ninety-per-cent subscription sales at its 900-seat Port-Royal theatre in the PLACE DES ARTS. Although its mandate is to provide theatre that will educate without distress and amuse without strain, there have been challenging productions, including Harold Pinter's *Le Gardien* (*The Caretaker*) and Dario Fo's *Mort accidentelle d'un anarchiste* (*Accidental Death of an Anarchist*). And in 1976 the company premièred Michel TREMBLAY's *Sainte Carmen de la Main*.

Nearly half the company's repertoire has been American, with heavy emphasis on Broadway shows; the rest has been divided between Canadian and European plays, with British drama being favoured. Favoured too are realistic and emotional plays such as *Charbonneau & le chef*, Peter Nichols's *Un Jour dans la mort de Joe Egg* (*A Day in the Death of Joe Egg*), John Pielmeier's *Soeur Agnès* (*Agnes of God*), and Arnold Wesker's *Des Frites, des frites, des frites...* (*Chips with Everything*). The standard model for the repertoire, however, is comedy, whether it deals with artists (Neil Simon's *Sunshine Boys*), the suburbs (*Les Voisins* by Claude Meunier and Louis Saia), or the tavern (*BROUE*). Such fare is regarded by some as shallow, but its popularity cannot be denied.

See Adrien Gruslin and Jean-Pierre Lamoureux, 'La Compagnie Jean Duceppe: un théâtre d'émotion et d'identification', *Jeu*, 29 (1983-84).

ADRIEN GRUSLIN

Compagnons de Saint-Laurent, Les. Founded in 1937 at Montreal's Collège Saint-Laurent by Father Émile LEGAULT—and directed by him until it disbanded in 1952—this amateur company reflected the Catholic Church's growing involvement in secular activities and, in particular, its response to the alleged immorality of the current professional theatre and the music hall. The company adopted the motto of a contemporary French group, Les Campagnons de Notre-Dame: 'Pour la Foi par l'art dramatique; pour l'art dramatique en esprit de Foi' (Faith through Dramatic Art; Dramatic Art in a Spirit of Faith).

Between 1937 and 1939 the company performed only edifying and semi-liturgical plays such as *Celle qui la porte fit s'ouvrir* by the Jesuit Louis Barjon and *Le Jeu de Saint Laurent du fleuve* by Henri Ghéon. Following a period of study in France (Sept. 1938 - Mar. 1939), during which Legault became more familiar with the work of Ghéon, Léon Chancerel, and Henri Brochet—all disciples of the Cath-

Compagnons de Saint-Laurent

Henri Ghéon's Le Noël sur la place, *Compagnons de Saint-Laurent, 1937*

olic convert and director Jacques Copeau—the Compagnons introduced into their repertoire such classical authors as Molière (*Le Misanthrope* in 1939 and *Les Femmes savantes* in 1940) and Racine (*Britannicus* in 1940 and *Athalie* in 1941). After moving into a hall in Montreal's Côte-des-neiges district that they renamed L'ERMITAGE (where they remained until 1945), the Compagnons continued to perform Christian authors (chiefly Ghéon) and Molière (*Les Fourberies de Scapin* in 1944, with Georges Groulx in the title role), but expanded their audience by adding contemporary plays, such as *L'Échange* and *L'Annonce faite à Marie* by Paul Claudel (directed by Ludmilla Pitoëff in 1942), *Noé* by André Obey, and *Orphée* and *Oedipe-Roi* by Jean Cocteau.

From 1945 to 1948 the Compagnons played at the GESÙ, a large theatre in the centre of the city, and continued to expand their repertoire. Besides Molière (*Le Médecin malgré lui, Les Précieuses ridicules, Le Bourgeois gentilhomme*) and Racine (*Andromaque*), they produced Shakespeare (*La Nuit des rois— Twelfth Night*—with sumptuous costume and set designs by the painter Alfred Pellan in 1946), Marivaux (*Le Jeu de l'amour et du hasard*), Beaumarchais (*Le Barbier de Seville*), Musset (*On ne badine pas avec l'amour*), and Rostand (*Les Romanesques*). In addition they discovered Jean Anouilh (*Le Bal des voleurs, Antigone*), Jean Giraudoux (*L'Apollon de Bellac*), and Garcia Lorca (*La Savetière prodigieuse*). During this period Legault created also *Les*

Cahiers des Compagnons, a magazine produced a dozen times between 1944 and 1947 that reinforced the teaching dimension underlying the Compagnons' entire theatrical enterprise—to educate their audiences and 'guide them towards intellectual development'. *Les Cahiers* established a precedent in the history of Quebec theatre; for the first time its practitioners openly posed questions about their art and its impact on society.

In 1948 the company turned professional, purchasing an Anglican church at the corner of Sherbrooke and Delorimier, which became the Théâtre des Compagnons. They also opened a training school and began producing shows for children. The number of productions jumped from six to fifteen a season, but the quality of work suffered. Several outstanding actors left to pursue careers elsewhere—Guy HOFFMANN, for example, after his triumph in *Le Malade imaginaire* in 1949 helped found the THÉÂTRE DU NOUVEAU MONDE in 1951; the casting and the directing were uneven; and the programming, despite some successes, seemed erratic. Standard plays such as *La Paix* by Aristophanes, Shakespeare's *Roméo et Juliette*, Corneille's *L'Illusion comique*, Goldoni's *La Locandiera*, and modern classics such as French translations of Tennessee Williams' *The Glass Menagerie*, Eliot's *Murder in the Cathedral*, Wilder's *Our Town*, Pirandello's *Henri IV*, and Garcia Lorca's *Bodas de sangre* (*Blood Wedding*) were produced along with such minor plays as *La Dame de l'aube* by Alejandro Casona, *Briser la statue* by Gilbert Cesbron, *La Première Légion* by Emmet Lavery, and *L'Honneur de Dieu* by Pierre Emmanuel. Unable to attract a large enough audience—although attendance reached 15,000 for some runs—and lacking government subsidy, the company was forced to close in 1952.

Les Compagnons nurtured many successful actors, directors, and designers—Pierre DAGENAIS, Jean-Louis ROUX, Jean GASCON, Charlotte Boisjoli, Guy Provost, Denise PELLETIER, Hélène LOISELLE, Françoise Faucher, Huguette OLIGNY, Gilles PELLETIER, Jean DUCEPPE, and Robert PRÉVOST, among others—while promoting thought-provoking theatre (filtered through the particular objective of a revived Christian spiritualism) from the best of the classical and modern repertoires, leaving an imprint on an entire generation of practitioners and theatregoers in Quebec.   GILBERT DAVID

Comus Music Theatre. While he was assistant artistic director to Jean GASCON at the STRATFORD FESTIVAL, Michael BAWTREE directed modern operas such as *Patria II: Requiems for a Party Girl* (R. Murray Schafer), *Exiles* (Raymond and Beverly Pannell), Gabriel CHARPENTIER's *Orpheus*, *Everyman* (Charles Wilson and Eugene Benson), and Gian-Carlo Menotti's *The Medium*, starring Maureen Forrester, at the Third Stage. Bawtree, Charpentier, and Forrester then combined talents with financial consultant Douglas Annett to found Comus Music Theatre in Toronto in 1975. Through productions, workshops, readings, and classes, Comus was designed to explore all forms of musical theatre from cabaret and revue to opera and multi-media events with the goal of creating a distinctively Canadian repertoire. Comus's first production, in 1976, was *Harry's Back in Town*, a traditional revue based on the music of film composer Harry Warren.

Bawtree supervised Comus until 1980, when he left to take over the BANFF CENTRE SCHOOL OF FINE ARTs' Musical Theatre Division. Billie Bridgman, concert singer and director, ran Comus from 1980 to 1985, succeeded by Stephen McNeff, a composer and former assistant artistic director of the Banff Musical Theatre Ensemble. Major Comus productions have included *The Shivaree*, by James REANEY and John Beckwith, in 1982; *Nightbloom*, adapted by Sean MULCAHY from James Joyce's *Ulysses* and featuring music by the Canadian Electronic Ensemble, in 1984; and, most notably, *Ra*, R. Murray Schafer's 1983 all-night epic tribute to Ancient Egypt staged at the Ontario Science Centre. During its first ten years, Comus presented thirty-seven musical theatre pieces, most of them Canadian, in various performance spaces around Toronto. In 1986, to celebrate its tenth birthday in typically eclectic style, Comus utilized the outdoor Greek-style amphitheatre at the Guild Inn in Scarborough, Ont., for a double bill of Joseph QUESNEL's seminal 1790 Canadian comic opera *COLAS ET COLINETTE*, resurrected by Godfrey Ridout, and John Milton's *Maske of Comus*, adapted by playwright James Reaney and composer Louis Applebaum. Unable, however, to establish a solid audience base for its eclectic repertoire, and encumbered by financial difficulties, Comus dissolved in 1988.   ROSS STUART

Cone, Tom (b. 1947). Born in Miami, he received his BA from Florida State University. After a year's study in Italy he moved to Vancouver in 1970, enrolling in Simon Fraser University's Communications Program, where he began the first of some thirty scripts for CBC radio. Playwright-in-residence for the West Coast Actors' Society in 1976 and for the STRATFORD FESTIVAL from 1978 to 1980, he is now based in New York, though he still regards Vancouver as his home and conducts workshops for the NEW PLAY CENTRE, with which he has been associated since 1973. His plays include *The Organizer* (produced by Simon Fraser University at the VANCOUVER EAST CULTURAL CENTRE in 1973), *Whisper to Mendelsohn* (produced by the New Play Centre at the ARTS CLUB Theatre in 1975), *Shotglass* (produced at the New Play Centre's du Maurier Festival in 1977), and *Veils* (published in 1974, produced at the Playwrights' Workshop, Montreal, in 1974). Cone's best-known work, *Herringbone* (1976), was first produced at the du Maurier Festival in 1975, and toured nationally en route to the Montreal Olympiad. It was also produced on CBC-TV, and—in a less satisfying two-act version—in New York and London.

In Cone's world rigid egoists brush against susceptible, open personalities. Influenced at first by Harold Pinter, Cone soon discovered his own style. The reminiscences of Alan and Ben in *There* (published in 1973, produced by Simon Fraser University at the Vancouver East Cultural Centre in 1972) reveal Alan's violent ego and Ben's free spirit. There is a similar interplay of reminiscence between the two women in *Cubistique* (published in 1975, produced at the du Maurier Festival in 1974). In *Herringbone* the protagonist, George Herringbone, a former trouper, acts out the events of his strange childhood in a resonant mad-cap vaudeville. In *Beautiful Tigers* (published in 1976, produced at the du Maurier Festival in 1976) Picasso and friends pay equivocal homage to Henri Rousseau as they seek to recreate in a tableau the innocent vision of *Le Douanier* expressed in his painting 'The Dream'. More recently Cone has moved from theatrical pyrotechnics towards life-as-it-is. The quartet in *Stargazing* (1978), produced at Stratford's Third Stage in 1978, search the night sky over Vancouver for falling stars. As Cone has said, they are 'characters who are desperate . . . trying to reach for something that might be too distant for them.' Cone's idiosyncratic word-music and theatricality signal a major talent.

Three Plays by Tom Cone (1976) includes *Cubistique, Herringbone*, and *Beautiful Tigers*.

ANTHONY JENKINS

Confederation Centre of the Arts. The idea of a national arts monument in Charlottetown, PEI—first proposed by Dr Frank MacKinnon to the Massey Royal Commission in 1950—finally materialized in Oct. 1964 with the opening of the Confederation Centre of the Arts by Queen Elizabeth. Officially named the Fathers of Confederation Memorial Building, the arts complex rises, monolithically, on Queen Square, where a large agricultural market had been the central gathering-place for over a hundred years. Built to commemorate the hundredth anniversary of the Charlottetown meeting of the Fathers of Confederation, the Centre was designated a national Centennial project, jointly financed by the federal government (with a grant of 2,800,000) and provincial governments with grants equalling fifteen cents per capita of their population. A nation-wide architectural competition was won by the Montreal firm of Affleck, Desbarats, Dimakopoulos, Lebensold, Michaud, and Sise, who had designed, among other notable buildings, the QUEEN ELIZABETH THEATRE in Vancouver and the PLACE DES ARTS in Montreal.

Constructed of sandstone from Wallace, N.S., and designed to complement the adjacent Province House—the location of the historic meeting that led to the birth of Canada—the $5,600,000 complex has a common concourse level concealed beneath a raised terrace. Out of this landscaped terrace rise a theatre, an art gallery, and a library. In the centre of the concourse is the most distinctive architectural feature: a glass-roofed Memorial Hall with interior walls sheathed in marble.

The theatre is the home of the CHARLOTTETOWN FESTIVAL, which has produced summer seasons of musical theatre there since 1965. The original theatre design created a flexible area that could be arranged—by a complex mechanical system that moved seats and walls—as a proscenium or semi-round performance space. Proving unreliable, however, this mechanism was abandoned in favour of a permanent proscenium theatre seating 1,108 (orchestra 942, balcony 166). The stage is 30' 6" deep, with a 58' wide x 24' 4" high proscenium opening. In 1982-3 box-office operations were computerized.

As well as being the home of the Charlottetown Festival, the Centre sponsors local

Confederation Centre, Charlottetown, Prince Edward Island

amateur and professional productions, and hosts concerts and touring companies throughout the year. During the Festival season it produces children's theatre in a smaller 300-seat lecture theatre and operates the Cameo Cabaret in the 200-seat David MacKenzie Theatre located across the street. When the Centre was first constructed, dwarfing its surroundings in a city of 20,000, many believed it would become a white elephant. It has, however, fully proven its entertainment and tourist potential, attracting over 250,000 visitors annually, 100,000 of whom purchase Festival tickets.

LINDA M. PEAKE

Conservatoire d'art dramatique du Québec, Le. Granted a charter in 1943, it opened in Montreal in 1954 under the direction of Jan Doat; its Quebec City conservatory opened in 1958 under Doat's successor, Jean Valcourt. Since 1962 both institutions have been under the jurisdiction of Quebec's Ministry of Cultural Affairs; they both provide free tuition but have adopted different educational mandates in accordance with their particular interests and the perceived artistic needs of the communities they serve.

In Montreal the conservatory emphasizes the acquisition of a solid technical foundation that enables the student to work in a variety of theatrical genres and styles, including radio and television. There are no classes in stagecraft, but students are obliged to participate in the technical aspects of production. The program teaches physical development through courses in gymnastics and dance; vocal development through courses in phonetics, diction, reading, and voice. Instruction in improvisation and interpretation encourages the development of individual acting styles, while various clinics, workshops, and seminars provide courses in theatre history and training in audio-visual techniques.

At the Quebec City conservatory the emphasis is on the concept of collective theatre. Formal teaching is given in technical theatre and design, and group activity is favoured over individualism. Students are judged more on development than on performance. Along with interpretation, improvisation, diction, voice, reading, poetry, and movement, there is instruction in mime, masque, clown, commedia dell'arte, white-faced pantomime, and the classical and modern chorus.

Graduates who have distinguished themselves include Catherine Bégin, Raymond Bouchard, Angèle Coutu, Nicole Filion, Robert Gravel, Gaston Lepage, Albert Millaire, Ghyslaine Paradis, Claire Pimparé, Yvan Ponton, Pascal Rollin, Louise Turcot, and Monique Spaziani. ODETTE GUIMOND

Conversion d'un pêcheur de la Nouvelle-Écosse, La. Elzéar LABELLE's play is the first example of playable political theatre in Quebec before the 1960s, and one of the most popular works of its day. The date of first performance is unknown, but certainly precedes June 1869. The text, words, and music were first published, undated, in 1869, and reprinted without music in *Mes Rimes*, a selection of the author's works published posthumously in 1876. Unlike the closet political drama that preceded it, *La Conversion* was a huge success on stage, continuing to draw enthusiastic audiences until at least 1899.

A comic operetta in one act, *La Conversion* has only two characters: the *habitant* Pierrichon and the Acadian fisherman Morufort. The Acadian enters first, codfish in hand. His long aria and monologue inform us he has walked all the way from Nova Scotia to protest against the ravages caused by Confederation: fish have left the shores, cows refuse to give milk, the provincial economy is in a mess. Pierrichon enters, carrying trade goods and a purse full of money. He describes how farmers in Quebec have prospered under the new system. The two engage in heated debate, but Pierrichon resolves their conflict amicably: he proposes to find the fisherman a good job in the new government as Inspector of Cod Livers.

La Conversion is full of malicious wit and puns, mostly untranslatable. The music, by Jean-Baptiste Labelle (a cousin), is derivative but serves as an excellent vehicle for Elzéar's satiric verve. The play's close resemblance to VAUDEVILLE and to topical revues, its amusing dialogue, slapstick action, and catchy songs provide a recipe that long remained popular in French Canada.

See L.E. Doucette, *Theatre in French Canada, 1606–1867* (1984), and *Theatre History in Canada*, 2 (1984) for the original text and music. L.E. DOUCETTE

Cook, Michael (b. 1933). Born in London, Eng., of Anglo-Irish Catholic parents, he worked as a waiter and farm labourer before joining the army at sixteen and serving twelve years in Korea, Japan, Germany, Malaya, and Singapore. As entertainment for the troops he wrote comic sketches and also directed John Arden's *Serjeant Musgrave's Dance*. After teacher-training in Nottingham, he immigrated to Canada in 1965, settling in Newfoundland and immediately feeling 'born again' in a challenging yet sympathetic environment. While teaching in Memorial University's Extension Department, he wrote a weekly television and theatre column for the *St John's Evening Telegram*, directed, and acted, winning a DOMINION DRAMA FESTIVAL award for his Common Man in Robert Bolt's *A Man for All Seasons* in 1970. The author of many radio plays, he has written for the stage since 1970. He joined Memorial University's English Department in 1969 and has had several extended leaves of absence for writing. In 1987 he was playwright-in-residence at the STRATFORD FESTIVAL.

Of about fifty radio plays, the most ambitious is the three-part *This Damned Inheritance* (broadcast in 1984), impressions of Newfoundland history from St Brendan, Eric the Red, and the Beothuk Indians to the present. Only two radio plays have been published. *Tiln* (1973), influenced by Samuel Beckett's *Endgame*, is about two keepers at an isolated lighthouse, on 'the edge of space and time'. One dies and the other preserves his corpse in salt and continues to talk to him. It was broadcast by the CBC in 1971. *The Terrible Journey of Frederick Douglas* (1981), broadcast in 1982, about the dreams and fantasies of a harassed professor, is light and playful, an unusual vein for Cook.

Of Cook's major stage plays three are historical and four concern present-day Newfoundland. The historical plays are large-cast epics. *The Gayden Chronicles* (1977) was first produced at the CAST Theatre, Hollywood, California, in 1980. Based on the diary of William Gayden, executed for murder, mutiny, and desertion at St John's in 1812, it depicts the psychology and motivation of the rebel and encompasses the early nineteenth-century British navy, the age of the French Revolution, the ideas of Tom Paine and William Blake, and attitudes to authority and conformity.

While *The Gayden Chronicles* has only slight links with Newfoundland, the Newfoundland setting is crucial in the other plays.

In *On the Rim of the Curve* (1977), first produced at the Newfoundland Drama Festival in 1977 by the Avion Players, Cook struggles to comprehend the genocide of the Beothuk Indians. On stage the Author appears, lamenting the difficulty of his task: 'How d'you write of a vanished people? Out of a bone? A book? A lock of hair? A litany of lies? Or simply honest confusion . . . I want you to help me piece the skeleton together.' He calls on a ringmaster to introduce the various characters who will perform: Sir Humphrey Gilbert; David Buchan and John Peyton, the last whites to see Beothuks (1811–19); the last three Beothuks; assorted dancers and furriers; a businessman. The resulting accounts invite audiences to share the writer's dilemma and gain their own understanding of the tragic story and its lessons.

Michael Cook's Colour the Flesh the Colour of Dust, *Neptune Theatre, Halifax, 1972, with l. to r. (foreground), Diane D'Aquila, Robert Reid, Ian Deakin, Donald Myers; (background) Margot Sweeney, Joan Hurley, Florence Paterson, Joan Orenstein*

Colour the Flesh the Colour of Dust (1972), the most powerful of the three historical dramas, first produced professionally by the NEPTUNE THEATRE in 1972, is set in 1762 when the French captured St John's and held it for a few months. Cook's large cast includes a magistrate; a corrupt merchant; a once-honourable Captain brought down by squalor, loneliness, and drink who goes insane; a Lieutenant who discovers he does not believe in values such as honour; and the common people—including a starving woman and a whore—unaffected by the change to French rule. The common people have a spokesman who concludes: 'One day we'll kill you all. Because there'll be nothing else left to do.' Yet the play starts with a corpse and ends with a baby; the common people survive—unlike the rebellious Gayden and the unfortunate Beothuks. *Colour the Flesh* is cold, joyless, fearsome: the audience, as in *On the Rim*, is asked to judge and to think.

Therese's Creed (1976), first produced in 1977 by Montreal's CENTAUR THEATRE, and *Quiller* (1975), first produced at Memorial University in 1975, are monologues about Newfoundland's people. Middle-aged Therese speaks of her Catholicism, of money, of her way of life, her children, and her dead husband, and of change—nylons, bingo, television, smoking, the telephone, electricity for the washing-machine. Quiller, an old man 'touched' by the death of his wife, is a more individualized portrait. His wandering mind mixes past and present as he addresses the Lord and drives away tormenting children.

Jacob's Wake (1975), first produced professionally by FESTIVAL LENNOXVILLE in 1975, is set in an outport at Easter during a great storm, and is ostensibly a family drama. Upstairs, Skipper, bedridden for thirty years, is dying: he was responsible for the death of his son (the Jacob of the title) on a seal-hunt. His other son depends on welfare and is mothered by his wife; his daughter is a teacher. Skipper's three grandsons have turned away from the sea and have found jobs in government, religion, and business. The seals—like men such as the Skipper—have gone, and the radio and welfare offer nothing to take their place. The old captain and the house-as-ship suggest comparison with Bernard Shaw's *Heartbreak House*. Cook attempts, as he writes in his notes to the play, to link 'symbolism and abstraction'. When Skipper dies, his death-mask lights up and he appears downstairs in his prime, crying out that 'Newfoundland is alive and well and roaring down the ice pack' just before 'the sound of a cosmic disaster, a ripping and rending and smashing.' Neil Munro's 1986 NATIONAL ARTS CENTRE production attempted to balance the play's naturalistic and supernatural elements through expressionist staging.

Another strong, tyrannical skipper who has outlived his time is central to *The HEAD, GUTS AND SOUND BONE DANCE* (1974), first staged in 1973 by the Open Group at the ARTS AND CULTURE CENTRE THEATRE, St

John's. The title refers to the parts of a fish (a sound bone is a backbone) discarded by humans, and the dance by three drunken old fishermen to a sad Newfoundland song about drowning is meant to suggest lost relationships. The underlying conflict of the play is the son-in-law's efforts to escape from old Skipper Pete's control. Cook's picture of the strengths and weaknesses of outport men and of the inevitable end to their way of life is at its most vivid in *Sound Bone Dance*.

As *Jacob's Wake* clearly shows, Cook's plays are not intended merely as Newfoundland documentaries. Cook's work commonly reveals admiration for the underdog (Quiller, Therese, Skipper Pete), a fear that Newfoundlanders' particular strengths will be lost through the impact of outside civilizations, and a belief that change may be damaging. The severity of traditional outport life, as he sees it, breeds tough, larger-than-life figures. Such people have lived fully; their language is distinctive, touched with poetry. 'Newfoundland had a growing language when I hit it,' Cook has stated,' . . . language was used as a stabilising force between themselves, experience and the universe . . . Newfoundland had a language that reflected the nature of its civilization . . . Alas, it's almost disappeared.' Cook feels for the Newfoundlanders and the bleak, inhospitable land and the ever-present sea that has made them what they are. His tone is elegiac; his vision near-tragic.

Cook has also written a children's play, *Fisherman's Revenge*. Produced by the Newfoundland Travelling Theatre Company in 1976, it tells of the struggle of Fisherman Joe, his daughter, and her sweetheart against Black Fred Black, the town merchant, and his wife.

Cook's plays have been collected in *Tiln and Other Plays* (1976), which contains *Tiln*, *Quiller*, and *Therese's Creed*, and in *Three Plays* (1977), which contains *The Head, Guts, and Sound Bone Dance*, *On the Rim of the Curve*, and *Therese's Creed*. See also *Stage Voices* (1978), ed. Geraldine Anthony; Brian Parker, 'On the Edge: Michael Cook's Newfoundland Trilogy', *Canadian Literature*, 85 (Summer 1980); and *The Work* (1982), ed. Robert Wallace and Cynthia Zimmerman.

MALCOLM PAGE

Corbett, Hilary (b. 1929). Born in Somerset, Eng., she studied painting at the Bath

Academy of Art and trained as a teacher at the Univ. of London. She joined the Sadler's Wells Opera as a seamstress and soon became a cutter, working subsequently in the opera houses of Covent Garden and Glyndebourne and—as a designer—for the BBC. She immigrated to Canada in 1964, quickly joining the STRATFORD FESTIVAL as a cutter. In 1967 she was appointed principal costume designer and wardrobe head at the SHAW FESTIVAL. As a costumier she strives to give actors a true feeling of character—whether in period or modern dress—and to make them comfortable, both aesthetically and physically, in costume. Among her most effective work at the Shaw Festival were designs in the 1970s for Shaw's *You Never Can Tell*, Ben Travers' *Thark*, and Brandon Thomas's *Charley's Aunt*. Her designs for Arthur Wing Pinero's *Trelawney of the 'Wells'*, staged in 1974 for Toronto Arts Productions at the ST LAWRENCE CENTRE, were a particularly satisfying evocation of period through costume.

Since 1975 Corbett has been a staff designer for CBC-TV, designing costumes for some thirty-five episodes of 'The Great Detective' series, among other productions.

MARTHA MANN

Corriveau, Joseph-Eugène (1885-1947). Born in Quebec City, he studied at the Séminaire de Québec and Laval University, and then began working at the Legislative Library of Quebec. His first play, *Le Secret des Plaines d'Abraham* (1909), is a four-act historical drama in which the heroine, Léa, disguises herself as a soldier to foil a plot to deliver Quebec to the British. *Le Roi des ténèbres* (1909), written in collaboration with actor Arthur Tremblay, is based on the legend of the clockmaker of Strasbourg who sells his soul to the devil in order to win a contest; it was performed successfully in Dec. 1910 at the THÉÂTRE DES VARIÉTÉS by the Julian DAOUST Company. Corriveau wrote other plays—mainly in collaboration with Arthur Tremblay, Ernest Nadeau, and Aimé Plamondon—but only two comedies were published. In the one-act *L'Anti-féministe* (1922), whose theme is the struggle for women's suffrage, a member of the Quebec legislature abandons his support for suffrage in order to win an 'old-fashioned girl'. It was performed on 26 Apr. 1922 during a concert presented by Botrel, the famous Brittany *chansonnier*. *Mon*

commis-voyageur (1926) recounts the rivalry of two suitors—one a salesman, the other a rich member of the legislature, who is blackmailing the girl's father; predictably, the salesman triumphs. A prolific playwright, Corriveau enjoyed little success, either in print or on the stage.

JOHN E. HARE

Coulter, Clare (b. 1942). Born in Toronto, the daughter of playwright John COULTER and Olive Clare Primrose, she moved with her family in 1950 to London, Eng., where she began her training as an actress. After the family returned to Toronto in 1956, she took a degree in English at the Univ. of Toronto. During these years she worked in the props department of the STRATFORD FESTIVAL and apprenticed there with some walk-on parts under the direction of Michael LANGHAM. In 1969 she joined Toronto's newly formed THEATRE PASSE MURAILLE, acting in some of its COLLECTIVE CREATIONS under the direction of Martin KINCH and Paul THOMPSON. Her breakthrough as an actress came when Bill GLASSCO invited her to audition for TARRAGON THEATRE; she became its most prominent actress and has appeared in over twenty productions there, including the English-language premières of four of Michel TREMBLAY's plays. She has performed at several other theatres in Toronto and across Canada, including the Stratford Festival, the NATIONAL ARTS CENTRE, the MANITOBA THEATRE CENTRE, and Montreal's CENTAUR THEATRE. She has also acted in films, radio, and television.

On stage Coulter combines extreme sensitivity with quiet strength, identifying fully with her roles in realistic plays, which are her forte. She received a Dora Mavor MOORE award for her performance in Caryl Churchill's *Top Girls* at Tarragon in 1984.

JAMES NOONAN

Coulter, John (1888-1980). Born in Belfast of Protestant parents, he attended the School of Art and Technology in Belfast and won a research scholarship to Manchester Univ. before returning to Belfast and Dublin, where he taught until 1919. Coulter had early plays produced in Belfast, Dublin, and London. He moved to London in 1920 and began contributing programs to BBC radio in both London and Belfast. In 1924 he became editor of the *Ulster Review* and in 1927 managing editor of John Middleton Murry's journal

The New Adelphi. In 1936 he married the Canadian Olive Clare Primrose in Toronto, where they raised two daughters, Primrose and Clare COULTER, who became a prominent actress.

Ireland, England, and Canada constitute John Coulter's triple heritage. He was directly influenced by the Irish literary renaissance but also by such major Northern Ireland dramatists as St John Ervine, Rutherford Mayne, Joseph Campbell, and George Shiels. When he was twenty-six Coulter moved to Dublin where the plays of Yeats, Synge, Padraic Colum, and Lady Gregory aroused his interest in mythological and historical cycles, supernatural and heroic tales, folklore, and peasant stories. His Irish plays include *The House in the Quiet Glen* (1937), a 1925 BBC radio play directed by Tyrone GUTHRIE under the title *Sally's Chance* and produced in Canada in 1937 by the Toronto Masquers under the original title as a stage play; *Father Brady's New Pig,* produced in 1937 on stage and radio in Belfast and Toronto; *Family Portrait* (1937), produced on BBC radio, Belfast, in 1935, at HART HOUSE THEATRE, Toronto, in 1938, and on CBC TV under the title *The Sponger* in 1956; *While I Live,* about Ulster gentry, produced on CBC radio in 1951; *Holy Manhattan,* about an Irish immigrant in New York, produced in 1940 as a stage play at the ARTS AND LETTERS CLUB, Toronto, as a CBC radio play in 1941, and on CBC TV in 1945, and revised as the novel *Turf Smoke* (1945); *The Drums Are Out* (1971), which premièred at the Abbey Theatre, Dublin, in 1948 and won the Sir Barry Jackson trophy for the best Canadian play at the DOMINION DRAMA FESTIVAL in Toronto in 1950; and *The Red Hand of Ulster,* a 1974 CBC radio play that portrays the formerly romanticized IRA as an unscrupulous band of terrorists struggling against an Ian Paisley-like Protestant leader in the still unresolved violence of Northern Ireland.

Of the Irish plays the best is *The Drums Are Out.* It revolves around the 'troubles' in Northern Ireland between the Catholic IRA and the Protestant police in the 1920-1 riots, and portrays a family sharply divided by political issues. A realistic play, it is a powerful revelation of the divisive but intensely human problems of the Irish people. Its weaknesses are a too-familiar plot and a lack of depth in character development; nevertheless, its attempt to bring together two warring fac-

tions resulted in highly favourable reviews in the Dublin newspapers.

Coulter's Canadian plays, which depict controversial historical issues, include the RIEL trilogy. *Riel* (1972), first produced in 1950, dramatizes hostilities in Canada between French and English, Catholic and Protestant, Irish and Scottish settlers, and between Métis and the English-Canadian government. Louis Riel, the enigmatic, powerful Métis leader and founder of Manitoba, captured Coulter's imagination and he went on to write *The Crime of Louis Riel* (1976), first produced at the Dominion Drama Festival, 1966, and *The Trial of Louis Riel* (1968), produced first in 1967 and annually given since then in Regina, where Riel was hanged.

Coulter wrote three historical plays about Quebec: *A Tale of Old Quebec,* commissioned by the BBC and sent from London in 1935 by shortwave to the CBC in Montreal as a salute to the founding of Quebec; *Quebec in 1670,* a 1940 radio play for CBS in New York as part of the 'Living History' series; and *François Bigot: A Rediscovery in Dramatic Form of the Fall of Quebec* (1978), a play depicting corruption of government officials, and written in the form of a television interview with historical characters, exposing the early causes of what was to become, two hundred years hence, the separatist movement in Canada. It was produced by CBC radio in 1970.

Another historical play of lesser interest is the CBC radio play *The Trial of Joseph Howe,* broadcast in 1942 to remind Canadians that the freedom they were fighting for in the Second World War had been hard won. *Mr. Churchill of England* (1944) was created as a 'living-newspaper' play by Coulter out of his deep respect for England's leader and was broadcast by the CBC in 1942. Later a stage play, it was also rewritten as a short biography (*Churchill,* 1945).

Coulter was fascinated not only by powerful leaders, but also by monomaniacs and great theatre personalities. He wrote a highly successful television adaptation (broadcast by the CBC in 1962) of the Russian novelist Ivan Goncharov's famous 1858 novel *Oblomov. A Capful of Pennies* (1967)—also titled *The Glittering Dust*—based on the life of Edmund Kean, was produced, not very successfully, on CBC radio in 1967 and on stage in Toronto.

Coulter

Coulter revealed in his plays a deep sensitivity to women and their problems, especially in *Sketch for a Portrait* (1943), *Green Lawns and Peacocks* (1951), and *Sleep, My Pretty One* (1954), a verse-drama about the rivalry between two women for the affections of father and husband.

Other work by Coulter includes libretti for radio operas composed by Healey Willan: *Transit Through Fire* (1944) produced in 1942 and revised for stage concert in 1943 and television in 1955; and *Deirdre of the Sorrows* (1944) broadcast by the CBC in 1946. A revised version, *Deirdre*, was produced by the Canadian Opera Company in 1967. A collection of poetry, *The Blossoming Thorn* (1946), is derivative of Yeats, but there is a haunting quality in the songs of this exiled man.

The accomplishments of John Coulter in Ireland and England where he learned his craft, and in Canada where he applied it, distinguish him as a Canadian immigrant who bequeathed to his adopted country a rich legacy of plays and a strong incentive to young playwrights to establish a national theatre for the production of Canadian work. The Coulter archives are in the Mills Memorial Library of McMaster University.

See Geraldine Anthony, *John Coulter* (1976); *Prologue to a Marriage: Letters and Diaries of John Coulter and Olive Clare Primrose* (1979); and John Coulter, *In My Day: Memoirs* (1980).   GERALDINE ANTHONY

Crabdance. Written between 1964 and 1968, Beverley Rosen SIMONS' absurdist comedy is a powerful and dynamic metaphor for the female human condition. The initial stimulus for the play arose out of the playwright's personal suffering and difficulties with older female members of her family. Thematically, *Crabdance* is a kind of endgame of universal womanhood. After the basic sexual relationships of mother to son, wife to husband, and mistress to lover have been acted out, nothing is left for widow Sadie Golden but to die and be carried into the existential void by her salesmen partners and the funeral director—the final service provided by the patriarchy to the used-up post-menopausal female.

Following its première at Seattle's A Contemporary Theatre on 16 Sept. 1969, directed by Malcolm BLACK, *Crabdance* was produced at the VANCOUVER PLAYHOUSE in Jan. 1972, directed by Frances HYLAND, and starring Jennifer PHIPPS; at NEPTUNE THEATRE's Second Stage in Aug. 1972; at the MANITOBA THEATRE CENTRE's Warehouse in May 1974; and at Toronto's Firehall Theatre in Nov. 1975. The most distinguished stage production to date was at the CITADEL THEATRE's Rice Theatre in Edmonton in Jan. 1977 (again directed by Malcolm Black), with Florence Paterson as Sadie, Thomas Hauff as Mowchuk, Roland Hewgill as Dickens, and Maurice Good as Highrise. Black also directed a CBC radio production in Apr. 1976.

Crabdance was first published in 1969 by In Press, Vancouver; a revised edition was published by Talonbooks in 1972. It has also been translated into Polish, Japanese, and Italian.   ROTA HERZBERG LISTER

Creeps. A long one-act play about the lives of men afflicted with cerebral palsy, its author, David FREEMAN, was born with the same handicap. Encouraged by director Bill GLASSCO to develop 'The World of Can't', an article Freeman had written for *Maclean's* in 1964 about workshops for CP victims, the resulting play was produced by Toronto's FACTORY THEATRE Lab on 5 Feb. 1971. Directed by Glassco, it was immediately hailed by critics and audiences. T.E. Kalem, writing in *Time* of a 1973 U.S. production, called the play 'powerful, harrowing, grimly humorous and altogether absorbing'.

The play's locale is the men's washroom of a workshop where five residents, all suffering from cerebral palsy, argue about their lives and their mindless work routine (folding boxes, sanding blocks). The slight plot turns on the efforts of Tom, a would-be painter, to persuade Jim, a potential writer, to leave the shelter for the outside world (as Freeman had done). The power of the play lies in its searing probing of the stricken men as they escape from their supervisor to the washroom and from an outside world that treats them as objects of pity or ridicule. This attitude is represented by the triple hallucinatory interruption of the Shriners and 'Miss Cerebral Palsy'.

The language of the play is brutal and obscene; however, if the contrast between these spastics and their constant talk of sex is disturbing, the play is surprisingly funny—Freeman has a good ear for humour. *Creeps* is not a balanced view of society's treatment of the handicapped, but Freeman's aim is to shock his audience into greater awareness of the common humanity that links the healthy and the disabled and to suggest that freedom is essential to health of body and mind.

Creeps won the 1971 CHALMERS Play Award and the New York Drama Desk Award for Outstanding New Playwright in 1973. Published in 1972 by the Univ. of Toronto Press, the play is also available in *The Penguin Book of Modern Canadian Drama* (1984), ed. Richard Plant.

See Mary Elizabeth Smith, 'Freeman's *Creeps* and *Battering Ram*: Variations on a Theme', *Canadian Drama*, 4 (1978).

EUGENE BENSON

Creley, Jack (b. 1926). An actor, singer, and dancer, he was born in Chicago and raised in California. He trained for the theatre in New York, but in 1951 joined the MOUNTAIN PLAYHOUSE Company in Montreal, later moving to Toronto to become one of the mainstays of the city's acting community. Equally at home in any of the performance media, Creley has been a busy radio and television actor, and has also appeared in over twenty-five films, including *The Canadians* (1961) and *Dr. Strangelove* (1963). His stage work ranges from Shakespeare to the 1961 New York production of Robert Bolt's *A*

Man for All Seasons with Paul Scofield, and includes a string of musical productions from revue to Offenbach and Gilbert and Sullivan.

NEIL CARSON

Crest Theatre, The. Founded in 1953 by brothers Donald and Murray DAVIS, with a mandate to 'provide repertory theatre in Toronto comparable with the best of British repertory companies' and to 'contribute to the cultural life of Canada by providing opportunities for the development of Canadian artistic directors, playwrights, designers, managers and technicians,' it occupied what was originally a movie theatre built in 1927 on Mt Pleasant Rd. The renovated space had a proscenium stage 29' wide and 19' deep and it seated 842. Further renovations took place in 1958 and 1963; in the latter renovation the stage was enlarged by some thirty-three per cent. Company members in the first 1954-5 season were the Davis brothers, their sister Barbara CHILCOTT, Max Helpmann (Chilcott's husband), Betty LEIGHTON, Mary Laura Wood, Eric HOUSE, George McCowan, Norma Renault, and Toby ROBINS. The inaugural production on 5 Jan. 1954 was Gordon Daviot's *Richard of Bordeaux*, directed by John Blatchley with Murray Davis in the title role. Other productions in the first season

Antony and Cleopatra, *Crest Theatre, 1956*

included Philip Barry's *Philadelphia Story*, Emlyn Williams' *The Light of Heart*, and Oscar Wilde's *Lord Arthur Saville's Crime*. When the Crest Theatre finally closed in 1966 it had presented thirteen seasons and some 140 plays, many of which received popular and critical acclaim: T.S. Eliot's *Murder in the Cathedral* (in 1954); Robertson DAVIES' *A Jig for the Gypsy* (1954, starring Barbara Chilcott); Jean Anouilh's *Antigone* (1956); Chekhov's *The Three Sisters* with Charmion KING, Amelia HALL, and Kate REID in 1956; Ray Lawler's *Summer of the Seventeenth Doll* (1959); Samuel Beckett's *Krapp's Last Tape* (1961, starring Donald Davis); and the company's final production in April 1966, Ibsen's *Hedda Gabler*, featuring Marilyn LIGHTSTONE, and directed by Murray Davis.

The Crest was always firmly committed to developing Canadian theatre. It produced plays (many of them premières) by Robertson Davies, John GRAY, Mary Jukes, Marcel DUBÉ, Ted ALLAN, and Bernard SLADE. Its directors included Robert GILL, Douglas CAMPBELL, John HOLDEN, Malcolm BLACK, Michael LANGHAM, Barry Morse, Mavor MOORE, David GARDNER, Leon MAJOR, John HIRSCH, Jean ROBERTS, Herbert WHITTAKER, Allan LUND, Kurt REIS, Marigold CHARLESWORTH, George McCowan, and the Davis brothers. It provided a stage, and important roles, for a new generation of Canadian actors, including Amelia Hall, John Vernon, Richard MONETTE, Frances HYLAND, Leo CICERI, Jackie BURROUGHS, Martha HENRY, Kate Reid, Charmion King, and Eric House. Throughout its life, however, the Crest was plagued with financial problems. It began as a limited-liability company, Murray and Donald Davis Ltd., with a public issue of $50,000. Losses up to 1957 were approximately $100,000. In that year the company was re-organized to become a non-profit foundation run by a board of directors. In 1958 the Crest began receiving annual support from the Canada Council; the Ontario Arts Council made its first grant in 1963 (the year the Council was founded). In Sept. 1964, however, the Canada Council refused to approve a requested grant of $20,000, and the OAC approved only $10,000 of a $30,000 request. The Canada Council, departing from its usual practice of not commenting on its treatment of grant applications, issued a press release that in its past two seasons the Crest had accumulated a deficit of $127,000, that attendance was only forty-four per cent of house, and that critical notices and 'Reports . . . from advisors' suggested that many of the Crest's productions were 'indifferent'. The Crest struggled on for two more seasons, amalgamating, in July 1966, with the CANADIAN PLAYERS under the name 'Canadian Crest Theatre'. But the new venture collapsed in the same year under the weight of accumulated deficits and no plays were ever produced. The Crest Theatre paid all its creditors in full.

The reasons for the collapse of the Crest are complex. Some have argued that its programming of plays was ill-suited to its potential audience, favouring the avant-garde and the contemporary—even though many popular and classical plays were produced; that it never cultivated a star system to attract an audience; that it was in a bad location; or that Nathan COHEN's sustained adverse criticism contributed to its downfall. Nonetheless the Crest's thirteen seasons represented an important contribution to Toronto's theatrical life, to which it brought a degree of professionalism more rigorous and enduring than that of the JUPITER THEATRE and the NEW PLAY SOCIETY; it promoted Canadian plays at a time when this was rare (its record in comparison to that of the STRATFORD FESTIVAL attests to its originality); and it presented many significant plays from the comtemporary international repertoire. The imaginative Crest Hour Company, founded by Barbara Chilcott to tour plays to schools, still continues to operate out of the ST. LAWRENCE CENTRE as the Theatre Hour Company.

See *Canadian Theatre Review*, 7 (1975) for several articles on the Crest Theatre.

HERBERT WHITTAKER

Critics and Criticism. Although knowledge of Canada's theatre history is based chiefly on thousands of reviews from the mid-eighteenth century to the present, dramatic criticism remains one of the most neglected areas of Canadian theatre studies. The belief persists that before the mid-1940s Canada had no competent theatre critics.

When journalism began in Quebec and Atlantic Canada in the mid-1760s, the theatre commentators' main concern was that live theatre be sustained; that it approximate the professional standards of excellence they associated with England, France, and the United States; and that it eventually develop into an indigenous theatre of Canadian artists and a national drama. Initially most theatrical notices—such as that of 11 Apr. 1765 in the *Quebec Gazette/Gazette de Québec* for a forthcoming amateur production of Molière's *Festin de pierre* (*Don Juan*)—simply provided factual information: the title of the play, time of production, and a brief synopsis of the evening's program. As critical judgement developed, it tended to be heavily influenced by British standards. Describing the first amateur performance in Saint John, N.B., in 1789 (Susannah: Centlivre's comedy *The Busy Body* and Hannah Cowley's farce *Who's the Dupe?*), the reviewer for the *Saint John Gazette* (31 Mar. 1789) asserted that 'some of the Company displayed comic talents which would have done honor to a British Theatre.' Reviewing Frederick Brown's visually splendid production of *Coriolanus* at Montreal's newly opened THEATRE ROYAL, the critic for the *Montreal Gazette* (21 Dec. 1825) declared that the production 'would have done credit to a London Theatre'.

Actors in Canada were thus commonly measured against famous stars of the British stage. 'We have often seen Kean in his favorite character of Richard', the critic for the *Colonial Advocate* (5 Jan. 1826) noted in his review of *Richard III* (performed in the Assembly Room of Frank's Hotel in Toronto), and proceeded to compare—not unfavourably—the vocal and physical skills of a local actor named Davis with Kean's. In the summer and fall of 1826 critics in Montreal and Quebec City were able to evaluate half-a-dozen Shakespearean performances by Kean himself. Some of the reviews show growing eloquence and perceptiveness. The critic for the *Montreal Herald* (2 Aug. 1826) lauded Kean's Richard III for the 'power of modelling his features into a concentrated expression of sneering malice, the effect of which . . . might be perhaps illustrated by imagining the sensation produced by having a razor drawn over the flesh, & lemon-juice sprinkled on the incision.'

Throughout the nineteenth century foreign professional TOURING STARS AND COMPANIES continued to set the standards and criteria for judging local performances and productions. Charles Kemble was praised for not having 'adopted the negligent system we have seen practised by some great, and some would-be-great, actors of dropping out of their part and standing listlessly on the stage

as soon as they have ceased to speak, depending solely on the hits they make in certain points and leaving the rest of the character in shadow' (*Quebec Mercury*, 8 Aug. 1833). Fanny Kemble's acting, said the same critic (20 Aug.), 'is of that school which pays attention to the whole piece, not content with making a few strong touches or eliciting a bright spark here and there; she treats a character as a skillful painter would a picture, and finishes it so that all parts shall bear examination.'

'Naturalness' was a quality particularly admired among British and U.S. touring professionals. The reviewer for the Saint John *Morning News* (8 July 1840) stated that in the production of *Romeo and Juliet* by the English tragedian John Vandenhoff 'we saw no *acting*; we saw *life* as it was some hundreds of years ago, as it is now, and ever will be—and nothing else. This is what we call "holding the mirror up to nature".' 'To be natural, simple, and yet as energetic as the character demands, is, to our mind, the highest excellence of the dramatic art,' opined the critic of the *New Brunswick Courier* (30 July 1859) in a review of the English actor C.W. Couldock. Naturalness was also sought in Canadian productions and performances. Reviewing J.W. LANERGAN, the actor/manager of Saint John's DRAMATIC LYCEUM, the critic for the *New Brunswick Courier* (18 July 1863) declared of his Iago that 'Mr. Lanergan exhibits the highest delineative power, which, aided by his fine physique and splendid voice, approaches the perfection of acting—which consists in the art of concealing art, and making the audience forget for the moment that the scene before them is not reality.'

Critics also became increasingly aware that the mirror held up to nature rarely reflected Canadian experience. When Samuel Thompson, editor of the Toronto *Daily Patriot and Express*, reviewed the first Canadian play produced at the ROYAL LYCEUM THEATRE in Apr. 1853, he criticized its English setting and characterization: George Simcoe LEE's 'New Canadian Farce', *Fiddle, Faddle, and Foozle*, was 'not a Canadian one', but 'English, both in its idea and its character . . . We expected to see the mirror held up in which we could see our own absurdities—not those of the mother country.'

In Quebec native dramaturgy was encouraged as early as 1790. On 11 Feb. 1790 the

Critics and Criticism

Gazette de Montréal called Joseph QUESNEL 'the Roscius of this little stage' for his comic opera *COLAS ET COLINETTE*, produced by the Théâtre de Société. In 1844 Antoine GÉRIN-LAJOIE was acclaimed as a Canadian Racine for his nationalist drama *Le JEUNE LATOUR*, and in June and July 1880 *Le Courier de Montréal*, *Le Nouveau Monde*, and *La Patrie* called Louis-Honoré FRÉCHETTE 'Father of the national theatre' in reviews of *Papineau*, his romantic drama about the 1837 Rebellion.

In Western Canada one of the most prominent of the early critics was the anonymous 'Touchstone', who wrote perceptively in the Vancouver *Province* in the mid-1890s. By then the art and profession of theatre criticism was relatively advanced in Winnipeg, where three important critics helped the city's theatre to evolve from its rough, pioneer-town saloon entertainments, melodrama, and variety theatre to legitimate drama capable of attracting more cultured middle- and upper-class audiences. Charles W. HANDSCOMB was the chief drama and music critic of the *Manitoba Free Press* and Charles W. Wheeler was drama critic for the rival *Winnipeg Daily Tribune*. At the end of the century they were joined by the independent-minded Harriet Walker, wife of the manager of the Winnipeg Theatre, who, as 'The Matinée Girl', wrote perceptive reviews in the weekly journal *Town Topics*, founded by Handscomb in 1898. Although united in their attempt to justify the moral and artistic worth of theatre in Winnipeg, Handscomb, Wheeler, and Mrs Walker did not always agree on how this could be brought about. Wheeler publicly accused Handscomb of being too eager to attract audiences to the Winnipeg Theatre, implying that he was a paid publicity agent for C.P. WALKER. 'So much advertisement, so much notice, seems to be the rule in dramatic matters to this day, even in progressive Winnipeg, and "woe" to that critic of independent mind who dares to thwart the growing autocratic tendencies of the local management,' Wheeler protested in the *Winnipeg Daily Tribune* on 22 Aug. 1903. 'If the dramatic critics were free to write what they thought of some of the productions at the Winnipeg Theatre, an end would soon be made to the despicable trash so often presented.' They also differed in their opinion of particular plays. Eager to champion Christian virtues and Victorian morality, all three were uneasy with drama that dealt frankly

with social problems: Handscomb dismissed Ibsen's *Ghosts* as 'unwholesome, degrading—disgusting . . . just plain smut' (*Manitoba Free Press*, 10 Mar. 1904), yet Mrs Walker called attention to the play's 'awful truths' (*Town Topics*, 19 Mar. 1904).

The influence of religious, moral, and political forces on theatre criticism was equally evident in Montreal in 1880. The first tour by the controversial Sarah Bernhardt sharply divided the French-language press; only the English-language *Gazette* provided detailed, objective reviews of her performances.

An even greater influence on theatre criticism than the Catholic Church's opposition to morally suspect stars such as Bernhardt resulted from increasing monopoly over North American theatres by New York booking agencies and touring trusts. Between 1880 and 1883, ninety per cent of all professional productions in Montreal came from New York. Theatre advertisements became a major source of revenue for newspapers and led to increased coverage of theatre productions. But critics were generally restrained by their papers from harshly criticizing their large advertisers; the practice of printing advance critical notices supplied by touring companies blurred the distinction between publicity and criticism. The Victoria *Colonist* (15 Nov. 1898) explained to its readers that these advance theatre notices were 'not the opinions of the newspaper printing them. They are as much a part of the advertisement as are the posters on the streets . . . Most engagements are for one night only, and this makes it impossible for the local newspapers to criticize the performance, so that we can be of any value to the readers.'

In larger cities such as Toronto, the great frequency of visits by touring companies and concert artists increased critical coverage in the daily papers. The English-born E.R. Parkhurst (1848–1924) was the first major music and drama critic of the Toronto *Mail* (from 1876 to 1898); he moved to the *Globe* and remained until 1924. By the 1880s both the *Mail* and the *Globe* featured regular 'Music and the Drama' columns, joined by the combined *Mail and Empire* in the 1890s.

In the first decade of the twentieth century critics began to emerge from their anonymity, and gradually reviews were initialled or signed with the critic's full name. They were no longer attributed to 'The Man in the

Front Row' (Toronto *Evening Telegram*, 23 July 1887) or to 'Mack', *Saturday Night*'s perceptive critic in 1895-6, although unsigned and pseudonymous reviews frequently appeared in smaller towns until the 1940s. Even B.K. Sandwell, known to readers of the *Montreal Herald* (1905-14) as 'Munday Knight', continued to write many of his influential *Saturday Night* reviews as 'Lucy Van Gogh' in the 1930s and 1940s. The greater assumption by critics of a public persona reflected their increasing involvement in Canada's theatrical and cultural life. The Earl Grey Musical and Dramatic Competition, for example, boasted such prominent critic-adjudicators as Samuel MORGAN-POWELL, theatre critic for the *Montreal Star*, who served as secretary in 1908; B.K. Sandwell, who adjudicated in 1910; and Hector Charlesworth (1872-1945), who adjudicated in 1910 and 1911.

Sandwell (1876-1954), who went on to found the *Canadian Bookman* in 1919, was a founder of the Canadian Authors' Association in 1921, and concluded his distinguished career not only as drama critic but as editor of *Saturday Night* (1932-51). Charlesworth began writing for *Saturday Night* in 1891, before becoming drama critic for the Toronto *World* and other papers. He rejoined *Saturday Night* in 1910, became its editor in 1926, served as Chairman of the Canadian Radio Broadcasting Commission from 1932 to 1936, and contributed music and drama reviews to *Saturday Night* and the *Globe and Mail* until his death in 1945. Besides reviewing plays, critics began to assume a major role in broader issues of cultural politics. Sandwell protested against American domination of Canadian theatres in his *Montreal Herald* reviews, in public speeches, and in articles, such as his Nov. 1911 *Canadian Magazine* essay, 'The Annexation of Our Stage'. The American-born Lawrence Mason (1882-1939), music and drama critic for the Toronto *Globe* and the *Globe and Mail* from 1924 until his death, travelled widely across Canada to stimulate both the burgeoning amateur theatre movement and indigenous playwriting. He also toured England and Europe in 1926, 1929, and 1931, examining the revival of drama there and possible theatrical models for Canada. In Quebec, critics such as Jean BÉRAUD, theatre critic of *La Presse* from 1931 to 1965, supported efforts to create a French-language national theatre.

Beginning in the 1920s prominent playwrights and directors joined the debate over theatrical developments in Canada. By the end of the decade Merrill DENISON had abandoned hope that Canada would ever develop a national theatre and drama or a distinct national character. In his essay 'Nationalism and Drama', published in the *Yearbook of the Arts in Canada 1928-1929*, he held that Canadian culture was by nature either colonial or American. Others, however, persisted in the belief that artists could forge a unique national theatre and character. In *Creative Theatre* (1929), Roy MITCHELL condemned the crass commercial touring productions from the U.S., calling on Canadians 'to build with native stone, to carve in native woods'. In his introduction to *Six Canadian Plays* (1930), Herman VOADEN called for the creation of 'a Canadian "Art of the Theatre" . . . that will be an expression of the atmosphere and character of our land as definite as our native-born painting and sculpture.' John COULTER—in his 1938 essay 'The Canadian Theatre and the Irish Exemplar', published in *Theatre Arts Monthly*—reaffirmed the central role of the playwright in the imaginative criticism and interpretation of national life and character. 'The most potent of all the theatre's activities,' he declared, 'is the expression of what is characteristic in the life of the community through plays written by, for and about the people of the community.' In Quebec Gratien GÉLINAS expressed a similar philosophy in his essay 'A National and Popular Theatre' (*Amérique français*, Mar. 1949). Robertson DAVIES' *Peterborough Examiner* reviews and other essays from 1940 to the 1980s exemplify the major contribution made to the analysis of Canadian theatrical culture by artists themselves.

Just as playwrights and directors have extended their interests to practical criticism and critical theory, so too have critics contributed to artistic practice. Augustus Bridle (1869-1952), the *Toronto Star* theatre critic from 1923 until his death, founded the Canadian National Exhibition Chorus in 1922 and for the next two decades intermittently experimented with dramatizing choral music. Roly Young, Lawrence Mason's successor as the *Globe and Mail*'s theatre critic, was producer for the Toronto Civic Theatre from 1945 until his death in 1948. In Ottawa Guy BEAULNE acted, directed, and produced for Le Caveau while writing criticism for *Le*

Droit from 1945 to 1948. Beaulne's successor at *Le Droit* since 1951, Edgard Demers, has also written a dozen scripts for children, has acted, and has directed or produced over 150 plays. Herbert WHITTAKER's work as a scene designer in Montreal in the 1930s complemented his critical career at the *Montreal Gazette* (1935-49) and the *Globe and Mail* (until his retirement in 1975). Because of his early involvement with theatre production and his awareness of the difficulties faced by Canadian artists attempting to establish an indigenous theatre, Whittaker generally accentuated whatever positive elements he could find in a performance. Hoping to elevate production standards gradually, he developed a style that presented adverse criticism by shading and implication. In Montreal Jean Béraud and other critics also faced the difficulty of criticizing and yet supporting the emerging indigenous French-language theatre.

Whittaker's critical philosophy was opposite to that of Nathan COHEN, Canada's most influential theatre critic in the 1950s and 1960s. Cohen believed that the critic should not be directly involved in professional theatre, since this was 'likely to alter the critic's point of view and put him on the side of the playmakers'. Throughout his career Cohen sought to establish international critical standards rather than what he called 'the widely elastic measurements of the Canadian theatre'. Critical evaluation, he thought, should be supported by an aesthetic and philosophic point of view, together with an appreciation of the wider social and cultural context from which the play emerged, and he directed pungent criticism not only at Canadian but at U.S. and European touring productions. Cohen described John Gielgud's 1964 pre-Broadway production of *Hamlet* at the O'KEEFE CENTRE, starring Richard Burton, as 'an unmitigated disaster. . . . The performance throughout is a parade of artistic horrors' (*Toronto Star*, 27 Feb. 1964). Nevertheless his high artistic expectations gave Cohen his critical authority.

For the past two decades Canadian theatre critics have followed variations of either Cohen's or Whittaker's philosophy. Urjo KAREDA, Cohen's successor on the *Star* (1972-6), championed the new wave of Canadian dramaturgy emerging from the ALTERNATE THEATREs at the beginning of the 1970s. His subsequent work as literary manager of the STRATFORD FESTIVAL, developing scripts for CBC Radio, and as artistic director of Toronto's TARRAGON THEATRE, continued a pattern of direct involvement by critics or ex-critics in professional theatre. The harsh criticism of Gina Mallet, who followed Kareda at the *Star* (1976-84), alienated many in the artistic community. Frequently as perceptive and pungent as Cohen, Mallet drew public protests from directors and playwrights with her application of Broadway and London West End critical standards. The reviews of her successor, Robert Crew, have followed Whittaker's more genial style of critical commentary. Ray Conlogue, the *Globe and Mail*'s theatre critic since 1977, has been a provocative analyst not only of production values but also of a play's wider artistic and social context.

In Quebec the relations between artists and critics have often been stormy. Beginning in the 1960s, a younger generation of artists and critics—represented most notably by Jean-Claude GERMAIN—frequently clashed with established figures such as Georges-Henri d'Auteuil, critic for the revue *Relations* (1956-78) and Martial Dassylva, the respected critic (1965-83) for Montreal's *La Presse*. Points of contention included the use of *joual* by Michel TREMBLAY and others, and the general importance of contemporary Québécois drama in relation to the classics and the international repertoire. Robert Lévesque's sometimes controversial theatre criticism since 1980 for *Le Devoir* continues to raise the question of whether the theatre critic is an integral organic part, or a detached observer, of the activity he assesses.

Criticism in journals such as the *Canadian Theatre Review* (founded by Don Rubin at York University in 1974) and *Les cahiers de théâtre Jeu* (founded by Gilbert David in Montreal in 1976) has attempted to stimulate an ongoing dialogue among creative artists, critics, and their public. Academic criticism in publications such as *Canadian Drama/L'Art dramatique canadien* and *Theatre History in Canada/Histoire du théâtre au Canada* has examined theatre production and the dramatic text from a literary and historical point of view. *Macleans*, *Saturday Night*, and other magazines have provided important outlets for critics such as Mark Czarnecki and Martin Knelman. Discussion of critical practice and theory occurs in the Canadian Theatre Critics Association, founded in 1980 (it sponsors the annual Nathan Cohen Award for criticism), and the Association québécoise des critiques de théâtre, founded in 1984 (it sponsors the annual Jean Béraud Award).

Unlike theatre practitioners, critics rarely have the opportunity of working outside their home towns for extended periods. Few critics transfer from one paper to another; respected journalists such as Max Wyman and Christopher Dafoe (theatre critics for the *Vancouver Sun* in the 1970s), Martine Corrivault (critic for *Le Soleil* in Quebec City, 1972-87), Brian Brennan (*Calgary Herald*, 1975-88), and Marianne Ackerman (*Montreal Gazette*, 1983-7) have only infrequently been heard in other parts of the country. Paradoxically, while both federal and provincial levels of government often pay foreign critics' travel expenses to major theatre festivals in Canada (particularly to the Stratford and SHAW FESTIVALs), no government programs enable Canadian critics to review productions in diverse regions of the country. The lack of critical forums on television as well as the everchanging arts programming by CBC Radio and Radio-Canada have also hindered the development of major national critical figures. Symbolic of the disappearance of national critical voices was the transfer of Jamie Portman—roving theatre critic for the Southam News Service from 1975— from his base in Calgary to an Ottawa political posting in 1987. (He had reviewed for the *Calgary Herald* from 1960 to 1975.) Portman's coverage of theatre in the Prairies, and of major productions around the country for twenty-five years, provided a national perspective on the great diversity of theatre activity in Canada's various regions.

See Jean Hamelin, *Le Renouveau du théâtre du Canada français* (1962); Yerri Kemph, *Les Trois Coups à Montréal: chroniques dramatiques 1959-1964* (1965); Martial Dassylva, *Un Théâtre en effervescence: Critiques et chroniques 1965-1972* (1975); Wayne E. Edmonstone, *Nathan Cohen: The Making of a Critic* (1977); *Whittaker's Theatre. A Critic Looks at Stages in Canada and Thereabouts 1944-1975* (1985), ed. Ronald Bryden with Boyd Neil; Pierre Lavoie, ed., 'La Critique théâtrale dans tous ses états', *Jeu*, 40 (1986); L.W. Conolly, ed., *Canadian Drama and the Critics* (1987).

ANTON WAGNER

Cronyn, Hume (b. 1911). Born in London, Ont., he studied at McGill University and the American Academy of Dramatic Art in New York. While at McGill he appeared with the MONTREAL REPERTORY THEATRE and the McGill Player's Club. He made his U.S. début in 1931 with the National Theatre Stock Company in Washington, D.C. in *Up Pops the Devil* and his Broadway début in George Abbott's *Three Men on a Horse* in 1935. After a series of Broadway roles in the 1930s, he made his film début in Alfred Hitchcock's *Shadow of a Doubt* in 1943 and in 1944 appeared with his wife Jessica Tandy in *The Seventh Cross*, for which he received an Academy Award nomination. There followed numerous film roles and a remarkable series of stage appearances with Tandy beginning in Jan de Hartog's *The Fourposter* (1951) and including Edward Albee's *A Delicate Balance* (1966); Samuel Beckett's *Happy Days* (1972); D.L. Coburn's *The Gin Game* (1977); and Cronyn's and Susan Cooper's *Foxfire* (STRATFORD FESTIVAL, 1980).

Hume Cronyn as Shylock, Stratford Festival, 1976

The artistic partnership of Cronyn and Tandy, characterized by an intimate rapport based on timing, nuance, and sympathetic anticipation, won them a 1986 Lifetime Achievement in the Theatre Award. Cronyn's crisp, finely delineated style of playing has brought him success not only in the commercial Broadway theatre, but also with the classical repertoire. His appearances at the GUTHRIE Theatre in Minneapolis and at the Stratford Festival (in such roles as Hadrian VII in Peter Luke's play in 1969, and as Shylock and Bottom in 1976) have been notable landmarks in his career, as was his memorable Polonius in John Gielgud's 1964 production of *Hamlet*, for which he received a Tony and a New York Drama Critics Award.　　　　　BRIAN SMITH

Cruel Tears. In the musical tradition of John Gay's *Beggar's Opera*, and indebted to Bertolt Brecht's *Threepenny Opera*, this 'country and western opera' by Ken MITCHELL and Humphrey and the Dumptrucks (a bluegrass group) is based on the plot of Shakespeare's *Othello*. (The title is from Othello's speech in Act 5: 'I must weep,/But they are cruel tears.') The music and characters are adroitly adapted to their Saskatchewan setting, and the result is one of the more popular musical works of the contemporary Canadian theatre.

The play was first performed at the Mendel Art Gallery in Saskatoon by PERSEPHONE THEATRE on 15 Mar. 1975. An instant hit, it was presented at Vancouver's Habitat Festival and Montreal's Cultural Olympics in 1976. In 1977 it had a successful national tour. A radio version was broadcast by the CBC in 1976 and a recording made by Saskatoon's Sunflower Records that same year. Memorable performances were given in these productions by Winston Rekert as Johnny Roychuck, David Stein and Alan Daikun as Jack Deal, Anne Wright as Kathy Jensen, and Janet and Susan Wright as Flora Deal. (The three Wrights are sisters.) The director throughout was Brian Richmond. The text was published by Pile of Bones (Regina) in 1976 and Talonbooks (Vancouver) in 1977.

Mitchell follows the plot of *Othello* closely but not rigidly, presenting a believable prairie setting that includes a conflict between the working-class truck drivers of Saskatoon and their employer Earl Jensen, the rise from trucker to foreman of the Ukrainian hero Johnny Roychuck, his love and marriage to Jensen's daughter, Kathy, and the destruction of their love by an envious fellow driver, the Iago-figure Jack Deal. The music ranges from tender love ballads ('Lady of the Prairie' and 'Die Aria') to blues songs ('Catalogue Blues') to parodies of country and western music ('It's One More for the Women', and 'Race Ballad'). The musical group remains on stage throughout the performance. Ukrainian folk dances enliven the wedding scene at the end of Act 1 and mime is used effectively at several points in the play.　　　JAMES NOONAN

Curtain Call, The. Canada's first magazine in English devoted to theatre and the arts began 9 Nov. 1929 under the aegis of HART HOUSE THEATRE as an eight-page fortnightly October-to-May publication distributed free. In Oct. 1931 it expanded to twelve pages and became a monthly. By 1932 it had added regular LITTLE THEATRE reports from across Canada and even 'A Glimpse at New York Theatres'. With its fifth volume (1933-4), *Curtain Call* severed its Hart House connection and became the 'Official Publication of the DDF', a relationship that lasted until 1940 when the DOMINION DRAMA FESTIVAL was suspended. In 1940 the now-independent 'Voice of the Arts in Canada' sold for 15¢ a copy or an annual subscription of $1.00. The final issue was Nov.-Dec. 1941. Throughout its twelve-year history *Curtain Call* was edited by Mona H. Coxwell, chief of Samuel French's Toronto office and responsible for their Canadian Playwright Series.

　　　　　DAVID GARDNER

Curzon, Sarah Anne (1833-98). Born in Birmingham, Eng., the daughter of an affluent manufacturer, George Phillips Vincent, she received a private education and contributed prose and verse to various family periodicals during her childhood and youth. She married Robert Curzon of Norfolk in 1858 and immigrated with him to Toronto in

Sarah Anne Curzon

1862. Her Canadian literary career includes contributions of verse, essays, and fiction to the *Canadian Monthly*, the *Dominion Illustrated*, *Grip*, *Week*, *Evangelical Churchman*, and the *Canadian Magazine*. She also published women's-suffrage articles in British and U.S. newspapers, and was a founding member in Nov. 1876 of the Toronto Women's Literary Club, which was based on the model of the American Society for the Advancement of Women. After her husband's death in 1878, she supported herself as a freelance journalist. In 1881 she was appointed associate editor of the *Canada Citizen*, the first Canadian prohibitionist paper,

writing a regular column on women's suffrage. She is best known for her verse drama *Laura Secord, the Heroine of 1812* (1887), a sentimental paean to Laura Secord's heroism in the War of 1812. Curzon's only other play, *The Sweet Girl Graduate* (published in the periodical *Grip-Sack* in 1882), deals with the topical issue of women's higher education; it contributed to the passing of an Order-in-Council on 2 Oct. 1884 admitting women to University College, Toronto.

Laura Secord and *The Sweet Girl Graduate* are reprinted in *Women Pioneers*, vol. 2 of *Canada's Lost Plays* (1979), ed. Anton Wagner. ROTA HERZBERG LISTER

D

Dagenais, Pierre (b. 1924). A theatrical prodigy who accelerated the development of Quebec theatre, he was born and raised in Montreal, educated at the Univ. de Montréal, and was only nineteen when he founded L'ÉQUIPE in Jan. 1943 to stage Julian Luchaire's *Altitude 3,200* at the MONUMENT NATIONAL. The critics hailed a major director, an opinion that was verified with the production in Sept. 1943 of *Tessa*, Jean Giraudoux's translation of Margaret Kennedy's English hit, *The Constant Nymph*. Dagenais further enhanced his reputation as 'the Orson Welles of Canada' by playing the lead in Emlyn Williams' thriller *Night Must Fall* (Jan. 1944). In 1945 he staged a passionate production of Shakespeare's *Le Songe d'une nuit d'été* (*A Midsummer Night's Dream*) in the gardens of L'ERMITAGE at the corner of Guy and Sherbrooke before English-speaking audiences in Montreal. His acclaim was now in two languages; but the Quebec government demanded $800 in unpaid amusement taxes, for which Dagenais languished proudly in jail for four days.

He quickly plunged into another crisis, staging in 1946 Jean-Paul Sartre's existentialist view of Hell, *Huis-Clos*, in the Salle du GESÙ, directly under the Jesuit Fathers' church on Bleury St. Despite protests, the

company repeated the performance at the old Windsor Hotel for Sartre, who was in North America on a lecture tour.

In 1946 Dagenais also directed *King Lear* in McGill University's Moyse Hall for the Shakespeare Society, an organization affiliated with the MONTREAL REPERTORY THEATRE. He worked with Charles RITTENHOUSE on text, Herbert WHITTAKER on design, and cast Christopher Ellis, a popular broadcasting personality, as Lear. Other English-language ventures followed, Dagenais playing Marchbanks in Bernard Shaw's *Candida* (opposite Betty Wilson) in 1946 and Richard in Christopher Fry's *The Lady's Not For Burning* (opposite John COLICOS) in 1954, both at the BRAE MANOR THEATRE. He also directed François Mauriac's *The Intruder* (*Asmodée*), with Wilson, Christopher PLUMMER, Adelaide Smith, and Rittenhouse at the Montreal Repertory Theatre in the 1946-7 season.

Dagenais ran L'Équipe until 1947, succeeding critically and financially with Armand Salacrou's *Les Fiancés du Havre* at Salle du Gesù in 1946, but failing with a production of Molière's *L'École des femmes* in 1947. By this time Dagenais was very much in debt, and his production of his own play, *Le Temps de vivre*, at the Monument National in 1947, was savaged by the critics. He was finally

Dagenais

forced to disband his company, having directed all but one of L'Équipe's thirteen productions—the exception being the 1946 successful production of Bernard Shaw's *Le Héros et le soldat* (*Arms and the Man*) in 1946.

While he never produced again, Dagenais wrote other plays, including *Le Diable s'en mêle* (1948), and he directed many plays, including Paul TOUPIN's *Brutus* at the Salle du Gesù in 1951. His voice was familiar as an actor on radio and he developed into a first-rate critic; but English- and French-language Quebec theatre, to which he had contributed notably, henceforth developed without his direct involvement. Dagenais has claimed that his success with English-language theatre harmed him in a separatist-influenced Quebec, a claim echoed by Jean GASCON when he returned from his years at the STRATFORD FESTIVAL. English-Canadian theatre, however, never fully recognized Dagenais's stellar talent.   HERBERT WHITTAKER

Daoust, Julien (1866–1943). Born near Montreal, he played his first role in 1883 beside Blanche de la SABLONNIÈRE in Victor Hugo's *Marie Tudor*; but it was in 1886, under the direction of Edmond Templé, that his career really began. He made his first tour in the U.S. between 1888 and 1890 with the Kate Claxton company, and spent a longer period there between 1894 and 1898 in New York and New Jersey. When he returned to Montreal he directed a production of Edmond Rostand's *Cyrano de Bergerac* at the MONUMENT NATIONAL. Determined to promote the development of a Canadian theatre, in 1900 he founded, with two friends, the THÉÂTRE NATIONAL, 'a theatre where Canadian talent will be able to flourish'. With Germain Beaulieu he wrote his first play in 1901, *La Passion*; said to have been inspired by the Oberammergau passion play, it was an enormous success. Subsequently Daoust flourished as a playwright of religious melodramas, including *Le Chemin des larmes*, *Le Triomphe de la croix*, and especially *La Conscience d'un prêtre* (a drama that inspired Alfred Hitchcock's film *I Confess*). He also wrote several revues, the best known of which, *La Belle Montréalaise*, featured personalities whose names would later become celebrated: Tizoune (Olivier GUIMOND) and La Poune (Rose Ouellette). Between 1900 and 1925

Julien Daoust dans Napoléon

Julien Daoust as Napoléon in Gaston Arman de Caillavet's and Robert de Flers's Le Roi de Rome, *Théâtre Nationoscope, Montreal, 1912*

Daoust was prominent as a manager, director, and actor throughout Quebec, but his works were seldom performed.

Except for *Le Triomphe de la croix* (first performed in 1904 at the Monument National and published in 1928), all Daoust's works (about twenty-seven plays) remain unpublished and a number have been lost. The surviving manuscripts are in the Bibliothèque Nationale du Québec.

See Jean-Cléo Godin, 'Julien Daoust, dramaturge, 1866–1943', *Theatre History in Canada*, 4 (1983); and 'Une Belle Montréalaise en 1913', *Revue d'Histoire littéraire du Québec et du Canada français*, 5 (1983).

JEAN CLÉO GODIN

David, Laurent-Olivier (1824–1926). Born in Sault à Récollet, Que., and educated as a lawyer, he was called to the Bar of Lower Canada in 1864 and took up practice in Montreal. During the 1870s he was an active journalist, and the co-founder and co-editor of three nationalist newspapers. Between 1877 and 1924 he wrote thirteen books in which he sought primarily to glorify French-Canadian heroes, both past and present. He nonetheless also supported Sir Wilfrid Laurier's policies of 'bonne entente' between French- and English-Canadians. In 1886 David was elected for one term as the Montreal East representative to the Legislative Assembly and in 1903 he was appointed to the Canadian Senate. He was president of the Société St-Jean-Baptiste, 1887–8.

David's only play, *Le Drapeau de Carillon*, is a nationalist domestic drama in five acts and two tableaux. It is his prescription for French-Canadian nationalism in the twentieth century and represents a synthesis of his political writings. Its initial performance in Dec. 1901, and publication in 1902, was part of the general nationalist program, 'Les Soirées de famille', organized by the Société St-Jean-Baptiste in Montreal. As part of the cultural and academic activities at the MONUMENT NATIONAL, *Le Drapeau* complemented the lectures in French-Canadian history that were offered that week. It was revived many times throughout the province until 1931. A second revised edition of the play (1923) expressed much more emphatically David's preference for closer relations with Britain. David framed his domestic drama with two decisive battles in French-Canadian history: the Battle of Carillon, otherwise known as Ticonderoga, and the Battle of St Foy. Two military heroes—the nationalist French-Canadian Capt. de Sérigny and the British Capt. Murray (modelled, says David in the first edition of the play, on General James Murray, first British governor of Quebec)—are suitors to sisters Alice and Blanche Dumas. Alice's relationship with de Sérigny symbolizes the potential for an independent French-Canadian state; on the other hand, Blanche's bond with Murray emphasizes the need to re-evaluate national animosities. When de Sérigny dies (shot, significantly, by a cowardly French merchant, his rival), the only viable union is that between Blanche and Murray.

Such a positive portrayal of a member of the enemy forces was unprecedented on the French-Canadian stage; David's allegiance to the dominance of French Canada by the British Empire was unequivocal. NATALIE REWA

Davies, Robertson (b. 1913). Born in Thamesville, Ont., to Florence and William Rupert Davies, editor, publisher, and, later, Senator (they moved to Renfrew in 1919 and to Kingston in 1926), Davies was educated at Upper Canada College, Queen's Univ., and Oxford Univ. (B.Litt., 1938). His Oxford thesis became his first book, *Shakespeare's Boy Actors* (1939). Davies acted in England briefly, notably at the Old Vic under Tyrone GUTHRIE, then returned to Canada in 1940 with his wife, Brenda Mathews, to begin a journalistic career. He joined the *Peterborough Examiner* in 1942, becoming editor in 1946. In 1960 he commenced teaching English and dramatic literature at the Univ. of Toronto, where from 1961 to 1981 he was the first Master of Massey College. He began publishing plays in 1949, novels in 1951. In addition to playwriting, Davies' contributions to Canadian theatre include much criticism, directing, and long service as a governor of the DOMINION DRAMA FESTIVAL and the STRATFORD FESTIVAL. In the 1970s and 1980s Davies' reputation as a playwright was eclipsed by his international reputation as a novelist. He is the recipient of many honorary degrees and literary prizes and is a Fellow of the Royal Society of Canada, a Companion of the Order of Canada, and the first Canadian honorary member of the American Academy and Institute of Arts and Letters.

Davies has had five one-act plays, two masques, a play for television, and nine full-length plays published or produced. All are comedies—ranging from romantic to satiric, from sombre to farcical—that wage battles against barriers to human fulfilment and celebrate human potential. His protagonists overcome their limitations by asserting their right to freedom from convention or by accepting some aspect of themselves that they had formerly feared.

Davies favours a theatre of grandeur, of heightened effects—he likes ritual and melodrama and seeks to avoid the constraints of realism. He relates theatre to dreams: its proper goal is not verisimilitude but psycho-

Davies

logical truth. Two of his earliest full-length plays, *The King Who Could Not Dream* (written in 1944, never published or produced) and *King Phoenix* (written in 1947, first performed in 1950 by the North Toronto Theatre Guild, published in 1972) are in the nature of myth or fairy-tale; another, *Benoni* (written in 1945, produced as *A Jig for the Gypsy* by Toronto's CREST THEATRE in 1954, and published the same year), features a gypsy and a conjurer in a romantic north Wales setting. When these failed to find a place on the London stage, Davies began to write simpler fare for the Canadian amateur theatre. His first one-act play was *Hope Deferred* (produced at the MONTREAL REPERTORY THEATRE in 1948, published in 1949), about the frustration of Count Frontenac's attempt to bring culture to seventeenth-century Quebec with a production of Molière's *Tartuffe*. Another on Canadian cultural poverty followed: *Overlaid*, probably the most popular of all Davies' plays, opposes an opera-loving farmer's yearning for a richer life and his middle-aged daughter's determined conventional respectability. It was first performed by the Ottawa Drama League in 1947 and published in 1948. *Eros at Breakfast* (1949) is

a fantasy about a young man afflicted with first love. *Overlaid* and *Eros at Breakfast* won the Ottawa Drama League's annual playwriting competition in 1947 and 1948 respectively, and *Eros* won the prize for best Canadian play in the 1948 Dominion Drama Festival. *The Voice of the People* (1949) is a farce about an opinionated, cocksure, uninformed writer of a letter-to-the-editor. Davies directed its 1950 première by the Peterborough Little Theatre. *At the Gates of the Righteous* (1949) depicts a gang of outlaws in 1860 that converts to respectability because their dubious values and goals are actually better accommodated by a conventional life. These five one-act plays—with which Davies first emerged as a noteworthy playwright—were published in *Eros at Breakfast and Other Plays* (1949).

Two full-length plays on Canadian cultural poverty followed, *Fortune, My Foe* (1949) and *AT MY HEART'S CORE* (1950). In the contemporary *Fortune*, two Canadian professors of literature, and an immigrant who hopes to offer Canadians his exquisite puppetry, battle the middle-class philistines who represent the Canadian national character. It was written for the Arthur Sutherland INTERNATIONAL

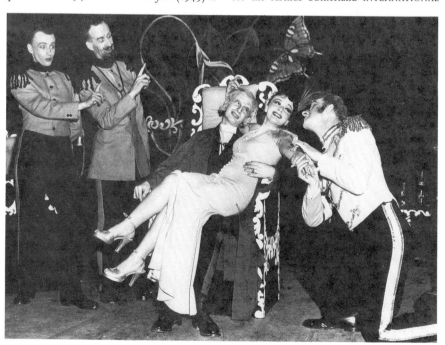

Robertson Davies' Eros at Breakfast, Ottawa Drama League, 1949, with (l. to r) Robert Rose, Michael Mieklejohn, Ian Fellows, Amelia Hall, Carl Lochnan

PLAYERS, whose summer-stock production in Kingston, directed by Davies in 1948, won rave reviews. A production by the Ottawa Drama League won the Dominion Drama Festival's top awards for Canadian drama in 1949. In the next twenty years it received over 100 productions. *At My Heart's Core*, written for Peterborough's 1950 centennial celebrations, depicts settlers whose cultural aspirations are sacrificed to the struggle for survival.

Davies' association with Donald and Murray DAVIS's Crest Theatre in Toronto made the mid-fifties the peak of his playwriting career. They produced *A Jig for the Gypsy* in 1954, and in 1955 a new play, *Hunting Stuart* (1972). Its protagonist, Ben Stuart, is a pleasant, colourless civil servant whose life is directed by his wife Lilian's aggressively middle-class aspirations and complicated by his friction with his dear, eccentric Aunt Clemmie. The main action is triggered by the arrival of two scientists who declare that Stuart is directly descended from Bonnie Prince Charlie, pretender to the throne of England. A powder transforms Ben into his ancestor and Lilian struggles comically to come to terms with the dominant, sensual man who is and is not her husband. Finally Ben, back to himself but fully aware of what has happened and emboldened by his newly discovered depths, uncharacteristically takes charge. The theme of the unfulfilled potential of the personality is typical of Davies' work, as are the opposing characters of the bizarre but appealing Clemmie and the priggish, utterly bourgeois Lilian. Also characteristic of Davies' writing are the magic of Stuart's transformation, a metaphor for the unrealized possibilities, and the satire of conventional Canadian values.

Davies' next play for the Crest was *General Confession* (1972), Davies' favourite and his most Jungian. Casanova, the central character, raises three spirits that prove to be facets of his own personality. In Jungian terms, which Davies does not use, they are Casanova's Shadow, his Anima, and his Wise Old Man. What begins as magic becomes the world of a man's mind, and the progress of the play, with its dreamlike flashbacks to episodes in Casanova's earlier life, is his psychic struggle to come to terms with himself. (*General Confession* was published with *Hunting Stuart* and *King Phoenix* in *Hunting Stuart and Other Plays* in 1972.) The play was

never produced, and another disappointment followed in 1960 with the failure on Broadway of *Love and Libel* (published as *Leaven of Malice*, 1981), Davies' adaptation of his novel *Leaven of Malice* (1954), which Tyrone Guthrie directed for the New York Theatre Guild. *A Masque of Mr. Punch* (1963), written for performance in 1962 by the boys of Upper Canada College, reflects Davies' disenchantment with theatre; in showing Punch's inability to find a place in contemporary Canada, it openly declared Davies' feeling that the theatrical vitality he liked was unfashionable. (Samuel Beckett and Tennessee Williams are both satirized in *Mr. Punch*.) This funny but bitter masque contrasts with the exquisite, lighthearted romp, *A Masque of Aesop* (1952), that Davies had written in 1952 for his old school.

Davies showed another burst of dramatic creativity in the mid-seventies, when he was riding the crest of success that followed the publication of his novels *Fifth Business* (1970) and *The Manticore* (1972) and when the national identity crisis created a greater demand for Canadian work. He wrote *Brothers in the Black Art* (1981), a drama about three friends in the printing trade at the turn of the century, broadcast by CBC television in 1974. *Question Time* (1975), his first entirely new full-length play in nearly twenty years, combined Davies' Jungian theme of the search for the self with the search for Canadian identity. Its protagonist is a prime minister who struggles for life after a plane crash in the Arctic. The struggle is unconscious; the question is whether his life is worth living. The multifold activity on the stage can be seen as his internal conflict made visible and audible. The key to his regaining consciousness is his acceptance of the primacy of his individual needs, which he had submerged in pursuit of the public good. The play is visually spectacular, written with an eye to the lavish 1975 production Davies knew the ST LAWRENCE CENTRE would give it. It may be considered the culmination of Davies' dramatic work, uniting themes and techniques of the earlier plays in a stunningly original piece of theatre. One more play followed, *Pontiac and the Green Man* (unpublished), written for and performed during the Univ. of Toronto's sesquicentennial celebration in 1975. Incorporating scenes from an eighteenth-century play about Canada into a musical play about the court-martial of its author, Major Robert Rogers, it explores heroism and drama as means of expressing an original outlook. It is an ingenious but not entirely successful attempt to integrate a new play with the old one.

Davies' dramatic strengths are witty dialogue, warm, humorous characterization, and thematic depth. In the 1970s and 1980s, however, when Canadian theatre blossomed fully, his plays seemed out of step with the times—optimistic, talky, and inclined towards bold effects in contrast to the bleak, understated drama deriving from Pinter and Beckett. But Davies' dramatic contribution to mid-century Canadian theatre surpassed that of any other playwright, and his dramatic quest for spiritual enrichment seems unlikely to go permanently out of date.

See Susan Stone-Blackburn, *Robertson Davies, Playwright* (1985); and *Canadian Drama*'s special Davies issue (vol. 7, no. 2, 1981), which contains Davies' adaptation of *Leaven of Malice*.   SUSAN STONE-BLACKBURN

Davin, Nicholas Flood (1843-1901). Born in County Limerick, Ireland, he trained as a lawyer at London's Middle Temple (1865-8) and worked as a journalist before immigrating to Canada in 1872. He first joined the *Globe* and, later, the *Mail*. His creditable but losing election campaign for the Conservatives in Haldimand in 1878 gained him a federal commission post, the first of several. In 1882 he settled in Saskatchewan, where he founded the *Regina Leader* (1 Mar. 1883) and was elected Conservative MP (Assiniboia West, 1887-1900). His principles were often at odds with party policy: he fought for the West, for women's rights, more support for artists, and urged the establishment of a national literature. He fathered two children out of wedlock with proto-feminist, poet, and playwright Kate Simpson-Hayes, married Eliza Jane Reid (1895), and following the sale of the *Leader* (1895) and his election defeat (1900), he wrote for the Toronto *Star* and the *West*. He met death by suicide.

Active in local amateur theatre, a poet and historian, Davin also wrote one play, *The Fair Grit; or, The Advantages of Coalition; a Farce* (1876). A short but entertaining and forceful attack on Canadian politics, the play involves the son of a Tory MP and the daughter of a Grit senator who fall in love but are opposed by their fathers—until the two politicians see opportunities for political advantage from the situation. Although Davin's Conservatism is evident in his satire of Prime Minister Alexander MacKenzie, the play's intense condemnation of political opportunism, patronage, and abuse of public office is non-partisan. No performance record of the play exists before the public reading by NDWT in 1978. A musical adaptation, *Love and Politics*, by Mavor MOORE—co-produced by Toronto Arts Productions and St Catharines' Press Theatre at Brock University—premièred in Oct. 1979. The play was reprinted in *Canada's Lost Plays*, vol. 1 (1978), edited by Anton Wagner and Richard Plant. An anonymously published satire about Davin, 'The Tribulations of N.F.D.', appeared in *Grip* (8 Mar. 1879).

Davin is the subject of Ken MITCHELL's play *Davin: The Politician* (1979). See C.B. Koester, *Mr. Davin M.P.* (1980).
                                    RICHARD PLANT

Davis, Donald (b. 1928). Born in Newmarket, Ont., he was educated at the Univ. of Toronto (BA, 1950). While there, he and his brother Murray appeared in 1947 in Robert GILL's first HART HOUSE THEATRE production: Shaw's *Saint Joan*, starring Charmion KING. Donald Davis made his professional début in 1947 as Henry Bevan in Rudolph Besier's *The Barretts of Wimpole Street* in summer theatre at the Woodstock Playhouse, N.Y. In 1948 the Murray brothers founded the Straw Hat Players in Muskoka, Ont. (see SUMMER STOCK); Donald Davis remained with the Players as co-artistic director until 1955. Between 1950 and 1953 he acted with the Glasgow Citizens' Theatre and the Bristol Old Vic. He made his STRATFORD FESTIVAL début as Tiresias in Tyrone GUTHRIE's 1954 *Oedipus Rex*, returning to the Festival in 1955, 1956, 1969, and 1970.

In 1953 Donald Davis and his brother Murray founded the CREST THEATRE, where Donald Davis's many roles included Thomas à Becket in T.S. Eliot's *Murder in the Cathedral* (in 1954); Jack the Skinner in Robertson DAVIES' *A Jig for the Gypsy* (1954); Malvolio in Shakespeare's *Twelfth Night* and Mr Stuart in Robertson Davies' *Hunting Stuart* (both in 1955); and Creon in Anouilh's *Antigone* and Vershinnin in Chekhov's *Three Sisters* (both in 1956). In 1957 he appeared in the world première of *The Glass Cage*, written by J.B. Priestley for the Davis brothers and their sister Barbara CHILCOTT. Tall, dark, and

Amelia Hall and Donald Davis in William Inge's *Come Back, Little Sheba*, Crest Theatre, Toronto, 1956

for the Gypsy, 1973), the Neptune (Gordon PINSENT's *John and the Missus*, 1976), the SHAW FESTIVAL (*The Royal Family*, 1972), Edmonton's CITADEL (James Goldman's *The Lion in Winter*, 1982) and the NATIONAL ARTS CENTRE (August Strindberg's *The Father*, 1978). In 1983 Davis returned to New York in an Alan Schneider production of *Beckett Plays*. The company was invited to the Edinburgh Festival and the Royal Court Theatre, London, and then embarked on a European tour. One of the most distinguished Canadian actors of his generation, Davis is active in Toronto theatre, appearing most recently in Michel TREMBLAY's *Bonjour, là, Bonjour* at CENTRESTAGE in 1986 and in Ian Weir's *The Idler* at THEATRE PLUS in 1988.   HERBERT WHITTAKER

Davis, Murray (b. 1924). Born in Newmarket, Ont., he served as a lieutenant in the RCNVR (1942-5) before attending the Univ. of Toronto (BA, 1948). He made his professional début in 1947 in summer theatre at the Woodstock Playhouse, N.Y. He was co-founder (with his brother Donald DAVIS) of the Straw Hat Players, Muskoka, Ont., in 1948, and co-artistic director until 1955. He also co-founded (again with his brother) the CREST THEATRE in Toronto; in its opening production in Jan. 1954 of Gordon Daviot's *Richard of Bordeaux* he assumed the title role. (He was co-artistic director until 1959 and artistic director from 1960 to 1966.) A polished actor, he appeared in 1952 in London's West End in William Inge's *Come Back, Little Sheba*, Guy Morgan's and Edward Sammis's *Albert, R.N.*, and other plays. He also played opposite Douglas CAMPBELL in the Crest's 1955 production of Bridget Boland's *The Prisoner*, was Iago in its 1955 *Othello*, and was also in *The Glass Cage* (in 1957), a play written by J.B. Priestley expressly for the Davis brothers and their sister Barbara CHILCOTT.

with a deep baritone voice, he usually played older character roles. Throughout the 1950s and 1960s he also appeared in many radio and television roles on the CBC and in the U.S.

In 1960 Davis played off-Broadway in Samuel Beckett's *Krapp's Last Tape*, directed by Alan Schneider, beginning a long identification with both Schneider and North American premières of Beckett's work. In the U.S. he has acted at New York's City Center, the Provincetown Playhouse, the American Shakespeare Festival, New York's Mermaid Theatre, Chicago's Goodman Theatre, and elswhere in parts ranging from Essex (opposite Judith Anderson) in Maxwell Anderson's *Elizabeth the Queen* to Robert Frost (in *An Evening of Frost*) and in plays as different as Shakespeare's *Troilus and Cressida* and Edward Albee's *Who's Afraid of Virginia Woolf?* Returning to Canada in 1971, Davis played many of the regional theatres—at FESTIVAL LENNOXVILLE in George RYGA's *Captives of the Faceless Drummer* in 1972, in the 1974 Toronto Arts Production of Solomon Ansky's *The Dybbuk*, in Theatre London's 1977 production of Molière's *School for Wives*, and in NEPTUNE THEATRE's 1983 production of George WALKER's *Filthy Rich*.

Davis began directing with the Straw Hat Players, and has subsequently directed at Festival Lennoxville (Robertson Davies' *A Jig*

Davis directed many productions at the Crest, including Agatha Christie's *The Mousetrap* (in 1958), Thornton Wilder's *The Matchmaker* (1959), Leslie Stevens' *The Marriage Go-Round* (1961), Arnold Wesker's *Roots* and *Roar Like a Dove* (1962), Shaw's *Arms and the Man* (1963), Garson Kanin's *Born Yesterday* (1963), Rolf Hochhuth's *The Deputy* (1964), Edward Albee's *Tiny Alice* (1965), Friedrich Dürrenmatt's *The Physicists*

Davis

(1965), and Ibsen's *Hedda Gabler* (1966), the Crest's last production.

Following the closing of the Crest, Murray Davis taught for three years at the NATIONAL THEATRE SCHOOL, Montreal. In 1969 he gave up the theatre and took up cattle-raising in Ontario. HERBERT WHITTAKER

Davis, Phyllis (b. 1891). Raised in Victoria and Vancouver, B.C., she starred in *Everykid*, a 1913 musical farce by Reginald Hincks and E.A.P. Hobday. She sang and danced in the *Follies of 1915* in Vancouver (15 Feb.-27 Mar.) and Victoria (29-31 Mar.). In New York she performed two dances in *Pom-Pom* at the George M. Cohan Theatre, Feb.-May 1916. After moving to England she married D'Oyly Rochfort in July 1916. She sang in and contributed the 'Powderpuff' sketch to *Hello Canada!*, a charity revue by Canadian artists (including Muriel Dunsmuir, Bessie Dunsmuir Hope, Margaret BANNERMAN, and Martha ALLAN) at His Majesty's Theatre, London, 11 May 1917 and at the Pavilion, Bexhill, 14 July 1917. By 1919 she was back in Victoria, where she performed in Reginald Hincks's *The Fool in the Family*, George H. Broadhurst's *What Happened to Jones*, and Cecil Clay's *The Pantomime Rehearsal* before leaving the stage for private life.
  ROBERT G. LAWRENCE

Day, Marie (b. 1933). Born in Toronto, she studied drawing and painting at the Ontario College of Art, where the quality of her painting suggested a career in theatre. Following a period of work at England's Mermaid Theatre, she returned to Canada in 1954 to be a design assistant to Tanya MOISEI-WITSCH at the STRATFORD FESTIVAL. She helped Jacqueline Cundall to create the famous masks for the Tyrone GUTHRIE and Moiseiwitsch production of *Oedipus Rex* in 1955. This led to her design of one of the first musical offerings at the Festival, Benjamin Britten's opera *The Rape of Lucretia* in 1956 (for which she won a Guthrie award), and to her co-design with Moiseiwitsch of *King Henry IV, Part I* in 1958; this work made her the first Canadian to design for the Festival stage. She was also resident designer at the CREST THEATRE for many years, her last production being J. B. Priestley's *The Glass Cage* in 1957.

Day's major achievements as a designer have been for the Canadian Opera Company in such productions as *La Bohème*, *Carousel*, and *Macbeth*. In collaboration with her husband Murray LAUFER she designed stunning costumes for the 1967 and 1973 première productions by the COC of *Louis Riel* by Harry Somers, Mavor MOORE, and Jacques LANGUIRAND and *Heloise and Abelard* by Eugene Benson and Charles Wilson. Her ability as a painter and knowledge of the great painters have always had a profound influence on her designs. She worked on Robertson DAVIES' *Love and Libel*, which was produced in Toronto and New York in 1960, and created costumes for the more enduring ANNE OF GREEN GABLES, first produced by the CHARLOTTETOWN FESTIVAL in 1965. It toured to New York, Japan, and London, and is still in the Festival's repertory. Her designs for *Major Barbara* at the 1978 SHAW FESTIVAL was her first assignment there. MARTHA MANN

Demers, Michel (b. 1949). Born in Quebec city, he was educated at the Univ. of Montreal, where (with Gilbert David) he co-founded the Centre d'essai des auteurs dramatiques and began his career as a set and costume designer—designing, for example, the set for Yves SAUVAGEAU's *Wouf wouf!* (produced at the university in 1971). He remained director of the Centre d'essai until 1979, also studying design at the NATIONAL THEATRE SCHOOL (until 1975).

Demers quickly made a reputation with many ALTERNATE THEATREs for whom he created imaginative, practical, and affordable sets. He was also soon in demand in established theatres, collaborating with director Claude Maher on plays such as *Inès Pérée et Inat Tendu* by Réjean DUCHARME in 1976, *Des Frites, des frites, des frites* (*Chips with Everything*) by Arnold Wesker in 1978, *Le Grand Poucet* by Jean BARBEAU in 1979, and *L'Histoire du soldat* by Igor Stravinsky in 1981.

Influenced by comic strips, movies, and television, Demers favours scenery that, like pop art, overflows with references to popular culture. Some of the most notable of his more than one hundred designs are those for Michel GARNEAU's *Les Voyagements* in 1975, Brecht's *Dans la jungle des villes* (*In the Jungle of Cities*) in 1981, Claude Poissant's *Passer la nuit* in 1983, Michel TREMBLAY's *À TOI, POUR TOUJOURS, TA MARIE-LOU* in 1984, *Camille C.* by Jocelyne Beaulieu and René Richard Cyr in 1984, and *Le Seigneur des Anneaux*, a giant PUPPET show adapted from J.R.R.

Tolkien's *Lord of the Rings*, produced by the Théâtre Sans Fil in 1985.   GILBERT DAVID

Denison, Merrill (1893-1975). Born in Detroit, he was educated at Toronto's Jarvis Collegiate Institute and the Univ. of Toronto. He studied architecture at the Univ. of Pennsylvania, Columbia Univ., and the American Army Art School, an adjunct of the École des Beaux Arts in Paris. After First World War service and further study of architecture in Paris, he became an architectural draftsman (1919-21) in Boston and New York. In 1921 Roy MITCHELL invited him to HART HOUSE THEATRE at the Univ. of Toronto as stage designer and art director. In 1932 Denison was invited to New York to work for CBS and NBC as a radio-drama specialist. For the next twenty-two years in New York he wrote stage plays, American and Canadian historical radio plays, corporate histories and biographies, and articles on conservation and forestry. After the death of his first wife, Jesse Muriel Goggin, he returned to Canada permanently in 1954, living in Montreal and on his estate, Bon Echo, in eastern Ontario with his second wife, Elizabeth Andrews, whom he married in 1957.

Denison was a master of the one-act play. His early plays are sharply defined vignettes of Canadian life, notably the four plays (the first three are one-act plays) included in *The Unheroic North: Four Canadian Plays* (1923): *Brothers in Arms, The Weather Breeder, From Their Own Place,* and MARSH HAY. *Brothers in Arms,* his first play, was performed at Hart House Theatre in 1921 and became Denison's most frequently produced play (over 1,500 performances by 1971). Its fiftieth-anniversary production was directed by Robert CHRISTIE at Hart House Theatre. Set in the Ontario backwoods, it is a clever and amusing satiric dialogue between a pompous Canadian major and an uneducated, likeable backwoodsman on attitudes towards war, industry, and responsibility. The major's wife is a foil, satirizing the popular viewpoint of women as being stupid and dependent. *The Weather Breeder,* also set in the Ontario backwoods, depicts a surly backwoods farmer and his daughter who plans to marry a young helper if the grain crop is successfully brought to market. The old farmer claims to be able to predict the weather. When the storm he predicts does not take place, he is thoroughly disgruntled. *From Their Own Place,* first produced by the ARTS AND LETTERS CLUB, Toronto, in 1922, is a satire on backwoods trappers attempting to hoodwink a young couple from Toronto. The tables are turned when the trappers are trapped by the young man's ingenuity. The dialogue is fast-moving, the plot full of suspense, and the climax witty and just, with each character getting his due reward. *Marsh Hay,* in four acts, is Denison's most serious drama—a powerful, naturalistic, social-problem play revealing the playwright's awareness of the dark side of the backwoods society he explores. The title of the collection, *The Unheroic North,* indi-

Merrill Denison's The Weather Breeder, *Hart House Theatre, Toronto, 1924*

Denison

cates Denison's wish to debunk contemporary attempts to idealize Canada's North.

In addition to these plays of the Canadian backwoods, Denison wrote *Contract* (unpublished), set in an upper-class drawing-room in Toronto. It is a good-natured comedy about a young woman who is bored by stock-exchange talk until she meets and marries a wealthy copper- and gold-miner from the North. Directed by Carroll AIKINS at Hart House Theatre in 1929, *Contract* was an immediate success.

Although neither profound nor subtle in theme, nor inventive in dramatic techniques, Denison's plays depict and interpret the Canadian scene in a critical and objective manner and with dramatic flair.

Denison was also a successful and prolific writer for radio. Under the direction of Tyrone GUTHRIE 'The Romance of Canada' series, commissioned in 1929 by the Canadian National Railways, Montreal, was broadcast in 1931-2 through CNRM over a chain of thirteen national and three associated stations. Six of these plays were subsequently published in 1931 as *Henry Hudson and Other Plays*: *Henry Hudson*, *Pierre Radisson*, *Montcalm*, *Seven Oaks*, *Laura Secord*, and *Alexander Mackenzie*. They reveal not only a solid knowledge of radio techniques, but also a considerable aptitude for presenting history in a fresh and colourful manner.

In New York Denison was commissioned to write a similar American series. He created 'Great Moments in History' (1932-3), forty weeks of half-hour programs on important historical events. He also wrote 'America's Hour' (1936) for CBS, a 13-week program that eventually became the highly acclaimed 'Cavalcade of America'. Other American historical radio programs include 'Democracy in Action' (1938-9), a CBS series produced in conjunction with the U.S. Office of Education; 'America in Action' (1941), twelve one-act plays on freedom and democracy; *The US vs Susan B. Anthony* (1941), a play; and 'The Forum of Liberty', a 1935 CBS 20-week series giving contemporary American leaders a chance to speak on air.

The Denison archives are housed at Queen's Univ. See also Dick MacDonald, *Mugwump Canadian: The Merrill Denison Story* (1973).   GERALDINE ANTHONY

Deschamps, Yvon (b. 1935). Quebec's most popular monologuist was born and grew up in the working-class district of St Henri in Montreal. At sixteen he left school and worked at odd jobs for Radio Canada from 1951 to 1958. From 1959 to 1964 he worked in television and film, also playing in sketches with, among others, Clémence Desrochers. Deschamps became an overnight celebrity in the 1968 Robert Charlebois/Louise Forestier production *L'Osstidcho*, revived in 1969 at the PLACE DES ARTS with additional monologues by Deschamps.

Deschamps toured in nine productions of his own monologues over the next fifteen years, averaging some 250 performances a year. His 1981-2 show *C'est tout seul qu'on est l'plus nombreux* had an unprecedented run of nearly four months at the Place des Arts. Since completing *Un Voyage dans le temps* (in 1984) he has reduced his stage appearances but has continued his involvement in radio and television. A strong Quebec nationalist, he has been concerned with social issues and has set up the Yvon Deschamps' Foundation for the handicapped.

His fame as an entertainer rests on close rapport with his audiences, who have seen in his characters and themes a reflection, albeit exaggerated, of themselves and their society. His earliest creation—the naïve little working man of 'Les Unions qu'ossa donne?' (1968) who is constantly taken advantage of by his boss and by his betters, and who is unaware of his pathetic situation at work and at home, yet waits for something better—was immediately successful. When Deschamps found his scope limited by the character he had created, he developed another, closely akin to the first: a neurotic, whose phobias were even greater. Increased use of music links the themes of these monologues, the humour is fast-paced, the cynicism apparent. The audience is very much his accomplice. Deschamps' satires and parodies have also sometimes aroused controversy ('Nigger black', 1968, 'L'Intolérance', 1971, 'La Libération de la femme', 1973).

When Deschamps appeared at the Théâtre de la Ville in Paris in Mar. 1983, critics found his comic interpretations bewildering and wordy. His form of humour, which is so closely allied with the Canadian or Quebec identity, may not be exportable, but his role as a provocative moralist and comic satirist of an era and a society has secured for him an unequalled position in the history of Quebec entertainment.

Most of Deschamps' texts have been published in *Monologues* (1973) and *Six Ans d'monologues* (1981).

See Jean-V. Dufresne, *Yvon Deschamps* (1971); E.G. Rinfret, *Le Théâtre canadien d'expression française*, I (1975); and L. Mailhot and D.-M. Montpetit, *Monologues québécois 1890-1980* (1980).   BARBARA McEWEN

Deverell, Rex (b. 1941). Born in Toronto, he grew up in Orillia, Ont., where both the theatre and the church captured his interest. After studies at McMaster Univ. and the Union Theological Seminary, New York, he became pastor of a Baptist church in St Thomas, Ont., where he combined church duties with playwriting, finally settling on the latter after two of his children's plays were professionally produced in 1971 and 1972. Associated with the GLOBE THEATRE, Regina, since 1972, he became its playwright-in-residence in 1975.

Deverell's adult plays, all first produced by the Globe Theatre, are overtly political, especially his docu-dramas. This group includes *Medicare!* (1981), produced in 1980, a historical piece about a crisis in health services in Saskatchewan, and *Black Powder: Estevan 1931* (1982), produced in 1981, a re-creation of the 1931 Estevan riots in which three union men were killed. Deverell stays close to historical fact in these works, yet manages to combine information with a sense of compassion for the working classes.

Deverell's other adult plays are different in kind but similar in their concern for history and for the struggles of the individual to survive physically and spiritually in a hostile world. Some combine his religious commitment with his interest in history: for example, *Righteousness* (1983), produced in 1983, about St Augustine, and *Beyond Batoche* (1985), produced in 1985, about Louis Riel. Plays with contemporary settings, like *Drift* (1981), produced in 1980, sometimes take up problems of moral ambiguity similar to those in the history plays. Deverell's most frequently produced adult play, *Boiler Room Suite* (1978), which premièred in 1977, concerns two down-and-out alcoholics—a failed poet who may be the devil or God and a failed actress—taking refuge in the basement of a vacant hotel and exercising their powers of imagination to revise their world. Humanitarian and political concerns blend with suggestions about the power, perhaps illusory, of art—an idea that has been growing in Deverell's most recent plays.

Most of his children's plays combine fantasy and didacticism: *Shortshrift* (1973), produced by the Globe Theatre for Youth on a school tour in 1972, shows how good a small town can be and how people can be made happy by being made to feel important; *Sarah's Play* (1975), produced by the Globe in 1974, and *You Want Me to be Grown Up, Don't I?* (1979), produced by the Globe Theatre for Youth in 1978, deal with the emotional survival of children. *Underground Lake* (1977), produced by the Globe in 1975, deplores prejudice. Other plays deal with such topics as pollution and war.

Springing from strong local and autobiographical roots, Deverell's plays address universal moral questions, sometimes in the tones of the teacher or preacher, sometimes in the authentic voice of the dramatist. His work includes musicals and scripts for both radio and television.

See *Canadian Children's Literature*, 8 and 9 (1977); R. Wallace and C. Zimmerman, eds., *The Work* (1982).   ANN MESSENGER

Deyglun, Henry (1903-71). Born in Paris to a family of the lesser nobility (barons of Aiglun) that included writers and artists, he moved with his family to Marseilles, where he met Edmond Rostand and became a student of Paul Mounet. Deeply affected by the First World War, in which several of his uncles and cousins were killed, he became extremely patriotic and enlisted in the navy at the age of sixteen. Six months later the war ended and Deyglun found himself in the Latin Quarter of Paris in the company of Paul Fort, Jules Romains, and other writers and artists. He obtained employment at Jacques Copeau's Le Vieux-Colombier, which made him decide on a career in the theatre, despite his father's opposition. There he met Charles Dullin and Gaston Baty, but he worked for Copeau—a master he would judge harshly as 'unbelievably biased', and with whom he would soon break. In fact, Deyglun later said that it was to escape Copeau's influence and 'tyranny' that he decided to leave France at the age of eighteen.

It was happenstance that led him to Montreal. With two of his friends he boarded a cargo ship bound for Bogota, but the ship changed course and anchored at Montreal on 3 Sept. 1921. Deyglun first found work as a barman, and then, a month later, was employed by Le THÉÂTRE NATIONAL, directed by Claude Gauvreau. For two years he toured as an actor, chiefly in Quebec. In May 1923 he returned to France to complete his military service; on a visit to Paris, Fred BARRY and Albert DUQUESNE persuaded him to come back to Canada after his demobilization in 1925, and Barry gave him a story-line that became Deyglun's first play, *Bonne Maman*, a melodrama that was successfully produced by Le Théâtre Arcade in 1925. Sometime later Deyglun saw the famous film *Over the Hill* and recognized the story that Barry had told him. Instead of trying to conceal his involuntary plagiarism, he profited by publicizing his play, renamed *La Mère abandonnée* (by the *La Presse* critic Adrien Arcand), as 'a French play, with our best French-Canadian artists, that is better than *Over the Hill*.' It was published in 1929.

Except for a short period of difficulty, Deyglun's career blossomed. Between 1925 and 1929 he wrote a new play every two weeks to keep up with the demand at Le Théâtre Saint-Denis, which offered fourteen performances a week, and in 1930 he founded Le THÉÂTRE STELLA, with Barry Duquesne. Although he rebelled against church censorship, he learned to live with the fact that his plays would be produced 'in parish halls and patronized by priests'. In 1933 he made his radio début, both at Radio-Canada and at CKAC where, with Mimi d'Estée (whom he married in 1928), he achieved great success with an amusing series called 'Nénette et Rintintin'. Between 1932 and 1940 he was responsible for several radio adaptations for important radio theatre series such as 'Lambert', 'Populaire', 'Lux', 'N.G. Valiquette', and 'Des Étoiles'. In 1936 his play *Coeur de maman* (1936) was broadcast in twenty episodes before being produced at l'Arcade; it was made into a film in 1953. In 1938 he created a series of 120 broadcasts under the title 'Vie de famille'. *Les Secrets du docteur Morhanges* (1944)—using themes and situations suggested by the war—followed, as well as other plays for stage and radio, of which the most famous was *Roman d'une orpheline* (1936), which was presented more than 1,500 times. (See also RADIO DRAMA IN QUEBEC.)

With the arrival of television (where he appeared several times as an actor), Deyglun devoted himself chiefly to journalism for var-ious Montreal magazines. In 1969, suffering from cancer, he decided to write a weekly diary for *Le Photo Journal* of his battle against death. He had also begun a 'brief history of show business' under the title 'Les années folles', which he never completed; his manuscript of 120 pages is in the National Archives of Canada.

Deyglun's works, written mostly between 1925 and 1950 when he played a dominant role in the theatrical life of Quebec, include seventeen plays and two published novels, over 32,000 pages of scripts written for radio (sketches, dramas, and serials), many magazine articles, and almost a thousand pages of writing on a variety of other subjects. Vol. 1 of *L'Annuaire théâtral*, published in 1985 by La Société d'histoire du théâtre du Québec, gives Deyglun a prominent entry, which includes six previously unpublished works and a bibliography.

RICHARD FAUBERT, JEAN CLÉO GODIN

Dinner Theatre. Closely related to the CABARET and CAFÉ-THÉÂTRE format, dinner theatre has combined food, performance, and alcohol to create a highly successful business. More formal than cabaret and café-théâtre, dinner theatre usually begins after the meal is finished, tables are cleared, and the bar is closed (it reopens during intermissions). First popularized in the U.S. in the 1950s, dinner theatre, which offers a complete evening of theatre in one location (usually suburban) at a set price, attracted many patrons who were not regular theatregoers. The show had to be familiar, usually a comedy or a Broadway musical; the star a well-known television or film performer (often a few years past stardom).

Canadian dinner theatre has developed two characteristics distinct from its U.S. counterpart. Whereas there was for many years in the U.S. a prejudice against acting in a dinner theatre, this was not the case in Canada, where performers are used to working in every available medium to remain professional. In addition, Canadian dinner theatre tended to develop in the city centre, not in the suburbs. The first Canadian dinner theatre, Toronto's Theatre in the Dell on Elm St, was opened in the upstairs banquet room of a downtown restaurant on 12 June 1962 by Sylvia Shawn and Ray Lawlor, who presented two one-act plays. Shawn offered plays at the Dell until 1964, when the restaurant's owners began a tradition of MUSICAL THEA-TRE revues including the long-running *Oh, Coward* (1970-1) and *Toronto, Toronto* (1980-3) that continued until 1986. In 1973 the improvisational Second City troupe occupied the Firehall restaurant on Lombard St in Toronto, but the first self-proclaimed 'authentic' dinner theatre in Toronto was the Teller's Cage in Commerce Court, which opened in Oct. 1974 with Howard Marren's and Charles Abbott's *Games* in a room combining a full-service restaurant and a well-equipped stage. The Limelight Dinner Theatre opened in 1979 in a church on Yonge St, after failing as a legitimate theatre; it still operates (in a new facility) as a dinner theatre.

All kinds of theatrical institutions in Canada use the dinner-theatre format for public relations, audience development, and fund-raising, and commercial dinner theatres in cities and resorts abound across the country. The most prominent commercial venture has been Stage West, begun in 1975 by Howard Pechet in Edmonton's Mayfield Inn. At first unsuccessful, Pechet found the right formula with a production of Mary Chase's *Harvey*, starring Gig Young (a familiar, but not recently seen, American movie actor). Pechet has continued to book a single star (Gale Gordon, Jamie Farr, Norman Fell, among many others) through agents in Los Angeles, forming a production around the star with local actors in light comedy. Stage West ran in Regina (1976-81) and Winnipeg (1980-5), and still operates successful franchises in Calgary (from 1981) and (from 1986) in Mississauga, Ont.   STEPHEN JOHNSON

Directing (English Canada). The uncertain and haphazard history of directing in English-Canadian theatre reflects a number of obstacles to its development. Training opportunities have been woefully inadequate; the NATIONAL THEATRE SCHOOL still offers no full director-training, a 'serious gap' according to the 1982 Applebaum-Hébert report. A few universities, such as the Univ. of British Columbia and the Univ. of Alberta, use their increasingly precious resources to provide Master's programs in directing, but with very restricted enrolments. Apprenticeships with major companies remain a potentially important means of acquiring experience, but the intensity and quality of the apprenticeship varies widely. Meanwhile, it remains difficult to make a livelihood from free-lance theatre

directing, without supplementing it with teaching or work in other media.

Not surprisingly, many of Canada's leading modern directors received their formative experience abroad: George LUSCOMBE with Joan Littlewood at Theatre Workshop, London; Paul THOMPSON with Roger Planchon at the Théâtre de la Cité, Villeurbanne, France; Guy SPRUNG at the Schiller Theatre, Berlin, and at the Half Moon Theatre, London; Jim GARRARD at the London Academy of Music and Dramatic Art; Bill GLASSCO at New York University; and Chris BROOKES at the Yale School of Drama. Meanwhile Canada has regularly recruited directors from abroad, especially to fill a key artistic directorship like that of the STRATFORD FESTIVAL, although such incumbents as Robin PHILLIPS have triumphantly overcome fears concerning their 'colonial' mentality.

The inadequacy of training opportunities is matched by an uncertainty (common to many countries) about what directing is, and consequently how to describe, teach, and evaluate it. While there has been considerable discussion, and indeed controversy, about actor-training, the methodology of director-training remains a largely unexplored field. Partly as a consequence of this, theatre criticism typically falls back on a haphazard lexicon of impressionistic terminology. Although increasingly aware of the centrality of the director in contemporary theatre, English-Canadian critics have focused resolutely on the actor and the playwright (and to a much lesser extent the designer) as the yardsticks of current theatrical achievement. Given such adverse conditions, Canada has been blessed with better directors than it has deserved.

Canada's first directors emerged in the LITTLE THEATRE movement, especially between the First and Second World Wars. At their best, the little theatres imitated the aesthetics and ideals of such European prototypes as the Théâtre Libre (1887), the Abbey Theatre (1904), and the Vieux-Colombier (1913). As early as 1905, Toronto's Margaret Eaton School of Literature and Expression emulated the Irish Literary Movement by staging plays by William Butler Yeats and Lady Gregory. That city's ARTS AND LETTERS CLUB began serious theatrical activity in 1908, led by Canada's first significant director, Roy MITCHELL (1884-1944), who as the first director of HART HOUSE THEATRE staged productions

Directing (English Canada)

marked by a spiritual, non-realistic emphasis on the visual, plastic elements of theatre (especially through creative lighting), inspired by the ideas of Edward Gordon Craig and Jacques Copeau; Mitchell's advanced ideas reached print most eloquently in *Creative Theatre* (1929). Some of his fervent idealism was carried across Canada by influential pupils like Elizabeth Sterling HAYNES, who taught and directed at the Edmonton Little Theatre and the Banff School of Theatre. Other outstanding directors in the little theatres included Edgar Stone and Nancy Pyper (at Hart House Theatre), Carroll AIKINS (at his Home Theatre in Naramata, BC), Martha ALLAN (founder of the MONTREAL REPERTORY THEATRE), E.G. Sterndale Bennett (with the Toronto Masquers), John Craig (with legendary productions of Shakespeare, Rostand, and Ibsen at the Winnipeg Little Theatre), and Herman VOADEN with his remarkable 'symphonic expressionist' productions in Toronto and Sarnia during the thirties and early forties. Many key directors of the pre-Centennial period (like Robert GILL at Hart House Theatre) were more important as teachers of acting than as directors *per se*.

The DOMINION DRAMA FESTIVAL formally recognized directorial achievement in 1949 with the Louis Jouvet Trophy, first won by Robertson DAVIES for his Peterborough Little Theatre production of *The Taming of the Shrew*; although later recipients included Herbert WHITTAKER, Tom KERR, and André BRASSARD, the DDF was not a major training-ground for directors, and their shortage was highlighted by the emergence of postwar professional companies: the Everyman Theatre Company, Vancouver (1946-7), the NEW PLAY SOCIETY (from 1946), and the CANADIAN REPERTORY THEATRE, Ottawa (from 1949). There was only partial improvement with the many cultural initiatives that followed the 1951 report of the Massey Commission: the Stratford Festival (1953), the CREST THEATRE and the CANADIAN PLAYERS (1954), the Canada Council (1957), the MANITOBA THEATRE CENTRE (1958), and the National Theatre School (1960). For example, although the Manitoba Theatre Centre was Canadian-led from the start, it was not until 1968 that the Stratford Festival acquired its first Canadian artistic director (Jean GASCON). The Canadian Players drew heavily on British directors, as did its successor THEATRE

TORONTO (1968-9). The key question for such companies was often whether a Canadian director was yet ready to tackle the British and European classics. The sheer authority with which Tyrone GUTHRIE and Michael LANGHAM worked at Stratford provided both a stimulus to Canadian directors and, paradoxically, an obstacle to their development.

A limited breakthrough for Canadian directors came in the small Toronto and Montreal theatres of the late fifties and early sixties, such as TORONTO WORKSHOP PRODUCTIONS (1959), where George Luscombe confronted the theatrical and socio-political status quo with provocative productions that laid the groundwork for the profusion of ALTERNATE THEATREs of the late sixties and seventies. Some of the latter, like THEATRE PASSE MURAILLE (1968), initially imitated U.S. experimental theatre; others, like FACTORY THEATRE Lab and the NEW PLAY CENTRE (both 1970) and TARRAGON THEATRE (1971), began with a mission to nurture and produce Canadian drama, directed by Canadian directors. These theatres brought to prominence such seminal directors as Bill Glassco (Tarragon Theatre), Paul Thompson (Theatre Passe Muraille), Pam HAWTHORN (New Play Centre), and Ken GASS (Factory Theatre Lab), who have continued to exert their very distinct influences on the alternate (and ultimately the mainstream) theatres of the seventies and eighties. Thanks to unusually active government funding in the early 1970s, they were joined by the leaders of new companies such as Martin KINCH (TORONTO FREE THEATRE), Nick Hutchinson (Caravan Stage), and Chris Brookes (the MUMMERS TROUPE), and by new directors in the regional theatres, such as Christopher NEWTON, Malcolm BLACK, John WOOD, Leon MAJOR, and Maurice PODBREY.

It is against this background that the tendency of some of Canada's major institutional theatres to recruit directors from abroad (Robin Phillips at Stratford; John NEVILLE and Peter Coe at Edmonton's CITADEL) aroused protest that Canadian directors were being denied adequate access to their leading cultural institutions. The 1980s, however, have seen important advances. Canadian directors who began in the alternate theatres lead major companies (Bill Glassco and Guy Sprung at the CANADIAN STAGE COMPANY; Larry Lillo at the VANCOUVER PLAYHOUSE;

Martin Kinch at THEATRE CALGARY); women directors are increasing in number (for example, Sharon Pollock, Martha HENRY, Janet AMOS, Mary Vingoe, JoAnn McIntyre, Kathleen Weiss); the newer alternate theatres can boast such strong directors as Richard ROSE and Patrick McDonald; and a significant number of actors and playwrights are making the transition to directing: Richard MONETTE, Neil Munro, George F. WALKER, to name only a few. After a slow, uncertain development, the prognosis for English-Canadian directing looks very healthy indeed.

HARRY LANE

Directing (Quebec). It was not until just before the Second World War that directing, in the modern sense, had any real meaning in Quebec francophone theatre. Until that time plays were prepared under the guidance of a member of the company, sometimes rather ambiguously called the 'stage manager' (régisseur), who was responsible in whole or in part for casting, props, and scenery, and for overall direction of the play—though rehearsal time seldom exceeded one week. The most prominent 'directors' of this period were Antoine Godeau, Paul CAZENEUVE, Fernand Dhavrol, Julien DAOUST, and Henry DEYGLUN, who established a European, romantic style that was occasionally balanced by influences from the American extravaganza.

Jean BÉRAUD's *Initiation au théâtre* (1936), with its critical and instructive chapter on the director, was a kind of plea for greater directorial control; his list of the skills expected of a good director, and his succinct analysis of the artistic merits of European directors such as André Antoine, Max Reinhardt, Adolphe Appia, and Jacques Copeau, led Béraud to conclude that the theatre must give up 'photographic' realism; it must not 'reproduce life' but 'interpret' it. The importance of the hermeneutic, poetic, and aesthetic dimensions of theatre was recognized by Father Émile LEGAULT. After a sojourn in France in 1938-9—during which he became initiated into the acting techniques of the followers of Jacques Copeau (Léon Chancerel, Henri Brochet, and Henri Ghéon)—Legault advocated a 'poetic transposition' of the dramatic text; fiercely opposed to naturalism (for reasons that were as much moral as artistic), the founder of the COMPAGNONS DE SAINT-LAURENT stressed that the actor

should produce a 'plastic and rhythmic interpretation' on a bare stage with highly stylized props. Legault's efforts to create artistic homogeneity through ensemble acting were supported by Gratien GÉLINAS—with his *FRIDOLINONS* revues and in his *TIT-COQ*—and by Pierre DAGENAIS at L'ÉQUIPE from 1943 to 1948.

The work of Jean GASCON at the THÉÂTRE DU NOUVEAU MONDE in the 1950s further raised the standards of theatrical performance in Quebec. Gascon held that the director is a 'catalyst' whose main task is to provide tempo and balance; that direction should serve the text with 'creative fidelity'; and that 'great theatre is theatre of thought'. Such concepts were advocated and practised by several other Quebec directors, including Jan Doat, Georges Groulx, Paul Buissonneau, Jean-Guy SABOURIN, Albert Millaire, Roland LAROCHE, Rodrig Mathieu, and, more recently, Guillermo de Andréa and Olivier Reichenbach.

The beginning of the 1970s, however, brought a re-examination of these ideas, now considered in some quarters to have become theatrical orthodoxy. The growth of COLLECTIVE theatre—with its merging of the normally separate functions of author, actor, and director and its emphasis on spontaneity, improvisation, and free expression—challenged the alleged authoritarianism of the director, replacing it with artistic egalitarianism. Directing based on the interpretation of text—whether classic or original—did not, however, disappear; it responded with new vigour to the collective ideology. Directors such as André BRASSARD—who from 1963 regularly produced brilliant work—Lorraine Pintal, Alexandre HAUSVATER, Daniel Roussel, and Téo Spychalski distinguished themselves from their predecessors and their contemporaries by their articulate and critical views of the relationship among text, actors, and audience. In this context Jean-Pierre RONFARD is an important example. One of the major creators and experimenters for the stage since 1960, he has wavered between collective creation and directing in the traditional sense, often working simultaneously as writer, actor, director, and producer.

Other approaches that had been marginal throughout the 1970s began to establish themselves in the 1980s. Not fitting comfortably into the usual categories, directors such as Gilles Maheu, Jean Asselin, and Robert Lepage have experimented with metaphorical productions, filled with images of the body and the environment.

GILBERT DAVID

Dixon, Frederick Augustus (1843–1919). Born in London, Eng., and educated at King's College, Canterbury, he immigrated to Canada in the 1870s and for a time worked as a journalist for the Toronto *Mail*. During the tenure of Lord Dufferin as Governor General at RIDEAU HALL (1872–8) he was appointed tutor to Dufferin's four sons, one of whom was born in Canada. Most of Dixon's dramatic work was done during these years. On the departure of the Dufferins he joined the civil service in Ottawa, where he spent the rest of his career.

Dixon wrote mainly children's plays for performance at Rideau Hall. *Pussy-Cat Mew-*

A contemporary impression of Frederick A. Dixon's The Maire of St Brieux *at Rideau Hall, Ottawa, 1875*

Mew (performed in 1875) was followed by the more sophisticated *Little Nobody: A Fairy Play for Fairy People* (1875; performed 1 Jan. 1876), *Maiden Mona the Mermaid: A Fairy Play for Fairy People* (1877; performed 1 Jan. 1877), and *Fifine, the Fisher-Maid; or, The Magic Shrimps* (1877; performed 1 Jan. 1878). He also wrote a libretto *The Maire of St. Brieux: An Operetta in One Act* (1875), for which Frederick W. Mills composed the music. This drama of love and intrigue, set in a Breton town when Napoleon was consul in France, was so well received at its Feb. 1875 Rideau

Hall première that it was remounted for a week at the GRAND OPERA HOUSE in Ottawa the following year. Dixon also wrote the libretto for *A Masque Entitled 'Canada's Welcome'* (1879) for the arrival of the next Governor General, the Marquis of Lorne, and his wife Princess Louise. With music by Arthur A. Clappé, it was also performed in the Grand Opera house, 24 Feb. 1879. It personifies each province, as well as Canada and the Indian population, as forming a welcoming party.

Dixon later published other dramas: a satire entitled *Ye Last Sweet Things in Corners, Being Ye Faithful Drama of Ye Artists' Vendetta* (1880); *Pipandor: A Comic Opera in 3 Acts* (1884), with music by S.F. Harrison; and *The Episode of the Quarrel between Titania and Oberon from Shakespeare's Midsummer Night's Dream* (1898) arranged for presentation with the Mendelssohn music.   JAMES NOONAN

Documentary Drama. Sometimes referred to as 'actuality drama' or 'drama of fact', this hybrid genre became a popular form of dramatic expression in the English-Canadian ALTERNATE THEATRE movement of the 1970s, largely among companies engaged in COLLECTIVE CREATION. The term 'documentary' was first applied to drama by Bertolt Brecht with reference to the political theatre of Erwin Piscator in the Berlin of the mid-1920s; soon after, it was independently coined by John Grierson for his new type of educative film-making, defined by him as 'the creative interpretation of actuality'. Since then, particularly in periods of heightened social and political consciousness, documentary drama has spasmodically re-emerged to combine the informational actuality of film (sometimes using film projection on stage) with authenticating performance techniques (paradoxically often borrowed from non-representational theatre such as music hall and political CABARET). Influential practitioners have included the U.S. Federal Theatre Project's Living Newspaper Unit of the 1930s, Joan Littlewood's Theatre Workshop of both the pre- and post-war periods in London, playwright Peter Weiss, and British director Peter Cheeseman of the Victoria Theatre, Stoke-on-Trent. In Canada the importance of documentary drama has been primarily cultural—in its development of new audiences for theatre and in its radical investigation of Canadian material.

George LUSCOMBE, who apprenticed with Littlewood in the 1950s and inherited her concern to develop a serious popular theatre, initially explored the mode at his TORONTO WORKSHOP PRODUCTIONS with *Gentlemen be Seated* in 1967, later revised as *Mr Bones* in 1969. In the manner of Littlewood's *Oh What a Lovely War!*, this production offered an iconoclastic corrective to American civil-rights history, depicting Lincoln, within the ironic structure of a minstrel show, as a reluctant emancipationist. Luscombe continued his satire of American politics in 1970 with *Chicago '70*, a combination of up-to-the-minute reportage and cartoon commentary on the trial of the Chicago Seven; here, as in Steven Bush's *Richard ThirdTime*, a lampoon on Watergate (produced at TWP in 1973), the documentary elements serve as a critique of the mass media, as advocated by Peter Weiss. In collaboration with playwright Jack Winter, Luscombe turned his attention to Canadian politics in 1975 with *You Can't Get Here from There*, a critical documentary analysis of Canadian foreign policy during the Chile-Allende crisis. He also developed theatrical adaptations of existing documentary works of social and political interest, notably *Fanshen* with Rick SALUTIN in 1972 (based on William Hinton's study of revolutionary China) and TEN LOST YEARS in 1974 with Jack Winter (from Barry Broadfoot's collection of Depression memories). In 1980 Luscombe used the episodic format of *Ten Lost Years* for *Mac-Paps*, his dramatization of a collection of CBC interviews on the Canadian experience of fighting in the Spanish Civil War.

The nationalistic drive towards the creation of a specifically Canadian theatre and drama was more directly served, however, in the collective documentary investigations of THEATRE PASSE MURAILLE under the direction of Paul THOMPSON. In marked contrast to Luscombe's authoritative directorial methods, Thompson involved his whole company at every stage of the play-making process. His most influential approach was to move into the community from which the company was to improvise its play in order to create, in Thompson's words, 'a kind of living community portrait or photograph, filled with things we observed and what they would like to say about themselves.' Such was the case for *The FARM SHOW*, 1972, based on a summer's stay in Clinton, Ont.; *Under the Grey-*

wacke, 1973, an investigation of the decline of the mining community of Cobalt, Ont.; and *Oil*, 1974, about the town and people of Petrolia, Ont. In 1975 the company attempted a more difficult project in its explorations of the past and present life of Saskatchewan in *The West Show*. Equally interested in Canadian history, Thompson and his company worked with Rick Salutin in 1973 on *1837: The Farmers' Revolt*, an interpretation reflecting the nationalistic bias of the day, particularly in its efforts to recover some of the forgotten or suppressed details of the rebellion of 1837-8. The earlier *Doukhobors*, 1971, offered a revisionist depiction of the oppression suffered by these immigrants at the hands of the Canadian government and people.

Companies that followed Passe Muraille's lead in the development of collective social and historical documentaries include 25TH STREET THEATRE, Saskatoon, notably with *PAPER WHEAT* in 1977; THEATRE NETWORK, Edmonton, with, for example, *Hard Hats and Stolen Hearts* in 1977; the MULGRAVE ROAD CO-OP of Guysborough, N.S., founded in 1977; and Theatre Energy, founded in 1976 in the Slocum Valley of the B.C. interior, which also began its work with the collective exploration of local material—for example, with *Renderings*, 1976, and *Voices: Echoes of the Past*, 1979.

Regional political documentary drama is represented in the work of the now-defunct MUMMERS TROUPE of St John's, Nfld, and the GLOBE THEATRE, Regina, Sask. Chris BROOKES, founder and director of the Mummers, established his activist intentions with *Gros Mourn* in 1973, designed to interrupt the inauguration ceremonies for Gros Morne National Park on the west coast of Newfoundland. Other Mummers plays include *Buchans: A Company Town*, a play protesting the effects of depleting mining resources, first performed in 1974, and the 1975 *I.W.A.: The Newfoundland Loggers' Strike of 1959*. Brookes' company later created two documentary revues for mainland audiences: *The Price of Fish*, 1976, and *They Club Seals, Don't They?* in 1978. At the Globe, playwright-in-residence Rex DEVERELL worked first in documentary with the collective creation *No.1 Hard*, a critical investigation of the contemporary grain industry, produced in 1978. Directed by Ken KRAMER, the play followed the strict principles of Peter Cheeseman in its

Documentary Drama

precise adherence to the language of the researched material (although within a revue format) with the intention of provoking serious discussion with its farm audiences. In 1980 Deverell wrote his own documentary reconstruction of the issues of the 1962 Saskatchewan physicians' strike, entitled *Medicare!*, demonstrating the dramatic possibilities of the mode within the confines of objectively observed recorded fact. His *Black Powder*, produced in 1981, is a freer, more partisan examination of the circumstances of the Estevan miners' riot of 1931. (See also POLITICAL AND POPULAR THEATRE.)

For commentary on documentary drama by its practitioners, see Rick Salutin, 'Documentary Style: The Curse of Canadian Culture', in *Marginal Notes* (1984); an interview with Paul Thompson in *The Work: Conversations with English-Canadian Playwrights* (1982), ed. Robert Wallace and Cynthia Zimmerman; Rex Deverell, '*Medicare!* as a one man collective', in *Showing West: Three Prairie Docu-Dramas* (1982), ed. Diane Bessai and Don Kerr. For critical analysis see Diane Bessai, 'Documentary Theatre in Canada: An Investigation into Questions and Backgrounds', *Canadian Drama*, 6 (1980); Robert C. Nunn, 'Performing Fact: Canadian Documentary Theatre', *Canadian Literature*, 103 (1984); and Alan Filewod, *Collective Encounters: Documentary Theatre in English Canada* (1987).   DIANE BESSAI

Dominion Drama Festival. On 29 Oct. 1932 a small group of theatre enthusiasts, led by the Governor General of Canada, the Earl of Bessborough, met at Government House, Ottawa, in response to critics such as John Edward Hoare, Herman VOADEN, and Lawrence Mason who had called for the creation of a centralized organization to co-ordinate the activities of the many LITTLE THEATRES spread across Canada. Among those attending were Vincent MASSEY, Martha ALLAN of the MONTREAL REPERTORY THEATRE, Col. Henry C. Osborne of the Ottawa Drama League, Ernest Sterndale Bennett of Lethbridge, Alta, Lady Margaret Tupper of the Winnipeg Little Theatre, and Rupert Harvey, a British actor-director who became the Festival's first adjudicator. The outcome of the meeting was a decision to hold an annual national drama festival each spring, entailing a series of regional competitions (judged by a single travelling adjudicator) and

Dominion Drama Festival organizers on the steps of Government House, Ottawa, May 1933, with (l. to r.) Sir Robert Borden (former Prime Minister), Col. H.C. Osborne (honorary director), the Earl of Bessborough (Governor General), Rupert Harvey (adjudicator), Vincent Massey (chairman)

then, on the basis of the regional adjudicator's recommendations, a week-long Festival competition held in a major city and adjudicated by a new judge. Prizes were awarded in a number of production categories—by 1950 they included the Bessborough Challenge Trophy for the best performance of a full-length play in either English or French; two other trophies for the best presentation of a full-length play in English and French respectively (excluding the winner of the Bessborough Trophy); the Louis Jouvet Challenge Trophy for the best director; the Martha Allan Challenge Trophy for the best visual presentation; the Henry Osborne Challenge Trophy for the best actor; and the Nella Jeffers Challenge Trophy for the best actress. Prizes were also awarded at the regional level, most notably the Sir Barry Jackson Challenge Trophy for the best presentation in the regional Festivals of a play (either full-length or short) written by a Canadian. The first Dominion Drama Festival was held in Ottawa in the week commencing 23 Apr. 1933 (Shakespeare's birthday); its inauguration was attended by Bessborough and Prime Minister Mackenzie King. Companies from eight provinces presented excerpts and one-act plays (full-length plays were allowed only after 1950).

Because of the national character of the Festival, adjudicators were expected to be proficient in both French and English and were usually (until after the Second World War) from Britain or France. Among the prominent European and Canadian adjudicators were J. T. Grein, Harley Granville-Barker, Philip Hope-Wallace, Michel SAINT-DENIS, Robert Speaight, Françoise Rosay, Pierre Lefèvre, Betty MITCHELL, David Peacock, David GARDNER, Guy BEAULNE, Sean MULCAHY, Robert GURIK, Leon MAJOR, and Herbert WHITTAKER. Michel Saint-Denis, who adjudicated on five occasions, returned to Canada to work with the Canadian Theatre Centre in founding the NATIONAL THEATRE SCHOOL in 1960. In his memoirs, *The Property Basket* (1970), Speaight mentions figures who caught his attention—Robertson DAVIES, William HUTT, and Frances HYLAND.

Although the DDF was an amateur organization, it gave experience to many actors who subsequently became prominent in the professional theatre—for example, John COLICOS, Kate REID, Brian Doherty (founder of the SHAW FESTIVAL), Douglas RAIN, Amelia HALL, Sean SULLIVAN, Gratien GÉLINAS, and André BRASSARD. Canadian playwrights such as Robertson Davies, Marcel DUBÉ, Robert Gurik, and Patricia JOUDRY gained national attention and valuable experience from DDF competitions.

There was also a political dimension to the DDF—Vincent Massey believed that it 'made no small contribution to the unity of the country'—and much time was spent placating sometimes tense relations between the English and French participants. It was something of a provocation in 1935 when the Governor General acquired a Royal Charter for the Festival signed by George V and witnessed by Bessborough himself. In Winnipeg in 1938 delegates from Quebec urged that there be two Festivals—one for French Canada and one for English Canada—but the Festival's Governors determined to maintain the bilingual mandate of a single organization.

Another political aspect of the Festival was its apparent nervousness about plays that seemed in any way to threaten the Festival's formality—the protocol, balls, and dinner parties that were an essential part of DDF Finals are mentioned by Speaight in his memoirs. The 1930s saw the rise of theatre groups such as the Theatre of Action, whose plays were usually of the agit-prop genre meant to challenge the ruling ideology (see POLITICAL

AND POPULAR THEATRE). When one such play—American playwright Irwin Shaw's anti-war *Bury the Dead*, produced by Toronto's Theatre of Action—did win its way to the 1937 Final in Ottawa, its director, David Pressman, still concluded that the DDF was likely to remain 'a conventional outlet for a drab and highly traditional one-act nightmare'.

Competition was suspended during the Second World War, and when it resumed the development of new professional theatres provided a potentially destructive challenge. Actors who achieved professional status—either through work on radio or television or in the new professional theatre—refused to work with amateurs, and their position was strengthened by the development of professional unions. When the Canada Council established its mandate in 1957 it limited support for the DDF to areas where professionals were hired. In 1970, recognizing that the Festival's original mandate was becoming irrelevant, the DDF was renamed Theatre Canada and the system of competition gave way to an emphasis on showcasing the country's best amateur groups. But the astonishing growth in professional theatre in Canada in the 1960s and 1970s spelled the end for Theatre Canada, which closed in 1978.

While the DDF can be faulted for emphasizing too strongly the values of foreign theatrical repertoires, it nonetheless made a great and significant contribution to Canadian drama and theatre. Unsubsidized, scattered across a vast country, the amateur theatre the Festival nourished was the bridge to the new professionalism of Canadian theatre of the 1960s and beyond.

See also LITTLE THEATRE AND AMATEUR THEATRE and Betty Lee, *Love and Whisky: The Story of the Dominion Drama Festival* (1973).   HERBERT WHITTAKER

Domino Theatre. An amateur company founded in Kingston, Ont., by Gordon and Valerie Robertson and others, it opened in Apr. 1953 with Jean-Paul Sartre's *No Exit* at the Odeon Theatre (a movie house). The following year Domino's production of J.M. Synge's *Playboy of the Western World* won an award for best actor (Roland Hewgill) in the Eastern Ontario Drama League (with Gordon and Valerie Robertson as runners-up for best actor and best actress) and went on to win the Calvert Trophy and best-actor award for

Domino Theatre

Gordon Robertson in that year's DOMINION DRAMA FESTIVAL finals. After ten years at inadequate locations, including 'The French Room' (a ladies dress shop), Portsmouth Town Hall, the Orange Hall, the Liberal Hall, a local high school, and the La Salle Hotel ballroom, Domino opened a theatre in Jan. 1964 at 8 Princess St. Subsequently Domino renovated a city-owned 1832 limestone stable, which it has occupied since Sept. 1974. With a repertoire leaning towards popular entertainment, Domino has served the interests of those seeking the values—chiefly social—inherent in community-based amateur theatre. It has also accommodated, somewhat uncomfortably at times, those who were used to more challenging fare or who had a professional orientation—including the Robertsons, who eventually left Domino to open their professional Theatre 5. A variety of programs—including plays for young audiences, a theatre school (1952–61), and drama workshops on radio (1955–63)—has offered further community enrichment.

RICHARD PLANT

Donation, La. The first play by a native Canadian to have been published *and* staged in this country, it was written by Pierre PETITCLAIR, and performed in Quebec City on 16 Nov. 1842 by Les Amateurs Typographes, a troupe founded and directed by the controversial Napoléon Aubin. It was published in successive issues of the biweekly newspaper *L'Artisan* in 1842, and was also included in J. Huston's *Répertoire national* (1848).

A two-act comedy of intrigue with strong melodramatic overtones, *La Donation* is surprisingly close to popular Parisian tastes of the 1840s. The central character, Bellire, a hypocritical swindler, has insinuated himself into the favour of a rich and credulous Quebec merchant, Delorval. He convinces Delorval that his trusted assistant Auguste, who was to marry his niece and receive title to the merchant's entire wealth, is a bigamous scoundrel. Delorval's rustic servants Nicodème and, especially, Suzette, are more perceptive than he. In a scene directly reminiscent of Molière's *Tartuffe*, Suzette positions her master behind a screen while Bellire and his accomplice gloat over their prospective spoils, mocking Delorval. The merchant summons a notary to formalize the legal donation of his wealth and, in an effective *coup de théâtre*, reads aloud the names of those to whom the donation will be made: his niece and her fiancé!

La Donation is tightly structured, the first act ending with a direct threat to the happiness of the young lovers, the second ending with the unexpected dissipation of that threat. Its defects are those of the melodramatic genre: abuse of soliloquy and asides and gross oversimplification of character. This is the first and one of the clearest examples of the influence of the melodramatic tradition on French-Canadian dramaturgy.

See L.E. Doucette, *Theatre in French Canada, 1606-1867* (1984).   L.E. DOUCETTE

Donkin, Eric (b. 1929). Born in Montreal, he began acting on radio at the age of eleven, and subsequently established a reputation as one of Canada's most versatile performers in roles that range from Lear to the transvestite comic Miss Rosalind Drool in his one-man show *The Wonderful World of Sarah Binks*. Renowned as a character actor, Donkin typically adopts a tone of self-effacing diffidence that can quickly become sardonic. A STRATFORD FESTIVAL stalwart, he has had many successes there, including Polonius in 1976, the Critic in Ferenc Molnar's *The Guardsman* in 1977, Dr Chasuble in Oscar Wilde's *The Importance of Being Earnest* in 1979, Farmer Gammon in John O'Keeffe's *Wild Oats* in 1981, and the title role in *Cymbeline* in 1986. Although Donkin lacks a singing voice, he has also performed effectively in a number of Gilbert and Sullivan roles at Stratford, beginning with his Rt Hon. Sir Joseph Porter in *H.M.S. Pinafore* in 1981 and most notably with his celebrated Ko-Ko in *The Mikado* in 1982—a much-revived production that played on Broadway in 1987.

Donkin also played Lear at Halifax's NEPTUNE THEATRE in 1977 and was an accomplished Theseus in *A Midsummer Night's Dream* at the NATIONAL ARTS CENTRE in 1983 and a highly praised Scrooge at Toronto's YOUNG PEOPLE'S THEATRE in 1985. In addition to *The Wonderful World of Sarah Binks*, he has also appeared as a solo performer as an eighty-two-year-old Jew in Charles Dennis's *Altman's Last Stand*, a holocaust memoir. His many television appearances include a continuing role in CTV's 1976 series 'Side Street'.   RAY CONLOGUE

146

Donnellys, The. James REANEY's three plays on the theme of a famous feud and murder at Biddulph, Ont., in 1880, were first staged between 1973 and 1975; they constitute both his most important work for the stage, and one of the most significant achievements of the modern Canadian theatre. The plays were developed over a period of eight years, during the earlier part of which the playwright conducted extensive historical research, gradually developing the story into dramatic form through workshops with actors, culminating in the summer of 1973 when Keith TURNBULL directed a group in Halifax, N.S. There it was decided to divide the complex story of thirty-six years into three parts, and the first of these was prepared for production.

Sticks and Stones opened on 24 Nov. 1973 at Toronto's TARRAGON THEATRE, where its energy and inventiveness met with an immediately enthusiastic response. The play deals with the early settlement of the Donnelly family in Canada and the origins of the feud. Reaney's literary form—episodic, moving back and forth freely through time, and 'alienating'—was married closely to a production style of forceful simplicity. Eleven actors, present on stage throughout, sang, danced, moved properties, and assumed characters as required; of these, five remained with *The Donnellys* throughout its subsequent career, including Jerry Franken (James Donnelly) and Patricia Ludwick (Judith Donnelly).

The St. Nicholas Hotel—Wm. Donnelly Prop. was produced in the same theatre a year later (16 Nov. 1974). The dramatic manner is more relaxed and discursive than that in either of the other two plays; it is in fact a recollection, through the consciousness of Will Donnelly, of the career of his family and of the deaths of two of his brothers in the 1870s, although everything that happens, the chorus reminds us, is merely a part of 'the stream of the time we all lie dreaming in'. Despite this elegiac note, the action of the play is predominantly brisk and lively. Where in the preceding play actual sticks and stones stand for the enmity of the land and of neighbours, and ladders for barriers and imprisoning lines, the physical symbols in *The St. Nicholas Hotel* are wheels and tops, figuring an energetic if ultimately futile movement.

Handcuffs was first presented at the Tarragon on 29 Mar. 1975. It deals with the central tragedy, the murder of five members of the family by a mob, and the burning of their home, an event that defines our understanding of the Donnellys from the beginning of the first play. The conflicts of the preceding action are brought to their bloody conclusion, depicted in shadow-play behind a curtain, as all the symbols of the plays—sticks, stones, roads, seeds, fire, wheels—are woven together in a rich conclusion.

Reaney's success in these plays arose not only from discovering, with the aid of actors and director, a fresh theatrical language, but also in setting a story of violence and brutality within symbolic patterns of fertility and sterility, and in conveying the significance of individual human existence within the flux of time. One of the most compelling scenes in the trilogy occurs in Act 2 of *Sticks and Stones* when Mrs Donnelly's ghost, outside time, is conjured from her and whispers to her of the futility of her life. Beyond such finely realized moments the larger structure is firmly controlled, resisting the dissipation of effect that threatens such extended treatment.

The enthusiasm generated by the first productions of *The Donnellys* led to the foundation, following the run of *Handcuffs*, of a company, NDWT, to tour the plays across Canada. It performed in most major centres from Vancouver to Halifax, and closed in Toronto with a performance in the Bathurst Street Theatre of all three plays on one day (14 Dec. 1975). Reaney has recorded his impressions of the tour in a lively journal, *Fourteen Barrels from Sea to Sea* (1977), which also includes a collection of reviews garnered during the tour. The fame of these original

James Reaney's The Donnellys, *Part II: The St. Nicholas Hotel,* Tarragon Theatre, Toronto, 1974

productions, paradoxically, may account for the lack of major realizations of the plays since 1975; their scope and complexity have proved too large a challenge to civic and festival companies.

Sticks and Stones was first published in the *Canadian Theatre Review* 2 (1974); it was published as a book by Press Porcépic in 1975, with photographs of the first production and a valuable essay by James Noonan. The same book format was followed for *The St. Nicholas Hotel* (1976) and *Handcuffs* (1977). In 1983 Press Porcépic reissued the three plays in one volume, *The Donnellys*, omitting the production photographs. Two of the plays appear in anthologies: *The St. Nicholas Hotel* in *Modern Canadian Plays* (1985), edited by J. Wasserman, and *Handcuffs* in *The Penguin Book of Modern Canadian Drama* (1984), edited by R. Plant. Selected criticism (including reviews) of all three plays is printed in *Canadian Drama and the Critics* (1987), edited by L.W. Conolly.   JOHN H. ASTINGTON

Donohue, Brenda (1950-79). Born and educated in Toronto, she acted in school productions but received no formal actor-training before appearing with THEATRE PASSE MURAILLE from 1970 to 1972, most notably in the COLLECTIVE CREATION *Vampyr* in 1972. In the short period before her death from cancer, Donohue became one of Canada's most admired actresses in the contemporary repertoire, with performances that combined emotional honesty with remarkable simplicity and clarity of focus. Of particular note were her appearances as Eva Braun in Bryan WADE's *Blitzkrieg* for TARRAGON THEATRE and Becky Lou in Sam Shepard's *The Tooth of Crime* at CENTAUR THEATRE (both in 1974), Dotty Sweeney in John PALMER's *The Pits* at TORONTO FREE THEATRE (in 1975), and Carla in Robert Patrick's *Kennedy's Children*, her only appearance at the STRATFORD FESTIVAL (also in 1975), and finally Carmen in Michel TREMBLAY's *Sainte Carmen of the Main* at Tarragon in 1978. The Brenda Donohue Award, established in her memory in 1980, recognizes distinguished contribution and achievement within the Toronto theatre community.   HARRY LANE

Drama in English. 1. *The Beginnings to the First World War*. The sixteenth-century introduction to Canada of European theatrical form—the dramatic mode whose history is charted here—was preceded by centuries of paratheatrical activities among North America's indigenous peoples. These performances often involved a variety of sophisticated 'stage effects' (e.g. magical disappearances, fire, voice, and sound tricks) and were enacted by specially endowed members of the tribes wearing elaborate costumes and skilfully carved masks. Anthropologists and theatre historians have cited the Corn Goddess tales of central Canada, the Mystery Play of the Kwakiutl Indians, and the Hamatsa (cannibal) ceremony on the West Coast as important examples of paratheatrical and paradramatic aspects of the highly developed native cultures. (See AMERINDIAN AND INUIT THEATRE.)

However, the extent to which European and indigenous expressions interpenetrated to influence the imported theatre and drama proves difficult to assess. Canada's earliest recorded theatrical event in a European mode shows evidence of a native presence. Typical of the period, on his 1583 expedition to Newfoundland the explorer Sir Humphrey Gilbert carried a small troupe of entertainers on his ship, who performed during anchorage in St John's. As explained by Edward Haies, 'we were provided of Musike in good variety: not omitting the least toyes, as Morris dancers, Hobby horsse and Maylike conceits to delight the Savage people, whom we intended to winne by all faire means possible'. As well, in 1606, the presence of Micmac Indians and Frenchmen dressed as Indians, in Marc LESCARBOT's masque, *Le THÉÂTRE DE NEPTUNE EN LA NOUVELLE-FRANCE* (1609), indicates that the cultural exchange was two-way from the beginning. From that time on, we can identify many occasions when European-based theatre and drama have been influenced by indigenous Canadian activity, but research has not yet been sufficient to warrant substantial discussion of the subject.

Similarly, although several studies trace the development of anglophone and francophone drama, and thereby offer implied, if not stated, comparative analysis, research has not extensively explored the relationship between French and English theatrical and dramatic activities. Considerable inter-cultural exchange existed in Montreal and Quebec immediately after 1763. Previously, the history of theatre and drama in all of Canada was that of the French. But records indicate that as early as 1743, British garrison officers and their ladies enjoyed a special Christmas celebration at Fort Anne, Annapolis Royal. With the establishment from the 1760s of British rule and settlement, activity among the English gradually increased to the point of dominance. But the relationship is complex: for instance, British rule created a climate in which the Roman Catholic Church was less able to control theatre, thus allowing francophone activity to increase during the early British regime.

Among the British, GARRISON THEATRE is recorded as early as 1773 when 'the gentlemen of the army and navy' produced Benjamin Hoadly's *The Suspicious Husband* at Halifax, and it continued wherever theatrically inclined personnel were stationed until the garrisons were recalled late in 1870. In addition to English plays, British officers sometimes staged French drama in translation, or in French, as was the case in 1774 at Montreal when the garrison amateurs presented Molière's *Le Médecin malgré lui* and *Le Bourgeois gentilhomme*. On many occasions the garrison thespians formed a bridge to local civilian communities, as in Saint John, N.B., in 1809, where their combined forces opened the DRURY LANE THEATRE, or in Kingston, Ont., where, between Jan. 1816 and July 1817 a company of officers and local gentlemen played nearly thirty mainpieces and thirty farces.

For the most part, practices and repertoire in civilian as well as garrison theatres imitated London and large American centres. Not surprisingly, then, the early plays we might speak of as indigenous were based on foreign models, especially when the officers were themselves the playwrights. Robert Rogers, a Massachusetts-born major in the British army who lived part of his life in Canada and was eventually stripped of his command of Fort Michilimackinac, wrote *Ponteach; or, The Savages of America* (1766). This five-act blank-verse drama offers heroic themes and a pre-Romantic image of native life crushed by 'civilization'. Ponteach, whose people have been misused by evil English and French traders, missionaries and soldiers, heads an Indian confederacy opposing the invaders. Treachery involving his bastard son, who seeks Ponteach's kingdom, defeats the great chief, but as the play ends, Ponteach remains noble and defiant, planning his flight to safety where he will beget more sons and collect more

troops. Lieutenant Adam Allan's *The New Gentle Shepherd* (1798) borrows title, form, and content from Allan Ramsay's *The Gentle Shepherd* (1725), a pastoral drama in Scottish dialect, 'reduced to English', by Allan.

Neither Rodgers' nor Allan's drama was staged, but George Cockings' *The Conquest of Canada; or, The Siege of Quebec* (1766) was produced in Philadelphia (17, 19, 22 Feb. 1773) by the American Company headed by Lewis Hallam Jr, the most famous professional troupe in the eighteenth-century United States. This dull patriotic tragedy, imitative of Dryden's *Conquest of Granada*, was valued enough to be printed three times: London 1766; Baltimore 1772; New York 1773. It also received a stage production by the British garrison in New York (4 Oct. 1783) and possibly several in Canada, the first of which was by the Edward Allen, John Bentley, and Wilson Moore Troupe (which they called the American Company on the basis of their earlier association with Hallam). They are recorded as staging *The Siege of Quebec: or, The Death of General Wolfe* (certainly the subject of Cockings' play) in Quebec (19 Oct. 1786), which could be Cockings' work under a slightly different name. The three-act *Acadius; or, Love in a Calm* is another eighteenth-century play staged by garrison performers (Halifax, 1774). Although the text is not extant, an advertisement (1 Feb. 1774), and lengthy abstracts of the first two acts, appeared in the *Nova Scotia Gazette and Weekly Chronicle* (12, 19 Apr. 1774) and indicate a stageworthy romantic adventure with moments of unsettling comedy and an anti-slavery sentiment. The play remains anonymous: the publication of detailed abstracts and its Halifax performance might argue for a local author, as might its anti-slavery stance; the prominence of a Boston merchant among its characters could, however, indicate otherwise.

Garrison activity has frequently been cited as a basis for the development of Canadian drama; but there was also civilian amateur and professional theatre in the eighteenth and early nineteenth centuries. By 1768 Messrs Giffard and Mills, leading an 'American Company of Comedians', played an autumn season in Halifax. The Allen, Bentley, Moore Company performed in Montreal and Quebec in 1786; Mr and Mrs Marriott from England (via the U.S.) managed the Halifax Theatre from 1798 to 1805, and, supplementing their company by local amateurs, played six months in Saint John in 1799; Toronto was visited by 'New York comic gentry' (amateurs?) in 1809, and in 1810 by Messrs Potter and Thompson, as well as a 'company of comedians from Montreal'; Kingston saw a touring troupe at Mr Poncet's 'large room' in 1812. Exactly how much of a role educational institutions had in developing indigenous drama in English is not known; however, as early as 1828 Toronto's Royal Grammar School performed Terence's *Adelphi* in Latin as part of its examinations.

Public performances often prompted anti-theatre reactions in the press and pulpit, which were engaged by pro-theatre views expressed not only in print but in attendance at the 'sinful' pastime. These anti-theatre attacks began as early as 1768 in the *Nova Scotia Gazette and Weekly Chronicle* and, unfortunately for the Canadian playwright, were a widespread and considerable deterrent. Theatres, though having a phoenix-like character, were generally make-shift and short-lived. The professional companies came from outside Canada and, like the amateur troupes, continued to present a non-Canadian repertoire.

By the turn of the eighteenth century, the interrelationship of an increasing Canadian population with businesses (including theatres) needing to sell products spurred the formation of a vigorous press, headed by enterprising editors concerned about individual rights in the face of government privilege and control. Twenty news sheets in 1813 grew to 291 newspapers in 1857, with many other short-lived ventures in the years between. As was the case for francophone writers in Quebec at the time, these avidly read publications, and the pamphlets from newspaper printing houses, offered another avenue for prospective dramatists seeking an audience: that of political satire using dramatic plots, characterization, and dialogue. These paratheatrical works contributed significantly to the development of a Canadian dramatic voice; they give evidence of a people for whom the dramatic metaphor was a natural conceptual framework for everyday reality.

In 1795 Edward Winslow's paradramatic pamphlet, *Substance of the Debates in the Young Robin Hood Society* (1795), entered the political controversy over a goverment plan to develop various inland areas of New Bruns-

wick. *The Niagara Gleaner*—after publishing for the first time a play in Upper Canada, *Rose and Nancy* (22 Jan. 1818), a reprint of one of Mary Leadbetter's *Cottage Dialogues among the Irish Peasantry* (1811)—carried an anonymous political satire, *The Convention: A Farce as Now Acting with Great Applause in Upper-Canada* (3 July 1818). During the 1820s Samuel Hull Wilcocke (the pseudonym of Lewis Luke MacCulloh) wrote and/or published several fierce satires in his paper *The Scribbler* (Montreal). These include *The Charrivarri* (vols. 3-4, 1823), which makes great fun in prose and verse of the celebration that took place in Montreal after the marriage of a lusty, rich widow and a well-known bachelor; *Dialogue at M'Killaway Lodge* (vol. 2, no. 74, 1822), in which Lord Goddamnhim and Sir Plausible Pompous M'Killaway rail against the editor of *The Scribbler* for ridiculing them in print; and *Domestic Economy* (vol. 4, no. 109, 1823), in which General Fleabite of Shamblee attacks 'Government City' extravagance and military ineffectiveness. By the 1830s the plays had become more ambitious, but because the hard-hitting satire remained, so did many pseudonyms. 'O.P.' (Robert Gowan) published a two-act, ten-scene prose satire, *The Triumph of Intrigue,* in the *New Brunswick Courier* (23 Feb., 2, 9 Mar. 1833), which showed villainy in official positions over Crown Land management and quitrents. In his paper *The British Colonist* (vol. 2, nos. 20, 21, 23, 25, 26, 1839), Hugh Scobie ('Chrononhotonthologos') skewered Upper Canadian graft and corruption in high circles with the *Provincial Drama Called the Family Compact*. Among editors who were also playwrights was Dr Edward Barker, founder of the *Kingston Whig*, and a drama critic to boot. Barker's opinionated reviews often led him into local controversy, as did his dramatic satires printed in the *Whig*. An immodest man, he published his one-act *The Bridegroom* (10 Feb. 1836) in the *Whig* with a note explaining that he had submitted it to the Park Theatre in New York where it was rejected by an 'American Dramatic Censor deficient in taste'.

Not until the mid-nineteenth century do we see any significant number of indigenous plays on the stage. Among the avenues open to prospective playwrights was poetic closet drama, which eliminated any need for live performance—with its perceived vulgarity and immorality—and which drew on a respectable literary tradition. Canadian poetic drama, however, was often a hybrid mix of closet literary elements, with character types and formulaic melodramatic plots taken from the popular stage. Hoping to see their work staged, Charles MAIR spoke of *Tecumseh* (1866) as a 'good acting play', William Wilfred Campbell offered his *Mordred* (1895) to Sir Henry Irving, and Charles HEAVYSEGE revised *Saul* (1857) with an eye to performance by Charlotte Cushman.

The existence of poetic dramas as printed texts—and their literary and philosophical 'weightiness'—has accorded a relatively small body of work excessive critical attention. The name most often associated with the sententious, prolix, and moralizing blank-verse dramas is Charles Heavysege, whose turgid six-act 10,000-line *Saul* is now considered unreadable—though it was reprinted twice in two years and modern scholars find isolated passages to admire. His melodramatic *Count Filippo* (1860) is deservedly unknown. Thomas Bush was equally ambitious in using a South American earthquake as the climax in *Santiago* (1866), a cautionary drama about religious corruption and papish idolatry. While engaging at times, the play suffers from obscure allusions, passages of incomprehensible verse, and a sprawling plot. Exotic settings were common, such as the mysterious forests of Portugal we see in John Hutchison Garnier's *Prince Pedro* (1877) or the mountains of Spain in John HUNTER DUVAR's *Enamorado* (1879). But the most exotic locale might be the gothic, outlaw-infested mountains of Hamilton, Ont., in George Washington Johnson's revenge tale *The Count's Bride*, published in Hamilton in 1864. Hunter Duvar also wrote *De Roberval* (1888), which struggles in vain to dramatize Sieur de Roberval's attempt to establish a settlement at Quebec. In Mair's *Tecumseh* the most interesting character is Lefroy, a poet who writes nostalgically of a beautiful vanishing wilderness and is in love with an Indian maiden. The quiet irony in Mair's treatment of Lefroy offers a reinterpretation of the white man caught between two worlds.

With a lesser poetic but greater dramatic talent than Mair, Sarah Anne CURZON also turned to poetic drama in *Laura Secord, the Heroine of 1812* (1887) to rescue a Canadian from obsurity—with limited success. Curzon's more significant achievement was in a different form, a lively prose comedy, *The Sweet Girl Graduate* (1882), which attacks discrimination against women at the University of Toronto. Earlier in the century, Eliza Lanesford Cushing had chosen the relatively private and lyrical voice of poetic drama to explore the subject of women, particularly creative women, in society. Among her ten plays published in various periodicals, often addressed to a female audience, was *Esther* (*Lady's Book*, 1838), an adaptation of the Biblical story of Queen Esther's fight to save her father from her husband's—the Persian King Ahasueras—decree of death to Jews. Esther's situation—Jewish herself and a victim of villainy by Haman, who was instrumental in establishing the decree—offers a loose parallel to that of nineteenth-century women as Cushing saw them. *Esther*'s blank verse of uneven quality and its overly moral tone are less evident in Cushing's more complex drama, *The Fatal Ring* (*Literary Garland*, 1840), in which a virtuous countess, stifled by the world she lives in, is seduced by the glory of court and an alluring, womanizing King, trapped by his public role.

By the 1850s most towns had a theatre, if only a long room and raised platform in the town hall. Cities had more elaborate structures and were beginning to be able to support professional resident stock companies on a long-term basis. This environment was somewhat more hospitable to the Canadian dramatist, and more Canadian plays began to appear; for instance, Graves Simcoe LEE, a Canadian-born actor in John NICKINSON's company resident at Toronto's ROYAL LYCEUM, wrote what was reported to be the first play by an Upper Canadian seen on a Toronto stage. *Fiddle, Faddle and Foozle* opened on 9 Apr. 1853 and was 'a most decided hit'. Nickinson's company also offered Lee's second farce, *Saucy Kate* (11 July 1853); a subsequent unnamed Lee composition; and Nickinson's own adaptation, *The Fortunes of War* (13 June 1854). None of these plays was published or preserved.

The paratheatrical dramaturgy that had so-far dominated political satire continued throughout the rest of the nineteenth century in numerous publications, including *Grip*, *Grip-Sack*, *Grinchuckle*, and the *Canadian Illustrated News*. But paratheatrical works crafted with greater assurance and skill, such as *Measure by Measure; or, The Coalition in Secret Session* (anon., New Brunswick, seven

Drama in English 1

instalments 25 Feb.-8 Apr. 1871)—one of several plays in the *New Dominion and True Humorist*—were joined by political satires written for and produced in the theatres. One of the first notable stage satires was *The Provincial Association; or, Taxing Each Other* (1845), written by Thomas Hill, editor of *The Loyalist* (Fredericton). Although no copy of the script has been recovered, it is well documented as the cause of a theatre riot in Saint John, N.B. Potentially even more volatile than Hill's satire, *The Female Consistory of Brockville* (1856, staged Dec. 1981), which was based on a contemporary occurrence, was understandably never performed in its own time. Its charges of a conspiracy by thinly disguised local women to drive their minister out of the church allegedly for beating his wife, and of corruption in the Presbyterian Synod at the minister's trial, would almost certainly have provoked furor in the small community. Instead, Caroli Candidus (an ungrammatical Latin pseudonym) published it privately. Also drawing on contemporary but less regional events, three of Sam Scribble's (pseud.) witty satires reached the stage of Montreal's THEATRE ROYAL. Two bear mention: *The King of the Beavers* (1865), first performed in 1865, 'A new original, political, allegorical, burlesque, extravaganza', in which the Queen of the Blue Noses and the King of the Beavers defeat Fenians attacking Beaverland; and *Dolorsolatio* (1865), first performed in 1865, in which various Canadian cities and localities bicker among themselves at Grandpapa Canada's house. Their squabbles are set against the intrusion of feuding Abe North and Jeff South, teaching the wisdom of family unity, useful when Santa Claus arrives with an elixir, 'Dolorsolatio', made of federation. Nicholas Flood DAVIN, a colourful MP, wrote a highly critical view of politics in his lively *The Fair Grit; or, The Advantages of Coalition* (1876), not performed (and only then in a public reading) until 1978, where the son of a Tory and the daughter of a Grit find their love opposed, until the Tory parent sees personal advantage in his joining the Grits. Davin's attack on opportunism and corruption in public office is fierce and non-partisan.

By 1870 Canada was entering a forty-year theatrical boom, marked by the building of numerous halls with stages and 'Grand Opera Houses' in large and small centres across the country: approximately forty theatres with a capacity of 1,000 or more were opened between 1873 and 1892. The force behind this activity was a combination of artistic impulse, civic pride, and financial gain. Profit was the impulse behind the touring circuits that were to bring to each centre professional combination troupes on a regular basis; in some years there were over 300 companies touring Canada. While this flourishing period reflected the presence of a large and interested Canadian audience, and while it made possible professional careers for many Canadian performers, back-stage workers, theatre owners, and producers, it offered little for the development of Canadian drama because the circuits and companies were American-dominated and almost exclusively non-Canadian in their repertoire. (See TOURING STARS AND COMPANIES.) Several Canadians gained prominence working out of the United States and writing the homogeneous commercial vehicles needed on the circuits. Among them was Arthur McKee RANKIN, a well-known actor whose name is associated with approximately two-dozen plays, most of which were co-written or worked on by play-doctors. Rankin starred over 2,000 times in Joaquin Miller's *The Danites*, and his *Abraham Lincoln*—the first play to recall the assassination—was performed five times in 1891, before Lincoln's son and others urged its withdrawal as being too soon after the event. Another well-known actor and director, Willard Mack (Charles McLaughlin), wrote popular commercial successes, the most famous of which was *Tiger Rose*, first performed in 1917, a melodramatic romance set in western Canada with a plot much like the later musical *Rose Marie*. For twenty years William A. TREMAYNE wrote pot-boilers, such as *The Secret Warrant*, first performed in 1897, and *The Black Feather*, first performed in 1916, published as *The Man Who Went* (1918). *Seats of the Mighty*, first performed in 1896, was adapted by expatriate Gilbert PARKER from his own popular novel. Simplified to a sensational romance in the historical setting of François Bigot's 'Little Versailles', *Seats of the Mighty* afforded opportunity for colourful period staging and a cloak-and-sword role for Herbert Beerbohm Tree, who took it on his second American tour and then used it to open Her Majesty's Theatre in London, Eng., in 1897.

The commercial theatre, which pragmatically made use of any element that might help fill the house, occasionally staged plays, especially musicals, with local appeal: this normally meant a Mountie here, a northern wilderness there, as in Willard Mack's *Tiger Rose*. However, some exceptions exist where Canada is included for its own sake rather than as atmospheric stereotype. Cashing in on the popularity of Gilbert and Sullivan, William Henry FULLER—who, ironically, may have been American (various claims have been made about his birthplace)—wrote what is likely the best-known nineteenth-century Canadian piece, *H.M.S. Parliament; or, The Lady Who Loved a Government Clerk* (1880). After opening *Parliament* in Montreal on 16 Feb. 1880, a few doors away from a production of *H.M.S. Pinafore*, American actor-manager Eugene A. McDOWELL's Shaughraun Company took this satirical account of Canadian politics on a successful national tour. Fuller was also the author of an amusing paratheatrical satire, *The Unspecific Scandal* (1874), and of several other stage pieces, including *A Barber's Scrape* (performed in 1886) and *Flapdoodle*. John Wilson Bengough, editor of *Grip*, also borrowed from Gilbert and Sullivan for *Bunthorne Abroad; or, The Lass That Loved a Pirate* (1883), which was first staged by the Templeton Star Opera Company in Hamilton in 1886: the crew of HMS Pinafore saves Bunthorne from the Pirates of Penzance who were driven to crime by his aestheticism. In Kingston the poet George Frederick Cameron combined with Oscar Telgman, a well-regarded local musician, for a 'military opera', *Leo, the Royal Cadet* (1889), first staged in 1889, in which a cadet from Kingston's Royal Military College goes off to fight the Zulus, eventually returning to his Nellie's loving arms with a Victoria Cross. Staged first by local amateurs, *Leo* was toured with some success by Telgman throughout Canada and the U.S.

Most plays concerned with Canadian issues or character were performed by amateur companies for local audiences. Jean Newton McIlwraith, and noted composer John E.P. Aldous, created *Ptarmigan; or, A Canadian Carnival* (1895), first performed in Hamilton in 1895, which satirically sketches the fate of the migrant Ptarmigan on his return from the United States where he signed papers to become an American citizen. While exploring Canadian identity, including artistic identity, the operetta makes clear that Ptarmigan's actions were lunacy when he

could have remained a citizen of British Canada. Like *Ptarmigan*'s topical connection with annexation, George BROUGHALL's *The 90th on Active Service; or Campaigning in the North West*, first performed and published in 1885, grew out of a crucial national event, the Riel Rebellion. However, his musical burlesque, performed in Winnipeg by the 90th Battalion, is a variety show on military camp life that makes almost no mention of issues or people in the rebellion they had been sent to quell. The same is largely true of Sergeant L. Dixon's *Our Boys in the Riel Rebellion. Halifax to the Saskatchewan*, first performed and published in 1886.

Another amateur theatre that aided the development of indigenous drama was under the vice-regal auspices of Lady Dufferin who included a theatre in her renovations of the Governor General's residence, RIDEAU HALL. Between 1873 and 1878 she organized dramatic performances there, frequently written by Frederick A. DIXON, tutor to her children.

2. The First World War to the Thirties. The years around the First World War brought major changes for drama in Canada. Facing rising costs and competition from the movies, the American-dominated touring business succumbed to the vapidity of its own commercial fare and to the disruptions caused by the War. Simultaneously, the growing power of nationalist voices called for the de-annexation of the Canadian stage—which ironically led to the deliberate importing of British touring companies for a brief time immediately before and after the War. Doubly ironic, several distinguished members of these companies urged the establishment of a Canadian national theatre, albeit a very British one. In cities during the twenties there was a flourishing of resident stock companies, less expensive to run and claiming a connection with the community, but they offered essentially the same fare as the touring professionals. When the Depression made money scarce, and radio entertainment arrived, these commercial ventures fell off.

At the same time, various initiatives helped shape a more supportive context for the Canadian dramatist. In 1906 the Margaret Eaton School of Literature and Expression in Toronto began to offer formal instruction in drama: Dora Mavor MOORE was among its early graduates. In 1907 Governor General Earl Grey began his national dramatic com-

Drama in English 2

petitions, which provided official backing for Canadian theatre activity. Performers included the likes of Mr and Mrs Stephen LEACOCK (in Shaw's *Arms and the Man*, 1907) and Dora Mavor Moore, who was praised in Catharine Nina Merritt's three-act comedy, *A Little Leaven*, during the 1910 competition at Toronto's ROYAL ALEXANDRA THEATRE. Merritt had previously published *When George the Third Was King* (1897), a competent but not very lively three-act historical drama that celebrated a romanticized United Empire Loyalist escape to southern Ontario from revolutionary United States. Of lasting importance, Toronto's ARTS AND LETTERS CLUB, founded in 1908, began its stage productions under Roy MITCHELL's supervision.

Prevalent in the early twentieth century were children's plays, and educational, temperance, and religious dramas, as were humorous dramatic sketches, such as adaptations from Dickens, and Stephen Leacock's burlesques of nineteenth-century theatrical modes. And there were still poetic dramas, such as Robert Norwood's *The Witch of Endor* (1916). All were staged by amateurs—amateur theatre was seen as a vital alternative for Canadian dramatists. Inspired partly by the art-theatre movement in Europe and the U.S., Canadian amateur groups eschewed the practices and commercial values associated with large and expensive professional companies. Ireland's Abbey Theatre was seen as an almost perfect model of a theatre dedicated to new dramaturgy and national expression. In 1919 HART HOUSE THEATRE opened as the beacon of this LITTLE THEATRE movement, offering an intimate performance-space for challenging plays that ranged from detailed psychological and social realism to the mythical, poetic, and expressionistic. Most important, Hart House had a mandate to include Canadian works among its productions. In its second season (Apr. 1921) it presented a bill of one-acts (the form itself an anti-commercial reaction): *Pierre*, by poet Duncan Campbell Scott, *The Second Lie* by Isabel Ecclestone MacKay, and *Brothers in Arms* by Merrill DENISON. Scott's play is a heavy-handed ironic tale in a realistic mode of a prodigal son who returns to his Quebec home and steals the family savings meant to send his sister to hospital. MacKay's realism explores the psychological tensions created by a husband who tricks his wife into poisoning him. *Brothers in Arms*, providing light comic

relief in exposing naive assumptions about character and rural Canadian life, continued to be staged for many years.

These three plays, with eight others from the early Hart House seasons, were published with a short but seminal introduction by Vincent MASSEY in *Canadian Plays from Hart House Theatre* (2 vols., 1926/1927), which gives a fair representation of the drama of the period. In Carroll AIKINS' *God of Gods* an Indian maiden, manipulated into becoming the tribe's priestess, reveals the trickery and hypocrisy behind their religious worship when she discovers her lover has been killed. Although in need of trimming, overly melodramatic and stilted, the play was exotic enough to be well-received not only at its première and revival by the Birmingham Repertory Theatre in 1919, but also in a production by London's Everyman Theatre in 1931. Massey's volumes also include Henry Borsook's *Three Weddings of a Hunchback*, first performed in 1923, a dark comedy centred on the youngest daughter, a hunchback, at three successive marriages in a Jewish family. Britton Cooke's *The Translation of John Snaith*, first performed in 1923, while suffering from faulty dramaturgy, has interesting thematic potential in its tale of an army deserter who secretly returns to his northern-Ontario town only to discover that the overseas man who bought his papers has been awarded a Victoria Cross. Haunted by his cowardice and deception, Snaith is led to suicide by a mysterious half-breed with whom he previously had a child. Cooke's other plays are shorter and display surer craft, while continuing to explore characters at odds with their community and conventional behaviour; for example, *Gloriana* (1916) reveals, on one hand, the disaster befalling a couple unsuited to the rigours of farm life, and on the other the love they shared: a triumph of the spiritual over the physical. Among the remaining plays in the Hart House volumes, Marian Osborne's mildly amusing *Point of View*, first performed in 1923, owes too big a debt to Shaw and English light comedies. Two others are ignorable: Leslie Reid's *Trespassers*, first performed in 1923, and Louis Alexander MacKay's *The Freedom of Jean Guichet*, first performed in 1925. In Merrill Denison's *Balm*, first performed in 1923, an elderly woman, denied her request to adopt a child, drives the insulting social worker from the house, and in his

The Weather Breeder, first performed in 1924, a cantankerous old farmer's reactions to the weather are humorously dramatized. Denison had six plays staged at Hart House. Among his achievements was the publication of the first significant collection of Canadian plays, *The Unheroic North* (1923), whose title derived from his urge to attack ill-founded ideas about Canadian life. The collection contains *Brothers in Arms*, *The Weather Breeder*, and *From Their Own Place*, as well as his strongest work, MARSH HAY.

There were other important writers and plays at Hart House in these years. Following their highly praised local production, the Montreal Community Players travelled to Toronto with Marjorie Pickthall's *The Woodcarver's Wife* (1920), first performed in 1921. This verse-play is a deceptively simple romantic melodrama in which a sculptor is unable to complete his half-Indian Pieta because the model, his wife, cannot express deep sorrow—until she is caught betraying him with an Indian lover. But the creative paradox, the poetic imagery, and the jealous husband's extreme revenge lead us to other possibilities where we see the way a role shapes female identity, and gain an indirect view of Pickthall herself as an artist confined by her identity as a female Victorian poet. Two short realistic plays by Mazo de la Roche also appeared at Hart House: *The Return of the Emigrant* (1929), first performed in 1928, and *Come True*, first performed and published in 1927. Another one-act, *Low Life*, first performed and published in 1925, was staged by Montreal's Trinity Players. It won first prize in competitions organized by the IODE and the Montreal Branch of the Canadian Authors' Association. Her *Whiteoaks*, first performed and published in 1936, is a conventional three-act drama adapted from her novels. Before the war *Whiteoaks* ran for over 800 performances in London, Eng.; an American production, starring Ethel Barrymore, played in Toronto, on Broadway for 112 performances, and then toured the United States.

Hart House resources and staff, and its pool of performers and young directors, were also available to those outside its scheduled programming. From the time it was founded by Leonora McNeilly in 1932 until 1941 the Playwrights Studio Group offered at least two annual bills at Hart House. As well as being one of the earliest organizations devoted to playwright development, the Group is an indication of the heavy involvement of women in the development of Canadian theatre. Among the Group's most important dramatists were Rica McLean Farquharson, Winnifred Pilcher, Marjorie Price, Virginia Coyne Knight, Dora Smith Conover, and Lois Reynolds KERR. Farquharson, editor of the *Canadian Home Journal* and wife of the editor of the *Globe and Mail*, contributed eight plays, as did Knight. Kerr has written some twenty-six plays, eight of which were staged by the Group. She won an IODE drama award for *Open Doors* (1930), first performed in 1931, in which the family of an immigrant worker, driven mad by poverty and exploitation on the job, is helped by the philanthropic daughter of a wealthy, exploitative industrialist. But much of Kerr's work was satirical comedy—in *Among Those Present* (1938), first performed in 1933, for example, she drew on her experience as a society writer for the *Globe and Mail* to attack social climbers.

The early twentieth century in Europe and the U.S. saw the conjunction of major advances in stage technology with an artistic community searching for new modes of theatrical expression: a move toward a director's theatre and the creation of anti-naturalistic, highly theatrical forms—symbolism, futurism, surrealism, dadaism, constructivism, among others. Canada, too, had its own experimental activity. Hart House had appointed as its first director Roy Mitchell, whose approach to staging, outlined in his inspirational book *Creative Theatre* (1929), placed emphasis on abstract visual images and sounds, and on the relationship between actors and the space in which they moved. Away from Hart House, Herman VOADEN—whose influences included Richard Wagner, Gordon Craig, the German Expressionists, and Eugene O'Neill—abandoned realism, as in *Wilderness* (1978), first performed in 1931, to write and stage works in a form he called 'symphonic expressionism'. His plays—such as the prototypical 'painter's ballet', *Symphony: A Drama of Motion and Light for a New Theatre* (written in 1930 with Lowrie Warrener, published in 1982), *Rocks* (an abstraction of *Wilderness*), first performed in 1932, and the much later *Murder Pattern* (1975), first performed in 1936—utilized evocative music, image-laden language, choral presentation, and the sculpting properties of highly directional light on abstract settings and balletic motion. Subject to a mixed reception, often by critics insensitive to their three-dimensional, non-literary values, the plays offer compelling theatricality but a naive, underdeveloped philosophy. Voaden brought his gift for impressive staging to works by other playwrights, such as the well-known abstract painter, critic, and businessman Bertram BROOKER. Both *Within* (1985), 'a drama of mind in revolt', first performed in 1930, and *The Dragon* (1985), 'a parable of illusion and disillusion', first performed in 1936, were produced at Voaden's Play Workshop and drew praise from reviewers who appreciated their allegorical, expressionistic representation of metaphysical questions.

Ideological commitment and experiments with the stage as a weapon in the battle for social, economic, and political reform characterised the left-leaning Workers' Theatre of the late 1920s and 1930s. As well as plays from the workers' movement in other countries, Progressive Arts Clubs across Canada performed their own drama aimed at educating and galvanizing the working class into action. In the process, they employed anti-illusionistic techniques similar to those of Erwin Piscator and Bertolt Brecht, and the presentational modes of agit-prop dramaturgy. In Oscar Ryan's 'mass recitation', *Unity*, first performed and published in 1933, four broadly drawn Capitalists in white spats, silk hats, and canes are defeated by a chorus of workers; Stanley Ryerson's *War in the East*, first performed and published in 1933, shows Japanese workers uniting in their opposition to Japan's assault on Manchuria; Dorothy Livesay's *Joe Derry*, first performed and published in 1933, is a narrated pantomime for children, urging unity and adherence to the principles of the Young Communist League. The most famous of the Workers' Theatre plays is EIGHT MEN SPEAK (1933), whose second Toronto performance was suppressed by a police 'Red Squad', as was the Winnipeg PAC's staging scheduled for the WALKER THEATRE. Written by Oscar Ryan, E. Cecil-Smith, Frank Love, and Mildred Goldberg, this five-act play culminates in the trial of Guard X, defended by his lawyer Capitalism, for attempting to assassinate Tim Buck, who was in Kingston Penitentiary with seven others as leaders of the outlawed Communist Party of Canada.

(See POLITICAL AND POPULAR THEATRE.)

After 1936 the Workers' Theatre became somewhat more conventional in its theatrical programming, even to the point where Toronto's Theatre of Action entered their production of Irwin Shaw's *Bury the Dead* in the 1937 DOMINION DRAMA FESTIVAL. That they were finalists indicates their level of skill; that they did not win has sometimes been seen as an indication of their non-Establishment status. For the Festival—another development of the 1930s with a major impact on Canadian drama—was Establishment: evening gowns, tails, and high society. In 1932 Governor General Bessborough—responding to his own love of drama, as well as to the enormous growth in Little Theatres, and repeated calls for a national theatre—drew together a small group of interested individuals, including Vincent Massey, to develop his plans for a national dramatic competition, not unlike the Earl Grey competitions in several respects but more ambitious. The Festival was renamed Theatre Canada in 1970 and ceased operations in 1978. The DDF succeeded in giving a national shape to amateur theatre (more to English than French), establishing overall standards (British, and inconsistently maintained), and providing opportunities for developing craft at the amateur level (for dramatists there was a Best Canadian Play award).

The Canadian Radio Broadcasting Commission, founded in 1932—it became the Canadian Broadcasting Corporation in 1936—also nurtured the development of Canadian drama. In its first thirty years the CBC produced some 3,000 original Canadian dramas; because they were mostly in short time slots, the one-act play—which was also so important to the Little Theatre movement and to the time-limits of the Dominion Drama Festival competitions—was the dominant form for nearly fifty years. (See RADIO DRAMA.) Early radio drama, broadcast from 1925 by the Canadian National Railway Radio Department, can be sampled in *Henry Hudson and Other Plays* (1931), which contains six of Merrill Denison's two-dozen scripts on Canadian history developed with producer Tyrone GUTHRIE for 'The Romance of Canada' series.

As for stage plays of the 1930s, the DDF newsletter, *CURTAIN CALL*, regularly printed short texts, such as Elsie Park GOWAN's *The

Royal Touch, first performed and published in 1935, an often-staged 'Ruritanian Fable' centred on a princess and other young people searching for values in life. As well, Samuel French Ltd launched its Canadian Playwrights Series in the mid-thirties, offering a variety of one-acts. *God Caesar*, first performed and published in 1935, is a DDF Best Canadian Play winner by Marjorie Price in which Cleopatra tempts Caesar while Calpurnia's slave, disguised as a statue, watches. Lois Reynolds Kerr's *Nellie McNabb* (1937), first staged by the Playwrights' Studio Group in 1934, is a society comedy that earned over $1,100 in royalties from more than one hundred different productions. But *Nellie McNabb* was edged out of a 1936 Best Canadian Play Award by Eric Harris's realistic *Twenty Five Cents*, first performed and published in 1936, which illustrates the demoralizing effects of the Depression on a working-class family. *Twenty Five Cents* was also printed by French in Margaret Mayorga's *Best One-Act Plays of 1937* (1938). *Summer Solstice* (1935) by Martha ALLAN, director of the MONTREAL REPERTORY THEATRE, is an anti-war play influenced by Shaw's *Heartbreak House*. Less serious fare, *The Lampshade* (1935), first performed in 1925, is an English murder mystery by W.S. Milne, a teacher whose playwriting was encouraged by Bertram Forsyth, director of Hart House, where *The Lampshade* was premièred. Lillian Beynon Thomas's amusing and popular light comedy *Jim Barber's Spite Fence* (1936), first performed by the Winnipeg Little Theatre in 1933, is about two neighbours feuding over a fence. Finally, French's *Plays of the Pacific Coast* (1935) collects Archibald Macdonald Duff Fairburn's four one-acts dramatizing the collision of white and west-coast native cultures. The famous Quebec legend of Rose's dance with the Devil is engagingly dramatized in the rhyming couplets of E.W. Devlin's *Rose Latulippe* (1935).

Among the masters of the one-act was Gwen Pharis RINGWOOD, who was a cornerstone of western Canada's extensive amateur theatre and a founder of modern Canadian drama. Inspired by Robert Gard's and Frederick Koch's ideas on 'folk drama', Ringwood wrote what is deemed a classic of Canadian theatre, STILL STANDS THE HOUSE (1938), a moving, realistic portrayal of spiritual starvation on the drought-stricken prai-

ries. Over her fifty-year career Ringwood wrote more than forty plays, ranging from the zany comedy of *Widger's Way* (1976), the sentimental folk history of *The Rainmaker* (1946), and the poignant wisdom of *Garage Sale* (1982), to the violence and echoes of Greek tragedy in her Indian trilogy, *Lament for Harmonica* (or *Maya*) (1975), *The Stranger* (1979), and *The Furies* (1982).

3. *The Birth of Professional Theatre*. The DDF suspended operation before a competition could be held in 1940, but many individual little theatres carried on limited, local activity throughout the Second World War, and remained vehicles for Canadian plays, although often only revues connected with the war effort. When the war ended, new energy filled the country, bringing changes eventually as important to Canadian drama as those following the First World War. In 1944 the federal government appointed a committee on Reconstruction and Re-establishment, and although nothing came immediately of its plan for a $10,000,000 subsidy to the arts, the same thinking informed the Massey Commission in 1951 that led to the formation of the Canada Council in 1957. The DDF, in 1947, despite internal problems (in particular shaky finances and francophone disaffection), launched a vigorous new Festival. But even before the war, signs of incipient change were discernible in an undercurrent of dissatisfaction with the standards and limitations of the DDF and in attempts at building professional companies, such as the John HOLDEN Players. The war experience for some people had included overseas' exposure to theatre of a type and quality they had not seen before, and that left them wanting more. In addition, a large pool of talent was forming in Canada who sought careers in a professional theatre. The group contained some imports, some new immigrants, Canadians who had been in stock companies during the twenties or thirties, or in the armed-forces' entertainment corps, radio performers, aspiring amateurs, and students from universities. This last body included those trained by Robert GILL at Hart House Theatre, and in programs at the Univ. of Saskatchewan (founded in 1945—the first in Canada), Queen's Univ., the Univ. of Alberta, and the Banff School of Fine Arts (see BANFF CENTRE). Fruitful drama-education programs, usually under extension

departments, had been pioneered in the West as early as the mid-thirties by people like the dynamic Elizabeth Sterling HAYNES, who greatly influenced the career of Gwen Ringwood.

Within eight years of the war's end, over two-dozen theatre companies (most of them short-lived) were established across the country with full professional status or clearly professional aims. Among them were the LONDON THEATRE COMPANY in St John's, the Montreal Repertory Theatre, Ottawa's CANADIAN REPERTORY THEATRE, the INTERNATIONAL PLAYERS, which ran seasons in Kingston and Toronto, the NEW PLAY SOCIETY, the JUPITER and CREST THEATRES in Toronto, Calgary's Workshop 14, the Western Stage Society, and Sydney RISK's Everyman Theatre in Vancouver. There were, as well, numerous summer stock companies, such as the Straw Hat Players, the Red Barn Theatre, BRAE MANOR THEATRE, and the Montreal MOUNTAIN PLAYHOUSE. The CANADIAN PLAYERS, a winter troupe, grew out of the STRATFORD FESTIVAL, the climax of this development.

Many of these companies, operating on a shoestring and mounting a different play every week, felt unable to risk untried Canadian fare or the time to develop it. But there were exceptions, such as the Everyman Theatre, which in 1947 toured Elsie Park Gowan's *The Last Caveman* (1987), a three-act comedy she termed 'a plea for international order'. Its dialogue is sometimes weak and its characters too thin to support her serious themes, but the plot deftly interweaves post-war humanitarianism with personal animosities and economic opportunism. Dora Mavor Moore's New Play Society, along with its bills of important international drama, ran a theatre school and staged forty-seven Canadian plays between 1946 and 1956, including works by Morley Callaghan, Mazo de la Roche, and Lister SINCLAIR. The most significant was *RIEL* (1962) by John COULTER, another founder of modern Canadian drama. His Irish plays were standards of the amateur theatre, especially a DDF award-winning light comedy, *The House in the Quiet Glen* (1937). *Riel*, first produced in 1950, which audiences found moving and provocative despite its weaknesses, highlighted the possibility in professional theatres of plays based on Canadian history. It also showed a degree of innovation: three years before Strat-

ford's thrust stage, this episodic drama, Coulter explains, was 'designed for presentation in the Elizabethan manner: a continuous flow of scenes on a bare stage. . . .'

The dominant playwright of the late forties and fifties was Robertson DAVIES, whose award-winning one-acts, such as *Overlaid* (1948) and *Eros at Breakfast* (1949), were popular with amateur theatres. The changes in Canadian theatre meant that Davies, like others, had access to professional stages: for instance, *Fortune, My Foe* (1949) was first produced by the International Players and, the following season, opened the Peterborough Summer Theatre; Peterborough staged another of his full-length plays, *AT MY HEART'S CORE* (1950), as did the Canadian Repertory Theatre. Influenced partly by the potential in this professional environment, such as Donald DAVIS's strong acting at the Crest where *A Jig for the Gypsy* (1954) and

Barbara Chilcott in Robertson Davies' A Jig for the Gypsy, *Crest Theatre, Toronto, 1954*

Hunting Stuart (1972) premièred, Davies developed the satirical attacks on philistine Canada, so eloquently stated in his early short plays, in the direction of the complex mythical and archetypal structures characteristic of his later novels. These plays include *General Confession* (1972), *Love and Libel* (1981), *Question Time* (1975), and *Pontiac and the Green Man*, staged in 1977 at the Univ. of Toronto.

The emergence of an indigenous professional theatre coincided with the 'golden age' of radio drama in the 1940s, and with the birth of television drama. Among the works of dramatists noted for their radio or television plays are a number that were produced in the theatre or have been otherwise influential in the development of Canadian drama. Len PETERSON's one-act BURLAP BAGS (1972), performed on radio, television, and the stage, is an important transition between the expressionism of the 1930s and post-war existentialism. Reliving the diary of a tramp driven to suicide, its characters place burlap bags over their heads, illustrating the individual's isolation in an absurd and insensitive world. Peterson went on to write *The Great Hunger* (1967), *Almighty Voice* (1974), and *Women in the Attic* (1972), all of which have had stage productions. The Jupiter Theatre produced two plays by the prolific radio dramatist Lister Sinclair: *Socrates* (in 1952) and *The Blood Is Strong* (in 1956), the latter about the different degrees of adaptation to Cape Breton life among three generations of a Scottish immigrant family. Applauded at the time, they now appear talky and dull. W.O. MITCHELL's *The Devil's Instrument* (1973) was also successful on radio but is underdeveloped as a serious stage drama about a prairie Hutterite youth rebelling against his religion. *The Black Bonspiel of Wullie MacCrimmon* (1965), popular with summer theatres, offers light humour in a curling match between Wullie and the Devil. *Back to Beulah* (1982), a more recent stage play, won a CHALMERS Award in 1976, but is only a sitcom lifted by Mitchell's gift for creating idiosyncratic characters. The poet Earle BIRNEY, who employed radio's power with words and its willingness to tackle controversial topics when he wrote *The Damnation of Vancouver* (published as *The Trial of a City*, 1952), adapted his clever dramatic poem for the theatre, but his uncompromising criticism of humankind's destruction of the natural environment kept the play from being given anything more than several staged readings. Radio producer John Reeves hit out at Canadian puritanism in *A Beach of Strangers* (1961), a verse-drama in the manner of Dylan Thomas's *Under Milkwood*. Among the most-adapted plays is Patricia JOUDRY's popular *Teach Me How to Cry*, a sentimental and psychologically naive tale of two adolescents fighting their parents and society for freedom to love. First produced on radio

(1953), followed by television (1953), it was staged professionally in New York (1955), won a DDF Best Play award (1956), and was retitled *Noon Has No Shadows* for London's West End, then *The Restless Years* as a movie. Joudry's more recent plays have not been well received. George RYGA's hard-hitting short play *Indian* (1962), produced first on television, then on radio and the stage, marked the beginning of his important career as a playwright.

The founding of the MANITOBA THEATRE CENTRE in 1958—with its mainstage, warehouse, and audience-development programs—introduced what is loosely called the 'regional' theatre movement. By the end of the sixties most urban centres had large professional houses, usually with resident companies but rarely with all three parts of the MTC mandate. Assisted by the Canada Council, as well as by local finances, they were better funded and better equipped than the early fifties' ventures. As a result, like the Stratford Festival, they provided stability, helped raise production standards, employed a large number of professionals, and came to be seen as the established theatres.

One contrast to these hierarchically structured institutions, with their bills dominated by mainstream international titles, was George LUSCOMBE's politically committed TORONTO WORKSHOP PRODUCTIONS. Begun in 1959, TWP staged plays by writers such as Garcia Lorca and Luigi Pirandello in the basement of a printer's shop in Toronto's industrial west end. They also produced Canadian writers, such as Len Peterson (*Burlap Bags*), and developed original plays using the company improvisational methods of England's Joan Littlewood, with whom Luscombe had worked. Over the years TWP has contributed to the Canadian canon many highly entertaining, often provocative DOCUMENTARY DRAMAs, such as *Hey, Rube!*, the company's first group creation, staged in 1961; *Chicago '70*, dealing with the Chicago Seven trial; *Mr Bones* (in 1969) about racial tensions; and TEN LOST YEARS (in 1974), developed by Luscombe and Jack Winter from Barry Broadfoot's oral history of the Depression. The collaborative method, the documentary approach, and the use of techniques that foregrounded the performance mode, made TWP important not only in itself, but as a herald of things to come in Canadian theatre.

Drama in English 3

Canada's Centennial (1967) gave rise to increased support for things Canadian, including the developing theatre. Centennial Year itself was highlighted by the appearance of four important plays focused on Canadian life. The Manitoba Theatre Centre staged Ann HENRY's *Lulu Street*, which dramatizes events in a boarding house during Winnipeg's 1919 General Strike. John HERBERT's *FORTUNE AND MEN'S EYES* had its first full production—but, ironically, in New York. It had received a workshop staging at the Stratford Festival in 1965, but its graphic depiction of the violent, homosexual, and exploitative world of Canadian prisons, which implied that the outside world was no better, was judged inappropriate for the Festival's regular program. In 1967, however, the Festival's Avon Theatre bill included *Colours in the Dark*, the first of James REANEY's plays to gain a major professional production. In *The Killdeer* (1962), *The Easter Egg* (1972), and *Listen to the Wind* (1972), which were staged by amateur groups, Reaney had created symbolic reflections of the way he perceived creativity being inhibited by insensitive puritanical forces. He had shaped his expression in accessible, though highly symbolic melodramatic plots that pitted good against evil in a battle for the safety of an innocent victim. *Colours* is a less conventional play, an arrangement of scenes tied together by the thematic relationships among various physical objects, colours, poems, and archetypal characters associated with a young boy growing up in rural Ontario. Audiences found it enjoyable but baffling.

The greatest impact in Centennial Year came from George Ryga's *The ECSTASY OF RITA JOE* in an outstanding VANCOUVER PLAYHOUSE production. This episodic drama takes the form of a trial of an Indian woman whose encounter with white urban society has separated her from native ways and forced her into crime and prostitution. Eventually, she is murdered, then raped. Ryga's multimedia *Grass and Wild Strawberries* (1971) was a second popular success at the Vancouver Playhouse. But when the commissioned *Captives of the Faceless Drummer* (1971) was being worked on, various members of the Playhouse Board were troubled by its alleged allusions to the 1970 FLQ hostage-taking. They refused to stage the play, which was presented instead at the Vancouver Art Gallery in 1971. Nearly two decades passed, during which *Captives*, the enormously popular *Rita Joe*, and Ryga's subsequent plays were produced in many theatres, before the Playhouse mounted its next Ryga work, a lavish first production (1987) of *Paracelsus*. It received scathing notices.

By the late sixties a generation of young people were seeking not only professional careers in the theatre, but their own drama. With only a couple of exceptions—such as Regina's GLOBE and Montreal's CENTAUR—regional theatres, as well as the Stratford and SHAW FESTIVALs, had built a reputation for offering few opportunities to Canadian plays, and for leaving Canadians out of major posts. With this as a spur, and with the international ALTERNATE THEATRE movement and counter-culture as influences, these young people founded their own theatres all across Canada, often funded by Local Initiatives or Opportunities for Youth grants. They ranged from writers' development groups, such as Vancouver's NEW PLAY CENTRE founded in 1970, through collectives, to more traditionally structured theatres; their productions ranged from workshops to full stage presentations of finished scripts. In almost all cases these theatres had a strong commitment to Canadian plays, with the result that Canadian drama flourished as never before. Its extent prompted the founding in 1972 of the Playwrights Co-op, now Playwrights Union of Canada, with a mandate to publish and distribute Canadian scripts.

One of the dominant dramatic modes in this explosion was a neo-naturalistic, detailed realism that explored the psychology of human action seen within the influences of specific Canadian environments. William Fruet's *Wedding in White* (1973), set in a small prairie town near the end of the Second World War, is close to the quintessential neo-naturalistic play, showing a heritage of repressive and hypocritical male-centred puritanism preying on a young victim's innate simple-mindedness. Fruet's play ran for eight weeks at Toronto's Poor Alex Theatre in 1972, and was later made into a film starring Donald Pleasence and Carol Kane. An even larger impact was registered by David FREEMAN's *CREEPS* (1972), first in a FACTORY THEATRE Lab workshop staging in Feb. 1971, then in a revised version as the opening play at TARRAGON THEATRE in Oct. 1971. Essentially a realistic play with surrealistic interjections, *Creeps* offers a searing, but at times hilarious look at life for a group of handi-capped people congregated in the washroom of their sheltered workshop. Freeman's sec-ond play, *Battering Ram* (1972), presents the sexual exploitation of a handicapped young man by a mother and her daughter, who are in turn exploited by him. But neither Free-man's *You're Gonna Be Alright, Jamie Boy* (1974), revealing the empty values of a family addicted to television, nor *Flytrap* (1976), live up to his two earlier works. *Leaving Home* (1972), David FRENCH's compassionate, humorous but lacerating portrayal of the psy-chological tensions in a Newfoundland fam-ily, the Mercers, living in Toronto, was the second hit of Tarragon Theatre's first season. When the well-crafted *Of the Fields, Lately* (1973), also about the Mercer family, was a second-season Tarragon success, French's playwriting career, which has placed him among the most important of Canada's play-wrights, was firmly established. Pool-room realism in the undistinguished *One Crack Out* (1975) preceded *Jitters* (1980), a popular and witty comedy satirizing Canadian theatre, and, through that, Canadian foibles in gen-eral. French's third play about the Mercer family, *Salt-Water Moon* (1985), staged at Tar-ragon in 1984, shows further refinement in his substantial skills, and his realism enhanced by a haunting lyricism, evident but not devel-oped in the early plays, that captures pro-found, bitter-sweet moments in the lives of his characters. A fourth Mercer play, *1949*, was produced in the fall of 1988. (See the MERCER PLAYS.)

In various forms realism has remained prev-alent since its early-1970s flourishing. The flamboyance of actor John Barrymore is matched by Ned Sheldon's reserve as the two face Ned's imminent death in Sheldon ROSEN's *Ned and Jack* (1979), a Stratford Festival production in 1979. *The Working Man* (1976), *The Jones Boy* (1978), and *Some-thing Red* (1980) are Tom WALMSLEY's graphic depictions of an anarchic subculture that expresses itself sensationally through drugs, sex, and violence. In *Cold Comfort* (1981), Jim GARRARD infuses the gothic tale of a travelling salesman and the closely guarded daughter of a prairie garage mechanic with an oblique humour that points up themes of spiritual, sexual, and cultural starvation. *Canadian Gothic* (1977) is the eponymous subject of Joanna GLASS's early one-act play, which dramatizes the haunting

memories of a young prairie woman, her mother, and her father. Glass is also the author of *Artichoke* (1979), whose first stag-ing (New York, 1975) starred Colleen Dewhurst, and of *Play Memory* (1987), win-ner of a 1984 Tony Award. There is a hint of prairie gothic also in Betty LAMBERT's *Jennie's Story* (1981), which dramatizes an incident concerning sterilization for the 'unfit' without the individual's consent. Through the clash between an Amish youth and his father, Anne CHISLETT's *Quiet in the Land* (1983) presents the larger conflicts exist-ing within the need for personal freedom, the will to seek change, and the adherence to wise tradition. A Marxist realism that sees the social and physical environments as the changing result of a class struggle has been characteristic of David FENNARIO's work. *On the Job* (1976) and *Nothing to Lose* (1977)—first staged at the Centaur Theatre in 1975 and 1976 respectively—are short, tough, but comic plays that show factory employees attempting to gain some control over their working conditions. BALCON-VILLE (1980) was also staged by the Centaur in a gritty, funny production that won wide acclaim. In it Fennario again demonstrates upper-class exploitation of the working poor who are united at the end to cope with a fire razing their tenement. One of *Balconville*'s distinguishing qualities is the vital, expressive bilingual dialogue spoken by the francophone and anglophone characters. Following *Balcon-ville*'s success in what he might call bourgeois theatres, Fennario wrote *Moving*, a Centaur première in 1984, notable for the develop-ment of the positive role played by the women in *Balconville*. *Joe Beef*, first per-formed in 1985, shows a major transition to the presentational techniques of agit-prop theatre. It reconstructs the history of the Black Rock area and attempts to effect social change by directly involving theatre in a working class community.

John MURRELL's realism has other dimen-sions, as is evident in *Farther West* (1985), about a prostitute pursued ever-westward on the Canadian frontier by a morally obsessive lover. In his *New World* (1985), the Chek-hovian comedy is overburdened by obvious metaphors derived from the relationships of several members of a WASP family to the new and old worlds—Canada, California, and England. In the simpler and widely pro-duced WAITING FOR THE PARADE (1980), episodes in the lives of five women in Calgary during the Second World War juxtapose the abstract impact of the distant war against the immediacy of racial and moral prejudice as well as fatal illness in their midst. *Memoir* (1978) gives us the layered realities of various moments in Sarah Bernhardt's colourful life, which are re-enacted by the aged Bernhardt herself and her secretary Pitou.

Documentary realism was central to one of the post-sixties' other major forms, documentary drama, in which the performance mode itself was foregrounded, and the dramatic action was authenticated by references to various records about the subject, such as court transcripts, newspaper accounts, photographs, and other historical artifacts. Many of these docu-dramas were created by the improvisational work of collective theatre companies, whose plays were characterised by topicality, polemicism, a vignette structure involving rapid changes of time and place, and an inventive, presentational performance style with actors taking multiple roles. Toronto's THEATRE PASSE MURAILLE under Paul THOMPSON's direction became synonymous with documentary drama and COLLECTIVE CREATION. Among Passe Muraille's important plays is The *FARM SHOW* (1976), developed in 1972 out of the company's research in the farming community around Clinton, Ontario. In 1975 Thompson took his troupe to Saskatchewan where they developed *The West Show* (1982), which dramatizes images and myths of prairie life. Influenced by Thompson's approach, 25TH STREET THEATRE in Saskatoon gained local as well as national attention with *PAPER WHEAT* (1977), about homesteading and the Co-operative and Wheat Pool movement on the Prairies. In Newfoundland the MUMMERS TROUPE, founded by Chris BROOKES, created issue-oriented plays, such as *They Club Seals, Don't They?*, which in 1978 defended the local sealing industry. Sometimes the collective documentary involved a writer, as in the case of *Far As the Eye Can See* (1977), scripted by the novelist Rudy Weibe with Theatre Passe Muraille. Here the collaboration of a writer gave the play a more complex structure: *Far As the Eye Can See* juxtaposes a contemporary farmers' protest against strip-mining on their land with Alberta history set against a background chorus provided by Princess Louise, Crowfoot, and William Aberhart—the 'Regal Dead'. Rick SALUTIN collaborated

with Theatre Passe Muraille on *1837: The Farmers' Revolt* (1975), the now-famous play about the Mackenzie Rebellion. *Les CANADIENS* (1977), produced in two versions in 1977, shows documentary and collective characteristics, but was scripted in a traditional manner by Salutin, with an 'assist from Ken Dryden', the Canadiens' goalie.

Medicare! (1982), which deals with the advent of socialized medicine in Saskatchewan, and *Black Powder* (1982), about the Estevan workers' riot in 1931, are two of Canada's purest documentary dramas. But while they possess traits typical of collective creations, they were written by Rex DEVERELL—who had been 'editor-in-chief' for the collective *No. 1 Hard*, an 'investigative documentary' about the grain industry staged in Regina by Ken KRAMER's Globe Theatre in 1975—as the Globe's playwright-in-residence. Deverell also wrote *Boiler Room Suite* (1978), produced by the Globe in 1977, a sensitive, lightly humorous drama about a pair of winos and the caretaker of a derelict building. When Carol BOLT was a young writer in Regina she was commissioned by the Globe to write a play. The result was *Next Year Country*, a documentary satire about a supposed Communist conspiracy, the Regina riot, and the 'On to Ottawa' march. Staged by the Globe in 1971, it was reworked by the Theatre Passe Muraille collective and produced in 1972 as *BUFFALO JUMP* (1972) in Toronto. Since then, Bolt has been a prolific dramatist, particularly for radio and television (as well as a strong presence in the establishment of rights for the Canadian playwright). Among her works for the stage are *Gabe* (1973), in which a hard-living young Métis searches for the spirit of Louis Riel, and *Red Emma* (1974), an episodic portrait of the anarchist, proto-feminist Emma Goldman. *One Night Stand* (1977) is a murder-thriller whose sensational melodrama dominates serious, although superficial, insights about isolation, loneliness, and high-rise living. Her more recent *Escape Entertainment* (1982) is a lightweight satire on Canadian culture; it was poorly received when staged by Tarragon in 1981.

As John Coulter's *Riel* foretold, Canadian individuals and events became the focus for a body of conventional history plays after the late sixties. *CHARBONNEAU & LE CHEF* (1968) by John Thomas McDONOUGH is an unjustifiably neglected drama centred on the battle against Maurice Duplessis and his government by the strikers of Asbestos, Quebec, led by Archbishop Charbonneau. Michael COOK revised several moments from early Canadian history, in a somewhat Brechtian way, to comment on present-day social and political injustices. For all their richness of theme and language, however, the dramatic effectiveness of *Colour the Flesh the Colour of Dust* (1972) and *The Gayden Chronicles* (1977) is muted by their diffuse focus. Cook's less historically oriented plays—including *The HEAD, GUTS AND SOUND BONE DANCE* (1974) and *Jacob's Wake* (1975)—offer a philosophical view of contemporary Newfoundland life. Other Canadian history plays that deserve mention include James NICHOL's *Sainte-Marie among the Hurons* (1977), Ron Chudley's *After Abraham* (1978), and Alden NOWLAN's and Walter LEARNING's *The Dollar Woman* (1981).

In the late-sixties and seventies an impulse to document, re-interpret, theatricalize, and often mythologize historical and contemporary Canadian reality found an imaginative correlative in James Reaney's idiosyncratic genius. His mythopoeic creativity flourished in conjunction with the innovative collective work of the NDWT company under director Keith TURNBULL, particularly in *The DONNELLYS* (*Sticks and Stones*, 1974; *St Nicholas Hotel*, 1976; *Handcuffs*, 1977), one of Canada's foremost dramas. As staged at Tarragon Theatre in 1973, 1974, and 1975 respectively, the trilogy became a focal-point for the new Canadian drama. Offering a hitherto unrealized complexity of theatrical experience, the trilogy is driven by the dramatic inevitability of the catastrophe befalling the Donnellys as well as by the complicated tensions among historical, mythical, and immediate stage realities, and among the resonant images found in the dialogue and its characters, stage action, setting, and props.

Just as documentary drama, collective creation, and Reaney's plays were challenges to established Canadian theatre and its conventional dramas, so the experimental work of many other playwrights and companies in the sixties and seventies extended the boundaries of Canadian drama. In Edmonton, award-winning poet Wilfred WATSON created a drama of 'radical absurdity', which he felt was demanded by the multi-consciousness of the post-modern world. In Vancouver between 1966 and 1972, John JULIANI's SAV-AGE GOD staged a variety of unconventional theatrical events, such as *A Celebration* (7 Jan. 1970), a ritualistic happening at the Vancouver Art Gallery that ended in Juliani's own wedding. Also in Vancouver, and part of the lively underground activity of the time, a group of UBC graduates, including John GRAY and Larry Lillo, founded TAMAHNOUS THEATRE as Theatre Workshop in 1971. They used a collective model in staging challenging contemporary works, such as *Dracula II* (Manchester's Stable Theatre, 1971) or adaptations of classics, such as Jeremy Long's Artaudian *Medea* (1973). They also produced original Canadian scripts—for example, Jeremy Long's *The Final Performance of Vaslav Nijinsky* (in 1972)—and developed a number of their own collective pieces, including *Vertical Dreams* (1979), an imaginative, drama-as-therapy performance based on the dreams and memories of the cast members.

The influential Tamahnous works remain unpublished, as do the stage versions of Michael Ondaatje's *The Collected Works of Billy the Kid* (1970), which has been adapted (sometimes collectively, sometimes by Ondaatje himself) at least twenty-one times. In each case the brilliant poetic narrative was given a dramatic form that juxtaposed short scenes in evocative prose and verse; the staged results (some more successful than others) were an ironic and imagistic theatre that urged viewers to take part in the creation of both mythical and realistic impressions of Billy and to question the nature of each, as well as the process by which they were formed. Probably less influential, yet important, have been the works of several other inventive playwrights. Lawrence Russell brought engaging surrealistic techniques to the theatre in *Penetration* (1972), first staged at the Univ. of Victoria (Dec. 1969), and the *Mystery of the Pig Killer's Daughter* (1975), a gothic mystery first staged at the Toronto Free Theatre (Nov. 1975). Also at Toronto Free (Oct. 1973) Michael HOLLINGSWORTH's *Clear Light* (1973) outraged many audience members and the Toronto Morality Squad with a crude, comic exaggeration of obscene acts. More recently, his wild satirical bent has been evident in *The History of the Village of Small Huts*, and in annual productions with VideoCabaret and Theatre Passe Muraille, which irreverently revise Canadian history in chronological segments. Hrant ALIANAK appears now to have stopped writing for the live stage, but in the early- and mid-seventies he created unconventional, if at times ephemeral, theatre-pieces, such as *Mathematics* (1973)—190 seconds without dialogue, during which six groups of carefully selected objects are thrown one-by-one onto the stage. Ken GASS—the author of a cartoon-like, anti-fascist *Hurrah for Johnny Canuck!* (1975), and founder of Factory Theatre Lab—raised controversy with *The Boy Bishop* (1976), a satirical extravaganza set in New France where a homosexual street-urchin is installed as Bishop of Quebec after the fashion of the Feast of Fools, until he proves as corrupt as Bishop Laval and the Order the boy displaced. Gass's more tightly crafted *Winter Offensive* (1978) has Adolf Eichmann's wife hosting a violent and sexually grotesque Christmas party for Hitler and other Nazi officials as bombs drop around them. Hitler and Eva Braun also indulge in sexual and power fantasies in Bryan WADE's *Blitzkreig* (1974). Larry FINEBERG's early plays show an exuberant imagination expressing a bleak vision of life. The macabre fantasy of *Hope* (1972) includes a young man who finds psychological and sexual comfort in bed with his dog, and a croquet game in which a mallet explodes blowing a player's hand into a bowl of mousse. *Eve* (1977), Fineberg's adaptation of Constance Beresford-Howe's novel *The Book of Eve*, provided a strong role for Jessica Tandy at the Stratford Festival (July 1976), and has been produced internationally. His version of Euripides' *Medea* (1978) proved oversimplified and dull.

Among the forces of change in English-Canadian drama have been productions of works by francophone playwrights and companies (usually in translation). As early as May 1950, an English-language version of Gratien GÉLINAS's *TIT-COQ*—and later of *Bousille and the Just* (*Bousille et les justes*) and *Yesterday the Children Were Dancing* (*HIER, LES ENFANTS DANSAIENT*)—presented to English-speaking audiences a hard-hitting drama that was a realistic, personal, and metaphorical reflection of Quebec identity. All three plays introduced to anglophones the presence of a dynamic francophone theatre and of firmly-established professional playwrights. Gélinas's influence was soon felt at a fundamental level when his plays were included in Canadian drama and literature courses. This type of influence was continued with the publication in 1972 of English trans-

lations of three exceptional French-Canadian plays: Robert GURIK's *The Hanged Man* (*Le PENDU*), Marcel DUBÉ's *The White Geese* (*AU RETOUR DES OIES BLANCHES*), and Guy DUFRESNE's *The Cry of the Whippoorwill* (*Le Cri de l'engoulevent*). But without question, the greatest impact on English-Canada has been made by Michel TREMBLAY, whose *Forever Yours, Marie-Lou* (*À TOI, POUR TOUJOURS, TA MARIE-LOU*) was staged in English by Tarragon Theatre in Nov. 1972. Since then, English translations of almost all of his plays have been widely produced—initially at Tarragon—and published. Tremblay has brought to English-Canada a multi-layered poetic drama, rich in imagery and centred around volatile issues and powerful emotions. His experiments with form, and his use of musical structures, interwoven aria-like monologues, and choruses are among the range of exciting possibilities he has shown to English-Canadian playwrights.

4. *The Pluralism of Contemporary Canadian Drama.* Following a period of re-thinking in Canadian theatres from the mid- to late-seventies—engendered to some extent by funding cut-backs, external pressure toward economic self-sufficiency, and by a natural pause for artists to regenerate their creative imaginations—theatre has moved into the late 1980s with renewed vigour, confidence, and immense variety. If any notable aspect has emerged as characteristic of recent years, it is the pluralism of a theatre that offers many types of drama and company structures, from the experimental to the staid and conventional, from interventionist theatre (CATALYST's *Stand Up for Your Rights*, for example) to DINNER THEATRE to large-scale musicals, from performance art to improvisational comedy clubs, such as THEATRE-SPORTS. But more than any time since the late nineteenth century, commercial viability has become a major consideration, and fostered a tendency in established theatres to avoid taking chances.

Within that framework, several conventional plays have become notable for their commercial success. Peter Colley's *I'll Be Back Before Midnight* (1974), a rural-Canadian murder-mystery, has had numerous productions since it premièred at the BLYTH FESTIVAL in July 1979. Equally popular is Allan STRATTON's situation comedy *Nurse Jane Goes to Hawaii* (1981). Stratton has employed his comic gifts in other, more insightful plays, such as the deceptively simple *Rexy!* (1981), centred on the complex personality of Prime Minister Mackenzie King. Probably leading the list of money-earners are Tom Wood's farcical parody, *B-Movie: The Play* (first staged in Edmonton, 1986), which has had lengthy runs in Toronto, and Sherman Snukal's moralistic sex comedy, TALKING DIRTY (1982). Plays such as these have demonstrated to Canadian dramatists the heretofore unimagined possibility of making a substantial living from their craft.

Interestingly, one of the most financially successful Canadian plays, John KRIZANC's TAMARA, is also among the most deconstructive of traditional dramatic forms. First staged in 1981, the production set-up of *Tamara* allows individual audience members to create their own plays, so to speak, by choosing a character to follow throughout the fascist-guarded estate of Italian poet Gabriele D'Annunzio. No individual, however, sees all the political and amorous intrigue occurring simultaneously in the many rooms, which results in a fragmented, incomplete experience emphasizing how political oppression and sensual obsession destroy the possibility of artistic creation. Krizanc's later and more traditional *Prague* (1987), which has the intricacy of Tom Stoppard's drama, is more successful in communicating to a general audience his views on the relationship between politics and creativity.

As 'environmental' theatre, *Tamara* looks back to other quite unconventional plays, such as the previously mentioned *A Celebration* by John Juliani. Other earlier examples include Theatre Passe Muraille's *Adventures of an Immigrant* (1974), which was presented in several community venues and on one occasion on a Toronto streetcar. More recently— among a range of environmental pieces that included the work of Quebec's CARBONE 14 and Théâtre Repère—David Fennario had the audience travel by bicycles to the various locations in his *Joe Beef on Bikes*.

The many one-person shows that occurred in the seventies and continued into the eighties—which in their very nature were a challenge to traditional dramatic action— were as much a response to economic rationalization, which induced a move to smaller-cast shows, as to the virtuosity of particular performers or to a limited, idiosyncratic skill in others. Inventive playwrights/performers

have often reacted to these conditions (eschewing such old devices as biographical chronology and dialogue by telephone) by developing new sources of dramatic tension for the solo performer. Newfoundland's Cathy Jones created the hilariously satirical *Wedding in Texas* (1986) by bringing together a number of her CODCO sketches with new material, such as the 'filmeo' *Outport Lesbians*, which follows LindyAnna Jones's trip across America to attend her lesbian friend's wedding. Jan Kudelka's script for *Circus Gothic* (1980, first staged in Mar. 1979) is like a long dramatic poem about a clown's experiences in a circus, and requires the extraordinary talents of a clown, such as Kudelka herself, to give it three dimensionality. *Herringbone* (1976), by Tom CONE, also the author of *Stargazing* (1978), requires vaudeville skills for the role of a ten-year-old whose parents pass him off as a thirty-five-year-old performing midget. Linda GRIFFITHS' clever playing of all three characters—Prime Minister Pierre Trudeau, Margaret Trudeau, and a journalist—added layered reality and virtuosity to the topical interest of *Maggie and Pierre* (1980). Griffiths' sizeable talent as a playwright is even more evident in *Jessica: A Transformation* (1987), a dense allegory that mixes everyday people with ancestral animal spirits in a young Indian woman's journey of discovery. Ken MITCHELL's *Gone the Burning Sun* (1985) presents an anguished, boisterous, and at times tender Norman Bethune in a carefully crafted, detailed allegory about a search for truth, beauty, and health, both physical and spiritual, for himself and as many people as possible. Just as it may be a misnomer to term *Gone the Burning Sun* a one-person show—since it employs throughout a musician whose oriental music and exquisite stillness are a powerful source of dramatic tension—BILLY BISHOP GOES TO WAR (1981) uses a pianist, primarily as accompanist for its many songs, whose presence similarly sets up dramatic tension. One of the most popular of Canadian plays, it explores the lethal nature of Bishop's achievements in the context of colonial Canada's perceived ties with Britain. These works might bear comparison with two-person cabaret scripts, such as Morris Panych's and Ken MacDonald's 'post-nuclear' *Last Call* (1983, first staged in Feb. 1982).

The francophone presence on the English-Canadian stage has also been evident in the one-person show: for example, Antonine MAILLET's *La SAGOUINE*, incomparably performed by Viola Léger; and Marshall Button's *Lucien: A Labour of Love in Two Acts* (1988, first staged by Contact Theatre, Mar. 1986) provides similar worldy wisdom in the person of an Acadian papermill worker, developed from a sketch by Comedy Asylum's *Maritime Mixed Grill* (Feb. 1984). The brilliant Albert Millaire revealed the fantastic reality of Roch CARRIER's *The Celestial Bicycle* (*La celeste bicyclette*) (staged on tour in English in 1982), where an actor, betrayed by his wife and committed to an asylum, tells us of his travels through the sky on his bicycle.

In addition to the interplay of anglophone and francophone worlds, English-Canadian theatre during the past two decades has seen an increase in drama dealing with minority cultures. Ryga's *Indian* and *Rita Joe*, for example, are joined by works such as Len PETERSON's *Almighty Voice* (1974, first staged 1970), Linda Griffiths' *Jessica* (all of which concern native Indians), and Herschel HARDIN's *Esker Mike and His Wife, Agiluk* (1969). Hardin's episodic play, centred on Agiluk, an Inuk driven to kill two of her children, shows the destruction of northern life by southern insensitivity to another culture. In contrast to the playwrights just mentioned, who are not from the minority peoples they have written about, a number of dramatists, fostered to a degree by the country's increased attention to its multicultural nature, have appeared on the scene addressing issues from inside their respective cultures. *A Little Something to Ease the Pain* (1981, first staged Nov. 1980), by René Aloma, dramatizes the psychological and political ties experienced by a young Cuban-born playwright returned home for a week from Canada, implicitly comparing Canadian and Cuban life. Rick Shiome uses a second-generation Japanese-Canadian private eye in *Yellow Fever* (1984) to parody the detective story and draw attention to racism at the same time. *Yellow Fever* opened in San Francisco (Mar. 1982), and has had subsequent productions in New York, Toronto, and Los Angeles, among other places. Marco Miconc's *Voiceless People* (1984)—in its original French version, *Les Gens du silence* (1982)—exposes fierce conflicts in an Italian-Canadian family coming to grips with the francophone and anglophone cultures in

Montreal. Among the original Canadian plays produced by Black Theatre Canada are Peter Robinson's *Changes* (staged Aug. 1984). Most recently, Tomson Highway's lyrical *The Rez Sisters* (1988, staged first in Dec. 1986)—which follows the humorous and deeply sad experiences of a group of northern-Ontario native Indian women who travel to Toronto for a gigantic bingo game—won a Dora Award (1986-7), was nominated for a Chalmers Award for Outstanding New Play (1986), and was invited to the Edinburgh Fringe Festival (1988). (See also MULTICULTURAL THEATRE.)

Recent years have also witnessed the continuing move away from dramatic forms that depend on Aristotelean linear plots and cause-and-effect psychological realism. These have been replaced by, or re-shaped into, forms that de-emphasize textuality and present experience as episodic and imagistic. They tend to emphasize theatre as process and affirm its interactiveness, taking account of the multiple dramatic tensions created by the audience's presence in the performing space, the performed reality itself (that evoked under the 'willing suspension of disbelief'), and the reality of theatre as art/artifice. One influence in this direction has been Canadians' increased exposure to contemporary theatre from outside Canada, facilitated by international festivals such as Montreal's Theatre Festival of the Americas, Toronto's du Maurier World Stage Showcase (which followed OnStage '81), and Quebec City's Quinzaine internationale du théâtre. Edmonton's Fringe Festival and, in Toronto, Factory Theatre's 'Brave New Works', Nightwood Theatre's festival of women writers ('Groundswell'), and the 'Rhubarb' festival from Buddies in Bad Times, a gay theatre, have contributed energy and venues for experiment. Again, francophone artists have been exemplary, with such electric productions as *Le Rail* (first seen in English Canada in 1986) by Carbone 14, an almost 'text-less' production inspired by D.M. Thomas's *The White Hotel*. Following what director Gilles Maheu calls 'abstract theatre', *Le Rail* presents rivetting images of beauty, sexuality, violence, and terror, which emerge from a stage fog, 'without the coherence of a connected story or even characters with personalities', to suggest what lies behind reality. *La Trilogie des dragons* (*The Dragons' Trilogy*, first seen in English Canada in 1986) by Robert Lepage's Théâtre Repère is equally spectacular and intellectually ambitious. With dialogue in French, English, and Chinese, and settings in Montreal, Toronto, and Vancouver, this imagistic production traces ideas and people associated over time with a plot of land that is now a Montreal parking-lot.

Individual successes of the order of Lepage's innovative works have not yet appeared in English Canada. *This Is for You, Anna* (1985) and *Smoke Damage: A Story of the Witch Hunts* (1985), however, have made a significant impact. The former, created by Susanne Odette Khuri, Ann-Marie MacDonald (also the author of the witty and complex *Goodnight Desdemona, Good Morning Juliet*), Patricia Nichols, Banuta Rubess, and Maureen White, was developed from a twenty-minute version in 1983 (involving Aida Jordao) and played a range of venues from Factory Theatre to women's shelters. Based on Marianne Bachmeier's shooting in court of her daughter's killer, *Anna* explores various myths and realities concerning violence, women, and revenge. *Smoke Damage*, first staged in Sept. 1983, was scripted by Banuta Rubess in collaboration with Peggy Christopherson, Ann-Marie MacDonald, Mary Marzo, Kim Renders, and Maureen White, and treats a group of women's radicalizing encounter with historic places where witches were burned. Whereas *Anna* is somber and profoundly emotional, *Smoke Damage* is darkly comic and exhilarating; both unfold in an imagistic fashion, fracturing chronological time and conventional perceptions of reality. Both were mounted with support from Nightwood Theatre and express a enlightened feminist perspective, which, it has been argued, links them with non-linear, non-hierarchical theatre, hence their imagistic mode and collective structure.

They draw attention to the higher profile earned by women dramatists in the past decade, whose way was marked by the work of writers such as Beverley SIMONS (*Preparing*, 1974) and Carol Bolt (*Red Emma*). Some of the most vital and challenging English-language theatre of the period has been created by women, who have often consciously broken down traditional dramatic modes. In *The Bible as Told to Karen Ann Quinlan* (staged in 1978), for example, the Hummer Sisters combine the technology of video and rock performance with satirical cabaret. The Clichettes (Janice Hladki, Johanna House-holder, Louise Garfield)—through their lip-synching, which sets up a variable tension between the image created by the performer and the text—offered a brilliant satire on sexuality in *She Devils of Niagara* (Nov. 1985). As well, English Canada has seen important plays in translation from the women's theatre movement in Quebec; for instance, Jovette MARCHESSAULT's highly imaginative *The Saga of the Wet Hens* (*Le SAGA DES POULES MOUILLÉES*) and Denise BOUCHER's controversial *The Fairies Are Thirsty* (*Les FÉES ONT SOIF*). (See also FEMINIST THEATRE.)

Ever Loving (1981), like other of Margaret HOLLINGSWORTH's plays—such as *The Apple in the Eve* (1977), a radio play given its first live stage presentation in 1983, *Mother Country* (1978), and *Alli Alli Oh* (1979)—is both feminist and much broader, demonstrating her skill at creating lively human characters and scenes loaded with tension and humour. In *AUTOMATIC PILOT* (1980), Erika RITTER demonstrates a rapier-like wit and a perceptive reading of life, but too often, by evoking an easy laugh, avoids probing deeply into the characters and issues she raises. Her later work, *Murder at McQueen*, although not well received in its only production (Nov. 1986), does dig deeper, but distances all with cynicism. Unfortunately Rachel WYATT's *Geometry* (1983) was given a weak production (Tarragon Theatre, Apr. 1983), which turned its brittle comedy into domestic psychological drama. The skilled author of some seventy radio dramas, Wyatt is a master of oblique, slightly fanciful satire.

Sharon POLLOCK and Judith THOMPSON are among the six major dramatists of the past decade, which include David French, George F. Walker, John Murrell, and Michel Tremblay. The versatile Pollock—an artistic director, administrator, and actress, as well as front-ranking playwright—has created a range of plays, including many for television and radio, that explore social, political, and metaphysical issues in a variety of dramatic styles. *Walsh* is episodic, juxtaposing scenes in different modes to dramatize the historical Major Walsh's anguish over the injustice that his compliance with orders brought on the great Sitting Bull. A side-show atmosphere and brothel setting shape an indictment in *The Komagata Maru Incident* (1978) of Canada's racist handling in 1914 of a shipload of Sikh immigrants. *BLOOD RELATIONS* (1981), which retells the Lizzie Borden story, inter-

Sharon Pollock's Walsh, *Stratford Festival, 1974, with (l. to r.) Jonathan Welsh, John Stewart, David Hemblen, Terry Judd (kneeling), John Bayliss, Michael Ball (as Walsh)*

weaves different time-periods and layers of reality (an actress playing an actress playing a character) to dramatize the social and patriarchal oppression of women as well as metaphysical questions about the nature of the self and of identity. Pollock draws more openly on her own history for *Doc* (1986), but again presents layered realities and time-frames as she focuses on social, personal, and metaphysical questions.

Whereas Pollock's career spans nearly two decades, Judith Thompson's began only in 1980 with *The Crackwalker* (1981), a graphic, compassionate presentation of emotionally dynamic young people operating under economic, social, and mental handicaps. While naturalistic in mode, it translates thoughts and feelings into physical stage metaphors that extend the dialogue, as when one character smashes an egg on his head in frustration over losing his job: 'Did you ever start thinkin' somethin' . . . ? And ya can't beat it out of your head?' *White Biting Dog* (1984) is an exuberantly metaphorical play whose emotional impact is strong. Thompson's most recent stage work, *I Am Yours*, disciplines her remarkably rich imagistic power, combining it with a clearer narrative or realistic base that appears to have made it more

accessible to audiences than *White Biting Dog*, while still retaining its power of emotion.

The other dominant playwright, George F. Walker, has a prolific career almost as long as Sharon Pollock's: his *Prince of Naples* (1972) was a Factory Theatre Lab production in July 1971. His plays, which have received many productions within and outside Canada, have used forms of popular culture, such as the 'B-movie' and television, as theatrical metaphors to express witty, humorous visions of society and art in a state of decline and confusion. Early works, such as *Bagdad Saloon* (1973), were part of the anti-naturalistic 'experimental' movement at the time. Later works, such as ZASTROZZI (1979) and *The Art of War* (1983), have continued to foreground theatrical forms, developing a more sophisticated, oblique expression of questions about the nature and function of art. At the same time they possess even wittier dialogue and comic invention, as well as deepened philosophical implications.

While Walker's relatively long career in the theatre links him with the first wave of Canadian professional dramatists—Reaney, Ryga, French, Pollock—the continuing experimental character of his work—together with that, for example, of Judith Thompson—serves as a beacon for a new generation of Canadian dramatists as they enter the last decade of the twentieth century.

5. *Selected anthologies of Canadian plays in English.* An increasing variety of English-Canadian plays is now available in anthologies. They include: Canadian Authors' Association, *One Act Plays by Canadian Authors* (1926); Vincent Massey, ed., *Canadian Plays from Hart House*, 2 vols. (1926-7); Stanley Richards, ed., *Canada on Stage* (1960); Rolf Kalman, ed., *A Collection of Canadian Plays*, 5 vols. (1972-8); Connie Brissenden, ed., *Now in Paperback: Canadian Playwrights of the 1970's* (1973); Connie Brissenden, ed., *West Coast Plays* (1975); John Stevens, ed., *Ten Canadian Short Plays* (1975); Marian Wilson, ed., *Popular Performance Plays of Canada*, 2 vols. (1976); Playwrights Co-op, *Five Canadian Plays* (1978); Diane Bessai, ed., *Prairie Performance: A Collection of Short Plays* (1980); Anton Wagner, ed., *Canada's Lost Plays*, 4 vols. (1978-82): vol. 1 (co-edited by Richard Plant) 'The Nineteenth Century', vol. 2 'Women Pioneers', vol. 3 'The Developing Mosaic', vol. 4 'Colonial Quebec'; Richard Perkyns, ed., *Major Plays of the Canadian Theatre 1934-1984* (1984); Richard Plant, ed., *The Penguin Book of Modern Canadian Drama* (1984); Jerry Wasserman, ed., *Modern Canadian Plays* (1985); Playwrights Union of Canada, *Four New Comedies* (1987); Playwrights Union of Canada, *New Works* (1987).

Important bibliographies include John Ball and Richard Plant, eds., *A Bibliography of Canadian Theatre History 1583-1975* (1976) and *Supplement 1975-1976* (1979); Anton Wagner, ed., *The Brock Bibliography of Published Canadian Plays in English* (1980); Patrick B. O'Neill, 'Unpublished Canadian Plays Copyrighted 1921-1937', *Canadian Drama*, 4 (1978) and 'A Checklist of Canadian Dramatic Materials to 1967', Parts I and II, *Canadian Drama*, 8 (1982) and 9 (1983).

See also Murray D. Edwards, *A Stage in Our Past. English-Language Theatre in Eastern Canada from the 1790s to 1914* (1968); William H. New, ed., *Dramatists in Canada: Selected Essays* (1972); Don Rubin, ed., *Canada on Stage: Canadian Theatre Review Yearbook*, 8 vols. (1974-82); Geraldine Anthony, ed., *Stage Voices. Twelve Playwrights Talk About Their Lives and Work* (1978); Don Rubin and Alison Cranmer-Byng, eds., *Canada's Playwrights: A Biographical Guide*, (1980); Robert Wallace and Cynthia Zim-

merman, eds., *The Work: Conversations with English-Canadian Playwrights* (1982); Anton Wagner, ed., *Contemporary Canadian Theatre: New World Visions* (1985); Eugene Benson and L.W. Conolly, *English-Canadian Theatre* (1987); L.W. Conolly, ed., *Canadian Drama and the Critics* (1987).   RICHARD PLANT

Drama in French. 1. *The French Regime.* The mariners and adventurers who accompanied Jacques Cartier, and those who continued to exploit his discoveries for the remainder of the sixteenth century, would certainly have celebrated successful crossings and landfalls, as well as individual, religious, and national anniversaries with traditional paratheatrical activities, on shipboard or ashore—much as Sir Humphrey Gilbert is known to have done in Newfoundland in 1583. But the first fully recorded performance of a play in French Canada (and in North America) took place at Port Royal (across the river from today's Annapolis Royal, N.S.) on 14 Nov. 1606: Marc LESCARBOT's *THÉ-ÂTRE DE NEPTUNE EN LA NOUVELLE-FRANCE*, a *réception* performed on the waters and shore surrounding the tiny settlement to celebrate the return of Port Royal's founders from a prolonged exploratory mission. Although the light, bantering tone of *Neptune* sets it apart from traditional formal *réceptions*, the political dimension of Lescarbot's play is important: it contains an earnest plea for continuation of the monopoly conceded by Henry IV to de Monts and Poutrincourt for colonization in the area.

Neptune is one of three dramatic texts that have survived from the French regime. The two others exhibit even more patently this political function. *La Réception de Mgr le vicomte d'Argenson par toutes les nations du país de Canada à son entrée au gouvernement de la Nouvelle-France* (1890) was composed at Quebec by the Jesuits and performed in 1658 by their pupils for the newly arrived Governor d'Argenson. There had been considerable dramatic activity in New France in the interval, mostly in dramatic forms less restrictive than the *réception*. In 1640, for example, the *Jesuit Relations* report the performance, directed by Governor Montmagny's secretary, Martial Piraubé, of a tragicomedy and a *mistère*, the latter featuring a sequence in Algonkian intended to edify Amerindian spectators. Corneille's *Héraclius*, *Le Cid*, and other fashionable plays were staged in the

1640s and '50s, as well as *réceptions* and pedagogic works supervised by the Jesuits. *La Réception de Mgr le vicomte d'Argenson* is even more strikingly local than Lescarbot's playlet, and more explicitly political. The classical allusions of *Neptune* here give way to earnest entreaty, couched in various Amerindian tongues with consecutive translation into French. The central figure is the 'Universal Spirit of New France', who introduces the others and underlines their message, which a second spokesman, the 'Spirit of the Forests', translates as each 'native' finishes. By the end of the short text the normal welcoming aspect of this reception has been supplanted by the Jesuits' political message to d'Argenson: he must throw the weight of his troops against the Iroquois, their common enemy.

Between 1658 and 1693 there are further references to religious-pedagogic theatre in the schools, more *réceptions* were performed, and, according to a later statement by Governor Frontenac, plays continued to be staged publicly in Quebec, especially in the pre-Lenten period. In the winter of 1693-4 Frontenac patronized performances of Corneille's *Nicomède* and Racine's *Mithridate*, but trouble arose when he announced that his amateur players would soon stage Molière's controversial *Tartuffe*. The Bishop of Quebec, Mgr de Saint-Vallier, denounced the plan from the pulpit, threatened excommunication for all who might attend, and began civil proceedings against the governor's director and principal actor. Charges and countercharges were hurled as tension mounted on both sides. Molière himself would have been hard pressed to find a more comic solution than that which put an end to the infamous *affaire Tartuffe*: Frontenac, out for a stroll with his intendant in late March 1694, encountered the bishop in the street. After an exchange of distant civilities, these two direct men came to direct terms: Saint-Vallier offered the governor 100 *pistoles* (roughly equivalent to some $5,500, in 1988 terms) not to stage *Tartuffe*. Frontenac, ever impecunious, pocketed the money and accepted. There is no further reference to public theatre of any sort for the rest of his governorship.

The solution was local, but the problem was European. In France in particular, the Church's opposition to public theatre was intensifying at precisely the same moment in a vigorous, effective campaign led by the eloquent Bishop Bossuet. But whereas in France there were too many dioceses and too many opinions for one firm policy to prevail, in New France the one all-powerful religious authority made compromise and equilibrium impossible. A few years later (1699) Saint-Vallier, for partisan reasons, extended his interdiction against theatre to the performances that had long been tolerated in the Jesuits' college. Only the modest *pastorales*, performed privately by the Ursulines' pupils, were permitted thereafter.

Consequently there are only four further references to theatre for the rest of the French regime. A musical or light opera was staged at the intendant's residence in 1706, bringing immediate condemnation from the Church. In Jan. 1727 the young female boarders at Quebec's Hôpital Général presented a *pastorale-réception* officially sanctioned by Saint-Vallier. There is an allusion to a 'comédie' staged for the Intendant Bigot in 1749, the first reference to theatre in Montreal; and, finally, there is an account of a comedy written for, and performed by, the troops stationed at Fort Niagara (N.Y.) in 1759, the first clear reference to GARRISON THEATRE. The text of the *pastorale-réception* of 1727—the third text to have survived from the French regime—was composed by the Jesuit Pierre de la Chasse at the request, ironically, of the ageing Saint-Vallier, ostensibly to welcome Governor Beauharnois, along with Intendant Dupuy and his wife, to the Hôpital; but it was also meant to urge these honoured guests to ensure financial support for the Hôpital after the bishop's death (in Dec. 1727). In form—carefully crafted verses recited in succession by the young actresses—the work is close to the tradition of the Ursulines' pastorales; its function and its political plea identify it as well with the *réceptions* of New France.

There is little doubt that even after Saint-Vallier's interdiction, more theatrical activity took place in New France than will ever be documented: any such activity would have had to remain private, to avoid the Church's intervention. But the opposition of the Church does not entirely explain theatre's low profile. Throughout the colony's history material conditions—particularly its small population dispersed over a vast area—were not conducive to the establishment of an enduring theatrical tradition.

2. *From the Conquest to Confederation*. In the decade following the formal cession of

New France in 1763 various forms of theatrical activity appeared in both Quebec and Montreal. Most visible were the performances in French by the British garrison—ironically, mainly of Molière. Garrison theatre continued well into the next century, with increasing participation by local civilians. College theatre returned in the 1770s, with ambitious semi-public performances of works chosen from the large repertory of French school classics. Students and staff at secondary institutions soon began to write or adapt plays suitable for the college setting, as witnessed by two manuscript texts from the early 1780s composed at the Séminaire de Québec. Carefully supervised and expurgated religious-pedagogic theatre of this sort is peculiarly important in the evolution of theatre in French Canada, for drama seems never to have disappeared entirely from the curriculum, even when public theatre was sparse or nonexistent. Collèges classiques, through which the entire intellectual élite would pass, continually introduced students to drama and to live theatre under the close supervision of the Church, thus developing a clientele and cultivating a taste that Quebec's amateur troupes would serve after graduation.

A third, particularly durable and particularly French-Canadian, type of theatre also emerged in the first decade after the Conquest: closet political drama, published in the earliest newspapers and soon thereafter in pamphlet form. Initially pale 'dialogues', they became rapidly more dramatic and more adversarial in tone as political awareness and activity quickened. Notable among these are a *Conversation au sujet de l'élection de Charlesbourg* (1792); and the anonymous *Le Canadien et sa femme* (1794), an attempt by the government to persuade francophones to join the militia. After the establishment of the first French-Canadian newspaper, *Le Canadien*, in 1806, these dramatized dialogues become more and more strident, culminating in the five *Status Quo Comedies* of 1834, in which all the political positions that would bring the battles and bloodshed of 1837-8 are rehearsed.

Non-military, non-pedagogic, and non-political theatre had a more timid re-awakening after 1763. There are sketchy references to performances by local amateurs as early as 1765, but no record of sustained activity until the winter of 1789-90, when eight separate plays were staged (in five double programs) in Montreal. The catalyst for this flurry of activity was the recent immigrant Joseph QUESNEL, who with six others founded a 'Society Theatre' (Théâtre de Société), based on models long popular in France. Their repertory included Molière and Jean-François Regnard, but also the contemporary *Deux Billets* by Jean-Pierre Florian, first performed in Paris in 1779, and, remarkably, a play by Quesnel himself, COLAS ET COLINETTE, first performed on 14 Jan. 1790.

The Church, insecure about its status in an occupied colony, did not at first react publicly. By 1789, however, some clergy felt confident enough to counterattack. The pastor of Quesnel's parish assailed the Théâtre

A contemporary newspaper illustration of a performance of Antigone *at the Petit Séminaire de Montréal, 1895*

de Société, its program, and theatre in general, threatening to withdraw sacraments from those who performed or attended. When Quesnel and his friends protested, the bishop intervened, advising his clergy to discontinue public attacks and to concentrate instead on the confessional as a more effective way of dissuading players and public. This ensured that almost to the end of the nineteenth century theatre in Quebec remained cyclical, disorganized, and amateur; meanwhile anglophone theatre moved steadily towards permanent, professional status, as reflected in the opening of Montreal's first THEATRE ROYAL in 1825.

Colas et Colinette was much applauded in its two performances in 1790 and critically acclaimed on its revival in Montreal in 1805 and in Quebec in 1807. Quesnel has left two other plays, a bitter satire of the French Revolution entitled *Les Républicains français* (1801?) and a humorous attack on his anglophile compatriots in Canada, *L'Anglomanie* (1803?), neither of which was performed or published in his lifetime. Between 1803 and 1837 virtually the only drama published in French Canada was the increasingly virulent political playlets appearing in newspapers, the exception being plays by recent French immigrants in the early 1830s, most notably *Valentine, ou La Nina canadienne* by Hyacinthe LEBLANC DE MARCONNAY, staged and published in 1836, a well-written urbane comedy that significantly modernized the local repertory. In 1837 Pierre PETITCLAIR's first play, *Griphon, ou La Vengeance d'un valet*, was published. It has traditionally been recognized as the first play published in Canada by a native French Canadian, a distinction that ignores the five *Status Quo Comedies* (1834) and their modest ancestors.

Griphon was never performed and its publication, like that of *Valentine*, went unnoticed in the fateful months preceding the Patriote Rebellion. Petitclair's second play, the melodrama *La DONATION*, was more fortunate, being acclaimed in its performances in Quebec City in 1842 and published in a local newspaper the same year. It thus represents a more important milestone: the first play by a Canadian-born author to have been published *and* performed. Two years later the separate streams of college and public theatre were conjoined momentarily in Antoine GÉRIN-LAJOIE's *Le JEUNE LATOUR*, performed for a large audience at the Collège de

Nicolet in July 1844 and published three times before the year was out. A historical tragedy in verse on a Canadian topic, it is again the first of its kind.

The 1850s saw the performance of Petitclair's third and last play, the satirical comedy *Une Partie de campagne* (1865), a critique of anglophile excesses that is reminiscent of Quesnel's *Anglomanie*. But the most visible development of the period is that of religious-pedagogic theatre. In the schools it is evidenced by plays such as Father H.-A. Verreau's *Stanislas de Kostka* (1878, first performed in 1855); in the public domain in dozens of unplayable propaganda pieces such as the anonymous *Soirées du village* (1860), leading to the epitome of the genre, Father A. Villeneuve's 500-page *La Comédie infernale, ou Conjuration libérale aux enfers* (1871-2). The 1860s brought a culmination in college theatre with *ARCHIBALD CAMERON OF LOCHEILL*, performed in 1865 and published in 1894 as *Les Anciens Canadiens*, by Fathers J.-C. Caisse and P.-A. Laporte.

Public theatre finally came of age in the decade of Confederation, principally with L.-H. FRÉCHETTE's *FÉLIX POUTRÉ* (1871, first peformed in 1862), the first drama to deal with the Rebellion of 1837-8 and the most popular play of the century. A solid foundation for indigenous dramaturgy had now been established, and it was further strengthened by the linking of two other disparate streams, the public and the political, in Elzéar LABELLE's *La CONVERSION D'UN PÊCHEUR DE LA NOUVELLE- ÉCOSSE* (1869), a hilarious non-partisan satire of both sides in the prolonged Confederation debate. Performed frequently to the end of the century, *La Conversion*, overflowing with irreverent satire and couched in popular speech, is a clear forerunner of the musical revue and of the topical monologues and burlesques that have remained so central to Quebec's theatrical tradition.

3. *From Confederation to the First World War*. A major influence on the evolution of theatre and drama in French Canada after Confederation was the increased number of visits by touring companies from France. Encouraged by improvements in transatlantic travel, professional troupes undertook regular tours to North America by mid-century. As the continent's railway system developed, these companies began in the late 1850s to add Montreal and, less frequently, Quebec

City to their itineraries. These visits soon disrupted the uneasy truce between church and stage, since the programs offered by most Parisian troupes seemed almost perversely calculated to offend local sensitivities. Led by Montreal's ultra-conservative Bishop Bourget, the hierarchy responded with a vigorous campaign against these 'godless' visitors and their 'immoral' repertory. There were memorable confrontations in 1859 and 1868, the latter provoked by a performance in Montreal of two 'adulterous' operettas by Offenbach. With Sarah Bernhardt's first tour in 1880 these condemnations multiplied, as they would for each of her five subsequent visits (the last in 1916).

These tours had an immediate and lasting effect on local dramaturgy and repertory. Sensation-dramas and lighter comedies, influenced by continental melodrama and Parisian *boulevard* theatre, became the vogue. They represent the majority of works written and, especially, performed from the 1860s on. Their influence is visible in the work of a future premier (1897-1900) of Quebec, F.-G. MARCHAND, whose five plays—from *Fatenville* (1869) to *Le Lauréat* (1899)—are lightweight comedies of unimpeachable morality, some with strong melodramatic elements, some enlivened with music and song. French-born Ernest Doin published nine insubstantial comedies and short farces between 1871 and 1879, adapting a dozen others for local amateurs such as the Cercle Dramatique, which he helped found in Montreal in 1859. Régis Roy, born in Ottawa, contributed another dozen *boulevards* for local tastes over his long career, from his adapted *Consultations gratuites* (1896, first performed in 1895) to *L'Oncle de Baptiste* (1930). Less creative playwrights—such as J.G. McGown, with thirty ephemeral titles to his credit—merely 'arranged' French works, expurgating all that might offend the ear or eye.

Partially because of the public's changing tastes, in the last third of the nineteenth century the rift between dramatic composition and performance widened. Of the forty-one plays published between 1868 and 1880, some eighteen (44 per cent) were performed; of the seventy-five published between 1881 and 1900, only twenty-two (29 per cent) are known to have been staged. Political and polemical theatre represents a large share of these unperformed titles: they deal with local politics, as in R.-E. Fontaine's *Un Parti de tire* (1871); provincial politics, as in Father S. Lemay's *Les Manifestes électoraux* (1909); national issues, such as the execution of Louis Riel in 1885, which inspired in the following year two plays (never performed) entitled *Riel*, one written in collaboration by two recent French immigrants, C. Bayèr and E. Parage, the other by Quebec-born Elzéar PAQUIN.

Another frequent source for dramatists was Canadian history: the heroic age of exploration and adventure, as in J.-L. ARCHAMBAULT's *Jacques Cartier, ou Canada vengé* (1879) and Father S. Corbeil's *Chomedey de Maisonneuve* (published and performed in 1899); the Conquest, in L.-O. DAVID's *Le Drapeau de Carillon* (1902) and J.-E. CORRIVEAU's *Le Secret des Plaines d'Abraham* (1909); the Patriote Rebellion, in Fréchette's *Félix Poutré* (1871) and his *Papineau* (1880), or in L. Guyon's *Denis le patriote* (n.d., first performed in 1902). In the 1880s Quebec's first two women dramatists appeared: Laure Conan (pseudonym of Félicité Angers), with her patriotic *Si les Canadiennes le voulaient!* (1886), and Joséphine Dandurand (daughter of F.-G. Marchand), author of several children's plays and of an adult comedy, *Rancune* (1896), which was staged in 1888 with considerable success.

In the midst of these divergent currents in dramaturgy, and to some extent independently of them, theatrical activity increased steadily in the 1880s and '90s. College theatre, little influenced by the public stage, prospered in virtually every institution, and talented dramatists ensured a steady supply of indigenous pedagogical works, mostly unpublished, to complement traditional student fare. Father J.-B. PROULX wrote one *réception* and four other college plays, and Father E. Hamon's *Exil et patrie* (1882, first performed in 1884) offers effective propaganda for colonization of Quebec's agricultural territories. Father S. Brault's proselytizing *Le Triomphe de deux vocations* (1898, first performed in 1897) returns to more traditional concerns of college theatre, such as recruitment for the priesthood.

The period 1898-1914 is frequently described as the 'golden age' of theatre in Montreal. Amateur theatre prospered there (and throughout the province), and new professional theatres and companies emerged: the Théâtre des Nouveautés, the THÉÂTRE DES VARIÉTÉS (under the leadership of Julien

DAOUST), and the THÉÂTRE NATIONAL, among others. Over a thousand performances are recorded in Montreal for 1898-9 alone, more than in the entire decade of the 1880s. But the works performed were, with rare exceptions, imported: no more than 3 per cent of plays staged by professional companies up to 1914 were written by French-Canadian authors. In 1903-4 the Théâtre National sponsored a competition for indigenous one-act plays, promising to have the winning entries performed. The response surprised the competition's organizers, attracting dozens of submissions, including Louvigny de Montigny's BOULES DE NEIGE. But a true golden age for French-Canadian dramaturgy would be another sixty years in coming.

By 1914 two other phenomena appeared that would greatly influence the course of dramatic arts for the next three decades: film, and American repertory. Movies came to Quebec in 1903 and immediately became wildly popular. Not recognizing the danger, theatre embraced the newcomer, even including film interludes for stage plays or abandoning drama to cinema entirely for a day or a week, as the Théâtre des Nouveautés did in 1907. By 1914 a noticeable change had occurred onstage as well, as the American popular genres of VAUDEVILLE, BURLESQUE, and revue combined to crowd out Parisian *boulevard* theatre and its derivatives.

4. 1914-39. The First World War brought an abrupt end to international tours and sent the numerous French and Belgian professionals still in Canada back to Europe. A massive decline in theatrical activity in French Canada ensued. Variety theatre on the American model continued in curtailed form for the extent of the war, and most locally written works were tub-thumping topical revues, four of them by Swiss-born Pierre Christe. In addition, J.-H. Lemay's *L'Espionne boche*, a Canadian military drama, and A. Plamondon's *Âmes françaises*, were both written and performed in 1916, and Anne-Marie Huguenin-Gleason's jingoistic *En pleine gloire* (performed and published in 1919) and *La Belge aux gants noirs* (1920) deal with the war itself. But the most notable work inspired by the war was Alexandre HUOT's *Le Songe du conscrit*. Focusing on the sensitive issue of compulsory military service, it was written in June 1918 and performed in Lévis on 24 July, only four months after Quebec's divisive conscription riots.

After the war professional companies from France returned occasionally, but the golden age of touring had come to an end. In fact by the 1920s public entertainment was largely confined to movies and to variety theatre, particularly burlesque.

Since burlesque sketches and comic monologues depended heavily on improvisation, few of the basic scripts have survived. The monologue form attracted local writers like Paul Coutlée, author of two collections, *Craches-en-un* (1920) and *Mes Monologues* (1926). Henri Letondal's *Fantoches* (1922) contains sixteen sketches of the type so much in vogue on the commercial stage, but the many annual revues and light comedies he wrote have remained unpublished. Other texts of the period are heavily influenced by variety theatre without following it slavishly. Oscar Séguin wrote a half-dozen such comedies, from *La Laveuse automatique* (1930, first performed in 1929) to *60 minutes ambassadeur au Japon* (1930, first performed in 1919) and *Le Français en une ronde* (1938). Of the approximately 130 dramatic texts published between 1919 and 1930, about fifty are visibly derivative of burlesque forms. And fully a quarter of the titles performed, some of them very frequently, never reached print. For example, despite the immense popularity throughout francophone North America of AURORE L'ENFANT MARTYRE, based upon a sensational crime that took place in a Quebec village in 1920, the play remained unpublished until 1982.

Many plays published between 1919 and 1939 belong to the category of patriotic-historical writing, a stubborn survival of another era. Many of these were not performed, and are well-nigh unplayable, although college, parish, and urban amateur companies staged a few. The strongly nationalistic approach to Canadian history exemplified by Father Lionel Groulx is directly responsible for a score of plays intended to reflect his stance and to resurrect some of the forgotten French-Canadian heroes he had identified or, as in the case of Dollard des Ormeaux, mythicized. Between 1920 and 1938 this seventeenth-century adventurer inspired seven plays, from H. Gagnier's *Dollard* (1922, first performed in 1920) to Father J. Perrin's *Gloire à Dollard!* (1923, first performed in 1922), A. Lavoie's *Dollard* (1937) and Father A. Giguère's play of the same title (1938), the latter two composed in alexandrine verse. Other historical figures are portrayed: *Charles Le Moyne* (1925, first performed in 1910), a college play by Brother Marie-Victorin (C. Kirouac), and *Brébeuf* by Father A. Poulin (published and performed in 1931) , a subject taken up also by Father J. Laramée in his *L'Âme huronne* (1931, first performed in 1930). J.-U. Voyer and A. Rousseau contributed a three-act opera, *L'Intendant Bigot*, which was critically acclaimed when first performed at Montreal's MONUMENT NATIONAL in Feb. 1929 and published the same year. The fall of Quebec remained a fertile subject for dramatists, from Georges Monarque's *Blanche d'Haberville* (published and performed in 1931) —a thorough reworking of Aubert de Gaspé's novel *Les Anciens Canadiens*—to Gustave LAMARCHE's 'drame choral', *Le Drapeau de Carillon* (published and performed in 1937). The Rebellion of 1837-8 is remembered in L.-N. Sénécal's *L'Aveugle de St-Eustache* (1928) and in P. Guillet's *Les Patriotes vengés* (1937). Contemporary Canadian politics resurface in A. Leclaire's *Laurier* (1921) and his *Le Petit Maître d'école* (1929), a provocative evocation of the plight of Ontario's francophones in the atmosphere of the province's infamous Regulation XVII curtailing French-language rights. (This play had been performed under the title *La Petite Maîtresse d'école* in June 1916, when the controversy was at its height, but the protagonist changed gender for the text's publication.) Collections of historical plays were published by Louvigny de Montigny, whose *Bouquet de Mélusine* comprises three short texts performed at the Festival de Québec in May 1928, and by V. Barrette, whose *Tableaux d'histoire* (1935) contains four plays intended for college performance, with male roles only. Traditionalist and agriculturalist ideology, dominant in French-Canadian literature of the period, is reflected in a dozen forgettable dramas: A. Cinq-Mars' and D. Potvin's *Maria Chapdelaine* (1919), an adaptation of Louis Hémon's novel; L.-N. Sénécal's *Terre de chez nous* (1923); C. Duguay's comedy *La Veillée de Noël* (published and performed in 1926); and P. Guillet's *La Terre conquise* (1935). Propagandistic drama with broader scope is represented by two anti-communist works by Catholic priests: A. Poulin's *Le Message de Lénine* (1934) and H. Trudel's *Le Signe de la bête s'efface* (1937, first performed in 1938).

A small minority of published plays that escape categorization are among the most interesting of the period: Jean-Aubert Loranger's *L'Orage* (1925), performed in Paris in 1923, the first Canadian play so honoured; Léopold HOULÉ's *Le Presbytère en fleurs*, performed more than 200 times throughout French Canada after its première in May 1929; Yvette Ollivier MERCIER-GOUIN's *Cocktail* (1935); and Arthur Provost's *Maldonne* (1943, first performed in 1938), winner of the Sir Barry Jackson Challenge Trophy at the 1938 DOMINION DRAMA FESTIVAL.

Forty-five published plays from the period 1919-39 are melodramatic in inspiration, modelled on nineteenth-century European melo, a genre whose influence had become so pervasive that many dramatists remained quite unaware they were composing in it— witness Rodolphe GIRARD's *Les Ailes cassées* (1921), described by the author as a 'comedy in four acts'. Alice Pépin (Mme E.-P. Benoît), under the pseudonym 'Monique', wrote *Le Mirage* (1923, first performed in 1921)—a 'tear-jerker' worthy of Dion Boucicault—and *L'Heure est venue* (published and performed in 1923). Both plays are interesting examples of pre-feminist writing, depicting the frustrated desires of two women who seek to lead more fulfilling lives.

As radio became established during the decade it produced two vigorous hybrids, virtually interchangeable between stage and airwaves: burlesque-like sketches, best exemplified by the annual revues of Henri Letondal, and the *Fridolinades* of Gratien GÉLINAS; and radio melodramas, minimally adapted to or from stage scripts. Some authors and performers worked concurrently for theatre and in RADIO DRAMA, passing with surprising ease from one medium to the other. Henri DEYGLUN, for example, wrote for and acted in both media, with occasional forays into cinema, completing over 3,000 radio texts and more than a dozen stage plays. Robert Choquette, a gifted poet and dramatist, also composed hundreds of radio plays and sketches, fifteen of them published in *Le Fabuliste La Fontaine à Montréal* (1935). Robert Charbonneau, Henri Letondal, Claude-Henri Grignon, and others wrote exclusively for radio, a financially more rewarding medium than stage or print.

While the BARRY-DUQUESNE troupe at the THÉÂTRE STELLA, the MONTREAL REPERTORY THEATRE, the COMPAGNONS DE SAINT-LAURENT, the Théâtre des Arts, and a few other groups attempted to sustain legitimate theatre in Quebec, the popularity of cinema and radio continued to increase. In 1932 Montreal had fifty-seven movie-houses with a total of 59,044 seats and three theatres with a total of 2,675 seats, plus a few buildings capable of staging amateur performances. By 1937 some 57 per cent of Quebec households possessed at least one radio receiver, a figure that had risen to more than 70 per cent by 1944. During the 1930s the audience rose from the few thousands a dramatist might hope to reach in the theatre (if a play were inordinately successful), to hundreds of thousands in the case of the most popular radio plays.

Little perturbed by cinema, variety theatre, or radio, the college stage expanded vigorously in Quebec after the First World War, and in the 1930s in particular began to seek a broader public, primarily through the efforts of writers and directors such as Fathers Laurent Tremblay, Gustave Lamarche, and Georges-Henri d'Auteuil. Lamarche is the outstanding religious-pedagogical dramatist in the history of French Canada, in quality as in quantity (his collected works include thirty-four plays in six volumes). In the 1930s and '40s his plays—frequently staged outdoors with hundreds of actors—attracted huge crowds, sometimes estimated at more than 100,000 for a single performance. The best known are vast pageant-plays, medieval in format and inspiration, usually based on biblical themes, such as his first work, *Jonathas* (1935); *La Défaite de l'enfer*, involving some 700 characters (1938); the 500-page *Notre-Dame-des-Neiges* (1942); and *Notre-Dame-de-la-Couronne* (1947). Considered marginal to the evolution of theatre by some historians, Lamarche's ambitious panoramic displays nonetheless exerted a profound and catalytic influence upon an entire generation of collegians and Catholic laity. Laurent Tremblay wrote and directed nearly two dozen plays (eighteen of them published) between 1935 and 1959, many of which he describes as 'social dramas', such as *L'Abonneux* (1936, first performed in 1935), *Hommage à la langue française* (published and performed in 1937), and *Le Curé Hébert* (published and performed in 1938). The Jesuit d'Auteuil has left no dramatic texts but much useful criticism. Like Émile LEGAULT, he was highly influential in directing college troupes, principally at Montreal's Collège Sainte-Marie.

5. *From the Second World War through the Quiet Revolution, 1939-68*. To the casual observer the state of dramatic arts in French Canada in 1939 must have appeared little different from that of two decades earlier. Continuing economic stagnation discouraged spending on all but life's necessities; radio and cinema, less expensive and more regularly accessible, continued to eclipse live performance. A more attentive analysis shows, however, that the seeds of change—as sown by the Théâtre Stella, by Gustave Lamarche, Henri Deyglun, and especially by Gratien Gélinas and Émile Legault—were about to bear fruit, awaiting only the improved economic conditions that the war would soon bring. For theatre professionals optimism was difficult: the early 1940s looked depressingly like the 1880s, with fewer active troupes and theatre buildings than in 1900. Amateur groups, on the other hand, flourished throughout Quebec, much of their repertory still blighted by *Aurore l'enfant martyre* and its imitations, but vigorous and expansive, as exemplified by Trois-Rivières's Compagnons de Notre-Dame, Hull-Ottawa's Le Caveau, and Sherbrooke's L'Atelier. For dramatists the war years were a carbon copy of 1914-18: few published texts and fewer local scripts performed, except for predictable revues and ubiquitous burlesque varieties. Deyglun, something of a minor war industry on his own, managed to publish nine plays between 1943 and 1945, notably his verse tragicomedy *La France vivra!* (1943), *Les Secrets du docteur Morhanges* (1944), and *Mariages de guerre* (1945), all adaptations of radio dramas—but he is an isolated exception.

During and after the war new professional companies—some short-lived, others more durable—were established, including Le Tréteau, Paul Langlais's Comédie de Montréal, L'ÉQUIPE, the Compagnie du Masque, the THÉÂTRE DU RIDEAU VERT, the THÉÂTRE CLUB, and the THÉÂTRE DU NOUVEAU MONDE. Although historians have been virtually unanimous in recognizing the staging of Gélinas's TIT-COQ on 22 May 1948 as the birth of modern Quebec theatre, this simple but compelling depiction of a foundling's search for identity is in fact the rich legacy of a century's evolution. Even if *Tit-Coq* now seems dated, one must give Gélinas his due:

one man, situated at the centre of his nation's theatrical activity, had been able to pull together disparate threads and weave a drama in which his nation saw itself, at least at that moment, depicted.

Between the production of *Tit-Coq* and the première of Marcel DUBÉ's *Zone* in 1953, dramaturgy in Quebec remained largely an avocation, as it had been before 1948. Poet-essayist Éloi de GRANDMONT wrote *Un fils à tuer* (1950); novelist Yves Thériault, *Le Marcheur* (1968, first performed in 1950); journalist-professor Paul TOUPIN, *Brutus* (1952); and singer-folklorist Félix LECLERC contributed seven sketches in his *Théâtre de village* (1951). A more committed and disturbing writer, Jacques FERRON, was learning his craft, with minor satirical works such as *Le Licou* (1953) and *L'Ogre* (1949), but the originality and real force of his dramaturgy would not be appreciated for another two decades. In drama and theatre the 1950s belong to Marcel Dubé, author of some three dozen plays to date, many of them written for TV and most of them visibly influenced by it.

Dubé began writing for radio in 1950 and for national TV two years later. His first stage play, *Le Bal triste*, was produced by a company he helped found, La Jeune Scène, in 1950; but he first attracted critical attention with *Zone* (1956), which won first prize at the Dominion Drama Festival in 1953. Before the decade was out he had added three more major plays to the Canadian repertory: *Florence* (1958, 1970), *Un SIMPLE SOLDAT* (1958, 1967), and *Le Temps des lilas* (1958).

Other dramatists had their first works published and/or performed in the 1950s: the novelist André Langevin—whose *Une Nuit d'amour* was, in 1953, the first Canadian play performed by the Théâtre du Nouveau Monde—added *L'Oeil du peuple* (1958), a political satire whose short run at the TNM in Nov. 1957 enlivened the first, and only unsuccessful, re-election campaign of Montreal mayor Jean Drapeau. Europe's pervasive Theatre of the Absurd reached Montreal in the works of Jacques LANGUIRAND, who had studied drama in Paris from 1949 to 1953. His *Les Insolites* (1962) was awarded the prize for best Canadian play at the DDF in 1956 and ran for weeks in Montreal that spring and summer. That fall his *Le Roi ivre* (1970) was staged, followed by a major work, *Les*

GRANDS DÉPARTS (1958), performed on TV in 1957, and on stage in 1958. His *Le Gibet* (1960) was performed in 1958. Pierre Perrault's poetic drama *Au Coeur de la rose* (1964) was highly praised on its production in 1958 but was not followed by any other stage play by this author. Two other landmarks of the 1950s are the publication in 1958 of Jacques Ferron's *Les Grands Soleils*, an attempt to de- and re-mythicize the Patriote Rebellion (still a few years ahead of its time, the play would not be performed until 1968); and Gélinas's *Bousille et les justes* (1960). Performed by the author's own company at Montreal's COMÉDIE-CANADIENNE, *Bousille* is a powerful, realistic depiction of a certain middle-class morality associated with the Duplessis era that was about to end.

Some of the events of the 1950s that had profound and lasting effects on theatrical activity took place offstage. In 1954 the CONSERVATOIRE D'ART DRAMATIQUE DU QUÉBEC was founded; in 1958 the Association Canadienne du théâtre amateur (ACTA) was organized by Guy BEAULNE, grouping together the many disparate francophone troupes; and in 1960 the NATIONAL THEATRE SCHOOL/École nationale du théâtre was created. 1956 saw the establishment of Montreal's Metropolitan Arts Council; the following year the Canada Council came into being, followed four years later by Quebec's Ministry of Cultural Affairs. By the very nature of these three agencies' decisions to fund one group and not another they have, deliberately or not, wielded much influence over the repertory chosen by theatrical companies, with the result that theatre managers and artistic directors have sometimes had to compromise their principles or risk losing funds.

Another important—and very visible—characteristic of the 1950s was the sudden birth of small *théâtres de poche*, often in direct opposition to the policies and repertory of 'establishment' troupes like the TNM. Of these the most noteworthy have been, in Montreal, Paul Buissoneau's THÉÂTRE DE QUAT'SOUS, Jacques Languirand's Théâtre de Dix Heures, Jean-Guy SABOURIN's APPRENTIS-SORCIERS, and Françoise Berd's Théâtre de l'Egrégore. In Quebec City, where ALTERNATE THEATRE had been represented only by Laval University's influential Troupe des Treize (1949), L'Estoc and Le THÉÂTRE DE

LA FENIÈRE were founded in 1957. Summer theatre also flourished in the wake of government funding, notably Marjolaine Hébert's THÉÂTRE DE MARJOLAINE.

The early 1960s are synonymous in Quebec with the Quiet Revolution, signalled by the election of Jean Lesage's Liberals in 1960 and the eclipse of Maurice Duplessis's Union Nationale after his death in 1959. In drama, and in theatrical activity in general, the 1960s proved to be the most remarkable decade in the history of Quebec, the period when theatre finally came of age. Although much of the vigour and novelty came from a new generation of writers, established dramatists like Dubé, Gélinas, Languirand, and Ferron contributed significantly to the maturing of native drama. Dubé's *Bilan* (1968), televised in 1960 and staged by the TNM in 1968, shows his movement away from Montreal's economically and culturally dispossessed towards the middle-class characters and concerns that have been concomitant with his own success. But his nuanced tragic vision remains in plays such as *Les Beaux Dimanches* (1968), a remarkable success in its performance by the TNM in 1965 and five years later on TV, and especially in what is often considered his finest work, *AU RETOUR DES OIES BLANCHES* (1969). Gélinas wrote only one stage play in the 1960s, *HIER, LES ENFANTS DANSAIENT* (1968), perhaps not his best but certainly his most topical, depicting a middle-class family riven by political forces that were then threatening to sunder Canada. The effervescent Languirand continued his career as director, impresario, actor, and author, adding the absurdist *Les Violons de l'automne* (1962), the musical comedy *Klondyke* (1971) and, like Dubé, having several of his plays performed in Europe. Jacques Ferron's fine satiric talent was again demonstrated in *La Tête du roi* (1953), dealing on intersecting historical and dramatic planes with the Riel Rebellion and with current revolutionary violence in Quebec—crystallized in the decapitation of the statue of King Edward VII, symbol of Empire. This play was not produced, but Ferron's equally iconoclastic *Les Grands Soleils* finally was produced by the THÉÂTRE POPULAIRE DU QUÉBEC in 1968, to critical reactions ranging from admiring applause to sheer bewilderment.

Among the newcomers was Françoise LOR-ANGER. Her reputation as a novelist and as a scriptwriter for radio and TV was already well established when her psychological drama *Une maison . . . un jour* (1965) was produced by the Théâtre du Rideau Vert in 1965. It was followed by the feminist *ENCORE CINQ MINUTES* (1967), broadcast in 1966 and staged by the Rideau Vert in 1967. As Quebec's revolution grew less and less quiet, Loranger's longtime political commitment grew less private, as evidenced by her savage political satire *Le Chemin du roy* (1969), written in collaboration with Claude Levac and staged by L'Egrégore in 1968. Thanks to rowdy behaviour by spectators at a performance in Feb. 1969, her enigmatic apolitical psychodrama *Double Jeu* (1969) caused unintended scandal. Another polemical play followed—*Médium saignant* (1970), focusing on the struggle for francophone rights in the atmosphere of Quebec's controversial Bill 63.

Robert GURIK's first play, *Le Chant du poète* (1963), attracted only local attention, but *Le PENDU* (1970) won the 1967 DDF prize for best play. His science-fiction drama *Api 2967* (1971) is, like the previous two works, apolitical, but *Hamlet, prince du Québec* (1968) is a polemical parody of the petty bickering between Quebec and Ottawa, reminiscent of much nineteenth-century political theatre.

Other authors attracted critical attention in the 1960s without going on to build a playwriting career: Guy DUFRESNE, with *Le Cri de l'engoulevent* (1969); Gilles Derome, with his witty *Qui est Dupressin?* (1963, first performed in 1961); André Laurendeau, with *Deux Femmes terribles* (1970, first performed in 1961); Réjean DUCHARME, with his parodic *Le Cid maghané*, unpublished but performed in 1968. New companies and organizations included the NOUVELLE COMPAGNIE THÉÂTRALE, the Théâtre Populaire du Québec, and the Centre d'essai des auteurs dramatiques (CEAD), committed to furthering dramatic arts at all levels, through public readings, lectures, and playwrights' workshops. In retrospect, however, the most important development of the 1960s was the production by the Rideau Vert on 28 Aug. 1968 of Michel TREMBLAY's *Les BELLES-SOEURS*. No play in the repertory of Quebec had ever aroused such spirited or varied reaction. Conservative critics were offended by its tawdry setting and even more tawdry characters, all seeking to enrich their drab lives at others' expense; and they were scandalized by the exclusive use of *joual*, the

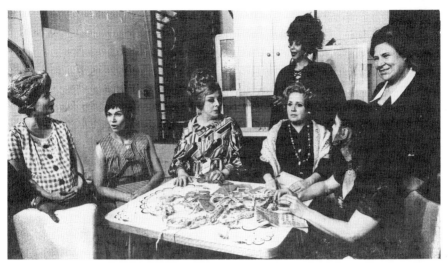

Michel Tremblay's Les Belles-Soeurs, *Théâtre du Rideau Vert, Montreal, 1970-1 season, with (l. to r.) Mirielle Lachance, Monique Mercure, Germaine Giroux, Eve Gagnier, Michèle Rossignol, Amulette Garneau, Sylvie Heppell*

impoverished, heavily anglicized dialect of the urban proletariat, hitherto considered too ugly for public display except in burlesque. But more perceptive critics responded both to the poignant lyricism Tremblay infused into his *joual* and to his stylized monologues and choruses—and their reaction has prevailed. As surely as *Tit-Coq* in 1948, *Les Belles-Soeurs* represents a watershed in the evolution of Quebec theatre. Performed in French across the province, on national TV, and in Paris, and staged in English or French in every major theatre in Canada, Tremblay's unlovely sisters-in-law now claim a central place in Canadian repertory.

6. *Theatre in Quebec since 'Les Belles-Soeurs'.* Tremblay's success galvanized the ever-present currents of creative dissidence in Quebec. There was a sudden flood of literature in *joual*, now taken as an affirmation of freedom from the constraints of European French literature and American culture. In 1969 the irreverent Jean-Claude GERMAIN founded his Théâtre du Même Nom (TMN), a parodic anagram of the Théatre du Nouveau Monde (TNM) and a gauntlet flung at the 'established' theatre it represents. His *Diguidi, diguidi, ha! ha! ha!*, produced by the TMN in 1969, set the tone, relying heavily on *joual* for its assault on theatre, religion, and social institutions, including the family. Germain added a string of exuberantly satirical works over the next decade, from *Le Roi des mises*

à bas prix (1972) to *Un Pays dont la devise est je m'oublie* (1976), *A Canadian Play/Une plaie canadienne* (1983), and a dozen others. In 1969 the GRAND CIRQUE ORDINAIRE—hostile to traditional theatre, theatre schools, and repertory—began its illustrious nomadic and collectivist assault on the economic and social structures of Quebec. These two companies typify the pervasive phenomenon known as 'Jeune Théâtre' (or alternate theatre) under the banner of which some of the most original theatre of the 1970s took place. Protesting against the authority of the dramatic text, against the 'well-made' play performed by subsidized practitioners for well-heeled spectators, TMN and GCO and a score of companies like them sought in the early 1970s to democratize the theatrical experience, to bring drama back to the people. Thus began a heady period of interventionist theatre, usually nationalistic, frequently Marxist or socialist in orientation, exemplified by the Théâtre Euh! (1970-8) and the Théâtre du 1er mai (1972-84).

As a result of this sudden proliferation of strongly nationalist companies, by 1970 half the annual dramatic production in Quebec was of indigenous works. This is an important milestone: it is not at all incidental that this nationalization of repertory took place during one of the most dynamic periods of nationalist fervour in the province's history. The decade 1970-80 represents a golden age of collective creation in Quebec. At present it is decidedly in eclipse, and there has been a general return to authored texts and rehearsed performance. (The most striking exception is the highly popular LIGUE NATIONALE D'IMPROVISATION, with two teams of actors in uniform who improvise competitively on a given topic and are then judged by audience response.) Most of the alternate companies disappeared because of economic factors, but also as a result of the internal divisions that have generally characterized COLLECTIVE CREATION.

Closer to traditional forms, the dramaturgy of Jean BARBEAU is an important component in the very mixed formula of Quebec theatre in the 1970s. Initially active in collective theatre, Barbeau, inspired by Tremblay's *Les Belles-Soeurs*, almost singlehandedly changed theatre's unhealthy preoccupation with Montreal and helped focus it on Quebec City. In the space of one year (Mar. 1970-Feb. 1971) he had eight new plays performed, five of them by a company he helped found, the Théâtre Quotidien de Québec. The most important of these plays are *Le Chemin de Lacroix* (1971), *Joualez-moi d'amour* (1972), *Manon Lastcall* (1972), and *Ben-Ur* (1971). Like Tremblay's plays, they rely on colourful *québécois* French, but Barbeau's is audibly different from the metropolitan *joual* of Tremblay. In black-humoured undertones, they portray the plight of francophone underdogs in a society that is culturally, economically, and linguistically schizoid.

Driven by a similar animus, the plays of Michel GARNEAU and Victor-Lévy Beaulieu exemplify the inundation of *joual* in the wake of Tremblay's success. Combining irreverent vulgarity with unexpected lyricism, Garneau has written some three dozen plays since 1970, eighteen of which have been published, including *La Chanson d'amour de cul* (1971); *Quatre à quatre* (1974); *Abriés désabriés* (1979); *Adidou Adidouce* (1977); and *Émilie ne sera plus jamais cueillie par l'anémone* (1981), a sensitive tribute to the poetry of Emily Dickinson. Beaulieu—better known as a novelist and publisher—espouses *joual* for philosophic reasons, in works such as *En attendant Trudot* (published and performed in 1974) and *Cérémonial pour l'assassinat d'un ministre* (published and performed in 1978), dealing with the assassination of Pierre Laporte in Oct. 1970. One of the few dramatists to resist the wave of *joual* was Roch CARRIER, whose *LA*

GUERRE, YES SIR! (1970), *Floralie* (1973), *Il n'y a pas de pays sans grand'père* (1977), and *Jolis Deuils* (1984) were successful novels or short stories before their transposition to the stage. The late 1970s and the '80s have witnessed a movement away from *joual*, but no return to the alienating constraints of 'standard' French now seems likely.

By the force of his talent and the sheer power of his vision, it is Michel Tremblay, however, who has continued to dominate Quebec's dramaturgy in the 1970s and '80s. For the first nine years after *Les Belles-Soeurs* he depicted the same dismal urban universe, with many characters resurfacing from one play to the next in works such as *En pièces détachées* (1970), *À TOI, POUR TOUJOURS, TA MARIE-LOU* (1971), *Hosanna* (1973), *Sainte Carmen de la Main* (1976), and *Damnée Manon, sacrée Sandra* (1977). But the sharp edge of his social criticism—like that of Bar-

Michel Tremblay's Hosanna, Théâtre de Quat'Sous, 1973, with (l. to r.) Jean Archambault, Gilles Renaud

beau and other politically committed writers—has been blunted since the election of the Parti Québécois government in 1976. As prolific as ever, Tremblay has turned to more general concerns, with no loss of dramatic power. His comedy of manners, *L'Impromptu d'Outremont* (1980), signals a new interest in middle-class characters, as does *Les Anciennes Odeurs* (1981). *Albertine, en cinq temps* (1984)—a moving portrayal of a woman at five different stages of her life—is considered his finest work by many, and by some the best play yet written in Quebec.

Among the newest generation of dramatists, Jean-Pierre RONFARD, René-Daniel DUBOIS, Marie LABERGE, Élizabeth Bourget, and Jovette MARCHESSAULT stand out. Ronfard is the author of some fifteen plays to date, the most notable being his monumental *Vie et mort du roi boiteux* (1981), a grotesque, bloody epic comprising six plays and an epilogue, with 210 characters and fifteen hours' playing-time. Dubois, one of the finest actors in today's theatre, has received much acclaim for several recent works, in particular *Ne blâmez jamais les Bédouins* (1985) and *Being at Home with Claude* (1986). Laberge, Bourget, and Marchessault are but three of the many talented female dramatists now active in Quebec. Laberge has written a dozen plays, the best known being *C'était avant la guerre à l'Anse à Gilles* (1981)—a poignant depiction of women's alienation in pre-war Quebec—and *Jocelyne Trudelle, trouvée morte dans ses larmes* (1983), which depicts a young woman driven to suicide by an insensitive society. Bourget, the first female graduate of the National Theatre School, has had eight plays performed, notably *Bernadette et Juliette ou La Vie, c'est comme la vaisselle, c'est toujours à recommencer* (published and performed in 1978) and *Bonne fête, maman* (published and performed in 1980). Marchessault—less tender, more literary, and more militantly feminist—created a minor sensation with her *La SAGA DES POULES MOUILLÉES* in 1981, a mordant depiction of five women authors from different periods of Quebec literature. Two other plays by her have attracted attention: *Alice & Gertrude, Natalie & Renée et ce cher Ernest* (1984) and *Anaïs dans la queue de la comète* (1986). Other women dramatists of note are Suzanne Aubry, Jocelyne Beaulieu, Marielle Bernard, Louise Bombardier, Diane Bouchard, Claire Dé, Jeanne-Mance Delisle, Louisette Dussault, Marie-Francine Hébert,

Maryse Pelletier, Marie-Thérèse Quintal, Louise Roy, and France Vézina. Many of their plays have been produced by women's companies such as Montreal's Théâtre des Cuisines and the Théâtre Expérimental des Femmes, or by Quebec City's Commune à Marie. Male dramatists of current interest are Christian Bédard, Michel-Marc Bouchard, Normand CHAURETTE—whose *Provincetown Playhouse, juillet 1919, j'avais 19 ans* (1981) was an outstanding success on its revival in 1985—Jean Daigle, Dominique de Pasquale, Georges Dor, Marc-F. Gélinas, René Gingras, Pierre Goulet, Louis-Dominique Lavigne, Roland LEPAGE, David Lonergan, Pierre Malouf, Serge Marois, Serge Mercier, Marco Micone, Pierre Morency, Claude Poissant, André Ricard, Claude Roussin, Marcel Sabourin, and Louis Saia.

In the late 1980s the state of dramatic arts in Quebec is a troubled one. Some observers are disturbed by the current popularity of CAFÉS-THÉÂTRES and comic monologuists like Yvon DESCHAMPS and Gilles Latulippe, seeing in them a potential rebirth of burlesque. Others are as distressed by the amazing popularity of 'trivial' collective creations such as *BROUE*. All observers agree that there are far too many companies competing in a market that has expanded only slowly: at the end of 1985 there were over 120 professional and at least 425 amateur companies in Quebec—more than that of the other nine provinces combined—most of them struggling for survival. By some Darwinistic process of popular selection, that number will have to be reduced drastically. Yet even after years of budgetary compression, with serious reductions in the funds available from municipal, provincial, and federal agencies, theatre in Quebec remains dynamic, colourful, and diverse.

7. *Anthologies of French-Canadian Plays*. No anthologies specifically devoted to drama in French were published in Canada before the 1970s. General literary anthologies occasionally included plays or excerpts from plays, notably James Huston's famous *Répertoire national* (4 vols, 1848-50), reproducing three inportant early dramas in their entirety. But it was more than a century before even such collections became common. The four-volume *L'Histoire de la littérature canadienne-française par les textes* (1968), edited by Gérard Bessette, Lucien Geslin, and Charles Parent includes extracts from six plays; André

Renaud's *Recueil de textes littéraires canadiens-français* (1969) has extracts from four. Gilles Marcotte's *Anthologie de la littérature québecoise* (4 vols, 1978-80) also has extracts from four plays, while Michel Le Bel's and Jean-Marcel Paquette's *Le Québec par ses textes littéraires, 1534-1976* (1979) selects from nine plays. The first anthology devoted exclusively to drama was Jean Doat's *Anthologie du théâtre québécois, 1606-1970* (1973), with brief extracts from ninety-seven plays. The two most useful collections to date are Etienne-F. Duval's *Anthologie thématique du théâtre québécois au XIXe siècle* (1978), with a scholarly introduction, biographical notes, and excerpts from fifty texts, followed by his pioneering *Le Jeu de l'histoire et de la société dans le théâtre québécois, 1900-1950* (1983), with 144 selections. Important recent collections outside the mainstream of traditional dramaturgy are Pierre Pagé's and Renée Legris's *Le Comique et l'humour à la radio québécoise: Aperçus historiques et textes choisis, 1930-1970* (2 vols, 1976, 1979), and *Monologues québécois, 1890-1980* (1980), edited by Laurent Mailhot and Doris-Michel Montpetit. In translation, the only significant anthology is the fourth volume of Anton Wagner's *Canada's Lost Plays*, entitled *Colonial Quebec: French Canadian Drama, 1606 to 1966* (1982), which includes seven complete plays.

See also QUEBEC, THEATRE IN; *Archives des lettres canadienne, vol 5: Le Théâtre canadien-français* (1976); *Dictionnaire des oeuvres littéraires du Québec*, vols 1-5 (1978-87); Jean Béraud, *350 ans de théâtre au Canada français* (1958); Beaudouin Burger, *L'Activité théâtrale au Québec, 1765-1825* (1974); Leonard E. Doucette, *Theatre in French Canada, 1606-1867* (1984); Jean Laflamme et Rémi Tourangeau, *L'Église et le théâtre au Québec* (1979); Chantal Hébert, *Le Burlesque au Québec: Un divertissement populaire* (1981); Pierre Lavoie, *Pour suivre le théâtre au Québec: Les Ressources documentaires* (1985); Elaine F. Nardocchio, *Theatre and Politics in Modern Québec* (1986).

L.E. DOUCETTE

Dramatic Lyceum. On 18 Mar. 1857 J.W. LANERGAN leased a 33' x 132' lot on King Square, Saint John, N.B., from broker John Ansley for ten years at a yearly rent of £80, and built the Dramatic Lyceum, which was designed by William Campbell, who had rebuilt London's Sadler's Wells Theatre. The 33' × 124' exterior was finished in an Ital-

ianate style; a 14' × 100' alleyway provided access on one side. Three ventilators in the roof were intended to overcome a problem of bad ventilation said to plague the city's other public buildings.

The stage was 30' deep, with a proscenium opening of 20' x 17'. The 78'-deep auditorium was divided into a parquet to seat 550, a dress circle (supported by eight heavy Doric birch columns) to accommodate 300, two private boxes for six persons each, and four family boxes each for nine persons. Inadequate sight-lines from the dress circle were corrected in 1860 when the auditorium was extensively altered. Lighting was by gas, and heating by two small stoves near the front of the theatre.

The first season, opening on 15 June 1857 with Edward Bulwer-Lytton's *Money* and a farce, *Mr. and Mrs. Peter White*, and ending on 1 Sept., included at least thirty-six different double bills. Lanergan offered annual summer seasons until 1871 and again in 1873 and 1874. The program included a judicious

Souvenir of the 1867 season of the Dramatic Lyceum, Saint John, N.B.

mixture of legitimate drama, old favourites, and pieces newly acclaimed in London and New York. Thus in 1864 *Fanchon the Cricket*, Augustin Daly's *Leah the Forsaken*, Tom Taylor's *Ticket-of-Leave Man*, and *Darrell Markham* shared the stage with Bulwer-Lytton's *Lady of Lyons*, Gilbert à Beckett's and Mark Lemon's *Don Caesar de Bazan*, John Tobin's *The Honeymoon*, *Camille*, *Othello*, and more. The strong stock company of from twenty to twenty-five members was regularly augmented by visiting stars such as E.A. Sothern, C.W. Couldock, Julia Bennett Barrow, E.L. Davenport, Carlotta Leclerq, F.S. Chanfrau, and Little Cordelia Howard; James and Caroline Lanergan frequently undertook major roles. Patrons paid 1s.3d. for the parquet, 2s.6d. for the dress circle (later 25c and 50c), and from $4.00 to $6.00 for a box. No intoxicating beverages could be sold on the premises, 'proper officers' were employed to enforce orderly deportment among the young, and ladies could not be admitted unless accompanied by a gentleman. The Lyceum provided strong encouragement to amateurs, some of whom, like H. Price WEBBER, turned professional. The Lyceum's success fostered a demand for a larger facility to remain open in winter, realized in the ACADEMY OF MUSIC. On 8 Oct. 1876 the theatre was sold to the Irish Friendly Society for $2,000; on 20 June 1877 it burned down in the fire that destroyed much of Saint John.

MARY ELIZABETH SMITH

Drury Lane Theatre. Sometimes known as the Theatre in Drury Lane or as the Saint John Theatre, Drury Lane, this was the first building in Saint John, New Brunswick, to be used solely as a theatre. Rebuilt from an existing structure on the corner of Union St and Drury Lane in fashionable York Point, the theatre contained a 56' × 26' auditorium with boxes, pit and gallery, a green room, workshops, and storage and meeting places. It was a co-operative venture between officers of the 101st Regiment at Fort Howe under Major George O'Malley and young men from the city, who formed a company called His Majesty's Servants. Joseph Holman's *Abroad and at Home* and Isaac Jackman's *All the World's a Stage* comprised the opening bill on 3 Feb. 1809. Tickets were 5s. for a box, 4s. for the pit, and 3s. for the gallery. After a three-month season of eighteenth-century comedies and melodramas—such as Thomas

Sheridan's *The Brave Irishman*, Thomas Morton's *Zorinski*, and George Colman's *The Poor Gentleman*—the regiment was transferred and the company disbanded. Except for C.S. Powell's *The Evening Brush for Rubbing Off the Rust of Care* in 1810, the theatre was unused until 1815-16, when another group of young lawyers and merchants presented a repertoire that included *Barnaby Brittle*, *The Soldier's Daughter*, Colman's *Heir at Law* and *John Bull*, Oliver Goldsmith's *She Stoops to Conquer*, and a locally written farce (anonymous), *The Sailor's Return; or Jack's Cure for the Hysterics*. The building was sold at auction on 16 July 1816 and later housed a school. When Addison B. Price's professional company came in 1819, it had to improvise a theatre in a new building on the corner of King and Studholm (now Charlotte) St.

MARY ELIZABETH SMITH

Dubé, Marcel (b. 1930). At the forefront of modern drama in Quebec, Dubé is its most prolific playwright, having written some forty plays for stage, radio, and television (including TV serials—'La Côte de sable', 'De neuf à cinq', 'Entre midi et soir'—and two memorable one-act plays, *L'Echéance du vendredi* and *Le Visiteur*), about one third of which he completed in the 1960s, his most productive period. Born in Montreal into a family of eight children, he studied at the Collège Sainte-Marie and, briefly, at the Université de Montréal, after a short stint in the Canadian army. He began writing poetry in his teens, but quickly moved to drama. In 1951, together with a group of friends (including Raymond Lévesque, Robert Rivard, and Monique Miller) he founded La Jeune Scène, a company that in 1952 staged his one-act play, *De l'autre côté du mur*. This was a forerunner of his highly successful full-length play, *Zone* (1956)—about a gang of cigarette smugglers—which initiated the use of music, usually of a plaintive variety, as a major component of Dubé's dramatic writing, and won prizes at the 1953 DOMINION DRAMA FESTIVAL for best production (by La Jeune Scène) and for best Canadian play. Dubé's career was thus launched at the very birth of Canadian television and at the first flowering of modern French-Canadian theatre. He was both a product of these developments and a catalyst for them.

Dubé's plays have usually been grouped into two basic periods—those written and staged before 1960 and after—that also correspond to a focus on two distinct milieus: a dead-end working-class district similar to the one where the author grew up, and *nouveau riche* suburban homes or established bourgeois dwellings of business, professional, and political élites. The first group highlights adolescent and young adult heroes, while the second, of necessity, features middle-aged characters, with their children somewhat in the background. In both, the young challenge their elders' outlook and behaviour, finding fault with their resignation, defeatism, crass materialism, hypocrisy, and political opportunism.

Major works of the first group include: *Zone*; *Florence* (1958), first performed on stage by the COMÉDIE-CANADIENNE in Oct. 1960; *Un SIMPLE SOLDAT* (1958), which has become a classic of the Quebec theatre; *Médée* (1973), performed on television in Feb. 1958; and *Le Temps des lilas* (1958), first performed at the Théâtre Orpheum in Feb. 1958. In the second group are *Bilan*, produced by THÉÂTRE DU NOUVEAU MONDE, Oct. 1968; *Les Beaux Dimanches* (1968), first performed by TNM at the Comédie-Canadienne in 1965; and *AU RETOUR DES OIES BLANCHES* (1969).

This scheme, however, is somewhat arbitrary, for a play like *Octobre* (1964), which by its ambience belongs to the second group, was first heard on the radio in 1954, while *L'Echéance du vendredi* (1972), a play about an unemployed mechanic, was shown on television in Feb. 1960. A more flexible grouping of Dubé's plays is by mode: tragic social realism; the *drames bourgeois* portraying the breakdown of the upper-middle-class family in Quebec; and a lighter vein of romantic, satirical, and humorous pieces, dominant in the last decade or so. *Le Réformiste, ou l'honneur des hommes* (1977), first performed in Feb. 1977 by the Théâtre du Nouveau Monde, marks a return to the tragic genre, albeit in a middle-class setting.

The first mode is reflected in the atmosphere of doom that hangs over the characters, particularly the younger ones who try to break out of the constraints of poverty and ignorance. The second is replete with marriage crises (infidelity, exchange of partners), in which women dissatisfied with mere accumulation of material possessions are the dynamic forces, although they are also often addicted to tranquillizers—like their partners who try to escape reality through alcohol.

The generations split along the lines of idealists/realists, or social and political reformers/upholders of the status quo. In both modes the family is in a state of tension and disorientation; the younger characters often engaged in a desperate search for truth and purity while the older ones, fearing reality, hide behind masks of self-righteousness and hackneyed answers to life's problems. The fundamental solitude of the characters (with a few exceptions, such as Blanche and Virgile, the nostalgic old couple of *Le Temps des lilas*) seems generalized in Dubé's world view, and is summed up by Olivier in *Les Beaux Dimanches*, usually taken as a spokesman for the author: 'You have to accept . . . that you're all alone in the world, that nobody—not ever—will give you a friendly hand to help you along the way.'

The third mode is made up of a variety of works. *L'Impromptu de Québec* (1974), first produced by THÉÂTRE DE MARJOLAINE in June 1974, an adaptation of Jean-François Regnard's late seventeenth-century comedy, *Le Légataire universel*, is a sexual satire of the money-grubbing frequently targeted by Dubé, although it is aimed here at marginal characters (a servant, a penniless would-be playboy). A serious note is counterpoised by the setting—just before, and just after, the 1929 stock-market crash. *L'Été s'appelle Julie* (1975) has a romantic tone, as well as recurring themes such as partner-swapping. The eponymous heroine is reminiscent of earlier pure young female characters such as Ciboulette (*Zone*), Cigale (*Le Naufragé*, staged by the THÉÂTRE CLUB in 1955), Fleurette (*Un simple soldat*), and Johanne (*Le Temps des lilas*), but she has more self-assurance and independence. This play (like *Pauvre amour*, produced at the Comédie-Canadienne in Nov. 1968, published in 1969) is also reflexive, the second major character, Ludovic, being a creative writer. *Dites-le avec des fleurs* (1976), written jointly with Jean BARBEAU, is a sometimes boring satiric romp, the butt of which is a counter-cultural commune, torn apart by egotism, lust, and suspicion. *L'Amérique à sec* (1986), Dubé's latest play, was first performed at the site of the action, at Saint-Jean-sur-Richlieu, near the U.S. border in June 1986, directed by the author. It is based on episodes in the life of, and dedicated to, the alcohol smuggler Conrad Labelle. His too-quickly-acquired, rather unlikely allies in his illicit trade are a priest and his attractive widowed niece who is about to enter a convent. They struggle against a hypocritical politician, and an assimilationist cleric who is a stand-in for an anti-francophone American bishop of Irish origin, Hildebrand McIntyre, thus giving the drama-turned-farce a nationalist ring (a progressively stronger *constante* in Dubé's plays since the late 1950s) and making Conrad a 'patriotic' hero. *L'Amérique à sec* contains more popular French-Canadian speech than any other Dubé play. Although some idiomatic prose and elisions occurred in his early plays, Dubé employed poetic and lyrical language as early as *Le Temps des lilas*, and consistently gives his characters international French, even in such proletarian dramas as *L'Échéance du vendredi* and the underworld-ridden *Paradis perdu* (produced on television in 1958, published in 1972). In a 1970 article, 'Dialogue imaginaire en guise de doléance, ou Les critiques sont aussi des êtres humains', Dubé defends his linguistic option in thinly veiled acerbic attacks on Michel TREMBLAY's *joual*, and the COLLECTIVE CREATIONs of Jean-Claude GERMAIN and the GRAND CIRQUE ORDINAIRE.

In *Florence*, Dubé's two major milieus—the working-class quarter, and the bourgeois world, here in the form of an advertising agency—interact. One of Dubé's strongest characters, Florence revolts against the passivity and sterility of her milieu, inspiring her father to become active in his union and her brother to regain interest in the extra-curricular life of his college. The meek delivery-boy, who is the title character of *Médée*, is another working-class figure who becomes resolute.

Le Temps des lilas mixes social realism with poetry and symbolism in its treatment of loneliness, disillusionment, and the fleeting nature of love. Of the three couples living in or near a rooming-house threatened with demolition, two break up, one of them violently through suicide, although the elderly landlords draw on memories of their first love for consolation.

Le Temps des lilas may be seen as a transition piece between the earthy realism of the plays that preceded it and the *drames bourgeois* that followed. *Bilan* ('balance sheet') was the first of these. The *arriviste* hero, William Larose, who is about to become chief organizer of a right-wing political party, finds his family in a state of turmoil as his daughter leaves her husband, a rebellious son dies in a car crash, another misappropriates funds from the family business, and William's neurotic wife declares her love for her husband's long-time friend and associate. A similar family crisis emerges in *Les Beaux Dimanches*, one of Dubé's biggest successes on stage and television (and adapted for the cinema in 1974 by Richard Martin). Victor Primeau, who has made a fortune in appliances, is left by his wife as his teen-age daughter is about to have an abortion—all of this against a background of his luxurious suburban home the day after an all-night party, followed by the gradual return of all the celebrants and the renewal of the endless drinking and exchange of partners. (The crisis of the bourgeois family in extremity is dramatized in *Au Retour des oies blanches*, Dubé's most clearly classical drama, with many reminders of Sophocles' *Oedipus the King*.) Through the political positions taken by Victor's daughter Dominique, and his friend, Olivier, a doctor, Dubé first shows a growing sympathy for the *indépendantiste* cause (and even for the imprisoned FLQ members). This is also expressed by Georges in *Pauvre amour* (1969), and echoes throughout *Un Matin comme les autres* (1971), produced by the Comédie-Canadienne in 1968, the year of the Parti Québécois's birth.

Dubé has indicated that his writings have been based on philosophical idealism and that he distrusts ideologies. Nevertheless, his work can be given an ideological reading, and certain of its contradictions elucidated. His most powerful proletarian plays certainly contain denunciations of alienation and exploitation, but rarely do his heroes envisage collective action to change their situation. (Unions are evoked briefly in *Florence*, quite artificially and fleetingly in *Un simple soldat*, and stereotypically in *Le Réformiste*.) Though he denounces the anti-Communist hysteria of the Duplessis era in *Florence* and in some of his essays, Dubé melodramatically characterizes the strange roomer Vincent in *Le Temps des lilas* as an ex-Communist still hounded by sinister accomplices. Étienne (in *Bilan*) is an admirable character who hangs posters of Ché Guevara in his room, but Dubé's one-act *Rendez-vous du lendemain* (1972) presents a right-wing caricature of successful Latin American revolutionaries. Contradictions are also evident in his treatment of nationalist and separatist themes. He flays the Québécois (again in *Florence*) for habitually blaming the stagnation of Quebec francophone society on 'les Anglais', and deftly satirizes anglophone capitalist scorn for francophone workers in *Un simple soldat*; yet his nationalism sometimes tends towards a reductionist definition of Quebec francophone society as an 'ethnic class', and generalized Manichean and chauvinistic elements creep into some plays, notably *L'Amérique à sec*.

Critics have found certain habitual weaknesses in Dubé's lesser works, and sometimes even in his major plays. These include melodramatic devices, sentimentality, a tendency to be overly discursive and rhetorical in key speeches, and the unconvincing presentation of background or explanation in order to establish or advance the action of the drama. Nevertheless his sensitivity to the complexities of the human condition and to that of Quebec society itself, his skilful use of dramatic tension, and his command of dramatic structure have achieved for him both success and distinction as well as an assured place among leading Canadian playwrights. With Gratien GÉLINAS he is the founder of modern Quebec dramaturgy.

Shortly after the Parti Québécois came to power, Dubé was appointed to the semi-official Conseil de la langue française, where he worked until 1979, when he became director-general of the organizing committee of the Rencontres francophones, another agency. A Fellow of the Royal Society of Canada and the Académie canadienne-française, Dubé won the Prix Victor-Morin in 1966, and the Prix David, Quebec's highest literary prize, in 1973, and the medal of the Académie canadienne-française in 1987.

See Laurent Mailhot and Jean-Cléo Godin, *Le Théâtre québécois*, I (1970), and Maximilien Laroche, *Marcel Dubé* (1971). Edwin C. Hamblett's *French-Canadian Dramatist Marcel Dubé* (1970) should be read with great caution, given its many factual errors and critical shortcomings. BEN-Z. SHEK

Dubois, René-Daniel (b. 1955). Born and raised in Montreal, he first wrote *Panique à Longueuil* (1980), a play that was premièred at Montreal's Café-théâtre Nelligan in 1980. Combining realism and fantasy, it is set in a modern building and dramatizes a descent into hell; Freudian complexes and various figures from history and literature are evoked, and the language alternates between that of everyday speech and that of literature. These features reappear in Dubois' subse-

quent works, where the figure of the dramatist tends to emerge as a character. Thus *Adieu, docteur Münch*, first produced in 1981 at the Café-théâtre Nelligan, and *26 bis, impasse du Colonel Foisy*, first produced in 1986 at the Café-théâtre de la Place in Montreal, place the creator in the foreground. These are complicated texts larded with historical and literary allusions, in which the relation between life and death, between actuality and dream (or theatrical illusion), seem to express an obsession with, or the manifestation of, a polymorphous identity.

Dubois has established his reputation mainly with *Ne blâmez jamais les bédouins* (1984)—in which the author played all the roles—and *Being at Home with Claude* (1986). *Ne blâmez jamais les bédouins*, first produced at the restaurant-théâtre la Licorne in Montreal, combines levels of language and evocation (political, geographical, and cultural) with unbridled fantasy in a superb but complex text. *Being at Home with Claude*, which deals with the murder of a homosexual by his lover, confines itself to a level of hyper-realism, except for the final intensely lyrical monologue. It was first produced by the THÉÂTRE DE QUAT'SOUS in 1985. The theme of homosexuality or transvestism appears, though less explicitly, in almost all Dubois's plays.

Several of Dubois's texts—including *Le récital-gala de Madame Célanyre Campeau, de la Scala de Milan* and *William (Bill) Brighton*—remain unpublished. His other plays have been published by Leméac. An English translation of *Panique à Longueuil* has had a reading in New York, but it has not been published. JEAN CLÉO GODIN

Duceppe, Jean (b. 1924). Born and raised in Montreal, he first acted professionally in 1942 at the Arcade. Since then he has acted with many Quebec theatre companies, including Les COMPAGNONS DE SAINT-LAURENT, THÉÂTRE CLUB, THÉÂTRE DU NOUVEAU MONDE, THÉÂTRE DU RIDEAU VERT (in Françoise LORANGER's *ENCORE CINQ MINUTES*, 1967), COMÉDIE-CANADIENNE (in the work of Marcel DUBÉ), THÉÂTRE DE QUAT'SOUS, NOUVELLE COMPAGNIE THÉÂTRALE, and THÉÂTRE DU TRIDENT, where he played Willie Loman in Arthur Miller's *Death of a Salesman* (*La Mort d'un commis-voyageur*) and 'le Chef' in John Thomas McDONOUGH's *CHARBONNEAU & LE CHEF* in

1971. In 1961 he founded the Théâtre des Prairies in Joliette and in 1973 the COMPAGNIE JEAN DUCEPPE. He has performed on radio since 1951, as host and actor in many serials, and on television since 1952, including the role of Stan Labrie in the long-running 'La Famille Plouffe'.

Duceppe has appeared in some twenty films, including *Mon Oncle Antoine* in which he played the title role. He has received numerous awards, including the Prix Victor-Morin in 1968, the Olivier GUIMOND trophy in 1974, the Molson Prize in 1978, the Prix Marc LESCARBOT, and the Prix Denise PELLETIER. In 1965 he launched a weekly magazine, *Le Miroir du Québec*.   PAUL HÉBERT

Ducharme, Réjean (b. 1942). Born near Sorel, Que., he spent a few months in the École Polytechnique, Montreal, and the RCAF before becoming an office clerk. His reticence about publicity became legendary after his first novel, *L'Avalée des avalés* (1966), was published in Paris (translated by Barbara Bray as *The Swallower Swallowed*, 1968). Praised in France and Canada, it won a Governor General's Award in 1966, and was followed by other novels—*Le Nez qui voque* (1967), *L'Océantume* (1968), *La Fille de Christophe Colomb* (1969), *L'Hiver de force* (1973), and *Les Enfantômes* (1976)—before his first dramatic work, *Inès Pérée et Inat Tendu*, was published in 1976. It was produced by Yvon Canuel at the Festival Sainte-Agathe in 1968, along with Ducharme's *Le Cid maghané* (unpublished). The verbal pyrotechnics, the unexpected puns and deformation of language, coupled with an uncompromising child-like innocence that is at odds with the adult world—all typical of his first novel—are also found in *Inès et Inat*. Ducharme's taste for parody and political satire, evident in his *Cid maghané*—a reworking of Corneille's *Le Cid* (in *joual*) to caricature both Corneille and Quebec society—is seen again in *Le Marquis qui perdit* (unpublished), directed at the THÉÂTRE DU NOUVEAU MONDE by André BRASSARD in 1970. Ducharme's most successful play, *HA! ha! . . .* (1982), directed at the TNM in 1978 by Jean-Pierre RONFARD, won Ducharme a second Governor General's Award. Here Ducharme combines his deconstruction of language with a tragic vision that focuses on the act of language itself, through adult characters who are always conscious of the cruel games they

impose on each other through language. Ducharme has also collaborated on two successful films with Francis Mankiewicz, *Les bons débarras* (1979) and *Les beaux souvenirs* (1981), as well as on popular songs with Robert Charlebois.

See Laurent Mailhot, 'Le Théâtre "maghané" de Réjean Ducharme', in *Le Théâtre québécois* (1970); *Réjean Ducharme: Dossier de presse 1966-1981*, Bibliothèque du Séminaire de Sherbrooke, 1981; E. Manseau, 'Bibliographie de Réjean Ducharme', *Voix et Images*, 8 (1983).   D.W. RUSSELL

Dufresne, Guy (b. 1915). Born in Montreal, he began his career in 1945 by winning the first Radio-Canada literary competition with a thirty-minute radio play, *Le Contrebandier*. From 1947 to 1955 he wrote the series 'Le Ciel par-dessus les toits'; close to 200 half-hour radio scripts on the religious history of Quebec; and from 1955 to 1958 'Cap-aux-Sorciers', a television series (parts of which were published in 1969) about a sea captain and his family, featuring the unforgettable Captain Aubert (played by Gilles PELLETIER). In the 1960s and 1970s Dufresne wrote further television serials, including 'Kanawio' (1960-1) about the Iroquois and Mohawks at the time of the founding of Montreal; 'Septième Nord' (1963-7), dealing with the world of physicians in Montreal in the same era; and 'Les Forges de Saint-Maurice' (1972-5), on Quebec's early eighteenth-century shipbuilding industry, published as *Ce maudit Lardier* (1975).

Dufresne's first stage play, *Le Cri de l'engoulevent* (1969), was presented at the COMÉDIE-CANADIENNE in Jan. 1960, directed by Jan Doat and Gratien GÉLINAS. It was produced for television under the title *Chemin privé*, and a third version was mounted by the THÉÂTRE POPULAIRE DU QUÉBEC in the winter of 1970-1. Dufresne's best-known play, *Le Cri*, is a domestic drama that pits father against daughter as she seeks her independence through a relationship with an American businessman. Pointing to Quebec's difficulties in moving from a rural to an industrial economy, the play also raises important questions about the province's political autonomy. It was translated by Philip London and Laurence Berard as *The Cry of the Whippoorwill* (1972). *Docile* (1972), a light comedy, was directed by Gratien Gélinas for the Comédie-Canadienne in 1968, and in 1969 the THEÂTRE DU NOUVEAU MONDE presented his *Les Traitants* (1969), directed by Albert Millaire—another historical chronicle, about the Montagnais and the Abenaki.

Dufresne has also adapted plays for stage and television, notably Luigi Pirandello's *As You Desire Me* (*Comme tu me veux*) and Chekhov's *Three Sisters* (*Les Trois Soeurs*), produced by Radio-Canada in Oct. 1962 and Nov. 1963 respectively. His splendid adaptation of John Steinbeck's *Of Mice and Men* (*Des Souris et des hommes*) was broadcast in Jan. 1971, and the COMPAGNIE JEAN DUCEPPE produced his version of Tennessee Williams' *A Streetcar Named Desire* (*Un Tramway nommé désir*) in 1974. Dufresne's 1976 film *Johanne et ses vieux* (written for television) was shown in France and at the Prague Film Festival. On the strength of its success he also wrote the scenarios for the films *Décembre* (1978), about the world of young musicians in Montreal, and *Le Frère André* (1987).

Dufresne's manuscripts are housed in the Bibliothèque Nationale du Québec. See also RADIO DRAMA IN QUEBEC and TELEVISION DRAMA IN QUEBEC.   PIERRE FILION

The Dumbells, France, 1917

Dumbells, The. One of several Canadian Army concert parties in France during the First World War, the original Dumbells—including Jack Ayre (pianist and musical director), Elmer A. Belding, Ted Charters, and Allan Murray—were organized by Merton W. Plunkett at Ferfay, France, in 1917 and entertained troops throughout France with collectively conceived skits and popular songs. In the summer of 1918 Plunkett added Ben Allan from the 16th Battalion's Party, 'Red' Newman and Charlie MacLean from the Y-Emmas, and Ross 'Marjorie' Hamilton from the Maple Leaf Concert Party and reorganized the Dumbells into a company of fifteen to perform in London at the Canadian YMCA's Beaver Hut, the Victoria Palace, and the Coliseum. In September of that year they performed seventy-one concerts for troops in France, before amalgamating at Mons with the Princess Patricia Canadian Light Infantry Comedy Company to produce a unique army version of Gilbert and Sullivan's *H.M.S. Pinafore*, beginning 11 Nov. 1918. They continued to entertain troops in France and England until June 1919.

On their return to Canada they reorganized as civilian entertainers. The new Dum-

bells included Plunkett (the impresario), Jack Ayre and Allan Murray from the original troop, and others from the London tour and the *Pinafore* production: Hamilton, Bert Langley, W.L. Tennent, Allan, Newman, MacLean, Fred Fenwick, and Al Plunkett. A dispute over profit-sharing in 1921-2 led to a temporary split into two companies: The Dumbells and The Maple Leafs. Immensely popular, the Dumbells toured Canada, the U.S., and England with *Biff, Bing, Bang* (1919, revised 1921), which played twelve weeks at the Ambassador in New York, *The Dumbells Revue of 1922, Carry On* (1922), *Cheerio* (1923), *Oh Yes* and *Ace High* (1924), *Lucky 7* (1925), *Three Bags Full, Joy Bombs, That's That* and *Let 'er Go* (1926), *Oo! La! La!* (1927), *Why Worry?* (1928), *Here 'Tis* and *Come Eleven* (1929), *As You Were* (1931), and *The Dumbells* (1933).

The Depression killed touring and ended the theatrical careers of the Dumbells, although they regrouped in Ottawa to sell War Bonds in 1939. Various members toured with shows such as *Lifebuoy Follies* (1945) to aid the war effort. In 1977 *The Legend of the Dumbells* was devised and staged by Alan LUND at the CHARLOTTETOWN FESTIVAL.

PATRICK B. O'NEILL

Duquesne, Albert (1890-1956). Born Albert Simard at Baie Saint-Paul, Que., he studied drama at the Conservatoire Lassalle in Montreal and made his début at the THÉÂTRE CANADIEN with the Fernand Dhavrol company. With Fred BARRY and Henri DEYGLUN he founded the Barry-Duquesne-Deyglun company in 1918. This group later became the Barry-Duquesne company, which director Antoine Godeau and his daughter, actress Marthe THIÉRY (whom Duquesne married), also joined. The company performed in a number of theatres in Montreal, in the province, and in the U.S. until 1929, when it purchased the Chantecler Theatre, which in the following year became the THÉÂTRE STELLA.

One of the most important French-Canadian actors of his generation, Duquesne played Grand Guignol, drama, and comedy. A radio commentator for CKAC, where he was a host of the 'Théâtre du sirop Lambert' in 1925 and of 'Les Nouvelles de chez nous' during the Second World War, he created the role of Alexis in the radio serial based on Claude-Henri Grignon's novel *Un Homme et son péché* for Radio-Canada. One of his last stage roles was that of the padré in *TIT-COQ* by Gratien GÉLINAS.   LUCIE ROBERT

E

Eagan, Michael (b. 1942). A native of St Stephen, New Brunswick, and a graduate of the Univ. of New Brunswick, he completed his design training at the NATIONAL THEATRE SCHOOL, and has since worked at virtually every major theatre in the country, as well as in New York. He has also designed for film and television and in 1979 represented Canada at the Prague Quadrennial.

More in the tradition of Oliver Messel, Desmond HEELEY, and Robert PRÉVOST than in that of Josef Svoboda, Eagan is a *trompe l'oeil* specialist, particularly with gouache. Dissatisfied with fragmented, asymmetrical approaches to design, he returned to classical forms, developing a style that applies neoclassical symmetry and grace to anything from a modern chamber opera (Peter Maxwell Davies' *The Lighthouse*, Guelph Spring Festival, 1986) to eighteenth-century French comedy (Marivaux's *Successful Strategies*, CENTAUR THEATRE, 1985). Believing that painterly productions can be highly evocative, Eagan artfully combines built and painted reliefs to provide an elaborately detailed environment that is never without a light, fantastic element. An iconographer of exquisite forms, as in Jean Herbiet's *De la manipulation de Dieu* (the NATIONAL ARTS CENTRE, 1975), and Strindberg's *A Dream Play* (TARRAGON THEATRE, 1977), he is also a precise architect. This fusion worked perfectly in *Oedipe Roi* in 1982 for Jean GASCON

at the NAC, which was staged in an unusual triangular configuration that obliged audiences to look at the play sometimes through a series of slatted blinds. This gave the lighting a stippled, Mediterranean quality and created a veiled or shrouded feeling appropriate to a tragedy. Eagan's skills also embrace lyricism (as in Edward Albee's *Tiny Alice*, THEATRE CALGARY, 1985, or Richard Wright's and George Forrest's *Kismet*, Rainbow Stage, Winnipeg, 1984); expressionism (Georg Büchner's *Woyzeck*, NAC, 1974); realism (John Steinbeck's *Of Mice And Men*, produced at the YOUNG PEOPLE'S THEATRE, Toronto, 1984); and parody (Charles Ludlam's *The Mystery of Irma Vep*, at Theatre Second Floor, Toronto, 1985). Eagan's innovative design for Pam Brighton's production of *Henry VI* at the STRATFORD FESTIVAL in 1980 gave the play futurist overtones.

Eagan has had one-man shows in Montreal (1975) and Toronto (1980) and has received Dora Mavor MOORE Award nominations for best costume design (*The Mystery of Irma Vep*, 1985) and best set design (Michel TREMBLAY's *Albertine, en cinq temps*, 1985). In 1987 he was appointed head of design at the National Theatre School.   KEITH GAREBIAN

Easton, Richard (b. 1933). Born and raised in Montreal, he played Hamlet in high school and studied theatre with Eleanor STUART.

He made his acting début with the BRAE MANOR THEATRE in June 1947, and subsequently joined the CANADIAN REPERTORY THEATRE, Ottawa, in 1951 and the STRATFORD FESTIVAL in its inaugural 1953 season, when he appeared as Sir Thomas Vaughan in *Richard III*. Following that season Easton (and Timothy FINDLEY) received financial assistance from Alec Guinness and Tyrone GUTHRIE for further training at the Central School of Speech and Drama in London. This led him into the H.M. Tennant stable of young actors, from which he emerged to play Edgar in the Shakespeare Memorial Theatre Company's so-called Kabuki *King Lear* in 1955, starring John Gielgud. He returned to Stratford in 1956, and also appeared at Toronto's CREST THEATRE. His first appearance in New York was in a classical season with the off-Broadway Phoenix Theatre in 1957, after which he appeared at the Stratford, Conn., Shakespeare Festival. A founding member of New York's APA (Association of Producing Artists) Repertory Theatre in 1960, he played many roles there, including Hamlet in 1961, Berenger in Eugène Ionesco's *Exit the King* in 1967, and Alceste in Molière's *The Misanthrope* in 1969.

Television success in the British series 'The Brothers' interrupted his stage career, but a variety of leading roles in British repertory led him back to Stratford-upon-Avon and the Royal Shakespeare Company, where he remained until 1986, when he joined Renaissance Theatre to play Jaques in *As You Like It* and Claudius in *Hamlet*.

HERBERT WHITTAKER

Ecstasy of Rita Joe, The. A landmark in modern Canadian theatre, George RYGA's drama was one of the first Canadian plays to win international recognition. Following the 1967 VANCOUVER PLAYHOUSE première, with Frances HYLAND as Rita Joe, it was restaged in Ottawa two years later as the first English-language production at the NATIONAL ARTS CENTRE. It was performed in London at the Hampstead Theatre Club, at the Kennedy Centre in Washington, and won an award for the best new production of the Edinburgh Fringe Festival in 1973. It also achieved considerable popularity in a 1971 version by the Royal Winnipeg Ballet (choreographed by Norbert Vesak) both in Canada and Latin America.

Like much of Ryga's dramatic work,

Ecstasy presents politics through a psychological perspective. It deals with a highly charged topical issue, the exploitation and degradation of the North American Indian by a supposedly liberal white society, and was based on newspaper reports about the deaths of Indian girls in Vancouver. But although the play contains the history of one such victim, from her childhood on a reservation through her repeated arrests to her murder by a gang of rapists, the chronological sequence is fragmented. On a multiple set past merges with present in episodic scenes framed by a recurrent courtroom trial. Given eight hours to find character witnesses, Rita Joe searches memories for an identity. A love of nature and family ties on the reservation—berry picking, a lacrosse game, her father's refusal to sell her to a white man whose child had died, her maternal protectiveness towards her sister—are set against the city where the cement makes her feet hurt. A job in a tire store leads to sexual harassment, the only setting for love is a graveyard, an Indian mother has to give her children away to survive, and imprisonment encapsulates her experience. Indicted for vagrancy, shoplifting, drunkenness, assault, and prostitution, Rita Joe receives no help from the uncomprehending or paternalistic white figures who are responsible for aiding the Indians through religion (the Priest), education (the Teacher), or social services (the Indian Centre). Traditional values in the person of her father (based on Chief Dan George, who played the role in Vancouver, Ottawa, and Washington) are too passive to offer a solution. Radicalism, represented by her lover who is killed by the rapists, seems equally powerless. The inherent injustice of the system is embodied in the legal process itself, and through the trial-format the society that sits in judgement is itself put on trial.

The brevity and dislocation of the episodes, and the juxtaposition of lyricism and brutality, mirror the protagonist's thought processes. The structural impression of a labyrinth, explicitly echoed in the setting, and the circular patterning of repeated actions represent the *status quo* that imprisons Rita Joe. Social reality, transposed into psychological terms, demonstrates the effect of political oppression on the non-conforming individual in a way that the audience can share emotionally. At the same time, the conventional liberal response is ruled out as self-indulgent romanticism through the figure of a singer, whose ballad rendering of the action is exposed as insensitive cliché. The interior nature of the drama and the repetitive trial sequences, in which all of Rita Joe's court appearances merge into a composite image, universalize the action. The protagonist not only represents the plight of Indian girls in general, but (in intention at least) all those exploited by the system. This archetypal quality gives the play considerable poetic power. However, it also tends toward the melodramatic, and the London and Washington productions demonstrated that the contrasting elements are difficult to balance successfully in performance. Overly naturalistic presentation in one case sensationalized the rape and double murder, lyrical emphasis sentimentalized the other.

Ryga's first major stage play, *Ecstasy* was developed in collaboration with the directors of the Vancouver and Ottawa productions, George Bloomfield and David GARDNER, respectively; the alterations it went through indicate Ryga's problems in creating his highly personal dramaturgy. The main elements were already present in the earliest sketch, as was the concept of 'a dream-night-mare type of movement and mood . . . played on a series of planes.' But the first four drafts experimented with mixtures of expressionism and realism, agitprop cartoon and documentary, each of which was discarded as Ryga defined his theatrical goals. The final version (which appears in *The Ecstasy of Rita Joe and Other Plays*, 1971, edited by Brian Parker) arrived at in the NAC production exemplifies Ryga's characteristic 'orchestrated composition' of thematic motifs interwoven on musical lines, which he has described as a 'ballad play'.

CHRISTOPHER INNES

Education and Training. In Canada and the U.S., theatre-in-education usually means practical or scholarly activity generated by academic theatre programs. Unlike Britain and Europe, Canada has not developed a strong core of private professional training schools separate from college campuses. There are few state-supported theatre schools or apprentice training programs available for the aspiring actor, designer, or director, and professional theatres have taken little responsibility for the training of the potential theatre artist. Most training takes place in a vacuum, with little communication between the institutions that study and train for the theatre and the theatres that practice theatre art. The change in the 1950s from a predominantly amateur to a professional theatre was paralleled by an equivalent growth in the study of theatre as an academic and practical discipline. Statistics in the Black Report ('Report of the Committee of Inquiry into Theatre Training in Canada', Canada Council, 1978) suggest that educational theatre programs in colleges and universities have become the largest theatre enterprise in Canada. This does not take into account the immense growth recorded in secondary-school theatre and recreational theatre.

1. *Quebec.* Although theatre in the province of Quebec faced continual opposition from the Catholic Church, the Jesuit practice of presenting intramural productions of the classics and morality plays in their colleges continued into the twentieth century. Formal training in theatre art in Quebec did not begin, however, until the 1950s; before that, French-speaking practitioners took courses at the Lassalle Conservatory (1907-), took classes from private teachers, or studied in France. The dynamic director-priest Father Émile LEGAULT, founder of the influential COMPAGNONS DE SAINT-LAURENT (1937), introduced a short-lived theatre school of good reputation in 1948.

The THÉÂTRE DU NOUVEAU MONDE opened an acting school in 1951 to give a more comprehensive training than that provided by the Lassalle Conservatory or private teachers. This was succeeded by the establishment of the CONSERVATOIRE D'ART DRAMATIQUE in Montreal in 1954 and a sister conservatory in Quebec City in 1958 following the closure of TNM's school for financial reasons in 1953. The NATIONAL THEATRE SCHOOL of Canada was founded in 1960 on the artistic principles of adviser Michel SAINT-DENIS. Located in Montreal, the NTS is still regarded as a major acting and design school offering separate training in French and English. The full-time faculty is usually about fifteen, supplemented by guest lecturers. The founders of the NTS had high hopes that the School would become a bi-cultural as well as a bilingual conservatory. The failure to realize either of these goals exemplifies one of the major problems facing any training institution that sets out to be national in character. Although the School has on several occasions

Education and Training

allied itself with professional theatres such as the STRATFORD FESTIVAL, and encouraged the formation of professional companies drawn from its own graduating classes, it has never been able to forge the necessary liaison with the profession. Furthermore, parsimonious federal funding has prevented the school from becoming a truly national institution.

By the end of the 1960s two schools at the CEGEPS (Community Colleges) of Sainte-Thérèse and Saint-Hyacinthe (on the outskirts of Montreal) were offering training to actors, technicians, and designers. In the 1970s the French-speaking universities began drama divisions, most notably Ottawa, l'Université de Québec à Montréal, and Sherbrooke.

2. *English Canada*. In the nineteenth century universities in English Canada offered almost no formal theatre courses. Anyone wishing to acquire the arts of the stage learned as an apprentice in the few resident professional companies or from a tutor in private academies, all of which were short-lived. The first half of the twentieth century was the golden age of the amateur in Canadian theatre. The birth of a vital Canadian professional theatre in the second half was greatly aided by the amateur theatre (educational and community) that preceded it. Canada's first professional actors, directors, and designers often had their training in amateur productions, and the teachers of these enthusiastic amateurs were often immigrant actors, directors, or painters who had forsaken a theatrical career in the old homeland for theatre as an avocation in the new.

Until the early 1960s there was no thorough training in theatre arts at the college level. Most universities followed the British tradition of offering credit courses in dramatic literature and criticism, while regarding practical training as an extra-curricular activity of the student drama society, or as the responsibility of the professional conservatory. Drama societies, departments of extension, and inter-collegiate festivals provided an opportunity for students wishing experience and training. There were many early signs of campus drama activity. The University Dramatic Club of Montreal, using mainly McGill personnel and alumni, staged Shaw's *Arms and the Man* for the first Earl Grey Dramatic Competition (Ottawa 1907). The Univ. of British Columbia Player's Club (1915-58) lasted for forty-three years as an all-student drama society with an unbroken record of continuing seasons. Play-reading groups were on the Univ. of Alberta campus as early as 1911, and during the winter of 1914-5 the Dept. of Extension at Alberta was distributing plays and dispensing production advice to Alberta communities. Campus drama organizations traditionally have offered opportunities to the beginning playwright when none were available from the profession. Campus support for young playwrights began as early as the 1921 HART HOUSE THEATRE production of Merrill DENISON's first play, *Brothers in Arms*.

The Univ. of Toronto's Hart House Theatre (1919) was a landmark theatre, for it had an endowment, a building, a budget, and a season dedicated in part to encouraging the development of amateur drama activities on the campus. Most importantly, it had an artistic director of vision, Roy MITCHELL, who between 1919 and 1921 established a semi-professional program. Incorporating many of the ideals and innovations of the ARTS AND LETTERS Players of Toronto, Hart House Theatre gave a sense of serious purpose to other campus and LITTLE THEATRE groups. Within the decade almost all universities had a student drama society. By 1930 McGill's Dept. of English was presenting plays for children. But it was not until 1941 that a few theatre courses were tentatively offered by the McGill department.

In central and eastern Canada it was often the English department that first provided academic respectability to courses in drama. Growth was much faster in the western universities. Following the U.S. pattern of offering degree programs that included some practical courses, the Univ. of Saskatchewan founded Canada's first Dept. of Drama in 1945, offering a BA in drama. The Univ. of Alberta followed with a Drama Division in 1947, and was the first to offer professional training programs: the four-year BFA in acting and in design (1966) and the two-year MFA in design and in directing (1968). The Banff School of Fine Arts (see BANFF CENTRE) has offered a wide spectrum of practical theatre courses since its founding in 1933. The first head of the theatre program, Elizabeth Sterling HAYNES, invited leading European and American teachers and artists to the School. In 1966 the Univ. of Toronto Graduate Centre for Study of Drama was founded, and Toronto became the first Canadian university to offer the Ph.D. in drama. As late as the 1960s, however, the majority of faculty in Canadian theatre departments and in professional training schools had received their training in England, France, or the U.S. By the late 1960s almost all French- and English-speaking universities had theatre departments offering a wide range of practical and theoretical courses. Nevertheless, the Black Report notes that only two private schools had met minimum requirements for actor training: the National Theatre School and the Vancouver Playhouse Acting School (1975). The latter, affiliated with the VAN-COUVER PLAYHOUSE, offers a course of two years of full-time study; only twelve students are accepted each year. Housed in the Firehall Theatre, the school has a full-time staff of three with a number of part-time and guest instructors. The Black Report established minimum requirements for acceptable professional training and rated anglophone Canadian university programs. Only the Univ. of Alberta qualified in the area of acting. No English-speaking school met the minimum requirements in design. In directing only the graduate programs of the Univ. of Alberta and the Univ. of British Columbia qualified. Stage-management requirements were achieved at the Univ. of Regina and at Toronto's Ryerson Polytechnical Institute, but no anglophone Canadian university met the minimum requirements for production management. Several regional professional theatres have teaching programs, but almost all cater for hobbyists. The possibility of an academy of classical acting attached to the Stratford Festival has often been raised, but has yet to materialize.

By the 1980s Canadian-trained drama faculty filled three-fifths of the university and college teaching positions, compared to one-tenth in the 1960s. Graduates of university drama-training programs are found in all professional theatre seasons—and many others make their mark in London, New York, and Hollywood.

In 1955 there were eight full-time instructors teaching 120 students in fledgeling drama programs at four universities. In 1977 twenty-two institutions offered professional or pre-professional training, and another fifteen offered programs with some form of drama specialization. In 1987, forty-eight programs, 280 faculty, and over ten thousand enrolments made up the educational theatre establishment in Canada. It is disappointing to note that even with the dynamic growth of university departments in the past thirty years, no Canadian department has become recognized for distinguished academic research or for significant innovative and experimental theatre presentation.

Prior to 1950 drama in the primary and high schools often meant merely putting on a play, although there were far-sighted teachers who attempted to integrate drama within the school curriculum in a more meaningful way. As early as 1948 the universities of Alberta and Saskatchewan offered a Bachelor of Education in drama for high school teachers. In 1968 the universities of Victoria and Calgary began four-year programs in drama education for teachers, and other universities soon followed suit. In the 1960s influential figures in British educational drama, such as Brian Way and Peter Slade, stressed the importance of drama in education as process rather than as finished product (the traditional school play). The training of teachers of school drama is, however, uneven. At least three provinces (in 1985) did not require teachers of drama to have specialization in this area. Efforts to improve drama-in-education are being pursued by such organizations as L'Association des professeurs d'expression dramatique du Québec and by the Council of Drama in Education.

GORDON PEACOCK

Edwards, Mae (1878-1937). Born in Lindsay, Ont., she worked in stock in Canada and the U.S. with such notables as Edward Everett Horton and Sydney Toler before founding, around 1914, the Mae Edwards Players with her husband, mentor, and stage partner Charlie T. Smith (a veteran vaudevillian and theatre manager for B.F. Keith). Noted for her elegant costumes and diction, Edwards led the company in a standard mixture of melodramas and light comedies. The company also doubled as a novelty orchestra, performing VAUDEVILLE numbers between the acts of its plays and at charity benefits. Appearing frequently in Ontario (once, in 1918, for a record twenty-nine-week run at the Family Theatre, Toronto) and on tour as far afield as Montana and the Carolinas, the Mae Edwards Players also performed in the Maritimes and northeastern New England. Summer rehearsals in June and three-night and one-week stands along the coast of Maine

Mae Edwards

banded in 1935. Edwards and her husband retired to Lindsay, Ont., where she died.

See Fred H. Phillips, 'The Mae Edwards Players', *Canadian Theatre Review*, 11 (1976). The Mae Edwards Collection is in the Metropolitan Toronto Library.   ROBERT SCOTT

Eight Men Speak. The most important play to emerge out of the Workers' Theatre movement of the 1930s, *Eight Men Speak* was the first play in Canada devised as a militant intervention in a political conflict. Produced on 4 Dec. 1933 at Toronto's Standard Theatre—a Yiddish theatre at the corner of Spadina and Dundas that subsequently became a BURLESQUE house and is now a Chinese movie theatre—it was written collectively by Oscar Ryan, Frank Love, E. Cecil-Smith, and Mildred Goldberg (all members of the Workers' Experimental Theatre) to protest the jailing of eight members of the Communist Party of Canada's Political Bureau. The focus of the play is the alleged attempted murder in prison of CPC leader Tim Buck by a prison guard.

The play's six acts embody a range of familiar agitprop techniques. Beginning with broad satire, the play centres around a Workers' Court in which Guard X, the would-be murderer, is brought to trial by the Canadian Labour Defence League. The court scenes alternate with mass chants and documentary satire. The action is unified by rhetorical performance structures, including expressionistic fugue techniques and extensive use of dramatic lighting and sound effects. Its emphasis on semiotic rather than literary techniques makes it an important predecessor to the political theatre of the present day.

The original benefit production of *Eight Men Speak* was performed by a cast of thirty-five unemployed workers, and played to a capacity audience of 1,500. A second performance was suppressed by the Toronto police Red Squad, and in Winnipeg the police revoked the licence of the WALKER THEATRE when its manager refused to cancel the show. In 1982 *Eight Men Speak* was revived for the first time by the Halifax activist troupe, Popular Projects Society, with one of the original authors, Oscar Ryan, in the audience. It was published in *Eight Men Speak and Other Plays from the Canadian Workers' Theatre* (1976), ed. Richard Wright and Robin Endres.

See also POLITICAL AND POPULAR THEATRE.   ALAN FILEWOD

and Massachusetts in July and August usually preceded an autumn season in the Atlantic provinces, with extended engagements in Halifax and St John's in early winter. The company continued to play small towns in Eastern Canada and New England into the 1930s, supplying many communities with their last taste of the 'real old-time travelling show'. The longest-lived of several touring stock companies operating in Ontario during the 1920s that headlined a female lead (the others being the Jane Hastings Players, the Marie Gladke Players, and the Arlie Marks Players), the Mae Edwards Players finally dis-

Eight Men Speak, *Standard Theatre, Toronto, 1933*

Elgin and Winter Garden Theatres. These double-decker theatres were built on Yonge St north of Queen in Toronto by the Marcus Loew circuit of New York as the flagship of its Canadian chain of 'small time' VAUDEVILLE and movie theatres. The complex was designed by the noted U.S. theatre architect Thomas W. Lamb.

The lower theatre opened as Loew's Yonge Street Theatre in Dec. 1913. The first Toronto theatre without a gallery, it seated 2,149 and shared a lobby, seven floors of dressing rooms, a backstage elevator, and its vaudeville and movie programs with the Winter Garden Theatre above, which opened in Feb. 1914. While the lower theatre offered a minimum of three continuous shows a day, the Winter Garden usually mounted one

The Winter Garden Theatre, Toronto, 1914

195

Elgin and Winter Garden Theatres

identical evening show, but with reserved seating and higher admission. The Loew's stage was 30′ 3″ deep, with a 39′ 6″ × 26′ proscenium opening.

Patron access to the Winter Garden was by one of three elevators or by a seven-storey grand staircase. The auditorium, with a single balcony, seated 1,410 and enjoyed a decorative scheme unique among Canadian theatres. Its ceiling and balcony soffit were hung with 10,000 fire-proofed and preserved beech boughs, supplemented by colourful leaded glass lanterns and cotton blossoms. Columns were rendered to resemble tree trunks, and garden murals decorated the walls. Its stage was built in front of the stage house of the theatre below, thus limiting its depth to 23′. From about 1921, the Winter Garden was generally open only on Saturdays and holidays; it closed in 1928.

Loew's Theatre below gave up vaudeville in 1930 but continued to show movies. It lost its proscenium arch and boxes to a Cinerama conversion in 1961. In 1970 the building was purchased by 20th Century Theatres, when the name was changed to the Yonge. In 1978 the name was changed again to the Elgin. It closed as a cinema on 14 Nov. 1981.

Both theatres were acquired in 1981 by the Ontario Heritage Foundation in order to revive and restore the complex, which has no known surviving counterpart dedicated to live performance. In 1985 the Andrew Lloyd Webber musical, *Cats*, opened in the Elgin for a two-year run. The entire complex is being restored for a planned reopening in late 1989.   HILARY RUSSELL

Empire Theatre (Edmonton). There were three Empire Theatres in Edmonton. The first was a small VAUDEVILLE house built on McDougall Ave (now 100 Street) in 1906 by O.C. Ross. Designed by A.M. Calderon, it measured 30′ × 80′ and seated 400 on chairs set out on its level floor. It opened shortly after the destruction by fire of Robertson Hall, the city's first purpose-built playhouse, but soon became a movie house (renamed the Bijou) and later a meat market. It was pulled down in the 1950s.

The second Empire, one of Edmonton's major theatres, opened on Third Street (now 103 Street) in Jan. 1909. Designed by H.D. Johnson and costing $4,000, it was converted from a warehouse and dancing academy. The building measured 110′ × 50′, with a stage 30′ deep; the main part of the auditorium was a brick-faced frame structure with a flat roof suspended from external trusses. The stage end was metal-clad, with a tall mansard

The second Empire Theatre, Edmonton

roof over the flies. The management first concentrated on vaudeville, and the theatre was briefly associated with the PANTAGES circuit, but by the end of the year it was offering touring shows. In 1911, under the management of W.B. Sherman, it joined the Orpheum vaudeville circuit, whose bills generally alternated with touring shows. In subsequent years most of the touring stars of the day performed there, including Johnston Forbes-Robertson, Lewis Waller, John Martin-Harvey, Maude Adams, Margaret ANGLIN, and Sarah Bernhardt, who appeared in 1913 as part of an Orpheum variety bill. The theatre stood until 1920.

Its replacement, the New Empire, opened on a site immediately to the north in Dec. 1920, and was Edmonton's most prominent theatre for the next two decades. It was 80' wide by 118' deep, with a seating capacity of 1,477—823 on the main floor, 510 in two balconies, 72 in boxes, and 72 in loges. The proscenium opening was 40' wide by 30' high, and the stage was 35' deep. The theatre housed road shows and vaudeville, and was occasionally used for the massive political rallies of the 1930s. After the war it was converted into the Trocadero Ballroom, and was subsequently used for bingo and office space. It was demolished in 1980.

See John Orrell, *Fallen Empires: Lost Theatres of Edmonton, 1881-1914* (1981).

JOHN ORRELL

Empire Theatre (Saskatoon). Designed by the Saskatoon architectural firm of Storey and Van Egmond for Joseph Sutton as part of his Empire Block on the corner of 2nd Ave and 20th St, the Empire opened on 29 Dec. 1910, under the management of David Douglas, with the Saskatoon Opera Society's production of Gilbert and Sullivan's *H.M.S. Pinafore*. Two balconies, ten dress boxes, and a large pit accommodated 800 patrons, and renovations in 1911 extended the seating capacity to 1,200. Supporting pillars and the boxes were upholstered and draped with gold plush; opera chairs in the latest style from Berlin, Ont., sat on fully carpeted floors. Safety features included fire doors on each level, a water safety system connected to the main water supply, and a 23' × 30' asbestos fire curtain. Electric lights in the dome, under the galleries, and in the boxes enhanced the comfort of the house, as did a four-foot rotary ventilator in the roof that created a

continual flow of fresh air. A 28' × 22' proscenium opened onto a stage 24' × 55', equipped with five drop curtains as well as the house curtain displaying painted advertisements.

Attractions were booked originally through Winnipeg's C.P. WALKER, and featured some of the great performers of the day: Sir John Martin-Harvey (1912, 1921, 1924), Robert Mantell (1913, 1924, 1926), Laurence Irving (1914), the Theatre Guild (1919), Fred Allen (1920), Ethel Barrymore (1922), the D'Oyly Carte Opera Company (1927), and Sir Harry Lauder (1929). Empire patrons welcomed Canadian favourites as well, including the MARKS BROTHERS (1911, 1912, 1913), the George H. SUMMERS Stock Company (1911, 1913), Margaret ANGLIN (1912), and numerous visits by the Oliver J. Eckhardt Players, Bert Lang's Juvenile Bostonians, and the DUMBELLS.

Competition from the new Capitol Theatre, which opened in 1929, proved disastrous and the Empire was sold in 1930. Renamed the Hub, the theatre operated as a movie house for twelve years; sold again in 1942 and renamed the Victory Theatre, it hosted a three-week VAUDEVILLE revival before reverting to a movie theatre. In June 1958 Canawa Holdings Limited purchased the theatre for $30,000 and demolished it to provide additional parking for the Empire Hotel.

PATRICK B. O'NEILL

Empress Theatre. Heralded as a new 'Opera House' that would be 'unsurpassed by any in the Province', the Empress Theatre, Fort Macleod, Alta., opened in 1912 at the height of the town's railway-boom years. The theatre has been in continuous use since its opening, playing an important role as the community's cultural centre for live theatre, concerts, lectures, and movies, and reflecting changing emphases in entertainment. Originally a franchise theatre of the Famous Players chain, the Empress was a road house for VAUDEVILLE and comic-opera tours from the eastern United States. Graffiti on the walls of the unaltered tiny basement dressing rooms attest to the stature and variety of the performers who have graced the Empress stage. Subsequently live performances gave way to motion pictures. Dramatic productions, which continued alongside the movies until the 1940s, made a comeback in the 1980s with productions by local groups such as the Fort Players and the resident Great West Summer Theatre Company, which runs throughout the summer. The Empress was built by local contractor J. S. Lambert for its first owner, T.B. Martin, and has remained surprisingly unchanged since. The approximately 2,400-square-foot rectangular three-storey structure is unadorned except for the front where the parapet's detailed and raised brickwork designs are repeated in the entrance archway. In 1937 Daniel Boyle purchased the theatre and completed renovations that remain today. Added were a 100-seat balcony to increase seating to 400 and a unique 'loveseat' staggered-seating arrangement. The orchestra pit was removed from the raked house and stairs were added to the sides of the 23' × 16.5' stage. To the pressed-metal tile ceiling, huge decorative neon tulips were added for enhancement of house lighting provided by small Tiffany-style lamps. Originally the fourth and now the only remaining theatre in Fort Macleod, it remains a valuable example of theatres of its period.

BRIAN C. PARKINSON

Encore cinq minutes. First presented on radio in 1966, Françoise LORANGER's play subsequently premièred on 15 Jan. 1967 at Montreal's THÉÂTRE DU RIDEAU VERT. It marks the end of what Loranger has called her 'first style'—a cycle of plays (*Une maison . . . un jour*, *Georges . . . Oh! Georges*) in the manner of bourgeois drama that portrayed an ossified family milieu of outdated middle-class comfort whose moral values stifled aspirations for happiness and freedom. Loranger's most successful drama, it won a Governor General's Award in 1967; it was published in the same year by the Cercle du Livre de France. A 1969 production by the THÉÂTRE POPULAIRE DU QUÉBEC toured Ontario, and there have been several revivals in France and Quebec.

The action is confined to a single setting, and centres on the character—one of the most powerful in Quebec drama—of Gertrude, a woman in her fifties. She is completely bound up in her possessive love for her family and especially for her son Renaud who, she sadly admits, wishes to control his own love life and has adopted a manner of speaking and a life style that do not conform to her conventional values. This conventionality is reflected in the décor of the house, which she has filled with beautiful antiques. A single crack in the wall declares that this order will soon be broken: it 'bores its way, stretches out, puts forth branches', which, at the end of the play, 'swarm over the whole wall'. When the curtain rises Gertrude is trying desperately to organize her enclosed but plainly unsatisfying world. Confrontations with her son and her husband force her to see the absurdity and emptiness of her existence. After smashing the objects that surround her and that symbolize middle-class family traditions, she announces that she is leaving the house, declaring that she has 'only five more minutes' (i.e. only a few more years) in which to live her own life.

JEAN CLÉO GODIN

Équipe, L'. Pierre DAGENAIS's French-language avant-garde theatre company was responsible for thirteen productions in Montreal over five years, beginning with Julian Luchaire's *Altitude 3,200* in Jan. 1943 at the MONUMENT NATIONAL. The company produced a dazzling array of plays, from Emlyn Williams' British thriller *Night Must Fall* (in 1944), in which Dagenais played the lead, to a production in the Salle du GESÙ of Jean-Paul Sartre's controversial *Huis-Clos* in 1946; and from Marcel Pagnol's *Marius* and *Fanny* (both in 1944) at the Monument National to an outdoor production of Shakespeare's *Le Songe d'une nuit d'été* (*A Midsummer Night's Dream*) in the gardens of L'ERMITAGE in 1945. Other notable productions included Ferenc Molnár's *Liliom*, 1946; Claude Puget's *Le Grand Poucet*, 1946; Shaw's *Le Héros et le soldat* (*Arms and the Man*), directed by Herbert WHITTAKER, 1946—the only Équipe production not directed by Dagenais; Armand Salacrou's *Les Fiancés du Havre*, 1947; and Dagenais's own *Le Temps de vivre*, 1947. All attracted widespread attention, and most received favourable notices from both French and English-language critics. *Le Temps de vivre*, however, was so badly received that, thanks to a history of poor financial management and the lack, at the time, of government subsidy, it ended L'Équipe's brief but influential existence.

L'Équipe complemented Gratien GÉLINAS's classical work at Les COMPAGNONS DE SAINT-LAURENT by introducing contemporary stagecraft and new international writing to Montreal. Dagenais's gift for producing exciting theatre developed many talented players: Denise PELLETIER, Yvette

BRIND'AMOUR, Guy Maufette, Denyse Saint-Pierre, Jean Deprez, Nini Durand, Jean-Pierre Masson, and Robert Rivard, among others.   HERBERT WHITTAKER

Ermitage, La Salle de l'. Built in Montreal, with an adjoining gymnasium, between 1911 and 1913 at 3510 Côte-des-Neiges for the Petit Séminaire de Montréal, on an estate belonging to the Saint-Sulpice order, the dimensions of L'Ermitage were 72' by 60' for the hall, 30' by 30' for the stage, 20' by 60' for the balcony, and 8' by 40' for the mezzanines—more spacious than those of the Crypt, a space beneath the chapel of the Petit Séminaire that had been fitted out for student performances in 1883. L'Ermitage was not opened for public performances until the mid-1930s, when it was used by a group of graduates of the Collège de Montréal that included, among others, Yves Bourassa and Gratien GÉLINAS. In 1941 the backstage area was enlarged by incorporating the side-aisles and part of the mezzanines, thereby attracting several professional companies: Les COMPAGNONS DE SAINT-LAURENT from 1942 to 1945 (with a memorable production of Paul Claudel's *L'Échange*, directed by Ludmilla Pitoëff); the Ludmilla Pitoëff company, which produced Ibsen's *La Maison de poupée* (*A Doll's House*) and Claudel's *L'Otage* in 1943 (with future stars Yul Brynner, Jean GASCON, and Jean-Louis ROUX); the Pierre DAGENAIS company, which offered a French production of Shakespeare's *Midsummer Night's Dream* (*Le Songe d'une nuit d'été*) in the gardens next to the theatre in 1945; and La Jeune Scène, which presented Marcel DUBÉ's *Le Bal triste* in 1951. Radio-Canada subsequently rented L'Ermitage for several years as a television studio. Although the stages of both the Crypt and L'Ermitage are intact, the halls are now used for recreation and sports.   ANDRÉ-G. BOURASSA

Eskabel L'. A theatre workshop founded in Montreal in 1971 by Jacques Crête, its name (which was not chosen until 1973) derives from the old French 'escabelle' (later 'escabeau'), a stepping-stool or step-ladder, reflecting the workshop's emphasis on actor training. Inspired by the work of Jerzy Grotowski and New York's Living Theatre Company, Crête concentrated on workshops in movement, voice, breathing, and improvisation for two years before producing his first show, *Création Collective I*, in 1973 at the 100-seat Conventum. This was followed by *Opéra-Fête* at the company's premises on rue Saint-Paul, after which it moved to a four-storey building on rue Saint-Nicolas, the ground floor of which was used for rehearsal and performance, while company members lived upstairs. This was the beginning of their ambulatory productions, when the audience (thirty or forty people) followed the action by moving from one room to another.

When the company moved to Pointe-Saint-Charles in 1979, it focused on creations and free adaptation (of Marguerite Duras, Thomas Mann, Marie-Claire BLAIS). In an enormous old vacant cinema L'Eskabel was able to expand its style of playing even further, becoming known for creating a theatre of atmosphere, of multiple spaces, and for highly visual and resonant productions. In the same year a group who wanted to return to the original Eskabel method left to found—under the direction of Pierre-A. Larocque—the Opéra-Fête company. In 1980 a new member, Serge Le Maire, introduced a strong musical component into the shows, and in 1983 Eskabel organized an impressive program called Forty Days of Experimental Theatre.

Obliged to leave their premises in Pointe-Saint-Charles when they were destroyed by fire, the company bought the Conventum, where they have since remained, producing two or three original plays each season.
                    MICHEL VAIS

Evelyn, Judith (1913-67). Born Judith Evelyn Morris in Seneca, South Dakota, she was taken when very young by her parents to Moose Jaw, Sask. She attended the Univ. of Manitoba (BA, 1932; MA in German, 1934) and acted there, and in the Winnipeg Little Theatre under the direction of Nancy Piper. In 1935, when Piper became director for a year of Toronto's HART HOUSE THEATRE, Evelyn followed her and acted in several productions and on CBC radio. She won the best-actress award of the DOMINION DRAMA FESTIVAL in 1936. After an eighteen-month association with the Pasadena Playhouse, California, she went to England in 1937 and acted on stage and radio there. In Sept. 1939, soon after war was declared, she left England on the *Athenia*, which was torpedoed. (After being abandoned for over five hours in a lifeboat that was destroyed by the rescuing ship's propeller, she and her friend Andrew ALLAN were among those who survived by clinging to some wreckage until they were rescued.) At the Hollywood Playhouse in Mar.-Apr. 1941 she performed the leading role of Mrs Manningham in Patrick Hamilton's *Gas Light*, about a man's attempt to drive his wife insane. In the New York production, called *Angel Street*—slated to be a vehicle for Vincent Price and his wife Edith Barrett—she assumed the female lead for the opening, to great acclaim, when Barrett became ill, and remained throughout the play's famous long run, from 5 Dec. 1941 to 1 June 1944. She won the Drama League Award in 1942 for the most distinguished performance of the season. Although tormented, or tormenting, female characters became a specialty, Evelyn also played highly intelligent, stable women. Her other Broadway appearances included starring roles in a revival of George Kelly's *Craig's Wife* in 1947 and in Joseph Kramm's *The Shrike* (1952) opposite José Ferrer. She toured in Howard Lindsay's and Russel Crouse's *State of the Union* (1946) and Tennessee Williams' *A Streetcar Named Desire* (1940-50) and appeared in several films, including Alfred Hitchcock's *Rear Window* (1954).

WILLIAM TOYE

F

Factory Theatre. One of Toronto's major ALTERNATE THEATRES, it was founded as Factory Theatre Lab in May 1970 by Ken GASS and Frank Trotz (who left the company a few months later). The Factory occupied a former candle factory above an auto body shop at 374 Dupont St, with environmental seating for 100 or more. Theatre classes were offered immediately, and its first production opened in July, a double-bill of Stan Ross's *Act of Violence* and Bill Greenland's *We Three, You and I*, both directed by Gass.

At its inception the Factory announced it would produce only Canadian plays, soliciting manuscripts with the slogan 'Discover Canada Before the Yankees Do'. Two productions attracted national attention in its first season: David FREEMAN's CREEPS (directed by Bill GLASSCO) and Herschel HARDIN's *Esker Mike and His Wife, Agiluk* (directed by Maruti Achanta). The fact that *Esker Mike* had been published (1969) but never produced supported Gass's contention that good Canadian scripts were being ignored by Canada's established theatres.

In 1971 two conferences on Canadian playwriting (sponsored by the Canada Council and the SHAW FESTIVAL respectively) brought greater attention to the Factory's programming policy, which began to be emulated in Toronto and elsewhere. While Glassco left the company that year to form TARRAGON THEATRE, Gass's devotion to new Canadian drama attracted and encouraged other talents, notably playwright George F. WALKER, directors Paul Bettis and Eric STEINER, and business manager Ralph Zimmerman, who also acted as agent for the Factory's playwrights. The Factory's 1971-2 season was its most energetic, fuelled by this new talent, by a current of cultural nationalism, and by federal job-creation grants. Productions included three plays by Walker: *The Prince of Naples*, *Ambush at Tether's End*, and *Sacktown Rag*; Larry FINEBERG's *Stonehenge Trilogy*; John PALMER's *A Touch of God in the Golden Age*; and the popular nostalgic comedies *Brussels Sprouts*, by Larry Kardish, and *Maybe We Could Get Some Bach*, by Louis Del Grande.

A series of setbacks began in Dec. 1972 with an exhausting 'Works' festival of thirteen short plays, including Michael HOLLINGSWORTH's *Strawberry Fields*. When Actors' Equity discovered that its members were being paid less than minimum, 'Works' was closed, an anticipated job-creation grant was forfeited, and the company all but collapsed. Special public and private grants were obtained to resolve the dispute with Equity and to finance a farewell production, Walker's

Bagdad Saloon, in Apr. 1973, after which public performances were forbidden at Dupont St because of inadequate safety standards. In Sept. 1973 the Factory received $42,000 from the Department of External Affairs for a three-week festival of Canadian theatre in London, England, featuring a repertory of *Bagdad Saloon* and *Esker Mike* along with 'fringe' activities of Canadian films, concerts, and lunchtime plays. Despite organizational problems, poor attendance, and a lack of critical attention in England, this tour further solidified the Factory's stature at home.

In May 1974, after three productions in rented premises, the Factory moved to another converted warehouse at 207 Adelaide St E. Although its capacity was greater (about 175), structural pillars dotted the space and caused severe staging difficulties. Important productions there included Walker's *Beyond Mozambique* in 1974 (remounted 1978), Gass's *Hurray for Johnny Canuck* in 1974, Bryan WADE's *Underground* in 1975, Walker's *Ramona and the White Slaves* in 1976, and Hrant ALIANAK's *Lucky Strike* in 1978. Perhaps the most effective production in this theatre was Gass's *The Boy Bishop* in 1976, an allegory of tarnished ideals set in New France. In Nov. 1977 the gratuitous sex and violence in Gass's *Winter Offensive*, set in Nazi Germany, prompted several critics to call for a cessation of public funding for the Factory and earned the company the nickname 'Nazi Theatre Lab'. Although he vigorously defended the artist's right to free expression, Gass resigned before the season ended. After a transitional year, artistic directorship passed to Bob White, who had worked as dramaturge with both the Factory and the Playwrights' Workshop of Montreal.

Under White and managing director Dian English, the Factory's slender resources were concentrated on fewer shows, while its reputation as a centre for script development was re-established. The company gave up its Adelaide St location in 1980, moved into the refurbished Adelaide Court Theatre until 1982, then operated without its own theatre for two years. The most important productions of this period were, in 1980, Walker's punk-rock musical *Rumours of our Death*, which was held over when the cast enlisted as co-producers; again in 1980, Cheryl Cashman's *Turning Thirty*, which was subsequently performed in several Canadian cities; in 1981, Walker's *Theatre of the Film Noir*, the

surprise hit of the Toronto Theatre Festival, which toured Britain the following year; and in 1983 Walker's *The Art of War* mounted at TORONTO WORKSHOP PRODUCTIONS. In Nov. 1984 the Factory moved to a new permanent home at 125 Bathurst St, a large Victorian house with a 230-seat auditorium attached. Productions there—under its new name, Factory Theatre—have included Walker's highly acclaimed *Criminals in Love* in 1984, Neil Munro's *Crossing Over* in 1986, and Walker's productions of his own ZASTROZZI and *Beautiful City* in 1987. White resigned as artistic director at the close of the 1986-7 season to pursue freelance directing, and was succeeded in July 1987 by Jackie Maxwell.

The Factory's greatest contribution to Canadian theatre has been a catalytic one, providing professional opportunities for new directors, designers, actors, and especially playwrights. Script development has always been a central activity, receiving public expression in the 'Works' festivals (1972, 1975, and 1976) and 'Brave New Works' series (annually since 1981). Factory dramaturges have included Palmer, Bettis, Walker, White, Maxwell, Alan Richardson, Connie Brissenden, and Rina Fraticelli. The Factory also developed, in opposition to Tarragon, an anti-realistic production style, associated at first with nationalist rhetoric, then with the theme of a Canadian cultural wilderness, and finally with Walker's witty indictments of ineffectual liberalism in an increasingly conservative society.

The archives of Factory Theatre are housed at the Univ. of Guelph. DENIS W. JOHNSTON

Farm Show, The. The definitive example of the work of Toronto's THEATRE PASSE MURAILLE, this COLLECTIVE CREATION was first performed in a barn near Clinton, Ont., in Aug. 1972, directed by Paul THOMPSON. After several weeks of immersion in the life of the farming community, the company created a series of monologues, sketches, songs, and visual images reflecting the vibrant yet vulnerable qualities of the community. In the tradition of Sunday School and Christmas concerts, skits at celebrations, parades and other festivities, *The Farm Show* spoke of and to a specific community—in its own patterns of speech and gesture—yet also succeeded in appealing to audiences throughout Canada and abroad, and it fused regionalism and

Farm Show

nationalism in a powerful and exemplary fashion. Intensely theatrical, though not technically complex, it directly influenced companies such as the MUMMERS TROUPE (Nfld) and 25TH ST THEATRE (Saskatoon), as well as the work of playwrights John GRAY, Linda GRIFFITHS, and Hrant ALIANAK. *The Farm Show* was also influential in encouraging the participation of actors in script development, and in drawing attention to unconventional performance venues and non-traditional theatre audiences.

The Farm Show was revived in the fall of 1972 (Toronto), 1973 (southwestern Ontario, and Ottawa's NATIONAL ARTS CENTRE), 1974 (Saskatchewan), 1975 (Petrolia, Ont.), 1976 (Vancouver), and 1979 (England and Wales). In 1985 the play returned to the Clinton area, where it was produced (with all but two of the original company) as part of Goderich Township's sesquicentennial celebrations. Versions were performed on CBC radio (1972) and television (1975). Michael Ondaatje's film, *The Clinton Special* (1974), chronicles the 1973 tour.

The published text (Toronto: Coach House Press, 1976) was prepared by Ted JOHNS, a native of the Clinton community, whose conversations with Thompson in 1972 gave rise to the idea of the play.   ROBERT C. NUNN

Faux Brillants, Les. Considered the best of Félix-Gabriel MARCHAND's five plays, this curious and largely successful blend of classical French comedy with the repertory favoured by late nineteenth-century Parisian *boulevard* theatre is composed in traditional alexandrine rhymed couplets, observes the classical unities, displays obvious melodramatic elements, and yet it was written, and set, in Quebec of the 1880s.

The plot focuses on a cunning, penniless swindler, Faquino, who convinces rich, gullible Dumont that he is an Italian nobleman about to recover an immense family fortune. He seeks to marry Dumont's daughter, Élise, and to have his accomplice marry her sister, Cécile. In anticipation of these marriages, Dumont lends money to Faquino and covers his debts, lauding his every excess. A cousin of Dumont's, Jean Brunelle, tries to undo Faquino's scheme and is nearly assassinated by hired thugs. But at the melodramatically opportune moment, when the marriage contract is about to be signed, Brunelle unmasks the imposter. Following the tradition of melodrama, there is no nuance, no depth of character. The plot is also traditional, recalling, among others, Molière's *Tartuffe*, Pierre PETITCLAIR's *La DONATION*, and Marchand's first play, *Fatenville* (1869).

Unlike the repertory offered by many French touring companies at the time, there is nothing in *Les Faux Brillants* to disturb the comfortable Quebec bourgeoisie to which Marchand, his readers, and his prospective audience belonged. It is comfortable theatre, chastened and domesticated for local tastes. The play was first published in full in 1885 (Montreal: Prendergast). The first production

Les Faux Brillants, *adapted by Jean-Claude Germain, Théâtre d'Aujourd'hui, Montreal, 1977*

was on 28 Feb. 1905, by an amateur group directed by J. Oscar Turcotte, at Montreal's MONUMENT NATIONAL. It was revived, with modest success—in an adapted version by Jean-Claude GERMAIN—in 1977.

See Louise Forsyth, 'Three Moments in Quebec Theatre History: *Les Faux Brillants* by F.-G. Marchand and by J.-C. Germain', *Theatre History in Canada*, 2 (1981).

L.E. DOUCETTE

Fées ont soif, Les. Denise Boucher's feminist play, first produced by the THÉÂTRE DU NOUVEAU MONDE on 18 Nov. 1978, directed by Jean-Luc BASTIEN, provoked a public outcry that earned it a place in Quebec's theatrical history. Because of the play's provocative subject matter the Montreal Arts Council refused to provide a production grant, and the ensuing controversy guaranteed the play's immediate success. While members of various religious groups—few of whom knew very much about the play—prayed at the theatre's doors, audiences flocked to this ritual of feminist liberation in large numbers. Subsequent attempts to suppress the production were unsuccessful, but the published text was temporarily banned by a Quebec Superior Court judge. Legal attacks on the play came to an end when the Supreme Court refused to hear charges of blasphemy in Feb. 1980.

The play is marked by evocative poetry and harsh realism. Assembled on the stage are three symbolic figures of feminine alienation: the Virgin, the Mother, and the Prostitute. They meet to proclaim their individual liberation as preparation for the liberation of Woman. Especially explosive was the depiction of the Virgin Mary, demythologized, laying claim to her status as a woman. Decrying the fact that her sexuality had been negated by the sublimation of her virginity, she drops, before the audience's eyes, the shackles that have made her a statue.

Through its exorcising incarnation of the Virgin, the play gave feminist demands a high profile in the theatre. At each corner of an obviously alienated triangle, three women finally 'pulled down their statues'.

Les Fées ont soif was published, with a file of press accounts on its CENSORSHIP, by Les Éditions Intermèdes in 1978.

See also FEMINIST THEATRE.

LORRAINE CAMERLAIN

Félix Poutré. The most popular play of the nineteenth century and one of the most frequently staged in the history of French Canada, Louis-Honoré FRÉCHETTE's play, based on the 1862 memoirs of a self-styled Patriote hero, was first performed by an amateur troupe at Quebec City's Salle de Musique on 22 Nov. 1862. Reviewers were unanimous in their praise for the production. It was revived two months later and became, after its publication in 1871 (Montreal: Beauchemin), a staple of amateur theatres throughout francophone North America, receiving countless performances.

The plot is simple: twenty-one year old Félix, recruiter of troops and arms for Patriote rebels, is betrayed by a spy, Camel. Imprisoned, he feigns madness in order to escape the gallows. Of the four acts of Fréchette's historical drama, the last three are merely a dramatization of the real Poutré's memoirs. Only Act I is original, and it is by far the best, creating perfectly the conspiratorial atmosphere of 1837-8. The text is balanced, carefully controlled, and an excellent vehicle for melodramatic actors. Most importantly, it allows the audience to identify strongly with the protagonist as, in his feigned madness, he pummels an anglophone doctor and his warders and insults the Queen, her judges, and her institutions.

Many contemporaries doubted Poutré's tale; historians have since proven he was a paid informer for the English cause. Fréchette, suspicious, allowed no edition of *Félix Poutré* to bear his name in his lifetime. It is unfortunate that for more than a century the very real merits of the first play to deal with the Rebellion have been obscured by the controversy surrounding the historical Poutré. The 1871 text was republished in 1974 by Editions Leméac.

See L.E. Doucette, *Theatre in French Canada, 1606-1867* (1984). L.E. DOUCETTE

Feminist Theatre. The first feminist playwright, although not the first woman to write for theatre in Canada, was Sarah Anne CURZON. A leader of the Toronto Women's Literary and Social Progress Club—the first Canadian women's rights group—she wrote her play *Laura Secord, the Heroine of 1812* (1887) 'to rescue from oblivion the name of a brave woman, and set it in its proper place among the heroes of Canadian history'. In a second play, *The Sweet Girl Graduate* (1882),

Feminist Theatre

Curzon ridiculed opponents of university education for women. In 1914, when women's right to vote in provincial and federal elections had still not been recognized, Nellie McClung and others in Manitoba's Political Equality League became the first to stage a feminist play, *Votes for Men*, which achieves its satiric effect through reversal of sex roles. Two contemporary feminist plays—Diane Grant and Company's *What Glorious Times They Had—Nellie McClung* (1976), performed in 1974, and Wendy Lill's *Fighting Days* (1985), performed in 1984—recount McClung's achievements. The struggles of early Quebec feminists were dramatized by Madeleine Greffard in *L'Incroyable histoire de la lutte que quelques-unes ont menée pour obtenir le droit de vote pour toutes* (1980) and *Pour toi je changerai le monde* (1981), performed in 1980 and 1981 respectively.

Prior to 1960 relatively little social criticism or protest was sustained in Canadian drama by women, with exceptions such as Gwen Pharis RINGWOOD, Grace Butt in Newfoundland, Lois Sweet in New Brunswick, and Lois Reynolds KERR in Ontario. In Quebec theatre women played a less important role since the moral climate did not encourage the dramatization of women's experience. Quebec's BURLESQUE theatre dealt irreverently with social practices and values but never challenged the role or image of women. Among journalists, a few feminist voices were heard: in *Le Mirage* (1923), performed in 1921, and *L'heure est venue* (performed and published in 1923), both by Monique (Alice Pépin-Benoît), the female protagonists oppose arbitrary male authority and seek self-realization. In Charlotte Savary's radio drama *La plus belle de céans*, broadcast in 1959, Mère d'Youville, the ethereal eighteenth-century Grey Nun of official history, is transformed into a woman of flesh, blood, and even sexuality.

Despite the major role played by women in the development of professional theatre in Canada since the 1950s, mainstream professional theatre, which receives the major share of government funding, has had little room for women. This 'Invisibility Factor' was studied in *Pour les Québécoises: égalité et indépendance* (1978) and in Rina Fraticelli's *The Status of Women in the Canadian Theatre* (1982). This exclusion has been more severe in English Canada than in Quebec, where radical feminist plays have been commissioned and performed at the THÉÂTRE DU NOUVEAU MONDE and the PLACE DES ARTS. It was outside the establishment, however, that contemporary feminist theatre in both English and French emerged in the early 1970s, often in cooperation with ALTERNATE, experimental theatre and playwrights' groups founded around the same time.

Plays by women writers in the 1960s tended not to advocate radical feminist social change, but often dealt with general social and moral issues such as nationalism, justice, and peace. Playwrights Marie-Claire BLAIS, Anne HÉBERT, Françoise LORANGER, Andrée Maillet, Antonine MAILLET, Mary Mitchell, Lily Pany, Aviva RAVEL, and Beverley SIMONS offered fresh perspectives on such issues as family politics, stereotypes, madness, violence, sexuality, and reproductive rights, but it was left to playwrights of the 1970s and 1980s to explore them in a more directly feminist way.

In English Canada such feminist playwrights include Gay Bell, Patricia Brown, Sally Clark, Grace Eamon, Anna Fuerstenberg, Maimie Hamer, Lezley Havard, Margaret HOLLINGSWORTH, Joan Hurley, Penny Kemp, Betty LAMBERT, Helen Lusting, Sharon POLLOCK, Janis Rapaport, Kelly Rebar, Erika RITTER, Elinore Siminovitch, Beverley Simons, and Betty Jane WYLIE.

Feminist playwriting in Quebec developed out of a climate of ferment during the Quiet Revolution of the 1960s and was consequently more radical. By the end of the 1970s it was recognized as a major cultural force. Some of the most successful works have been monologues or variations on that form, which is particularly well suited to presenting the conflict between normal social discourse and what women's inner voices are saying. Quebec playwrights developing feminist themes include Michelle Allen, Anne-Marie Alonzo, Suzanne Aubry, Marielle Bernard, Micheline Bernard, Marie Chouinard, Sonia Côté, Jeanne-Mance Delisle, Clémence Desrochers, Louisette Dussault, Jocelyne Goyette, Michèle Lalonde, Monique LEPAGE, Marthe Mercure, Maryse Pelletier, Ghyslaine Poirier, Claudine Raymond, Nicky Roy, Louise Roy, Francine Ruel, Louis Saïa, Marie Savard, Suzanne Tétrault, Francine Tougas, Manon Vallée, and France Vézina.

As in English Canada, the works of the best-known playwrights in French (Elizabeth Bourget, Marie LABERGE) have not been consistently feminist, although they have often treated feminist themes. The plays of Acadian playwright Antonine Maillet, despite their strong female characters, are nationalist and feminine rather than feminist. Much stronger in that regard is Denise Boucher's Les FÉES ONT SOIF (1978), around which public controversy exploded because of its dramatization of women's angry rejection of the traditional roles and images imposed by social practice and such patriarchal institutions as family and Church. Jovette MARCHESSAULT has written the most significant body of radical feminist theatre work yet produced in Canada. Her characters are frequently writers from the past whose creative expression and energy Marchessault draws upon to celebrate images, tales, and myths of women, thus proclaiming the historical reality of women's culture.

Quebec's first theatre company composed entirely of women, Le Théâtre des Cuisines, believes in the primacy of social action. Born of the struggle for access to safe contraception and abortion in the late 1960s, this militant group wished to reach ordinary women who may not often attend established theatres. Its first production, Nous aurons les enfants que nous voulons (1975), first performed in 1974, was twice featured in Montreal's International Women's Day Celebration. Subsequent plays of Le Théâtre des Cuisines include Moman travaille pas, a trop d'ouvrage, first performed and published in 1976, and As-tu vu? Les Maisons s'emportent (1981), first performed in 1980. In recent years feminist theatre has also flourished in Montreal cafés— for example with works such as Jovette Marchessault's Les faiseuses d'anges (1980), first performed in 1982, and Marie Savard's Journal d'une folle (1983), first performed in 1982. Pol Pelletier, Louise Laprade, and Nicole Lecavalier of the Théâtre Expérimental de Montréal (see NOUVEAU THÉÂTRE EXPÉRIMENTAL DE MONTRÉAL) produced two feminist plays with that company—Finalement in 1977 and À ma mère, à ma mère, à ma mère, à ma voisine (1978) in 1978, which led to the founding in 1979 of an autonomous women's theatre— Montreal's Théâtre Expérimental des Femmes, a collective whose role in presenting and encouraging new play production, challenging theatrical tradition and practice, offering training, and organizing festivals and workshops has made it the most important feminist company in Quebec. La Peur surtout

was the first production by the TEF, followed by regular seasons offering both COLLECTIVE CREATIONs and the work of single dramatists. Of particular interest were Pol Pelletier's La Lumière blanche in 1981 and Lise Vaillancourt's Ballade pour trois baleines in 1982. The TEF has collaborated with the feminist community and other theatre groups, including Toronto's Redlight Productions and Nightwood Theatre.

In Quebec City Le Centre d'essai des femmes, founded in 1977, gave rise to La Commune à Marie in 1978, which has often workshopped Marie Laberge's plays. In Enfin Duchesses! (1983), first performed in 1982, Les Folles Alliées satirized the annual practice during the Quebec Carnival of electing a Queen or 'Duchesse'. The same group's Mademoiselle Autobody, in 1985, was a biting satire on pornography.

Winnipeg's Nellie McClung Theatre, founded in 1968, is Canada's oldest continuing feminist troupe. An amateur group doing both commissioned and collective creations, it maintains a focus on social problems and on bringing 'the spirit and message of the women's movement to wide audiences'. In Vancouver—despite the city's strong tradition of women working in both mainstream and experimental theatre, where important feminist plays have been written and produced, and where the Women's Theatre Cooperative (1973) was founded—no feminist theatre company currently exists. The situation is similar in the Maritimes and Newfoundland, where regional companies, especially alternate theatre groups, have been receptive to feminist themes, but where there are no feminist companies. On the Prairies the collective If We Call This 'The Girlie Show' Will You Find It Offensive?, produced at Regina's GLOBE THEATRE in 1984, has not elicited sustained interest in feminist theatre. In Montreal, Melanie, which sought to be a feminist theatre, workshop, and school, is probably best known for its 1975 production of Charlotte Fielden's One Crowded Hour (1976).

Toronto's oldest continuing feminist theatre company is Redlight Productions (1974) which, among other plays, has produced Elinore Siminovitch's Strange Games and Hollingsworth's Alli, Alli, Oh!. In collaboration with the Théâtre Expérimental des Femmes, Redlight created Wild Gardens in 1983, performing it in both Toronto and Montreal.

Feminist Theatre

Such collaboration among anglophone and francophone feminist theatre companies has been frequent in the 1980s. For example, an English version of Denise Boucher's *Les Fées ont soif* was twice presented in Toronto in 1981. In 1979 Keltie Creed founded the Toronto lesbian theatre group Atthis, which has created new plays and sponsored performances in translation of Quebec lesbian works, such as Pol Pelletier performing Jovette Marchessault's *Night Cows* in 1980.

The most influential feminist theatre company in Toronto has been Nightwood Theatre. Its first production, the 1979 *The True Story of Ida Johnson*, an adaptation of Sharon Riis's novel about women's friendship, was an innovative mixed-media performance. Nightwood has organized festivals and workshops, commissioned scripts, and collaborated in CHILDREN'S DRAMA AND THEATRE. The company's collective creation, *This is for you, Anna* (1985), first performed in 1980, based on an actual event—a woman's shooting of the man who murdered her small daughter—explores the troubling ambiguities that arise when women must handle power and violence. Another notable production, Banuta Rubess's *Pope Joan*, performed in 1984, is based on a historical incident—the election of a female Pope.

The development of feminist theatre has been encouraged by festivals and playwriting competitions. In 1980 a National Women's Playwriting Competition and Theatre Festival was held in Toronto, offering professional workshop presentations of new scripts. The same year 'Faces of Women' was organized in Newfoundland, presenting *Mom* by Grace Butt. Other festivals include the Women & Words Conference (Vancouver, 1983); Celebration of Women in the Arts (Edmonton, 1983); the ongoing Edmonton Fringe Festival; Women's Cultural Building in Toronto (offering performance, slide shows, cabaret, narrative art, film, dance, panels, discussions, installations, and theatre events); Women's Perspective Festival (Toronto, 1983); 'The Next Stage: Women Transforming the Theatre' at Festival of Theatre of the Americas (Montreal, 1985); and Four-Play Festival of lesbian/gay theatre, produced by Toronto's Buddies in Bad Times (1985-7).

Current feminist theatre is experimental in theme, technique, and medium, and ranges in outlook beyond linguistic and national boundaries. It has been encouraged by feminist periodicals, publishing houses, and by feminist theatre criticism. New radical companies include Toronto's Company of Sirens, and Mean Feet, which aims 'to give visibility to the problems women encounter as a result of gender stereotyping, and to create opportunities for female directors and playwrights, as well as helping them to develop the skills required to capitalize on those opportunities'. Special groups have formed in Ontario to use theatre as an educational medium, such as Tomorrow's Eve and Theatre Direct. Other groups—the Hummer Sisters and the Clichettes—offer irreverent comedy in CABARET.

See Anton Wagner, ed., *Women Pioneers. Canada's Lost Plays*, vol. 2 (1979); Pol Pelletier, 'Petite Histoire du théâtre de femmes au Québec', *Canadian Women's Studies/Les Cahiers de la femme*, 2 (1980); Rina Fraticelli, *The Status of Women in the Canadian Theatre* (1982); Ann Saddlemyer, 'Circus Feminus: 100 plays by English-Canadian Women', *Room of One's Own*, 8 (1983); 'Feminism and Canadian Theatre', *Canadian Theatre Review*, 43 (1985); Jane Moss, 'Women's Theatre in Quebec', *Traditionalism, Nationalism, and Feminism: Women Writers of Quebec* (1985), ed. Paula Gilbert Lewis; 'Les Femmes dans le théâtre du Québec et du Canada/Women in Quebec and Canada Theatre', *Theatre History in Canada*, 8 (1987).   LOUISE H. FORSYTH

Fennario, David (b. 1947). Born David Wiper, one of six children, in Pointe-Saint-Charles—a Montreal working-class district where he still lives—he witnessed and experienced the poverty and misery that led him to embrace Marxism and that permeate his plays. He left school at sixteen and was part of the hippie scene in the 1960s.

His first published work, *Without a Parachute* (1972)—a largely autobiographical account of life in the Pointe—reveals an unusual gift for lively dialogue. It is not surprising, therefore, that Fennario's greatest contribution has been to the theatre. His first two published plays, both in one act, with all male casts, are highly political, the characters and incidents recalling those of *Without a Parachute*. *On the Job* (1976) was first performed, directed by David Calderisi, on 29 Jan. 1975 at Montreal's CENTAUR THEATRE, where Fennario was writer-in-residence. As is usual with Fennario's plays, *On the Job* has a simple plot: some packers in a dress factory

David Fennario's Nothing to Lose, *Centaur Theatre, Montreal, 1978, with (l. to r.) Don Scanlan, Peter MacNeill, Simon Malbogat, Raymond Belisle, Lubomir Mykytiuk*

refuse to work overtime on Christmas Eve and walk off their jobs, emboldened by the consumption of a large quantity of alcohol. (Most of Fennario's characters drink an inordinate amount in order to escape from their boredom and misery.) The theme of *Nothing to Lose* (1977), commissioned by the Centaur and directed by Guy SPRUNG when first performed there on 11 Nov. 1976, resembles that of the previous play. The scene is a tavern, across from the Sunnybrook Farms' warehouse. Incensed at the arrogance of the foreman and at their working conditions in general, the truckers decide to strike. While alcohol again plays an important part in triggering their rebellion, the grievances of the men are real enough. In both plays they receive no help or encouragement from their unions; in fact the union boss in *On the Job* is more obnoxious than the employers.

The characters in these plays apparently gain no positive results from their rebellion. What Gary says in *On the Job* applies to all of them: 'We have only begun to lose . . . and lose . . . And lose and lose and lose and keep on losing.' But he does add: 'Until

overwhelmed by our defeats, we shall win.' Instead of fighting with one another, 'hitting the wrong people', they find unity in action and are at least conscious of who their enemies are.

BALCONVILLE (1980), Fennario's most popular play, was billed as Canada's first bilingual play and received the 1979 CHALMERS Award. True to his principles, Fennario gave his prize money to workers' organizations.

Fennario's three published plays end on an inconclusive note. The fate of the workers in *On the Job* and *Nothing to Lose* can only be surmised; the last words of *Balconville* are 'Qu'est-ce qu'on va faire?'. Like Irene, one of his most intelligent and sensitive characters, the author believes that the conditions of the working class can be improved only through political action, but few of his characters have the awareness or energy required for it. When they act, they do so on impulse, often in a drunken fury.

Several unpublished Fennario plays have also been produced at the Centaur. *Toronto*, first performed on 2 Feb. 1978, was inspired by a day he spent auditioning in a hotel room

Fennario

for the Toronto production of *Nothing to Lose*. *Toronto* was poorly received and the character of Jerry Nines, Fennario's alter ego, which already seemed out of place in *Nothing to Lose*, is unconvincing. *Without a Parachute*, performed by amateurs at the Centaur in Sept. 1978, is an adaptation from his journal. *Moving*, produced for the first time in 1983, once again tackles the problem of Anglo-French relationships in Quebec.

Disillusioned with mainstream theatre (which Fennario considers bourgeois and out of touch with social realities), Fennario has lately been working with a community group of amateur actors, the Black Rock Theatre, from Pointe-Saint-Charles. For them he wrote *Joe Beef*, which, after undergoing several transformations, was performed in its final version at the Players Theatre, McGill Univ., on 14 Dec. 1985. A series of sketches, some of them musical, the play looks at Canadian history from a Marxist point of view and is a ferocious attack on the rich Montreal families that Fennario blames for the plight of the poor. *Doctor Neill Cream*, about the Montreal physician and mass murderer who was hanged in London, Eng., in 1892, opened at Toronto's Theatre Centre in Nov. 1988. The opening of *The Murder of Susan Parr*—which reflects on the fragmentation and disintegration of the Point-Saint-Charles community—at Centaur in Jan. 1989 marked Fennario's return to mainstream theatre.

Fennario's success has generally been attributed to his gift for dialogue and his ability to create convincing characters who respond vociferously, if ineffectively, to their conditions. His loud-mouthed workers, eager to quarrel with their peers, hiding their despair under a cloak of aggression, and his disgruntled women, whose men are a burden rather than a help, are often deeply moving. Even though Fennario firmly believes art must bear a message, his chief weakness is perhaps the heavy-handed manner in which that message is delivered.

See Robert C. Nunn, 'The Interplay of Action and Set in the Plays of David Fennario', *Theatre History in Canada*, 9 (1988).

PAULETTE COLLET

Ferron, Jacques (1921-85). Born in Louiseville, Que., he was educated in Trois Rivières at Collège Brébeuf and at Laval Univ., graduating in medicine. After a brief period in the Canadian army, he practised medicine in the Gaspé Peninsula, Montreal, and Longueuil. Actively involved in politics, he founded the Rhinoceros Party in 1963 and in 1970 was a key figure in negotiations with the FLQ during the October Crisis. His literary works include short stories, novels, essays, and dramas—though his twenty plays achieved only limited success.

Ferron's early plays—from *L'Ogre* to *Le Cheval de Don Juan* (1957), which was revised as *Le Don Juan Chrétien* (1968)—recall the comedies of Molière, Marivaux, Beaumarchais, and Musset. Light, subtle, and ironic, they feature valets, chambermaids, young lovers, and old fogies—as in *Le Dodu; ou Le prix du bonheur* (1956), *Tante Elise: ou Le prix de l'amour* (1958), and *Cazou; ou Le prix de la virginité* (1963).

More serious in tone and subject are Ferron's two political plays: *Les Grands soleils* (1958) and *La Tête du roi* (1963). Not performed until 1968—at Montreal's THÉÂTRE DU NOUVEAU MONDE—*Les Grands soleils* concerns the 1837 Patriote rebellion, with frequent allusions to the present. The central complex symbol of the sunflower suggests fecund sacrifice, cyclical resurrection, perhaps even national revolution. There is certainly hope—not despair—in the death of the hero Chénier. In *La Tête du roi* the feast of Corpus Christi—a popular liturgy that spills out of the churches into the streets—forms the core of the setting and the action. Historical events such as the Riel rebellions, the Quebec conscription crisis, and the violence of the 1960s again bring into focus the political problems and dilemmas facing French-Canadians.

Systematic comment on the nature of theatre itself is the dominant feature of other Ferron plays—particularly *L'Impromptu des deux chiens* (written in 1967, published in 1975) and *Le Coeur d'une mère* (1969). In *L'Impromptu* the playwright Ferron debates openly with his director, Albert Millaire, about their respective roles. In *Le Coeur d'une mère* the author, this time called Pope, explains to his two characters (who can be split into an infinite number) that they are not 'real', that this is 'not actually about the theatre': 'You're under my control, mine are the only roles you can play', declares this Brechtian playwright.

See Jean-Cléo Godin and Laurent Mailhot, *Le Théâtre québécois: introduction à dix drama-*

turges contemporains (1970); Jean Marcel, *Jacques Ferron malgré lui* (1978); and Pierre Gobin, *Le Fou et ses doubles: figures de la dramaturgie québécoise* (1978).

LAURENT MAILHOT

Festival Lennoxville. The first professional theatre to devote itself entirely to Canadian work, Quebec's Festival Lennoxville, founded at Bishop's Univ. in 1971 by William Davis and David Rittenhouse, produced over thirty shows in its ten-year existence (1972–82). The company gave festival-calibre productions of a repertory that included revivals of old plays (Lister SINCLAIR's *The Blood is Strong*, 1974, Robertson DAVIES' *Hunting Stuart*, 1975), re-stagings or co-productions of recent plays (Michel TREMBLAY's *Forever Yours, Marie-Lou*, 1977, J. Ben Tarver's *The Murder of Auguste Dupin*, 1979), and premières of new or unproduced plays (George RYGA's *Sunrise on Sarah*, 1973, Ted ALLAN's *The Secret of the World*, 1976). The mix was challenging for a summer theatre, and artistic results were often exciting. At its best the Festival celebrated the talent of Canadian writers, actors, directors, and designers, and made its contribution to the nationalization of professional theatre in this country. But ever-present financial problems, coupled with an increasing lack of creative focus and, finally, administrative mismanagement, led to the Festival's collapse.

In the early years artistic director Davis and administrative director Rittenhouse had significant support from the community and the University. With this founding energy and the credibility provided by such early critical successes as Ann HENRY's *Lulu Street*, 1972, Robertson Davies' *A Jig for the Gypsy*, 1973, and Donald HARRON's *Adam's Fall*, 1974, the Festival won substantial public- and private-sector funding. Until 1976 the Canada Council and the Quebec government significantly increased their grants. Private-sector fund-raising was equally successful, in particular with a commitment from the McConnell Foundation. With such encouragement the Festival decided to extend its visibility outside the province. To this end it professionalized its administrative staff in 1975 and added to the Board influential people from outside the region.

Two critically successful seasons in a row (Davis's last in 1977 and Richard OUZOUN-IAN's first in 1978), ought to have ensured the Festival's security. But with federal wage-and-price controls in place, arts money—public and private—was frozen; in reaction to the election of a Parti-Québécois Government, the anglophone population of Quebec dwindled, and the Festival, never strong at the box office, felt the strain. As well, the Festival's provincial grants were cut. Such fiscal pressures made simple survival of paramount importance.

Artistic director Ouzounian, who as a director had created great commercial successes at the Festival (Betty LAMBERT's *Sqrieux-de-Dieu*, 1976, and Lezley Havard's *Jill*, 1977), attempted to solve the Festival's financial difficulties by concentrating on the one area where growth was possible: box office attendance. He extended the season, produced four instead of three plays, and selected more typical summer fare. The formula worked in 1978 but failed artistically and financially in 1979.

In crisis management from then on, the Festival cut back its season in 1980 and canvassed for a new artistic director. Now in a sort of limbo, with small local support, an increasingly diffident landlord in the University, and a decreasing national profile, the Festival needed new direction. Heinar Piller was hired, but his ambitious plans were found unrealistic by the Board. He left and the Festival went dark for a season.

During the following year, however, the local community rallied to the Festival and raised money. With the help of the federal government's debt-clearing 'Strategic Initiatives Program', the Festival Board eliminated the accumulated deficit. A new Board, more locally based, sought an artistic director to revitalize Festival Lennoxville for the summer of 1982. Scott Swan was hired, but failed. The last season was an administrative fiasco. In less than one year the Festival ran up a deficit of over $250,000, and in mid-summer 1982 the season was abruptly cut short. This time Festival Lennoxville was not resurrected.

Great promise and ambitious plans had not been fulfilled. Yet over the years good theatre, even great theatre, had been produced: the hit of the first season, John HIRSCH's production of *Lulu Street*; Betty Lambert's modern comedy of manners, *Sprieux-de-Dieu* in 1976; and the first-ever English-language production of Tremblay in Quebec, *Forever Yours, Marie-Lou* in 1977. Festival Lennoxville aimed high, and to some degree its final failure was a measure of how much it wished to create, of how far it hoped Canadian drama and theatre could progress.

Its archives are housed at Bishop's University.

See also SUMMER STOCK.

JONATHAN RITTENHOUSE

Findley, Timothy (b. 1930). Born and educated in Toronto, he began his career as an actor with Kingston's INTERNATIONAL PLAYERS during their first winter season in Toronto (1951-2). In 1953 he became a member of the original STRATFORD FESTIVAL Company. Directed by Tyrone GUTHRIE, Findley played Catesby to Alec Guinness's Richard III and an officer in *All's Well That Ends Well*. Findley and fellow actor Richard EASTON received financial assistance from Guinness and Guthrie to attend classes at London's Central School of Speech and Drama, graduating in 1954.

Guthrie cast Findley in Thornton Wilder's *The Matchmaker* for the Edinburgh Festival première in 1954 with Ruth Gordon and Alec McCowen. Findley then worked as a contract artist for the Tennent organization, acting in numerous secondary roles, culminating in the 1956 Paul Scofield/Peter Brook season at London's Phoenix Theatre, where he played Osric to Scofield's Hamlet. As a resident of the UK, however, Findley was enlisted for National Service. An avowed pacifist, he returned to Canada in 1956.

After several years of acting for stage and television in Canada and the U.S., Findley gave up performing to become a writer. A short story, 'About Effie', in the first issue of the *Tamarack Review* (Autumn 1956), marks the starting-point of this new career. While working at radio station CFGM, Richmond Hill, as a copy-writer, he wrote two novels: *The Last of the Crazy People* (1967) and *The Butterfly Plague* (1969). Throughout this period Findley wrote scripts for various media: 'The Paper People' (CBC-TV, 1967), 'Don't Let the Angels Fall' (NFB, 1969), and 'Gold', 'River Through Time', and 'Missionaries' (for 'Ideas', CBC Radio, 1971-3). The journal *Canadian Drama* has published *The Paper People* (1983) and *The Journey: A Montage for Radio* (1984).

The period 1971-80 was a particularly productive time for Findley as a writer for television. He wrote 'Whiteoaks of Jalna' for CBC (1971-2); the ACTRA-award-winning series 'The National Dream' (CBC, 1975), written in collaboration with William Whitehead; '1832' and '1911' for 'The Newcomers' (CBC, 1978-9); the Anik-Award-winning 'Dieppe 1942' (CBC, 1979), with William Whitehead; and 'Other People's Children' (CBC, 1980).

Findley was the first writer-in-residence at the NATIONAL ARTS CENTRE, Ottawa, 1974-5, when he wrote his major play *Can You See Me Yet?* (1977), first presented in 1976 at the NAC under the direction of Marigold CHARLESWORTH, with Frances HYLAND in the role of Cassandra. Telling the story of Cassandra Wakelin, an inmate of an asylum in southern Ontario in 1938, it is a psychodrama that portrays in a documentary fashion common to much of Findley's writing the Wakelin family's collapse and Cassandra's own breakdown. The voices of Aimée Semple McPherson and Hitler drift in between scenes and the Wakelin family resonates with that same Edwardian stiffness and faded grandeur that Findley has written into the Ross family in his novel *The Wars* (1977).

The success of *The Wars* resulted in a film version scripted by Findley (1983) and directed by Robin PHILLIPS. The film contains some remarkable performances from an ensemble of major actors including, among others, William HUTT, Martha HENRY, Jackie BURROUGHS, Brent CARVER, and Domini BLYTHE.

In his second play, *John A. Himself!*—performed at Theatre London in 1979 under the direction of Peter Moss, with William Hutt in the title role—Findley uses a full range of theatrical tricks to present the 'real' person behind the political mask of Canada's first prime minister.

Findley's short story collection, *Dinner Along the Amazon* (1984), contains 'Out of the Silence', an extract from a play about T.S. Eliot and Vivien Eliot that was written in 1983 and abandoned when Michael Hastings' play *Tom and Viv* appeared in 1984. The same collection contains an extract from a play-in-progress, 'Daybreak at Pisa', about Ezra Pound, who figures prominently in Findley's novel *Famous Last Words* (1981). The Stratford Young Company, under the direction of Robin Phillips, workshopped Findley's novel *Not Wanted on the Voyage* (1986) in the 1987 season, but scheduled public performances were cancelled. Findley's adaptation of *Famous Last Words* was broadcast by CBC radio in five one-hour segments in 1988.

KEVIN BURNS

Fineberg, Larry (b. 1945). Born and raised in Montreal, he attended McGill Univ. and Emerson College, Boston (BA, 1967), after which he was hired as an assistant director by Frank Loesser's production company in New York. In 1972 he moved to Toronto, where three of his plays were produced within twelve months—*The Stonehenge Trilogy* (1972) and *Death* (1972) at FACTORY THEATRE Lab, and *Hope* (1972) at TORONTO FREE THEATRE.

The Stonehenge Trilogy—three loosely linked one-act plays—is essentially a young Jewish male's satire on suffocating Jewish mothers (and their head-hunting daughters). Significantly rewritten in a way that stresses a menacing sense of the absurd, it was remounted as *Stonehenge* at VANCOUVER EAST CULTURAL CENTRE in 1974 and published in 1978. *Hope*—set on a country estate complete with heaths, crypts, towers, and missing wills—lacks focus and complicates its tone with large dollops of the comic grotesque, the surreal, and parodic exaggeration of gothic conventions. More impressively crafted, with economical dialogue and highly compacted blackout scenes, is the one-act *Death*, which plays skilled Pinter variations on a theme by Beckett. In *Human Remains* (1976), produced by Toronto's NEW THEATRE in 1975, Fineberg adheres to the discipline of essentially naturalist conventions, and the result is a fine, coherent play. Three disillusioned idealists from the sixties—two bisexual men and the woman they have shared in addition to each other—engage in a psychological dissection of their personal relationships and family backgrounds.

Fineberg's career took an unexpected turn when Robin PHILLIPS commissioned an adaptation of Constance Beresford-Howe's novel, *The Book of Eve*. As one of the few experiments with original Canadian work at the STRATFORD FESTIVAL, the play was under enormous pressure to succeed. Produced at the Avon Theatre in 1976, starring Jessica Tandy, *Eve* (1977) not only set box-office records but won a CHALMERS Award for its run in Toronto. (It was also successfully produced in London, starring Constance Cummings, and in St Louis and Amsterdam.)

Another adaptation, *Medea* (1978), played the Third Stage at Stratford in 1978. During this period Fineberg also wrote two musicals, *Waterfall* (1974) and an adaptation of Homer's *Odyssey*, *Fresh Disasters* (unpublished), both for Toronto's YOUNG PEOPLE'S THEATRE, produced in 1973 and 1976 respectively.

In *Life on Mars* (unpublished), produced by Toronto Free Theatre in 1979, Fineberg returned to the personal concerns he had explored in *Human Remains*, but with less success. Reviewers were impatient with the narcissism of its three charmless characters. His love of parody appears again in the political satire *Montreal* (1982), produced by TORONTO TRUCK THEATRE in 1981, which plays the dangerous game of satirizing racial and religious stereotypes by exaggerating them.

Devotion, produced at MAGNUS THEATRE, Thunder Bay, in 1985, is perhaps Fineberg's best work to date; it is certainly his most complete and accessible treatment of the case history that in one way or another informs so much of his writing. Arthur, the bisexual artist figure, returns home from a psychiatric institution after his domineering, alcoholic mother commits suicide. Jealous of her husband's mistress and eager to protect her interests in the family's therapeutic wrangles, the irrepressible mother haunts the proceedings as a very vocal 'blithe spirit'. Her presence allows Arthur to work through his alienation from his emotions and his fear of love. *Human Remains* also begins with a mother's suicide as the occasion for its artist-hero's self-exploration. Both plays combine good comic dialogue with dramatically deferred psychological revelations.

Fineberg has been important politically because of his frank portrayals of homosexual experience; on the other hand, as his adaptations demonstrate, he has a broad range of human experience within his grasp. He has been important artistically because he practised and championed a disruptive, experimental theatre; but to this point his best dramas have been those that honour the spirit of naturalism even though they play fast and loose with some of its laws.

Stonehenge, *Death*, *Hope*, and *Human Remains* are collected in *Four Plays by Larry Fineberg* (1978).

See Wallace and Zimmerman, eds., *The Work* (1982).

LARRY McDONALD

Fitzallan. The first play by a Canadian-born author produced in Canada. Masking his probable authorship behind 'a Halifax native', William Rufus BLAKE premièred *Fitzallan* at the Halifax Theatre on 27 Apr. 1833. Audience and critics did not respond favourably and no further performances were advertised.

Although no script survives, a plot summary appeared in the *Nova Scotian* on 3 May 1833. Lord Montauban murders Lord Fitzallan, seizes his lands, and beggars his child. Twenty years later young Fitzallan has married a handsome wife and fathered a son. Montauban sees the young wife and determines to have her. Fitzallan is lured into a midnight ambush and imprisoned. The young wife and her son are also entrapped in the castle. When Lady Fitzallan rejects Montauban's advances, he promises certain death to Fitzallan. Fitzallan, however, escapes and reappears as the mock priest at the wedding of Montauban and Lady Fitzallan. Throwing off his disguise, Fitzallan stabs Montauban, whose confession and remorse conclude the melodrama.   PATRICK B. O'NEILL

Forget, Florent (1918-85). Born in Montreal, he was educated at the Collège Sainte-Marie and the Univ. of Ottawa (1938-41). After training with Les COMPAGNONS DE SAINT-LAURENT in 1942, he worked extensively as an actor in the 1940s and 1950s, subsequently turning to directing (from 1957) with Le THÉÂTRE DU RIDEAU VERT, La POUDRIÈRE, Le Centre Dramatique du Conservatoire, and at several summer theatres. His principal career, however, was as a producer, both in radio (1945-50) and television (1950-84). He produced over forty television plays for Radio-Canada, of which about half were Québécois works, including *Illusions*, 1954, by Yves THÉRIAULT; *Faux Départs*, 1956, and *Le Véridique procès de Barbe-Bleue*, 1966, by Louis Pelland; *Le Refuge impossible*, 1958, by Jean Filiatrault; *La Vie de Chopin*, 1950, by Eugène Cloutier; *Ta Nuit est ma lumière*, 1970, by Robert Choquette; and *L'Homme aux faux diamants de braise*, 1973, by Jean-Robert Rémillard. In the series 'Le Monde de Marcel DUBÉ' (1973) he directed a new version of Dubé's *Le Temps des lilas* as well as Dubé's *Le Naufragé*, and in 1973 he produced a new version of Dubé's *Un SIMPLE SOLDAT*. He also directed six television episodes in the serial 'Monsieur Lecoq', 1964-

5, using writers such as Jean-Louis ROUX and Claude JASMIN. Forget also taught theatre history at Studio Quinze, 1947-9, and radio and television at Université Laval, 1948-50; after 1967 he taught at the CONSERVATOIRE D'ART DRAMATIQUE DU QUÉBEC, retiring in 1984.   RENÉE LEGRIS

Fortune and Men's Eyes. This prison drama by John HERBERT was first workshopped at the STRATFORD FESTIVAL in Oct. 1965 but was not produced because its subject and language were judged to be unsuitable for Stratford audiences. It premièred in a full production at the Actors Playhouse, New York, on 23 Feb. 1967; the first full professional Canadian production took place only in 1975 at Toronto's PHOENIX THEATRE and won the CHALMERS Award as best Canadian play of the Toronto season.

While *Fortune and Men's Eyes* draws upon Herbert's openly professed homosexuality and on his experiences in a Canadian reformatory on a charge of gross indecency (a charge he has always denied), its primary theme is human relationships and how denial of love can warp young lives. The play is about the 'education' of a new inmate, Smitty, whose 'teachers' are his fellow inmates: Rocky, a pimp and homosexual (who professes to hate homosexual behaviour); Queenie, a transvestite; and Mona, an eighteen-year-old boy, the victim of repeated gang rapes. In the course of the play Smitty is raped by Rocky, taught the politics and power structure of prison life by Queenie, and offered a redemptive love by the Christ-like Mona. Mona's 'quality of mercy' speech from *The Merchant of Venice* trial scene and the references to Shakespeare's sonnet 29 ('When in disgrace with fortune and men's eyes / . . . Haply I think on thee . . . ') are balanced against the raw and obscene language of the other characters. The hope implied by the Shakespearean allusions is undercut, however, by the brutal whipping of Mona by the prison guards and by the progressive moral degeneration of Smitty. At the play's close he has given himself over to violence and a criminal future.

Although its subjects—homosexuality, gang rapes, physical abuse—are unpalatable, Herbert's play is leavened by humour and raw energy. Queenie's Christmas drag routine is a comic theatrical *tour de force* and all

John Herbert's Fortune and Men's Eyes, *Manitoba Theatre Centre, 1969, with (l. to r.) Don Sutherland, Jim Sutherland, Wendell Smith, and (on floor) Michael O'Regan.*

the characters are compelling in their rage to survive.

Fortune and Men's Eyes quickly became internationally famous—in its first ten years it was performed in more than 100 countries in some forty languages. It led to the founding of the Fortune Society, which seeks to bring about prison reform. The play was published by Grove Press in 1967 and a film version by MGM was released in 1970.

EUGENE BENSON

Fox, David (b. 1941). Born in Swastika, Ont., he taught high school from 1963 to 1972. In 1972 he joined THEATRE PASSE MURAILLE's *The FARM SHOW*, playing several roles, including Bruce Pallett, whose passionate and moving words capture the dilemma of the Canadian farmer. Other such strong rural characters Fox has played include Anton Kalicz in *Far As The Eye Can See*, by Rudy Wiebe in collaboration with Theatre Passe Muraille, and the Father in *Boys and Girls*, the short TV film adapted by Joe Wiesenfeld

from the story by Alice Munro. Fox has had a long association with Theatre Passe Muraille, acting in a number of productions, including the COLLECTIVE CREATIONS *The West Show, 1837: The Farmers' Revolt, Studhorse Man, Les Maudits Anglais*, and *Them Donnellys*, Betty Jane WYLIE's *The Horseburgh Scandal*, and Rick SALUTIN's *The False Messiah*. Other important roles include Seward in John MURRELL's *Farther West* directed by Robin PHILLIPS at THEATRE CALGARY in Apr. 1982; Christie in *Quiet in the Land* by Anne CHISLETT at the BLYTH FESTIVAL and the MANITOBA THEATRE CENTRE in 1981; John Hackman in *The Art of War*, written and directed by George WALKER, at Toronto's FACTORY THEATRE in Feb. 1983; and Telespore Tremblay in *Le Temps d'une vie* by Roland LEPAGE at Toronto's TARRAGON THEATRE in May 1978. Fox has acted in television and film for directors Gillian Armstrong, Allan King, and Claude Jutra.

JAMES DEFELICE

Fréchette, Louis-Honoré (1839-1908). Born near Lévis, Que., he graduated from the Collège de Nicolet in 1859, then studied law at Laval Univ. From 1859 he published occasional poems in newspapers and took a keen interest in theatre. Two of his plays— *Les Notables du village* and his most popular dramatic text, FÉLIX POUTRÉ—were written and performed in 1862 while he was still a student. His first volume of poetry, *Mes Loisirs*, was published in 1863, and his remarkable literary career was then launched.

Little attracted by the practice of law, Fréchette helped found two unsuccessful Liberal newspapers and became closely identified with the *Rouges* and their ageing hero, Papineau, an identification that would frequently prove detrimental to him later. Disillusioned by current politics, he left for Chicago in 1866, where he was active in journalism and continued to write drama and poetry, notably the polemical poems entitled *La Voix d'un exilé*, directed against Canadian federalists. The Great Chicago Fire of 1871 destroyed many of his manuscript works, including the five-act drama *Tête à l'envers*, staged by amateurs in 1868, and the five-act satirical comedy, *La Confédération*. He returned to Canada that year, ran unsuccessfully in provincial and federal elections, and was eventually elected for one term, 1874-8, as Liberal MP for Lévis. Most important for the security of his

Fréchette

Louis-Honoré Fréchette

literary career, in 1876 he married a wealthy heiress. By 1880 he had published two more volumes of verse, *Pêle-Mêle* (1877) and *Les Fleurs boréales/Les Oiseaux de neige* (1879), the latter earning for him France's prestigious Prix Montyon in 1880 and establishing his reputation as Canada's leading poet. His last two books of verse, *La Légende d'un peuple* (1887) and *Feuilles volantes* (1890), confirmed that reputation; but thereafter he wrote mainly prose, notably *Originaux et détraqués* (1892) and *La Noël au Canada* (1900).

Throughout this period, Fréchette continued to write plays. *Le Retour de l'exilé* and *Papineau* were both staged and published in 1880. Three unpublished works followed: the comedy *Un Dimanche matin à 'l'Hôtel du Canada'*, performed in Quebec in 1881; *Hamderbold*, a historical drama staged in New York in 1883; and a one-act VAUDEVILLE piece, *Change pour change*, performed by students at the Collège de Nicolet in 1886. His last play, *Veronica*, was performed in 1903 and published in 1908, a few months after his death.

Of his four published plays, by far the most popular was *Félix Poutré* (1871); it was performed hundreds of times by amateur groups throughout French Canada and New England well into the twentieth century. The two

1880 plays won praise at first, but this was quickly tempered. *Le Retour de l'exilé*, a five-act drama performed at Montreal's ACADEMY OF MUSIC on 25 and 27 June 1880, evoked controversy when it was learned, soon after the play's publication, that the plot had been borrowed from a novel, *La Bastide rouge*, by the French author Élie Berthet. Fréchette's many enemies, led by the poet William Chapman and right-wing author-editor Jules-Paul Tardivel, seized the occasion to discredit not only this play but his work in general, in a bitter campaign that continued for the rest of the century. The real value of Fréchette's adaptation has thus been totally obscured: like *Félix Poutré*, it is an excellent dramatization of someone else's text. Fréchette changed the setting to the village of Sillery, near Quebec, and made the hero a political exile of 1837-8; he seized upon the dramatic potential in Berthet's tale, of a dispossessed man's struggle to regain his property, and made it an effective melodramatic vehicle.

Inevitably *Papineau*, staged in Montreal in June 1880—alternating with *Le Retour de l'exilé*—suffered from the campaign led by literary and political rivals of the author and his hero. A 'Canadian historical drama in four acts', it is panoramic in scope and epic in intent, tracing the main events leading to the Battle of St-Denis in 1837, the Patriote victory, and Papineau's controversial flight to the U.S. The author's portrayal of his avowed idol is uneven: his Papineau is distant and indecisive, the many lengthy quotations gleaned from his published speeches slow down the action and make of him a character much too close to the two-dimensional caricatures that people Quebec's closet political drama. Fréchette stitched onto the historical canvas a fictive sub-plot reminiscent of that which animates Aubert de Gaspé's *Les Anciens Canadiens*, the best known Quebec novel of the nineteenth century: Hastings, a young English nobleman, is in love with the sister of one of Papineau's principal supporters. He is suspected by the Patriotes of betraying their cause; that suspicion is finally dispelled by the fortuitous discovery of a lost letter; bicultural love and amity prevail just as the Patriote leader reaches safety. Modern sensitivities are perhaps confused by this mixture, but contemporary reaction was exceptionally favourable. The province's newspapers—even those whose policies differed radically from the author's—lauded the performances. But Tardivel and Pascal Poirier dissected the play, magnifying every defect and ridiculing the author. When a revival was attempted at Montreal's Théâtre des Nouveautés on 20 Oct. 1905, it proved a disaster. *Papineau*, in an English translation by Eugene Benson and Renate Benson, appears in *Canada's Lost Plays*, vol. IV (1982).

Fréchette's last play, *Veronica*, has an even more controversial background. A five-act drama in verse, it was read at a public session of the École littéraire de Montréal on 29 Dec. 1899, performed at the Théâtre des Nouveautés on 2 Feb. 1903, and first published in full in vol. III of his *Poésies choisies* (1908). A romantic melodrama much influenced by the theatre of Victor Hugo, it too was initially well received. But correspondence discovered after Fréchette's death revealed that the entire plot had been written by a minor French author, Maurice de Pradel, at the request of the Canadian poet, and had then been transposed to alexandrine verse by Fréchette. *Veronica* adds nothing to the author's stature.

Fréchette is truly an enigmatic figure in the history of Canadian dramaturgy, though *Félix Poutré* demonstrated his genuine dramatic talent, his ability to seize upon and develop the innate theatricality of a given text. Fascinated by the stage, Fréchette continued to write regularly for it, but apparently with no confidence in his ability to devise original plots. Yet even if his contribution is limited to *Félix Poutré* and *Papineau*, his role in the evolution of native dramaturgy in Quebec is considerable.

See articles by Paul Wyczynski in *Archives des lettres canadiennes*, I (1961), V (1976), and Jean-Marc Larrue, 'Les Créations Scéniques de Louis-Honoré Fréchette: Juin 1880', *Theatre History in Canada*, 7 (1986). *Félix Poutré*, *Le Retour de l'exilé*, *Papineau*, and *Veronica* were reissued separately in 1974 by Leméac Press.   L.E. DOUCETTE

Freedman, William (b. 1929). Born and raised in Toronto, and educated at the Univ. of Toronto, after theatre experience at HART HOUSE THEATRE, the NEW PLAY SOCIETY, and the CREST THEATRE he produced Julian Slade's *Salad Days* in Toronto and in New York in 1958. He continued a career in production with Gore Vidal's *Visit to a Small Planet* (starring Barry Morse) in 1958, Wil-liam Gibson's *Two for the Seesaw* in 1959, and Albert Meglin's *The Four Faces of Two People* in 1963, all at the Crest, after which he moved with his wife, actress Toby ROBINS, to London, Eng. There he produced Marcel Achard's *The Love Game* in 1964, Charles Dyer's *Staircase* (in co-operation with the Royal Shakespeare Company) in 1966, Peter Luke's *Hadrian VII* in 1968, Don HARRON's adaptation of L.M. Montgomery's ANNE OF GREEN GABLES in 1969, and Claire Luckham's *Trafford Tanzi* in 1981, among other plays. With his Maybox organization, Freedman controls six West End theatres.

HERBERT WHITTAKER

Freeman, David (b. 1947). Born in Toronto, a victim of cerebral palsy, he spent his formative years at the Sunnyview School for the Handicapped. At seventeen he began writing freelance articles for *Maclean's*, the Toronto *Star*, and *Star Week*; one article published in *Maclean's* in 1964, 'The World of Can't', about the frustrations of CP victims trying to live in a society unable to accept them on equal terms, led to a CBC commis-

David Freeman

sion to adapt it for television. Judged too unpleasant for national viewing, the script was rejected. In 1966 Freeman enrolled at McMaster University, graduating with a degree in political science in 1971. At the suggestion of Bill GLASSCO he rewrote 'The World of Can't' for the stage. The production of CREEPS (1972) at Toronto's FACTORY THEATRE Lab on 5 Feb. 1971, directed by Glassco, was an immediate critical and box-office success. The play has won many awards and has received numerous productions in Canada and abroad.

In his second play, Battering Ram (1972), produced at Factory Theatre Lab in Apr. 1972, Freeman again dramatizes the situation of a handicapped person. Irene, a 'professional volunteer', offers the crippled Virgil a room in her home. She and her young daughter prey upon him and are, in turn, preyed upon by Virgil in a macabre sexual and emotional exploitation. In You're Gonna Be Alright, Jamie Boy (1974), first produced at Toronto's TARRAGON THEATRE in Jan. 1974, directed by Glassco, Freeman draws on memories of a period he spent in Toronto's Clarke Institute of Psychiatry in 1972. The play dramatizes the return of Jamie, who has had a nervous breakdown, to his home, where his recovery is threatened by his family's addictions to alcohol and television. While both Battering Ram and Jamie Boy are well written and seek to widen the narrow and claustrophobic world of Creeps, they are conventional in structure and ideas and lack the power and insight of Freeman's first play.

In 1975 Freeman moved to Montreal where his fourth play, Flytrap (1980), opened at the SAIDYE BRONFMAN CENTRE in 1976. It is a disappointing domestic drama about a childless husband and wife who invite a young man to live with them as a tenant (and surrogate son) in the hope of rescuing their marriage. Although the play enjoyed some success, it is too slow-paced and derivative (of Albee especially).

See Geraldine Anthony, ed., Stage Voices (1978), for Freeman's own account of his career.   EUGENE BENSON

French, David (b. 1939). Born in Coley's Point, Nfld, he moved when he was seven with his family to Toronto. He began to write short stories in his mid-teens, but after training as an actor in Toronto and at the Pasadena Playhouse in California he per-

David French

formed in CBC radio plays between 1960 and 1965. In 1962 his one-act play Beckons the Dark River (unpublished) was broadcast on CBC-TV. Leaving Home (1972) was also first written as a television play (The Keeper of the House), but after seeing Bill GLASSCO's production of David FREEMAN's CREEPS at TARRAGON THEATRE French offered it to Glassco.

The development and first production (in 1972) of Leaving Home, about the Mercer family in Newfoundland (see the MERCER PLAYS), was the beginning of the long working relationship between French and Glassco (who has directed the premières of all but one of French's subsequent stage plays)—a playwright-director collaboration of a sort rare in Canadian theatre history. It made Leaving Home a success throughout Canada. Of the Fields, Lately, his second play about the Mercers, produced the following year, was only slightly less successful. It established French's pre-eminence among English Canadian dramatists, and Canadian drama thereafter achieved new presence in the public consciousness: the two plays did much to convince audiences that seeing Canadian experience on stage could be exciting and moving.

With his third full-length play, *One Crack Out* (1976), produced at Tarragon in 1975, French left a familiar world in which domesticity is mixed with violence in a ratio of about two to one, and entered an underground world of Toronto pool hustlers, con-men, loan sharks, pimps, and prostitutes in which the ratio is reversed. The middle-aged protagonist, Charlie Evans, gets into trouble by allowing a family problem to affect his professional life: Charlie's failure in bed with Helen wrecks his concentration at the pool table and drives her to the sinister loan enforcer, Bulldog, for solace. Jack the Hat lends Charlie money to bet on the horses, but Charlie spends it on a prostitute with the hope that his confidence—sexual and professional—will be restored. Bulldog takes over the debt and demands repayment or blood. Charlie and his sidekick, Suitcase Sam, undertake a series of scams to try to raise the money, but fail. Helen intercedes with Bulldog on Charlie's behalf, and Charlie, reassured of his woman's love, regains his confidence and prepares to beat Bulldog at the pool table, wiping out both debts.

Although it enjoyed some commercial success, *One Crack Out* was less well received than the Mercer plays. The dialogue is often unconvincing, and French has not found an efficient dramatic shape for the plot twists. Discouraged by the lukewarm reception, he considered abandoning the theatre until Glassco persuaded him to translate Chekhov's *The Seagull*, with the assistance of Russian scholar Donna Orwin. The 1977 Tarragon production was a success, the text was published in 1978, and French, his confidence restored, turned to a long-held ambition to write a comedy.

Jitters (1980), produced at Tarragon in 1979, is his most commercially successful play, with over a hundred professional productions in Canada and abroad; it is considered by a number of critics the equal of the Mercer plays, and possibly the best Canadian comedy ever written. It is certainly the definitive Canadian comedy about theatre, and the most effective exploitation of the play-within-a-play structure. Like the Mercer plays, *Jitters* has strong autobiographical elements: the small alternate theatre producing the new Canadian play, *The Care and Treatment of Roses*, is very much like Tarragon, and the nervous playwright does resemble French in some respects. Furthermore, the play is a vehicle for French's complaints about the place of theatre in Canadian society: the playwright character remarks, 'They hate success in this country. They punish you for it'—an attitude that at least one reviewer described as 'whining'.

In the play's central conflict a fading actress's attempts to make a come-back, to impress a visiting New York producer, and to repeat her Broadway triumphs are sabotaged by her own insecurities and by a cynical Irish-Canadian actor who secretly fears that the play will go to New York where his inadequacies will be exposed. In the play-within-a-play they are lovers, and French expertly exploits the ironies of this and other truth-and-illusion dichotomies through the three acts: a disastrous last rehearsal before preview; an even more disastrous first night seen from the perspective of the dressing room; and the day after, with the actors back on the set reading the reviews (which gives French an opportunity for a hilarious parody of pompous, wrong-headed reviewing) and reaching a precarious reconciliation. The fragility of a life in the theatre has seldom been evoked so well.

French's next attempt at comedy, *The Riddle of the World*, first performed in 1982, was less happy. As in *One Crack Out*, he uses male sexual insecurity to animate the play: Bethany joins an Eastern religion that demands celibacy, and when her lover, Ron, cannot accept this, she goes to an ashram in India. Left behind in Toronto, Ron alternates between unsuccessfully attempting to seduce other women and debating the nature of sexual and spiritual love with his friend Steve, an ex-priest also abandoned by his woman. After failing to dissuade Steve from converting to homosexuality, Ron considers taking up the spiritual life himself as the play ends. Some lines are very funny in their own right, and some jibes at contemporary values are telling, but too often comic confrontation is avoided, and quotations from scripture and T.S. Eliot obscure rather than illuminate issues. However, any suspicion that French's powers might be waning were dispelled three years later with the appearance of the third Mercer play, the lyrical and bittersweet *Salt-Water Moon* (1985), a play judged by some critics to be his best so far.

French returned to adaptation with his version of Alexander Ostrovsky's *The Forest*, based on a translation by Samuel Cioran; it

French

was produced in 1987 at CENTRESTAGE in Toronto. That the production's two-dimensionality obliterated Ostrovsky's subtlety and diminished his humour was blamed more on Guy SPRUNG's direction than on French's writing; one reviewer praised French's wit and 'sure craftsmanship'.

French's fourth play about the Mercers, *1949*, set on the eve of Newfoundland's joining Confederation, was co-produced by the CANADIAN STAGE COMPANY and the MANITOBA THEATRE CENTRE in 1988, again directed by Glassco.

See Edward Mullaly, 'Canadian Drama: David French and the Great Awakening', *The Fiddlehead*, 100 (1974); Richard Horenblas, '*One Crack Out*: Made in His Image', *Canadian Drama*, 2 (1976); Geraldine Anthony, ed., *Stage Voices* (1978); Robert Wallace and Cynthia Zimmerman, eds., *The Work* (1982); Albert-Reiner Glaap, '*Noises Off* and *Jitters*: Two Comedies of Backstage Life', *Canadian Drama*, 13 (1987); Anne Nothof, 'David French and the Theatre of Speech', *Canadian Drama*, 13 (1987).

CHRIS JOHNSON

Fridolinons. This satirical revue by Gratien GÉLINAS derives its title from the theme song that conjugates the central character's name, 'Fridolin'—the Chaplinesque character (impersonated by Gélinas), who was first heard on CKAC, Montreal, 23 Sept. 1937, as part of a weekly radio series, 'Le Carrousel de la gaîeté' (later 'Le Train de plaisir'). In 1938 the sketches were expanded to a full stage revue. For two-and-a-half years the radio and stage show ran parallel—a *tour de force* for the author-producer-director-actor. Gélinas subsequently abandoned the radio show for an annual three-hour satirical revue at the MONUMENT NATIONAL theatre, 1941-6, with a retrospective reprise in 1956. The revue emphasized social and political satire and domestic comedy; *Les Fridolinades '46*, for example, contains Gélinas's most scathing satire of French-Canadian society, 'The Edifying Life of Jean-Baptiste Laframboise', as well as 'Le Retour du conscrit', the sketch

on which his play *TIT-COQ* was based. With the various stage manifestations of Fridolin, Gélinas laid the foundation for a 'national and popular' theatre.

Publication of the Fridolin revues is underway at Les Quinze. *Les Fridolinades*, a compilation of material from the revue series, was produced at the NATIONAL ARTS CENTRE in Jan. 1987 and at Toronto's Premiere Dance Theatre in Feb. 1989. See Renate Usmiani, *Gratien Gélinas* (1977).   RENATE USMIANI

Fuller, William Henry (fl. 1870–98). Born and educated in England, he spent some years in India in banking before joining the Ontario Bank in Canada in 1870. On retirement he devoted his time to mining investments and writing. A frequent contributor to magazines and newspapers, he gained some notoriety with satirical pieces such as *The Unspecific Scandal* (1874) and *Ye Ballad of Lyttel John A.* (1873). He is best known for his comic opera *H.M.S. Parliament; or, The Lady who Loved a Government Clerk* (1880), a satirical attack on John A. Macdonald and his government, particularly his 'National Policy'. It opened in Montreal on 16 Feb. 1880 to laudatory reviews. One critic praised the performance as one that 'may not ineptly be considered as marking a new departure in the theatrical world as far as Canada is concerned.' The play was toured by E.A. McDOWELL and Company, playing mainly in eastern Canada. Forgotten for many years, it was revived at University College, Univ. of Toronto, in April 1983. The play's success encouraged Fuller to continue his career as playwright, but further success eluded him.

His musical comedy *Off to Egypt; or, An Arab Abduction* was produced by the American entrepreneur Augustus Pitou in the U.S. and Canada, appearing in Toronto on 22 Dec. 1884. Unlike *H.M.S. Parliament*, this play has little social or political significance. Fuller's *A Barber's Scrape*, a musical burlesque, was produced in Montreal in 1886, and *A Fair Smuggler*, a curtain-raiser, is also attributed to him.   MURRAY D. EDWARDS

G

Galay, Ted (b. 1941). Born in Beauséjour, Man., he earned a Ph.D. in mathematics at the Univ. of British Columbia and has taught at Brandon Univ. and Vancouver City College. His three one-act and two full-length plays present his first-hand experience of Manitoba's Ukrainians. In *After Baba's Funeral* (1981) a Ukrainian family mourns the passing of Baba, their grandmother, who is the last of her generation, while resolving familial differences. *Sweet and Sour Pickles* (1981) dramatizes a discussion between two older Ukrainian-Canadian women about traditional values. A third one-act play, *The Grabowski Girls*, portrays three sisters in their sixties who consider reviving an annual churchyard picnic. The character Netty Danischuk, who appears in both *After Baba's Funeral* and *Sweet and Sour Pickles*, belongs to an in-between generation. Baba was the last to be Ukrainian-born; Netty's university-educated son has moved away; Netty has left a farm and fears nursing-homes. All three plays were produced by Vancouver's NEW PLAY CENTRE, in 1979, 1980, and 1983 respectively.

Galay extended his range with two full-length plays: *Primrose School District 109* (produced by the BLYTH FESTIVAL in 1985 and the PRAIRIE THEATRE EXCHANGE, Winnipeg, in Oct. 1986) about the first woman teacher to come to a small Ukrainian community in 1930; and *Tsymbaly* (New Play Centre, 1985; MANITOBA THEATRE CENTRE, 1986) in which, over a twenty-five year period, the protagonist grows away from his roots only to rediscover them. The title is the name of a hammer dulcimer and the production includes a chorus, dancers, and musicians introducing traditional Ukrainian songs.

MALCOLM PAGE

Galloway, Pat (b. 1933). Born and educated in London, Eng., this versatile actress trained at the Royal Academy of Dramatic Art in London and the Conservatoire d'Art Dramatique in Paris, France. She gained her first acting experience in English repertory theatre, musicals, and music hall and has lived in Canada since 1957. Best known for her strong performances at the STRATFORD FESTIVAL, she excelled in the title role in John Webster's *Duchess of Malfi* in 1971 and as the male lead in Alfred de Musset's *Lorenzaccio* in 1972. Also highly praised were her portrayals of two famous actresses: Mrs Patrick Campbell in Jerome Kilty's *Dear Liar* at the SHAW FESTIVAL in 1979 and Sarah Bernhardt in John MURRELL's *Memoir* at Victoria's BASTION THEATRE in 1982. Galloway has also starred in U.S. productions, and has directed for the NATIONAL THEATRE SCHOOL in Montreal and at the Stratford Festival.

ROTA HERZBERG LISTER

Galvin Players, The. Opening at the Capitol Theatre, Ottawa, on 28 Feb. 1927, they began the longest and most successful engagement of any resident stock company in Canada during the 1920s—over 120 weeks. The company was one of five theatrical troupes operated primarily in the U.S. by the Galvin Producing Company, a family enterprise that grew out of James A. Galvin's original production company at the National Theatre, Philadelphia, and prospered under the direction of Galvin's son-in-law, A.H. McAdam, a seasoned theatre manager, formerly of Toronto. The Ottawa company was a family affair. McAdam himself appeared on occasion in 'heavy' roles; his daughter, Irene Galvin, was leading lady; and her uncle, Johnny Galvin (a comic character actor who had performed with three generations of Galvins), was the mainstay of the acting corps. Solid management practices and production methods, a carefully considered selection of recent Broadway hits, and elaborate but tasteful advertising were all important factors in the company's success. Encouraged by the reception of the Ottawa troupe, the parent company set up a second troupe in Hamilton in Oct. 1928, but the venture unaccountably failed after only a few weeks. The Ottawa company continued until 8 Dec. 1929.

The Galvin Producing Company was one of several large U.S. theatrical conglomerates that sought in the 1920s to replace the declining touring system in Canada with high-class resident stock theatre. However, despite their centralized organization, integrated production and publicity methods, stable casts, and standardized repertoires, they were forced by the Wall Street crash of 1929 to retrench and withdrew to the U.S.

The Galvin Theatre Diary for 1927-8 is in the Theatre Collection, Ottawa Public Library.   ROBERT SCOTT

Gard, Robert E. (b. 1910). Born in Kansas, he graduated from the Univ. of Kansas (1934) and Cornell (MA, 1938). His work at Cornell in folk drama with A. M. Drummond led to his appointment, from 1942 to 1944, as director of the summer folk-playwriting program (established by Frederick Koch) at the Banff School of Fine Arts (see BANFF CENTRE). In Sept. 1943 he helped establish the Alberta Folklore and Local History Project at the Univ. of Alberta, funded by the Rockefeller Foundation for 'the growth and development of native culture' through 'the creation and preservation of folklore and stories dealing with the early history and settlement of the province.' From 1943 to 1945 Gard collected Alberta folk material, and stimulated others. This led to the creation of a rich archive, now at the university, a collection of tales, *Johnny Chinook* (1945), and two volumes of *The Alberta Folklore Quarterly* (1945-6).

In the project's second year (1944-5), inspired by the summer Banff program, a provincial competition was held for original plays based on the collected material, and three plays were commissioned from Gwen Pharis RINGWOOD: the one-acts *The Jack and the Joker* and *The Rainmaker*, and her full-length *Stampede*. Gard's own playwriting contribution included *Johnny Dunn* (1944), of interest both for its subject and its staging—it deals with the origin of Alberta's strange town names, and utilizes a chorus to mimic the sound of the wind and an assortment of animals.

Gard's appointment to the Univ. of Wisconsin in 1945 ended this project prematurely. He subsequently ran the Wisconsin Idea Theatre, in addition to his teaching duties. See his memoir, *Grassroots Theatre* (1955).

MOIRA DAY

Gardner, David (b. 1928). Born in Toronto, he graduated from the Univ. of Toronto (BA, 1950; MA, 1974; Ph.D. in Drama, 1983). His acting career began at HART HOUSE THEATRE, under Robert GILL, when he was a student and continued in the 1950s with the Straw Hat Players, the CREST THEATRE, and the NEW PLAY SOCIETY,

among other companies. A member of the STRATFORD FESTIVAL company in 1955, 1956, and 1986, he won the Tyrone GUTHRIE Award in 1956; in London he acted at the Royal Court Theatre (1957) and with the Old Vic Company (1958-9). Since then he has pursued a busy and varied acting career on stage, radio, TV, and in film, combining this with work as a director, teacher, and theatre historian. Gardner was chairman of the 1960 Canadian Theatre Centre Committee, which established the NATIONAL THEATRE SCHOOL, and has been a CBC drama producer (1959-69), theatre officer for the Canada Council (1971-2) and artistic director of the VANCOUVER PLAYHOUSE (1969-71), resigning when the board would not allow him to produce George RYGA's *Captives of the Faceless Drummer*, about the FLQ crisis in Quebec.   WILLIAM TOYE

Garneau, Michel (b. 1939). Born in Montreal into a cultured, upper-middle-class family, he was educated at L'Académie Saint-Germain des Clercs de Saint-Viateur, Le Collège Brébeuf, Le Collège Sainte-Marie, and Le Collège Saint-Denis, but abandoned formal studies after the 1953 suicide of his poet-brother Sylvain. He trained briefly at the THÉÂTRE DU NOUVEAU MONDE's theatre school and the CONSERVATOIRE D'ART DRAMATIQUE, later working as a radio and TV announcer and scriptwriter in Quebec and Ontario. Garneau writes poetry, plays, music, film scripts, and 'tradaptations' (translations of the classics or contemporary plays into the popular language of Quebec). A teacher, performer, and director, he has been called both the Quebec troubadour and a Jack-of-all-arts. His preferred mode of writing for the theatre is 'sur commande'—that is, as a sort of dramaturge commissioned by a student or professional group of actors with whom he collaborates in a workshop situation. His dramatic writing derives its vitality from the strengths and constraints inherent in such conditions, and draws on the creative and improvisational potential in the group, as well as on individual and collective experiences. The published text therefore reflects the performance experiences; many of his plays exist in several versions and much of his work remains unpublished.

Garneau wrote his first plays—*Le Pierrot de cette Colombine* and *Un Verre d'eau*—in 1956, but considered himself primarily a poet until the late 1960s, when he began to take a keen interest in social questions and to participate actively in Quebec's dynamic theatre scene with *Les Grands Moments*, produced in 1967 by Les Jeunes Comédiens of the TNM and then by students of the NATIONAL THEATRE SCHOOL; *Who's Afraid of General Wolfe?* (written in 1967 for Toronto television but rejected); *Le Ravi*, given a dramatic reading in 1969 under the auspices of the Centre d'essai des auteurs dramatiques in Montreal and Paris; *Des Chevaux, des rois, des dames et des fous*, which Les Jeunes Comédiens toured in Quebec and across Canada in 1970; and *Chrisporlipopette et Saperlipochrist*, *Hostay de croum*, and *Beu-meu*, produced by the THÉÂTRE POPULAIRE DU QUÉBEC in 1971. Garneau's social commitment crystallized definitively at the time of his arrest during the October Crisis of 1970.

In general Garneau's plays are characterized by simplicity of staging and action. He makes frequent use of song and music, both directly—by using his own and others' compositions—and also by incorporating the principles of rhythm and composition into theme, plot, and form. Several plays resemble what he has called 'permutations', or complex fugues for multiple voices and instruments. Characterization is usually flat, with little psychological complexity. Proper names are usually irrelevant; roles can and should be exchanged; sex distinctions are crossed and blurred; doubling is encouraged; characters repeat and echo each other's lines. In *Petipetant et le monde* (1982), for example, a dog offers his particular perspective on humans' vexing problems. Originally conceived for students at the National Theatre School in 1971, this play has been variously titled *Dix-sept*, *Seize*, and so on, according to the number of actors available; the published version is an adaptation made by Lorraine Pintal in 1975 for ten actors. Garneau's first published play, written 'sur commande', was *Sur le matelas* (1974), first produced in 1972. It humorously presents the relentless invasion of a couple's intimacy by a series of characters, each representing one of society's inescapable institutions. The same year he produced a dialogue version of an earlier monologue, *La Chanson d'amour de cul* (1971), in which an animated conversation between two employees of an advertising agency underlines the arbitrary nature of sexual taboos and reveals how traditional moral standards and the practices of a materialistic society make love between the sexes impossible, leaving pornography as a poor alternative.

Garneau's best-known play, *Quatre à quatre* (1974), first produced in 1973 and published in an English translation by Christian Bédard and Keith TURNBULL in 1978, has received hundreds of performances in many countries, including France's Festival d'Avignon and the Théâtre National de Chaillot in Paris in 1977. Four generations of Quebec women appear on stage, each representing a specific historical moment. The youngest explores the ambiguity of her feelings about her foremothers and what they mean to her. She has the difficult task of restoring bonds with her problematic heritage, while retaining full personal autonomy in her present life. *Strauss et Pesant (et Rosa)*, produced and published in 1974, offers a grotesque portrait of the traditions of three Quebec institutions in the face of death—family, Church, justice—while the theme of *Le Bonhomme Sept-Heures* (1984), first produced in 1974, is the joyous, poetic exorcism of human fear.

Garneau's 'tradaptations' include Shakespeare's *The Tempest* (*La Tempête*), Garcia Lorca's *House of Bernarda Alba* (*La Maison de Bernarda Alba*), and the American Oyam O's *The Resurrection of Lady Lester* (*La Résurrection de Lady Lester*). His most personal adaptation to date is that of the Sumerian epic poem *Gilgamesh* (1976), first performed in 1974, which recounts the initiatory passage into adulthood of two brothers, one of whom dies. His translation of Shakespeare's *Macbeth*, produced and published in 1978, uses the language of rural Quebec rather than standard French.

Other Garneau plays include *Les Voyagements* (1977), produced in 1975—in which four characters on exercise bicycles strip off layers of transparent masks as they search for their dynamic selves—and *L'Usage du coeur dans le domaine réel* (1979), produced in 1975, a reflection on Utopia. *Abriés desabriées* (1979), produced in 1975, uses the incantatory language and ritualistic structure of the traditional square dance to explore themes of self-knowledge and love, while in *Rien que la mémoire* (1977), produced in 1976, five old people evoke their memories of the past, confront the dullness of the present, and face death. *Les Célébrations* (1977), produced in 1976, portrays a couple gently working out

Garneau

the almost insurmountable difficulties of sustaining their love for each other. *Adidou Adidouce*, produced and published in 1977, also analyses the pursuit of love and happiness, impeded in this instance by the institutions and values of traditional Quebec—Church, family roles, and social stereotypes.

Les Neiges (1984), produced in 1978, is a series of variations on the subject and language of snow as an intimate part of the Quebec experience. *Nasopodes et autres bêtes merveilleuses*, produced in 1980, is a dramatization of poems from *Les Petits Chevals amoureux* (1977) and *Elégie au génocide des nasopodes* (1979). *Émilie ne sera plus jamais cueillie par l'anémone*, produced and published in 1981, evokes in delicate poetic terms the inner life of Emily Dickinson through a dramatic dialogue with her musician-sister Uranie. In contrast, *Le Groupe* (1982), produced in 1981, satirizes the clichés of the consumer society.

As a writer of 'théâtre sur commande' and in the various aspects of his work as an educator for the theatre, Garneau has produced a number of unpublished scripts in the past ten years. He has also contributed a short play, *Une Fête* (1985), to a collection marking the twentieth anniversary of the Centre d'essai des auteurs dramatiques, of which he is currently president. He collaborates widely with Quebec theatre projects—for example in *Parce que c'est la nuit* at the Théâtre expérimental des femmes in 1980—and with international groups.

Garneau published important theoretical statements in *Le Théâtre sur commande* (1975) and *Pour Travailler ensemble* (1978). See also *Michel Garneau. Dossiers de presse* (1985).

LOUISE H. FORSYTH

Garrard, James (b. 1939). Born in Englehart, Ont., and educated at Queen's Univ. and the London Academy of Music and Dramatic Art, he founded THEATRE PASSE MURAILLE in 1968 at Rochdale College, Toronto, an educational experiment of which he was later president. Obscenity charges arising from TPM's first public performance, Rochelle Owens' *Futz*, in Mar. 1969, brought sudden notoriety to ALTERNATE THEATRE in Toronto. Garrard's other productions that year included Paul Foster's *Tom Paine* (like *Futz*, inspired by New York's La Mama Experimental Theatre Club) and an environmental version of Jean Genet's *The Maids*. Garrard's subsequent experiments in

British Columbia with 'survival theatre', an improvisational form analogous to jazz, culminated in his production of Frank Powley's *The Black Queen is Going To Eat You All Up* at Theatre Passe Muraille in 1972, and led to the founding of Supernova Productions (fl. 1972-7) and Salon Theatre (fl. 1981-6) to continue such experiments. Garrard's plays include *Dead Heat* (produced at the University College Playhouse, Toronto, 1974), *Getting Even* (produced at Theatre Second Floor, 1979, published 1983), *Spencer's Mom* (Salon Theatre, 1981), and the gothic comedy *Cold Comfort* (produced by Saskatoon's 25TH STREET THEATRE in 1981 and published the same year in *Canadian Theatre Review*). He calls these four plays 'Bondage Plays for My Country'. Another play, *Peggy's Song*, opened at Theatre Passe Muraille in Feb. 1988.

DENIS W. JOHNSTON

Garrison Theatre. The term refers primarily to the theatrical activities of the British and French army and navy contingents stationed in Canada prior to the twentieth century—either private performances by the ranks, or public ventures by the officers. While theatricals served a social function under both the French and British regimes (and can often be characterized as parapolitical), the British garrisons' encouragement of local amateur and touring professional theatre did not contribute significantly to Canadian theatre history.

The first record of a garrison performance in Canada is the elaborate nautical pageant, Marc LESCARBOT's *Le THÉÂTRE DE NEPTUNE EN LA NOUVELLE-FRANCE* in Nov. 1606. Derived from the French tradition of *réceptions*, it was an elaborate presentation conceived to celebrate the return of the colony's leader, Jean de Biencourt de Poutrincourt, to the habitation at Port Royal. Subsequently the only documented garrison theatrical activity of the French regime took place under the auspices of the Governor of New France, Count Frontenac, in his private theatre during the winter of 1693-4. The season culminated in a spectacular confrontation between Bishop Saint-Vallier and the Governor over a planned production of Molière's *Tartuffe*, which was banned by Saint-Vallier. The next account of garrison theatricals appears in General Montcalm's journal for 1756-9. A performance of the locally written *Le Vieillard dupé* at Fort Niagara was allowed as a diversion for the soldiers when bad weather made work on the fortifications difficult.

These scattered examples suggest that theatre activity during the French regime was largely limited to private performances within the precincts of the garrison. Moreover, the confrontation between Saint-Vallier and Frontenac in 1694 indicates the strongly negative impact of the Catholic Church on garrison theatricals.

On the other hand, evidence of theatrical performances has been found for almost every British garrison resident in Canada from 1758 to 1870. British colonial officials apparently encouraged public theatricals as a means of creating civil stability and asserting—albeit unobtrusively—British cultural and political supremacy. Officers who had ambitions for a professional career on stage often viewed these theatricals as semi-professional occasions. John NICKINSON is perhaps the best-known example of a professional actor who came from the ranks of regimental amateurs. A garrison's contribution was not limited to performance. Military patronage and private support by individual officers helped build theatres for use by civilian and professional companies, and the English plays produced by garrisons served as models for many of the initial efforts of indigenous playwrights.

The earliest documentation of garrison the-atricals in British North America is found in the *Nova Scotia Weekly Chronicle* for a performance in 1773 of Benjamin Hoadly's English comedy *The Suspicious Husband* by the 'Gentlemen of the Army and Navy' in Halifax. Records of Edward William, Commander of the Royal Artillery in Montreal, show receipts for the lease of a hall between 1774 and 1776; additional documents indicate that at least two plays by Molière were performed there by officers, most likely in French. A 1783 garrison that performed in Quebec City is mentioned in the letters of military surgeon Adam Mabane. The first recorded theatrical performance in Saint John, N. B., occurred in the ballroom of Mallard's tavern in Feb. 1789. Although it is not known whether the performers were officers of the garrison, Thomas Mallard, the owner, had been a lieutenant of the 37th Company of the Militia. The building of the first permanent theatre in Saint John—the DRURY LANE, which opened in Feb. 1809—was assisted by the officers of the 101st Regiment under Major George O'Malley. Navy theatricals took place as early as 1853 aboard the *HMS Trincomalee* in Esquimault Harbour, B.C., and in Arctic waters (see ROYAL ARCTIC THEATRE).

An increase in garrison theatrical activity, as well as greater encouragement of civilian amateurs, frequently occurred in periods of

The Lady of Lyons Burlesque, *presented by officers of the Halifax Garrison, 1872*

political or cultural crisis: in Quebec City during the late eighteenth and early nineteenth centuries, probably in response to the Napoleonic threat overseas; in London and Quebec City following the 1837 Rebellions; in Montreal and Kingston when U.S. threats challenged British sovereignty; and in the 1860s when Britain was withdrawing military support of British North America. In Quebec City and Montreal garrisons appear to have used theatre as a velvet-glove method of cultural assertion. French-Canadian amateurs often performed in an English-language theatre, frequently under the patronage of the Governor or officers. By encouraging public theatricals, the British challenged the traditional censure by the Catholic Church of such activity.

The garrison repertoire consisted largely of English comedies and farces, with an occasional translation of Molière or Marivaux for the benefit of a French-speaking milieu. The original component was usually a prologue written for the benefit of a particular audience.

The tradition of garrison theatricals died after Confederation, with three notable Canadian military exceptions. *Leo, the Royal Cadet* (1889), a military opera about the Royal Military College written by G. F. Cameron, with music by Oscar Telgmann, was produced in 1889 in Kingston; and in Winnipeg Staff Sergeant George BROUGHALL wrote *The 90th on Active Service; or, Campaigning in the North West* (1885), 'a musical and dramatic burlesque', and *The Tearful and Tragical Tale of the Tricky Troubadour; or, The Truant Tracked* (1886), a satirical burlesque of Verdi's *Il Trovatore*. Both of Broughall's works were produced at Winnipeg's PRINCESS OPERA HOUSE, providing an effective means of highlighting military presence in the West during the Riel Rebellion.

The purpose of military theatrical performances during the First and Second World Wars was different from that of the previous century. In the First World War concert parties—often using material developed by the soldiers themselves—fulfilled the need for entertainment and morale boosting, as did the ARMY SHOW and NAVY SHOW during the Second World War.   NATALIE REWA

Gascon, Jean (1921-88). Born in Montreal, he enrolled in the Univ. of Montreal in 1939 to study medicine. But he began acting with Émile LEGAULT's COMPAGNONS DE SAINT-LAURENT, and in 1945 gave up his medical studies to pursue a stage career. Influenced by the great French actress and teacher Ludmilla Pitoëff, whom he met in Montreal, Gascon left for Paris in 1946 to study under Julien Bertheau at L'École du Vieux-Colombier. After touring with Pitoëff's company in France, he spent a season acting at the Centre Dramatique de l'Ouest in Rennes before returning to Paris to work with La Compagnie Grenier-Hussenot. In 1951 Gascon returned to Montreal, where he helped found the THÉÂTRE DU NOUVEAU MONDE, remaining as its artistic director for the next fifteen years. He was also the theatre's principal director and one of its leading actors, performing many memorable roles, including the title role in Molière's *Don Juan* in 1952, the Doge in Thomas Otway's *Venice Preserved* in 1959, and Macheath in the 1961 production of the Brecht/Weill *Threepenny Opera*. Under Gascon's artistic leadership the TNM became one of the country's leading theatres.

In 1956 the TNM first appeared at the STRATFORD FESTIVAL, presenting three farces by Molière at the Avon Theatre; company members played the French courtiers in Michael LANGHAM's production of Shakespeare's *Henry V*, with Gascon as the Constable of France. Two years later the company returned to Stratford with Molière's *Le Malade imaginaire*. In 1959 Gascon was invited to direct *Othello* on the Festival Theatre stage.

Instrumental in founding the NATIONAL THEATRE SCHOOL in Montreal in 1960, Gascon became its first director general (1960-3). In 1963 at Stratford, Gascon directed a *commedia Comedy of Errors*, with splendid designs by Mark Negin and Robert PRÉVOST; despite a generally unfavourable press the production was a box-office hit. His 1964 Stratford production of Molière's *Le Bourgeois gentilhomme* was well received on tour in Chichester, England. Gascon also staged operas at the Avon theatre—Mozart's *The Marriage of Figaro* in 1964, and the North American première of the Brecht/Weill *The Rise and Fall of the City of Mahagonny* in 1965. In 1966 he directed and acted in August Strindberg's *The Dance of Death*, playing Edgar to Denise PELLETIER's Alice—generally regarded as one of the finest non-Shakespearean productions at the Festival.

After the 1967 season Gascon was

appointed executive artistic director of the Stratford Festival with John HIRSCH as associate artistic director. In his initial season, 1968, Gascon directed a respectable production of Anton Chekhov's *The Seagull* and a superb production of Molière's *Tartuffe*. This was followed in the next season by Ben Jonson's *The Alchemist* and Peter Luke's *Hadrian VII*, with Hume CRONYN, which toured the U.S. for thirty-eight weeks. At the end of the 1969 season Hirsch resigned and Gascon assumed sole artistic responsibility for the Festival. Gascon's productions in 1970 included *The Merchant of Venice* and a brilliant staging of the rarely seen *Cymbeline*. At the Avon Theatre he introduced a season of contemporary plays, which included Fernando Arrabal's *The Architect and the Emperor of Assyria*, Arnold Wesker's *The Friends*, and Slawomir Mrozek's *Vatzlav*. While the choice of these plays showed a great deal of artistic courage, they failed to attract audiences. The 1971 season, however, was marked by two more remarkable Gascon productions: John Webster's *The Duchess of Malfi* at the Festival Theatre and Georges Feydeau's *There's One in Every Marriage* at the Avon. His two 1972 shows—Alfred de Musset's *Lorenzaccio* and *The Threepenny Opera*—were both controversial.

In Jan. 1973, when the Festival visited Holland, Denmark, Poland, and the Soviet Union, Gascon's new production of *The Taming of the Shrew* was in the repertoire. He directed *Pericles* in 1973 at the Festival Theatre, and in 1974—his final season as artistic director—Molière's *The Imaginary Invalid* (which was one of the productions the Festival took to Australia in 1974) and Jacques Offenbach's *La Vie parisienne*.

Under Gascon's leadership the Stratford Festival grew both in size and reputation, and his efforts to make it into a genuinely bicultural and national institution, though limited in success, were very much in keeping with the dominant political direction of the time. Gascon then freelanced for two years as a director and actor. Most significant was a production of John COULTER's *RIEL* at the NATIONAL ARTS CENTRE, Edmond Rostand's *Cyrano de Bergerac* at the MANITOBA THEATRE CENTRE, and a double bill of Molière farces for the THÉÂTRE POPULAIRE DU QUÉBEC: *The Flying Doctor* and *The Doctor in Spite of Himself*. He also returned to the TNM to direct a French adaptation of Eugene

O'Neill's *Long Day's Journey into Night*—he played the part of James Tyrone—and *Les Rivaux*, a French adaptation of R.B. Sheridan's *The Rivals*.

In 1977 Gascon was appointed director of theatre at the National Arts Centre, where he participated as director and actor in the work of both the NAC English and French companies. His first production was the English première of Roch CARRIER's *Floralie, Where Are You?*. The next season he gave a memorable performance as the Captain in Strindberg's *The Father*, which he also directed. This was followed by Carlo Goldoni's *Arlequin, serviteur de deux maîtres*. His subsequent seasons at the NAC included Corneille's *Le Cid*, an English-language production of Molière's *Don Juan*, and Feydeau's *La Puce à l'oreille*. When it became apparent that inadequate funding, internal administration problems, and indifferent public support would foil Gascon's ambition of making the NAC the country's national theatre, he welcomed the opportunity to work at other theatres, such as the Théâtre Populaire du Québec and Stratford, to which he returned in 1981 to direct Molière's *The Misanthrope* and Friedrich Dürrenmatt's *The Visit*. Gascon also accepted an offer from Joseph Shoctor to become the consulting artistic director of the CITADEL THEATRE in Edmonton. He maintained his association with the Citadel for the next two years. Among his productions there were Shakespeare's *The Comedy of Errors*, Bernard Pomerance's *The Elephant Man*, and Molière's *The Miser*. Serious illness in 1984 forced Gascon to resign from the NAC and curtail his other activities, but he was active again in 1985, directing Arthur Schnitzler's *La Ronde* at Montreal's Encore Theatre. At L'Opéra de Montréal he directed *The Barber of Seville* in 1986 and *Tosca* in 1987. After performing in Chekhov's *The Cherry Orchard* at TNM, he returned to Stratford once again in 1988, where he died of a heart attack while directing Lerner and Loewe's *My Fair Lady*.

Throughout his career Gascon also performed in film and on television. He was a Companion of the Order of Canada and recipient of the Molson Award, the Royal Bank Award, and the Prix du Québec.

MICHAL SCHONBERG

Gass, Ken (b. 1945). Born and raised in Abbotsford, B.C., he earned an MA in theatre and creative writing at the Univ. of

Gass

British Columbia before moving to Toronto in 1968. Working as a free-lance director at John HERBERT's Garret Theatre and THEATRE PASSE MURAILLE, he became interested in the possibilities that new and experimental theatre held for Canadian drama. In 1970 he helped organize Toronto's Festival of Underground Theatre (F.U.T.), which many locate as the origin of the ALTERNATE THEATRE movement that dominated Toronto theatre for most of the 1970s. FACTORY THEATRE Lab, which he founded in 1970, became an early focus for this activity, with its mandate to 'pursue unconventional programming and . . . search for something indigenous and unique.' As the Factory's first artistic director, Gass devoted himself to an all-Canadian production policy that helped hone his dramaturgical, administrative, and directorial skills but left little time for writing. That many leading Canadian playwrights owe much to his tutelage during this period—notably, David FREEMAN, Bryan WADE, George F. WALKER and Larry FINEBERG—accounts for his continuing recognition; but it is his design of the Factory as a 'research and development' facility for the creation of new plays that is his most important legacy. During his tenure, this 'home of the Canadian playwright' became the prototype for the small, nationalistically inclined theatres that sprang up across the country as alternatives to the larger and more solvent regional theatres.

By the time Gass resigned his Factory position in 1977 to pursue his interest in writing, Canadian theatre had become more comprehensive and complex. However, conservative audiences, cautious funding policies by governmental arts councils, and the high cost of maintaining theatre spaces made Gass pessimistic about the future of theatre in Toronto. In an article he wrote for *Canadian Theatre Review* 21 (Winter 1979), he suggests that what had begun as alternative theatre had become mainstream. 'Toronto may be a bustling, chic metropolis with abundant resources and an active theatre industry, but it is also thoroughly conservative and not the most conducive environment for serious theatre work. It is this realization that has caused me, for one, to plan my future theatre work elsewhere.' In *Winter Offensive* (1978), the last play he wrote before leaving the Factory and produced there in 1977, Gass seemed intent to shock the audience out of its per-

The Boy Bishop *by Ken Gass, Factory Theatre Lab, Toronto, 1976*

ceived apathy; but, as with *The Boy Bishop* (1976), the other major play he wrote during this period (also produced at Factory Theatre Lab in 1976), the script revealed more about his own frustrations than the socio-historical situation it dramatized.

After leaving the Factory, Gass taught acting and directing for six years at the Univ. of Toronto, and wrote a number of radio and television plays—notably *Terror*, in 1983, which he also adapted for the stage. In 1984 he began to investigate the possibility of opening a new theatre that not only would produce new Canadian work but also would remount plays from Canada's past. Despite financial difficulties, he opened Canadian Rep Theatre, Toronto, in 1985 to pursue these goals, and within two years managed to present such early Factory hits as Herschel HARDIN's *Esker Mike and His Wife, Agiluk* and Hrant ALIANAK's *Lucky Strike* in major new productions. While it is too soon to evaluate the significance of this theatre, certainly its mandate provides an important mechanism for the understanding and reappraisal of Canadian plays, and it confirms Gass's continuing importance to Canadian theatre.

ROBERT WALLACE

Claude Gauvreau's Les Oranges sont vertes, *Théâtre du Nouveau Monde, Montreal, 1972, with (l. to r.) Robert Lalonde, Robert Gravel, Michelle Rossignol*

Gauvreau, Claude (1925-71). Born and educated in Montreal, he was a prolific, polemical supporter of Paul-Émile Borduas and the avant-garde Automatistes, to whose manifesto *Refus global* (1948) he contributed three short dramatic pieces. Although Gauvreau worked in RADIO DRAMA and published experimental poetry (*Brochuges*, 1956) and drama (*Bien-être*, 1947, *Sur fil métamorphose*, 1956, *La jeune fille et la lune* and *Les Grappes lucides*, 1959), his work attracted little public attention until his suicide in 1971.

The first major production of a play by Gauvreau, *La Charge de l'orignal épormyable* (1977), by the Groupe Zéro in 1970 at the Salle du GESÙ in Montreal, closed on the fourth night; a new production by Jean-Pierre RONFARD at the THÉÂTRE DU NOUVEAU MONDE ran for a month in 1974. *La Charge* examines institutionalized cruelty in a psychiatric ward, and the boundary between sanity and madness. Gauvreau's best-known play, *Les Oranges sont vertes* (1977), produced in 1972 at TNM, is typical of his work: there are passages of 'langage exploréen' (surrealistic automatic speech), polemical debates on modern art, attacks on censorship, and explicit erotic fantasies, in dramatic form influenced by both Samuel Beckett and Antonin Artaud. The central character, Yvirnig—who has much in common with Gauvreau—is a 'poète assassiné', killed by other artists.

Most of Gauvreau's creative work remained unpublished until the 1,500-page *Oeuvres créatrices complètes* was published posthumously in 1977. It includes drama, poetry, opera, and a novel, all of which defy convention. A section of twenty-six dramatic pieces called 'Entrailles' (*Entrails*, 1981, translated by Ray Ellenwood)—which includes those first published in *Refus global*—shows an evocative fantasy similar to that of Rimbaud's *Illuminations*, and surrealistic settings more suited to presentation on radio than on stage. In both drama and poetry Gauvreau frequently experimented with pure sound, attempting to express a reality beyond rational speech.

See the NFB film *Claude Gauvreau, poète* (1975); J. Marchand, *Claude Gauvreau, poète et mythocrate* (1979).   D. W. RUSSELL

Gélinas, Gratien (b. 1909). Born in Saint-Tite, Que., he moved with his family to Montreal in infancy. His graduation from the classical studies program at the Collège de Montréal coincided with the onset of the Depression, which scuttled his dreams of a law degree, and he went to work as a department store salesman. Two months later he joined an insurance company, where he worked for eight years. In 1935 he married Simone Lalonde; they had six children.

A childhood fondness for dramatic activity had become a passion during Gélinas's stay at the Collège and devoured most of his subsequent leisure time. He organized a theatre group, La Troupe des Anciens du Collège de Montréal, comprising alumni of his former school, and presented three productions annually; he played roles in both English and French at the MONTREAL REPERTORY THEATRE; and he appeared in small parts in radio plays. In 1934 he performed regularly in Robert Choquette's successful radio serial 'Le Curé de village', and two years later joined Jean BÉRAUD and Louis Francoeur in their satirical stage revue Télévise-moi ça in which his one-man sketches 'Le Bon Petit Garçon' and 'Le Méchant Petit Garçon' were an instant success. Thereafter his original monologues were in steady demand at CABARETs, charitable functions, and social events throughout Montreal.

When in 1937 a local radio station, CKAC, offered Gélinas $75 weekly to write and perform a half-hour comedy, he began a full-time career as a professional entertainer. The program, first titled 'Le Carrousel de la gaîté' and later 'Le Train de plaisir', marked the start of a decade-long love affair between Quebec audiences and Gélinas's Fridolin, a street-smart adolescent from Montreal's East End slums. Week by week Fridolin's shrugging acceptance of the facts of provincial and national life, his cocky determination to survive and dream in the face of hardship and disillusion, and his capacity for optimism and laughter in life's gloomiest moments came to epitomize for audiences all that was best in the French-Canadian character. Not the least of Fridolin's charms was his frankly colloquial Quebec French.

In 1938 Gélinas made Fridolin the star of an annual stage revue, titled FRIDOLINONS, which in its first season ran for a week at the MONUMENT NATIONAL to popular and critical acclaim. Three years later Gélinas terminated the radio program to devote more time to the stage version, which grew in popularity. In 1946-7, its final season, fifty-five performances were presented in Montreal and fifteen in Quebec City to an audience of over 100,000. Box-office receipts totalled $150,000.

Well before the last Fridolinons performances, it was apparent that Gélinas had out-grown the revue format: his situation comedy sketches were now longer, their mood more sombre, and their structure more complex than was appropriate to variety. Fridolin's satire, too, became harder-edged, almost bitter at times. That Gélinas would turn to the writing of full-length plays was inevitable. TIT-COQ, a three-act drama that premièred in 1948, proved to be a landmark in the artistic evolution of both Gélinas and Quebec theatre. This darkly comic account of a brash young army private's attempt to transcend his lonely illegitimacy by marriage into a large family, his subsequent betrayal and disillusion, and his ultimate reassertion of selfhood, captured on stage for the first time with trenchant symbolism Quebec's profound sense of alienation and marginality, a theme later to fascinate Marcel DUBÉ, Michel TREMBLAY, and others.

Gélinas began a brief flirtation with television in 1954. A weekly comedy series, 'Les Quat'fers en l'air' ('Anything Goes'), featuring a loquacious East End barber, Exubert Lajoie, played by Gélinas, lasted only one season. In 1956 he was back on stage with a nostalgic reprise of Fridolinons in Montreal and guest appearances in Henry V and The Merry Wives of Windsor at the STRATFORD FESTIVAL, Ontario.

Throughout this period Gélinas found himself perplexed by the dearth of home-grown Canadian theatre: 'Did our public really see itself in the theatre?' he asked. 'Instead of its own reflection, wasn't it rather being offered the portrait of another?' As an antidote to the colonial complex and as a gesture of faith in an indigenous Canadian stage, he purchased and renovated (with the financial aid of governments and a brewery) a midtown VAUDEVILLE house that he rechristened La COMÉDIE-CANADIENNE and dedicated to the creation of Canadian plays. Despite Gélinas's generous patronage, the only major hits during the lifetime of the Comédie-Canadienne were his own plays: Bousille et les justes in 1959 and HIER, LES ENFANTS DANSAIENT in 1966.

Bousille et les justes (Bousille and the Just), a tragicomedy that premièred on 17 Aug. 1959, is a savage indictment of Pharisaism in a small-town family. The Grenon clan, pillars of society in Saint-Tite, are determined to have their son and brother Aimé avoid a murder conviction, not out of belief in his innocence, but because a criminal record in the family would lower its social status. The sole witness to Aimé's murder of Bruno Malthais is Bousille, a God-fearing, simpleminded cousin, whom two family members physically torture until he agrees to commit perjury. While Madame Grenon and her offspring rejoice in their freshly purged honour, Bousille, devastated by the betrayal of his convictions, hangs himself.

The play's momentum derives primarily from Gélinas's relentless juxtaposition of Bousille's artless Christianity with the self-seeking hypocrisy of the rest of the family; the cumulative effect is shattering. At times, however, the dramatist's predilection for revue tempts him into superficiality: characterization degenerates into caricature, rampant witticisms mar the tone and weaken the thrust of key sequences, and complex ethical issues assume a deceptive simplicity. Nevertheless Gélinas's uncompromising attack on provincial religiosity on the eve of the Quiet Revolution awakened modern Québécois theatre to its role as social critic; few francophone Canadian dramatists of the past quarter-century have escaped *Bousille*'s influence. With the playwright in the title-role, the play enjoyed some three hundred performances in the course of long English and French runs in Montreal and a national tour of twenty-six cities.

Hier, les enfants dansaient (*Yesterday the Children Were Dancing*) premièred at La Comédie-Canadienne on 11 Apr. 1966. Amid mounting political pressure for independence for Quebec and intensified random violence, Gélinas limns poignantly the intellectual and spiritual havoc wreaked within a family by the separatist dilemma. The play met with considerable critical reserve in Quebec. The subject was judged relevant, but Gélinas's handling of the federalist-separatist debate was thought to be undramatic and simplistic. The English première at the CHARLOTTETOWN FESTIVAL (5 July 1967), on the other hand, was a remarkable success.

In 1969 Gélinas was appointed chairman of the Canadian Film Development Corporation. Widowed in 1967, he married the distinguished actress Huguette OLIGNY in 1973. On his retirement in 1978 he settled in Oka, a rural community near Montreal; after eight years of relative inactivity, however, he returned to the stage in *La Passion de Narcisse Mondoux* (*Narcisse Mondoux's Passion*), a play he wrote for himself and his wife. A romantic comedy, teetering on the brink of farce, *Narcisse Mondoux* lightheartedly explores the sexuality of the elderly as revealed in the efforts of a retired plumber to woo his lifelong love, the recently widowed Laurencienne Robichaud. It premièred at Toronto's THÉÂTRE DU P'TIT BONHEUR on 2 Oct. 1986, and transferred to Montreal's THÉÂTRE DU RIDEAU VERT on 19 Jan. 1987. The script and the performances of Gélinas and Oligny enjoyed a mellow critical and popular reception in both cities.

During the run of *Narcisse Mondoux* the NATIONAL ARTS CENTRE mounted a reprise of excerpts from *Les Fridolinades* (12-14 Nov. 1986), which later played for a month (18 Nov.-19 Dec.) at Théâtre du Rideau Vert and in Feb. 1989 at Toronto's Premiere Dance Theatre.

The superficial contemporaneity of *Narcisse Mondoux* apart, Gélinas's major dramas are now undeniably dated. The very topicality that prompted their initial success has been their undoing. *Tit-Coq*'s dilemmas have little relevance in an era of easy divorce and sexual permissiveness; the churchgoer—the social target of *Bousille*—is today an almost invisible minority; while the introverted cultural rhetoric of *Hier, les enfants dansaient* strikes contemporary economic nationalists as downbeat and naïve.

As a pioneer of contemporary Canadian theatre, however, Gélinas's importance can hardly be overestimated, and has been recognized by a Fellowship in the Royal Society of Canada (1959), the Order of Canada (1967), a series of honorary degrees, and numerous cultural prizes.

See Yves Bolduc, 'Gratien Gélinas', *Archives des Lettres Canadiennes*, 5 (1976); *Gratien Gélinas: dossiers de presse, 1940-1980* (1981); Donald Smith, 'Gratien Gélinas, rénovateur du théâtre québécois', *Lettres québécoises* 36 (1984-85); Renate Usmiani, *Gratien Gélinas* (1977).   JOHN RIPLEY

Gérin-Lajoie, Antoine (1824-82). Born at Yamachiche, Que., the eldest of sixteen brothers and sisters, he attended local schools and the Collège de Nicolet. In 1842, while still a student, he wrote the words to the well-known folksong 'Un Canadien errant', dedicated to the exiled leaders of the Patriote Rebellion, and, two years later, a verse play, *Le JEUNE LATOUR* (1844), the first tragedy written and published in Canada. Graduating

Gérin-Lajoie

Antoine Gérin-Lajoie

the same year, he helped found the controversial Institut Canadien, becoming its first secretary and, in 1845, president of its Montreal branch while serving at the same time as secretary to the fledgeling Société St-Jean-Baptiste.

After working for Montreal's *La Minerve* he abandoned journalism to study law. Called to the Bar in 1848, he soon gave up law to accept a position with the civil service, going on to a career as copyist, translator, and, eventually, parliamentary librarian in Toronto, Quebec, and Ottawa. Throughout his life he retained his lively interest in literature, history, and politics, although he did not return to drama. He helped found the two most important literary reviews of his time, *Les Soirées canadiennes* (1861-5) and *Le Foyer canadien* (1863-6), to both of which he contributed frequently. He wrote three historical works, the most important being *Dix ans au Canada, de 1840 à 1850*, an account of the struggle for responsible government, published posthumously. Gérin-Lajoie is best known, however, as the author of *Le Jeune Latour* and of the two *Jean Rivard* novels: *Jean Rivard, le défricheur*, in *Les Soirées canadiennes* (vol. II, 1862) and its sequel, *Jean*

Rivard, économiste in *Le Foyer canadien* (vol. II, 1864). These novels advocate the return to a land-based economy and rural values, a theme that would dominate Quebec literature for the next three generations.

See René Dionne, *Antoine Gérin-Lajoie, homme de lettres* (1978).   L.E. DOUCETTE

Germain, Jean-Claude (b. 1939). Born on rue Fabre, a working-class area of Montreal, he studied history at the Univ. de Montréal, founded the Théâtre Antonin Artaud, which survived only briefly, and worked for three years as a grocer. During the 1960s he was drama critic for *Le Petit Journal*, *Dimensions*, and *Digest Éclair*, continuing through the 1970s with contributions to *Le Magazine Maclean* and to various theatre magazines in both French and English Canada, as well as founding the journals *L'Illettré* (1970-1) and *Le Pays théâtral* (1977-80). He was co-founder and artistic director of the Centre du THÉÂTRE D'AUJOURD'HUI (1969-82), and has taught at the NATIONAL THEATRE SCHOOL since 1972.

In 1969 Germain founded the Théâtre du Même Nom (TMN) and its company Les Enfants de Chénier; the acronym deliberately parodied that of the establishment theatre, the THÉÂTRE DU NOUVEAU MONDE, which rarely produced Quebec work. TMN's first play, performed at the Centre du Théâtre d'Aujourd'hui, was the collective *Un Autre grand spectacle d'adieu*, which satirized borrowed foreign culture and bid a joyous 'adieu'—in the form of a boxing-match—to the great masters of the international repertory who have monopolized the Quebec stage. (Although unpublished, a recording of this play, along with recordings of most other Germain productions, is available in the archives of the Audiovidéothèque of the Univ. de Montréal.) Germain and Les Enfants de Chénier continued experimental improvisation with *Diguidi, diguidi, ha! ha! ha!* (1970) on the theme of the dehumanizing and debilitating effect of tradition on family life in Quebec. Their next work, *Si Aurore m'était contée deux fois*, is in two parts: *Le Grand rallye de canonisation d'Aurore l'enfant-martyre* and *La Mise à mort d'la miss des miss*, both performed in 1970. Its point of departure is the gruesome story of the tortured child Aurore, the subject of Léon Petitjean's and Henri Rollin's popular play *AURORE L'ENFANT MARTYRE*. Germain's play suggests

Jean-Claude Germain

told. Offers of friendship and understanding prove illusory. The play offers Farnand a choice between obedience and revolt. After several revivals, a new version of *Le Roi des mises* was toured in 1976 by the THÉÂTRE POPULAIRE DU QUÉBEC under the title *La Reine des chanteuses de pomme.*

The first production of Les P'tits Enfants Laliberté, the new name taken by Les Enfants de Chénier in Sept. 1971, was Germain's *La Garde montée, ou Un épisode dans la vie canadienne de Don Quickshot*, a satire on the forces of law and order. Since 1971 Les P'tits Enfants has produced a number of significant (but unpublished) works by Germain: *Nous autres aussi on fait ça pour rire*, 1972, celebrating humour and creativity; *Dédé mesure*, 1972, exploring the unreality of fashion-designed images; *La Charlotte électrique, ou Un conte de Noël tropical pour toutes les filles pardues dans a'brume, dans a'neige ou dans l'vice*, 1972, satirizing the artificiality of materialistic society; *Les méfaits de l'acide*, 1973; *L'Affront commun*, 1973, a fable on union ritual arising out of the strike by the Front Commun in 1973; the unsuccessful *Beau, bon, pas cher, ou La transe du bon boulé*, 1975; and *Sot d'Ostie*, 1981, satirizing the policy of subsidizing and encouraging imported culture.

In the highly successful *Les Hauts et les bas d'la vie d'une diva: Sarah Ménard par eux-mêmes. Une Monologuerie bouffe*, performed in 1974 and published in 1976, a diva—partially identified with both Emma Albani and Sarah Bernhardt—illustrates with devastating humour that none of the arias of the world's repertory are right for her, since none let her sing her own (Quebec) song. Using the same character, Germain further explores the problem of the absence of a specifically Quebec culture on the Quebec stage, this time in a darker light, in the sequel *Les Nuits de l'indiva: une mascapade*, performed in 1980, published in 1983.

Les Hauts et les bas begins a cycle of plays in which Germain attempts to recapture in today's terms some of the cultural vitality of the past, though for Germain history is a living contact with the present implying no commitment to preserving a dead past. In *Un Pays dont la devise est je m'oublie. Une grande gigue épique*, a parody of the provincial motto 'Je me souviens', performed and published in 1976, itinerant comedians stroll through great moments of the past, which they see in a fresh and humorous perspective, seeking

that in a climate of religious and political oppression, where free expression is impossible, only grotesque and perverted cultural forms, such as that of *Aurore*, are able to survive. With *Rodéo et Juliette*, first performed in 1970, a lively parody of American popular culture and the cult of classical traditions, music and musicians assumed a vital role in Germain's work.

Les Tourtereaux, ou la vieillesse frappe à l'aube (1974) satirizes mass culture and government manipulation of the media. First performed in 1970, the play reflects directly on the October Crisis. A short play, *Le Pays dans l'pays*, was performed in 1971 as a benefit for 'the defence of Quebec political prisoners', while *Si les Sansoucis s'en soucient, ces Sansouci-ci s'en soucieront-ils? Bien parler c'est se respecter!*, performed in 1971 and published in 1972, takes a broader critical look at Quebec culture, ridiculing families that unquestioningly follow meaningless traditions. The central figure of *Si les Sansoucis*—Farnand, a representative Québécois spending his time between tavern and apartment—reappears in *Le Roi des mises à bas prix*, performed in 1971, published in 1972. Farnand is made to understand, by the many authoritarian voices surrounding him, that he has no right to claim or own anything and must go where he is

Germain

to make sense of the world today. The same two characters return in *L'École des rêves. Une jonglerie*—performed in 1977, published in 1979—along with an ingenuous female character whose quest for truth and knowledge is a joyous celebration of the myths and the dreams of the common people of Quebec. *Les faux brillants de Félix-Gabriel Marchand, paraphrase*, performed and published in 1977, is a brilliant re-creation of Félix-Gabriel MARCHAND's neglected comedy of manners *Les FAUX BRILLANTS*, while *Mamours et conjugat. Scènes de la vie amoureuse québécoise*—performed in 1978, published in 1979—presents complex and carefully woven tableaux drawn from five historical events. In *A Canadian Play/Une plaie canadienne*, performed in 1980, published in 1983, Germain suggests that Canada suffers from a collective inferiority complex, with the voices of political leaders and artists speaking from a defensive position. It is a darkly humorous ritual of exorcism ending in the ceremonial execution of les Anglais.

From the beginning of his career Germain has actively participated in experimental and innovative theatre in Quebec. He played a major role in creating the Centre d'essai des auteurs dramatiques; he has written about the new dramaturgy and experimental theatre; he has worked with many writers, actors, musicians, and directors in developing collective work; and he has been an important educator in many forums. Germain's entire career to date shows his fervent belief that the people of Quebec possess the basis of a rich culture that urgently needs recognition and support.

See *Jeu*, 13 (1979), a special issue on Germain; Laurent Mailhot and Jean-Cléo Godin, 'Les p'tits enfants de Germain par eux-mêmes', *Théâtre québécois II. Nouveaux auteurs, autres spectacles* (1980); and *Voix et Images*, 6 (1981), a special issue on Germain and Le Théâtre d'aujourd' hui.

LOUISE H. FORSYTH

Gerussi, Bruno (b. 1928). Born in Medicine Hat, Alta, he won a scholarship to the Banff School of Fine Arts (see BANFF CENTRE) in 1946 and subsequently studied acting and performed at the Seattle Repertory Theatre. He acted at the Totem and Avon theatres in Vancouver from 1951 to 1953 before his first appearance at the STRATFORD FESTIVAL in 1954: as Grumio in *The Taming of the Shrew*

and a Chorus member in *Oedipus Rex*. He remained a regular member of the Stratford Company until 1965, playing Feste in *Twelfth Night* (1957), Romeo (1960), Ariel in *The Tempest* (1962), and Edmund in *King Lear* (1964), among other major roles. A founding member of the CANADIAN PLAYERS, Gerussi played the title role in their 1956 production of Ibsen's *Peer Gynt* (as well as in the 1957 CBC-TV/Stratford Festival production). In 1959 he toured the U.S. in Schiller's *Mary Stuart* and in the early 1960s also appeared at Toronto's CREST and CENTRAL LIBRARY theatres. An athletic, emotional, and immensely popular actor, Gerussi left the theatre in 1965 for radio and television, hosting a CBC radio talk-show until 1971 and then creating the role of Nick Adonidas in CBC-TV's adventure series *The Beachcombers*, which has run continuously since 1972 and has been broadcast in over thirty countries. L. W. CONOLLY

Gesù, La Salle du. Attached to the Jesuit Collège Sainte-Marie on rue Bleury, the oldest operating theatre in Montreal opened on 10 July 1865. It occupies the basement and ground floor of the church of the same name, designed by Brooklyn architect Patrick C. Keely and built in 1864. The Gesù—intended for academic debates and student meetings—is 110' long and 80' wide, with a semi-circular seating plan and a stage area (including backstage) measuring 50' by 60'.

Open to the public from the beginning, the hall was not used for theatrical performances until 1925, when Father Joseph Paré and his Anciens du Gesù performed Racine's *Athalie* on 27 May. Among the company were Hector Charland and Paul Langlais, who subsequently enjoyed successful stage careers. In Paré's production of Edmond Rostand's *L'Aiglon* the company was supplemented by several students, including Jean GASCON and, in the title role, Jean-Louis ROUX.

For the centenary of the College in 1945 the theatre was modernized with new lighting and a revolving stage. The removal of a row of pillars allowed for an increase in seating from 875 to 1,000. Companies using the Gesù included Les COMPAGNONS DE SAINT-LAURENT in 1945, L'ÉQUIPE in 1946, le THÉÂTRE DU RIDEAU VERT and Le Théâtre d'Essai in 1949, Le THÉÂTRE DU NOUVEAU MONDE in 1951, Le THÉÂTRE CLUB in 1956, and La NOUVELLE COMPAGNIE THÉÂTRALE

232

in 1964. Important productions at the Gesù include Gratien GÉLINAS's *TIT-COQ* in the fall of 1948, Félix LECLERC's *Le P'tit Bonheur* in 1949, Lomer Gouin's *Polichinelle* in 1950, and several DOMINION DRAMA FESTIVAL productions, such as Marcel DUBÉ's *De l'autre côté du mur* in 1952, Jacques LANGUIRAND's *Les Insolites* in 1956, and Robert GURIK's *Le Pendu* in 1967.

Since the closing of the College in 1969 and the departure of La Nouvelle Compagnie Théâtrale in 1977, the Salle du Gesù has been used chiefly for conferences and sermons, though scheduled renovations should ensure that theatre will continue to be offered in this historic hall.   ANDRÉ-G. BOURASSA

Gilbert, Edward (b. 1937). Born in Austria and educated at Oxford University, he worked with the Royal Shakespeare Company, Sadler's Wells, and the Oxford Playhouse before Michel SAINT-DENIS arranged for him to come to Canada as assistant artistic director of the English acting section of the NATIONAL THEATRE SCHOOL. His long association with the MANITOBA THEATRE CENTRE began when he directed Shaw's *Heartbreak House* in its 1964-5 season. He stayed on as resident director, succeeding John HIRSCH as artistic director in 1966. Gilbert's two terms at MTC (1966-9 and 1972-5) were marked by conservative programming with an emphasis on articulate plays of ideas, many of them English in origin. He enjoyed particular success with Shaw (*Major Barbara*, 1967, and *You Never Can Tell*, 1973, both co-productions with the SHAW FESTIVAL), and with contemporary plays such as Joe Orton's *What the Butler Saw* (MTC, 1971) and Peter Shaffer's *Equus* (MTC, 1976). His apparent preference for American rather than Canadian actors and his refusal to promote Canadian plays on MTC's mainstage tended, however, to isolate him from the increasingly nationalistic Canadian theatre of the 1970s.

After a period of freelance work, Gilbert was appointed director of Toronto Arts Productions (see CENTRESTAGE), 1980-4, where failure of his first production, *Macbeth*, starring Len CARIOU, was blamed on the inadequacies of the ST LAWRENCE CENTRE theatre. However, when the rebuilt theatre reopened with an equally disastrous Gilbert production of Tom Stoppard's *On the Razzle*, it became clear that the artistic principles that had served him well in Winnipeg would not

suffice in Toronto, and he resigned to pursue a career of freelance directing. ROSS STUART

Gill, Robert (1911-74). Born in Spokane, Washington, of a Canadian father, he was educated at Pittsburgh's Carnegie Tech (BA, MFA), where he later taught. He acted and directed with the Pittsburgh Playhouse and Opera Society, as well as with the Woodstock Playhouse, New York, before being invited in 1945 to reopen HART HOUSE THEATRE, Univ. of Toronto. As its director until 1965 he trained a postwar generation of Canadian actors and directors that included Anna Cameron, Barbara CHILCOTT, Donald and Murray DAVIS, Ted Follows, David GARDNER, Barbara HAMILTON, Eric HOUSE, William HUTT, Charmion KING, Leon MAJOR, George McCowan, Kate REID, and Donald SUTHERLAND. He also taught at the Royal Conservatory of Music, Toronto, the Banff School of Fine Arts (see BANFF CENTRE), and the Univ. of British Columbia. With the Davis brothers, Gill helped found the Straw Hat Players in Muskoka (1947) and Toronto's CREST THEATRE (1954). The Robert Gill Theatre, Univ. of Toronto, is named in his honour.   DAVID GARDNER

Girard, Rodolphe (1879-1956). Born in Trois-Rivières, Que., he moved in 1891 with his family to Montreal, where he attended the Académie Commerciale Catholique de Montréal and the Collège de Montréal. A reporter with *La Presse*, he was fired in 1904, following the Archbishop of Montreal's denunciation of his novel *Marie Calumet* (1904). Girard then moved to Ottawa and became a translator for the House of Commons, a position he held until retirement. A prolific journalist, essayist, and short story writer, Girard also wrote many plays, some of which were published and performed. His historical drama *Fleur de lys* (unpublished) was performed at Montreal's MONUMENT NATIONAL in Dec. 1902. This romanticized account of Madeleine de Verchères, who repulsed a band of Iroquois in 1692, was followed by a five-act dramatization of the legend of the golden dog, *Le Chien d'or*, unproduced and unpublished. A short piece, *Le Conscrit impérial*—in which Napoleon outwits a jealous rival—and the three-act *À la conquête d'un baiser* were both published in the journal *Mosaïque* (1902), a collection of short stories and these plays. *À la conquête d'un baiser* is a witty comedy about four young men who try to steal a kiss from a Parisian beauty.

A leading member of the Institut canadien-français of Ottawa, Girard wrote a few plays between 1907 and 1912 for amateur players, including *Dialogue sur les morts* (1912), a conversation between a widow and a childhood friend, and *Le Doigt de la femme* (1912), a one-act comedy, in which a medical student falls in love with a friend of his sister, performed on 24 Apr. at the Institut canadien-français at a gala under the patronage of the Governor General, Lord Grey. For the 75th anniversary of the Institute, Girard wrote a melodrama, *Le Sacrifice* (1912), performed on 17 Nov. 1912 in the Château Laurier. Marked by the effective use of language to define class distinctions, *Le Sacrifice* is otherwise a conventional story of sibling rivalry and sacrifice. *Les Ailes cassées* (1921), first performed in 1932 at the Monument National, has a melodramatic ending, but this satire on opportunistic marriages contains some interesting characters and allusions to Ottawa politicians.

JOHN E. HARE

Giroux, Antoinette (1899-1978) and **Germaine Giroux** (1902-75). Born in Montreal, the Giroux sisters began acting at a young age (Germaine played in *Madama Butterfly* when she was only three), subsequently studying at the Conservatoire Lassalle and appearing at the ORPHEUM and the MONUMENT NATIONAL in Montreal and at the Imperial in Quebec City.

In 1923 Antoinette won a Quebec government grant to study in Paris with Denis Dinès. This was followed by tours with the Théâtre de la Porte-Saint-Martin, the Comédie-Française, and other companies in Europe, the Orient, and North America. Responding to appeals by Fred BARRY and Albert DUQUESNE, she returned to Montreal in 1930 to join the Barry-Duquesne company at the THÉÂTRE STELLA, serving as director of the theatre in 1934-5. In 1931 Germaine Giroux—after a successful career in New York, including Broadway—also returned to Montreal to work at the Stella.

After the closing of the Stella in 1935 Antoinette and Germaine appeared with other companies throughout Quebec, as well as on radio, in films, and in popular television series such as 'Le Survenant', 'Les Belles Histoires des pays d'en Haut,' and 'Rue des pignons'.

PIERRE LAVOIE

Glaser, Vaughan (1872-1958). Born in Cleveland, Ohio, he acted in the U.S. and occasionally in Canada from 1893. He was in touring companies with Mrs Patrick Campbell, 1902-3, and with Mrs Minnie Maddern Fiske, 1903-4. His stock company, the Vaughan Glaser Players, performed regularly in Toronto from 1921 to 1928 and was briefly revived in 1930 and 1932; the company was known as the Vaughan Glaser English Players in 1926 and 1928. Enormously popular at both Loew's Uptown Theatre (1921-6) and the Victoria Theatre (1926-8 and 1932), the company gave approximately 2,200 performances of 214 different plays. The varied weekly repertoire reflected Toronto tastes. American comedies predominated: *Smilin' Through, Daddy Longlegs, Are You a Mason?, Mrs. Wiggs of the Cabbage Patch,* and many others. English comedies and pantomimes were also popular: among them *Charley's Aunt, The Better 'Ole, The Private Secretary, Bunty Pulls the Strings, Grumpy, Cinderella, Babes in the Wood, Mother Goose and the Gingerbread Man,* and *Babes in Toyland.* In addition, the Players presented musicals (*Buddies, Irene, Tangerine*), mysteries (*Within the Law, The Green Goddess, The Bat, Sherlock Holmes*), and dramas (*St. Elmo, East Lynne, The Sign of the Cross, The Man Between*). Regular company members were principally American (Ruth Amos, Basil Loughrane, Elmer Buffham, Corinne Farrell, and others) and English (Anne Carew, Eugene Wellesley, Barry Jones, Alison Bradshaw, Lambert Larking), with a few Canadians (Catherine Procter, May Belle MARKS, Lois Landon—whom Glaser married in 1927). By 1928 public interest in repertory theatre had declined as a result of the popularity of VAUDEVILLE, films, radio, cars, bridge, tennis, and daylight saving time; consequently Vaughan Glaser retired, returning to Toronto theatres only twice, with limited success. He performed in several films in the U.S.

See Robert G. Lawrence, 'Vaughan Glaser on Stage in Toronto 1921-1934', *Theatre History in Canada,* 9 (1988).

ROBERT G. LAWRENCE

Glass, Joanna (b. 1936). Born Joan McClelland in Saskatoon, she developed an interest in theatre as a high-school student. After graduation in 1955 she performed with the Saskatoon Community Players while working as an ad writer and broadcaster at a local radio station. She soon moved to Calgary to join Betty MITCHELL's Workshop 14, supporting herself as a television continuity writer. Her lead role in Maxwell Anderson's *Anne of the Thousand Days*, the Calgary entry in the 1957 DOMINION DRAMA FESTIVAL, won her a scholarship from the Alberta Cultural Activities Branch to study acting for the summer at the Pasadena Playhouse, Calif. She next enrolled in Warner Brothers Drama School, but soon left for New York. There she met Alexander Glass, whom she married in 1959.

In the following years Glass acted at Yale, where her husband was a student, but after her three children were born she turned to writing. In 1966 she completed an early version of the play that was eventually to become *ARTICHOKE*. A second work, *Santacqua*, was accepted at the Herbert Berghof Studio, New York, for workshop production in late 1969. Further workshops of her plays were conducted soon after: *Artichoke* at the Long Wharf Theatre, New Haven, Conn., in 1970, and the one-act plays *Trying* and *Jewish Strawberries* in 1971 at the Hilberry Theatre, Wayne State Univ., Mich.

Glass's breakthrough as a professional dramatist came in 1972 with the production of the companion one-act pieces *Canadian Gothic* and *American Modern* (published jointly in 1977) at the off-Broadway Manhattan Theatre Club under the direction of Austin Pendleton. Set in a small prairie city and a New York suburb respectively (and usually produced together), the one is a sombre study of a failing struggle against emotional repression, the other a tragicomic sketch of eccentric accommodation to marriage breakdown. The first of many Canadian productions followed in 1973 at the Pleiades Theatre, Calgary, under the direction of Ken Dyba. The premières of *Artichoke* (1979)—at the Long Wharf Theatre in 1975 and Toronto's TARRAGON THEATRE in 1976—drew critical attention from both sides of the border to Glass's talent for piquant dialogue and her facility for countering the expectations of established literary norms.

Glass's next two plays premièred in New York: *To Grandmother's House We Go* (1981), starring Eva Le Gallienne, in 1981, and *Play Memory* (1984), directed by Harold Prince in 1984; although the latter earned a Tony nomination, critical response to both plays was lukewarm. The former, in a contemporary American setting, reverses the usual generational conflict in its comic-ironic exploration of the question, 'Is there life after children?' *Play Memory*, set in the Saskatoon of the playwright's youth, is a largely autobiographical study of the decline of a proudly unrepentant alcoholic as recollected years later by his daughter. The play has its origins in a short story, 'At the King Edward Hotel', written in 1975 and published in *Winter's Tales 22* (1976); its first dramatic version, entitled *The Last Chalice*, was commissioned by the MANITOBA THEATRE CENTRE for its twentieth-anniversary season in 1977. Glass was awarded a Guggenheim Fellowship in 1981 for the extensive revision of the play, which had its Canadian première at 25TH STREET THEATRE, Saskatoon, in 1986, directed by Tom Bentley-Fisher and was produced in 1987 at Toronto's THEATRE PLUS, directed by Malcolm BLACK. In 1985 Glass was awarded a Rockefeller grant to work at the Yale Repertory Theatre, New Haven, on a new farce, *Towering Babble*. As playwright-in-residence (1987-8) at CENTRESTAGE, Toronto, she completed a new prairie comedy, *Yesteryear*, which premièred at the ST LAWRENCE CENTRE in Jan. 1989.

Glass has written two novels: *Reflections on a Mountain Summer* (1974) and *Woman Wanted* (1985). She now lives in Toronto. The Univ. of Calgary has published an inventory of its Glass holdings with a biocritical essay by Diane Bessai.

See Hetty Clews, 'Kindred Points: The Twin Worlds of Joanna M. Glass', *Atlantis* (Autumn 1978), and John Parr, 'Reflections of Joanna Glass', *Journal of Canadian Fiction*, 20 (1977).

DIANE BESSAI

Glassco, Bill (b. 1935). Born in Quebec City, he grew up in Toronto and was educated at Ridley College, St Catharines, Ont., Princeton, and Oxford. From 1962 to 1967 he taught English at the Univ. of Toronto and directed student productions there. He left his position to study acting and directing at New York University's School of the Arts. On his return to Canada in 1969 Glassco directed plays at community theatres in Jackson's Point, Toronto, and Kingston. With his wife Jane Gordon he founded TARRAGON THEATRE in Toronto in the fall of 1971, opening with a production of David FREEMAN's

Bill Glassco

the Maggie Bassett Studio, to house a new script-development program and professional development classes.

In 1975-6 Glassco took a year away from the Tarragon, returning to direct, in 1978, another Chalmers Award winner, Roland LEPAGE's *Le Temps d'une vie* (translated by Sheila Fischman as *In a Lifetime*), with Clare COULTER in the leading role. In 1982 Glassco resigned as artistic director to take up free-lance directing. Appointed artistic director of Toronto's CENTRESTAGE in 1985, he had a limited success with his first season, though it included a record-breaking revival of David French's *Jitters*, first produced at Tarragon in 1979.

Glassco has directed across Canada as well as in New York, New Haven, and Philadel-phia. His acclaimed 1985 production of Michel Tremblay's *Albertine, in Five Times* at Tarragon was revived the following year at Tarragon and went on to the Edinburgh Festival, London (England), and western Canada, including Vancouver's Expo '86. In Mar. 1988 CentreStage merged with Guy SPRUNG's TORONTO FREE THEATRE to become the CANADIAN STAGE COMPANY, where Sprung and Glassco are co-artistic directors. Final artistic decisions will alternate between them every two years.

See Denis W. Johnston, 'Diverting the Mainstream: Bill Glassco and the Early Years of Tarragon Theatre', *Canadian Drama*, 13 (1987).   JAMES NOONAN

CREEPS, which Glassco had directed in Feb. 1971 at the FACTORY THEATRE Lab.

Glassco's aim at Tarragon was to produce new Canadian plays in close collaboration with their authors and actors, and to intro-duce English-Canadian audiences to the work of Quebec playwrights. He championed the work of important new playwrights such as David Freeman and David FRENCH, and directed several of Michel TREMBLAY's plays at Tarragon, six of which he co-translated with John Van Burek. In the first three years of Tarragon's operation it won the CHAL-MERS Award for the best play in the Toronto region for *Creeps* (in 1972), French's *Of The Fields, Lately* (in 1973)—both directed by Glassco—and James REANEY's *The St. Nicho-las Hotel* (in 1974), directed by Keith TURN-BULL. Glassco's determination to encourage new Canadian playwrights was shown by his establishment in 1974 of a playwrights-in-residence program under Bena Shuster, which continued until 1977. In 1980 he opened another space at the newly renovated theatre,

Globe Theatre. This Regina-based company was founded by Ken KRAMER and Sue KRA-MER in 1966, with a loan from the Saskatch-ewan Arts Board. Originally conceived in order to produce Brian Way's participation plays for children, the company employed arena staging—a type of theatre-in-the-round—to present Way's plays, which are designed for an audience of no more than 240 children, seated on four sides of the stage action. Kramer says arena staging is demo-cratic, but it is also economical, requiring little scenery—an important consideration for a troupe travelling thousands of kilometres through Saskatchewan winters. In the Globe's first twenty years more than 4,900 performances were presented in more than 2,700 communities to over a million young people. (See also CHILDREN'S DRAMA AND THEATRE.)

When the Globe added an adult season in

1970 it also acquired its first permanent playing space, in the Saskatchewan Centre for the Performing Arts. Arena staging was preserved there, as it was in 1981 when the Globe moved into a 400-seat theatre on the second and third floors of a renovated downtown Regina landmark—formerly Old City Hall. The Globe has remained loyal to theatre for children through its School Company—which tours to schools in the fall and spring—and produces family Christmas shows. At first Way's plays predominated, but since 1972 Rex DEVERELL, as playwright-in-residence, has contributed the most plays to the Globe's repertoire for the young. In 1985 Brian Way was appointed associate director; he has been a frequent guest director, was in residence in 1983 to establish 'The Alternate Catalogue', an outreach program, and he now directs adult plays and is responsible for the School Company, which his pioneer work in England inspired.

Box-office receipts at the Globe account for only one-quarter of the theatre's annual budget, which exceeded a million dollars in the 1986-7 season; provincial and federal subsidies provide the rest. Kramer's populist stance, which is shared by Rex Deverell, is reflected in the playwright's large body of work, and Kramer's belief in the importance of political theatre emerges in Deverell's *Medicare!* (produced in 1980), about the physicians' strike of 1962, and *Black Powder* (produced in 1981), written to commemorate the thirtieth anniversary of the Estevan coal-mine riots. Other playwrights who have contributed plays based on regional or politically charged materials are Carol BOLT, whose *Next Year Country* premièred in the 1970-1 season and was subsequently rewritten and published as *BUFFALO JUMP* in 1976, and Rod Langley, who wrote *Tales from a Prairie Drifter* (produced in 1973), *Bethune* (produced in 1974), and *Two Gun Cohen*, workshopped at the BANFF CENTRE in 1986 and produced in the 1986-7 season.

Although the Globe's seasons have in general been adventurous, plays with explicit violence and offensive language have seldom been produced, automatically eliminating many contemporary plays from consideration. But the Globe—which resembles a repertory company with its attendant advantages of ensemble, authority, maturity, and trust, and occasional disadvantages of predictability, complacency, and arrogance—truly reflects its

region. Continuity is important to the company; Ken Kramer is still artistic director, and Sue Kramer, who died at thirty-nine, left behind a rich legacy of performance and principle.

See 'Next Town Nine Miles: the Globe Theatre of Saskatchewan', in *A Mirror of Our Dreams: Children and the Theatre in Canada* (1979), by Joyce Doolittle and Zina Barnieh.

JOYCE DOOLITTLE

Gobeil, Pierre (b. 1938). Born and raised in Sherbrooke, Que., he became in 1959 a founding member of l'Atelier, where, under the guidance of Roger Thibault, he was trained as an actor and director. He completed his training at the Paris Conservatoire in 1961, and at the École Supérieure d'art dramatique in Strasbourg in 1965.

Gobeil has always worked in the Eastern Townships of Quebec, where he was an influential figure from 1960 to 1972. He distinguished himself as an actor (winning four major awards), as a director, and as artistic director of l'Atelier from 1967 to 1980. Gobeil's most important accomplishment was to break with the classical French theatrical tradition. He introduced new authors such as Samuel Beckett, Eugène Ionesco, Roger Vitrac, Boris Vian, Fernando Arrabal, Murray Schisgal, Edward Albee, and Neil Simon; he produced the works of important Quebec authors; and he staged collective creations, notably *El Théâtre c't'un ben grand mot* and *Maudit qu'c'est platte à T.V. à soir*, both of which achieved enormous local success.

Since 1972 Gobeil has pursued a parallel career as an actor on Quebec television in serials, dramas, and educational programs and in fourteen Quebec films, the most important being *La Gammick* (1973) by Jacques Godbout and *La Quarantaine* (1981) by Anne-Claire Poirier.

HERVÉ DUPUIS

Godin, Jacques (b. 1930). Born in Montreal, he was educated at Les Hautes Études Commerciales and l'Université de Montréal and trained as an actor at the THÉÂTRE DU NOUVEAU MONDE and with Georges Groulx. He has appeared in many television productions for Radio-Canada, including Guy DU-FRESNE's adaptation of John Steinbeck's *Of Mice and Men* (*Des Souris et des hommes*), Arthur Miller's *Death of a Salesman* (*La Mort d'un Commis voyageur*), Garcia Lorca's *Blood Wedding* (*Noces de sang*), Ben Jonson's *Vol-*

pone, and Strindberg's *Miss Julie*. He has also appeared in several television series, notably 'Radisson', '7e Nord', and 'Les belles histoires'.

Godin is equally adept in both English and in his native French. He played Mountjoy in Shakespeare's *Henry V* at the STRATFORD FESTIVAL in 1956, but his stage reputation has been established primarily in Montreal, where he has played in Samuel Beckett's *Endgame (Fin de partie)* and *Waiting for Godot (En attendant Godot)*, and Edward J. Moore's *Seahorse*.

An accomplished film actor, Godin has appeared in some twenty films, including *La Quarantaine* (directed by Anne-Claire Poirier), *Pouvoir intime* (Yves Simoneau), *Equinoxe* (Arthur Lamothe), *Mario* (Jean Beaudin), and several international co-productions, including *The Amateur* and *The Man Inside* (Canada-U.S.A.), and *Le Sang des autres* (France-Canada-Italy). His television films include *L'Ile au trésor* (Germany-France-Canada), and *Sébastien et la Mary Morgane* (France-Canada).

JACQUES LEBEL

Goldby, Derek (b. 1940). Born in Australia, he was educated at Cambridge Univ. and began his professional directing career at London's Royal Court Theatre. He worked at various UK repertory theatres and firmly established his reputation as a leading director of comedy and farce with the première of Tom Stoppard's *Rosencrantz and Guildenstern Are Dead* for the National Theatre in 1967 (taken to Broadway the same year) and the original Broadway production of Joe Orton's *Loot* in 1968. Goldby's first Canadian season was in 1976-7 at the VANCOUVER PLAY-HOUSE, where he directed Molière's *Tartuffe*, Shaw's *Pygmalion*, and Brecht's *A Respectable Wedding*—a production he repeated (with the addition of a controversial rape scene) at the SHAW FESTIVAL in 1980. His brilliant staging of Feydeau's *A Flea in Her Ear* in the same season initiated a successful partnership at the Shaw with actor Heath LAMBERTS in a series of farces and in a memorable version of Edmond Rostand's *Cyrano de Bergerac* in 1982 (revived in 1983). His productions of a violent *Julius Caesar* at the STRATFORD FESTIVAL in 1982, a seamy *Delicatessen* (by François-Louis Tilly) at TORONTO FREE THEATRE in 1984, and a sexually explicit *Spring Awakening* (by Frank Wedekind) at Toronto's ST LAWRENCE CENTRE in 1986 reflect Goldby's conviction

that theatre should be provocative as well as entertaining. Goldby has also directed at the NATIONAL THEATRE SCHOOL, Toronto's TARRAGON THEATRE, the NATIONAL ARTS CENTRE, and London's Grand Theatre (see GRAND OPERA HOUSE), as well as in Belgium and Holland.

L.W. CONOLLY

Goodier, Robert (b. 1912). Born in Montreal, he worked during the 1930s in local revues and night clubs, with the BRAE MANOR THEATRE, and in radio drama. During the Second World War Goodier had a leading role in the NAVY SHOW. He returned to Canada in 1943 and for the next ten years performed with the MONTREAL REPERTORY THEATRE and in radio and film in Canada and the U.S. In 1953 he joined the first STRATFORD FESTIVAL company, playing Richmond in *Richard III* and Dumain in *All's Well That Ends Well*. In 1954 he was Creon in *Oedipus Rex* and an outrageous Barnardine in *Measure for Measure*, followed by Antonio in *The Merchant of Venice* in 1955. From 1956 Goodier pursued other stage and film work, but returned to Stratford in 1960 and 1961. Since then he has concentrated on film and television work, with an occasional small role in Toronto's alternate theatre.

HERBERT WHITTAKER

Gowan, Elsie Park (b. 1905). Born in Scotland, Elsie Park Gowan (née Young) moved to Edmonton in 1912. She attended the Univ. of Alberta (BA, 1930) where, like Gwen Pharis RINGWOOD, she came under the influence of Elizabeth Sterling HAYNES, who directed her in three campus productions. When her rural teaching career (1922-6, 1930-3) ended in 1933 with her marriage to Edward Gowan, a physics professor, she immediately became active in the Edmonton theatre scene.

Gowan's talents as an actress and teacher, like Ringwood's, have been overshadowed by her playwriting. She first attracted notice in the Carnegie Foundation playwriting competitions (administered by the Univ. of Alberta for Albertans), in which her first three plays—*Homestead* in 1932, *The Giant Killer* in 1933, and *The Royal Touch* in 1934—won honourable mention, first, and second place respectively. *The Royal Touch* was published in 1935. Most of Gowan's stage plays were written between 1932 and 1941 and performed by the Edmonton Little Theatre or the Co-operative Commonwealth Youth Movement. While capable of folk tragedy (*God Made the Country*, produced in 1935) and social protest in a serious vein (*Glorious and Free*, co-written with Jim S.C. Wright and produced in 1937), Gowan more often leavened her pacifist, socialist views with wit and humour. Both *You Can't Do That!*, co-written with William Irvine (produced and published in 1936), and her full-length comedy *The Last Caveman*, produced in 1938, were well received, the latter being toured by Sydney RISK's Everyman Theatre in 1946-7. Gowan's comedies remain charming and worthy of production by reason of their dry, urbane wit.

However, with the exception of *Breeches from Bond Street* (produced in 1949, published in 1952), and several civic pageants—including *Who Builds a City* (Edmonton), produced in 1954, and *The Jasper Story*, produced in 1957—Gowan turned mainly to radio writing in the 1940s and 1950s.

Commissioned by the University station CKUA, Gowan's first two series of historical plays for radio—*New Lamps For Old*, co-written with Ringwood, broadcast in 1936-7, and *The Building of Canada*, broadcast in 1937-8—were quickly picked up by the CBC. Between 1939 and 1958 she wrote over 100 scripts for local and national radio, some of which went out over American, British, Australian, and Caribbean airwaves. Many of her series had an educational focus, dealing with Canadian history (*This is Our Heritage*), social concerns or structures (*The Town Grows Up*, *In Search of Mental Health*), or ordinary family life (*The Barlows of Beaver Street*).

Gowan's writing career effectively ended with her husband's death in 1958 but she has continued to serve the city as an actress, speaker, and instructor. Active in Edmonton's theatrical life for over fifty years, Gowan received the Canadian Drama Award in 1942, a provincial Achievement Award for Excellence in Literature in 1977, and an honorary doctorate from the Univ. of Alberta in 1982 for her services as teacher, historian, and playwright.

See Anton Wagner, 'Elsie Park Gowan: Distinctively Canadian', *Theatre History in Canada*, 8 (1987).   MOIRA DAY

Grainger, Tom (b. 1921). Born in Lancashire, Eng., he left school at age fourteen to work in a textile mill. After a stint in the

RAF, he immigrated to Canada in 1956. His first two plays, *Daft Dream Adyin'* (1969) and *The Action Tonight* (1965), won national playwriting prizes in 1964. In 1965 Grainger was awarded a fellowship to the Yale School of Drama. He returned to Canada in 1970, settling permanently in Vancouver.

Between 1964 and 1974 six of Grainger's plays won awards, yet only *The Helper* (1975) received a full professional production—in 1972 at Vancouver's NEW PLAY CENTRE, which also mounted *The Great Grunbaum* (in 1974) and *Roundabout* (in 1976). *Down There* had a major production in Bolton, Eng., in 1975, and *The Injured* (1976), winner of the first Clifford E. Lee Award, was staged semi-professionally at the Univ. of Alberta in 1975. Though critical responses to Grainger's work were almost always enthusiastic, the Canadian professional theatre has largely ignored him. None of Grainger's plays has been produced a second time, and many have not been produced at all.

In the 1960s and early seventies, when Canadian content had come into vogue, Grainger's eclectic dramatic imagination remained focused on England, which provided the setting for the working-class political drama of *Daft Dream Adyin'* and *Down There*, the Pinteresque ironies of *The Helper*, the gothic melodrama of *The Injured*, and *Roundabout*'s Pythonesque comedy. Along with their rich verbal texture, all these plays reveal Grainger's sense of spiritual exile and disillusion, the present unhappily parodying the past and the future mocking the present. Only in *Roundabout* is the characteristic bitterness subsumed in a sprawling comic vision ('imagine Billy Liar as Coco the Clown impersonating Don Quixote in search of Guinevere,' suggested critic Max Wyman), making it the most successful of Grainger's unduly neglected plays.

See Geraldine Anthony, ed., *Stage Voices* (1978).   JERRY WASSERMAN

Grand Cirque Ordinaire, Le. Although a relatively short-lived undertaking, the Grand Cirque Ordinaire was probably the most representative of Quebec's ALTERNATE THEATRE companies. It began in 1969 when the entire graduating class of the NATIONAL THEATRE SCHOOL withdrew in protest against the School's perceived conservatism to set up their own COLLECTIVE CREATION company. Led by Raymond Cloutier, an NTS graduate

Grand Cirque Ordinaire

who had worked with avant-garde companies in Europe, the group included Paule Baillargeon, Lyse Bédard, Jocelyn Bérubé, Suzanne Garceau, Claude Laroche, Marie-Josée Lippens, Hélène Prévost, Jean-Pierre Roy, and Guy Thauvette. They called their productions 'spectacles socio-poétiques', a combination of Brechtian fable and Artaudian communion, and referred to themselves as 'comédiens-créateurs', although Cloutier often provided a basic outline ('canevas') for their improvisations.

The group's first production together was a collection of ten short skits, *POT T.V.*, performed for a student audience at the Université de Montréal in 1968-9. The company's first official performance was *T'es pas tannée, Jeanne d'Arc*, which had a successful run of 180 performances in 1969. Based on Brecht's radio play, the GCO version linked the Joan of Arc story with the historical and contemporary realities of Quebec. The production included skits, monologues, MIME, songs, and giant puppets (see PUPPET THEATRE) to represent the forces of oppression (Church, Justice, Invader). *La Famille transparente*, 1970, attacked the key bourgeois values and power structures of family and consumerism. While each actor drew up his own outline and wrote the songs for his own character, so close was the relationship within the group that these individual scenarios appeared perfectly meshed. The GCO next embarked on straight political theatre with *T'en rappelles-tu, Pibrac, ou le Québecoi?* (*Do You Remember, Pibrac, or the Quebec-What?*). They moved into the small community of Pibrac, attempting with their show to help redress economic grievances. It failed on all levels, and was closed down by the government for bad taste in portraying public figures. The company's next shows, *L'Opéra des pauvres* (*The Poor People's Opera*), 1973, and *La Tragédie Américaine de l'Enfant Prodigue* (*The American Tragedy of the Prodigal Child*), 1975, probed the individual and collective problems of the once close-knit company. Some women in the group seceded to create a show of their own; in 1974, Paule Baillargeon, Suzanne Garceau, and Luce GUILBEAULT produced *Un Prince, mon jour viendra* (*A Prince, My Day Will Come*), a satirical reversal of the traditional fairy tale, ending with a DOCUMENTARY on rape. Although the GCO had lost momentum by 1975, it produced two more shows: *Le Steppette impossible* (*Impossible High-step-*

ping), and *Mandrake chez lui* (*Mandrake at Home*), both in 1976. By 1978 the activities of the GCO had ceased. Cloutier has since commented on the usefulness of oral theatre at that particular time in Quebec, but he has also called for a return to authored plays.

See Michel Belair, *Le Nouveau théâtre québecois* (1973); *Jeu 5* (1977), a special issue on GCO; and Renate Usmiani, *Second Stage: The Alternative Theatre Movement in Canada* (1983).   RENATE USMIANI

Grandmont, Eloi de (1921-70). Born in Baie-du-Febvre, Que., he attended Montreal's École des Beaux-Arts before pursuing studies in Paris from 1946 to 1948. Playwright, poet, screen-writer, storyteller, songwriter, art critic, translator, travel-writer, humorist, scriptwriter, and a radio and television commentator, he was also one of the founders and the first general secretary of the THÉÂTRE DU NOUVEAU MONDE.

De Grandmont's first play, *Un Fils à tuer* (1950), directed by Jean-Louis ROUX, premièred at Montreal's Salle du GESÙ on 4 Oct. 1949. Set in New France, it depicts the struggle between a courageous but inflexible father—blinded by traditional, authoritarian patriotism—and a son eager to seek freedom and adventure in Paris, culminating in the father's murder of his son. Although somewhat contrived, the play has powerful psychological, moral, social, and political overtones. Apart from *Le Temps des fêtes* (1952)—a macabre, cynical, absurdist drama about a murderous mother and daughter who commit suicide one Christmas night while awaiting the return of the prodigal son—de Grandmont's other plays provide lighter fare. *La Fontaine de Paris* (1953), staged in 1954 by the Théâtre du Nouveau Monde, is a farce set in a mythical Middle Ages. *Doux temps des amours* (unpublished), a light musical comedy written in collaboration with Louis-George Carrier, was produced in 1964 at the THÉÂTRE DE MARJOLAINE. A clever adaptation-translation for TNM of Bernard Shaw's *Pygmalion*—which has been produced several times since its première at Expo 67—plays light-heartedly with the varieties of French (notably *joual*) spoken in Quebec.

See Jean-Cléo Godin and Laurent Mailhot, *Le Théâtre Québécois: introduction à dix dramaturges contemporains* (1970).

LAURENT MAILHOT

Grand Opera House (Hamilton). Designed by Toronto architect George Lalor (who also designed the Toronto GRAND OPERA HOUSE), it opened on James St at Gore on 29 Nov. 1880 with a performance of *The Brook* by the Salisbury Troubadours. The second legitimate theatre in Hamilton (the first, the Theatre Royal, burned down in 1868), it was initially managed by a board of directors, but after one unsuccessful season the actor J. R. SPACKMAN was hired as manager. In the early 1880s American impresario C.J. Whitney purchased the Grand and in 1886 made the first of many alterations, increasing seating capacity to 1,226. Tom Reche succeeded Spackman as manager in 1891, immediately prior to extensive renovations that included the installation of cherry-wood seats upholstered in Moroccan leather, marble fittings, an electric switchboard, signal bells, and speaking tubes. In 1895 Reche was succeeded by E.D. Stair. Between 1880 and 1895 the Grand hosted European and American stars Edwin Booth, Sarah Bernhardt, Henry Irving, and John Martin-Harvey, and Canadians Julia ARTHUR and May Robson. The repertoire was generally imported from London and New York, but in 1895 the Canadian play *Ptarmigan* by Jean McIlwraith and John Aldous was produced. Annual visits by the McDOWELL and TAVERNIER companies were also popular with Hamilton audiences.

In 1904 A.J. SMALL bought the Grand for $25,000 and appointed A.R. Loudon as manager. Further renovations were made in 1905; the seating capacity was increased to 1,780. The Grand survived competition from the Savoy Theatre (1906) and Bennett's Theatre (1907), but Small sold the Grand to Trans-Canada Theatres in 1919. As the touring era declined, it fell into disuse as a live theatre and was eventually converted into a movie house, the Granada, before being demolished in Jan. 1962.   KATHLEEN FRASER

Grand Opera House (Kingston). Kingston's first legitimate theatre, William Martin's Opera House opened on 6 Jan. 1879 to capitalize on the period's lucrative touring business. Although its exterior was unprepossessing, the building's 110′ × 64′ interior accommodated a 60′ × 33′ stage with a 30′ wide by 14′ high proscenium fronted by an elaborately frescoed arch. The drop curtain, a scene of St Goar on the Rhine, was designed by William Heney, who also decorated the auditorium, which was lit by chandeliers. There were six dressing rooms, a green room, property room, and four private boxes with chandeliers, damask curtains, and velvet upholstery. The theatre boasted a scene stock that included a snow scene, a street, forest, parlour, garden, prison, and landscape. The acoustics enabled 'the merest whisper . . . [to] be heard in any part of the house'. But after nearly two decades of popular fare—a mix of touring shows, locally-written entertainments, and visits by touring stars—Martin's burned to the ground on 6 Dec. 1898. A joint stock company was formed on 13 Sept. 1899 to build the new Grand Opera House on the same site. It opened on 15 Jan. 1902, leased by Ambrose SMALL. Approximately the same size as Martin's, the Grand had two galleries, four boxes, and modern facilities, including a lighting board capable of controlling 650 electrical instruments. For thirty years the Grand presented professional touring companies (VAUDEVILLE to serious drama) and local amateur productions. As touring declined, however, so did the fortunes of the Grand. From 1938 to 1961 it was a movie house and then remained closed until extensive renovations enabled it to reopen on 26 Apr. 1967 as a live theatre, though devoid of its original character. Since then, with two subsequent renovations, the Grand has operated with a professional management staff booking visiting professional and local amateur shows.   RICHARD PLANT

Grand Opera House (London). Built as part of a Masonic Temple by architects Tracy and Durand, and modelled after the recently opened Madison Square Theatre in New York, it opened on 8 Sept. 1881 under lessee and manager C.J. Whitney of Detroit as part of his expanding theatre-circuit in Ontario, Michigan, and Ohio. Seating 2,070 on the third and fourth floors of the temple, the Grand's proscenium measured 28′ high by 30′ wide; the stage was raked and equipped with spring traps. There were eight dressing-rooms, a luggage and property elevator, a 40′-by-60′ property room and scene dock, and ample lobby space. The building was illuminated by gas, with a specially designed ventilation system.

Because of its excellent rail connections to Detroit, Buffalo, Port Huron, and Toronto, the Grand quickly became a major touring-house, hosting in the 1890s as many as 300 performances annually. Popular entertainments included the minstrel group Thatcher, Primrose, and West; *Uncle Tom's Cabin* with George C. Howard and his wife and daughter; Gilbert and Sullivan productions by the D'Oyly Carte Company; and Barnum's circuses. Major actors who appeared at the Grand included Thomas W. Keene, Lawrence Barrett, Hortense Rhea, Emma Albani, Helena Modjeska, Lily Langtry, Henry Irving and Ellen Terry, Julia ARTHUR, and Sarah Bernhardt.

On 23 Feb. 1900 a major property-room fire destroyed the theatre, and a new building—called the Grand Theatre, four blocks north of the original—was built, opening on 8 Sept. 1901 under the continuing management of Whitney, now in partnership with Canadian impresario Ambrose J. SMALL. According to the *London Free Press* (4 Sept. 1901), it had 'the appearance of a car barn with a cold storage at the rear. Beauty of outline has been slaughtered for business results.' The new Grand was typical of contemporary touring houses, having an ornate proscenium stage of substantial proportions, box seats, and two balconies. The lobby was small, and there was no rehearsal or administrative space. Seating for 1,850 ranged from upholstered seats in the orchestra to wooden benches in the second balcony. But it boasted one stunning feature (both then and now): a

magnificent proscenium arch decorated by an Italian fresco.

From 1901 to 1919 the Grand presented melodramas by the MARKS BROTHERS and the George SUMMERS Stock Company; revues by the DUMBELLS; and syndicated touring shows from the Shubert, Frohman, and Klaw and Erlanger groups in New York. After Whitney's death in 1903, Small sold the Grand, as part of a $1.75 million deal, to Trans-Canada Theatres on 2 Dec. 1919, who in turn sold it to Famous Players in 1924. Small disappeared a few hours after the sale (his ghost is said to haunt the Grand). After twenty years as a movie-house, the Grand was sold by Famous Players to the London Little Theatre, an active and successful amateur group (the losing bidder was a businessman who wished to convert the theatre into a bowling alley).

By the late 1960s, after years of great popularity, the London Little Theatre was in an artistic rut, with declining ticket sales, and decided to turn professional. This was achieved over a three-year period and coincided with Heinar Piller's term as artistic director from 1971 to 1976, when it became known as Theatre London (its corporate name) and The Grand Theatre (its public name). In 1975 a major restoration and reconstruction project was undertaken at a cost of $5.5 million, $3 million of which was raised

The Grand Theatre, London, Ont. (following 1970s restoration)

before construction began, such was the popularity of the theatre. The proscenium arch and boxes were preserved, but the rest of the theatre is new, and includes ample rehearsal and administrative space as well as a substantial lobby and bar. The seating was reduced to 829, with the new McManus Studio Theatre in the basement accommodating a further 300. The theatre re-opened in 1978 with a production of Cole Porter's *Kiss Me Kate*. William HUTT, the artistic director from 1976 to 1980, was succeeded by Bernard Hopkins (1981-3).

Since turning professional, theatre at the Grand has on the whole benefited from its proximity to the SHAW and STRATFORD FESTIVALs, some of whose actors and directors have worked at the Grand. The 1983-4 season was under the artistic direction of Robin PHILLIPS. He ignored a subscription system that had been in place for over forty years— a serious miscalculation—and, though artistically splendid, his season was a financial disaster, incurring million-dollar losses. Phillips was succeeded by Don Shipley (1984-6), Larry Lillo (1986-8), and Martha HENRY (1988-). The Grand now offers a balanced repertoire of drama and musicals, showcasing Canadian plays whenever possible.

KATHLEEN FRASER

Grand Opera House (Ottawa). Also known as Gowan's New Opera House, it was built in 1875 to replace a hall on Sparks St known as Gowan's Opera House (later St James Hall). The new $40,000 brick structure at 134 Albert St, near Metcalfe, had a capacity of 1,000, the same as HER MAJESTY'S THEATRE, which the Grand succeeded as the centre of cultural entertainment in the capital (with the exception of RIDEAU HALL).

The gala opening on 1 Feb. 1875—a performance by the Toronto-based HOLMAN Opera Company of Michael Balfe's opera *The Bohemian Girl*—was attended by the Governor General and Lady Dufferin. Bellini's *La Sonnambula* opened the second night, followed by four subsequent Holman productions that week.

The theatre brought to Ottawa some of the finest actors and companies of the English, French, Canadian, and American stages: tragedian T.C. King, who played seven lead roles in one week in 1875, including Macbeth, Hamlet, and Othello with the HERNDON Opera Troupe; Mrs Scott-Siddons; the come-

dian E.A. Sothern; Mary Anderson; Charlotte MORRISON; Charlotte Thompson; James O'Neill; Lawrence Barrett; Clara MORRIS; the Parisian Company (performing plays in French); the E.A. McDOWELL Company; the Soldene Company; J.T. Raymond and his Superb Dramatic Company; the Shaughraun Company; and General Tom Thumb and his Wife. In 1876 the Grand remounted a Rideau Hall success of the previous year, F.A. DIXON's and F.W. Mills's *The Maire of St. Brieux*; in 1879 it hosted Dixon's and Arthur A. Clappé's masque, *Canada's Welcome*, for the new Governor General Lord Lorne and Princess Louise; and in 1880 W.H. FULLER's *H.M.S. Parliament* was produced. Shakespeare, Tom Taylor, T.W. Robertson, Dion Boucicault, and Gilbert and Sullivan were among the Grand's most popular playwrights.

Gowan sold the Grand in 1877, and it subsequently changed hands several times; John Ferguson was manager for a time until 1898. When the RUSSELL THEATRE was built in 1897, the Grand went into decline; melodramas and VAUDEVILLE featured more prominently among its fare, and then came BURLESQUEs, bioscopes, motion pictures, and wrestling.

On 5 July 1913 the Grand Opera House was destroyed by fire, along with the Nickel Theatre, which was beside it. Its age of elegance had been over for some time, yet it served the Ottawa community longer than its predecessor, Her Majesty's, or its successor, the Russell.

See Mary M. Brown and Natalie Rewa, 'Ottawa Calendar of Performance in the 1870s', *Theatre History in Canada*, 4 (1983).

JAMES NOONAN

Grand Opera House (Toronto). In Mar. 1873 the Toronto Opera House Company, which included Charlotte MORRISON and leading members of the community, was incorporated with a mandate to build a larger and more modern theatre than the existing ROYAL LYCEUM. The Grand Opera House opened on Adelaide St, west of Yonge, on 21 Sept. 1874 with a performance of Sheridan's *School for Scandal* under the patronage of Lord Dufferin and the management of Charlotte Morrison. The four-storey building, seating 2,196, was designed by the Toronto firm of Lalor and Martin in consultation with Thomas R. Jackson, the American architect

Grand Opera House (Toronto)

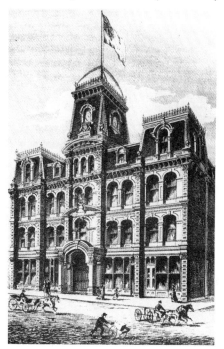

Grand Opera House, Toronto

Grand Opera House lost many major American touring attractions. According to critic Hector Charlesworth, the Grand 'lost its ancient glory from the very day Small entered its doors as proprietor, and never recovered it.' The theatre, however, remained part of the largest touring circuit in Canada, controlled by Small, in association with C.J. Whitney of Detroit.

In 1928, after the Grand had been empty for several years, it was demolished. For approximately thirty years it had been an important source of Toronto entertainment, presenting significant companies that developed touring in Canada—the McDOWELLS, the HOLMANS, the TAVERNIERS, Denman THOMPSON, and McKee RANKIN; international stars such as James O'Neill and Edwin Booth; and some Canadian plays, including W.H. FULLER's *H.M.S. Parliament* (8–13 Mar. 1880) and Clay M. Greene's *Louis Riel; or, The North-West Rebellion* (5 Jan. 1886)—though American and British melodramas and comedies dominated its repertoire.

KATHLEEN FRASER

of New York's Academy of Music. It burned down in 1879, but a new theatre, similar in design, was completed within fifty-one working days, opening on 9 Feb. 1880 with a performance of *Romeo and Juliet* starring English actress Adelaide Neilson. The stage measurements—35′ wide by 50′ deep—were the same as those of the original structure, but the proscenium arch was increased from 30 to 50 feet; 'chaste and ornate' in design, the arch was elliptical, panelled, and supported by six Corinthian columns. The interior was decorated in white, gold, and pink, and dressing rooms, property rooms, and business office were provided.

Oliver Barton Sheppard was appointed business manager in 1876 by the theatre's owner, Alexander Manning; Augustus Pitou succeeded Charlotte Morrison in 1878 as manager. In 1903 the theatre was purchased by Ambrose SMALL, who ousted Sheppard in 1906; Sheppard took his experience, along with his booking rights with the New York Klaw and Erlanger touring agency, to the rival PRINCESS THEATRE. When the New York Shubert organization took its business to the ROYAL ALEXANDRA THEATRE, the

Grands départs, Les. Jacques LANGUIRAND's most accomplished play, written in 1957, was strongly influenced by the Theatre of the Absurd. The plot concerns a family's vain and trying wait for movers to transport them to smaller, poorer living-quarters. With suitcases packed, furniture scattered about the room, the paralysed grandfather lying somewhere on a mattress among the luggage, the family quarrel and talk, marking time before death, the only possible departure. Nothing happens in the play and no one really leaves.

Hector, the father, is a contemptible intellectual, an unsuccessful writer who lives off his wife's savings. Systematically he uses his intelligence to destroy his family's last illusions. None of the characters are defined physically, psychologically or socially. They are weak, silly, unable to relate to each other—puppets bearing witness to a pathetic and ridiculous humanity.

Although considered Languirand's best play, *Les grands départs* has had limited impact. It questions the ability of language to communicate, implying through its satire that all words are mendacious. Such an attitude ran counter to the mood of Quebec's writers at the time when poets like Anne HÉBERT and Gaston Miron were affirming the omnipotence of the word and when playwrights Gratien GÉLINAS and Marcel DUBÉ had reached the Quebec public with their socio-realistic dramas written in a popular French-Canadian idiom.

Commissioned by Radio Canada, *Les grands départs* was written in approximately three weeks and was televised on 1 Oct. 1957. It premièred on stage at the summer theatre in Percé, on 8 July 1958, with Languirand's own company. It has been produced at the Théâtre de Poche in Geneva (Feb. 1960), in London (as *The Departures*), notably at the Royal Court Theatre, and by the CANADIAN PLAYERS (in 1966). In 1966 it was also broadcast in Spanish on Mexican television.

First published in 1958 (Montreal: Cercle du livre de France), the play has also been edited and annotated by Renald Bérubé (1970). An English translation, *The Departures*, by Albert Bermel, was published in *Gambit*, 5 (1966).   MONIQUE GENUIST

Grand Théâtre de Québec, Le. Built as a 1967 Centennial project for Quebec City, and opened on 16 Jan. 1971, it was designed by architect Victor Prus for a site on Quebec's Parliament Hill. The building houses two theatres—the Louis-Fréchette Theatre and the Octave-Crémazie Theatre—as well as rehearsal rooms, an art gallery, and the premises of the Conservatoire de musique de Qué-

bec. With its 1,800 seats, thirty boxes, 1,200-square-metre stage, and its sophisticated lighting and sound facilities, the Louis-Fréchette theatre is by far the best equipped in Eastern Quebec for large presentations such as opera and ballet. More flexible and adaptable, the Octave-Crémazie theatre can accommodate between 200 and 800 people, depending on the type of performance. The stage can be oblong, thrust, or converted to theatre-in-the-round.

The mandate of La Société du Grand Théâtre de Québec—the theatre's governing body, whose members are appointed by the Quebec government—is to present a broad and balanced spectrum of cultural events to a wide cross-section of the public, including young audiences. By 1986 some six million spectators had seen 7,000 performances of 2,400 different shows. About sixty per cent of the shows are given by resident companies: the Quebec Symphony Orchestra, le THÉÂTRE DU TRIDENT, l'Opéra de Québec, and le Club Musical de Québec. Le Grand Théâtre also produces its own shows as well as presenting those by visiting companies.

                      CHANTAL HÉBERT

Gray, Jack (b. 1927). Born in Detroit, Mich., he studied playwriting with Robert GILL at Toronto's HART HOUSE THEATRE

Le Grand Théâtre de Québec

245

from 1948 to 1950 before becoming assistant editor of *Maclean's* (1953-7). After the production of two of his early plays at Toronto's CREST THEATRE—*Bright Sun at Midnight* in 1957 and *Ride a Pink Horse*, with music by Louis Applebaum, in 1959—he went to England to write television and stage dramas, including the revue *Clap Hands* (produced in 1962). On returning to Canada he became the first playwright-in-residence at the NEPTUNE THEATRE in Halifax, writing the historical drama *Louisbourg*, directed by Leon MAJOR in Mar. 1964 and later published as *Chevalier Johnstone* (1972). His *Emmanuel Xoc* (unpublished) was produced at the Crest in 1965; *Susannah, Agnes and Ruth* (1972) remains unproduced. Traditional in form and sceptical in tone, Gray's plays reveal an almost sentimental admiration for the underdog breaking free from social, religious, and psychological oppression.

During the 1960s Gray wrote for both Canadian and British television, and also taught at the Univ. of Waterloo (1969-71) before taking a BA (1972) and MA (1973) at the Univ. of Toronto. During the 1970s he had an active career as a cultural administrator: Secretary General of the Canadian Theatre Centre (1971-3), Canadian President of the International Writers Guild (1974-84), Chairman of the Writers' Council of the Alliance of Canadian Cinema, Television and Radio Artists (ACTRA) (1972-7), and then National President of ACTRA (1977-82). Meanwhile his comedy *Striker Schneiderman* (1973) was produced at the ST. LAWRENCE CENTRE in Feb. 1970. He wrote the screenplay adaptation of Andrew Angus Dalrymple's stage play *Quiet Day in Belfast* (1973-4) and he edited a Canadian drama series for the Univ. of Toronto Press (1972-5). A vigorous advocate of Canada's cultural independence, he has helped write policy documents for the Canadian Conference of the Arts, including *A Strategy for Culture* (1980) and *The Third Strategy* (1984), and has been a consultant and speech-writer for the Minister of Communications.   DENIS SALTER

Gray, John (b. 1946). Born in Ottawa into a musical family, he was raised in Truro, N.S. In 1968 he graduated from Mount Allison Univ. with a BA in English. While a student he played organ and trumpet with a local band, an experience that became the basis for his musical *Rock and Roll*. He trained as a

director at the Univ. of B.C., graduating in 1972 with an MA in theatre.

Until 1975 Gray worked in Vancouver theatres and was a founding member of TAMAHNOUS THEATRE. When he moved to Toronto he joined Paul THOMPSON and Eric PETERSON at THEATRE PASSE MURAILLE as a director. He composed incidental music for many plays, including Rick SALUTIN's *1837: The Farmers' Revolt* and *The False Messiah*, and Herschel HARDIN's *Great Wave of Civilization*. Gray's own musical drama, *18 Wheels*, premièred at Theatre Passe Muraille in 1977, with subsequent productions at Tamahnous, FESTIVAL LENNOXVILLE, Toronto's TARRAGON THEATRE, and throughout Canada. An unsentimental series of vignettes on the lives of truckers, *18 Wheels* was followed by *BILLY BISHOP GOES TO WAR*, Gray's greatest success to date.

Rock and Roll (1982) was a co-production of the VANCOUVER EAST CULTURAL CENTRE and the NATIONAL ARTS CENTRE, where it premièred in 1981. Based on a 1978 reunion concert of Gray's band in Truro, the semi-autobiographical story is set in the fictional town of Mushaboom, N.S. It captures the spirit of the rock groups of the 1960s, without glamorizing the difficulties and insecurities of such a life. It toured B.C. in 1981 and was revived for a national tour in 1983; it was also presented on CBC radio in 1982. Gray adapted the musical for a quite different but successful film version entitled *The King of Friday Night*, which premièred on CBC television in 1985.

Gray's nostalgia for Canadiana was emphasized again in his 1985 musical *Don Messer's Jubilee*, based on the life and television career of the famous PEI fiddler. Halifax's NEPTUNE THEATRE production went on national tour that year. Gray's major non-musical production, a farce-thriller entitled *You Better Watch Out, You Better Not Die*, premièred at Neptune Theatre in 1983. He is currently working on a screen adaptation of Erika RITTER's comedy *AUTOMATIC PILOT*.

Gray has written children's plays, notably two commissioned by the Vancouver Children's Festival, *Bongo from the Congo* (with Eric Peterson), and *Balthazar and the Major Star*. For the B.C. Pavilion at Expo '86 he composed eighteen eight-minute musicals.

His writings include two novels: *Dazzled* (1984), an uproarious but far-fetched satire on marriage breakdown, business enterprise, television, and the consumer society of the 1970s, and *Stage Fright* (unpublished), about the backstage life of a regional theatre company. An outspoken nationalist, Gray writes in the introduction to *Billy Bishop Goes to War*: 'We export natural resources and we import culture—that's our lot in life.' While Gray's forte is his music and lyrics, he has not yet combined this with carefully developed plot or complexity of character. His musical theatre has usually been based on well-known stories and individuals rather than original material.

See Robert Wallace and Cynthia Zimmerman, eds., *The Work* (1982), and *Local Boy Makes Good: Three Musicals by John Gray* (1987), which contains *18 Wheels*, *Rock and Roll*, and *Don Messer's Jubilee*.

JAMES NOONAN

Great Canadian Theatre Company. It was founded in Ottawa in 1975 by a group of teachers and students from Carleton University, including Bill Law (artistic director, 1976-8), Robin Mathews, Larry McDonald (artistic director, 1978-81), Greg Reid, and Lois Shannon. The company performed in various halls until 1982, when it converted an industrial garage into a 218-seat theatre at a cost of nearly $400,000, met by government grants and 700 private donations. GCTC's mandate has been to mount only Canadian plays, to use local Canadian talent, and whenever possible to produce works on local subjects or dealing with significant political or social issues. Since opening on 29 July 1975, the company has staged an average of four plays annually and conducted workshops and an extensive children's program. About one-third of the productions have been premières, including *Yonder Lies the Valley*, 1975, by Bernie Bedore; *Chaudière Strike*, 1977, by Gerald Potter; *Selkirk*, 1976, and *For Love—Quebec*, 1978, by the first playwright-in-residence, Robin Mathews; and *Cheap Thrill*, 1985, and *Zero Hour*, 1986, by Arthur Milner, also playwright-in-residence. GCTC has also demonstrated its left-wing and populist orientation through a number of revues and COLLECTIVE CREATIONs, as well as agit-prop works performed at labour rallies and meetings of organizations such as the Canadian Civil Liberties Association. By far the most important and ambitious work of this nature has been *Sandinista!*, a 1982 collective based on the Nicaraguan revolution

and directed by artistic director Patrick McDonald (1981-8). Despite the critics' initial, hostile reaction to the social orientation of its programming, GCTC has become the longest-lived professional anglophone theatre in Ottawa. Steven Bush became artistic director in 1988.

See also POLITICAL AND POPULAR THEATRE; Léa V. Usin, ' "A Local Habitation and a Name'': Ottawa's Great Canadian Theatre Company', *Theatre History in Canada*, 7 (1986) and a 'Response' by Robin Mathews, *Theatre History in Canada*, 8 (1987).

LÉA V. USIN

Green Thumb Theatre for Young People. Founded in 1975 in Vancouver by Dennis Foon and Jane Howard Baker, this touring company performs only new plays. To date some one million children in Canada, the United States, England, Germany, and Australia have seen Green Thumb shows. Early repertoire was unorthodox, lively, and eclectic. Foon contributed *Heracles* (1978), a dark look at heroes; *Raft Baby* (1978), in which two British Columbia lumberjacks 'adopt' an abandoned baby; and *The Windigo* (1978), a vivid dramatization of an Ojibway tale of cannibalism. 1977's *Shadowdance*—developed by director Yurek Bogajewicz, his cast, and playwright Sheldon ROSEN—was an evocation of medieval times called by Foon 'a sort of *Seventh Seal* for kids'. The unusually high interest in Joe Wiesenfeld's candid comedy about divorce, *Hilary's Birthday*, produced in 1979, convinced the company to specialize in drama that reflects the direct experience of the audience. In 1977 director/playwright Campbell Smith created the popular musical *Juve* (1980), after interviewing three hundred adolescents. *New Kid* (first produced in 1981 as *New Canadian Kid* and published in 1982) and *Invisible Kid* (1985), playing as a double bill in London, won Foon the British Theatre Association prize for best playwright for young people in 1986. Both plays treat the trauma of being foreign; *NewKid* reverses the immigrant experience by having newcomers speak English and natives gibberish. Colin Thomas's *One Thousand Cranes* (1983) is a lyrical but disturbing play about nuclear war in which a Canadian boy's naive idealism is contrasted with a Japanese girl's death from radiation sickness. It won the CHALMERS Award for Best Children's Play in 1984. The National Film Board's 1984 documentary of

247

Green Thumb Theatre

Green Thumb's *Feeling Yes, Feeling No* (first produced in workshop, 1982) has become a widely used and highly praised teaching tool in the prevention of child sexual abuse. In 1988 the company toured Foon's *Liars* (1986) and John Lazarus's *Night Light* (1987)—about the problems of alcoholism in the family and childhood fears, respectively—across Canada and into the U.S. Patrick McDonald, formerly of the GREAT CANADIAN THEATRE COMPANY, succeeded Foon as artistic director, also in 1988.

See *Canadian Theatre Review*, 37 (1983), 39 (1984), and 41 (1984). See also CHILDREN'S DRAMA AND THEATRE IN ENGLISH.

JOYCE DOOLITTLE

Robert Christie, Lorne Green, Donald Davis, and Lloyd Bochner in Julius Caesar, *Stratford Festival, 1955*

Greene, Lorne (1915-87). Born in Ottawa, he earned a BA from Queen's Univ. in 1937 and studied at the Neighborhood Playhouse School of the Theatre in New York, returning to Canada to become the chief newscaster for CBC Radio (1939-42) as well as acting in CBC radio plays. After serving in the Canadian army during the war, he returned to Toronto where he again worked in radio. He started the Academy of Radio Arts (1946-53) in Toronto, helped found and act with the short-lived JUPITER THEATRE, and acted with the Earle GREY Players and the NEW PLAY SOCIETY. Frustrated by Canada's limited opportunities for professional actors, he went to New York, where he appeared with Katharine Cornell in *The Prescott Proposals* (by Howard Lindsay and Russel Crouse) in 1953 and with José Ferrer in Milton Geiger's *Edwin Booth* in 1958. He fulfilled a lifelong interest in classical acting by playing Brutus in Michael LANGHAM's 1955 production of *Julius Caesar* at the STRATFORD FESTIVAL, making a strong impression with his 'massive presence' and 'big voice', followed in the same season by a stately Prince of Morocco in Tyrone GUTHRIE's *The Merchant of Venice*. However much they admired Greene's physical gifts, influential critics (e.g. Brooks Atkinson of the *New York Times*) found his interpretations lacklustre, and his classical career did not flourish. His handsome face, rugged dignity, and deep throaty voice, however, brought him international acclaim as the patriarch Ben Cartwright in the highly successful American television serial 'Bonanza' (1959-73); he also gave creditable performances in other television dramas and on film.

DENIS SALTER

Grey, Earle (1892-1978). A Dublin-born actor and director, he and his wife, actress Mary Godwin, came to Canada as performers on a 1939 British tour and decided to stay. Noting the success of the occasional summertime Shakespearean productions at Toronto's ROYAL ALEXANDRA THEATRE, where they had performed, Grey and Godwin formed the Earle Grey Players and made their début in the summer of 1946 with a production of *Twelfth Night*, performed outdoors for two nights in the quadrangle at Trinity College, Univ. of Toronto. Other productions—both indoors and outdoors—followed, but it was not until 1949 that they formally established the Earle Grey Shakespeare Festival, which continued to present professional productions of three or four of Shakespeare's plays for up to five weeks each summer until 1958. School productions toured throughout Ontario and (in 1957 and 1958) into the Maritimes as well. In order to train a new generation of actors experienced in the classics, Grey established the Festival Drama School in 1953 under voice specialist Lillian Graham.

Like the actor-managers of the nineteenth century, Grey starred in most productions and directed many of them, sharing that work with stage director Charles Palmer. Grey strove for historical accuracy and high professional standards, eschewing the eccentric and vowing to 'perform Shakespeare's plays in the closest possible accord with the original intention and spirit of the dramatist.' The simple platform stage at Trinity College, used since 1946, was rebuilt in 1954 in the Elizabethan manner. With ten entrances on

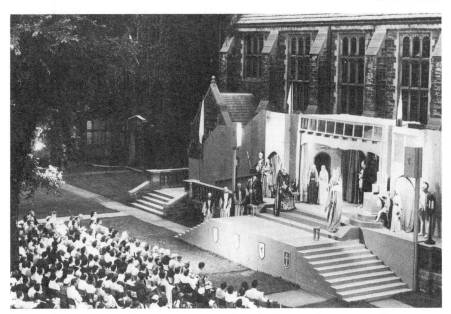

The Earle Grey Players performing The Winter's Tale *in the quad of Trinity College, University of Toronto, 1957*

three levels, the new stage enabled Grey to present productions with the speed and flow of those at the STRATFORD FESTIVAL. However, the Earle Grey Shakespeare Festival could not compete with Stratford for the limited pool of talented classical actors in Canada in the 1950s. His productions inevitably suffered in comparison with Tyrone GUTHRIE's highly publicized productions at Stratford, with their professional gloss and well-known stars. After struggling on for six years in a losing battle with Stratford, the Earle Grey Shakespeare Festival dissolved after the 1958 season when it lost the use of its Trinity College space and was unable to find another suitable location. Earle Grey returned to England in 1960 and there continued his profession as an actor and director for the BBC and organized the Stage Cricket Club for performers. He died at the age of 86. ROSS STUART

Griffiths, Linda (b. 1953). Born in Montreal, she attended Dawson College and the NATIONAL THEATRE SCHOOL, before earning a teacher's diploma from McGill Univ. After early acting experience with Saskatoon's 25TH STREET THEATRE, she became well known as co-author (with Paul THOMPSON) of, and actress in, *Maggie and Pierre* (1980), a one-person play about Pierre and Margaret Tru-

deau. First performed at Toronto's THEATRE PASSE MURAILLE in Nov. 1979, *Maggie and Pierre* won Griffiths Dora Mavor MOORE awards for best new play and outstanding performance, 1979-80. Griffiths is also one of the original writer-performers of *PAPER WHEAT* (1978), a collective about the Saskatchewan Co-operative movement, first performed by 25th Street Theatre in Mar. 1977. She has participated in many of Paul Thompson's COLLECTIVE CREATIONs, including *Les Maudits Anglais* (1984; produced by TPM, Nov. 1978), and *Shakespeare for Fun and Profit: A Canadian Dream* (TPM, Sept. 1977, unpublished). Griffiths is co-author with Patrick Brymer of *O.D. on Paradise* (TPM and 25th Street Theatre co-production in Feb. 1982, unpublished), winner of a Dora for best new play, 1982-3, and of *Jessica* (TPM, Mar. 1986, unpublished), also a Dora winner for best new play, 1985-6. She has also appeared in film and on television. JUDITH RUDAKOFF

Guilbeault, Luce (b. 1935). Born in Montreal, she was educated at the Conservatoire de la Province de Québec and the Université de Montréal, where she took a BA in philosophy. Her acting career—which began in earnest in 1971—includes over twenty Canadian films, including Denys Arcand's *La Maudite*

Guilbeault

Galette, Francis Mankiewicz's *Le Temps d'une chasse*, and Anne-Claire Poirier's *Albedo*. Her theatrical repertoire comprises roles in such diverse plays as Pirandello's *Six Characters in Search of an Author*, Maeterlinck's *The Blue Bird*, Réjean DUCHARME's *Le Cid maghané*, Racine's *Britannicus*, and Denise Boucher's *Les FÉES ONT SOIF*. In 'Des Dames de coeur', a 1986 Canadian television series written by Lise Payette, Guilbeault played a fiercely competitive and overly adoring mother—one of many singular women she has portrayed.

Guilbeault studied at the Cité International des Arts in Paris in 1978-9, when she also trained as a trapeze artist at the École Pierre Bergham. She has taught at the NATIONAL THEATRE SCHOOL and at the Université du Québec à Montréal. In 1976 she won a Canadian Film Award for best actress in *Bargain Basement*, and in 1977 she founded the film production house, Les Reines du foyer.

KENNETH W. MEADWELL

Guimond, Olivier (1914-71). Son of dancer Effie Mac and Olivier Guimond *père* (the most famous comic of the 1920s and 1930s in Montreal), he made his début in the St Catherine Street cabarets in 1932 playing the straight man. In 1933 he joined his father's company and took the name 'Exhaust'. Several months later he established himself in the comic role that made him famous, adopting his father's stage name, Tizoune. From 1935 he was with the Jean Grimaldi troupe, and from 1948 to 1957 with the Théâtre Radio-Cité, where he shared the spotlight with Manda Parent and Paul Desmarteaux. From 1958 to 1970 he played several roles on CFTM-TV, notably in the series 'Cré Basile', which ran from Sept. 1965 to June 1970; his performance in 'Bye-Bye '70' for Radio-Canada was equally memorable. During the same period he made a cabaret appearance in the revue 'Pique Atout', and played at the THÉÂTRE DES VARIÉTÉS.

First trained by his father, from whom he acquired several small 'turns', Tizoune developed a visual style of comedy in which his 'funny faces' and physical gestures had a remarkable effect. His most popular creations were as a drunkard and in a number of 'drag' roles. It is noteworthy that, unusually for burlesque artists, his exceptionally fine acting was recognized by the CBC.

See also BURLESQUE (Quebec).

JEAN CLÉO GODIN

Robert Gurik

Gurik, Robert (b. 1932). Born in Paris of Hungarian parents, he has lived in Montreal since 1950. While still a practising professional engineer, he published his first play, the one-act *Le Chant du poète* (1963). Co-founder and several times president of the Centre d'essai des auteurs dramatiques, he has written some twenty plays (several of them unpublished).

Strongly influenced by French playwright Armand Gatti, Gurik is interested in the environment, communications, and the overconsumption of the post-industrial age. Satirical farces, fables, and parables, his plays develop into scientific, mathematical, or technical games: of numbers in *Les Louis d'or* (1966); of blocks in *Le Tabernacle à trois étages* (1972); and of an interminable chess match in *Lénine* (1975).

Of the early plays, *Les Louis d'or*—an examination of human identity that is both Pirandellian and Brechtian, with a cast of two men and one woman playing multiple roles—is a mix of boulevard light comedy and *commedia dell'arte*, while *Api 2967* (1971), which premièred at Le Théâtre de l'Egrégore in 1967 and was subsequently performed in Paris and Vienna, predicts a technological aseptic future that denies humanity. Two characters, A (Adam?) and E (Eve?) find an old manuscript and attempt to understand forgotten words and concepts such as love, pleasure, and sin. *Le PENDU* (1970), which treats Judeo-Christian myth and the Bible, was judged best Canadian play at the DOMINION DRAMA FESTIVAL finals in 1967.

Hamlet, Prince du Québec (1968), first produced in 1968 by Montreal's L'Escale, is unquestionably Gurik's most successful play. Gurik brilliantly adapts Shakespeare to comment on contemporary Quebec politics: Hamlet represents Quebec; Horatio, René Lévesque; Polonius, Lester Pearson; Ophelia, Jean Lesage; Laertes, Pierre Trudeau; Rosencrantz and Guildenstern, Jean Marchand and Gérard Pelletier; and Charles de Gaulle appears as the Ghost. As Hamlet dies, a new social and political order for Quebec is ready to emerge. Compared to *Hamlet*, other overtly political plays such as *À coeur ouvert* (1969), first produced by Le THÉÂTRE DE QUAT'SOUS in 1969, about organ transplants and the imperialist appetites of the U.S., and *Les Tas de siège* (1971) (a pun on 'l'état de siège', state of siege), which deals with the October Crisis of 1970, are more journalistic than theatrical.

Le Procès de Jean-Baptiste M. (1972), first produced in 1972 at Le THÉÂTRE DU NOUVEAU MONDE, is based on the 1971 assassination of three executives of a Montreal company by a paranoid employee. It skilfully exploits the contradictions of capitalism, the dilution of the concept of responsibility ('society cannot be guilty'), and society's fear of success.

In the 1980s Gurik turned his attention to 'practical literature': eye-witness accounts, documentaries, and dramatizations of social problems.

Gurik has published two novels, *Spirales* (1966) and *Jeune Délinquant* (1980). Some of his plays have been collected in *Les Tas de siège* (1971) and *Sept courts pièces* (1974).

See Hélène Beauchamp-Rank, 'Pour un réel théâtral objectif—le théâtre de Robert Gurik', *Voix et images du pays 8* (1974); and Jean-Cléo Godin and Laurent Mailhot, *Le Théâtre québécois II: nouveaux auteurs, autres spectacles* (1980).   LAURENT MAILHOT

Guthrie, Tyrone (1900-71). Born in Tunbridge Wells, Eng., great-grandson of the

Tom Patterson, Tanya Moiseiwitsch, Tyrone Guthrie, Stratford Festival, 1953

Irish actor Tyrone Power (and a fourth cousin of the film star of that name), he attended a military school, Wellington, but at Oxford was drawn into amateur acting and on graduation joined J.B. Fagan's Oxford Playhouse company. Too tall (6′ 4″) to succeed as an actor, he moved to the infant British Broadcasting Corporation, and at its Belfast station acquired a reputation as a radio producer and playwright. In 1930 the Canadian National Railway hired him to produce for its radio network a historical series, 'The Romance of Canada', by Merrill DENISON. As a bonus for his winter in Montreal, the CNR gave him a return trip next spring to Victoria, B.C. In Toronto he met Dora Mavor MOORE, cousin of his friend James Bridie; twenty-two years later she was instrumental in bringing him to the STRATFORD FESTIVAL.

In England Guthrie was recruited by Lilian Baylis, manager of the Old Vic, as its resident director, first for a trial year in 1933-4, then on a continuing basis from 1936. He mounted three brilliant seasons before the Second World War, notable for Laurence Olivier's Hamlet, Henry V, and Coriolanus. In 1940, when the Vic was bombed, Guthrie moved operations to Lancashire and toured the provinces for four years. In 1944 he assembled the great company led by Olivier and Ralph Richardson that opened at the New Theatre in his production of Ibsen's *Peer Gynt*. It was instantly recognized as the seed of a national theatre, but before the postwar Labour government announced plans for this in 1946,

Guthrie had resigned, exhausted by differences with Olivier and Richardson and with the Vic's governors. Following the dismissal of Olivier and Richardson from the Vic in 1948, Guthrie returned briefly but unhappily (1951-2). This was when a cable from Dora Mavor Moore brought him back to Canada to advise on the formation of a Shakespeare Festival at Stratford.

It seems clear that Guthrie's intention was to create a national theatre for Canada. In 1945 he had discussed with his friends Brenda and Robertson DAVIES how a company might tour Canada by train, playing under a circus tent. He had long believed that Shakespeare's plays work best on a naked platform, with the audience on three sides, as in the Elizabethan theatre. Canada, with its postwar oil wealth and cultural ambitions, seemed ideal for an experiment testing this belief. As artistic director of the Stratford Festival, with his designer Tanya MOISEIWITSCH, he devised the wooden platform onto which Alec Guinness sidled as Richard III on 13 July 1953, the opening night.

That winter, Stratford's success established, emissaries attempted unsuccessfully to persuade Calgary or Vancouver to build a second similar stage. Guthrie's hopes of sustaining a year-round ensemble faded when his spectacular revival of Christopher Marlowe's *Tamburlaine the Great*, with Stratford actors, flopped in New York in 1956. Deciding that the best hope for a permanent North American classical theatre lay in the U.S., he handed over Stratford to his protegé Michael LANGHAM and launched the campaign that culminated in the opening of the Guthrie Theatre in Minneapolis in 1963. After 1957, apart from two Gilbert and Sullivan operettas, he did not work again at Stratford, though he continued to direct in the U.S. and Britain. Guthrie's six productions on the Festival stage, however, included some of his finest work, and illustrated what a national theatre might do: display a nation's history, as in *Richard III* (1953); discuss its public morality, as in his *Merchant of Venice* (1955); imagine happy endings (*All's Well That Ends Well*, 1953); tell family jokes (*The Taming of the Shrew*, 1954); purge in ritual mankind's deepest fears and passions (*Oedipus Rex*, 1954-5), or simply celebrate life's joy and brevity (*Twelfth Night*, 1957). Hoping his stage would engender an equally ambitious Canadian drama, confronting man and cosmos on its timeless platform, Guthrie overlooked the preference of young national dramatists for local realism, as well as the difficulty his stage posed for directors less skilled than he in maintaining focus amid shifting three-dimensional groupings. He also failed to confront the problem of creating a national theatre for a nation with two languages. Nevertheless he gave Canada what Harley Granville-Barker called an 'exemplary theatre': a school and model for theatres across North America, and a superb theatrical instrument that was to be copied around the world.

Guthrie published his autobiography, *A Life in the Theatre*, in 1960, and was knighted in 1961. See James Forsyth, *Tyrone Guthrie* (1976).   RONALD BRYDEN

Guy, Jean (b. 1940). Born in Quebec City, he was educated at various schools there and the CONSERVATOIRE D'ART DRAMATIQUE DU QUÉBEC, graduating in 1964. He became assistant to Jean Valcourt that year at the Conservatoire in Montreal, returning to the Quebec City's Conservatoire in 1966 to teach modern theatre; he became director of the Conservatoire in 1971.

Guy has played light comedy in SUMMER STOCK and more serious work at Quebec City's L'Estoc, Le THÉÂTRE DU TRIDENT, and other theatres in plays by Samuel Beckett, André RICARD, Marc Doré, and Bertrand Leblanc, *et al*. He has also appeared in his own plays, including *Rex, le dernier des romantiques*, based on the life of Mackenzie King. For Laval University's Troupe des Treize he directed Jean BARBEAU's early plays, winning a DOMINION DRAMA FESTIVAL award in 1968 for directing Barbeau's *Et caetera*.

Guy has founded several small theatre companies, including La Grenouille, Le Théâtre de Maintenant, and Le Théâtre du Carnaval. He also founded Le Théâtre du Vieux Québec in 1966. Dissolved in 1970 when it merged with other companies to form Le Trident, TVQ was revived in 1975 as a CABARET theatre. In 1978 Guy retired from the Conservatoire and in 1981 mounted his one-man show, *De fil en aiguille*, in Quebec City. He has since founded another company, Les Productions Desmaures (1983), has appeared on television and in film, and has returned to teaching at the Conservatoire.

MARTINE CORRIVAULT

H

Halford, Allan (1838-88). Beginning in 1859, this Toronto-born actor learned his craft under successive managers at Toronto's ROYAL LYCEUM, and later toured with J. C. Myers and the HOLMANs. He appeared intermittently at the three theatres that replaced the Royal Lyceum, and acted for varying periods in Buffalo, Rochester, Montreal, and Hamilton. Possessed of a fine stage presence, he played leading roles, including the gentlemanly villain in Dion Boucicault's *Formosa* and the gallant sailor William in Douglas Jerrold's *Black-Eyed Susan*. Although he had neither poetic nor comic talent, and was often criticized for stiffness and obtrusive mannerisms, a wide circle of friends invariably welcomed his appearances. A daughter, Ollie, went on the stage as a child in such roles as Little Eva in *Uncle Tom's Cabin*.

MARY SHORTT

Hall, Amelia (*c*. 1916-84). One of the most distinguished and versatile figures in Canadian theatre, she was born in Leeds, Eng., and brought to Hamilton, Ont., at the age of five. She studied at McMaster University (BA, 1938) and taught school in Ottawa for eight years, but became increasingly involved in theatre, helping to found the Junior Theatre of the Ottawa Drama League. She studied movement with Frances Robinson Duff in New York and voice with Clara Salisbury Baker at the Toronto Conservatory of Music, and acted at the BRAE MANOR THEATRE in 1945 and 1947, and with Joy Thomson's Canadian Art Theatre in 1948, before leaving teaching to work full-time in the theatre. At the MONTREAL REPERTORY THEATRE in the spring of 1949 she played Amanda in Tennessee Williams' *The Glass Menagerie* and directed Ronald Duncan's *This Way to the Tomb*. In the summer she toured with the Canadian Art Theatre, and in the autumn of 1949 travelled to Edinburgh with the Ottawa Drama League's production of Robertson DAVIES' *Eros at Breakfast* (playing Hepatica). In Nov. 1949 she joined the CANADIAN REPERTORY THEATRE in Ottawa, serving as artistic director from 1950 to 1954. During this period she appeared in most of its 150-odd productions and directed about forty of them—including an adaptation by John Col-

Amelia Hall and Alec Guinness in Richard III, *Stratford Festival, 1953*

ton and Clemence Randolph of Somerset Maugham's *Rain* (with Christopher PLUMMER and Betty LEIGHTON), Oliver Goldsmith's *She Stoops to Conquer*, and Robert Sherwood's *The Petrified Forest* (with Richard EASTON). In the summers she acted with the Canadian Art Theatre, touring Quebec (1950); the Red Barn Theatre (1951); the Straw Hat Players (1952); and at the newly formed STRATFORD FESTIVAL in 1953, where she was the first woman to speak on the stage, as Lady Anne opposite Alec Guinness's Richard III.

Hall became a valued member of the Stratford company, playing a wide range of roles, from the Widow in *All's Well That Ends Well* (in 1953) to the nurse in *Romeo and Juliet* (1968) and Mrs Hardcastle in *She Stoops To Conquer* (1973). Based in Toronto from 1954, she appeared regularly with the CREST THEATRE (1954-7, 1959-60)—notably in Graham Greene's *The Living Room* (in 1954), William Inge's *Come Back, Little Sheba* (1956), and Chekhov's *The Three Sisters* (1956-7)—and toured with the CANADIAN PLAYERS (1955, 1963-5). She appeared on Broadway in Robertson Davies' *Love and Libel* in 1960, directed by Tyrone GUTHRIE. Most of Hall's career, however, was spent acting in Canadian theatres, including the MANITOBA THEATRE CENTRE (1965-6, 1970), Ottawa's TOWN THEATRE (1969), THEATRE TORONTO (1968-9), the SHAW FESTIVAL (1970, 1978), and the NATIONAL ARTS CENTRE (1970, 1975-7)—in James REANEY's *The Easter Egg* (1970) and *The Killdeer* (1975), and in Timothy FINDLEY's *Can You See Me Yet?* (1976). At Queen's Univ. in 1960 she created the role of Emily Carr in Herman VOADEN's *Emily Carr*.

Hall's career included work in film, radio, and especially television. She appeared in CBC drama during the 1950s, and, as she had done in 1950, in Mazo de la Roche's *The Whiteoaks of Jalna* in the early 1970s. Her last appearance on the stage was in Terence Rattigan's *Separate Tables* for the Stratford Festival at the ROYAL ALEXANDRA THEATRE, Toronto, in 1984.   HERBERT WHITTAKER

Hamilton, Barbara (b. 1921). Born in Toronto and educated in Coburg, Ont., she played at HART HOUSE THEATRE before getting her first major role in 1943 in Joseph Kesselring's *Arsenic and Old Lace* at Toronto's ROYAL ALEXANDRA THEATRE (where she has played in more productions—thirteen in all— than any other actor in the theatre's history). After a role in a 1951 Broadway revue, *Razzle Dazzle*, which folded quickly, she toured with the CANADIAN PLAYERS before working for three seasons with a stock company in Bermuda. She joined the cast of SPRING THAW in 1958, establishing a reputation as 'The Funniest Woman in Canada' in her seven-year association with the revue. She starred in her own revue *That Hamilton Woman* at Toronto's CREST THEATRE, where she also acted in Alexander Ostrovsky's *Diary of a Scoundrel* (in 1955), Eugene O'Neill's *Ah, Wilderness!* (1957), Jean Giraudoux's *The Madwoman of Chaillot* (1961), and other plays. A frequent performer at the CHARLOTTE-TOWN FESTIVAL, she created the role of Marilla in ANNE OF GREEN GABLES in 1965, confirming that she could play serious parts (as she had demonstrated when she played Amanda in a Canadian Players' production of Tennessee Williams' *The Glass Menagerie* in its 1965-6 season). When she repeated the role of Marilla in London, Eng., in 1970, she won the London drama critics' award for best actress. Notable performances since then include the two-woman feminist revue *Sweet Reason*, with Sandra O'Neill, and Nikolai

Erdman's *The Suicide*, both in 1976; Anthony Marriott's and Alistair Foot's *No Sex Please, We're British*, 1985; and, in 1987, the role of Lady Catherine de Bourgh in David Pownall's adaptation of Jane Austen's *Pride and Prejudice* at the Royal Alexandra Theatre.

EUGENE BENSON

Handscomb, Charles Wesley (1867-1906). Born in Dover, Eng., he immigrated to Clinton, Ont., in the early 1870s, and moved to Winnipeg in 1879. In 1886 the E.A. McDOWELL Company presented his melodrama *The Big Boom* at the PRINCESS OPERA HOUSE in Winnipeg; the play (not extant) satirizes the real-estate boom in Manitoba in the early 1880s. He became a journalist, and by the mid 1890s was chief drama and music critic for the *Manitoba Free Press*. In 1898 he founded a weekly magazine of social and artistic comment, *Town Topics*.

Handscomb was a close friend of Winnipeg's leading theatre manager, C.P. WALKER, and strongly supported his efforts to win acceptance for theatre among Winnipeg's church-going mercantile élite. Handscomb's reviews emphasized the virtues of morally uplifting plays and attacked any that might draw criticism from Winnipeg's Protestant pulpits. Thus he condemned Sardou's *Tosca* and Tolstoy's *Resurrection*, and called Ibsen's *Ghosts* 'smut—just plain smut'. Handscomb attributed the immorality of some of the plays he reviewed to the 'decadence' of the American and European cities from which Winnipeg imported its theatre, and emphasized the special standards drama must submit to in 'this morally healthy western community'. Handscomb's concern to distance himself from the values of the international theatre reinforced the strain of Canadian nationalism in his criticism. He warned of the dangerous effects of American patriotic dramas on Canadian youth, and strongly supported Harold Nelson SHAW in his efforts to create a uniquely Canadian school of dramatic art, looking toward the day when Winnipeggers might see 'dramas telling Canadian stories, with Canadian heroes and extolling our own Canadian flag.' DOUGLAS ARRELL

Hardin, Herschel (b. 1936). Born and raised in Vegreville, Alta, he graduated in philosophy from Queen's Univ., Kingston, in 1958, after which he toured northern Europe for two years before settling in West Vancouver, where he currently lives. The author of four plays, Hardin is best known for *Esker Mike and His Wife, Agiluk* (1973), an episodic play that uses sixteen 'scenes from life in the Mackenzie River Delta' (the play's subtitle) to depict the economic destruction of Canada's North. Although written in 1967 and published in *The Drama Review* (14, Fall 1969), the play was not produced until 1971, by Toronto's FACTORY THEATRE Lab. Subsequently, one of Hardin's earlier plays, *The Great Wave of Civilization* (1976), written in 1962, was produced by FESTIVAL LENNOX-VILLE in 1976, directed by Paul THOMPSON. The generally Brechtian style of these two plays is more overtly developed in the other play Hardin wrote prior to *Esker Mike*: an adaptation of Brecht's *Threepenny Opera* entitled *School for Swindle*, which, like *William Lyon Mackenzie, Part I*, written in 1968, remains unpublished and unproduced.

Hardin's reputation as a playwright rests almost entirely on the acclaim accorded *Esker Mike* by critics and scholars, and on its wide circulation in Canadian high schools and universities. Focusing on Agiluk, an Inuit woman who murders two of her children to compensate for her exploitation by her husband, Hardin creates a stark and desperate metaphor for a village culture doomed to extinction by Southern opportunism and deceit. The merits of the play were reappraised when it received a major revival at Toronto's World Stage Festival in May 1986. Generally unfavourable reviews called into question the play's reputation as an important contribution to Canadian theatre.

Hardin continues to write, but not for the stage. His two most important books are *A Nation Unaware* (1974), a study of Canadian economic policy, and *Closed Circuits: The Sellout of Canadian Television* (1985).

ROBERT WALLACE

Harron, Donald (b. 1924). Born in Toronto, he served in the RCAF in the Second World War before taking his BA at the Univ. of Toronto. While still a student he appeared in NEW PLAY SOCIETY productions, and in Feb. 1950 performed in and directed the NPS première of John COULTER's *Riel*. In 1950 he also appeared (with Vivien Leigh) in Tennessee Williams' *A Streetcar Named Desire* at the Aldwych Theatre, London. He made his Broadway début in Oct. 1951 in Christopher Fry's *A Sleep of Prisoners*, and was a member of the first STRATFORD FESTIVAL company in 1953. In 1953-4 Harron acted and studied at the Bristol Old Vic. His American career continued with the American Shakespeare Festival in the 1950s, and in 1958 he toured the U.S. as Jimmy Porter in John Osborne's *Look Back in Anger*. Despite Harron's talents as a leading man and character actor, his stage appearances since then have been sporadic.

Harron wrote scripts for NPS's SPRING THAW, and his farce, *The Broken Jug* (adapted from Heinrich von Kleist), premièred in London, Ont., in Feb. 1958. His stage adaptation of L.M. Montgomery's ANNE OF GREEN GABLES (music by Norman Campbell) premièred at the CHARLOTTETOWN FESTIVAL in 1965. He has performed and written for radio and television throughout his career. He has had great success impersonating, and writing the monologues of two comic characters of his own invention: Charlie Farquharson, the hayseed from Parry Sound, and Valerie Rosedale, the Toronto matron. Farquharson's malapropisms and creative misuse of language combine in witty social and political satire and have spawned several popular books. In 1969 Harron married his third wife, singer Catherine McKinnon.

See Martha Harron, *Don Harron: A Parent Contradiction* (1988).   L.W. CONOLLY

Hart House Theatre. When Hart House in the Univ. of Toronto was built in 1919 by the trustees of the Massey Foundation under the direction of its administrator, Vincent MASSEY, to provide for the non-academic interests of the university's undergraduates, a theatre was built in its basement, although it had not been included in the original plans. The architects of Hart House and the new theatre were Sproatt and Rolph of Toronto, and the theatre was planned and equipped under the close supervision of Vincent Massey and his wife Alice. In later years Massey would both direct and act in the theatre, as did his brother Raymond MASSEY.

Seating up to 500, with a proscenium opening 30' wide by 15' high and the stage 22' deep, and technically very advanced (the stage switchboard was the third largest in North America), the theatre had facilities for constructing its own scenery, properties, and costumes. Under director Roy MITCHELL (1919-21) the first season consisted of Lord

Hart House Theatre

Hart House Theatre stage and auditorium

Dunsany's *The Queen's Enemies*, the anonymous *The Farce of Master Pierre Patelin*, Ben Jonson's *The Alchemist*, the Chester Mysteries of *The Nativity* and *The Adoration*, Euripides' *The Trojan Women*, Basil Hastings' *The New Sin*, and Shakespeare's *Love's Labour's Lost*. Generally a season consisted of eight or nine plays, each running for a week, and each season (after the first) included at least one play by a Canadian author. Merrill DENISON's *Brothers in Arms*, for example, was produced in the 1920-1 season, and Carroll AIKINS' *The God of Gods* in 1921-2. (Vincent Massey subsequently edited two volumes of *Canadian Plays from Hart House Theatre* (1926-7).) The first season's productions were representative of the ambitious nature of the theatre's programming—in the next decade plays by Ibsen, O'Casey, Synge, Maeterlinck, Yeats, and particularly Shaw were regularly offered, putting Hart House Theatre at the forefront of the LITTLE THEATRE movement in Canada. Directors before the Second World War were Mitchell, Bertram Forsyth (1921-5), Walter Sinclair (1925-7), Carrol Aikins (1927-9), Edgar Stone (1929-37), and Nancy Pyper (1937-9).

Before the Second World War, Hart House Theatre's activities were dominated by aspiring or accomplished actors and not by students. They included Ivor Lewis, Raymond Massey, Lorna McLean, George Patton, Rauff Acklom ('David Manners'), Randolph Crowe, Alfred J. Rostance, Freddie Mallett, Andrew ALLAN, Frank Peddie, H.E. Hitchman, Agnes Muldrew, Kirby Hawkes, Elaine Wodson, Grace Webster, Florence McGee, Judith EVELYN, and Jane MALLETT. Healey Willan was director of music; Group of Seven members Lawren Harris, Arthur Lismer, A.Y. Jackson, and J.E.H. MacDonald designed and painted sets for plays in the 1920s.

In 1946 control of Hart House Theatre was transferred from a Board of Syndics to the Univ. of Toronto and greater student involvment was encouraged, though only as an extra-curricular, non-credit activity. Robert GILL was appointed director; his opening production of the 1946-7 season was Shaw's *Saint Joan* with Charmion KING creating headlines in the title role. Post-war students at the theatre included Donald DAVIS and Murray DAVIS, William HUTT, Kate REID, Anna Cameron, Henry Kaplan, Ted Follows, Eric HOUSE, David GARDNER, Donald SUTHERLAND, Araby LOCKHART, Donald HARRON, George McCowan, Bea Lennard, and Jack GRAY. Attracted by Gill's professionalism, they were exposed to the classics as well as to contemporary masterpieces—Shakespeare, Shaw, Chekhov, Cocteau, Thornton

Wilder, and Tennessee Williams.

In 1966 the Senate of the Univ. of Toronto approved the establishment of the Graduate Centre for Study of Drama, which assumed control of Hart House, using it to stage its major productions, often under such guest directors as David Gardner, William Hutt, Leon MAJOR, Desmond Scott, and Herbert WHITTAKER. Major was director of productions from 1968 to 1970. On 1 May 1986 the Graduate Centre severed its administrative links with the theatre, which is now available, on a rental basis, for student, community, and professional productions. The spread of professional theatre in Toronto in the 1970s diminished the importance of Hart House Theatre, but it has an illustrious place in the development of Canadian theatre as 'a dynamic force in the artistic life of the community' (Merrill Denison).

HERBERT WHITTAKER

Hart's Opera House. This wooden structure originally served as a roller-skating rink in Port Moody, British Columbia, during the construction of the Canadian Pacific Railway, fulfilling the same purpose when transferred to the terminus of the railroad, Vancouver, in 1886. When, in Dec. 1887, it opened as a theatre and assembly hall known as Hart's Opera House it had the distinction of being the first building in the city to be explicitly identified as a theatre. Its location on Carrall St placed it in the heart of the original townsite; nearby buildings included a saloon, an opium factory, and a gambling hall. Its owner, Frank William Hart, was an entrepreneur of Swedish extraction who had emigrated from the United States. The building measured 50′ × 130′, and its seating (and standing) capacity varied according to the occasion. Performances on the makeshift stage included a mixture of local amateur productions and brief visits from touring companies presenting minstrel shows, musicals, opera, variety-vaudeville, and legitimate theatrical productions. Hart's did not long survive the opening of the IMPERIAL OPERA HOUSE in Apr. 1889. The last recorded performance featured Lucille B. Griffin in 'Lifelike Imitations and Mimicry' in June of that year.

R.B. TODD

Hausvater, Alexandre (b. 1949). Born in Bucharest, Romania, he immigrated to Israel with his mother at the age of twelve. At twenty he moved to Ireland, where he studied theatre and joined the Abbey Theatre, soon becoming director of its experimental Peacock Theatre. He returned to Israel, founded a troupe, and during the 1967 war presented political theatre from a truck that travelled from village to village. These performances, considered offensive by the authorities, were suppressed and Hausvater, disenchanted with Israel, came to Montreal in 1971. Starting with his own English-Canadian companies Neo-Mythos and the Montreal Theatre Lab, he quickly became a bilingual free-lance director.

Hausvater's work, noted for its bold stage imagery and shock tactics, invariably arouses extreme reactions from both audiences and critics. His two major goals are to create productions that are strongly, if not overtly, political and to breathe new life into accepted masterpieces. Like Brecht, he looks to the classics to provide him with the raw material for a personal vision of the present: 'The masterpieces are there to survive . . . one has to find through the text a modern way to stage them.' Hausvater's concept of a 'modern way' often leads to theatrical *tours de force*, such as *Solzhenitsyn* done in Noh style, *The Decameron* set in a concentration camp, *The Seagull* beginning with Act Four. Some of his most interesting work has been done at the tiny THÉÂTRE DE QUAT'SOUS in Montreal; it includes an adaptation of Kafka's *Metamorphosis* (performed in 1980) that used a giant net strung across the stage as the central image. Hausvater's interpretation hinted at incest between Gregor and Grete, his sister. The controversial *Decameron* drew parallels between the physical plague and fascism; the director's main interest lay in exploring 'what happens to comedy when you have a gun pointed at your head.' Hausvater has directed other notable productions in Montreal, Buffalo, and Ottawa. His production of Peter Handke's *Kaspar* toured Ontario in 1977.

Some of Hausvater's adaptations—*The Crime and Punishment Show* (1978), *Solzhenitsyn* (1979), *Comrade Pioneer* (1980), and *The Decameron* (1982)—have been published by Playwrights Canada.

RENATE USMIANI

Hawthorn, Pam (b. 1939). Born in Trail, B.C., she attended the Univ. of British Columbia and Yale Drama School (MFA). After two years teaching in the U.S., she was co-associate director of HOLIDAY THEATRE, Vancouver, in 1968-9. In 1972 she became artistic and managing director of Vancouver's NEW PLAY CENTRE, where she has promoted substantial growth. For the Centre she directed Sheldon ROSEN's *Ned and Jack* in Nov. 1977, Tom CONE's *Beautiful Tigers* in May 1976, Eric NICOL's *Ma* in Apr. 1981, Leonard ANGEL's *The Unveiling* in May 1982, and Betty LAMBERT's *Under the Skin* in Nov. 1985. Her directing elsewhere reflects her commitment to Canadian works: Joe Weisenfeld's *Jack Spratt* for the VANCOUVER PLAYHOUSE, John MURRELL's *WAITING FOR THE PARADE* for West Coast Actors, and Dennis Foon's *Raft Baby* for GREEN THUMB THEATRE FOR YOUNG PEOPLE. As well as directing at the GLOBE, Regina, she has directed twice at the STRATFORD FESTIVAL: Cone's *Stargazing* in 1978 and Shakespeare's *The Taming of the Shrew* in 1979. Also an actress, Hawthorn has taught both acting and playwriting.   MALCOLM PAGE

Haynes, Elizabeth Sterling (1897-1957). Born in England, she immigrated in 1905 to Ontario, where as a Univ. of Toronto student she came under the influence of Roy MITCHELL. In the 1919-20 season she acted in two of Mitchell's HART HOUSE THEATRE productions and was profoundly impressed by his philosophy of theatre. She moved with her dentist husband to Edmonton in 1922 and over the next decade established herself as a theatrical force in the province as director of the Univ. of Alberta's Dramatic Society productions (1923-4, 1927-32), first artistic director of the Edmonton Little Theatre (1929-32), founding member of the Alberta Drama League (1929), and drama instructor for the Department of Education Summer School (1929, 1931-2).

In 1932, with the help of a Carnegie Foundation grant, Haynes became the first drama specialist for the Dept. of Extension, Univ. of Alberta. From 1932 to 1937 she travelled extensively across the province, helping with school and community productions, lecturing, demonstrating, teaching, adjudicating, writing, and broadcasting. Through the Banff School of Fine Arts (see BANFF CENTRE), which she co-founded with E.A. Corbett in 1933, her influence as an educator spread to the rest of Western Canada. Her influence was also evident in Alberta's becoming the first province to put drama on the secondary-school curriculum in 1936. In 1937-8 she worked with the New Brunswick Dept. of Education, supervising the dramatic and literary phases of their new education program.

Haynes was also a director, actor, and supporter of the Univ. of Alberta's Department of Drama and Studio Theatre in the early 1950s. However, she is primarily remembered as an important pioneer in the educational and community drama movements of the 1920s and 1930s.

See Moira Day and Marilyn Potts, 'Elizabeth Sterling Haynes: Initiator of Alberta Theatre', *Theatre History in Canada*, 8 (1987).
                    MOIRA DAY

Head, Guts and Sound Bone Dance, The. Michael COOK's play was first performed at the ARTS AND CULTURE CENTRE, St John's, Nfld, on 4 Mar. 1973, and subsequently at the SAIDYE BRONFMAN CENTRE, Montreal; THEATRE NEW BRUNSWICK; the GLOBE, Regina; and on CBC television. The head, guts, and sound bone (i.e. backbone) are the parts of a fish discarded by humans; the dance is both the ritual of gutting fish and an actual drunken step-dance that briefly makes the men in the play 'all one, all free'. The subtitle, 'a controversial play that deals with Newfoundland's future,' is ironic: the men are old, there are no fish to catch, a child drowns. If Newfoundland *has* a future, the play predicts a bland, safe future of television and electric blankets, a far cry from the harsh, heroic tradition represented by its fishermen.

The drama occurs in the course of a single day in a 'splitting room on a fishing stage' in an outport, where Skipper Pete, a heroic but despotic captain in his mid-80s, and his son-in-law, Uncle John, work. Pete is decisive, John a would-be rebel. Pete knits nets and John attaches twine to a stone-anchor—a futile activity when the fish are gone and the two men are so old. These 'elaborate rituals' are part of the 'presentational' techniques that fascinate audiences by their precision and skill. Act I concludes with a child calling for help for a drowning boy. The old men, sunk in reverie, wilfully ignore the child's plea and the boy drowns. Critics have seen this scene as either a gratuitous piece of violence or as 'a thin device' to arouse Uncle John to escape the Skipper's control.

In Act 2 Pete's retarded only son, Absalom, returns with a catch of six cod that are gutted; they celebrate, drinking 'shine' and dancing. Absalom recovers the body of the drowned child and John, realizing his responsibility, leaves. Pete, alone at the end, sings and eats the fish.

Apart from the distinctive Newfoundland language, the drama's strength is in the portrait of Pete—tyrannical, powerful, pathetic. Though he is wrong, much is lost when the world has no use for men with his traditional values and abilities. Cook has commented that his aim was to achieve 'classic tragedy . . . When [Pete] shuts the door at the end, he shuts out the world, and he shuts himself in forever. That defiant song that rises from his mouth is meant to be tragic. He has failed to adapt.' (R. Wallace and C. Zimmerman, eds., *The Work*, 1982.) The play was published in *Canadian Theatre Review*, 1 (1974), by Breakwater Press (1974), and in Michael Cook, *Three Plays* (1977).   MALCOLM PAGE

Heavysege, Charles (1816-1876). Born 16 May 1816, probably in Liverpool, Eng., he spent his childhood in a poor home. Leaving school at nine, he was apprenticed to a woodcarver. Heavysege later remembered that he was 'what is usually styled religiously brought up . . . and taught to consider not only the theatre itself, but dramatic literature, even in its best examples, as forbidden things.' He was largely self-educated, developing an admiration for Milton and Shakespeare. When he saw *Macbeth* on the stage he conceived a never-fulfilled ambition to become an actor. With the Bible, one has the sum of Heavysege's early literary influences; Byron was added later. Heavysege eventually set up his own woodcarving shop in Liverpool, but increasingly diverted his energy to poetry. His first work, *The Revolt of Tartarus*, a mock-Miltonic epic, appeared in 1852. The following year Heavysege immigrated to Montreal, continuing as a woodcarver until 1860; then he became a newspaper reporter, and eventually city editor of the *Montreal Witness* until 1874, two years before his death of 'nervous exhaustion'.

During his Canadian years, Heavysege published a bad novel, *The Advocate* (1865), *Sonnets* (1855), which contains some of the most powerful Canadian Victorian verse, some narrative poems, and two plays, *Saul* (1857) and *Count Filippo; or, the Unequal Marriage* (1860). Neither play was produced in Heavysege's lifetime. He prepared an acting version of *Saul*, which the American actress Charlotte Cushman talked of producing, but nothing came of the idea, though it may have been this abridgement that Heavysege himself read publicly in 1862 at the Nordheimer Hall, Montreal, the only semblance of a production either of his plays got in his lifetime.

Heavysege's contemporaries accepted his plays as closet dramas to be read, not seen; Hawthorne, Longfellow, and Coventry Patmore praised their literary merits. *Saul* is an immense and clumsily constructed play; the second (and best) edition (1859) runs to 328 pages. Like *Count Filippo*, it has no relation to the Canadian world Heavysege adopted or the English world he left behind, though it was certainly influenced by the revival of Elizabethan and Jacobean dramatists in which Charles Lamb and William Hazlitt were active during his boyhood. While in form *Saul* belongs among Victorian closet dramas, in its archaic and orotund language it relates to the pre-Commonwealth seventeenth century and in concept to the Satanic succession that runs from Milton through Byron. The struggle between God and devil in *Paradise Lost* is transmuted—under the perceptible influence of Byron's *Cain*—into the struggle between arbitrary God and compassionate man. Critics have debated how far *Saul* consciously defies Christian orthodoxy; observing Heavysege's close involvement in Saul's predicament, it is hard to read it without suspecting that Heavysege was of the devil's party (as Blake said of Milton) and knew it.

Count Filippo, an Italianate morality about marriage—especially marriage between generations—is a much lesser work, a tragi-comedy with occasional flashes of surprising wit, influenced by Vittorio Alfieri in plot—he also wrote a play called *Filippo*—and Beaumont and Fletcher in diction.

Count Filippo and *Saul*, abridged by Peter Howarth, were broadcast by CBC Radio in 1968 and 1973 respectively. Director Norman Newton claimed, with some justice, that *Saul*, 'in spite of its flaws,' was 'the only significant religious drama written in English since *Samson Agonistes*.' *Saul* and *Filippo* were reprinted in 1973 in facsimile editions; Sandra Djwa's introduction to *Saul and Selected Poems* (1976) and George Woodcock's *Charles Heavysege* (1987) are the fullest essays on Heavysege to date. GEORGE WOODCOCK

Hébert

Anne Hébert

Hébert, Anne (b. 1916). Born at Sainte-Catherine-de-Fossambault, Que., she was encouraged to write by her father, who was a literary critic, and in her youth she was strongly influenced by her cousin, the poet Hector de Saint-Denys Garneau. In 1942 Hébert published her first volume of poems *Les Songes en équilibre*, for which she won the Prix David. *Le Torrent*, a collection of short stories, appeared in 1950. A 1954 grant from the Royal Society of Canada enabled her to visit Paris, which became her second home. A succession of rich novels followed: *Les Chambres de bois* (1958), *Kamouraska* (1970), *Les Enfants du sabbat* (1975), *Héloïse* (1980), *Les Fous de bassan* (1982), and *Le premier jardin* (1988). Hébert won Governor General Awards for *Poèmes* in 1960 and for *Les Enfants du sabbat* in 1975 and the Prix Femina for *Les Fous de bassan*.

Although her theatrical work is less well known, it is an integral part of her *oeuvre*. Hébert developed an avid interest in theatre long before she became a scriptwriter for the National Film Board of Canada and for Radio Canada, 1950-4. Her first play, *L'Arche de Midi* (written in 1944-5, unpublished, not produced), which she calls a 'poème drama-

tique en trois actes', unfolds in an unspecified place and time during war and is concerned primarily with a mother, Elisabeth, and her daughter Marie. Elisabeth, 'la complaisante', is at peace with herself; Marie, however, has been marked by the teachings of a puritanical society and her sexuality is crippled. When she finally seeks happiness with a suitor, she is killed. Typically, Hébert suggests that love is destined to be thwarted and that happiness is illusory.

Hébert's next three plays—*Les Invités au procès*, *La Mercière assassinée*, and *Le Temps sauvage*—were published in a single volume, *Le Temps sauvage*, in 1967. *Les Invités au procès*, another 'poème dramatique', was written for radio and was first broadcast on 20 July 1952 by Radio Canada in the series 'Le Théâtre du Grand Prix'. The trial in the play—the 'procès'—is presided over by a traveller, the Voyageur, who turns out to be Satan. The key characters represent mankind, corrupted by a primal and inexplicable crime that is symbolized by an extraordinary black flower. In this play the fantastic and the surreal intermingle, cause and effect are irrelevant, and montage replaces plot and conventional structure.

La Mercière assassinée, a television play, is a detective story that examines an individual's right to a dignified existence. A Canadian journalist travelling through France becomes involved in, and solves, a mysterious crime— the seemingly motiveless murder of an elderly haberdasher, Adélaïde Menthe. A series of flashbacks reveal that Adélaïde had been deeply humiliated by degenerate friends and members of an upper-class family, and had dedicated her life to executing them; eventually she is murdered by Olivier, the last member of the family. The play was first televised in four parts in July and August 1958 by Radio Canada in the series 'Quatuor', and was first published in *Écrits du Canada français*, 4 (1958). An English translation of *Les Invités au procès* and *La Mercière assassinée* by Eugene Benson and Renate Benson was published in *Canadian Drama*, 9 (1983) and 10 (1984).

Le Temps sauvage was first performed on 8 Oct. 1966 by the THÉÂTRE DU NOUVEAU MONDE at the Palais Montcalm, Quebec City. This more conventional four-act play is set in an isolated mansion in the mountainous Quebec countryside, and portrays a dramatic struggle between a domineering mother,

Agnès, and her children, who seek freedom and education away from the stifling atmosphere of their home. Agnès is typical of Hébert's embittered female figures damaged by a male- and clergy-dominated society. Her niece Isabelle, who is guided by instinct and her love for life, is likewise a typical protagonist. Agnès's final consent to allow her children to leave the maternal home is analogous to Quebec's liberation from a repressive past.

L'Île de la demoiselle, a radio play first published in *Écrits du Canada français*, 42 (1979), but not produced, dramatizes the 1542 expedition of de Roberval from France to Canada when he fell in love with his niece, Marguerite de Nontron. She rejects him for her lover, Nicolas, and de Roberval abandons them on a desert island with Marguerite's confidante, Charlotte. Charlotte, Nicolas, and Marguerite's baby die; but Marguerite survives to become a symbol of all the women who faced and overcame the dangers of the New World.

Hébert's numerous awards include membership in the Royal Society of Canada (1960), the Prix Duvernay (1958), and the Molson Prize of the Canada Council (1967).
RENATE BENSON

Hébert, Paul (b. 1924). Born at Thetford Mines, Que., and educated at the Collège de Lévis and Université Laval, he made his acting début with the Comédiens de la Nef de Québec in 1945. In 1949 he received a grant from the British Arts Council to study at London's Old Vic, followed by further training in Europe.

In 1952 Hébert moved to Montreal, where for twenty years he acted in radio, television, and film, and acted, directed, and wrote for the stage. He helped found the Anjou Theatre in Montreal in 1954 and, with Albert Millaire, the Chanteclerc summer theatre at Sainte-Adèle in 1956, which featured works from the international repertoire as well as Canadian plays by Yves THÉRIAULT, Marcel DUBÉ, Félix LECLERC, Gratien GÉLINAS, Jacques LANGUIRAND, and Françoise LORANGER.

In 1959 Hébert became assistant director to Gratien Gélinas at the COMÉDIE-CANADIENNE and in 1961 he founded the Esterel Theatre in the Laurentians. He taught at the NATIONAL THEATRE SCHOOL from its inception, was a member of the board and vice-president of the NATIONAL ARTS CENTRE,

and in 1969 became director of both the Montreal and Quebec City CONSERVATOIRES D'ART DRAMATIQUE.

Hébert left Montreal in 1970 to devote his time entirely to the Conservatoire in Quebec City, where he also founded the THÉÂTRE DU TRIDENT. He was artistic director there until 1974, and again in 1976 and 1978. In 1982 he founded the Paul Hébert Theatre, on l'Île d'Orléans, where he has lived since the mid-seventies.

As a screen actor Hébert works in both English and French. In 1965 he appeared in Gilles Carle's *La Vie heureuse de Léopold Z*, which marked the beginning of fictional cinematic works in Quebec. He played in a half-dozen other films, including *Les Beaux souvenirs*, a 1982 film by Frank Mankiewicz, and Denise Benoit's 1985 *Le Dernier havre*, adapted from a story by Yves Thériault.

Hébert's work as a director includes Shaw's *Pygmalion*, Arthur Miller's *Death of a Salesman* (*La Mort d'un commis-voyageur*), and Thomas McDONOUGH's *CHARBONNEAU & LE CHEF*. In 1973 he received the Victor-Morin prize from the Saint-Jean-Baptiste Society in Montreal for his contribution to Quebec culture, and in 1984 he was awarded an honorary doctorate by the Université du Québec.
MARTINE R. CORRIVAULT

Heeley, Desmond (b. 1930). Born in England, he began his career in Birmingham and Stratford-upon-Avon, where he designed costumes for a production of *Toad of Toad Hall* at the Memorial Theatre in Dec. 1948. He subsequently designed sets and costumes for numerous productions in Stratford-upon-Avon and London throughout the 1950s and 1960s. In 1957 he immigrated to Canada and in the same year designed *Hamlet*, starring Christopher PLUMMER, for the STRATFORD FESTIVAL, thus beginning a long association with the Festival. A brilliant and innovative designer of sets and costumes, Heeley created a sumptuous *Cyrano de Bergerac* at Stratford in 1962 and 1963 (designed with Tanya MOISEIWITSCH), a colourful *Troilus and Cressida* (1963), and an evocative *The Country Wife* (1964). His lighthearted *The Three Musketeers* (1968) found its opposite in a stern, strong, and dark *The Duchess of Malfi* (1971). His designs for *She Stoops to Conquer* (1972) were reused the following year.

In 1968 Heeley won two Tony awards for costumes and sets for the New York production of Tom Stoppard's *Rosencrantz and Guildenstern are Dead*. He is also well known for his work in ballet, having designed for the National Ballet of Canada, the Australian Ballet, the Royal Swedish Ballet, the Stuttgart Ballet, and the American Ballet Theatre. In 1978 Heeley designed *Don Pasquale* for New York's Metropolitan Opera, followed by *Manon Lescaut* in 1980 and other operas. He now makes his home in New York.

MARTHA MANN

Heide, Christopher (b. 1951). Born in Summerside, PEI, he was educated mainly in Ottawa before moving to Nova Scotia. His plays were first produced by CBC radio, Halifax, in 1976: *Pawn's Promotion* (unpublished), broadcast nationally, and *Two Sisters/The Scream* (1977), a striking expressionistic experiment. He was writer-in-residence in 1976-7 at Toronto's TARRAGON THEATRE, which produced *On the Lee Shore* (1978), a naturalistic family drama, in 1977.

Heide's interest in local social and economic issues led him to reject naturalism in favour of the more episodic folk play containing scenes of Nova Scotian life, interspersed with music and song. He returned east to work with the MULGRAVE ROAD CO-OP in Mulgrave, N.S., on the collectives *The Coady Co-op Show* and *Road Reviews* in 1979 and 1982 respectively, and he wrote *Bring Back Don Messer* for the company in 1980. His most successful play in this folk style is *Pogie* (first performed 1980, published in 1981), depicting with humour and compassion the effects of unemployment on working-class people.

Heide frequently portrays elderly and eccentric characters: Jill the Red in *The Flood*, Cora Scott in *The Sound of Sirens*, the Stuarts in *The Waiting's Over* (all radio plays broadcast by CBC in 1977, 1979, and 1981 respectively) and the Grandmother in *I Ain't Dead Yet* produced by the MERMAID THEATRE, in Wolfville N.S., in 1985. *Going Back* was also presented by the Mermaid Theatre in 1987. Heide co-founded the Dramatists' Co-op of Nova Scotia in 1976 and in 1978 began a 'Writer-in-Community' program through the Writers' Federation of Nova Scotia. The most active and talented playwright currently working in Nova Scotia, in 1987 he was appointed artistic director of Mulgrave Road Co-op, which produced his latest play, *The Promised Land*, in 1988.

See Denyse Lynde, 'Christopher Heide: Canadian Playwright of the Nineteen Eighties', *The Proceedings of the Theatre in Atlantic Canada Symposium* (1988), ed. Richard Paul Knowles.   RICHARD PERKYNS

Hendry, Tom (b. 1929). Born and raised in Winnipeg, and educated (in accounting) at the Univ. of Manitoba, his theatre career spans acting, playwriting, and administration. While still a student he acted in television and radio drama, including the ongoing role of Buddy Jackson in the CBC radio serial 'The Jacksons and their Neighbours'. In 1952 he joined John HIRSCH's Muddiwater Puppet Company, beginning a long working relationship with Hirsch, who directed Hendry's first stage play, *Do You Remember?* (unpublished) in 1957 at Winnipeg's Rainbow Stage. The play was a revision of a TV script earlier broadcast by CBC Winnipeg in 1954. In 1957, while still practising as a chartered accountant, he and Hirsch founded Theatre 77, which the next year merged with the Winnipeg Little Theatre to become the MANITOBA THEATRE CENTRE. In 1958 Hendry began three years as producer at the Rainbow Stage and, by 1960, had sold his accountancy firm to work full time in theatre. MTC produced his next play, *Trapped* (unpublished), in 1961, followed in 1964 by *All About Us* (unpublished), a musical review written in collaboration with Len PETERSON and Allan Laing that toured Canada in 1964-5.

From 1964 to 1969 Hendry served as the first full-time Secretary-General of the Canadian Theatre Centre, organizing in 1967 'Colloquium 67: the Design of Theatres', an international conference on theatre architecture. In the same year his contribution to Canadian theatre was recognized by the award of the Centennial Medal.

In 1969 Hendry became literary manager of the STRATFORD FESTIVAL, and his *Satyricon* (unpublished), a 'disposable opera' (with music by Stanley Silverman), was produced at the Avon Theatre. The same year his 1966 television play, *Fifteen Miles of Broken Glass* (1968), was adapted and produced by the Toronto Central Players (the adaptation was published in 1972). Winner of the 1970 Ontario Lieutenant-Governor's Medal, the play concerns the disappointment felt by an Air Force cadet too young to go to war. The bombing of Hiroshima ends his heroic fantasies, however, maturing his attitudes. The play introduces the figure of the outsider—'the non-participant' as Hendry has called him, a figure who populates many of his plays. The outsider becomes representative of Canada in *Fifteen Miles*, reappearing more strongly in *Gravediggers of 1942* (1973), first produced in 1973 at the TORONTO FREE THEATRE, which Hendry had co-founded (with Martin KINCH and John PALMER) in 1971. *Gravediggers*, a musical collaboration with Steven Jack, suffers from sometimes clumsy lyrics and an inconsistent integration of song and plot. It attempts to combine a sub-plot of camp musical-comedy satire with the tragic events of the Dieppe Raid. In the main plot Canada is the outsider, sacrificed by stronger powers, while in the sub-plot well-intentioned Canadian kids try to mount a show to sell War Bonds. In *How Are Things with the Walking Wounded?* (1972), first presented in 1972 by Toronto Free Theatre, the action takes place in Montreal at a party given by Willie, a successful English-speaking businessman, for his homosexual and French-Canadian lover René, to celebrate a two-year relationship about to dissolve. The play presents a brittle world of clever dialogue, liquor, and drugs—the same world seen in *You Smell Good to Me* (1972), produced in workshop at the FACTORY THEATRE Lab, 1972, and *The Missionary Position* (1972), presented at Vancouver's Noon-Hour Theatre in fall 1972. Although the characters change personalities and even gender from play to play, they work out similar patterns of hustler and victim.

In 1974 Hendry helped to create the Playwrights Colony at the Banff School of Fine Arts (see BANFF CENTRE), where several of his unpublished plays have been workshopped. From 1976 to 1979 he wrote scripts for the CBC television series 'The King of Kensington'.

Hendry's *Byron* (1976)—first presented by Toronto Free Theatre in 1976 with music by Steven Jack—dramatizes an imagined meeting between Harriet Beecher Stowe and Byron, whom she admonishes for his aristocratic humanitarianism, demanding instead genuine heroic action. The central characters of *Hogtown: Toronto the Good* (1981) are also historical figures, and the thesis—a dialectic on the legislation of public morality—is again presented in a struggle between the governing power (a Toronto mayor) and an outsider

(Belle Howard, a famous brothel keeper). The form is again that of the musical (music by Paul Hoffert). First produced at TORONTO TRUCK THEATRE in 1981, the play closed early.

In his role as administrator, Hendry has been treasurer of Playwrights Canada and president of the Toronto Free Theatre. Since 1983 he has worked as a consultant for the Toronto Arts Council, writing *Cultural Capital: The Care & Feeding of Toronto's Artistic Assets* (1985), a comprehensive consideration of the economic benefits of the arts. He was also chairman of the Task Force on the NATIONAL ARTS CENTRE, whose report was presented in 1986. His children's play, *East of the Sun; West of the Moon*, was produced by Toronto's Inner Stage in Dec. 1986. Hendry is currently working on a film adaptation of *Fifteen Miles of Broken Glass*.

REID GILBERT

Henry, Ann (b. 1914). Born in Winnipeg, where her father was a former evangelist who became a labour activist, her early life is vividly described in her autobiography *Laugh Baby Laugh* (1967). In the 1950s she became a journalist, and from 1954 to 1964 was drama, film, and television critic for the *Winnipeg Tribune*. In 1967 her play *Lulu Street* was presented at the MANITOBA THEATRE CENTRE, directed by Edward GILBERT. It was subsequently revised with the assistance of John HIRSCH and presented under his direction at FESTIVAL LENNOXVILLE in 1972. Both versions of the play were published by Playwrights Co-op (1967, 1972); the Talonbooks edition (1975) incorporates a few further revisions. Other productions included the VANCOUVER PLAYHOUSE (1973), ALBERTA THEATRE PROJECTS (1974), and CBC radio and television.

Lulu Street is set in an old house in central Winnipeg during the Winnipeg General Strike of 1919. Matthew Alexander, a charismatic labour speaker, is so caught up in his reformist activities that he neglects his young daughter Elly. Though in debt himself, he fills the house with an odd assortment of hangers-on he feels he must help. At the climax the play's political and domestic themes coincide as Matthew is forced to choose between the cause of the strikers and his daughter's love. Even in its revised version the play has weaknesses in structure, characterization, and language; but the author's use of her memories of her father and childhood gives rise to moments of striking vividness and vitality.

Henry is also the author of *All The Men On The Moon Are Irish*, a children's play; the radio plays *Isabel* and *Travels With Aunt Jane*, both written in 1977-8; and *It's All Free on the Outside* (1975), a novel.

DOUGLAS ARRELL

Henry, Martha (b. 1938). Born Martha Buhs in Detroit, Michigan, she often visited Stratford, Ont., as a child, and while studying at Pittsburgh's Carnegie Institute of Technology acted in summer stock with the Sun Parlor Players of Leamington, Ont. She moved to Canada in 1959 to perform at Toronto's CREST THEATRE, where she met Powys THOMAS, who persuaded her to attend the newly founded NATIONAL THEATRE SCHOOL in Montreal. She subsequently played Jennet Jourdemayne in Christopher Fry's *The Lady's Not for Burning* at the MANITOBA THEATRE CENTRE in 1961, beginning her long association with John HIRSCH as well as meeting her first husband, actor Donnelly Rhodes, son of playwright Ann HENRY, whose name she took and retained.

In more that forty performances at the STRATFORD FESTIVAL—débuting in 1961 as Miranda in *The Tempest*—Henry achieved a reputation as an actress whose technical assurance enabled her to master successfully a wide variety of roles. Notable successes include her Elmire in Molière's *Tartuffe* in 1968 and her Isabella in *Measure for Measure* in 1975, directed by Robin PHILLIPS. Henry's unfortunate experience as one of the Stratford Festival's interim directorate of 1980, the 'Gang of Four', resulted in her withdrawal from Stratford for a number of years. She returned as associate director of Robin Phillips' production of *Cymbeline* in 1986, and was an associate director in 1987 and 1988.

Henry has also acted with the Lincoln Centre Company in New York, and at several other Canadian theatres, including Toronto's CENTRESTAGE and TARRAGON, and THEATRE CALGARY, where she created the role of May Buchanan in John MURRELL's *Farther West* in 1982. Her first venture into musical comedy resulted in an electrifying rendering of Vera in Rodgers' and Hart's *Pal Joey* in 1986.

Henry has appeared on television in the BBC production of George Eliot's *Daniel Deronda* and in the CBC mini-series *Empire, Inc.* Her Canadian film appearances include the roles of Mrs Ross in Timothy FINDLEY's *The Wars* in 1983, directed by Robin Phillips, and of Edna Cormick in Leon Marr's production of Joan Barfoot's *Dancing in the Dark* in 1986. She won Genie Awards for both roles.

Henry has recently devoted her talents to directing, taking on Eugene O'Neill's *A Moon for the Misbegotten* for Tarragon Theatre in 1985, Neil Simon's *Brighton Beach Memoirs* for Theatre London in 1986, and Colleen Murphy's *All Other Destinations are Cancelled*, for Tarragon in 1987. In 1988 she was appointed artistic director of Theatre London (see GRAND OPERA HOUSE, London).

Henry's many honours include a 1979 GUTHRIE Award, a Theatre World Award (1970), and an LL D from the University of Toronto. She was made an Officer of the Order of Canada in 1981.

ROTA HERZBERG LISTER

Herbert, John (b. 1926). Born John Herbert Brundage in Toronto, where he was educated, he served a six-month sentence in the Guelph reformatory in 1946 on a charge of gross indecency, a charge he has consistently denied. He attended the Ontario College of Art (1947-9) and studied acting, directing, and production at the NEW PLAY SOCIETY School of Drama (1955-8) and ballet with the National Ballet School (1958-60). He was artistic director of Toronto's Adventure Theatre (1960-2) and New Venture Players (1962-5) before founding and running the Ganet Theatre Studio (1965-70), subsequently founding the Medusa Theatre Club (1972-4). He became writer-in-residence and associate director of the Smile Company, Toronto, in 1984. He was associate editor (1975-6) of the Toronto newspaper *Onion*, which serialized his novel *The House that Jack Built* in 1975-6.

The most famous of Herbert's plays is *FORTUNE AND MEN'S EYES* (1967), a drama about the dehumanizing effects of prison life on young people. Raw in its language and unsparing in its portrayal of violence and homosexuality, the play justifiably gained Herbert international fame and led to the formation in many countries of the Fortune Society, which seeks to bring about reform of the prison system. In its first ten years the play received more than 100 professional productions in some forty languages.

Although Herbert has written many plays, few have been published. Like *Fortune and Men's Eyes*, the other plays often deal with the betrayal of a relationship, which leads to the destruction of the protagonist. *Omphale and the Hero* (1974) is a melodramatic full-length play in which Antoinette, an ageing French-Canadian whore, a former librarian, falls in love (improbably) with a young drifter. The drifter also falls in love (again improbably) with another woman, and Antoinette—who has rejected the police chief for the drifter—is murdered by him. The language of the play is gratuitously offensive and the characterization one-dimensional and stereotypical. The play was first performed at Toronto's Forest Hill Chamber Theatre in 1974. *Born of Medusa's Blood* (unpublished), produced in 1972, also portrays a whore-virgin figure who is destroyed by a corrupt society.

Some Angry Summer Songs (1976) is a collection of four short pieces—*Pearl Divers, Beer Room, Close Friends*, and *The Dinosaurs* — first performed in 1974 at the Forest Hill Chamber Theatre. *Pearl Divers* is a slight sketch in which Queenie, a flamboyant homosexual, lands a job as a dishwasher; *Beer Room* chronicles the goings-on in a Toronto gay bar; in *Close Friends* two former male lovers meet again, discuss their break-up, and part; *The Dinosaurs* sets an ageing world-famous actress against a Canadian drama critic who has destroyed her Canadian career. These plays are inferior work—Herbert's tendency towards melodrama is unchecked, the language is banal, the characterization mere caricature. The power and imagination of *Fortune and Men's Eyes* rightfully won it critical applause; the other plays demonstrate that Herbert is an all-too-common literary phenomenon: a writer known primarily for one work.

The John Herbert papers are in the Univ. of Waterloo Archives. See Geraldine Anthony, ed., *Stage Voices* (1978), for Herbert's own account of his career.

EUGENE BENSON

Her Majesty's Theatre (Montreal). One of North America's most elegant playhouses, Her Majesty's, located on the east side of Guy Street above St Catherine, was for the first half of the twentieth century Montreal's premier venue for road companies. Erected in 1898 as a public service by a chartered corporation—which included in its membership Senator A.A. Thibaudeau, Mayor Raymond Préfontaine, William Mann, William Barclay Stephens, and William Strachan—the building was designed by the fashionable New York theatre architects J.B. McElfatrick and Son. Its conservative exterior of pressed red brick relieved with Ohio buff stone gave little hint of its lavish interior—a mixture of Italian Renaissance and rococo styles highlighted by red plush seats, brass fixtures, heavy velvet curtains, and crystal chandeliers.

The auditorium had a large orchestra, two galleries, and ten boxes on either side of the stage, six of which were incorporated into the proscenium arch, and accommodated 1,704. The stage, equipped with up-to-date machinery, was 45' deep and 65' high from the stage floor to the rigging loft. The proscenium opening was 34' wide and 32' high.

The theatre opened on 7 Nov. 1898 with E.E. Rice's musical comedy *The Ballet Girl*. The original lessees, Mr and Mrs Frank Murphy, booked grand opera, lavishly costumed melodrama, and musical comedy for the first two years. The 1898–9 season featured productions of Ludwig Englander's *The Little Corporal*, J.M. Morton's *The Highwayman*, an adaptation of Alexander Dumas's *The Three Musketeers*, Edmond Rostand's *Cyrano de Bergerac*, and a three-week season by the Grand Opera of New Orleans. The 1899-1900 season brought visits by Alice Neilson, the Sousa Band, and the Grand Opera Company of New York. In Apr. 1900 the theatre came under the management of John A. Gross, who operated a stock company there for six months with only middling success. In Mar. 1901 it was leased by F.F. Proctor, the American VAUDEVILLE magnate, who promptly renamed it Proctor's Theatre. Performers appearing during this period included young Buster (then Francis) Keaton, who with his parents offered a display of acrobatics. After promoting vaudeville with indifferent results for a year, Proctor installed a stock company. In 1904 the J.B. Sparrow Theatrical and Amusement Company purchased the property, remodelled it somewhat, restored its original name, and dissolved the stock company. From this point onwards Her Majesty's became Montreal's leading house for touring attractions. Over the next quarter-century British and American road shows made the theatre a regular port of call:

Her Majesty's Theatre (Montreal)

dramas, musicals, BURLESQUEs, travelogues, even small circuses—all were welcomed. Solo recitals, symphony concerts, and opera and ballet productions were also featured. One of the more unusual events was a debate on capital punishment in 1924 between Montreal lawyer Robert L. Calder and the legendary Chicago attorney Clarence S. Darrow. Among the artists appearing under the Sparrow management were Sarah Bernhardt, Enrico Caruso, Gertrude Lawrence, Harry Lauder, Sir Henry Irving, Robert Mantell, Sir John Martin-Harvey, Nellie Melba, Anna Pavlova, Basil Rathbone, Ellen Terry, and Sir Herbert Beerbohm Tree.

In 1929 the theatre was bought by Consolidated Theatres Corporation, which maintained the high production standards set by the Sparrow organization. First-class shows from London's West End and Broadway tryouts accounted for a good part of its bookings. In 1938 Phil Maurice, a prominent local impresario, was appointed manager. Artists presented under Consolidated Theatre's management included Katharine Cornell, Ruth Draper, Edith Evans, Maurice Evans, John Gielgud, Louis Jouvet, Charles Laughton, and Donald Wolfit.

Consolidated Theatres sold Her Majesty's in 1958 to British American Enterprises Ltd., who closed it in 1963. The last event in the theatre, a concert by Billy Eckstein, took place on 27 May 1963. In Nov. 1963 the building was bought by Hermaj Investments Ltd., who demolished it shortly afterwards. The seats and stage equipment were transferred to the Capital Theatre; and the role of Her Majesty's as host to touring attractions was assumed by the newly erected PLACE DES ARTS. JOHN RIPLEY

Her Majesty's Theatre (Ottawa). Construction of this first legitimate theatre in the capital began in 1854 on Wellington St, just west of O'Connor, facing Barrack (now Parliament) Hill, on a site currently occupied by the National Press Building. By early 1856 the only section of the building open for business was a tavern, the Shakespeare Saloon, but on 4 Oct. it was ready for a gala opening. Built in stone at a cost of $7,500 by a group of local businessmen, it had a seating capacity of about 1,000. A lease was taken by Joseph Lee, the first of several managers.

Her Majesty's, which featured mainly vis-

Her Majesty's Theatre, Ottawa, c. 1867

iting British and American troupes, was renamed The Prince of Wales Theatre in 1860 on the occasion of the Prince's visit to lay the cornerstone of the Parliament Buildings, but its original name was restored in 1866. Improvements were made in 1870: the chandelier was replaced by gaslights, and a new lessee, W.J. Marshall, enlarged the orchestra pit and reupholstered the seats. For much of 1870 Marshall's London Comedy & Burlesque Company—which included comedian Harry LINDLEY and his wife Florence Webster, Nellie Nelson, Johnnie Ward, and O.D. Byron—performed a repertoire of English plays. There were only one or two performances in 1871 before the Times Printing and Publishing Company occupied the building on 29 Aug. 1871.

It was replaced as the home of legitimate theatre for a brief time by the Rink Music Hall and then by the GRAND OPERA HOUSE in 1875. On that theatre's opening, the *Ottawa Times* paid tribute to Her Majesty's, 'which did duty as a playhouse when Bytown was in the zenith of its turbulent glory.'

See Eric Minton, *Ottawa: The Way We Were* (1975); Mary Brown, '''Pepper's Ghost Is Tearing Its Hair'': Ottawa Theatre in the 1870s', *Theatre History in Canada*, 4 (1983). JAMES NOONAN

Herndon, Thomas J. (1831–93). This American-born actor-manager toured extensively in Ontario from 1870 to 1882 with his popular Opera House Company. On 11 Feb. 1874 he opened Hamilton's New Mechanics' Hall, to which he drew enthusiastic crowds for a record five-week season. On 11 May 1874 he opened the Queen's Theatre, Toronto, where his company, supplemented by many old Toronto favourites, achieved three months of unbroken success. His 1874-5 season included visits to Belleville, Kingston, and Ottawa with the English tragedian T.C. King. In support of King, the company substituted *Macbeth*, *Othello*, and *Hamlet* for its usual melodrama repertoire of *East Lynne* and Charles Foster's *Bertha the Sewing Machine Girl*. As an actor Herndon was acclaimed chiefly for comedy: according to one Hamilton critic, 'his every look was a joke and his every action a glorious burlesque.' Herndon's most memorable role was Rip van Winkle in the stage adaptation of Washington Irving's tale.   MARY SHORTT

Heron Family, The. Based in Philadelphia after emigrating from Dublin, Ireland, in 1847, this talented musical group toured major centres in Canada West and East, the Maritimes, and Newfoundland between 1851 and 1855, giving farces and short musical plays combined with concerts of Irish, sacred, and operatic songs. The parents, John and Frances, were manager and accompanist respectively, and the eldest daughter, Mary Ann (1833-1905), who had been a child prodigy in Ireland and London, played the leading roles. Fanny (1835-91) had a fine contralto voice, and Agnes (1837-89), a soprano, was the troupe's irresistible comic. In 1851 the family scored a series of triumphs beginning in Hamilton, Toronto, and Kingston, and including engagements in Montreal and Quebec City. After tours of New Brunswick, Nova Scotia, and Newfoundland in 1852 and 1853, Mary Ann retired to marry R.W. Scott, mayor of Bytown (Ottawa), who became a cabinet minister under Sir Wilfrid Laurier. By 1853 a fourth sister and two brothers had joined the company, which in 1855 again toured the Maritimes. A few years later— unable to survive the loss of Fanny and Agnes to concert and operatic careers—the troupe dissolved, and the remaining members settled in Ottawa. The youngest brother (1848-1914) using the stage name Alfred Hudson, joined the Myers and HOLMAN companies at Toronto's ROYAL LYCEUM, and later played two seasons at Charlotte MORRISON's GRAND OPERA HOUSE, Toronto, before moving to the Boston Museum Company in 1878.
                MARY SHORTT

Hier, les enfants dansaient (*Yesterday the Children Were Dancing*). Gratien GÉLINAS's third play was the first major Quebec stage work to deal with the federalist-separatist dilemma, and inaugurated a decade of intense political theatre activity throughout the province. Set in a comfortable Montreal living-room, Gélinas's drama poignantly depicts the misery wreaked within a middle-class family, and symbolically within Quebec society at large, by the political choices morally responsible people find themselves obliged to make regarding Quebec's national destiny.

Pierre Gravel, a successful Montreal lawyer and long-time Liberal, is offered the opportunity to run for a federal parliamentary seat with the promise of a cabinet post if he succeeds. As he is about to announce his candidacy, his elder son, André, a recent law graduate, admits to the leadership of a terrorist group dedicated to Quebec's independence. A bomb has been planted, he claims, which he or his alternate will explode within an hour or two. While André's parents and uncle argue with him against the clock in an effort to salvage the careers of both father and son, the bomb is detonated by André's younger brother Larry. At curtain-fall André goes to the police-station to admit responsibility for the crime, leaving Pierre Gravel to contemplate the wreck of both his family and his political hopes. Gravel's curtain lines, part of a speech he will deliver next day to the Canadian Club in Toronto, remind English Canada of the bleak fact that Quebec's nationalist anguish is far from irrelevant to their own interests. 'For my divided house will not go down,' he warns, 'without shaking yours to its very foundations.'

The play is in two acts: the first deals with Gravel's decision to enter federal politics, and the second with André's devastating announcement and the impassioned debate that follows. The structure of neither act is entirely satisfactory. Act 1 is largely without conflict, while Act 2 is overweighted with intellectual cut-and-thrust. Gélinas's summary of both the federalist and *indépendantiste* positions is admirably precise and even-handed, but ultimately undramatic. Beneath the political rhetoric, however, one cannot fail to sense Gélinas's concern with the human dimension of Quebec's nationalist struggle, and the play's finest moments are those in which family members blindly grope towards each other out of a love that tran-

Hier, les enfants dansaient

scends, but can never deny, the freedom and responsibility to make political decisions.

The play premièred on 11 Apr. 1966 at Montreal's COMÉDIE-CANADIENNE, with Gélinas as Pierre Gravel and his son Yves as André. The production ran for eighty-five performances to mixed notices. Some critics faulted Gélinas for failing to take a firm political position on the independence issue, and others found the piece intellectually bourgeois and lightweight; but most reviewers applauded the playwright's courage in dealing frankly with a crucial Quebec and national problem.

An English version of the play, translated by Mavor MOORE as *Yesterday the Children Were Dancing*, premièred at the CHARLOTTE-TOWN FESTIVAL, 5 July 1967. Again Gélinas and his son played Gravel and André. Festival audiences gave the piece standing ovations, and anglophone critics were more enthusiastic than their francophone confrères. Nathan COHEN, for example, considered *Yesterday* 'the most jolting play in the experience of the Canadian Theatre'. It has since received some twenty-five revivals by professional and amateur companies, including a 1973 production, sponsored by the Quebec government, which opened at Montreal's PLACE DES ARTS, went on to the NATIONAL ARTS CENTRE, and concluded its tour at the Théâtre de la Renaissance in Paris.

The federalist-separatist issues raised by Gélinas are as real today as they were two decades ago, and not much nearer solution. Now, however, the play's pivotal concern—the legitimacy of violence in pursuit of national sovereignty—finds little sympathy among those who endured the 1970 October Crisis. Contemporary Québécois youth, convinced that Quebec's national survival depends more on economics than politics, prefer to wage the nationalistic struggle in the boardrooms of corporations. To buoyant young graduates of the École des Hautes Études Commerciales and other business schools, André's defeatist cultural rhetoric seems dated and naïve.

Mavor Moore's translation of the play was published in 1967 by Clarke, Irwin & Co., Toronto. The first French edition appeared in 1968 (Les Editions Leméac).

See Mavor Moore, *Four Canadian Playwrights* (1973), and Renate Usmiani, *Gratien Gélinas* (1977).   JOHN RIPLEY

Hill, Charles (1805-74) and **Anne (Russell)** (1810-90). Born into prominent English theatrical families, the Hills played in London and the provinces before immigrating to the U.S. in 1840. Although Anne was 'an excellent comedienne . . . dancing with exquisite grace and lightness', Charles, somewhat pompous and given to rant, was less popular, and the couple failed to establish themselves in the U.S. Retreating to Montreal in 1843, they acted in summer with visiting professionals and in winter with local amateurs, together with their daughter Rosalie. When their son, (Charles) Barton Hill (1828-1911), joined them in 1846 the family toured many towns in Canada West with programs of short comedies, dance, and song. In 1849 they moved to Toronto, where Anne ran a Dancing and Calisthenics Academy, as she had in Montreal. After 1851 the senior Hills and Barton joined a succession of American stock companies, returning to Canada West for brief engagements. Charles retired and died in the U.S. but in 1861 the more resilient Anne resumed acting in Montreal, where, except for a mid-1870s tour with the HOLMAN company, she spent her remaining years. Barton, who built a distinguished career on the American stage, returned occasionally to play leading roles with companies in Toronto and Montreal.   MARY SHORTT

Hirsch, John (1930-89). Born in Siofok, Hungary, the sole member of his immediate family to survive the Holocaust, he immigrated to Canada in 1947. After being adopted by a family in Winnipeg, he learned English and graduated from the Univ. of Manitoba. His early theatre work included the founding of a touring PUPPET THEATRE, the writing of children's plays, and the beginning of a long association with the Winnipeg Little Theatre, where he directed his first play, William Saroyan's *The Time of Your Life*, in 1951 and worked as production manager from 1953 to 1957. He also joined CBWT Winnipeg, first as production assistant and then as TV producer.

Hirsch and Tom HENDRY founded Theatre 77, which merged with the Little Theatre in 1958 to form the MANITOBA THEATRE CENTRE. Under Hirsch, who became its first artistic director, the MTC became a model for regional theatre development in Canada and the U.S. Between 1958 and 1966 he directed Tennessee Williams' *A Streetcar Named Desire*, Thomas Heggen's and Joshua Logan's *Mister Roberts*, Gore Vidal's *Visit to a Small Planet*, Len PETERSON's *Look Ahead*, James REANEY's *Names and Nicknames*, Edward Albee's *Who's Afraid of Virginia Woolf?*, and the first Canadian production of Bertolt Brecht's *Mother Courage* with Zoë CALDWELL in the leading role. Hirsch also helped establish the Rainbow Stage, an outdoor summer theatre where he directed musical comedies. His reputation as a highly imaginative and demanding director led to his staging of Tennessee Williams' *Cat on a Hot Tin Roof* at Toronto's CREST THEATRE and a highly acclaimed *Mother Courage* (*Mère Courage*) starring Jean GASCON and Denise PELLETIER for Montreal's THÉÂTRE DU NOUVEAU MONDE in 1964. In 1965 he directed his first play at the STRATFORD FESTIVAL, Chekhov's *The Cherry Orchard*. This was followed by *Henry VI* in 1966, and by a controversial production of *Richard III* starring Alan Bates and Zoë Caldwell in the 1967 season. Although critics questioned Hirsch's view of the King's psychological motivation as well as his interpretation of the play's politics, they acknowledged the theatrical force and originality of his approach. An undisputed artistic success of the 1967 season, however, was Hirsch's direction of the première of Reaney's *Colours in the Dark*. That same year he was appointed associate artistic director of the Festival (with Jean Gascon) and made his directorial début in New York with Garcia Lorca's *Yerma* and Brecht's *Galileo* at the Lincoln Centre for the Performing Arts.

Hirsch's first production of Stratford's 1968 season, *A Midsummer Night's Dream*, disturbed traditionalist critics, particularly for what they saw as the gratuitous decadence of the court of Theseus. His *The Three Musketeers*, however, was a feast of romantic theatricality that demonstrated Hirsch's mastery of the thrust stage and his penchant for melodrama. After that season Hirsch made his Broadway début, directing Joseph Heller's *We Bombed in New Haven*.

The harmony and enthusiasm of the Hirsch-Gascon collaborative leadership ended in 1969. On the Festival stage Hirsch directed *Hamlet*, which was generally rejected by the critics, though it sold out; but his second production—Tom Hendry's adaptation of

Petronius's *Satyricon*—scandalized the Festival purists. The ensuing furore illustrated the incompatibility between Hirsch's confrontational style and the aims and objectives of the Festival's Board of Governors. At the end of the season he resigned and moved to New York.

Hirsch spent the next five years working primarily in the U.S. At Lincoln Centre he directed Marc Connelly's *Beggar on Horseback*, Synge's *The Playboy of the Western World*, and Sophocles' *Antigone*. In 1970 he directed Chekhov's *The Seagull* for the opening of the new National Theatre of Israel, received an Obie Award for his direction of *AC/DC* at the Chelsea Theatre in Brooklyn, and was named Off-Broadway's Best Director of the Year. Twice during this period Hirsch returned to Canada: in 1971 for Brecht's *A Man's a Man* at the MTC, and in 1973 to direct Ann HENRY's *Lulu Street* at FESTIVAL LENNOXVILLE.

As head of CBC Drama for English-language television from 1974 to 1977—where he established the successful situation-comedy series 'The King of Kensington'—he continued directing; his production of Ansky's Yiddish classic *The Dybbuk* at the MTC in the 1973-4 season was one of his best. Three separate productions of this play—at the MTC, the ST LAWRENCE CENTRE for the Arts in Toronto in 1974, and in 1975 at the Mark Taper Forum in Los Angeles—were highly acclaimed. In 1976 Hirsch returned to Stratford to direct *The Three Sisters* with Maggie Smith, Martha HENRY, and Keith Baxter, and in 1979 he was appointed consulting artistic director of the Seattle Repertory Theatre.

In Dec. 1980 Hirsch accepted the artistic directorship of the Stratford Festival. His five-year tenure, based on a strong acting company and a varied and colourful dramaturgical plan, was artistically productive, his personal contribution consisting of five mainstage productions—*The Tempest*, *As You Like It*, Molière's *Tartuffe*, *A Midsummer Night's Dream*, and *King Lear*—and Friedrich Schiller's *Mary Stuart* and Tennessee Williams' *The Glass Menagerie* at the Avon Theatre. The Shakespearean productions were marked by a strong directorial concept, textual clarity, and by Hirsch's highly personal vision of the plays. Of the other plays, *Tartuffe*—with brilliant performances by Brian

Bedford and Douglas CAMPBELL, and Tanya MOISEIWITSCH's exceptional design—was likely his best. Hirsch also established the Young Company, a training scheme for young professional actors at the Third Stage.

After leaving Stratford Hirsch continued to coach and teach at several American universities. He was awarded the Order of Canada in 1967 and the Molson Prize in 1976 for outstanding contributions to the arts in Canada. MICHAL SCHONBERG

Hoffmann, Guy (1916–86). Born in France, where he worked as a cameraman for the Pathé-Natan studios, he immigrated to Canada in 1948. His theatrical career began in 1949 as an actor with the COMPAGNONS DE SAINT-LAURENT. In 1951 he helped found the THÉÂTRE DU NOUVEAU MONDE, appearing in its inaugural production of Molière's *L'Avare* and in a 1953 production of Molière's *Tartuffe* as Madame Pernelle in drag. One of his greatest successes was in Molière's *Trois Farces* in Montreal in 1953-4 and in Paris in 1955. His spectacular interpretation of Sganarelle was praised by French critics and brought Hoffmann offers from the Comédie Française and the Théâtre National Populaire in Vilar, France.

Though best known as an interpreter of Molière, Hoffmann played in numerous other works ranging from Shakespeare (at the STRATFORD FESTIVAL) to Shaw's *Pygmalion* and a French version of James Goldman's *The Lion in Winter* (*Le Lion en Hiver*) at the THÉÂTRE DU RIDEAU VERT (in 1977 and 1978 respectively). He also designed for the stage, produced dramas and children's programs for television, and acted in over one hundred 'télé-théâtres' for Radio-Canada. He appeared as a judge in the 1985 film *Agnes of God*, and also played a judge in 1986 in his last television performance in Claude Vermorel's *Jeanne avec nous*, a play about Joan of Arc's trial.

One of the most active performers in the history of classical theatre in Quebec, Hoffmann has been described as Quebec's first major comic actor and the best interpreter of Molière in North America.

RAMON HATHORN

Holden, John Porter (d. 1967). Born in the U.S. and raised in Toronto, he was introduced to the theatre at the College St Presbyterian Church; but after attending the

John Holden, c. 1936

Univ. of Toronto he studied business at the Univ. of Michigan, where he later taught theatre. One of his productions drew the attention of actress Mary Robson, and he toured opposite her with the Jessie Bonstelle stock company. He also played in stock with Vaughan GLASER and on Broadway. He worked extensively in Toronto radio and, from 1942, as stage and production manager for Broadway tours. He became an important figure in the development of Canadian theatre when, in 1934, he founded in the resort town of Bala, Ont., the Actors' Colony—a stock company called, in their first season, the Good Companions and, after 1937, the John Holden Players.

Holden's 1934 season was mounted at the Bala Town Hall (with four performances at the nearby Gravenhurst Opera House), using paper scenery, and tin cans as footlights. The repertoire included a satirical review, *So This is Canada* by W.S. Atkinson, and *City Limits*, written by Holden under the pseudonym of 'John Porter'.

The Actors' Colony included Isabel Price (Palmer), Eric Clavering, and Catherine Proctor. When they moved to Toronto in the early 1930s for their first winter at the Margaret Eaton Hall, these artists were joined by Jane MALLETT, among others, and, in subsequent seasons, Robert CHRISTIE.

By 1937 Holden's company had a set routine: summers in Muskoka, playing at the Bala Town Hall and at the Bigwin Inn resort; fall and winter in Winnipeg at the Dominion Theatre; and a brief run at Margaret Eaton Hall in the spring before returning to Muskoka. By 1938 Holden was producing twenty-seven plays during his thirty-week season in Winnipeg.

Holden's dream of an all-Canadian national repertory company was realized in the summer of 1939 when the CBC began to broadcast weekly half-hour segments of the Actors' Colony in performance.

The Second World War drained both the company's manpower and the size of the audience, and in 1941 the company produced its final complete season of live repertory theatre. Though Holden, Isabel Price, and Everett Staples returned to Bala in 1942, they presented only film and musical evenings, often donating the box-office returns to local wartime organizations. However, after the war the Straw Hat Players, and more recently the Muskoka Festival, continued the tradition established by Holden.

In the 1940s Holden worked as production manager for the Shubert Organization; in the 1950s he directed on a freelance basis in the U.S. and Canada.

See also SUMMER STOCK.

JUDITH RUDAKOFF

Holiday Theatre. The first professional theatre for young people in Canada, it was founded in 1953 in Vancouver by Joy COGHILL and Myra Benson. Its twenty-four-year history reflects both Canadian and international post-Second World War philosophy, style, and fashion in this specialized theatrical genre. Early repertoire featured family entertainment based on fairy tales and children's-literature classics. Many of the plays were by American authors, particularly the pioneering teacher, director, and playwright Charlotte Chorpenning, of Chicago's Goodman Theatre, who had inspired Joy Coghill as a student. Works by local writers, such as Margaret Adelberg, were also produced. In 1967 the company sponsored a playwriting contest to celebrate Canada's Centennial. The winner was Eric NICOL for his nationalistic fantasy *Beware the Quickly Who*, which, along with Betty LAMBERT's science-fiction drama *The Riddle Machine*, toured nationally in 1967-8.

In 1966 Coghill left to become artistic director at the city's adult regional theatre, the VANCOUVER PLAYHOUSE, and was replaced by Hutchison Shandro; in 1969 Holiday joined the Playhouse and became Holiday Playhouse. While Joy Coghill remained as artistic director, work for children continued to flourish; but when she left, artistic leadership floundered. The $50,000 that Holiday had brought to the merger was absorbed in general funds and the company's name changed to Playhouse Holiday, reflecting the diminished importance attached to children's plays. The prestige and vitality of the company were nevertheless acknowledged in 1972 when it was chosen as one of five Canadian companies to appear in Montreal for the Fourth General Assembly of ASSITEJ (Association internationale du théâtre pour l'enfance et la jeunesse). New directions for the company were sought by Don Shipley when he became artistic director in 1972. In England he discovered Theatre-in-Education, in which actor/teachers (known as 'Tie Teams') created dramas about social or historical issues for classroom audiences. Shipley, and his successor Gloria Shapiro-Latham, produced for Holiday timely and provocative pieces in the TIE style, but some problems emerged. Actors with teaching experience were hard to find and the cost per student was prohibitive for many institutions.

For most of its artistic life Holiday continued its two kinds of theatre: large-cast proscenium plays for Metro Vancouver and smaller touring shows for British Columbia schools. But in 1973 the large-cast shows were cancelled and the name changed, once more, to the Playhouse Theatre Centre of B.C. Theatre-in-Education and Holiday as it was first conceived virtually went out of existence. Ironically the last piece performed by the first company for children was for adults—Vancouver teachers. During its twenty-four years of service and metamorphoses, Holiday Theatre established the concept of professional theatre for young people, initiated the first school tours of live plays to remote areas, commissioned and performed dozens of new Canadian plays, and gave many young professionals their first job. Its influence is still felt through published scripts of plays it premièred and by the work of its 'graduates', many of whom continue to devote part of their mature professional life to theatre for children and young people.

Holiday Theatre

See also CHILDREN'S DRAMA AND THEATRE IN ENGLISH.   JOYCE DOOLITTLE

Hollingsworth, Margaret (b. 1942). Born in London, Eng., she immigrated to Canada in 1968, having decided to come to a place, as she puts it, 'where they didn't automatically say "no".' While studying creative writing at the Univ. of British Columbia (MFA, 1974), she became involved with Vancouver's NEW PLAY CENTRE, which subsequently workshopped several of her plays. She has written a number of one-act plays, as well as radio plays that have been broadcast in Canada and abroad.

Hollingsworth's most produced plays are *Mother Country* (1980), her first full-length play, produced by Toronto's TARRAGON THEATRE in 1980, and *Ever Loving* (1981), first produced by Victoria's BELFRY THEATRE in 1980. In her own words she writes about 'what happens when you violate someone's space.' Her characters 'live on a knife edge' where one leap in the wrong direction causes catastrophe. The inhabitants of *Mother Country*, set on a west-coast island, are caught in a web of cultural and familial tensions that are orchestrated in a style that has often caused Hollingsworth's critics to regard her as a mere mood-maker. *Ever Loving*, the story of three Canadian war brides, dramatizes with humour and pathos the shattering and reconstitution of the self. In *War Babies* (1985), first produced by the Belfry Theatre in 1984, Hollingsworth confronts multiple realities through the play-within-a-play technique to express a female sensibility that broods darkly, 'I don't even like men. They're alien beings.'

Hollingsworth's short plays—including *Apple in the Eye*, *Diving*, and *Islands* (all produced in 1983 at the New Play Centre, and published with *Ever Loving* and *War Babies* in *Willful Acts*, 1985)—are full of precise, often violent, imagery, and usually isolate a woman who articulates the dark, complex world of the female. Hollingsworth works in an experimental mode necessary to her vision, but remains largely unappreciated; her difficult drama has yet to be fully understood by her public and fully developed by its author. Four experimental plays—*The House that Jack Built*, *It's Only Hot for Two Months in Kapuskasing*, *Poppycock*, and *Prim and Duck, Mama and Frank*—were published as *Endangered Species* (1988).

See also Robert Wallace and Cynthia Zimmerman, eds., *The Work* (1982).

PATRICIA KEENEY

Hollingsworth, Michael (b. 1950). Born in Swansea, Wales, he immigrated with his parents in 1956 to Toronto where he continues to live. Greatly influenced by the counter-culture of the late 1960s, he left school after grade twelve to pursue his interest in rock 'n' roll music, which quickly impressed him with its theatrical potential. His first play, *Strawberry Fields* (1973), depicting the violent aftermath of a rock concert—John Lennon's lyric gave the play its title—introduced the themes that characterize his early work, best presented in *Clear Light* (1973), where a group of characters affected by LSD, the Watergate crisis, and urban ennui self-destruct to the wailing improvisations of a saxophone-player. While both plays premièred in 1973 (at FACTORY THEATRE Lab and TORONTO FREE THEATRE), the latter gained the greater notoriety, being closed by the Morality Squad for alleged obscenity. In 1976 Hollingsworth's interest in integrating videotape, music, and theatre led him to collaborate with the Hummer Sisters, a Toronto political cabaret troupe, with whom he co-founded Video Cabaret International. After remounting *Strawberry Fields* in 1976 as a rock-drama, VideoCab (as it soon became known) produced in 1977, in conjunction with various Toronto theatres, *Punc Rok*, *Cheap Thrills*, and *White Noise* (all unpublished), which, although receiving poor critical notices, solidified Hollingsworth's reputation as a theatrical *enfant terrible*. In 1978 Toronto Free Theatre produced *Trans World* (1979). With the première that same year (at A Space, Toronto) and a subsequent tour of *Electric Eye* (unpublished), a media extravaganza based on the Son of Sam slaughter in New York and the murder of a Toronto shoe-shine boy, his experiments with the interaction of live performers and videotape achieved a sophistication that inspired him to create his major works of the seventies: complex musical adaptations of George Orwell's *Nineteen Eighty-Four*, produced in 1978, and Aldous Huxley's *Brave New World*, presented at Toronto's International Theatre Festival in 1981. In 1985 Toronto's THEATRE PASSE MURAILLE premièred his *The History of the Village of the Small Huts, Part 1: New France*. Conceived as twenty one-act plays to be presented in five parts over five years, *History* is an irreverent historical satire in which Hollingsworth traces the evolution of the Canadian psyche as a comedy of manners. While the 1986 *Part 2: The British* failed to garner the critical and commercial success of the first instalment, it confirmed that the cycle, even unfinished, is a major contribution to Canadian theatre.

See R. Wallace and C. Zimmerman, eds., *The Work* (1982). ROBERT WALLACE

Holmans, The. This acting and singing family appeared in Canada and the U.S. from about 1854 to about 1885. Mrs Harriet Holman (born in England 1824; died in London, Ont., 1897), a contralto, was also the piano accompanist and musical director; her husband, George W. Holman, Jr (born in England 1821; died in London, Ont., 1888), a tenor and occasional actor, was the artistic manager; his brother Alfred Holman (1830-82) was the business manager. The children formed the company's nucleus: Sarah or Sallie (*c*. 1849-88), a lively performer with a 'strong, flexible and well-toned soprano voice'; Julia (*c*. 1854-79), a contralto, second only to her sister in popular acclaim; and Alfred D. Holman, Jr (*c*. 1853-1918), a baritone specializing in comic and dramatic roles. A son from Mrs Holman's first marriage, Benjamin Phillips Holman (1844-64), played the comic parts eventually assumed by the popular American comedian William H. Crane. First called the Holman Juvenile Opera Troupe, they expanded rapidly to include some of the period's most accomplished performers—the actors George H. Barton, Denman THOMPSON, and Allan Halford; the actress Blanche Bradshaw (wife of Alfred D. Holman, Jr); the comedians Joe Banks, William Davidge Jr, and Harry LINDLEY; the French-Canadian tenor Joseph Brandisi; and the English baritone James T. Dalton (husband of Sallie Holman).

As the Holman English Opera Troupe they were the resident company at Toronto's ROYAL LYCEUM THEATRE from 1867 to 1872 where success depended on a mixed repertoire of *opéra bouffe* (Balfe's *The Bohemian Girl*, Auber's *Fra Diavolo*, Donizetti's *La Fille du Régiment*, and Offenbach's *Orpheus in the Underworld*), grand opera (Verdi's *Il Trovatore*, Bellini's *La Sonnambula*, and Weber's *Der Freischütz*), and 'legitimate' drama (an adaptation of Charles Dickens' *Dombey and Son*, Dion Boucicault's *Formosa* and *The Streets of New York*). After a brief period (1872-3) at Montreal's THEATRE ROYAL, Holman renovated the Music Hall in London, Ont., opening it as the Holman Opera House on 25 Dec. 1873 with Offenbach's *La Grande Duchesse de Gérolstein*. Apart from regular tours to places as far apart as Halifax, N.S., and Richmond, Virginia, the Holmans remained in London until 1881. On 13 Feb. 1879, however, less than a year after its première in London, Eng., they presented Gilbert and Sullivan's *H.M.S. Pinafore* at the Royal Opera House in Toronto, where it received an enthusiastic popular and critical reception and ran for several weeks before touring the U.S.

In the 1880s the company gradually declined as members died or left and as the public grew weary of their kind of mixed repertoire. In their heyday the Holmans trained a new generation of performers and gave Canadian audiences the pleasure of seeing a traditional and contemporary repertoire performed to exacting standards. The critic 'Chaudière' of the *Canadian Illustrated News* (13 Feb. 1875) gave a telling patriotic and artistic explanation for their popularity: 'I have always been a stickler for the Holmans, because they are so painstaking, conscientious, and because they are Canadian.'

DENIS SALTER

Houlé, Léopold (1883-1953). Born in Montreal, he was for twenty years assistant editor of *La Presse* and then of *La Patrie*, where he was also drama critic. From 1936 to 1948 he was director of public relations for Radio-Canada. Houlé wrote a dozen plays that were performed during his lifetime, though none have worn well.

Houlé's plays reflect a society dominated by a God-fearing élite and theocratic concepts at a time of economic crisis during the 1930s. Essentially idealistic—naively so—they feature characters that lack substance and life, victims of moralizing themes. Thus in *Le Presbytère en fleurs* (1933)—his most popular play, with over 200 performances after its première at the MONUMENT NATIONAL in 1929—the good priest of Saint-Alme, by means of a very transparent subterfuge, persuades a doctor to allow his daughter to marry a boy from an inferior social class. In *Matines et laudes; ou, Du bal au cloître* (1940), first performed in 1933, a fashionable young woman visits her friend who has fled to the convent after being deceived by her lover; this meeting is the pretext for a Jansenist critique of wordly attitudes and of polite society. Other plays that achieved fleeting success include *Monsieur ne danse pas*, first performed in 1927, and *Bien fol qui s'y fie*, first performed in 1934.

Houlé is also the author of *L'Histoire du théâtre au Canada* (1945), a pioneering work that extols the classical French repertoire, while still recognizing the importance of an indigenous theatrical tradition.

See *Dictionnaire des oeuvres littéraires du Québec*, 2 (1980) and 3 (1982).   GILBERT DAVID

House, Eric (b. 1923). A skilful comic actor, he is able to convey the seriousness, even the sadness behind his comic roles. A graduate of the Univ. of Toronto, where he appeared in several HART HOUSE THEATRE productions, House gained his early experience in the Straw Hat Players (1948-50), the CANADIAN REPERTORY THEATRE (1951), and CBC television (from 1952). He was one of the original members of the STRATFORD FESTIVAL and the CREST THEATRE, and appeared in the 1956 Stratford production of *Henry V* at the Edinburgh Festival. He then went to London where he appeared in the West End in Will Glickman's and Joseph Stein's *Mrs. Gibbon's Boys* in 1956 and in the Arts Theatre Club production of Jean Genet's *The Balcony* in 1957. Since the early 1960s he has acted in most parts of Canada as well as in New York, Boston, and Minneapolis. He has also appeared in films, directed widely in this country, and written for television.

NEIL CARSON

Hull's Opera House. The first theatre in Calgary, it was constructed in 1893 by Calgary cattleman William Roper Hull to provide facilities for touring companies and local amateurs. The exterior was a decorative red brick, and the interior consisted of a large hall (seating approximately 700) with a small stage, gas lighting, and balconies extending the full length of the building.

From its opening on 22 Mar. 1893 a wide variety of events were presented: concerts, dances, political forums, public auctions, boxing matches, Calgary's first motion pictures, and even church services. Local organizations—such as the Calgary Amateur Orchestra, the Calgary Amateur Dramatic Club, the Fire Brigade Band, and the Calgary Operatic Society—performed there. Melodrama, VAUDEVILLE, musical comedy, grand opera, Shakespeare, and religious pageantry were produced by touring companies such as the Clara Mathes Company, the Harold Nelson SHAW Company, Shipman's Comedians, C.P. WALKER's Comedians, the Australian Comedy Company, the Sherman-Platt Company, and the Tom MARKS Company.

Remodeled by W.B. Sherman, the theatre was reopened on 30 Jan. 1905 as Sherman's Opera House, now featuring permanent raked seating, improved heating, and new scene-changing equipment. Sherman offered repertory performances five days a week at the Opera House until his interest shifted to the newer LYRIC THEATRE which he acquired in 1905. After thirteen years as the focus of culture in Calgary, the theatre was closed, replaced by retail space on the ground floor and rental rooms above. The building was demolished in 1963.

See also the SHERMAN GRAND THEATRE.

JEFFREY GOFFIN

Hunter Duvar, John (1821-99). Born John Hunter in Newburgh, Scotland, he became a reporter and agent in England for the Associated Press of New York and in 1848 married Anne Carter—an illegitimate first cousin of Queen Victoria, according to Hunter's will. In 1857 the couple immigrated to Prince Edward Island, where they created an estate at Hernewood on the northwest part of the island. In 1861 the Lieutenant Governor approved an act to change Hunter's surname to Hunter Duvar. Between 1860 and 1868 he served as an officer in the militia of PEI and Nova Scotia, and was appointed Justice of the Peace for Prince County, PEI, in 1868. He was editor of the Summerside *Progress* (1875-9) and Dominion Inspector of Fisheries (1879-89).

Although PEI theatrical groups such as the Charlottetown Dramatic Club and the Fortune Bay Colony of American actors were active during Hunter Duvar's career, he chose to write closet dramas, none of which—as was his wish—have been performed. The first, *Ten Years*, was published in the *Maritime Monthly* in Aug. 1873. A three-act romantic melodrama, it depicts the adventures of three English merchants who are captured and enslaved by Barbary pirates before escaping with the help of a Moorish princess. *The Enamorado; A Drama* (1879), a verse-tragedy dedicated to Swinburne, dramatizes the life of Mazias of Gallicia, a fifteenth-century Spanish soldier-poet who is unhappy and unsuccessful in love and marriage. Hunter Duvar explores the association between poetic inspiration and madness and concludes—as Bernard Shaw does in *Candida*—that women, at least, prefer the security of conventional marriage to divine frenzy and grand passion.

The title piece of *De Roberval, A Drama; also The Emigration of the Fairies, and The Triumph of Constancy, A Romaunt* (1888) is another verse-drama, based on the life of Jean François de la Roque, Sieur de Roberval, Viceroy and Lieutenant-General of Francis I, a soldier and administrator who in accounts of the colonization of New France is overshadowed by his rival Jacques Cartier. Taking considerable liberties with historical accuracy, Hunter Duvar downplays de Roberval's cruelty, alters the circumstances of his death, and mitigates his conflicts with the Iroquois by inventing his love for the warrior-maiden Ohnawa, who dies saving de Roberval from her kinsmen's arrows.

See *Hernewood. The Personal Diary of Col. John Hunter Duvar June 6 to September 17, 1857. The Story of Anne of Hernewood a Fascinating Lady and the Emigration of the Fairies* (1979), ed. L. George Dewar, and Mark Blagrave, '"O Brave New World": Colonialism in Hunter Duvar's *de Roberval*', *Canadian Drama*, 13 (1987).   ROTA HERZBERG LISTER

Huot, Alexandre (1897-1953). Born at Lévis, Que., he attended the Collège de Lévis and Université Laval. In 1918, while still at Laval, he wrote his first and most unusual play, *Le Songe du conscrit*. Joining the staff of Quebec City's *L'Événement*, he worked as journalist and editor for the rest of his life, moving to Montreal in 1925. Throughout his busy career Huot found time to write popular fiction—publishing three 'thrillers' and collaborating on another—and, in addition to *Le Songe*, three plays: *La Pipe de plâtre* (1923), *Les Pâmoisons du notaire* (1926), and *Le Reporter* (1930).

The one-act *Le Songe du conscrit* was first performed by amateurs at the Cercle Chevalier de Lévis on 24 July 1918 and published that year, under Huot's pseudonym 'Paul Verchères'. The fourteen-page text has one realistic character (the young Conscript) and two phantoms that appear to him in his dream: the infamous Intendant Bigot and heroic Champlain. Bigot rails against the young man's cowardice and that of Quebec in resisting compulsory service. The Conscript protests; Champlain appears, comforts him and supports his people's attitude, assuring him that all will be well with Canada when the war ends. The tone is balanced, the message moderate. *Le Songe* is unique in its topicality, with the Great War still raging and Quebec's conscription riots of March-April 1918 a very recent memory.

La Pipe de plâtre, a one-act comedy, was first staged by amateurs at the Théâtre Parisien in Montreal on 26 Jan. 1923, under the patronage of the Association des Auteurs Canadiens. It turns on a wager a doctor has made as to who can best break in a new clay pipe in a five-day period. The bickering between him and his wife (she accidentally breaks the pipe), the rapid entries and exits, the *quiproquos*, and mistaken identities produce intensive but predictable comic action. *Les Pâmoisons du notaire*, first performed in 1925, is Huot's longest and best-constructed play. The forty-six scenes in this 'comédie-vaudeville en 1 acte' succeed each other with a rapidity that is reminiscent of Feydeau. A newly qualified notary, Maurice Rivard, celebrates his status by borrowing his father's car without permission. It breaks down in the little town of Berthier. He and his companions, two of them female, seek lodging for the night while the police and his parents come looking for them. Mistaken identities, elaborate lies, and unlikely coincidences conspire to produce a rollicking farce in the best *boulevard* tradition.

Huot's last play, *Le Reporter*, apparently never performed, depicts in rhymed alexandrine couplets the curious and heroic deeds of a small-town newspaper reporter as he rescues women and children, unmasks political incompetence and corruption, and wins the hand of the woman he loves.

Huot's theatre is light, amusing, and fast-paced, reflecting—apart from *Le Songe du conscrit*—both the regionalistic vogue in Quebec literature at the time and, paradoxically, the pervasive influence of light Parisian *boulevard* theatre.   L.E. DOUCETTE

Huston, Walter (1884-1950). Born Walter Houghston in Toronto, he took classes at the Shaw School of Acting and the Toronto College of Music, and made his début in 1900 in a musical show at Massey Hall. From 1901 to 1905 he acted in both Canada and the U.S. with several leading companies including Rose Coghlan's, George SUMMERS' and Richard Mansfield's. He then worked as an engineer until 1909, when he began touring in VAUDEVILLE, eventually teaming up with Bayonne Whipple, whom he married in 1914. In 1924 he acted his first important Broadway role in Brock Pemberton's production of Zona Gale's *Mr. Pitt*. Subsequent Broadway successes included parts in Eugene O'Neill's *Desire Under the Elms* in 1924, Ring Lardner's *Elmer the Great* in 1928, Sydney Howard's dramatization of Sinclair Lewis's *Dodsworth* in 1934, and Maxwell Anderson's and Kurt Weill's *Knickerbocker Holiday* in 1938, in which he introduced 'September Song'. He perfected a detailed, powerful, and distinctively American style of realistic acting, learning clear diction from Mansfield, split-second timing, inventiveness, and versatility from vaudeville, and understatement and concentration from a long career in films, which included *Abraham Lincoln* (1930), *Dodsworth* (1936), and his son John's *The Treasure of the Sierre Madre* (1948) in which he gave an Academy-Award-winning performance.

DENIS SALTER

Hutt, William (b. 1920). Born and raised in Toronto, he saw service in the Second World War for which he was awarded the Military Medal. He developed an interest in acting at the Univ. of Toronto, performing at HART HOUSE THEATRE, and began his professional career in Ontario's summer theatres, at Bracebridge (1948) and subsequently at Peterborough and Niagara Falls. In the early 1950s he performed with Ottawa's CANADIAN REPERTORY THEATRE for two seasons, becoming associate director in the second year. He joined the STRATFORD FESTIVAL's inaugural company in 1953, and was the first winner of the Tyrone GUTHRIE Award (1954). Since then he has been almost continuously associated with the Festival as an actor (appearing in more than sixty productions), director, and associate director. During the 1950s Hutt also starred in several tours with the CANADIAN PLAYERS as Macbeth (1955), Hamlet (1956-7), an Eskimo Lear (1961-2), and Elyot in Noël Coward's *Private Lives* (1962-3). Equally at home in formal tragedy or knockabout farce, this

William Hutt in Timothy Findley's John A. Himself!, *Theatre London, 1979*

urbane and versatile leading player is distinguished by an excellent voice, which ranges easily from clipped English to rural Canadian. While a master of the daring moment and the onstage pause, his basic playing style draws an audience to him through its unforced simplicity and generosity of spirit.

Hutt's New York début was in Stratford's production of Christopher Marlowe's *Tamburlaine* in 1956, followed by Friedrich Schiller's *Mary Stuart* and Karel Capek's *The Makropoulos Secret* at New York's Phoenix Theatre in Dec. 1957. In 1964 he created the role of the lawyer in Edward Albee's *Tiny Alice* on Broadway and returned again in 1968 as Warwick in Bernard Shaw's *Saint Joan* at Lincoln Center. In Britain he fulfilled important engagements with the Bristol Old Vic in 1959 as James Tyrone in Eugene O'Neill's *Long Day's Journey Into Night* and in London's West End in Noël Coward's *Waiting in the Wings* in 1960. That same year he was in the pre-Broadway tour of Coward's *Sail Away*. At Stratford during the 1960s and 1970s Hutt demonstrated his prodigious range as Prospero, 1962; Richard II, 1964; Gaev in Chekhov's *The Cherry Orchard*, 1965; Feste, 1967; Tartuffe and Trigorin, 1968; Epicure Mammon in Ben Jonson's *The Alchemist*, 1969; Volpone, 1971; Lear, 1972-3; Lady Bracknell in Oscar Wilde's *The Importance of Being Earnest* and the Duke in *Measure for Measure*, 1975; Vanya, Falstaff, and Titus Andronicus, 1978; and the Fool opposite Peter Ustinov's Lear, 1979-80. After a four-year absence, 1982-5, in which he played Timon of Athens and Claudius at the Grand Theatre, London, Ont. (see GRAND OPERA HOUSE), 1983-4, Hutt returned triumphantly to Stratford as Wolsey in Shakespeare's *Henry VIII* and Thomas More in Robert Bolt's *A Man For All Seasons* in 1986. With the Stratford company he has toured to New York and Edinburgh (1956), Chichester (1964), and he led the company from Copenhagen to Moscow in 1973 and throughout Australia in 1974. Hutt was the first member of the Stratford company to direct at the Festival. His productions include Samuel Beckett's *Waiting For Godot* (1968); *Much Ado About Nothing* (1971); *As You Like It* and Betty Jane WYLIE's *Mark* (1972); Turgenev's *A Month in the Country* (1973); and Shaw's *Saint Joan* (1975). From 1976 to 1979 he was artistic director of Theatre London, overseeing the rebuilding of the Grand Theatre.

Hutt's contemporary work in the 1980s includes leading parts in Peter Shaffer's *Equus*, Ronald Harwood's *The Dresser*, Bernard Pomerance's *The Elephant Man*, David W. Rintel's *Clarence Darrow*, and John MURRELL's *New World*. In films he has been featured in *Oedipus Rex* (1956), *The Fixer* (1967), and Timothy FINDLEY's *The Wars* (1981). On television he won both ACTRA and Canadian Film Awards in 1975 for his portrayal of John A. Macdonald in *The National Dream*, and the CBC's Prix Anik Award for playing Bernard Shaw in Richard Huggett's *The First Night of Pygmalion*. Other honours include the Centennial Medal (1967), Companion of the Order of Canada (1969), and honorary doctorates from the Universities of Ottawa, Guelph, and Western Ontario.

See Keith Garebian, *William Hutt, a Theatre Portrait* (1988).   DAVID GARDNER

Hyland, Frances (b. 1927). Born in Shaunavon, Sask., she studied acting as a child with Mary Ellen Burgess, making her début (at about age ten) in Stuart Walker's adaptation of Oscar Wilde's *The Birthday of the Infanta*. She studied at the Univ. of Saskatchewan (BA, 1948) before entering London's Royal Academy of Dramatic Art on a scholarship in 1948. She won the silver medal at

RADA and made her London début as Stella in Tennessee Williams' *A Streetcar Named Desire* at the Aldwych Theatre in June 1950. Among the roles she played as a contract player for producer H.M. Tennant were Perdita in *The Winter's Tale* in 1951 and Gelda in Christopher Fry's *The Dark is Light Enough* in 1954, both directed by Peter Brook.

Hyland returned to Canada in 1954 to play Isabella, opposite James Mason, in *Measure for Measure*, and Bianca in director Tyrone GUTHRIE's Western-style *Taming of the Shrew* at the STRATFORD FESTIVAL. She spent eight of the next thirteen summers at Stratford (1955, 1957-9, 1964-7), playing a wide variety of Shakespearean roles, including Portia (1955), Ophelia (1957), Desdemona (1959), Goneril (1964), Doll Tearsheet (1965), Queen Margaret (in *Henry VI*, 1966, and *Richard III*, 1967), and Mistress Ford (1967). She also played Varya in John HIRSCH's 1965 production of Chekhov's *The Cherry Orchard*. During the winter months she toured with the CANADIAN PLAYERS (1955-7, 1962-3), most notably as Shaw's Saint Joan in 1955. She

James Mason and Frances Hyland in Measure for Measure, *Stratford Festival, 1954*

Hyland

acted with Toronto's CREST THEATRE (1954-5, 1958-9, 1964, 1965), starring for that company in the North American première of Graham Greene's *The Living Room* (in 1954), as Eliza in Shaw's *Pygmalion* (1958-9), and Cleopatra in his *Caesar and Cleopatra* (1964). During this period she also acted in American regional theatres (e.g. the Goodman Theatre, Chicago, 1958-9), on Broadway (making her début in Thomas Wolfe's *Look Homeward, Angel* in 1957), and again in London. In the 1960s she increasingly worked at Canada's expanding network of regional theatres, including the MANITOBA THEATRE CENTRE, where she played Catherine in Bertolt Brecht's *Mother Courage* in 1964 and Ariel in *The Tempest* in 1966. In the 1968-9 VANCOUVER PLAYHOUSE season Hyland played Blanche in *A Streetcar Named Desire*, created the title role in George RYGA's *The ECSTASY OF RITA JOE*, and directed Orson Welles' adaptation of *Moby Dick*.

Since then Hyland has worked steadily as a leading actress and as a director across Canada. She has played roles in Michel TREMBLAY's *Forever Yours, Marie-Lou* (in 1975) and Tennessee Williams' *Night of the Iguana* (1978) at Edmonton's CITADEL THEATRE; Timothy FINDLEY's *Can You See Me Yet?* at the NATIONAL ARTS CENTRE in 1976; Thomas Dekker's *The Shoemaker's Holiday* for Toronto Arts Productions at the ST LAWRENCE CENTRE in 1977; and frequent appearances at the SHAW FESTIVAL, in Shaw's *Heartbreak House* (in 1968), *Candida* (1970), and *Back to Methuselah* (1986), and in Ibsen's *John Gabriel Borkman* (1978) and Nöel Coward's *The Vortex* (1985). She has performed frequently on radio and television. Her extensive directing credits include Harold Pinter's *The Birthday Party* at THEATRE CALGARY in 1970, *Othello* at Stratford in 1979, Euripides' *The Trojan Women* and Shaw's *Arms and the Man* at the Citadel in 1979 and 1980 respectively, and Strindberg's *Playing With Fire* at the Shaw Festival in 1987. An actress of unusual versatility whose mannered style is often characterized as 'aristocratic', Hyland has received numerous awards, holds two honorary doctorates, and is a member of the Order of Canada.

HERBERT WHITTAKER

I

Imperial Opera House. The first building in Vancouver specifically constructed for theatrical performances, it was built at a cost of $10,000 by local architect William Crickmay and financier Hugh Robson, and was located at the intersection of Abbot and Pender Streets, close to the original townsite. A wooden structure 120' × 50', it had a stage measuring 30' × 49' and the proscenium opening was 23' wide and 15' high. Seating capacity was 600, including a gallery for 280. Equipped with footlights, raked stage, and six dressing rooms, it opened on 25 Apr. 1889 with a recital by the Mendelssohn Quintet of Boston. A few weeks later, on 13 May 1889, there was a 'grand opening and dedication' with a performance of *The Pearl of Savoy* by the Thomas Keene Theatre Company. It remained the city's main theatre for touring companies as well as for amateur performances until 1892, when it began to be superseded by the recently opened VANCOUVER OPERA HOUSE, a larger theatre in a more fashionable location. It was last used as a theatre in 1894. Thereafter it served a variety of purposes before being converted into a livery stable in 1903. R.B. TODD

Imperial Theatre. Built for the Keith-Albee VAUDEVILLE and movie interests of New York on the persuasion of Walter H. Golding (1876-1945), Saint John's Imperial Theatre opened on 19 Sept. 1913. The architect was Albert E. Westover of Philadelphia, principal contractor was H.L.Brown, and the building was supervised by W.S. McKenny, who had supervised the building of the 'sister' Imperial Theatre in Montreal. Overall dimensions of the building were 168' × 78', a 24' depth across the front being occupied by offices and shops. The heavily ornamented proscenium arch (34' × 26') was crowned by a frescoed soffit. The stage (76' × 26'), fronted by an orchestra pit, boasted a full fly gallery and the 'first real fire curtain in Canada'—450 lbs. of asbestos. Stock scenery was imported from New York. Seating capacity on opening was 1,800. The house was done in old rose and moorish tints and featured remarkable Italianate decorative plasterwork on box cornices, balcony front, and around the central electrolier.

Managed by Golding, a pioneer of live orchestral accompaniment to silent films, the Imperial maintained its own orchestra. Although designed primarily as a movie house, the theatre (renamed the Capitol in 1929) also served large professional touring attractions and local amateurs. Touring performers included Ethel Barrymore, John Martin-Harvey, Gracie Fields, John Philip Sousa and his band, the DUMBELLS, the ARMY SHOW, and the NAVY SHOW. Walter Pidgeon, a native son of Saint John, played on the Imperial's stage as a youth. In 1952 the Capitol hosted the DOMINION DRAMA FESTIVAL.

The conversion of the building in 1957 to a church largely preserved its theatrical appointments; in Nov. 1983 it was purchased by the non-profit Bi-Capitol Project Inc., to be restored as a performing arts centre.

MARK BLAGRAVE

International Players, The. Founded in Kingston in 1948 by Arthur Sutherland—who had previously founded New York's Imperial Players—the company opened on 29 June 1948 at the La Salle Hotel ballroom for a ten-week season that culminated with the première of Robertson DAVIES' *Fortune, My Foe*. After a second summer season (of fifteen weeks) in Kingston, Sutherland opened a winter-spring season at Toronto's Leaside Collegiate, continuing in both cities for the rest of the Players' history. In 1952 and 1953 the Players performed for part of each week in towns near Kingston (Gananoque, Napanee, Prescott), and for one period in 1952 operated separate companies simultaneously in Kingston and Toronto. On 6 Sept. 1953 the Players recorded their 1,000th perfor-

mance, but Sutherland died of a heart attack later that month. Drew Thompson—who had been with the company from the beginning and had served as co-producer from 1950—ran a final season in 1954.

The repertoire of the International Players normally consisted of light comedy, melodrama, and domestic drama, occasionally including more challenging fare such as Jack Kirkland's *Tobacco Road* and Tennessee Williams' *The Glass Menagerie*. Critical reaction was not uniformly favourable, especially in Toronto, but the Players helped establish SUMMER STOCK in post-war Canada. They also offered opportunities to Canadian playwrights (Davies' *Fortune, My Foe* and *AT MY HEART'S CORE*, and Clifford Braggins's *Look What's Doin'*, for example) and to many other Canadians who went on to significant careers in Canada and the U.S.—including Joy COGHILL, Donald DAVIS, Timothy FINDLEY, William HUTT, Charmion KING, William NEEDLES, Bernard SLADE, and Neil Vipond.

RICHARD PLANT

Irwin, May (1862-1938). Comedienne ('a female Falstaff') and singer, she was born Georgia Campbell in Whitby, Ont., where she sang in the Episcopal choir and attended high school. At thirteen her father died and she ventured into VAUDEVILLE with her sister Ada. Changing their names to the Irwin Sisters (May and Flora), they made their début on 8 Feb. 1875 at the Theatre Comique, Rochester, N.Y., and joined Daniel Shelby's variety circuit. Two years later they were on Broadway performing songs and sketches for Tony Pastor (1877-83), followed by supporting parts in Augustin Daly's stock company (1883-7). After extensive touring (including England in 1884) and engagements with Charles Frohman, May formed her own management (1894-1908). Her roles evolved from saucy soubrettes (she was blonde and blue-eyed) to buxom countesses and good-natured widows. Her prolonged kissing sequence from *The Widow Jones* became one of Edison's early one-reel films (*The Kiss*, 1896). Alternating between farce and vaudeville, 'Madame Laughter' wrote many songs and helped popularize, among white audiences, the rag-time music and cake-walk dances of black America.

DAVID GARDNER

J

Jackson, Brian (b. 1926). Born in Bournemouth, Eng., he attended the Bournemouth College of Art and the Old Vic Theatre School. After army service he began his career in the properties department of the Old Vic in 1947. He came to Canada as head of properties at the STRATFORD FESTIVAL in 1955, a position he held until 1963 while gradually establishing himself as a designer. For the CANADIAN PLAYERS he designed Shaw's *Man and Superman* in 1957 and in following years Shaw's *Arms and the Man*, Shakespeare's *Twelfth Night*, Synge's *The Playboy of the Western World*, and Eliot's *Murder in the Cathedral*. His first design credit at Stratford was for *The Beggar's Opera* in 1958, followed by *A Midsummer Night's Dream* in 1960. He collaborated with Tanya MOISEIWITSCH on the remodelling of the Festival stage in 1962, and his designs for *Timon of Athens* (1963) featured in the company's British tour in 1964. Jackson's *H.M.S. Pinafore* (1960), *The Pirates of Penzance* (1961), and *The Mikado* (1963) matched in their designs the new spirit breathed into the Savoy operettas by Tyrone GUTHRIE, although his sets for Chekhov's *The Seagull* in 1968 and Ivan Turgenev's *A Month in the Country* in 1973 at the Avon Theatre also showed a sympathy for the realistic scenic convention. He continues to work at Stratford, and designed *Two Gentlemen of Verona* in 1988.

Jackson created a memorable design for Wilde's *The Importance of Being Earnest* at the MANITOBA THEATRE CENTRE in 1965, and from 1968 to 1972 he was resident designer at the VANCOUVER PLAYHOUSE, where his *The Royal Hunt of the Sun* (by Peter Shaffer) was notable. Jackson has also worked at the NATIONAL ARTS CENTRE—designing *Cosi Fan Tutte*, *Oh, What a Lovely War!*, and *Twelfth Night* in 1973, *Man and Superman* and *Don Juan in Hell* in 1977.   MARTHA MANN

Janson, Astrid (b. 1947). Born in Germany, she grew up in Canada and attended Waterloo Lutheran Univ. and the Univ. of British Columbia, where she earned her MFA in theatre design in 1972. After a short period in 1972 as costume designer for the Toronto Dance Theatre, she became resident designer for TORONTO WORKSHOP PRODUCTIONS (1973-7), where her notable designs included those for the première of TEN LOST YEARS. From 1975 to 1984 she designed costumes for CBC-TV, while maintaining an active freelance career in theatre design. Her startling perspex set design for Ibsen's *The Master Builder* at Toronto's TARRAGON THEATRE in 1983 contrasted with a delicate lace-tablecloth effect for Chekhov's *The Cherry Orchard* at the SHAW FESTIVAL in 1980. For YOUNG PEOPLE'S THEATRE in Toronto she designed Mordecai Richler's *Jacob Two-Two Meets the Hooded Fang* in 1984 (revived in 1987) and *Richard III* in 1987. A lavish *Cabaret* for CENTRESTAGE in Toronto in 1983 was balanced by the more intimate *The Grace of Mary Traverse* (by Timberlake Wertenbaker) at TORONTO FREE THEATRE in 1987. At the STRATFORD FESTIVAL she designed costumes for Gilbert and Sullivan's *H.M.S. Pinafore* in 1981 and *Othello* in 1987.

Extremely versatile, Janson helped create the Ontario pavilion at Expo '86 in Vancouver, and worked with the Desrosiers Dance Company on *Incognito* at the 1988 Calgary Olympics. She designed *The Tales of Hoffman* for the Canadian Opera Company in 1987.

Janson has exhibited at the Prague Quadrennial, has won several Doras for her Toronto designs, and in 1980 received the Toronto Drama Bench Award for distinguished contributions to Canadian theatre.

MARTHA MANN

Jasmin, Claude (b. 1930). Born in Montreal, he obtained a diploma in ceramics from the École du Meuble in 1951, subsequently working as a commercial artist and in children's theatre before becoming a set designer for Radio-Canada in 1956, a position he still holds.

Jasmin has been a prolific novelist, essayist, journalist, and pamphleteer, as well as a playwright for radio, television, and the stage. His earliest dramatic works include five radio plays broadcast between 1953 and 1955, but his later television serials gained him a wide popular following: 'La Petite Patrie' (weekly

1974–6) and 'Boogie-Woogie 47' (1980–1) are based on his autobiographical sketches *La Petite Patrie* (1972), *Pointe-Calumet Boogie-Woogie* (1973), and *Sainte-Adèle-la-vaisselle* (1974), which are sympathetic evocations of the people and the neighbourhood of his childhood.

Jasmin's individual plays for television have been less well received. *La Rue de la liberté*, produced in 1960, is an overly symbolic work dealing with freedom and power. *La Mort dans l'âme* (1971), first produced in 1962, now seems a clichéd treatment of drug addiction. *Les Mains vides*, produced in 1963, uses a murder trial to reveal the hidden side of the characters. *Blues pour un homme averti* (1964), produced on television in 1964 and on stage in 1966, repeats the main theme of his novel *La Corde au cou* (1960)—the search for a father figure by a violent mythomaniac. *Tuez le veau gras* (1970), produced in 1965, deals with a young intellectual's attempt to unionize the pulp-and-paper workers of his home town; though effective as social commentary, it has weak secondary characters that impair its dramatic quality. Jasmin's later television plays—*Un certain chemin de croix*, 1968, and *Procès devant juge seul*, 1977—remain unpublished, though *La Cabane du skieur*, produced in 1972, was published as *C'est toujours la même histoire* (1972); it is the story of the ill-fated love of a bourgeois girl for an American hippy.

Jasmin's stage plays compare unfavourably with his television work. *Le Veau dort* (1979), written in 1955 and produced (at the DOMINION DRAMA FESTIVAL) in 1963, consists of ten Brechtian tableaux criticizing western society. The experimental *La Tortue* and *Tuer-Kill*, both produced in 1967 (at Sir George Williams University and at Expo '67, respectively), are unsuccessful explorations of war and violence.

See Mireille Trudeau, *Claude Jasmin*. Dossiers de documentation sur la littérature Canadienne-Française (1973). See also RADIO DRAMA IN QUEBEC and TELEVISION DRAMA IN QUEBEC.   D.W. RUSSELL

Jeune Latour, Le. Antoine GÉRIN-LAJOIE's play, the first tragedy written and published in Canada, was composed in 1843 and performed at the Collège de Nicolet (where Gérin-Lajoie was a student) on 31 July 1844, with the author playing the title role. Newspaper accounts were glowing, one comparing the young author to Racine. The text was published in 1844, in two newspapers and in a separate edition (Montréal: Cinq-Mars). The plot, drawn from Michel Bibaud's *Histoire du Canada sous la domination française* (1837), is a heroic tale of a military family, the De Latours, and their struggle for the little Acadian outpost of Cape Sable in 1629–30. As in Bibaud's history, the father, Claude, is a traitor, trying to win for the English the little garrison captained by his son Roger. Unable to persuade him to yield, the elder Latour leads an armed assault against the outpost, but his son's valiant resistance wins the day. Repentant, Claude throws his lot in with his son, who receives him with generous forgiveness.

Gérin-Lajoie's style emulates that of Corneille, including his sonorous rhymed alexandrine couplets and attempts at pithy, sententious aphorisms. His vocabulary, too, is that of Corneille and Racine, with a strong penchant towards preciosity. *Le Jeune Latour* is static and verbose, its three acts repetitive, its characters devoid of psychological depth or development. Its saving grace is the passionate sincerity, the ardent patriotism in which the text is steeped. Six years after the Patriote Rebellion, when many participants were still in exile, the young author's heroic sentiments and lofty ideals moved Lower Canada's élite profoundly, and indeed certain passages cannot leave a modern reader unmoved.

Gérin-Lajoie never again turned his hand to drama, and later dismissed *Le Jeune Latour* as 'college theatre, of the type that should remain there.' It does, however, represent an important step in the evolution of theatre in French Canada, and has been so recognized by generations of critics. It was revived at the Collège de Nicolet in 1916. An excellent English translation by Louise Forsyth was published in *Canada's Lost Plays* (1982), vol. 4.

See René Dionne, *Antoine Gérin-Lajoie, homme de lettres* (1978) and L.E. Doucette, *Theatre in French Canada, 1606–1867* (1984).
                    L.E. DOUCETTE

Johns, Ted (b. 1942). Born in Seaforth, Ont., he was educated at the Univ. of Toronto, and taught at Brock Univ. before beginning a long association with Toronto's THEATRE PASSE MURAILLE in 1972 as an actor in *The FARM SHOW*. With his wife, Janet

AMOS, he acted in numerous plays for the company, including the collectives *Far As the Eye Can See* (written with Rudy Wiebe), *The West Show, Them Donnellys, The Horsburgh Scandal, Under the Greywacke, The Oil Show*, and *Shakespeare for Fun and Profit*. (See COLLECTIVE CREATION.) Johns' plays include *Naked on the North Shore* (1976), produced at TPM in Mar. 1977, based on his experiences as a teacher in a one-room school in a remote fishing village; *The School Show* (1978), produced at the BLYTH FESTIVAL in Aug. 1978, about the Huron County teachers' strike; and *St Sam and the Nukes* (1980), produced at Blyth in July 1980, an examination of the pros and cons of nuclear power. Johns' *Country Hearts*, an unpublished musical, was produced in Aug. 1982 at the Blyth Festival, and in May 1985 at THEATRE NEW BRUNSWICK. His *Garrison's Garage* (1984) was produced at Blyth in June 1984 and TNB in Oct. 1985.

JAMES DEFELICE

Joudry, Patricia (b. 1921). Born in Spirit River, Alta, and raised in Montreal, Joudry had written over 250 radio scripts (see RADIO DRAMA) by 1954, including three situation-comedy series: 'Penny's Diary' (CBC, 1941-5); 'The Aldrich Family' (NBC, 1945-9); and 'Affectionately Jenny' (CBC, 1951-2). *Teach Me How To Cry* (1955), produced by Andrew ALLAN for CBC's 'Stage' on 19 Apr. 1953, explores the joys and pains of adolescence and first love. When produced in New York on stage, 5 Apr. 1955, critics judged the play as 'everywhere marked by talent' and 'one of the best plays of the season.' The UNIVERSITY ALUMNAE DRAMATIC CLUB of Toronto staged the Canadian première on 12 Mar. 1956 and Universal Studios adapted the play as the movie *The Restless Years* (1959).

The Sand Castle (1981), a comedy satirizing Freudian psychoanalysis, was produced in a television adaptation (CBC, 12 Apr. 1955), and by the Margo Jones Theatre in Dallas. After *Three Rings For Michelle* (1960), a morality play decrying fundamentalist religious dogma, failed commercially at the Avenue Theatre, Toronto, in Nov. 1956, Joudry and her family moved to England where *Teach Me How To Cry*, now titled *Noon Has No Shadows*, was produced in July 1958 in London's West End with an all-Canadian cast.

Two stage plays followed: *Semi-Detached* (New York, 10 Mar. 1960), which explores the bigoted relationships between two households in Montreal, one Protestant and English, the other Catholic and French; and *Walk Alone Together* (London, 7 June 1960), a lively comedy concerning child-rearing. Neither play enjoyed a long run.

Joudry's plays for television (see TELEVISION DRAMA) enjoyed considerable success. They include *The Song of Louise In The Morning* (1960), broadcast on CBS; *Something Old, Something New* (CBC, 11 June 1961); *The Dinner Party* (London, ATV, 9 July 1961); and *Valerie* (CBC, 18 Oct. 1961).

A number of plays written under the influence of Spiritualism have not been produced or published. Joudry's writings in England include the plays *Toe of Clay, God Goes Heathen, Think Again*, and *I Ching*. Only *Think Again*, a delightful science-fiction comedy, was produced (1982) and published (1979). She returned to Canada in 1973, and presently resides in St Denis, Sask. *A Modest Orgy* (1982) was Joudry's first stage play to be produced in Canada in twenty-four years, in 1981 by 25TH STREET THEATRE, Saskatoon. A comedy, the play satirizes sexual experimentation while defending the traditional family framework.

Joudry's finest dramatic work has been for specific radio programs, a familiar audience, and under the guidance of a sympathetic director or producer. In these she writes perceptively and expresses a variety of contemporary social concerns with clarity and insight. Many of her observations on marriage, child-rearing, and woman's identity were clearly in advance of her time.

AVIVA RAVEL

Juliani, John (b. 1940). Born in Montreal, this avant-garde director trained in acting at the NATIONAL THEATRE SCHOOL, worked two seasons at the STRATFORD FESTIVAL, and was hired in 1966 to teach theatre at Simon Fraser Univ., B.C., where he began the SAVAGE GOD series of experiments in theatre, emphasizing the principles of 'economy, flexibility and mobility'. After holding a 1973-4 Canada Council grant, during which he travelled and studied world theatre, he helped create the graduate program in drama at York Univ., Toronto. He directed it for two years before moving in 1976 to Edmonton, in both places producing further Savage God work. In 1981 Juliani returned to Vancouver, where he works as a CBC radio-drama producer and freelance director of stage, television, and film drama. In Sept. 1986 he directed George RYGA's *Paracelsus* for the VANCOUVER PLAYHOUSE; both his direction and the play were severely criticized.   JAMES HOFFMAN

Jupiter Theatre. Founded in Toronto in 1951 by a group of CBC Radio actors—including Lorne GREENE, John Drainie, and Len PETERSON—it set out 'to produce plays of repute, both classic and contemporary, and to promote the production of plays by Canadian dramatists'. In addition, it hoped 'to establish a professional theatre which . . . would be self-sustaining, and sufficiently remunerative to Canadian artists to preclude their loss to Canada through their departure for greener fields.'

Jupiter's first season opened on 14 Dec. 1951; forty-one performances of four plays were given in the Museum Theatre of the Royal Ontario Museum: Bertolt Brecht's *Galileo*, directed and designed by Herbert WHITTAKER; American playwright Dalton Trumbo's *The Biggest Thief in Town*, directed by Roeberta Beatty; Lister SINCLAIR's *Socrates*, directed by Esse LJUNGH, the surprise success of the season; and Jean-Paul Sartre's *Crime Passionel*, directed by Edward Ludlum.

The ambitious second season ran for 103 nights, from Oct. 1952 to May 1953, with seven plays: Eugene O'Neill's *Anna Christie*; Tennessee Williams' *Summer and Smoke*; George Kelly's *The Show-Off*; Christopher Fry's *A Sleep of Prisoners* (produced in St Andrew's Church) and *The Lady's Not For Burning* (starring Christopher PLUMMER and revived late in the season by popular demand at HART HOUSE THEATRE); and two Canadian plays, Ted ALLAN's *Money Makers* and Nathan COHEN's *Blue is for Mourning*.

The Museum Theatre—occupied by the NEW PLAY SOCIETY—was unavailable for the 1953-4 season, forcing the new executive producer, Leonard Crainford (formerly of Britain's Shakespeare Memorial Theatre), to seek alternative venues. Two productions were presented at the Ryerson Theatre—Luigi Pirandello's *Right You Are* and Lister Sinclair's *The Blood is Strong*. The ROYAL ALEXANDRA THEATRE was used for Jean Anouilh's *Ring Round the Moon* (starring Douglas RAIN) and Noël Coward's *Relative Values*. Four further plays were announced, two of them Canadian—Len Peterson's *Never Shoot a Devil* and Ted Allan's *Answer to a Question*—but a financial crisis prevented their production and the company disbanded.   STEPHEN JOHNSON

K

Kam Theatre. Founded in 1974 as the Kaministiquia Theatre Laboratory in Kaministiquia, Ont., near Thunder Bay, it has aimed at presenting COLLECTIVE CREATIONs of particular relevance to Northern Ontarions. At first exclusively a touring organization, it has for several years presented a regular season at the Ukrainian Labour Temple in Thunder Bay, from which it makes extensive annual tours. The company is known for its production of issue-oriented musical collectives (*Dancing with the Daughters of Radon* in 1975-6, about uranium mining), *commedia dell'arte* satires (*Nothing Like A Rock/Rien comme une roche* in 1975-6, from

a scenario by John Book), and plays of interest to a northern rural audience (Herschel HARDIN's *Esker Mike and His Wife, Agiluk* in 1975-6, George RYGA's *Ploughmen of the Glacier* in 1980-1, and *Stars in the Sky Morning*, by Rhonda Payne, Jan Henderson, and Jane Dingle, about Newfoundland women, in 1985-6). In 1981 Kam commissioned Ryga's *A Letter to My Son* to celebrate the ninetieth anniversary of Ukrainian settlement in Canada, and in the same year hosted 'Bread and Circuses', a national festival of ALTERNATE THEATRE. Its name was changed to Kam Theatre Lab in 1979 and to Kam Theatre in 1981.   STEPHEN JOHNSON

Kareda

Kareda, Urjo (b. 1944). As critic, dramaturge, radio commentator, and artistic director, he has been a central figure in the development of indigenous Canadian dramatic writing during the 1970s and 1980s. Educated at the Univ. of Toronto and King's College, Cambridge, the Estonia-born writer was a university lecturer and free-lance writer prior to becoming film critic and then drama critic for the *Toronto Star*.

Kareda's tenure as the *Star*'s drama critic, 1971-5, coincided with the explosion of theatrical activity that Toronto witnessed in the early 1970s. His reviews, imbued with the excitement of this period, articulated a compelling personal response to new voices like David FRENCH, Paul THOMPSON, and Michel TREMBLAY.

In 1975 Kareda became literary manager of the STRATFORD FESTIVAL. There he experienced his first opportunity to commission and work collaboratively with such writers as Edna O'Brien, John MURRELL, and Tom CONE, while also participating in the selection and casting of the Festival's programs and co-directing a number of productions with artistic director Robin PHILLIPS, including Murrell's new versions of Chekhov's *Uncle Vanya* and *The Seagull*.

Kareda returned in 1980 to Toronto where, after working as director of script development for CBC Radio Drama, he succeeded Bill GLASSCO in 1982 as artistic director of TARRAGON THEATRE. Working with both established and unproduced writers, either individually or in playwrights' units, Kareda has been involved in the development of thirty or more scripts each year. Under his guidance as many as seven world premières have been staged at Tarragon in a single season.

Although catholic in his dramatic tastes, Kareda has evinced a strong literary sensibility, preferring plays that achieve their impact more through the power of language and characterization than through physicality or post-expressionist techniques. His efforts have contributed greatly to the development of such young writers as Judith THOMPSON, Steve PETCH, and Don Hannah, and have increased and enriched the repertoire of original Canadian works.　　　　IRA A. LEVINE

Kerr, Lois Reynolds (b. 1908). Born in Hamilton, Ont., and educated at the Univ. of Toronto, she won a national playwright's competition with her one-act play *Open Doors* (1930), first produced in 1931 by Toronto's Little Playhouse. This led to her appointment with the Toronto *Globe*'s women's department, where she worked from 1930 to 1937. In 1933 she was invited to join the Playwrights' Studio Group, founded in 1932 by Dora Smith Conover, Rica McLean Farquharson, and Leonora McNeilly. Committed to staging original Canadian plays, the Group's membership also included Marjorie Price, Virginia Coyne Knight, Winnifred Pilcher, Arthur Burrows, Jameson Field, and Margaret Ness. The Group wrote and produced over sixty plays, most of them comedies, and most at HART HOUSE THEATRE, between 1932 and 1940.

The newspaper profession shared by a number of these playwrights provided the background for many of Kerr's plays. *Among Those Present* (1938) and *Nellie McNabb* (1937), her most popular play, were produced at Hart House Theatre in 1933 and 1934 respectively. Like *Guest of Honour* (produced in 1936), they deal with the world served by the women's department of a thirties' newspaper, and represent the escapist social comedy typical of that period. The production of Kerr's espionage comedy *X.Y.7.* in 1939 was her last full-length dramatic work with the Playwrights' Studio Group, but she did contribute to the wartime revues *Well, Of All Things* and *Keep It Flying*, staged by the Group in 1940 to raise funds for the war effort.

After moving in 1950 to Vancouver, where she still lives, she was prevented by family responsibilities and the lack of an outlet for producing from working in the theatre again until the 1960s. Plays written in Vancouver include *No Reporters Please!* and *O Woman!*, which were produced by the University Women's Club, Vancouver, in 1969 and 1972 respectively. *No Reporters Please!* won honourable mention at the 1970 Pacific Writers Conference in Seattle.　　PATRICK B. O'NEILL

Kerr, Tom (b. 1929). Born in Scotland, he trained at the Univ. of British Columbia, before earning such recognition as the Louis Jouvet Trophy for best director at the 1964 DOMINION DRAMA FESTIVAL. He was founding artistic director of the Western Canada Youth Theatre (later the Western Canada Theatre Company) in Kamloops from 1969 to 1976, winning an Edinburgh Festival

Fringe First Award for his 1973 production of George RYGA's *The ECSTASY OF RITA JOE*, its British première; he won again in 1979 with a production of David FREEMAN's *CREEPS* from the Univ. of Saskatchewan, where he was head of the Department of Drama from 1976 to 1983. His successful free-lance directing career and reputation for capable financial management led to his appointment as artistic director of Halifax's NEPTUNE THEATRE from 1983 to 1986, and (less successfully) as director of the 1986 STRATFORD FESTIVAL's Third Stage, after which he resumed his career as an educator and free-lance director on the west coast. It was announced, however, in Dec. 1988 that he would return to the Neptune as guest director for the 1989–90 season.

HARRY LANE

Kinch, Martin (b. 1943). Born in London, Eng., he immigrated to Canada in 1948. After graduating in English from the Univ. of Western Ontario in 1966, he studied directing with the Birmingham Repertory Theatre in 1967-8 before founding with John PALMER in 1969 the Canadian Place Theatre at Stratford, Ont., a low-budget and short-lived enterprise noteworthy as one of the first theatres to adopt an all-Canadian production policy. Although he held various directorial positions during the late 1960s, including two seasons as an assistant director at the STRATFORD FESTIVAL, it was not until he co-founded TORONTO FREE THEATRE with Palmer and Tom HENDRY in 1971 that his talents as a director and playwright fully emerged.

Best known for his première productions of plays by Canadian playwrights such as Palmer, Carol BOLT, Michael HOLLINGS-WORTH, and Michael Ondaatje, Kinch is also important for the image and direction he provided TFT as its first artistic director. Beside introducing controversial new plays in high quality productions, he developed a company of fine young actors, of whom many—Saul Rubinek, Clare COULTER, R.H. THOMSON, and David Bolt, for example—have made important careers. Of the four plays that Kinch wrote and directed during this period, only one is published—*Me?* (1975)—which perhaps accounts for his negligible reputation as a playwright. First produced at TFT in 1973, then remounted in 1977, *Me?* nevertheless is worthwhile if only for its carefully drawn portrait of Toronto's

artistic community. The play also suggests the types of problems that may have led Kinch to resign from TFT in 1978 to pursue a career in television drama with the CBC. Although he produced a prestigious six-part series of tele-films, *Some Honourable Men*, commissioned from Canadian playwrights, his work at the CBC failed to sustain his enthusiasm and he resigned in 1985 to accept the position of artistic director of THEATRE CALGARY on the eve of its moving into the Calgary Centre for the Arts, a position he continues to hold.

See Robert Wallace and Cynthia Zimmerman, eds., *The Work* (1982).

ROBERT WALLACE

King, Charmion (b. 1925). Born and educated in Toronto, she first achieved critical acclaim in 1947, while a student at the Univ. of Toronto, with her performance of the title role in Shaw's *Saint Joan* at HART HOUSE THEATRE. She was a member of the original Straw Hat Players and in 1953, after two years of study in England, she performed at Toronto's CREST THEATRE, where she achieved particular success in the title role of Jean Giraudoux's *Madwoman of Chaillot* in 1961 and in Chekhov's *Three Sisters*. At the STRATFORD FESTIVAL King played opposite Jason Robards Jr and Christopher PLUMMER in 1958, and on Broadway in Tyrone GUTHRIE's production of Robertson DAVIES' *Love and Libel* in 1960. She created the role of Jessica Logan in David FRENCH's *Jitters* at Toronto's TARRAGON THEATRE in 1979. Her film credits include *Nobody Waved Goodbye* (1964) and *Who Has Seen the Wind* (1977) and she played Aunt Josephine in CBC-TV's *ANNE OF GREEN GABLES* in 1985. King won a Nellie Award as best radio actress of 1985. She is married to Gordon PINSENT.

ROTA HERZBERG LISTER

King, Jack (1930-1987). Born in Chatham, Ont., he began his theatrical career as an actor in amateur theatre at the age of fourteen. After seasons in SUMMER STOCK in Leamington, Ont., and Erie, Pennsylvania, he moved to Toronto in 1963, where he worked in the properties departments of the Canadian Opera Company and the National Ballet. In 1964 he joined the props department of the STRATFORD FESTIVAL, where his talents as a dyer and painter of costumes attracted the attention of Leslie Hurry, the prominent Stratford designer. For the next ten years King worked as Hurry's principal assistant at Stratford and at the SHAW FESTIVAL. In 1969—on a Tyrone GUTHRIE scholarship from Stratford—he went to England's Slade School to study painting, a discipline that became the principal influence on his work as a designer.

King had a long association with the London Little Theatre, for which he designed Peter Weiss's *Marat/Sade* (the North American première), Julian Moore's, David Heneker's, and Monty Norman's *Irma La Douce*, and Oscar Hammerstein's and Jerome Kern's *Show Boat*, among many other shows. With Ed Kotanen he supervised design at Theatre London (see GRAND OPERA HOUSE, London) from 1979 to 1982. Particular accomplishments at Theatre London were his designs for Eric NICOL's *Gwendolyn*, Molière's *The Misanthrope*, and *The Incredible Murder of Cardinal Tosca* by Walter LEARNING and Alden NOWLAN.

Sue and Ken Kramer at the conclusion of a performance of Macbeth, *Globe Theatre, Regina, 1972*

King's capacity for lyric theatre took him frequently to Winnipeg's Rainbow Stage where Lionel Bart's *Oliver* (1978), Lerner and Loewe's *My Fair Lady* (1973), and Cole Porter's *Kiss Me Kate* (1981) were perhaps his outstanding designs. In Ottawa he created *Moralities* for Theatre Ballet and in Toronto his designs for the National Ballet—*Mad Shadows* (1976), *Brown Earth* (1971), and *Washington Square* (1979)—were widely acclaimed.

In 1985 King and Ed Kotanen opened the first independent scenic studio in Toronto.
MARTHA MANN

Kramer, Ken (b. 1940) and **Sue Kramer** (1939-78). Co-founders of the GLOBE THEATRE, Regina, Canadian-born Ken Kramer met and married Sue Richmond in England while acting in Brian Way's Theatre Centre touring company. When they moved to Canada in 1965, they dreamed of establishing a populist theatre company (staged in-the-round), based on Way's philosophy and on that of Peter Cheeseman's Victoria Theatre in Stoke-on-Trent. Attempts in Vancouver and in Edmonton, however, failed. When Sue Kramer accepted a summer teaching job in Charlottetown in 1966, the couple's separation forced them to reassess their options. They decided to try once more to find support for a theatre company. A positive response came from the Saskatchewan Arts

Board, and in the autumn of 1966 the Globe Theatre was launched as a touring company presenting Way's participation plays to school children. The company soon added an adult season. With Ken Kramer directing and acting and Sue Kramer teaching and acting, they shared administrative responsibilities. In 1978 Sue Kramer died of cancer. Her many outstanding performances include roles in Brecht's *The Good Woman of Setzuan* (Oct. 1968), in *Macbeth* (Apr. 1972), and in Rex DEVERELL's *Boiler Room Suite*, Jan. 1977, as Aggie, a role written specially for her. Since his wife's death Ken Kramer has continued his triple job as artistic director, director, and actor with productions, for example, of *Macbeth* (Nov. 1985), Edmond Rostand's *Cyrano de Bergerac* (Apr. 1986), and *King Lear* (Nov. 1986). In 1987 he was named to the Order of Canada.
JOYCE DOOLITTLE

Krizanc, John (b. 1956). Born in Lethbridge, Alta, he was raised in Lethbridge, Edmonton, Sudbury, and Toronto, where he now lives. Krizanc's plays include *Crimes of Innocence*, produced by the Theatre Dept. of York Univ. in 1976; *Uterine Knights*, produced in 1979 by Toronto's Necessary Angel Theatre Company; the award-winning *TAMARA* (1987), first produced by Necessary Angel in 1981; and *Prague* (1987), first produced in 1984 at TARRAGON THEATRE, Toronto, and awarded the Governor General's 1987 Award for Drama. Krizanc, all of whose work has been directed by Richard ROSE, also contributed to Necessary Angel's COLLECTIVE CREATION, *Desire*, produced at TORONTO FREE THEATRE in 1985. He is chairman of the publishing committee of the Playwrights Union of Canada.

Krizanc's plays reflect his middle-class liberal distrust of dogmatism, tinged with a consciousness of the danger of either non-commitment or individual heroism. *Tamara*, for example, concerns itself with the failure of artists and intellectuals to respond to fascism in Italy in the 1920s, while *Prague* treats the futility of the heroic public gesture in post-1968 Czechoslovakia. His plays are characterized by a metadramatic exploration of the role of the artist, by experiments with simultaneous staging, and by an innovative use of space that allows Krizanc to explore the fundamental lie of theatre itself, and to reassert the individual responsibility of artists and others as people.

RICHARD PAUL KNOWLES

L

Labelle, Elzéar (1843-75). Born in Montreal, he attended the Collège de l'Assomption and the Collège des Jésuites before being admitted to the Bar in 1862. With his brother Ludger, one of the founders of the Conservative newspaper *Le Colonisateur* and of the first Union Nationale Party, Elzéar turned more and more to politics. Unlike his brother, he never ran for office, preferring to snipe from the sidelines and to satirize elected politicians, soon acquiring a reputation as the foremost wit of his day. He contracted tuberculosis at an early age and died at thirty-two after a long struggle with the disease. Labelle was a playwright, a journalist, and a poet, and his collected works (mainly occasional poems and satirical songs) were published posthumously in 1876 by his brother-in-law A.-N. Montpetit, with the title *Mes Rimes*. Included is the text, without music, of Labelle's most important work, *La CONVERSION D'UN PÊCHEUR DE LA NOUVELLE-ÉCOSSE*.   L.E. DOUCETTE

Laberge, Marie (b. 1950). Born in Quebec City, she studied at Laval Univ. prior to enrolling in the acting section of the CONSERVATOIRE D'ART DRAMATIQUE. She directed several productions and wrote her first plays in Quebec City before moving to Montreal, where she still lives. The author of some sixteen plays, she brings her experience as an actress and director to playwriting; her works are noted for their strong characterization, crisp dialogue, and skilful use of space.

Her earliest plays show feminist sympathies in a gently satirical mode, her targets being subservient women as well as the men they encounter. *Profession: je l'aime* (unpublished) offers a wry picture of the reactions of three women to marriage: servility, frustration, and resignation. *Éva et Évelyne* (1986) shows two ageing sisters reviewing with touching unconscious humour their unfulfilled lives. Both plays were first produced at the Théâtre du Vieux Québec, Quebec City, in Jan. 1979. *T'sé veux dire*, produced by Productions Germaine Larose in Jan. 1980, presents an entertaining picture of inarticulate young men and women anxious to preserve an air of nonchalance while desperately seeking to impress others with their sexual strategies.

Laberge came to prominence in 1980 with *C'était avant la guerre à l'Anse à Gilles* (1981), which won a Governor General's Award. First produced by Montreal's NOUVELLE COMPAGNIE THÉÂTRALE in Jan. 1981, the play depicts a self-employed young widow and laundress—Marianna—who rejects the patient image of womanhood advocated in *Maria Chapdelaine*; when her orphan friend Rosalie is sexually abused by her employer, Marianna decides she must seek a freer life for them both elsewhere. The play pits Marianna's views against those of her conventional aunt, who is profoundly influenced by her church—but the real antagonist is the closed world of l'Anse à Gilles, for which the aunt and Rosalie's employer become metaphors. This tightly constructed work makes imaginative use of stage resources—such as the changing patterns of Marianna's laundry-décor to indicate the passing seasons and the introduction of a radio to convey the attractive presence of the outside world.

Laberge's documentary drama, *Ils étaient venus pour . . .* (1981), produced by Le Théâtre du Bois de Coulonge, Quebec City, in July 1981, depicts the creation and demise of a mill town, Val-Jalbert, using techniques reminiscent of Bertolt Brecht and Jacques FERRON. Laberge abandoned this approach in more recent plays, which tend to explore the stress of human relationships. *L'Homme gris* (1975), produced by Productions Marie Laberge in Montreal in Sept. 1984, centres on a garrulous, dominant father, given to drinking, and his near-aphasic daughter. The claustrophobic motel-room setting, the storm outside, even the colours visible on stage, intensify the aggression in the text, which culminates in a violent act of revolt. The play enjoyed two runs in Paris in 1986, reaching 120 performances at the Petit Marigny on the Champs-Elysées. It was produced in English at TORONTO FREE THEATRE in Mar. 1988. *Jocelyne Trudelle trouvée morte dans ses larmes* (1983), produced by the Commune à Marie, Quebec, in Oct. 1986, is a moving study of a suicide. *Le Night Cap Bar* (unpublished)—produced by Le Théâtre de la Manufacture, Montreal, in Apr. 1987—is a gripping excursion into a sordid world of drug addiction and alcoholism in which three characters re-enact their versions of events steeped in deceit and treachery. It marked Laberge's return to acting.

The chief strengths of Laberge's plays lie in their ability to build dramatic tension within a variety of frameworks and in their subtle, compelling characters. Laberge moves easily beyond the boundaries of her Québécois idiom to examine contemporary human problems with humour and compassion.

BRIAN POCKNELL

La Guerre, Yes Sir! Adapted by Roch CARRIER from his novel of the same name (1968), the play was first produced in French at Montreal's THÉÂTRE DU NOUVEAU MONDE on 19 Nov. 1970. It toured France, Belgium, Luxembourg, and Czechoslovakia in 1971 and received its English-language première at the STRATFORD FESTIVAL on 4 Aug. 1972. The French text was published by Éditions du jour, and the English by Anansi (translated by Sheila Fischman), both in 1970.

Through a series of short, amusing but poignant sketches, the first half of the play shows the effects of the Second World War on village life in Quebec. The second half takes place primarily at the home of Anthyme and Mother Corriveau during the wake of their soldier son, accidently killed in the early days of the war. In the midst of the drinking, eating, dancing, and story-telling of the village guests, the English soldiers who have brought the son's body home stand guard over it and the Union Jack. Several fights break out, first between two villagers, then between the soldiers and the villagers. The play ends at the cemetery with the parish priest exhorting the villagers to honour their Catholic heritage while Corriveau's grave-digger remarks sadly that war has finally struck the village.

Critics have seen this piece as a microcosm of Quebec in transition. Torn between their own world and the obtrusive outside world, the French-Canadians portrayed here cannot disregard the destructive elements within their own ranks. The play's nationalist overtones are thus tempered with self-criticism. While the English are a negative force to be reckoned with, the quaint and naïve French-Canadians must also change if they are to survive in modern times.

ELAINE F. NARDOCCHIO

Lamarche, Gustave (1895-1987). Born in Montreal and educated at Collège Bourget in Rigaud, he entered the Saint-Viateur order in 1913 and was ordained a priest in 1920. After obtaining a degree in classical literature from the Institut catholique and the Sorbonne in Paris (1926), and a degree in political science from the Université de Louvain (1927), he returned to Canada and taught humanities at the Séminaire de Joliette (1927-31), the Collège Bourget (1931-4), and at a theological college, Le Scolasticat Saint-Charles, in Joliette, where he lived for most of his life.

Lamarche revealed his talent as a dramatist in 1933 with *Jonathas* (1933), which was produced—with a musical score by Gabriel Cusson—at Collège Bourget, and with *La Défaite de l'Enfer*, a choral play for 700 voices, presented on the mountain at Rigaud before 10,000 spectators on 28 and 29 May 1938. In 1939 he started a school company, 'Paraboliers du Roi', for which his brother, Antonin Lamarche (1909-67), a member of the same order, mounted some daring productions.

The six volumes of Lamarche's *Oeuvres théâtrales* (1972-5) contain thirty-five plays, in verse and prose, on biblical, evangelical, historical, and mythological subjects. Inspired by medieval mystery plays, and also by the works of Paul Claudel and Henri Ghéon, these plays show man confronted by fate, forced to choose between sin and grace, in situations that give evidence of divine intervention. Requiring elaborate staging, with choirs and musicians, most have been presented in boys' colleges and convents, at assemblies, or on the modest stage of the Saint-Charles theological college in Joliette.

One of the founding members of the Académie canadienne-française in 1944, he also published a large number of poems, which were reprinted in *Oeuvres poétiques* (1972).

ALONZO LE BLANC

Lambert, Betty (1933-83). Born in Alberta, she settled in Vancouver at the age of twenty, studying creative writing at the Univ. of British Columbia. She wrote one novel (*Crossings*, 1979), and many plays, including (in the late 1950s and the 1960s) over thirty radio plays, usually directed by Gerald Newman in Vancouver. Four were published in the *West Coast Review*. They include *The Good of the Sun* (1975) and her last and most ambitious, *Grasshopper Hill* (1985), chosen best radio play of 1979. She wrote three childrens' plays for HOLIDAY THEATRE, Vancouver, 1966-70, making sex and murder the unlikely subjects. Lambert's first adult stage play, *The Visitor* (1969), was followed by *Sqrieux-de-Dieu* (1975). This sex-comedy, subtitled 'a nasty play about nice people' and turning on a domesticated mistress and extrovert wife, played at the VANCOUVER EAST CULTURAL CENTRE, 1975, at FESTIVAL LENNOXVILLE in 1976 and 1977, and at the NATIONAL ARTS CENTRE in 1977. *Clouds of Glory* (1979) is a satire dealing with the turbulent history of Simon Fraser Univ., British Columbia, where Lambert taught English from 1965.

Lambert achieved what she saw as her true personal voice, that of feminist anger, only in her last two dramas. *Jennie's Story* (1984) is based on a true story about an Alberta teenage girl, mistress of a priest who has her sterilized as a moral defective. When Jennie finds that she cannot have children, she kills herself. *Under the Skin* (posthumously performed in 1985), also based on fact, tells of a man who kidnaps a twelve-year-old girl and holds her prisoner for six months, of his wife's gradual discovery of this, and of her friendship with the child's mother. Both plays are grim and painful. MALCOLM PAGE

Lamberts, Heath (b. 1941). Born James Langcaster in Toronto, he entered the first class at the newly opened NATIONAL THEATRE SCHOOL in 1960. After graduating in 1963 and winning the *Toronto Telegram* Award as 'Most Promising Newcomer', he was a member of the MANITOBA THEATRE CENTRE company from 1963 to 1967, appearing in such roles as Puck in *A Midsummer Night's Dream* and Andri in Max Frisch's *Andorra*. He also appeared at the STRATFORD FESTIVAL from 1964 to 1967, winning two Tyrone GUTHRIE Awards, and first appeared at the SHAW FESTIVAL in 1967. Lamberts then freelanced in many Canadian regional theatres before beginning a series of important performances at the VANCOUVER PLAYHOUSE in the late 1970s, including Tartuffe in Molière's *Tartuffe* in 1976, the Fool in *King Lear*, 1977, and Tristan Tzara in Tom Stoppard's *Travesties*, 1979. From 1972 he was a regular member of the Shaw Festival company, where he developed a specialization in farce, very often involving multiple roles or other demands for rapid physical transformation. His appearance in Ben Travers' *Thark* in 1977 was followed by Georges Feydeau's *A Flea in Her Ear* (1980), Will Evans' and Valentine's *Tons of Money* (1981), Philip King's *See How They Run* (1982), Travers' *Rookery Nook* (1983), and Ray Cooney's and Tony Hilton's *One For the Pot* (1985). In a somewhat similar vein he won a Dora Mavor MOORE Award in 1981 for his performance as Pseudolus in Stephen Sondheim's *A Funny Thing Happened on the Way to the Forum* for Toronto Arts Productions. The common perception that Lamberts was an actor of much greater depth than such roles suggested was triumphantly realized in his superb Cyrano in Edmond Rostand's *Cyrano de Bergerac* at the 1982 Shaw Festival (revived by the Festival in 1983, and then at Toronto's ROYAL ALEXANDRA THEATRE in 1985, when Lamberts won a second Dora Mavor Moore Award). In 1986 he extended his range even further with a tormented (if slightly mannered) portrayal of Shelley Levene in David Mamet's *Glengarry Glen Ross* for CENTRESTAGE and TORONTO FREE THEATRE. He was named to the Order of Canada in 1987.   HARRY LANE

Lane, William (b. 1951). Born in Ottawa and educated at Carleton Univ., he joined TORONTO FREE THEATRE as dramaturge in 1975, also serving as associate artistic director, 1977-9, under Martin KINCH, and as acting artistic director 1979-80. At Toronto Free Theatre he directed ten productions, including the premières of Lawrence Russell's *The Mystery of the Pig Killer's Daughter* in 1975, Tom WALMSLEY's *The Jones Boy*, 1977, and George F. WALKER's *ZASTROZZI*, 1977, and *Filthy Rich*, 1979. Lane's own play, *The Brides of Dracula*, was produced there in 1978. Elsewhere Lane has directed premières of Michael HOLLINGSWORTH's *Trans World* (Eneraction Theatre, 1978), Larry FINEBERG's *Montreal* (TORONTO TRUCK THEATRE, 1981), Walker's *Science and Madness* (TARRAGON THEATRE, 1982), and Erika RITTER's *AUTOMATIC PILOT* (NEW THEATRE, 1980) and *The Passing Scene* (Tarragon, 1982). He joined the CBC in 1982 as a producer of radio drama.
                    DENIS W. JOHNSTON

Lanergan, James West (1828-86). Born in Taunton, Mass., he began his career in Portland, Boston, and New York. In 1856, as manager of the Star Company with Edward Sandford and Moses W. Fiske, he toured the New England coast to Saint John, N.B., where in 1857 he opened his DRAMATIC LYCEUM theatre. Combatting prejudice, he gave theatre a respectable image while drawing large, profitable houses. Between regular summer seasons to 1874 he toured his company to Newfoundland, the West Indies, and cities in the American mid-west. A theatrical entrepreneur with a keen business sense and a talent for public relations, he was known as an able and gentlemanly manager, appreciated for his integrity, his well-organized company, and for the high quality of his diversified repertoire of standard and new plays. With his own company he acted dozens of leading roles, most of them opposite his wife Caroline. He was particularly favoured as Don Caesar (in an adaptation of P. Dumanoir's and A.P. Dennery's French play, *Don Caesar de Bazan*), as Nathan in Augustin Daly's *Leah* (Niblo's Garden, New York, 1863), and as Iago (to Charles Dillon's *Othello*, Broadway Theatre, New York, 1866). As an actor he was praised for intelligence, gentility, versatility, careful study, a splendid voice free of rant, and a sense of fun. Although after 1866 he continued to introduce new material into his company's repertoire, he did not himself learn new roles, and he performed much less often. Following the sale of the Dramatic Lyceum in 1876 he acted only infrequently in Boston and on tour and briefly managed the Lawrence (Mass.) Opera House. Ill health plagued him from 1852; he died penniless in Boston.
                    MARY ELIZABETH SMITH

Lang, (Alexander) Matheson (1879-1948). Born into a clerical family in Montreal and taken to Scotland at the age of four, he was originally destined for the church, but was attracted instead to the theatre. He made his professional début in 1897 with Louis Calvert's troupe and subsequently appeared extensively with Frank Benson and with the Vedrenne/Granville-Barker management in their famed Royal Court Theatre seasons in London, Eng., 1904-7. A tall, handsome, classical actor, Lang then formed his own company, which introduced Shakespeare to the Old Vic and toured such Commonwealth countries as South Africa, India, Australia, Canada (in 1926-7), and Barbados, where he eventually retired and died. In addition to triumphs as Romeo, Hamlet, Othello, Benedick, Petruchio, and Shylock, Lang created in 1913 the Chinese character of Mr. Wu in the play of the same name, written by Harry Vernon and Harold Owen, with which he was always associated. He wrote an autobiography, *Mr. Wu Looks Back* (1941).
                    DAVID GARDNER

Langham, Michael (b. 1919). Born in England and raised in Scotland, he first acted under an assumed name while studying law in London. During six years as a prisoner of war he produced plays for fellow officers. At the end of the war he became assistant director of Beatrice Lehmann's Midland Theatre Company in Coventry, staging his first professional production, *Twelfth Night*, in

1946 and in the next three years directing a mixed repertory of more than twenty plays. Tyrone GUTHRIE—who was to play a decisive role in Langham's career—saw and admired his work at Coventry on a 1947 visit.

In Nov. 1948 Langham joined the Birmingham Repertory Theatre, and in May 1950 he directed *Julius Caesar* at the Shakespeare Memorial Theatre in Stratford-upon-Avon, which confirmed his reputation as an up-and-coming classical director. After engagements in Europe, he spent a year (1953-4) as director of the Glasgow Citizens' Theatre. Langham's North American association began at Toronto's CREST THEATRE—at Guthrie's instigation—in Feb. 1955 with productions of Alexander Ostrovsky's *The Diary of a Scoundrel*, James Bridie's *Meeting at Night*, and J.B. Priestley's *When We Are Married*. Although his directorial début at the STRATFORD FESTIVAL in 1955 with *Julius Caesar* was marred by difficulties in casting and rehearsal, Langham was appointed Guthrie's successor as artistic director of the Festival. In his first season, 1956, he staged a brilliant *Henry V* with Christopher PLUMMER in the lead and members of Montreal's THÉÂTRE DU NOUVEAU MONDE company as the French courtiers. The production was highly praised by U.S. critics, less so by the Canadian critics, notably Nathan COHEN (who had opposed Langham's appointment). During Langham's second season the Festival moved out of the tent and into the new Festival Theatre. Langham returned from London to direct the Festival's first *Hamlet*, once again with Plummer in the lead. This production was not highly regarded by the critics, save for the designs of Desmond HEELEY, whom Langham had brought from England.

During the next two seasons Langham expanded the Festival, initiating touring, the first televised Stratford production, a film festival, training projects, and, most importantly, school performances. Nevertheless he found himself continually criticized, especially for importing too many British artists. Matters were not helped when Langham fell seriously ill and had to miss all of the 1959 season. Returning to work in 1960 (after having first directed *The Merchant of Venice* at Stratford-upon-Avon) he directed a highly successful *Romeo and Juliet* at the Stratford Festival.

In 1961 Langham directed two productions at the Festival: *Coriolanus*, with Paul Scofield and John COLICOS, and *Love's Labour's Lost*, regarded by many as one of the finest productions ever mounted at the Festival. In the winter of 1962 he directed Max Frisch's *Andorra* on Broadway and then returned to Stratford to stage *The Taming of the Shrew* and Edmond Rostand's *Cyrano de Bergerac*, both to great acclaim. He followed this in 1963 by directing two of Shakespeare's most problematic plays, *Troilus and Cressida* and *Timon of Athens*. Both productions drew plaudits from critics and indifference from audiences.

In 1964 two of Langham's productions—a revival of *Love's Labour's Lost* and a modern-dress *Timon of Athens*—were successfully presented during the Stratford Festival's tour to Chichester, England. There followed a brilliant *King Lear* that same season at Stratford, with John Colicos, and an irreverent production of William Wycherley's *The Country Wife*.

After a sabbatical in 1965, Langham returned to Stratford for two uneven seasons marked by financial difficulties. 1966 saw an indifferent production of *Henry V* at the Festival Theatre, and Michael BAWTREE's new play *The Last of the Czars* at the Avon Theatre; a disastrous *Antony and Cleopatra* and an excellent *Government Inspector* (by Nikolai Gogol) concluded Langham's long term as artistic director.

On leaving Stratford Langham freelanced in England and the U.S. He became artistic director of the Guthrie Theatre in Minneapolis in 1971, and in 1979 director of New York's Juilliard School of Theatre. Langham returned to Stratford in 1982 to direct Shaw's *Arms and the Man* on the Festival stage, to great critical and audience acclaim. In 1983 he became director of the Stratford Festival's Young Company, teaching, and staging *Love's Labour's Lost* and *Much Ado About Nothing*. In 1984 he re-staged *Love's Labour's Lost* on the Festival stage and also directed the Young Company in *Henry IV, Part I*. Since 1985 Langham has spent most of his time teaching and consulting for a number of theatrical organizations in the U.S.

MICHAL SCHONBERG

Languirand, Jacques (b. 1931). A native of Montreal, he was educated at the Collège Saint-Laurent, Montreal, and the Classical

College of Sainte-Croix. Detesting the politics of the Duplessis regime, he moved to Paris in 1949, remaining there until 1953 and returning again in 1954-5. While in Paris he worked for the French Radio network; studied drama with Charles Dullin, Michel Vitold, and Etienne Decroux; and wrote his first radio plays, *Le Roi ivre* and *Noël sur ruine*.

Languirand was in Paris when the Theatre of the Absurd developed in the early fifties. Upon his return to Quebec in the fall of 1956 he established Le Théâtre de Dix Heures, where he produced Samuel Beckett's *En attendant Godot* and Jean Genet's *Les Bonnes (The Maids)*, as well as his own play *Les Insolites* (1962), which had been performed on 9 Mar. 1956 with great success at the Salle du GESÙ in the regional competitions of the DOMINION DRAMA FESTIVAL. At the DDF finals in Sherbrooke it received the prize for best Canadian play. Translated into English by Donald Watson, the translator of Eugène Ionesco's plays, it was produced in Birmingham in 1960.

Les Insolites began as an experiment in automatic writing, which may explain the play's surrealist atmosphere. It takes place in a bar where four men drink and share memories of women they have loved. When an old woman enters, they all recognize in her the girl they had loved under different names. The old woman is murdered during a power failure, and the play, parodying a murder story, ends with the innocent barman's arrest and the men resuming their positions at the bar. The dialogue of the changing incoherent characters is interspersed with misunderstandings, plays on words, clichés, proverbs, and popular sayings. The play denounces the superficiality of ordinary language, exposing the difficulty of establishing meaning or valid communication among human beings. Despite this metaphysical aspect, farcical elements prevail, turning the play into a light, witty comedy. The cyclical structure, the main themes—derisive love and justice, senseless life and death—the eccentric characters, and distinctive language all reappear in Languirand's later plays.

Le Roi ivre (1970), originally broadcast in France in 1950, had a short run at Le Théâtre de Dix Heures in fall 1956. It centres on the tyrannical figure of a bored and cruel king appropriately called Coeur-de-fer; he brings to mind Alfred Jarry's Ubu as well as the politician Duplessis, exploiting their peoples. The play remains a grotesque farce that finally succeeds neither as tragedy nor as comedy.

Les GRANDS DÉPARTS (1958), Languirand's most accomplished play, was produced by his own company at Percé in 1958 with his two short fantasies—*Diogène* (1965), a one-act farcical tragi-comedy, and *L'École du rire* (1982), a ballet-comedy. In *Le Gibet* (1960), produced at La COMÉDIE-CANA-DIENNE in 1958, Languirand also performed the lead role of Perplex, an idealistic but pathetic figure trying in vain to break the world pole-sitting record. The plot was suggested by a local news item; the setting is a Quebec suburb and the main character an archetypal, average Québécois. A mixture of several moods and genres—lyrical, farcical, detective story, musical comedy—the play is also a political satire.

Les Violons de l'automne (1962) ridicules a triangle of old people hopelessly wanting to live up to their lost illusions about love. Though it received a Governor General's Award in 1962 (with *Les Insolites*) it was a failure on stage both in Montreal, where it ran for about two weeks in May 1960 at the THÉÂTRE CLUB, and in France where it was presented at the Comédie de Paris in Mar. 1963. While preparing for the latter production in Paris, Languirand wrote *Les Cloisons* (1966), a one-act dialogue. 'He' and 'she', two strangers, fall in love with each other without ever meeting, separated by the partition of their hotel room. It was staged only in English (translated by Albert Bernel) as *The Partition* at Le Théâtre de la Place in Montreal in 1966 and as *Keyhole* in Toronto by the CANADIAN PLAYERS at the CENTRAL LIBRARY THEATRE in 1960.

Languirand turned to epic theatre with the musical *Klondyke* (1971), documenting life in the Yukon during the Gold Rush. It was produced in 1965, with music by Gabriel CHARPENTIER, at Montreal's Le THÉÂTRE DU NOUVEAU MONDE, and in the same year at the Commonwealth Arts Festival in London, England. His last work for the stage, *L'Âge de Pierre*, a multi-media show, was produced in English (as *Man, Inc.*) at Toronto's ST LAWRENCE CENTRE in 1970.

Since 1972 Languirand has been teaching at McGill University, but continues to write. The host of a number of radio and television shows, he has also published a novel, *Tout compte fait* (1963), which sums up his involvement with the Theatre of the Absurd. Other works include *De McLuhan à Pythagore* (1972), *La Voie initiatique* (1978), *Vivre sa vie* (1979), and *Mater Materia* (1980). He was appointed a member of the Order of Canada in 1987.   MONIQUE GENUIST

Laroche, Roland (b. 1927). Born and raised in Sainte-Hyacinthe, Que., he studied at the National Academy of Theater Arts (1950-1) and the Theater Artistic School (1951-3) in New York, before spending three years at Montreal's THÉÂTRE DU NOUVEAU MONDE's theatre school. He then studied in Paris, at the Jacques Lecoq school of mime, l'École du Théâtre de l'Oeuvre, l'École de Tania Balachova, and l'Université du Théâtre des Nations.

The co-founder, with Françoise Berd, of Théâtre de L'Egrégore in 1959, Laroche made his début as a director there in the same year with Dostoevsky's *Une Femme douce*, which toured Europe in 1966. He has since directed over sixty productions, several from the international repertoire, but chiefly Québécois plays. They include: *Api 2967, Hamlet, Prince du Québec, Le Procès de J.B.M.*, and *Le Pendu* by Robert GURIK, for which he won the Louis Jouvet Trophy in 1967; *L'Auberge des morts subites* by Félix LECLERC; *La Maison des Oiseaux* by Gilles Derome; *La Mariaagélas, La Contrebandière*, and *Garrochés au Paradis* by Antonine MAILLET; *La Débacle* by Jean Daigle; *La Collection de Mde Suzanne* by François Beaulieu; *Wonderland* and *Michael et Aléola* by Gaetan Charlebois; *Pontiac* by Pierre Goulet; and *J'attends de tes nouvelles* by Claire Dé.

In 1972-3 Laroche was executive secretary of Le Centre d'essai des auteurs dramatiques. One of Canada's foremost directors of Quebec plays in English translation, particularly at the London Little Theatre and the GLOBE THEATRE in Regina, he has also directed over thirty operas in Quebec. Laroche has taught all aspects of theatre at the NATIONAL THEATRE SCHOOL, the Conservatoire de Musique in Montreal and Quebec, l'Option Théâtre Sainte-Thérèse et Sainte-Hyacinthe, the Univ. of Toronto, and elsewhere. He also frequently appears on stage as an actor.
                    RENÉE NOISEAUX-GURIK

Laufer, Murray (b. 1929). Born in Toronto, he studied drawing and painting at the Ontario College of Art. After further study abroad, he worked for CBC television and subsequently at Toronto's CREST THEATRE, where he rose from set painter to designer (of John Osborne's *Epitaph for George Dillon* in 1960).

Laufer began his association with the Canadian Opera Company in 1959 when he designed Prokofiev's *The Love for Three Oranges*. He soon became the Opera's principal designer, displaying his talent for large, sculptured, spatial sets, that often included extensive use of projections—sometimes collages of images, sometimes photographs of abstract forms, sometimes of colours and organic forms, but always totally integrated into the shape and style of the physical set. Among his most memorable sets were those for *Louis Riel* (1967), *Fidelio* (1973), *The Flying Dutchman* (1974), and *Bluebeard's Castle* (1974).

For ten years Laufer created startling sets at the ST LAWRENCE CENTRE as principal designer for plays by Michel TREMBLAY, Brecht, Sean O'Casey, and others. His 1965 set for ANNE OF GREEN GABLES at the CHARLOTTETOWN FESTIVAL has been seen around the world. For the same festival he designed *Johnny Belinda* in 1968. At the STRATFORD FESTIVAL he designed Nikolai Gogol's *The Marriage Brokers* in 1973 and Gilbert and Sullivan's *H.M.S. Pinafore* in 1981. A member of the Order of Canada, Laufer was the first stage designer to be elected to the Royal Canadian Academy (in 1974). He was the first recipient of the Pauline McGibbon Award for artistic excellence in Ontario in 1975, and in 1979 he was appointed commissioner general of Canada for the Prague Quadrennial.   MARTHA MANN

Leacock, Stephen (1869-1944). Born in England, he immigrated with his family to Canada in 1876. Leacock was educated at the Univ. of Toronto and the Univ. of Chicago (Ph.D., 1903) and was appointed lecturer in Economics and Political Science at McGill Univ., Montreal, in 1903. His first published work was *Elements of Political Science* (1906), but *Literary Lapses* (1910) introduced him as a humorous writer of genius. He had a lifelong interest in theatre, attending plays frequently, arranging private theatricals at his summer home on Old Brewery Bay, Lake Couchiching, in the 1920s and 1930s, and writing a number of full-length and one-act plays.

Behind the Beyond (1913), a three-act play, satirizes the popular modern 'problem play'. It was first performed by the Cambridge Univ. Dramatic Society in 1922. In Oct. 1916 Michael Morton's four-act play, *Jeff*, an adaptation of a story from Leacock's *Sunshine Sketches*, toured briefly before folding in Montreal. Leacock's own four-act adaptation, *Sunshine in Mariposa*, was published in *Maclean's*, May, June, and July 1917.

Leacock's 'Q' (published as a 'Psychic Pstory of the Psuper Natural' in *Nonsense Novels*, 1911) was adapted for the stage in collaboration with Basil MacDonald Hastings and performed at the London Coliseum, England, 24 Nov.-4 Dec. 1915, as part of a weekly variety show. His original one-act plays are generally amusing burlesques. *Damned Souls* (1923) and *The Sub-Contractor* (1923), for example, poke fun at the contemporary vogue for Russian plays and Ibsen respectively. *The Raft* (1923), a burlesque melodrama, was performed by the Player's Guild of University College in HART HOUSE THEATRE, Toronto, in Oct. 1924. Mavor MOORE's musical comedy *Sunshine Town*, based on Leacock's *Sunshine Sketches*, played Toronto and Montreal in Jan. 1955 and was revived at the CHARLOTTETOWN FESTIVAL 29 July-31 Aug. 1968. Leacock's plays and dramatic sketches are collected in *Behind the Beyond and Other Contributions to Human Knowledge* (1913), *Over the Footlights* (1923), and *Funny Pieces: A Book of Random Sketches* (1936).   ROBERT G. LAWRENCE

Learning, Walter (b. 1938). Born in Quidi Vidi, Nfld, he studied philosophy at the Univ. of New Brunswick (MA, 1963) and at the Australian National Univ. (1963-6). His theatrical interests were first fostered during his years at UNB (1957-63) by Professor Alvin Shaw, a graduate of Robert GILL's HART HOUSE THEATRE productions, who guided the Student Drama Society from 1952 to 1971. From 1966 to 1968 Learning lectured at Memorial University.

In 1968 he was appointed general manager of the Beaverbrook Playhouse, Fredericton. The following year he founded THEATRE NEW BRUNSWICK, remaining its artistic director until 1978. In 1974 he founded TNB's Young Company. From 1978 to 1982 he was head of the Canada Council's Theatre Section, and from 1982 to 1986 artistic director and chief executive officer of the VAN-COUVER PLAYHOUSE. Learning's achievements there were mixed: subscriptions increased, audience size nearly doubled (from 70,000 in 1981 to 130,000 in 1985), and a number of eastern-Canadian actors, such as William HUTT and Gordon PINSENT, were reintroduced to Vancouver audiences; at the same time, the Playhouse deficit rose from $300,000 to $600,000. When Learning departed at the end of 1986, he said he did so in order to avoid 'the fur-lined coffin' of theatrical complacency that he feared after twenty years of administering and directing theatres. Nonetheless in 1987 he accepted the artistic directorship of the CHARLOTTETOWN FESTIVAL.

While artistic director of TNB, Learning produced three plays he co-authored with Alden NOWLAN: in 1974 *Frankenstein: The Man Who Became God* (1976), in 1977 *The Dollar Woman* (1981), and in 1978 *The Incredible Murder of Cardinal Tosca* (1978). Learning has also written, directed, and edited for CBC television, especially for the series 'Up at Ours'. He directed his first STRATFORD FESTIVAL production, Robert Bolt's *A Man for All Seasons*, in 1986.   EDWARD MULLALY

Leblanc de Marconnay, Hyacinthe-Poirier (1794-1864). Born in Paris to an ancient noble family, he came to Canada in 1834, remaining in Montreal for six years. Editor of four newspapers during his stay in Canada, he wrote several brochures dealing with political events, and two plays.

Before leaving France, Leblanc de Marconnay had collaborated on a comic opera, *L'Hôtel des princes*, staged successfully in Paris in 1831. Music plays an important part in his *Le Soldat* (1836) and *Valentine, ou La Nina canadienne* (1836). *Le Soldat* is a one-person interlude in two parts, interspersed with songs, probably written in collaboration with Napoléon Aubin. In Part I a jingoistic French soldier extols the glories of the military; in Part II, wounded and dying, he recites from a long, bathetic letter to his beloved. The title-page states that the play was performed at Montreal's THEATRE ROYAL in 1835 and 1836, but only one performance, on 6 Feb. 1836, can be verified. *Valentine* is a more substantial work, representing an important step in the evolution of theatre in French Canada. Familiar with current Parisian taste and stage techniques, the author has skilfully constructed a play that is clearly Canadian in setting, with frequent references to Canadian history and politics and an astute use of local speech patterns and traditional French-Canadian folksongs. He has been falsely accused of plagiarizing an operetta by B.J. Marsollier des Vivetières, whose *Nina, ou La Folle par amour* (1786) had enjoyed much success in Paris. The indebtedness is minimal, and sufficiently acknowledged in Leblanc de Marconnay's title. The play was performed at least twice at the Theatre Royal in Feb. 1836, but as with *Le Soldat*, no critical reaction is known.

See L.E. Doucette, *Theatre in French Canada, 1606-1867* (1984).   L.E. DOUCETTE

Leclerc, Félix (1914-88). Born in La Tuque, Que., where his father was a lumber dealer, he spent much of his childhood in the out-of-doors, and grew up to be a non-conformist and a lover of wildlife. After six years of classical studies in Ottawa (four at the Juniorat du Sacré-Coeur and two at the Univ. of Ottawa), during which time he developed a taste for theatre, he was forced by lack of funds to leave school. He found work as a radio announcer in Quebec City (1934-7) and then in Trois-Rivières (1938-9). His broadcasts, embellished with his own sketches, opened doors for him in 1939 at Radio-Canada, where he worked seven years as an actor and scriptwriter, meanwhile publishing several works of poetry.

From 1942 to 1945 Leclerc acted with the COMPAGNONS DE SAINT-LAURENT, which produced his three-act play *Maluron* in 1947; although never published, *Maluron* received twenty-five performances, a record for the period. Encouraged by this success, Leclerc wrote *Le P'tit bonheur* the following year; by the time this collection of sketches and songs was published in 1959 it had been performed over 300 times—following its 1956 première at the THÉÂTRE DU RIDEAU VERT—of which 120 performances took place overseas. Meanwhile he published two collections of the best of his radio sketches, *Dialogues d'hommes et de bêtes* (1949) and *Théâtre de village* (1951). In addition Leclerc honed his talents as a singer-guitarist: after three years' training in Paris (1950-3), he became an international star in this field, returning only sporadically to literature: several sketches for Canadian television (1956-7), and four plays: *Sonnez les matines* (performed at the Rideau Vert in 1954, published in 1959), *L'Auberge des morts*

Guy Beaulne and Juliette Béliveau in Félix Leclerc's Sonnez les matines, *Théâtre du Rideau Vert, 1959*

subites (1964), *Les Temples* (unpublished), and *L'Enfant en pénitence* (performed in 1987, unpublished).

Leclerc was a pioneer in the revival of Quebec theatre, thanks to his discovery of a formula for popular plays that reflected reality and dealt with matters of concern to the general public. He was among the first Quebec dramatists to anchor his work in the affairs and traditions of his compatriots. Leclerc's favourite themes are nature, life, death, human suffering, solitude (which can be banished in dreams), and love (often drowned in sorrow and broken by disillusionment). His plays, however, are threaded with humour, lightheartedness, and sharp irony about some of the taboos that still flourished in Quebec prior to the Quiet Revolution.

Critics have been harsh on Leclerc's plays, detecting unevenness of style, superficiality of content, disjointed and langorous plots, and ill-defined conclusions. Nonetheless, the plays have been highly prized by a large public who have enjoyed the verve of his popular style and his delightful flashes of inspiration, and whose emotions have been stirred by

Leclerc

Guy L'Écuyer and Jean Lajeunesse in Jacques Ferron's Les Grands Soleils, *Théâtre du Nouveau Monde, 1968*

Leclerc's portraits of Quebec life. His death in Aug. 1988 on the Île d'Orléans, where he lived, was an occasion for many tributes.

JEAN LAFLAMME

L'Écuyer, Guy (1931-85). Born and educated in Montreal, he joined Les COMPAGNONS DE SAINT-LAURENT in 1949, moving in 1951 to the THÉÂTRE DU NOUVEAU MONDE, where he studied with Jean GASCON and acted in many productions over a fifteen-year period. In 1954 he founded, with Marcel Sabourin, the short-lived Compagnie de Montréal, successfully mounting Jacques LANGUIRAND's *Les Insolites* and earning the Best Actor's Award in the 1957 DOMINION DRAMA FESTIVAL for the title role in Molière's *Le Médecin malgré lui*.

L'Écuyer appeared in some twenty Shakespearean productions at the STRATFORD FESTIVAL, but he was equally interested in Québécois plays. Jean-Claude GERMAIN wrote *Un Pays dont la devise est je m'oublie* with L'Écuyer specifically in mind. His favourite character—the one that best suited his personality and political inclinations—was the Patriote, Mithridate, in Jacques FERRON's *Les Grands Soleils*.

L'Écuyer also contributed to the development of early Quebec television and cinema. His portrayal of Parfait, the plump baker in the serialized novel by Germaine Guèvremont, *Le Survenant*, and his lead role in Gilles Carle's film *La Vie heureuse de Léopold Z* won him critical praise and popularity.

When L'Écuyer died, Gilbert Lepage, director of the THÉÂTRE D'AUJOURD'HUI, suggested that this memorable comic actor should be ranked with Jean-Louis ROUX and Jean Gascon as 'one of the pillars of modern Québécois theatre'.

RAMON HATHORN

Lee, Graves Simcoe (1828-1912). Born in London, Ont., he played an unknown female role in a barn theatre in London in 1844, before moving to Toronto where from 1853 to 1857 he was a member of John NICKINSON's ROYAL LYCEUM companies, appearing as Laertes, Orlando, the twins in Dion Boucicault's *The Corsican Brothers*, and in other parts. He is remembered for writing *Fiddle, Faddle and Foozle*, the first indigenous play to be performed in Toronto. This 'New Canadian Farce', concerning three suitors pursuing a young widow (Lee played the victorious Fred Foozle), opened on 9 Apr. 1853 and was seen again on 6 July, 13 July, and 2 Dec. Although no text has survived, the plot is summarized in *The Daily Patriot and Express* (13 Apr. 1853) where editor Samuel Thompson declared it 'a most decided hit' but lamented that it held the mirror up to British rather than Canadian absurdities.

Lee's second original farce, *Saucy Kate*, was seen at the Lyceum on 11 July 1853. The itinerant Lee made his New York début on 26 Sept. 1856 as Claudius and joined J.W. Wallack's company in the same year. In 1859 he appeared in Pittsburgh and in 1861-2 was back in Toronto and London. Subsequently, he performed major roles in Rochester, Buffalo, Detroit, Cleveland, and Columbus, Ohio. On 16 May 1864 he opened again in New York in *An English Tragedy* and during the 1878-9 season was featured at Niblo's Gardens. From 1886 to 1888 he was in Edmonton, where he staged and participated in 'Literary and Musical Entertainments' and became the first director of the city's amateur Drama Society. After a farewell concert on 3 May 1888 he travelled north-east to Fort Saskatchewan and then to the coast. His last recorded appearance is in London, Ont., on 5 Aug. 1889 when he read Trowbridge's *The Vagabond* as part of a local testimonial minstrel performance. Edgar Allan Poe's *The Raven* was another favourite recitation. By the turn of the century he was ensconced in the Edwin Forrest Home for Aged Actors in New York, where he was amused to read his obituary notice prematurely published in the

New York Dramatic Mirror. About 1902 he returned to Canada, residing in Kingston, where he died at the age of eighty-four.

DAVID GARDNER

Lee, Joseph Smith (fl. 1835-70). A leading member of early amateur companies in Toronto and Montreal, and a would-be theatrical entrepreneur, English-born Lee founded a Shakespeare Club in Toronto in the 1830s and one in Montreal in the 1840s, and lectured on Shakespeare and other literary subjects in those cities as well as in Kingston and Ottawa. As an amateur actor he won praise as Mrs Malaprop in Sheridan's *The Rivals*. When Montreal's Dalhousie Square Theatre Royal closed in 1851, Lee unsuccessfully urged the building of a replacement to be part of a Canadian circuit, and later proposed converting Toronto's Old Gaol into an opera house. After this scheme too collapsed, Lee acted professionally in 1852-3 with John NICKINSON's company in Utica and in New York City. Regaining a post with Customs in Ottawa, Lee attempted to provide that city with a much-needed theatre, and after strenuous fund-raising efforts opened the still-unfinished HER MAJESTY'S in 1856, but did not long retain the lease. MARY SHORTT

Legault, Émile (b. 1906). Born in the village of Saint-Laurent (now suburban Montreal), and educated at the seminaries of Quebec and Sainte-Croix, he was ordained in 1930 and worked first as a teacher at the Collège de Saint-Laurent, then as director of the *Journal d'Action Catholique*. Shortly after becoming a priest in his native parish of Saint-Laurent in 1937, he founded an amateur theatrical group, Les COMPAGNONS DE SAINT-LAURENT. Legault spent the academic year 1938-9 in London and Paris on a grant to study contemporary drama; he saw the work of most of the leading theatre people in Paris—including Henri Ghéon, Louis Jouvet, Charles Dullin, Gaston Baty, Jean-Louis Barrault, and Jacques Copeau—and gained a working knowledge of the professional and technical aspects of theatre. His application of these new ideas, both theoretical and practical, to his work with the Compagnons is credited with creating the birth of modern drama in French Canada.

Although the Compagnons initially presented only religious drama (particularly that of Henri Ghéon), their production of

Molière's *Le Misanthrope* in 1939 was the start of a shift towards secular theatre. The Compagnons played in the Collège de Saint-Laurent until 1942; then in the more central Montreal theatre, the ERMITAGE, at the Collège de Montréal, 1942-5; in the GESÙ theatre, 1945-8; and finally in their own Théâtre des Compagnons, 1948-52. The repertoire grew from the seventeenth-century French classics to embrace Marivaux, Beaumarchais, Musset, Cocteau, Giraudoux, and Anouilh, and finally international theatre—Shakespeare, Lorca, Pirandello, Wilder, and Williams. The evolution of the repertory also reflected a growing professionalism in the performers and an increasingly large, sophisticated and stable audience. The move to the Théâtre des Compagnons also marked a change from amateur to professional status for the troupe—a change about which Legault was ambivalent. Although this period (1948-52) saw some of the Compagnons' most successful productions (Wilder's *Notre Petite Ville* (*Our Town*), Pirandello's *Henri IV*), when faced with a financial setback the Compagnons disbanded in 1952, leaving the way clear for other new companies such as the THÉÂTRE DU NOUVEAU MONDE, founded in 1951 by several former Compagnons. Legault's contribution to theatre was sustained by the many professionals who had first begun with the Compagnons—including Jean GASCON, Jean-Louis ROUX, Georges Groulx, and Guy HOFFMANN.

Legault returned to religious theatre in the mid-1950s with an amateur troupe based at the Oratoire Saint-Joseph, dedicated to serving a small public of pilgrims and visitors. But his legacy of renewed appreciation for the craft of theatre, as well as of modern drama, is recognized as the most important element in the rebirth of theatre in Quebec.

See Legault's autobiography, *Confidences* (1955), and Anne Caron, *Le Père Émile Legault et le théâtre au Québec* (1978).

D.W. RUSSELL

Leighton, Betty (b. 1923). Born and educated in London, Eng., she immigrated to Canada in 1942 to join her husband, Geoffrey Leighton, an electronics engineer on loan from the RAF to the RCAF. 'A product of the Ottawa Little Theatre and Ottawa's Stage Society', as she has characterized herself, she was a leading lady with the CANADIAN REPERTORY THEATRE between 1949 and 1952, when she was spotted by Tyrone GUTHRIE in a CRT production of Chekhov's *Three Sisters*. This led to the role of Queen Elizabeth in his 1953 *Richard III*, the STRATFORD FESTIVAL's inaugural production. Other firsts included the opening play of Toronto's CREST THEATRE—Gordon Daviot's *Richard of Bordeaux* in 1954—and the first full Equity year of the SHAW FESTIVAL, 1964, when she played Lady Utterword in Shaw's *Heartbreak House*. Leighton has acted in most major Canadian theatres in a variety of roles from the classical repertoire. Her remarkable versatality is evident in some of her early favourite roles—Liza in Shaw's *Pygmalion*, Blanche in Tennessee Williams' *A Streetcar Named Desire*, and Phoebe in John Osborne's *The Entertainer*—and was notably demonstrated in two THEATRE CALGARY productions of 1970 when she played both the comical Lady Bracknell in Wilde's *The Importance of Being Earnest* and the tragic Mary Tyrone in O'Neill's *Long Day's Journey into Night*. In 1981 Leighton was reunited with actor Donald DAVIS (he had directed her in the Crest Theatre's 1964 production of Molière's *The Imaginary Invalid*) in a ST LAWRENCE CENTRE production of Ernest Thompson's *On Golden Pond*.   EUGENE BENSON

Lepage, Monique (b. 1930). Born and raised in Montreal, she trained in singing and classical dance at the École du Doux Parler, founded by her mother. In 1950 she played Celimène in Molière's *Le Misanthrope* with Les COMPAGNONS DE SAINT-LAURENT. Three years later she and Jacques Létourneau founded a worker-controlled theatre company, Le THÉÂTRE CLUB, which she managed until 1965.

Lepage has played award-winning roles on television and in the theatre, appearing in such well-received television series as 'Le Survenant', 'Les Filles d'Ève', 'Rue de l'Anse', 'Le Paradis terrestre', 'Le Bonheur des autres', and 'La Vie promise', as well as in several television plays. On radio she was a regular member of the cast of 'Sur toutes les scènes du Monde', and in the theatre she played Martha in Edward Albee's *Qui a peur de Virginia Woolf?* (*Who's Afraid of Virginia Woolf?*), Mirandoline in *La Locandiera*, Portia in *Le Marchand de Venise* (*The Merchant of Venice*), and Viola in an unforgettable version of *La Nuit des Rois* (*Twelfth Night*), produced by the Théâtre Club.

For four years (1966-70) Lepage managed The Piggery, a summer theatre at North Hatley, Quebec. She has directed at many theatres, including Le THÉÂTRE DE QUAT' SOUS, Le THÉÂTRE POPULAIRE DU QUÉBEC, and Le Patriote, with productions of Shakespeare, Michel de Ghelderode, Arnold Wesker, and many Québécois plays including Claude GAUVREAU's *Métamorphoses*, which was Canada's entry at the Festival of Nancy in 1977. Lepage has also acted in both English and French films and in musical comedies. Since 1969 she has taught at the CONSERVATOIRE D'ART DRAMATIQUE in Montreal.
                              SOLANGE LÉVESQUE

Lepage, Roland (b. 1928). Born in Quebec, he received his training as an actor at the Centre dramatique in Bordeaux, France. He settled in Montreal in 1956, working mostly in television for Radio-Canada, where he played in the series 'Ouragan' and 'San Yorre'. In 1962 he wrote his first scripts for the series 'Marcus', while collaborating as actor and author on scripts for the popular children's programs, 'La Ribouldingue' (in which he played the important role of Monsieur Bedondaine), 'La Boîte à surprises', and 'Marie Quat-poches'. He drew on these experiences for his first stage play, *La Toilette de gala*, an unpublished work for children, written in 1974. His best known work for children is *Icare* (1979), first produced in Dec. 1979 at Montreal's Théâtre Maisonneuve. In this play Lepage retells the legend of Icarus, but he changes the ending: the young hero is transported in the stomach of a whale to Cumes in Italy, where he is reunited with his father, Daedalus.

Almost all of Lepage's other plays are commissioned works. For the NATIONAL THEATRE SCHOOL (where he teaches theatre history) he translated and adapted texts in the Paduan dialect to create *L'alphabet des paysans*, produced in 1972, which gave him his first opportunity to use the popular language of Quebec. After completing another adaptation—of Edgar Lee Masters' *Spoon River Anthology*, translated as *Le Chant des morts*—Lepage wrote a farce with a political flavour, *La Pétaudière* (1975), which sets in opposition the supporters of 'barley soup' and those of 'pea soup'. Produced in the spring of 1974 by the students of the National Theatre School, *La Pétaudière* coincided with the political debate surrounding the famous Bill

22 on the status of French in Quebec. *La Complainte des hivers rouges* and *Le Temps d'une vie*, written for the students of the NTS, were also produced in 1974. The first, conceived as an oratorio with singing parts or chants, is a reworking of a student piece written at the age of thirteen, based on L.O. DAVID's *Patriotes*, a dramatization of the history of the dozen Patriotes of 1837 who were hanged at Pied du courant. The play had a professional run at Le GRAND THÉÂTRE DE QUÉBEC in Jan. and Feb. 1978.

Le Temps d'une vie (1974) remains Lepage's best-known play, and the only one to have been produced internationally. Described as an 'intimate chronicle in eight tableaux and eight scenes', it follows the life, from birth to old age, of Rosana Guillemette. The popular speech, with its archaic and musical flavour, functions more effectively in this play than in Lepage's other works. The author achieves the right balance between realistic anecdotes and evocations, in a static and serious presentation. As in *La Complainte*, he inserts some 'choral-poems' that suggest the influence of Apollinaire, but they reflect tenderness, nostalgia, and a poetry that suits the character. Ably performed by the actresses Murielle Dutil and Marie Tifo, the play had its first success at Montreal's THÉÂTRE D'AUJOURD'HUI in Sept. 1975, before playing in English at Toronto's TARRAGON THEATRE in 1978. That production, in a translation by Sheila Fischman, won the CHALMERS Award for the author—the first time this award was given to a French-Canadian. In 1979 the play was successfully performed in Belgium and in France.

La Folle du Quartier-latin, an adaptation by Lepage of Jean Giraudoux's *La Folle de Chaillot*, was produced at Le Grand Théâtre de Québec in Oct. 1976. This play—along with *Thérèse est souffrante*, written in 1978, and *Trois livraisons*, a radio script written in 1979—remains unpublished.

JEAN CLÉO GODIN

LePage, Sue (b. 1951). Born in Toronto, she graduated from the Univ. of Guelph in 1973 before joining the STRATFORD FESTIVAL as an assistant in the paint shop. Since then she has designed productions for many of Canada's leading theatres and festivals.

Her first major assignment was that of design co-ordinator for James REANEY's *The DONNELLYS* for NDWT's national tour in

Sue LePage

1975. In 1976 she designed Tennessee Williams' *The Glass Menagerie* and *Brecht on Brecht*, compiled by George Tabori, for Halifax's NEPTUNE THEATRE, where as head scenic artist she designed many other shows. Other notable achievements include her designs for the premières of David FRENCH's *Salt-Water Moon* and Judith THOMPSON's *White Biting Dog* at Toronto's TARRAGON THEATRE in 1984. At Stratford her first design was for Steve PETCH's *Victoria* in 1979; her most memorable work there includes costumes for John Gay's *The Beggar's Opera* (1980), set and costumes for the twinned *Hamlet* and Tom Stoppard's *Rosencrantz and Guildenstern are Dead* in 1985, and for Brecht's *Mother Courage* (1987).

For both classical and new scripts LePage's designs reflect the meaning of the play rather than a personal style, though texture is a vital element in her work, whether conveyed through a wealth of detail or with extreme simplicity.

EUGENE BENSON

Lescarbot, Marc (1570?-1642). Born at Vervins, France, he studied at the Collège de Vervins, the Collège de Laon, and the Univ. of Paris, graduating in 1598 with a degree in law and an exceptional foundation in classical studies. Lescarbot was accredited by the Parlement de Paris as a lawyer in 1599, and remained in the capital to practise his profession until 1606 when, disillusioned by the venality of a judge in a case he was defending, he accepted a proposal from Jean de Biencourt de Poutrincourt to accompany him on a colonizing voyage to Acadia. They left France in May 1606, reaching Port Royal in July and spending the winter there. Lescarbot returned to France in the summer of 1607. This was his only voyage to North America, but he retained throughout his life a passionate interest in subsequent attempts at colonization in the New World.

Historian, poet, and skilled translator from Latin to French, Lescarbot is best known for his *Histoire de la Nouvelle-France* (1609), which saw three editions in his lifetime and which, translated into English and German, was to have considerable influence on later European colonization. Included in this *Histoire*, in a collection of poems entitled 'Les Muses de la Nouvelle-France', is the text of a short verse play Lescarbot composed to celebrate the return of Poutrincourt and his men from a dangerous expedition along the uncharted coast of what is today New England. Performed by members of the little colony on the waters and the shore at Port Royal, this nautical *réception*, entitled *Le THÉÂTRE DE NEPTUNE EN LA NOUVELLE-FRANCE*, is the first dramatic text known to have been composed and performed in North America.   L.E. DOUCETTE

Levine, Michael. (b. 1961). Born in Toronto, he spent a year at the Ontario College of Art before studying theatre design at the Central School of Art and Design in London, Eng. After graduating in 1983, he worked with the Glasgow Citizens' Theatre, but achieved his first major success as co-designer for Eugene O'Neill's *Strange Interlude* in London and on Broadway, for which he received both Olivier and Tony nominations. Levine has subsequently designed for major theatres on both sides of the Atlantic, including the Old Vic, the English National Opera, and the Royal Shakespeare Company in England, and TARRAGON THEATRE, CENTRESTAGE, the Canadian Opera Company, and the SHAW FESTIVAL in Canada. He won a Dora Mavor MOORE Award for his set and costume designs for Frank Wedekind's *Spring*

Awakening at CentreStage in 1986, and his designs for the Shaw Festival—particularly for *Heartbreak House* in 1985—have been widely praised. Among the country's most innovative designers, Levine favours the surrealistic over the realistic, though his bold and imaginative designs rarely fail to capture the mood and atmosphere of the play.

L. W. CONOLLY

Lightstone, Marilyn (b. 1941). Born and educated in Montreal, she studied at McGill Univ. (BA, 1961) where she acted in the university's Red-and-White revues. After three years at the NATIONAL THEATRE SCHOOL—where her voice coach was Eleanor STUART—she moved to Toronto in 1964 to appear at the CREST THEATRE's *Brecht on Brecht*, but the season was terminated for lack of funds. Only in 1965 did Lightstone play the Crest, taking the lead role in Ibsen's *Hedda Gabler* in the Crest's swansong production. She played at the STRATFORD FESTIVAL in 1967 (Ikas in *Antony and Cleopatra*) and 1968 (Masha in Chekhov's *The Seagull*), and at the 1971 CHARLOTTETOWN FESTIVAL she created the title role in the musical *Mary, Queen of Scots*. In 1976 she was named best actress for her leading role in the film *Lies My Father Told Me* at both the Canadian Film Awards and the ACTRA Awards. Lightstone appeared in the long-run Los Angeles production of John KRIZANC's *TAMARA* and also in the New York production, which opened in 1987.   EUGENE BENSON

Ligue Nationale d'Improvisation, La. Founded by Robert Gravel and Yvon Leduc in 1977 and presented for four years under the aegis of the Théâtre Expérimental de Montréal (see NOUVEAU THÉÂTRE EXPÉRIMENTAL DE MONTRÉAL), it has since become more commercially oriented, with an international focus.

Parodying the National Hockey League and its colourful rituals, the LNI features two teams of six actors (three women, three men) and a coach who confront each other on a skating rink (without ice) for three thirty-minute periods. A referee and his assistants ensure that the rules of play are obeyed, while a master of ceremonies and an organist stir up the crowd. Cards, selected at random and read out by the referee, contain all the necessary instructions for the development of each dramatic improvisation: the subject; the number of players; the category (free, pantomime, in the style of Kafka or Michel TREMBLAY, for example); and the length (from thirty seconds to twenty minutes). At the end of each improvisation the audience votes for the winner. After an initial season of friendly encounters, LNI began in 1978 to organize championship matches in which several companies competed for the Coupe Charade. The live telecast by Radio-Québec of the 1982 finals created a mania for this sort of theatre in schools, social clubs, and professional organizations, such as the Bar Associations of Montreal and Quebec City.

Since 1981 the show's numerous tours of Europe have led to the birth of Ligues d'Improvisation in France, Belgium, and Switzerland, and to international tournaments (the first World Cup of improvisation took place in Montreal and Quebec City in 1985).

Created to demonstrate not only the result but also the process of improvisation, and to make this important theatrical technique more accessible and appreciated, LNI has moved further away from theatre and closer to sport. Unfortunately the demand for repetitive entertainment does not always promote the best in exploratory theatre.

PIERRE LAVOIE

Lillie, Beatrice (1894-1989). Born and raised in Toronto, she first performed with her sister and mother in Ontario, before moving to London, Eng., where she quickly became the leading revue-comedienne of her generation, starring there (from 1914) and in New York, where she made her début in 1924. Readily identified by her Eton crop, petite figure, and often androgynous costumes, she never lost her ladylike composure, no matter how risqué the double-entendre or preposterous the sketch. A genius at comic timing and improvisation, she relied on eccentric, occasionally 'naughty' bits of pantomime to ridicule her favourite targets: social hypocrisy, bad manners, and middle-and upper-class pomposity. As the vulnerable yet resilient 'little person' in a world intent on self-destruction, she was enormously popular with the Allied Armed Forces in the Second World War and on her world-tour, *An Evening With Beatrice Lillie* (1952-6). Her 'intelligent' clowning and 'clear, fresh voice' were at their sophisticated best in Noël Coward's *This Year of Grace!* in 1928, *Set to Music*, 1939, and *High Spirits*, 1964.

See her autobiography, *Every 'Other' Inch a Lady* (1972).   DENIS SALTER

Lindley, Harry (1839-1913). Born in Ireland, he immigrated to America about 1866 with his first wife, the actress Florence Webster, and came to Canada in 1869 with Marshall's London Comedy Co. Following two seasons with the HOLMANS and brief engagements with Charlotte MORRISON (1871 and 1872), he took his own company on tour. After a financially disastrous term as manager of Montreal's THEATRE ROYAL, he returned to touring, but he again tried management in 1879 at Halifax's ACADEMY OF MUSIC. During 1880 and part of 1881 Lindley toured Charlottetown, Saint John, and other centres, and opened a new theatre in Halifax. In the 1880s and 1890s he was a familiar and popular figure in many small Ontario towns. Heading west in 1897, he performed in Edmonton, Vancouver, Victoria, and the interior of B.C. for three years. His repertoire consisted chiefly of standard comedies and melodramas, but included a few plays, such as *The Castaways*, of which he claimed authorship. As an actor Lindley's greatest strength lay in comedy, and he won special acclaim as Micawber and the Artful Dodger in stage adaptations of Dickens' novels. His six children—notably Ethel, who starred for several years as Little Lord Fauntleroy—all joined their father's companies. Lindley's amusing memoir, *Merely Players* (1892?), provides a valuable picture of theatre in late nineteenth-century Canada.   MARY SHORTT

Little Theatre and Amateur Theatre. Community theatres in Canada can be traced back nearly four centuries to the single performance of Le *THÉÂTRE DE NEPTUNE* in 1606, but it was only during the 1913-50 period that, as part of the international Little Theatre movement, they began the process of reclaiming the theatre in Canada from foreign domination and sowed the seeds for the post-Second World War emergence of a truly national expression. All theatre during the French colonial regime (1605-1763) was amateur, whether produced by the Jesuit and Ursuline Schools for pedagogical purposes, by the military garrisons, or by high society. These three indigenous traditions extended into the British colonial era (1763-1867) and well beyond, paralleling the arrival of professional touring companies.

Little Theatre and Amateur Theatre

Although pedagogic theatre continues today in Drama-in-Education programs at all levels of Canadian schooling, until 1945 performance opportunities at secondary schools and universities followed the European pattern of extra-curricular activity. Notable early university drama societies in Canada included the University College (Toronto) Glee Club (1879-), which even ventured in 1882 to produce *Antigone* in its original Greek; the Queen's Dramatic Club (1899-) (renamed 'Guild' in 1925), which began with scenes from Shakespeare; the Univ. of Toronto Players' Club (1913-21), the first tenant of HART HOUSE THEATRE; the Univ. of British Columbia Players' Club (1915-), which toured annually for three weeks; Toronto's still excitingly experimental UNIVERSITY ALUMNAE DRAMATIC CLUB (1918-); and Wolfville's Acadia Dramatic Society (1919-). By the 1930s theatre and drama studies had entered the curricula via Department of Extension and summer courses. Finally, in 1945 the Univ. of Saskatchewan followed the American educational example by establishing a Chair of Drama and subsequently granting the first BA in the British Commonwealth to include credit courses in theatre practice. There have also been a number of Inter-Varsity and High School Drama Festivals, the latter patterned after Simpson's (now Sears) Ontario Collegiate Festival launched in 1946, which still attracts 150-200 one-act play entries. More specialized training for the profession was available in elocution courses and conservatories as early as the 1880s, culminating in 1960 with the founding of the NATIONAL THEATRE SCHOOL in Montreal. (See also EDUCATION AND TRAINING.)

Garrison productions (see GARRISON THEATRE) often achieved high production standards, while bolstering colonial morale and raising funds for charity. Their repertoire was drawn essentially from the British comedies of the time, but some original works were devised to celebrate special events (see ROYAL ARCTIC THEATRE). Occasionally service personnel—such as actor/manager John NICKINSON—were emboldened to leave the army and venture into professional careers. Between Confederation and the Boer War, the British troops were gradually replaced, first by the North-West Mounted Police and then by Canadian military units. The Garrison Club of Toronto, for example, was still active in 1907. During two world wars the garrison tradition survived in troop entertainments such as the DUMBELLS, and the ARMY, NAVY, and Air Force (see BLACKOUTS) shows.

But the third amateur stream, the society tradition, had the greatest eventual impact. The role of the French governors and fur-trading officials in charge of seventeenth- and eighteenth-century evenings of drama, ballet, and opera can be traced forward through the RIDEAU HALL theatricals, inaugurated in 1873 by Lord and Lady Dufferin, to Governor General Earl Grey's Musical and Dramatic Competitions (1907-11), and the eventual landmark achievement of the DOMINION DRAMA FESTIVAL.

Perhaps the oldest continuously running civic dramatic society in Canada is Toronto's Dickens' Fellowship, which has been active since it mounted Albert Smith's dramatization of *The Cricket on the Hearth* in 1905. The Hamilton Players' Guild (1929-) traces its roots back to 1875 when a group of wealthy lawyers, merchants, and bankers founded the Garrick Club of Hamilton (1875-1910), with the Governor General, the Marquis of Lorne, as their patron. The Garrick Club produced plays and musicals and sponsored fancy-dress balls, all for charity. After it disbanded, Caroline Crerar—daughter of K. C. John Crerar, the Garrick's first vice-president—revived the idea of community theatre in Hamilton with the Players' Guild.

French-speaking equivalents of these dramatic societies existed throughout the nineteenth century. Joseph QUESNEL delivered an 'Address to the Young Actors of the Théâtre de Société' in Quebec City in 1805, and towards the end of the century a series of private literary-*cum*-theatrical circles extending from Hull to Lotbinière were established. One of the earliest was Montreal's Cercle littéraire de Saint-Henri, founded in 1878. Others in the Montreal area were the Cercles Jacques Cartier (started in 1875), Talma (1889), Ville-Marie (1890), and Crémazie (1895). On 13 Nov. 1898 the Saint-Jean-Baptiste Society instituted 'Les Soirées de famille' on Sunday evenings at Montreal's MONUMENT NATIONAL under the direction of 'the Canadian Coquelin', thirty-year-old Elzéar Roy. These 'Family Evenings' combined French classics, tasteful comedies, and some original historical dramas with orchestral and choral music. Movies and magic were often interspersed between the acts. To avoid church censure they were presented under the guise of public recitals given by students of declamation. The *soirées* permitted the intermingling of the sexes and served as a rallying point for French-Canadian culture; to many they represented the birth of Québécois theatre. They lasted until 1901, when the youthful acting ensemble even ventured a tour to New England.

In 1908—probably in response to Earl Grey's primarily anglophone competition—eighteen Cercles on Montreal Island entered the first all-French amateur festival, the Concours de l'Île. Organized by the French-born artistic director of the THÉÂTRE NATIONAL, Paul CAZENEUVE, in association with the journal *La Patrie*, it was spread over three weeks, a different Cercle playing each night, prior to the regular entertainment at the National, before a panel of adjudicators. In the 1908-9 period some sixty amateur troupes were active in Quebec, including the Cercles St Louis, Laval, and Champlain in Quebec City. The Laval Club, formed in 1899, ran into CENSORSHIP problems in 1904, but was reinstated in 1906 after agreeing to have its plays vetted by a church committee. French amateur societies were often highly religious and sexually segregated—Omer Godbout's Union Dramatique of Quebec City (1907-36) and Father Gustave LAMARCHE's all-male touring troupe, Les Paraboilers du Roi (1938-40), were prime examples. Father Émile LEGAULT's famed amateur COMPAGNONS DE SAINT-LAURENT (1937-52) not only had an immense impact on the Dominion Drama Festival, but in its apprenticing of Jean GASCON, Jean-Louis ROUX, Pierre DAGENAIS, and others, it proved a dynamic catalyst for Quebec's post-Second World War professionalism.

Outside Quebec francophone amateur theatre in New Brunswick was established at Collège Saint-Joseph (today's Univ. of Moncton) in 1864. Important early groups in Moncton included Le Cercle Beauséjour (c.1899-1914) and Le Cercle Dramatique (1910-20). In Manitoba the CERCLE MOLIÈRE, founded in 1925, remains Canada's oldest francophone company. Other French-language amateur societies were founded in Edmonton (Le Cercle Dramatique Jeanne d'Arc, c.1913), Vancouver (La Troupe Molière, 1946-68), Ottawa (Le Caveau), and Northern Ontario.

Despite their contribution to the development of Quebec culture, some of the 'aimless social dramatic clubs' were criticized by the distinguished Montreal director Rupert Caplan (in the *Canadian Forum*, Jan. 1929) for not producing worthwhile plays that would foster a native drama in preparation for the 'Ultimate National Canadian Theatre'. The criticism was answered by the glorious age of Canada's amateur theatre—the between-the-wars flowering of *la petite scène*, the Little Theatre movement.

The Little Theatre movement began in Europe during the 1880s, soon becoming an international theatre-as-art groundswell. As a reform movement it drew its first inspiration from the historically accurate ensemble productions of the Duke of Saxe-Meiningen's resident court company. Its 1870-80s tours of Europe influenced the creation of such seminal Little Theatres as André Antoine's Théâtre Libre (Paris, 1887), Otto Brahm's Freie Bühne (Berlin, 1889), J. T. Grein's Independent Theatre Club (London, 1891), and Konstantin Stanislavsky's and Vladimir Nemirovich-Danchenko's Moscow Art Theatre (1898). Soon disciples like Jacques Copeau, Max Reinhardt, Harley Granville-Barker, and Vsevolod Meyerhold modified the vision and extended it into the twentieth century, as poetic naturalism gave way to symbolism, psychological realism, and expressionism. Of immense impact were the abstract design and lighting theories of Edward Gordon Craig and Adolphe Appia, and the folkloric grassroots example of Dublin's Abbey Theatre. William Butler Yeats, co-founder of the Abbey, lectured in Canada in 1904-5, and Lady Gregory accompanied the Irish Players on their North American tours between 1911 and 1914.

The Little Theatre movement was spurred by its almost evangelical opposition to the commercial theatre, exemplified in Canada and the U.S. by the crass melodramas, spectacles, and comic VAUDEVILLE of syndicated touring. Canada's own prophet of theatrical change, Roy MITCHELL, led the crusade to drive out the 'money-changers' in his brilliant analytical treatise *Creative Theatre* (1929).

In 1912 Maurice Browne, one of the fathers of Little Theatre in America, opened his tiny 93-seat Chicago playhouse. In Canada, Carroll AIKINS patterned his short-lived 100-seat Home Theatre (1920-3) in Naramata, B.C.,

Little Theatre and Amateur Theatre

after Browne's Chicago and Seattle experiments. In contrast to the commercial road-houses, most Little Theatres were indeed little; they were not, however, links in a continental distribution chain but indigenous theatres located in a particular community. It was no accident that the Community Players of Winnipeg (later The Winnipeg Little Theatre) (1921-58) chose as their motto 'The greatest art has always been communal' (from Roger Fry's *Vision and Design*). In contrast, Leonard Young's Community Players of Montreal (1920-3) failed because they tried to compete by playing in commercial theatres like His Majesty's.

Although enlightened Canadians absorbed developments in Europe, more direct influences came from the U.S. The American Drama League, formed in 1909, began publishing its quarterly, *The Drama*, in 1911. On its masthead was George Pierce Baker, with whom Canada's Herman VOADEN studied playwriting at Yale in 1930-1. In 1913 the Ottawa Drama League (renamed the Ottawa Little Theatre in 1952) became Canada's first branch of the Drama League of America (although it declared its independence during the First World War and later affiliated with the British Drama League).

The crucible for change in English Canada, however, was Toronto's ARTS AND LETTERS CLUB. Established in 1908, this men's club brought together artists from the Group of Seven with writers and critics of the time. Their after-supper theatricals were in the capable hands of 'Prankmeister' Roy Mitchell who, from 1910 to 1916, introduced Maeterlinck, Yeats, and *commedia dell'arte* to this appreciative private audience. When Toronto's Hart House Theatre was opened in 1919, Vincent MASSEY invited Mitchell to be its first stage director and together they turned Hart House Theatre into the flagship of Canada's Little Theatre movement. With its eclectic European repertoire of Euripides, Shakespeare, Sheridan, Wilde, Ibsen, Shaw, Synge, Molnár, Rostand, and Claudel, Hart House became a model for Little Theatres across Canada. Its annual bill of Canadian one-act plays quickened thoughts of a national drama and set the pattern that Toronto's NEW PLAY SOCIETY and the ALTERNATE THEATREs would complete. Novice playwrights Merrill DENISON, Mazo de la Roche, Fred Jacob, Marjorie Pickthall, and Duncan Campbell Scott were given a showcase. In 1927 Macmillan published two volumes of *Canadian Plays from Hart House Theatre*, preceded by the Canadian Authors' Association's *One-act Plays by Canadian Authors* (1926), which sold 900 copies. Further incentives came from CAA and IODE playwriting contests held between 1925 and 1928, and another contest devised by Herman Voaden in 1929. Influenced by the Group of Seven, Voaden asked contestants to set their works in the Canadian North and write out of a northern vision of the land. Forty-nine entries were received and a half-dozen were published under the title *Six Canadian Plays*

Hart House, University of Toronto

304

(1930). Voaden's own plays, together with those of Bertram BROOKER, were probably the most avant-garde to come out of the Little Theatre movement. Samuel French's more commercially minded *Canadian Playwright Series*, introduced in 1935, published one-act titles on a regular basis and even made them available for international distribution. It was an era when the one-act play reigned supreme, perhaps symptomatic of the more manageable scale that could be encompassed by new writers. The Ottawa Little Theatre's annual one-act Canadian Play Writing Competition has been held continuously since 1939.

The Little Theatres succeeded in filling the vacuum caused by the gradual collapse of mainstream touring in the 1920s and in meeting the mass-audience challenge of cinema and radio broadcasting. A vast grassroots network of indigenous companies rapidly blossomed, cultivating a different kind of theatregoing in Canada and providing essential training for a generation of actors, dramatists, and technicians. Because of their non-professional status, these 'dramateurs' were able to survive the economic devastation of the 1930s and to provide the continuity that allowed Canada to bridge the gap between the imported commercial entertainments of the 'road' and the post-Second World War appearance of a native professional theatre.

Hundreds of Little Theatres were active between the wars. In the Atlantic provinces the Halifax and Saint John (N.B.) Theatre Guilds were formed in 1931. The Haligonian company endures in its Pond Playhouse on the outskirts of the city. For forty years it was guided primarily by H. Leslie Pigot (1885-1971), a professional actor stranded in 1924 after the Frances Compton tour folded in the Maritimes. Today Nova Scotia boasts approximately eighty community groups. In New Brunswick the various university drama clubs dominated the post-Second World War festivals, along with Moncton's excellent Stage Door '56, while the earlier Theatre Guilds of Fredericton and Saint John (1931-56) slowly faded in importance. The now-defunct Charlottetown Little Theatre Guild was set up in 1935 and the St John's Players of Newfoundland in 1937. Amateur societies in other Newfoundland cities included the Amateur Players and the Playmakers Company in Corner Brook, the Northcliffe Drama Club in Grand Falls, and the Avion Players of Gander, among others.

Some of Montreal's finest anglophone community theatres were the Trinity Players (1911-61), established by the Rev. Robert Norwood of Trinity Anglican Church, and Rupert Caplan's YM-YWHA Players. Montreal's major amateur company was the MONTREAL REPERTORY THEATRE. Begun in 1930 by Martha ALLAN as the Theatre Guild, it was quickly retitled to avoid confusion with its New York namesake. In 1933 it opened a French section that saw Yvette BRIND'AMOUR, Gratien GÉLINAS, and Guy BEAULNE, among many others, acting or directing either in French or English. On 5 Mar. 1952 their Guy Street headquarters went up in flames. For another decade they struggled on, even flirting with Equity status. There were perhaps another twenty Montreal clubs over the years, of which the Shakespeare Society (1945-7) was probably the most memorable.

In Toronto, Hart House Theatre set the pace up to the Second World War and the University Alumnae after. Some of the most exciting ensemble productions were those mounted by the Stanislavsky-oriented Theatre of Action (1935-40), a less radical spinoff of the coast-to-coast left-wing Progressive Arts Clubs. Artistic direction came from two successive Americans, David Pressman (1936-8) and Daniel Mann (1938-40). In addition to these workers' clubs were the Imperial (Oil's) Players Guild (Toronto) and the T. Eaton Company's Masquers Clubs with branches in Montreal, Toronto, Hamilton, Winnipeg, and Calgary. The Masquers distinguished themselves in several Dominion Drama Festivals and especially during the Second World War, producing concert party revues for the troops in Canada and overseas. Of scholarly interest was Toronto's Shakespeare Society (1928-40) in which, from 1931-40, the noted English academic G. Wilson Knight used Hart House Theatre as a laboratory for many of his published interpretations of Shakespeare's plays. Similarly, at Queen's Univ., G. B. Harrison corroborated his theories while teaching and staging Shakespeare between 1943 and 1949.

One of the most remarkable Ontario organizations was the London Little Theatre (LLT), a 1934 amalgamation of four earlier clubs. In 1945 it was able to buy the Grand Theatre (see GRAND OPERA HOUSE, London), becoming the first amateur group to own

Little Theatre and Amateur Theatre

Leslie Chance and Lord Duncannon in Romeo and Juliet, *Ottawa Little Theatre, 1933; photograph by Karsh*

and operate a year-round legitimate, unionized house. Professionals were hired to direct an amateur roster of six productions, while the summers were given over to an Equity stock company. Commercial touring productions were also integrated into the season and the Grand even served on occasion as a tryout theatre for Broadway shows. By 1953 the LLT had cleared off its mortgage and boasted an annual subscription of 11,000, more than ten per cent of the city's population. In 1971 the LLT commenced the rare transition from amateur status to a resident professional company, first called Theatre London, later the Grand Theatre Company. The Ottawa Little Theatre (OLT) also purchased its own real estate, its members raising $60,000 to convert an Eastern Methodist Church into a T-shaped playhouse that opened on 3 Jan. 1928

and lasted until fire destroyed it in 1970. Two years later, on 11 Feb. 1972, a modern proscenium house opened on the old site. In 1988 the OLT celebrated seventy-five years of operation. Theatre Ontario now reports approximately 240 community groups in the province.

In western Canada the Winnipeg Little Theatre went professional in 1958, uniting with John HIRSCH's Theatre 77 to become the MANITOBA THEATRE CENTRE, the prototype for Canada's eventual chain of regional/civic theatres, while the Penthouse Players (1961-)—inmates of the Stoneybrook Penitentiary and Winnipeg residents—remains one of Canada's most innovative amateur groups. The Regina Little Theatre, founded in 1926, carried on when the earlier Community Players (1921-34) went under. Since 1967 John COULTER's historic reconstruction of *The Trial of Louis Riel* has been their annual summer tourist attraction. Saskatoon's Little Theatre Club evolved out of a play-reading group in 1922, but never had a proper home and disbanded in 1949. After the war the Saskatoon Community Players (1952-9) took the spotlight briefly, but it was the Gateway Players who emerged successfully in 1967, followed by the Strolling Players (1971-) and a second version of the Western Stage Society (1972-). The Saskatchewan Drama League was incorporated in Mar. 1933 and became one of the most vital in the country, promoting three kinds of drama festivals: the regular DDF regional playoff for established clubs, a unique Class B festival for less-experienced adult groups, and Junior festivals for the schools. When the DDF stopped operating during the Second World War, the various provincial Leagues followed suit, except for those of Saskatchewan and British Columbia in the Western Canada Theatre Conference. As a result, in 1945, when the others struggled to reorganize, the Saskatchewan Drama League had 120 active member societies and conducted twenty-four separate festivals. It was fitting that for the return of the DDF in 1947 Emrys Jones, Professor of Drama at the Univ. of Saskatchewan, was named Finals adjudicator. He was the second Canadian to be so honoured. (Toronto-born Barrett H. Clark, who coined the phrase 'non-professional theatre', was the first, in 1938.) The government of Saskatchewan also established its own Arts Board in 1948, nine years before the Canada Council was created. Although superseded by a governmental Ministry of Culture and Youth in 1972, it continues as an autonomous funding body.

Calgary's amateur theatre was launched in 1912 with the Paget Players (1912-28), succeeded by the Calgary Little Theatre (1923-8) and the Green Room Club (1929), which amalgamated into the Theatre Guild in 1932. The founding treasurer of the 1929 Green Room Club, a young teacher named Betty MITCHELL, was destined to become Calgary's most important theatrical figure. In 1944 she gathered a quartet of her Western Canada High School alumni around her and formed Workshop 14 (1944-66), named after the number of the classroom provided for them. In their first golden years they won nine out of the eleven regional festivals they entered, and participated in the Blue Flame Theatre, a radio series sponsored by the Calgary Gas and Power Co. With the 1957 opening of the Southern Alberta Jubilee Auditorium, they withdrew from amateur competition and began to play in the larger theatre. Financial difficulties, however, forced a merger with the Musicians and Actors Club of Calgary in 1966, and the new MAC 14 group evolved, two years later, into THEATRE CALGARY, the third non-profit regional theatre to grow logically out of amateur beginnings.

Little Theatre in Edmonton began with Ethel Reese-Burns's Forbes-Robertson Amateurs (1916-20), a group she reformed when she moved to Victoria. The Edmonton Little Theatre (1929-45) owes its existence to another remarkable woman, Elizabeth Sterling HAYNES, one of the first products of Roy Mitchell's Hart House regime. (In 1988 Edmonton's 'Sterling' Theatre Awards were named after her.) The Edmonton Little Theatre was succeeded by the Community Players (1945-51), the Mercury Players (1952-6), Circle 8 (1955-61), and, finally, by the Edmonton (or Walterdale) Theatre Associates (1959-), who have made a name for themselves with their annual melodramatic contribution to 'Klondike Days'.

In British Columbia the still-flourishing Vancouver Little Theatre Association (VLTA) was founded on 3 Nov. 1921 and still operates in the 465-seat Alcazar/Palace theatre (opened in 1913), which it purchased in 1923 and rechristened the York in 1940. Isabel Ecclestone MacKay in the 1920s and A.M.D. Fairbairn of Victoria in the 1930s were perhaps the West Coast's outstanding dramatists at the time. (Several of Fairbairn's one-act plays deal with the Indian in white society and were published in a Samuel French collection called *Plays of the Pacific Coast*, 1935.) On 24 Apr. 1962, in response to the rise of professionalism in Vancouver, the VLTA joined ten other amateur groups to form the Metropolitan Co-operative Theatre Society. Collectively they purchased the 450-seat Marpole Theatre in 1963 and converted it to the Metro, with the hope of using it as a showcase for the many community theatres that circle the city. By 1966, however, administrative problems dictated that the Metro become, instead, an independent amateur theatre with a subscription season, drawing its casts from the collective talent pool.

On Vancouver Island, Victoria's Amateur Dramatic and Operatic Society began in the 1880s and the operatic side was still active in the 1920s. The Univ. of Victoria's Players Club dates from 1923 and the Victoria Theatre Guild from 1930, the latter moving into their Langham Court Playhouse in 1949. Some of the leading lights of Victoria in the 1930s were Ethel Reese-Burns (the Forbes-Robertson Players), Archie MacCorkindale (Punch and Judy Theatre), and Llewelyn BULLOCK-WEBSTER, the Welsh actor, director, playwright, historian, and teacher who was associated with the Beaux-Arts Club, director of the B.C. Dramatic School (1921-32), and originator of the Canadian Drama Award in 1935. This award—perhaps the first Canadian theatre award outside of competitions—recognized national service in the Little Theatre. Montreal Repertory Theatre's Martha Allan was its first recipient.

Provincial or district umbrella organizations were usually called Drama Leagues (the Central, Eastern, and Western Ontario Drama Leagues, etc.) and tended to be patterned after the British example formed in 1919. In the *Canadian Forum* (Dec. 1928), Herman Voaden made a first plea for 'a National Drama League' to provide technical advisers, library loans, and to arrange for conferences, exhibitions, lecture tours, and, most significantly, play competitions. With its national and regional infrastructure, the idea would translate into the Dominion Drama Festival.

By 1928 the Little Theatre movement was glowing brightly. The flames were fanned by

Little Theatre and Amateur Theatre

Barry Jackson's National Council of Education cross-Canada lecture tour in 1929-30, extolling the writing of original Canadian plays and preaching the concept of a national theatre that would flourish in a dozen different cities. The *Canadian Forum* instituted a regular column called 'The Little Theatres' with its Nov. 1928 issue, and a year later Hart House Theatre's CURTAIN CALL (1929-41), Canada's first theatre magazine, was born. Other Little Theatres published newsletters such as *Callboard* (Nova Scotia Drama League), *Cue* (MRT), *Play-Time* (Woodstock Little Theatre), *Call-Boy* (LLT), *The Prompter* (Manitoba Drama League and Saskatoon's Gateway Players), and *Rôle Call* (Edmonton Little Theatre).

The rise of several theatres for children can also be attributed to the amateur movement: the Toronto Children's Players (1931-); the Punch and Judy and Strolling Puppet Players (1935-) on the west coast; Yvonne Firkins' Children's Theatre of Canada in Vancouver (1936-); and Josephine Barrington's Juveniles in Toronto (1936-). (See also CHILDREN'S DRAMA AND THEATRE IN ENGLISH.)

One sour note was Merrill Denison's famous and salutary 1928-9 essay 'Nationalism and the Drama' (*Yearbook of the Arts in Canada*, 1929), in which he derided the 'introspective patriotism that recognizes nationhood most easily in folk songs and native dances' and challenged the regional concept of a national theatre by arguing that great theatre was 'the most centrifugal of the arts' and has existed only 'at the capital centre of a people'. Paying due respect to the Irish renaissance and the writings of Gordon Craig, he tilted at the 'lofty intentions' of the Little Theatre idealists and their waning influence.

During the Depression much of the initial idealism evaporated as the Little Theatres drifted back to being community theatres. The move towards festivals and competitions also provided a new focus that killed Little Theatre as an art form. As early as May 1929 in the *Canadian Forum* R.K. Hicks suggested that 'Ontario has an established system for the conduct of rural dramatic competitions', and by Feb. 1930 E. Sterndale Bennett of the Playgoers' Club of Lethbridge (1923-) had organized, in Calgary, Canada's first-ever provincial drama-league festival. On 29 Oct. 1932 the organizational meeting of the Dominion Drama Festival was convened at Rideau Hall. A few years later, in his 'Reflections on the Decline of the Little Theatre' (*Curtain Call*, Nov. 1939), Professor Laughlin Campbell responded to the news that his Theatre Guild in Windsor would be producing *Petticoat Fever* by reminding his readers that the movement had begun as a protest and now had succumbed to being what it attacked, 'a second-hand commercial venture' and 'a box office panderer'. 'Let the curtain come down on another in the long line of lost causes,' he concluded.

The DDF may have killed the Little Theatre as an art movement, but until at least 1950 it was Canada's national theatre expression, a unique moveable feast that brought together French and English, and devotees from the Atlantic to the Pacific, in one heightened week of excitement and camaraderie. It planted and nurtured the seed of a National Theatre in Canada's cultural consciousness. Whether this would culminate in a building in Ottawa, a cross-country touring company, a chain of civic theatres, or a body of original drama, no one could yet agree. In the decades to come, Canadian theatre would embrace all of these alternatives, plus the professional machinery and government commitment that would see them carried through on a consistent, qualitative level. It is not that the DDF failed to achieve professional standards. It did, frequently, and attracted fashionable audiences. But its attitudes were non-professional, and perhaps because it was a national organization spread across the country and meeting only occasionally it was slow to move with the times. By 1950 the tatty curtain backdrops had gone and productions were often splendidly designed. It had become a three-act festival and by 1960 had shuffled off enough colonial coils to hire Canadian professionals on a regular basis to adjudicate the regional festivals and even occasionally the finals. But the first 1947 talk of an all-Canadian festival was (rightly enough) deemed immature, and the further suggestion of a non-competitive showcase festival (such as today's fringe festivals) would have to wait until 1971.

The Second World War marked the watershed between amateur and professional theatre in Canada. Just as the amateurs had filled the vacuum created by the departure of the touring companies in the 1920s, so the burgeoning Canadian professionals filled the vacuum created by the cessation of DDF activities between 1939 and 1947. In less than a decade Canada had changed from an agricultural to an industrial nation, and returning troops and a wave of European immigrants brought with them new cultural demands: they wanted outdoor cafés, wine with meals, and more urbane entertainments. With the establishment of the STRATFORD FESTIVAL in 1953, professional theatre had its touchstone. In hailing Tyrone GUTHRIE's achievement, Robertson DAVIES turned his back on 'the seedy amateurism which has afflicted the arts here for so long', and declared that it 'is not good enough for our new place in the world'. The Canada Council agreed and the pattern was set—cultural funding would go to the professionals.

Since the collapse of DDF/Theatre Canada in 1978, Canada's amateur theatre has been represented internationally by the National Multicultural Theatre Association (1975-), and it is significant that Canadian amateur theatre has been given new focus by a rainbow of multicultural expression. (See MULTICULTURAL THEATRE.) Provincially there are a number of umbrella organizations—like Theatre B.C., Theatre Ontario, or l'ACTA (Association canadienne de théâtre amateur), which in 1972 became AQJT (Association québécoise du jeune théâtre)—that speak for community theatre in their region and organize festivals. Canada is also a member of the International Amateur Theatre Association (headquartered in The Hague since 1968), which sponsors festivals that rotate every two years to a different country, with Monaco the host country every fourth summer. Calgary hosted the 'World Theatre Mosaic' in 1983, and the Great Canadian Theatre Festival in Halifax in July 1988 selected Powerhouse Theatre from Vernon, B.C., as Canada's representative to Monaco in 1989.

Amateur theatres today continue to flourish. In 1983 Samuel French estimated there were 700-800 community theatre groups in Canada and 300-400 college and university societies. There were also 7,000 high schools on its mailing list. With the arrival of professional theatre, the amateur movement did not go underground but moved out into the suburbs of the larger cities, or found welcome in smaller communities not served by the mainstream. While amateur productions still evince a noticeable London or Parisian accent, they increasingly embrace Canadian plays and venture into original writing.

The amateur theatre has been criticized for letting its social predilections dull its artistic principles and for prolonging Canada's colonial ties, but as Robertson Davies pointed out in his Foreword to Betty Lee's *Love and Whisky* (1973), 'thanks to the Dominion Drama Festival, Canada was never without a theatre.' Even though only a few groups made the actual transition to professional status, the roots of Canada's National Theatre and the beginnings of its National Drama were indisputably amateur. DAVID GARDNER

Ljungh, Esse W. (b. 1904). Born in Malmö, Sweden, he studied law at the Univ. of Upsala for two years before immigrating to Manitoba at age twenty-three. He farmed there until 1930 when he became editor of the *Swedish Canada News*, a Winnipeg weekly. After free-lance work for the CBC in the late 1930s he became a producer at Station CJRC. In 1942 he joined CBC Winnipeg full-time as Prairie Region Drama Producer.

While in Winnipeg, Ljungh learned all aspects of radio production (see RADIO DRAMA) and pioneered many new techniques. After his transfer to Toronto in 1946 he worked on productions ranging from such classic series as 'CBC Wednesday Night' to soap operas like 'Brave Voyage' and 'Search for Tomorrow'. In 1955 he became producer of the prestigious 'Stage' series, created by Andrew ALLAN, whom he officially succeeded as National Supervisor of Drama in 1957, a position he held until his retirement in 1969. Subsequently he occasionally directed radio plays for the CBC.

Ljungh's production style was characterized by simplicity and naturalness; he often went to great lengths to achieve realistic sounds—like building partial sets to provide the right acoustical background and having the actors use cutlery in an eating scene. Ljungh saw his role as a co-ordinator of the work of others—playwrights, actors, technicians, musicians. He produced many programs based on Canadian content before it was fashionable to do so. Unfortunately none of Ljungh's early work, and only a little of his work from the late 1950s and 1960s, has been preserved on tape. SHARON BLANCHARD

Lockhart, Araby (b. 1926). Born in Toronto and educated at the Univ. of

Lockhart

Toronto, she began acting at the Belmont Theatre in Toronto in 1945 and at HART HOUSE THEATRE under Robert GILL. She made her professional début in tours in Brian Doherty's productions of the Victorian melodrama *The Drunkard*, 1948-9, and the revue *There Goes Yesterday*, 1949-50. In the late 1950s, she produced and starred in a series of annual revues called *Clap Hands* at Hart House, and in the 1960s toured in England. She has acted with most major theatres in Canada, her notable roles including Betty in Allan STRATTON's *Nurse Jane Goes to Hawaii* at Toronto's PHOENIX THEATRE in 1981, Maureen in Anne CHISLETT's *The Tomorrow Box* at the Muskoka Festival in 1985, and Lulu in Suzanne Findlay's *Gone to Glory* at the BLYTH FESTIVAL in 1985. Lockhart chaired the Jane MALLETT Theatre Fund Committee for the ST LAWRENCE CENTRE, and since 1985 she has been President of The Actors Fund of Canada.   HERBERT WHITTAKER

Gilles Pelletier and Hélène Loiselle in Antigone, *Nouvelle Compagnie Théâtrale, 1975*

Loiselle, Hélène (b. 1928). Born in Montreal, she made her début with Les COMPAGNONS DE SAINT-LAURENT as a walk-on in Léon Chancerel's *Pichrocole*. Shortly afterwards she appeared there as Rosette in Musset's *On ne badine pas avec l'amour* in 1945, and subsequently as Junie in Racine's *Britannicus* in 1949, and as Juliette in Shakespeare's *Roméo et Juliette* in 1950. On radio she played in the series 'Jeunesse dorée' by Jean Desprez. Throughout her career Loiselle's acting has been marked by an ability to communicate the complexities of human situations while enhancing her interpretations with a remarkable range of physical effects.

Between 1952 and 1954 Loiselle studied acting in Paris, and on her return she became well known for her roles in the television serials 'Cap-aux-Sorciers' (1955-6), 'Les Forges de Saint-Maurice' by Guy DUFRESNE (1973-5), and 'Rue des Pignons' by Louis and Mia Morrisset (1966-73), as well as for roles in some thirty television plays, including works by Molière, Wilde, Chekhov, Gorky, Lorca, and Ionesco. She appeared in Arthur Miller's *Les Sorcières de Salem* (*The Crucible*) at Le THÉÂTRE DU NOUVEAU MONDE, Chekhov's *Oncle Vania* (*Uncle Vanya*) and Marcel Aymé's *Les Maxibules* at L'Egrégore, and Chekhov's *Les Trois Soeurs* (*The Three Sisters*) at Le THÉÂTRE DU RIDEAU VERT. She also played in works by Québécois playwrights, including Françoise LORANGER

(*Le Chemin du roy*, 1968, and *Médium saignant*, 1970) and Michel TREMBLAY: Lisette de Courval in *Les BELLES-SOEURS*, 1968, Robertine in *En pièces détachées*, 1969, and an unforgettable Marie-Lou in *À TOI, POUR TOUJOURS, TA MARIE-LOU*, 1971. Her other major roles include Blanche Dubois in Tennessee Williams' *Un Tramway nommé désir* (*A Streetcar Named Desire*) for La COMPAGNIE JEAN DUCEPPE in 1974, Lady Macbeth for La NOUVELLE COMPAGNIE THÉÂTRALE in 1976, and Madame in Jean Genet's *Les Bonnes* (*The Maids*) at the Café de la Place in 1981. In 1980 she directed a brilliant production of Pavel Kohout's *Pauvre assassin* for La Compagnie Jean Duceppe. Loiselle has appeared in many films—notably Claude Jutra's *Mon oncle Antoine* (1971) and Denys Arcand's *Réjeanne Padovani* (1973)—and from 1975 to 1982 was administrative and artistic co-director (with her husband, Lionel Villeneuve) of Le Théâtre Beaumont-Saint-Michel.

PIERRE MACDUFF

London Theatre Company, The. Formed in St John's, Nfld, in 1951 by Leslie Yeo and Hillary Vernon—who were subsequently joined by Oliver Gordon and George Paddon-Foster—Newfoundland's first professional resident company operated out of a high-school auditorium for six years, producing approximately one hundred plays. The company's objective was to present plays from the classical and modern repertoire of the kind being produced in the major theatres in London, Eng., using mainly British actors. In 1952 the company toured to Corner Brook, Halifax, Saint John, Moncton, and several cities in southern Ontario. They also contributed to radio shows and school broadcasts in Newfoundland, though their most important achievement was to establish professional theatre as an integral part of the cultural life of the capital.   C.J. SKINNER

Loranger, Françoise (b. 1913). Born in Saint-Hilaire, Que., Loranger spent most of her childhood in Montreal's east end and was raised in an intellectual climate of philosophical awareness and ideological tolerance. Financial circumstances forced her to leave school at fifteen. Although best known as a writer for the stage, she spent much of her career in radio and television, becoming the first woman in Quebec theatre to earn her living as a writer.

Loranger began her career in radio in 1938 as secretary and co-writer for Robert Choquette, leaving in 1939 to work independently as an author and a director at CKAC and CBF—the first woman to direct radio drama in Quebec. She continued to write for radio until 1955, when CENSORSHIP of her texts and the use of radio for propaganda became intolerable to her.

During the 1930s Loranger also published short stories. Her only novel, *Mathieu* (1949), revolves around the activities of a theatre company based perhaps on the experiences of childhood friends Denise PELLETIER and Gilles PELLETIER and of actors she knew through her radio work, such as Pierre DAGENAIS and his company, L'ÉQUIPE. *Mathieu* was adapted for broadcasting on CBF in 1951 in the series 'Les Grands Romans canadiens'.

Loranger moved easily from radio to the writing of television drama, which includes *L'École des vieilles filles*, broadcast in 1958, and published in 1965 under the title *Georges . . . oh! Georges*. This well-constructed play is Loranger's first clear dramatization of the difficulty and the necessity of escaping from a stifling bourgeois home and the dead weight of its traditional values. In 1961 'Sous le signe du lion', a critically acclaimed serial, again challenged middle-class family values. *Un Cri qui vient de loin* (1966) was the only original television serial broadcast in Quebec during the 1964-5 season. *Un si bel automne*

(1971), written as a television serial, dramatizes the situation of native Indians in Quebec at the time of the October crisis. Considered too controversial for Radio-Canada, it received only an amateur stage performance (in 1972).

Loranger's first stage play, *Une Maison . . . un jour* (1965), was an immediate success. Produced by Le THÉÂTRE DU RIDEAU VERT in 1965, it toured the same year to Quebec City, Sherbrooke, Leningrad, Moscow, and Paris, where it was produced at the prestigious Odéon. It presents a day in the life of three generations of an established bourgeois family for whom everything is falling to pieces. Despite the characters' efforts to avoid reality, the crumbling family home is due for immediate demolition. Suffering and death hover over the stage as relationships disintegrate.

ENCORE CINQ MINUTES (1967), first presented on radio in 1966 and then on stage in 1967 by Le Théâtre du Rideau Vert, won a Governor General's Award. A new production in 1969 by the THÉÂTRE POPULAIRE DU QUÉBEC at the THÉÂTRE DES VARIÉTÉS toured Ontario. Like *Une Maison . . . un jour*, the play depicts the impossibility of love and the hell of family life. Yet whereas the first play presents a number of more-or-less equally interesting characters, *Encore cinq minutes* is sharply focussed on a mother's quest for self-knowledge and control. In the end she realizes she must leave home in order to move into a social space where she can live more productively. The play eloquently portrays the meaninglessness and powerlessness of the life of a woman who exists solely for her husband and children. The role of the mother is one of the best yet written in Quebec for an actress. The television series 'Les beaux dimanches' presented *Une Maison . . . un jour* in 1970, and *Encore cinq minutes* in 1971.

Political questions and technical experimentation dominate Loranger's next three plays. *Le Chemin du roy, comédie patriotique* (1969), written in collaboration with Claude Levac and produced by L'Egrégore in 1968, was inspired by the 1967 visit of Charles de Gaulle to Quebec, his journey from Quebec City to Montreal, and his famous 'Vive le Québec libre!' speech. Characters in the play are real figures—René Lévesque, Daniel Johnson, Jean Lesage, Pierre Bourgault, and Eric Kierans, for example—formed into two opposing teams: federalists and nationalists. Director

Françoise Loranger's Une Maison . . . un jour, *Théâtre du Rideau Vert, Montreal, 1965, with (l. to r.) Geneviève Bujold, François Tassé, Benoit Girard, André Cailloux, Gérard Poirier, Monique Miller, Yvette Brind'Amour*

Paul Buissonneau, after improvisational work with the actors, staged the play as a mock hockey game.

Double jeu (1969), produced in 1969 by the COMÉDIE-CANADIENNE, and directed by André BRASSARD as a participatory happening in the style of the Living Theatre, drew criticism both from those favouring traditional theatre techniques and from those who felt Loranger had not gone far enough. The controversy culminated in 'L'affaire Paradis' (15 Feb. 1969), in which a small group in the audience, wishing to test the authenticity of the actors' improvisation and the spectators' participation, removed their clothes on stage and slit the throats of two doves and a rooster. *Double jeu* is a psychodrama in which a group of night students and their professor, improvising on the story line of a quest, gain greater awareness of themselves and their sexuality, of personal goals and values, and of the destructiveness of arbitrary social convention.

Médium saignant (1970), which once again shows Loranger's innovative approach to drama, is also militantly nationalistic, a dramatic rendition of real events: Bill 63 and the language controversy in St-Léonard (1968-9). First produced at the Comédie-Cana-

dienne in 1970, the play presents a meeting of municipal councillors held in a cultural centre where a group of young people, representing the voice of counter-culture, is preparing a show for Mardi Gras. Dialogue takes the form of a contrapuntal rhythm between the two groups. The specific topic of the play is the danger of bilingualism for Quebec. Related to this is the reaction to language regulation in the anglophone and immigrant community. The play's main theme is debilitating fear and how to overcome it through new awareness. It ends with a ceremony—resembling the final cry in *Un Cri qui vient de loin*—through which collective fear is exorcized. A new production of *Médium saignant* in Nov. 1976 at the PLACE DES ARTS, where Loranger modified the ritualistic ending of the first version, was successful, although certain critics complained of the play's potential for cheap propaganda and its caricatured presentation of ethnic types.

The first woman playwright to have had significant impact on the evolution of Quebec society and its theatre, Loranger chronicles the painful decline of a past whose values, practices, and structures stand as a barrier to awareness, freedom, acceptance of responsibility, and full enjoyment of the present. Her themes are fear, self-knowledge, social injustice, memory, communication, creativity, freedom, and action. The initial situation of all her plays shows characters who are individually or collectively constrained by the weight of the past, deluded about present reality, and unable to act effectively in it.

See J.P. Crête, *Françoise Loranger. La Recherche d'une indentité* (1974); *Québec français*, 28 (1977), a special issue on Loranger; and C.F. Coates, 'From Feminism to Nationalism: The Theatre of Françoise Loranger, 1965-1970', in Paula Gilbert Lewis (ed.), *Traditionalism, Nationalism and Feminism. Women Writers of Quebec* (1985).

LOUISE H. FORSYTH

Lunch Theatre. Lunch Theatre in Canada resulted from the realization that a large segment of the population, trapped in an urban environment at lunchtime, could form a new and potentially large theatre audience. Among the early groups to exploit this potential was Toronto's 190-seat Colonnade Theatre, built in 1964 in the second storey of a downtown shopping mall as a venue for a variety of entertainments. In May 1965 director Jan Steen offered two one-act plays to shoppers at a cost of fifty cents; this was reported as 'the birth of lunchtime theatre', and referred to as 'Instant Theatre'. In Montreal Mary Morter's Instantheatre flourished briefly in the late 1960s, presenting original English-language works in a 99-seat venue at Place Ville Marie; but Morter's successor, Maurice PODBREY, successfully lobbied for the dissolution of the Instantheatre in favour of an evening venture, the CENTAUR THEATRE. Vancouver's CITY STAGE, Canada's most influential Lunch Theatre, was founded in 1972 by Ray Michal and George Plawski (who had worked at the King's Head Pub in London, also a Lunch Theatre). After moving from their original venue, a former doughnut shop, to new facilities in 1976, Michal became increasingly interested in evening fare and abandoned the lunchtime format. Several companies, however, were inspired by the initial success of City Stage. Edmonton's NORTHERN LIGHT THEATRE opened in 1975 as a lunch theatre, but by 1980 had moved entirely to an evening repertoire. In Calgary, Lunchbox Theatre, located in a 100-seat theatre in Bow Valley Square, has offered the local labour force a diet of musicals and comedy—much of it

Canadian—since 1975 under artistic director Bartley Bard. The Solar Stage has been operating in the heart of Toronto's banking district since 1978 under artistic director Gene Tishauer. In contrast to the usual evolution, it began as an evening theatre in North Toronto (1976), moving to Lunch Theatre and its present location to serve an untapped audience with short plays, musical satires, soap operas, and dance.

While light comedy and musical revues are most likely to please Lunch Theatre audiences, the repertoire is wide-ranging. One-act plays by Bernard Shaw, Noël Coward, Jules Feiffer, and even August Strindberg and Harold Pinter are offered, along with selections by Canadian playwrights such as Tom CONE, Peter Colley, and John Lazarus, and many satirical COLLECTIVE revues. Venues are usually very small, and the atmosphere intimate and informal—audiences are encouraged to eat lunch during the performance.

Lunch Theatre is also produced by established theatre companies in an attempt to extend their normal evening audiences, though only companies near a business district have been able to do this. Halifax's NEPTUNE THEATRE under John NEVILLE succeeded with such a program, as did Montreal's THÉÂTRE DU NOUVEAU MONDE under Jean-Louis ROUX, who established the Théâtre-midi in 1973. It produced two lunchtime plays a season on TNM's main stage, including topical sex comedies by Jean BARBEAU and François Beaulieu. Other than Roux's experiment, French-language Lunch Theatre has been uncommon; its nearest equivalent was the CAFÉ-THÉÂTRE, which sought a different, more sophisticated audience.

STEPHEN JOHNSON

Lund, Allan (b. 1927). Born in Toronto, he began formal dance studies at the age of eight. During the Depression he regularly won five dollars a week at tapdancing contests in BURLESQUE theatres. At thirteen he formed a professional association with Blanche Harris (whom he married in 1943), and they modelled themselves on their idols, Ginger Rogers and Fred Astaire. They appeared in the original Second World War Canadian NAVY SHOW, *Meet the Navy*, touring Europe and Canada.

After the war they spent five years on the nightclub circuit in the U.S. but returned to Canada, where Lund emerged as a leading choreographer. He transformed Quebec's amateur Feux Follets into Canada's first professional musical dance company. Pioneers in Canadian variety television, the Lunds were the first performers to sign contracts with the CBC, dancing in such shows as *Parade, Showtime*, and *Mister Showbusiness*.

From 1960 Lund was associated with sixteen productions at the STRATFORD FESTIVAL, ranging from Shakespeare and Molière to Brecht's *Rise and Fall of the City of Mahagonny*. With the founding of the CHARLOTTETOWN FESTIVAL in 1965 he moved to Prince Edward Island, first as director and choreographer and from 1968 to 1986 as artistic director. He has occasionally directed for other companies and has been associated with the BANFF CENTRE SCHOOL OF FINE ARTS since 1983.

Lund's Charlottetown Festival musicals were based on literary, historical, and pastoral themes, with a strong eye to family entertainment. The most successful shows dealt with innocent waifs teaching a moral lesson to their elders: ANNE OF GREEN GABLES, *Johnny Belinda, Joey*, and *Little Lord Fauntleroy*. Lund worked in close co-operation with community theatres on the Island, dedicating himself to the development of amateur talent to professional standards. He added a second and third stage to complement the main Festival productions, as well as children's productions.

In spite of the Festival's commercial success under Lund (ninety per cent attendance was not unusual), he was criticized for favouring excessively 'saccharine' productions, as well as producing 'Broadway clones'.

RENATE USMIANI

Luscombe, George (b. 1926). The founder of TORONTO WORKSHOP PRODUCTIONS in 1959, he was its only artistic director until the end of the 1985-6 season. Luscombe's twenty-seven years at TWP was by far the longest tenure of any artistic director in Canada, and the application of his ideas in a consistent body of work over a long period enabled him to perfect a distinct and complex 'group theatre' technique that gave Toronto some of its greatest theatrical successes. Luscombe's productions are characterized by highly skilled ensemble improvisation and brilliant use of the physical stage.

Luscombe was born and raised in Toronto and trained in commercial art at Danforth Collegiate. From the first his work in the theatre reflected his commitment to left-wing politics. His first encounter with theatre came after the Second World War as a member of the Toronto Co-operative Commonwealth Federation drama club, directed by Ann Marshall, whom he would later claim as one of his two mentors (the other being Joan Littlewood). While working with Marshall, Luscombe wrote and organized variety shows for the Co-operative Commonwealth Youth Movement, and put together a song-and-dance troupe to perform for striking workers on picket lines. His first professional experience came in 1948 as a member of E.G. Sterndale Bennett's Peoples' Repertory Theatre, which toured such plays as Valentine's and Will Evans' *Tons of Money* and J.B. Priestley's *Dangerous Corner* to small towns in Ontario.

In 1950 Luscombe went to Great Britain where he got a job as second lead with a provincial 'fit-up' troupe touring Wales. In his two seasons with the troupe, he underwent a rigorous apprenticeship, often learning a new role every day. A chance encounter led to a meeting with Joan Littlewood, who accepted him into her Theatre Workshop troupe just prior to the company's move to Stratford East.

Luscombe's five apprentice years with Littlewood set the course of his later work, imparting a commitment to Stanislavsky on the one hand and to the disciplined physical techniques of Rudolf Laban on the other. His stagecraft, like Littlewood's, relies heavily on mime, lights, and sound effects to create spectacular images supported by documentary material and larger-than-life ensemble playing—all devised as strategies for renewing classic texts and adapting non-dramatic material for the stage. Two years after his return to Canada in 1957 Luscombe began his own Workshop Productions group. After four years of working on a part-time basis, he chose six actors as the beginning of a permanent ensemble in 1963. Although unable to realize his initial dream of an ongoing company (to critics who held this against him, he retorted that he had trained instead 'several companies'), he nonetheless succeeded in gathering a nucleus of actors who would reappear in many of his shows.

Although his work at TWP heralded the ALTERNATE THEATRE movement in Toronto, Luscombe has always remained somewhat

Mr. Bones, *co-authored and directed by George Luscombe, Toronto Workshop Productions, 1969*

apart from it, showing little interest in the nationalism of the theatres that followed him. Nor has he been especially interested in the new wave of Canadian playwrights. His belief that the text exists only in performance, and his insistence that the author is merely one collaborator among several, has made him unpopular with many playwrights. Luscombe has been criticized for the fact that no major playwrights have come out of TWP; his most frequent writer, Jack Winter, is more of a dramaturge than an author. Such criticism overlooks the precepts of the group-theatre approach, in which the performances and the *mise-en-scène* are inseparable from the spoken text. In that sense, Luscombe's theatre is non-literary, although it is often highly literate and poetic. His signature play is *Hey Rube!*, an acrobatic, behind-the-scenes look at circus life. First performed in 1961, it was revived several times, most recently in 1983. *Hey Rube!* is the least political of Luscombe's plays, but perhaps the most revealing, with its delight in theatricality and its sentimental attachment to the world of the performer.

Luscombe's most popular shows have been those in which his theatrical brilliance has been matched by his passion for politics. His ideological affiliation with the traditional left-wing issues of trade unionism and internationalism was expressed in a trilogy of documentaries on working-class history: TEN LOST YEARS (1974), *The Mac-Paps* (1979),

and *The Wobbly* (1983). His first major hit was also his most overtly political: *Chicago '70*, a living newspaper about the trial of the Chicago Seven, ran for close to a year, a record broken only by *Ten Lost Years*. By the time *Ten Lost Years* was revived as a recognized classic in 1981, critics had begun to complain that Luscombe's work had a sameness about it.

In 1986 Luscombe was succeeded by Robert Rooney as artistic director, while remaining as artistic director emeritus, but in the theatre's 1988 budget crisis his position was eliminated; Luscombe subsequently launched a lawsuit against TWP for wrongful dismissal.   ALAN FILEWOD

Lyceum Theatre (Edmonton). The Lyceum was the most prominent stock playhouse in Edmonton before the First World War. Originally called the Edmonton Opera House, it was built by Alexander W. Cameron in 1906 at what is now 10320 Jasper Avenue. The architect was H.A. Magoon, and the cost some $8,000. The structure was 48' wide by 150' deep, with a stage measuring 48' x 22', later extended to 40'. It was a metal-clad frame building with a flat roof over the auditorium suspended from exposed external trusses and a tall mansard roof over the stage for fly space. At first the auditorium floor was level, equipped with rows of wooden chairs that could be pushed back against the walls to allow roller-skating in the afternoons. There was a gallery supported by posts.

The theatre opened in Oct. 1906, initially booking road shows. In 1907 its floor was raked to give the audience a better view. In the same year Cameron opened another smaller theatre, the Kevin, in a warehouse immediately to the north on Third Street. This soon burned down, but was reconstructed as the Dominion, with a capacity of 390. The Opera House was then run in tandem with the smaller playhouse as part of a theatre complex.

In 1910 W.B. Sherman became manager of the Opera House, changing its name to the Lyceum. He encouraged resident stock companies—such as the Winnipeg Stock Co., the New Lyceum Co., and the Toronto Stock Co.—to stay for extended periods, during which they built up a loyal audience, thereby giving the house a firmer local identity than that achieved by Edmonton's other major

Lyceum Theatre (Edmonton)

theatre, the EMPIRE (also managed by Sherman), which booked in road shows. In 1914 the control of both theatres passed to C.P. WALKER of Winnipeg, and the Lyceum's last booking, before closing forever, was the A.B. Basco Co. with tabloid musicals in December of that year.

See John Orrell, *Fallen Empires: Lost Theatres of Edmonton, 1881-1914* (1981).

JOHN ORRELL

Lyceum Theatre (Halifax). Located on Starr St, the 75' × 70' heavy frame building, styled after a Greek temple, opened as the Temperance Hall on 3 Dec. 1849. On the lower floor were club rooms for the Sons of Temperance, and on the second an auditorium intended 'to be a Public Hall—open to exhibitions and meetings of every description not of an immoral tendency.' Until 1867 touring companies presenting legitimate drama were disqualified, although band concerts, vaudeville entertainments, and minstrel shows were allowed. Briefly known as the Olympic Theatre during T.C. Howard's occupation in the 1868-70 seasons, it was purchased in May 1880 for $4,825 by the St Vincent's Dramatic Club (afterwards called the Young Men's Literary Association). After renovations, it re-opened as the Lyceum Theatre on 8 Dec. 1880.

Contemporary estimates of seating on the benches in the level auditorium and in the single U-shaped gallery vary from 1,000 to 2,000 (1,250 is a reasonable estimate). In 1869 Howard enlarged the lecture-platform stage; in 1880 it was rebuilt to measure 23' × 20'. New scenery was fitted, dressing-rooms were added on each side, and a new proscenium arch was constructed. Because of the lack of fly space, rolled drop scenes had to be used. Heating was by stove and lighting by gas. In 1874 William NANNARY installed chairs on the orchestra floor and cushioned the balcony seats.

Inadequate facilities made the Lyceum unattractive to professional repertory companies, most of which preferred the ACADEMY OF MUSIC (opened 1877). Consequently bookings by minstrel, vaudeville, and amateur companies predominated, along with occasional bookings by repertory companies such as the Boston Comedy Co., the Lindley

Comedy Co., and the P.A. Nannary Co. In the 1890s the Lyceum was unoccupied for increasingly long periods of time; it burned down on 15 Mar. 1899.

MARY ELIZABETH SMITH

Lyric Theatre. The pre-eminent theatre in Calgary from 1904 until the opening of the larger SHERMAN GRAND THEATRE in 1912, it was a more opulent theatre than its predecessor, Sherman's Opera House, with larger seating capacity (over 700), permanent opera chairs, boxes, and a spacious foyer. Located in downtown Calgary (126 8th Ave SW), the Lyric served as a regular venue for international stars and community events.

The Lyric opened on 5 Sept. 1904 with a production by Miss Jessie Shirley & Company of Arthur Wing Pinero's melodrama *The Ironmaster*. From then on the major attractions were touring performers presenting classics, grand opera, concerts, stock melodramas, and VAUDEVILLE. Appearing at the Lyric were the Harold Nelson SHAW Company, C.P. WALKER's Comedians, Stuart's Comic Players, the R. Buchanan Company, the San Francisco Opera Company, the MARKS BROTHERS, the Partello Stock Company, and the George H. SUMMERS Company—as well as two resident repertory companies: the Lyric Stock Company (1905) and the Sherman-Platt Company (1905-6). In Oct. 1905 W.B. Sherman took over management of the Lyric, renaming it Sherman's Lyric Theatre. Vaudeville troupes, combining novelty acts and short silent movies, dominated the bill.

When the lavish Sherman Grand opened in Feb. 1912, the Lyric was forced to change management again, becoming part of the PANTAGES vaudeville circuit. It reopened on 23 Feb. 1914 as the Pantages Theatre. In addition to regular vaudeville, the Pantages periodically hosted political rallies and benefit concerts for local charities as well as patriotic concerts during the First World War.

After the war competition from movies caused a decline in Pantages' audiences, and the theatre closed in June 1921. The building was remodelled to accommodate several shops, a beauty parlour, and a dining-room, before demolition some years later.

See also HULL'S OPERA HOUSE.

JEFFREY GOFFIN

M

McAnuff, Des (b. 1952). Born in Princeton, Ill., to a Canadian father, he was raised in Guelph and Scarborough, Ont. While at Ryerson Polytechnic he wrote *Leave it to Beaver is Dead* (1976), first produced in 1975 at Toronto's Theatre Second Floor and later workshopped at New York's Public Theater in its 1978-9 season. As assistant director for TORONTO FREE THEATRE, he developed (with John PALMER and the cast) *The Pits*, first produced by TFT in 1975.

Following the lukewarm reception of his May 1976 adaptation of *Dr. Faustus* at THEATRE PASSE MURAILLE, McAnuff moved to New York where he worked at the Chelsea Theater before becoming associate director of the Dodger Theater at the Brooklyn Academy of Music, scoring a great success with his 1978 production of Barrie Keeffe's *Gimme Shelter*. In 1980 he directed Keeffe's *A Mad World, My Masters* for Toronto Arts Productions (see CENTRESTAGE) and in 1981 Wolfgang Heldesheimer's *Mary Stuart* at the Public Theater. He wrote the book, music, and lyrics for *The Death of Von Richthoven As Witnessed from Earth* produced at the same theatre in 1982 to poor reviews. In 1983 he directed *Macbeth* at Ontario's STRATFORD FESTIVAL.

In 1982 McAnuff was appointed artistic director of La Jolla Playhouse, San Diego, where his first season included *Big River*, a musical based on Mark Twain's *Adventures of Huckleberry Finn* whose Broadway production in 1985 won seven Tony Awards, including one for McAnuff's direction.

EUGENE BENSON

Macdonald, Brian (b. 1928). Born and raised in Montreal, he began dance training in 1944. After graduating from McGill University he was music critic for the *Montreal Herald* for two years before joining the National Ballet of Canada as a dancer in 1951, its inaugural year. After sustaining a severe injury in 1953, he turned to choreography and teaching. In 1956 he founded the Montreal Theatre Ballet, dedicated to the creation of dance based on Canadian music and choreographed by Canadian artists; in 1957 he helped create McGill's enormously successful student revue MY FUR LADY. Beginning in 1958 he choreographed a series of ballets for the Royal Winnipeg Ballet, including *Rose Latulipe*, first performed in 1966, and *The Shining People of Leonard Cohen*, first performed in 1970, with music for both by Harry Freedman. Macdonald was artistic director of the Royal Swedish Ballet (1964-7), the Harkness Ballet of New York (1967-8), the Batsheva Ballet of Israel (1971-2), and Les Grands Ballets Canadiens (1974-7), and has created ballets and directed operas for companies throughout the world. In 1978 he began directing Gilbert and Sullivan operettas at the STRATFORD FESTIVAL. His Stratford *Mikado* went on to play London's Old Vic and New York's City Centre. In 1987 he directed the musical *Cabaret* on the Festival main stage.

All Macdonald's work—dance, opera, operetta—is distinguished by a choreographer's feeling for design combined with an opera director's response to music (he memorizes the scores of the works he directs). 'I love speed and I love richness of texture,' he says. Macdonald received the Order of Canada in 1967, the Molson Prize in 1983, and the 1985 Dance in Canada Award.

EUGENE BENSON

McDonough, John Thomas (b. 1924). A native of Ottawa, he studied at Laval, Toronto, and Oxford Universities and at the Dominican College in Louvain, Belgium. He became a Dominican monk in 1950 but left the order and the priesthood in 1968. His religious concerns are manifested in the one play for which he is known, CHARBONNEAU & LE CHEF (1968), a realistic portrayal of the conflict over social justice in the Asbestos workers' strike of 1949 between Archbishop Charbonneau of Montreal and the Premier of Quebec, Maurice Duplessis. An unpublished and unproduced play, *The Social Gospel of Jim Crow, According to Matthew*, was written as a Centennial project. McDonough now teaches Greek philosophy at Centennial College in Scarborough, Ont., and is completing a book on Socratic philosophy.   JAMES NOONAN

McDowell

E. A. McDowell in Dion Boucicault's The Shaughraun.

McDowell, Eugene A. (1845-93). Born in South River, New Jersey, he spent most of his career managing stock and touring companies in Canada. He started as an actor, making his début in St Louis in 1865, and appearing in New York with Helena Modjeska, Edwin Booth, Clara MORRIS, James O'Neill, and Fanny Davenport. Beginning in romantic roles, he quickly became adept at comic parts and was particularly well known for his rendition of Conn in Dion Boucicault's *The Shaughraun*.

After a successful summer season in 1874 in Halifax managing a stock company with William NANNARY, McDowell brought his own company to Canada in the spring of 1875, concentrating on *The Shaughraun*. This early success led to a period (1875-7) as manager of the Montreal ACADEMY OF MUSIC with a resident stock company supplemented by international performers that included Adelaide Neilson, George F. Rowe, Joseph Murphy, and Oliver Doud Byron. The seasons in Montreal were not financially suc-

cessful and thereafter he managed touring companies almost exclusively. During fourteen seasons in Canada, McDowell produced over 200 plays, contemporary and classical. Notable productions of Canadian plays included William Henry FULLER's *H.M.S. Parliament*, in which McDowell toured Canada (Saint John to Winnipeg) in the winter and spring of 1880. McDowell's own company played as far west as the Dakotas, as far east as Newfoundland, and as far south as the West Indies. In 1879 it became the first professional stock company to play in Winnipeg. The company contributed significantly to the training of a number of Canadian artists, including Julia ARTHUR and Albert TAVERNIER. Other notable company members included Annie Russell, Neil Warner, Harry LINDLEY, and Felix Morris.

In 1877 McDowell married actress Fanny Reeves (1852-1917); their daughter Claire (1878-1966) was also an actress. McDowell died in Bloomingdale, N.Y.

KATHLEEN FRASER

McLeay, Franklin (1864-1900). Born in Watford, Ont., he was educated at the Univ. of Toronto and became a teacher in Woodstock, Ont. He later moved to Boston to study acting with James E. Murdoch, who recommended him to English actor-manager Wilson Barrett. McLeay returned to England with Barrett's company, making his London début in 1891 at the Olympic Theatre in *The People's Idol*, by Barrett and Victor Widnell. He played several other roles in Barrett's melodramas, winning particular acclaim as the grotesque cripple in the Egyptian melodrama *Pharoah* in 1892; his Iago was also much praised. After five years with Barrett he joined Herbert Beerbohm Tree's company at Her Majesty's Theatre, where, among other roles, he shone as Cassius to Tree's Brutus. In June 1900 McLeay organized a benefit performance—attended by Queen Victoria—at Drury Lane Theatre for the victims of the great 1900 Ottawa fire. He died three weeks later from, it was said, 'brain fever brought on by overwork'—more likely from pneumonia.

Versatile and intelligent, McLeay was one of the earliest Canadian actors to make an impact abroad. He was, said one British critic, 'one of the very few real artists of the stage, one of the very few worthy to join the ranks of Irving.' L. W. CONOLLY

McNamara, Ed (1921-86). Born in Chicago, he was educated in a seminary before he left the U.S. in 1939 to join the Canadian army. After various jobs on the West Coast, he joined Sydney RISK's Everyman Theatre to play Bill Sears in the 1946-7 tour of Elsie Park GOWAN's *The Last Caveman*. Moving to Toronto in 1951, he became a regular CBC actor, on both radio and television. In the sixties and seventies McNamara was increasingly occupied in television and films (especially those of Allan Kroeker), winning such recognition as a 1976 Canadian Film Award (for the National Film Board's *For Gentlemen Only*) and a posthumous 1987 Gemini Award for 'Another Point of View', an episode of CBC's 'Seeing Things'. In his long stage career two outstanding performances at Toronto's TARRAGON THEATRE epitomized his seemingly effortless ability to combine enormous inner strength with warm, open generosity and charm: as Gabriel in Michel TREMBLAY's *Bonjour, là, Bonjour* in 1975 and as Old Eddy in Sharon POLLOCK's *Generations* in 1981; for the latter he won a Dora Mavor MOORE Award.   HARRY LANE

Magnus Theatre Northwest. Northern Ontario's first professional theatre company, it was founded in Thunder Bay by British director Burton Lancaster. Early in 1972 he received a Local Initiatives Project grant for school tours of children's plays, using actors from Lakehead University and Confederation College. Further grants allowed him to rent the 181-seat former Slovak Community Hall—renamed Magnus Theatre—and, beginning in Jan. 1973, he presented his first full-length adult season. Until 1976 Lancaster offered a repertory of entertaining, if unadventurous, commercial fare, while improving the standards of the company and building an audience. He also offered Shaw and Shakespeare, provocative plays such as Charles Dyer's *Staircase* (1974-5 season), and Canadian plays—including David FRENCH's *Of the Fields, Lately* (1975-6 season). Maurice Evans was artistic director for the 1977-8 season, presenting the première of a play set in Thunder Bay—Michael John Nimchik's *Leonard Brady* (directed by Lancaster)—and a successful production of Peter Shaffer's *Equus*, directed by Tibor Feheregyhazi, who became artistic director that autumn. He remained until 1983, expanding the season, broadening the audience base with a flamboyant personal style, and increasing the number of Canadian plays produced—by French, John MURRELL, Erika RITTER, and Michel TREMBLAY.

Brian Richmond was artistic director from 1983 to 1987. Under his direction Magnus continued to present Canadian plays, several of which were premières: *I Love You, Ann Murray* by Paul Ledoux and David Young and *Gone the Burning Sun* by Ken MITCHELL, co-produced with the Guelph Spring Festival (1983-4 season); *And When I Wake* by James W. NICHOL, *Shipbuilder* by Mitchell, and *Fire* by Ledoux and Young (1984-5); Larry FINEBERG's *Devotion* and Ledoux's and Young's *As Time Goes By* (1985-6). Since 1987 Michael McLaughlin has been artistic director; in his first season three of five productions were Canadian plays.

STEPHEN JOHNSON

Maillet, Antonine (b. 1923). A dramatist, novelist, story-writer, and literary scholar, she was born in Bouctouche, N.B., and edu-

Antonine Maillet

cated at the Université de Montréal and at Laval. A realist with a central focus on the people of Acadia, she stands at the crossroads of the rich oral and written traditions that have been preserved in the words spoken and shared among Acadians in their unique idiom, and has made the voice and language of Acadia heard. Maillet's drama and fiction use this idiom not merely to preserve folklore but to dispel romantic myths and reveal harsh but proud realities. Maillet considers herself a political writer, whose work affirms human dignity and freedom, and protests against inequality and injustice. She has evolved a theatrical practice and invented a theatrical language that are uniquely suited to the creation of theatre and drama for Acadia.

Maillet's first plays, *Entr'acte* and *Poire-acre*, were performed at Le Collège Notre-Dame d'Acadie in Moncton in 1957 and 1958 respectively, where both she and Viola Léger were teaching. An important collaboration has been sustained between Maillet and Léger, who has subsequently played a decisive role in creating for the stage all Maillet's dramatically powerful heroines. *Entre'acte* was presented at the provincial drama festival in Bathurst, and *Poire-acre* was named the best original Canadian play in the 1958 DOMINION DRAMA FESTIVAL. During this early period, Maillet also wrote children's plays. None of these early plays have been published.

In *Les Crasseux* (1968), produced by Montreal's COMPAGNIE JEAN DUCEPPE in 1974, Maillet creates a living tableau of Acadia, dividing her characters into two opposing camps of the poor and the rich. While the upper-town characters are known only by their position in society—the mayor's wife, the doctor—those of the lower town have the colourful names and the long family associations Maillet uses in her work to give a sense of Acadian genealogy. Like Michel TREMBLAY, Maillet has her characters speak the language of their class and region. While these people are poor and have little education, Maillet's empathy with them and the irony of the title (The 'Grubby') are clear. The leader of the group, Don l'Orignal, a giant of a man, reappeared as the title figure in her novel *Don l'Orignal* (1972), in the same way that La Sagouine, in her forties in *Les Crasseux*, was soon to appear—alone and much older—in her own play. A new and considerably revised version of *Les Crasseux* was published in 1974.

La SAGOUINE, pièce pour une femme seule (1971), the play for which Maillet is best known, is a collection of sixteen monologues delivered by a seventy-two-year-old charwoman who ekes out a living scrubbing the floors of the rich. The repository of Acadia's heritage and of the dignity of its people, she also serves as a vehicle for Maillet's biting commentary on a society where Acadians continue to be underprivileged and risk losing their language and traditions. Through Gapi, husband of La Sagouine, Maillet continued the same thematic development and social commentary. A man of the sea, he is a lighthouse keeper who remains true to his light and to the magic of the sea, though modern technology threatens him with redundancy. *Gapi et Sullivan* (1973), commissioned by Théâtre Jean Duceppe, but not produced, shows Gapi alone in the first act, speaking to the gulls out on a sand dune, establishing his own philosophy and reminiscing about La Sagouine, now dead. In the second act his old friend Sullivan appears to encourage him to travel, to abandon Acadia. The second version of the play, *Gapi* (1976), was produced by the THÉÂTRE DU RIDEAU VERT in both Quebec and Montreal in 1976.

In *Évangéline Deusse* (1975), produced by Théâtre du Rideau Vert in 1976, Maillet rewrites the old romantic myth. An eighty-year-old but still vigorous Évangéline is in a Montreal park with three men who, like her, are dispossessed and in exile. A touching love story with Le Breton parallels, it subverts the Longfellow romance. Rejecting despair and a surrender to futile tears, the characters triumph in their own modest way through their words, their strength, their attachment to their heritage and to each other.

La Veuve enragée (1977), produced by Théâtre du Rideau Vert in 1977, based on Maillet's novel *Les Cordes-de-bois* (1977), derives its dramatic conflict from dissension between rival village factions. The rich, powerful, and bigoted widow is opposed to three generations of squatter women who represent love, wisdom, and vitality, as well as bootlegging, prostitution, and witchcraft. The scheming widow is thwarted in her attempts to put an end to the women's illegal activities. Both novel and play stand as high points in Maillet's career. *Le Bourgeois Gentleman* (1978), produced by Théâtre du Rideau Vert, in which Maillet sought to adapt the Molière play to the Acadian situation and to her own satirical purposes, was not well received.

In 1974 Le Rideau Vert presented a dramatic adaptation of Maillet's novel *Maria-agélas* (1975), the story of an energetic Acadian woman and members of her village during the 1930s who preferred the dangerous adventures of using their lobster pots for rum-running to seeking work in American canning plants. This adaptation featured Michelle Rossignol and Denise PELLETIER. Mariaagélas is yet another strong Maillet heroine who, in her fight against a debilitating status quo, spontaneously chooses to act in opposition to established moral and legal standards. She is opposed in this by the same bigoted widow figure who violently campaigned for her own view of propriety and who was finally defeated in *La Veuve enragée*. As in *La Veuve*, the crusading role of the widow was performed by Viola Léger in *La Contrebandière* (1981), a revised version of the initial dramatization of *Mariaagélas* produced in 1981.

A dramatization of the novel *Emmanuel à Joseph à Dâvit* (1979), which shows the Nativity as occurring among the poor of an Acadian village, was presented at Le Rideau Vert in 1979. *Les Drôlatiques, horrifiques et épouvantables aventures de Panurge, ami de Pantagruel d'après Rabelais* (1983), produced by Le Rideau Vert in 1983, is Maillet's version of the travels of Rabelais's Panurge and his companions in Acadia, where the language is familiar and where the old traditions still retain the promise of youth and vigour. *Garrochés en Paradis*, produced in Nov. 1986 by Théâtre du Rideau Vert, is about a group of poor workers 'thrust into Heaven' after a Christmas Eve explosion. The same theatre produced her *Margot la Folle* in Oct. 1987 featuring Yvette BRIND'AMOUR and Jean Dalmain.

Maillet has created a gallery of characters who vividly evoke the lived reality of the Acadian people. Her plays reflect their courageous tenacity and the imaginative devices they have used in order to survive. They have also, particularly through their use of the language unique to the Acadian people, greatly strengthened the sense of community and the will to prevail as a culture. Both Canada and France have granted her their highest honours. The English version of *La Sagouine* (1979) received the CHALMERS Canadian Play Award in 1980.

See L. Léger and C. Maillet, 'Dossier Antonine Maillet', *Revue de l'Université de Moncton*, 7 (1974); B. Drolet, *Entre dune et aboiteaux ... un peuple. Étude critique des oeuvres d'Antonine Maillet* (1975); M. Lacombe, 'Breaking the Silence of Centuries', *Canadian Theatre Review*, 46 (1986).

LOUISE H. FORSYTH

Mair, Charles (1838-1927). A prominent poet of the Confederation era, Mair is also known today for his only dramatic work, the blank-verse tragedy *Tecumseh* (1886), in which he tried to give dramatic form to the pro-Empire, anti-American, and anti-francophone nationalism of the Canada First movement, of which he was a co-founder. It was an attempt to establish a Canadian drama by infusing the British literary tradition with a 'taste of the wood'. The story of the Shawnee chief who allied his people with the British forces in the war of 1812 provided Mair with the material of a national myth. The character of Tecumseh, however, is merely a shadow of the play's real hero, Isaac Brock, the British general who rallies the Canadian volunteers to victory. Mair's picture of the war is a parade of melodramatic characters: a Byronic artist, an innocent Indian maid, a genocidal shaman, stout-hearted Canadians, and villainous Americans. These characters are tied together with an episodic plot that betrays Mair's inexperience with theatre. Despite its pretensions to literary form, *Tecumseh* is in fact a pageant celebrating Mair's dubious thesis that Canadian nationhood was won on the slopes of Queenston Heights.

Tecumseh is today read as a historical document. Its Imperial ideology is quaint and its patronizing treatment of native peoples repugnant to modern sensibilities, although the lyric passages are occasionally moving, and certain scenes display a talent for lively satire. Mair's hopes for a professional production were unrealized until 1971, when Ken GASS mounted a much-changed adaptation at FACTORY THEATRE as *The Red Revolutionary*. ALAN FILEWOD

Major, Leon (b. 1933). Born and raised in Toronto, he studied at the Univ. of Toronto and began directing professionally at Toronto's CREST THEATRE in the 1950s. An assistant to Michael LANGHAM at the STRATFORD FESTIVAL in 1961, he directed Gilbert and Sullivan's *The Gondoliers* there the next year. He co-founded the NEPTUNE THEATRE in

Major

Halifax, serving as artistic director from 1962 to 1967, was director of productions for HART HOUSE THEATRE (1968–70), and a frequent stage director for the Canadian Opera Company, where he directed Canadian operas *Louis Riel* by Harry Somers and Mavor MOORE (produced in 1967) and *Heloise and Abelard* by Charles Wilson and Eugene Benson (produced in 1973).

In 1969 Major was named director of theatre for the new ST LAWRENCE CENTRE in Toronto, succeeding Mavor Moore as general director in 1970. As artistic director of Toronto Arts Productions there, Major directed some highly regarded productions—notably Arthur Wing Pinero's *Trelawny of the 'Wells'* (in 1974), Alexander Solzhenitsyn's *Article 58* (in 1975), Bertolt Brecht's *Caucasian Chalk Circle* (in 1976), and Thornton Wilder's *The Matchmaker* (in 1979)—all stylish large-cast shows. Major left the company in 1980, resuming his free-lance career (including assignments at the Stratford and SHAW FESTIVALS) in theatre and opera. He taught at York University from 1984 to 1987, when he was appointed head of a new professional opera training program at the Univ. of Maryland.

Major was awarded an honorary LL D by Dalhousie University in 1971, and was made a Member of the Order of Canada in 1981.

DENIS W. JOHNSTON

Mallard's Long Room. On 28 Feb. 1789 Mallard's Long Room, King St, Saint John, was the scene of the first dramatic representation in New Brunswick, when Susannah Centlivre's *The Busy Body* and Hannah Cowley's *Who's the Dupe?* were performed for public charity by a company of young gentlemen amateurs. Two productions completed that short 1789 season; five were presented in the winter of 1795. Among the plays presented during these early seasons were Edward Moore's *The Gamester*, Arthur Murphy's *The Upholsterer*, Elizabeth Inchbald's *Everyone Has His Fault*, Henry Brooke's *The Imposter*, and *All the World's a Stage* (with localized setting). Three of the actors are known: Jonathan and Stephen Sewell (lawyers) and Ebenezer Putnam (merchant). Two spectators present at the first production, Colonel Edward Winslow and the Hon. Ward Chipman, Solicitor General, are probably representative of the social class of the audience.

Mallard House, Saint John, N.B.

Thomas Mallard, formerly a lieutenant with the Thirty-Seventh Company of Militia, owned the inn that contained the large room usually designated as The Theatre, King St. It held also the first meeting of the provincial Legislative Assembly in 1786 and sessions of the Saint John Common Council from 1785 to 1797. The room contained a stage and scenery. Numbered tickets, at a uniform price of 3s., corresponded to seats (numbered in an effort to provide orderliness). There appears to have been an attempt to incline the seating, but the ceiling was too low to allow sufficient elevation at the back; consequently ladies were requested to 'come with their heads as low dressed as possible.' Plays were not given there again, and the Mallard House was demolished 7 June 1851.

MARY ELIZABETH SMITH

Mallett, Jane (1899–1984). Born Jane Keenleyside in London, Ont., she grew up in Regina and then studied at Victoria College, Univ. of Toronto. In 1926 she married Frederick Mallett. As Jane Aldred she acted with Toronto stock companies, playing a variety of roles at the Empire Theatre under George Keppie, the Victoria Theatre under Vaughan GLASER, and the Actors' Colony Theatre at Bala, Ont., under John HOLDEN. In the 1930s she appeared with the HART HOUSE Players Club and won a 1936 DOMINION DRAMA FESTIVAL acting award as Viola in *Twelfth Night*. Having a pronounced gift for comedy, she began a long association with revue, a form in which she excelled, starring in the NEW PLAY SOCIETY's *SPRING THAW*, and in *Town Tonics*. When Toronto's new ST LAWRENCE CENTRE company celebrated Hart House Theatre's half-century in 1969, Jane

Mallett starred in Slowomir Mrozek's *Tango*. Her last stage performance was in THEATRE COMPACT's production of Hugh Leonard's *Da* in 1976.

Jane Mallett was also well known as a radio and television actress. She became nationally known for her work in such series as 'Carry on, Canada', 'Soldier's Wife', 'The Craigs', and the 'Shakespeare Series', and she was featured often in Andrew ALLAN's 'Wednesday Night' and 'Stage' series on CBC radio. Her films include *Sweet Movie*, *Love at First Sight*, *Cosmic Christmas*, and *Utilities*. Active in many professional organizations, notably the Actors' Fund, she was the recipient of several awards; the main auditorium in the St. Lawrence Centre is named after her.

HERBERT WHITTAKER

Manitoba, Theatre in (English). 1. *The Beginnings*. Because of its dominant role in the economic and cultural life of Manitoba, Winnipeg has always been the hub of theatrical activity in the province. The history of professional theatre in Manitoba is largely a Winnipeg story, and the amateur movement, while often widespread and vigorous, has depended greatly on Winnipeg resources for organization, technical and artistic guidance, and inspiration.

GARRISON THEATRE productions and other amateur dramatic activities took place in Winnipeg from 1867 on, but the first professional troupe, the 'Cool' BURGESS company, appeared on the stage of the City Hall auditorium on 24 July 1877. Access to Winnipeg before 1878 was by river-boat, but in that year a rail-link was established with St Paul, Minnesota, and more and more theatre companies began to find their way north to the small but lively frontier settlement.

In May 1883 the PRINCESS OPERA HOUSE opened, and managers William Seach and Charles Sharpe set out to book touring companies systematically through an agent in St Paul. Although fire destroyed the Princess in May 1892, Seach and Sharpe continued their theatrical enterprises, sometimes separately and sometimes in collaboration. Seach, for a time, was manager of the Bijou Theatre, where he hosted such major American touring attractions as James O'Neill's production of Alexandre Dumas's *The Count of Monte Cristo* and Thomas Keene's Shakespearean repertory company.

2. *C.P. Walker and the Theatrical Syndicate.*

In 1895 a syndicate of powerful New York producers and managers established monopolistic control of North American touring arrangements. In 1897 Fargo theatre manager C.P. WALKER, with encouragement from Northern Pacific Railway officials and with Theatrical Syndicate affiliation assured, moved to Winnipeg and assumed management of a remodelled Bijou Theatre. Renamed the Winnipeg Theatre, it became the leading house in Walker's Red River Valley Circuit, a string of theatres along the Northern Pacific route from Fargo to Winnipeg. Earlier that year Seach and Sharpe had opened a new Winnipeg theatre, the Grand Opera House, on McDermot St. Because of Walker's New York connections and his superior business acumen, the Grand was unable to compete successfully, and by 1900 Walker had secured an entertainment monopoly in Winnipeg.

Important, but by no means impartial, critics and commentators in this period were Walker's enemy, W.H. Wheeler of the Winnipeg *Tribune*, his close friend Charles HANDSCOMB of the *Free Press* (also editor of the society journal *Town Topics*), and Mrs C.P. Walker, who wrote drama criticism for *Town Topics* under a pseudonym. Battles in the press about Walker's business methods were open and fierce.

Walker's entertainment monopoly was challenged in 1904 with the building of Winnipeg's first VAUDEVILLE theatre, the Dominion, and repeatedly thereafter as other touring interests (such as New York's Shubert Organization) tried to encroach on Syndicate territory. An unsuccessful attempt was made in 1904 to close down Walker's operation on the grounds that the Winnipeg Theatre was in violation of fire-safety regulations.

In 1906 Walker built a modern fire-proof theatre, the WALKER THEATRE, and the Winnipeg Theatre was purchased by an American theatre chain, Drew and Campbell. W.B. Lawrence came from Cleveland, Ohio—with his own stock company—to manage the Winnipeg. Until the end of the 1920s Winnipeg legitimate theatre, stock, and vaudeville operations were dominated by Walker and Lawrence, sometimes in competition with each other, but often in discreet collaboration. By the outbreak of the First World War Winnipeggers had access to a rich and varied theatrical diet. The city boasted a Syndicate touring house, a major legitimate stock house, a minor stock house, an Orpheum vaudeville house, a Sullivan-Considine vaudeville house, a PANTAGES vaudeville house, and a number of other small theatres specializing in vaudeville. After the war this system of commercial theatrical entertainment continued, though somewhat diminished in scope, until the the arrival of the Depression and the motion-picture industry in the early 1930s.

3. *The Community Players/Winnipeg Little Theatre.* In 1921 the Community Players of Winnipeg, an amateur art theatre, was established. Its aims were to produce the work of Canadian authors; to present quality plays not suited to commercial production; to lay the foundations for a Canadian theatre; to develop arts and crafts ancillary to the drama; to encourage dramatic appreciation in the public; and to provide facilities for the study of theatrical technique. Original organizers were lawyers H.A.V. Green and Alan Crawley. Dr Fred A. Young was the first chairman. The Community Players operated their own small theatre at the corner of Selkirk Ave and Main St in Winnipeg's North End and produced a number of original works, including Green's own *The Death of Pierrot* (in May 1923), *A Game at Mr. Wemyss* (Mar. 1924), and *The Land of Far Away* (Dec. 1928), as well as plays by Calderón, Shaw, Synge, O'Neill, Granville-Barker, Ibsen, Lennox Robinson, Ashley Dukes, Pirandello, and other dramatists not regularly included in the fare of commercial touring companies.

Prominent among the Community Players were John Craig, Nancy Pyper, Edith Sinclair, O.A. Eggertson, and Lady Margaret Tupper, all of whom acted and directed. Painters Lemoine Fitzgerald and W.J. Phillips were both active in the design and decoration of sets. Robert Ayre and Arthur Phelps edited *The Bill*, a theatre program in the form of a 'little magazine'. Out of the efforts of the enthusiasts of the Community Players grew the Manitoba Drama League, which fostered a vigorous amateur theatre throughout the province through lectures, workshops, and a system of adjudicated drama festivals. In the 1930s the MDL worked closely with the DOMINION DRAMA FESTIVAL, and the activities of the two organizations became more and more integrated. The work continued on this basis until the demise of the DDF in 1970.

In 1930, when the commercial touring system began to disintegrate, Craig was hired as full-time director of the Community Players. The name was changed to Winnipeg Little Theatre, and Craig set about reshaping the repertoire to capture the mainstream audience that had been left without access to live theatre by the collapse of the touring system.

Craig's production of Ibsen's *A Doll's House* in Mar. 1931, starring Nancy Pyper, and his *Othello* (Aug. 1932), starring George Waight, were particularly admired and drew large houses. Winnipeg Little Theatre operations began to attract comment in the national press. *Othello* was shown to the new Governor General, Lord Bessborough, on his 1932 national tour.

In 1933 the Winnipeg Little Theatre moved from its Selkirk Ave theatre to the Dominion—owned by grain merchant and financier James Richardson—at a nominal rent. Arguments about artistic policy broke out between Craig, now moving in a more professional and commercial direction, and Lady Tupper, who favoured an amateur company aligned with the newly formed Dominion Drama Festival. Lady Tupper eventually formed her own Players' Guild to produce Shakespeare, Celtic operas, verse dramas, and ethnic dance plays, and became a major force in the DDF. Craig continued to work towards the creation of an ambitious professional-level organization geared to what he conceived to be the social, cultural, and entertainment needs of a broadly based local theatre audience.

Craig's production of Ibsen's *Peer Gynt* in Feb. 1936, with Esse LJUNGH in the title role, drew an audience of over 3,000. Unfortunately for Craig, the success of this production convinced the owners of the Dominion that theatre could once again be commercially viable in Winnipeg. They invited the Holden Players, a company of young Toronto professionals directed by John HOLDEN, to the Dominion, leaving the Winnipeg Little Theatre without a home. Holden's company operated successfully at the Dominion Theatre until the Second World War, but the Winnipeg Little Theatre ceased operations early in 1937. The Players' Guild broke up at about the same time, as Lady Tupper turned her attention to the problems of the struggling Winnipeg Ballet Club, which would grow, partly through her efforts, to become the Royal Winnipeg Ballet.

During the 1930s the Progressive Arts Club Workers' Theatre and its offshoot, the

Manitoba Theatre Centre's 1959 production of Frances Goodrich's and Albert Hackett's The Diary of Anne Frank

New Theatre, produced plays ranging from agit-prop collectives to such classics of social satire as Ben Jonson's *Volpone*.

4. *Rebirth of the Little Theatre Movement.* In 1948, under the leadership of George Brodersen and Robert Jarman, a group of academics, CBC radio actors, and remaining members of the old Little Theatre and the Players' Guild re-established the Winnipeg Little Theatre. Productions were staged at the Playhouse Theatre (formerly the Pantages vaudeville house), which the city now owned. A number of other amateur groups also operated out of the Playhouse Theatre, among them the Winnipeg Dramatic Society, the Teachers' Dramatic Society, and the Winnipeg Repertory Theatre. During the 1950s several semi-professional ventures were also launched, notably Peggy Green's Actors' Guild, the Junior League Children's Theatre, and the Musical Comedy Guild.

5. *Rainbow Stage.* In July 1954, largely through the efforts of James Duncan, an outdoor theatre, Rainbow Stage, was opened at Kildonan Park. In 1956 Rainbow Stage presented its first full summer season: Irving Berlin's *Annie Get Your Gun*, directed by Duncan and Syd Perlmutter; *The Wizard of Oz*, directed by John HIRSCH; Thornton Wilder's *Our Town*, directed by Hirsch and Moray Sinclair; and Cole Porter's *Kiss Me Kate*, directed by Peggy Green.

Also in 1956 the Winnipeg Little Theatre hired a full-time artistic director, Arthur Zigouras, a graduate of the Yale School of Drama, and began a search for a permanent home. The family of financier James Richardson anonymously made the Dominion Theatre available, and the Little Theatre prepared for reorganization and expansion.

Rainbow Stage's 1957 season consisted of Cole Porter's *Can-Can*, directed by Hirsch; John van Druten's *I Remember Mama*, directed by Sinclair; *Do You Remember?*, a musical review by Tom HENDRY and John Hirsch, and directed by Hirsch; Anita Loos's and John Emerson's *Gentlemen Prefer Blondes*, directed by Jack Phillips; *The Pitfalls of Pauline*, directed by George Werier; and Oscar Asche's *Chu-Chin-Chow*, directed by Hirsch, which was an overwhelming critical and box-office success.

6. *Manitoba Theatre Centre.* In the fall of 1957 Hirsch and Tom Hendry, together with people they had worked with at Rainbow Stage, founded Theatre 77, a professional company formed to take advantage of the Little Theatre's willingness to rent the Dominion Theatre at reasonable rates in the periods between their own shows. Theatre 77 and Winnipeg Little Theatre produced alternate shows at the Dominion Theatre in the 1957–8 season. In the spring of 1958 Zigouras resigned, and the Winnipeg Little

Manitoba, Theatre in (English)

Theatre joined with Theatre 77 to form the MANITOBA THEATRE CENTRE, while retaining their separate artistic programs. Hendry became the Centre's administrator, while Hirsch remained director of Theatre 77. A New York director, Zara Shakow, was hired to direct the Little Theatre productions. At the end of the first season, however, the distinction between the two companies was eliminated and Hirsch became artistic director of the Manitoba Theatre Centre. Under Hirsch's leadership MTC became a model for Canadian regional theatres, the first of a string of such theatres to be established across the country.

7. *The Present Situation*. Under the leadership of Jack Shapira (general manager and producer, 1966–87), Rainbow Stage adopted a policy of producing two well-known musical-comedy classics each summer with a cast of established Canadian stars and local semi-professionals and amateurs, a policy that creates regular sell-out business.

PRAIRIE THEATRE EXCHANGE (founded in 1972) produces full seasons of commissioned Manitoba plays, while Agassiz Theatre, incorporated in 1980 to produce plays by its individual member artists and constituent small theatre groups, has recently become a subscription-based company with a season of new Manitoba and small-scale American plays performed by local actors. Actors' Showcase, founded in 1965 by Daphne Korol as an alternative adult theatre and incorporated in 1977 as a CHILDREN'S THEATRE under artistic director Tony Pydee, has become, under the leadership of Leslie Silverman (artistic director since 1983), a nationally recognized professional children's theatre specializing in child-advocacy and other educational drama. The mid-1980s saw a resurgence of independent professional theatre projects, amateur groups, and university theatre.

The Manitoba Association of Playwrights (formed in 1979) provides dramaturgical advice and organizes workshops, and with the existence of theatres willing to produce local plays it has brought Manitoba to the verge of what promises to be an exciting period of dramatic exploration.

See E. Ross Stuart, *The History of Prairie Theatre* (1984).　　REG SKENE

Manitoba, Theatre in (French). French theatre in Manitoba began at the Grey Nun's school in Saint-Boniface with occasional productions of European and Quebec plays. The first Manitoba francophone play—Sister Malvina Colette's *Un Dernier souvenir de la patrie*—was produced there in 1870. The Oblate Fathers also produced plays at their boys' school in Saint-Boniface, as did the Sisters of the Holy Names of Jesus and Mary at the Académie Sainte-Marie in Winnipeg and the Académie Saint-Joseph in Saint-Boniface. The Académie Sainte-Marie was eventually converted to an anglophone institution, but the Académie Saint-Joseph continued its French theatrical activities until 1960.

Under Jesuit direction from 1885 to 1970 the Collège de Saint-Boniface became a pillar of francophone theatre in Manitoba. At first it chose plays by authors such as Lebardin and C.-T.-P. Lévesque, as well as extracts from Molière, Racine, and Corneille; but later it attempted the work of a wider variety of playwrights, including Courteline, Eugène Labiche, François Coppée, Théodore Botrel, Henri de Bornier, Charles LeRoy-Villars, Henri Ghéon, Grégoire Leclos, Marcel Pagnol, and André Obey. Plays currently popular in Europe and Quebec also became part of its repertoire. Both teachers and students considered theatre one of the most important methods of promoting French culture in an anglophone milieu. Their amateur productions in the Collège's theatre occasionally reached professional calibre and attracted a widespread audience. Unfortunately, when the Jesuits left, theatrical activity at the Collège died out.

Other early theatre developed outside of Winnipeg and Saint-Boniface, thanks largely to the enthusiasm of teachers and lay groups—including Swiss, Belgian, and French immigrants—who used school auditoriums for their shows. In a rural environment where solitude was often a hardship, theatre gave people a chance to congregate. In 1890 the Cercle dramatique de Saint-Alphonse was already established; in 1892 amateur performers from the village of La Broquerie presented their first play; in 1895 Saint-Léon boasted a theatre; and by the turn of the century Lorette was also involved in theatre. Thus not long after Manitoba was founded in 1870, French-language theatre had taken root in the province. Several religious and cultural organizations consolidated these beginnings, both for entertainment and as a means of protecting language rights in the face of the provincial government's refusal to regard the French-speaking minority as a separate and distinct community. Many theatre companies—including L'Union des Secours Mutuels, Le Cercle Provencher, La Brigade de Feu, Le Club Dramatique de Saint-Boniface, Les Forestiers Catholiques, La Gauloise, L'Union Sainte-Cécile, Le Cercle LaVérendrye, and Le Cercle Dramatique de Winnipeg—were founded between 1877 and 1914.

The golden age of francophone theatre in Manitoba, however, was between the wars. Some seventeen groups—including L'Union Jeanne d'Arc, Le Club Belge, Le Club 'Le Canada', Le Cercle Dramatique de Saint-Boniface, Les Amis de Riel, Le CERCLE MOLIÈRE, La Société Dramatique Langevin, and Le Cercle Ouvrier—strove to sustain French culture and language. Unfortunately, as people began to accommodate themselves to the language situation and made less effort to protect their rights, French-language theatre began to wither away. By 1939 only two active companies were left: Le Cercle Dramatique de Sacré-Coeur and Le Cercle Molière.

Currently the reputation of Le Cercle Molière tends to overshadow the efforts of other amateur groups in the francophone community. Though it is complemented and nourished by Le Festival Théâtre-Jeunesse, founded in 1970, and the CM2, founded in 1974, the Cercle Molière is the official voice of francophone theatre in Manitoba. It has done more than any other company to nurture the growth of francophone theatre in the province.

See Annette Saint-Pierre, *Le Rideau se lève au Manitoba* (1980) and the Société historique de St-Boniface, *Chapeau bas: Réminiscences de la vie théâtrale et musicale du Manitoba français* (1980).   ANNETTE SAINT-PIERRE

Manitoba Theatre Centre. The model for the Manitoba Theatre Centre was Roger Planchon's innovative Théâtre de la Cité in Lyon, France. The MTC's objectives are summarized by co-founder Tom HENDRY in a 1965 souvenir program: 'Main-Stage major productions. . . . Touring productions travelling eventually around a Manitoba circuit of some thirty or forty centres. . . . An entire area devoted to the formation of taste in children and students, beginning with a school of the theatre in which several hundred of our eventual audience could . . . absorb some of the theatre tradition they had been denied because they lived in Manitoba.' Although these objectives have not been consistently maintained—the school was closed in 1972, not to reappear until 1987, and the provincial tours have grown, diminished, disappeared, come back in a truncated form—the idea that the MTC should be more than just a theatre has persisted and has provided the model for other regional theatres across the country.

The MTC was formed by an amalgamation of the Winnipeg Little Theatre and John HIRSCH's semi-professional Theatre 77; the inaugural 1958-9 season, presented in the 800-seat Dominion Theatre, was divided into a Little Theatre series, directed by Zara Shakow, and a Theatre 77 series, directed by Hirsch. The distinction disappeared the following season when Desmond Scott was brought in as resident director, sharing directorial duties with Hirsch. The first season saw productions of Michael Gazzo's *A Hatful of Rain*, Noël Coward's *Blithe Spirit*, Patricia JOUDRY's *Teach Me How To Cry*, Tennessee Williams' *The Glass Menagerie*, Jean Anouilh's *Ring Round the Moon*, Frances Goodrich's and Albert Hackett's *The Diary of Anne Frank*, and John Steinbeck's *Of Mice and Men*. It set the pattern for what critic Brian Brennan later described as the standard regional mainstage season, chosen to appeal to the broadest possible audience.

The Hirsch-Hendry years (Hendry, the administrator, left in 1963; Hirsch in 1966)

Cré-Sganarelle, *adapted from Molière's* Le Médecin malgré lui, *Le Cercle Molière, 1984, with (l. to r.) Louis Dubé, Vincent Durault (standing), Claude Dorge (kneeling), Pierre Trudel*

are often regarded as the MTC's 'golden years'. Mainstage premières of Canadian work included *Bonfires of '62*, an original revue; *A Very Close Family* by Bernard SLADE in 1963; and Len PETERSON's *All About Us* in 1964. Productions remembered as exceptional include John Osborne's *Look Back in Anger* (1959-60), directed by Desmond Scott, the first fully professional MTC production; Scott's production of J.M. Synge's *Playboy of the Western World* with Zoë CALDWELL, Len CARIOU, and Adrian Pecknold (1960-1); Hirsch's production of Jean Anouilh's *Thieves' Carnival* with Eric DONKIN (1961-2); Brecht's *Mother Courage* with Caldwell in the title role and Frances HYLAND, Cariou, and Paul Hecht as the children, directed by Hirsch (1964-5); Hirsch's *The Taming of the Shrew* with Leon Pownall, Heath LAMBERTS, and Pat GALLOWAY (1964-5); and Hirsch's production of Edward Albee's *Who's Afraid of Virginia Woolf?* with Kate REID and Donald DAVIS (1964-5). The MTC acquired the nickname 'Stratford West' because so many Stratford actors worked there in the winter. To this group were added Winnipeg actors of comparable talent: Evelyne Anderson, Vic Cowie, Robert Trudel, and Cariou.

The school and a second stage were early developments, the second stage initially a studio series at the Dominion with later seasons of new and experimental plays in various locations in the downtown area. Memorable productions included *Jocasta Is At It Again* in 1960-1 (an unauthorized and re-titled production of Arthur Kopit's *Oh Dad, Poor Dad, Mamma's Hung You In the Closet and I'm Feelin' So Sad*) and Desmond Scott's 1961 production of Samuel Beckett's *Waiting for Godot* with Eric CHRISTMAS and Ted Follows. Saturday theatre classes were offered in 1958, with the school proper opening in 1960 under Esme Crampton. Provincial tours started in 1961, and tours to schools began in 1962. Canada Council funding was obtained in 1964, establishing a precedent for the regional-theatre system.

The years remembered as 'golden' extended into the tenure of Hirsch's successor, Edward GILBERT, whose first term of three seasons ran from 1966 to 1969. Under Gilbert there were fewer productions of Canadian plays, although Ann HENRY's *Lulu Street* premièred in 1967. Productions earning praise were Chekhov's *The Three Sisters* directed by Gilbert, with Ann Firbank, Martha HENRY, and Deborah Kipp, and a spectacular *A Funny Thing Happened On the Way to the Forum*, co-directed by Hirsch and Marvin Gordon.

In 1968 the Dominion was razed, but the planned new home for the MTC was not ready for another two seasons. Gilbert's 1968-9 season was presented in the Centennial Concert Hall on Main St, a huge facility not at all suitable for the sort of theatre the MTC audience had come to expect. A season designed to fill the space and appeal to the lowest common denominator failed to solve the problem, and Gilbert left in 1969.

His successor, Kurt REIS, had one strong card to play: the Warehouse, the MTC's second stage located at 140 Rupert Ave, a block away from the present mainstage. The facility accommodated 232 in slightly curved seating facing an open stage 48' wide and 32' deep. (Renovations in 1988 raised seating capacity to 300; the rebuilt, proscenium arch stage is 73' wide wall to wall, 33' deep with the removable thrust, 25' without.) Limited free height, 12½', the absence of proper wings, and unpredictable acoustics were the theatre's major problems, but it was a comfortable space in which Reis mounted a season of five plays (including David Halliwell's *Hail Scrawdyke!* and Sam Shepard's *La Turista*) to supplement a five-play mainstage season (ranging from Gilbert's production of Peter Weiss's *Marat/Sade* to Kaufman and Hart's *You Can't Take It With You*). While Reis's programming looks relatively conservative, his goals for the MTC were not; conflict with an already nervous board ensued and Reis was let go after only one season, 1969-70.

The new mainstage at 175 Market Ave was ready for the 1970-1 season. Principal architect was Allan Waisman. To minimize distance between stage and auditorium, the asymmetrical balcony, seating 254, extends down on the left almost to the orchestra level, also asymmetrical to compensate; the orchestra seats 531 for a total of 785. The house faces a very large stage, 108' wide wall to wall and 49' deep. The proscenium opening is huge—62' wide, 32' high—dwarfing smaller plays and widening the gap the designers had hoped to close. While backstage facilities are generally considered to be excellent, the building's appearance—cold and forbidding, raw concrete everywhere—has dated quickly.

The Manitoba Theatre Centre, Winnipeg

The first artistic director in the new building was Keith TURNBULL, and the first production Brecht's *A Man's a Man*, directed by Hirsch. Although Turnbull was committed to Canadian plays and the development of new work, his two-year term saw only his own production of James REANEY's *The Sun and the Moon*, and his own adaptation, *Alice Through the Looking Glass*, on the mainstage, and an original revue, *Head 'Em Off at The Pas*, in the Warehouse. Nonetheless because Turnbull, like Reis, had plans that were more radical than his programming, the board let him go at the end of the 1971-2 season. Critics said that because the board was not drawn from all sectors of the community it was not interested in theatre that came from and spoke to the community as a whole.

At the same time the theatre school was closed for financial reasons, and with it went much of the MTC's claim to be a 'theatre centre'. Theatre for Young Audiences continued until 1981, and an Elementary School Program is still in place, but much of the young audience development in the province has been taken over by other Winnipeg theatres, such as PRAIRIE THEATRE EXCHANGE and Actors' Showcase.

Gilbert returned to the MTC for three seasons, 1972–5. Most observers consider his second term less distinguished than his first, but Hirsch's production of Frank Loesser's *Guys and Dolls* (1972-3) and Sholem Ansky's *The Dybbuk* (1973-4), as well as Gilbert's

productions of Shaw's *You Never Can Tell* (1973-4) and Chekhov's *The Cherry Orchard* (1974-5), are remembered fondly.

Gilbert was succeeded by Len Cariou, who stayed only one year, 1975-6, before leaving Winnipeg to resume his international career. Cariou did very little directing (Steinbeck's *Of Mice and Men*), but played the title role in Jean GASCON's production of Rostand's *Cyrano de Bergerac* and Dysart in Gilbert's production of Peter Shaffer's *Equus*. The season is remembered as a fine one.

Arif Hasnain's tenure (1977-80) began with a production of a commissioned Canadian play, Joanna GLASS's *The Last Chalice*, but audience reaction was so hostile that no other Canadian play appeared on the mainstage until 1979, when her *ARTICHOKE* did little better. Hasnain's *A Midsummer Night's Dream* and Reis's *Death of a Salesman* are usually considered the highlights of his tenure, and in the 1977-8 Warehouse season he initiated a Plays in Progress series of Winnipeg plays. But the MTC was increasingly accused of being out of touch both with its own community and with developments elsewhere in Canadian theatre.

Richard OUZOUNIAN's four-season term, 1980-4, confirmed for some his reputation as the 'Noël Coward of the Pepsi generation', but Ouzounian was responsible for some substantial productions, among them a fine *As You Like It* and his own adaptations of Dickens' *Nicholas Nickleby* and *A Tale of Two*

Cities. Ouzounian also undertook a number of innovations intended to reduce the MTC's isolation from the community. He established a resident company, made extensive use of the city's acting pool, and took an unusual interest in local playwriting, appointing a resident playwright. Three of Alf Silver's plays—*Thimblerig, Climate of the Times,* and *Clearances*—were produced at the Warehouse. After Ouzounian went to Toronto's CENTRESTAGE, MTC co-operated with the Association of Community Theatres to offer courses to amateur actors, directors, and technicians in a summer theatre camp, reviving some of the MTC's educational function and restoring frayed ties with amateur theatre in the province.

Ouzounian's successor, James Roy, quickly revealed his populist bias: half his first Warehouse season and all but one of the second consisted of light Canadian plays. On the mainstage he presented his wife Anne CHISLETT's *Quiet in the Land* and his populist triumph *Tsymbaly,* a new play commissioned from Ted GALAY celebrating the Ukrainian community; that community responded in huge numbers, making the show the MTC's biggest box-office success. But the board did not renew Roy's contract after the 1985-6 season.

The current artistic director, Rick McNair, like many of his predecessors, is pursuing the elusive idea of a theatre 'centre', and achieving more success than most. Canadian plays produced on the main-stage during the first two years of McNair's tenure were Sharon POLLOCK's *Doc* (1986-7), W.O. MITCHELL's *Royalty is Royalty,* and the première of Allan STRATTON's *The 101 Miracles of Hope Chance* (1987-8); only the Pollock play was received with great enthusiasm. The 1988-9 season will include Tom Wood's *B Movie: The Play* and the première of David FRENCH's *1949,* an MTC/CANADIAN STAGE COMPANY co-production. Perhaps the most memorable production of McNair's tenure so far has been Athol Fugard's *The Road to Mecca,* with Charles McFarland directing Joy COGHILL and Susan Coyne in Mar. 1988. While McNair has yet to produce an original local play, the MTC is once again involved in new play development. The organization has also tried to improve community out-reach through re-establishing the theatre school and opening a youth theatre, and by involving rural community theatres in the mounting of

MTC touring productions. In an attempt to restore the MTC's role as a theatrical innovator, McNair initiated a Winnipeg Fringe Festival, sponsored by the MTC, in the summer of 1988. The first Fringe was an enormous success, with fifty companies performing in six venues in Winnipeg's Exchange District; attendance topped 30,000, many times the first year numbers at the Edmonton and Vancouver fringe festivals, suggesting that the event will become an annual fixture and raising hopes that the Fringe will encourage the development of a Winnipeg alternative theatre scene.

CHRIS JOHNSON

Marchand, Félix-Gabriel (1832-1900). Born at St-Jean d'Iberville, Que., he attended the Séminaire de St-Hyacinthe. He qualified as a notary but was early attracted to journalism and to politics, devoting his energy to public affairs after 1867 and serving in various cabinet posts before becoming, in 1892, leader of the provincial Liberal party and, from 1897 to his death, premier of Quebec. One of the last of the *rouge* Liberals, he helped found the newspaper *Le Franco-Canadien* in St-Jean and was for a time editor of Montreal's *Le Temps.* President of the Royal Society of Canada and an officer of France's Légion d'Honneur, he was also active in the militia, commanding a regiment that fought against the Fenians in 1870.

Despite his many activities, Marchand found time to write occasional poetry and five plays, all of them published in a catchall volume, *Mélanges poétiques et littéraires* (1899). *Fatenville,* printed in *La Revue canadienne* in 1869, is the first of these. A light comedy in one act, it depicts a penniless, boorish schemer, Fatenville ('Fop-in-town'), who tries unsuccessfully to impress a rich French-Canadian merchant with his social standing and connections in order to gain his daughter's hand. The intriguer is inevitably unmasked and virtue triumphs. Never performed, *Fatenville* is clearly influenced by Parisian *boulevard* comedy, one of the first examples of that influence in Canada. The use of authentic rural Canadian speech by minor characters is notable, as is the decidedly anti-urban tone that prevails: Fatenville's superior attitude is based as much on his urban background as on his claimed social standing. *Erreur n'est pas compte; ou Les Incon-*

vénients d'une ressemblance (1872), a 'vaudeville in two acts', is light fare also, its main comic device being the reiterated confusion of one identical twin with another, one of them a desirable match for the daughter of a rich banker, the other a bankrupt drifter. Again the resolution is predictably rosy, the airy tone enhanced by a half-dozen musical interventions (new words sung to familiar airs, as implied by the French term 'vaudeville'). *Erreur n'est pas compte* was a modest success when first staged on 15 May 1872 at St-Jean, and was revived in Jan. 1922 at Quebec's Théâtre de l'AUDITORIUM.

The next two plays are verse comedies, rare examples of the genre in French Canada. *Un bonheur en attire un autre* (1883) demonstrates even more clearly the influence of repertory imported by touring professional companies: as with many a Parisian comedy the focus of its one act is apprehended conjugal disloyalty. But the recipe is the only possible one for French Canada at the time, for the suspicion is unfounded and true marital love prevails. It was first performed at St-Jean on 21 June 1883 and revived at Quebec's Académie de Musique on 27 Mar. 1889. *Les FAUX BRILLANTS* is Marchand's best-known work, although it was not performed until after his death. His last dramatic work, the comic opera *Le Lauréat*, unlike the other four, was not published elsewhere before inclusion in *Mélanges*, and was also performed posthumously—at Quebec's Théâtre de l'Auditorium on 26, 27 Mar. 1906. The lively music composed for it by Joseph Vézina probably accounts for much of its success, because the plot of *Le Lauréat* is sketchy: a recent university graduate wants to choose a poor orphan as his fiancée, despite strenuous objection from his family. In melodramatic fashion, all is resolved by the appearance of the girl's long-lost father, who has acquired millions of dollars in California. Yet the two acts are nicely balanced, the verses pleasant, and the atmosphere appropriate to an opéra-comique where verisimilitude is hardly important.

A dilettante playwright, Marchand's significance is nevertheless considerable: at a time when native dramatists were drawn to unplayable polemical dialogues, to proselytizing pedagogic-religious theatre, or to heavy historical and patriotic drama, he consistently sought a disengaged, humorous style, unashamedly influenced by popular continental fare. His work—with that of Ernest Doin, J. G. W. McGown, and Régis Roy—demonstrates the effect of the more and more frequent tours by French professional troupes after the late 1850s, when the development of a North American railway network allowed Montreal and Quebec to be added to their itinerary.

See L. Fortin, *Félix-Gabriel Marchand* (1979).
                                    L. E. DOUCETTE

Marchessault, Jovette (b. 1938). Born in Montreal, she left school at thirteen and is largely self-taught. A novelist and playwright—and a painter and sculptor, whose work has been exhibited in Quebec, Ontario, Paris, Brussels, and New York—she is a radical feminist who has lived for many years in the country, northwest of Montreal, surrounded by what she calls her 'therapy group'—her dogs, cats, ducks, guinea-fowl, and geese.

Marchessault won the Prix France-Québec in 1976 for her first novel, *Comme une enfant de la terre* (1975). A second novel, *La Mère des herbes* (1980), confirmed her reputation. *Tryptique lesbien* (1980) is a 'lesbian history of medieval Quebec'. *Lettre de Californie* (1982) is a pamphlet poem that recalls the radical American feminist Meridel Le Soeur.

After 'Les Vaches de nuit' (a monologue from *Tryptique lesbien*) was staged in 1979 by actor and set-designer Pol Pelletier in an evening of readings sponsored by Montreal's THÉÂTRE DU NOUVEAU MONDE, Marchessault turned to drama. Her plays examine feminist issues while asking questions about the nature of writing and providing a biographical view of a number of female writers. *La SAGA DES POULES MOUILLÉES* (1981), first performed in 1981 at the Théâtre du Nouveau Monde, concerns the life of four Quebec writers: Laure Conan (Félicité Angers), Germaine Guèvremont, Gabrielle Roy, and Anne HÉBERT. *La Terre est trop courte, Violette Leduc* (1982), first performed by Montreal's Théâtre Experimental des femmes in 1981, dramatizes the life of Violette Leduc, a writer and friend of Jean-Paul Sartre, Jean Genet, and Simone de Beauvoir. *Alice et Gertrude, Nathalie et Renée et ce cher Ernest* (1984), first performed by Les Productions Vermeilles, Montreal, in 1984 and *Anaïs dans la queue de la comète* dramatize—from the viewpoint of women artists—events in the lives of Alice B. Toklas,

Marchessault

Gertrude Stein, Nathalie Barney, Renée Vivien, Ernest Hemingway, Anaïs Nin, and Henry Miller.   ANNE-MARIE ALONZO

Marks Brothers, The. A family of performers who remained based at their family farm near Christie Lake, Ont., the Marks Brothers' touring organization operated successfully from the 1870s until the 1920s. First to enter 'show business' was Robert William Marks (1853-1937), the eldest boy in a family of seven. While selling mouth organs in Maberly, near Perth, Ont., about 1870 he met a magician called 'King Kennedy, the Mysterious Hindu from the Bay of Bengal'. Intrigued by the novelty of show business, Marks introduced himself and a partnership was formed. After a year's tour with the magic act, Marks returned to his family convinced that he had found his life's work. Actors were hired, a repertoire developed, and with the aid of his brothers he organized a theatrical touring company that by 1879 had reached as far west as Winnipeg.

By the 1890s three companies had been established and the name Marks Brothers had won recognition on the Canadian 'road'. Robert Marks was the manager of one company, his wife May A. Belle the leading lady, and brother George Marks the company's treasurer and theatrical 'heavy'. The second company was managed by Ernie Marks, with his wife Kitty as leading lady. Joe and Alex Marks were also members. The third company was led by Tom Marks. Composed of approximately twelve members—including a stage manager, business manager, musical director, and property man—each company toured the country for about forty-two weeks a year, returning in mid-June to the Christie Lake farm to rehearse and plan the next year's itinerary. The plays were chosen and distributed among the companies and the routes were planned in detail. Although all three companies opened their seasons at approximately the same time, they took care to begin at an appropriate distance from each other. In 1902, for example, when Tom Marks was opening in Battle Creek, Michigan, Bob Marks began his operation close to home at Peterborough, Ont., and Ernie Marks started at Morrisburg, Ont.

Their repertoire included versions of such melodramas as *A Celebrated Case, East Lynne,* Henry Pettitt's *The Black Flag,* Harriet Beecher Stowe's *Uncle Tom's Cabin,* John Oxenford's *The Two Orphans,* and William Pratt's *Ten Nights in a Bar-Room*—the com-

The Marks Brothers

mon stock-in-trade for many touring companies. The Marks Brothers took little interest in new movements in theatre and were conservative in play selection and production styles. In several other respects, however, they were innovative. Recognizing the need for colour and excitement in the small towns they frequented, they invariably made their entrance with a brass band and a parade down 'Main' street. In order to attract as many people as possible, they often rented a three-storey building and put a variety show on the first floor, drama on the second, and an exhibit of curiosities (or 'dime museum') on top. Their slogan, 'ten-twenty-thirty', drew attention to the different prices of admission.

The Marks Brothers also lavished considerable attention on costumes and sets. Unlike many touring companies of the time, which would merely reshuffle the flats to give the appearance of a new scene, the Marks Brothers took pains to create expensive and elaborate scenery. On occasion a scene painter would accompany the troupe and, on short notice, create a completely new scene. This practice was particularly employed by Bob Marks when he was playing for an extended period in one town.

While the Marks Brothers could never be credited with promoting indigenous drama, they can be seen as a prototype of a Canadian theatre industry. During the period of their greatest success, live theatre in North America was controlled by a virtual monopoly based in New York City, and the trend of that monopoly was to abandon touring to smaller cities and towns in favour of longer runs in larger cities and of drama suited to urban tastes. In the face of this, the Marks Brothers conducted a prosperous and competitive business that filled the void left by the monopoly in smaller communities with appropriate entertainment, particularly melodrama. They remained rooted in their region, a summer employer in their local community while preparing for the next season's tour and loyal to their longstanding small-town clientele.   MURRAY D. EDWARDS

Marsh Hay. A four-act play by Merrill DENISON, first published in 1923 (in his *The Unheroic North: Four Canadian Plays*), it was not produced until 1974 (HART HOUSE THEATRE, Toronto), directed by Richard Plant. Denison examines not only the inhumane

conditions of farm life in the Ontario backwoods but also the sociological and economic factors causing them. Set in the dirty kitchen of a backwoods farmhouse, *Marsh Hay* depicts the aimless existence of the Serang family. The parents, Lena and John, in their early forties, are worn-out, crushed by their hopeless twenty-year struggle with poor land. Lena blames John for not going west; John blames Lena for not wanting to leave relatives and friends. Of their twelve children, five are dead and three have run away. Those remaining are intent only on avoiding work. The neighbours are narrow and uneducated—with the exception of Andrew Barnood, a placid, kindly man. He and William Thompson—an elderly lawyer who comes for the hunting season—are foils against which the family's deterioration is emphasized.

Naturalism, in which heredity and environment so determine life that nothing one can do can alleviate or change the pattern, is clearly the philosophy behind *Marsh Hay*. There is no hope for the future. The misery of the Serang family is climaxed by the unwanted pregnancy of fifteen-year-old Sarilin, a subsequent abortion, and her return to sexual promiscuity. The title of the play is symbolic of destitution. The wild marsh hay growing in the cedar swamps, so vital for the cattle's winter fodder, is often destroyed by beavers building their dams. The atmosphere of despair is heightened by Serang's criticism of a government that in his view pays more attention to immigrant farmers than to native Canadian farmers. He also condemns the lumber companies for their ruthless harvesting of all the white pine, so reducing the land to bare rock and scrub.

A powerful statement of the ills of Ontario farmers in the early twenties, *Marsh Hay* is a tightly constructed play with sharp dialogue and powerful characterization, especially the portrait of John Serang—although the character of Mrs Serang is weakened by her puzzling motivation in so willingly accepting her pregnant, unwed daughter. That the play had to wait fifty years for its première is probably explained by the reluctance of the country's amateur theatres to promote such a bitter and bleak view of Canadian rural society.
                        GERALDINE ANTHONY

Massey, Vincent (1887-1967). The eldest son of Chester Massey and grandson of Hart Almerrin Massey, a wealthy industrialist and

Massey

Vincent Massey as the Pope in Paul Claudel's The Hostage (L'Otage)

philanthropist, Charles Vincent Massey was educated at the Univ. of Toronto and Balliol Coll., Oxford, for which he formed a lifelong attachment. A period as Dean of Residence and lecturer in history at Victoria Coll., Univ. of Toronto, 1913-5, was followed by military service, 1915-8. He served as president of Massey-Harris Company from 1921 to 1925, when he entered politics, unsuccessfully as a parliamentary candidate but with notable success as a member of the Imperial Conference in London (1926) and as first Canadian minister to the United States (1926-30). From 1935 to 1946 he was Canadian High Commissioner in London. In 1949 he was appointed chairman of the Royal Commission on National Development in the Arts, Letters and Sciences in Canada, presenting an influential Report (followed by a supplementary volume of essays) in 1951 that called for 'a vigorous and distinctive cultural

life' in Canada. Appointed governor general of Canada (1952), he held office until 1959, discharging it with distinction and exercising considerable influence in the development of the arts. This culminated a life-time concern with the artistic growth of Canada. He and his wife (Alice Stuart Parkin) conceived and carried through the building of Hart House, including HART HOUSE THEATRE in the Univ. of Toronto (1919), a theatre that has been strongly influential in the creation and preservation of a national theatrical tradition. Massey edited two volumes of *Canadian Plays from Hart House Theatre* (1926-7) containing eleven plays. The Masseys' patronage was also extended to music (the Hart House String Quartet 1923-48) and to painting, and their home, 'Batterwood', near Port Hope, was a focus for musicians, painters, and theatre folk at a time when such encouragement was uncommon. Massey was a patron of the DOMINION DRAMA FESTIVAL from 1932 until his death, and when governor general he intervened decisively to save the STRATFORD FESTIVAL in 1953. He was a patron of all the arts and education; his gifts to the Univ. of Toronto (Hart House and Massey College, 1963) were munificent. But it was in the theatre that his chief interest lay. He was in his younger days a fine amateur actor at Hart House and his sense of ceremony, when he became governor general, gave evidence of a subtle but sure touch in dramatic effect. His manner could be austere, but never forbidding, and in private life he was genial and exhibited a fine wit and a distinctive sense of humour. It is not without significance that he kept on his desk until his death a photograph of himself as Pope Pius VII in Paul Claudel's *L'Otage*.

See his memoirs, *What's Past is Prologue* (1963), and Claude Bissell's *The Young Vincent Massey* (1981) and *The Imperial Canadian* (1986).   ROBERTSON DAVIES

Massey, Raymond Hart (1896-1983). The brother of Vincent MASSEY, he was educated at Appleby School, the Univ. of Toronto, and Balliol Coll., Oxford. While serving in the First World War in France and Siberia, he organized a Canadian Army minstrel troupe and following the war he acted at HART HOUSE THEATRE. His first professional appearance was at the Everyman Theatre, London, in 1922 as Jack in Eugene O'Neill's *In the Zone*. His stage career was mainly centred in New York, where he had his first great success in 1936 in *Ethan Frome*, by Owen and Donald Davis. He became associated with the figure of Abraham Lincoln (to whom he bore some resemblance) and played in Robert Sherwood's *Abe Lincoln in Illinois* from 1938 to 1940, and in the subsequent film, and also in Norman Corwin's *The Rivalry*, 1960. His homely but attractively masculine appearance and fine voice won him rapid advancement as a leading man. His powerful and contemporary style was seen to advantage in New York revivals of three plays by Bernard Shaw; he was notable as Ridgeon in *The Doctor's Dilemma* (1941), Morell in *Candida* (1942), and Higgins in *Pygmalion* (1946). His Broadway début as Hamlet (1931) was accounted a failure, a judgement in which he concurred. After serving briefly in the Second World War in the Canadian Army (he was invalided out in 1942), he had a great success in the U.S. with his readings from Stephen Vincent Benét's epic *John Brown's Body*. His movie career, begun in 1930, comprised seventy films, and he made many appearances on television, the best-known being as Dr Gillespie, the wise mentor of the hero in the series *Dr. Kildare*. He was thrice married—to Margery Fremantle, Adrienne Allen, and Dorothy Ludington Whitney. Two of his children, Daniel Massey and Anna Massey, are prominent English actors. He became an American citizen in 1944.

See his autobiographies *When I Was Young* (1976) and *A Hundred Different Lives* (1979).

ROBERTSON DAVIES

Matthews, Cameron (1884-1958). Born in England, where he began his acting career, he immigrated to the U.S. in 1916, appearing with the Henry Jewett Players in Boston from Oct. 1916 to Apr. 1920. First known in Canada as an actor with the Vaughan GLASER Players in Toronto, 1921-2, he formed the Cameron Matthews English Players in 1923, a repertory company at the PRINCESS THEATRE, Toronto, offering classics and popular comedies, such as Oscar Wilde's *The Importance of Being Earnest*, Bernard Shaw's *Pygmalion* and *Arms and the Man*, John Hay Beith's *Tilly of Bloomsbury*, and Harold Brighouse's *Hobson's Choice*. The company included Anne Carew, Deirdre Doyle, Nella Jefferis, Alison Bradshaw, Lambert Larking, Barry Jones, and Leonard Mudie. It began

another season in Sept. 1923 at the Regent Theatre, Toronto. In Jan. 1924 it joined forces with the Maurice British Company and moved to the Comedy Theatre on Richmond St. After Matthews left in May 1924, the company continued the season as the Comedy Players.

Matthews ran another season in Toronto, again at the Comedy, Jan. to Apr. 1925, still with a repertory of standard successes: J.M. Barrie's *What Every Woman Knows*, Shaw's *Major Barbara*, Anthony Hope's *The Prisoner of Zenda*, A.A. Milne's *The Dover Road*, Horace Hodges' and T.W. Percival's *Grumpy*, and others. Several actors from previous seasons remained with him, together with newcomers Sheila Hayes, Hugh Buckler, Violet Paget, and Charles Hampden. Matthews and six of the actors toured across the continent to British Columbia and Seattle between Oct. 1925 and Jan. 1926, but the plays that had been successful in Toronto (*The Dover Road*, *Three Live Ghosts*, and W.S. Maugham's *Too Many Husbands*) did not draw large audiences. In Mar. and Apr. 1927 Matthews and a small company took Ralph Spence's *The Gorilla* on a short western tour.

Subsequently Matthews performed with various companies in the U.S. and Canada; he twice revived the Cameron Matthews English Players in Toronto: 21 Sept. to 12 Dec. 1931 at the Empire Theatre; and 19 Sept. to 29 Oct. 1932 at the Victoria Theatre. The times were not auspicious for stock companies, and plays like *Pygmalion*, *The Dover Road*, *The Importance of Being Earnest*, Barrie's *The Admirable Crichton*, St John Ervine's *The First Mrs Fraser*, and Eden and Adelaide Phillpotts' *Yellow Sands* did not prove popular, although an uncut *Strange Interlude* by Eugene O'Neill ran for two weeks from 26 Sept. at the Victoria. Matthews also organized the short-lived Toronto Repertory Theatre Company (Dec. 1934-Jan. 1935) and the Cameron Matthews Canadian Players (June 1936). During the last twenty years of his life he occasionally worked with LITTLE THEATRE groups and acted on radio, finally retiring to a farm at Barry's Bay, Ont.

ROBERT G. LAWRENCE

Maxwell, Roberta (b. 1942). Born in Toronto, she made her professional début in 1956 at the CREST THEATRE in Chekhov's *Three Sisters* (starring Kate REID). Appointed the STRATFORD FESTIVAL's first apprentice actor in 1957, she appeared there in 1958 and 1959 before spending three years in England working in repertory theatres and on television. In the mid-1960s she appeared at Halifax's NEPTUNE THEATRE, the MANITOBA THEATRE CENTRE, and at Stratford (where she won a GUTHRIE Award in 1966). Her career in the U.S. was initiated at the Guthrie Theatre in Minneapolis in 1968, the year she also made her Broadway début in Michael LANGHAM's production of *The Prime of Miss Jean Brodie* (adapted from the novel by Muriel Spark). Maxwell's career has subsequently been divided between Canada and the U.S. Notable successes include the role of Jill in the North American première of Peter Shaffer's *Equus* in 1974 (opposite Richard Burton), the lead in an off-Broadway production of Schiller's *Mary Stuart* in 1979 for which *Time* named her 'one of the ten best actresses in America', and a triumphant Nina in Chekhov's *The Seagull* at Stratford in 1980. Once known primarily for her *ingénue* roles, she is now one of North America's most adaptable and experienced actresses. The winner of two Obie awards (for off-Broadway performances) and a Drama Desk Award, Maxwell has also appeared extensively on U.S. and Canadian television and in several films, including *The Changeling, Rich Kids, Popeye,* and *Psycho III*.   L. W. CONOLLY

Mercer Plays, The. The importance and influence of David FRENCH's Mercer plays as a body of connected works is rivalled in Canadian drama only by James REANEY's DONNELLY trilogy and George F. WALKER's Power plays. *Leaving Home*, the first Mercer play, is credited with consolidating the reputation of TARRAGON THEATRE in Toronto, raising the credibility of Canadian drama in the opinion of the general public, and encouraging the development of a Canadian neorealistic 'school'. As a whole, the Mercer plays document a Canadian social phenomenon, the culture shock experienced by 'immigrants' moving from one region to another.

Leaving Home, French's first full-length play for the stage, opened at Tarragon on 16 May 1972. French has said that the piece is in many respects autobiographical. Set in a Toronto working-class household in the late 1950s, *Leaving Home* pits Jacob Mercer, the patriarch carpenter, against his eldest son, Ben, while the long-suffering mother, Mary, tries to keep the peace. The father/son conflict is both extended and localized by the clash between the values of outport Newfoundland and those of Toronto. The Mercers moved to Ontario from Newfoundland when their sons were small. The boys have grown up as urban North Americans and resent Jacob's old outport standards, especially those that define a 'man'. Most of the characters 'leave home' in the course of the play. Billy and Ben leave physically, Billy to marry a girl pregnant by him, Ben to escape his father's tyranny, while Jacob spiritually leaves home by abandoning the values of the fishing village he left physically many years before. With his sons gone, there is no one to whom he can pass on his values.

Father/son conflict is paralleled and reinforced by mother/daughter tension between Kathy, Billy's fiancée, and her mother Minnie, a flamboyant former flame of Jacob's. Much of the play's comedy is provided by Minnie and her silent undertaker boyfriend, Harold, while contrast between the old and the new is given vivid aural presence through the sharp contrast between the Newfoundland accents of the older generation and the Torontonian speech of the younger.

Champions of the play praise *Leaving Home* for its structure, the poetic resonance arising from selective naturalism, and its archetypal implications; negative critics accuse it of sentimentality and point to the playwright's imbalanced treatment of the central conflict and to the somewhat arbitrary conclusion. There is no arguing, however, with the play's popular success: it received over thirty productions across the country in the season following its première.

Of the Fields, Lately opened at Tarragon on 29 Sept. 1973. Two years after the events depicted in *Leaving Home*, Ben returns from Regina to attend an aunt's funeral. Father and son are as far apart as ever, but in the course of the play Ben discovers that Jacob has suffered a heart attack. He decides he will find work in Toronto so his father will not have to return to his potentially dangerous job. However, Ben does come to some understanding of his father's values, and knowing that the work is necessary to Jacob's sense of self, changes his mind and once again leaves home.

The play is a 'memory play', framed by direct address to the audience, placing the events proper in the past. *Of the Fields, Lately* is a slower, more sombre play than *Leaving*

David French's Of the Fields, Lately, *Tarragon Theatre, 1973, with (l. to r.) Sean Sullivan, Florence Paterson, Sandy Webster, Tim Henry*

Home: the imminence of death and the passage of time sharpen the poignancy of Jacob's and Ben's inability to communicate. The core of the play is to be found in three scenes between father and son, marvellously detailed but oblique—among the most effective uses of sub-text to be found in Canadian dramatic literature.

Again, critical opinion was divided, some preferring *Of the Fields, Lately* to its predecessor because it is a cleaner play with fewer characters and plot developments; others consider the second play inferior, finding fault with what they consider its inappropriate language, convincing neither as dialect nor as timeless poetic speech. While *Of the Fields, Lately* did not achieve the commercial success of its predecessor, it won the CHALMERS Award for 1973.

French did not return to the Mercers for eleven years, writing several other plays in the interim. *Salt-Water Moon* opened at Tarragon on 2 Oct. 1984. This long one-act two-hander is a 'prequel' set in Coley's Point, Nfld., in 1926. Jacob has returned from a year in Toronto to discover that his former sweetheart, Mary, is engaged to Jerome McKenzie, a school teacher Jacob despises.

Jacob finds Mary in the yard of the house where she works as a domestic, looking at the stars through a telescope; in the course of the evening he woos her back. While the essence of the play is this lyrical courtship, we get insight into social conditions of place and time. Jacob left Newfoundland because he could not endure the humiliation suffered by his father when he was employed by Jerome's father 'in collar', and Mary is determined to rescue her sister, Dot, from a home for indigent children.

While *Salt-Water Moon* stands on its own, it acquires additional resonance from *Leaving Home* and *Of the Fields, Lately.* We see more of the motivations of the older Mercers, and of the reality behind Jacob's 'mythic' Newfoundland.

A fourth Mercer play, *1949*, premièred at Toronto's ST LAWRENCE CENTRE on 20 Oct. 1988 in a CANADIAN STAGE COMPANY/MANITOBA THEATRE CENTRE co-production. The play has a cast of twelve, is set on the eve of Newfoundland's entering Confederation, and incorporates a number of the characters seen or mentioned in the previous Mercer plays.

Leaving Home was published by Samuel French and by New Press, Toronto, in 1972;

Mercer Plays

Of the Fields, Lately by Playwrights Co-op in 1973 and New Press in 1975; and *Salt-Water Moon* by Playwrights Canada in 1985.

Selected criticism of *Leaving Home* and *Of the Fields, Lately* is included in *Canadian Drama and the Critics* (1987), ed. L.W. Conolly.   CHRIS JOHNSON

Mercier-Gouin, Yvette (1895-1984). Born and educated in Quebec City, she married in 1917 Léon Mercier-Gouin—a future senator and the son of the then-premier, Sir Lomer Gouin—and moved to Montreal. A philanthropist, painter, lecturer, actress, short-story writer, and novelist, she also wrote radio plays and over a dozen stage plays, all of which were produced, though only two—*Cocktail* (1935) and *Le Jeune Dieu* (1937)—were published.

Mercier-Gouin belongs to the new generation of French-Canadian playwrights that appeared in the 1930s. Turning away from the historical figures that had haunted the Quebec stage, she searched the Montreal high society that was familiar to her—that of celebrated physicians, brilliant lawyers, wealthy industrialists, ambitious politicians, and their well-born wives. The situation most frequently exploited by Mercier-Gouin in her unpublished works is that of two women in love with the same man; this occurs, for example, in *Ma-Man Sybille*, first produced by the MONTREAL REPERTORY THEATRE in 1933; in *La Réussite*, which played at the Théâtre Daunou, Paris, in 1939; and in *Le Plus bel amour, ou Zone libre*, first produced at the Théâtre de l'Arcade, Montreal, in 1941. But in the three-act *Cocktail*, first produced at the THÉÂTRE STELLA in 1935, the situation is reversed. Here two men are in love with the same woman: Dr François Normand wishes to marry Nicole Beaudry, a widow who is hesitant because her daughters are jealous of being deprived of their mother's love, and also because of the reticence of their English tutor Charles Black, who has never dared to declare his love for their mother. At the play's end—after a series of complications—the tutor has left, the doctor has been banished, calm has been restored to the Beaudry household, and the daughters are lovingly reunited with their mother. Well received by the critics, *Cocktail* reveals Mercier-Gouin's gift for plot construction and for witty dialogue, but the play lacks dramatic invention and relies on a formula based on French popular theatre.

This is also true of the three-act *Le Jeune Dieu*, first performed in 1936 at Montreal's Théâtre Imperial, which also deals with amorous rivalry and inappropriate marriage. To the great sorrow of Dr Jacques Martin, his cousin Lisette Martin, with whom he is secretly in love, has married a 'young god'—le Comte Didier Prémontel de la Grand'Ville—and goes to live disconsolately in Paris. After a series of events—a confrontation with the mother-in-law, a visit from cousin Jacques, and the pregnancy of Lisette—the couple decide to reside in Canada. When the mutual love of Lisette and Jacques is admitted, Jacques heroically decides to move to New York, telling his cousin that she must never leave her husband. *Le Jeune Dieu* captivated the critics with its 'psychological acuity', the brilliance of the acting, and the opulence of the sets. The audience must also have been aware of the traditional ideals upheld by the play. Despite some structural clichés—anticipated scenes, an obvious balancing of comedy and pathos, and a rather pat conclusion—*Le Jeune Dieu* showed unusual playwriting skill for its time.

If Mercier-Gouin's plays did not exhibit originality, they were nevertheless milestones in the evolution of Quebec theatre, paving the way for other dramatists to explore the local scene further.

See Edouard-G. Rinfret, *Le Théâtre canadien d'expression française. Répertoire analytique des origines à nos jours*, 3 (1977).

NORMAND LEROUX

Mermaid Theatre. Formed in 1972 at Acadia University in Wolfville, the company was originally committed to touring plays for young audiences in rural Nova Scotia. Acadia's director of drama Evelyn Garbary, artistic director Tom Miller, and administrator Sara Lee Lewis built a solid repertory of plays based on local history and Micmac Indian legends. These productions combined Miller's rod puppets, constructed of foam rubber and ranging in size from eighteen inches to ten feet, with masked actors and dancers, live music, and vibrantly coloured designs.

While the company continued to tour rural Nova Scotia, national tours became part of the theatre's mandate. In 1977 Mermaid made the first of its many international tours, visiting Wales and England (including a three-day Royal Court Theatre engagement). The use of guest actors, a new reliance on scripted plays, and the development of plays dealing with problems relevant to young audiences (*Running the Red Lights*) demonstrated the theatre's willingness to experiment and develop. The Micmac plays remained popular, however; the company was invited to the 1980 World Puppet Festival in Washington, D.C.

In 1982 Graham Whitehead replaced Miller as artistic director. Whitehead's 1983 productions—*Sam Slick the Clock Maker* (script, based on the Haliburton book, and music by Paul Ledoux) and *Just So Stories* (adapted from Kipling by Whitehead)—continued using music, multiple but simple sets, puppetry, and imaginative properties and doubling. This style was continued in the 1984 *Peter and The Wolf* (adapted by Whitehead) which used motorized wolf, puppets, and actors interchangeably, and synthesizer music based on Prokofiev's score. The company visited Mexico in 1984 and the Smithsonian Institution in Washington, D.C., in 1985. It has been located in Windsor, N.S., since 1987.

See Denyse Lynde, 'Wolfville's Mermaid Theatre: the First Fifteen Years', *Theatre History in Canada*, 9 (1988). See also PUPPET THEATRE.   DENYSE LYNDE

Mess, Suzanne (b. 1928). Born in Toronto and raised in Ottawa, she studied drawing and painting at the Ontario College of Art before pursuing her first interest, the theatre. In New York she apprenticed with the Broadway designer Helene Pons before returning to Toronto, where she made costumes for a television show and assisted with costumes at the fledgeling Canadian Opera Company, soon becoming head of wardrobe and principal costume designer there—a post she still holds. In this capacity she has become a designer of international stature, and her costumes have been seen all over North America and in Europe.

Outside the world of opera, Mess designed costumes for the NEW PLAY SOCIETY's SPRING THAW for several years and, since 1960, she has been a staff designer for CBC television—working on such memorable series as 'A Gift to Last', 'Chasing Rainbows', and 'Love and Larceny'.

MARTHA MANN

Milton-St Clair Resident Players, The. After two years in the movie business and five years with American actor and producer George M. Cohan, Jack Milton (also known as Jack Tuthill, and born James M. Tuthill) joined with Robert St Clair (juvenile actor with the St Clair Stock Co. in California) to form their own company at the Imperial Theatre, Kitchener, in the summer of 1921 (after a brief membership in Kitchener's Marie Gladke Stock Co.). There followed engagements in Stratford, Kitchener, Guelph, Chatham, Woodstock, and Hamilton over the next year. The company was seen for the last time in Ontario in Kitchener between Jan. and Mar. 1923. Like most stock companies of the day, the Milton-St Clair company provided a repertoire of well-worn Broadway hits with VAUDEVILLE numbers between the acts. Milton and St Clair brought in several actors from the Pacific Coast (where they had previously worked together) including leading-lady Alma Bunzell, Peter J. Kelly, Ada Burriss, Helen Howarth, and Irene and Harry St Clair. The presence in Ontario of performers from the West Coast provides evidence of the desperate search for new fields of operation in a shrinking market as the movies and radio (which could bring theatre into the home) became the dominant forms of entertainment. Although little is known of Milton's later career (he died on 31 Oct. 1952), Robert St Clair went to Hollywood and acted with such stars as Boris Karloff and Victor Jory, but he became better known as a screen writer. He died on 17 June 1967.

ROBERT SCOTT

Mime. Largely a transplanted form from France, Canadian mime (apart from a few individual performers) dates from the late 1960s. The most marked influence on Canadian mime has been that of Jacques Lecoq. Graduates of his Paris school have founded many Canadian companies whose principal feature is the white-faced mime artist with expressive hands presenting a program of several short sketches of idiosyncratic human movement and behaviour (often combined with clown and mask performances). Although mimes trained by Lecoq mount shows with serious themes, their approach is usually comic and their style is often deemed appropriate for young audiences. Corporal mime—as taught by Étienne Decroux in Paris and using voice, music, and lighting to supplement body movement, in contrast to the

Mime

normally silent performance of the Lecoq tradition—is much less widespread in Canada, its greatest impact having been in Quebec. Often referred to as the theatre of images, corporal mime is rarely performed for children.

The first professional Canadian mime artist of note was Claude St Denis. After studies with both Lecoq and Decroux in Paris and at the Piccolo Theatre in Milan, he founded Le Théâtre de Mime in Montreal in 1965, remaining as artistic director until 1970. Since then he has worked primarily outside Canada; between 1970 and 1973 he performed in Samuel Beckett's *Act Without Words* at Theatre Kaleidoscope in Paris and has subsequently toured and taught in Europe. His performances in Canada are now limited chiefly to festivals of mime.

Red Noses, *Canadian Mime Theatre, 1976, with (l. to r.) Adrian Pecknold, Larry Lefebvre, Frank Rader*

Canada's main advocate for mime in the late 1960s was Adrian Pecknold. His book, *Mime: The Step Beyond Words* (1982), remains the only Canadian practical mime manual. After training with Lecoq he founded the Canadian Mime Theatre (CMT) at Niagara-on-the-Lake, Ont., in 1969. In 1974 the company established the Canadian Mime School—under the direction of Myra Benson—in the newly renovated Royal George Theatre. (Three graduates of the school founded Arété Physical Comedy Company of Calgary in 1976.) In 1977 Pecknold left CMT. Harro Maskow and several other members also left CMT and in 1977 formed Theatre Beyond Words, which continues to work in Niagara-on-the-Lake and to tour nationally and internationally. Their work with large white masks has replaced the traditional make-up of French mime; their signature is the Potato People. Pecknold was succeeded at CMT by English mime Wayne Pritchett, who remained for two years. The company closed in 1979.

Mime Theatre Unlimited was established in Toronto in 1975 by Ron East, another Lecoq student; in 1978 the company began offering a two-year professional training course. Vancouver's Axis Mime—founded by Wayne Specht in 1975—also offers training courses and tours its productions in Canada and abroad. Other Canadian professional companies in the Lecoq tradition include the Paul Gaulin Company (1968), the Canadian Silent Players (1972), Les Mimes Électriques(1974), Canadian Theatre of the Deaf (1976), Mime-Light (1976), Cirque Alex-

ander (1977), Théâtre de l'entrecorps (1977), and the Deaf Gypsy Mime Company(1976).

Corporal mime was first promoted in Canada by Jean Asselin and Denise Boulanger who, after working with the Omnibus mime company in Montreal in the early 1970s, studied in Paris from 1972 to 1977. They returned to Canada with several pieces choreographed for them by Decroux and quickly founded L'École de mime corporéal de Montréal. In 1985 members of the company established Le Pool, which further explores and experiments with corporal mime. Montreal's CARBONE 14 (formerly Les Enfants de paradis, founded in 1975) is similarly devoted to experiment, particularly the exploration of text through corporal mime. Their productions—such as *Le Rail*, adapted from D. M. Thomas's novel *The White Hotel*, and *Hamlet-Machine*, adapted from Heiner Müller's play—reject traditional narrative structure in favour of a strong series of arresting theatre images.

To foster better communication among mime companies, the Association of Mime was formed in 1978, the year of Canada's first festival of mime in Toronto. Festivals have subsequently been held in Vancouver (1980), Montreal (1983), and Vancouver and Montreal in 1986. An International Festival of Contemporary Mime was held in Winnipeg in 1983, 1985, and 1986. As well as showcasing Canadian and foreign mime artists, each festival offered workshops and seminars on professional development.

NATALIE REWA

A puppet version of August Strindberg's A Dream Play, *adapted by Jean Herbiet, designed by Felix Mirbt, Tarragon Theatre, Toronto, 1977, with (l. to r.) Robert Pot and Felix Mirbt*

Mirbt, Felix (b. 1931). Born in Breslau, Germany, he studied at the Univ. of Göttingen, where he developed an experimental puppet group, the 'Dach-Kammer-Spiele', and worked on figure animation for film. He immigrated to Canada in 1953.

Drawing on Japanese Bunraku puppetry, Mirbt designs highly stylized puppets of various sizes with mask-like heads and stylized hands attached to a flowing cloth body. Initially he concentrated on productions for children—Henry BEISSEL's *Inook and the Sun*, which premièred at the STRATFORD FESTIVAL in 1973, was written specifically for Mirbt puppets—but subsequently moved to adult scripts. He has designed puppet productions of Georg Büchner's *Woyzeck* (NATIONAL ARTS CENTRE, 1974), Strindberg's *A Dream Play* (National Arts Centre, 1977), Samuel Beckett's *Happy Days* (Canadian tour, 1981), Jean Cocteau's *Wedding on the Eiffel Tower* (Stratford, 1982), Jean-Guy SABOURIN's *Rose Rose Roose* (THÉÂTRE DU P'TIT BONHEUR, 1986), and the collective *Wild Child* for Ground Zero Productions at the 1986 Quinzaine Internationale and the 1986 Montreal International Puppet Festival.

Mirbt's work has been acknowledged internationally at the Prague Quadrennial and by the Union Internationale des Marionnettes.

See also PUPPET THEATRE. NATALIE REWA

Mirvish, Edwin (b. 1914). Born in Colonial Beach, Virginia, he immigrated with his parents to Toronto at the age of nine. At fifteen he inherited the small family grocery business, which—through flamboyant advertising—he developed into a successful retail business known as 'Honest Ed's'. He also built a chain of restaurants. In 1962 he purchased Toronto's ROYAL ALEXANDRA THEATRE for $215,000 and restored it to its former Edwardian splendour. He chose the theatre's productions from successful plays and musicals originating in London's West End and on Broadway, usually featuring an international star. In 1983-4 the subscriber list was 50,000. Mirvish's most notable venture into theatre was marked by his purchase in 1982 of London's Old Vic for $1.3 million; after a £2 million renovation it opened in Nov. 1983.
HERBERT WHITTAKER

Mitchell, Betty (1896-1976). Born in Sandusky, Ohio, she moved to Canada as a child and grew up in Saskatchewan, becoming a teacher in rural schools before entering the Univ. of Alberta. Although her 1924 degree was in Botany, her enthusiasm was theatre. She directed her first play in Edmonton, John Galsworthy's *Punch and Go*. She became Director of Drama at Calgary's Western Canada High School in 1936, and a Rockefeller Fellowship (1942) allowed her to study and lecture at the State Univ. of Iowa, where she earned an MA in Theatre (1944). Her thesis was a thorough and sensitive account of important Broadway plays and players, seen and interviewed while she held a National Research Fellowship from the Cleveland Playhouse. When she returned to her Calgary position, some of her students founded an amateur theatre, Workshop 14, and continued to produce plays, directed by Betty Mitchell, after their graduation. Workshop 14 was a leader in amateur theatre for the next generation, winning many awards in DOMINION DRAMA FESTIVALs and leading directly to the establishment of professional theatre in Calgary. Betty Mitchell was recognized for her pioneer work with an honorary Doctor of Laws from the Univ. of Alberta (1958), an Alberta Achievement

341

Award (1972), and two Calgary theatres were named after her: one in the former Allied Arts Centre (1962), the other in the Southern Alberta Auditorium (1984).

See Kenneth Dyba, *Betty Mitchell* (1986).

JOYCE DOOLITTLE

Mitchell, Ken (b. 1940). Born and raised in Moose Jaw, Sask., he studied (and failed) journalism at Toronto's Ryerson Polytechnical Institute. After graduating from the Univ. of Saskatchewan (MA in English, 1967), he joined the Dept. of English at the Univ. of Regina, where he remains as a professor of Canadian literature and creative writing.

Mitchell's love of travel has given a broad perspective to his writing, which nevertheless retains a definite prairie identity. He has worked as an actor and performed at folk festivals with the musical group Humphrey and the Dumptrucks, who collaborated with him on CRUEL TEARS (1976). Travel and performance were combined in 1982-3 when he received a Canada Council grant to research a major project on China; he gave performances in China of his play-in-progress on Norman Bethune, *Gone the Burning Sun* (1985).

Mitchell's prolific output includes radio and television plays, film scripts, stage plays, short stories, novels, history, criticism, and poetry. Most of this work is set in Saskatchewan but its vision and zest for life can be appreciated anywhere. His first play, *Heroes* (1973), won the Ottawa Little Theatre's one-act playwriting competition in 1971. A comic satire on the displacement of heroes, specifically of Superman and the Lone Ranger, the play had its first professional production at the GLOBE THEATRE in Regina in 1975 directed by Esse LJUNGH, and has been performed widely in Canada and the U.S. *Wheat City*, originally titled and published as *This Train* (1973), a one-act play produced at Toronto's TARRAGON THEATRE in Mar. 1973, is a realistic evocation of the loneliness of a man and a woman on the platform of a small Saskatchewan railway stop. *The Medicine Line* (1976), first produced in Moose Jaw in 1976, is a somewhat sketchy evocation of attempts by Major James Walsh to save Sitting Bull and his Sioux Indians from a forced return from Canada to the U.S. and their deaths. *Showdown at Sand Valley: A Western Entertainment* (1977), first produced at the

Univ. of Regina in 1975, is a parody of the classic western story of the arrival of a gunfighter in a strange town. *Cruel Tears*, subtitled 'a country opera', is Mitchell's most successful play to date. Based on the plot of Shakespeare's *Othello*, it is a tale of love and jealousy among the truckdrivers of Saskatoon.

Many of Mitchell's plays are about proud and independent men faced with insuperable odds. Such characters appear in *Davin: The Politician* (1979), a panoramic treatment of the life of the flamboyant Irish-born western Conservative politician who killed himself in 1901. It premièred at the Globe Theatre, Regina, in 1978. *The Shipbuilder* (1979)—the story of a Finnish immigrant who decided to build a ship on the prairies, transport it seventeen miles to the Saskatchewan River, and then sail back to his homeland—was first produced by the Univ. of Regina in 1978. *The Great Cultural Revolution* (1980) ran at the ARTS CLUB, Vancouver, in 1979. It effectively uses the play-within-a-play device to show the excesses of China's cultural revolution of the 1960s. Mitchell continued to show his versatility in other one-act plays: *Chautauqua Girl: A Musical Show for Young People* (1982), produced at the Carousel Theatre, Vancouver, in Feb. 1982, and *Little Nooton* (1979, unproduced).

Gone the Burning Sun had its Canadian première at the Guelph Spring Festival in 1984 with David FOX in the role of Dr Norman Bethune, and oriental music by David Liang played on stage by the Chinese musician Pan Hui-zhu. An unheroic but energetic portrait of Bethune in fourteen scenes, it received the Canadian Authors Drama Award for 1985 and toured the People's Republic of China for four weeks in 1987. Mitchell has several unpublished plays, including *Pleasant Street*, produced in 1972 at Saskatoon's 25TH STREET THEATRE; *Genesis*, first performed in 1975 at the Univ. of Saskatchewan; and *Gabriel Dumont: The Plainsman* and *Melody Farm*, a play about the mentally handicapped, both of which premièred at 25th Street Theatre (in 1985 and 1987 respectively).

Mitchell's fiction, while not as successful as his drama, is more rooted in his western-Canadian experience. He has published three novels: *Wandering Rafferty* (1972), *The Meadowlark Connection: A Saskatchewan Thriller* (1975), and *The Con Man* (1979), the most ambitious yet least satisfying of his novels.

Everyone Gets Something Here (1977) is a collection of short stories. *Ken Mitchell Country* (1984), ed. Robert Currie, is a selection from his drama, poetry, short stories, and novels, including the complete texts of *Wheat City* and *The Meadowlark Connection*, and excerpts from *Gone the Burning Sun*. JAMES NOONAN

Mitchell, Roy (1884-1944). Born in Fort Gratiot, Michigan, he was raised and educated in Toronto (Univ. of Toronto, 1902-4). He spent thirteen years in Canada and the U.S. as theatre critic, drama editor, and press agent. In 1908 he began directing plays for Toronto's ARTS AND LETTERS CLUB, with visits to New York where he studied design, stage managed on Broadway, and worked at the Greenwich Village Theatre. He was also deeply interested in comparative religion, mysticism and philosophy, and had close links with the Theosophical Society of Toronto. During the First World War, he worked as Director of Motion Pictures for the Federal Department of Public Information in Ottawa. When HART HOUSE THEATRE opened in 1919, he became its first director, subsequently using it as an experimental lab to test his theories on motion, 'mutable settings', and colour systems. The results of these experiments were later incorporated into his book *The Creative Theatre* (1929). In 1926 he married Margaret C. (Jocelyn) Taylor, an artist and sculptor who collaborated with him in his work.

Because Mitchell encountered a great deal of indifference, if not resistance, to his avant-garde views, he moved to New York in 1927, becoming Professor of Dramatic Art at New York Univ. (1930). Besides teaching and writing, he also developed a type of singing based on phonetics to enable his group, the Consort Singers, to perform folk songs in any language.

Member of a Canadian avant-garde that included Lawren Harris, Arthur Lismer, and Bertram BROOKER among others, Mitchell represents the most prophetic voice in Canadian theatre history, anticipating the work of Antonin Artaud, Tyrone GUTHRIE, Peter Brook, and Jerzy Grotowski in Europe as well as developments in Canadian theatre of the 1960s. In *Creative Theatre* he condemns the commercialism of contemporary American theatre as a 'betrayal', and a 'Dance of Death'. The ideal theatre he envisions will include exhibition space for art and sculpture,

a library, museum, and, most important, training facilities for actors. He emphasizes the importance of the audience ('the audience is the consummation of the theatre') and the need for native, original plays ('Art is a native growth which . . . must arise generation by generation from its native soil'). The experience of theatre should be a revelation, with the actor 'a celebrant of a mystery' which only live performance can create. This is to be brought about by de-emphasizing the verbal element and Aristotelian structure in favour of movement, shape, and form ('the stage is not a picture: it is a place'). He concludes the book with a plea for a dramaturge/director to replace the traditional producer to bring about once more 'miraculous theatre'.

Mitchell also wrote *Shakespeare for Community Players* (1919) and *The School Theatre: A Handbook of Theory and Practice* (1925). *Through Temple Doors: Studies in Occult Masonry* (1923) and *The Exile of the Soul* (1983), edited by John L. Davenport, deal with Mitchell's religious and philosophical ideas.

See Renate Usmiani, 'Roy Mitchell: Prophet in Our Past', *Theatre History in Canada*, 8 (1987). RENATE USMIANI

Mitchell, W.O. (b. 1914). A native of Weyburn, Sask., he was educated at the Universities of Manitoba and Alberta. After some years of teaching he settled in High River, Alta, to write full time. Apart from three years in Toronto as fiction editor for *Maclean's* (1948-51), he lived in High River until 1968, when he became writer-in-residence at the Univ. of Calgary. He has since held that position at three other universities, most recently at Windsor.

Mitchell's first publications were stories, the best known being his small-town prairie chronicles of Jake and the Kid, which appeared in *Maclean's* over two decades beginning in 1942. A selected volume, *Jake and the Kid* (1961), won the Stephen LEACOCK Medal for Humour. His first full-length work of fiction, *Who Has Seen the Wind* (1947)—to date the all-time best-selling Canadian novel—was followed by two relatively undistinguished works, *The Kite* (1962) and *The Vanishing Point* (1973). But Mitchell's novelistic reputation revived with the publication of *How I Spent My Summer Holidays* (1981), a dark sequel to *Who Has Seen the Wind*, and *Since Daisy Creek* (1984).

As a dramatist he first gained success in radio and television. 'Jake and the Kid' ran as a popular weekly series on CBC radio, 1950-6, in more than 200 half-hour episodes, establishing Mitchell as one of Canada's pre-eminent folk humorists. In Jake, the farm-hand *cum* philosopher whose colourful tall tales constitute the Kid's real education, Mitchell celebrates the vitality of a liberating, non-conformist imagination battling the restrictive tendencies of the community. Though lighter and more anecdotal than most of his other treatments of this theme in drama and fiction, *Jake and the Kid*, with its emphasis on the eccentric comic voice as purveyor of truth, remains a paradigm of Mitchell's writing.

As *Jake and the Kid* evolved from print to radio, the bulk of the episodes Mitchell wrote for the CBC were original scripts. His stage plays, in contrast, have nearly all been adaptations of works he wrote for other media. His first stage production, *The Devil's Instrument* (1973), produced by the Ontario Youth Theatre in 1972, was broadcast on radio in 1949 and on television in 1956. With uncharacteristic earnestness it depicts a Hutterite boy straining to escape the narrow-minded morality of his elders. Like the majority of Mitchell's stage plays it only half-succeeds. In the transition from one medium to the other it suffers structural flaws (the fragmentation of one act into twenty-eight scenes) and a flatness of character that show up throughout Mitchell's work for the theatre.

His two most popular and critically successful plays also had previous incarnations on radio and TV. *Back to Beulah* (1982), produced by the VANCOUVER PLAYHOUSE New Series Company in 1976, and winner of the CHALMERS Award in 1976, is a hybrid of melodrama and comedy pitting three female mental patients against their repressed and hypocritical psychiatrist, also a woman. The play is dramatically effective until its third act, where characterization gives way to caricature, satire to overstatement, and plot to message. *The Black Bonspiel of Wullie MacCrimmon* (1966), first produced by THEATRE CALGARY in 1978, directed by Guy SPRUNG, with none of the ambitions of *Beulah*, is at once Mitchell's funniest and most theatrical play. The audacious concept of a curling match in depression-era Alberta between a local rural rink and the Devil (with Guy Fawkes, Judas, and Macbeth rounding out his fearsome foursome) allows Mitchell to work in the broad lines and bright colours of the humorist's art without having to worry about depth of character or consistency of theme. This will likely prove his most enduring play.

Both the strengths and weaknesses of Mitchell's playwriting are epitomized in *The Kite* (1982), produced by Theatre Calgary in 1981. It showcases his most memorable character, 117-year-old Daddy Sherry, existential acrobat and mocker of conventional wisdom. Earthy, ornery, and larger than life, Daddy survives the journey from novel to stage (again via radio and TV) fully intact. But in every other respect *The Kite* pales as a play, reaffirming the widely held impression that theatre is not Mitchell's natural medium.

Mitchell has been awarded a number of honorary degrees as well as the Order of Canada. The above stage plays and *For Those in Peril on the Sea* are collected in *Dramatic W.O. Mitchell* (1982).

See Diane Bessai, 'A Literary Perspective on the Plays of W.O. Mitchell', *Canadian Drama*, 10 (1984). JERRY WASSERMAN

Moiseiwitsch, Tanya (b. 1914). Born in London, Eng., daughter of the pianist Benno Moiseiwitsch, she was encouraged towards a musical career but chose art instead, training at London's Central School of Arts and Crafts. She apprenticed as a scene-painter at Tyrone GUTHRIE's Old Vic in 1933-4, then became assistant designer at the Westminster Theatre, designing John Masefield's *The Faithful* in 1934. In 1935 Hugh Hunt, its director, persuaded her to follow him to the Abbey Theatre, Dublin, where she designed sets and costumes for over fifty productions.

For much of the war she was resident designer at the Oxford Playhouse. In 1944 Tyrone Guthrie asked her to join the Old Vic's wartime company in Liverpool, where she designed Ben Jonson's *The Alchemist* in Jan. 1945. Thereafter, until his death in 1971, she was Guthrie's chosen designer, working with him on more than thirty productions in Britain, Canada, Israel, and the U.S.. Their first London collaborations were Edmond Rostand's *Cyrano de Bergerac* at the Old Vic in 1946 and Benjamin Britten's opera

Peter Grimes at Covent Garden in 1947. The former established Moiseiwitsch's mastery of seventeenth-century costume and painting; the latter was her first experiment with Guthrie in clearing the stage of sets and properties, building stage pictures with bodies and costumes alone. Another, more important, experiment followed at Stratford-on-Avon in 1949: a setting for Guthrie's *Henry VIII* on a simple Elizabethan stage that, in a modified version, became the design of Ontario's STRATFORD FESTIVAL stage in 1953.

Probably the most visually memorable of the Guthrie/Moiseiwitsch productions were *Oedipus Rex* at Stratford, Ont. (1954-5), and *The House of Atreus* at the Guthrie Theatre, Minneapolis (1967), bold recreations of the monumental scale of the masked and buskined Greek tragic theatre. Perhaps the most delightful were their exercises in turn-of-the-century nostalgia, Thornton Wilder's *The Matchmaker* (London, 1954; New York, 1955) and their Ruritanian *All's Well That Ends Well* (Stratford, Ontario, 1953; re-designed for Stratford-on-Avon, 1959). Some of Moiseiwitsch's finest work was also done for other directors at Stratford, Ontario: *Love's Labour's Lost* and a Napoleonic *Coriolanus* for Michael LANGHAM in 1961; *Cymbeline* (1970) and Molière's *The Imaginary Invalid* (1974) for Jean GASCON; another *All's Well*, after Velasquez, for David Jones in 1977; Friedrich Schiller's *Mary Stuart* (1982) and Molière's *Tartuffe* (1984) for John HIRSCH; and Nikolai Gogol's *The Government Inspector* for Ronald Eyre in 1985.

Guthrie warned that the success of his open stage would depend on superb costuming, creating by its detail the density of reality lost by forfeiting settings, and preventing by its splendour any sense of visual starvation. Moiseiwitsch gave what he demanded. Her costumes, meticulously exact, were sumptuous without drawing attention from the actors. Her rich, subtly modulated colours turned the canvases of her favourite seventeenth-century masters into the three-dimensional living sculpture that the bare, polished, wooden platform required. Her special brilliance as a designer has been her architectural sense of theatrical space. Much of the Stratford Festival's early success can be credited to its designers; no matter how uneven the acting, the designs always stood up to the best in the world. Moiseiwitsch gave it that

standard, and has helped to maintain it over thirty years. RONALD BRYDEN

Monette, Richard (b. 1944). Born and educated in Montreal, he has acted professionally in both the classical and contemporary repertoires since 1964. Trained by Eleanor STUART, and winner of best-actor awards at the Inter-Varsity Drama Festival (1962, 1963), Monette worked at the CREST (a precocious Hamlet in 1964), the STRATFORD FESTIVAL, and THEATRE TORONTO before leaving Canada in 1969 for England, where he appeared with the Welsh National Theatre, Regent's Park Theatre in London, and in the West End production of *Oh! Calcutta!* Returning to Canada in 1972, Monette established himself as a major actor through his tour-de-force performance in TARRAGON THEATRE's production of Michel TREMBLAY's *Hosanna* and his significant work at Stratford under Robin PHILLIPS in such roles as Caliban, Romeo, Hamlet, and Berowne in *Love's Labour's Lost*.

Highly successful in contemporary plays as on-the-edge, intense characters, his success in the classics has been more with comic or ironic rather than tragic characters. In recent years Monette has produced and directed while continuing to act. In 1988 he made his directorial début at Stratford with *The Taming of the Shrew*. JONATHAN RITTENHOUSE

Montreal Repertory Theatre. An amateur company founded in 1930 by Martha ALLAN—with the support of Margaret ANGLIN and Sir Barry Jackson, who were visiting Montreal at the time—as the Theatre Guild of Montreal, the company's first production was A.A. Milne's *The Perfect Alibi*. Because of a dispute with the New York Theatre Guild over rights to produce *Candida*, the company changed its name to the Montreal Repertory Theatre to secure permission to mount Shaw's play, which became its second production. During its first two seasons rehearsals were conducted in the coach house of the Allan family estate, and productions were presented in McGill University's Moyse Hall and elsewhere. Although it was a bilingual company, the MRT received its initial support from the anglophone communities of Montreal and Ottawa, including the then Governor General, Lord Bessborough, who designed the sets for a 1933 co-production with the Ottawa Little Theatre of *Hamlet*, in which his son played the title role. A strong staff headed by Allan, and including Rupert Caplan and Lorne Pierce, set high production standards, despite having no permanent theatre.

In 1932 the MRT acquired a headquarters on Union St, including an abandoned indoor golf course that became the MRT's Workshop (later called the Studio), a venue to try out new talent and experimental plays. The first Workshop season (1932-3) consisted of original Canadian plays, half of them in French. Experimentation and education became as important to the company as its full productions. In 1933 a School of Theatre was formed under the leadership of Filmore Sadler.

A concerted effort to appeal to both French and English communities continued through the 1930s. In 1933 André Obey's *Noë* was given a full production in French at the Salle du GESÙ, and original French-Canadian plays continued to be produced at the Workshop. By 1938 a separate but affiliated organization, Le Mont-Royal Théâtre Français (to retain the initials MRT), had its own associate producing director, but shared technical and production staff with the English-language company. In 1938 it won the Sir Barry Jackson Trophy at the DOMINION DRAMA FESTIVAL with an original play, Arthur Prévost's *Maldonne*.

During the war the MRT continued to present a season of full productions, and toured its *Tin Hat Revue* to troops across eastern Canada until 1946. In 1942 three major changes occurred in the organization: the purchase, renovation, and expansion of the rented quarters on Union St; the acquisition of a permanent theatre on Guy St, with a 19′ × 15′ stage and seating for about 200; and the untimely death of Martha Allan.

During the 1950s, under the direction of Mildred Mitchell and then Doreen Lewis, a graduate of the MRT's school, the bilingual and experimental mandate of the company was much less visible. Seasons consisted primarily of serious drama from the New York theatre and proven classics. Particularly important during this period was the work of directors Roeberta Beatty and Pierre DAGENAIS. MRT director Charles RITTENHOUSE and director and designer Herbert WHITTAKER together produced an annual Shakespearean play under the auspices of the Shakespeare Society of Montreal. The school, which had closed during the war, was reopened in 1947 by Sadler and remained in operation, affiliated with the BRAE MANOR THEATRE, until Sadler's death in 1952.

In that year a fire gutted the Guy St theatre, destroying all the MRT's possessions. Subsequently, under Patricia Coe and Julia Murphy, MRT seasons were presented in various local school auditoriums. In 1956 the company turned professional, beginning with a production of Christopher Fry's *The Lady's Not For Burning*, and in 1957 it became resident in the Navy League building on Closse St, shared with opera and ballet companies. In 1961 that building was sold. Debt-ridden and forced to vacate, the MRT ceased operations.

A major force in the country's LITTLE THEATRE movement and a winner of many DDF prizes, the MRT helped develop the careers of numerous Canadian theatre professionals, including (among many others) Gratien GÉLINAS, Yvette BRIND'AMOUR, Fred BARRY, Denise PELLETIER, Eleanor STUART, Robert GOODIER, Christopher PLUMMER, Richard EASTON, Amelia HALL, John COLICOS, Eric DONKIN, and William SHATNER.

HERBERT WHITTAKER

Monument National, Le. Built in 1893-4 on rue Saint-Laurent (near Dorchester) in Montreal as the headquarters of the Société Saint-Jean-Baptiste de Montréal, this four-storey building featured a metal superstructure and stone walls decorated with recesses and Romanesque windows. It was designed by the firm of Perrault, Mesnard, and Venne. Both eclectic and naïve in architectural style, it contained a hall accommodating 1,496 spectators; on the ground floor were shops, and on the upper floors, offices, classrooms, and reception rooms. The Monument National was officially inaugurated on 24 June 1893, but the building was not completed until June 1894.

Devoted to popular education, and offering practical courses in various subjects (from mechanics to elocution), the Monument National was also host—from 13 Nov. 1898 to 14 May 1901—to 'Soirées de famille', theatrical presentations organized by Elzéar Roy and Jean-Jacques Beauchamp. In 1902 projectionist Ernest Ouimet showed some short films there, and national figures such as Wilfrid Laurier, Henri Bourassa, and Canon

Groulx spoke there. World-famous musicians also appeared, such as the Polish pianist Ignace Paderewski in Feb. 1909.

The Monument National was used by various theatrical groups, both established and occasional. From 1921 to 1945 it was the home of the 'Veillées du Bon Vieux Temps' under the direction of Conrad Gauthier, with such stars as Ovila Légaré and Mme Édouard Bolduc (Mary Travers), who made their début in 1927. In 1921 Honoré Vaillancourt founded 'La Société canadienne d'opérette', which—after thirteen years' activity—gave way to the 'Variétés lyriques'. From 1936 to 1956, under the direction of Charles Goulet and Lionel Daunais, this company gave 128 different shows at the Monument. From 1915 to 1950 the local Jewish community presented Yiddish theatre there, and Gratien GÉLINAS's annual revue Les Fridolinades (see FRIDOLINONS) appeared from 1938 to 1946. The opening of Gélinas's TIT-COQ on 22 May 1948 was an instant success and marked the birth of contemporary Quebec theatre. Maurice Duplessis and Archbishop Joseph Charbonneau attended the hundredth performance. During the 1950s the immediate neighbourhood of the Monument National acquired a bad reputation and in 1960 the Société Saint-Jean-Baptiste moved its offices to Sherbrooke St and put the building up for sale. In Nov. 1971 it was bought for $350,000 by the NATIONAL THEATRE SCHOOL, which converted the rooms to studios and workshops, while keeping the main hall for their productions.

On 19 Nov. 1976 the Quebec National Assembly declared the Monument National a cultural building, and in 1985 a confidential preliminary report by the provincial and federal governments, co-ordinated by the Montreal Heritage Society and with the approval of the National Theatre School, stressed the importance of restoring the building. It was to be devoted primarily to theatrical and cultural activities, without excluding the commercial, which were included in the founders' original intentions. The co-operation of Hydro-Québec, a powerful neighbour and potential patron, would seem essential in achieving such a restoration.

ALONZO LE BLANC

Moore, Dora Mavor (1888–1979). One of several post-Second World War teacher-directors who helped establish Canada's professional theatre, Dora Mavor was born in Glasgow but was brought to Toronto at the age of four and educated at Havergal College, Bishop Strachan School, and abroad. In 1911 she graduated from Toronto's Margaret Eaton School of Expression and won an acting scholarship to RADA, the first Canadian to be enrolled there. She made her professional début in 1912 with Ottawa's Colonial Stock Company and then went to New York to join Ben Greet's Pastoral Players on their CHAUTAUQUA tours. Other American appearances were in Edward Sheldon's Romance on Broadway in 1913, in C.R. Hopkins's How Much is a Million in Chicago in 1913, and in the silent-film version of Anna Karenina (1915). In 1916 she directed Maurice Maeterlinck's The Blue Bird for the Central Neighbourhood House in Toronto's Cabbagetown, and accompanied her army-chaplain husband, Captain Francis Moore, overseas. She became the first Canadian to perform at London's Old Vic when she played Viola in Greet's production of Twelfth Night in 1918. Returning to Toronto with one son, Francis, she bore two more, James Mavor MOORE and Peter.

Dora Mavor Moore continued to act at HART HOUSE THEATRE during the 1920s and early 1930s, but her interests shifted towards teaching and directing. She founded the Univ. of Toronto Extension Players in 1930 and the Hart House Touring Players in 1931. A third group, the Village Players (1938–46), became the prototype for her NEW PLAY SOCIETY. Remembered for its annual satiric revue SPRING THAW (1948–71), the NPS also ran a theatre school (1950–68). Mrs Moore was instrumental in bringing Tyrone GUTHRIE to the STRATFORD FESTIVAL. Honours included the Centennial Medal and Canadian Drama Award (1967); honorary doctorates from Ohio University (1969) and the Univ. of Toronto (1970); the Order of Canada (1970); Toronto's Award of Merit (1977) and first Drama Bench Award (1978). Since 1981 Toronto's annual theatre awards have been named after her. DAVID GARDNER

Moore, Mavor (b. 1919). One of three sons of the Rev. Francis John Moore and Dora Mavor MOORE, he was born and educated in Toronto. In 1938 he and his mother co-founded the Village Players (Toronto), a community theatre located in a barn on their property at Bathurst and Eglinton in Toronto that gave early experience to Lorne GREENE, Don HARRON, Toby ROBINS, Fletcher Markle, William NEEDLES, Lister SINCLAIR, and other theatre and broadcasting professionals. Moore also co-founded with his mother in 1946 Toronto's NEW PLAY SOCIETY, and served as manager, writer (most notably of its annual review SPRING THAW), director, and actor. He has since been general director of the Charlottetown CONFEDERATION CENTRE (1963-5), founding artistic director of the CHARLOTTETOWN FESTIVAL (1964-8), and founding general director of Toronto's ST LAWRENCE CENTRE (1965-9).

Moore was a pioneer in Canada's broadcasting industry. At the age of twenty-two he was the CBC's youngest radio feature producer (1941-2), becoming chief producer for the CBC International Service, Montreal (1944-5), after service overseas in the psychological warfare branch of the Canadian Army (1943-5); from 1950 to 1954 he was chief producer of the new CBC-TV English network. He also served two terms as executive producer of the United Nations Information Division, New York (1947 and 1949). He has held key administrative and artistic positions with the CANADIAN PLAYERS, the Canadian Opera Company, CREST THEATRE, the Vancouver Festival, the VANCOUVER PLAYHOUSE, and NEPTUNE THEATRE, and has been adviser and consultant to Expo 67, Hamilton Place, the Newfoundland ARTS AND CULTURE CENTRE, the NATIONAL ARTS CENTRE, THEATRE CALGARY, and the Ontario Arts Council. He served on the first Board of Governors of the STRATFORD FESTIVAL (from 1953 to 1974), and was also a Governor of the NATIONAL THEATRE SCHOOL (1960-73), the founding chairman of the Canadian Theatre Centre (1960), founding chairman of the Guild of Canadian Playwrights (1977), and a member of the Canada Council (1974-9) as well as its chairman (1979-83).

A professional actor since the age of fourteen, Moore's many stage, radio, television, and film roles in Canada, the U.S., and England include Macbeth, King Lear, Caesar in Shaw's *Caesar and Cleopatra*, and roles in several feature films, including *Thresholds* (1982) and *The Killing Fields* (1983). He was host for the CBC-TV series 'Performance' (1981-4).

Moore has written over a hundred produced plays, musicals, and operas, including the libretti for the opera *Louis Riel* (produced in 1967) with Jacques LANGUIRAND and composer Harry Somers, and the musicals *Johnny Belinda* (Charlottetown Festival, 1968) and *Fauntleroy* (Charlottetown, 1980). His most widely produced play is *The Ottawa Man* (1958), a Canadian version of Nikolai Gogol's *Inspector General*, first produced at the Crest Theatre in 1958, and subsequently on CBC-TV in 1959, the Charlottetown Festival in 1967, and in FESTIVAL LENNOXVILLE's inaugural season in 1972. Several of his short radio plays—including *Getting In* (1969), *The Pile* (1973), *Inside Out* (1973), *The Store* (1973), and *Come Away, Come Away* (1973)—have also been produced on stage and on television. Together with the four-act documentary, *The Roncarelli Affair* (1976), they resemble Harold Pinter's comedy of menace and, in their testing of realities and illusions, the improvisational characteristics of Luigi Pirandello. *Customs* (1977), a one-act dream-like treatment of customs and immigration procedures, perhaps epitomizes Moore's dramaturgical preoccupations with the elusiveness of identity and the unpredictability of public and private interactions.

Moore was theatre critic for the *Canadian Commentator* (1956-7) and the *Toronto Telegram* (1959-60), and from 1984 to 1989 wrote a weekly cultural affairs column for the Toronto *Globe and Mail*. He has lectured extensively and was Professor of Theatre at York Univ. from 1974 to 1984, becoming Professor Emeritus in 1984. His many honours include three Peabody Awards (1947, 1949, 1957), the Centennial Medal (1967), the John Drainie Award for lifetime service to broadcasting (1982), the Diplôme d'honneur of the Canadian Conference of the Arts (1985), and five honorary doctorates. In 1973 he was made an Officer of the Order of Canada. *Three One-act Plays by Mavor Moore* (1973) contains *Inside Out*, *The Pile*, and *The Store*.   ROTA HERZBERG LISTER

Morgan-Powell, Samuel (1867-1962). Born in London, Eng., he travelled the Middle East and South America before joining the *Montreal Star* in 1907, where he was the drama and literary critic for thirty-five years and a prolific writer of sketches, poems, and articles. He became the *Star*'s senior editor during the Second World War and retired in 1953, but continued to contribute reviews.

As a drama critic Morgan-Powell was dogmatic, outspoken, and intolerant of shoddy acting and staging. In the 1920s and 1930s, when Montreal was used as a 'dog town' or try-out centre for Broadway productions, his incisive comments often determined the fate of a play. Though fond of British plays and actors, Morgan-Powell supported the development of a Canadian theatre, particularly through his encouragement of LITTLE THEATRE groups. He acted as secretary of the Earl Grey Music and Dramatic Competition in 1908, supported the fledgeling DOMINION DRAMA FESTIVAL, and worked closely with Martha ALLAN in the establishment of the MONTREAL REPERTORY THEATRE.

Morgan-Powell's columns included interviews with famous actors, evaluations of contemporary playwrights, and comments on productions in New York, London, and Moscow. He frequently praised the efforts of French-Canadian actors in Montreal, urged the creation of a children's theatre, and deplored CENSORSHIP of plays and films.

On his death New York's 'Outer Circle', a society of drama critics, praised Morgan-Powell as an 'outstanding stalwart of the stage'. He remains one of the few Canadian drama critics with a truly international reputation. His book *Memories That Live* (1929) won Quebec's Prix David.

RAMON HATHORN

Morris, Clara (Clara Morrison, née La Montagne, *c*.1848-1925). Born in Toronto, the future 'Queen of Melodrama' was soon spirited south by her mother to escape her bigamous French-Canadian father. Settling eventually in Cleveland, she became a 'ballet-girl' with John Ellsler's family theatre and by 1869 achieved stardom with a Cincinnati company. In July 1870 she played a short season in Halifax, N.S. (Ophelia, Juliet, Lady Macbeth) before winning a three-year engagement with Augustin Daly in New York. An emotional actress, she was an overnight sensation in Wilkie Collins's *Man and Wife* and hailed in Dion Boucicault's *Jezebel*, as mad Cora in *L'Article 47* (anon.) and subsequently, under A.M. Palmer, in Dumas's *Camille* and Augustus R. Cazauran's *Miss Multon*. Recurring spinal problems curtailed her performances after 1885, but in 1892 she appeared in Montreal in Victorien Sardou's *Odette* and in 1904 in an all-star Broadway

revival of John Oxenford's *The Two Orphans*. She wrote three volumes of theatrical reminiscences, notably *Life on the Stage* (1901).

DAVID GARDNER

Morrison, Charlotte (1832-1910). Born Charlotte Nickinson in Quebec City, she grew up in New York, where at the age of fourteen she joined her father, John NICKINSON, in Mitchell's Olympic Co. On tour with him, she first appeared in Toronto in Apr. 1851, scoring an immediate success. In 1853 her father leased Toronto's ROYAL LYCEUM, with Charlotte—who excelled in light, witty, and graceful characters such as Lady Teazle, Rosalind, and Portia—as his popular leading lady. She also appeared with the Nickinson troupe in Hamilton and other nearby cities, and starred with the local companies in London, Quebec City, and elsewhere. In 1858 she married Daniel Morrison, a journalist, and in the next decade moved with him to Quebec City, London, New York, and finally Toronto. Left a widow with four children in 1870, she returned to the stage in 1871 and 1872, producing short summer seasons at the Royal Lyceum. In 1873 she became a director of the Toronto Opera House Co., formed to build a theatre worthy of the growing city, and was appointed the first manager of the GRAND OPERA HOUSE, known during her regime as 'Mrs Morrison's Grand Opera House'. On its opening night (21 Sept. 1874) she appeared in her favourite role of Lady Teazle; an immense crowd, including the most prominent Torontonians, and large parties from Montreal, Ottawa, Hamilton, London, and other cities attended. Morrison continued to play leading roles in stock productions, as well as handling the duties of manager. Unfortunately the Grand proved unprofitable and was sold in 1876 to a new owner who in 1878 replaced Mrs Morrison as manager. In retirement she continued the public-spirited activities that had won her so much respect and affection, directing entertainments for charity, and serving as president of the Toronto Relief Society.

MARY SHORTT

Motion Pictures, Canadians in. It has long been an accepted truism of Canadian artistic life that Canadians can more readily find fame and fortune by working outside Canada—usually in the U.S., but also in Britain and

Motion Pictures

France. This was perhaps truer in the early twentieth century, when there was limited professional theatre and film activity in Canada, but it remains a pattern in recent decades for those who, having begun their professional careers in Canada, later sought the promise of more lucrative rewards abroad—especially in Hollywood. Many actors, actresses, directors, producers, cinematographers, and designers have taken this route to success.

Prior to the First World War most Canadians seeking professional film careers were, of necessity, forced to do so in the U.S. Among them were Mary Pickford (b. Gladys Mary Smith, 1893-1979), and her brother and sister, Jack and Lottie; Marie Dressler (b. Leila Marie Koerber, 1869-1934); Berton K. Churchill (1876-1940); Lew Cody (b. Louis Cote, 1884-1934); Jonathon Hale (1882-1965); Walter HUSTON (1884-1950); May IRWIN (1862-1938); Florence Lawrence (1886-1938); Vivienne Osborne (b. 1900); Walter Pidgeon (1897-1984); Marie Prevost (b. Marie Pickford Dunn, 1898-1937); Nell Shipman (b. Helen Foster Barham, 1892-1970); Norma Shearer (1900-83); Ned Sparks (1883-1957); and Lucille Watson (1879-1962). Others who left Canada for Hollywood were several pioneer directors, including Sidney Olcott (b. John S. Olcott, 1874-1949), a major contributor to the development of the Kalem Company; Allan Dwan (1885-1981), a major director over a sixty-year career from 1909, with credits that include the classic Douglas Fairbanks films; the famous producer/director of comedies, Mack Sennett (b. Mikall Sinnott, 1880-1960); and some lesser names—John Murray ANDERSON, Henry MacRae, Del Henderson, Harry Edwards, Joseph De Grasse, J. Gordon Edwards, and John Robertson. Other Canadians who worked in Hollywood include writers W. Scott Darling and George White; cinematographers Osmond Borradaile (who worked in both Hollywood and Britain), James Crosby, and Alvin Knechtel; and sound engineer Douglas Shearer (1899-1971), brother of Norma Shearer. Though Hollywood producer Jack L. Warner (of Warner Brothers) was Canadian-born, and Louis B. Mayer (of MGM) immigrated to Canada from Russia with his parents, both left Canada at too young an age for Canada to have left an imprint on their consciousnesses. However, producer Al Christie (1886-1951)

became a rival to Mack Sennett in Hollywood after 1914 and producer Ernest Shipman had considerable success as an independent film producer following a career as a theatrical promoter in Canada and the U.S.

From 1914 to 1922 the Canadian film industry experienced its first major period of growth when about twenty feature-length dramas were produced (including seven by Ernest Shipman). Though some of the people involved (especially lead performers and directors) were American, many were Canadian, and these productions allowed them their first real experience in the film industry. This period also saw the (short-lived) return of a few expatriates, including producer Ernest Shipman; his then wife, the actress/writer/director Nell Shipman—one of the world's first women film makers; director Henry MacRae, who later became famous in Hollywood as 'king of the serial makers'; and actresses Pauline Garon and Vivienne Osborne.

Though the feature-film industry in Canada collapsed in 1923, there remained sporadic production of film dramas through the 1920s and 1930s alongside continuing production of short films by government agencies and commercial companies. This, together with a growth in theatrical activity, effectively altered the pattern of emigration by artists. Cinematographers and other technicians now tended to remain in Canada, while performers, producers, and directors who went abroad tended to do so after at least some training or experience in Canada—even if that hardly gave them an established reputation. Among them were Robert Beatty (b. 1909) who often played American roles in British films; Raymond Burr (b. 1917), who played many Hollywood villains before achieving fame as Perry Mason in the television series of that name; Western star Rod Cameron (b. Nathon Cox, 1910); comic actor Jack Carson (1910-63); exotic actress Yvonne de Carlo (b. Peggy Yvonne Middleton, 1922); Fifi d'Orsay (b. 1907); character actor Douglas Dumbrille (b. 1890); comedian Jonathon Hale; Barbara Kent (b. 1908), featured Hollywood actress of the 1930s; writer and character actor Gene Lockhart (1891-1957); Raymond Lovell (1900-53), who played numerous stage and screen villains in Britain; Wilfrid Lucas (1871-1940); stage and screen performer David Manners (b. Rauff de Ryther Duan Acklom, 1901); Raymond MAS-

SEY (1896-1983), who worked in both Britain and Hollywood in roles from Sherlock Holmes to Abraham Lincoln; cabaret singer and occasional screen actress Helen Morgan (1900-41); Douglass Montgomery (1908-66), who worked on both stage and screen in Britain and the U.S.; former child stage star, then Hollywood actress, Ann Rutherford (b. 1920); character actress Madeleine Sherwood (b. 1926); Jay Silverheels (1920-85), the Canadian Indian actor who appeared in many Westerns but was best known for his role as Tonto in the 'Lone Ranger' movies; stage and occasional film actor Joseph Wiseman (b. 1919); and Donald Woods (b. 1906), who played lead roles in minor Hollywood films of the 1930s and 1940s. Some of the most famous Canadian-born Hollywood stars of this period cannot be truly considered 'expatriates', since they were raised and educated in the U.S.: Deanna Durbin (b. Edna Mae Durbin, 1921), whose family moved to California in 1922; Glenn Ford (b. Gwyllyn Samuel Newton Ford, 1916), who grew up in Santa Monica; John Ireland (b. 1915), who moved with his family as a child to the U.S.; Ruby Keeler (b. Ethel Keeler, 1910), whose family moved to New York in 1913; director Mark Robson (b. 1913), who was educated in California; and Alexis Smith (b. 1921) and Fay Wray (b. 1907), who were both educated at Hollywood high schools. In addition, director Edward Dmytryk (b. 1908) ran away from home to the U.S. at the age of fourteen.

The pattern of emigration continued and even intensified in the forties, fifties, and sixties, though it became increasingly true that those leaving Canada already had well-established reputations. In the 1940s and 1950s such reputations had been developed in Canadian RADIO DRAMA; in later years they were increasingly developed in Canadian TELEVISION DRAMA and in the theatre. The reasons for emigration at this time were not simply to find work on stage and screen that was unavailable in Canada, but to seek better financial rewards and wider career opportunities—not to mention the potential for international stardom. Lorne GREENE (1915-87) notably followed this pattern. Others departing in this period to settle permanently abroad include stage and screen actors Arthur Hill (b. 1922), Christopher PLUMMER (b. 1927), and William SHATNER (b. 1931); and the less well-known Lee Patterson (b. 1929),

who played lead roles in many minor British and U.S. films after 1951.

Sydney Newman (b. 1917), former CBC supervisor of TV dramas and National Film Board producer, had a major influence on British TV drama between 1958 and 1968; he returned to Canada in 1970. Fletcher Markle (b. 1921), an influential CBC radio drama producer and writer, played a similar role in relation to U.S. television dramas in the early 1950s; he also directed several Hollywood features before returning to Canada as producer and host of CBC's 'Telescope'. Other expatriate directors with initial Canadian television experience include Sidney Furie (b. 1933), who also directed two Canadian feature films in the late 1950s before moving to Britain; Norman Jewison (b. 1926), who produced CBC variety programs before moving to Hollywood and who continues to direct U.S. films while residing mainly in Canada; Ted Kotcheff (b. 1931) and Silvio Narrizzano (b. 1925), who both worked in British TV dramas and who continue to work abroad, though both have also directed Canadian feature films; Daryl Duke (b. 1930), who moved to Hollywood in 1970 and continues to direct U.S. films while residing in Canada; and three producer/directors for CBC's 'Festival'—Harvey Hart (b. 1928), who moved to Hollywood in 1963 and directed feature and TV dramas before returning to Canada in 1970; Arthur Hiller (b. 1924); and Eric Till (b. 1929), who has directed features in Canada, Britain, and the U.S. Daniel Petrie (b. 1920) is another Canadian-born director who gained stage and television experience before directing Hollywood features.

Producer/director Ivan Reitman (b. 1947) (*Ghostbusters*) and director Clay Borris (b. 1950) (*Alligator Shoes*) are more recent expatriates. Other Canadians in Hollywood include writers Al Rogers (b. 1936), David Brandes (b. 1944), and Bernard SLADE (b. 1930), and director Steven Stern (b. 1937). Alvin Rakoff (b. 1937) has worked primarily in British TV ('Paradise Postponed'), but has also directed features in Canada.

Expatriate performers in recent decades represent something of a variation in earlier patterns, since many of them have either returned to Canada after time spent abroad or have continued to work in Canadian theatre, television, and film. Though the following list is far from exhaustive, they include: Lloyd Bochner, Geneviève Bujold, Barbara

CHILCOTT, Susan Clark, Elizabeth Cole, Anne Collings, Larry Dane, James Doohan, Don Franks, David Greene, Peter Kastner, Margot Kidder, Larry Mann, Barry Morse, Kate REID, Donnelly Rhodes, Michael Sarrazin, Helen Shaver, Donald SUTHERLAND, John Vernon, and Austin Willis. Over the years these actors, together with others mentioned above, have formed a clearly defined Canadian 'colony' in Hollywood.

In the 1980s the earlier patterns of emigration have continued. Michael J. Fox and Shannon Tweed gained their initial reputations in Hollywood. Among those who first gained experience and a reputation in Canada and then went on to Hollywood are comedians Dan Ackroyd, John Candy, Martin Short, Eugene Levy, and others who worked with Second City and 'SCTV' and who moved on to either 'Saturday Night Live' and then Hollywood, or directly to Hollywood from 'SCTV'. PETER MORRIS

Mountain Playhouse. This English-language summer theatre—the old Toboggan and Ski Club on the western slopes of Montreal's Mount Royal, converted into a 200-seat proscenium auditorium—flourished from 1950 to 1961. Run during its first season by the Canadian Art Theatre, it produced popular comedies typical of the 'Straw Hat' circuit in the U.S. that were chosen by founder Joy Thomson and her assistant Norma SPRINGFORD. They began with Garson Kanin's *Born Yesterday*, but in the first season also produced Mazo de la Roche's *Whiteoaks* with Amelia HALL as Adeline and Christopher PLUMMER as Finch. Other leading Canadian actors—Jack CRELEY, Barry Morse, Jane MALLETT, Budd Knapp, and Corinne Conley, among others—appeared regularly in starring roles, and promising young Montreal actors were cast in supporting roles. When Thomson retired in 1951 Norma Springford carried on as producing director until 1961. The charm of the setting, overlooking Beaver Lake, the theatre's close relationship with the nearby Open-Air Theatre, which produced Shakespeare *al fresco* as an added inducement to make the excursion up the mountain, and the proximity of both theatres to a large urban audience help to explain the box-office success of the Mountain Playhouse; in addition, the standard of production was high

compared to that of other summer theatres of the period.

See also SUMMER STOCK.

HERBERT WHITTAKER

Mulcahy, Sean (b. 1930). Born and educated in Ireland, he first acted professionally at the age of fourteen. He studied privately with the famous Irish actor W.G. Fay, best known for his work with the fledgeling Abbey Theatre. After service with the Royal Air Force, Mulcahy spent three years with the Cheltenham Repertory Theatre before immigrating to Canada in 1957. Following some years of radio and television work, he became associate director from 1963 to 1965 of the SHAW FESTIVAL where his 1964 production of Sean O'Casey's *Shadow of a Gunman* won acclaim. He was artistic director of Montreal's Instant Theatre (1964-6), Edmonton's CITADEL THEATRE (1968-73), St Catharines' Press Theatre (1974-6), and associate director of Fredericton's Beaverbrook Playhouse (1966-7). In 1988 he was appointed artistic director of the Stephenville Festival, Nfld.

A gifted actor, Mulcahy favours Shaw, O'Casey, Brian Friel, and Hugh Leonard, whose plays he has frequently directed—especially at Halifax's NEPTUNE THEATRE and Saskatoon's 25TH STREET THEATRE. He won an ACTRA Nellie Award in 1986 for his role in the CBC-TV production of Friel's *Philadelphia, Here I Come!* Mulcahy has appeared in several films, including *Stepdance* and *Educating Rita*. EUGENE BENSON

Mulgrave Road Co-op Theatre. Founded in 1977 in the town of Mulgrave, N.S., by Robbie O'Neill, Michael Fahey, Gay Hauser, and Wendell Smith, and registered as a legal co-op in 1978 as The Mulgrave Road Co-op Theatre Company, it is a small, collectively run touring company dedicated to the production of new Nova Scotian plays, with special emphasis on plays about Guysborough County and the province's northeast. The Co-op moved to the town of Guysborough in 1979, and in 1985 changed its name to the Mulgrave Road Co-op Theatre. It owns no performance facility, opening each of its shows in community or parish halls, and touring throughout the county, Nova Scotia, the Maritimes, and beyond.

While the direction of the company is collective, it was decided in 1983 that artistic directors would be elected annually from among the membership to implement policies on the group's behalf. Ed McKenna has been full-time general manager of the company since 1978.

Mulgrave Road has developed and produced more than twenty scripts since *The Mulgrave Road Show* opened on 13 July 1977, including such other collectives as *Let's Play Fish*, 1978, *One on the Way*, 1980, and *Another Story*, 1982; collectives with writers, such as *The Coady Co-op Show*, 1979, with Christopher HEIDE, *Bring Back Don Messer*, 1980, also with Heide, *Occupational Hazards*, 1985, with Lesley Choyce and Wendy Lill, and *A Child is Crying on the Stairs*, 1985, with Nanette Cormier; annual Christmas shows since 1980; and, since 1983, fully scripted plays such as Mary Vingoe's *Holy Ghosters*, 1983, Robbie O'Neill's *In My Father's Footsteps*, 1984, Cindy Cowan's *Spooks: The Mystery of Caledonia Mills*, 1984, *A Woman From the Sea*, 1986, and *Beinn Bhreagh*, 1986, and Robert Kroll's *Cry for the Moon*, 1986. The company also won praise for its 1982 collective stage adaptation of Alistair MacLeod's stories *The Lost Salt Gift of Blood*, and for its production of Robbie O'Neill's one-man show, *Tighten the Traces/Haul in the Reins*, which toured in Canada and abroad between 1981 and 1985.

The company's productions are rooted for the most part in popular theatre traditions such as minstrel shows and *commedia* as well as the story-telling and musical traditions of the region, and they deal with social and cultural issues of particular significance to rural Nova Scotia audiences.

See Richard Paul Knowles, 'The Mulgrave Road Co-op: Theatre and the Community in Guysborough County, N.S.', *Canadian Drama*, 12 (1986); see also COLLECTIVE CREATION. RICHARD PAUL KNOWLES

Multicultural Theatre. Several common traits—particularly the wish to preserve the culture and language of the mother country and to instil a sense of community ties—link early twentieth-century ethnic theatre groups (or 'multicultural' groups, as they are termed today) formed by new immigrants with later ones formed after the Second World War. Early ethnic theatre groups rarely moved beyond their community core, or saw their dramatic presentations as anything other than enjoyable offerings for their own immediate circles. Later groups, attempting to draw wider audiences, were able to present more sophisticated entertainment, largely because many professional artists immigrated to Canada after the Second World War. Moreover, political and socialist drama, which had reached its peak in the 1930s, gave way to a more traditional theatrical repertoire better suited to the post-Depression generation.

This progression is illustrated particularly well in the theatre of the Ukrainians, Hungarians, and Finns, all of whom inherited a strong amateur tradition from their homelands. Ukrainian theatre began in Canada as early as 1906 in the mining areas of the Sudbury Basin and in Manitoba, which was the main centre of Ukrainian dramatic activity in the early days of settlement in Canada. The steady development of Ukrainian theatre continued through the 1930s and 1940s, diminishing somewhat after the war. Today a handful of Ukrainian companies engage in more specialized dramatic work. The Canadian Ukrainian Opera Association (CUOA, formed in 1974) produces spectacular operas, such as *Natalka Poltavka* at Toronto's MacMillan Theatre in 1984, featuring international performers along with groups such as the Canadian Ukrainian Opera Chorus and the Vesnianka Dance Ensemble. The CUOA has also appeared in gala concerts at Massey Hall, Roy Thomson Hall, Hamilton Place, and Carnegie Hall, New York. Ukrainian children's theatre has become an important educational tool in both Winnipeg and Edmonton where the Ukrainian Story Theatre for Children, founded in 1979, takes its content from Ukrainian folklore and integrates Ukrainian and English. In Toronto, productions of the Ukrainian Dramatic Ensemble 'Zahrava', founded in 1956, still attract a loyal following.

Hungarian theatre in Ontario experienced a flurry of activity in the 1930s with major presentations organized by the Catholic Circle and by Hungarian left-wing organizations in Toronto. In the mid-1950s Sàndor Kertész, a professional actor and director for many years in his native Budapest, immigrated to Canada and formed the Hungarian Art Theatre in Toronto in 1958. Although the audience has dwindled, the company is still producing two shows yearly and remains the

Multicultural Theatre

only Hungarian theatre group in North America. Kertész's repertoire is varied and has included the operettas of Emmerich Kalman, Franz Lehar, Johann Strauss, and Franz Schubert, the occasional modern European drama such as Peter Müller's *Gloomy Sunday*, and the comedies of Neil Simon and Bernard SLADE translated into Hungarian.

The community support given to Finnish theatre through the Depression until the present day has resulted in one of the strongest surviving ethnic theatres in the country. The venerable Finnish Social Club, founded in 1932, which still produces four shows a year from its own community hall in Scarborough, Ont., is a testament to the Finns' historic love of theatre. Their repertoire has contained an interesting cross-section of Canadian, British, American, and Finnish drama, including Gratien GÉLINAS's *Bousille and the Just* and *The Heiress* (based on Henry James' *Washington Square*), as well as plays by the Finnish playwright Mika Waltari. Other Finnish theatre groups are active in Vancouver, Sault St Marie, Sudbury, and Thunder Bay.

While Toronto's once vibrant Italian theatre companies—Piccolo Teatro (1949-76), founded by Bruno Mesaglio, and La Compagnia dei Giovani (1969-82), founded by Alberto di Giovani—no longer exist, Italian theatre is still represented by Montreal's excellent Le Maschere, founded in 1974. The group presents only one production a year, but its six-month rehearsal period testifies to the care and quality of its shows. For the fiftieth anniversary of Luigi Pirandello's death (1986) the company's splendid presentation of *Sei personaggi in cerca d'autore* (*Six Characters in Search of an Author*) represented Quebec in the National Multicultural Festival held in Toronto. An important new voice in Montreal's multicultural scene is that of Marco Micone, whose plays speak forcefully about the Italian immigrant experience. Under the influence of Bertolt Brecht and Dario Fo, Micone's realistic works have met with considerable success in both the original French and in English translation. Micone's first play, *Gens du Silence*, was presented as staged readings before its full production at La Licorne Theatre in 1983 and again in 1984 by La Manufacture theatre company. An English version, *Voiceless People*, was presented in 1986 by the Italian Cultural Institute in Vancouver. Micone's next play,

Addolorata, about a young Italian girl trying to free herself from her father's authority, was a box-office success at La Licorne in 1983. It has also been translated into English.

Toronto's Latvian D.V. Theatre Company—active for over thirty years—uses theatre as a teaching vehicle for the Latvian language, taking advantage of the drama groups in Toronto's Latvian high school as well as conducting its own student theatre. The group has toured to Latvian communities in Canada and the U.S. and presents a mixed program of four to five plays a year, ranging from the classical to the avant-garde.

Hamilton's Lithuanian drama group, Aukuras, was founded by Elena Kudaba, who has been producing plays and concert programs since 1950, a record achieved by no other North American Lithuanian theatre company. The Toronto Lithuanian drama group, Aitvaras, while younger (1971), has toured to cities in the American midwest, earning awards at the Lithuanian Theatre Festival in Chicago.

Equally distinguished is the Yiddish Theatre, founded in Montreal in 1956 by Dora WASSERMAN. She produces two plays a year at the SAIDYE BRONFMAN CENTRE, the company's home since the early 1970s. Other contemporary Jewish theatres present only English-language productions that reflect a Jewish consciousness, sensitivity, and flavour. They include the Jewish Heritage Theatre, founded in 1972 in Vancouver, which presents plays such as Isaac Bashevis Singer's *Yentl* and the Judd Woldin musical *Petticoat Lane*, and the Leah Posluns Theatre, founded in 1977 by the Jewish Community Centre in North York, Ont. Some of the outstanding productions seen in the Leah Posluns' annual five-play subscription series include the Canadian première of William Gibson's *Golda* in 1978, the world première of Eric Blau's *Dori*, 1985—a musical based on the life of Theodore Herzl, the founder of modern Zionism—and *Raisins and Almonds*, a specially commissioned musical adaptation of Fredelle Bruselle Maynard's delicate novel of prairie life, produced in 1984.

Montreal's Deutsches Theater (formerly the German Academy Theatre, founded in 1952 by Sasha Djabadary) was one of the theatre groups that occupied the Montreal International Theatre, La POUDRIÈRE, specifically set up in 1958 to present multicultural theatre. When La Poudrière encountered financial difficulties in 1976, the group took the name of Deutsches Theater and has since presented two productions yearly at Montreal's CENTAUR THEATRE, in addition to touring across Canada and to Germany. Among their classical and contemporary fare are plays by Brecht, Friedrich Dürrenmatt, Max Frisch, Ferenc Molnár, Goethe, Nikolai Gogol, and Peter Handke. The Deutsches Theater of Toronto, which experienced a rebirth in 1979 when it reached out into the community for performers from its base at the Univ. of Toronto German Dept., has produced (in German) such plays as *It Was the Lark* (in 1984), a comedy by Israeli playwright Ehpraim Kishon about Romeo and Juliet thirty years later, Peter Weiss's *Marat/Sade* (in 1980), and a challenging production of Christian Dietrich Grabbe's nineteenth-century satire, *Wit, Satire, Irony and Deeper Meaning*. Other established German theatre groups are Winnipeg's Deutsche Bühne, founded in 1959, which produces mainly comedies, the German Theatre of Vancouver (founded in 1971), whose mandate is to introduce German authors to Canadian audiences, and the Winnipeg Mennonite Theatre (founded in 1972), which produces classics and large-scale operas such as Puccini's *Gianni Schicchi*, presented at the Warehouse Theatre during the 1981 Manitoba Multicultural Theatre Association annual festival, and the little-known *Galileo* by German composer G. Dahlwitz.

While Anglo-Irish drama is no stranger to Canadian professional stages, there are also several Irish theatre groups whose goal is to preserve their Gaelic heritage, among them Edmonton's Shamrock Players, Winnipeg's Tara Players, British Columbia's Stage Eireann Dramatic Society, the Toronto Irish Players, and the Irish Newfoundland Association.

Although the majority of Canadian ethnic theatre companies perform western-style drama, the Chinese United Dramatic Society of Toronto has been performing Cantonese opera since 1933. Its elaborate productions are presented twice yearly and feature lavish costumes, designed and made in Hong Kong, and professional actors brought from the U.S. and Hong Kong to augment the mainly amateur (but highly skilled) local casts. Other Chinese opera societies exist in Montreal and Vancouver.

Black theatre groups have existed since the early nineteenth century in Vancouver and Halifax and in small communities, such as Ontario's North Buxton and Amherstburg. The first major breakthrough, however, occurred in 1942 in Montreal with the Negro Theatre Guild's production of Marc Connolly's *The Green Pastures*, produced by Don A. Haldane with stage design by Herbert WHITTAKER. The show was first produced at Victoria Hall, then transferred to HER MAJESTY'S THEATRE. In 1949 the group's production of Eugene O'Neill's *The Emperor Jones* won a DOMINION DRAMA FESTIVAL best-actor award for Percy Rodriguez, who is now a respected Hollywood film actor.

The late 1960s and early 1970s saw the formation of several black theatre companies. One of the first was Montreal's Black Theatre Workshop, which devoted itself both to presenting the experiences of blacks living in a predominantly white society and to promoting black playwrights and artists. Their première production was Loris Elliott's *How Now Black Man?* in 1968 at the Centaur Theatre. In addition to presenting new and contemporary Canadian works, such as Hector Bunyan's stinging drama *Prodigals in a Promised Land* (which opened at Toronto's THEATRE PASSE MURAILLE in 1982), the now-professional company also presents non-Canadian plays such as Joseph A. Walker's *The River Niger* and David Westheimer's *My Sweet Charlie*. Two other noteworthy black theatre companies are Toronto's Theatre Fountainhead, founded in 1974 by Jeff Henry, and Black Theatre Canada, founded in 1973 by Vera Cudjoe. Following Henry's intention to develop and produce the works of black playwrights, his professional company has performed the works of Wole Soyinka, Errol Sitahel, and Henry's own play, *Africa in the Caribbean*. More recent productions have included the delightful *Cold Snap* in 1983 written by prairie-born Linda Ghan, which deals with the dilemma of a West Indian immigrant adjusting to Canadian life; the musical fantasy *The Obeah Man*, produced in 1985, written by and starring Richard Keens-Douglas in a role that won him a Dora nomination; and Athol Fugard's *The Blood Knot* in 1986. Cudjoe's goal in pioneering black theatre in Toronto was to share the culture of black people with the larger community. To this end BTC has taken productions into the schools and has run successful workshops. BTC's theatrical milestones have

Multicultural Theatre

Robin Breon's The African Roscius, Black Theatre Canada, *Toronto, 1987, with Doug Kier and Michael Danso*

included many new works, among them *School's Out*, which introduced Jamaican playwright Trevor Rhone to Canada; Peter Robinson's *Dem Two in Canada* in 1979; and Daniel Caudiron's multi-ethnic foray into the 'new' Toronto, *More About Me* in 1979. BTC's recent productions have included Leon Bibb's *One More Stop on the Freedom Train*, a musical about the early underground-railroad period in Ontario. Produced in Toronto in 1984, it was revived in 1985, toured the country, and played at Vancouver's Expo '86 in the Canada Pavilion. Lisa Evans' *Under Exposure*, a play about South Africa, was mounted as part of the 1986 Arts Against Apartheid Festival. Financial difficulties caused Black Theatre Canada to suspend operations in 1988. Two other interesting black theatre companies are Winnipeg's Caribbean Theatre Workshop, which generally produces the works of new West Indian playwrights, and the only black theatre company in the Atlantic provinces, New Brunswick's 'Kwacha' (Zambian for 'Dawn of a New Day'), incorporated in 1984 in Saint John under the artistic direction of Walter Borden. Borden's company opened with a 1927 gospel musical, *God's Trombones*, by James Weldon Johnson. *Tight Rope Time*, Borden's own work about the quest of black people for a place in the Canadian mosaic, won critical acclaim at the 1984 National Multicultural Theatre Festival in St John's, Nfld.

The New Czech Theatre in Toronto, founded in 1970, has an annual subscription season of six productions, ranging from Czech classics to adaptations of contemporary American classics. Montreal has two energetic Hispanic companies: the Teatro Valle Inclàn, founded in 1974, and the Théâtre Latino-americain Horizontes founded in 1977, dedicated to performing South American plays, many of a political nature, in Spanish, French, and English. The latter group represented Canada in the Latin American Theatre Festival in Nicaragua in June 1983, and at the International Festival of Havana, Cuba, in 1984. The company also organized the Montreal Festival Latino 86, an extension of Joseph Papp's Festival Latino in New York.

Newer groups that stand out because of their youth and singlemindedness are Winnipeg's Gujuarti East Indian theatre group (the only East Indian one in North America); Toronto's Canasian Artists Group, whose two productions at TORONTO FREE THEATRE, Rick Shiomi's *Yellow Fever* in 1983 and David Henry Hwang's *F.O.B.* (Fresh Off the Boat) in 1984, were both well received; the Toronto Jewish Theatre, founded in 1983, which organized the annual Jewish Theatre Festival and appeared at Expo '86; and the Carlos Bulosan Cultural Workshop in Toronto. While the Workshop engages in a number of activities, a highlight of their 1986 year was a presentation of the Philippine Educational Theater Association's production of *An Oath to Freedom*, a COLLECTIVE CREATION that dramatizes the last twenty years of social and political conditions under the Marcos regime.

In recent years several plays that premièred in a multicultural community setting have gone on to professional productions and wider audiences. The Ukrainian plays of Ted GALAY, for example, have received successful professional productions in Toronto and Winnipeg, and Nika Rylski's engaging comedy revue, *Just a Commedia*, about growing up in Ukrainian Canada, toured the country and went to Expo '86 in Vancouver after its première at the St Vladimir Institute, Toronto, in 1984.

The first provincial multicultural theatre association was founded in Ontario in 1970, and OMTA remains the oldest and largest of the provincial theatre associations, representing sixty multilingual companies. In 1985 the

Toronto Operetta Theatre, a professional company dedicated to the production of European operettas, was formed as a subsidiary of the OMTA. Two full-scale productions have since been presented: Franz Lehar's *The Count of Luxembourg* in 1985, and Emmerich Kalman's *Countess Maritza* in 1986. The National Multicultural Theatre Association (NMTA) was founded in 1975 and now comprises some 350 community theatre groups, many of them French and English. The NMTA acts as liaison for its provincial associations, disseminating ideas and news, promoting the exchange of productions, personnel, and material, and publishing a newsletter, *Multicultural Theatre News*. The annual NMTA Theatre Festival is held in a different province each year and is the only national event of its kind in Canada. The NMTA also organizes national playwriting competitions through which it searches for children's plays dealing with tolerance, co-operation, and multiculturalism. Since 1979 the NMTA has officially represented Canadian amateur theatre, replacing the defunct Theatre Canada. In addition, the Association sponsored Canada's first Indigenous Theatre Celebration in 1980, and in 1983 organized the 'World Theatre Mosaic' in Calgary, the first international community-theatre festival ever held in Canada.

JENIVA BERGER

Mummers Troupe, The. Founded in 1972 by Christopher BROOKES, Lynne Lunde, and John Doyle, this Newfoundland ALTERNATE THEATRE company adopted a collective approach that concentrated on presenting socio-political issues relevant to the people of Newfoundland and Labrador, in unconventional spaces such as shopping malls and union halls. From 1972 to 1975 (when the troupe received Canada Council funding) it was subsidized by various *ad hoc* grants and by Brookes (who was artist-in-residence with Memorial University's Arts Extension program).

The inaugural show of the Mummers Troupe was a revival of the traditional Newfoundland Mummer play of St George, which had been played into the early twentieth century. The 1973 production of *Gros Mourn*—which explored the dilemma of the residents of the small village of Sally's Cove who were being resettled by Parks Canada to make room for the national park Gros Morne—

was, however, overtly political. The company developed a documentary style that incorporated local dialogue and imagery to present the problems of other Newfoundland communities: COLLECTIVE CREATIONs such as *Buchans: A Mining Town*, 1974; *Dying Hard*, 1975; *IWA Loggers Strike*, 1975; *Silakepat Kissiane: Weather Permitting*, 1977; and, perhaps their most controversial, *They Club Seals, Don't They?*, 1978. In their determined exploration of indigenous Newfoundland material through theatrical means, the Mummers created over twenty shows, ranging from agit-prop presentations on economic and social injustice to musical fantasy.

In 1978 a group of actors broke away from the Mummers Troupe to form Rising Tide Theatre. Controversy broke out in 1979 over Brookes's management, and he resigned in 1980. When the Mummers closed in 1982 it had firmly established itself as the most vital and productive Newfoundland theatre company of its time.

See Chris Brookes, *A Public Nuisance. A History of the Mummers Troupe* (1988) and Alan Filewod, 'The Life and Death of the Mummers Troupe', *The Proceedings of the Theatre in Atlantic Canada Symposium* (1988), ed. Richard Paul Knowles. See also POLITICAL AND POPULAR THEATRE.   C.J. SKINNER

Murphy, Arthur Lister (1906–85). Born in Dominion, Cape Breton Island, N.S., Murphy's life-long interest in theatre was sparked in the 1920s by the English companies that toured Halifax, where he was a medical student at Dalhousie University. Returning to Halifax in 1935 after completing his residency at Montreal General Hospital, he established his writing career, preparing radio scripts for a local children's show, 'Cousin Henry'. In the 1950s he also wrote plays for television, including *The Death Around Us* (CBC, 1957), about an antibiotic-resistant epidemic in a hospital. While pursuing a busy medical career, Murphy also wrote scripts for the 'Ben Casey' and 'Dr. Kildare' TV series on American networks. Realizing in the late 1950s that Canadian playwrights had little chance of production, he chaired a Theatre Feasibility Committee for the city of Halifax and served as Founding President and Director of the NEPTUNE THEATRE Foundation. His community status and theatrical knowledge helped to overcome all obstacles to the new theatre. Four of Murphy's plays—*The*

Diary of a Scoundrel, *The Sleeping Bag*, *Charlie*, and *Tiger! Tiger!*—were produced at Neptune during its first seven seasons. His other stage plays include *The First Falls on Monday*, *A Virus Called Clarence*, *The Breadwinner* (1979), *To The Editor: Sir* (1984), *You'll Be Calling Me Michael* (1984), *Keeper of the Gold* (1975), and *Thy Sons Command*. (Texts of his plays are available from Dramatists' Co-Op of Nova Scotia.) After retiring from medicine, Murphy taught playwriting at Dalhousie University until his death.

PATRICK B. O'NEILL

Murrell, John (b. 1945). Born in Texas, Murrell was raised in the western United States. He received a BFA from Southwestern Univ., Georgetown, Texas (1966) and a B.Ed. from the Univ. of Calgary (1969). After graduation he worked for some years as a teacher, but increasingly dedicated himself to writing. He has also worked as an actor, and occasionally directs plays. One of Canada's most literate and technically accomplished playwrights, he has been playwright-in-residence with ALBERTA THEATRE PROJECTS, Calgary (1975-6), an associate director with the STRATFORD FESTIVAL (1977-8), dramaturge at THEATRE CALGARY (1981-2), and head of the BANFF CENTRE SCHOOL OF FINE ARTS Playwrights Colony (1986). In Dec. 1988 he was appointed head of the Theatre Section of the Canada Council.

In 1975 Murrell won the Clifford E. Lee Playwriting Award, sponsored by the Univ. of Alberta, for *Power in the Blood*, which deals with a crisis in the life of a woman evangelist, and in 1976 Alberta Theatre Projects presented *A Great Noise, A Great Light*. Set in Alberta in 1937, the play views the political phenomenon of William Aberhart through the experience of a group of vagrants. Other early plays that received professional productions are *Haydn's Head*, 1973, *Teaser* (with Kenneth Dyba), 1975, and *Arena*, 1975. All five remain unpublished.

Murrell came to the attention of eastern Canada, and subsequently to international fame, with *Memoir* (1978). Having won a prize in a Univ. of Regina playwriting competition, it was produced at the Guelph Spring Festival, Ont., in May 1977. The play is technically very simple: it has one setting and two characters, the old and dying Sarah Bernhardt and her absurdly devoted amanuensis, Georges Pitou. The action concerns

the determined efforts of the aged actress to continue her memoirs. A meticulous and painstaking writer, Murrell worked on the play for four years, slowly reducing a drama that covered Bernhardt's career to a concentrated two-act piece dealing with the end of her life. Siobhan McKenna, who created the role of Sarah, with Gerard Parkes as her secretary, Pitou, took the play to successful productions in Dublin (1977) and London, England (1978). It has since been produced throughout Canada, on CBC radio in 1980, has been translated into many languages, published in German (1979) and in French (1983), and performed in over twenty-five countries. The most outstanding foreign production has been of the French version by the actor and director Georges Wilson: *Sarah et le cri de la langouste* (1982). This one-act condensation of the original play ran in Paris for three years, with Delphine Seyrig, and Wilson himself as Pitou; the production toured to the Edinburgh Festival in 1984.

If the Bernhardt legend partly explains the international popularity of *Memoir*, the play also appeals as a quietly moving and comic episode. Humour and emotional truth are also apparent in Murrell's next major play, *WAITING FOR THE PARADE* (1980), another thorough success. Subsequently Murrell turned his attention for some years to translations, and to projects that did not lead to finished scripts (including an adaptation, for Stratford, of John Ford's *'Tis Pity She's a Whore*). His knowledge of French and Italian, fostered by his love of opera, has allowed him to translate directly Machiavelli's *Mandragola* (Theatre Calgary, 1978), Racine's *Bajazet* (TARRAGON THEATRE, Toronto, 1979), and Sardou's *Divorçons* (Theatre Calgary, 1983); but in the case of Chekhov, one of his favourite writers, Murrell worked from a literal translation, aided by dictionaries. *Uncle Vanya* (1978) was produced at Stratford in 1978, and *The Seagull* in 1980. In 1983 his version of Ibsen's *Bygmester Solness, Master Builder*, was produced at Tarragon, and his version of Sophocles' *Oedipus the King* was acted at Stratford in 1988.

In 1982 Murrell's next major play, *Farther West* (1986), was produced by Theatre Calgary, directed by Robin PHILLIPS, with Martha HENRY as May Buchanan. Here Murrell moves from the quieter, atmospheric style of some of his earlier work to a story of violence and sexual obsession, but without abandon-

Sketch by Cameron Porteous of costumes for John Murrell's
Farther West, *Tarragon Theatre, Toronto, 1986*

ing his characteristic wit and sense of rhythm. The westward drift of the independent-minded prostitute May ends in horrific scenes of murder and mutilation, which perhaps place too great a strain on modern stage technique. It won the CHALMERS Award in 1986. Murrell followed this play with *New World* (1986), again directed by Phillips, produced in Ottawa in 1984 and Toronto in 1985. It is a rather bitter comedy, with ironic allusion to Shakespeare's *The Tempest* and its sea-born blessing of a new start in life. Murrell wrote the play as an essay in Chekhovian style, but the brittle hysteria of its characters has rather more affinity with another such essay, Shaw's *Heartbreak House*. Murrell's latest play, *October*, dramatising a meeting between Eleonora Duse and Isadora Duncan, was produced at Tarragon in Nov. 1988, directed by the playwright. JOHN H. ASTINGTON

Musical Theatre. The first theatrical performance in Canada (in 1606)—Marc LESCARBOT's *Le THÉÂTRE DE NEPTUNE EN LA NOUVELLE-FRANCE*—was a masque with music; and one of the rare Canadian works performed in Quebec during the eighteenth century (1790), Joseph QUESNEL's *COLAS ET COLINETTE*, was an operetta. Most Canadian plays written for the stage in the nineteenth century were musical burlesques—parodies with original lyrics set to borrowed tunes, such as William H. FULLER's *H.M.S. Parliament*, a topical satire on Canadian government set to the pirated music of Arthur Sullivan.

Canadians have excelled at writing revues, usually satirical programs of songs and skits like those created by the DUMBELLS, the famous First World War soldier entertainers who continued to perform through the 1920s. This originally all-male troupe, under the direction of Merton Plunkett and Jack McClaren, triumphed on Broadway in 1921 with *Biff, Bing, Bang*. At the beginning of the Second World War, a few of the Dumbells regrouped to perform in *Chin Up* and established the model for the service shows—the ARMY SHOW, the NAVY SHOW, and the RCAF *BLACKOUTS*—that gave professional experience to entertainers such as Blanche Lund and Alan LUND, Johnny Wayne, and Frank Shuster.

More intimate satirical revues developed from informal shows in private clubs. Toronto's ARTS AND LETTERS CLUB, for example, presented an annual Spring Revue (organized by Napier Moore) beginning in 1930. More biting musical satires of the 1930s—*We Beg to Differ* in Montreal and the *Beer and Skits* evenings in Winnipeg—played in workers' clubs. Gratien GÉLINAS's annual FRIDOLINONS revues entertained Quebec audiences from 1938 to 1946 with the views of a cocky kid in a Montreal Canadiens' hockey sweater. Canada's most celebrated revue, SPRING THAW, lasted twenty-four years and toured extensively. The original director, Mavor MOORE, set the pattern for its enduring success in the initial 1948 edition (produced by Toronto's NEW PLAY SOCIETY), mixing song and dance with low comedy and high satire, and emphasizing Canadian topics. Its greatest legacy was a generation of skilled performers that included Dave Broadfoot, Jack Duffy, Robert Goulet, Barbara HAMILTON, Don HARRON, Eric HOUSE, Rich Little, Jane MALLETT, and Toby ROBINS. *MY FUR LADY*, a 1957 McGill Univ. student show that toured Canada, was indebted to *Spring Thaw*; Galt MacDermot, who went on to compose the music for *Hair*, wrote songs for *My Fur Lady*. Other shows encouraged by the success of *Spring Thaw* include John Pratt's *There Goes Yesterday* and *One for the Road* (both on

Musical Theatre

tour, 1949-51); Araby LOCKHART's *Clap Hands* in Toronto (1958-62); *Bonfires of 1962*, at Winnipeg's MANITOBA THEATRE CENTRE; and *Squeeze* in Montreal during the early 1970s.

In the 1960s Toronto's Theatre in the Dell and Old Angelo's became the first of many licensed CABARETs in Canada to offer light, small-scale professional revues. Many were pastiches—of music of the 1940s in *Blue Champagne* at Anthony's Villa, Toronto, in Oct. 1976, for example—or collections—such as *Indigo*, Salomé Bey's history of Black songs, performed at the Basin Street Cabaret, Toronto, in Oct. 1978. Other Toronto revues concentrated on one composer (Roderick Cook's *Oh Coward* at the Theatre in the Dell, May, 1970) or one performer (Sneezy Waters' impersonation in *Hank Williams: The Show He Never Gave* at the Horseshoe Tavern, Dec. 1977). Successful contemporary all-Canadian revues have included Clémence Desrochers' *La grosse tête* (at Montreal's Le Patriote à Clémence in 1967) and *C'est pas une revue, c't'un show* (at Montreal's Le Dell, Feb. 1972); Sandra O'Neill's and Barbara Hamilton's *Sweet Reason* (Teller's Cage Dinner Theatre, Toronto, July 1975), a celebration of women's liberation; Jacqueline Barrette's *Heureux Celui qui meurt* (Le Patriote, 1976-7); Mark Shekter's and Charles Weir's ribald view of their hometown, *Toronto, Toronto* (Theatre in the Dell, Oct. 1980); the satirical guide to Montreal's anglophone community, *Anglo* (La Diligence, Montreal, 1984); and *Sex Tips for Modern Girls* (Touchstone Theatre at the Firehall Theatre, Vancouver, Feb. 1985), with music by John Sereda, which ran for over a year.

Most Canadian theatres favour Broadway musicals: Vancouver's Theatre Under the Stars (1940-63), Toronto's Melody Fair (1951-4), and the Rainbow Stage in Winnipeg (which adopted an all-musical format in 1966) have produced mainly imported musicals and operettas. *Hair* (in 1970) and *Cats* (1985-7) set new records for long runs in Toronto. Nevertheless Canadians continue to write musicals. Mavor Moore's *Sunshine Town* (based on Stephen LEACOCK's *Sunshine Sketches of a Little Town*) toured Canada in a New Play Society production in 1955, and Moore subsequently helped to found the CHARLOTTETOWN FESTIVAL in 1964, which his successor Alan Lund dedicated to Canadian musicals. Charlottetown's most widely

Mavor Moore's Sunshine Town, *New Play Society, 1955*

produced musical has been ANNE OF GREEN GABLES. Also popular were *Johnny Belinda* (an adaptation by John Fenwick and Mavor Moore of Elmer Harris's play); *The Legend of the Dumbells*, which used the troupe's original songs; *Fauntleroy*, adapted by Mavor Moore, using the music of American composer Johnny Burke; and the much-produced mini-musical for four performers, *Eight to the Bar* (by Joey Miller and Stephen Witkin). Charlottetown has been a showcase for some of Canada's most talented musical writers, such as Jim Betts (*On a Summer's Night*), David Warrack (*Windsor*), and Cliff Jones (*Kronborg: 1582*, a rock version of *Hamlet*). Jones's other Charlottetown shows include *The Rowdyman* (based on Gordon PINSENT's novel), *Babies, Alexandra—the Last Empress*, and the mini-musical *Love in the Back Seat*, which was later staged at the CITADEL THEATRE in Edmonton in Nov. 1980. The Citadel also premièred Jones's *Hey Marilyn!* (Jan. 1980), an opulent tribute to Marilyn Monroe.

The burgeoning theatrical scene across Canada in the 1960s and 1970s provided other outlets for original musicals in a range of styles. Dolores Claman—whose *Timber!* was one of the rare Canadian works performed at Theatre Under the Stars in Vancouver (summer 1952)—collaborated with Richard Morris and Ted Wood on *Mr. Scrooge*, an adaptation of Dickens' *A Christmas Carol*, for the CREST THEATRE (Dec. 1963). In Quebec *chansonnier* Claude Leveillée wrote several musicals for Marjolaine Hébert's summer THÉÂTRE DE MARJOLAINE in Eastman, Que., including *Doux Temps des amours* and *Il est un saison*, produced in 1964 and 1965 respectively. Jacques LANGUIRAND's and Gabriel CHARPENTIER's *Klondyke*, (THÉÂTRE DU NOUVEAU MONDE, Feb. 1965), provided a Brechtian view of the Gold Rush. Composer Morris Surdin collaborated with W.O. MITCHELL to turn a *Jake and the Kid* story into *Wild Rose* (Southern Alberta Jubilee Auditorium, June 1967) for Calgary's Centennial celebrations. Ann Mortifee wrote a folk-oriented score for George RYGA's ECSTASY OF RITA JOE (VANCOUVER PLAYHOUSE, Nov. 1967), and the West Coast rock band The Collectors transformed Ryga's *Grass and Wild Strawberries* (Vancouver Playhouse, Apr. 1969) into a joyous celebration. Tom HENDRY's and Stanley Silverman's *Satyricon* (STRATFORD FESTIVAL, June 1969), was a lush extravaganza directed by John HIRSCH. In May 1970 Toronto's Global Village staged Robert and Elizabeth Swerdlow's *Justine*, a long-running rock counterculture allegory, which, under the title *Love Me, Love My Children*, played Off-Broadway for seven months—the longest run for any Canadian musical. THEATRE CALGARY commissioned the science-fiction musical *Trip* (Jan. 1971) by Allan Rae, who later collaborated with Tink Robinson on *Festival!* for Theatre Calgary in Feb. 1977. Tom Hendry's and Steven Jack's *Gravediggers of 1942* (TORONTO FREE THEATRE, June 1973) effectively contrasted cheerful music with the horror of the Dieppe raid.

Recent Canadian musicals have been equally eclectic in style and subject matter. The much-performed Vancouver show *Last Call* (TAMAHNOUS THEATRE, Jan. 1982) by Morris Panych and Ken MacDonald featured a musical encounter between two survivors who meet in a post-nuclear cabaret. For Calgary's ALBERTA THEATRE PROJECTS William Skolnik collaborated with Paddy CAMPBELL on *Hoarse Muse*, about the legendary newspaper editor Bob Edwards (Mar. 1974). In Mar. 1975 Saskatoon's PERSEPHONE THEATRE had an unexpected hit with Ken MITCHELL's *Cruel Tears*, a prairie *Othello*, with music by the blue-grass band Humphrey and the Dumptrucks. The Manitoba Theatre Centre

premièred Patrick Rose's, Merv Campone's, and Richard OUZOUNIAN's *Jubalay* (May 1974), a revue-like 'entertainment in song' that later played in revised form across Canada and in New York under the title *A Bistro Car on the C.N.R.* MAGNUS THEATRE produced two Paul Ledoux and David Young musicals: *I Love You, Anne Murray* (Apr. 1984) (later retitled *Love is Strange*) about a farmer obsessed with a famous singer; and *Fire* (Dec. 1986), which juxtaposes rock-and-roll music and fundamentalist religion. George F. WALKER's and John Roby's *Rumours of our Death* (FACTORY THEATRE Lab, Jan. 1980) is a bizarre, almost punk, comedy, and Phil Schreibman's, Gordon Stobbe's, and Nancy White's *I Wanna Die in Ruby Red Tap Shoes* (NDWT, Sept. 1976) provided a song-and-dance perspective on Canadian theatre. Steven Bush's and Allen Booth's *Life on the Line* (produced by the Mixed Company at Toronto's YOUNG PEOPLE'S THEATRE in Apr. 1983), a biting new-wave comment on unemployment, contrasts with the sentimentality of Joey Miller's and Grahame Woods' musical adaptation of Gordon Pinsent's *A Gift to Last* at YPT in Dec. 1986 (after a summer tryout at Barrie's Gryphon Theatre).

Montreal's Théâtre du Nouveau Monde produced Claude Roussin's and James Rouselle's comic *Marche, Laura Secord!* in Dec. 1975, with music by Cyrille Beaulieu. But one of the most spectacular contemporary musicals in Quebec has been *Starmania* (at Montreal's Comédie Nationale, Sept. 1980), a rock fantasy about stars—both celestial and performing—by French composer Michel Berger and Quebec lyricist Luc Plamondon. Contemporary Maritime musicals have continued to favour the loose revue format. The Acadian folk entertainer Calixte Duguay wrote music and lyrics for Jules Boudreau's *Louis Mailloux*, produced by the Théâtre Populaire d'Acadie in 1976, and the Steel City Players' *The Rise and Follies of Cape Breton Island* (June, 1977 at College of Cape Breton Theatre, Sydney) was a local triumph. In Newfoundland Roy Hynes provided songs for several MUMMERS TROUPE productions, and Brian R. Sexton wrote *The Newfie Bullet* (ARTS AND CULTURE CENTRE, St John's, May 1981)—an affectionate tribute to the island railway—for Rising Tide Theatre and the Newfoundland Symphony Orchestra.

Vancouver composer, lyricist, and librettist

Musical Theatre

John GRAY has become Canada's dominant force in musical theatre with four successful mini-musicals: *Eighteen Wheels* (Tamahnous Theatre, June 1977), a truckers' musical; BILLY BISHOP GOES TO WAR (VANCOUVER EAST CULTURAL CENTRE Nov. 1978), a *tour de force* about the First World War flying ace; *Rock and Roll* (Vancouver East Cultural Centre, Mar. 1981), an ironic commentary on the faded dreams of a popular small-town band; and *Don Messer's Jubilee* (Neptune Theatre, Jan. 1985), a tribute to the legendary Maritime entertainer.

The Guild of Canadian Musical Theatre Writers (which grew out of workshops conducted in Toronto by Broadway's Lehman Engel), formed in 1982, continues the challenging task of developing a distinctively Canadian musical theatre.   ROSS STUART

Music Hall, The. Financed by l'Association de la Salle de musique de Québec—a group of public-spirited music-lovers headed by Archibald Campbell—the Music Hall, Quebec City, accommodating 1,500, was designed by architect Charles Baillargé and erected on the rue Saint-Louis. It opened on 5 Feb. 1853 with a concert by La Société harmonique that was attended by Lord Elgin. Although intended primarily as a music facility, the house possessed a stage equipped for dramatic productions, and throughout its life was used as much for theatre as for music.

For its first two years the Music Hall hosted local amateur companies, garrison theatricals (see GARRISON THEATRE), music concerts, a season by J.W. Wallack Jr's touring company, jugglers, acrobats, and itinerant lecturers. In 1855 J.W. BUCKLAND, co-proprietor of Ford's Theatre in Washington, acquired the lease, hired a stock company, and recruited a number of visiting stars. The 1855-6 season featured Louisa Howard of the Haymarket Theatre, London, and Henry Farren, comedian and former manager of London's Olympic Theatre. In the spring of 1856 Farren became proprietor of the Music Hall and renamed it the Olympic Theatre, sometimes advertising it as the Royal Olympic Theatre. J.W. Buckland reassumed the management in the autumn, however, and two years later formed a partnership with W.W.

Wheeler. Over the next few years tightrope-walkers, ventriloquists, opera, and a smattering of legitimate drama formed the repertoire. The most distinguished artists to appear under the Buckland-Wheeler management were the English actors Mr and Mrs Charles Mathews in 1858.

Throughout the second half of the century the Music Hall, latterly known as the Academy of Music, remained Quebec City's primary venue for variety shows, concerts, VAUDEVILLE, minstrels, military balls, amateur theatricals, and touring dramatic attractions. International visitors included Blondin (1859, 1860), the Italian Opera Company (1860), Charles Dillon (1861), the Christy Minstrels (1861), and Emma Albani (1889). Although it was predominantly an English-language theatre, on 4 Dec. 1872 audiences saw productions of two original Canadian works—M. Tanguay's *L'Intendant Bigot* and Félix-Gabriel MARCHAND's *Erreur n'est pas compte, ou Les Inconvénients d'une resemblance.*

The theatre underwent extensive renovations in the summer of 1899, and on 18 Mar. 1900 burned to the ground.   JOHN RIPLEY

My Fur Lady. Produced by the Red and White Society, McGill University, in 1957 (punning on the title of the 1956 Broadway hit *My Fair Lady*), this gentle, political musical satire on Canada's need for a cultural identity was devised by Timothy Porteous, Donald MacSween, and Erik Wang. Direction and choreography were by Olivia and Brian MACDONALD, with music by pianist-producer James de B. Domville, Galt MacDermot (composer for *Hair*), and Harry Garber, plus additional songs by Roy Wolvin and orchestral arrangements by Ed Assaly. It opened on 7 Feb. 1957 for eleven sold-out performances at McGill's Moyse Hall. Quince Productions remounted and recorded it in May. It gained national attention as a STRATFORD FESTIVAL fringe attraction (forty performances at the Avon Theatre) and then triumphantly toured Canada in 1957-8, playing 402 times in eighty-two centres. The original student cast was supplemented by professionals. The profits, nearly a million dollars, were re-invested the following year in another touring revue, *Jubilee*, which unfortunately failed.   DAVID GARDNER

N

Nannary, William (1839-after 1887). Born of Irish immigrant parents, dry-goods clerk Nannary was a member and manager of the amateur Saint John Dramatic Club (frequently associated with J.W. LANERGAN and his DRAMATIC LYCEUM in Saint John), then business agent for the Lyceum, box-office agent for the ACADEMY OF MUSIC, and editor of the program *Footlight Flashes*, which included theatrical news. In 1874 and 1876, in partnership with E.A. MCDOWELL, he managed the Star Company at the Academy, concentrating on new plays; in 1875 he presented with Lanergan a program of standard repertoire and new works such as Augustin Daly's *The Big Bonanza* and Lester Wallack's *Rosedale*. Stock companies under his management were the mainstay of the Saint John Academy of Music and of the Halifax ACADEMY OF MUSIC until mid-1879; they also toured to St John's (Nfld.), Charlottetown, Moncton, Amherst, Yarmouth, Montreal, and Ottawa. Nannary saved the Saint John Academy from bankruptcy soon after opening, introduced the first winter season offered by a professional company resident in Saint John, and helped to restore the cultural life of that burned-out city in 1878 by bringing touring companies to the Mechanics' Institute. He pressed for construction of the Halifax Academy where his company gave the first dramatic performance, and he attempted to maintain companies simultaneously in Halifax and Saint John, penetrating the entire Maritime region from these centres. He claimed to pay as much as $4,700 a week in salaries, and to have over 100 people employed in various theatres at one time. Unfortunately poor box office, expensive new spectacles, recruiting difficulties, and changing audience tastes led to financial difficulties that caused Nannary's resignation from the management of both companies in 1879.

In the 1880s Nannary briefly shared management of the Lindley Comedy and Opera Co. on tour and his companies occasionally appeared under his management in various Maritime centres until 1887, when he moved his family to California. Nothing is known of his subsequent years. His brother Patrick was an actor and three of his children (May, Genevieve, and Edward) became actors.

MARY ELIZABETH SMITH

National Arts Centre, The / Centre National des Arts, Le. The most prestigious and controversial performing arts centre in Canada, it was completed in 1969 in Ottawa at a cost of forty-six million dollars, with a mandate 'to develop the performing arts in the National Capital region, and to assist the Canada Council in the development of the performing arts elsewhere in Canada.' The seating capacity of each of the performance spaces operated by or associated with the Centre is as follows: Opera, 2,326; Theatre, 969; Studio, 350; Salon, 150; L'Atelier (a warehouse theatre in Ottawa), 100; La Maison du Citoyen (at the City Hall in Hull, Que.), 225.

The NAC has been only moderately successful in carrying out its mandate for theatre, partly because of the lack of a consistent policy, and partly because of a decrease in government funding in the 1980s. It set the following priorities among its programming guidelines: professional rather than amateur presentations; resident rather than visiting companies; Canadian rather than foreign productions; NAC presentations rather than rental presentations. It toured many of its plays throughout Canada and abroad from 1978 to 1981, but the cost of these tours became prohibitive and government support for them was discontinued. Another victim of cost-cutting was the position of archivist, held by Anthony Ibbotson from 1979 to 1985.

The NAC has had various resident theatre companies since its opening, and a shifting administrative hierarchy. Hamilton Southam was its director general from 1967 to 1977. During this time Jean-Guy SABOURIN ran a short-lived French theatre group, Théâtre du Capricorne in 1969-70, and the STRATFORD FESTIVAL wintered in Ottawa under the name Stratford National Theatre in 1969-71. For one season the Centre Studio, with a French and English component, produced experimental work under, respectively, Jean Herbiet and Michael BAWTREE (1970-1). In 1971 a

National Arts Centre

National Arts Centre, Ottawa

separate division of Theatre was created under the direction of Jean ROBERTS, with Jean Herbiet named as associate director in charge of French Theatre; in 1975 a movement towards separate French and English administrations and companies was completed with the naming of Roberts and Herbiet as artistic directors of English- and French-language drama respectively. During this period the NAC occasionally staged original productions, but more often brought in shows from across Canada. It also funded a playwright-in-residence (1974–7) and a French young company, L'Hexagone, which toured plays for young people from the Centre's early years until 1982.

In 1977 Southam was replaced by Donald MacSween; Jean GASCON became director of Theatre, and John WOOD artistic director of English Theatre, succeeding Roberts. In 1978 both sections were given funds to organize resident companies, which for seven years produced a mix of international and Canadian works, both at the NAC and on tour. Unfortunately budget constraints took a heavy toll on the English-Theatre division during the 1980s; when Gascon and Wood left in 1984, both their positions were eliminated, and the resident company Wood had formed in 1978 was disbanded. Andis Celms, who had been administrator of Theatre from 1972, was appointed producer of Theatre, and he has since concentrated on filling the theatrical season at the NAC with touring productions and co-productions with companies across Canada. The French administration has fared somewhat better. L'Hexagone was disbanded

in 1982, but Herbiet was immediately succeeded as artistic director of French Theatre by André BRASSARD, who still serves in that capacity, presenting a seasonal mix of productions, co-productions, and tours. MacSween left the post of director general in March 1987. His successor, Yvon Des-Rochers, was finally appointed in May 1988 after much indecision on the part of the directors.

The initial prosperity and optimism of the Centre under its first director, and the lack of careful planning and organizational structures in theatre, left it unprepared for the cost-cutting that MacSween faced during his tenure. In his time the Centre was scrutinized by three separate federal task forces, which resulted in three reports—the 1982 Applebaum-Hébert report; and two in 1986, the Nielsen report and the HENDRY report. Two of these recommended the cessation of in-house theatre production so that the NAC could concentrate on its role as a showcase for the arts in Canada.

Although these task-force recommendations were rejected by MacSween, in practice the Centre has been forced to reduce its own theatre production and rely more on plays from visiting companies. MacSween nevertheless was hopeful, as he ended his association with the NAC, that the setbacks during his tenure would be temporary, and that the National Arts Centre would some day be able to fulfil its original mandate.

See James Noonan, 'The National Arts Centre: Fifteen Years at Play', *Theatre History in Canada*, 6 (1985).   JAMES NOONAN

National Theatre School of Canada, The/L'École Nationale de Théâtre du Canada. The movement to found a national school for the training of professional Canadian theatre artists was heavily influenced by Michel SAINT-DENIS, the French actor, director, and theatre educator who first appeared in Canada as the adjudicator of the DOMINION DRAMA FESTIVAL finals in Ottawa in 1937. It was during the 1950s as a DDF adjudicator and adviser that Saint-Denis's ideas made the greatest impact on Canadian theatre artists, patrons, and administrators. At Saint John, N.B., in 1952 he proposed the idea of a professional theatre school for both English and French Canadians, advocating it again on his next visit to Canada in 1958 (for the DDF finals in Halifax).

Subsequently—at meetings in Quebec City, Montreal, and Toronto with Canadian theatre artists, members of the Canada Council, and the DDF—Saint-Denis stressed that he would not be able to run such a school, but that he would be willing to offer advice and guidance. It was agreed that the proposed school should be bilingual, national in scope, and conceived along the lines of Saint-Denis's principles of training. Questions of financing and location proved more contentious, and it was not until the establishment of the Canadian Theatre Centre in 1959 that the school moved significantly towards realization. Under the umbrella of the CTC a pilot committee was formed to investigate the planning of the proposed school and report its findings to the Centre. Chaired by David GARDNER, the committee included Powys THOMAS as artistic adviser, and noted Canadian theatre artists such as Donald DAVIS, Jean GASCON, Gratien GÉLINAS, Michael LANGHAM, Mavor MOORE, Jean-Louis ROUX, and Herbert WHITTAKER, with Saint-Denis as special adviser. The committee selected Montreal as the school's location, with the opening scheduled for fall 1960. Jean Gascon was named director general, with Powys Thomas and Jean-Pierre RONFARD as heads of the English and French sections respectively. The committee's recommendations were ratified by the Board of Directors of the Canadian Theatre Centre on 8 Feb. 1960 and the National Theatre School opened on schedule that fall in three rented rooms in the Canadian Legion Building on Mountain Street.

Although emphasis and definition have changed with successive administrators, the practices of the school have remained essentially faithful to the Saint-Denis model. He believed that a theatre school must address the student's ethical, imaginative, and technical capacities, and advocated the slow growth of student artists over a three-year program in three fundamental branches of theatre: acting, production, and design. Although 'classical' training was at the core of the program, Saint-Denis hoped that indigenous North American realism would collide with classical discipline in a reciprocally beneficial manner and invigorate, indeed renovate, the existing theatre with a continuous reinvestigation of the meaning of theatrical style. Technique—which for Saint-Denis existed solely for the purpose of liberating the imagination and serving dramatic necessity—would provide the disciplined freedom essential to the staging of plays of any given period or style.

This pragmatic and empirical approach to theatre training was steadfastly upheld by successive administrators of the school (James de Domville, 1963-8; a 1968-70 triumvirate; David Peacock, 1970-2; Donald MacSween, 1973-7; Richard C. Dennison, 1978-81; Jean-Louis Roux, 1982-7; Paul THOMPSON, 1988-) as the sure way of preventing the training from being jaundiced by theory and isolated from the actuality of theatre practice. It invited, indeed begged, vital connection with a living theatre, and although the initial intimate rapport of the National Theatre School with the STRATFORD FESTIVAL and the MANITOBA THEATRE CENTRE was eventually severed, certain fundamental assumptions and structures in the school's program have guaranteed an on-going association with the professional Canadian theatre. Admission to the school (sixty students were admitted in 1987) is determined solely by auditions, interviews, and portfolios. No formal degrees are granted to students completing their NTS training; it is assumed that on graduation students will find work in the professional theatre.

From the beginning teachers in the school have been engaged in professional theatre activities; there is no system of tenure that might encourage recalcitrance towards change. A tradition of visiting professional artists has allowed for continuous exposure to fresh ideas within the existing structure, and dialogue between the faculty and student body—viewed by Saint-Denis as vital to any school's evolution—has produced significant changes in the school's curriculum: for example, the closer alignment of the French section with contemporary Quebec culture, the inclusion of a French playwriting section, and the introduction of a directing program in the English program.

Well-known NTS graduates include Martha HENRY, R.H. THOMSON, Michael EAGAN, Heath LAMBERTS, Judith THOMPSON, Jean-Luc BASTIEN, Yves SAUVAGEAU, René-Daniel DUBOIS, Michel CATUDAL, and Michel DEMERS. Although the early vision and promise of artistic reciprocity between the two language groups has not been borne out, the National Theatre School remains a functionally colingual institution, funded by a variety of federal, provincial, and private agencies.

After numerous temporary locations, the school moved in 1987 into its own facilities on rue St Denis.

See L'École/The School (1985), ed. Jean-Louis Roux, Michel Garneau, and Tom Hendry.   BRIAN SMITH

Navy Show, The. After opening on 2 Sept. 1943 at Toronto's Tivoli Theatre, produced by the Royal Canadian Navy under the supervision of Captain J.P. Connolly, *Meet the Navy* moved to Ottawa for its official première at the Capitol Theatre, 15 Sept. 1943. After two non-stop cross-Canada tours, the company performed overseas at the London Hippodrome, throughout Britain, and in France, Belgium, Holland, and Germany. In 1946 *Meet the Navy* was filmed as backdrop to a Hollywood-style musical of the same name. In 1980 and 1981 it was revived by Alan LUND and Blanche Lund for performances in Eastern Canada.

Built around a series of elaborate production numbers, *Meet the Navy* was influenced by the Hollywood musical in format and direction. The music and dance ensembles were staged by Hollywood musical director Louis Silvers and former Broadway producer Larry Ceballos. Sets by Broadway designer Paul Dupont were executed by Canadian Leonard Brooks. Hollywood costumier Billy Livingston designed the costumes.

Patrick E. Quinn composed original music for the show. Scripts were by R. William Harwood, Noel Langley, and Henry Sherman. Robert GOODIER, John 'You'll Get Used To It' Pratt, and Lionel Murton—all

products of the MONTREAL REPERTORY THEATRE and its 'Tin Hat Revue'—and Phyllis Hudson were comedians with the company. The Terrible Trio (Dixie Dean, Bill Richards, and Tony Stechyshyn), which had formed a Navy concert party in Halifax, were incorporated as a unit into the show. Ivan Romanoff, already popular with radio audiences, brought his Russian Choir. Dancing talent included Torontonian Louise Burns from the Radio City Music Hall 'Rockettes', and Blanche Harris and Alan Lund. The company numbered 135, including forty WREN dancers and a thirty-piece orchestra under Eric Wild.

Although few Canadian productions ever equalled *Meet the Navy* as spectacle, *Saturday Night* felt that the show lacked the 'warm colour and breathtaking pace . . . of the [equivalent] army production' (i.e. the ARMY SHOW).   PATRICK B. O'NEILL

NDWT (Ne'er-Do-Well Thespians). This innovative theatre company developed from the association of playwright James REANEY, director Keith TURNBULL, and a number of actors who had worked together in London, Ont., Halifax, and Toronto on several of Reaney's plays, especially the DONNELLYS trilogy. NDWT was formed in Apr. 1975 specifically to tour Canada with the trilogy as well as a production of *Hamlet*. Based in Toronto, it remained active until 1982, dedicated to producing new Canadian plays, to collaborative work among playwright, director, and actors, to involvement through street festivals, drama workshops, and study guides in the social and cultural life of the communities in which they performed, and eventually to the development of theatre by and for Canada's native Indians. Keith Turnbull, artistic director of the group, was later joined by actor-director Jerry Franken as associate director.

Following the *Donnellys* tour, NDWT moved into Toronto's Bathurst St Theatre (where a memorable one-day presentation of the trilogy took place on 14 Dec. 1975), producing a season of plays there and in other locations until 1980. Productions included premières of several of Reaney's plays—*Baldoon* (written with Marty Gervais, in Nov. 1976), *Wacousta!* (Apr. 1977), *The Dismissal* (at HART HOUSE THEATRE in Nov. 1977), and a workshop of *The Canadian Brothers* at the Univ. of Western Ontario in Nov. 1977.

Baldoon and *Wacousta!* successfully toured Ontario, but in Toronto both received a mixed critical reception, as did much of NDWT's other work.

The company then became alienated from Toronto and grew interested in native theatre, producing plays with and for native people, and eventually organizing a native theatre group called Northern Delights under the direction of Jim Morris, a native Indian. *Northern Delights* was the title of the group's first production, a COLLECTIVE CREATION about life in the North. While this, and another play about native people—*Radio Free Cree* by Paulette Jiles—were well received on 1978 and 1979 tours of northern Ontario, they failed in Toronto. A second play by Jiles, *Northshore Run*, was not produced in Toronto, though it toured in 1981. Several of the native actors from Northern Delights, however, have established professional careers in the theatre.

NDWT's alienation from Toronto, combined with an ongoing deficit of $13,000 from the *Donnellys* tour, forced the company to leave the Bathurst St Theatre in 1980. It continued to produce plays at other venues in Toronto—Reaney's *Gyroscope* at TARRA-GON THEATRE in May 1981 and Gordon Pengilly's *Swipe* at TORONTO FREE THEATRE in Dec. 1981. But by that time much of the energy and several of the actors had left the company.

In 1982 Turnbull announced a suspension of operations for one year, but NDWT never resumed operation. The NDWT archives are housed at the Univ. of Guelph.

JAMES NOONAN

Needles, William (b. 1919). Born in Yonkers, N.Y., and raised in Kitchener, Ont., he was educated at the Goodman School of Drama in Chicago. His acting career has spanned both Canada and the U.S., including most STRATFORD FESTIVALs since 1953, the CANADIAN PLAYERS, the CREST THEATRE, TARRAGON THEATRE, and CENTRESTAGE. His acting is marked by apparently effortless intellectual and moral authority, combined with ironic playfulness and rich vocal sensitivity. One of Canada's most skilled Shakespearean actors, he has also given important performances in plays by Shaw (whose Inquisitor in *Saint Joan* he has played in three different productions), Brecht (including a

much-admired Chaplain in *Mother Courage* at the MANITOBA THEATRE CENTRE in 1964), Chekhov, and Slawomir Mrozek; his roles in contemporary drama include the Minister in the 1968 Buffalo, N.Y., world première of Edward Albee's *Box—Mao—Box*. Since 1975 he has also been artist-in-residence and lecturer in the Dept. of Drama, Univ. of California at Irvine. HARRY LANE

Nelligan, Kate (b. 1951). Born and educated in London, Ont., she studied at York Univ. before entering the Central School of Speech and Drama in London, Eng., graduating in 1972. She made her professional début with the Bristol Old Vic as Corrie in Neil Simon's *Barefoot in the Park* that same year. Other parts in that 1972-3 season included Hypatia in Shaw's *Misalliance*, Stella in Tennessee Williams' *A Streetcar Named Desire*, Pegeen Mike in Synge's *Playboy of the Western World*, and Sybil in Noël Coward's *Private Lives*. In 1974 she won the London critics' Most Promising Actress Award for her work in David Hare's *Knuckle* at London's Comedy Theatre. A year later she joined England's National Theatre, where she soon became a leading member of the company. Critics noted her intelligence, wit, beauty, and her 'aristocratic spikiness'. Her 1977 Rosalind in *As You Like It* for the English Shakespeare Company was hailed as the finest since Vanessa Redgrave's a decade earlier. In 1978 she won the British theatre's premier award—the *Evening Standard* award for best actress—for her role as Susan Traherne in Hare's *Plenty*, a role she reprised to critical acclaim at New York's Public Theatre in 1983. In 1984 her portrayal of Josie Hogan in Eugene O'Neill's *A Moon for the Misbegotten* at New York's Cort Theatre won plaudits for creating the illusion of O'Neill's 'great ugly cow of a woman'. At the Public again in 1985 she played the role of Virginia Woolf in Edna O'Brien's *Virginia*. She subsequently appeared in a successful off-Broadway production of Michael Weller's *Spoils of War* in which she also made her suprisingly late Canadian stage début at Toronto's ROYAL ALEXANDRA THEATRE in Sept. 1988.

Nelligan also appeared in television plays and films in England, notably a dramatization of Zola's *Thérèse Raquin*. She left England in 1981 for the U.S. hoping to become a movie star, but her films—*The Romantic English-*

woman, *Dracula*, *Eye of the Needle*, *Mr. Patman*, *Without a Trace*, *Eleni*—have not shown her talents to best effect.   EUGENE BENSON

Neptune Theatre. The Neptune Theatre Foundation—following a report by Leon MAJOR, Tom Patterson, and Jack GRAY favouring the establishment of a repertory company in Halifax, N.S.—opened its first season in July 1963 in a former vaudeville theatre and cinema, the Garrick, at Sackville and Argyle Streets. For its opening the renamed Neptune Theatre was renovated, to the specifications of resident designer Les Lawrence, to its present 521-person capacity: 336 in the orchestra and 185 in the balcony of an auditorium measuring 58′ × 47′, and with a stage approximately 30′ deep and 42′ wide. Major became the company's first artistic director in 1962, and Gray its first resident playwright and administrator. The first company included Diana Leblanc, Dawn Greenhalgh, Ted Follows, Bernard Behrens, Norman Welsh, and four whose association has continued until the 1980s: David Renton, Joan Gregson, Mary McMurray, and designer Robert Doyle. The first season opened with Shaw's *Major Barbara*, directed by George McCowan and starring Mavor MOORE. Productions ranged from modern light comedy and farce to Shakespeare and Anouilh. Gray advocated repertory seasons with the best plays of the past in balance with the new, especially Canadian, works. He himself wrote the historical *Louisbourg* for the company, and Arthur L. MURPHY, the Foundation's first President, had three plays premièred: *Charlie*, *Tiger! Tiger!*, and *The Sleeping Bag*, the last of which toured Canada with Sean O'Casey's *Juno and the Paycock* in the 1967 Centennial year.

Despite government subsidy the theatre soon suffered several financial crises; in 1966 the province contributed $250,000 to help eliminate accumulated debts. John Hobday, business administrator, 1967-71, established a balanced budget with the start of subscription series, and in 1969 Major's associate, Heinar Piller, became artistic director. In 1971 winter-season repertory was abandoned for stock, as the theatre was ill-equipped for constant set changes. Highlights of Piller's tenure were Joan Gregson in Frederick Knott's *Wait Until Dark*, Jack Medley in Robert Bolt's *A Man for All Seasons*, Linda Livingston in Jean Giraudoux's *Ondine*, and Lynn Gorman in

Edward Albee's *Who's Afraid of Virginia Woolf?*

Robert Sherrin was Neptune's artistic director from 1971 to 1974. Among the outstanding productions of this period were James REANEY's *Listen to the Wind*, directed by Keith TURNBULL; David Dodimead in Eugene O'Neill's *Long Day's Journey Into Night*, directed by William Davis; David Renton in Eric Salmon's production of Pinter's *The Caretaker*; Roger Rees in Shaw's *Candida*, directed by Andrew Downie; and Sherrin's own productions of Ibsen's *Peer Gynt* with Heath LAMBERTS, and of David FRENCH's *Leaving Home* and *Of the Fields, Lately* (of the MERCER PLAYS) with Florence Paterson. Sherrin also directed Carlo Goldoni's *The Servant of Two Masters* and Michael COOK's *Colour the Flesh the Colour of Dust*, both of which were presented at the NATIONAL ARTS CENTRE, Ottawa, during a national tour. Sherrin established Neptune's experimental Second Stage, 1971-4, which presented early performances of Beverley SIMONS' *CRABDANCE*, Michel TREMBLAY's *Forever Yours, Marie-Lou* (*À TOI, POUR TOUJOURS, TA MARIE-LOU*), and David FREEMAN's *CREEPS*; James Reaney conducted his Donnellys workshop there for two summers (see *The DONNELLYS*).

John WOOD, with associate directors Alan Laing, Hamilton McClymont, David Renton, and Christopher Banks, succeeded Sherrin in 1974. He mounted some colourful productions, such as Shaw's *Misalliance* and Peter Shaffer's *Equus*; *Hamlet*, with Neil Munro, and *King Lear*, with Eric DONKIN, were less successful. He staged several musicals, which required structural alterations to the stage, reducing the apron size and number of seats to provide orchestral space. When Wood left Neptune in 1977 the theatre's deficit had risen to $200,000.

In an attempt to restore budgetary stability and strong artistic leadership, the theatre board appointed John NEVILLE to succeed Wood as theatre director. David Renton, acting artistic director until Neville was able to take over in May 1978, arranged a well-balanced season that achieved a modest profit. With control over both artistic and fiscal policies, Neville—assisted by general managers Lynne Dickson (1977-8), Christopher Banks (1978-81), and Denise Rooney (since 1981)—was able to reduce the deficit dramatically and finally produce a profit; subscrip-

Neptune Theatre production of King Lear, *1977, with (l. to r.) Patricia Gage, Frank Maraden, Eric Donkin, Stephen Russell, Denise Fergusson*

tions rose from just over 3,000 in 1977 to about 9,500 by 1982-3. Corporate sponsorships helped to subsidize all productions and tours.

Neville was prominent as actor as well as administrator; in his first season he played the lead in *Othello*, which toured Nova Scotia. He gave notable performances in Shaw's *The Apple Cart*, Charles Dyer's *Staircase*, Ibsen's *The Master Builder*, and Beckett's *Endgame*, as well as directing many plays, including Chekhov's *The Sea Gull*, in which Tony Randall played Trigorin, and Tennessee Williams' *The Night of the Iguana*. Other leading artists at Neptune during this time included actors Roland Hewgill, Fiona REID, Douglas CAMPBELL, Ann Casson, Eric HOUSE, Joan Orenstein, and Joseph Rutten; directors Leslie Yeo, Richard OUZOUNIAN, Denise Coffey; and designers Arthur Penson, Phillip SILVER, and Robert Doyle. Neville instituted a successful lunchtime theatre (see LUNCH THEATRE) with some fine productions, notably Brian Friel's *Winners*, David Mamet's *Reunion*, and Pinter's *The Lover*. The Young Neptune Company also flourished under Neville, with the assistance of Irene Watts and Bill Carr.

Neville was succeeded as theatre director in 1983 by Tom KERR who, in conjunction with general manager Denise Rooney, maintained the theatre's financial stability. Kerr retained the Young Neptune Company and started a theatre school, directed first by Irene

Watts and later by Jennette White. The Cunard Street Theatre provided a home for a second stage, Neptune North; this company, directed by Glen Cairns, in its first season (1985-6) mounted some striking experimental productions, notably Maxim Mazumdar in Harvey Fierstein's *Torch Song Trilogy*. Main-stage productions were workmanlike, if rarely inspiring. Most interesting was a single-cast staging of Shakespeare's *Romeo and Juliet* and Leonard Bernstein's *West Side Story* in 1983.

Under both Neville and Kerr several Canadian plays were staged, though few were as memorable as productions of works by French, Reaney, and Tremblay in the early seventies. Richard Ouzounian, appointed artistic director in May 1986, included several Canadian works, notably Sharon POLLOCK's *Doc*, in his first two seasons, which contained no fewer than seven world premières. He staged his own adaptations of Molière's *Tartuffe* and Hugh MacLennan's *Barometer Rising*, as well as *Shine Boy* by Halifax playwright George Boyd. Most striking was Eric STEINER's second stage production at the Dunn Theatre of playwright-in-residence Kent Stetson's *Warm Wind in China*. Ouzounian gave many opportunities to Nova Scotian actors, but in the face of economic problems performance standards sometimes wavered and there was a dearth of high-quality traditional or modern plays. In Dec. 1988 it was announced that Ouzounian would leave Neptune at the end of his contract in May 1989, Tom Kerr returning as guest director for the 1989-90 season.

After the company's failure to acquire a new building on the Halifax waterfront in 1983, negotiations are continuing to expand Neptune Theatre on its present site. In spite of its vicissitudes, Neptune remains one of Canada's most successful and interesting regional theatres.

See Richard Perkyns, 'Two Decades of the Neptune Theatre', *Theatre History in Canada*, 6 (1985), and Richard Perkyns, *The Neptune Story: Twenty-Five Years in the Life of a Leading Canadian Theatre* (1989). The Neptune Theatre archives are housed at Dalhousie University.   RICHARD PERKYNS

Neville, John (b. 1925). Born in Willesden, a suburb of London, Eng., he trained at the Royal Academy of Dramatic Art and served

Neville

his apprenticeship at the Birmingham Repertory Theatre and the Bristol Old Vic before joining the Old Vic in London in 1953, the same year as Richard Burton. Their first season set a pattern Neville struggled to escape: while Burton played Hamlet—dark, passionate, and self-tormenting—Neville played Fortinbras—calm, Nordic, and single-minded; while Neville played Ferdinand in *The Tempest*, Burton played Caliban. Critics began to stereotype: Burton as Olivier's successor, all earthy intensity, and Neville as Gielgud's heir, all music and nobility. Neville had to fight to persuade directors that he could play not only Orlando and Romeo, but Hotspur, Autolycus, and Thersites in *Troilus and Cressida*.

He won his point in 1955-6, when he and Burton alternated opposite each other in the roles of Othello and Iago. By general consent Neville's was the finer Iago—crop-haired, currish, and venomously common. When Burton left for Hollywood, Neville stayed only long enough to play a muscular, sardonic Hamlet—a far cry from Gielgud's—before forsaking the Vic to kick up his heels in a West End musical, *Irma La Douce*, and Bill Naughton's saga of a Cockney seducer, *Alfie*—the first character he had ever played who might have been born in Willesden. In 1962 Olivier gave him leading roles in the Chichester Festival company from which he recruited his National Theatre players a year later, but instead of joining Olivier's team, Neville chose to head his own as artistic director of the Nottingham Playhouse. Under Neville's leadership Nottingham became the foremost British provincial repertory, but his commitment to political theatre caused disputes with some board members that led to his departure in 1968. The role of Humbert Humbert in Alan Jay Lerner's musical *Lolita*—another flight from stereotyping—brought Neville to North America in 1971. The show collapsed on tour, but Jean ROBERTS at the NATIONAL ARTS CENTRE, in Ottawa, seized the opportunity to invite him to direct Sheridan's *The Rivals*. A guest appearance at the MANITOBA THEATRE CENTRE followed, prior to his appointment as artistic director of Edmonton's CITADEL THEATRE (1973-8). In addition to opening a new theatre for the Citadel, Neville became a Canadian citizen and a partisan of Canadian playwriting, directing Michel TREMBLAY's *Hosanna* and playing the title role in Rod

Langley's *Bethune*. His years as artistic director of Halifax's NEPTUNE THEATRE (1978-82), were less happy, coinciding as they did with an economic recession that prevented the building of a promised new theatre.

Since 1983 Neville has been associated with the STRATFORD FESTIVAL, first as an actor and as director of the Young Company (1983-4), and from 1985 as artistic director. Stratford has given him the opportunity of acting in a company worthy of him. Even in an inadequate production, his Solness in Ibsen's *Master Builder* at the Neptune showed a larger actor than British audiences knew, with more knowledge of the greed, fear, and cruelty of Ibsen's character than the prince of the Old Vic could have dreamed of. In Michael LANGHAM's revival of *Love's Labour's Lost* for Stratford in 1983-4, Neville's Don Armado was a superb, flawless performance. Admirers regret that such appearances have been few. As a director his taste has been less sure, political passion sometimes leading him into over-stated simplification, such as a nuclear explosion toward the end of his production of Bertolt Brecht's *Mother Courage* in 1987. Nonetheless, Neville's achievement at Stratford—following some uncertain years for the Festival—has been to revive both artistic standards and financial stability.

RONALD BRYDEN

New Brunswick, Theatre in. *1. Beginnings: 1789-1855.* Susannah Centlivre's comedy *The Busy Body* and Hannah Cowley's farce *Who's the Dupe?* formed the bill for the first recorded dramatic presentation in New Brunswick, given on 28 Feb. 1789, six years after the arrival of the Loyalists. Performed for public charity in MALLARD'S LONG ROOM, Saint John, as the first program in a short winter season, its significance in the cultural life of the province is suggested by the fact that Colonel Edward Winslow travelled from above Fredericton to attend. The 1789 program and further seasons in Saint John in 1795, 1801, 1815, and 1816, and in Fredericton in 1803, were given by gentlemen amateurs, sons of Loyalist and pre-Loyalist families and the occasional Scottish merchant—the élite class who also provided the audience.

In 1809 there took place the only close association between the amateurs and the garrison in Saint John, in the co-operative construction and operation of the DRURY LANE THEATRE. Otherwise officers sometimes

370

THEATRE,

KING-STREET.

On *FRIDAY* the 10th *Inst.*

WILL BE PERFORMED,

A COMEDY, called

" *Every One has his Fault;*"

To which will be added,

A FARCE, called

" *All the World's a Stage.*"

Between the 4th and 5th Acts, will be introduced a New Scene, reprefenting *Partridge Ifland,* the *Light Houfe,* &c. with a Song called *Heaving the Lead.*

And by particular defire, previous to the Farce, will be fpoken, Mr. *Garrick's* celebrated Prologue to *Barbaroffa;* in the Character of a *Country Boy.*

Every precaution will be taken to render the Theatre comfortable.

☞ TICKETS to be had at Mrs. Mallard's.

Doors to be opened at Six, and the performance to begin precifely at Seven o'clock. *St. John, April.* 7, 1795.

Advertisement from the Saint John Royal Gazette, *7 April 1795*

assisted both amateurs and professionals, as in a re-enactment of the Battle of Waterloo in 1830 that resulted in a soldier's death on stage. In Fredericton the relationship among the garrison, the amateurs, and the professionals was closer. The 33rd Regiment was active in theatricals between 1844 and 1847, and the 72nd Regiment in 1853; both the amateurs and the garrison worked with H.W. Preston at his Olympic Theatre from Dec. 1844 to Feb. 1845. (See also GARRISON THEATRE.)

Apart from variety artist Mr Hackley (1794), the earliest professionals were Mr & Mrs Marriott, who arrived via Edinburgh, Boston, New York, Philadelphia, and Halifax to perform, with the assistance of lady and gentlemen amateurs, in Saint John's Exchange Coffee House and their own amphitheatre from Feb. to Aug. 1799, introducing John Home's popular tragedy, *Douglas,* to New Brunswick. Mr Robertson, the 'Antipodean Whirligig' (1808), ventriloquist Rannie (1809), Marriott's colleague C.S. Powell (1809), and Addison B. Price's Company (1817) followed. Weather, illness, economic depression, a small population base, and the view of the *City Gazette* that the theatre endangered morality, were some reasons the professionals failed to succeed financially at this time.

Opposition from the *City Gazette* also plagued Hopley's Golden Ball Theatre during its first three years, 1828-30—the first two under actor-manager Cornelius A. Logan and the third under W.C. Forbes. Hopley's, usually known simply as The Theatre, fronted 40' on the south side of Union St in Saint John, extending back 100' to the Old Burial Ground. Built in time to house the first circus to visit Saint John in Aug./Sept. 1824, it was purchased by Joseph Hopley, an Irishman and mariner who also owned the inn next door where the actors stayed. A wooden building with plank flooring laid over sawdust and tanbark, it had bench seating for about 800 in the pit and boxes. Its loose construction allowed access by unauthorized persons, and poor lighting offered the possibility of rowdiness without detection. The strongest members of Logan's company were the Riddle family, Arthur Keene, and Frederick BROWN, and of Forbes' company Thomas Cooper, Mr and Mrs W.H. Smith, and Mr and Mrs William Pelby. Plays such as *Forty Thieves,* Charles Jeffers' *Thérèse,* Matthew G. Lewis's *Timour the Tartar,* and William Moncrieff's *Cataract of the Ganges,* reflected the growing taste for spectacle and romantic melodrama. Prices that on the 2 June 1828 opening were 5s. and 2s.6d. dropped in 1830 to 2s.6d. and 1s.3d., reflecting both the economic depression of the times and the scanty means of the largely Irish working-class audience. During an interlude in his nine-month season, Forbes toured to Fredericton and the Miramichi.

The image of Hopley's was elevated considerably under the management of W.S. Deverna in 1838 and of Henry W. Preston in 1839-41 and 1845. Deverna, with stage manager John NICKINSON, opened with the support of the mayor and lieutenant-governor, and offered plays like *Othello* and George Lillo's *George Barnwell* for 4s. and 2s. Preston rebuilt the interior of the theatre in 1840, raised the stage, turned the pit into a parquet, and banished the pitters to the gallery. He invited stars John Vandenhoff, Junius Brutus Booth, George H. (Yankee) Hill, James H. Hackett, and Fanny Fitzwilliam, and was also

New Brunswick, Theatre in

responsible, in 1845, for the production of Thomas Hill's controversial *The Provincial Association*, whose alleged satire of local people sparked rioting in the theatre. Preston finished the 1845 season in the Prince of Wales Theatre on Sydney St, newly remodelled from a church (opened 23 June, burned 4 Dec.). Critics complained about the unevenness of a company that mixed professionals and amateurs.

Between 1845 and 1856 only scattered popular entertainers came to Saint John—Rockwell & Stone's Circus, Signor Blitz, General Tom Thumb, Giant Angus McCaskill—and Fredericton saw no professional entertainment apart from the HERON FAMILY in 1853. Neither city had a theatre; Hopley's was unused after its owner's death in 1845, was damaged by fire in 1854, and consumed in 1874. Economic depression was severe as Saint John coped with overcrowding, poverty, and violence caused by a tide of Irish immigration.

2. 1856-1877. An unprecedented prosperity and the arrival of the energetic, discreet, and talented American actor-manager J.W. LANERGAN reversed the situation in Saint John, making that city the theatre centre of the Maritimes. Realizing that Saint John 'offered a good & profitable field for permanent dramatic business,' Lanergan returned on 24 Dec. 1856, following the successful summer season of the Lanergan-Sanford-Fiske Star Company, to give nightly performances in the Saint John Hotel while his own DRAMATIC LYCEUM was under construction. Soon after its opening on 15 June 1857 the press lauded it as a 'fashionable place of public resort' whose audience, representing a cross-section of society, indulged in none of the hissing and stamping that had plagued Hopley's. Until the autumn of 1867 Lanergan's was the only company to spend an extended time in Saint John, apart from E.A. Sothern's company in Aug. 1858. Wilson and Clarke's turn in the Mechanics' Institute between 26 Oct. and 18 Dec. 1867, the first of several visits, overcame a prejudice against touring companies. T.C. Howard's Olympic Company came to the Mechanics' Institute in the spring of 1868 and Flora Myers' Company in 1870, both with a repertoire of familiar pieces similar to Lanergan's, such as Tom Taylor's *The Ticket-of-Leave Man*, Augustin Daly's *Under the Gaslight*, and F. Schuler's *Fanchon*. Until 1872 no

company challenged Lanergan in the summer months. Although by 1867 his Lyceum could not accommodate its overflowing audiences, he ignored exhortations to build a larger one. Accordingly in Apr. 1870 a group of citizens sought approval from the Legislature for incorporation of a company to erect an ACADEMY OF MUSIC. As well, in Sept. 1870 Otis Small began construction of a modestly priced ($8,900) complex on Dock Street that included a large hall. From the opening of the two new facilities on 6 May 1872 until the Great Fire of 1877, Saint John had three theatres, each capable of seating 800-1,000 spectators, offering a choice of repertoire at comparable prices. Leased first by Bishop's Serenaders and then by Pete Lee, Small's Hall was the centre for variety—comic sketches, farces, gymnastics, and character songs. As managers of the Academy of Music, William NANNARY and E. A. McDOWELL took advantage of its more modern facilities to stage new spectacular pieces, while Lanergan continued to produce a proven repertoire at the Lyceum. In 1874 dramatic entertainment was available year-round and sometimes at more than one theatre, but by 1875 a depressed economy caused Lanergan and Nannary to consolidate their efforts into one season at the Academy of Music, and led Lee to allow his lease of Small's Hall to lapse in mid-July. In 1876 the Dramatic Lyceum was sold. The burning down of the theatres in 1877 once more left Saint John without a proper facility.

3. 1878-1929 (Saint John). The Mechanics' Institute, opened on 9 Dec. 1840, whose directors had long prohibited plays, now became Saint John's chief facility for theatre. It was in financial difficulty in 1877 and its directors welcomed increased rentals. The original 55'-square second-storey lecture hall had been enlarged in 1856 to 95' × 60' at a cost of nearly $1,000. Architect John J. Munroe raised the platform, enlarged the doors, and installed two stoves for heating. The old hard unpadded benches with armrails remained in semi-circular form on an inclined plane in the front and on the sides, and additional seats were added behind on the level floor. In 1881 the Institute was remodelled again. Opera chairs replaced the benches, except in the gallery, making seating for about 900. A new 9'-wide grand staircase was intended to eliminate congestion, and an exterior portico provided protection from the weather. The 33' × 54' stage was not improved, though William Gill provided new scenes for the re-opening. Finally in 1887 a furnace was installed. William Nannary was the first manager, then in June 1880 a group of citizens formed the Micawber Club, whose purpose was to provide first-class dramatic entertainment. For one year, in 1884, the Irving Club assumed management. Other halls in use were Berryman's Hall (renamed the New Academy of Music), Victoria Rink, and especially Dockrill's Hall, which functioned essentially as a Dime Museum.

Coincident with the 1877 fire, the resident stock company virtually disappeared from Saint John and professional theatrical productions were furnished mostly by travelling companies, of which Kit Carson's was the first. A fondness for light opera in the 1880s was satisfied by Wm. T. Carleton's Opera Company, the Corinne Opera Troupe, Dora Wiley's Boston English Opera Company, the HOLMAN and Brignoli Opera Companies, and others. A fondness for novelty and sensation was fed by productions such as Snyder and Lytell's of Paul Merritt's and Henry Pettitt's *The World*, which included scenes of a raft at sea and a fiery explosion aboard ship. Dramatic fare of diverse kinds was offered by repertory companies such as those of E.A. McDowell, Charlotte Thompson, the Lingards, Lily Langtry, Albert TAVERNIER, George Miln, Mme. Rhea, and the Boston Museum.

In 1887 new American railway legislation made tours in the eastern Canadian cities expensive, which led to a temporary reduction in the number of entertainers visiting and a corresponding reduction in rentals. The Mechanics' Institute was advertised for sale, causing the Micawber Club to use alternate facilities in the Lansdowne Rink. The Bennett-Moulton and Levy Opera Companies performed there in 1888, and McDowell completed an eight-week season in 1889, despite the difficulty of paying Broadway salaries on Saint John receipts. No buyer having emerged, the Mechanics' Institute was again refurbished in 1890. Entertainments were also being given in the Palace Theatre (Rink), McCann's Lyceum (Jack's Old Hall), and the St Andrew's Rink. By this time, however, subscriptions for a proposed new Opera House (see SAINT JOHN OPERA HOUSE) were well underway. Disputes about its site were settled, and with the 21 Sept. 1891 opening the city once more had a suitably designed

and elegant theatre. In the 1890s more than eighty different dramatic companies played mostly in repertory, though just over a third were one-play companies. The taste towards comedy and variety continued. There was little Shakespeare, but many attempts at realism: real horses, real buzz saws, real water. The company of *The Evil Eye*, with its fifty people and two cars of scenery, particularly pleased its patrons. Pieces such as *Side Tracked* and George H. Broadhurst's *Why Smith Left Home* packed the Opera House 'almost to suffocation', and Lewis Morrison's supernatural tale of *Faust* earned the highest box-office receipts of 1896. One-time visitors such as James O'Neill and Tyrone Power had difficulty attracting a following despite their reputations, while frequent visitors H. Price WEBBER and W.H. Harkins and the long-staying Valentine Company won support with familiar plays and reliable standards.

By 1911-12 debate over the legitimacy of moving pictures *v.* live theatre had reached a climax. Several motion-picture houses were operating in Saint John: the Gem, Star, Unique, Lyric, Empress (or Carleton's), and chiefly the Nickel (formerly the Mechanics' Institute and now owned by Keith and Albee). The Saint John *Globe* estimated weekly attendance between 25,000 and 30,000. With the opening of the Keith-owned Imperial on 19 Sept. 1913 Saint John had a movie palace of which it was immensely proud, and the Opera House had a formidable competitor. Through the 1920s the Opera House, under manager F.G. Spencer, attempted to hold its own, first with its own stock company and then with frequent touring companies; but after 1929, when Albee leased the Imperial to Famous Players Canada, who renamed it the Capitol, the Opera House was used infrequently, and apparently closed in 1938. The Capitol then became host to visiting stars such as John Martin-Harvey, Ethel Barrymore, Gracie Fields, Edgar Bergen, and Saint John native Walter Pidgeon.

4. 1875-1929 (outside Saint John). Until 1875 the towns in New Brunswick were served by amateur dramatic societies and the occasional professional specialty act, which performed in makeshift quarters such as temperance halls, Orange lodges, and masonic halls. Fredericton's City Hall Opera House, in use from 1870, was the most adequate facility outside Saint John. It contained wooden seats for 836 persons and had a 30′ × 40′ stage with a 24' proscenium. In 1875 Pete Lee's variety troupe visited Chatham, Kingston, Moncton, Richibucto, and Shediac. In 1875-6 Price Webber's Boston Comedy Company performed in Bathurst, Campbellton, Chatham, Dalhousie, Newcastle, and Woodstock as part of a tour that included all three Maritime provinces. In 1876 John H. Murray took his Railroad Circus to Bathurst, Campbellton, Newcastle, St Andrews, Shediac, and Woodstock, and in 1877 Kit Carson visited Chatham, Moncton, and Sackville. These beginnings created a heightened consciousness of dramatic activity that expressed itself in a move towards improved facilities. In 1876 a new masonic hall was constructed in Newcastle containing a stage, and a 21' × 36' enlargement of an existing masonic hall in Chatham was undertaken 'for the purposes of securing an ample stage accommodation.' When Ruddick's New Hall (formerly a Methodist church) opened in Moncton in Dec. 1878 it was called the largest and best-equipped theatre outside Saint John and Fredericton, but by 1881 it was outshone by Tait's Hall in Shediac (a second-storey hall over a potato warehouse). In 1882 James Carr converted the Woodstock Rink into a temporary summer theatre with a 61' × 32' stage, sixteen footlights, ninety-three pieces of scenery, and 200 easy chairs; the Town Hall was used in winter. The second-storey Sackville Music Hall, opened in 1883, had a 25' × 45' stage with a 14' × 22' proscenium. Most elaborate of all was the Moncton City Hall Opera House, opened in 1885. Seating in the 65' × 60' auditorium was in the shape of a horse-shoe, each row of seats rising six inches higher than the last. Six hundred hinged opera chairs, exact replicas of those in the Halifax ACADEMY OF MUSIC, stood on the main floor, and 150 less comfortable seats were available in the gallery. The 35' × 60' stage was equipped with 'every necessary accommodation'. In 1907 the Hayden-Gibson Theatre, seating 900, was erected in Woodstock.

The most frequently visited centres were Fredericton, Moncton, Woodstock, and Chatham; but even small villages had visitors, such as General Tom Thumb's 1879 tour to Dorchester, Petitcodiac, Shediac, and Sussex, and Harry LINDLEY's 1880 tour to Hopewell Corner, Dorchester, Hillsboro, Salisbury, as well as Campbellton, Moncton, Sackville, and Sussex. H. Price Webber's Boston Com-

edy Company was the most frequent visitor. His company's reputation for a well-executed performance and his ability to familiarize himself with rural audiences and local situations earned him a consistently appreciative following. Some troupes—like those of W.H. Lytell, Albert Tavernier, Wm. Nannary, W.H. Harkins, Bennett-Moulton, and C.H. Smith—visited two or more times, whereas others, including Kittie Lougee, Katherine Rogers, Eugenie Legrand, and the Holman Opera Company, made only one rural tour. Fredericton sometimes saw companies (including those of Mme. Rhea, Mme. Janauschek, Alvin Joslin, Kate Claxton, Charlotte Thompson, Stafford-Foster, Redmund-Barry) that visited Saint John also, but not the rest of the province. Appearances by professional companies were intermittent. No centre outside Saint John had regular entertainment, and sometimes a town or village was without a visit for a year or more. Fredericton saw no professional shows between Price Webber's season in Jan. 1890 and Cyril Spear's in May 1899. Performances of amateur societies and of professional 'burnt-cork' companies continued to supplement the touring dramatic companies everywhere.

5. 1930-1985. Largely because of the enthusiasm of Major H. Christie, editor of the *Telegraph Journal and Evening Times Globe*, the Saint John Theatre Guild was established in 1931, partly to compensate for the gradual disappearance of touring companies. This was not the first time that Saint John amateurs had stepped into the breach; the Histrionic Society had attempted to alleviate some of the silent years at Hopley's (1842-5), and indeed the amateur tradition had always been strong in the city and in the rest of the province.

The objectives of the Saint John Theatre Guild were enlightened and comprehensive, including stimulation of appreciation for, and participation in, drama; experimentation within practical limits; encouragement of British and Canadian work; competition; and maintenance of an amateur character. True to these goals for more than twenty years, until it faded away following the 1953-4 season, it offered productions yearly (except during the war) in makeshift theatres or school auditoriums, competed annually in regional drama festivals, several times represented New Brunswick in the DOMINION DRAMA FESTIVAL, and routinely performed plays by its own members and other Canadian playwrights. The establishment of the Dominion Drama Festival in 1933 provided incentive to amateur societies throughout New Brunswick, particularly the Univ. of New Brunswick's Dramatic Society, under Professor Alvin Shaw's direction, which won more than forty regional awards. Although numerous amateur companies existed in the province during the life of the Saint John Theatre Guild and after—including the Sackville Theatre Guild, the Saint Andrews Music, Art and Drama Club, the Rexton-Richibucto Dramatic Society, the Miramichi Summer Theatre, Moncton's Stage Door '56, and the Saint John Fundy Players—none had anything approaching its staying power and influence.

From the opening of the PLAYHOUSE in 1964 domination in theatre passed from Saint John to Fredericton. Initially a rental hall, a temporary home to amateurs and visiting professionals, and from 1966 to summer stock companies, the Playhouse became in 1968 the launching pad for a daring experiment in theatrical entrepreneurship. Since that year, when Walter LEARNING established THEATRE NEW BRUNSWICK, the story of English-language theatre in the province has been largely the story of that professional company. From its inception, Theatre New Brunswick has been committed to two principles: to make available live professional theatre to as many communities as possible throughout the province; and to encourage local actors and actresses to participate in productions, where appropriate under Equity agreement.

In addition to Theatre New Brunswick, three other professional English companies are active from time to time, all based in Fredericton: the Comedy Asylum, Enterprise Theatre, and the Callithumpians. There are also three French-speaking professional companies. The Théâtre Populaire d'Acadie has performed in the Boîte-Théâtre at Caraquet since the mid-1970s and also tours its productions of original ACADIAN plays and classics to fifteen francophone centres around New Brunswick. La Co-operative de Théâtre L'Escaouette, based in Moncton, is the Acadian equivalent of TNB's Young Company. Established in 1978, it tours to French schools in the Atlantic region with locally written pieces that frequently stress the Acadian heritage. In the early 1980s Le Théâtre du Bord

d'la Côte was founded in Shippegan.

6. Playscripts. Nineteenth-century newspapers published a number of political satires in dramatic form, including *The Triumph of Intrigue* (1833), *Northumbria* (1869), and *Done in Darkness* (1879). *The Sidewalks of Saint John* (1870) and *A Farce in One Act* (1870) attacked rival newspapers and ladies' boarding schools respectively. Closet dramas include Lt. Adam Allan's adaptation *The New Gentle Shepherd* (1798), Peter John Allen's romantic fragment *Pygmalion, Prince of Cyprus* (1853), William Murdoch's verse play (imitative of the dialect of Burns) *A Fireside Drama* (1876), and theologically oriented works by George Henry Hammond: *Two Offerings* (1890) and *Crowning Test* (1901). Unfortunately, except for some of John CARLETON's plays, no performed scripts are extant. Lost are Thomas Hill's riot-producing *The Provincial Association* (1845), Beatrice Jones's allegedly unladylike tale of love, kidnapping, and crime in Mexico, *The League of Sierra Madre* (1868), and the temperance plays of the 1880s. Known only by their names are many original works by members of the Saint John Theatre Guild and other amateur societies of this century, although Jean Sweet's award-winning *Small Potatoes* (best play, Dominion Drama Festival, 1938) and several of novelist Dan Ross's plays have survived. Walter Learning's tenure at TNB saw successful productions of three pieces co-authored by Learning and Alden NOWLAN: *Frankenstein* (produced in 1977), *The Dollar Woman* (produced in 1977), and *The Incredible Murder of Cardinal Tosca* (produced in 1978). Malcolm BLACK continued to encourage local writing with commissions for Dan Ross's *Murder Game* (produced in 1981-2), and Norm Foster's *Sinners* (produced in 1983-4) and *The Melville Boys* (produced in 1984-5). The best-known English-language playwright from New Brunswick is perhaps Sharon POLLOCK, who was appointed artistic director of TNB in 1988. The best-known French-language playwright from the province is undoubtedly Antonine MAILLET, whose *La SAGOUINE* made both Maillet and actress Viola Léger household names.

See Mary Elizabeth Smith, *Too Soon the Curtain Fell: A History of Theatre in Saint John 1789-1900* (1981); Edward Mullaly, *Desperate Stages: New Brunswick's Theatre in the 1840's* (1987); and Mark Blagrave, 'Community Theatre in Saint John Between the Wars',

New Brunswick, Theatre in

The Proceedings of the Theatre in Atlantic Canada Symposium (1988), ed. Richard Paul Knowles.   MARY ELIZABETH SMITH

Newfoundland, Theatre in. In the sixteenth and seventeenth centuries theatre as it existed in Europe was unknown in Newfoundland; however, beginning in the eighteenth century performances and presentations were common to most communities during the few holidays the fishing industry afforded the people. The most popular form of drama was associated with mummering, a custom of the Christmas season that has its roots in medieval Europe and entails disguising oneself both physically and vocally and seeking admittance to homes within the community. Another form of this ancient custom, the mummer play of St George and the Dragon, was performed in a number of centres throughout the Island. Dealing with death and resurrection, the folk drama was peopled with a cast of diverse characters such as St George, St Patrick, Turkish Knight, and Father Christmas; it died out after the First World War, although there have recently been revivals by professional theatre groups. As was the case with mummering in the Middle Ages, the Newfoundland practice incurred the wrath of the authorities and in 1861 was legislated against to prevent the rowdiness that came to be associated with the custom in St John's and the larger communities on the Avalon Peninsula.

In the nineteenth century formal theatrical activity, widespread and produced in all communities throughout the Island, was represented by the Community Concert, which consisted of songs, recitations, dialogues, short plays, and readings. These productions were organized and directed in the villages usually during the Christmas season and were intended to raise money to provide financial assistance to the poor and needy, and to maintain the upkeep of churches and schools. Community concerts encouraged self-sufficiency in the field of entertainment and contributed to the cohesiveness of the community as a whole.

Until 1950 the production of full-length plays was confined primarily to St John's, which was visited frequently by travelling troupes from Canada, the U.S., and Great Britain. Since it was a major port of call for transatlantic traffic, many of the acts were representative of the popular fare of the time.

Records show that the first professional company to perform in Newfoundland was a group from Quebec—the Ormsby company made up of Walter Davids, Michael Henry, and James and Mary Ormsby—who, in 1806, received permission to 'exhibit their Theatrical Representatives'. They performed with license from the governor along with the caveat that the four performers conduct themselves in an orderly and decent manner. Perhaps the most famous performer to visit St John's in the nineteenth century was Jean Davenport, the celebrated child actor who performed from a repertoire of Shakespeare, Restoration drama, and melodrama during a three-month stay in St John's in 1841. The Henry W. Preston Company visited St John's regularly between 1841 and 1843 and performed in the Amateur Theatre (opened in 1823). It presented such plays as Douglas Jerrold's *Black-Eyed Susan* and Edward Bulwer-Lytton's *The Lady of Lyons* and in 1842 travelled to Harbour Grace and Carbonear. The J.W. LANERGAN Company performed in St John's from 1857 to 1860, and the Wilson and Clarke Company from Boston, known as the New Provincial Theatre, performed from the 1860s to 1872 melodramas such as *Uncle Tom's Cabin* and *Ten Nights in a Barroom*, and Dion Boucicault's *The Colleen Bawn*. Other visiting companies included the Woodward/Whitman Company, 1900; the Lyceum Company, 1900; the Robinson Opera Company, 1900; the W.S. Harkins Company, 1901-7; the Bixley Comedy Company, 1908; the Klark/Urban Company, 1909; and the Merkle/Harder Company, 1909.

Row's Warehouse, a warehouse adapted for theatricals, was used from 1817 to 1822. The Amateur Theatre, a thirty-foot high wooden building, opened on 17 Feb. 1823 with a production of M.G. Lewis's melodrama *The Castle Spectre*. Following the fire of 1846, when much of St John's was destroyed, most performances—particularly by touring companies—took place in makeshift buildings; it was not until the Mechanics' Hall was built in 1857 that a suitable performance space existed in St John's. In 1861 The Fisherman's Hall opened as a theatre and continued to be used as such until 1873, when it was taken over by the Roman Catholic Church.

In 1873 the Total Abstinence Hall was opened and was used as a theatre by travelling

376

and local companies until it was destroyed by the fire of 1892. A new hall was constructed, this time with a properly equipped theatre: the stage was 26' high by 25' deep by 56' wide; there were two private boxes, and seating capacity for about 1,400. Eventually the Total Abstinence Hall was renamed, in turn, the Casino, the Metropolis, and the People's Theatre; it finally became the Capitol Movie Theatre in 1935. St Patrick's Hall, built by the Benevolent Irish Society, also housed the BIS Dramatic Company and hosted touring companies. Foran's Opera House, a converted skating rink, opened in 1888 and was capable of seating 3,000.

It was not until the 1960s, when ARTS AND CULTURE CENTRES were built in St John's, Corner Brook, Grand Falls, and Stephenville, that Newfoundland could claim permanent theatres for use by professional and amateur companies.

Amateur theatre has been a popular pastime since the first show in 1817 when The Gentlemen of the Navy performed Nicholas Rowe's *The Fair Penitent* in Row's Warehouse. As with community concerts and other such theatrical events, amateur theatre was produced to assist the destitute. A prologue to *The Fair Penitent*, written especially for the St John's production, painted a grim picture of life in the city and asked that the actors' 'noble objective' might excuse their lack of skill. Following this successful production the same group presented Charles Kemble's *The Point of Honour*, along with David Garrick's farce *Bon Ton; or High Life*

Above Stairs, and they, and other amateur groups (such as The Benevolent Irish Society and The Dorcas Society) continued to offer similar dramatic fare throughout the nineteenth century. Most of the amateur and professional theatrical activity in Newfoundland during the nineteenth century took place in St John's. It was not until 1950, with the formation of the Newfoundland Drama Society, that regular amateur productions took place in centres outside the capital city. Again, these were confined to the larger towns, with the smaller communities continuing to be restricted to mummering, concerts, and the occasional school or church production.

In 1951 the first professional repertory company, the LONDON THEATRE COMPANY, was formed in St John's by British actors who had played there with the Alexandra Theatre Company of Birmingham for twelve weeks in 1947-8. From 1951 to 1957 it produced 100 plays representing primarily the kind of theatre that was popular at the time in London. From St John's the company toured to the west coast of Newfoundland, to major centres in the Maritimes, and even to southern Ontario. It made a considerable contribution to theatre in Newfoundland, not only through its productions but, after it was dissolved, through many of its performers who continued to work and live in the province and became active in the Newfoundland Drama Society.

The MUMMERS TROUPE, founded in 1972 by Chris BROOKES, Lynne Lunde, and John

Joey, *Rising Tide Theatre*, St John's, Nfld, 1982, with (l. to r.) Sheilagh Guy, Jeff Pitcher, David Fox, Kevin Noble, Brian Downey, David Ross

377

Doyle, developed most of its own material as COLLECTIVE CREATIONs, focusing on socio-political issues that affected the people of Newfoundland and Labrador. Until its demise in 1982 the Mummers Troupe successfully carried out its objective—'to explore indigenous Newfoundland material in a theatrical context'—while introducing theatre to many parts of the province.

Newfoundland subject-matter, and particularly the stereotypical image many mainland Canadians have of Newfoundlanders, provided material for the Newfoundland group CODCO, which was formed in Toronto in 1973 and premièred with their collective *Cod on a Stick*. After a successful run sponsored by THEATRE PASSE MURAILLE, the company returned to St John's and toured the province. Since then Codco's comic treatment of contemporary and traditional Newfoundland culture has established for them a national reputation. Although the original Company disbanded in 1979, Codco Productions is still active and works out of St John's.

Current professional theatre companies include THEATRE NEWFOUNDLAND AND LABRADOR, which operates out of Corner Brook, and The Rising Tide Theatre, which was formed in 1978 and operates out of the Arts and Culture Centre, St John's. Rising Tide's initial successes were with collective shows such as *Joey* (about former Newfoundland premier Joey Smallwood), but their repertoire now encompasses a broad range of modern plays, collectives, and children's shows. The Stephenville Festival was founded in 1979 by Bombay-born actor, playwright, and director Maxim Mazumdar (who died in 1988); it produces six plays each summer and runs a year-round drama academy. Its mixed Canadian and international repertoire has attracted prominent Canadian actors such as Gordon PINSENT, Barbara CHILCOTT, Wendy Toye, and Edward Atienza. Sean MULCAHY was appointed artistic director in 1988. The Resource Centre for the Arts (RCA) in St John's runs a 200-seat theatre in the Longshoremen's Protective Union (LSPU) Hall, offering an eclectic mix of community, experimental, and collective theatre.

Since 1950 a number of Newfoundland playwrights have had their work produced by professional and amateur groups; foremost among these is Michael COOK (born in England), whose plays explore the Newfoundland character in relation to the environment and the conflicts resulting from the clash of traditional and contemporary cultures. Plays by Tom Cahill, Grace Butt, Ted Russell, and Cassie Brown are popular with Newfoundlanders because of their use of Newfoundland speech and attention to Newfoundland issues.

Under the auspices of the Newfoundland Drama Society, amateur theatre continues to play a significant role in theatre in the province. There is an annual drama festival that brings together seven community theatre companies in competition and presents a varied program of contemporary plays as well as original works by Newfoundland playwrights.

Outside St John's and Corner Brook the populations are not large enough to support professional theatre, but traditions related to community concerts, and the interest sparked by the Mummers and Codco, have helped widen the appeal of theatre throughout Newfoundland.   C.J. SKINNER

New Play Centre, The. The mandate of the New Play Centre, founded in Vancouver in 1970 by Douglas Bankson and Sheila Neville, has been to encourage the production of Canadian plays. Dissatisfied with the efforts of the DOMINION DRAMA FESTIVAL, with which Bankson and Neville were both affiliated, and working on a small Koerner Foundation grant of only five hundred dollars, they created the New Play Centre to seek out and develop dramatic writing in B.C.

The original plan was to invite scripts from local playwrights who wanted informed criticism of their work, and to encourage professional companies to look at the best of these for possible production. To present this work to the theatre community, the Society staged public readings. The popularity of these readings, and the large number of scripts submitted during the first eighteen months, made clear the need for full-time co-ordination. In Jan. 1972 Pamela HAWTHORN joined the company as managing director, which allowed for a significant increase in the volume and diversity of its activities. The Centre operates from offices at 1405 Anderson St on Granville Island, in space shared by a number of small theatrical companies and conveniently close to the Waterfront Theatre, which NPC co-owns and operates with Carousel Theatre.

In 1972, under Hawthorn's direction,

Waterfront Theatre (New Play Centre), Vancouver

NPC began to mount productions and to advertise its activities nationally. It now enjoys a national reputation and receives some 150 scripts a year from all regions of the country. Of these, thirty-five are dramatized in a workshop format and five to ten are presented in full productions. The Centre issues catalogues of its scripts, and distributes them on request.

The première season of such productions, in the summer of 1972, included Sharon POL-LOCK's first play, *A Compulsory Option*, and Tom GRAINGER's *Helper* (1975). These early productions, at the old Vancouver Art Gallery, were extremely simple: Equity minimum was paid to the actors; and Hawthorn, Neville, and two helpers handled all backstage and production details. Productions were later mounted at the VANCOUVER EAST CULTURAL CENTRE, and the company now performs in the Waterfront Theatre. Readings are still held in a variety of locations.

Since 1974 the Centre has taken a more active role in developing scripts. Acting out of Hawthorn's concern that there was still no 'strength in the undergrowth', it established competitions to attract new writers and to encourage writing by women. A Women's Playwriting Competition in 1975 discovered *Rites of Passage* by Anne CAM-ERON (Cam Hubert), and in 1985 a 'Short Takes for Women' Competition developed five scripts by women writers.

The NPC has not been without criticism. Some feel that the choice of plays is too conservative; Pamela Hawthorn replies that a conscious effort has been made to showcase a variety of differing styles, but that 'most of the experimental material received is less skillful, somehow . . . less exciting . . . highly derivative.'

In 1985 NPC also extended its interest to writing for television. Initially, each of four playwrights was asked to adapt a play of his own into a short TV script. In a manner comparable to the full productions given selected theatrical scripts, these plays have since been treated to a full shoot by a professional television crew. In 1986 NPC received three CBC commissions to develop scripts and two of these were filmed in the 1986-7 season. In the same year another Vancouver television station funded the Centre to create a series of short dramas.

Since its inception, the New Play Centre has produced some ninety plays and remains a central force in the development of new Canadian writing for the theatre, film, and television. Beginning in 1974 NPC has received du Maurier sponsorship for its annual Festival of Plays, and in 1985 won the Vantage Arts Academy Award.

REID GILBERT

New Play Society, The. Toronto's first indigenous professional theatre company after the Second World War was also the first to produce Canadian plays on a regular basis. In 1946 Dora Mavor MOORE's amateur Village Players (1938-46) voted to incorporate themselves into the NPS, 'to establish a living theatre in Canada on a professional but non-profit basis.' Utilizing her savings and her sons' war bonds, Mrs Moore rented the non-union 450-seat Royal Ontario Museum Theatre. She opened a Fall series on 11 Oct. 1946 with J.M. Synge's *The Playboy of the Western World*, followed by an imported Chinese production, *Lady Precious Stream*; Somerset Maugham's *The Circle*; Eugene O'Neill's *Ah, Wilderness!*; and, at Christmas, the Coventry Nativity Play. Productions were presented fortnightly on Fridays and Saturdays. Actors and technicians alike were paid $15 per week. By 1948-9 the shows ran a week; but only with the advent of the annual SPRING THAW revue (opening on 1 Apr. from 1948 to 1971) did extended runs become possible. The golden seasons were between 1946 and 1950. From the international repertoire there were memorable productions of William Saroyan, Sean O'Casey, Sophocles, R.B. Sheridan and G.B. Shaw. Less memorable were the attempts at Shakespeare. The first Canadian play staged by the NPS was Lister SINCLAIR's *The Man in the Blue Moon* (1-3 May 1947); the second, Morley CALLAGHAN's *To Tell*

New Play Society

The Truth (14-22 Jan. 1949), which was transferred to the ROYAL ALEXANDRA THEATRE (7-12 Feb.). The extraordinary 1949-50 season saw five original Canadian works: *Who's Who* (Sept. 1949) by Mrs Moore's son Mavor MOORE; Harry Boyle's *The Inheritance* (Nov. 1949); Andrew ALLAN's *Narrow Passage* (Jan. 1950); John COULTER's *RIEL* (Feb. 1950); and Callaghan's *Going Home* (Mar. 1950). When the Museum Theatre became a union house, the NPS discontinued its regular seasons and opened its Theatre School in the Boris Volkoff building on Yonge St. There were occasional Museum presentations—Shaw's *Arms and the Man* (Mar. 1952), its 50th production, and Mazo de la Roche's *Mistress of Jalna* (Sept. 1953)—but the unsubsidized NPS was obliged to go commercial in larger theatres. The Coventry Nativity gave way to Christmas pantomimes like *Mother Goose* (1949) and *Babes in the Wood* (1950) at the Royal Alexandra, and *Peter Pan* (1952) and *Cinderella* (1953) at the Eaton Auditorium. Mavor Moore assumed leadership in 1954 but lost money with his 1955 touring musical *Sunshine Town*, based on LEACOCK's *Sunshine Sketches*, and *The Optimist*, which he based on Voltaire's *Candide*, mounted in 1956 at the Avenue Theatre. Also seen there was Don HARRON's adaptation of Earle BIRNEY's *Turvey* in 1957. However, hopes that this re-converted cinema might become their permanent playhouse were dashed when the building was demolished in 1957 to become a parking lot. The Theatre School (1950-68) catered primarily for children. At its height there were 200 students. In its final decade, the NPS presented a Mexican Night (1958); a 1959 Director's Stage series of unusual European dramas (Obey, Brecht, and Anouilh); a production of Marc LESCARBOT's *Theatre of Neptune* (*THÉÂTRE DE NEPTUNE EN LA NOUVELLE-FRANCE*) (1962); and an all-Canadian play festival (1965) introducing ten short works. Over the years the NPS also sponsored important lecture series on Television (1955), Canadian Plays (1956), New Directions (1958), and Theatre Management (1956). In 1971, on its 25th anniversary, the NPS was dissolved, free of debts. As Nathan COHEN said, it had been a company full of 'passion, artistic focus and an elated rage for identity.'

The archives of the New Play Society are housed at the Univ. of Toronto.

DAVID GARDNER

New Theatre. The first of Toronto's second wave of ALTERNATE THEATRES, it was founded in 1971 by Jonathan Stanley and Adolf Toman, who had been colleagues in a summer youth project called Theatre-Go-Round. Their first production was Oscar Wilde's *The Importance of Being Earnest* in 1971 at the Colonnade Theatre. The Stanley/Toman partnership dissolved the next year. Toman subsequently founded Classical Stage Productions (1972-3), Aladdin Theatre (1975-), and Limelight Dinner Theatre (1977-), all in Toronto. Stanley re-established New Theatre in a disused 220-seat church hall on Bathurst St, producing a challenging range of modern international plays, beginning in 1973 with Wilde's *Salomé*, Sam Shepard's *The Tooth of Crime*, and Heathcote Williams' *AC/DC*. New Theatre attained its greatest critical success with Picasso's *Four Little Girls* (in 1975), Peter Handke's *The Ride Across Lake Constance* (also 1975), and a popular production of Robert Patrick's *Kennedy's Children* (in 1976). Original productions included Larry FINEBERG's *Human Remains* in 1975 and Michael HOLLINGSWORTH's *White Noise* in 1977.

New Theatre then embarked on two financially debilitating projects: a 1977 commercial production of Tom Stoppard's *Travesties* at the ST LAWRENCE CENTRE and, in co-operation with OPEN CIRCLE THEATRE and Le Théâtre du P'tit Bonheur (see THÉÂTRE FRANÇAIS DE TORONTO), the conversion of a heritage court-house into the Adelaide Court Theatre, which opened in 1978. New Theatre mounted only four productions there, including John PALMER's *The Pits 1979*, in 1979, and in 1980 Erika RITTER's *AUTOMATIC PILOT*, which was a huge success. Stanley remounted *Automatic Pilot* twice before the company closed. Despite a reputation for dubious business practices and uneven production standards, New Theatre was admired for presenting unusual European and American plays at a time when new Canadian drama dominated Toronto theatre.

DENIS W. JOHNSTON

Newton, Christopher (b. 1936). Born of Welsh parents in Deal, Eng., he took a BA at Leeds University, prior to graduate work in the U.S. at Purdue and the Univ. of Illinois (MA, 1959). At Illinois he took up acting and, after a year's teaching at Bucknell University, Pennsylvania, he came to Canada in

1961 to audition for the STRATFORD FESTI-VAL. Rejected, he nonetheless secured roles in a 1961-2 cross-country tour by the CANA-DIAN PLAYERS of Shakespeare's *Julius Caesar* and Shaw's *Saint Joan*, which he later described as his education as an actor.

In 1963 he played Algy in Mike Nichols' VANCOUVER PLAYHOUSE production of Oscar Wilde's *The Importance of Being Earnest*. Two years later Nichols summoned him to New York to take over the role of Tom in Ann Jellicoe's *The Knack*. He then spent three seasons (1966-8) with the Stratford Festival, playing among other roles Orsino in *Twelfth Night*, Oberon in *A Midsummer Night's Dream*, and Aramis in *The Three Musketeers*. In 1968 he was invited to become the founding artistic director of THEATRE CAL-GARY, before moving in 1973 to succeed Paxton WHITEHEAD as artistic director of the Vancouver Playhouse. In his six-year term he made it one of the liveliest regional theatres in Canada, with a permanent core of resident actors, a distinctive company style, and its own acting school, launched with Powys THOMAS in 1975.

In 1980 Newton became artistic director of the SHAW FESTIVAL, inheriting an accumulated deficit of $600,000. Within four years the debt had been liquidated, the Festival put into profit, and Newton offered a further five-year contract. This success could be traced to a two-pronged strategy. On the one hand Newton took even further than before the Shaw Festival's habit of sugaring its main pill with undemanding sideshows: antique British farces and pocket versions of old musicals. On the other hand, he took the same kind of liberties with Shaw's plays that directors had long taken with Shakespeare's. Shavians complained of his high-handed ways with Shaw's texts. Defenders argued that he did only what a Shaw Festival presumably existed to do—treat Shaw's plays not as period pieces, but as works for all times. He also succeeded in displaying, as seldom before, Shaw's immense powers of theatricality.

Influenced by the anti-illusionist techniques of the Glasgow Citizens' Theatre, Newton's productions are often heavy with parody and camp, but at their best—*Heartbreak House* in 1985, *On The Rocks* in 1986, or *Major Barbara* in 1987—they evoke a surreal, spectacular theatricality that makes Shaw seem once more avant garde.

Newton has also written several plays, including *Slow Train to St Ives*, staged in the MANITOBA THEATRE CENTRE studio in 1966, and *The Sound of Distant Thunder*, staged in the Vancouver Playhouse studio in 1977. He has been awarded honorary degrees by Brock Univ. and the Univ. of Guelph.

RONALD BRYDEN

Nichol, James W. (b. 1940). Born and raised in Paris, Ont.—the locale known as 'Kingforks' in all his work—he is the author of over fifty produced radio dramas, ten television scripts, and a dozen stage plays.

Many of his plays dramatize extreme mental states. The working-class husband in *The House on Chestnut Street* (1972), produced by THEATRE CALGARY in 1972, is hounded into a crippled state of mind and body by an upper-class wife, whose thwarted sense of ambition is expressed in anguished sexual projections. In *Sainte-Marie Among the Hurons* (1977), produced by Theatre London in 1974, the Jesuit protagonist is plagued by an obsessive martyr complex, which is dramatically portrayed.

James Nichol's Sainte-Marie Among the Hurons, *National Arts Centre, 1977, with (l. to r.) Wayne Barnett, Hugh Webster, Colin Fox*

Nichol

This emphasis on the psychological is often accompanied by a treatment of the socio-sexual ethos of the small town. *Gwendoline* (1978), set in 1907, features an unstable heroine and a town whose repressed emotional life makes it fearfully hypocritical about sex and intolerant of difference. Nichol's most popular play to date, it subverts the social and dramatic cliché of the neurotic spinster, who in this case emerges triumphantly healthy. It was first produced by the BLYTH FESTIVAL in 1978.

Gwendoline's structure is typical of most of Nichol's plays, including *Child* (1979), produced at the Blyth Festival in 1979, in which two couples work out their attitudes to abortion and parenthood, and *Relative Strangers* (1983), produced by Theatre London in 1983, in which an actress returns to her childhood home and exorcizes ghosts that have energized her career and haunted her personal relationships. The problems of Act 1, complicated or disguised by the distorting pressures of repressed childhood traumas, are honestly confronted, if not always solved, by the full revelation of the determining past in Act 2. *Sonny* (1982), produced by Victoria's BELFRY THEATRE in 1982, a darkly bittersweet satire of the Beatles generation and its middle-American parents, and *And When I Wake*, a modern Gothic thriller produced by MAGNUS THEATRE, Thunder Bay, in 1984, are both structured around the interplay of present action and past re-enactment. Any tendency towards melodrama is usually countered either by the characters' ironic sense of 'play' or by the witty, sometimes cutting dialogue. *The Three True Loves of Jasmine Hoover*, produced by Magnus Theatre in 1986, marks an interesting stylistic departure for Nichol at mid-career. The expressionistic elements often felt as part of the subtext in Nichol's naturalist dramas are here released and symbolized by exaggerated props and stage images.   LARRY McDONALD

Nickinson, John (1808-64). Born in England, he was posted to Canada with the 24th Regiment, but his success in GARRISON theatricals led him to abandon the army for the stage. After a season in Albany (1836-7), he went to New York, playing at the Franklin, the Park, and from 1841 to 1850 at Mitchell's Olympic, where he won renown as a comedian and character actor. When the Olympic closed in 1850, he and his eldest daughter Charlotte MORRISON toured the Northeastern States and the British Provinces, appearing for the first time in Toronto in Apr. 1851. In 1852 he returned with a full company for five weeks of crowded houses before resuming a tour that ended in Utica, N.Y., where he remained as manager for the fall season. On 28 Mar. 1853 Nickinson launched his first season as lessee of Toronto's ROYAL LYCEUM. His company, which included his four daughters—Charlotte, Eliza, Virginia, and Isabella—and other talented young actors offered a repertoire ranging from Goldsmith's *She Stoops to Conquer* to popular melodramas such as *Uncle Tom's Cabin*. His annual Christmas spectacle (*Cinderella, Aladdin*, etc.) was an innovation in Toronto, where it became a gala holiday tradition. Nickinson himself was most effective in dialect parts and in the portrayal of military characters, especially Havresac in Boucicault's *Napoleon's Old Guard*. In addition to the Royal Lyceum, he managed Hamilton's Metropolitan Theatre, taking his Toronto company there each year for short seasons. Five prosperous years ended in 1858, when hard economic times drastically cut theatre receipts; salaries were unpaid, actors departed, and in 1859 Nickinson gave up as manager. He returned to the Royal Lyceum in Mar. 1860, but lasted only one brief and profitless season. After touring smaller centres with a few faithful associates, he joined the company at Pike's Opera House, Cincinnati, as stage manager and died in that city.   MARY SHORTT

Nicol, Eric (b. 1919). Born in Kingston, Ont., and educated at the Univ. of British Columbia and at the Sorbonne, he settled in Vancouver after a period in England (1950-1), writing comedy for the BBC. He has written a syndicated column for the *Vancouver Province* since 1951. More than a dozen collections of satirical essays and comic 'histories' have won him three LEACOCK Medals for Humour.

Like Father, Like Fun (1973) is Nicol's most commercial play. Its plot—a businessman's attempt to have his son initiated into sex—becomes the vehicle for comment on the rough business practices that built Vancouver and the very different values represented by the 'flower children' of the 1960s. The play enjoyed a huge success when produced at the VANCOUVER PLAYHOUSE in Mar. 1966 and, despite negative criticism, long runs in Toronto and Montreal. Its disastrous one-day 'run' in New York (as *A Minor Adjustment*) became the subject of a witty journal, *A Scar is Born* (1968). *The Fourth Monkey* (1973) is a thinly disguised allegory about a writer whose island (Canada) is invaded by outsiders. It opened at the Vancouver Playhouse on 10 Oct. 1968. *Pillar of Sand* (1975), first performed at the same theatre during the 1972-3 season, has a more universal theme in which Nicol contrasts the rationality of a Roman soldier with the excesses of a Christian saint—excesses that have a decidedly contemporary ring.

Nicol's children's plays continue his preoccupation with national and cultural issues. In *Beware the Quickly Who* (1972), produced at the HOLIDAY THEATRE, Vancouver, in 1967, a boy embarks on a journey to discover his name. That his name turns out to be Johnny Canuck may strike some as straining a too-obvious analogy. This early play is perhaps Nicol's most original experiment in dramatic effect, employing clever doubling and a highly theatrical use of actors as puppets, totems, and even as scenery. *The Clam Made a Face* (1972), produced at the same theatre in Dec. 1967, uses a potlatch as a frame device. A participation play, it dramatizes five West Coast Indian legends. (See also CHILDREN'S DRAMA AND THEATRE IN ENGLISH.)

While Nicol's plays do have a serious dimension, the overall emphasis is on the easy laugh. A facile treatment of women, voyeuristic humour, and a marked theatrical conventionality now date most of Nicol's work. *Three Plays by Eric Nicol* (1975) contains *Like Father, Like Fun*, *The Fourth Monkey*, and *Pillar of Sand*.   REID GILBERT

Northern Light Theatre. Inspired by the success of CITY STAGE in Vancouver, Scott Swan (artistic director), Allan Lysell (administrative director), and Angela and Merrilyn Gann (actresses) founded a similar LUNCH THEATRE in Edmonton. On 6 Mar. 1975 Northern Light opened in the Edmonton Art Gallery with *Love and Drollery*, a collage of Elizabethan music, prose, and poetry compiled by Swann and Lysell. Three more collages, two of them by Swan and Lysell, completed the first season.

Meeting with immediate critical and popular success, the theatre developed rapidly from 1975 to 1980. A $12,000 grant in 1975 was used to improve the small Art Gallery Theatre and costs were kept down by adhering to the 'company system' that Swan had encountered at the Bristol Old Vic School in Britain; by the fall of 1978 the theatre had a core company of fourteen people who simultaneously served as production team, board of directors, and office staff. It offered a mixed program of classics, new work, musicals, and light comedy marked by the company's self-described 'house style'—an amalgam of ensemble playing and lyrical and emotional intensity of acting. While this general approach remained constant, two significant expansions occurred. A 1976 decision to begin offering two evening shows a week allowed the company to present full-length plays, while a 1977 decision to become the first Edmonton company to hire a full-time dramaturge, Frank Moher, led to the establishment of a 'playwrights' unit' for the reading and workshopping of new scripts. Plays by Gordon Pengilly, Tony Bell, Frank Moher, and Ben Tarver were first developed in the unit, with Northern Light doing premières of James DeFelice's *Take Me Where the Water's Warm* (1978) in 1979 and Frank Moher's *Down for the Weekend* (1981) in 1980. Occasional summer seasons and the founding of a Young Company were other experiments during these years.

Between 1980 and 1982 the theatre underwent crisis and change. At the end of the 1979-80 season, Northern Light moved completely into the full-length evening format, sought a permanent theatre space, and launched an ambitious summer repertory theatre out of a tent in a local park. The 1980 summer season was successful, but the company's large debts forced cancellation of all but one play of their proposed 1980-1 season, and the expanded 1981 summer season was financially disastrous. The 1981-2 season started with a debt of $130,000 and the news that artistic director Scott Swan would move to FESTIVAL LENNOXVILLE at the end of the season.

Nonetheless in 1982-3, under artistic director Jace van der Veen, formerly of Vancouver's NEW PLAY CENTRE, Northern Light moved into a period of recovery. With careful budgeting, smaller seasons, and an intense fund-raising campaign, the company's debt was completely cleared by 1983 and a new home found in the Kaasa Theatre in the Northern Alberta Jubilee Auditorium. By the

Northern Light Theatre

spring of 1988 Northern Light Theatre was functioning successfully with mixed seasons of classical, new, and Canadian works, and preparing to welcome a new artistic director, Gyllian Raby, formerly of Calgary's One Yellow Rabbit Theatre.   MOIRA DAY

Northwest Territories and Yukon, Theatre in the. Early explorers left little documentation about the theatrical practices of the Inuit. We do know, however, that through the nineteenth and early twentieth centuries the Inuit told dramatic stories using puppets made from whale-bone and fibre threads, a tradition that has now disappeared. In ceremonies witnessed by early explorers, dancers assumed the personae of animals, or re-created battles. The drum dance, the oldest continuing native theatrical tradition in the Arctic, is still regularly performed in the communities of the Keewatin mainland, north Baffin Island, and the Kitimeot region (in the Central Arctic). A recent attempt has been made to revive and preserve Inuit tradition by the Igloolik/Pond Inlet Theatre Group, composed of Inuits who produce plays in English and Inuktitut based on Inuit legends. (See AMERINDIAN AND INUIT DRAMA AND THEATRE.)

European theatrical influence began with whalers and explorers on the Arctic coast. During the 1750s British whalers in Davis Strait performed 'crossing-the-line' ceremonies or 'the play of Neptune' as they crossed the Arctic Circle. This quasi-theatrical ceremony, much like a mummers' play, continued until the 1870s and the advent of steampower. Whalers wintering in Canada's Arctic waters also sponsored variety entertainment: first at Cumberland Sound (1853-4), then at Marble Island in Hudson Bay (1862-3), and finally in the Beaufort Sea. In Sept. 1864 American whalers built the first permanent Arctic theatre on Marble Island. Its inaugural performance on 17 Oct. 1864 included a presentation by the Hudson Bay Minstrels and a play, Henry Fielding's *The Mock Doctor* (based on Molière). The theatre continued operations until the 1880s; local Inuit still refer to its ruins as 'The Theatre'. When whaling vessels reached the Beaufort Sea in 1889, they brought theatre with them: one ship in the fleet, the *Beluga*, was specially fitted for theatricals, primarily variety entertainment and minstrel shows.

Theatricals were a regular feature of British Arctic expeditions in the nineteenth century, a period of extensive naval exploration in the Arctic, beginning with the 1819 expedition of Captain William Edward Parry, which wintered on the south coast of Melville Island. Undertaken primarily to boost morale, amateur productions were eagerly accepted by the ships' crews and resulted in at least three original scripts: *The North-West Passage; or, The Voyage Finished*, partially written by Captain Parry himself and performed aboard the *Hecla* on 23 Dec. 1819; the pantomime *Zero; or, Harlequin Light*, written by Charles Ede and performed aboard the *Assistance* on 9 Jan. 1851; and *King Glumpus*, written by John Barrow for performance at Melville Island on board the *Resolute* on 1 Feb. 1853. (See also ROYAL ARCTIC THEATRE.) American explorers also produced plays during the winter months, including at least one original script, *Pantomime*, performed aboard the *Advance* on 30 Jan. 1852. The American Army expedition, led by Lt Adolphus W. Greely, which wintered at Fort Conger at Discovery Harbour on Ellesmere Island between 1881 and 1883, named their troupe the 'Lime-Juice Club' and performed at the 'Dutch Island Opera House'. This venue witnessed the first and undoubtedly the only performance of a Wild West Show in the Arctic when nine performers staged a representation of an Indian Council and war-dance.

Inland, European theatrical influence was transmitted by missionaries who travelled north from Western Canada in the mid-nineteenth century to establish missions and schools. By the 1860s the Grey Nuns had opened mission schools on Lake Athabasca and Great Slave Lake, where plays and playlets were performed regularly. On 1 July 1912, to mark the golden jubilee of the Oblate Mission of Notre Dame de la Providence, eight missions—including Fort Rae, Fort Nelson, and Arctic Red River—sent children to perform an original playlet.

With the discovery of gold in the Yukon, theatre became a more regular feature of inland Arctic life. Even before gold was discovered at Bonanza Creek in 1896, small canvas or wood-frame shanty theatres had existed in places like Circle City and Fortymile. Such buildings were divided into two rooms, a saloon and combination theatre/dance hall with a small stage. During the winter of 1896, the Tivoli Theatre in For-

St Andrew's Night, Palace Grand Theatre, Dawson City, 1899

tymile produced *The Pallyup Queen* for seven straight months because the actors had failed to get out before freeze-up. Finally the audience shouted the performers off the stage.

Dawson. The first permanent wooden theatre in Dawson was a log building called the Opera House. During 1898 three more theatre/dance halls opened: the Monte Carlo, the Pavillion, and the Combination (later the Tivoli). In 1899 a fire at the Bodega saloon spread, destroying the Opera House and the Tivoli, and damaging the Monte Carlo, but later that year they were replaced by the Amphitheatre and the Novelty.

Alexander PANTAGES, a Greek immigrant, had begun his Dawson career as a waiter, but around the turn of the century he began operating the Orpheum Theatre, Dawson's most successful VAUDEVILLE house (opened *c.* 1897). Using his Dawson capital and experience, he later built a North American theatre chain into a fifteen-million-dollar empire.

The major theatre in Dawson was, and remains, the Palace Grand Theatre, built in 1899 and seating 600–700 patrons. Known as the Grand Opera House during its first four-month season, its name was changed to the Palace Grand Theatre (1899–1900), the

Savoy (1900–1), the Old Savoy (1901), the Auditorium (1901–38), the Nugget Dance Hall (1938–40), and the Auditorium (1940–62), until its reconstruction as the Palace Grand Theatre in 1962. Designed and built by C.H. Albertson for 'Arizona Charlie' Meadows, who had formerly toured Europe and Asia with a Wild West Show, the Palace Grand featured demonstrations of Meadows' shooting skill as he shot glass balls from between the fingers of his wife until the night he shot a finger off and she insisted they drop the act. Four months later Meadows hired George Hillyer, a manager who attempted to run 'a strictly legitimate house', opening with Goethe's *Faust*. In Jan. 1900, Eddie O'Brien became manager, offering such popular works as *Marriage Is Sublime*, *Human Hearts*, Denman THOMPSON's *Old Homestead*, Martha Morton's *A Bachelor's Romance*, and Harriet Beecher Stowe's *Uncle Tom's Cabin*. In 1901 Meadows sold the Palace Grand for $17,000 to the mining magnate James Hall, who renamed it the Auditorium and installed the Bittner Stock Company for the 1901-2 season. The next year his wife Lillian Hall established her own stock company at the Auditorium.

In 1902 the Auditorium was assessed at $26,500. After 1902, however, the passing of the Gold Rush drastically reduced the variety of entertainment. In 1902 occasional amateur productions were presented at the Auditorium, including the Dawson Amateur Society's *Mikado*; but by 1903 Dawson had been taken off the professional vaudeville circuit. In 1907 the Auditorium was assessed at only $2,500. The first moving-picture was shown there in 1900; by the end of the First World War the major form of entertainment throughout the North was the movies.

The Klondike Visitors' Association purchased the Auditorium in Dawson City in 1960 and Parks Canada undertook its reconstruction. On 1 July 1962 the newly reconstructed Palace Grand Theatre opened with the world première of Robert Emmett Dolan's *Foxy*, a musical version of Ben Jonson's *Volpone* set in the Klondike Gold Rush, starring the American comic Bert Lahr. Since that time the theatre has served primarily as a tourist attraction during the summer months, staging such shows as *The Gaslight Follies*.

Palace Grand Theatre, Dawson City, 1899

Whitehorse. The Whitehorse Little Theatre was formed in 1946 and continues today as the Whitehorse Drama Club, which assisted in the establishment of the Frantic Follies in the 1960s, a professional troupe performing at various locations during the tourist season. In 1977 the Frantic Follies travelled on a twenty-seven-centre tour through rural B.C., the Prairies, and Ontario, highlighted by a performance at the West Block of Parliament Hill for 300 politicians, journalists, and civil servants.

Citadel-on-Wings. The Citadel-on-Wings program, an outgrowth of Citadel-on-Wheels and Edmonton's CITADEL THEATRE, took professional theatre to the Canadian Arctic from 1969 to 1971 and from 1977 to 1984. Among the 1970-1 offerings *A Dream of the Sky People*—based on the Cree creation legend, which has parallels in Inuit legend—excited interesting audience response. In her diary of the two-week tour, director Irene Watts noted that 'the beat of a drum in the play will start an almost imperceptible chant from the audience'. In all, the Citadel-on-Wings visited over twenty-five communities, including Arctic Bay, Cambridge Bay, Coppermine, Gjoa Haven, Hall Beach, Holman, Nanisivik, Pelly Bay, and Spence Bay in the Northwest Territories, and Whitehorse, Car-

macks, Elsa, Mayo, Dawson City, Pelly Crossing, and Faro in the Yukon.

Yellowknife. The major theatrical achievement of the 1980s in the North has been the building of the Northern Arts and Cultural Centre in Yellowknife. Attached to the high school, this 313-seat theatre opened in May 1984 at a cost of $1.3 million, raised largely by Roy Megarry, publisher of the Toronto *Globe and Mail*; Richard Doyle, its editor-in-chief; and Yellowknife Mayor Michael Ballantyne. The Centre's première performance included an Indian prayer, Inuit singers, Dene drummers, Caroll Baker, John Allan Cameron, and the Famous People Players. *Trying Out*, an original musical with music by Bill Gilday and libretto by Carolyn Czarneck, which explored the lives of contemporary children growing up in Yellowknife, has probably been the most memorable production offered in this new theatre space.

PATRICK B. O'NEILL

Nouveau Théâtre Expérimental de Montréal, Le. Founded in May 1975 by Robert Gravel, Pol Pelletier, and Jean-Pierre RONFARD as Le Théâtre Expérimental de Montréal, it espoused a mandate—shaped by its four principal directors, Ronfard, Gravel, Robert Claing, and Anne-Marie Provencher—to offer audiences a repertoire marked by lyricism, satire, eclecticism of form, the bloody, the grotesque, and the scatological. Between 1975 and 1978 the company was intent on challenging all formalities and conventions, conveying fantasy and the fantastic, and emphasizing a physical, improvisational style of acting. They offered workshops, readings, 'happenings' (twelve- and twenty-four-hour improvisations, and Le Théâtre des Deux Couilles—a smutty PUPPET theatre—for example), and productions such as *Zoo*, La LIGUE NATIONALE D'IMPROVISA-TION, *Orgasme I*, and *Orgasme II*. With the exception of *Lear*, a hybrid anti-adaptation of Shakespeare's play by Jean-Pierre Ronfard, all shows from this period were COLLECTIVE CREATIONs. The company also published the magazine *Trac*.

At the end of 1978 the company split into two groups: Le Théâtre Expérimental des Femmes—founded by Pol Pelletier, Louise Laprade, and Nicole Lecavalier—and the Nouveau Théâtre Expérimental. After producing plays at the Atelier Continu and the Studio Theatre of the NATIONAL THEATRE SCHOOL (*Treize Tableaux* and *Où est Unica Zurn?*, both about the relations between theatre and painting) NTE collaborated with CARBONE 14 and Omnibus in 1981 to convert an old fire-hall into L'Espace Libre. The company's most remarkable achievement during this period, however, was its production of Jean-Pierre Ronfard's magnificent historical epic *VIE ET MORT DU ROI BOITEUX*, presented in its entirety on 24 and 26 June 1982 on the open-air stage of Montreal's Expo Theatre.

Following the acquisition of L'Espace, the company suffered a period of artistic stagnation. The updating of texts such as *Les Mille et une Nuits* (*The Thousand and One Nights*) and Euripides' *Le Cyclope* was one focus, and collective creations remained important— including one (*À Beloeil ou ailleurs*) spread out over four months and modified from one evening to the next, an ambitious project that failed because of the show's weak structure and the banality of many of its sketches. More recently NTE has adopted an artistic identity defined chiefly in terms of the personal projects of its directors: the textual experiments of Robert Claing (in his *Le Temps est au noir* and *Des Nouvelles pour le théâtre*); investigations of the connections between the performance and audience in *La Tour* by Ann-Marie Provencher (a show for a single spectator), and *Les Objets parlent* by Jean-Pierre Ronfard (a show without actors); and an examination of myth and tragedy in

Marilyn ou le Journal intime de Margaret MacPherson and *Mao Tsé-Toung ou Soirée de musique au consulat*, two plays by Ronfard. Since *Vie et Mort du Roi Boiteux*, however, NTE has lacked creative resources and a common artistic vision. The passion that once animated the company has been dissipated in productions that too often have been—even if daring—slapdash and rife with platitudes and clichés.   PIERRE LAVOIE

Nouvelle Compagnie Théâtrale, La. Founded in Montreal in 1964 by Françoise Graton, Georges Groulx, and Gilles PELLE-TIER, it favoured during its first five seasons the production of major European plays by Corneille, Molière, Racine, Marivaux, Musset, Sophocles, Shakespeare, Ben Jonson, Carlo Goldoni, and Chekhov. The 1969 production of Marcel DUBÉ's *Un SIMPLE SOLDAT* was an exception. Between 1964 and 1969 audiences grew from 32,000 annually to more than 85,000. On the strength of this support the company initiated a playwriting competition that lasted for three years (1969-72). It also diversified its activities in 1972 by creating a program designed for young people aged twelve to fourteen, featuring mainly commissioned works. (See also CHILDREN'S DRAMA AND THEATRE IN FRENCH.) Between 1969 and 1977 twenty-one out of thirty-eight productions were from the twentieth century, including sixteen Québécois works: there were important revivals of Michel TREMBLAY's *À TOI, POUR TOUJOURS, TA MARIE-LOU* in 1974, Réjean DUCHARME's *Inès Pérée et Inat Tendu* in 1976, and Tremblay's *Les BELLES-SOEURS* in 1984. The company continued, however, to produce plays from the classical repertoire: Euripides, Calderón, Tirso de Molina, Shakespeare, Il Ruzzante (Angelo Beolco), Edmond Rostand, Molière, Ibsen, and Strindberg.

In 1977—after thirteen years of performing at le GESÙ—NCT purchased an east-end Montreal cinema, converting it into a 900-seat theatre named Le Théâtre Denise-PEL-LETIER. A small rehearsal and performance space—La Salle Fred-BARRY—was designated for productions of new Quebec plays under the direction of Jean-Luc BASTIEN. After several seasons of small-budget NCT productions, it became a venue for visiting ALTERNATE THEATRE companies; since 1986 Pierre MacDuff has been artistic director of La Salle Fred-Barry.

Nouvelle Compagnie Théâtrale

Between 1977 and 1987 the percentage of Québécois productions by NCT dropped, but still accounted for over a third of the forty-six productions, of which twenty-nine were twentieth-century works. In 1982 Pelletier and Graton resigned as artistic directors and were succeeded by Bastien, whose innovations included inviting new talented directors such as Lorraine Pintal and Daniel Roussel to NCT, mounting bold productions such as the 1984 québécois version of Brecht's *Mother Courage and Her Children*, and hosting guest productions by other companies: in 1983 Le Théâtre de la Vie from Brussels presented a modernized version of Molière's *Le Médecin malgré lui*; La Comédie de Genève from Switzerland offered *L'Oiseau vert* by Carlo Gozzi in 1985; and Le Théâtre Sans Fil, a québécois troupe working with giant puppets, performed an adaptation of Tolkien's *The Lord of the Rings* (*Le Seigneur des anneaux*) in 1986.

From the beginning NCT has exercised a particular responsibility to young audiences; the company's bond with the educational milieu has, however, left the company open to pressures concerning the moral content of the plays. In order to maintain a continuing dialogue with both teachers and students, the NCT publishes *En scène!* (begun in 1966 as *Cahiers de la NCT* by Gilles Marsolais), which for each of the three major annual productions provides extensive background material in order to encourage better understanding of the plays.

See Jean-Luc Bastien and Pierre MacDuff, eds., *En scène depuis 25 ans; la Nouvelle Compagnie Théâtrale* (1988).   GILBERT DAVID

Nova Scotia, Theatre in. *1. Beginnings to 1850*. Theatrical history for Nova Scotia, and for Canada, begins on 14 Nov. 1606 with the production of Marc LESCARBOT's masque *Le THÉÂTRE DE NEPTUNE EN LA NOUVELLE-FRANCE*. Written ostensibly to welcome the governor, the Sieur de Poutrincourt, and Samuel de Champlain, its primary purpose was to raise the morale of the French settlers in Port Royal. Nearly 150 years later, residents witnessed the first performance of a play in English in Canada during the winter of 1743-4 when Paul Mascarene, Lieutenant-Governor of Nova Scotia, translated Molière's *Le Misanthrope* and staged it at least twice. The second performance on 6 Jan.

1744 coincided with celebrations to mark the birthday of Frederick, Prince of Wales.

Theatricals were probably performed by the French at Louisbourg as well at this time, but dramatic presentations certainly occurred during the British occupation of the town in 1758-9. The diary of Nathaniel Knapp, a New England carpenter working in Louisbourg during and after the second siege, states that on Friday 9 Mar. 1759, 'At night went to ye play acting' and on 7 May 1759, 'and had Play Day to day.'

The history of theatre in Halifax is better documented, although lacunae in the early period remain. The passenger list of the thirteen transports of the Cornwallis expedition in 1748 included William Paget, formerly 'a comedian in the House of Drury-Lane and Covent Garden'. It seems likely that Paget would have entertained members of the expedition prior to his death in Halifax on 23 Mar. 1752.

The first professional company to appear in Canada performed in Halifax between 26 Aug. and 28 Oct. 1768 under the name of the American Company of Comedians, also known as Mr Mills and Henry Giffard's Company, which had previously performed in North Carolina. Mills and Giffard prepared 'a large and commodious House' for their productions in what most sources suggest was the Pontac Inn; more likely, however, the plays were staged at the Wolfe Inn on Granville St opposite Province House. A debate about the morality of theatregoing raged in the *Nova Scotia Gazette* during the company's presence in Halifax. Similar newspaper debates in successive issues of the *Nova Scotia Chronicle and Weekly Advertiser* of Jan. 1770 suggest theatrical activity at that time, but no details of actual productions survive.

Newspapers of the 1770s provide a few theatrical references. By 1772 the amateurs of the town had established a yearly theatre at the Pontac Inn in Halifax and in Feb. 1774 they staged the anonymous *Acadius; or, Love In a Calm*, probably the first English-language play written in Canada. By the end of the decade Loyalists were arriving from the U.S.; one of them, Jacob Bailey, wrote *The Humors of the Committee; or, the Majesty of the Mob*, chronicling his own experience as a Loyal American living in Maine. It was apparently never published or performed.

Used primarily for amateur productions, the Pontac Coffee House was also occupied by a touring professional actor, William Moore, for productions of his *Fashionable Raillery* and *The Court of Momus* in May and June 1785. Prior to appearing in Halifax, Moore had given the same presentations at Mr Steel's long room in Shelburne on 13 May 1785.

The Grand Theatre on Argyle St, which opened on 26 Feb. 1789, continued operations until 1814, when it became the Royal Acadian School. The 500-seat theatre was known successively as the New Theatre, the Halifax Theatre, and the Theatre Royal. Although records are incomplete, Haligonians witnessed over four hundred plays and farces at this theatre. Primarily used by amateurs, it also played host to a number of professionals—Mr MacPherson from Lewis Hallam's American Company, Mrs Mechtler, and Mrs Anne Hatton. In the fall of 1797 Charles Stewart Powell arrived from Boston to assume the management of the theatre until his death in 1810. Powell's wife and two daughters supported the company in female roles.

The Freemason's Hall built on Grafton St in 1800 was occasionally used for concerts and theatricals. It was probably here that the American company of Addison B. Price produced their first season of 1816-7. About this time William Rufus BLAKE managed a group of amateurs at an improvised theatre in an old barn on Water St. In 1816 the amateurs fitted up a theatre at Fairbank's Wharf. In Mar. 1817, after the failure of a subscription to raise $5,000 to build a new theatre, Price moved his company into the Fairbank's Wharf Theatre for his two remaining seasons. During the last season Blake joined the company and began his professional career. The Fairbank's Wharf Theatre was used by amateurs and professionals until 1821, when it was converted to a warehouse. In 1821 an old building called the Red Store, opposite Starr's Liverpool Market at the foot of Hurd St on Upper Water, was converted into a theatre for use by the army and navy for their amateur performances. By the end of the 1820s the Masons' Hall had again been pressed into service as a theatre, billed as the Theatre Royal, and the navy had taken to staging plays on board ships in Halifax harbour. Halifax desperately needed a new theatre.

In 1829 the New Theatre opened on Grafton St. Even for its time it was a small theatrical space: 'Altogether it was much like performing in a sentry box', writes a contemporary observer; 'we were so close to the performers that a darkened eyebrow or rouged cheek could be easily detected and the prompter's voice was heard in every sentence.' Nevertheless, it remained in operation until July 1844, when the building was auctioned and removed. During its fifteen-year career it welcomed a number of performers whose names were familiar to Maritime audiences: William Rufus Blake, who brought his company for two years ending in June 1833; the Henry W. Preston Company from Saint John in 1839 and 1840; Master John (1840); the Vanden Hoffs (1840); Fanny Davenport (1841); Mrs Fanny Fitzwilliam and J.B. Buckstone (1842). The last two performers found the New Theatre so lacking in amenities that they moved their performance to the Halifax Hotel. In the first half of the 1840s the Halifax Hotel and the Masons' Hall, which had been enlarged in 1839, became the centres of dramatic activity.

2. 1850 to 1914. Theatrical activity in Nova Scotia had been sporadic before 1850 and was limited largely to Halifax. Mid-century brought increased activity across the province, especially after the opening of the Inter-Colonial Railway in 1876, and professional entertainers began to appear on a more regular basis until the First World War in the many theatre spaces built to accommodate them. At first, these spaces were social halls—Mechanics' Institutes, Temperance Halls, Orange Halls, or other multi-purpose spaces—built by local businessmen to serve each community's needs.

In Dartmouth the Mechanics' Institute Building, constructed in the 1840s, was purchased by the town in 1877 and became the Town Hall, complete with auditorium. For over forty years it provided space for touring groups, but primarily served local amateurs. The Mechanics' Hall in New Glasgow also underwent a transformation. Opened in the 1860s, it long welcomed amateur and professional companies. Leased by N.M. Mason and F.G. Spence in 1907, the building was refurbished as the Empire Theatre and for five years was the centre of theatrical activity in New Glasgow.

Temperance Halls were built in North Sydney and in Sydney, Cape Breton, in 1849; the Sydney Hall was renamed the Theatre Royal after use by the 76th Regiment for the theatrical season of 1854. Even small towns built Temperance Halls—Middle Musquodoboit built one in 1850; destroyed by fire in 1880, it was replaced by a second Temperance Hall in 1889 that welcomed both touring and local productions. The town of Brookvale's Temperance Hall, which opened in 1875, served as the cultural centre of the area for over 100 years.

Local businessmen also opened multi-purpose spaces to welcome musicians, performers, lecturers, and theatre companies. In Dartmouth McDonald's Hall provided an alternative to the Mechanics' Hall from the 1840s until after Confederation. In Yarmouth T.B. Dane opened a 300-seat concert hall in Jan. 1848. Another auditorium in the Ryerson block opened with a promenade concert on 13 July 1866.

The Colonial Troupe brought their production of 'The Ethiopian Burlesque Minstrels' to the new Victoria Hall in Bridgetown in 1853. By the 1870s Bridgetown welcomed a number of touring companies on a regular basis; the Boston Comedy Company, for example, performed there in 1875 and 1876 with such productions as J.B. Buckstone's *Flowers of the Forest*, John Oxenford's *East Lynne*, Harriet Beecher Stowe's *Uncle Tom's Cabin*, and William Pratt's *Ten Nights In a Bar Room*.

In North Sydney the Caledonian Hall, built in 1861 on the north corner of Commercial and Caledonia Sts, competed with the Temperance Hall for theatrical bookings. In 1889 the Terra Nova Hall was opened, but a year later the Royal Albert Hall became the centre of dramatic activity for the next decade. In 1901 St Joseph's Parish built a large two-storey building known as the Empire Hall at a cost of $3,745. Primarily a centre for parish activities, it also welcomed touring productions such as Arthur Wing Pinero's *Dandy Dick* on 2 Oct. 1907. In 1914 Lew Acker opened his Family Theatre but sold it a few years later, whereupon it became the Strand movie house.

In Sydney the Catholic Episcopal Corporation financed the building of the Lyceum, a multi-purpose facility designed by the Chappell Brothers of Sydney at a cost of $37,000, which housed a gymnasium and dressing-rooms in the basement, a 900-seat theatre on the main floor, and a library and club rooms on the second floor. Completed on 23 May 1904, the Sydney Lyceum was the venue for

professional productions of *Between Love and Duty*, Mark Quinton's *In His Power*, Cosmo Gordon Lennox's *The Marriage of Kitty*, Bartley Campbell's *My Geraldine*, and Leonard Grover's *Lost in New York*; but the Lyceum was better utilized by amateur groups, such as that which presented a nine-act production of *Domhnull-Nam-Trioblaid* in Gaelic on 24 Apr. 1919. During the Second World War the Lyceum was an entertainment centre for troops stationed in Sydney. Fire destroyed the inner shell of the Lyceum on 7 Mar. 1951, but the Lyceum Society, which purchased the building in 1982 for $100,000, has begun its renovation.

Another noteworthy Cape Breton theatre, the Royal Theatre in Dominion, opened in 1909, welcoming touring companies such as H. Price WEBBER's, along with the new moving pictures. It continues its uninterrupted career today as a movie house.

The theatre on the third floor of H.L.P. McNeil's Hall, New Glasgow, later known as the Green Lantern, provided competition for the Mechanics' Hall/Empire Theatre from the 1870s. By the 1890s touring players performed there regularly. Norman W. Mason produced plays at the McNeil Hall from his arrival in 1896 until his purchase of the Mechanics' Hall in 1907. In 1912, with local capital, Mason built the Academy of Music, the first purpose-built theatre space in Pictou County, which served the community for thirty-four years. After a 1945 fire destroyed much of its stage scenery, the theatre was renovated as a movie house, which it remained until 1961; demolition followed in 1964. Although McNeil's Hall, the Empire, and the Academy of Music were the principal theatres in the county, travelling companies also performed at the Opera Houses in Pictou and Stellarton and at the Comet in Westville.

In Amherst the Second Baptist Church (built originally in 1863) was converted to the Academy of Music in 1894; it measured 82' × 40' with a balcony 30' × 40'. Replacing it as the principal touring house after 1900, the Empire Theatre—a brick building measuring 92' × 58' with a stage measuring 28' × 58'—welcomed touring shows until the DUMBELLS' tour of Apr. 1931.

The theatrical fare offered in all these centres varied from Sir John Martin-Harvey and the Dumbells to Professor Crocker's '25 Educated Horses', which performed on 31 July 1905 at Sydney's Lyceum. The highlight of the show was a final tableau in which a horse patriotically held aloft the Union Jack amid a blaze of lights.

In contrast to the general mediocrity of the companies visiting Nova Scotia, three names stand out: H. Price Webber, Mae EDWARDS, and Norman Mason. Although already elderly when they first arrived in the 1890s, H. Price Webber and his wife, Edwina Grey, performed throughout the province with a repertoire of melodramas that included *Uncle Tom's Cabin*, *Ten Nights In a Bar Room*, *East Lynne*, and *Under Two Flags*. Both their theatrical fare and their community service ensured their popularity in the small communities that were their market; attending the Anglican church every Sunday, they offered the assistance of a benefit for any local disaster. The Mae Edwards Players performed for the first time in Halifax at the Strand Theatre in 1926. Great favourites in the Pictou area, their yearly performances gave them the status of locals. A Nova Scotian from St Margaret's Bay, Norman Mason had settled in New Glasgow in 1896, where he first staged Denman THOMPSON's *The Old Homestead* at McNeil's Hall in 1906. He revived the production regularly until his death in 1945. His 1909 tour played at twenty-five Maritime stops in a six-week period.

Halifax acquired two new theatre spaces at mid-century that would serve for the next twenty-five years: the THEATRE ROYAL and the Temperance Hall. The Theatre Royal on Queen St, which opened in 1846, was converted from a barn by the 23rd Royal Welsh Fusiliers for their productions. It had a deep apron, proscenium doors, and gas lighting. Isherwood and Stewart's company from Wallack's Theatre in New York appeared there for the summer of 1856. Their eight-week run reportedly netted £900. At the end of the summer, English actor E.A. Sothern (who had been acting under the name D.B. Stewart) announced that he had leased the theatre for seven years. Following renovations during the season 1856-7, it re-opened as Sothern's LYCEUM in June 1857. After a less successful second summer season, Sothern attempted a winter season that proved financially disastrous. For the summer of 1858 he brought Agnes Robertson, wife of Dion Boucicault, to star with his company. With Robertson, Boucicault's *Jessie Brown; or, the Relief of Lucknow* ran for five nights and recouped some of Sothern's losses. For the summer season of

1859 he brought stars such as Joseph Jefferson, Mary Gladstone, Matilda Heron, and Barry Sullivan. The star system had reached Nova Scotia.

The outbreak of the American Civil War curtailed touring, and the theatre reverted to amateur use. After the war, H.W. Fiske, the popular American comedian, brought his company from Boston at various times between 1865 and 1867, but the days of the Theatre Royal were numbered; it was abandoned after the 60th Rifles used it for their production of Mark Lemon's *Self-Accusation* in Feb. 1874.

The Temperance Hall superseded the Theatre Royal. Originally opened in Dec. 1849 on Starr St, it refused to lease to drama companies (E.A. Sothern tried to lease it), but did allow variety performers to use its facilities. After the Civil War this policy was discontinued and touring companies opted for the more spacious (1,200-seat) Temperance Hall in preference to the Theatre Royal. In 1868 the Sons of Temperance leased the Hall to T. Charles Howard for $2,100. Renaming the space the Olympic Theatre, Howard returned in 1869 and 1870 for additional seasons. Other managers at the Temperance Hall included William NANNARY, J.W. LANERGAN, and E.A. McDOWELL, and visiting stars included Mr and Mrs E.L. Davenport, Clara MORRIS, and Marietta Ravel. With the opening of the ACADEMY OF MUSIC in 1877 the Temperance Hall lost its appeal and was sold in 1880 to the Young Men's Literary Association, which, after six months' renovation, reopened it as the Lyceum in December. For the next decade the Lyceum became the centre for variety, minstrel shows, and amateur productions until it was destroyed by fire on 15 Mar. 1899.

In spite of numerous attempts to launch a new theatre in Halifax, the city had to wait until 9 Jan. 1877 when the Academy of Music, designed by the English architect T.R. Jackson, opened. The first legitimate company to use the facility was William Nannary's for a six-week run beginning 16 Jan. 1877. William Gill, a Halifax native, who painted scenery for the Academy of Music in its first season, eventually became well known as a scenic artist at the Tremont Theatre in Boston.

The Academy of Music flourished in an era of touring companies that included the Kirk Brown Company, the Klark-Urban Company, W.S. Harkins, F. James Carroll, May Howard, and E.A. McDowell. Between 1880 and 1900 a large number of touring opera companies also appeared at the Academy: the Boston English Opera, the Italian Opera Company, the Hess Opera Company, the Anna Granger Dow Opera, the Pollard Juvenile Opera, and the Grau Opera Company, to name but a few. When not leased to legitimate drama or opera companies, the theatre was used by minstrel and variety shows, or by speakers such as Oscar Wilde, William Jennings Bryan, and Henry Ward Beecher. In 1910 the theatre was renamed the Majestic, and although occasional dramatic companies such as those of F. James Carroll, Florence Glossop-Harris, and Sir John Martin-Harvey played there, VAUDEVILLE, musical comedies, and revues were the usual fare.

It was difficult to fill the Academy/Majestic's 1,200 seats. Most amateur productions therefore used the smaller vaudeville/movie houses, including the Orpheus Hall (1886-1947); the Strand Theatre (1915-present); the Empire Theatre (1900-7); the King Edward Theatre (1907-37)—also known as Acker's New Theatre (1926); the Scotia Theatre (1927); the Gaiety Theatre (1935); and the Dreamland Theatre (1908-21)—also known as the Empire Theatre (1909-11, 1914-18), Gault's Theatre (1912-14, 1920-21), and the Gaiety Theatre (1919-20). Of these the Strand merits special mention. Opened on 23 Oct. 1915, it operated primarily as a vaudeville house, but with the onset of the Depression it was converted to movies as the Garrick Theatre. On 1 July 1963 it reopened as the NEPTUNE THEATRE and remains the home of Halifax's major professional theatre.

3. French-language, University, and Amateur Theatre to 1962. Beginning in the late 1870s Acadian communities organized amateur clubs. The impetus came from the four Acadian colleges: St Joseph's, Saint Louis, St Anne's, and Sacred Heart. Both St Joseph's and St Anne's produced plays for Nova Scotia audiences. Although based in New Brunswick, students from St Joseph's toured in Nova Scotia and inspired Le Cercle dramatique français d'Amherst. The Amherst production of *Les Crochets du Père Martin* (first produced at Moore's Hall, Amherst) played in Moncton on 1 Feb. 1912.

St Anne's College at Church Point, founded in 1890, had two societies producing theatre on campus: the St Patrick Literary and Dramatic Society and the Société littéraire Saint-Joseph. The latter group produced its first play, *La Malediction d'un père*, on 8 May 1893. Notable productions at St Anne's included *Les Derniers Martyrs du Colisée* in 1898 and *Supercase* in 1902, both written by the Rev. A. Braud, professor of rhetoric at the college; *La Passion de Nôtre Seigneur* in 1928 and *L'Évangeline* in 1930, written by Father Jean-Baptiste Jégo; *Joseph* in 1929; and *Le Drame du peuple acadien* by Émile Lauvrière in 1930. (See also ACADIAN THEATRE.)

English universities were also active in theatre. St Mary's University took C.H. Chambers' *Captain Swift* to the first Earl Grey Competition in 1907. Dalhousie University travelled throughout the province in the summer of 1914 with its production of *The College Widow*, with original words and music by Owen B. Jones, depicting life on the Dalhousie campus. The first LITTLE THEATRE Guild in the Maritime provinces was organized by five Acadia University students in Wolfville in Nov. 1924. After this club closed, Acadia organized the Playmakers Dramatic Club in 1934 and staged Euripides' *The Trojan Women* on the south portico of University Hall.

Although the universities played the major role in the formation of theatre groups in this period, other organizations were also active. The Halifax Dramatic and Musical Club, which presented Victor Herbert's *Fortune Teller*, the last production at the Majestic Theatre before its demolition in June 1929, merged with the Garrison Dramatic Club in 1931 to form the THEATRE ARTS GUILD, which is still active.

Throughout the Depression amateur theatre groups were active in the province, but the enlistment of younger members in the armed forces and the influx of military personnel brought changes to amateur theatre during the Second World War. The Theatre Arts Guild was reorganized into the Halifax Concert Parties Guild to entertain service personnel throughout the Atlantic Provinces and to tour England, Holland, Germany, and Belgium immediately after the war. Donald Wetmore, who had been active in Acadia theatricals during the 1930s, served with the YMCA and organized concert parties at Debert, N.S., and St John's, Nfld. In Sydney the Lyceum became the cultural centre for armed forces personnel in Cape Breton, and in Pictou the employees of the Pictou shipyard formed a concert party to entertain troops at the Parkdale Military Training Centre.

With the end of the war the emphasis of

amateur theatre underwent a radical shift. In 1949 Wetmore chaired a meeting to found the Nova Scotia Drama League; although the meeting's aim was the promotion of amateur theatre within the province, the League was also influential in promoting a professional theatre. In the years immediately following the war a number of amateur groups were formed: Dartmouth's Club '46 in 1946, Robert Alban's Theatre-In-The-Round in 1951, the reconstituted Theatre Arts Guild in 1950, the Lunenburg Little Theatre Group in 1950 (opening with Wetmore's *Incident on the Border*), the Gaspereau Drama Club in 1951, and the Wolfville Players in 1957.

Some of these groups won national recognition. In May 1952 the Robert Alban Players were invited to demonstrate their Theatre-in-the-Round production of Oscar Wilde's *The Importance of Being Earnest* at the DOMINION DRAMA FESTIVAL in Saint John. The NSDL sponsored the Nova Scotia Players, a travelling repertory company, which toured to forty-three communities. The Travelling Players, formed in 1956, won the best-play award for their production of John Osborne's *Look Back in Anger* at the DDF in 1962. Evelyn Garbary and Michael Sinelnikoff won the best-direction award for the same production.

The NSDL also encouraged the production of Nova Scotia scripts. *Halifax 1749*, book and lyrics by Will R. Bird, celebrated the city's bicentennial in 1949. Donald Wetmore's *The Londonderry Heirs* did the same for Truro in 1959. Wetmore's best-remembered works are *The Highland Heart in Nova Scotia* and *Dashing through the Years*. In addition, the NSDL published the newsletter *Callboard* to promulgate news and information about its member groups.

4. Professional Theatre, 1950 to the Present. Various Canadian professional companies toured the province in the 1950s: the Earle GREY Players (1951, 1958), the LONDON THEATRE COMPANY of Newfoundland (1951-6), *MY FUR LADY* (1958), the National Ballet of Canada (1958), the Toronto Opera Festival's production of *The Barber of Seville* (1958), the CANADIAN PLAYERS (1959, 1960, 1961), Les Grands Ballets Canadiens (1962), and the COMÉDIE-CANADIENNE with a production of Gratien GÉLINAS's *Bousille and the Just* starring Gélinas (1962). In part because of this increased emphasis on professional theatre, by the mid-1960s membership in the NSDL had diminished to only nine groups: the Acadia

Dramatic Society, the Dartmouth Drama Club, the Theatre Arts Guild, the Annapolis District Drama Group, the Cathedral Players, the Breton Players, the Colchester Players, Saint Mary's University Drama Society, and the Travelling Players.

This move toward professionalism is seen in Robert Alban's departure from Theatre-in-the-Round to CBC television and the establishment of a theatre-training school by Halifax's Theatre Arts Guild in 1957, and culminates in the establishment of the Neptune Theatre in 1963. Supplementary support across the province was found in the Festival of the Arts at Tatamagouche; in Jack Sheriff's work with the Acadia Summer Playhouse in 1961; the Theatre Arts Festival International in 1970; the Kipawo Showboat Theatre in 1972; and the founding of the MERMAID THEATRE in Wolfville by Evelyn Garbary and Tom Miller in 1972. Dalhousie's Theatre Department, founded in 1968, specifically aims to prepare its graduates for professional acting careers.

The 1970s and 1980s have been marked by attempts to provide a professional alternative to the Neptune Theatre, enhanced recently by the NSDL's provision in Halifax of the Cunard Street Theatre as a playing space. The first

The Brothers, *Micmac Indian folklore, Mermaid Theatre,* N.S.

of these was Pier One, the only experimental theatre group in the Maritimes up to its demise in 1974. Others include Portus (1976), founded by David Renton, a long-time regular with Neptune; Seaweed Theatre (1975-82); the MULGRAVE ROAD CO-OP and the Rise and Follies of Cape Breton Island Company (1977-present), two of the few to enjoy continuing success across the province; Theatre 1707 or the Bit Players (1978-80), successful in Cape Breton but failing after its move to Halifax; Stage East (1979); Pop Productions at Stages (1980-1); Another Theatre Company (1982-6); Theatre Nova Scotia (1983); and the Ship's Company at Parrsboro (1984-present).

These companies and others have filled a continuing need. Even after almost 400 years of settlement the population of Nova Scotia remains small—at 850,000 too small and diffuse to support a wide range of continuous theatrical activity. The history of theatre in the province, however, reflects the compulsion of its residents to support theatre and augurs well for a continuing lively theatrical culture.   PATRICK B. O'NEILL

Nowlan, Alden (1933-83). Born near Windsor, N.S., he left school at fifteen shortly after starting grade five. He worked as a labourer until 1952 when he took a job with a New Brunswick newspaper. From 1963 to 1968 he worked for the *Telegraph- Journal*, Saint John, as a reporter and night editor.

From 1968 to his death he was writer-in-residence, Univ. of New Brunswick, Fredericton.

Nowlan was already a much-published poet—he won a Governor General's Award in 1967—and short-story writer when he started writing plays with Walter LEARNING in 1975. This collaboration gave birth to *Frankenstein: The Man Who Became God* (1976), first produced by THEATRE NEW BRUNSWICK in 1977; *The Dollar Woman* (1981), first produced by Theatre New Brunswick in 1977; *The Incredible Murder of Cardinal Tosca* (1978), first produced by Theatre New Brunswick in 1978; *A Gift To Last* (an unpublished stage adaptation of the pilot episode of Gordon PINSENT's television series of the same name), first produced by the VANCOUVER PLAYHOUSE in 1982; *Svengali*, a radio play broadcast by the CBC in Jan. 1983; and three episodes for 'Up at Ours', a CBC-TV series, 1979-82.

These plays, all set in the nineteenth century, exhibit a strong humanistic streak informed by an idiosyncratic sense of humour. Using the form of the 'well-made play', a wide range of social, moral, and spiritual questions is explored. In *The Dollar Woman* society's responsibility to its poor and uneducated is examined; *Tosca* demonstrates the distinction between what is legal and what is just; *Svengali* examines what it costs an artist to achieve the best in his chosen field.   WALTER LEARNING

O

O'Keefe Centre, The. Built in Toronto by the O'Keefe Breweries at a cost of twelve million dollars, this multi-purpose theatre building opened on 3 Oct. 1960 with the musical *Camelot* by Alan Jay Lerner and Frederick Loewe, starring Richard Burton, Julie Andrews, and Robert Goulet. Located at the corner of Front and Yonge Streets, the theatre was designed by Toronto architects Earle C. Morgan and Page and Steele. It seats 3,223—2,200 on the main floor, 1,023 in the balcony.

The house can be reduced to 1,100 seats by drawing an acoustic curtain in front of the balcony. The stage measures 125' by 60' with a 60' by 30' proscenium that can be reduced to 36' by 18'. The orchestra pit, which normally has space for fifty musicians, can be enlarged to accommodate an orchestra of ninety. Because of the size of the auditorium (700,000 cubic feet), sound amplification is extensively used.

From its opening the O'Keefe has catered

primarily for large-scale spectacles, such as Russia's Kirov Ballet and the Metropolitan Opera of New York, and to such Broadway musicals as *My Fair Lady*, *The King and I*, *Hello Dolly*, *Porgy and Bess*, *Fiddler on the Roof*, and *Sugar Babies*. Solo entertainers have included Marlene Dietrich, Danny Kaye, Maurice Chevalier, Lena Horne, Judy Garland, and Harry Belafonte. The theatre has proved less successful for legitimate theatre, but the National Theatre of Great Britain and the Comédie Française have appeared there, as have Vivien Leigh, Ralph Richardson, Laurence Olivier, John Gielgud, and other stars of the legitimate stage.

The O'Keefe became home to the Canadian Opera Company and the National Ballet of Canada when both companies, seeking larger audiences, moved there from the ROYAL ALEXANDRA THEATRE in the early 1960s. Both companies, however, have been pressing for a separate facility designed specifically for opera and ballet. Should that happen, the O'Keefe is likely to concentrate even more on presenting Broadway musicals and Las Vegas-type variety shows. While the theatre has been subjected (justifiably) to criticism for its poor acoustics, its ill-designed space, and its populist programming, it has nonetheless enriched Toronto's cultural life, particularly as home to its ballet and opera companies.   HERBERT WHITTAKER

Oligny, Huguette (b. 1922). Born in Montreal, she began acting at an early age, and in 1940 appeared in *Les Jours heureux* by Claude-André Puget at the MONTREAL REPERTORY THEATRE. In the first play produced by Pierre DAGENAIS at L'ÉQUIPE in 1943—*Altitude 3200* by Julien Luchaire—she created an unforgettable Magali. She subsequently played the role of Marie-Ange in Gratien GÉLINAS's TIT-COQ. Oligny directed Yves THÉRIAULT's *Le Marcheur* in 1950, and also acted in the première—both in Montreal and in Paris—of *Le Temps des lilas* by Marcel DUBÉ.

In addition to appearing in numerous radio and television programs for Radio-Canada, Oligny played the major roles of the classical French repertoire for the THÉÂTRE DU NOUVEAU MONDE—including Toinette in Molière's *Le Malade imaginaire* in 1956, Elmire in Molière's *Tartuffe* in 1968, and the title role in Racine's *Bérénice*. In French-lan-

guage productions of two famous dramas, she played Laure in Peter Shaffer's *Equus* for the Théâtre du Bois de Coulonges in Quebec City (1981), and Maria in Chekhov's *Uncle Vanya* in 1982, a role that she repeated in André BRASSARD's production at the NATIONAL ARTS CENTRE in Ottawa and at the TNM in 1983. She has performed in English—notably in *Saint-Lazare's Pharmacy* by Niklos Laszlo in Chicago in 1945. In 1973 she married Gratien Gélinas following the death of his first wife. He wrote *La Passion de Narcisse Mondoux* for himself and Oligny; the play premièred at the Théâtre du P'tit Bonheur (see THÉÂTRE FRANÇAIS DE TORONTO) in 1986, and played again at the THÉÂTRE DU RIDEAU VERT in Montreal in 1987.   DOMINIQUE ROY

Ontario, Theatre in. In 1798, five years after its founding as the town of York, Toronto numbered 250 inhabitants. Only half a century later, when its population had grown to 23,500, were economic and cultural conditions sufficiently advanced to sustain a permanent professional theatre, the ROYAL LYCEUM, built in 1848. At the beginning of the century York gentry had amused themselves with home entertainments such as parties, play readings, and dances. Public events included a puppet show in 1800 and the visit of a 'Learned Pig' in 1802. The first professional company, a group of 'New York comic gentry', performed Sheridan's *School for Scandal* on 11 Feb. 1809. A year later the York *Gazette* recorded the first visit by British actors, the Messrs Potter and Thompson, from London. On 7 May 1809 they presented a 'theatrical performance consisting of Songs, Recitations, and Ventriloquism' at Miller's Assembly-Room, a former coffee-house.

After the opening of the Erie Canal in 1825—which provided a direct transportation route between New York City, Albany, and the lower Great Lakes region—York became part of an American professional theatre circuit that included Albany, Oswego, Rochester, Buffalo, Niagara, York, Kingston, and Montreal. In 1836, two years after the incorporation of the town of York as the City of Toronto, an American company managed by Charles Robert Thorne and Reuben Meer established the 'Theatre Royal' in a former carpentry shop on the northeast corner of King and York Streets. Until it burned down in 1840 it provided a more respectable performance venue than the previous converted rooms in taverns such as Frank's Hotel.

The increased importance of Toronto as an economic centre and the emergence of a larger middle class in the 1840s led businessman John Ritchie to erect the 750-seat Royal Lyceum in 1848, which succeeded James Mirfield's 500-seat Lyceum Theatre (1846-47), a former stable located near the present site of the ROYAL ALEXANDRA THEATRE. In its first decade the Lyceum's most successful resident company was led by the actor-manager John NICKINSON, whose thirty-four-member company—including his daughters Virginia, Eliza, Isabella, and Charlotte MORRISON—first appeared at the theatre in 1852. That year Nickinson staged, over a thirty-one-night period, seventy pieces, primarily British comedies and farces, twenty-three of which had never been seen before in Toronto. In 1853 he took over the management of the Royal Lyceum and presented a twenty-week season in which the most popular production, *Uncle Tom's Cabin*, ran for nine nights. Nickinson managed the Lyceum until the summer of 1859, winning critical and audience approval and attracting prominent American and British actors to the city. The first building in Toronto specifically erected as a theatre, the Royal Lyceum continued in operation until it burned down in 1874.

Theatre developed in a similar pattern in other Ontario towns and cities in the first three-quarters of the nineteenth century. A 'large Room . . . fitted up for the purpose' in Poncet's Inn served as a venue for visiting troupes in Kingston in 1812. In Hamilton the Burlington Hotel Ballroom served the same function in 1828. A small temporary theatre was built at the rear of the Kingston Hotel in 1826 and in a stable behind Mrs Walker's Hotel in the same city in 1829. Toronto's 1836 'Theatre Royal' was soon joined by other Theatre Royals in London (1840) and in both Hamilton and Kingston (1844).

British garrisons (see GARRISON THEATRE) provided a major stimulus to theatre activity throughout the province until troops were withdrawn from Canada in 1871. The Kingston Amateur Theatre, consisting of officers and a few Kingston gentry, performed nearly sixty comedies, farces, and dramas over an eighteen-month period in 1816-17. Other 'Gentlemen' and 'Garrison Amateurs' performed in York in 1818, staged the first recorded performances in Ottawa in 1837, and were active in London from 1838 to 1845. Though producing sporadically—depending on the theatrical interest of the commanding officer and troop movements—Garrison Amateurs encouraged the formation of civilian amateur companies, which attempted to emulate the sometimes considerable dramatic skills of the officers. Amateur societies, sometimes with the assistance of Garrison Amateurs, began to be active in York and Ancaster (1826), Kingston (1837), Hamilton (1840), Galt (1843), Cobourg (1845), and Ottawa (1850).

British garrisons provided the first form of government subsidy for theatre in Canada, funding the construction of temporary stages and paying the salaries of actors. Any profits from performances were usually donated to local charities. The first municipal subsidy for theatre activity came from the building of city and town halls throughout the province, most of which contained a large assembly room on the second floor with a small stage suitable for dramatic performances. Town halls often served as performance venues for local amateur societies such as those in Hamilton (1840-1) and Ottawa (1850). Other city and town halls used for dramatic performances opened in Kingston (1844), St Catharines (1848), Toronto (1850), London (1855), Galt and Stratford (both 1857), Brockville (1858), Guelph (1867), Ancaster (1871), Millbrook and Port Perry (both 1873), Aylmer, Ameliasburgh and Niagara-on-the-Lake (all 1874), Paisley and Demorestville (both 1876), Clinton (1880), Cannington (1887), Wingham (1890), St Mary's (1892), Embro (1893), and Carleton Place, Hastings, and Walkerton (all 1897).

By the middle of the nineteenth century growing audiences, improved transportation, and an increase in performance venues encouraged producers and artists to organize tours within Ontario. One of the first of these new entrepreneurs was the actor-manager T.P. BESNARD, whose spring 1848 tour of Upper Canada included Niagara, St Catharines, Port Hope, Cobourg, and Toronto. When he became manager of the Royal Lyceum (Dec. 1849-1852), he used his Toronto base to tour companies to other cities. In 1851, for example, Besnard managed the HERON FAMILY company tour to Montreal, Ottawa, Kingston, Toronto, Hamilton, Brantford, Dundas, and London. His successor at the Royal Lyceum, John Nickinson, opened a second theatre in Hamilton in 1853, the Royal Metropolitan Theatre, and performed with his stock company in both cities, as well as in Brantford and London, until he disbanded his company in 1858. Through greatly increased railroad transportation by the end of the 1850s, Ontario cities became accessible to touring companies not only from Toronto but also from other theatrical centres such as New York and Detroit (via the American Great Western Railroad) and Montreal (via the Grand Trunk Railway). By 1875 Ontario's larger cities were becoming profitable stops on the international touring circuit. For the next half-century foreign touring companies were attracted by, and helped to fill, the larger permanent theatres in the province. These included, in Ottawa, the 1,000-seat HER MAJESTY'S THEATRE (1856–71), the 1,000-seat GRAND OPERA HOUSE (1875–1913), and the 1,700-seat RUSSELL THEATRE (1897–1928); in Kingston, Martin's Opera House (1879–98) and the GRAND OPERA HOUSE (1902–38); in Hamilton, the 1,200-seat GRAND OPERA HOUSE (1880–1930s); in London, the 2,070-seat GRAND OPERA HOUSE (1881–1900); and,

in Toronto, the 1,000-seat Queen's Theatre (1874–83)—which specialized as a VAUDE-VILLE and variety house promising 'more amusement for less money than any theatre in America'—the 1,450-seat Royal Opera House (1874–83), and the 1,300-seat GRAND OPERA HOUSE (1874–1928). By the turn of the century Opera Houses (generally seating about 1,000) in Barrie, Berlin (Kitchener), Brantford, Brockville, Chatham, Cobourg, Galt, Gananoque, Guelph, Peterborough, Stratford, St Thomas, Windsor, and Woodstock served as brief stop-overs for touring companies on the way to longer, more profitable runs in larger centres such as Toronto, Ottawa, Montreal, and U.S. cities.

But even in Toronto, operating a resident stock company on a permanent basis was still financially precarious. Despite much critical and public support, Charlotte Morrison, the most talented and popular of John Nickinson's four actress daughters, was only able to manage the Grand Opera House and her own stock company from 1874 to 1878. Referring to the competition for audiences between the Grand and the Royal Opera House, an editorial in the Toronto *Mail* (19 Feb. 1876) maintained that 'there is no room

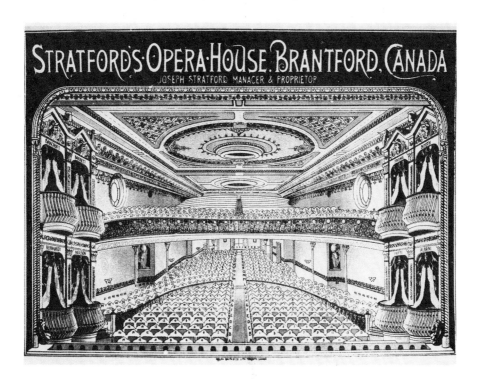

Ontario, Theatre in

here for two legitimate performances on the same evening'. Yet in 1884, when Toronto's population was still less than 100,000, five theatres competed for audience support. Despite the frequent folding of local companies and theatres, however, Toronto audiences in the last quarter of the century enjoyed a greater variety of theatrical fare and international stars than did audiences a century later. The former ranged from popular musical comedy and melodrama to farce, BURLESQUE, vaudeville, variety, Irish and German ethnic comedies, 'Ethiopian Delineators' (black-faced white performers in minstrel shows), and all forms of legitimate drama. Productions were not only in English but included, for example, Italian actor Tomasso Salvini—supported by an English cast—performing the title role of *Othello* in Italian, the all-French productions of Sarah Bernhardt (at the Grand Opera House in 1881), and the accented delivery of Hortense Rhea, Helena Modjeska, and Francesca Janauschek.

With the great number of foreign touring productions available, producers soon discovered that it was much more profitable to rent out theatres than to manage their own local companies. Among this new breed of entrepreneurs was Augustus Pitou, who had been an actor in Charlotte Morrison's stock company at the Grand in 1874. Pitou not only became the manager of the Grand (1879-81), but by 1880 gained control over a large part of the central and eastern Ontario circuit: besides the Grand in Toronto, he held the leases of the ACADEMY OF MUSIC in Montreal; the Grand Opera House in Ottawa; the Opera Houses in Brockville, Kingston, and Belleville; the Holman Opera House in London; and the Mechanics' Hall in Hamilton. This gave him considerable leverage when booking shows from producers in New York. Pitou eventually left Canada to embark on a major career as a New York producer.

An even greater theatrical empire was established by the Canadian impresario Ambrose J. SMALL. In 1919 he sold all his theatrical assets to the short-lived Montreal consortium Trans-Canada Theatres Ltd. for $1,750,000. His A.J. Small circuit toured primarily American, British, and a few Canadian productions. He was the outright owner of Grand Opera Houses in Toronto, Hamilton, London, St Thomas, Kingston, and Peterborough, and leased other theatres in Barrie,

Brantford, Brockville, Galt, Lindsay, Midland, North Bay, Orillia, Pembroke, Renfrew, St Catharines, Sarnia, Stratford, Sudbury, and Trenton.

While foreign TOURING STARS AND COMPANIES provided Ontario audiences with a rich diversity of dramatic fare, they also impeded the development of indigenous professional theatre and drama. As early as the 1850s John Nickinson's stock company at the Royal Lyceum became increasingly dependent on visiting stars to attract audiences. Local actors were gradually relegated to playing supporting roles to itinerant stars repeating the same limited repertoire in all the U.S. and Canadian towns on their circuit. Resident stock companies soon came to lack the artistic and financial resources to mount new productions.

By the late 1870s stock companies such as Charlotte Morrison's were further threatened by the hundreds of 'combination companies' touring from New York. These were fully cast companies supporting a star actor, usually in just one production, with lavish sets, costumes, and stage effects. Audiences naturally preferred the greater scenic splendour and superior acting of these well-rehearsed travelling companies to the quickly assembled productions (with usually less than a week's rehearsal) of resident stock companies. New York became the giant talent and financial centre from which productions toured all over North America. The Theatrical Syndicate, founded in 1896, purchased or leased theatres across the continent and by 1905 achieved a virtual monopoly over touring productions in the U.S. and Canada. With Canadian stages dominated by American and British actors and companies, there was little possibility for the emergence of an indigenous national drama. Less than one per cent of nineteenth-century productions were Canadian. Graves Simcoe LEE's farces, *Fiddle, Faddle and Foozle* and *Saucy Kate*, were staged at the Royal Lyceum on 9 Apr. and 11 June 1853; John Nickinson's *Fortunes of War*, adapted from the French, appeared at the same theatre on 13 Jan. 1854, as did the anonymous *The Poor of Toronto; or The Great Money Panic of 1857* on 19-21 Jan. 1858; and *Ottawa Firemen* (Rink Music Hall, Ottawa, 10 Apr. 1873) and *The Poor and Proud of Toronto* (Royal Opera House, Toronto, 29 Jan. 1875) were adapted from foreign plays to provide local settings. But few professionally produced Canadian plays achieved more than an occasional performance. The most successful was William Henry FULLER's *H.M.S. Parliament*, adapted from Gilbert and Sullivan's *H.M.S. Pinafore*, which trenchantly satirized Sir John A. Macdonald's protectionist National Policy. Following its première at the Academy of Music in Montreal on 16 Feb. 1880, the Eugene McDOWELL Comedy company toured the play throughout Ontario.

One of the few ways in which theatre professionals in Ontario could compete with the heavily capitalized American and European touring companies, particularly outside the large urban centres, was to work in family units: the Nickinsons in the 1850s; the Herons in the 1850s, '60s, and '70s; the musical HOLMAN family in the 1860s, '70s, and '80s; the husband-and-wife team of Ida VAN CORTLAND and Albert TAVERNIER in the 1880s and '90s; and the ubiquitous MARKS BROTHERS from the late 1870s to the early 1920s. Ontario-born actresses Julia ARTHUR, Marie Dressler, Clara MORRIS, May IRWIN, and Margaret ANGLIN established international careers after leaving Canada. In the larger centres such as Toronto, new theatre buildings—the Academy of Music (1889-1895), the PRINCESS THEATRE (1895-1930), the Majestic Theatre (1903-20), the Royal Alexandra (1907-), Loew's Yonge Street Theatre (1913-28), the Winter Garden (1914-28, see ELGIN AND WINTER GARDEN THEATRES), and Shea's Hippodrome (1914-56)—continued to provide performance venues for large-scale foreign touring productions.

At the beginning of the twentieth century, however, many Canadians were no longer content to remain passive consumers of American and British commercial theatre. They wanted to create their own productions, particularly classics of world drama ignored by commercial producers, and plays written by Canadians with Canadian settings, characters, and subject matter. In 1906 Timothy Eaton financed the construction in Toronto of the Margaret Eaton School of Literature and Expression in an attractive grey stone building on the west side of North (Bay) St south of Bloor known as The Greek Temple. Its productions of works from the Irish Literary movement, directed by Mrs Scott Raff, mark the beginning of the LITTLE THEATRE movement in the city. Little The-

atres anticipated the ALTERNATE THEATRE movement of the late 1960s and early 1970s in their experimentation with production methods and repertoire of modern international and Canadian works. The programming policy of HART HOUSE THEATRE, for example,—'No plays which have been done in Toronto before' and 'No plays which are likely to be done in Toronto in the near future'—was to stage high-quality drama neglected by the commercial companies. At a time when there was no direct government financial support of the arts, patronage by wealthy Ontario families such as the Eatons and the Masseys played a major part in encouraging indigenous artistic self-expression. The Massey family had already donated Massey Hall to Toronto in 1894. In 1919 Vincent MASSEY supervised the building of Hart House Theatre at the Univ. of Toronto, one of the best equipped university playhouses in North America.

Another important non-commercial company, still producing today as the Ottawa Little Theatre, was the Ottawa Drama League, founded in 1913. In 1915 the Dominion Government loaned the League the auditorium of the Victoria Memorial Museum, leading a number of journalists to announce prematurely the birth of a 'Canadian National Theatre'. When the Parliament Buildings burned the following year, the League lost the Museum to the politicians until 1923. But in 1927, with a membership approaching 1,700, the League was able to convert a Methodist church into its own permanent 500-seat theatre. Other Little Theatres with over half-a-century of continuous ongoing production include the Sarnia Little Theatre, founded as the Sarnia Drama League in 1928, and Toronto's UNIVERSITY ALUMNAE DRAMATIC CLUB, established in 1918.

After the First World War few Canadian professional companies existed. The all-male army revue, The DUMBELLS, entertained troops in France and England from 1917 to 1919 before embarking on successful tours of Canada and the U.S. as a civilian revue from 1919 to 1933. The Vaughan GLASER Players performed a repertory of popular American and English comedies, pantomimes, musicals, and dramas in Toronto from 1921 to 1928 and in 1930 and 1932, and Cameron MATTHEWS managed another repertory company in Toronto, the Cameron Matthews English Players, 1923-7 and 1931-2. In 1934 John

HOLDEN founded the Actors' Colony, a stock company in Bala, and continued to operate the company as the John Holden Players in Muskoka, Winnipeg, and Toronto from 1937 to 1941. Other professional companies in Ontario between the wars included the REX STOCK COMPANY, which toured in the early 1920s, the Mae EDWARDS Players, and the GALVIN PLAYERS in Ottawa.

But more important in the long run than these isolated attempts at sustaining professional theatres was the DOMINION DRAMA FESTIVAL, which brought together amateur companies in regional and national competitions from 1933 to 1939 and, following a Second World War hiatus, until 1970. Companies were encouraged to improve artistic standards through adjudications by leading figures from both European and American professional theatre and by seeing the best work from other regions in the country. Many theatre artists who subsequently achieved professional success in Canadian theatre made their start through the DDF.

Of the new companies established after the Second World War, the NEW PLAY SOCIETY, founded in Toronto in 1946 by Dora Mavor MOORE, was one of the most influential. The company grew out of Moore's amateur Village Players (1938-46) and was financed by her personal savings and her sons' war bonds. The aim of the NPS was 'to establish a living theatre in Canada on a professional but non-profit basis.' Though essentially only semi-professional, the NPS was noted for high-quality productions of works by Synge, Maugham, O'Neill, Saroyan, O'Casey, and Shaw. It also produced Canadian plays by Lister SINCLAIR, Morley Callaghan, Mavor MOORE, Harry Boyle, Andrew ALLAN and, most notably, John COULTER. The NPS's most popular success was the annual SPRING THAW revue (1948-71). Also founded in 1946, Toronto's Earle GREY Players and their Earle Grey Shakespearean Festival (1949-58) were precursors of the STRATFORD FESTIVAL, which in turn gave birth to the CANADIAN PLAYERS (1954-66), founded by Tom Patterson and actor/director Douglas CAMPBELL, the first twentieth-century indigenous professional company to tour widely in Canada and the U.S. In Ottawa the CANADIAN REPERTORY THEATRE, founded in 1949 and led by Amelia HALL from 1950 to 1954, produced a repertoire of classical and modern plays in the 700-seat auditorium of the La Salle Academy.

Unable to generate sufficiently large audience support for its financial needs, the company disbanded in 1956. It was succeeded in 1967 by the TOWN THEATRE, which produced modern international plays until it was eclipsed by the opening of the NATIONAL ARTS CENTRE in 1969.

Toronto also supported a series of professional companies before the opening of its substantially subsidized civic theatre complex, the ST LAWRENCE CENTRE, in 1970. JUPITER THEATRE—organized by a group of actors, playwrights, and directors who had worked together for CBC radio—produced plays by Brecht, Sartre, O'Neill, Pirandello, Coward, Williams, and Fry from 1951 to 1954. It also staged a few Canadian works by Lister Sinclair, Ted ALLAN, and Nathan COHEN. The most important of the post-war Toronto companies was the CREST THEATRE, founded in 1954 by Donald DAVIS and Murray DAVIS. In its thirteen seasons the Crest presented over 140 productions, generally of a high artistic standard, in its 822-seat theatre on Mt Pleasant Road: classics, popular contemporary European and American plays, and a small percentage of Canadian works by Robertson DAVIES, Marcel DUBÉ, John GRAY, Ted Allan, Mavor Moore, Bernard SLADE, and others. THEATRE TORONTO, an amalgamation of the Crest Theatre and the Canadian Players, had two seasons at the Royal Alexandra Theatre in 1968-9 until financial difficulties forced it to amalgamate with the St. Lawrence Centre for the Arts. In contrast to the Crest, George LUSCOMBE's TORONTO WORKSHOP PRODUCTIONS, founded in 1959, emphasized political drama, actor-centred COLLECTIVE CREATIONs, and free adaptations of the classics. While it anticipated many of the political and aesthetic concerns of Toronto's alternate theatre companies a decade later, TWP's progressive political orientation and repertoire—in addition to its small houses (100 seats until 1967, 300 at present)—prevented it from developing into a recognized civic theatre.

At Stratford, founding artistic director Tyrone GUTHRIE imported designer Tanya MOISEIWITSCH, leading British administrative and technical staff, and actors Alec Guiness, Irene Worth, Douglas Campbell, and Michael Bates for his inaugural 1953 season. But his two 1953 productions—Richard III and All's Well That Ends Well—also displayed some of the best Canadian acting talent:

Members of the 1956 Stratford Festival Company. Back row (l. to r.): William Shatner, Christopher Plummer, Richard Easton, Ted Follows, Donald Davis, William Hutt. Front row (l. to r.): David Gardner, Max Helpmann, Amelia Hall, Eric House, Bruce Swerdfager

Lloyd Bochner, Robert CHRISTIE, Robert GOODIER, Amelia Hall, Donald HARRON, Eric HOUSE, William HUTT, Betty LEIGHTON, Peter Mews, William NEEDLES, Douglas RAIN, Eleanor STUART, and Bruce Swerdfager. The Canadianization of the company continued under artistic directors Michael LANGHAM (1956-67), the co-directorship of Jean GASCON and John HIRSCH (1968-9), and Gascon (1970-4). In 1957 Stratford's original canvas tent was replaced by Robert Fairfield's Festival Theatre, which maintained Guthrie's and Moiseiwitsch's novel thrust stage in close proximity to the audience. In 1963 the proscenium Avon Theatre, already used for Guthrie's striking productions of *H.M.S. Pinafore* and *The Pirates of Penzance* in 1960-1, was purchased as a permanent performance venue. Jean Gascon added the 250-seat Third Stage as an experimental theatre in 1971.

While the Stratford Festival helped to make stars out of William Hutt, Douglas Rain, Kate REID, Frances HYLAND, Martha HENRY, Pat GALLOWAY, and others, it has had much less success in developing Canadian directors capable of mastering the large-scale productions of the Festival and Avon stages. In 1974 the appointment of English director Robin PHILLIPS to succeed Jean Gascon as Stratford's artistic director (1975-80) generated protests from the Canadian theatre community. Phillips' frequently outstanding and highly popular productions, many featuring imported stars such as Brian Bedford, Maggie Smith, and Peter Ustinov, silenced critics, however. A more serious crisis developed in 1980 when the Stratford Festival Board of Directors initially hired, and then quickly fired, a committee of four artistic directors—Martha Henry, Urjo KAREDA, and directors Peter Moss and Pam Brighton—to succeed Phillips. The Board's subsequent attempt to appoint British director John Dexter as artistic director caused such nation-wide public controversy that the federal Department of Immigration refused to issue Dexter a work permit. While John Hirsch eventually agreed to return as artistic director in order to prevent the cancellation of Stratford's 1981 season, his tenure (1981-5) was marked by financial and artistic instability. John NEVILLE's contribution as artistic director (1986-9) has been to restore public confidence, sound financial management, and the overall artistic quality of the Festival.

The SHAW FESTIVAL's artistic and financial growth since its beginnings in Niagara-on-the-Lake in 1962 has been almost as impressive as Stratford's. Following its founding by Brian Doherty, successive artistic directors Andrew Allan (1963-5), Barry Morse (1966), Paxton WHITEHEAD (1967-77), and particularly Christopher NEWTON (1980-) have transformed the Festival into an internationally recognized showcase for the works of Shaw and his contemporaries, several of its productions surpassing Stratford's in critical and audience appeal. Unlike Stratford, the Shaw Festival has also succeeded in establishing a presence in Toronto through a series of co-productions or transfers with YOUNG PEOPLE'S THEATRE, TORONTO FREE THEATRE, Toronto Workshop Productions, and the Royal Alexandra Theatre. The most popular of these have been Tom Wood's *B-Movie* at TWP in 1987 and Edmond Rostand's *Cyrano de Bergerac* and Claire Booth Luce's *The Women* at the Royal Alex in 1983 and 1987.

In Ottawa the prestigious National Arts Centre, opened in 1969, contains a 2,326-seat opera house, a 969-seat theatre, a 350-seat studio, and a 150-seat salon. Because of high operating costs and insufficient government subsidies, the NAC has had only limited success in fulfilling its legislative mandate to promote the performing arts within and beyond the National Capital Region. The Centre's English-language theatre company, headed by John WOOD since 1978, was disbanded in 1984, and to cut costs Andis Celms, director of theatre, co-produces or imports productions by other companies. French-language theatre has been consistently more successful at the NAC under the artistic direction of Jean Herbiet (1971-82) and particularly André BRASSARD (1982-). The only ongoing English professional producing company in Ottawa, since the demise of the Penguin Theatre Company (1978-83) and Theatre 2000 (1979-83), has been the GREAT CANADIAN THEATRE COMPANY, founded in 1975. In its 218-seat theatre the GCTC produces exclusively Canadian plays dealing with local subjects or significant political or social issues. (See POLITICAL AND POPULAR THEATRE.)

The National Arts Centre's difficulties in operating both an expensive physical plant and professional resident companies with roots in the local community had already been encountered by regional theatres in major urban centres across the country in the late 1960s and early 1970s. Even before Mavor Moore's and Leon MAJOR's unpopular inaugural season at the St Lawrence Centre in 1970—consisting of poorly chosen Canadian plays and Canadian translations of European works—an ALTERNATE THEATRE movement had developed in Toronto to challenge the artistic policies of the regional theatres and the government cultural agencies that funded them. THEATRE PASSE MURAILLE was founded by Jim GARRARD at Rochdale College in 1968; FACTORY THEATRE Lab by Ken GASS in 1970; TARRAGON THEATRE by Bill GLASSCO in 1971; and Toronto Free Theatre by Tom HENDRY, Martin KINCH, and John PALMER in 1972. Theatre Passe Muraille built its reputation on actor-centred collective creations and mythmaking DOCUMENTARY drama, most notably *The FARM SHOW* in 1972. Factory Theatre has developed the careers of several playwrights, notably George F. WALKER, while Tarragon—both under founding artistic director Bill Glassco and his successor Urjo Kareda—has favoured literary drama by David FRENCH, James REANEY, Judith THOMPSON, and others. Tarragon has also been a major showcase for leading Québécois playwrights in English translation, particularly Michel TREMBLAY. Toronto Free Theatre has produced the works of dozens of leading Canadian and foreign playwrights, while giving greater prominence to directors and designers. Other alternate companies included John HERBERT's 35-seat Garret Theatre (1967-70), Robert and Elizabeth Swerdlow's Global Village (1969-75), and Louis Capson's Creation 2 (1969-77). Ernest Schwarz's STUDIO LAB THEATRE, founded in 1965 as a children's theatre company emphasizing improvisational techniques, achieved a previously unprecedented twelve-month run in adult programming with *Dionysus in '69* and *Dionysus in '70*.

In contrast to the regional theatres, Theatre Passe Muraille, the Factory, Tarragon, and Toronto Free produced almost exclusively contemporary Canadian plays to small but appreciative audiences. These Toronto theatres were soon joined by a second wave of alternate companies such as Jonathan Stanley's NEW THEATRE (1971-80), Sylvia Tucker's and Ray Whelan's OPEN CIRCLE THEATRE (1973-82), the feminist Red Light Theatre (1974-77), Paul Bettis's Theatre Second Floor (1975-79), Graham Harley's PHOENIX THEATRE (1975-83), Keith TURNBULL's NDWT company (1975-82), and Michael BAWTREE's COMUS MUSIC THEATRE (1975-86). Collectively this second wave favoured Canadian works, socially relevant drama, and investigations of different aesthetic styles, but also staged contemporary plays from the international repertoire. Lacking the special grants—Local Initiatives Projects, Opportunities for Youth, and other government programs—available to the early alternate theatres, and unable to generate the artistic identity and audience loyalty of Passe Muraille, Factory, Tarragon, and Free, the second wave of alternates did not survive.

By the mid-1970s the original alternate theatres in Toronto began to lose much of their earlier artistic radicalism and, partly for economic reasons, became part of the establishment mainstream. A third wave, however, continued the tradition of artistic experimentation and the search for new audiences, led in Toronto by directors such as Richard ROSE (Necessary Angel Theatre), Jim Millan (Crow's Theatre), Leah Cherniak and Martha Ross (Theatre Columbus), and director/playwright Sky Gilbert, whose Buddies in Bad Times company is a voice for Canada's gay and lesbian communities. Kate Lushington's Nightwood Theatre gives creative expression to feminist concerns.

These companies, and several dozen like them, have found it difficult to outgrow their fringe-theatre status, partly because of the great increase in theatre activity all across Ontario since the 1960s. New professional companies now must compete for audiences not only with civic theatres such as the SUDBURY THEATRE CENTRE, MAGNUS THEATRE (Thunder Bay), THEATRE AQUARIUS (Hamilton), Press Theatre (St Catharines), and two dynamic regional theatres—the Grand Theatre (see GRAND OPERA HOUSE, London) and the CANADIAN STAGE COMPANY (Toronto)—but also with hundreds of amateur-theatre companies, multi-cultural theatres, and theatres for young people, which collectively attract audiences in the hundreds of thousands annually. Experimental theatre companies in Toronto also no longer serve as the prime production venue for Canadian playwrights, as they did in the 1970s. Canadian plays are now popular attractions at civic and regional theatres, at other alternate companies outside of Toronto—such as KAM THEATRE in Thunder Bay—and at amateur, community, and university theatres. Since the founding in Toronto of THEATRE PLUS by Marion ANDRE in 1973, summer theatres such as Arbor Theatre (Peterborough), the all-Canadian BLYTH FESTIVAL, Huron Country Playhouse (Grand Bend), Kawartha Summer Theatre (Lindsay), the Muskoka Festival, and the Petrolia Summer Theatre have greatly increased in importance as producers of Canadian plays. Native Indian performers and playwrights have found a public voice through Native Earth Performing Arts. *The Rez Sisters*, a moving comedy-drama about the lives of seven women on a Manitoulin Island reserve, by Native Earth artistic director Tomson Highway, premièred in Toronto in 1986, toured Canada in 1988, and was warmly received at the Edinburgh Festival the same year.

French-language theatre in Ontario, like its English counterpart, has also made remarkable progress since the founding of the Théâtre du P'tit Bonheur in Toronto in 1967. Companies such as P'tit Bonheur (renamed THÉÂTRE FRANÇAIS DE TORONTO in 1987), Le Théâtre du Nouvel-Ontario (Sudbury, 1970-), Le Théâtre des Lutins (Vanier, 1971-), Le Théâtre d'la Corvée (Vanier, 1975-), and Le Théâtre de la Vieille 17 (Ottawa, 1979-) have become important cultural institutions assisting Ontario francophones in preserving their language and cultural identity. Besides mounting major works by Quebec dramatists, these and other French-language companies have produced a number of important playwrights and collective creations dramatizing Franco-Ontarian life. Some of the most important of these include André Paiement's *Lavalléville* (Théâtre du Nouvel-Ontario, 1974); the collective creations *La Parole et la loi* (Théâtre d'la Corvée, 1979) and *Les Murs de nos villages* (Théâtre de la Vieille 17, 1979); *Hawksbury Blues* (Brigitte Haentjens and Jean-Marc Dalpé, Théâtre de la Vieille 17, 1981); *Nickel* (Jean-Marc Dalpé and Brigitte Haentjens, TNO, 1984); *Le Nez* (Robert Bellefeuille and Isabelle Cauchy, Théâtre de la Vieille 17, 1984); *Les Rogers* (Robert Belle-

Ontario, Theatre in

feuille, Jean-Marc Dalpé, and Robert Marinier, TNO and Théâtre de la Vieille 17, 1986); *Little Miss Easter Seals* (Lina Chartrand, Théâtre Français de Toronto, 1988); and Jean-Marc Dalpé's powerful drama *Le Chien* (TNO and National Arts Centre French Theatre, 1988).

Paradoxically, theatre in Ontario became a publicly recognized 'cultural industry' in the 1980s, just as the third wave of alternates in Toronto was suffering from severe financial constraints. A 1987 study on the economic impact of the arts in Ontario, commissioned by the Ontario Arts Council, indicated that already in 1981 arts-related employment in Canada was almost as large as that in agriculture, and that the estimated attendance for the performing arts in Ontario in 1986 was more than six million. That theatre is big business in Ontario was demonstrated by producers Marlene Smith, Tina VanderHeyden, and Ernie Rubenstein, who capitalized a 1985 Toronto production of Andrew Lloyd Webber's musical *Cats* with a pre-opening ticket sale of nearly $4 million. By the end of its Toronto run and Canada-wide tour, *Cats* had grossed in excess of $40 million. Smith and Rubenstein were subsequently chosen by the Ontario Heritage Foundation as producers for the Elgin and Winter Garden theatres, the former vaudeville complex on Toronto's Yonge St renovated by the provincial and federal governments at a cost of $23 million.

The financial and artistic success of *Cats*, and competition for even bigger West End/Broadway musical spectacles such as Webber's *The Phantom of the Opera*, are causing major changes in commercial theatre production in Toronto. Ed MIRVISH and David Mirvish, who, as owners of the Royal Alexandra Theatre, are the biggest commercial theatre producers in Toronto, proposed building a $6-million theatre next to the Royal Alex specifically to house *Phantom* before rival producer Garth Drabinsky won the show for the converted Imperial Six movie house on Yonge St, the former 2,000-seat vaudeville PANTAGES theatre. Competing with these major commercial ventures is the subsidized Canadian Stage Company, a 1988 merger between Toronto Free Theatre and CENTRESTAGE, Toronto's civic theatre. Joint artistic directors Bill Glassco and Guy SPRUNG have merged the financial and artistic resources of their respective companies to provide a greater talent pool and more capital for the production of Canadian and foreign works. The merger of a leading alternate with a former establishment regional theatre, in the face of strong competition from commercial theatre producers, neatly symbolizes the current condition of Ontario theatre.   ANTON WAGNER

Open Circle Theatre. Founded in Toronto in 1973 by Sylvia Tucker and Ray Whelan, it aimed to present theatre that reflected the social and political concerns of its immediate community. Inspired by the performance techniques of Bertolt Brecht, *commedia dell'arte*, and the San Francisco Mime Troupe, the company's early COLLECTIVE productions (frequently based on taped interviews with local residents) dealt with such issues as welfare and unemployment (*No Way José*, Mar. 1973), police power (*Cop*, Nov. 1973), and lead pollution (*Business as Usual*, a musical comedy, July 1974). Local Initiatives Program and Opportunities for Youth grants provided funding for Open Circle productions in community performance venues (church halls, schools), helping to attract many spectators who had never attended a conventional theatre event.

As funding sources tightened in the late 1970s, Open Circle turned more to scripted shows, but maintained its radical stance. Plays by Athol Fugard, David Hare, Pablo Neruda, and Dario Fo were produced, but the biggest critical and popular success was Israel Horowitz's *The Primary English Class*, which ran in Toronto in 1977 and went on national tour in 1978. This show's commercial success, and the company's move to the well-appointed Adelaide Court Theatre in the fall of 1978 called into question Open Circle's activist mandate. Ray Whelan left, Sylvia Tucker resisted administrative change, and the first show at Adelaide Court—Horowitz's *Mackerel* in Oct. 1978—failed. A surplus of $10,400 at the end of the 1977-8 season fell to a deficit of $43,600 a year later, increasing to $60,000 by 1982. In March 1982 a production of Fo's *Mother's Marijuana is the Best* was halted at dress rehearsal when there was no money to pay the actors, and the company closed.

The archives of Open Circle Theatre are at the Univ. of Guelph.   L.W. CONOLLY

Orpheum Theatre (Montreal). It was built on rue St Catherine in 1905 as a VAUDEVILLE

404

house. By 1914 a summer stock company featuring Lillian Kemble and Charles Mackie proved a popular addition to the regular vaudeville shows and a growing number of movies. In the 1920s winter stock companies—known as the Orpheum Players, starring Margaret Knight and later Victor Sutherland and Mildred Mitchell—attracted a faithful following, giving nine performances a week and changing shows weekly. In contrast to the typical New York road shows that dominated Montreal theatre at this time, the Orpheum Players offered unsophisticated fare such as George M. Cohan's romantic comedy *A Prince There Was* (in Sept. 1920). When the Depression and the popularity of movies and radio brought a decline in the audiences for stock companies, the theatre became a cinema until 1957, when the THÉÂTRE DU NOUVEAU MONDE leased it. The Orpheum was demolished in May 1966, after TNM decided to move to the PLACE DES ARTS, thence to Gratien GÉLINAS's COMEDIE-CANADIENNE across the street, to which it gave its own name. HERBERT WHITTAKER

Orpheum Theatre, Vancouver

Orpheum Theatre (Vancouver). The third Vancouver theatre of this name (see ALHAMBRA THEATRE and VANCOUVER OPERA HOUSE), it opened on Granville St on 8 Nov. 1927, financed by a local entrepreneur, Joseph Francis Langer, at a cost of around $1,000,000. Architect B. Marcus Priteca of Seattle designed it in the palatial fashion of the 1920s, a combination of structural eclecticism and bold colours. Priteca's most outstanding achievement, however, was the superb acoustics that remain a lasting legacy. Originally part of the Orpheum VAUDEVILLE circuit, the theatre yielded to motion-picture conglomerates RKO and Famous Players, and from the early 1930s to 1973 it was primarily a movie house. Films were punctuated by occasional vaudeville performances, variety shows provided by local talent, and the early concerts of the Vancouver Symphony Orchestra. There were also occasional performances by visiting opera singers, classical musicians, actors, and ballet companies, including the Ballet Russe de Monte Carlo in 1936, which performed at midnight after the conclusion of the film program.

The theatre's manager from 1935 to 1969 was Ivan Ackery, whose promotional energy and efforts to make a commercial operation also serve civic interests undoubtedly contrib-

uted to the public outcry that followed a plan proposed by the owners in 1973 to gut the theatre and insert a number of smaller cinemas. Eventually, in 1974, the city of Vancouver purchased the Orpheum, with the help of a well-supported fund-raising campaign, and it joined the QUEEN ELIZABETH THEATRE as an additional civic auditorium. Following extensive restoration work, it re-opened on 2 Apr. 1977 as the home of the Vancouver Symphony Orchestra. It also serves as a general concert hall whose rich setting has proven aesthetically as well as acoustically popular with every kind of audience. In its present form it has a seating capacity of 2,788; its proscenium is 57' wide and 40' high, dimensions almost exactly corresponding to those of the stage itself. In 1983 a new foyer known as Westcoast Hall was completed. The federal government has declared the Orpheum a National Historic Site.

See Ivan Ackery, *Fifty Years of Theatre Row* (1980), and Douglas McCallum, *Vancouver's Orpheum* (1984). R.B. TODD

Ouzounian, Richard (b. 1950). Raised in New York, he was active in Vancouver between 1970 and 1977 as an MA student at the Univ. of British Columbia, where he played a butch Olivia in an all-male *Twelfth Night*, and as Theatre Resident at Simon Fraser University (1974-6). Ouzounian wrote book and lyrics for, and directed, several musicals: *Merry Wives*, in which he starred as Falstaff, and *Love's Labour's Lost*, both of which had scores by Marek Norman; *Macbeth*, a rock-opera set during the Vietnam war, with only thirteen lines from Shakespeare, again with music by Norman; *Olympiad*, marking the 1976 Olympics; and *A Bistro Car on the C.N.R.*, written with Merv Campone. Pat Rose was composer for these last two, which were for the most part songs with no linking material. Ouzounian's five plays include *Come Out, Come Out, Whatever You Are* (performed 1974), a comedy of the sex-lives of students, and *British Properties* (performed 1977), a gentle, satirical farce about the rich, re-named *Westmount* when performed at FESTIVAL LENNOXVILLE in 1979. The former was published in *Canadian Theatre Review* (1984), the latter in *New Canadian Drama I* (1980).

In Vancouver Ouzounian directed as many as fourteen shows a year. Successes included *Jacques Brel*, Stephen Schwartz's *Godspell* (in Christ Church Cathedral), and Molière's *Scapin*. He made a reputation for glitzy and visually extravagant productions: a compilation about St Joan at Simon Fraser Univ., for example, ended with the door behind the stage opening to reveal Joan burning at the stake.

As artistic director of Festival Lennoxville (1978-80), Ouzounian turned the Festival to lighter summer fare. He was briefly director of YOUNG PEOPLE'S THEATRE, Toronto (1979-80), then artistic director of the MANITOBA THEATRE CENTRE (1980-4), achieving record season-ticket sales. His directing was by now confined to musicals and Shakespeare—his *Tempest* featured a five-foot boa constrictor, his *Taming of the Shrew* was set in an affluent Winnipeg suburb. In 1984-5 he was producer at CENTRESTAGE, Toronto, and in 1986 he became artistic director of the NEPTUNE THEATRE, Halifax, where in 1987 he translated and adapted Molière's *Tartuffe* as *What Happens at the No Nancy Summit*, representing Orgon as Prime Minister Brian Mulroney and Tartuffe as President Ronald Reagan.

MALCOLM PAGE

P

Palmer, John (b. 1943). Born in Sydney, N.S., he was raised in Ottawa where, at Glebe Collegiate, his interest in writing and directing for the theatre first emerged. While studying English at Carleton Univ. during the mid-1960s, he began to direct professionally, first at Le Hibou Coffee House, then at the Black Swan in Stratford, Ont. After winning prizes in the Canadian University Drama League Playwriting Competition in both 1965 and 1966, he received his first professional production in 1969 with the première of *Memories For My Brother, Part 1* (1972) at Stratford's Canadian Place Theatre, which he co-founded with Martin KINCH that same year as an alternative to the STRATFORD FESTIVAL. His production of this play in a revised version at Toronto's fledgeling THEATRE PASSE MURAILLE later the same year introduced Palmer to Toronto, where he co-founded TORONTO FREE THEATRE with Kinch and Tom HENDRY in 1971.

Although Palmer continues to write and direct sporadically, it is his contribution to Toronto theatre during the early to mid-1970s for which he is most recognized. His flamboyant productions of new Canadian plays at Theatre Passe Muraille, such as *Charles Manson a.k.a. Jesus Christ* (1972) by Fabian Jennings and Allan Rae, in 1971, and at Toronto Free Theatre—notably Larry FINEBERG's *Hope* (1972) in 1972—helped to stimulate interest in indigenous scripts and to spread enthusiasm for the small theatre companies working outside mainstream structures. His work as a director achieved its apotheosis with *The Pits*, a 1975 COLLECTIVE CREATION produced by Toronto Free Theatre in which the denizens of a dilapidated rooming-house were displayed in a multiple set, open to the audience that moved around and above its periphery. A *cause célèbre* with both audiences and critics, the production capitalized on Palmer's interest in the details of eccentric behaviour and the audience's fascination with bizarre personalities. Other noteworthy productions that he directed during this period include the 1977 revival of *Me?* by Martin Kinch in an elaborate environmental set, and *Gossip* in 1977, the first of three plays by George F. WALKER to be produced at Toronto Free Theatre.

During the 1970s Palmer's interest in directing declined in proportion to his disenchantment with the increasingly conservative Canadian theatre audience. Productions of his plays also declined as the theatres he had helped to create attracted more playwrights and larger audiences. A one-act monologue, *Henrik Ibsen On the Necessity of Producing Norwegian Drama* (1976), produced at FACTORY THEATRE Lab in 1976, best expresses the cynicism about Canadian culture that typifies his plays during this period. In 1979 he wrote and directed *The Pits '79* for NEW THEATRE, Toronto, before going to New York. He returned to Toronto in 1981. Because his recent work remains unpublished and unproduced, it is the early plays that shape his reputation as a playwright. Of these, *The End* (1972) and *A Touch of God in the Golden Age* (1972) are the most worthwhile, the former illustrating Palmer's agility with farce and comic characterization and the latter revealing his considerable ability with poetic reverie. They were produced at Toronto Free Theatre in 1972, and Factory Theatre Lab in 1971, respectively. His *A Day at the Beach*, two inter-related one-act plays produced by the Canadian Rep Theatre at Toronto Free Theatre in 1987, directed by Eric STEINER, received poor reviews.

See R. Wallace and C. Zimmerman, eds., *The Work* (1982).   ROBERT WALLACE

Pantages, Alexander (1871–1936). Born Pericles Pantages, he left his native Greece at age nine for America. Before he made his way to Dawson at the height of the 1897 Klondike Gold Rush, he had worked as cabin boy, bootblack, labourer (on the Panama Canal), restaurant manager, and professional boxer. Pantages had no formal education, and although he eventually controlled one of the largest and most successful of the American-owned VAUDEVILLE circuits, he apparently remained illiterate.

An extraordinary businessman, Pantages' first theatre venture (with the help of 'Klondike Kate' Rockwell) was the Orpheum, a dancehall-saloon in Dawson City. The Orpheum formed the first link in what became North America's largest privately owned chain of vaudeville playhouses. By 1910 Pantages was successfully established in Seattle, where he owned and operated three vaudeville houses, besides having controlling interest in twenty-six theatres extending from Vancouver to Los Angeles.

In 1912 Pantages announced plans to construct several vaudeville houses in Canada. They were built in Edmonton and Vancouver in 1913, and in Winnipeg in 1914, but elsewhere (Calgary, Saskatoon, Moose Jaw) the plans never materialized and the Pantages circuit played in leased houses. All the theatres built for Pantages were characterized by the elaborate classical baroque interior stylings of architect B. Marcus Priteca, whose Corinthian-columned proscenium arches and ornately plastered ivory and gold auditoriums formed a style of theatre embellishment coined 'Pantages Greek'.

By 1914 the Pantages theatre empire extended in a giant crescent from Chicago through Winnipeg and Edmonton, to Vancouver and Seattle, and as far south as San Francisco. Unlike some of his competitors, Pantages adjusted to wartime stringencies and emerged with one of the most secure vaudeville circuits on the continent.

The wit, glitter, and spectacle of lively paced vaudeville shows provided a tempo matching that of the rapidly expanding western-Canadian cities selected to have Pantages playhouses. But Pantages vaudeville palaces were not built as an outlet for Canadian talent, nor can Alexander Pantages be credited with fostering any indigenous dramatic expression. However, the Pantages circuit entertainments remain a significant facet of popular entertainment in Canada.

See Theodore Saloutes, 'Alexander Pantages, Theatre Magnate of the West', *Pacific Northwest Quarterly* (Oct. 1966).
GEORGINA KRAVETZ

Paper Wheat

Paper Wheat, *Toronto Free Theatre, 1980, with (l. to r.) Lubomir Mykytiuk, Maja Ardal, David Francis, Skai Leja, (background) Bill Prokopchuk, Peter Meuse*

Paper Wheat. A COLLECTIVE CREATION of 25TH STREET THEATRE in Saskatoon, it opened in Sintaluta, Sask., on 18 Mar. 1977, had a two-week run in Saskatoon that spring, and was remounted for a Saskatchewan tour in the fall and a national tour between June and Dec. 1979. It toured eighty Canadian communities, was performed over 200 times to an estimated audience of 65,000, and was televised by the CBC; the second national tour formed the basis for a film by Albert Kish of the National Film Board.

Paper Wheat was originally created by Andras Tahn, founder and artistic director of 25th Street Theatre, and six actors: Bob Bainborough, Catherine Jaxon, Brenda Leadley, Sharon Hughes, Linda GRIFFITHS, and Michael Fahey. From interviews with Saskatchewan rural people, they fashioned a rough-and-ready episodic play that was considerably refined in subsequent productions. There are two substantially different versions: the original, and a revision by Guy SPRUNG with a partially new cast. It is the latter

version that toured and that has been published.

Act 1 is a series of folk episodes and parables about the settlement of western Canada and the need for co-operation. Its best-known episodes include a farmer and his wife folding and squeezing a blanket to describe their harsh years on the land; two scenes in which co-operation wins—'The marriage proposal' and 'The broken plough'; a comic song of woman's work, 'Old Bessie'; and a scene where an elevator agent cheats farmers when weighing their grain. Act 2 is a selective version of farming co-operative history, starting with Ed Partridge of Sintaluta and the Territorial Grain Growers' Association of 1905, and including the founding of the wheat pools in 1924, a speech by Louise Lucas in the 1930s, a 1960s co-op family, and closing with old people who remember the heroic past. 'I'd give it all to be young again and feel that I could change the world,' is the play's last line.

Several factors account for *Paper Wheat*'s

success. It presents a heroic story—the struggles of ordinary people on the Prairies to gain more control over their own lives—and tells it with clarity and economy. It combines its heroic elements with a saving humour so that the sentiment inherent in the story is controlled. The direct and episodic style, not unlike that of small-town Christmas concerts, appealed to audiences nationwide. Finally, in political terms the play is more utopian than critical.

The text of the unpublished first version is in the 25th Street Theatre collection in the Univ. of Saskatchewan archives. The touring version was published in *Canadian Theatre Review*, 17 (1978). The final version of *Paper Wheat* was published by Prairie Books in 1982.

See Robert C. Nunn, 'Performing Fact, Canadian Documentary Theatre', *Canadian Literature*, 103 (1984) and Alan Filewod, *Collective Encounters: Documentary Theatre in English Canada* (1987).   DON KERR

Paquin, Elzéar (1850-1947). Born at St-Raphaël, Que., he received his MD from Laval University in 1878. He lived in the U.S. between 1883 and 1897. Journalist, author, and advocate of francophone and Catholic causes, he wrote three books on medical topics, several politico-religious brochures, and one play, *Riel*, published in 1886.

Riel was never intended for performance. Defined by its author as a 'tragedy in four acts', it is a rambling, panoramic epic with some seventy-five characters, purporting to illustrate Louis Riel's career between 1869 and his death in 1885. To underline its propagandizing intent, each act is preceded by a lengthy synopsis, providing background and allocating blame for the action to be portrayed. Act 1 recounts events leading to the first Métis Rebellion; Act 2 focuses on Riel's domestic life and precarious mental state during his long exile. In Act 3, sought out by a delegation of his countrymen, Riel agrees to lead their struggle for justice. This act ends with the Battle of Batoche and his surrender. The last act is the most heterogeneous, the first scenes depicting a heroic, almost saintly Riel accepting his martyrdom for the good of his nation, the rest attacking, with long verbatim accounts from no less than forty-eight newspapers from Canada and abroad, the Macdonald government, its advisers, the Orange Lodge and the press it controls, and

especially the Conservative ministers from Quebec. *Riel* is a classic example of armchair political drama, a genre whose roots in Quebec go back to the French regime and which remained, with religious-pedagogic theatre, the sturdiest genre of nineteenth-century drama in Quebec. Translated into English by Eugene Benson and Renate Benson, *Riel* appears in vol. IV of *Canada's Lost Plays* (1982).

See L.E. Doucette, 'Louis Riel sur scène: L'État de la dramaturgie québécoise en 1886', *Theatre History in Canada*, 6 (1985).
                                        L.E. DOUCETTE

Pardey, Herbert O. (1808-65). Born in England, he acted in Montreal amateur productions shortly after immigrating to Canada in 1838. As 'Mr Pardey from Canada' he joined a professional company in Boston for the 1844-5 season. Returning to Montreal, he played in George SKERRETT's 1846 and 1847 summer companies, and toured with them to Hamilton, Toronto, and Kingston. At least two of his plays, *The Canadian Settlers* and *The Rights of Age*, were produced during these years. Between 1848 and 1852 he acted at several New York theatres, where some of his plays were performed. In the 1853-4 company in Providence, R.I., he found his most memorable role, that of Uncle Tom in *Uncle Tom's Cabin*. Two more seasons in Boston and one in Provincetown preceded his final drink-sodden years in a Philadelphia almshouse.   MARY SHORTT

Parker, Sir Gilbert (1860-1932). Born Horatio Gilbert George Parker in Camden East, Ont., he was educated at the Univ. of Toronto. His early career was as a teacher, part-time curate, and lecturer in elocution at the Univ. of Toronto and Queen's University, Kingston. In Australia from 1886, he worked as a journalist and dramatized Goethe's *Faust* for a well-received production by George Rignold at Her Majesty's Theatre in Sydney; the next year he adapted, also for Rignold, A.C. Gunter's best selling novel *Mr. Barnes of New York*, retitled *The Vendetta*. Neither script is extant.

In 1890 Parker left for England, where he established himself as an internationally successful novelist and short-story writer. His playwriting career was less successful. A comedy, *The Wedding Day*, written for Willie Edouin, expired at the Strand Theatre after only a performance or two, and plays written for theatre managers George Alexander and Augustus Harris failed to reach the stage. None of these scripts survive.

Parker's adaptation of his own 1896 novel, *The Seats of the Mighty*, enjoyed better success; Herbert Beerbohm Tree premièred the drama in Washington on 27 Nov. 1896, with himself in the role of Doltaire, to inaugurate his second American tour. Despite mixed reviews Tree opened his new theatre, Her Majesty's, with it on 28 Apr. 1897, making it the first Canadian play to be staged in London's West End. Reviews were unenthusiastic and the production was withdrawn after a six-week run.

Thereafter Parker directed his energies exclusively to literature and politics. He was knighted in 1902. He died in London, Eng., and was buried in Belleville, Ont.

Dramatizations of two of Parker's novels by more experienced playwrights enjoyed considerable success. *The Right of Way*, dramatized by Eugene W. Presby, premièred at Wallack's Theatre, New York, in 1907 to excellent notices. *Pierre of the Plains*, an adaptation by Edgar Selwyn of *Pierre and His People*, enjoyed a similar reception at New York's Hudson Theatre in 1908.

See John Coldwell Adams, *Seated with the Mighty: A Biography of Sir Gilbert Parker* (1979), and John Ripley, ed., *Gilbert Parker and Herbert Beerbohm Tree Stage 'The Seats of the Mighty'* (1986).   JOHN RIPLEY

Pelletier, Denise (1929-76). Born in Saint-Jovite, Que., the daughter of literary critic Albert Pelletier and the sister of actor Gilles PELLETIER, she studied with Sita Riddez and made her acting début with Les COMPAGNONS DE SAINT-LAURENT. She subsequently gave memorable performances in such plays as Eugene O'Neill's *Long voyage vers la nuit* (*Long Day's Journey into Night*), Brecht's *Mère Courage* (*Mother Courage*), Samuel Beckett's *Oh les beaux jours* (*Happy Days*), and Michel TREMBLAY's *Bonjour, là, bonjour*. A few months before her death she performed in English in Jacques Beydenwellen's *La Divine Sarah*. Indisputably Quebec's most distinguished actress of her time, she also starred in several television series—notably 'Les Plouffe', in which she created the role of Cécile. She won the Molson Prize in 1975, and in 1977 both the Quebec prize for theatre

Denise Pelletier

artists and the new theatre of the NOUVELLE COMPAGNIE THÉÂTRALE took the name of Denise Pelletier.   JEAN CLÉO GODIN

Pelletier, Gilles (b. 1925). Born in Saint-Jovite, Que., he began his acting career in radio in 1945, after a short stint in the French navy, and turned to the theatre after studying with Sita Riddez and Eleanor STUART. Pelletier made his stage début with Pierre DAGENAIS's L'ÉQUIPE and with Les COMPAGNONS DE SAINT-LAURENT. In 1958 he created the role of Joseph Latour in Marcel DUBÉ's *Un SIMPLE SOLDAT* and also played in the 1971 première of Michel TREMBLAY's *À TOI, POUR TOUJOURS, TA MARIE-LOU* and the 1976 première of *Gapi* by Antonine MAILLET. In 1964, with Georges Groulx and Françoise Graton, he founded La NOUVELLE COMPAGNIE THÉÂTRALE, which he directed until 1982. He appeared in Alfred Hitchcock's *I Confess* (1953), among other films, both English and French, and has acted in some thirty television productions, including Chekhov's *Oncle Vania*, Emanuel Roblès' *Montserrat*, Ibsen's *Hedda Gabler*, Paul Claudel's *Partage de midi*, Molière's *Don Juan*, and Shakespeare's *La Nuit des Rois* (*Twelfth Night*). Pelletier received an honorary doctorate from the Université de Sherbrooke in 1984.   JEAN CLÉO GODIN

Pendu, Le. Robert GURIK's play—first produced at the DOMINION DRAMA FESTIVAL on

24 Mar. 1967 and published in 1970 (Montreal: Editions Leméac)—is a socio-evangelical humanitarian fable, with more resonances (biblical, mythical, psychoanalytical) than is common in Gurik's work.

An unemployed miner, old and paralysed, sits in his shack subsisting on illusions and schemes. Decayed and foul-smelling, he scratches himself and writhes like a mangy dog; he crawls, sniffs, whines, collapses. He seeks not to live, but to survive. His son Yonel, a fake blind man just recovering from a pit-gas explosion, is unable to bring home a penny, despite his placard, his dark glasses, and his white cane. The unscrupulous father persuades Yonel to tie a noose around his neck in an apparent plan to hang himself and sell pieces of the rope as good-luck charms. The son outdoes himself in this profitable role of victim—becoming a hero, a prophet, and a miracle-worker—as he manipulates merchandising techniques to force the wicked into paying dearly, while the good thrive and become rich. Believing himself to be a new Messiah, 'a great sun that shines on everyone', Yonel dreams of justice. But those he has helped insist that the hanging occur; the final scene is a parody of the Last Supper, reminiscent of Bunuel, in which the poor devour both the rope and the hanged man. Beginning as a tale of epic proportions, the play ends as a lesson in political realism.

Le Pendu was translated into English as *The Hanged Man* (1972) by Philip London and Laurence Bérard. See Rémi Tourangeau, 'Le Pendu de Robert Gurik; ou Le jeu illusoire du bonheur', in *Archives des lettres canadiennes 5, Le Théâtre canadien-français* (1976).
LAURENT MAILHOT

Pennell, Nicholas (b. 1939). Born in Devon, Eng., he trained as an actor at the Royal Academy of Dramatic Art and quickly established a successful career in provincial theatres, the West End, and on television—particularly as Michael Mont in the BBC's acclaimed series *The Forsyte Saga*. He first appeared in Canada at the STRATFORD FESTIVAL in 1972 playing Orlando in *As You Like It*, Tebaldeo in Alfred de Musset's *Lorenzaccio*, and Young Marlow in Goldsmith's *She Stoops to Conquer*. Pennell has performed in every subsequent Festival season in a wide range of Shakespearean roles—Jaques, Hamlet, Macbeth—and non-Shakespearean roles, including Jack Worthing in Wilde's *The Importance of Being Earnest*, Oswald in Ibsen's *Ghosts*, and Leonard Woolf in Edna O'Brien's *Virginia* (which transferred to London's Theatre Royal, Haymarket, in 1980). His one-man show, *A Variable Passion*, premièred at Stratford in 1982, and he has since toured it extensively in Canada and the U.S. Other work outside of Stratford includes a memorable Norman in Ronald Harwood's *The Dresser* (opposite Douglas CAMPBELL) at Toronto's Bayview Playhouse in 1983, and his directing of Shakespeare at the Cleveland Playhouse and Chicago's Court Theatre. An exceptionally articulate actor, deeply sensitive to textual nuance, Pennell has also taught acting in universities and acting schools. His films include *Only When I Larf* (1968), *Isadora* (1969), *The Battle of Britain* (1969), and *David Copperfield* (1970).
L. W. CONOLLY

Pennoyer, John (b. 1949). Born in Montreal and educated at McMaster Univ., he worked in 1972 as property apprentice at the STRATFORD FESTIVAL, where he was influenced by Leslie Hurry and Desmond HEELEY. After experience in England and the U.S., he returned to Stratford as assistant to such designers as Daphne Dare, Susan BENSON, Robin Fraser Paye, and Michael Annals. He was the first recipient of the Tom Patterson Award (1977) for excellence in a designer in training.

Pennoyer's reputation is based largely on costume design. Of his thirteen Stratford productions, most notable were *Hamlet* (1976), with its feeling of a youth returning to a stuffy world of pinstripes and wool; *Julius Caesar* (1982), an amalgam of togas and the contemporary fashions of Giorgio Armani and Gianni Versace, which reflected the terrorism of contemporary Rome; and *Love's Labour's Lost* (1983, 1984), influenced by Diana Vreeland's 'La Belle Époch' exhibition at the Metropolitan Museum, New York.

Pennoyer's set designs range from the soft-edged, fairy-tale Arthur Rackham quality of *Beauty and the Beast* (1981) and the toy-theatre decorativeness of *Alice* (1983), both produced at the YOUNG PEOPLE'S THEATRE, to the cinematic Renoir-like *L'École des femmes* (1983) and the spray-paint impressionism of *L'Avare* (1985), both Molière plays produced at the Théâtre du P'tit Bonheur (see THÉÂTRE FRANÇAIS DE TORONTO). In 1986 he executed a mannerist design (in a silver, grey, and black palette) for Philip Barry's *Holiday* at the SHAW FESTIVAL. The texture of an engraving accentuated the production's dark tones and sense of oppressive materialism. A six-time Dora Award nominee, Pennoyer has worked on all three Tyrone GUTHRIE stages: Stratford, Minneapolis, and Sheffield.

KEITH GAREBIAN

Persephone Theatre. Saskatoon's main professional theatre company was founded in 1974 by director Brian Richmond and two Saskatoon actresses, Janet and Susan Wright, who had already achieved acclaim elsewhere and who wanted to perform in their own city. Their first three-play season defined the kind of theatre Persephone would feature: a recent American hit, Lanford Wilson's Hot l Baltimore; a classic, Ibsen's A Doll's House; and a Canadian première, Ken MITCHELL's CRUEL TEARS.

Richmond remained artistic director for two seasons (1974-6), followed by Howard Dallin (1976-8), Ron McDonald (1978), Tom Kerr (1978-80), and Eric Schneider (1980-2). Tibor Feheregyhazi has been artistic director since 1982.

Premières of Canadian plays at Persephone have included Mitchell's Cruel Tears, 1974; Frank Moher's Stage Falls, 1978; Ronald Mavor's A House on Temperance, 1980; Geoffrey Ursell's Saskatoon Pie, 1982 (remounted for a Saskatchewan tour in 1986); and Barbara Sapergia's Matty and Rose and The Great Orlando, both in 1985.

Persephone performed its first season at the Mendel Art Gallery and its second at the University's Greystone Theatre before moving in 1976 to St Thomas Wesley Church Hall, where it remained until 1983. When 25TH STREET THEATRE joined Persephone in that space in 1981, it became known as the Saskatoon Theatre Centre. In 1983 Persephone purchased the Westgate Alliance Church and transformed it into the first permanent home for a Saskatoon professional theatre company.

The Persephone Youth Theatre has operated since 1982, first with Ruth Smillie as director, succeeded by Paul Lampert in 1984. New Canadian plays have included Ruth Smillie's Teenage Moms, 1983; Geoffrey Bilson's Goodbye Sara, 1983; Barbara Sapergia's and Geoffrey Ursell's The Willowbunch Giant, 1983; and Barbara Sapergia's The Skipping Show, 1986; as well as important COLLECTIVE productions with the Saskatoon Native Sur-

vival School: Uptown Circles in 1983 and Papihowin in 1984. In 1985-6 the Youth Theatre played to 42,000 students in seventy-two schools in Saskatoon and Saskatchewan. In that season the main stage had 2,400 subscribers.

DON KERR

Petch, Steve (b. 1952). Born in Vancouver and raised in Ontario, he was writing for the Kitchener Little Theatre at the age of sixteen. A degree in psychology from the Univ. of Waterloo, and travels in Mexico and the Mediterranean, help explain the neurotic souls and exotic locales of plays like The General (1973), workshopped by FACTORY THEATRE Lab in 1972, Turkish Delight (1975), produced by Theatre Second Floor in 1976, and The Island, produced by TARRAGON THEATRE in 1986. Success in Toronto led to a commission from the STRATFORD FESTIVAL, where Victoria (1979) appeared on the Festival's Third Stage in 1979. Swell was showcased during Toronto's first International Theatre Festival, 1981. After Tarragon's 1984 production of Cousins, Petch cycled back to Vancouver on a fund-raising marathon for that theatre.

Tumble-down rooms and war-torn or deserted landscapes symbolize the untidy, fractured relationships Petch's characters achieve. The ravaged frontier-post in Passage (1974), workshopped at Factory Theatre Lab in 1974, guards a land whose history is impenetrable and whose inhabitants cheat, kill, and adopt false identities in order to survive the region's ghosts and wandering magicians. In Turkish Delight Ana and her mother warm to Istanbul despite its dirt and hostile charm. But Victoria offers less reassurance. Its characters move in paranoid fits and starts; their confrontations have scarcely begun when one of the protagonists abruptly flits away. On the other hand there is little resonance to the amusing games of Sight Unseen (1979), produced by Tarragon Theatre in 1979; here motives are explained, but they turn out to be a predictable collection of sexual hangups. When Petch's plays maintain a balance between obliqueness and dramatic energy they are evocative and haunting mood-pieces. However, as evidenced by the divided critical response to Another Morning (1987), produced at the Granville Island stage of the ARTS CLUB, Vancouver, 1987, and Service, presented by Vancouver's NEW PLAY CENTRE at the Waterfront Theatre, 1988, those who insist on a significant message are apt to find these enigmatic, disturbing encounters claustrophobic, undramatic, and annoying.   ANTHONY JENKINS

Peterson, Eric (b. 1946). Born in Indian Head, Sask., he studied acting at the Univ. of Saskatchewan for two years, worked in England as a stage manager, and performed in Alberta children's theatre before moving to Vancouver in 1970. After a year at the Univ. of British Columbia he co-founded TAMAHNOUS THEATRE, an alternative, collective company in whose experimental versions of *The Bacchae* and *Nijinsky*, both directed by John GRAY, Peterson had his first major roles. He moved to Toronto in 1974, joining THEATRE PASSE MURAILLE and becoming one of its feature performers. Its collective, improvisational style showcased his versatility and imagination. Appearing in such seminal Passe Muraille works as *The FARM SHOW*, *The West Show*, and *Them Donnellys*, Peterson gained his highest profile in the roles of William Lyon Mackenzie and Lady Backwash in *1837: The Farmers' Revolt*.

From 1976 to 1978 Peterson and John Gray put together their musical play *BILLY BISHOP GOES TO WAR* (1981). It was modelled closely on the formula of a two-man musical they had done in Vancouver in 1975—Tom CONE's *Herringbone*—in which Peterson played more than two dozen roles, with Gray directing and accompanying him on piano. Peterson's virtuoso performance in *Billy Bishop* earned him critical superlatives throughout Canada, Britain, and the U.S. In New York he won the Clarence Derwent Award for most promising performer (1980), as well as Best Actor nominations from London's Society of West End Theatres (1982) and Canada's ACTRA (1983).

Another *tour de force*, Peterson's solo performance in Patrick Suskind's *The Double Bass* at Toronto's TARRAGON THEATRE in 1985 suggests that his acting has gained depth to go along with the extraordinary breadth revealed in his previous work.
                    JERRY WASSERMAN

Peterson, Len (b. 1917). Born in Regina, Sask., he was educated at Northwestern Univ., Ill. (B.Sc., 1938). In Toronto in 1938 he sold his first play, *It Happened in College*, to the CBC. Following infantry service in the Canadian Army, 1942-3, he wrote docu-

Len Peterson receiving a 1984 ACTRA award

mentaries—about army life and the war—for the radio section of NDHQ in Ottawa. In 1944 he joined a group of writers associated with Andrew ALLAN, head of drama at the CBC, preparing scripts for the new 'Stage' series. Peterson's first contribution was *Within the Fortress*, a sympathetic portrayal of the Germans trapped in their Nazi stronghold, which raised less of a storm than his second 1944 play, *They're All Afraid*, about office bullying and fear. This won Peterson his first international award—the Columbus Award of the Ohio Radio Institute. In 1946 the CBC broadcast Peterson's best-known work, *BURLAP BAGS* (1972), a play that anticipates the Absurdist drama of Beckett, Ionesco, and Pinter; its disregard for convention caused an uproar, but it won another Columbus award. Several of his plays—including *Adolescent Rebellion*, *Brotherly Hatred*, *The Careful Boy*, and *Sex Education*—were broadcast in the late 1940s on the CBC's 'In Search of Ourselves' series.

Peterson's first full-length stage play, *The Great Hunger* (1967), produced by the Arts Theatre, Toronto, in 1960, integrates issues of social justice, Inuit myths, and social customs into the formal structure of the Elizabethan revenge tragedy. Two children's participation stage plays, *Almighty Voice* (1974) and *Billy Bishop and The Red Baron* (1975)—both commissioned and produced by Toronto's YOUNG PEOPLE'S THEATRE in 1970 and 1975 respectively—explore heroic death and survival in familiar language and recognizable settings. A children's participation play about creation myths—*Let's Make a World* (1973)—was produced at YPT in 1971. Peterson's feminist drama, *Women in the Attic* (1972), was first produced by Ken KRAMER at Regina's GLOBE THEATRE in 1971, as was his version of the Regina Riot of 1935, *The Eye of the Storm*, in 1985.

Peterson is the author of more than one thousand works—plays, musicals, films, stories, and a novel—and they have included many firsts, such as the first trilogy broadcast on Britain's BBC: *Prairie Town, Big City,* and *Quebec*, in 1943; the first RADIO DRAMA series in Canada on mental health, 'In Search of Ourselves', from 1948 to 1954; the first dramatizations in Canada in English of works by Albert Camus and Knut Hamsun; the opening show of CBC-TV's national network, *Memo to Champlain*, on 1 July 1958. His chamber opera, *Clear Sky and Thunder*, with music by Ruth Watson Henderson, was performed by the Toronto Children's Chorus at Vancouver's Expo '86.

In addition to several Columbus awards, Peterson's honours include the John Drainie Award for distinguished contribution to broadcasting (1974) and ACTRA Awards for best drama in radio and television for *The Trouble With Giants* (1973) and for best radio drama for *Evariste Galois* (1984).

ROTA HERZBERG LISTER

Petitclair, Pierre (1813-60). Born to an illiterate farming family at St-Augustin de Portneuf, Que., he attended the Petit Séminaire de Québec before working as a copyist and notary's clerk for several years; but, by his own later account, he spent most of his time reading. In the winter of 1837-8 he accepted a position as tutor to the twelve children of a family engaged in the fish and fur trade in Labrador. He spent most of the rest of his life on the remote North Shore, returning only occasionally to Quebec City, yet he continued to contribute short stories and occasional poems to newspapers in the capital. He is the author of three published plays, *Griphon* (1837), *La DONATION* (1842), and *Une Partie de campagne* (1865).

Griphon, ou La Vengeance d'un valet has long been identified as the first published play by a native French-Canadian (the 1834 *Comédies du statu quo* are anonymous). *Griphon* was never performed, and its publication in the year of the Patriote Rebellion went virtually unnoticed. A comedy in three acts with strong farcical elements, it draws heavily for situation, characters and sometimes dialogue on Shakespeare's Falstaff plays, and on David Garrick, Jean-François Regnard, Philippe Destouches, and especially Molière. A lively, fast-moving first act is followed by two others that merely reproduce, with diminishing effect, the same devices. The central character, Griphon, is an interesting portrayal. Nearly eighty years old, he is an inveterate womanizer and religious hypocrite. To avenge a perceived wrong, his valet, Citron, with the help of another, disguises himself as a woman and arranges a tryst with the old man. Griphon is humiliated, beaten, and robbed. Impenitent, he is lured again, with the same result. Only a contrived resolution ends the plot. Modern sensibilities find the valets sadistic, their 'revenge' exaggerated. *Griphon* is a beginner's play, demonstrating real potential in its manipulation of scene and character, but lacking depth and structure. The setting is Quebec City, but only an occasional reference reveals this. Curiously the servants in the play speak the same standard French as their masters, with the sole exception of the maidservant Florette, whose earthy, genuine dialect is the first, and one of the best, instances of québécois French in Canadian drama.

La Donation, performed and published in Quebec City in 1842, represents a more important milestone than *Griphon*: it is the first play by a native author to have been published *and* performed in Canada. Petitclair's third play, *Une Partie de campagne* (only the titles of two other comedies, *Qui trop embrasse mal étreint* and *Le Brigand*, survive) was first performed in Quebec in 1857 and published posthumously in 1865. The most specifically Canadian of his plays, it is set in the countryside near Quebec City and deals with a perennial concern of French Canada—the temptation to adopt English manners, dress, and especially language. (The theme is thus identical to Joseph QUESNEL's *Anglomanie*, a play Petitclair could have consulted in manuscript during his years at the Séminaire de Québec.) The main character has even anglicized his name from Guillaume to William. Returning to his native village from studies in the city, William scornfully rejects rural values, the loyal friends he had known, and the French language. He is of course made to pay dearly for these excesses. Structurally, the work shows much progress in Petitclair's development as a playwright, with near-perfect balance between its two acts, the first winding tight the springs of action, the second releasing their tension. Dialogue is much more natural, with fewer asides and monologues (the bane of *La Donation*). Four different levels of French, appropriate to the social and educational status of each character, are used, and much fun is derived from the rustic dialect and foot-stomping music of local peasants.

Petitclair's importance is that of a self-taught pioneer, applauded by his contemporaries, then virtually forgotten for more than a century after his death.

See L.E. Doucette, *Theatre in French Canada, 1606-1867* (1984).

L.E. DOUCETTE

Phillips, Elizabeth Jane (1830-1904). Known throughout her long career as Miss (occasionally Mrs) E.J. Phillips, she was born in Chatham, Upper Canada, and gained her early acting experience at the ROYAL LYCEUM, Toronto, and on tours of Canadian cities, before moving to the U.S., where she built a distinguished career in character roles. In 1849—when women amateurs were almost unknown—she acted with the Hamilton Amateur Theatrical Society at the Royal Lyceum. Graduating from amateur to professional, she joined John NICKINSON's Utica company in 1852, and became a valuable member of his Toronto company from 1853 to 1858, playing a wide range of supporting roles with increasing success. Her connection with Nickinson lasted until his death in 1864, when they were both acting at Pike's Opera House, Cincinnati. Later she played for many seasons at the Chestnut St Theatre, Philadelphia, and the Union Square Theatre and Palmer's Theatre, New York. Not a beautiful woman, she was rarely cast for romantic leads, but excelled as spinsters, aristocrats, and 'women of convictions'. Her personal dignity and gracious manner earned her the affectionate title of 'Lady' Phillips among her many theatrical friends.

MARY SHORTT

Phillips, Robin (b. 1942). Born in England, he trained at the Bristol Old Vic Theatre School under Duncan Ross. He was associate director of the Bristol Old Vic in 1960, and acted in Laurence Olivier's first Chichester season in 1962. In 1965 he was assistant director with the Royal Shakespeare Company, and in 1967-8 associate director of the Northcott Theatre, Exeter. He returned to the RSC in 1970 and to Chichester in 1972 before helping to found the Company Theatre, Greenwich, where he was appointed artistic director in 1973. His most notable early productions were of Edward Albee's *Tiny Alice* (RSC, 1970), Ronald Millar's *Abelard and Heloise* (London and Broadway, 1970), Shakespeare's *Two Gentlemen of Verona* (RSC, 1971), Shaw's *Caesar and Cleopatra* (Chichester, 1971, with John Gielgud), Jean Anouilh's *Dear Antoine* (Chichester, 1971, with Edith Evans), and Christopher Fry's *The Lady's Not For Burning* (Chichester, 1972, with Richard Chamberlain).

In 1974, despite nationalist objections, Phillips was appointed artistic director of the STRATFORD FESTIVAL. He spent his first year observing at the Festival and touring the country to familiarize himself with Canadian theatre. In the next six years he directed or co-directed twenty-nine new productions and six revivals. There were significant productions of Shakespeare's *Measure for Measure* (1975-6), *A Midsummer Night's Dream* (1976-7), *Richard III* (1977), *As You Like It* (1977-8), *The Winter's Tale* (1978), and *King Lear* (1979-80); Oscar Wilde's *The Importance of Being Earnest* (1975, 76, and 79); William Congreve's *The Way of the World* (1976); Noël Coward's *Private Lives* (1978); Chekhov's *Uncle Vanya* (1978) and *The Seagull* (1980), both in new translations by John MURRELL; and the première of Edna O'Brien's *Virginia* (1980, restaged at the Haymarket Theatre, London, England, 1980-1).

During his tenure at Stratford, Phillips significantly increased revenues, numbers of productions and numbers of performances, as well as greatly enhancing the artistic reputation of the Festival. His departure in 1980, however, like his arrival six years earlier, was plagued by controversy. The Festival board first refused to acknowledge or act upon his resignation; then approved and later rescinded approval of a collective directorate; tried to hire British director John Dexter, but was prevented by a Canadian Immigration ruling; and finally appointed John HIRSCH as Phillips' successor.

Since his departure from Stratford, Phillips has directed in England and Canada, including a production of Shakespeare's *Antony and Cleopatra* (Chichester, 1985); première productions of John Murrell's *Farther West* (Calgary, 1982) and *New World* (NATIONAL ARTS CENTRE, Ottawa, 1984, and CENTRESTAGE, Toronto, 1985); and of Noël Coward's *Tonight at 8:30* (Centrestage, 1984). He was also artistic director for one artistically brilliant but financially disastrous repertory season at the newly inaugurated Grand Theatre, formerly Theatre London (GRAND OPERA HOUSE), in London, Ont., 1983-4, where he directed seven productions. In 1986 he returned to Stratford to direct a notable production of *Cymbeline* at the Festival Theatre, after which he was appointed director of the Young Company at Stratford's Third Stage.

Phillips' film credits include directing Timothy FINDLEY's *The Wars* and Strindberg's *Miss Julie*, and acting in *Decline and Fall*, *Tales from the Crypt*, and *David Copperfield* (in which he played the title role). He has also appeared on television as Wilfred Desert in *The Forsyte Saga* and as Konstantin in *The Seagull*, both for the BBC.

Known as an actor's director, Phillips is respected for his sensitivity to the actor's process and for his ability to draw on actors' unconscious motivations. This, together with careful and intelligent textual work, results in productions of extraordinary clarity of text and interpretation. With the assistance of his favourite designer Daphne Dare, he is also known for the visual clarity and beauty of productions that derive their unity less from an externally imposed intellectual concept than from a contextual approach that has its origin in design. He surrounds a largely exploratory rehearsal process with very specific visual images, period metaphor or scenic locations, and he structures his productions around brilliantly staged tableaux.

Phillips' directing vocabulary and the style of his productions are largely filmic. He blocks and achieves focus through the use of upstage actors, crosses, and patterning that lead the audience's eye in ways consciously analogous to the zooms, pans, and variable depth-of-field of a camera; and he employs an almost continuous and often subliminal cinematic soundscape to underscore the action

and to feed the imagination and emotional involvement of the actors.

In 1988 Phillips turned down the offer of another term as artistic director at Stratford, subsequently accepting the artistic directorship at the Chichester Festival.

RICHARD PAUL KNOWLES

Phipps, Jennifer (b. 1934). Born in England, she trained as an actress at the Royal Academy of Dramatic Art and worked throughout the 1950s in British repertory theatre, the West End, and in radio, television, and film. After marrying Canadian actor Peter Boretski, she moved with him to Winnipeg in 1960, appearing at the MANITOBA THEATRE CENTRE in Sean O'Casey's *Juno and the Paycock*, Patrick Hamilton's *Gaslight*, and Ray Lawler's *Summer of the Seventeenth Doll*. She taught in 1961 at Hollywood's Academy of Theatre Arts, but returned in 1962 to Canada, where she has since performed regularly at the STRATFORD FESTIVAL, the SHAW FESTIVAL, and most of the country's regional theatres. A strong character actress, known for her intelligent and intuitive performances and her resonant voice, Phipps became in the 1970s leading lady at Toronto Arts Productions (see CENTRESTAGE), playing roles as varied as Clytemnestra, Mrs Malaprop, and Mother Courage. She has also appeared in a number of contemporary Canadian and U.S. plays, including Jovette MARCHESSAULT's *Saga of the Wet Hens* (*SAGA DES POULES MOUILLÉES*) at Toronto's TARRAGON THEATRE in 1982, Christopher Durang's *Sister Mary Ignatius Explains It All For You* at Tarragon in 1983 (for which she won a Dora Mavor MOORE Award), and Marsha Norman's *'Night Mother* at Edmonton's PHOENIX THEATRE in 1984.

L. W. CONOLLY

Phoenix Theatre (Edmonton). It was founded by Keith Digby in June 1981 when legal difficulties forced Edmonton's THEATRE 3 to close. Theatre 3's collapse came at a time when attendance and subscriptions were at record highs, and Digby, artistic director of Theatre 3 since 1978, felt a new organization dedicated to the same aesthetic mandate could rise like a 'Phoenix' out of its ashes.

While losing the Theatre 3 space to creditors, Phoenix was able to raise enough money to mount a season of four productions, including a TAMAHNOUS THEATRE production on tour, in the Univ. of Alberta's Students' Union Theatre for the 1981-2 season. Digby's original aims for Phoenix were to continue those of Theatre 3: to perform a combination of new Canadian works, noncommercial contemporary plays, and seldom-seen classics. Under Digby's successor, Bob Baker (1982-7), the theatre turned more sharply towards contemporary work featuring strong elements of social satire, dance, music, and the visual arts, and mounted successful productions of John GRAY's *18 Wheels* (in 1983), Caryl Churchill's *Cloud 9* (1984), Harvey Fierstein's *Torch Song Trilogy* (1985), and the première of Tom Wood's *B-Movie: The Play* (1986). During Baker's tenure subscriptions rose from 200 to 2,200, and Phoenix found a permanent, main-stage home in the Kaasa Theatre in the Northern Alberta Jubilee Auditorium (1983-4) and, the year after, an additional intimate studio space in a downtown business building for more experimental projects.

Since 1984-5 Phoenix's activities have been divided between doing regular season performances in the Kaasa, and featuring or sponsoring such varied fare as classes in movement and dance, special performances by local or touring artists, a weekly improvisational soap opera ('Soap on the Rocks'), and avant-garde summer productions in the Phoenix Downtown space. In 1987 Jim Guedo became artistic director, mounting a season of plays by Sam Shepard, Beth Henley, René-Daniel DUBOIS, and David Rabe, as well as experimental productions in the new 90-seat Phoenix Downtown in Edmonton's Chinatown.

MOIRA DAY

Phoenix Theatre (Toronto). It opened its first season in Apr. 1975 in a 135-seat space on Dupont St with Simon Gray's *Butley*, directed by Desmond Scott. Subsequent productions, under artistic director Graham Harley, included an eclectic array of mainly British, American, and Canadian works. The 1977 production of Edward Bond's *The Sea* established the theatre's artistic reputation, and in 1978 David Rudkin's *Ashes* and the Canadian première of David Mamet's *American Buffalo* further enhanced its standing. In 1979 a production of Sir John Vanbrugh's Restoration comedy, *The Relapse* (another Canadian première), attracted 87 per cent attendance and then toured Canada and the U.S. Allan STRATTON's *Rexy!* and *Nurse Jane*

Goes to Hawaii and John Ibbitson's *Mayonnaise* formed an all-Canadian season of premières in 1980-1, but further progress was hampered by the inadequacies of the Dupont St theatre. Some renovations had taken place in 1977 (increasing seating capacity to 166), but a larger and better-equipped facility was essential. The company did not renew its lease after the 1980-1 season, and from 1982 it shared space with other companies at Adelaide Court Theatre. However, the move raised operating costs and, despite significant increases in Canada Council support (from $1,800 in 1976 to $55,000 in 1983), the company had a $60,000 deficit by the summer of 1983 and ceased operations.

In eight years Phoenix mounted some forty productions, including several world and North American premières, but its failure to find a suitable theatre and its inability to secure adequate box-office and corporate support proved its undoing.

The archives of Phoenix Theatre are at the Univ. of Guelph.   L.W. CONOLLY

Photographers, Theatre. Theatre photography generally falls into three categories: photos for publicity; photos for records and archives; and portraits of individual artists. Before the rise of professional theatre in Canada, theatre photography made up a very small portion of photographers' business. Scattered theatre-related photos may be found, for example, in the extensive archives of William Notman (1826-91) of Montreal (some 400,000 items in Montreal's McCord Museum) and of William James Topley (fl. 1867-1924) of Ottawa (some 150,000 items in the National Archives of Canada), mostly portraits of actors and dramatic clubs. Even today very few theatre photographers do as much as half their business in the performing arts.

With technical advances in lighting in this century, the artistic potential of theatre attracted photographers from other specialties. An invitation to join the Ottawa Little Theatre in the 1930s had an enormous impact on the career of Yousuf Karsh (b. 1908), who has written: 'The experience of photographing actors on the stage with stage lighting was exhilarating. . . . Moods could be created, selected, modified, intensified. I was thrilled by this means of expression, this method of interpreting life; a new world was opened to me.' After the Second World War

Photographers

Lord Duncannon (son of the Governor General, the Earl of Bessborough) and Julia MacBrien in Romeo and Juliet, *Ottawa Little Theatre, 1933; photograph by Karsh*

professional theatre attracted other photographers such as Ken Bell (b. 1914)—already renowned for his wartime photos—and Robert C. Ragsdale (b. 1928), who worked in journalism. Bell was associated with the National Ballet for twenty-five years (1951-76), and Ragsdale became Canada's pre-eminent theatre photographer through his production photos for CBC-TV (since 1952), the CREST THEATRE (1957-66), the CANADIAN PLAYERS (1960-6), the SHAW FESTIVAL (1964-80), the Canadian Opera Company (since 1970), and the STRATFORD FESTIVAL (since 1972).

In recent years the proliferation of smaller theatre companies has given opportunities to a new generation of theatre photographers, including Michel Lambeth (1923-77), an art photographer who worked at TORONTO FREE THEATRE; Robert Barnett (b. 1944), whose production photos of Toronto's TARRAGON THEATRE are now in the Univ. of Guelph Theatre Archives; Nir Bareket (b. 1939), Barnett's successor at Tarragon; Andrew Oxenham (b. 1945), a former dancer

who succeeded Bell at the National Ballet and also photographed several theatre companies; and Glen Erikson (b. 1946), a long-time photographer for the ARTS CLUB in Vancouver. At present, along with Ragsdale, Canada's busiest theatre photographers are probably David Cooper (b. 1952), whose clients include the Shaw Festival and the VANCOUVER PLAYHOUSE, and his brother Michael Cooper (b. 1958), who shoots for the Stratford Festival, the CANADIAN STAGE COMPANY, and several other theatres.

DENIS W. JOHNSTON

Pinsent, Gordon (b. 1930). Born and raised in Grand Falls, Nfld, he gained his early acting experience at Winnipeg's Theatre 77 and the MANITOBA THEATRE CENTRE (1954-60), and subsequently in Toronto with the Straw Hat Players, NEW PLAY SOCIETY, and CREST THEATRE (1960-9), and at the STRATFORD FESTIVAL (1962 and 1975). He first achieved national prominence in the title role in the CBC-TV series 'Quentin Durgens, M.P.' (1966-9) and gained further national

Gordon Pinsent in Michael Gazzo's Hatful of Rain, *Theatre 77, Winnipeg, 1958*

recognition through writing and acting in nearly all of the episodes of another CBC-TV series, 'A Gift to Last' (1976-9), for which he received an ACTRA Award in 1979.

Pinsent has appeared in films created and directed by others—such as Allan King's *Who Has Seen the Wind* (1977) and *Silence of the North* (1981), and the CTV-CBS *Escape from Iran: The Canadian Caper* (1980-1), in which he portrayed Canadian diplomat Ken Taylor—but his most successful film work has grown out of his own writing. *The Rowdyman* (1972) is a study of a dangerously irresponsible Newfoundlander, Will Cole, played by Pinsent, which earned him another ACTRA Award and also resulted in a novel (1973) and a 1976 musical at the CHARLOTTE-TOWN FESTIVAL, with music by Cliff Jones and Pinsent co-directing and playing the title role. In the film *John and the Missus* (1987)—based on his 1974 novel and directed by Pinsent—he portrays the intransigent copper-miner John Munn, a folk-hero who resisted former Newfoundland Premier Joey Small-wood's resettlement program, a performance that won him a 1987 Genie for Best Actor.

A stage version premièred at Halifax's NEPTUNE THEATRE in 1976. In 1986 Gryphon Theatre, Barrie, Ont., produced his *A Gift to Last* and his most recent play *Easy Down Easy* in 1987. Pinsent is an Officer of the Order of Canada (1978) and holds honorary degrees from three Canadian universities. He is married to actress Charmion KING.

ROTA HERZBERG LISTER

Place des Arts. Located on the north side of Sainte-Catherine St at the corner of Saint-Urbain, this tri-theatre complex is home to Montreal's leading musical groups and also hosts international touring drama, variety, dance, and music attractions.

The first phase of the project, the large, multi-purpose Salle Wilfrid-Pelletier, was commissioned by the Sir George-Etienne Cartier Corporation—a non-profit group representing the province, the city, and potential patrons—and opened in 1963. Designed by the Montreal architectural firm Affleck, Desbarats, Dimakopoulos, Lebensold, Michaud, and Sise, the theatre is built of reinforced concrete with a steel roof. It accommodates an audience of 2,952 with no patron further than 135 feet from the stage. The stage measures 155' × 53', with a proscenium opening 69' wide and 33' high. The Salle Wilfrid-Pelletier's permanent tenants include the Orchestre symphonique de Montréal and the Opéra de Montréal.

In 1967 two theatres were added, designed by Montreal architects David, Barott, Boulva, Dufresne and constructed one above the other. The Théâtre Port-Royal, which is entirely below ground, was originally built as a flexible venue for recitals and experimental dramatic productions, but was remodelled during the 1984-5 season into a traditional proscenium house seating 747 patrons. The stage is 140' wide and 52' deep, with a proscenium opening 65' wide and 25' high. It is the permanent home of the COMPAGNIE JEAN DUCEPPE. Directly above is the Théâtre Maisonneuve, a third proscenium space, seating 1,278, with a stage measuring 56' wide, 27' high, and 48' deep. The orchestra pit holds fifty musicians, and can be covered to provide a 20' forestage. This theatre is particularly suitable for classical theatre, ballet, and musical-comedy performances. It is currently the permanent home of the McGill Chamber Orchestra and the Société Pro Musica.

Original construction costs totalled

Place des Arts

Place des Arts, Montreal

$20,000,000, mostly financed by various levels of government. The complex is administered by a non-profit corporation, La Société de la Place des Arts, the nine members of which are appointed by the Quebec government in consultation with the Montreal Urban Community.

See Fred Lebensold, 'Place des Arts, Montreal, P.Q.', *Canadian Architect*, 8 (1963), and 'Edifices des théâtres Maisonneuve et Port-Royal', *Architecture-Bâtiment-Construction*, 22 (1967).   JOHN RIPLEY

Plaxton, Jim (b. 1942). Born and raised in Winnipeg, he was employed in an architectural office for five years and in 1966 began working on the sets of films (making twenty-five in the next four years). He worked as a set painter at the MANITOBA THEATRE CENTRE before moving to Toronto, where he became resident designer for the Toronto Dance Theatre while also designing for theatre. In 1980 he won a Dora Mavor MOORE award for Outstanding Lighting Design and again in 1981 for his work on George WALKER's *Theatre of the Film Noir* and Michael Weller's *Loose Ends*, for which he was awarded Outstanding Set Design. Plaxton's designs for Shaw's *Too True to be Good* (1983) at the SHAW FESTIVAL represented Canada at the 1983 Prague Quadrennial. He also designed the operas *Curlew River* (in 1983),

The Prodigal Son (1985), and *The Lighthouse* (1986) for the Guelph Spring Festival. In 1982 he became associate artistic director of Toronto's THEATRE PASSE MURAILLE and was responsible for the complete renovation of the theatre in 1983-4. Plaxton, who thinks of his designs as machines for actors, is especially interested in novel ways of using materials.   MARTHA MANN

Playhouse, The. A gift of Lord and Lady Beaverbrook (the latter acting for the Sir James Dunn Foundation), the Playhouse stands at 686 Queen St, Fredericton, NB, across John St from the Legislative Buildings. When it opened on 26 Sept. 1964 the 1,000-seat facility was the only adequately equipped theatre in New Brunswick. Under the first two directors, Alexander Gray and Brian Swarbrick, performances were given by amateurs (Gray founded the Company of Ten); in addition the Patrons of the Playhouse sponsored visits by the NEPTUNE THEATRE, the CANADIAN PLAYERS, the Canadian Opera Company, the STRATFORD FESTIVAL, and the Royal Winnipeg Ballet. In 1972, while Walter LEARNING was artistic director (1968-78), Sir Max Aitken underwrote a $1.5 million renovation by Arcop Associates of Montreal that added a 69' fly tower, moved the stage forward to provide greater intimacy between actor and audience, enlarged the lobby, installed new lighting and sound systems, and provided rehearsal space larger than the stage, as well as new workshop, storage, and administrative areas. Lord Goodman, chairman of the Arts Council of Great Britain, presided at the reopening on 16 May 1972. Currently the Playhouse seats 763 (236 balcony, 527 orchestra). The stage is 35' wide and 35' from the front of the apron to the rear wall, with five traps and a maximum flying height of 59'. Walter Learning extended the professional summer seasons that had begun under Brian Swarbrick in 1966 and, most important, in 1968 founded THEATRE NEW BRUNSWICK, a professional company based at The Playhouse whose mandate is to tour its productions throughout New Brunswick, thereby realizing Lord Beaverbrook's intention to provide a theatre for the people of the province. Malcolm BLACK (1979-83) and Janet AMOS (1984-) succeeded Walter Learning as artistic director.

MARY ELIZABETH SMITH

Christopher Plummer (as Sir Andrew Aguecheek) and Douglas Campbell (as Sir Toby Belch) in Twelfth Night, *Stratford Festival, 1957*

Plummer, Christopher (b. 1927). Born in Toronto and educated in Montreal, he began his professional career in 1950 with Ottawa's CANADIAN REPERTORY THEATRE, playing Faulkland in Sheridan's *The Rivals*. In the next two years he played some 100 roles for CRT, while also performing in both English and French on CBC radio. After two further years with a repertory company in Bermuda, he made his Broadway début in 1955 as Count Peter Zichy opposite Katharine Cornell in Christopher Fry's *The Dark is Light Enough*. In the same year, at the Stratford Festival, Connecticut, he played Mark Antony in *Julius Caesar* and Ferdinand in *The Tempest*. Plummer made his début at Ontario's STRATFORD FESTIVAL in 1956 in the title role of *Henry V* and played Hamlet and Sir Andrew Aguecheek (in *Twelfth Night*) in 1957. He returned in 1958, 1960, 1962, and 1967. Throughout the 1960s and 1970s he starred with several major U.S. and British companies, including the Royal Shakespeare Company and the National Theatre Company. His 1982 Iago on Broadway (opposite Earl Jones as Othello) was highly praised, but his 1988 Macbeth (opposite Glenda Jackson) received mixed reviews in both Toronto and New York. Noted for his good looks, aristocratic bearing, and commanding voice, he received a 1973 Tony Award as best actor in a Broadway musical—Anthony Burgess's adaptation

of Edmund Rostand's *Cyrano de Bergerac*. Along with extensive television work he has made many films, including *The Silent Partner*, *The Pyx*, and the enormously successful *The Sound of Music*.

In 1970 Plummer was made a Companion of the Order of Canada.   EUGENE BENSON

Podbrey, Maurice (b. 1934). Born in Durban, South Africa, he graduated from Witwatersrand Univ. in 1956. After professional theatre studies in England at the Rose Bruford College of Speech and Drama, he joined the Dundee Repertory Theatre in 1959, subsequently acting with other provincial companies. In 1964 he became artistic director of Chester Playhouse, and later acted in London's West End and in a number of television dramas.

Podbrey came to Montreal in 1966 as assistant director of the English Section of the NATIONAL THEATRE SCHOOL. During breaks from teaching he directed and acted in Regina with the GLOBE THEATRE and in Montreal at Instantheatre (the lunchtime playhouse of the Centaur Foundation for the Performing Arts) and the SAIDYE BRONFMAN CENTRE. In 1969 he became artistic director of Instantheatre. Finding himself limited by the theatre's objectives and facilities, he and the Centaur foundation president, Dr Herbert Auerbach, persuaded the board to lease space in the Old Stock Exchange for a full-scale professional venture—the CENTAUR THEATRE—which opened in 1969, with Podbrey as artistic director. Under his skilled administration it has matured into a major Quebec cultural institution.

Podbrey has achieved distinction at the Centaur as both director and actor. Among his directing successes are three plays by his South African compatriot, Athol Fugard— *Sizwe Bansi is Dead* in 1977, *The Island* in 1978, and *Master Harold . . . and the Boys* in 1985; several Canadian plays, including David FREEMAN's *CREEPS* in 1973, Beverly Lockwood's *Weeds* in 1979, and Michel TREMBLAY's *Albertine, in Five Times* in 1985; and works from the contemporary British and American repertoire, such as Aleksei Arbuzov's *The Promise* in 1974, Tom Stoppard's *Night and Day* in 1981, and Marsha Norman's *'Night Mother* in 1985. His performances of the title role in Chekhov's *Uncle Vanya*, 1971, of Willy Loman in Arthur Miller's *Death of a Salesman*, 1972, of Morris in Fugard's *The Blood Knot*, 1972, and of Stalin in David Pownall's *Master Class*, 1986, were all praised. From 1979 to 1983 Podbrey served as chairman of the Professional Association of Canadian Theatres.   JOHN RIPLEY

Political and Popular Theatre. Despite such precedents as Napoléon Aubin's didactic theatrical group, Les Amateurs Typographes, founded in 1839, and an active tradition of political BURLESQUE in English Canada (of which William Henry FULLER's *H.M.S. Parliament* is the most famous example), there are no records of Canadian equivalents to the nineteenth-century radical labour theatres of Europe and the United States.

Following the pioneering example of German director Erwin Piscator, Canadian political theatre has tended to advocate working-class and socialist causes, although the two have not always coincided. The first proletarian theatres in Canada surfaced in immigrant communities in the first decades of the twentieth century. Fiercely divided by the Russian Revolution, the Finnish and Ukrainian communities in particular sponsored both Red and White amateur troupes, such as the Ukrainian Workers' Theatre of Winnipeg, which achieved professional status briefly in 1919. Although sponsored by political organizations, these troupes performed plays that were more nationalistic than revolutionary.

In English-speaking Canada political theatre began as an agitprop voice of the organized Left during the 1930s, although there were rare instances of right-wing political performances; in Alberta, William Aberhart used a form of agitprop as part of his Social Credit campaign. In Quebec, because of the conservative influence of the Church and the weak position of the Communist Party, an active political theatre did not develop until after the Quiet Revolution. By the 1980s, however, Québécois political troupes were more numerous and notably more radical than their anglophone counterparts.

The Workers' Theatre movement of the 1930s was made possible by the founding of Progressive Arts Clubs in major cities across Canada. For the most part, groups such as Toronto's Workers' Experimental Theatre adapted the agitprop techniques current in Europe and the United States. The texts that have survived (printed in the movement's journal, *Masses*) suggest that the most common form of agitprop was the choral mass chant. The most developed of the texts, and the most sophisticated theatrically, is the collective work *EIGHT MEN SPEAK*.

The troupes normally consisted of unemployed workers for whom the highly formalized performance conventions provided a way to act without experience or training. More sophisticated performance techniques and texts gradually developed. The Theatre of Action (1935–40), for example, was an important left-wing presence in the DOMINION DRAMA FESTIVAL. Under the guidance of New York director David Pressman, the Theatre of Action set a standard of commitment and professionalism in its productions of such left-wing plays as Clifford Odets' *Waiting For Lefty*, Irwin Shaw's *Bury the Dead*, and Sergei Tretiakof's *Roar China*, and in its regular series of workshops and CABARETs. More moderate in its political line than the Workers' Experimental Theatre, the Theatre of Action attracted a number of aspiring professionals, including such later stars as Lorne GREENE, Johnny Wayne, and Frank Shuster.

Following the Second World War the radical left was unable to regain popular support and no longer sponsored political theatre. There were occasional instances of political performance from more moderate groups

Workers' Theatre poster

of Newfoundland, which was the first English-Canadian professional company to use theatre to intervene in community political struggles. In such plays as *Gros Mourn*, produced in 1973, and *Buchans: A Mining Town*, produced in 1974, the Mummers created a unique form of activist documentary; with its later political revues, which toured mainland Canada, the troupe addressed topical issues rather that specific communities. *They Club Seals, Don't They?*, produced in 1978 in defence of the Labrador seal hunt, was one of the most controversial productions in Canadian theatre history.

The most recent evolution in Canadian political theatre was signalled in 1981 at the Bread and Circuses Festival of Popular Theatre, sponsored by Thunder Bay's KAM THEATRE. There participants founded the Canadian Popular Theatre Alliance to bring together troupes that 'work to effect social change'. The CPTA has since sponsored three more festivals: Bread and Roses (Edmonton, 1983), Bread and Dreams (Winnipeg, 1985), and 'Standin' the Gaff' (Sydney, 1987). One of the most innovative of the CPTA companies is Edmonton's CATALYST THEATRE, which creates audience-intervention shows for social welfare and development agencies. In the course of its work with handicapped and prison audiences, Catalyst has evolved a performance style that parallels Brazilian director Augusto Boal's Theatre of the Oppressed. In Boal's 'forum theatre' the audience intervenes by replacing the protagonist to test solutions to a scenario of oppression. Vancouver's Headlines Theatre, Toronto's Second Look Community Arts Resource, and Quebec's Théâtre Sans Détour are three notable groups that have successfully adopted Boal's techniques in recent years.

In the 1980s companies as diverse as Ottawa's GREAT CANADIAN THEATRE COMPANY, Toronto's Ground Zero, and Regina's GLOBE THEATRE have produced investigative and agitprop plays for organized labour; and numerous non-professional groups, among which women's groups figure prominently, have adapted popular theatre techniques as a form of developmental education.

Political theatre in French Canada is described under THEATRE ENGAGÉ, but certain aspects bear comparison with the English-Canadian experience. The rapid growth of the *jeune théâtre* movement was character-

such as George LUSCOMBE's song-and-dance troupe that performed from the back of a truck to picket lines at the 1948 Hamilton Strike, but these were rare.

The growth of contemporary political theatre can be divided into two overlapping phases: the evolution from confrontational guerilla theatre to populist political documentary (see DOCUMENTARY DRAMA) in the 1970s, and a subsequent development of popular theatre for marginalized and oppressed audiences. The guerilla theatres of the late 1960s, such as the Vancouver Street Theatre, modelled themselves on the American troupes that took to the street to oppose the war in Vietnam. Giant puppets (see PUPPET THEATRE) and quick agitprops became familiar parts of Canadian demonstrations as well.

During the 1970s political theatre was inextricably part of the ALTERNATE THEATRE's attempt to 'decolonize' the theatre by promoting Canadian plays and rejecting foreign, chiefly British, influences. In this, Canada's oldest politically committed theatre, TORONTO WORKSHOP PRODUCTIONS, was an exception, with its emphasis on internationalist politics. The most radical of the alternate theatres was the MUMMERS TROUPE

Political and Popular Theatre

ized by a widespread use of political agitprop, marked by a close association with left-wing political groups. If in English Canada the alternate theatres of the 1970s embraced a vaguely socialist populism, in Quebec the politically committed troupes frequently advocated revolutionary platforms. Perhaps the most radical was Théâtre Euh!, which affiliated itself with the Marxist-Leninist party En Lutte and led the controversial walk-out of radical troupes from l'Association québécoise du jeune théâtre in 1975. More typical of the political theatres of the 1970s was Le GRAND CIRQUE ORDINAIRE, one of the first theatres committed to working-class audiences. Influenced by Bertolt Brecht in its earlier work, GCO created a form of community intervention theatre when in 1971 it created a play—*T'en rappelles-tu Pibrac?*, about the economically depressed town of Pibrac—in three days.

T'en rappelles-tu Pibrac? and Théâtre Euh!'s *L'Histoire du Québec* (inspired by Léandre Bergeron's popular history) offer useful comparisons to the work of the Mummers Troupe. As was the case with GCO in Pibrac, the Mummers created *Gros Mourn* in ten days while touring *Newfoundland Night*, a populist history of the province inspired by the example of Bergeron's book. The Mummers Troupe provides the closest English-Canadian equivalent to the Québécois model of political theatre, perhaps because, like Quebec, Newfoundland preserves a strong sense of independent culture.

For the most part, English-Canadian political theatres have tended to rely on a form of documentary realism that draws upon oral traditions of storytelling, whereas Québécois political theatres have tended to a more flamboyant and metaphorical theatricality based on strong intellectual analysis. In this they more closely resemble the general rule of American political theatres. During the 1970s, Québécois and English-Canadian troupes were for the most part ignorant of one another. Only in recent years have political troupes from English and French Canada met to compare their work; in this regard the participation of two Québécois troupes in the 1983 CPTA festival in Edmonton was a significant development.

See R. Endres, ed., *Eight Men Speak and Other Plays from the Canadian Workers' Theatre* (1976); Toby Ryan, *Stage Left: Canadian Theatre in the Thirties* (1981); Gerald Sigouin,

Théâtre en Lutte: le Théâtre Euh! (1982); Alan Filewod, 'The Changing Definition of Canadian Political Theatre', *Theatrework* (1983), and *Collective Encounters: Documentary Theatre in English Canada* (1987); Elaine Nardocchio, *Theatre and Politics in Modern Québec* (1986).

ALAN FILEWOD

Pollock, Sharon (b. 1936). Born in Fredericton, N.B., the daughter of esteemed physician and long-time MLA Everett Chalmers, Mary Sharon Chalmers attended the Univ. of New Brunswick, but dropped out in 1954 to marry Ross Pollock, a Toronto insurance broker. After their separation in the early 1960s she returned to Fredericton with her five children where she worked at various theatre jobs, including acting, at the PLAYHOUSE in Fredericton, later THEATRE NEW BRUNSWICK. In 1966, having moved with actor Michael Ball to Calgary, she won a DOMINION DRAMA FESTIVAL best actress award for her performance in Ann Jellicoe's *The Knack*, directed by Joyce Doolittle. Her first stage play, *A Compulsory Option*, a black comedy about paranoia, won an Alberta Culture playwriting competition in 1971 and was given its first production in 1972 by Pamela HAWTHORN at Vancouver's NEW PLAY CENTRE. In 1973 Harold Baldridge premièred her historical play *Walsh* (1973) at THEATRE CALGARY; John WOOD's production of this play at the STRATFORD FESTIVAL's Third Stage in 1974 first drew Pollock to national attention. Now living in Vancouver, she wrote a number of children's plays for production by Playhouse Holiday (formerly HOLIDAY THEATRE), and Playhouse Theatre School; in these years she was also writing for CBC radio.

Pollock's next three adult plays were first produced in the Vancouver area: *And Out Goes You?* (unpublished), a satiric comedy on contemporary B.C. politics, and the *Komagata Maru Incident* (1978) at the VANCOUVER PLAYHOUSE in 1975 and 1976 respectively, and *My Name is Lisbeth*, an unpublished early version of the Lizzie Borden story, at Douglas College, Surrey, B.C. in 1976, in which Pollock played the lead. After a year in Edmonton as a playwriting instructor at the Univ. of Alberta, Pollock returned to Calgary in 1977 where she made her home until 1988. All her later plays have had their premières in either Edmonton or Calgary: *One Tiger to a Hill* (1981) in 1980 at the CITADEL THEATRE; *BLOOD RELATIONS* (1981) at THEATRE

3 in 1980 (winner of the Governor General's Award for 1981); *Generations* (1981) at ALBERTA THEATRE PROJECTS in 1980; *Whiskey Six Cadenza* (1987) at Theatre Calgary in 1983; and *Doc* (1986) at Theatre Calgary in 1984.

Over the past ten years Pollock has also been active in theatre as dramaturge, administrator, director, and actor. She was head of the Playwrights Colony at the BANFF CENTRE SCHOOL OF FINE ARTS (1977-80); playwright-in-residence at Alberta Theatre Projects, Calgary (1977-9) and at the NATIONAL ARTS CENTRE (1980-2); briefly artistic director at Theatre Calgary (1984), and writer-in-residence at the Regina Public Library (1986). In 1988 she was appointed artistic director of Theatre New Brunswick. She has directed in a number of Canadian theatres, including productions of her own plays—*One Tiger to a Hill* at the NAC in 1981 and *Doc*, under the revised title of *Family Trappings*, at Theatre New Brunswick in 1986. She played the role of Miss Lizzie in Theatre Calgary's production of *Blood Relations* in 1981, and Mama George in her own radio adaptation of *Whiskey Six Cadenza* for CBC radio in 1983.

In her plays of the 1970s Pollock shows a strong concern for political and social issues related to both the past and contemporary Canadian life. In *Walsh* and *The Komagata Maru Incident* she uses historical events to challenge racism. The first blames the abuse of indigenous peoples on the Macdonald government's political expediency of the 1870s. Major Walsh of the North-West Mounted Police is caught between personal honour and public obligation in the infamous Sitting Bull incident following the Sioux flight to the Canadian North West after their defeat of General Custer. The second play exposes racism against Asians as evidenced by legislation passed in 1914 that prevented a boat-load of Sikh immigrants from landing in Vancouver harbour. A confrontational narrator representing the 'system' interrupts brief cinematic scenes to implicate the audience directly in what is presented as a clear matter of legalized racial injustice. The public servant in the case, immigration officer William Hopkinson, is caught in a web of self-interest; his characterization suggests a tragic potential that remains undeveloped. Pollock's most ambitious issue-oriented play is *One Tiger to a Hill*, an indictment of the modern

prison system. The work is loosely based on a New Westminster penitentiary hostage incident of 1975 when a female classification officer was killed by the prison's tactical squad in a botched rescue attempt. While multiple perspectives on prison life are skilfully integrated with dramatic action, their polemical impact is partly diverted by the sentimental characterization of the two principals.

From *Blood Relations* on, Pollock's interest in issues is subsumed in her fuller focus on conflicts in private lives. In *Blood Relations* the playwright is less concerned with historical analysis of the famous and unresolved Fall River, Mass., murders than with the implications of Lizzie Borden's story (or hypothetical story) for a contemporary audience. The play seeks to determine why such a crime could be committed, then or now. In *Generations*, ultimately a more positive analysis of family values, *Blood Relations'* concerns about matters of dependence and identity crisis are put into a modern context where, unlike Lizzie, the young people are free to make their own choices but must learn how to do so. The specific issue in this naturalistic play is the traditional tie of the land as it affects three generations of an Albertan farm family.

In *Whiskey Six Cadenza* Pollock again tackles a historical issue, the oppressive prohibition laws of the 1920s, but here the issue reinforces characterization and avoids the overt polemics of her earlier work. Rum-running in a southern Alberta mining community is the background to a curious emotional triangle consisting of a flamboyant gospeller of free will who is also the local bootlegger, his adoptive daughter, and the rebellious son of a local temperance zealot. The polarities of controversy over the public jurisdiction of personal choice dissolve into the half-hidden complexities of sadly destructive personal relationships. In *Doc* Pollock continues to examine the destructive elements of family in her most intricate dramatic structure to date. Its subject, partly autobiographical, is the conflict between a compulsively dedicated physician and his alcoholic wife, with particular emphasis on the impact of their discord on a growing daughter. In a further step from *Blood Relations'* retrospective time frame, this play rejects linear time, directly engaging the audience in the two present-time characters' associational memory patterns.

One Tiger to a Hill, *Blood Relations*, and *Generations* are published in *Blood Relations and Other Plays* (1981), with a critical introduction by Diane Bessai; *Whiskey Six Cadenza* appears in *NeWest Plays by Women* (1987). See also M. Page, 'Sharon Pollock: Committed Playwright', *Canadian Drama*, 5 (1979); R.C. Nunn, 'Sharon Pollock's Plays', *Theatre History in Canada*, 5 (1984); S.R. Gilbert in *Canadian Profiles*, 6 (1986); and R. Wallace and C. Zimmerman, eds., *The Work* (1982).   DIANE BESSAI

Porteous, Cameron (b. 1937). Born in Rosetown, Sask., he trained as a designer at the Wimbledon School of Art in London, Eng. (1967–9), and has subsequently become one of Canada's leading scenic artists. He spent ten years at the VANCOUVER PLAY-HOUSE—where he designed productions as diverse as *King Lear*, Tom Stoppard's *Travesties*, and David FRENCH's *Jitters*—before becoming head of design at the SHAW FESTIVAL in 1980. Porteous has taken advantage of the Shaw's sophisticated technical capabilities in spectacular productions of plays such as Noël Coward's *Cavalcade* (1985, revived 1986) and J. M. Barrie's *Peter Pan* (1987, revived 1988), but he has also designed more restrained sets for Shaw and other playwrights, both at the Shaw Festival and at the

Cameron Porteous

NATIONAL ARTS CENTRE, TARRAGON THEATRE, YOUNG PEOPLE'S THEATRE, the CITADEL THEATRE, and the GLOBE THEATRE. He has taught design at the BANFF CENTRE (where he was appointed director of design for the Music Theatre Ensemble in 1981) and the Univ. of British Columbia, and has worked extensively in film and television. A designer who successfully combines vision and practicality—guided by the principle that design should be a metaphor for the production as a whole—Porteous has exhibited at the 1979 Prague Quadrennial and other venues.   L. W. CONOLLY

Poudrière, La. An early nineteenth-century structure located on Ile Ste-Hélène near Montreal, La Poudrière theatre was originally a powder magazine. Renovated as an intimate 180-seat theatre with a nineteen-feet-wide revolving stage, it opened on 11 July 1958 with a production of N. Richard Nash's *The Rainmaker*.

From 1958 to 1982 the multilingual La Poudrière (officially Le Théâtre International de Montréal) presented, spring through fall, seasons of professionally produced plays in English and French, and also regularly offered amateur productions in German and Spanish. Until 1979, the company averaged around 200 performances a year under founder and artistic director Jeanine Beaubien, including professional and amateur plays, a series of mini-operas, a Christmas season of marionette plays, and occasional tours of successful productions—Edward Albee's *Qui a peur de Virginia Woolf?* (*Who's Afraid of Virginia Woolf?*) in 1966, and Alan Ayckbourn's *Relatively Speaking* in 1974.

Beaubien's programming for both anglo- and francophone audiences provided an eclectic mix of popular and serious American, British, French, and European dramas. Beaubien successfully secured the rights to such plays as Albee's *A Delicate Balance*, Ayckbourn's *Absurd Person Singular*, and E.A. Whitehead's *Alpha Beta* (done in French and English). She also produced in translation (English and French, or both) such challenging European playwrights as Friedrich Dürrenmatt and Ugo Betti.

Beaubien's French-language productions utilized such talent as François Cartier, Louise Marleau, Jacques LANGUIRAND, Denise PELLETIER, and Jean-Pierre Ferland in productions that included *Les Bozos en Vacances* and

Dostoevsky's *Crime et Châtiment (Crime and Punishment)*, in 1959; *La Folle Nuit* in 1961; Samuel Beckett's *Oh, les beaux jours (Happy Days)* in 1973-4; and Molière's *Le Misanthrope* in 1976. Her English-language productions—particularly in the 1960s, when La Poudrière was one of the few Quebec theatres producing in English—helped keep alive English-language drama in Montreal.

For twenty years La Poudrière was supported with funding from various sources: the City of Montreal, the Quebec government, the Canada Council, the German Embassy, and the Goethe Institute. Eventually, however, it fell victim to a devastating combination of factors: the recession of the late seventies; the granting agencies' increased emphasis on Canadian work; and internal administrative problems. Unable to survive reduced funding and Beaubien's departure, La Poudrière, which had provided Montreal with an interesting and unique experiment in multicultural theatre for over twenty years, closed in 1982.

JONATHAN RITTENHOUSE

Prairie Theatre Exchange. This theatre-resource organization was founded in Winnipeg in 1972 as the Manitoba Theatre Workshop in response to the MANITOBA THEATRE CENTRE's dissolution of its theatre school and abandonment of much of its community outreach program. Charles Huband, a judge of the Manitoba Court of Appeals, was the first board chairman, and provided leadership throughout the organization's existence. Colin Jackson served as director of MTW from its beginning until Mar. 1976. During its early years MTW ran a theatre school, maintained a vigorous outreach program in the schools, and fostered a wide range of theatrical ventures. It was instrumental in launching the Manitoba Puppet Theatre, Manitoba Drama Festivals, the Confidential Exchange, Agassiz Productions, the Manitoba Association of Playwrights, the television program 'Lets Go!', and the Neighbourhood Theatre, a professional children's theatre company operated by Deborah Quinn, who was MTW artistic director from 1977 to 1981. In 1981 Colin Jackson returned as executive producer, and Gordon McCall became artistic director of the newly named Prairie Theatre Exchange. Emphasis shifted to full-scale professional adult theatre, specializing in Canadian plays. McCall's production of

George RYGA's *The ECSTASY OF RITA JOE* in Nov. 1981, with native actors, attracted national attention. In the summer of 1983 Kim McCaw replaced McCall as artistic director and he and Jackson announced a policy of 'populist theatre'. Production of such plays as Wendy Lill's *The Fighting Days* (Mar. 1984) and *Section 23* (Feb. 1985), a revue based on the Manitoba language question co-produced with CERCLE MOLIÈRE, gave PTE a reputation for thoughtful, entertaining work and subscription sales soared. The 1985-6 season consisted entirely of original plays commissioned by PTE. These included Patrick Friesen's *The Shunning* (Oct. 1985), Sharon Stearns' *Enemy Graces* (Nov. 1985), David Arnason's and Gerard Jean's *Welcome to Hard Times: The Cultural Cabaret* (Jan. 1986), and Wendy Lill's *The Occupation of Heather Rose* (Feb. 1986). Prairie Theatre Exchange is located in Winnipeg's historic Grain Exchange Building, at 160 Princess Street. REG SKENE

Prévost, Robert (1927-82). Born in Montreal, he studied at the Collège Sainte-Croix and at the Université de Montréal. He first attracted attention with his set and costume designs for the COMPAGNONS DE SAINT-LAURENT's productions of Beaumarchais's *Le Barbier de Seville*, Tennessee Williams' *La Ménagerie de verre (The Glass Menagerie)*, and Jean Anouilh's *Le Bal de voleurs (The Thieves' Carnival)*.

As a costume, set, and lighting designer, and later as a director, he worked for over thirty years with principal theatre, dance, and opera companies in Montreal and at the STRATFORD FESTIVAL. From 1949 to 1952 he designed sets for Montreal Festival productions of Puccini's *Manon* and *Tosca*, Gounod's *Faust* and *Roméo et Juliette*, and other operas. After 1970 he also worked for L'Opéra du Québec on Puccini's *La Bohème* and *Il Trittico*, Verdi's *Falstaff* and *Otello*, and Mozart's *Don Giovanni*.

From 1952 to 1962 Prévost designed sets and costumes for Radio-Canada. He also designed over seventy-five productions by major authors for Le THÉÂTRE DU NOUVEAU MONDE: Molière, Brecht, Beckett, Chekhov, Albee, O'Neill, Pirandello, Claudel, Racine, Guitry; and Quebec authors such as Marcel DUBÉ (*Le Temps des lilas*), François Moreau (*Les Taupes*), Jacques LANGUIRAND (*Klondyke*), Félix-Antoine Savard (*La Dalle-des-morts*), Guy DUFRESNE (*Les Traitants*), and

Eugene O'Neill's Désir sous les ormes (Desire Under the Elms), *Théâtre du Nouveau Monde, 1970-1 season, designed by Robert Prévost*

Réjean DUCHARME (*Le Marquis qui perdit*). For the THÉÂTRE DU RIDEAU VERT he designed over thirty productions, including Marivaux's *L'Heureux stratagème*, Feydeau's *La Dame de chez Maxim*, Calderón's *L'Alcalde de Zalaméa*, Giraudoux's *Ondine* and *La Guerre de Troie n'aura pas lieu*, and Antonine MAILLET's *Emmanuel, à Joseph, à Davi* and *Evangéline Deusse*.

For the Stratford Festival Prévost designed sets for Shakespeare's *The Comedy of Errors* in 1964; Molière's *Le Bourgeois gentilhomme*, 1964, and *Tartuffe*, 1968; and Brecht's *The Threepenny Opera*, 1972. Notable designs for the Grands Ballets Canadiens included Carl Orff's *Carmina Burana* in 1968 and Stravinsky's *Les Noces* in 1972. Prévost was also responsible for a number of television dramas, such as Roger Lemelin's series 'Les Plouffe'. He taught set design at the NATIONAL THEATRE SCHOOL and won awards from the Royal Society of Canada, the Canada Council, and the Cultural Institute of Rome. Prévost received the Order of Canada in 1972 and became an Officer of the Order in 1978.

Versatile and flexible, believing that a designer must have the ability to respond to the stylistic demands of each show, Prévost was the most important designer in the history of Quebec theatre. CLAUDE SABOURIN

Primrose, George Henry (1852-1919). Born in St Catharines, he grew up in London, Ont., where he early cultivated the talent that was to bring him fame by practising dancing in the basement of a hotel where he worked as a bell-boy. While still in his mid-teens, he performed in Western Ontario towns, prophetically billed as the 'celebrated clog dancer', with small troupes such as Murphy's Minstrels. Moving to Buffalo, N.Y., he joined a succession of circus and minstrel companies and teamed up with William H. West, who was to be his song-and-dance partner and business associate for the next thirty years. Their enormously popular act was a major attraction of the successive minstrel troupes to which they belonged: Haverly's (1874-7); Barlow, Wilson, Primrose, and West (1877-82); Thatcher, Primrose, and West (1882-9); and their own company, Primrose and West (1889-98). In 1898 the long-time partners broke up over differences of artistic style, West favouring new ideas while Primrose held to blackface traditions. A new company, Primrose and Dockstader, billed as 'The only true exponent of blackface comedy', toured with great financial success from 1898 to 1903. For over a year, 1903-4, Primrose danced in VAUDEVILLE, but in Nov. 1904 he launched his own minstrel company of over 100, offering spectacular extravaganzas. Primrose joined Dockstader again for two seasons (1912-14) and in 1914-15 toured with an old associate, George Wilson. Returning to the vaudeville circuit, Primrose offered a popular demonstration of soft-shoe dancing as late as the summer of 1918.

An elegant master of clog and soft-shoe, forerunners of modern tap-dancing, Primrose was the Fred Astaire of his day, the idol and inspiration of young dancers. During the decades of minstrelsy's decline this 'Millionaire Minstrel' continued to draw crowded houses in cities and towns across the continent, delighting audiences with his supremely graceful, seemingly effortless routines. Although active in every region of the U.S., Primrose also toured regularly in Canada— to Montreal, Toronto, Hamilton, London, and smaller centres. MARY SHORTT

Prince Edward Island, Theatre in. The first evidence of any theatrical activity in PEI dates from 1800 (thirty-two years after it became a British colony), when the Char-lotte-Town Amateur Theatre was formed. For three decades it was the sole provider of theatre during the winter months; in fact amateur theatre remained for most of the century the wintertime fare, when commu-nication with the other British North Amer-ican colonies virtually ceased. This dedicated group of amateurs, comprised of garrison personnel and local citizens, produced a rep-ertoire consisting, for the most part, of Eng-lish comedies and farces popular with London audiences at the turn of the century. Farces such as James Kenney's *Raising the Wind* and John Till Allingham's *Fortune's Frolic* were frequently mounted as afterpieces to plays such as George Colman the Younger's *John Bull* and Isaac Pocock's *The Miller and His Men*. During its thirty years of production, the company often made public its intention to build a permanent theatre, but this never came to fruition and the Charlotte-Town Amateur Theatre continued to use whatever space was made available to them.

A few other theatrical groups operated for a season or two; between 1866 and 1876 the Charlottetown Amateur Dramatic Club mounted two to four productions annually. Established by Mrs Wentworth Stevenson, the Dramatic Club continued the tradition of mounting popular British and European works and added Shakespeare to its reper-toire. *The Merchant of Venice* or *Hamlet* could be found on the same bill at St Andrew's Hall or the Market Hall with John Maddison Morton's *Box and Cox* or *Fortune's Frolic*. No group, however, endured as long as the Char-lotte-Town Amateur Theatre, partly because after 1850 fraternal societies and other orga-nizations included theatre as a part-time activity. In the 1880s and 1890s the Benev-olent Irish Society sponsored Irish plays, such as William Travers' *Kathleen Mavourneen* or

Walter Reynolds' *The Shamrock and the Rose* in celebration of St Patrick's Day, and the Independent Order of Oddfellows concen-trated on light opera, particularly Gilbert and Sullivan's *H.M.S. Pinafore*, for their annual Natal Days. Such organizations provided not only regular entertainment during the winter months, but—aside from the Charlottetown Market Hall, opened in 1867—the only suit-able physical facilities for touring profession-als in the summer. The Sons of Temperance Hall opened in 1851; it eventually became the Academy of Music, under the management of Harry LINDLEY, who in 1880 operated the province's first resident stock company. The Benevolent Irish Society opened the 900-seat Lyceum Theatre in 1886 and the Masons built an elegant Opera House, complete with dress circle, parquet, and horse-shoe balcony, in 1893; both survived into this century as con-verted movie houses.

By 1850 family concert companies began to include PEI on their itinerary during the sum-mer. The HERON FAMILY twice toured the province, in 1852 and 1855, with musical and dramatic programs. The number of dramatic troupes increased during the next decade, including brief engagements by J.W. LANER-GAN's company from Saint John (1858), M.W. Fiske's Dramatic Corps of Actors (1867), and T.C. Howard's Olympic Theatre Company (1868). The 1869 and 1870 tours by Wilson and Clarke's Provincial Boston Theatre were noteworthy forerunners of

Prince Edward Island Theatre, Charlottetown, 1893

larger troupes, such as the Boston Comedy Company, W.S. Harkins' Company, and many others, who carried their own scenery and costumes and whose repertoire could fill a two-week engagement. The shipwreck suffered by the Wilson and Clarke Company while enroute from Newfoundland to Charlottetown in 1870 is a reminder of the sometimes perilous journeys undertaken by theatre companies.

Throughout much of the nineteenth century, crossing the Northumberland Strait to PEI was often unreliable, hazardous, and rarely comfortable. The short touring season, June through September, was determined by the conditions of the Strait and the frequency of steamer crossings. Companies rarely arrived outside this period, since few could sustain the financial burden of interrupted schedules if stranded or delayed in the province. By the 1880s, however, the Intercolonial Railway allowed companies travelling by either steamer or rail from Boston and New York to connect with the railway at Saint John or Halifax. A more efficient steamer service joined PEI to this network.

The expansion of PEI's own railway system made other parts of the province more accessible. Although Charlottetown remained the heart of theatrical activity, outlying communities began to enjoy an increase in visiting troupes. Improved transportation also lengthened the touring season itself. For example, an Island audience in the 1890s could witness in a single season Joseph Murphy in The Kerry Gow, Josie Mills in John Oxenford's East Lynne, Harry Lindley in his own The Castaways, Edwina Grey and H. Price WEBBER's Boston Comedy Company in Fanchon, the Cricket or other standard melodramas, a mammoth production of Uncle Tom's Cabin, or a recent New York success performed by W.S. Harkins' Company. This represented a great increase over the average of two touring companies a year between 1850 and 1880.

By the end of the 1920s motion pictures and the Depression forced American touring to retrench and to abandon small markets like PEI. The revival of theatre on the Island was, like the beginning of theatre in the nineteenth century, due to the efforts of amateurs. LITTLE THEATREs sprang up in many communities throughout the province. The Charlottetown Little Theatre Guild, for example, lasted as long as its nineteenth-cen-

tury counterpart, the Charlotte-Town Amateur Theatre. Founded in 1935, it continued to operate until the building of the CONFEDERATION CENTRE of the Arts in 1964. Since then the CHARLOTTETOWN FESTIVAL has been the primary producer of theatre, albeit musical theatre. Two other summer repertory theatres also draw their audiences from the tourist population: the King's Playhouse at Georgetown, and the Victoria Playhouse at Victoria-by-the-Sea.

The King's Playhouse, originally the Town Hall (though it was never used as such), was designed by Island architect William C. Harris and built in 1897. It housed tours until the demise of road companies and amateur productions in the 1940s. In 1966, this 200-seat theatre was leased by Georgetown to Beth McGowan, a local theatre enthusiast, who refurbished the interior, maintaining the Victorian style, and mounted a season of SUMMER STOCK. King's Theatre, as it was then known, closed at the end of its second season in 1967. But in 1974 it continued to struggle for survival, mounting standard fare like The Owl and the Pussycat, The Odd Couple, Dracula, and an occasional Canadian play—Carol BOLT's One Night Stand and Peter Colley's I'll Be Back Before Midnight. In 1981 its name was changed to King's Playhouse with the establishment of the King's Playhouse Foundation, a non-profit organization aimed at revitalizing and providing support for community theatre in Georgetown. Although it continues to produce a 'straw hat' repertoire, it includes a greater variety of Canadian works and a broad spectrum of entertainments—the National Multicultural Theatre Festival, concerts, and variety shows. After the theatre was destroyed by fire while under renovation in 1983, a larger structure—adhering to the Vic-

The Town Hall (King's Playhouse), Georgetown, PEI

torian exterior and Harris's architectural style—was built and reopened in July 1985.

The Victoria Playhouse, housed in a converted community hall, began operation in 1981. Like the King's Playhouse, it produces plays that appeal to a tourist audience, which is somewhat easier to attract because the Victoria is closer to Charlottetown. Under artistic director Erskine Smith, the Victoria Playhouse offers a broad variety of Canadian plays, such as Warren Graves's *The Hand that Cradles the Rock*, Betty LAMBERT's *Jennie's Story*, and George F. WALKER's *The Art of War*; and whenever possible it produces works by Island playwrights. Both the Victoria Playhouse and the King's Playhouse have begun to develop established audiences. They now have the flexibility to experiment (each has mounted original plays with Island themes), and are in the process of establishing year-round operations.

The Island Community Theatre in Charlottetown, under artistic director Ron Irving, is also an active producer during the winter season. Established in 1981, the ICT acts as a resource organization through its mandate to provide leadership, to co-ordinate the resources necessary for teaching the fundamentals of theatrical production, and to provide a stimulus for the production of plays by local groups. ICT regularly produces and tours Island works and hosts an annual playwriting competition entitled 'New Voices'.

To a great extent theatre in PEI remains seasonal. Winter continues to be the domain of the amateurs and summer that of the professionals. In the nineteenth century the determining factor was transportation; in the twentieth it is tourism.　　LINDA M. PEAKE

Princess Opera House. Built by local businessmen D. Cowan and T.B. Rutledge to accommodate the growing number of touring companies visiting Winnipeg after the Pembina Branch rail line that connected the city to the east was completed in 1878, the Princess opened on 14 May 1883 with the C.D. Hess Opera Company's presentation of Gilbert and Sullivan's *Iolanthe*. Situated at Princess St and Ross Ave, the theatre's exterior—with its veneer of white brick, mansard roof, and domed tower—suggested urban refinement and old-world culture. Underneath this imposing façade the Princess was a wooden frame building supported by piles and posts. The theatre was on the second

Princess Opera House, Winnipeg

floor over shops which originally included a restaurant, saloon, and billiard parlour. The building covered an area of 75' × 100' with an auditorium about 72' × 72'. The stage was 75' wide and 33' deep, with over 30' from wing to wing. The proscenium arch was a little over 24' high. Total seating capacity of the parquet, dress circle, boxes, and gallery was 1,376. Performers appearing at the Princess in the first five years of its operation included Thomas Keene in a short season of Shakespeare, Katie Putnam, W.H. Lytell, Mlle. Rhea, Eugene McDOWELL, Kate Castleton, Sol Smith Russell, and McKee RANKIN.

In July 1883 the Princess was taken over by the newly incorporated Northwest Opera House Company, formed by a group of Winnipeg businessmen including Charles Wallace Sharp, a plasterer and contractor, who assumed responsibility for its day-to-day management. Recognizing the difficulties in attracting high-quality touring companies to Winnipeg, Sharp and his associates decided to present a mixture of stock and touring attractions. Their plan was to tour the stock company to the towns around Winnipeg whenever touring companies could be booked for the Princess. They also hoped to build theatres in such centres as Brandon and Portage la Prairie as an added inducement to companies to make the detour to Winnipeg.

A downturn in the economy of the 1880s, problems with heating the Princess in winter, and the difficulty of booking good companies made the opera house an unprofitable venture. In 1887, however, Sharp succeeded in acquiring a resident company for the Princess. Managed by Frank G. Campbell, who had been to Winnipeg as Frederic Bryton's stage

Princess Opera House

manager, it opened with George R. Sims' and Cecil Raleigh's *The Guardsman* on 12 Dec. 1887. In their first season Campbell and his company received a warm welcome, the highlight of the season being a spectacular production of Dion Boucicault's *The Colleen Bawn*. The following year support fell off, although Campbell did his best to woo audiences back with ambitious productions of Boucicault's *The Streets of New York*, and adaptations of Jules Verne's *Around The World in Eighty Days* and *Michael Strogoff*. The third season began on 4 Nov. 1889 with the popular Fanny Reeves in Sheridan's *The School For Scandal*, but despite critical praise support was still inadequate. One reason for this may have been controversy over the safety of the Princess.

During the summers, and when other companies were booked for the Princess, Campbell and his company toured. Except for a financially disastrous tour to Port Arthur and Sault St Marie in the summer of 1888, and an extensive tour in 1889 across the Canadian West and to some American centres, most of these tours were in the area around Winnipeg. Between Jan. 1888 and May 1890 Campbell and his company made at least ten such forays.

The management of the Princess changed during these years. Sharp gave way to his friend, William H. Seach, and at the start of the 1888-9 season Campbell and Seach were joint lessees of the theatre. At the end of Dec. 1889, when their lease expired, they dissolved their partnership. Seach retained control of the Princess and ran it successfully as a house for touring attractions until it was destroyed by fire on the morning of 1 May 1892.   CAROL BUDNICK

Princess Theatre (Montreal). Located on the south side of Sainte-Catherine St, at City Councillors, it was designed by D.J. Spence and erected in 1908 as a burlesque house. The brick structure, accommodating 2,300 patrons, featured a stage approximately 30' deep, 70' wide, and 74' high (from the stage floor to the grid). The Princess opened on 5 Oct. 1908 with *A Night on Broadway*, 'a Musical Play with 40 Artists', followed by a series of vaudeville turns. Throughout the first season BURLESQUE and VAUDEVILLE were staple attractions, although a presentation of comic opera by the Robinson Opera

Company enjoyed some success in the spring of 1909.

A few months later the theatre was taken over by the U.S. Shubert organization. Enlarged by 200 seats, it reopened in Sept. 1909 as a major venue for touring theatre, opera, and musical-comedy companies. Visiting stars included George Arliss (1909), Gertrude Elliott (1910), Albert Chevalier (1910), William Faversham (1910), Alla Nazimova (1910), Robert Mantell (1911), Margaret ANGLIN (1912), Al Jolson (1913), and Marie Tempest (1914).

Late in 1915 the house was once more refurbished, and subsequently featured mainly musical comedy and opera until 1917, when it was sold to Canadian United Theatres Ltd. After substantial alterations by the original architect, the theatre resumed its identity for nine years as a vaudeville house in Dec. 1917, offering B.F. Keith's High Class Vaudeville twice daily. A highlight of this period was a gala performance for the Prince of Wales on 29 Oct. 1919.

The Shuberts again leased the building in 1926 and mounted musical comedy, revue, and occasional legitimate theatre until 1929. George Arliss, Katharine Cornell, and Sacha Guitry were among the Shubert headliners. The Stratford-upon-Avon Festival Company, under the direction of W. Bridges Adams, visited in Oct. 1928, closely followed by the Théâtre de la Porte Saint-Martin de Paris. Appearances by the American Opera Company and the Lyric Musical Comedy Company, both from New York, enlivened the early months of 1929.

On 1 June 1929 Consolidated Theatres, which had bought the building a year earlier, terminated the Princess's live-stage career. Two weeks later it re-opened as a motion picture house. In 1963 it became an exclusively French-language cinema and was renamed Le Parisien. At the same time the capacity of the auditorium was reduced to 1,000. Le Parisien was purchased in 1966 by Famous Players Corporation and altered to a 'fiveplex' that currently features first-run French films.   JOHN RIPLEY

Princess Theatre. (Toronto). Opened in 1889 as the Academy of Music, this music hall on King St W. between York and Simcoe was the first public building in Toronto with electric lights. In addition to the auditorium, it contained a banquet hall, art gallery, drawing-room, reception rooms, and a ballroom. Early musical and dramatic productions included Gounod's *Faust* and T.W. Robertson's *David Garrick*, but in 1895 alterations—a new gallery, new promenades, a smoking room, an enlarged stage, and an improved foyer—transformed the theatre into a rival of the GRAND OPERA HOUSE. The stage measured 35' × 45' and seating was increased to 1,800. Renamed the Princess, the new theatre opened in Aug. 1895. Under the management of O.B. Sheppard, it housed stock companies, but in 1901 it became a higher-priced theatre featuring visiting stars: Sarah Bernhardt, Robert Mantell, Henry Irving, and Ellen Terry, among others. Having supplanted the Grand as Toronto's leading theatre, it remained so until the ROYAL ALEXANDRA THEATRE opened in 1907. In May 1915 the Princess burned, reopening as the New Princess in Oct. 1917 as part of the Detroit-based Whitney circuit of twenty-one theatres in Ontario, Michigan, and Ohio. A decline in the quality of productions was noted by reviewers in the early 1920s with occasional exceptions, such as Shaw's *Saint Joan* in 1924, starring Julia ARTHUR. The Princess was demolished in 1930 to accommodate the University Avenue extension.

KATHLEEN FRASER

Professional Organizations.

Associated Designers of Canada. Formed in 1965 to improve the status of the Canadian design artist, the ADC negotiates, on behalf of its some 120 members, a minimum-conditions contract with the Professional Association of Canadian Theatres as well as with commercial producers, opera and ballet companies, and industrial shows. It has also published 'Standards and Recommended Working Procedures' to assist designers. Other activities include the presentation of national and international design exhibitions and a membership directory.

Canadian Actors' Equity Association. CAEA is the professional organization of performing artists, directors, choreographers, and stage managers engaged in theatre, opera, and ballet. Originally a branch of the U.S. Actors' Equity Association, it became independent in 1976 and now has an active membership of some 3,200 across Canada. Within its jurisdiction the Association negotiates all agreements, minimum salaries, and working conditions for its members, monitors all contracts, ensures that every member is bonded while under contract, and mediates disputes between its members and producers. It also administers a retirement savings plan and insurance plan for its members and publishes a monthly newsletter.

Canadian Theatre Critics Association/Association des critiques de théâtre du Canada. Founded in 1980, it is composed of professional critics, entertainment writers, and journalists employed in electronic, broadcast, and print media, and has the following primary objectives: to enhance national and international awareness of Canadian theatre by means of theatre criticism, and to promote excellence in criticism through improved training opportunities and working conditions for critics through the development of a code of ethics for both critics and their employers. The Association publishes regular newsletters, organizes an annual conference, and administers the Nathan COHEN theatre criticism award.

Centre d'essai des auteurs dramatiques. Since 1965 this Montreal-based organization has worked to cultivate and promote French-language playwriting in Quebec and to increase international awareness of Quebec theatre. Each year the Centre organizes a series of workshops, showcases, and readings for the purposes of script development. It also operates a script-lending service to facilitate the distribution of indigenous scripts throughout the theatre community. Its promotional activities overseas have included stage readings of Quebec plays in France and Switzerland, and a translation-workshop exchange with the New Dramatists, a New York-based playwrights' organization. In order to increase the number of local plays available in translation, the Centre also administers jointly with Playwrights Workshop Montreal a program entitled 'Transmissions', which is designed to bring together, in a workshop environment, a Quebec playwright, a translator, and a team of actors. The Centre publishes a bibliography of plays available in English translation and a quarterly newsletter, *Théâtre Québec*. It also publishes a catalogue of works by playwright members every two years.

Dramatists Co-operative of Nova Scotia. Founded in 1976, the co-operative is a self-governing branch of the Writers' Federation of Nova Scotia. Its organizational objectives

Professional Organizations

are to enhance the skills of provincial playwrights, to disseminate information about their works, and to communicate with theatre, film, and television producers throughout the Atlantic community. It conducts a variety of programs, including informal at-home readings of members' scripts and a series of province-wide two-day workshops, or 'Round Tables', during which the scripts of both members and the general public are given professional direction. Other activities include week-long workshops of selected scripts, a monthly newsletter, public readings, and a catalogue of members' works published every three to four years.

Guild of Canadian Musical Theatre Writers. Organized in 1982 to promote the development of musical theatre in Canada, to facilitate communication between musical-theatre writers and composers, and to develop minimum contracts between writers and producers, the Guild holds bi-weekly workshops during which members present songs, scenes, and outlines of work in progress in order to benefit from the comments and criticism of their colleagues. In addition it offers introductory classes in musical-theatre writing and updates annually its Directory of Musical Works, originally published in 1984. Each year the Guild hosts a trade forum where its members' work is showcased before an invited audience of theatre producers.

Manitoba Association of Playwrights. It was formed by a group of Manitoba playwrights in 1979 to foster the development of Manitoba plays, to be a resource centre for all provincial writers, and to maintain contacts with other regional and national playwrights' organizations. The Association sponsors the Playwrights Development Program, an ongoing series of readings, private and public workshops, and public presentations of Manitoba plays. It also holds a Playwrights' Colony, publishes a newsletter, sponsors a speakers' series, distributes scripts, maintains a library, and participates in the Artists-in-the-Schools program of the Manitoba Arts Council. The organization has arranged exchanges of playwrights for workshop purposes with other centres in Saskatchewan and in Minneapolis.

Playwrights Union of Canada. A national association of Canadian playwrights, it was established in 1983 as a result of the merger of Playwrights Canada (previously Playwrights Co-Op, founded in 1971) and the Guild of Canadian Playwrights. Membership is open to any Canadian who has a minimum of one professionally produced play. The Union, of approximately 270 dramatists, publishes between twenty and thirty of its members' scripts in paperback annually as well as a bi-monthly newsletter (*CanPlay*), and offers many more scripts in photocopied playscript format. It also files all members' scripts on computer disk and issues two annual catalogues.

Professional Association of Canadian Theatres. Based in Toronto, PACT was incorporated in 1976 to serve as the national service and trade association for the non-profit professional theatre community in Canada. Approximately eighty professional theatre companies from coast to coast constitute its current membership. Foremost among PACT's activities is the negotiation, every three years, of a collective agreement with the Canadian Actors' Equity Association. It has also been active in developing contractual guidelines with the Associated Designers of Canada and the Playwrights Union of Canada. PACT engages in political advocacy on its members' behalf with government agencies and departments. The organization's Communications Centre publishes a monthly newsletter, a monthly bulletin (*Artsboard*) of employment opportunities, a reference guide to Canadian theatres and theatre-related resources (*Behind the Scenes*), and an illustrated yearbook (*Canada on Stage*). PACT has also published a textbook, *Financial Management for Canadian Theatres*. It serves as the Secretariat of the Canadian Centre of the International Theatre Institute (English-language) and hosts a World Theatre Day celebration each year.

Theatre Ontario. Founded in 1971, this province-wide organization provides a broad range of programs and services to a membership of more than 200 professional, community, and educational theatre companies and over 2,000 individual members. It administers a professional theatre-training program that subsidizes career upgrading in the form of 'on-the-job' training with established theatre companies, a community training program that provides financial assistance for community groups to hire professional trainers, and a youth program that enables young people to train with theatre professionals. Each year Theatre Ontario produces a festival of community theatre and presents the Maggie Bassett Award for a significant contribution to the development of theatre in Ontario.

Toronto Theatre Alliance. Founded in 1979, it is an umbrella organization composed of more than 190 performing-arts organizations, commercial producers, venues, artist-management agencies, dance companies, and businesses serving the theatrical community in the Toronto area. Throughout its history the Alliance has endeavoured to articulate the problems and needs of its constituency to governmental agencies and task forces. It works to enhance the profile of theatre in the local community through an array of promotional projects and, most importantly, through its annual production of the Dora Mavor MOORE Awards.   IRA A. LEVINE

ASSITEJ Canada. When ASSITEJ (Association international du théâtre pour l'enfance et la jeunesse) was founded in 1964, Canada was represented by Myra Benson, co-founder of HOLIDAY THEATRE of Vancouver. Four years later a Canadian Centre for ASSITEJ was established at the Univ. of Calgary under the direction of Joyce Doolittle. Its aims were to provide information to foreign centres of ASSITEJ regarding Canadian professional theatre for young audiences, and to provide similar information to Canadian companies about developments and opportunities abroad. In Montreal in 1972 the Canadian Centre co-hosted (with the American centre) the Fourth International General Assembly of ASSITEJ, and in 1984 it co-sponsored an international conference in Toronto. After the first Vancouver Children's Festival in 1977, many of the Centre's functions were taken over by professional theatre companies for young audiences, and the next year the Centre moved to Montreal. In 1987 ASSITEJ Canada decided to split into two centres, one anglophone (at GREEN THUMB THEATRE in Vancouver) and one francophone (at La NOUVELLE COMPAGNIE THÉÂTRALE in Montreal).

Association for Canadian Theatre History/ Association d'histoire du théâtre au Canada. Founded in 1976, the ACTH/AHTC is a non-profit organization dedicated to promoting research into, and publication of, Canadian theatre history. It publishes (since 1980) a semi-annual academic journal entitled *Theatre History in Canada/Histoire du théâtre au Canada*, and (since 1977) a semi-annual newsletter. It also created and administers the Heather McCallum Scholarship for research

projects in Canadian theatre history, first awarded in 1988. A member of the Canadian Federation of the Humanities, the ACTH/ AHTC meets each year as part of the Federation's Learned Societies conference.

Association of British Columbia Drama Educators. Formed in 1970, the ABCDE is a provincial specialists' association for drama educators, operating under the umbrella of the B.C. Teachers Federation. It publishes a semi-annual newsletter and a semi-annual journal, both entitled *Abracadabra*, and sponsors an annual teachers' conference and an annual high-school drama festival.

Canadian Centre for the International Theatre Institute. The two Canadian centres of the ITI form a national service organization that represents Canadian theatre world-wide. It began in 1956, on a volunteer basis, as the Canadian Theatre Centre. In 1965 it acquired new funding to expand its operations; under the leadership of Tom HENDRY, its first full-time Secretary-General, the CTC embarked on an ambitious national program of publishing, communications, and administrative consulting based in Toronto. The CTC was disbanded in 1973, largely because of its inability to serve both francophone and anglophone interests at the same time; but in 1977, through the Canada Council, the ITI invited Canada to rejoin. In 1979 two separate but equal centres were established for the two language groups, in Montreal and Toronto, called (respectively) Le Centre Québécois de l'Institut International du Théâtre and the Canadian Centre of the International Theatre Institute (English-language); they provide their members with training and festival information, and contacts with theatre professionals abroad. The first two presidents were Hélène Dumas (1979-) and Curtis Barlow (1979-86). In 1985 the Canadian centres hosted the World Congress of the ITI in Montreal and Toronto, with over 400 theatre professionals attending from sixty countries.

Canadian Child and Youth Drama Association. The CCYDA is a national umbrella organization for educational drama in Canada. Inspired by the work of British educators Peter Slade and Brian Way in the 1950s, the CCYDA was formed in 1962 under the leadership of Donald Wetmore. Originally emphasizing children's participation in dramatic activity, such as the group improvisations led by adult actors in Way's celebrated 'participation plays', it now aims to support

Professional Organizations

and develop both drama-in-education and children's theatre in Canada. It publishes a regular newsletter, and maintains informal connections with provincial drama teachers' groups and with ASSITEJ Canada.

Council of Drama in Education. Formed in 1970, CODE is dedicated to promoting drama-in-education in Ontario. It provides regional workshops, sponsors an annual conference, promotes Ontario's drama and theatre-arts curricula, and facilitates communications and professional development among drama teachers. CODE publishes a newsletter several times yearly, and an annual journal entitled *Drama Contact*.

Nova Scotia Drama League. An alliance of community, educational, and professional theatre companies dedicated to promoting the growth and quality of theatre arts in Nova Scotia, the NSDL offers educational and technical services to members, and publishes a quarterly magazine (*Callboard*) and a monthly Calendar/Newsletter. Founded in 1949 and incorporated in 1951 (under the leadership of Donald Wetmore), the NSDL is funded by membership fees and private donations, and by an operating grant from the provincial government. In 1985 it opened the Cunard Street Theatre in Halifax to provide an inexpensive rental house for a variety of companies.

Prologue to the Performing Arts. It began in 1966 as a booking service for Toronto's YOUNG PEOPLE'S THEATRE, the Canadian Opera Company, and the National Ballet for their touring shows for young audiences. Prologue grew into an independent non-profit organization that handles Ontario bookings for some thirty other companies as well, mostly for school performances, with audiences totalling about 700,000 annually. Its board functions as a jury, each year auditioning companies and individual performers in dance, mime, story-telling, puppetry, and theatre in both French and English, and occasionally commissioning new work.

Vancouver Professional Theatre Alliance. Formed in 1973, the VPTA is an informal organization of some sixteen professional theatre companies, dedicated to promoting professional theatre in Vancouver. To be eligible for membership a company must have operated continuously for at least two years, and must have obtained Canada Council funding. The VPTA sponsers two major programs each year: a professional tour of four shows (called the Package Deal tour) and the Jessie Richardson Awards for excellence in Vancouver theatre.

See Carla Wittes, ed., *Behind the Scenes: A Guide to Canadian Non-Profit Professional Theatres and Theatre-Related Resources* (1986).
DENIS W. JOHNSTON

Proulx, Jean-Baptiste (1846-1904). Born at Sainte-Anne-de-Bellevue, Que., and educated at the Séminaire de Sainte-Thérèse, he was ordained a priest in 1869, working in Manitoba missions between 1870 and 1874. He became a teacher of literature and modern history at the Séminaire de Sainte-Thérèse and at Université Laval de Montréal, where he was named vice-rector in 1888 and wrote travelogues, academic pamphlets, and a novel. Under the pseudonym Joannès Iovhanné he published four plays for his students. In these plays for adolescents, which had no female roles, he preached saintliness (*Edouard le confesseur, roi d'Angleterre*, 1880), denounced alcoholism (*L'Hôte à Valiquet; ou le Fricot sinistre*, 1881), made fun of student customs (*Le Mal du jour de l'an; ou Scènes de la vie écolière*, 1882), and fought against emigration to the United States (*Les Pionniers du lac Nomininigue; ou les Avantages de la colonisation*, 1883). His treatment of secular subjects, his use of Quebec folklore, and his sense of humour somewhat redeem these didactic plays, making Proulx one of the more interesting Quebec dramatists of the nineteenth century.
LUCIE ROBERT

Publishers: English-Language drama. Publication of plays in English Canada did not occur until the proliferation of literary periodicals and newspapers during the nineteenth century. Short scenes on local topical themes by anonymous authors can be found in most early newspapers, while full-length plays were often serialized over several issues—such as Hugh Scobie's satire of the Family Compact in ten issues of the *British Colonist* in 1839 under the pseudonym Chronohotonthologos and J. W. Bengough's ten instalments of his 'farcical tragedy' *The Edison Doll* in *Grip* in 1894. Plays derived from British models were published in Montreal's *Literary Garland* (1838-51) and occasionally reprinted in local newspapers. Anonymous paratheatrical political satires, the more popular form of indigenous playwriting, particularly after Confederation, were featured in

Grip (1874-94), *Grip's Almanac* (1881), *Grinchuckle* (1869), *Acta Victoriana* (1888-), and the *Canadian Illustrated News* (1869-81). Individual plays were also published privately, often in collections of the author's poetry—J.H. Brown's poetic drama *A Philosopher*, for example, was published in his *Poems: Lyrical and Dramatic* (1892).

Samples of plays from this early period have been republished in volume I of the four-volume series of *Canada's Lost Plays* (1978-82), edited by Anton Wagner and in several annotated editions of early works published by the Univ. of Toronto Press. *Theatre History in Canada/Histoire du théâtre au Canada* has published articles about and excerpts from early paratheatrical plays and in two cases fully annotated scripts—the operetta *La CONVERSION D'UN PECHEUR DE LA NOUVELLE-ÉCOSSE* by Elzéar Labelle and Jean-Baptiste Labelle and John Richardson's *The Miser Outwitted* in vols 5 (1984) and 7 (1986) respectively.

Early in the present century established companies such as Hunter Rose, William Briggs, John Robinson, and Macmillan in Toronto, and John Lovell in Montreal published individual editions of plays and, by the mid 1920s, the first anthologies began to appear. The Canadian Authors' Association published *One-Act Plays by Canadian Authors* (1926); the first volume of Vincent MASSEY's *Canadian Plays from Hart House Theatre* appeared in 1926, the second in 1927; and in 1930 Herman VOADEN edited *Six Canadian Plays*. In this period scripts were being published in theatre journals such as the *Educational Review*, *Acadian Athenaeum*, *CURTAIN CALL*, and *Callboard*. And during the 1940s the Univ. of Alberta published scripts for the Western Canadian Theatre Conference.

Since the 1960s there has been a significant effort to make Canadian plays more accessible. Numerous anthologies have been published, among them *A Collection of Canadian Plays* (5 vols, Simon & Pierre, 1972-8), ed. Rolf Kalman; *Now in Paperback* (1973) and *The Factory Lab Anthology* (Talonbooks, 1974), ed. Connie Brissenden; *Eight Men Speak and Other Plays from the Canadian Workers' Theatre* (New Hogtown Press, 1976), ed. Richard Wright and Robin Endres; *Encounter: Canadian Drama in Four Media* (Methuen, 1973), ed. Eugene Benson; and in 1984 and 1985 three anthologies—*The Penguin Book of Modern Canadian Drama* (Penguin, 1984), ed.

Richard Plant, *Major Canadian Plays of the Canadian Theatre, 1934-1984* (Irwin, 1984), ed. Richard Perkyns, and *Modern Canadian Plays* (Talonbooks, 1985), ed. Jerry Wasserman—appeared almost simultaneously. *Eight Plays for Young People* (NeWest Press, 1984), ed. Joyce Doolittle, and the fourth volume of Kalman's collection contain the majority of published plays for children.

Publication of individual plays has been largely the domain of the Playwrights Union of Canada, based in Toronto, which began publishing typescripts in 1972. In 1985 PUC commenced publishing paperback editions of plays but continues to make unpublished typescripts available upon request. In Vancouver, Talonbooks began publishing scripts in 1972, the New Play Centre in 1971; in Edmonton NeWest Press began in 1977; in Halifax the Dramatists' Co-op, established in 1977, began publishing scripts. In addition Coach House Press and Simon & Pierre of Toronto both carry a significant list of plays. Translations of French-language plays have been published by almost all the publishers mentioned above and since 1987 by Le Centre d'essai des auteurs dramatiques. New scripts are also regularly published in *Canadian Theatre Review* and other journals. The only comprehensive record of published Canadian plays, *The Brock Bibliography of Published Canadian Plays in English 1766-1978* (1980), ed. Anton Wagner, has been supplemented by Patrick B. O'Neill's 'A Checklist of Canadian Dramatic Materials to 1967', published in *Canadian Drama*, 8 and 9 (1982, 1983), which lists more than 5,000 titles.

NATALIE REWA

Publishers: French-language drama. A 1776 reprint of the French play *Jonathas et David; ou le triomphe de l'amitié* by Pierre Brumoy was the first play to be published in French Canada; it was brought out in Quebec City by Fleury Mesplet and Charles Berger, a printer who had just arrived from France. In the 1790s printers Samuel Nelson and John Neilson of Quebec City published a number of political dialogues, thus initiating what was to become an important dramatic tradition in Quebec. Satirical dialogues were either printed separately or in newspapers. The first play performed and published in Quebec was Joseph QUESNEL's *COLAS ET COLINETTE*, published by John Neilson in 1812 (but bearing the imprint '1808').

Another printer, William Cowan, published the first play by a Quebec-born author, Pierre PETITCLAIR's *Griphon, ou la vengeance d'un valet* (1837). Petitclair's *La DONATION*—the first play by a native-born Québécois to be published and performed in Quebec—was published in *L'Artisan* in 1842. Antoine GÉRIN-LAJOIE's *Le JEUNE LATOUR* was published by two newspapers, *L'Aurore des Canadas* and *Le Canadien* in 1844. Several important early plays—including *Colas et Colinette*, *La Donation*, and *Le Jeune Latour*—were made more widely available in James Huston's four-volume *Le Répertoire national* (Montreal, 1848-50).

During the second half of the nineteenth century the role of publisher was assumed primarily by printers like Charles Payette, Darveau, Eusèbe Sénécal, Chapleau & Lavigne, and especially Beauchemin, who published the works of Ernest Doin, J.G.W. McGown, Louis-Honoré FRÉCHETTE, Philippe Aubert de Gaspé, Félix-Gabriel MARCHAND, and Laure Conan.

During the second half of the nineteenth century a number of periodicals published dramatic texts, beginning with *La Revue canadienne*, founded in 1860. By the end of the century popular magazines such as *La Vie illustrée* were also publishing plays. In the first half of the twentieth century *La Revue populaire*, *La Revue moderne*, *La Revue musicale*, and *Le Théâtre populaire français* published plays directed to both popular and specialized audiences.

The first serious attempt to produce a bibliography of Quebec plays was George-H. Robert's *L'Annuaire théâtral* (1908), listing 172 titles; Robert also published Germain Beaulieu's *Fascination* and Louvigny de Montigny's *La Gloire*. *Le Monde illustré* published de Montigny's *Les BOULES DE NEIGE* (1903) and other original plays. However, despite the efforts of Robert and a number of writers and actors who were part of a major renewal of French-language theatre in Montreal, few original Quebec plays were published in this period.

During the first half of the twentieth century the Catholic Church in Quebec had its own printing, publishing, and distribution facilities, as well as its own journals, which regularly published dramatic texts: *Les Carnets viatoriens*, La Librairie Saint-viateur, Les Éditions des Paraboliers (which published the texts of Gustave LAMARCHE and Rina Lasnier), *Le Pays laurentien*, L'Imprimerie de l'Action catholique, La Bibliothèque de l'Action française, Éditions de la Ligue missionnaire étudiante, L'Action sociale, and *La Revue franciscaine*.

During this same period, when Quebec's amateur theatre was quite lively, newspapers in all major cities and towns of the province published a significant number of short plays—Les Éditions du *Bien Public* of Trois-Rivières, for example, published several plays. Only one independent publishing house between the 1920s and the 1940s published a significant number of dramatic works: Les Éditions Édouard Garand, whose list of authors included Jules Ferland and Henry DEYGLUN. During the 1940s small publishing houses devoted to new creative work were established to counteract the domination of the publishing industry by a conservative ideology whose primary purpose was to produce school texts. These included Les Cahiers de la file indienne and Les Éditions de Malte, which offered important new works by Jacques FERRON, Gilles Hénault, and Eloi de GRANDMONT. Les Éditions Beauchemin played an important role at this time, publishing plays such as Gratien GÉLINAS's *TIT-COQ* (1950) and Félix LECLERC's *Le P'tit Bonheur* (1959). Beginning in the early fifties, Fides published works by Leclerc, Émile LEGAULT, and Félix-Antoine Savard and has continued to play an important role in publishing works of theatre history and criticism. At the same time, established publishers—Pierre Tisseyre and Le Cercle du Livre de France, L'Institut littéraire du Québec—took new initiatives to encourage Quebec writers. Since the beginning of the 1950s *Les Écrits du Canada-français* have given first publication to important plays by Marcel DUBÉ, Claude GAUVREAU, Anne HÉBERT, Jacques Ferron, Françoise LORANGER, and others. Other small publishing groups—Éditions Erta, Éditions d'Orphée, Éditions Pierre DAGENAIS—usually founded by the writers themselves, have made new theatrical works available.

The world of publishing was completely transformed in Quebec during the 1960s. Many general publishers—Hurtubise HMH, Les Éditions du Jour, Les Éditions de l'Homme, L'Hexagone, Stanké, Quinze—have also published dramatic texts and criticism. The need for specialized theatre publishers was recognized by the creation in 1966 of the Centre d'essai des auteurs dramatiques and its Théâtre vivant series. Théâtre vivant published seven volumes, including first editions of important works such as Antonine MAILLET's *Les Crasseux* (1968) and Michel TREMBLAY's *Les BELLES-SOEURS* (1968).

The founding of Éditions Leméac in 1968—its first title a new edition of Marcel Dubé's *Zone* (1955)—marked a radical new departure in the publication of dramatic texts in Quebec. Leméac's success has been astonishing. It has published more than 250 Quebec plays, representing almost all the major dramatists of the past twenty years, and eleven translations/adaptations into French. Three of its titles have sold over 100,000 copies, and another ten titles have sold over 50,000. In all, it has sold more than 2,000,000 copies. Several of its titles have won major literary awards provincially, nationally, and in France. Leméac's standard practice of publishing texts with performance photos, serious introductory material, and extracts from critical notices enhances the utility and attractiveness of each volume.

In the 1970s Éditions de l'Aurore published a number of avant-garde dramatic texts. In 1976 this venture merged with VLB (Victor-Lévy Beaulieu) Éditeur, a publishing house whose titles include plays by Michel GARNEAU, Jean-Claude GERMAIN, Marie LABERGE, Elizabeth Bourget, and Maryse Pelletier.

Two feminist publishing houses were founded in Montreal in the 1970s: Éditions de la Pleine Lune and Éditions du Remue-ménage. Pleine Lune has published five plays, including three by Jovette MARCHESSAULT. Remue-ménage, with origins in COLLECTIVE CREATIONs and theatre integrated with social action, has published six plays, all collaborative work. In 1983 a feminist theatre group in Quebec City founded a publishing house: Les Éditions des Folles alliées.

French-language drama has, of course, also been published outside Quebec. In Manitoba Le CERCLE MOLIÈRE, founded in 1925, has served as a focal point—although playwrights of the 1920s and 1930s, such as A. Castelein de la Lande and Auguste-Henri de Trémaudan, still published in Quebec (with *La Revue populaire* and E. Garand respectively). Since its founding in 1974 Les Éditions du Blé has published five volumes of plays. Two plays have also been published in the 1980s by Les Éditions des Plaines. In all, fourteen plays have been published by Franco-Manitobans.

In New Brunswick the newspaper *L'Evangéline* began to publish titles in the 1930s and Les Éditions d'Acadie has published four plays since 1974. In Ontario, where French-language theatre activity has been growing over the past two decades, the publication of original plays has been centred almost exclusively at Prise de parole in Sudbury, founded in 1972 in conjunction with Le Théâtre du Nouvel-Ontario and CANO (Cooperative Association of Northern Ontario), following the earlier example of Quebec's L'Hexagone. Prise de parole has published twelve plays, including authors André Paiement, Jean-Marc Dalpé, Brigitte Haentjens, and Robert Marinier.   LOUISE H. FORSYTH

Puppet Theatre. Artefacts and early Jesuit documentation indicate the use of puppetry in Amerindian shamanic ritual of the Kwakiutl, Inuit, and Iroquois peoples. Puppet figures and elaborate masks were means of connecting the spiritual and mortal worlds. Evidence of these early forms of puppetry can be found in the Museum of Anthropology in British Columbia and the Museum of Civilization in Ottawa. (See also AMERINDIAN AND INUIT THEATRE.)

Puppetry before the early twentieth century is difficult to document fully but, according to the *Mémoires* (1866) of Philippe Aubert de Gaspé, a puppet theatre was established in Quebec City as early as 1775 by Père Marseille and his wife for performances at the Seminary and on private occasions. Productions in French continued until 1837 when the British regime apparently withdrew its approval of such activity. Nineteenth-century memoirs attest to occasional marionette and puppetry performances, both through local initiative and as part of North American tours by English and American artists.

In the twentieth century, puppetry in Canada developed as an integral part of theatre for young audiences, and during the 1920s it began to gain professional status. The New York-trained Rosalynde Osborne Stearn established a troupe in Hamilton, Ont., in 1923; two years later David Keogh and his wife began mounting productions in Toronto.

By the 1930s there were amateur companies in most large Canadian cities—Kay's Puppets (Toronto), the Maycourt Club (London), the Junior League Puppets (Winnipeg), the Strolling Puppet Players (Vancouver)—as well as individual puppet artists, such as T. Cohen in Edmonton and H. H. Stansfield in Huntsville, Ont. Some of these troupes toured the U.S. as well as Canada, presenting adaptations of popular English fairy-tales and stories for children. Enthusiasm for puppetry led to the addition of a puppetry workshop at the MONTREAL REPERTORY THEATRE's School in 1941.

Rosalynde Stearn was chiefly responsible for drawing public attention to puppetry in English Canada. After her U.S. training under Lilian Owen—an assistant to New York puppeteer Tony Sarg—Stearn returned to Canada. Between 1932 and 1941 she contributed a regular column to the theatre magazine CURTAIN CALL with news of puppet activity in Canada, brief instalments on international puppet history, and instruction and commentary on the art. As the director of the King Cob puppets, she mounted shows in Hamilton, Toronto, and Montreal. In 1939 she participated in the Canadian Puppet Conference in Hamilton. The Rosalynde Stearn Puppet Collection at McGill University is a comprehensive resource for the study of puppetry, containing both scripts and puppets.

From the 1940s to the 1970s companies proliferated throughout the country. One of the first major contributions after the Second World War was that of Munich-born Albert Wolff. His puppet production of Mozart's opera *Bastien et Bastienne* for the 1945 Mozart Festival in Montreal remains an important landmark in the development of puppetry in Canada. Wolff's work inspired the founding of Les Marionnettes de Montréal in 1948 by Micheline Legendre. In 1953, under the auspices of the municipal government of Montreal, Le Théâtre Vagabond, a summer touring company in the parks, was formed. Local and touring puppet productions were hosted at La POUDRIÈRE on Île-Sainte-Hélène in Montreal from 1958. In 1950 in Ontario Dora and Leo Velleman founded the Canadian Puppet Festivals, a professional company that by 1972 had established its own permanent theatre in Chester, N.S. In Hamilton the Keoghs established the Canadian Puppet Theatre after the Second World War, and by 1963 they were presenting a summer season in a permanent puppet theatre on the Toronto Islands; in 1964 they also performed in Charlottetown, PEI. On the West Coast the South Burnaby Puppeteers (founded in 1954) were joined in 1961 by the Vancouver Guild

of Puppetry, and in 1966 by the Coad Puppet Theatre—a company that has toured extensively in Canada and internationally. During the 1960s there was also sporadic puppet activity in Winnipeg, Saskatchewan, and Edmonton.

The immigration of professional European puppeteers to Canada, beginning in the 1950s, prompted experimentation in the presentation and scripting of puppet plays. English actress Evelyn Garbary and Acadia Univ. professor Tom Miller established the MERMAID THEATRE in Wolfville, N.S., in 1972 and mounted plays based on Micmac and other local legends. German-born Felix MIRBT collaborated with Henry BEISSEL on Beissel's *Inook and the Sun*, performed at the STRATFORD FESTIVAL in 1973, and Mirbt's puppetry for Georg Büchner's *Woyzeck* and Strindberg's *A Dream Play* at the NATIONAL ARTS CENTRE (1974 and 1977) won popular and critical acclaim. George Merton, a professional puppeteer from Great Britain, was instrumental in establishing the Ontario Puppetry Association in 1957. (The association maintains a library and performance venue in Toronto.) Johan Vandergun from the Netherlands collaborated with American-born

Lampoon Puppettheatre

Niki Tilroe in productions by the Frog Print Theatre (founded in 1969 in London) until 1973, when he founded his own company, Lampoon Puppettheatre, in Toronto. Eric Merinat, from Switzerland, worked in Montreal until his appointment to the Univ. of Calgary in 1978. Peter Shuman's Bread and Puppet Theatre of Vermont was an important influence during the 1970s on such companies as the Breadbaker's Puppet Theatre in Vancouver and the Wholeloaf Theatre in Toronto.

During the 1970s and 1980s there was an increase in experimentation with puppet shows for adults. The MUMMERS TROUPE of Newfoundland politicized puppets with its *Once a Giant* (1974), a play about U.S. imperialism. Théâtre sans fil (founded in Montreal in 1971) used Ojibway legends as the basis of *Tales from the Smokehouse*, which toured Canada in 1979. Like Mermaid Theatre, Théâtre sans fil has experimented with masks and life-size puppets in an attempt to capitalize on the theatrical aspects of indigenous legends and rituals. The Coad Canada Puppets of Vancouver, the Famous People Players and the Puppetmongers Powell of Toronto, and Théâtre de l'oeil of Montreal have also experimented with the theatricality of native materials. The Manitoba Puppet Theatre, founded by Chris Hurley in 1973, was perhaps the most experimental puppet company in the 1970s. Besides performing plays in schools, Hurley developed a DOCUMENTARY and COLLECTIVE puppet theatre, travelling through the Canadian West with plays on specifically Canadian issues.

Canadian puppet companies have gained international prominence through participation in festivals in Europe, South America, the U.S., and the Orient. In 1986 a successful puppetry festival in Montreal enabled Canadians to see the work of many international companies.

Puppetry has also made a significant contribution to the development of children's television programming. Since 1952 puppets have been a major component of such CBC shows as 'Uncle Chichimus', 'Pépinot et Capucine', 'The Friendly Giant', and 'Mr. Dress Up'.

See Christopher Hurley, *The Fat Clowns at the Circus and Other Plays for Puppets* (1977); K. McKay, *Puppetry in Canada* (1980); R. Tilroe, *Puppetry and Television* (1981); M. Legendre, *Marionnettes, Art et tradition* (1986); Luman and Ailyn Coad, *Producing for the Puppet Theatre* (1987).   NATALIE REWA

Q

Quebec, Theatre in (English). Although theatre in Quebec, both professional and amateur, was largely English until the middle of the twentieth century, the increasing social and cultural dominance of the growing francophone majority made the movement to indigenous theatrical professionalism after the Second World War a predominantly francophone phenomenon. English-language theatre—once a significant presence in Quebec City, the Eastern Townships, and, to a lesser degree, in the Ottawa Valley and Gaspé—has become increasingly limited to Montreal.

The British garrisons in Quebec City and Montreal entertained themselves sporadically in French and English during the first generation of English rule (see GARRISON THEATRE). In 1780 Governor Haldimand allowed the head of the Montreal garrison, General Allan Maclean, the use of the Jesuit residences for performances. From 1783 to 1786 amateur groups in Quebec City gave some forty performances at the Thespian Theatre, activities that were reinforced by the visiting English company of Edward Allen and William Moore, who presented the first professional theatre in the province in 1786-7. Performing usually once a week on Friday, this company had successful seasons in both Montreal and Quebec City, giving command performances of Oliver Goldsmith's *She Stoops to Conquer* for Prince William in Quebec City in Aug.

Quebec, Theatre in (English)

1787, and reopening in Montreal in Nov. 1787 under the patronage of Lord Dorchester.

During this period professionals visiting the province had to contend with poor facilities. The American actor Noble Luke Usher, who offered seasons in Montreal and Quebec City before the war of 1812, brought in Noble Allport from London's Covent Garden to provide the latest in scenic painting, and in 1818 John Turnbull hired John Milbourne—a student of the famous German designer Philip de Loutherbourg—to inaugurate the opening of the New Montreal Theatre, which operated for two seasons before it was destoyed by fire on 4 May 1820. Facilities remained makeshift, however, until the opening of the THEATRE ROYAL in Montreal in 1825. Intended as an 'embellishment of the City' and 'a source of instruction as well as of amusement', this elegant and well-equipped 1,000-seat theatre—built by steamboat proprietor and brewer John Molson—offered an ambitious repertory under manager Frederick BROWN. A company of fifty (including orchestra) staged some seventy performances during the first winter season. Edmund Kean played there in the summer of 1826, and before the theatre was razed in 1844 it hosted various amateur and professional companies. Manager Vincent DeCamp brought Halifax-born Rufus BLAKE in the summer of 1831, Charles Kean in 1831, and Charles and Fanny Kemble in 1833. Charles Dickens appeared with the Garrison Amateurs in 1842, and William Macready closed the theatre with his July 1844 engagement.

In Quebec City the American producers William West and C.W. Blanchard opened the Royal Circus in 1824. Built as a combined equestrian and legitimate theatre, it was renovated and reopened in 1832 as the THEATRE ROYAL, becoming the city's major theatre until it was demolished in 1846.

British and American immigration increased the English-speaking proportion of Quebec's population to twenty-five per cent in the pre-Confederation era. New theatres were built to accommodate the greater audiences—the Royal Olympic (1845), Hay's (1847), and a new Theatre Royal (1852) in Montreal; the Près de Ville (1852) and the Academy of Music in Quebec City—presenting regular winter amateur seasons (by, for example, the Garrick Club in Montreal) and summer professional seasons. John BUCKLAND provided stability for the professional

Interior of the Theatre Royal, Montreal

offerings in Montreal, managing the new Theatre Royal almost continuously through to Confederation. His summer seasons—which often featured his common-law wife Kate Horn—gave Montrealers the chance to see such major stars as Dion Boucicault and his common-law wife, Agnes Robertson, Barry Sullivan, John McCullough, and Charles Kean. The noted American actor Barton Hill was the featured star for most of the 1860s. In Quebec City John NICKINSON, a former soldier who had acted at the old Theatre Royal in Montreal, inaugurated the Près de Ville with Charlotte MORRISON, his Quebec-born daughter, while amateur groups, such as the Quebec Histrionic Club and the Young Irishmen's Literary and Dramatic Club—which had been important in Quebec City since early in the century when Thomas Cary, editor of the *Quebec Mercury*, was a noted amateur actor—still flourished up to Confederation.

From Confederation to the First World War the anglophone population of Quebec increased to over 300,000, but declined to sixteen per cent of the total population. By 1914 almost half the English-speaking population was located in Montreal, which then became the focus of theatrical construction and performance. The 2,000-seat ACADEMY OF MUSIC opened in 1875 and the 1,700-seat HER MAJESTY'S in 1898. Other new Montreal theatres included the New Dominion (1873), the Lyceum (1880), and the Queen's (1891). In the Eastern Townships, despite a decline in population, school and community theatre became established and American touring companies frequently visited small-town halls and the opera houses of larger centres. With railroads now providing easier access, professional touring companies and stars began to appear year-round in the Montreal theatres. The American Shakespearean actor Thomas W. Keene first performed in Montreal in May 1882 and Henry Irving made the first of many visits in Oct. 1884. An important figure who stands out as a link between the professional theatre and Montreal's amateur fare was playwright, actor, and director William TREMAYNE. He wrote successfully for the U.S. stage, and American star Robert Mantell performed in his *The Secret Warrant* at the Academy of Music in Jan. 1898. Tremayne was also an active participant in the burgeoning LITTLE THEATRE movement, most importantly in directing the Trinity Players from 1908.

From the First World War to 1960, and the onset of the Quiet Revolution in Quebec, the English-speaking population more than doubled to 700,000, yet its proportion of total population continued to decrease, to thirteen per cent. The development of Little Theatres—particularly the establishment of the influential MONTREAL REPERTORY THEATRE (MRT) in 1930—was the dominant trend of the era in English-language theatre. Imported professional theatre continued, but on an occasional rather than a seasonal basis, especially after the failures of the British Canadian Theatrical Organization and Trans-Canada Theatres Ltd. (See TOURING STARS AND COMPANIES.)

Attempts to establish a community theatre in Montreal failed until the charismatic Martha ALLAN launched the Montreal Repertory Theatre. At its height—under the leadership of Allan and, later, Doreen Lewis—the MRT produced subscription seasons of from four to eight shows, experimental studio offerings, and theatre classes. The DOMINION DRAMA FESTIVAL spurred the development of other groups, such as the 16-30 Club of Montreal, led by Herbert WHITTAKER and Charles RITTENHOUSE. The Lakeshore Summer Theatre, the MOUNTAIN PLAYHOUSE, and the Open Air Playhouse—all semi-professional summer anglophone companies of the 1940s and 1950s—did not have long lives, unlike the BRAE MANOR THEATRE at Knowlton, in the Eastern Townships, run by Filmore and Madge Sadler for twenty years (1936-56).

The anglophone population of Quebec has not increased in the past thirty years and now comprises about eleven per cent of the population. Significant numbers of unilingual anglophones, primarily from Montreal, left the province during the turbulent language debates of the 1970s. With the development of a pervasive French identity in Quebec, anglophone culture has been significantly overshadowed. Despite this apparent marginalization, however, three important professional English-language theatres were born in this period: the SAIDYE BRONFMAN CENTRE, CENTAUR THEATRE, and FESTIVAL LENNOXVILLE. The establishment of the NATIONAL THEATRE SCHOOL in Montreal enhanced training for both anglophone and francophone students, as did the creation of new theatre programs in the province's colleges and universities.

Quebec, Theatre in (English)

The Jewish community's long-standing support of local amateur theatre—dating back to Rupert Caplan's YMHA productions in the 1910s and 1920s—was transferred to professional theatre when Montreal's Saidye Bronfman Centre inaugurated a full-scale subscription season in 1967 under Marion ANDRE. The Centaur, founded in 1969, has become anglo-Montreal's flagship theatre. Under its founding artistic director, Maurice PODBREY, it slowly built up a solid base of local subscribers in the tradition of the MRT. Centaur has produced an eclectic blend of popular and serious drama and has been notably successful with Podbrey's productions of Athol Fugard's plays. The Centaur nurtured and developed the talent of Montrealer David FENNARIO, mounting excellent productions of *On the Job* in 1975, *Nothing to Lose* in 1976, and *BALCONVILLE* in 1979. Continuing the tradition of summer theatre in the Townships, Festival Lennoxville began in 1972 with the novel concept of an all-Canadian festival. Under artistic directors William Davis (1972-7) and Richard OUZOUNIAN (1978-80), and administrative director David Rittenhouse, it ambitiously sought to become an all-Canadian version of the STRATFORD and SHAW FESTIVALs. The Piggery, near North Hatley, offered in turn a SUMMER STOCK alternative to Lennoxville. Founded in 1964 as an amateur theatre, it turned professional in 1972.

Small audience bases and severe funding cutbacks eventually led to the demise of Festival Lennoxville and the Saidye Bronfman Centre's theatre seasons in the early 1980s. Centaur Theatre survived and now has two theatres in continuous operation. The past five years have also seen a growth in anglophone DINNER THEATRE, ALTERNATE THEATRE, and companies—such as Black Theatre Workshop—that portray the reality of Montreal's varied cultural communities. Playwrights' Workshop, and the revitalized Quebec Drama Festival, have also given a boost to English theatre in Quebec.

JONATHAN RITTENHOUSE

Quebec, Theatre in (French). A precarious francophone enclave in a predominantly anglophone North America, Quebec society (now numbering some 5 million francophones) has nevertheless been able to preserve its distinct cultural character since the arrival of the French colonists. Under the French colonial regime (1534-1760), New France—which soon extended from Acadia to Louisiana—maintained sporadic theatrical activity that depended primarily on imported plays. Corneille's *Héraclius*, for example, was performed in Quebec City in 1652, scarcely four years after its Paris première, and his *Le Cid* may have been staged there as early as 1646. And in the winter of 1693-4 Governor Frontenac arranged for productions of Corneille's *Nicomède* and Racine's *Mithridate*. But in 1694, when he decided to produce Molière's *Tartuffe*, he ran into fierce opposition from Mgr de Saint-Vallier, the bishop of Quebec, who considered the play an intolerable attack on religion; the affair ended with the withdrawal of the project after the bishop agreed to pay the expenses already incurred by the governor. This first conflict between the theatre and the Church presaged the many restrictions placed on Quebec theatre right up until the 1950s. (See CENSORSHIP.)

Réceptions—such as Marc LESCARBOT's *THÉÂTRE DE NEPTUNE EN LA NOUVELLE-FRANCE*, performed at Port Royal on 14 Nov. 1606—and religious and pedagogic drama (in the Jesuit colleges) also occurred sporadically in the seventeenth and early eighteenth centuries (see DRAMA IN FRENCH), but given the opposition of the Catholic Church and the sparse population (approximately 55,000 French settlers in a vast territory *c.* 1763), it is hardly surprising that there were relatively few theatrical presentations and no permanent theatres during the French era.

Following the Conquest and the Treaty of Paris (1763), Quebec's largest cities—Montreal and Quebec—were dominated by an English-speaking administrative and commercial class; now a political and economic minority, French Canadians had to wait until the 1890s before their own professional theatre began to take root. It is one of the ironies of francophone culture in Quebec that it was the English who first performed Molière in Montreal—by English officers in Montreal in 1774 and 1776 of *Le Bourgeois gentilhomme* and *Le Médecin malgré lui* respectively.

From 1770 to 1825, when the first theatre worthy of the name opened in Montreal, amateur companies such as the Société des Jeunes Messieurs Canadiens and other théâtres de société, both in Montreal and Quebec City, performed irregularly in whatever space they could find, presenting plays from the French repertoire (Molière, Regnard, Voltaire, Beaumarchais), and inevitably incurring the wrath of the clergy—notably from Quebec City's Mgr Plessis, who waged a campaign against the theatre from the early 1790s to 1825. Joseph QUESNEL, a French immigrant, wrote three original plays: COLAS ET COLINETTE, OU LE BAILLI DUPÉ, an operetta, first performed in 1790, Les Républicains français; ou La Soirée du cabaret, composed about 1801, and L'Anglomanie; ou Dîner à l'anglaise, a one-act verse comedy, probably written in 1803.

On 21 Nov. 1825 the THEATRE ROYAL opened in Montreal. Accommodating 1,000 spectators, it attracted foreign actors such as Edmund Kean in the summer of 1826, and the following year a French touring company under the direction of Scévola Victor. After it closed in 1844 a second Theatre Royal (or Hays Theatre) produced shows from 1847 to 1851. A third Theatre Royal opened in 1852; directed until 1875 by J. W. BUCKLAND and his wife, it remained active until 1913.

Beginning in 1831, Firmin Prud'homme, a student of the great French actor François-Joseph Talma, worked assiduously with amateurs in Montreal and Quebec, gave courses, and attempted, without success, to establish the first professional francophone company in Canada. Over a period of a dozen years he produced among other plays Hamlet and Othello in translations by Jean-François Ducis, Molière's Georges Dandin, and a historical play, Napoléon à Sainte-Hélène. Original Québécois plays also began to appear. Pierre PETITCLAIR's Griphon, ou la Vengeance d'un valet was published in 1837, but not performed; his later La DONATION (1842) and Une Partie de campagne (1865) were, however, first performed in 1842 and 1857 respectively.

In 1844 Le JEUNE LATOUR by Antoine GÉRIN-LAJOIE, a tragedy in alexandrines and a pastiche of motifs from Corneille, was both performed and published. In 1862 Louis-Honoré FRÉCHETTE mounted FÉLIX POUTRÉ in Quebec City, and in 1880 Papineau in Montreal, two plays about the Patriote rebellion of 1837. Félix-Gabriel MARCHAND presented a VAUDEVILLE piece, Erreur n'est pas compte, in 1872, and published Les FAUX BRILLANTS, a melodramatic comedy of intrigue, in 1885, though it was not produced until 1905.

The dearth of French-Canadian plays performed in this period is a consequence of the strict control over theatrical productions maintained by the Church. Theatre was certainly offered in the colleges, but its function was didactic (lessons in declamation); short plays written for special occasions were fundamentally edifying. French touring companies were also condemned by the bishops—Mgr Taschereau in Quebec City and Mgr Bourget in Montreal. Nevertheless the tours—American and British, as well as French—multiplied, indicating that a francophone audience, hungry for theatre in any language, had been established despite clerical disapproval. Among the early touring companies were Alfred Mayard in 1871 with a program of operetta and comic opera, and Achille Fay-Génot and his Société dramatique française in 1874; in 1878 the Troupe Saint-Louis of New Orleans, directed by Alphonse-Victor Brazeau (whose forebears were French-Canadian), visited the province. A series of eight important tours by Sarah Bernhardt began in 1880 (the others took place in 1891, 1896, 1905, twice in 1911, 1916, and 1917) in a contemporary romantic repertoire that included Victor Hugo, Victorien Sardou, and Alexandre Dumas fils. Other tours that made their way to Montreal, and occasionally to Quebec City, included the Coquelin l'aîné company (1889, 1893, and 1896), the company of Comédie-Française actor Jean Mounet-Sully in 1894—whose classical repertoire of Racine, Shakespeare, and Hugo had only a limited success—and that of the actress Réjane (1895), offering contemporary plays such as Sardou's and Emile Moreau's Madame Sans-Gêne.

In the 1890s professional francophone theatre made its début in Quebec, and the first career-actors appeared. During this decade over 340 francophone shows were produced—in 1,575 performances—which contrasts sharply with preceding decades. These figures amounted respectively to fourteen and eighteen per cent of the total theatrical activity at the time. From 1893 on, Montreal's Empire Theatre, although managed by anglophones, was the province's principal French-language theatre; the Compagnie Franco-Canadienne (founded in 1887) offered one season there (1893-4) without much success, after which the Théâtre de l'Opéra français played there for three seasons. The Société Saint-Jean-Baptiste established a precedent by funding the construction of a francophone theatre in Montreal, the MONUMENT NATIONAL, which opened in 1894 and featured mainly amateur companies, such as that

Quebec, Theatre in (French)

of Elzéar Roy, which from 1898 to 1901 offered its popular *Soirées de famille*. After the short-lived venture of Antoine Godeau's and Léon Petitjean's THÉÂTRE DES VARIÉTÉS (1898-9), the THÉÂTRE NATIONAL, founded by actor/playwright Julien DAOUST, became in 1900 the principal centre of dramatic art in Montreal. When Paul CAZENEUVE, a French actor who had been influenced by American theatre, took over as artistic director in 1901, he opened the way for a repertoire whose variety compared favourably with the offerings of the touring companies. At the same time, from 1902 to 1908, the Théâtre des Nouveautés was presenting contemporary French plays, such as *La Rafale* by Henri Bernstein, which was subsequently banned by Mgr Bruchési in 1907. And in 1903 it was Quebec City's turn to acquire an important theatre, L'AUDITORIUM (later Le Capitol), which attracted professional shows from Montreal as well as local amateur groups. Francophone theatre continued to develop, despite the arrival of silent films, until the Depression in the 1930s. Theatres and companies multiplied: the Nationoscope (1912), the Canadien-Français (1912), the Saint-Denis (1916), the Chantecler (1918), and the Arcade (1918). Eugène Lassalle, a French-born actor, opened a private conservatoire, still active, in 1907. And in 1923 the Quebec government gave its first grant for the study of professional acting to Antoinette GIROUX, who promptly headed for Paris.

After 1922 many more French companies began touring in Quebec: Maurice de Feraudy's in 1922 and 1924; the Théâtre de la Porte Saint-Martin in 1924 and 1928; the Théâtre de l'Odéon (directed by Firmin Gémier) in 1924; the Cécile Sorel company, the company of Sacha Guitry and Yvonne Printemps, as well as that of Gabrielle Dorziat-Georges Mauloy in 1927; and the Eve Francis company in 1928 and 1929.

The quantity and quality of French-Canadian drama during this period was minimal, though actor-authors such as Julien Daoust, Henry DEYGLUN, Léon Petitjean, and Henri Rollin can be said to have paved the way for the next generation. Petitjean's and Rollin's 1921 melodrama *AURORE L'ENFANT MARTYRE* enjoyed a long stage life.

This period also saw the appearance and the flowering of improvisational burlesque theatre—a direct descendant of American variety theatre—that was initially entirely anglophone but became francophone after 1920 with the troupe of Olivier GUIMOND *père*. Despite the legitimate theatre's disdain for it, burlesque continued to attract large audiences until the 1950s, when it was hard hit by the arrival of television. (See BURLESQUE.)

During the Depression theatrical activity slowed down considerably, but two new companies helped professional theatre survive: the THÉÂTRE STELLA (1930-5), started by the Barry-Duquesne company, and the MONTREAL REPERTORY THEATRE (1930-46), directed by Martha ALLAN, which opened a French-language section under Mario Duliani. In Quebec City a group of professionals established Les Artistes Associés (1936-42). During these difficult years actors and playwrights turned to radio (see RADIO DRAMA IN QUEBEC).

Few new plays for live theatre made any impact. Playwrights such as Léopold HOULÉ (*Le Presbytère en fleurs*, 1929) and Yvette MERCIER-GOUIN (*Cocktail*, 1935; *Le Jeune Dieu*, 1936) scarcely created anything beyond pleasant fare. More ambitious was Gustave LAMARCHE, a Saint-Viateur priest who drew his inspiration from the Bible and from the works of Paul Claudel; but since his plays focused on ideology or spiritual themes, and indeed mysticism, they were of little influence outside religious circles.

Nevertheless, in 1937 three initiatives helped to reshape the theatrical landscape and to provide the climate for a great leap forward. First, the founding of the Union des Artistes gave theatre artists professional status and a lever for negotiating with producers. Second, the radio début of Gratien GELINAS's Fridolin character, which led to a long series of annual shows (*FRIDOLINONS*, 1938-46) at the Monument National, for the first time provided a large francophone audience from all walks of life with a genuine mirror of their society—an unassuming one, but one in which they could recognize themselves. These revues represented, in a satirical vein, a new control by French Canadians of the socio-cultural reality of Quebec and signalled an irreversible change in their attitudes. Finally, Father Émile LEGAULT, a Sainte-Croix priest who was also a first-class director, founded Les COMPAGNONS DE SAINT-LAURENT (1937-52), an amateur company that was destined to play a decisive role in the search for a more effective language for Quebec theatre.

In the 1930s and 1940s the theatre began to gain social legitimacy, thanks to the help of enlightened priests who, while advocating caution and staying within the bounds of moral orthodoxy, challenged anti-theatrical obscurantism. It is also clear that the times were ripe for change and that ecclesiastical veto no longer had its previous power. Taking advantage of the freedom in the air, three professional companies were founded in 1941 alone: La Comédie de Montréal (1941-3), Le Jeune Colombier (1941-44?) in Montreal, and Les Comédiens de Québec (1941-57). From 1943 to 1948 Pierre DAGENAIS led L'ÉQUIPE in Montreal, mounting some brilliant productions, including Shakespeare's *Songe d'une nuit d'été* (*A Midsummer Night's Dream*) in 1945, performed in the gardens of l'Ermitage, and in the following year the North American première of Jean-Paul Sartre's *Huis Clos*.

In 1946 there were some 6,000 regular theatregoers in Montreal, a number that meant that new companies could expect to last longer than their predecessors. Thus the THÉÂTRE DU RIDEAU VERT, founded by Yvette BRIND'AMOUR in 1948, is still active. In 1951 the THÉÂTRE DU NOUVEAU MONDE set up shop—permanently, as it turned out, thanks to the joint efforts of two of its founders, Jean GASCON and Jean-Louis ROUX. These two companies also contributed to the establishment of new production standards for Quebec theatre, putting them on a par with those of major European companies. Their repertoires favoured classical and well-known contemporary playwrights.

It was at this time that painter Paul-Émile Borduas's controversial manifesto *Refus Global* (1948) accused traditional French-Canadian culture of stifling creativity and urged artists to adopt a libertarian program. The subsequent avant-garde movement— composed of painters, choreographers, and of poet and playwright Claude GAUVREAU— foreshadowed the cultural changes that would occur in Quebec during the 1960s and beyond. Gauvreau's own theatrical career proved difficult and his intensely dramatic plays did not attract much attention until after his suicide in 1971. 1948 also saw the première of Gratien Gélinas's *TIT-COQ*, the success of which stimulated other play-

Calderón's La Vie est un songe, *Théâtre du Rideau Vert, 1966, with Yvette Brind'Amour and Gérard Poirier*

wrights, including Marcel DUBÉ, Jacques LANGUIRAND, Jacques FERRON, and Françoise LORANGER.

In Montreal theatrical activity continued to develop and expand. The THÉÂTRE-CLUB, founded by Monique LEPAGE and Jacques Létourneau, operated from 1953 to 1964. Paul Buissonneau, who directed the first shows by La Roulotte, a children's theatre created by the Montreal Parks Commission, founded in 1955 his own company, the THÉÂTRE DE QUAT'SOUS, which is still active. In 1958 Gratien Gélinas purchased a cinema, refurbished it, and named it the COMÉDIE-CANA-DIENNE; until 1969 he sought—with mixed results—to produce only plays by Canadian authors, both in English and in French. From 1958 until 1982 La POUDRIÈRE adopted an international program, producing plays in English and French, and occasionally in German and Italian. From 1959 to 1968 Françoise Berd directed a Little Theatre, l'Egrégore, which offered an avant-garde contemporary repertoire. In 1963 the Quebec government created the THÉÂTRE POPULAIRE DU QUÉ-BEC, with a mandate to tour all the regions of the province; it is still in operation. In 1964 Françoise Graton, Georges Groulx, and

Quebec, Theatre in (French)

Gilles PELLETIER founded the NOUVELLE COMPAGNIE THÉÂTRALE, which since its inception has been devoted to theatre for high-school students. The COMPAGNIE JEAN DUCEPPE, named for its founder, has offered since 1973 a repertoire drawn mainly from Quebec translations of successful New York and London plays. In Quebec City the founding of L'Estoc in 1957 gave a boost for more than a dozen years to professional theatre; but it was not until 1970, with the founding of the THÉÂTRE DU TRIDENT, installed in the new GRAND THÉÂTRE DE QUÉBEC complex, that Quebec City was able to offer theatrical amenities comparable to those of Montreal.

The first regular summer theatres also began to appear in the 1950s: Le Chanteclerc and Le THÉÂTRE DE LA FENIÈRE in 1957, Le THÉÂTRE DE MARJOLAINE in 1960. Their productions, featuring mainly light comedies, caught on quickly, especially since the 1970s, and today there are about fifty such seasonal companies. (See SUMMER STOCK, QUEBEC.)

Theatre in general gained strength during this period with the founding of specialized schools and the creation of government-funded programs. In 1954 Jan Doat, from France, became the first director of the CONSERVATOIRE D'ART DRAMATIQUE de Montréal, set up by the Quebec government; four years later a sister conservatory was created in Quebec City. And in 1960, this time with the support of the federal government, the NATIONAL THEATRE SCHOOL opened in Montreal. Regular funding from three levels of government—municipal, provincial, and federal—was assured by the creation of the City of Montreal Arts Council in 1955, the Canada Council in 1957, and the Quebec Ministry of Cultural Affairs in 1961.

Another important phenomenon that took root in the 1950s was the remarkable dynamism of amateur theatre. The best of these companies—Les APPRENTIS-SORCIERS (1955-68) and Les SALTIMBANQUES (1962-9) in Montreal, and La Troupe des Treize (1949-73?) at Université Laval in Quebec City—were imbued with a spirit of innovation that was soon reflected in the theatre as a whole; their explorations in European avant-garde theatre and their constant inventiveness (despite limited resources) attracted the attention of the critics and enthusiastic public support. In 1958 the founding of L'Association canadienne du théâtre amateur (ACTA) by Guy BEAULNE enabled many of these companies to combine their efforts and to offer research services and workshops. In 1972 ACTA became l'Association québécoise du jeune théâtre (AQJT), which until it disbanded in 1986 was party to the theatrical revival led by numerous alternate professional companies. (See ALTERNATE THEATRE.)

With the launching in 1960 of the Quiet Revolution, which helped link Quebec with other liberal industrialized societies, a strong current of neo-nationalism began to inflame the post-war 'baby-boom' generation, giving rise to many new plays and COLLECTIVE CREATIONS. In 1965 Le Centre d'essai des auteurs dramatiques was founded to promote the growth of contemporary Quebec dramaturgy and to encourage established companies to recognize the need for greater creativity. These advances were not long in producing results: between 1965 and 1980 an average of fifty-five creations were produced annually, the majority of them by alternate companies. Thus the winds of revolt began to blow through theatrical practice, challenging the socio-political and cultural *status quo* by denouncing the 'white niggers of America' condition of French Canadians.

The production in 1968 of *Les BELLES-SOEURS* by Michel TREMBLAY had an explosive effect on Quebec theatre, with its raw presentation of a microcosm of women expressing themselves frankly in the language of the streets—*joual*—and its portrayal of a culture and a society that had dispossessed themselves. Since this first amazing feat Tremblay has delved ever deeper. His prolific output of plays, whose incisive writing and deconstructed realism depict a heartbreaking and tragic world, has won international recognition. Another voice of the 'new Quebec theatre' was Jean-Claude GERMAIN, who directed the THÉÂTRE D'AUJOURD'HUI (founded in 1968) from 1969 to 1983 and also enriched the contemporary repertoire with some twenty-five plays—fierce satires that relentlessly analyse the history of Quebec from its founding to the present day. Other authors—Robert GURIK (*Hamlet, prince du Québec*, 1968), for example, and the prolific Jean BARBEAU (*Ben-Ur*, 1971)—have written plays that examine the collective destiny of the Quebec people and advocate their political independence. The plays of André Ricard, Michel GARNEAU, Réjean DUCHARME, and

Jeanne-Mance Delisle have expanded this probing of the collective experience, creating dramatic worlds whose impact is derived from stylistic invention and emotional intensity.

In collective creations, groups such as the GRAND CIRQUE ORDINAIRE (1969-77) and Le Théâtre Euh! (1970-8), despite their dependence on rather idiosyncratic ideologies, have contributed to the politicization of theatre. Following in their footsteps, but with a viewpoint that is more community-oriented than socially radical, are groups such as Le Théâtre Parminou and Le Théâtre de Quartier, both founded in 1975, which work willingly with citizens' groups and will perform theatre to order. (See POLITICAL AND POPULAR THEATRE.)

Along with the agitation surrounding the *séparatisme* question and the fringe activities of theatrical groups involved in specific sociopolitical problems in the 1970s, there was an affirmation of experimental theatre that to some extent espoused the surreal aims of the *Automatistes* twenty years earlier. A company like L'ESKABEL (1971), for example, called attention to itself by turning to complicated dream-like environments and a bizarre ritualistic performance style. Internationally known MIME companies such as Omnibus (1970) and CARBONE 14 (1975) gradually integrated speech about the postmodern condition into their shows. The Théâtre Expérimental de Montréal (1975), which became the NOUVEAU THÉÂTRE EXPÉRIMENTAL DE MONTRÉAL in 1979, experimented in many directions, notably by playing in a style of mockery and second-rate kitsch; it also gave birth to the LIGUE NATIONALE D'IMPROVISATION, an improvisational show based on the rules of ice hockey that has become very popular. Le Groupe de la Veillée (1973) intensely and rigorously explores the role of the actor, based on the principles of Jerzy Grotowski.

The contributions of women to Quebec theatre in the past fifteen years are noteworthy. In the wake of militant feminism, but not always identifying with it entirely, authors such as Elizabeth Bourget, Denise BOUCHER, Maryse Pelletier, and Marie LABERGE (who has also enjoyed success in Europe) have written plays that are imbued with the preoccupations of contemporary women's lives. Other playwrights, such as

France Vézina, Jovette MARCHESSAULT, Pol Pelletier, Michelle Allen, and Lise Vaillancourt, have taken a more radical approach to form and theme in their work, which bears the stamp of a heightened symbolic system. Since 1979 the Théâtre Expérimental des Femmes has been a spur to women in their search for an appropriate place in playwriting and drama. (See FEMINIST THEATRE.)

Since the 1970s important developments have also occurred in children's and youth theatre, which had previously been rather marginal, even though several companies had tried—despite a repertoire that was often shallow—to establish a tradition in this field. The founding in 1973 of the THÉÂTRE DE LA MARMAILLE, the Théâtre de l'Oeil (a puppet theatre), and the Théâtre de Carton, and in 1975 of the Théâtre du Quartier and Théâtre le Carrousel launched a very productive movement that changed methodologies, themes, and staging. (See CHILDREN'S DRAMA AND THEATRE IN FRENCH and PUPPET THEATRE.)

Since 1980 a new generation of playwrights and directors has made a name for itself by moving away from the nationalist and sociopolitical themes of the preceding decade. Although suggesting a certain disenchantment with the *indépendantiste* cause (after the defeat of the referendum on Quebec autonomy in 1980), this return to values centred on individual and personal problems—the need to think about metaphysical rather than sociological matters—also identified a fundamentally existential questioning that had its own sense of urgency.

In its own way the carnival-like but extremely parodic saga conceived by Jean-Pierre RONFARD under the title *VIE ET MORT DU ROI BOITEUX* (1981-2)—a series of six plays that took fifteen hours to present—forcibly demonstrated that under this wider freedom Québécois theatre could plunge unafraid into new artistic adventures. In 1980, with *Panique à Longueuil*, René-Daniel DUBOIS had already shown that henceforth it would be necessary to be open-minded about oddities of language and mental confusion, and that he was interested in the image of an individual living in a society that, though affluent, is increasingly policed and pre-programmed. Other new authors—such as René Gingras, Normand CHAURETTE, Claude Poissant, Michel-Marc Bouchard, and, more

Quebec, Theatre in (French)

recently, Anne Legault and Normand Canac-Marquis—have written plays in the past few years that portray, in a style that wavers between philosophical meditation and impassioned action, the dead-ends in which many of their rather stunned contemporaries find themselves.

During the 1980s several young and not-so-young companies turned to well-known international authors, such as Marguerite Duras, Rainer Fassbinder, Yukio Mishima, Peter Handke, Thomas Bernhard, Franz Xaver Kroetz, Botho Strauss, and others. This reinstatement, so to speak, of foreign drama contrasts with the desire, rampant in the preceding decade, to operate in near-self-sufficiency. It seems as if the theatrical implosion of the 1970s was succeeded by a kind of fission of the constituent atoms of Québécois theatre that impelled all the theatre people into a tremendous chain reaction. Le Théâtre Repère, founded in Quebec City in 1980, is a good example of this basic tendency in recent Quebec theatre. Headed by the versatile director Robert Lepage, this company—particularly with *Circulations* (1984) and *La Trilogie des dragons* (1985-7)—has managed to forge a link between collective creation and powerful scripts, drawing images from everyday objects, which are transformed by their dramatic function and become freighted with cross-cultural dimensions.

In barely twenty years the number of theatrical productions in Montreal has quintupled—from thirty in 1961 to over 150 per season in the 1980s; altogether nearly 300 are given in the province each year. There are now five theatre schools in Quebec, not counting degree programs in theatre at the Université du Québec à Montréal. In 1980-1 an estimated three million people attended the theatre. Scarcely fifty years after the renewal began in the 1930s, Québécois theatre is vibrant, spreading its influence not only throughout Canada but on the international scene as well. Two major biennial international festivals, La Quinzaine internationale du théâtre of Quebec City begun in 1984 and the Festival de théâtre des Amériques in Montreal begun in 1985, have also helped Quebec theatre to gain exposure.

Approximately 100 theatres received funding in 1986 from various levels of government, sharing a total of about $11 million. In a stagnant financial situation, however, with the state encouraging unprofitable companies to woo private enterprise for the support the government refuses to give, the theatrical milieu is bound to react. Theatre artists and companies have given much time and energy to organizing themselves since the 1970s. Since the États généraux du théâtre professionnel au Québec in 1981—which led to the creation of the Conseil québécois du théâtre (1983)—theatre professionals, actors and producers alike, have at their disposal a valuable instrument for creating debate and applying pressure to try to steer government administrators towards more generous cultural policies. Obtaining a suitable level of public funding for an art that has reached maturity but whose requirements are still not understood by the community is the challenge that awaits Quebec theatre on the threshold of the 1990s.

See also DRAMA IN FRENCH; Jean Béraud, *350 ans de théâtre au Canada français* (1958); Jean Hamelin, *Le Renouveau du théâtre au Canada français* (1962); Michel Bélair, *Le Nouveau théâtre québécois* (1973); Baudoin Burger, *L'Activité théâtrale au Québec (1765-1825)* (1974); Jacques Cotnam, *Le Théâtre québécois, instrument de contestation sociale et politique* (1976); *Le Théâtre canadien-français* (1976), ed. Paul Wyczynski, Bernard Julien, and Hélène Beauchamp (*Archives des lettres canadiennes*, vol. 5); Jean Laflamme and Rémi Tourangeau, *L'Église et le théâtre au Québec* (1979); Adrien Gruslin, *Le Théâtre et l'État au Québec* (1981); Jean-Marc Larrue, *Le Théâtre à Montréal à la fin du XIXe siécle* (1981); Leonard E. Doucette, *Theatre in French Canada: Laying the Foundations 1606-1867* (1984); Pierre Lavoie, *Pour suivre le théâtre au Québec. Les Ressources documentaires* (1985); and *Répertoire du Centre d'essai des auteurs dramatiques. Des auteurs, des pièces: portraits de la dramaturgie québécoise* (1985), ed. Chantale Cusson.

GILBERT DAVID

Queen Elizabeth Theatre. An all-purpose auditorium built and owned by the City of Vancouver, it opened on a site at Hamilton and Georgia Streets, on the periphery of the downtown core, in July 1959, following many years of campaigning by local groups (notably the Junior League and Community Arts Council) for the city's first major auditorium since the loss of the VANCOUVER OPERA HOUSE in 1912. Designed by Affleck and Associates of Montreal, the theatre seats 2,815 in a severely undecorative auditorium quite without roots in any tradition of theatrical architecture. The stage measures 114' × 64', and the proscenium is 70' wide and 30' high. The QET has had to combine the essentially incompatible roles of concert hall and theatre-cum-opera house. Its acoustics were thought to be particularly inappropriate for music and orchestral conductors were reluctant to locate the orchestra on the stage in an acoustical shell, preferring an extended platform. Critics were silenced only by the conversion of the acoustically superb ORPHEUM THEATRE into a concert hall in 1977. The QET continues as home to the performances of the Vancouver Opera Association, and to the larger theatrical, dance, and musical touring companies. Its very size makes it a theatre for special occasions rather than for regular theatrical activities.

R.B. TODD

Quesnel, Joseph (1746–1809). Born in St-Malo, France, to a prosperous merchant family, he received a solid classical education at the Collège St-Louis before entering the family business. After travelling extensively to India, Africa, the Caribbean, and South America, his ship, carrying supplies for the rebellious American colonies, was intercepted off Newfoundland by the Royal Navy in 1779. Family connections with Governor Haldimand may explain his release from custody, his naturalization, and his immediate establishment in Montreal where, in April of the following year, he married into a successful fur-trading family. Quesnel was soon actively involved in that trade, travelling to the West and American Southwest. He visited France in 1788–9, but the Revolution made it impossible to return thereafter. In the 1790s he retired to an estate in Boucherville, near Montreal, to lead the life of a cultivated *seigneur*. Most of his poetry and two of his three completed plays stem from this period.

Soon after his arrival in Montreal, Quesnel had become involved in local theatrical and musical activity. On his return from France in 1789 he helped found a group of amateur players in a 'Society Theatre'. But even before its first performance the company, and theatre in general, were bitterly attacked from the pulpit by the *curé* of the parish to which Quesnel belonged. The seven members of the troupe protested to the diocesan hierarchy and were partially upheld, the Bishop counselling discreet intervention by the clergy through the confessional rather than public attacks. In their brief season Quesnel's troupe presented six plays, among them his own best-known work, *COLAS ET COLINETTE; OU, LE BAILLI DUPÉ*, the first operetta written in North America.

First performed on 14 Jan. 1790, *Colas et Colinette* was a distinct success. The warm reception it received in an 1805 revival led Quesnel to write a didactic 'Adresse aux jeunes acteurs', published in the *Quebec Gazette* on 7 Feb. 1805, in which he counsels budding actors to seek verisimilitude, naturalness of diction and gesture, and (obviously mindful of the Church's opposition) above all to avoid the slightest hint of immorality in the texts they choose. Quesnel completed two other plays, *Les Républicains français* and *L'Anglomanie*, and began another operetta, *Lucas et Cécile*, part of the score of which survives.

Les Républicains français, subtitled *La Soirée du cabaret*, is a savage polemic in prose, a bitter parody of the worst excesses of the French Revolution, which had ruined the Quesnel family's business and caused the execution of some of his relatives. As with his first play, there is a significant musical component, his six characters borrowing popular French airs to intone their lampoons. The play falls clearly within the category of political theatre, the most vigorous and most original genre to appear in Lower Canada. Although it seems never to have been performed, and was not published until 1970, it was probably written in 1801 and circulated in manuscript. *L'Anglomanie; ou, Dîner à l'anglaise* has a similar history. Probably written in 1803, it is a short verse-comedy that ridicules the attempt by some members of French-Canadian society to adopt British manners, customs, and speech. The topical content of *Les Républicains français* no doubt militated against its publication or performance in the author's lifetime. *L'Anglomanie* remained in manuscript—it was first published in 1932–3 in *Le Canada français*—because the characters it portrays were copied from well-known, identifiable originals in the little society of Boucherville. This is a pity, for it is a good-humoured satire of a perennial

Quesnel

French-Canadian problem, and is as astute as it would have been effective when performed.

Joseph Quesnel was the outstanding author of his age in French Canada, the first playwright after the French regime whose works have survived. The short-lived troupe he helped found in 1789 modernized the repertory performed by local players; its example would be followed by the amateur groups that succeeded it.

See Baudoin Burger, *L'Activité théâtrale au Québec (1765-1825)*, I (1974).

L.E. DOUCETTE

R

Radio Drama in English. Since the late 1920s English-language radio drama on the Canadian Broadcasting Corporation has offered Canadian and international drama to listeners across the nation, and for two decades (from the early 1940s) it was Canada's first genuine national theatre. Twice a week the CBC Drama Department presented plays to national audiences in the millions; and for regional audiences there were weekly series of local plays. Through these activities the CBC provided a showcase, training, and financial support for the vast majority of Canadian directors, authors, composers, and technicians. Theatre professionals trained in the Radio Drama Department made significant contributions to the development of theatre in other forms starting in the early fifties, including CBC TELEVISION DRAMA. Many of the major roles in the early years of Ontario's STRATFORD FESTIVAL were filled by radio actors such as Frances HYLAND, Douglas RAIN, William SHATNER, John COLICOS, Lorne GREENE, and Christopher PLUMMER. Other CBC radio drama professionals—such as Fletcher Markle, Bernard Braden, and Robert Allan—eventually moved into the radio, television, stage, and film industries in both Britain and the U.S.

Unlike drama on the U.S. radio networks, which had its golden age in the 1930s and virtually disappeared when American sponsors switched to television in the mid-1940s, the CBC Drama Department has provided a crucial continuity for Canadian audiences, actors, and writers for more than half a century. Almost every Canadian playwright in

Lorne Greene performing on radio

the last fifty years has had plays produced on the CBC; some, like George RYGA, have had many more CBC productions than stage productions. Many Canadian playwrights and actors still earn part of their income from radio drama. For six decades radio drama has been inextricably interwoven with the history of Canadian theatre.

Radio Drama as Theatre. The ability to communicate multiple layers of meaning simultaneously—facilitated in television, film, and live theatre by visual resources—is limited on radio because of the danger of confusion in the aural medium. On the other hand, the simplicity of radio commands the listener's close attention through vocal expression, accent, narrative description, sound effects, and music. Radio drama enjoys an extraordinary freedom compared with stage, film, and television drama, since it can move instantaneously from place to place and time to time, and from the external to the internal world.

Although the production of a radio drama takes place in a control room and one or more soundproof studios, it was from the beginning until the end of the golden age a live performance, including members of an orchestra who provided the background, atmosphere, and bridges. With the coming of electronic tape and new recording techniques in the 1950s, live performance was replaced by a very different method that involved canned music and sound effects, a non-chronological production schedule approximating a film-shooting schedule, and the mixing and editing of the final product in a manner similar to that used in the film industry. The earlier sense of immediacy and performance was replaced by a greater flexibility of effect, and greater control of the final product. Despite the difference between the two techniques and the resulting products, some aspects of the radio play did not change: the directness of the communication, and the need to provide the listener's imagination with aural cues in order to follow the action of the play.

Early History. From 1919—when the first public radio station in North America, Montreal's XWA, began broadcasting—radio in Canada paralleled the commercial organization of American radio. The distinctiveness of Canadian radio began with the establishment in Canada of the first North American radio network. This 'commercial' network was begun by Canadian National Railways in 1924, several years before NBC, the first U.S. network. The CN Radio Department was not commercial in the American sense: there was no program sponsorship or selling of program time. (CN Radio broadcast commercials only for its own transportation services.) The CN chose to broadcast programs mainly of a cultural and service nature: music, drama, and information. The first CN radio station, CNRA, opened at Moncton in 1924, and its network was complete by the end of 1925, with stations in Halifax, Montreal, Toronto, Ottawa, Winnipeg, Calgary, and Vancouver. At first most of the programs were local, with network broadcasts for only one hour daily.

CNRA broadcast the first Canadian radio play, *The Rosary* (author unknown), in 1925. Like the other CN radio stations, CNRA continued to broadcast occasional plays for the next few years—often popular American stage plays such as Winchell Smith's comedy *The Fortune Hunter* and James Montgomery's farce *Nothing but the Truth*—though there was little attempt to adapt them to the new medium. The broadcast schedules occasionally offered the printed 'program' of a production, including descriptions of characters, plot, and scenes—a helpful aid to the audience's understanding of the radio production, which lacked the visual elements of theatre.

The first CN radio-drama series—that is, a weekly anthology series of individual plays—was created and produced in 1927 by Jack Gillmore, a Vancouver writer, actor, and opera singer, and broadcast over the Vancouver station, CNVR, which gave his company and the series their name: the 'CNVR Players'. (This series anticipated the first serious American radio-play series, the 'NBC Radio Guild', by two years.) Gillmore invented the basic techniques of communicating drama in sound: part of his method was to produce plays in which the text was central. He produced over a hundred plays in the four years of the CNVR series: adaptations from the European and American theatre repertory, the first Shakespeare play on radio in North America, and original Canadian plays. The 'CNVR Players' series, however, did not survive the nationalization of the CN network in 1932, which created the first Canadian government-controlled broadcasting network, the CRBC (Canadian Radio Broadcasting Commission).

'The Romance of Canada' radio drama series, broadcast in 1931, helped push the government towards the nationalization of broadcasting by convincing Canadians of the value of a national radio network. The first complete series of original Canadian plays on a national network, it consisted of documentary dramas on Canadian historical themes, written by Merrill DENISON and produced and directed by Tyrone GUTHRIE. Denison had suggested Guthrie as director after reading Guthrie's own radio plays, written in the late 1920s while he was a producer with the

Radio Drama in English

fledgeling BBC. Guthrie's ideas on radio drama, first tested at length on 'The Romance of Canada' series, greatly influenced his later theories on the staging and acting of Shakespeare. The popularity of the fourteen-play series induced CN to schedule a second season. Production was taken over (Guthrie having returned to England) by one of Guthrie's repertory actors on the series, Rupert Caplan, a young Montreal actor who had worked in New York with Eugene O'Neill at the Provincetown Playhouse. Caplan's career as the senior drama producer in Montreal spans the periods of the CN network and the CRBC as well as the CBC (the publicly owned broadcasting corporation that was created in 1936, replacing the CRBC), where from 1936 to his retirement in 1968 he was Montreal director of drama.

The most impressive Drama Department among 'private' stations in the 1930s was that of CKUA, Edmonton, the station of the Extension Department of the Univ. of Alberta, which broadcast an influential drama series from 1928 to 1941. This ambitious series, part of CKUA's cultural programming, had no equal in Canada or the U.S. for much of the 1930s. Directed from 1929 by Sheila Marryat, it included many original plays by local dramatists, including Elsie Park GOWAN and Gwen Pharis RINGWOOD (who took over production briefly on Marryat's departure in 1939). CKUA was the active centre of an unofficial Western 'network' of stations (including CNVR) that spread CKUA's productions throughout the prairies and B.C.

In Winnipeg, Esse W. LJUNGH, a Swedish-trained theatre professional, organized, wrote, and produced radio dramas on station CKY from the mid-1930s. Ljungh became head of drama for CBC Winnipeg in 1939. One of his well-known productions, on which the actor Tommy TWEED worked, was the serial of small-town Canadian life, 'The Youngbloods of Beaver Bend'. In 1947 Ljungh moved to Toronto to work with Andrew ALLAN in the CBC's National Drama Department. He became national supervisor after Allan's retirement in 1955.

A number of Toronto stations produced radio dramas in the 1930s. The local CRBC station, CRCY, increased the number of its series, including popular shows, documentaries, and serious dramas, many of them for the expanded national service. Among playwrights, the work of Horace Brown is significant. Beginning as the CN Drama Department script editor, Brown also wrote many plays from the late 1920s for CN, CRBC, CBC, and (in the 1950s) for Ontario Hydro Radio. Radio drama also emanated from the private Toronto station CFRB, where John HOLDEN performed in the early 1930s. Holden's professional repertory company provided several live radio-drama broadcasts to the CBC. The producer who directed Holden at CFRB was the young Andrew Allan, soon to make his mark in the CBC.

The Golden Age of CBC Radio Drama. At CFRB Allan gained much valuable writing, editing, production, and on-air announcing experience between 1933 and 1938, while occasionally writing plays and adaptations for the CRBC and CBC. In 1938 he travelled to London to work in offshore commercial British radio, returning to Canada in 1939 as director of drama at CBC Vancouver. There he gradually built up a repertory team of actors, writers, and technicians, including Lister SINCLAIR and John Drainie, as well as Fletcher Markle, whose experimental scripts for the series 'Baker's Dozen' in 1942 made his and Allan's reputation. Allan succeeded Rupert Lucas as CBC's national supervisor of Drama in 1943. His goals were: to create a genuine national Canadian theatre across the country; to promote original and experimental drama; and to produce plays that would help bring about his perception of a better world—a goal stimulated by the Depression and the war. Gathering his repertory group around him—many from his earlier Vancouver team—in Jan. 1944 he began the hour-long national drama series 'Stage 44', the country's first 'national theatre', as well as a showcase for Canadian playwriting and acting talents.

In 1947 CBC Toronto's second important national series began: 'CBC Wednesday Night'. Unlike the 'Stage' series, which featured Canadian plays in at least half of its productions, 'Wednesday Night' concentrated on British and European classics, as well as on the best of modern American, British, and European plays, in a prime-time slot of up to four hours. The guiding force behind the 'Wednesday Night' series was Allan's administrative superior, Harry Boyle. Production of this series was shared by the four senior CBC producers: Allan, whose major interests were Canadian plays, Shakespeare and the Elizabethans, and Greek drama; Esse Ljungh, who contributed mainly modern European plays, especially Scandinavian and German drama; Frank Willis, who had earlier come to Toronto from Halifax to become head of Features, and was primarily interested in drama-documentaries and epics; and Rupert Caplan, who, from his base in Montreal, concentrated on modern American and Canadian playwrights, as well as modern French drama.

Though Allan and the CBC administrators were determined to have a strong central 'national theatre' base in Toronto, from as early as 1939 the CBC had also been setting up regional drama production centres across the country, a network that was completed during the war. In each of these centres there was a weekly regional drama series, though they were at most a half-hour in length. These series ('Halifax Theatre', 'Vancouver Theatre' and so on) were showcases for local writing and acting talent, and, like the national series in Toronto, a source of training and income for local theatre professionals.

By 1947, with Allan at the helm and strong national and regional drama institutions on the air, the CBC was well into its golden age of radio drama. In addition to his three senior production colleagues, Allan's team included a national script editor, Alice Frick, who vetted scripts from across the country and distributed them to the appropriate producers. Among Allan's many talented playwrights were Len PETERSON (*BURLAP BAGS*, 1946, *Man with a Bucket of Ashes*, 1952); Joseph SCHULL (*The Jinker*, 1955); W.O. MITCHELL (*The Devil's Instrument*, 1949); Allan King (*Who Killed Cock Robin?*, 1952); Patricia JOUDRY (*Mother is Watching*, 1952); Fletcher Markle (*Baker's Dozen*, 1942); Gerald Noxon (*Mr Arcularis*, 1948); Lister Sinclair (*Socrates*, 1947, *Hilda Morgan*, 1949); Harry Boyle (*The MacDonalds of Oak Valley*, 1949); and Reuben Ship (*The Investigator*, 1954—a brave and trenchant satire on Senator McCarthy).

The golden age of Canadian radio drama lasted for more than a decade after the Stratford Festival, other new Canadian stage companies, and television superseded it in the early 1950s. In fact the number of CBC drama productions increased in the 1960s, and though Allan retired as national drama supervisor in 1955, his colleagues Caplan, Willis, and Ljungh continued their radio

work until the end of the sixties.

Later Radio Drama. Beginning in 1952, the development of CBC television drama—which competed with radio for funding, professional actors, and audiences—eventually damaged the Radio Drama Department. The growth of the legitimate stage, supported by the newly created (1957) Canada Council, exacerbated the loss of radio audiences. With the arrival of new technology and of electronic tape, producers experimented both in theme and technique, influenced by the new radio drama of Germany, Italy, and elsewhere.

Of the radio-drama producers who made their reputation in the late 1950s and the 1960s two stand out as exceptional: John Reeves and Gerald Newman. Reeves, who continues to produce in Toronto, began in 1957 with 'Wednesday Night'. He was the last producer of 'Stage' in the mid-1970s. His interest in poetic experimental theatre is evident both in the works he produced and in his own plays, such as *A Beach of Strangers* and *Triptych*. Gerald Newman was CBC Vancouver region drama supervisor from the early 1950s until he took a position at Simon Fraser University in 1965. During his time at CBC he was responsible for the Western Region's major drama series, 'Pacific Playhouse', while creating productions not only for the 'Wednesday Night' series but also for his western variant, 'CBU Sunday Night'. Newman's productions included classical and modern European drama, as well as modern Canadian plays. His experiments emphasized the text, produced usually without music and sound effects; he made full use of the possibilities of taping and editing of his productions in contrast to the earlier tradition of live performance.

Radio drama broadcasting in the last two decades has undergone a radical transformation, the most crucial change being the shift from live to taped performance. Whereas a golden-age 're-broadcast' was normally a new live performance, plays on tape can be held back for many months before broadcast; they can be cut up, or used on different series; or they can be re-broadcast by simply replaying the original tape. The effect of a dramatic performance is thus not only transformed by new production methods, but modified by new broadcasting practices. There have also been important changes in the nature of radio in general, and in its audiences: it has lost its original function as the country's main entertainment and advertising medium, and the content has become mainly music programs, not drama. Many of the regional series of individual dramas had disappeared by the 1970s, and regional producers' work began to be slotted into national series. An excellent regional series of serious plays from Vancouver, 'The Hornby Collection', continued but it was not heard on the national network.

At the beginning of the 1980s, however, there was a resurgence of interest in radio drama. Under the new national drama supervisor, Susan RUBES, appointed in 1980, the CBC gave new life to the 'Stage' series under the title 'Sunday Matinée', offering original Canadian plays. Furthermore, in 1980 new drama series were created: 'Audience' and 'Celebration', both of which followed the cultural formula of 'Wednesday Night'. A new mystery-fantasy series, 'Nightfall', also premièred that year. In 1982 the anthology series 'Saturday Stereo Theatre' began, and, in 1983, 'Sunday Stereo Theatre'. A daily interview show, 'Morningside', began to broadcast Canadian plays in five parts. These series broadcast seventy new plays between 1981 and 1983, about fifty of which were original Canadian plays. In 1983 the CBC completed a million-dollar refurbishing of CBC Toronto's radio-drama Studio G, adding the latest in electronic equipment; the same has recently been done in Halifax. Unfortunately, because of CBC budget cuts a number of the series were cancelled by the end of 1984.

Nevertheless, what remains is encouraging. The 'Sunday Matinée' anthology series of original Canadian plays still exists, produced in turn in the drama studios in Toronto, Vancouver, Halifax, and Calgary. The 'Saturday Stereo Theatre' series also remains, offering mainly serial plays, but also original Canadian works. A fascinating mystery-fantasy series called 'Vanishing Point' began in 1984, produced by William LANE in Toronto, and a popular documentary series, 'Scales of Justice', has been produced since 1982. 'Morningside' continues to offer Canadian plays in daily episodes. And the 'Royal Canadian Air Farce', a Canadian comedy show (recorded live), continues season after season, showing in the most basic way how radio can create drama out of pure sounds.

Canadian radio drama, then, remains healthy. The new formula combines entertainment and experiment. Though much changed in response to current tastes in radio, the long tradition of the first national theatre on the air continues.

See Howard Fink and Brian Morrison, *Canadian National Theatre on the Air 1925-1961. CBC-CRBC-CNR Radio Drama in English: A Descriptive Bibliography and Union List* (1983); *All the Bright Company. Radio Drama Produced by Andrew Allan* (1987), ed. Howard Fink and John Jackson; N. Alice Frick, *Image in the Mind. CBC Radio Drama 1944-1954* (1987).   HOWARD FINK

Radio Drama in Quebec. Since 1930 radio—principally stations CKAC, CBF, and CBF-FM—has made a major contribution to the development of Québécois dramatic literature, acting, and directing. In the 1930s many programs on CKAC depended on adaptations of stage plays, but subsequently some 300 Quebec authors have written over 3,000 plays for radio.

Radio-Canada: CBF and CBF-FM. Unquestionably the leading Quebec radio dramatist is Robert Choquette, who began his radio career with a series of plays on Quebec folklore, followed in 1934 by a series of moralistic one-act social comedies for CRCM, 'Le Fabuliste La Fontaine à Montréal' (rebroadcast on CBF in 1951). In 1935 he wrote his first radio serial, 'Le Curé de village', and a summer series, 'Vacances d'artistes'—about vacationing artists, actors, and musicians—that featured a great deal of extravagant clowning and witty dialogue. Other summer series included 'Théâtre de ma guitare' by Félix LECLERC, directed by Florent FORGET (1946), and 'Théâtre Estival', directed by Paul Leduc (June-Sept. 1946).

Meanwhile Judith Jasmin directed 'Entrée des artistes' (1944-5), which included plays by Gérard Bessette, Henriette Giroux, Léopold HOULÉ, J. Laroche, and Mario Duliani. A series directed by Pierre DAGENAIS in 1946-7, 'L'Équipe aux quatre vents', offered plays by Guy Saint-Pierre, S. Gentillon, C.-H. Grignon, Pierre Dagenais, and Carl Dubuc. An epoch-making series, 'Les Voix du pays' (1945-8), directed by Judith Jasmin and Armand Plante, focused on works by Claude Aubry, Gérard Bessette, Dominique Perret, Hélène Frechette, Guy DUFRESNE, J. Gilbert, Cecile Chabot, Alfred Rousseau, Jeanne Frey, Jeanne Daigle, Charlotte Savary, Yvette

Naubert, Germaine Guèvremont, Vanna Ducharme, Françoise LORANGER, Guy Saint-Pierre, Yves THÉRIAULT, Michelle Thériault, Claude Robillard, Paul Dumont-Frenette, Jean-Louis Béland, and Jean Léonard. These weekly half-hour broadcasts promoted Quebec playwrights in a field formerly dominated by French authors. The late 1940s also saw a popular series of detective plays, 'Qui est le coupable?', broadcast from 29 Apr. 1947 to 15 Oct. 1948, written by several authors, including Claude GAUVREAU.

The 1950s opened with 'Le Théâtre des nouveautés' (1950), directed by Nöel Gauvin; 'J'ai rêvé cette nuit' (1951-2), a series of fanciful and humorous plays by Eugène Cloutier; 'Le Théâtre canadien' (1953-5), which produced works by Henri Letondal, Ernest CHOQUETTE, Lomer Gouin, Hubert Aquin, and Louis-Georges Carrier; and 'Le Théâtre d'été', directed for many years by Ollivier Mercier-Gouin. Short series such as 'Zone interdite' (1950), 'Le Théâtre du grand prix' (1952), 'Flagrant délit' (1955), 'Billet de faveur' (1955), and 'Les Ineffables' (1956) introduced authors Jacques LANGUIRAND, Jean-Marie Poirier, Louis Pelland, Luan Asllani, and Marcel Blouin and provided opportunities for innovation in theme—especially absurdism—and experimentation with radio aesthetics.

The most important drama series of the 1950s was 'Nouveautés dramatiques', begun by Guy BEAULNE in 1950. It was a radio-drama lab for writing and for exploring sound-effects and broadcasting aesthetics. From 15 Oct. 1950 to 15 Apr. 1962, 374 half-hour plays were presented on CBF. Following the example of France's ORTF, which during the fifties carried out extensive research into radio broadcasting and whose *Cahiers d'études de la radio-télévision* (1954-60) helped advance this research, Beaulne stimulated, through his work with young authors, a new awareness of the value of radio drama and of the rapport the director could establish between writer and audience.

During its first two years (1950-1) 'Nouveautés dramatiques' was sustained chiefly by a small group of five playwrights, principally Yves THÉRIAULT (13 of whose plays were produced), Yvette Naubert (14), Félix Leclerc (4), Charlotte Savary (3), and Marcel DUBÉ (3). Between 1952 and 1958 Thériault (25 plays) and Dubé (11) continued to write for the series. Other playwrights included Louis-

Georges Carrier (12 plays), Bernard Daumale (16), Jean Faucher (4), Luan Asllani (13), Noel Guyves (5), Louis-Martin Tard (5), Claude JASMIN (4), Claude Gauvreau (4), Marcel Cabay (10), François Moreau (20), Jacques Godbout (4), Jacques Antoons (9), Maurice Champagne (4), and Jean-Raymond Boudou (4). During this period the directors were Lorenzo Godin, Paul Legendre, and Jean-Guy Pilon. The period from 1959 to 1962 included Thériault again (7), along with Jean-Raymond Boudou (6), Maurice Champagne (2), and François Moreau (2), and several new authors: François de Vernal (4), Patrick Straram (4), Maurice Gagnon (4), Ollivier Mercier-Gouin (6), and Hubert Aquin. Ollivier Mercier-Gouin, Jean-Guy Pilon, and Gilles Delorme were the directors.

Faced with competition from television, radio-drama production in Quebec declined significantly in the 1960s and 1970s, but some important series were still broadcast. André Giroux wrote a dozen plays in 1960 for 'Le Théâtre de Québec', while 'Studio d'essai' was directed by Madeleine Gérôme from 1968 to 1970. The long-running (1971-85) 'Premières' on CBF-FM produced plays by a host of playwrights under directors Madeleine Gérôme, Roger Citerne, and Ollivier Mercier-Gouin. The experimental series 'Escales' and 'La Feuillaison', however, were both dropped in the 1980s, despite their success in developing the skills of directors such as Gérard Binet, Jean-Pierre Saulnier, and Jean Piché—with contributions as well from directors from across the CBF network: Guy Lagacé (Ottawa), Michel Gariépy (Quebec City), Bertholet Charron (Moncton), and Richard Labrie (Matane). Among the new authors of this period were Monique LaRue, Yolande Villemaire, Louise Nantel, and Hélène Ouvrard, as well as winners of the Radio-Canada drama competition established in 1972.

Like some of the private radio stations, CBF also broadcast dramatic series based on historical characters and events, such as Guy Dufresne's 'Le Ciel par-dessus les toits' (1947-55) and Charlotte Savary's 'Les Visages de l'amour' (1955-70). Robert Choquette's 'Promenades en Nouvelle-France' was produced by CRCM in 1933-4, Jean Laforest's 'L'Histoire du Canada' on CKVL, 1957-60, and Jean Monté's 'L'Histoire de Dieu' also on CKVL, 1951-61.

CKAC, 1938-50. Radio station CKAC

Radio Drama in Quebec

launched its first major dramatic series, 'Le Théâtre de chez nous', in 1938. It closed in 1947, but others followed. 'Studio d'essai de CKAC' (1947), directed by Félix Bertrand, presented works by Aimé Grandmaison, Roger Marien, Jean Desprez, and Paul Gélinas, while 'Théâtre du printemps', also broadcast in 1947, was written by Roger Marien and Ernest Pallascio-Morin. 'Le Théâtre de chez nous', however, remains CKAC's most important achievement in radio drama. For over eight years, from 31 Oct. 1938 to 22 May 1947—with only two interruptions, 4 July 1940 to 14 Feb. 1941 and 14 Nov. 1941 to 1 Jan. 1942—it had continuing success. Produced by Paul L'Anglais, it was the first radio series to commission original works. From 1938 to 1943 Henri Letondal was the sole author; in all he wrote 190 half-hour plays for the series on a wide range of subjects: war, politics, religion, as well as light romantic comedy. Between 1944 and 1947 several other writers contributed plays: Jean Laforest, Vanna Ducharme, René-O. Boivin, Aliette Brisset-Thibaudeau, Mario Duliani, Odette Coupal, Laurier Lebrun, Simon L'Anglais, Gérard Vlémincks, Alice Gastice, and Marie-Eve Liénart. From 1938 to 1942 the plays were directed by Yves Bourassa. In 1942–3 direction alternated among Gabriel and Simon L'Anglais, and Paul Guèvremont, succeeded in 1943–4 by Jacques Desbaillets and in 1944–5 by Clément Latour. Gabriel L'Anglais shared the 1946–7 season with Jean Laforest. These various directors worked with highly skilled actors, most of whom had previous radio experience. Led by Jacques Auger, the principal actors were Gaston Dauriac, Armand Leguet, Pierre Durand, Nicole Germain, Sita Riddez, Liliane Dorsenn, Jeanne Maubourg, and Antoinette GIROUX. Other excellent actors gradually enriched the original group: Albert Cloutier, Paul de Vassal, Jacques Catelain, René Coutlée, Camille Ducharme, Henri Poitras, Teddy Burns, André Treich, and François Rozet. After 1941 Clément Latour, Albert DUQUESNE, Antoine Godeau, Arthur Lefèvre, and Fred BARRY joined the company. The most important actresses between 1938 and 1942 were Marthe THIÉRY, Rose Rey-Duzil, Jeanne Demons, Juliette Huot, Marcelle Lefort, Olivette Thibault, Blanche Gauthier, and Sita Riddez. Subsequently Huguette OLIGNY, Germaine Giroux, Bella Ouellette, and Andrée Basilières joined. From 1944 to 1946 Jean-Pierre Masson, Guy Mauffette, Denis Drouin, Lucie Poitras, and Muriel Guilbaut—the principal radio actors of the period—appeared on both CBF and CKAC.

In addition to its regular drama productions, 'Le Théâtre de chez nous' also broadcast special programs on historical figures or national events. Letondal wrote dramatizations such as *Louis Fréchette*, broadcast on 23 Nov. 1939; *Terre de nos aieux*, 1 Feb. 1940—the sixty-first anniversary of the national anthem; *L'Hommage du Canada français à Lord Tweedsmuir*, 15 Feb. 1940; *Hommage à Branly*, 28 Mar. 1940; and *Malheureux Joko*, 6 June 1940, inspired by the tragic death of Mazurier, the celebrated mime. War plays were common in the early 1940s: Letondal's *Nuit à Palerme*, 13 Oct. 1943; *Dans L'ombre, ou le Coeur d'un soldat*, 27 Oct. 1943; *Le Monastère prisonnier*, 1 Mar. 1944; Jean Laforest's *Torpillage en mer*, 15 Mar. 1944, and *Le Coup d'archet*; and Aliette Brisset-Thibaudeau's *La Leçon de français*, 21 Feb. 1945. Christmas and the New Year featured seasonal plays, while Church holy days emphasized religious drama.

Although the audience for radio drama was smaller than that for the radio serials and musical and variety shows, its importance to Quebec's cultural development was immense. It created its own dramatic tradition independently of the theatre and created a corps of writers, actors, and directors who later made a vital contribution to the expansion of legitimate professional theatre, beginning in the 1960s.

See Pierre Pagé and Renée Legris, *Répertorie des oeuvres de la littérature radiophonique québécoise, 1930-1970* (1975); 'Le Théâtre à la radio et à la télévision au Québec', in *Archives des lettres canadiennes*, 5, *Le Théâtre canadien-français* (1976); *Comique et l'humour à la radio québécoise* (2 vols., 1976, 1979); Renée Legris, *Robert Choquette: romancier et dramaturge de la radio-télévision* (1977); Louise Blouin and Raymond Pagé, 'Le Phénomène des adaptations à la radio québécoise (1939-1949)', *Theatre History in Canada*, 7 (1986).   RENÉE LEGRIS

Rain, Douglas (b. 1928). Widely regarded as one of Canada's finest classical actors, he was born in Winnipeg where he began acting on radio at the age of eight. Studies at the Univ. of Manitoba and the Banff School of Fine Arts (see BANFF CENTRE) led to a scholarship at the Old Vic Theatre School in London. He returned to Canada in the early 1950s and performed on CBC and at Toronto's JUPITER THEATRE before playing Dorset and understudying Alec Guinness in *Richard III* at the STRATFORD FESTIVAL in 1953. He subsequently appeared in some forty-five Festival productions between 1953 and 1978.

Sometimes referred to as 'an actor's actor', Rain is particularly admired for the clarity of his speech and the subtlety and incisiveness of his performances, attributes that have served him particularly well in the classical repertoire. At Stratford he has been equally at home in Shakespeare—Malvolio (1957), Prince Hal (1958 and 1965), King John (1960), Iago (1959 and 1973), and Macbeth (1978)—and such non-Shakespearean classics as Molière's *Le Bourgeois gentilhomme* (1964) and *Tartuffe* (1968 and 9), or Ben Jonson's *Volpone* (1971).

Rain has also acted abroad: in Peter Barnes' *The Ruling Class* in Washington, 1971, and in New York in Robert Bolt's *Vivat! Vivat Regina!*, 1972, for which he received a Tony Award nomination. He performed in London in Peter Luke's *Hadrian VII* in 1968 and in Morris West's *The Heretic* in 1970. In Canada he has had particular success in works by Ibsen, including *Hedda Gabler* (MANITOBA THEATRE CENTRE, 1972), *The Master Builder* (TARRAGON THEATRE, 1982); by Shaw, including *Arms and the Man* and *Heartbreak House* (SHAW FESTIVAL 1967 and 1985); and by Arthur Miller (*The Crucible*, Stratford, 1975). Rain demonstrated his versatility in light comedy in D.L. Coburn's *The Gin Game* (Stratford, 1980).

Rain has also directed plays and was Head of the English Acting Division of the NATIONAL THEATRE SCHOOL, 1974-7.

NEIL CARSON

Rankin, Arthur McKee (1841-1914). Actor-manager and dramatist, he was born in Sandwich, Ont. In 1861, after a family disagreement, he fled Toronto's Upper Canada College to become an actor in Rochester, N.Y., briefly calling himself 'George Henley'. Blessed with 'piratically handsome' good looks, he was soon *jeune premier* with Mrs John Drew's Philadelphia company, and in 1866 made both his London and Broadway débuts. He played in melodrama and farce at A.M. Palmer's Union Square Theatre (1873-5), but had his greatest success touring with

his wife, Kitty Blanchard (m. 1869), principally in Joaquin Miller's *The Danites*. Their three daughters acted with them and eventually married important actors: Gladys (Sidney Drew), Phyllis (Harry Davenport), and Doris (Lionel Barrymore). By 1887 his Macbeth was accounted 'portly' and spoken with a voice 'full of whiskers'. Rankin had a success in 1890 with *The Canuck*, which he helped dramatize from his brother George's novel *Border Canucks* (1890). Separated from his wife around 1889, Rankin teamed first with Mabel Bert and then with rising star Nance O'Neill, touring North America, England, and Australia from 1897 to 1909. Rankin ended his career in VAUDEVILLE, abnormally fat, performing scenes from past hits. He died in San Francisco.

DAVID GARDNER

Ravel, Aviva (b. 1928). Childhood memories of Montreal's garment-district, the importance of education, and family ties activate most of Ravel's stories and plays. As a teenager she acted in Montreal community theatre, an interest that continued after she and her husband, eluding the British blockade, settled on an Israeli kibbutz. Returning to North America in 1959, she studied playwriting at New York's Actors' Studio before returning to Montreal and school-teaching. In 1967 *Mendel Fish* (unpublished, produced at HART HOUSE THEATRE in 1967) won the Canadian Women's Press Club Award for Humour; that same year she earned a BA from Loyola College. Many of her subsequent plays show the choices women face in their marriages and careers, a theme that reflects her own shifting roles as mother, writer, graduate student, university lecturer, and wife.

When Ravel draws characters she knows completely, their Jewish idiom and constraining traditions surround dramatic choices with comic pathos. Her strongest plays, however, are distanced from her own circumstances, focusing on ebullient, combative older women whose will has nevertheless been shaped by social convention. The irony emerges when, like the dying mother in *The Twisted Loaf* (1973), produced at the SAIDYE BRONFMAN CENTRE, 1973, or the deserted wife in *Listen I'm Talking* (1978), broadcast by CBC radio, 1982, they are forced to take stock of their lives. In plays that lack such distancing, plot tends to over-ride character:

Ravel

for example, the brisk comedy of *Second Chance* (1982), produced at the Kawartha Festival Theatre, 1981, ends unconvincingly, and *Soft Voices* (1973), produced at the Centre d'art canadien, Montreal, 1966, seems even more contrived—despite the sexual tension between the housewife and the career woman, and their sudden shifts into fantasy, the two remain pale stereotypes. At its best, Ravel's dialogue lifts realism into ritual. Accordingly the down-and-outs of *Dispossessed* (1976), produced at the Saidye Bronfman Centre, 1977, take on a nobility and vision far beyond their seemingly depressing and narrow personalities. These localized figures are magnificently universal and deserve to be better known outside Eastern Canada and Israel.

See an interview with Patricia Morley in *Canadian Drama*, 5 (1979).

ANTHONY JENKINS

Reaney, James (b. 1926). Born in South Easthope, near Stratford, Ont., he began writing while a student at local schools. In 1944 he commenced studies at University College, Univ. of Toronto, graduating in 1948, and completing an MA in English the following year. During this five-year period he published poems and stories in various journals and magazines, and in 1949 issued his first volume of poetry, *The Red Heart*, which won a Governor General's Award. He was married in 1951 to Colleen Thibaudeau, also a poet; they have a son and a daughter. From 1949 to 1956 Reaney taught English at the Univ. of Manitoba, returning to Toronto in the latter year for doctoral study under Northrop Frye; his thesis, 'The Influence of Spenser on Yeats', was successfully defended two years later. A second volume of verse, *A Suit of Nettles* (1958), an ironic variation on Spenser's *The Shepherd's Calendar*, also received a Governor General's Award, as did *Twelve Letters to a Small Town* (1962). Reaney returned to his teaching position in Winnipeg, but in 1960 moved to the Univ. of Western Ontario in London, Ont., where he is Professor of English.

The late fifties and early sixties mark the beginning of Reaney's mature interest in dramatic writing, which has gradually come to absorb the major part of his creative attention, but one further book of poetry, *The Dance of Death at London, Ontario* (1963), was followed by the collected *Poems* (1972) and

James Reaney

by two selections of shorter and longer poetry (1975, 1976), all edited by Germaine Warkentin. For ten years, beginning in 1960, Reaney edited and published the theoretical and critical magazine *Alphabet*, dedicated to 'the iconography of the imagination', and he has also issued the occasional newsletter *Halloween* in various journals. He is a Fellow of the Royal Society of Canada; in 1975 he was made an Officer of the Order of Canada, and he received an honorary D. Litt. from Carleton University.

Reaney's interest in the theatre began in high school, but was later stimulated by a variety of influences and associations. A reader of his poems might observe a natural tendency to the dramatic: they are frequently in the form of monologue or dialogue. *One-Man Masque* (1962), first performed by Reaney himself in 1960, is an extended setting of individual poems. His collaboration with the composer John Beckwith on opera and on other musical settings of texts (still continuing), began in the early 1950s and drew him further towards a form in which the sense of words is qualified by their sound

460

and movement. Reaney has written of the excitement generated by the foundation of the STRATFORD FESTIVAL in his native district in 1953; his first play, *The Rules of Joy*, later revised to become *The Sun and the Moon*, was entered in a contest for new plays to be staged at Stratford. In the same period he was urged by Pamela Terry, then John Beckwith's wife, to write a play for production by the University of Toronto's UNIVERSITY ALUMNAE DRAMATIC CLUB. The result was Reaney's first major success in drama, *The Killdeer*, produced at the Coach House Theatre in January 1960, directed by Terry. Subsequent productions, on CBC television in 1961, and at the Glasgow Citizens' Theatre, Scotland, in 1965 consolidated the successful first impression made by the play in performance. *The Killdeer and Other Plays* (1962)—which includes *One-Man Masque* and *The Sun and the Moon*—won a further Governor General's Award. In 1962 Pamela Terry also directed the first performance of *The Easter Egg* (1972), a play recognisably similar in manner to *The Killdeer* and *The Sun and the Moon*.

If the early plays exhibit an elaborate, literary quality, Reaney's wide-ranging interests in theatrical style soon led him to other kinds of drama and to other collaborators. Various plays for children, for performance by actors and by marionettes, liberated Reaney's instinct for fun and energy in the theatre; in 1963 John HIRSCH, whom Reaney had met while in Winnipeg, mounted a celebrated production of *Names and Nicknames* (1973) at the MANITOBA THEATRE CENTRE, and the connection between them culminated in the commissioning for a 1967 Stratford production at the Avon Theatre of *Colours in the Dark* (1969), one of Reaney's most accomplished plays. His interest in a bare, presentational style had also been stimulated by a visiting performance by the Peking Opera (Toronto, 1962), while his immersion in directing and in theatrical workshops at his own university was to produce what he has called 'more whirling and fluid plays'. His initiation into the practice of theatre was helped by Keith TURNBULL, whose association with Reaney's plays began with the 1965 London, Ont., summer theatre production of *The Sun and the Moon*, and continued through the famous productions between 1973 and 1975 of his trilogy of plays, *The DONNELLYS*, to further collaboration in productions of Reaney's plays by the NDWT

Company. Following the July 1966 London, Ont., production of *Listen to the Wind* (1972), a play that remains rather bogged down in literary encumbrances, Reaney began his 'Listeners' Workshops' with volunteer groups of amateurs, in which he experimented with improvisation, choric effects, and the translation of myth into simple but striking theatrical symbols. Such work lies behind nearly all his subsequent plays.

Since the success of *The Donnellys* Reaney has been very active in the theatre, but his plays have not approached the quality of his trilogy. Attempts to give similar treatment to other nineteenth-century stories produced *Baldoon* (1976, with C.H. Gervais), *The Dismissal* (1978), and two dramatisations of Major John Richardson's melodramatic romances, *Wacousta!* (1979), and *The Canadian Brothers* (1984). In *Gyroscope* (1983) he seemed to return rather to the style of his earlier plays, while his involvement with local and amateur groups has resulted in *King Whistle* (1980), a dramatic treatment of a strike during the Depression in Stratford; *Antler River*, on the history of London; *Traps*, a mime play suggested by experiments in sensory deprivation; *I, the Parade*, commissioned by the Univ. of Waterloo to mark its twenty-fifth anniversary; and *Cloud Shadows*, written for old people, on conflict and contact between generations. His current projects include (in collaboration with John Beckwith) a 'doll opera' based on the murder-novel *Crazy to Kill* by Anne Cardwell; it will be premièred at the Guelph Spring Festival in 1989. He has completed the libretto to an opera, *Serinette*, with music to be composed by Harry Somers, on life at Sharon, Ont., commissioned by Music at Sharon, and scheduled for performance in 1989. He is at work on a music drama to do with the Brontë children and their legends, in addition to beginning work in the media of video and film.

The length of Reaney's career, and the breadth and variety of his achievement mark him as a leading figure in the Canadian theatre. His work typically displays an interesting mixture of the arcane and the literary with 'rough' and broad theatricality; this can either prove very powerful or can stall the dramatic motor disastrously. In the earliest plays certain symbolic patterns may be discerned, and these recur, in one way or another, throughout his drama. The children or child-like adults of the plays are Blakean

Reaney

innocents confronting worlds of experience that appear confusing or ambiguous, but that are revealed to be simply divided into conflicting powers of light and darkness—'Uncle Good and Aunt Evil' (*Colours in the Dark*). The early plays also display Reaney's characteristic modes, those of melodrama and ironic comedy, with abrupt and arbitrary shifts of tone that can easily puzzle readers or audiences. In essays and interviews Reaney, drawing on Frye and Jung, places great faith in the unifying power of pattern in dramatic structure, but in his own plays he is not always successful in anchoring a large design in concrete theatrical symbols that connect with one another. Dialogue and character frequently seem to be adrift, and the patterning lost in erratic arabesques. In response to such criticism of *The Killdeer*, Reaney revised the original three-act play into a two-act version (1972, in *Masks of Childhood*, ed. B. Parker)—but exuberance, for better or worse, has remained a mark of his writing. As early as 1964 Michael Tait characterised Reaney's unique style as a 'capacity to write for the stage at once so badly and so well', and a survey of his work since then tends to confirm such a judgement. *The St. Nicholas Hotel*, the second of the Donnelly plays, was hailed in 1974 as displaying 'the confidence of a writer who has found his own voice' (Urjo KAREDA, the *Toronto Star*), but such a voice has not been maintained in work that has followed Reaney's major artistic success.

The most intellectually challenging criticism of Reaney remains Louis Dudek's essay 'A Problem of Meaning', *Canadian Literature* 59 (1974); other studies of interest are S. Dragland, ed., *Approaches to the Work of James Reaney* (1983); J. M. Heath, ed., *Profiles in Canadian Literature* 4 (1982); and A. A. Lee, *James Reaney* (1968). Two essays on Reaney's plays by Michael Tait are contained in *Dramatists in Canada* (1972), edited by W.H. New; W.J. Keith's remarks on Reaney's dramas in *Canadian Literature in English* (1985) are judicious and well-balanced.   JOHN H. ASTINGTON

Regina Theatre. Built for $18,000 by Whitmore Bros., a local architectural firm, the Regina Theatre opened on 7 Feb. 1910 with a performance by the Regina Philharmonic Society. Measuring 60' × 100', the theatre seated 870 in a raked auditorium,

eight boxes, and a gallery that circled the house from two upper boxes flanking the 27' proscenium. Dressing rooms were located under the 30' stage, which was equipped with the first dimmer board in Saskatchewan. An orchestra pit in front of the stage accommodated 'eight players and a piano'. Other facilities included a cloakroom adjoining the box office, a gentlemen's smoking room, and toilets in the basement.

Barney Groves, agent for C.P. WALKER's circuit, was manager for nine years. For 28 Mar. 1910 he booked Walker's tour of Ben Jerome's *The Royal Chef* as the theatre's first theatrical performance. Many leading performers and companies of the touring era appeared at the Regina Theatre: Nellie Melba, Lewis Waller, Laurence Irving, Johnston Forbes-Robertson, Marie Tempest, Sophie Tucker, Maude Adams, the Stratford-Upon-Avon Players, and the DUMBELLS. Local favourites—such as Bert Lang's Juvenile Bostonians and the Oliver J. Eckhardt Players, who performed ninety-three weeks at the theatre during the First World War—also entertained theatre patrons. The Operatic Society produced A. Baldwin Sloane's *The Mocking Bird*, and Lionel Monckton's *The Country Girl* and *The Toreador*; the Regina Amateur Society performed Gilbert and Sullivan's *The Mikado* and Somerset Maugham's *Lady Frederick*. Production standards of local companies often outshone those of the third-rate American companies which, on the whole, supplied the basic fare. With the opening of the Capitol Theatre on 19 Mar. 1921 the Regina Theatre ceased to be the most important theatre in the city. Under the management of Oswald W. Power theatrical attractions diminished and the Famous Players Canadian Corporation acquired the theatre, appointing P.D. Egan manager in 1927. Inactive from 1928, the building was demolished in 1939.   PATRICK B. O'NEILL

Reid, Fiona (b. 1951). Born in England, she immigrated to Canada in 1964. After graduating from McGill Univ. in 1972, she began her acting career in revue in Toronto and summer stock in Muskoka before attracting national attention in 1975 in the popular CBC-TV series 'The King of Kensington'.

Reluctant to become stereotyped as a light comedienne, she left the series in 1978 to devote more time to her stage career. Her affinity for comedy has been evident in styles

462

ranging from Restoration comedy (William Congreve's *Love for Love*, CENTRESTAGE, 1985) to theatre of the absurd (N.F. Simpson's *One Way Pendulum*, NATIONAL ARTS CENTRE, 1976). She is no less at home in more serious drama—both contemporary (David Rudkin's *Ashes*, PHOENIX THEATRE, Toronto, 1978) and classical (*The Trojan Women*, Toronto Arts Productions, 1978). She was featured in the premières of both Erika RITTER's *AUTOMATIC PILOT*, at the Adelaide Court Theatre in Jan. 1980, and John MURRELL's *WAITING FOR THE PARADE*, at TARRAGON THEATRE in 1979. She has performed at many Canadian theatres, including the STRATFORD FESTIVAL, and since 1983 has been a regular member of the SHAW FESTIVAL Company.   NEIL CARSON

Reid, Kate (b. 1930). Born Daphne Kate Reid in London, Eng., she was educated at Havergal College, Toronto, the Royal Conservatory of Music, and the Univ. of Toronto. She also studied with Uta Hagen in New York. Her career began with appearances at HART HOUSE THEATRE, Univ. of Toronto, under Robert GILL. Professional engagements followed, with roles on CBC radio and TV and at Toronto's CREST THEATRE, starring in such plays as Patrick Hamilton's *Gaslight*, Lillian Hellman's *The Little Foxes*, and Chekhov's *Three Sisters*.

She first appeared at the STRATFORD FESTIVAL—playing Celia in *As You Like It* and Emilia in *Othello*—under artistic director Michael LANGHAM in 1959. In subsequent Stratford seasons she played the Nurse in *Romeo and Juliet*, Cassandra in *Troilus and Cressida*, Katherina in *The Taming of the Shrew*, and Lady Macbeth. In Chekhov's *The Cherry Orchard*, directed by John HIRSCH in 1965, she gave her most accomplished interpretation of a classic role. Her luminous Ranevskaya followed on the heels of New York appearances as Martha in Edward Albee's *Who's Afraid of Virginia Woolf?* in 1962 and as Caitlin Thomas opposite Alec Guinness in Sidney Michael's *Dylan* in 1964. These two complex and brilliantly-written women offered Reid the opportunity to hone her craft and mature as an actress. She emerged as one of North America's finest and most admired theatre artists. Roles were now being written specifically for her, notably by Tennessee Williams (*Slapstick Tragedy*, 1966), Arthur Miller (*The Price*, 1968), and

Kate Reid

Edward Albee (*A Delicate Balance*—in which she was able to perform only in the film version, 1973).

During the 1970s Kate Reid appeared at the SHAW FESTIVAL, Niagara-on-the-Lake; the Long Wharf Theatre, New Haven; the Stratford Festival (under Robin PHILLIPS), as well as in Philadelphia, Houston, Vancouver, and Stratford, Conn. Among her roles in this decade were Gertrude in *Hamlet*; Juno Boyle in Sean O'Casey's *Juno and the Paycock*; Lily in Brian Friel's *The Freedom of the City*, and Big Mama in a highly successful New York revival of Tennessee Williams' *Cat on a Hot Tin Roof*.

Her film work includes major roles in *This Property is Condemned* (1966), *The Andromeda Strain* (1971), and *Atlantic City* (1981).

Her interpretation of Linda Loman in the 1985 New York revival of Arthur Miller's *Death of a Salesman* showed Ms Reid at the height of her considerable powers. Happily, *Salesman* has been preserved by means of a video recording. In it, all the disciplined energy of the mature artist is brought to bear on her performance. It sums up the reasons why this actress is held in such high esteem both outside and within the theatrical profession.

She received an honorary Ph.D. from York Univ. in 1970 and she was inducted into the Order of Canada in 1974.

TIMOTHY FINDLEY

Reis, Kurt (b. 1935). Born in Vienna, he has lived in Canada since 1944, graduating from the Universities of Toronto and Wisconsin and Chicago's Goodman Memorial Theatre School. Reis had directed over eighty plays—at such theatres as the CREST in Toronto, the NEPTUNE in Halifax, and the CITADEL in Edmonton—by the time he was appointed artistic director of the MANITOBA THEATRE CENTRE in 1969. Following a lengthy dispute with his board and the frustration of trying to build a company in difficult circumstances (MTC did not have a permanent theatre at that time), Reis resigned after one season. Since then he has been an extremely active freelance director in Canadian and American regional theatres. In 1975 he founded the Centre for Actors' Study (CAST) in Toronto. Modelled after the Actors' Studio in New York, CAST is a place for professional actors to perfect their craft with the help of a master teacher.

ROSS STUART

Rex Stock Company, The. Named after owner-manager Rex Snelgrove, an expatriate Englishman who had previously managed the Wilson Avenue Theatre, Chicago, the company first appeared in Ontario in Oct. 1920 at the Savoy Theatre, Owen Sound, for an eleven-week season. For the next four years, it played short seasons in Kingston, Peterborough, St Catharines, and Chatham initially as part of a venture by Trans-Canada Theatres Limited to offer a first-rate alternative to the American touring system that dominated Canada's professional theatre. The company split its season between two communities within easy travelling distance of each other, performing from Monday to Wednesday in one city and then moving to the other with the same play for the Thursday-through-Saturday run, before returning on Sundays to the first city to prepare a new production. The repertoire was pragmatic but intelligent and included Salisbury Field's *Wedding Bells*, Maude Fulton's *The Brat*, Brandon Thomas's *Charley's Aunt*, Bayard

Villiers' *Within the Law*, James Forbes's *The Travelling Salesman*, Edward Peple's *A Pair of Sixes*, and George Broadhurst's *Bought and Paid For*. The company was headed by Snelgrove and his wife Zana Vaughn (who had performed in stock in Regina, Saskatoon, and on the West Coast), supported by Herbert Lewis, Grant Martin, Betty Leslie, Ethel Van Orden, Mark Cole, and Fred Dampier. Canadian actors included William Yule of Kingston and Gloria Machan, daughter of Joe Machan of the original Machan Associate Players.

The company's visit to Chatham in Mar. 1925 marked its final engagement in Ontario. The sporadic appearances of the company over its five years in Ontario give evidence of the increasing difficulty of obtaining bookings as more and more theatres were being converted into movie houses. But in spite of the extraordinary demands on cast members, its system of alternating seasons between two cities offered an ingenious method of maintaining full employment for its cast and of bringing live theatre to towns and cities otherwise no longer served by professional companies.

The Rex Snelgrove Collection is in the Metropolitan Toronto Library, and related material is in The Robinson Locke Collection, New York Public Library.

ROBERT SCOTT

Ricard, André (b. 1938). Born in Sainte-Anne-de-Beaupré, Que., he attended Laval University and the Quebec CONSERVATOIRE D'ART DRAMATIQUE. He was one of the founders of the Théâtre de l'Estoc (1957-68, Quebec City), and was its artistic director from 1963 to 1968. He has written numerous scripts for film and radio and in 1976 was awarded the 'Court Métrage' prize for his radio play, *Le Tue-Monde*.

Ricard has written several one-act and six full-length plays. Most of his characters seek to acquire power in one form or another; money is usually the means to that end. For example, *La Vie exemplaire d'Alcide 1er le pharamineux et de sa proche descendance* (1973), first performed in Quebec City by the THÉÂTRE DU TRIDENT on 6 Jan. 1972, directed by Albert Millaire, is an epic play with fifty-four characters and twelve scenes depicting the rise and fall of a Mafia-type family. *La Gloire des filles à Magloire* (1975), directed by André BRASSARD at the Trident, 11 Sept.

1975, tells of the revenge of women driven to prostitution. *Le Casino voleur* (1978), also first produced at the Trident, 20 Apr. 1978, directed by Michel Gariépy, is a story of petty swindling. *Le Tir-à-blanc* (1973), directed by Luce GUILBEAULT when first performed at the THÉÂTRE DU NOUVEAU MONDE, 18 Feb. 1983, is about sexual domination. *La Longue Marche dans les Avents* (1985), first presented on 3 May 1983 by NATIONAL THEATRE SCHOOL students, directed by Michelle Rossignol, is about life in New France at the time of the Conquest with parallels to Quebec of the 1970s. His most recent play, *Le déversoir des larmes*, premièred at Théâtre du Café de la Place in 1988 and won Montreal's Place des Arts prize.

There is (often rather bitter) humour in all Ricard's plays, but his chief quality is a versatile style. He is equally at ease with the elegant, sometimes stilted language of aristocrats or refined crooks, the racy dialogue of ladies of easy virtue, and the colourful speech of the Beauce.   PAULETTE COLLET

Lady Dufferin and an unidentified actor in W.S. Gilbert's Sweethearts, *Rideau Hall, 1878*

Rideau Hall. The original house that is now the official residence of the Governor General was built by Thomas McKay in Ottawa in 1838. In 1864 he leased it to the Canadian government as a residence for the Governor General, and extensive additions were made between 1865 and 1868 (when it was purchased by the government). With the appointment in 1872 of Lord Dufferin, great-grandson of the playwright Richard Brinsley Sheridan, the first theatrical activity took place there. Dufferin and his wife brought with them the tradition of private theatricals, and had a proscenium stage installed in a new ballroom constructed in 1873. Theatricals were inaugurated on 13 Mar. 1873 with a performance of Tom Taylor's one-act comedy *To Oblige Benson*. Under Dufferin, such entertainments were important social occasions in Ottawa; two to four plays were presented each year, usually during Lent, followed by dinner for some 300 guests. The repertoire consisted of contemporary social comedies and farces by such authors as Taylor, Tom Robertson, J.M. Maddox, J. Palgrave Simpson, J.R. Planché, and W.S. Gilbert. Lady Dufferin, and members of the staff, as well as Ottawa friends with theatrical experience, performed in them. An original Canadian work was presented in 1875, *The Maire of St. Brieux*, an operetta by F.A. DIXON with

music by F.W. Mills. Dixon—tutor to the Dufferins' sons—wrote several children's plays with parts for the Dufferin family; they were performed each New Year at Rideau Hall from 1874 to the end of the Dufferins' tenure in 1878.

This theatre tradition continued intermittently under succeeding Governors General: the Lornes (1878-83) presented a series from 1879 to 1882 that included J.M. Morton's *Woodcock's Little Game* and *Betsy Baker*, M.W.B. Jerrold's *Cool as a Cucumber*, H.J. Byron's *Old Soldiers*, and William Brough's and Andrew Halliday's *The Area Belle*; the Stanleys (1888-93) included two plays—S.T. Smith's *Cut Off with a Shilling* and Walter Gordon's *Dearest Mama*—on an entertainment program in 1891; the Aberdeens (1893-8), more interested in historical balls and pageants, gave theatrical adaptations of Dickens's *David Copperfield* and Jane Austen's *Pride and Prejudice* in 1894. Tableaux vivants were also a popular form of entertainment under several of these early Governors General.

Despite the replacement of the permanent stage with moveable panels in 1897, the Mintos continued the theatre tradition at Rideau Hall, especially with a series of British-style pantomimes written and directed by aide-de-camp Captain Harry Graham, with the Minto children taking part: *Babes in the Wood*

Rideau Hall

in 1899; *The Princess and the Pauper* in 1900; *Alice in Wonderland* in 1902; and *Bluebeard* in 1904. Subsequent plays at Rideau Hall were few: a musical revue, *Oriental Ottawa*, written by Lord Byng (1921-6) was performed *c.* 1925; and a version of the musical *Heaven Will Protect the Working Girl* (with the original cast—who collectively created the show—from Toronto's Solar Stage) under the Schreyers (1979-84) in 1979.

JAMES NOONAN

Riel Trilogy, The. John COULTER's trilogy of plays on Louis Riel consists of: *Riel*, an epic stage play of Elizabethan proportions; *The Crime of Louis Riel*, a free adaptation of the same play for less-experienced companies to produce; and *The Trial of Louis Riel*, a documentary drama of Riel's trial.

Riel was first performed on 17 Feb. 1950 by the NEW PLAY SOCIETY, Toronto, at the Royal Ontario Museum Theatre, with Mavor MOORE in the title role, Donald HARRON directing. A revised version was produced on CBC radio's 'Wednesday Night' series on 4 Apr. and 9 May 1951, and in Apr. 1961 another revised version was televised in Canada, Britain, Europe, and the U.S., with Bruno GERUSSI as Riel. *Riel* was published by Ryerson in 1962 and by Cromleck Press, Hamilton, in 1972. But not until 13 Jan. 1975 (at the height of the separatist movement in Quebec) was it given the major Canadian stage production it deserved, when it was performed at the NATIONAL ARTS CENTRE, Ottawa, directed by Jean GASCON, with French-Canadian actor Albert Millaire as Louis Riel. The large cast was drawn from both English- and French-Canadian theatre.

The action of *Riel* takes place in 1869 and 1885 in the section of the Northwest Territories that is now Manitoba. Part I is concerned with Riel's claim that the land belongs to him and his Métis people. He has no wish to establish a new country under a new flag, and respects the British flag as long as the British respect the Métis rights to the land. In the ensuing uprising of 1869, incited both by the British attempt to take over their land and by Riel's decision to have the Ontario Orangeman Thomas Scott executed, Riel and his Métis followers are defeated. Part I ends with Riel's escape to Montana, where he settles down, marries, and raises a family. Part II takes place in 1885 when the Métis send a delegation to Riel begging him to

Mavor Moore (centre) as Riel in John Coulter's Riel, *New Play Society, Toronto, 1950*

return and lead another uprising against the British. He does so and is again defeated. This time the British, determined to capture him, dupe him into meeting with their leader by promising Riel a peaceful settlement. Instead he is imprisoned, put on trial, and condemned to death. The play ends with his hanging.

Riel is a highly dramatic representation of a figure of heroic proportions: a leader, a victim, and a martyr. Part I identifies Riel's strengths and weaknesses. There are echoes of the New Testament in the dialogue, with allusions to Riel as a Christ figure. Coulter imbues Riel's 'voices' with overtones of Joan of Arc, thus inviting comparisons between the two revolutionaries. In Part II Coulter hints at mental instability as Riel imagines himself to be an infallible religious leader, divinely inspired to lead his people to victory. The trial scene gives Coulter the opportunity to show his considerable gifts for depicting victims of injustice; as an Ulsterman, Coulter knew political unrest at first hand. The actual testimony of Louis Riel (who insisted on defending himself) pales in contrast to that written by Coulter, which is more dramatic, though based on the substance of Riel's actual speech. Riel's subsequent hanging, accompanied by liturgical chanting, is strongly suggestive of the crucifixion and its aftermath.

Riel is a combination of epic, myth, legend, pageant, documentary, and montage. As epic it dramatizes the deeds of a historical hero in a series of events expressed in elevated language; as myth it is an allegory of a Christ-like prophet who symbolizes the larger and deeper beliefs of a nation; as legend it is the story of a Canadian hero who has assumed larger-than-life proportions; as pageant it is a procession of stylized events leading to a rich climax; as documentary it is a substantially accurate account of events and personalities; as a montage it is a composite picture of many elements produced through a rapid succession of scenes.

Many theatre groups were eager to perform *Riel* but found it beyond their capabilities. Accordingly Coulter wrote *The Crime of Louis Riel* (1976), a shortened version for small-cast, non-professional groups. It was commissioned by the Canada Council in 1966 and won an award at the DOMINION DRAMA FESTIVAL in 1967. It consists of a continuous flow of scenes set in motion by the 'Actor', who plays the part of the Crown Prosecutor. Functioning much like the stage manager in Thornton Wilder's *Our Town*, the 'Actor' also serves the same role as a Greek chorus. The audience is invited to join the jury to determine whether Riel will live or be hanged. *The Trial of Louis Riel* was commissioned by the Chamber of Commerce, Regina, Sask., in 1967 to mark Canada's Centennial and to be an annual tourist event. It is a one-act documentary of the actual court scene in which Coulter takes Riel's own words and weaves them into a lively debate featuring twenty-eight characters. The play is performed in a replica of the original courthouse, where the audience, ushered in, as in a real courtroom, is scrutinized by the Constable as the Court assembles. Among the spectators are ladies of social prominence, colourfully dressed in period costume, and officers of the North West Mounted Police in scarlet uniforms. Once the counsel, witnesses, and jurymen arrive to take their seats the play begins with the usual formalities of a trial. Louis Riel, shackled with ball and chain, is placed in the dock, and the trial progresses as on the actual day.

The Trial of Louis Riel is a highly moving play, direct and shocking in its re-creation of an infamous trial. The text, published in 1968 by Oberon Press, has been reprinted several times.

While the *Riel* trilogy brought the plays of John Coulter to the attention of the Cana-

dian public, it also provided the inspiration for contemporary scholars and historians to research and re-evaluate the role of Louis Riel in Canadian history. The still unresolved grievances of the Indian and the Métis peoples are powerfully emphasized by this trilogy. Many of the tensions plaguing Canadian society are mirrored in Riel, who has become a symbol for both native-rights groups and French Canadians. Merrill DENISON termed *Riel* 'the first Canadian play of genuine stature.'

Selected criticism of *Riel* is included in *Canadian Drama and the Critics* (1987), ed. L. W. Conolly.   GERALDINE ANTHONY

Rinfret, Jean-Claude (b. 1929). Born at Shawinigan, Que., he studied at l'École des Beaux-Arts in Montreal (1948–53) and at l'École Supérieure Nationale des Arts décoratifs in Paris (1953–4). Between 1954 and 1967 he designed sets for over seventy-five Radio-Canada productions of opera, ballet, and drama, including the operas *Oedipus Rex*, *Dialogues des Carmélites*, *Orpheus and Eurydice*, *Roméo et Juliette*, *Le Château de Barbe bleue* (*Bluebeard's Castle*); the ballet *Daphnis et Chloé*; and the plays *Marie Stuart* by Friedrich Schiller and *Un Mois à la campagne* (*A Month in the Country*) by Ivan Turgenev—which won the prize for best set design in Quebec for 1959. He was head of design for Radio-Canada from 1967 to 1974, and from 1974 to 1985 director of French television programming.

Rinfret has also designed extensively for major theatre, ballet, and opera companies. Among his most memorable productions have been Valentin Kataev's *La Quatradure du cercle* (*Squaring the Circle*), Jacques Audiberti's *Le Mal Court*, and Jacques LANGUIRAND's *Les Violons de l'automne* for Le THÉÂTRE CLUB; Racine's *Les Plaideurs* (*The Litigants*), Anna Bonnaci's *L'heure éblouissante*, Languirand's *Le Gibet*, Marcel DUBÉ's *Les Beaux dimanches* and *AU RETOUR DES OIES BLANCHES*, Shakespeare's *Le Marchand de Venise* (*The Merchant of Venice*), and William Faulkner's *Requiem pour une nonne* (*Requiem for a Nun*) for La COMÉDIE-CANADIENNE; Brendan Behan's *Un Otage* (*The Hostage*) and Eugène Labiche's *Un Chapeau de paille d'Italie* (*An Italian Straw Hat*) for Le THÉÂTRE DU RIDEAU VERT; *Don Giovanni*, *Otello*, *Tosca*, *Madama Butterfly*, and *Samson et Dalila* for L'Opéra du Québec; as well as other operas for the Montreal Opera Guild, the Canadian Opera Company, the Vancouver Opera Association, and Colorado's Central City Opera House; and *Première Classique* and *La Reine* for Les Grands Ballets Canadiens. Rinfret has taught design at L'École des Beaux-Arts in Montreal and Quebec City, the NATIONAL THEATRE SCHOOL, and the BANFF CENTRE SCHOOL OF FINE ARTS.

CLAUDE SABOURIN

Ringwood, Gwen Pharis (1910-84). Born in Anatone, Washington, she moved with her family to a farm near Lethbridge, Alta, in 1913. In 1917 the family moved to Magrath, Alta, and in 1926 to a farm in Valier, Montana, where Ringwood completed high school. She then attended the Univ. of Montana, but left when her father's farm failed in 1928, and worked as a bookkeeper on the Blackfoot reservation. Her father was forced to sell the farm in 1929, and the family returned to Magrath, where both parents worked as teachers, while Ringwood studied at the Univ. of Alberta in Edmonton.

In 1933 she became secretary to Elizabeth Sterling HAYNES, the director of drama for the Extension Department of the Univ. of Alberta, and the recipient of a Carnegie Foundation grant to give direction to community drama groups in Alberta and assist with the development of drama-in-education. Ringwood attended the First Annual School of Drama offered by Haynes and Edward A. Corbett at Banff in Aug. 1933, and after receiving her BA in 1934 became the registrar of the Banff School of Fine Arts in 1935 (see BANFF CENTRE). Her first stage play, *The Dragons of Kent*, was produced there that year. In 1936 she contributed ten radio plays to the Univ. of Alberta's CKUA 'New Lamps for Old' series, dealing with the lives of Beethoven, Cromwell, Socrates, Henry the Navigator, Florence Nightingale, Nansen of the North, and Christopher Columbus.

In 1937, with the help of Professor Frederick Koch, chairman of the Department of Drama, Univ. of North Carolina, who taught playwriting at Banff in the summer, she won a Rockefeller Foundation grant to enter the MA program in drama at North Carolina. In the fall of 1939 she married J.B. Ringwood and returned to Alberta, having completed her MA and written six plays at North Carolina. Five of them have been pro-

Gwen Pharis Ringwood, 1939

duced; one of them, STILL STANDS THE HOUSE (1938), is perhaps the most popular of all Canadian one-act plays.

Ringwood worked as director of drama for the Univ. of Alberta Department of Extension until the fall of 1940, when the Ringwoods moved to Goldfields in northern Saskatchewan. Her successful northern comedy, *The Courting of Marie Jenvrin* (1941), which owes its inspiration to a local character, was produced at Banff in Aug. 1941.

A versatile combination of work in community theatre and theatre education was to persist throughout Ringwood's life. When living in Edmonton in 1943-5 with her two children while her husband served in the Canadian army overseas, she received a grant from Robert GARD of the Alberta Folklore and Local History Project to write Alberta folk plays, which resulted in three regional folk comedies: *Jack and the Joker* (1944), dramatizing the life of Bob Edwards, the outspoken editor of the *Calgary Eye-Opener*; *The Rainmaker* (1946), which deals with a drought-related Medicine Hat episode of 1921; and *Stampede* (1946), the saga of 'Nigger John', cowboy and rancher. *Jack and the Joker* and *The Rainmaker* were produced at Banff in 1944 and 1945 respectively, *Stampede* at the Univ. of Alberta in Mar. 1946.

While teaching playwriting and short-story writing at Banff, Ringwood also wrote *A Fine Coloured Easter Egg; or, The Drowning*

468

of *Wasyl Nemitchuk* (1946), a comedy that drew on her experience of the Ukrainian community, and *Widger's Way* (1976), an Alberta version of the classical story of the miser and his gold, produced at the Univ. of Alberta in Mar. 1952.

In 1953 the Ringwoods moved to Williams Lake, B.C., where she spent the rest of her life, writing and maintaining her involvement in community theatre. Historical musicals such as *Look Behind You, Neighbour* (1961), with music by Chet Lambertson, commissioned for the fiftieth anniversary of Edson, Alta, and *The Road Runs North* (1967), with music by Art Rosoman, commissioned for the Williams Lake centennial, are influenced by the rich mix of cultural activities she experienced when she attended the CHAUTAUQUA festival at Magrath as a child. The three parts of her trilogy *Drum Song* (1982)—*Maya, The Stranger*, and *The Furies*—express her strong sympathy for native people and were first produced at the Univ. of Victoria in June 1982.

Ringwood's many honours and awards include a Governor General's Medal for outstanding service in the development of Canadian drama in 1941, the Eric Hamber Trophy of the B.C. Drama Association (1973), and honorary doctorates from the Univ. of Victoria (1981) and the Univ. of Lethbridge (1982). *The Collected Plays of Gwen Pharis Ringwood* (1982) includes twenty-five of her plays. See also Geraldine Anthony, *Gwen Pharis Ringwood* (1981).

ROTA HERZBERG LISTER

Risk, Sydney (1908-85). Born in Vancouver, he acted in the Players Club at the Univ. of British Columbia, succeeding Frederic Wood as director after graduation in 1930. In 1933 he went to London to study acting at the Old Vic, then under Tyrone GUTHRIE's direction, and trained under Murray McDonald. Working with the Worthing and Coventry repertory companies and in a Shakespearean touring company, he learned to admire the English repertory system, especially the small, innovative club theatres, such as the Everyman in Hampstead, which were fertile training-grounds for young actors and playwrights. In 1938 Risk returned to Canada and joined the Univ. of Alberta Extension Department as director of drama, where he taught, gave workshops, adjudicated, and, in

the summers, headed the theatre division of the Banff School of Fine Arts (see BANFF CENTRE). During 1942-3, on a Rockefeller Foundation Fellowship, he obtained his MA in theatre at Cornell University. In 1946 he resigned his university post to found in Vancouver the Everyman Theatre Company based on European models, with fourteen members—many former students from Alberta. Commencing in Jan. 1947 he successfully toured three plays—including Elsie Park GOWAN's *The Last Caveman*—from Vancouver to Winnipeg. Financial problems and lack of a home theatre led the company to concentrate on school productions for the next three years, but in the fall of 1950 Everyman moved into a studio theatre on Main St where, for two years, much of its finest work was done. Notable productions included Peter Ustinov's *The House of Regrets*, Jean-Paul Sartre's *The Flies*, T.S. Eliot's *Murder in the Cathedral*, the popular *Will the Mail Train Run Tonight?* (a musical comedy by Malcolm L. LaPrada), and, under co-director Joy COGHILL, well-received children's plays. In 1952 the company moved into the 800-seat State Theatre, a former BURLESQUE house, and renamed it the Avon. However, it then lost its youthful, co-operative spirit when 'stars' were brought in and the 'run' replaced the repertory system. There were some hits—*Macbeth* and Sidney Howard's *The Late Christopher Bean*—but Risk faced mounting debts. He chose Jack Kirkland's adaptation of Erskine Caldwell's *Tobacco Road* to open the new year, hoping to recoup losses. Though well received, both critically and at the box-office, police responded to a complaint and closed the production in the second week, walking onstage and arresting five of the cast. The resulting strain of publicity and litigation, and divisive changes in the company, led Risk to withdraw himself and the name Everyman from the venture. He subsequently taught drama at the Univ. of British Columbia, retiring in 1966. He was a man of great integrity who dedicated his life to the development of professional theatre in western Canada; many of his actors—Ted Follows and Bruno GERUSSI, for example—went on to important careers.   JAMES HOFFMAN

Riske, Douglas (b. 1945). Born in Calgary, he attended the BANFF CENTRE SCHOOL OF FINE ARTS and the Univ. of Alberta before beginning his professional career in 1966 as an actor with the GLOBE THEATRE, Regina. With his wife Paddy CAMPBELL he co-founded in 1967 the Calgary Allied Arts Company, Alberta's first fully professional theatre company for children. Riske's 1968 production of *Chinook*, a participation play for young audiences written by Paddy Campbell, was representative of the work championed by the company. As co-founder (with Lucille Wagner) of ALBERTA THEATRE PROJECTS in 1971, and as its first artistic director, Riske encouraged new Canadian plays on regional historical themes. ATP's play-development program, while assisting many emerging playwrights, also resulted in world premières of two internationally acclaimed plays by John MURRELL: *WAITING FOR THE PARADE* in 1977 and *Memoir* (the new version, 1981), both directed by Riske. He also co-founded the Playwrights Colony at the Banff Centre in 1974. Since leaving ATP in 1983, Riske has directed at Banff, Stratford, and Calgary, and acted and produced for film, stage, and radio.   ZINA BARNIEH

Rittenhouse, Charles (1909-82). Born in Montreal and brought up in Winnipeg, he had a long career in Montreal as a teacher and as an educational administrator for the Protestant School Board of Greater Montreal. From 1939 to 1969—as Supervisor of Speech Arts, Supervisor and then Co-ordinator of English—Rittenhouse initiated and organized a broad program of theatrical productions in both the primary and secondary school systems of Montreal. By encouraging talented teachers and by hiring professionals and aspirants, he co-ordinated a comprehensive system of high-quality classical and contemporary theatrical productions in Montreal's school system. Professionals who worked for him include Marion ANDRE, Eric DONKIN, Doreen Lewis, Ron Singer, Kay Tremblay, and Herbert WHITTAKER.

Along with his significant contributions and achievements in drama-in-education, Rittenhouse was a talented director and actor and expert producer for Montreal's lively LITTLE THEATRE movement in the thirties, forties, and fifties, playing a major role in the encouragement and development of English-language theatre in Montreal. As a director Rittenhouse was particularly successful with Shakespeare. Between 1933 and 1937 he directed four Shakespeare plays at West Hill High School, notably a highly acclaimed

Romeo and Juliet in 1935. From 1945 to 1947 he was producer for the ambitious Shakespeare Society of Montreal, which did *Much Ado About Nothing, King Lear,* and *Romeo and Juliet* (which he directed) at Moyse Hall. These productions brought together much of Montreal's theatrical talent.

Rittenhouse also adjudicated, acted, wrote or adapted stage and radio dramas, and composed original music.

JONATHAN RITTENHOUSE

Ritter, Erika (b. 1948). Born in Regina, she was educated at McGill and the Univ. of Toronto. After teaching for three years at Loyola College, Montreal, she moved to Toronto and became a full-time writer.

Ritter's four major plays—*The Splits, Automatic Pilot, The Passing Scene,* and *Murder at McQueen*—are comedies about the stresses of being an intelligent, independent woman in today's urban society. *The Splits* (1978), first produced at TORONTO FREE THEATRE in Jan. 1978, covers a few days in the life of Megan, a would-be serious writer for television, dealing in turn with Hal, her lover; Joe, her tough, drunken but appealing ex-husband, also a writer; and the weak David, her present writing partner. *AUTOMATIC PILOT* (1980), Ritter's greatest success, was followed by *The Passing Scene* (TARRAGON THEATRE, Jan. 1982). This clever comedy of male-female relationships discusses journalistic ethics—a Canadian woman who writes 'lifestyle' pieces marries an American investigative reporter; the time is 1971-6, with Watergate the central issue. *Murder at McQueen* (Tarragon, 1986), weakest of the four, looks at four thirty-ish professional women—a lawyer, a crime novelist, a free-lance writer, and the owner of the club of the title—and their relations with a chauvinist male. The play has no actual murders, only the little murders of betrayal—and an abortion.

These four plays successfully combine Ritter's gift for comedy with serious examinations of modern relationships and artistic integrity. To feminists who criticize her for showing women too dependent on men, Ritter replies that 'Drama is about the way people are, not the way they should be,' and argues that 'the best way to serve women in the theatre [is] to write straightforwardly, assuming that women are important, not soap-boxing for it.'

Her early plays include *A Visitor from Charleston* (1975), produced at Loyola in 1974 and at the MANITOBA THEATRE CENTRE in 1976, in which the main character tries to avoid dealing with her problems (ex-husband and ex-boyfriend) by escaping into a fantasy world suggested by *Gone with the Wind*, a movie she has seen forty-eight times. In *Winter 1671* (1979), performed at the ST LAWRENCE CENTRE, Toronto, in 1979, Ritter portrays a group of *filles de roi* sent from France to Quebec. Esperance, a whore, is desperate to return to France; Renée has run away from a husband and wants to find a way of marrying the landowner, Philippe; Madelaine is pregnant and married to a soldier-turned-farmer who dislikes her. The play ends with the murder of two men, and Renée's flight to the wilderness. Ritter's radio play, *Miranda* (1985), concerns a nineteenth-century Englishwoman who successfully impersonated a man so that she could be an army surgeon.

Urban Scrawl (1984) and *Ritter in Residence* (1987) are collections of Ritter's shrewd, amusing essays on city life. She was the first playwright-in-residence at the STRATFORD FESTIVAL, 1985, and host of a daily CBC radio show, 'Dayshift', from 1985 to 1987.

MALCOLM PAGE

Roberts, Jean (b. 1926). Born in Perth, Scotland, she was educated in Belgium and at the Univ. of Edinburgh (1944-7). Early jobs backstage led to an extended engagement (1949-54) with the Stratford Memorial Theatre (now the Royal Shakespeare Company), where she served as assistant stage manager, stage manager, and, on European tours, as interpreter (she speaks Flemish, Dutch, German, French, and English). After a year in television production, she returned to Stratford in 1955 as an assistant director.

In 1956 Roberts immigrated to Canada with her partner Marigold CHARLESWORTH, with whom she was ultimately to produce many plays. At first she worked as production manager at the CREST THEATRE, Toronto (1959-62), establishing at the same time, with Charlesworth and William Fredric Whitehead, a company at the Red Barn Theatre, Jackson's Point, Ont. In 1962 this same partnership produced a winter repertory season of plays at Toronto's CENTRAL LIBRARY THEATRE, leading directly to the appointment of Roberts and Charlesworth as co-artistic directors of the CANADIAN PLAYERS (1965-6).

From 1967 to 1971 Roberts was theatre officer and dance officer at the Canada Council, and from 1971 to 1977 director of theatre at the NATIONAL ARTS CENTRE, Ottawa. Here she introduced several innovations, including a Young Company ('Hexagon') and a playwright-in-residence program. She was also responsible for the Centre's first project involving both the English- and French-speaking theatre communities: Jean GASCON's 1975 production of John COULTER's *RIEL*. No other NAC director has succeeded in presenting such a wide range of successful productions, nor has any other matched the attendance records achieved during Roberts' tenancy.

From 1978 to 1983 she was director of Program Development and Production for CBC-TV Drama and, since 1983, as well as teaching, she has been a freelance producer and director.

Jean Roberts became a Canadian citizen in 1973. Her various honours include the Maggie Bassett Award (1984) and a Toronto Theatre Alliance Award (1984) for her distinguished contribution to the theatre.

TIMOTHY FINDLEY

Robins, Toby (1931-86). Born and educated in Toronto, she studied at the Royal Conservatory of Music and made her professional stage début as Miranda in the NEW PLAY SOCIETY's 1948 production of Shakespeare's *The Tempest*. Many other roles with this company followed, including Ellie Dunn in Shaw's *Heartbreak House* and Cordelia in *King Lear* (both in 1950) and Peter Pan (1952), leading to work with the CREST THEATRE (including the role of Cleopatra in Shaw's *Caesar and Cleopatra* in 1962) and at the STRATFORD FESTIVAL in 1954 and 1962. Robins, however, was most widely known as a charming and well-informed panelist on the popular CBC-TV panel show 'Front Page Challenge' from 1957 to 1961. In 1964 she moved permanently, with her husband William FREEDMAN, to England, where she worked successfully with the Royal Shakespeare Company, at the Mermaid, Apollo, and Haymarket theatres, at the Hampstead Theatre Club, and at a number of provincial theatres.

HARRY LANE

Ronfard, Jean-Pierre (b. 1929). Born and educated in France, he was from 1953 to 1960 an itinerant actor, director, and teacher in Algeria, Greece, Portugal, and Austria. He immigrated to Canada in 1960, becoming artistic director of the French section of the NATIONAL THEATRE SCHOOL in Montreal, a post he held until 1964. As secretary-general of the THÉÂTRE DU NOUVEAU MONDE (1967-70), an organizer of the Théâtre de Rues in Paris (1968-9), and director of Les Jeunes Comédiens du Théâtre du Nouveau Monde (1969-74), he directed productions by many playwrights, both from Quebec and abroad, including Jean BARBEAU, Réjean DUCHARME, Claude GAUVREAU, Eugène Ionesco, Alfred Jarry, Arthur Miller, and Chekhov. Since 1981 he has been a driving force behind Montreal's L'Espace libre.

In May 1975 Ronfard helped found the Théâtre Expérimental de Montréal, which in 1979 became the NOUVEAU THÉÂTRE EXPÉRIMENTAL DE MONTRÉAL. The activities of the NTEM—which was chiefly concerned with exploring new avenues of improvisation, outrageousness, the sublime, the grotesque, and parody—led Ronfard to compose a cycle of seven plays inspired by Shakespeare: VIE ET MORT DU ROI BOITEUX (1981), which parodies the great myths of the western world, its literature, traditions, and history. This cycle was followed by his reinterpretations of masterpieces from the classical repertoire: Machiavelli's La Mandragore (1982), produced at TNM in Nov. 1982; Les Mille et une nuits (1984), produced at NTEM in June 1984; and Cervantes' Don Quichotte (1984), produced at the THÉÂTRE DU TRIDENT in Nov. 1984.

Ronfard's translations of King Lear and Euripides' Le Cyclope were produced at TEM and NTEM in Jan. 1977 and Mar. 1985 respectively, and he has also collaborated with Robert Claing, Patricia Nolin, and Alice Ronfard on other plays, some of which remain unproduced.   GILLES LAPOINTE

Rose, Richard (b. 1955). Born in Maracaibo, Venezuela, he took a theatre degree at York Univ. and in 1978 founded the Necessary Angel Theatre Company in Toronto. The first production, Agamemnon, failed, but the company has subsequently established a reputation for addressing contemporary issues in a style encompassing absurdism, clowning, clever manipulation of spatial and temporal reality, and a strong visual element. The company's most notable success has been John KRIZANC's TAMARA, directed by Rose in 1981, but there have been other interesting achievements, including the 1983 production of Censored (adapted by Rose from the book A Cabal of Hypocrites by Mikhail Bulgakov)—about the censorship of Molière's plays—which took place in Toronto's St Paul's Church, and Rose's own play, Mein (a Dora Award-winner, in 1984), in which six identically dressed actors portray the internal conflicts in a businessman's mind. From 1982 to 1984 Rose's Necessary Angel and Thom Sokoloski's Theatre Autumn Leaf collaborated as the Autumn Angel Repertory Company, successfully workshopping Krizanc's Prague (among other projects), which received a full production, directed by Rose, at Toronto's TARRAGON THEATRE in 1984. Rose also worked as associate director at the STRATFORD FESTIVAL in 1983 on Guy SPRUNG's production of Arthur Miller's Death of a Salesman.   RAY CONLOGUE

Rosen, Sheldon (b. 1943). Born in New York, he was educated at Rochester and Syracuse Universities before working briefly in television. In 1970 he left the U.S. Army and moved to Toronto, where in June 1971 his one-act fantasy play Love Mouse (1972) was successfully produced at the Learning Resources Centre of Toronto Public Libraries; in Aug. 1971 it was performed again, with his Meyer's Room (1972), at the Poor Alex Theatre. These were followed in Apr. 1972 by The Wonderful World of William Bends Who is Not Quite Himself Today (1972) and in Dec. 1972 by The Stag King (an unpublished adaptation of Carlo Gozzi's play), both at TARRAGON THEATRE. In 1973 Rosen moved to Vancouver, where he became affiliated with the NEW PLAY CENTRE, which in Mar. 1974 produced his The Box (1975) and Frugal Repast (1978), and in May 1975 his Like Father, Like Son, later rewritten as The Grand Hysteric (1978). His Ned and Jack (1979), written while he was Playwright-in-Residence at the NATIONAL ARTS CENTRE in 1976-7, about a fictional encounter between John Barrymore and the American playwright Edward Sheldon, was well received at the New Play Centre in 1977, and, after much rewriting, ran for two seasons at the STRATFORD FESTIVAL in 1978 and 1979; it won the Canadian Authors' Association Literary Award for Drama in 1980.

Rosen was Chairman of the Guild of Canadian Playwrights in 1979-80. He moved in 1981 to New York City, where a further revised version of *Ned and Jack*, directed by Colleen Dewhurst, closed on opening night at the Little Theatre in Feb. 1981. His next full-length play *Souvenirs* (1985), dealing with social responsibility and commitment among a group of tourists on a politically troubled tropical island, was first staged at the Cubiculo Theatre, New York, in 1984, and was produced by the SHAW FESTIVAL (with FACTORY THEATRE) in Toronto in Dec. 1985.

HARRY LANE

Ross Hall. This was the first and most important purpose-built theatre in South Edmonton, which subsequently became the City of Strathcona and was eventually merged with Edmonton. Until 1913, when a high-level bridge was built, rail travellers approaching Edmonton from the south had to detrain near the south bank of the Saskatchewan. Touring theatrical troupes took the opportunity to perform for a night or two in the local community before crossing the river by ferry to the larger audiences in Edmonton. An Orange Lodge built over a hardware store in 1894 served as an early auditorium; it was named Fergusson's Hall after the proprietor of the store. Three years later the building was bought by W.E. Ross, who in 1898 added a new playhouse in an upper room, 35' × 60', at the back of the

previous one. Ross Hall seated 300 people in rows of wooden chairs set out on its level floor. It was visited by many of the touring companies of the day, including the Tom MARKS Co. and Harold Nelson SHAW. Known variously as the Strathcona Opera House or the Grand Opera House, the theatre became inactive in 1911 with the development of local movie houses. Nevertheless it still stands, and has been restored. The interior has been refitted as an auditorium, and the playhouse is used in the annual Edmonton Fringe Festival for musical and theatrical performances.

See John Orrell, *Fallen Empires: Lost Theatres of Edmonton, 1881-1914* (1981).

JOHN ORRELL

Roux, Jean-Louis (b. **1923**). Born in Montreal, he received a classical education at Collège Sainte-Marie. On receiving a scholarship from the French government, he abandoned his medical studies at the Université de Montréal to train as an actor in France (1946-50). In 1950 he married Monique Oligny, sister of actress Huguette OLIGNY.

On his return to Montreal in 1950 Roux established Le Théâtre d'Essai de Montréal to produce Eloi de GRANDMONT's *Un Fils à tuer* and his own first play, *Rose Latulippe*, a folktale in two scenes with epilogue. In 1951 Roux and fellow-actor Jean GASCON, also recently returned from Paris, founded Le THÉÂTRE DU NOUVEAU MONDE, of which

Molière's Don Juan, *directed by Jean-Louis Roux, Théâtre du Nouveau Monde, 1980*

Roux

Roux became secretary-general (1953–63) and artistic director (1966–82). In the thirty years he was associated with this prestigious company he directed more than fifty plays, ranging from Racine, Molière, and Marivaux to Claudel, Shaw, Lanoux, and Jean BARBEAU.

A classical actor, fluent in French and English, Roux has played a wide spectrum of roles, including Thomas Diafoirus in Molière's *Le Malade imaginaire*, Cassius in Shakespeare's *Julius Caesar*, Almaviva in Beaumarchais's *Mariage de Figaro*, Doctor Dysart in Peter Shaffer's *Equus*, and Le Général in Jean Genet's *Le Balcon* (*The Balcony*). At the STRATFORD FESTIVAL he has played Orleans and Burgundy in Shakespeare's *Henry V* (1956) and *Henry VI* (1966), and Kurt in Strindberg's *Dance of Death* (1966). As an actor and director he has toured widely abroad as well as across Canada.

Roux's career in radio, television, and film as actor and writer is long and impressive. In 1947, while in Paris, he played Néoptolème in a radio production recording of André Gide's *Philoctète*, in which Gide himself played Ulysses. Roux's first film, made in Paris, was René Delacroix's *Docteur Louise*. He later played parts in films by Otto Preminger, Harvey Hart, Lionel Chetwind, George Bloomfield, Jean-Claude Lord, Jean Beaudin, Tony Richardson, and Fernando Arrabal, among others. His outstanding career with the CBC's French and English television networks won him national acclaim. For seven years he starred as Ovide Plouffe in the weekly series 'La Famille Plouffe' written by Roger Lemelin. Other remarkable performances include the Count in Jean Anouilh's *La Répétition, ou L'Amour puni* (*The Rehearsal*); Gregers in Ibsen's *Le Canard sauvage* (*The Wild Duck*); Vershinin in Chekhov's *Les Trois Soeurs* (*The Three Sisters*); Velchaninov in Dostoevsky's *L'Éternel Mari* (*The Eternal Husband*); Lanctôt in Denis Arcand's *Duplessis*; and Lui in Jacques LANGUIRAND's *Les Violons de l'automne*.

In addition to numerous articles for magazines and newspapers, Roux has written many radio and television plays and adaptations for the Société Radio-Canada. In 1963 his account of the CBC French radio and television producers' strike (1959) was published in book form under the title *En Grève! Radio-Canada 1959*. His second play, *Bois Brûlés* (1967), an epic account of the revolt of the Manitoba Métis people under the visionary leadership of Louis Riel, was first produced by Le Théâtre du Nouveau Monde in 1958. In 1968 he directed his own translation of Shakespeare's *Twelfth Night* for Le Théâtre du Nouveau Monde. His translation of *Julius Caesar* was published in 1972, followed by translations of *Hamlet* and *Othello* in 1976. *Othello* was given a lavish production in 1986 by TNM director Olivier Reichenbach. Roux's translations show respect for the style of the original writing and use a vocabulary pleasing to the listener and natural for the actor.

Roux has also made a distinguished administrative contribution to Canada's cultural life. From 1953 to 1964 he was president of the Société des Auteurs (Montreal), and in 1960 he became a member of the board of l'Union des Artistes (Montreal). He was Chairman of the Canadian Conference of the Arts (1967–71), a member of the board of the National Film Board (1968) and its vice-chairman (1968–74). In 1981–2 he served on the Applebaum-Hébert federal cultural policy review committee. He was executive secretary of the Canadian Theatre Centre (International Theatre Institute/UNESCO), 1959–64; president, 1965–8, and Chairman of the Board, 1970. From 1966 to 1971 he was on the executive committee of the International Theatre Institute, was chairman of the Board of Governors of the NATIONAL THEATRE SCHOOL from 1976 to 1979 and the School's director general from 1981 to 1987.

Roux has been awarded many distinctions. In 1960 he received the Best Actor award from Le Congrès du Spectacle in Montreal. He was honoured with the Centennial Medal (1967), the Prix Victor-Morin of the Société Saint-Jean-Baptiste de Montréal (1969), the Order of Canada (1972), and the Molson Award of the Canada Council (1977). In 1982 he was elected to the Royal Society of Canada.   GUY BEAULNE

Royal Alexandra Theatre. Built in 1906–7 by the 23-year old Cawthra Mulock (known as 'Toronto's youngest millionaire') to plans by Toronto architect John M. Lyle, this 1,525-seat touring house on King St W., Toronto, opened on 26 Aug. 1907 with Anna Loughlin starring as Kokomo in the pantomime *Top o' the World*. The front of the building is devoted to reception and administration and the remaining two thirds are given over to the auditorium, the stage, and the back-

Royal Alexandra Theatre, Toronto, 1907

stage area. The auditorium consists of main floor, balcony, and gallery, with dimensions—75' wide by 66' deep—that bring the audience close to the stage. There are four boxes, two on the main floor and two on the balcony floor, on each side of the proscenium stage. The stage is 42' wide by 37' 6" deep, the proscenium 38' wide by 40' high. There are four fly galleries, two on each side, and a gridiron 70' above the stage floor. The original colour scheme was yellow and old gold, the walls hung with silk and panelled with oak. Construction costs were some $750,000 (though figures vary).

In its early years the Royal Alex (as it came to be known) was the home of several stock companies: the Royal Alexandra Players starring Elfreda Lasche in 1907; Miss Percy Haslam's Stock Company from 1910 to 1915; the Jessie Bonstelle Players from Detroit in 1914; the Edward H. Robins Players (the biggest stock company in Canada) during the war years.

The 1923-4 season was typical of the eclectic programs offered by the Royal Alex. It included *David Copperfield*, a dramatization by Bransby Williams of Dickens' novel, Bernard Shaw's *The Devil's Disciple*, Ibsen's *Peer Gynt* by the Theatre Guild of New York, and Sir John Martin-Harvey's season, which included *Hamlet*. As a prominent venue for touring companies, and sometimes for pre-Broadway try-outs, the Alex has presented many of the great names in twentieth-century theatre, including the Barrymores (John, Ethel, and Lionel), Alfred Lunt and Lynn Fontanne, Katharine Cornell, Helen Hayes, Judith Anderson, Ruth Gordon, Frederic March, Florence Eldridge, Ruth Draper, Cornelia Otis Skinner, Tallulah Bankhead, Paul Robeson, José Ferrer, Jessica Tandy, Hume CRONYN, Beatrice LILLIE, Gertrude Lawrence, Edith Evans, John Gielgud, Ralph Richardson, Donald Wolfit, and Michael Redgrave.

When Montrealer Ernest Rawley became manager in 1939 (Lawrence Solman was manager from 1907 to 1937, when he was replaced by William Breen), he favoured ballet, bringing such companies as the Ballet Russe de Monte Carlo, Colonel de Basil's Ballet Russe, the Mordkin Ballet, the Jooss Ballet, and the Sadler's Wells Ballet, whose visit in Oct. 1949 helped inspire the founding

475

of the National Ballet of Canada, which made its home for many years at the Royal Alex before moving to the O'KEEFE CENTRE. Opera companies have also played the Alex. In 1916, for example, the Boston Grand Opera Company combined with the Ballet Russe Company, starring Anna Pavlova, for three performances. The Canadian Opera Company (founded in 1959) used the Royal Alex for many seasons before it too moved to the larger O'Keefe Centre.

Large-scale musicals, normally from Broadway, were always popular. A typical year was 1915 when the theatre offered *Dancing Around* (with Al Jolson) and *The Mikado*. The 1935-6 season offered *The Ziegfeld Follies of 1935* and Irving Berlin's and Moss Hart's *As Thousands Cheer*. During the Second World War the Alex presented productions of the major revival of Gershwin's *Porgy and Bess*, the Oscar Hammerstein II/Georges Bizet *Carmen Jones*, and Katherine Dunham's *Tropical Revue*, which originated on Broadway in 1942, 1943, and 1943 respectively. The 1953 *South Pacific* (by Hammerstein and Richard Rodgers) broke box-office records, grossing a quarter of a million dollars in a six-week run. The pattern has continued into the 1980s with productions, for example, of *Damn Yankees* (by Richard Alder and Jerry Ross) in 1988 and Alain Boublil's and Claude-Michel Schönberg's *Les Misérables* in 1989.

Although the theatre is not suited for movies, it has occasionally shown art films—Walt Disney's *Fantasia*, and *Romeo and Juliet* starring Canada's Norma Shearer, and Leslie Howard, for example.

When the Cawthra Mulock estate put the Royal Alex up for sale, it was purchased by Toronto businessman Ed MIRVISH in 1963 for $215,000. He refurbished the theatre with crimson 'French Baroque' wallpaper, a new stage curtain, and a new grand chandelier. The installation of larger seats reduced seating capacity from 1,525 to 1,497. Mirvish arrested the 1960s slide in attendance with productions of contemporary musicals such as *Hair* in 1970 and a very successful *Godspell* in 1972, and through vigorous marketing he developed a healthy subscription series (42,000 subscribers in 1987-8). In 1986 he appointed his son David as producer and the Alex entered into co-productions with other Canadian companies, including the MANITOBA THEATRE CENTRE, TORONTO FREE THEATRE, Marlene Smith Productions, the SHAW FESTIVAL, and Edmonton's CITADEL THEATRE. In an ambitious move David Mirvish invited the Berliner Ensemble in 1986 on their first visit to North America to present Bertolt Brecht's *The Threepenny Opera* and *The Caucasian Chalk Circle*.

Although the Royal Alex has never stressed Canadian content, it has presented the DUMBELLS, the NAVY SHOW, the ARMY SHOW, and the finals of the DOMINION DRAMA FESTIVAL (in 1949 and 1959). Gratien GÉLINAS brought his English version of *TIT-COQ* twice in 1951. The NEW PLAY SOCIETY staged Morley Callaghan's *To Tell the Truth* there in 1949 and Mavor MOORE's *Sunshine Town* in 1955. JUPITER THEATRE's final production was Noël Coward's *Relative Values* at the Alex in 1954. Previously it had presented Christopher Fry's adaptation of Jean Anouilh's *Ring Round the Moon*. SPRING THAW has appeared at the theatre and the STRATFORD FESTIVAL tried out its 1956 *Tamburlaine the Great* there before going to Broadway. *Love and Libel*, a dramatization of Robertson DAVIES' novel *Leaven of Malice*, was produced there in 1960 prior to its opening on Broadway (where it was unsuccessful). THEATRE TORONTO had a hit at the Alex in 1968 with its production of Rolf Hochhuth's *Soldiers*.

Still a roadhouse and still operating without government subsidy, the Royal Alex continues to offer its subscribers a popular mix of musical hits from London or Broadway, serious drama, comedy, and star performers. The 1987-8 season, for example, consisted of George Abbott's and John Cecil Holm's *Three Men on a Horse*, Gilbert and Sullivan's *H.M.S. Pinafore*, Neil Simon's *Biloxi Blues* and *Broadway Bound*, N.F. Simpson's *One-Way Pendulum*, Tennessee Williams' *Sweet Bird of Youth*, and George Abbott's and Douglass Wallop's *Damn Yankees*.

HERBERT WHITTAKER

Royal Arctic Theatre. Intermittently between 1819 and 1876 plays were performed, by the officers and crews of ships wintering in the Canadian Arctic, on makeshift stages built either aboard the sailing vessels frozen in the ice or in 'snow-theatres' alongside. Although these venues were variously named, the term 'Royal Arctic Theatre' has come to serve as an umbrella title.

Following the establishment in 1818 of the British Navy's Arctic Service to search for a northern route to Asia, Lieut. Wm. E. Parry inaugurated the 'North Georgia Theatre' on the upper deck of HMS *Hecla* in 1819. Tarpaulins enclosed the space, and heat was first provided by red-hot cannonballs and later by ducts conducting warmed air from below. Depending on the latitude, temperatures ranged from −30°F to −45°F. Parry's theatre opened on 5 Nov. 1819 with David Garrick's *Miss in Her Teens*, and on 23 Dec. (repeated 2 Feb. 1820) it presented an original work optimistically titled *The North-West Passage; or, Voyage Finished*, which Parry co-authored. Sets and costumes were constructed from materials at hand, but for his second voyage (1821-2) Parry borrowed drop-scenes and wing-pieces, possibly from Halifax, where he performed in 1821.

The second wave of arctic theatre occurred in mid-century when forty different search parties (spurred by a £20,000 reward) tried for ten years to discover the fate of Sir John Franklin's doomed 1845-8 expedition. HMS *Assistance* advertised its seasons on playbills (sometimes printed on silk) and HMS *Resolute* included pictures and articles in their *Illustrated Arctic News* (printed between 30 Oct. 1850 and 14 Mar. 1851). Plays included J.R. Planché's *Charles XII*, W.B. Rhodes's burlesque *Bombastes Furioso*, and Garrick's adaptation of *The Taming of the Shrew*, as well as farcical afterpieces. The men of HMS *Pioneer* played Act 1 of *Hamlet* in an onshore ice-theatre on 21 Dec. 1852, although the actors were hardly visible in the clouds of vapour caused by the condensation of breath (perhaps a godsend for the gentleman who doubled the roles of Hamlet and Ophelia). The harlequinade *Zero; or, Harlequin Light* was given its world première on 9 Jan. 1851 and repeated at least twice. Written by assistant surgeon Charles Ede, it depicted the defeat of winter's perpetual darkness by Harlequin and Columbine disguised as Sun and Daylight. A second original, 'the laughable extravaganza' *King Glumpus*, by John Barrow, had its first performance on 1 Feb. 1853.

The British arctic theatre came to a close in 1875-6 during several attempts to reach the North Pole. A burlesque pantomime, H.J. Byron's *Aladdin; or, the Wonderful Scamp*, was performed below decks on HMS *Alert* on 23 Dec. 1875. Further south, in an Ellesmere Island snow-theatre, the officers and ordinary seamen of HMS *Discovery* took turns alternating productions every fortnight.

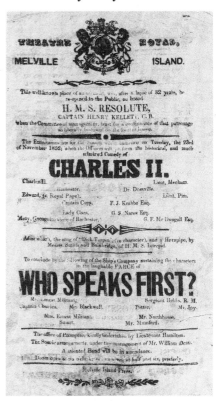

Playbill from HMS Resolute, *1852*

Sometimes the native Inuit population attended performances of the Royal Arctic Theatre and often reciprocated with drum dances and representations of hunting exploits.
DAVID GARDNER

Royal Lyceum Theatre. Toronto's first purpose-built theatre, it was the city's entertainment centre for a quarter of a century, 1848-74, providing the leading local stage not only for plays, operas, and musical comedies but also for minstrels, magicians, and gymnasts. It opened on 28 Dec. 1848 with a Philharmonic Society concert, and offered its first dramatic program (three short plays performed by Toronto and Hamilton amateurs) on 16 Jan. 1849. Designed and constructed by John Ritchey (or Ritchie), a local builder, it was a substantial brick building on a lot 36' by 94', seating 750 persons in boxes, gallery, and pit, and lighted by gas. Its awkward location behind shops on the south side of King St, between Bay and York, allowed access only by Theatre Lane or through an opening between 99 and 101 King St West. So bad was the theatre's design—cramped stage, clumsy pillars, poor sightlines, miserable dressing rooms, and inadequate ventilation—that lessees customarily began their tenure with extensive alterations. Of some dozen lessees, most failed because of hard times, incompetent management, or untalented stock actors; only John NICKINSON (1853-9 and 1860) and George HOLMAN (1867-72) achieved success. There were two temporary changes of name: to the Prince of Wales Theatre in 1860, in honour of the Prince's visit to Toronto, and the New Royal Lyceum in 1872-3, marking the takeover from Holman by John L. Saphore and DeWitt C. Waugh.

During its quarter-century, the theatre's dramatic fare was transformed from a limited range of London-spawned plays to a riotous succession of melodramas and spectacles, chiefly American. Such famous artists as James W. Wallack, William E. Burton, and Matilda Heron played at the Royal Lyceum in its first decade, but later the inferior stage facilities and limited capacity deprived Toronto of visits from first-rate stars. In 1859 Ritchey sold his theatre to James French, a provision merchant, who was still the owner on 30 Jan. 1874, when it was totally destroyed by fire.   MARY SHORTT

Rubes, Susan (b. 1925). Vienna-born Zuzka Zenta arrived in the United States at age fourteen and grew up to become a popular actress on stage, screen, radio, and television with a new name, Susan Douglas, picked from the Manhattan telephone book. She appeared on Theatre Guild of the Air, Studio One, and ABC Playhouse, and played Kathy in 'The Guiding Light' for ten years. She received the Donaldson Award for Best Supporting Performer in Tyrone GUTHRIE's Broadway production of Leonid Andreyev's *He Who Gets Slapped*. Her films include *Forbidden Journey*, shot in Montreal and featuring a young Czech actor-singer, Jan Rubes, whom she married. In 1960 they moved to Toronto with their three small sons.

Reacting to the absence of regular live theatre for children in Toronto, Susan Rubes borrowed $250 from ten friends in 1964 and was immediately successful with her Museum Children's Theatre. In 1966 she founded YOUNG PEOPLE'S THEATRE, a multi-faceted enterprise with weekend performances, tour-

ing companies, and a theatre school. In 1977 Young People's Theatre moved into its present location at 165 Front St, Toronto.

In 1980 Rubes returned to her 'first love', RADIO DRAMA. She was Head of CBC Drama for six years, initiating a training program for young directors, commissioning new scripts, and generally raising the profile of the department. Since leaving the CBC she has remained active in the arts, helping to manage the thriving acting career of her husband. Her many honours include the B'nai B'rith Women's Council 'Woman of the Year' Award (1979), the Toronto Theatre Bench Award for Achievement (1975), and the Order of Canada (1975). In 1988 the mainstage theatre of YPT was named the Susan Douglas Rubes Theatre.
                                        JOYCE DOOLITTLE

Russell Theatre. Located on Ottawa's Queen St at Elgin, beside the elegant Russell Hotel, it opened on 15 Oct. 1897. Designed by J.B. McElfatrick & Son of New York in Italian Renaissance style, it had 1,733 seats, including two balconies, ten private boxes, and four loge boxes. The stage was equipped with a large curtain, fifty adjustable scenic panels, and an elaborate lighting system; the proscenium arch was surmounted by a large painting, 'The Triumph of Drama', by Toronto artist Frederick Sponton Challener that was acquired by the National Gallery of Canada after the demise of the theatre. Destroyed by fire on 7 Apr. 1901, it was immediately rebuilt to the original plans and reopened on 5 Oct. 1901 as the New Russell Opera House under the management of Ambrose J. SMALL.

The Russell superseded the GRAND OPERA HOUSE as the home of legitimate theatre and music in Ottawa. It was patronized by Governors General and Prime Ministers, the élite and the ordinary, and was host to touring groups and actors from Canada, the U.S., England, and France. During its decline in the 1920s it presented VAUDEVILLE and motion pictures.

The last performance at the Russell was by the DUMBELLS. On 14 Apr. 1928 the adjoining Russell Hotel, which had been vacant since 1925, burned down; although the theatre was not damaged, it remained dark until its demolition in August to make way for Confederation Park (now Square). Ottawa then had no legitimate theatre for professional drama until 1969, when the NATIONAL ARTS CENTRE opened on almost the same site.

See Hilary Russell, *All That Glitters: A Memorial to Ottawa's Capitol Theatre and Its Predecessors* (1975).   JAMES NOONAN

Ryga, George (1932-87). The author of fifteen stage plays—in addition to over ninety scripts for radio, television, and film; three oratorios and two albums of folk songs; as well as a volume of poetry, four novels, sixteen short stories, and a documentary travelogue—Ryga was both one of the best-established and least-performed Canadian dramatists. A controversial figure in Canadian drama in the late sixties and early seventies, he progressively withdrew from mainstream theatre in Canada, although the strong moral commitment and radical socialism of his work won him a continuing reputation in Germany and Russia.

Ryga's Ukrainian family background and formative years spent on a farmstead bordering a Cree reservation in northern Alberta not only shaped the themes of his mature work but gave him the perspective of an outsider. Forced by poverty to leave school at thirteen, he continued his education by correspondence while working as a manual labourer. In 1949, and again in 1950, he won one of the two annual scholarships to the Banff School of Fine Arts (see BANFF CENTRE), where he became involved in protests against the Korean War. Such activism was again demonstrated in a 1953 Remembrance Day program for the Edmonton radio station CFRN, which used poems and songs from the trenches to make an anti-war statement. This caused a public outcry (the first of many in his career) and Ryga was forced to resign from CFRN after leading a protest rally over the Rosenberg treason case.

From these early experiences came his identification with the working classes; his perception of the need for a unifying cultural mythology drawn from popular sources (the exploited masses) to replace official history (limited to public figures); and his focus on protagonists who define themselves in opposition to an oppressive and alienating social structure, which turns all its citizens into displaced persons. In his first plays these figures are the poor or the exploited, while subsequent works include counter-culture

George Ryga

drop-outs and representatives of the Establishment.

Indian—produced by CBC television in 1962, published in 1971—depicts the spiritual emptiness of a materialistic society in its portrayal of the conflict between a government official and a symbolically anonymous Indian labourer in which the despised and degraded outcast dominates through the force of his despair. The plight of the dispossessed and their moral ascendancy is developed to tragic proportions in Ryga's best-known work, *The ECSTASY OF RITA JOE* (1970), first produced at the VANCOUVER PLAYHOUSE in 1967. Dealing with the martyrdom of an Indian girl, who is forced by city life into crime and prostitution and is caught in the mesh of a legal system that interprets justice as the maintenance of the status quo, and is murdered by a gang of rapists, the action exposes the dichotomy between liberal ideals and the behaviour that society condones. Although the specific dramatic situations relate to racial questions, on a deeper level these Indians stand as an extreme example of exploitation, which is seen as endemic and as affecting all ethnic groups. The Indian

Ryga

'Everyman' of a proposed television series (*Born of Man*) is an almost exact equivalent to the protagonist in Ryga's first full-length play, *Nothing But A Man*, unpublished, but performed at Walterdale Playhouse, Edmonton, in 1966: a migrant worker of Polish background whose search for his roots, and for the future through an unborn son, provides a panorama of Canadian society. Reflecting the search for a Canadian identity, this heroic symbol of proletarian labour both challenges an exploitative system and serves as a catalyst in changing the attitudes of those with whom he interacts.

Grass and Wild Strawberries (produced at the Vancouver Playhouse in 1969, published in 1971) uses psychedelic staging and rock music and deals with teenage life and the generation gap. Intending to offer a positive alternative to the social system portrayed in the preceding plays, Ryga sets up a political triangle between an old socialist, whose gradualism leads him to capitulate to the most reactionary element of the Establishment, a 'partisan of chaos' representing the anarchic preconditions for social change, and the young protagonist, who has a mystical vision. This positive alternative was given a new dimension in the next two major plays. *Captives of the Faceless Drummer* (produced at the Vancouver Art Gallery and also published in 1971) is the most immediately political of Ryga's works, with its analogies to contemporary FLQ kidnappings in Quebec: it centres on the relationship between a revolutionary leader and his diplomat hostage, who form a bond of common identity. Against a projected future of ecological disaster and the complete breakdown of urban society, the Establishment representative (the diplomat) comes to affirm a new morality of sexual liberation. Political argument is intercut with memory scenes, and this psychological level forms the whole action in *Sunrise on Sarah*, (a 1972 Banff School of Fine Arts production, published in 1973). Here the protagonist is a composite of middle-class women interviewed by Ryga; the other figures are projections of suppressed desires or socially conditioned fears. Sarah gains the insight to reject both her reduction to a sex object and the self-destructive urge to conform. The ending, however, is ambiguous: although the final statement is one of liberation, the absence of any tangible reality in the play means that it can be seen as a retreat into isolation, madness being preferable to the 'cure' offered by an insane society.

Such a political standpoint equates artistic success with co-option by the system, and Ryga's concern about public acceptance is reflected in the character of a self-indulgent ballad singer in *The Ecstasy of Rita Joe*, as well as in early drafts of *Grass and Wild Strawberries* (where the popularity of *Rita Joe* is seen as transforming serious social concern into entertainment in a way that inhibits rather than promotes change) and in *Captives of the Faceless Drummer* (where the central figure, initially a playwright, substitutes literary accomplishment for political action, his moral values having been undermined by success). The relations between art and politics also form the main theme of a short play, *Just an Ordinary Person* (produced at Metro Theatre, Vancouver, in 1968, but unpublished), which takes one of Ryga's poems about Garcia Lorca's death as its starting-point. Here the strongly autobiographical poet-protagonist is challenged by a proletarian figure from the audience to redefine his art so that it can become the voice of the masses. The later period in Ryga's work is an attempt to find ways of doing this.

The plays from 1966 to 1972 are structurally complex, using expressionistic elements in an 'orchestrated composition' to present dream states or to merge past and present in a largely interior drama. Their large casts, choreographed action, and scenic demands mark them as main-stage work. From 1972 on, however, Ryga's plays were increasingly shaped for alternate-theatre and working-class audiences. Techniques for connecting interior monologue with social reality are explored in *Portrait of Angelica* (Banff, 1973; unpublished), in the political morality play *Seven Hours to Sundown* (Univ. of Alberta, 1976; published 1977), and in *A Letter To My Son* (KAM THEATRE, Thunder Bay, 1981; published 1982); while *Last of the Gladiators* (Giant's Head Theatre Company, Summerland, B.C., 1976), an adaptation of Ryga's novel *Night Desk* (1976), and *Ploughmen of the Glacier* (Western Canada Theatre Co., Kamloops, B.C.; published 1977) return to the stark simplicity and symbolic realism of *Indian*. These later plays move from defining the absence of authentic Canadian culture to attempting to create prototypes of a national mythology embodied in unsophisticated but heroic figures. These prototypes range from an old-age pensioner who encapsulates the socialist immigrant experience (in *A Letter to My Son*) to a broken-down wrestler (in *Last of the Gladiators*) or legendary figures like Volcanic Brown, the prospector who discovered Cooper Mountain in *Ploughmen of the Glacier*. Apart from *Portrait of Angelica* (commissioned by the Banff Centre), these plays were designed for performance by theatrical co-ops or local touring companies. Oriented to working-class audiences, their subject matter reflects on a populist level the background and concerns of labourers, farmers, and miners in rural B.C. Though the simpler and more realistic of these plays (in particular, *Ploughmen of the Glacier*) have been highly successful in that context, more poetic myth-making attempts have not—whether exploring history for positive role models, as in *Paracelsus* (produced at the Vancouver Playhouse in Sept. 1986, and published in 1974), or celebrating the archetypes of class struggle, as in Ryga's oratorios *Twelve Ravens For The Sun* (written in 1972-3, not produced) and *A Feast of Thunder* (produced in Massey Hall, Toronto, in 1973).

Ryga's themes show a remarkable consistency, though his style has been eclectic and his use of different media unusually wide. A script may have been written for television, then revised for radio before being adapted to the stage. The same material may form the basis for a novel or a play. But Ryga's anti-establishment stance, which led him to reject main-stage drama for 'people's theatre', may explain the critical neglect his work has suffered.

Indian, however, has been republished in several anthologies. *The Ecstasy of Rita Joe*—which had an exceptionally favourable response and inspired a ballet version that was first produced by the Royal Winnipeg Ballet in 1971—was hailed as a landmark in Canadian drama; reviews testified to its emotional power in performance. The Vancouver production of *Grass and Wild Strawberries* became a cult event, although its identification with the hippie movement of the late 1960s dates it badly. With the production of *Captives of the Faceless Drummer*, however, Ryga was labelled a narrowly ideological playwright in the light of the intensely political controversy that surrounded it, with the result that the wider themes of this and Ryga's subsequent works have been generally overlooked. The poetic vision and social commitment of all his theatrical works give them considerable force, and his technical experimentation—unusual in Canadian drama—was truly innovative in the way it sought to extend the range of the stage, even if it was not always successful stylistically.

See Christopher Innes, *Politics and the Playwright: George Ryga* (1985).

CHRISTOPHER INNES

S

Sablonnière, Blanche de la (c. 1855-?). Born Angéline Lussier in Saint-Hyacinthe, Que., she first performed as a teenager with an amateur group, Les Artisans, in *Pierre Lenoir et les chauffeurs* at Montreal's ACADEMY OF MUSIC. Her professional début was in *Marie Jeanne; ou la femme du peuple* in Mar. 1887 at the Bijou Theatre, with Louis Labelle and Madame Larcher. She subsequently appeared with several touring companies before returning to Montreal in the late 1890s. From 1900 to 1916 de la Sablonnière was a leading member at the THÉÂTRE NATIONAL, enjoying great success in plays such as Alexandre Dumas *fils'* *Le Conte de Monte Cristo*, Alexandre Dumas *père's* *Les Trois Mousquetaires*, Prosper Mérimée's *Carmen*, M. Dumanois's and A.P. Dennery's *Don César de Bazan*, and Dennery's *Martyr*. Her husband Jos Tremblay owned several theatres, including the THÉÂTRE DE LA PLACE JACQUES-CARTIER in Quebec City, and also founded a company for her called the Théâtre de la Sablonnière. After the First World War, when theatrical activity had declined, the couple bought a hotel in Quebec City and 'la Sarah Bernhardt canadienne'—one of the most important of the early generation of French-Canadian professional actors—retired after a thirty-year career.   JOHN E. HARE

Sabourin, Jean-Guy (b. 1934). Born at L'Orignal, Ont., he attended the Collège Sainte-Croix in Montreal, the Univ. of Montreal, and the Univ. of Ottawa. He taught at Collège Sainte-Croix from 1957 to 1968, and since 1970 has taught at the Univ. of Quebec.

In 1955 Sabourin co-founded Les APPRENTIS-SORCIERS in Montreal, serving as artistic director from 1956 to 1966 and directing over twenty plays there, mainly from the contemporary European repertoire—Claudel, Brecht, Ionesco, Dürrenmatt, Gorki, Synge, and Adamov. After a year as head of drama for the Quebec Ministry of Cultural Affairs (1966-7), he ran Le Théâtre du Capricorne at the NATIONAL ARTS CENTRE (1968-70) before assumimg the artistic directorship of Le THÉÂTRE POPULAIRE DU QUÉBEC (1972-6), where he emphasized the production of Quebec works such as Jean BARBEAU's *Le Chant du sink*, André Major's *Une Soirée en octobre*, Jean-Robert Rémillard's *La Vie éjarrée de Dollard des Ormeaux*, and Roch CARRIER's *Ce Soir on improvise*. In 1976 he founded Le Théâtre de la Grande-Réplique (which he still runs), where—with productions such as Brecht's *La Vie de Galilée* (*Galileo*) in 1980—he has confirmed his reputation as an inventive and energetic director.
                                MADELEINE GREFFARD

Saga des poules mouillées, La. First produced on 24 Apr. 1981 at Montreal's THÉÂTRE DU NOUVEAU MONDE, directed by Michelle Rossignol, this powerful feminist play by Jovette MARCHESSAULT pays homage to creative works by women, especially four French- Canadian women—Laure Conan (Félicité Angers), Germaine Guèvremont, Gabrielle Roy, and Anne HÉBERT—who meet 'in the northern regions of the Promised Land of America, in the heart of a mythical vortex.' An apparently rambling conversation on a variety of subjects, *La Saga* gradually works its way towards its main objective: the revenge of women on history and literature. It is clear, however, that there is little resemblance between Marchessault's characters and

their historical counterparts. From the first tableau ('The Awakening'), the historically pious Laure Conan, for example, uses the coarsest of language to dispel the myths she was subjected to in her time.

The first two tableaux consist of conversations—one between Laure Conan and Germaine Guèvremont, the other between Anne Hébert and Gabrielle Roy. The third tableau anachronistically unites the four women, who stay together to the end of the play. The fourth tableau establishes the idea developed in the fifth ('How forceps came to man')—that a book be written jointly by the four women to 'overcome legend, myth, and history', as Roy puts it in the sixth and final tableau, which concludes with a list of distinguished women that the book will rescue from the oblivion imposed by men.

The use of time-travel to unite the four famous authors affords the opportunity for penetrating commentary on their critics, the public response to their works, and the image of women writers. The light, comical, and iconoclastic tone of the opening tableau is quickly succeeded by a more lyrical one in which Marchessault's diction recalls the richness of the poetic imagery in her novels *Comme un enfant de la terre* (1975) and *La Mère des herbes* (1980).

La Saga des poules mouillées (1981) was published by Les Éditions de la Pleine Lune, and in an English translation (by Linda Gaboriau) as *The Saga of the the Wet Hens* (1982) by Talonbooks, following a 1981 première at Toronto's TARRAGON THEATRE.

See also FEMINIST THEATRE.
                                ANNE-MARIE ALONZO

Sagouine, La. This one-woman play, for which Antonine MAILLET is best known, is a collection of sixteen monologues delivered by La Sagouine, a seventy-two-year-old Acadian woman, who recalls her life as the wife and daughter of fishermen, and as a prostitute when sailors were in port, and who now earns a meagre living as a scrubwoman. The name 'La Sagouine', a nickname and the only one by which she has ever been known, ironically suggests that its bearer belongs to a somewhat unclean lower order of being. In fact she has beauty and dignity earned through a life of work and suffering.

The thematic and documentary interest of *La Sagouine* is closely linked to the language of its only character. She uses a roughened

Viola Léger as La Sagouine

version of the popular speech, specific to Acadia, brought to New France in the seventeenth century by her ancestors (the first time these authentic accents were used in a literary work). The play is also important for its social commentary on discrimination and injustice arising from race, class, and gender. Rarely does La Sagouine get angry herself or criticize the hypocrisy and injustice of which she is so obviously a victim. Instead, while she evokes—often with humour—the rich flavour of her existence, it is left to her absent husband Gapi, or to the audience, to name the guilty and to accuse them of cruelty, exploitation, and base self-interest. Through La Sagouine, Maillet rejects the attitude of sweet and quiet submission—as symbolized by Acadia's traditional heroine, Evangeline—in favour of awareness, protest, and action.

La Sagouine first appeared as a character in Maillet's play *Les Crasseux* (1968). Here she is only forty, but her language, social condition, and character are already established. La Sagouine subsequently appeared in a series of fifteen-minute texts written and read by Maillet on radio station CBAF in Moncton. In 1970 the Centre d'essai des auteurs dramatiques sponsored a dramatic reading by Monique Joly at the MONUMENT NATIONAL, Montreal, of some of the monologues and

then collaborated with Les Éditions Leméac in their publication in 1971.

La Sagouine has been synonymous with the name of Viola Léger who created the title role. Directed by Eugène Gallant, she toured as La Sagouine through the Maritimes in 1971-2 and in 1972, as New Brunswick's entry to the DOMINION DRAMA FESTIVAL, performed *La Sagouine* in Saskatoon where, despite controversy and mixed reactions, it won the adjudicators' unqualified praise. In 1972-3 *La Sagouine* ran in Montreal at the THÉÂTRE DU RIDEAU VERT, first as part of its experimental program on Monday evenings and then as part of the regular program for two successive seasons. The sixteen-episode series was presented on Radio-Canada in 1972. In 1973 Léger gave four performances in Paris at the Canadian Cultural Centre and toured the play in the Maritimes, Quebec, and Ontario. In 1974 six of the book's remaining episodes were performed at the NATIONAL ARTS CENTRE and then at the Rideau Vert as *La Sagouine II*.

Published in France in 1976, the play toured some twenty-five major European cities in the same year, including a successful run in Paris at Jean-Louis Barrault's Petit Orsay theatre. It was taken to the Festival artistique d'Avignon in 1978. The English version of *La Sagouine*, translated by Luis de Céspedes (1979), received the 1980 CHALMERS Award. Still in the title role, performing in English, Viola Léger toured English Canada in 1980.

See Laurent Mailhot, 'La Sagouine', *Études françaises*, 8 (1972); G. Chesneau, 'Les modalités de socialisation du *Je* de la récitante dans *La Sagouine* d'Antonine Maillet', *Le Théâtre canadien-français. Archives des lettres canadiennes*, 5 (1975); Micheline Tremblay, 'Interview d'Antonine Maillet sur *La Sagouine*', *Canadian Drama*, 2 (1976).

LOUISE H. FORSYTH

Saidye Bronfman Centre. Founded in 1967 by the YM-YWHA with funding from the Bronfman family, Montreal's Saidye Bronfman Centre has served as both a Jewish community centre and a cultural resource to diverse communities. Along with services in fine arts, music, and education, the production of professional theatre in the functional 230-seat auditorium has been given high priority since its inception: until 1982, when

Saidye Bronfman Centre

financial problems forced closure, the Centre mounted its own productions.

Under its three artistic directors—Marion ANDRE (1967-72), Muriel Gold (1972-80), Per Brask (1980-82)—the Centre provided anglophone Montreal with quality theatre, producing over sixty plays from the international and Canadian repertoire, both serious drama and stylish comedy or musicals. Ibsen's *A Doll's House* (1970), Neil Simon's *The Gingerbread Lady* (1974), Michel TREMBLAY's *Bonjour, là, Bonjour* (1977), *Side by Side by Sondheim* (1978), and Harold Pinter's *Betrayal* (1982) are representative examples.

During Andre's tenure the Centre instituted a four-play season of international fare, producing plays by Brecht, Athol Fugard, Joe Orton, Paddy Chayefsky, and others. In one notable production of *A Doll's House* Louise Marleau played a Québécois Nora to an obviously Anglo Torvald. Unfortunately the Centre received its greatest publicity during this period for the event that led to Andre's resignation: the cancellation by the Centre's Board, in Feb. 1972, of Robert Shaw's controversial play *The Man in the Glass Booth*, in response to pressure from holocaust survivors and the YM-YWHA board.

After Andre resigned the Centre seemed willing to let the professional theatre disappear; but the extraordinary efforts of Muriel Gold, who reorganized the 1972-3 theatre season, and of the Centre's new executive director Nahum Ravel, who helped smooth relations between the Centre and the YM-YWHA board, averted closure. Subscriptions, which in 1972-3 had collapsed from 2,000 to 200, mounted to over 3,000 in 1973-4.

Gold, who produced rather than directed, brought the Centre both popular and critical success. Her commitment to producing English- and French-Canadian plays each year was particularly important: English versions of John T. McDONOUGH's *CHARBONNEAU & LE CHEF*, Michel GARNEAU's *Quatre à Quatre*, and Tremblay's *Bonjour, là, Bonjour* were singularly successful. Gold also supported local artists and dramatists by sponsoring Théâtre Rencontre (a project of allied Jewish Community Services, Playwrights' Workshop, and Centre d'essai des auteurs dramatiques), where short English and French plays were produced on the same evening; by establishing the Second Stage, an alternative, experimental company primarily made up of local

theatre graduates; and by bringing Dora WASSERMAN's Yiddish Theatre under the wing of the Centre.

Through the 1970s subscriptions rose to 6,000. In 1979-80 the Centre's season expanded to six shows, but it was plagued by internal and financial problems and was not successful. An ambitious venture to stage Arnold Wesker's *The Merchant* at Place des Arts was cancelled when the Y board feared the production would be too costly. Despite the critical success achieved by Per Brask, Gold's successor as artistic director, the theatre's fortunes continued to wane. In May 1982, as subscriptions dipped to 1,600 and the projected deficit rose to over $100,000, the YM-YWHA decided to close down the professional company. Since then the theatre has served as a roadhouse, and in 1983-4 as the auditorium for the independent Encore Theatre.

Following extensive renovations—which increased seating capacity to 325—the SBC theatre re-opened in Jan. 1987 with a commitment to produce Quebec and Jewish plays, but with no provision for a resident professional company.

JONATHAN RITTENHOUSE

Saint-Denis, Michel (1897-1971). This French actor, director, educator, and writer apprenticed with his uncle, Jacques Copeau, at the Théâtre du Vieux-Colombier in Paris, and later (1924-9) worked with Copeau as writer and actor at Les Copiaus in Burgundy. In 1929 Saint-Denis founded La Compagnie des Quinze, whose annual visits to London from 1931 to 1934 initiated Saint-Denis's career in Britain as a director and educator. With the establishment of the London Theatre Studio in 1935, Saint-Denis created the blueprint of a theatre-training program that provided the foundation of London's Old Vic Theatre Centre, Strasbourg's L'École Supérieure d'Art Dramatique, New York's Juilliard School Drama Division, and Montreal's NATIONAL THEATRE SCHOOL, founded in 1960. As an adjudicator for the DOMINION DRAMA FESTIVAL (1937, 1950, 1952, 1958, 1959), Saint-Denis made a lasting contribution to the development of professional theatre in Canada and the training of young professional actors. BRIAN SMITH

Saint John Opera House. Opened on 21 Sept. 1891 with the New York Stock Company's presentation of *The Marble Heart*, the Opera House replaced the ACADEMY OF MUSIC (burned 1877). Built on land leased from Richard H. and John F. Dockrill, its 60′ long grand lobby was entered through the front of a store on Union Street. Plans drawn by J.C. Dumaresque in 1883 called for a 62′ × 101′ building (exclusive of two vestibules 24′ × 24′ and 26′ × 34′ and a 37′ × 38′ wing for 6 dressing rooms), and for a stage 58′ × 35′. *Julius Cahn's Official Theatrical Guide* (1906) gives the stage dimensions as 60′ × 40′, with a proscenium opening of 29′6″ square. The depth under the stage was 9′ (there were 5 traps). The height to the fly gallery was 23′, to the rigging loft 51′, and the distance between fly girders 39′6″. There were no grooves. There were twenty footlights and three rows of border lights on reflectors, twenty in a row. The house was lit by electricity (seven different circuits controlled from a switchboard on the stage), and heated by steam. Sidney Chidley was scene painter. The structure took advantage of the natural slope of the site, with the horseshoe-shaped auditorium being at street level and the balcony and gallery rising with the incline. Seats were of oak, upholstered in crimson plush, each with its own hatrack (304 orchestra, 258 dress circle, 302 balcony, and 400 gallery).

In the first half of the 1890s the board of directors, under President Alfred O. Skinner, struggled against inadequate financing, high transportation costs, and duties on theatrical equipment. In 1893 the theatre lost about $300 on the Standard Opera Company, and the floating indebtedness increased to about $12,000. On the other hand 1900 saw a cash credit of over $1,570. Ticket prices varied in the 1890s from the 10¢, 20¢, and 30¢ charged by Ethel Tucker, Mora Williams, the John S. Moulton Co., and others to the 25¢, 35¢, 50¢, 75¢, and $1.00 asked by Lewis Morrison. His $571.35 earnings for one evening of *Faust* in August 1896 were the highest of that year. By 1913 opera tickets could cost as much as $2.00. The Opera House attracted both 'the elite and commonalty of St John' to watch a succession of touring companies: repertory companies such as those of Thomas Shea, W.S. Harkins, H. Price WEBBER, Frankie Carpenter, Arthur Rehan, Katherine Rober, Mme. Janauschek, Mme. Rhea, Tyrone Power, James O'Neill, Robert Mantell, Mae EDWARDS, Arlie Marks, F. James

Carroll, Florence Glossup-Harris, the Valentine Co; one-play companies offering staples like *Side-Tracked*, Frank Tannehill's *Nancy Hanks*, Sutton Vane's *The Span of Life*, and H. Grattan Donnelly's *Darkest Russia*; opera companies such as the Jaxon, Robinson, New York Bijou, and Jules Grau Companies; and minstrel and VAUDEVILLE companies. Former Saint Johners like Margaret ANGLIN, Ethel Mollison, Grace Hunter, and Owen Coll returned to adorn the stage. Amateur companies sometimes rented the theatre and after 1900 movies were commonly shown. From 1929, when touring companies stopped coming, the Opera House was used only sporadically, the newer IMPERIAL having taken its place. It burned down in 1954.

MARY ELIZABETH SMITH

Saltimbanques, Les. An avant-garde amateur company, it was founded in Montreal on 12 July 1962 by former members of Les APPRENTIS-SORCIERS. Under the direction of Rodrig Mathieu, the new company opened on 8 Mar. 1963 with Romain Weingarten's *Akara* in a 50-seat theatre in a converted warehouse on rue Saint-Paul. The stage measured 33′ × 26′ with a height of 21′; seating capacity was increased to 94 in 1964.

For six years Les Saltimbanques presented an international repertoire of plays, often North American premières. Among the playwrights whose works were produced were Jean Genet, René de Obaldia, Fernando Arrabal, Armand Gatti, Boris Vian, Murray Schisgal, Slawomir Mrozek, and two Québécois: Roger Huard and Michel Vaïs. Romain Weingarten's *Les Nourrices* was the company's most popular production, attracting an audience of 2,500.

Although amateur, Les Saltimbanques operated with professional discipline, offering regular seasons of six or seven plays on a subscription or single-sale basis. Working (or studying) during the day, its members performed four evenings per week (Thursday to Sunday) and rehearsed the next play on the other three evenings, as well as during the day on Saturdays and Sundays. To sustain the company financially, each member paid a weekly fee throughout the year. This income was supplemented by occasional government grants, mostly for special projects, and private fundraising. Members who subsequently became established actors include Claude Gai,

Saltimbanques

Jacques Crête, Robert Toupin, and Carol Laure.

The theatre faced two major crises in its brief history. It had to close for three months in 1966 for renovations ordered by the Montreal Fire Department. And in 1967 the morality squad of the Montreal police arrested nine of the twelve actors appearing in *Équation pour un homme actuel* at Expo 67 as part of the Festival des Jeunes Compagnies. Accused of taking part in an indecent performance, the actors were convicted by the municipal court of Montreal, but won their appeal to the Quebec superior court a year later. Written by company member Pierre Moretti and directed by Mathieu, *Équation*—a fresco of the human condition—consists of sixteen tableaux, one of which, 'Erotomanies', is sexually suggestive. Despite the prosecution and the banning of the play (see also CENSORSHIP), the company received a $20,000 grant from the Quebec Ministry of Cultural Affairs to take *Équation* to the Festival de Nancy in France in 1968. On its return, however, when the company was evicted from its theatre (allegedly for late rental payments), it merged with Les Apprentis-Sorciers and André BRASSARD's Mouvement Contemporain to form Le Centre du THÉÂTRE D'AUJOURD'HUI.

See Michel Vaïs, 'Les Saltimbanques (1962–1969)', *Jeu*, 2 (1976).   MICHEL VAIS

Salutin, Rick (b. 1942). On completing degrees at Brandeis and Columbia, he abandoned his doctoral work in philosophy at New York's New School for Social Research and returned to his native Toronto, in 1970, after reading Harold Innis's *The Fur Trade in Canada*, which Salutin claims 'made sense of the present by making sense of the past.' He worked with labour leaders Kent Rowley and Madeleine Parent, learning from them what he calls 'a welcome antidote to the rather abstract politics with which I'd emerged from the American New Left.' Moral passion colours all his writing—journalism, satire, and plays—and has charged his varied roles as trade-union agitator for the Artistic Woodwork strike in Toronto in 1970; satirist for the CBC radio series, 'Inside from the Outside'; journalist for *Harper's*, *Today*, *Weekend*, and *Maclean's*; editor and contributor for *This Magazine*; and dramatist.

Salutin's first play, *Fanshen*, produced in 1972 by TORONTO WORKSHOP PRODUC-

TIONS, was an adaptation of William Hinton's study of the effects of the Chinese Revolution on the life of a small village, from which Salutin drew an analogy with the October Crisis in Quebec. Subsequent unpublished plays showed a concern for the underprivileged: *The Adventures of an Immigrant* (THEATRE PASSE MURAILLE, Toronto, 1974); *I.W.A.* (MUMMERS TROUPE, St. John's, 1975); *Money*, a one-act musical (YOUNG PEOPLE'S THEATRE, Toronto, 1976); and *Maria*, a CBC television drama (1977) about a young woman struggling to unionize factory workers.

Salutin's first published play, *1837: The Farmers' Revolt* (1975), was created in collaboration with Paul THOMPSON and the actors of Theatre Passe Muraille in 1973. It is a collage of DOCUMENTARY DRAMA, expressionist symbolism, and satire about William Lyon Mackenzie's aborted rebellion in colonial Canada. Later revised, the play's regionalism was broadened, its rhetoric toned down, its dramatic focus sharpened. The new version, a runner-up for the CHALMERS Award for Best Canadian Play, toured Canada and Scotland and was produced on CBC television in 1975.

Salutin's most popular play, written with assistance from NHL goalie Ken Dryden, is *Les CANADIENS* (1977), which premièred at the CENTAUR THEATRE, Montreal. Winner of the 1977 Chalmers Award, *Les Canadiens* continued Salutin's preoccupation with interpreting the present in the light of the past.

Salutin's commitment to social reform has not always found a suitable theatrical form. *The False Messiah: a Messianic Farce* (1981), produced at Passe Muraille in 1975, is so contrived in characterization, dialogue, and plot that its ultimate argument for philosophic humour in the face of persecution seems unconvincing. *Nathan Cohen: a Review* (published in the *Canadian Theatre Review*, Spring 1981) celebrates a critic (q.v.) who espoused the cause of indigenous theatre, but its lame musical segments—overblown in their sympathy for its brash, egotistical, opinionated subject—trivialize the issue. The 1981 Passe Muraille production was not a success. *Joey*—a 1982 portrayal of the life of Joseph Smallwood, former premier of Newfoundland, written in collaboration with the Rising Tide Theatre, St John's—does not move beyond a superficial presentation of Smallwood's personality.

A winner of two National Magazine Awards for comment and criticism, Salutin has written for media other than live theatre: with Murray Soupcoff and Gary Dunford, *Good Buy Canada!* (1975), a collection of satirical humour; a 1980 biography of Kent Rowley, labour leader; and a collection of his journalism, *Marginal Notes: Challenges to the Mainstream* (1984). His CBC television script, *Grierson and Gouzenko*, was broadcast in 1986. KEITH GAREBIAN

Saskatchewan, Theatre in. 1. *1878-1900.* Native people provided the first entertainment for settlers in the Northwest. These performances—such as one at Hay Station on Christmas Day 1878 in which 'several native performers' took part—were probably 'thirst' or 'Sun' dances, some of which were recorded photographically by Geraldine Moody at the Battlefords in 1895.

During the early years of white settlement the impetus toward theatricals came primarily from the North West Mounted Police in the form of minstrel shows and one-act afterpieces. Especially active was Trumpeter Harry Walker, who organized the Star Minstrels and Variety Troupe in Battleford in 1878, and groups in Qu'Appelle and Regina in the 1880s. After 1885 the military took over minstrel shows, and the NWMP turned their attention to dramatic evenings: Prince Albert audiences in May 1886 witnessed J.M. Morton's *Box and Cox* by the 'F' Division Dramatic Club, and in Feb. 1887 H.T. Craven's *The Chimney Corner* and T.J. Williams' *Ici on Parle Français* at the police barracks.

Although the theatrical laurels graced the police and military barracks, the settlers were not inactive. The Presbyterian Mission House in Prince Albert featured local entertainment by 1878, followed by the Lone Hand Minstrel Troupe at Richard's Hall, and J.J. Campbell's Penny Readings in 1879. Notices of entertainments in the Battlefords date from 1879, and by 1881 private theatricals were a regular occurrence at Government House.

The Pioneer Society initiated Saskatoon's theatrical history with a concert on 1 Dec. 1884 at the Lake Building. James Hambley's minstrel shows appeared in Regina in the 1880s, but the driving theatrical force in the town was Catherine Simpson Hayes, who wrote and produced *A Domestic Disturbance* in 1892, *T'Other from Which* (1894), *Slumberland Shadows* (1894 and 1895), *Fairyland*

(1896), *The Duplicate Man* (1897), and *Cinderella* (1898 and 1899). The Regina Musical and Dramatic Society was organized in 1897 with John S. Dennis as its conductor. Failure to pay royalties on a production of Gilbert and Sullivan's *Pirates of Penzance* in 1899 led to a lawsuit and a $1,000 fine; a series of benefit performances raised the funds necessary to pay the fine.

2. *1900-14.* With the new century and confederation with Canada in 1905, new towns and theatres sprang up; by 1915 nearly 400 licensed theatres and halls existed, many of them incorporated into town-hall complexes. The Regina Town Hall housed theatricals between 1886 and 1909. In addition, the Auditorium Rink was used as a summer theatre (1905-8), where both Madame Albani (1906) and Minnie Maddern Fiske (1907) appeared in defiance of Marc Klaw's and Abe Erlanger's Syndicate, a growing American touring monopoly. With the building of a new City Hall and theatre in 1908, the old Town Hall was leased to Barney Groves and C.P. WALKER as the Regina Theatre. When they were unable to renew their lease, they built a new REGINA THEATRE, which opened on 7 Feb. 1910, and switched allegiance from Klaw and Erlanger's Syndicate to the Shuberts. The Majestic Theatre, opened in December 1911, offered VAUDEVILLE.

In Saskatoon, R. Dulmage built in 1900 the Saskatoon Music Hall, where the Dramatic Club, founded by D. Harry Williams, made its début with *The Noble Outcast* on 19 Mar. 1903. The opening of the SASKATOON OPERA HOUSE later that year forced the closure of Dulmage's Hall. In 1906 a second Saskatoon Opera House opened, operating under a variety of names until 1916. In the Kevin Theatre, opened in 1907, John Pringle, a local businessman, unsuccessfully attempted to form the first permanent stock company in Saskatchewan. A second attempt in 1908 also failed, and the Kevin became primarily a movie house, known as the Bijou and subsequently as the Starland. With the opening of the EMPIRE THEATRE, which received first-rate touring attractions, on 29 Dec. 1910, the Starland Company bought the Lyric (originally the Saskatoon Opera House) for $18,000 and renamed it the Starland. (The former Kevin/Bijou/Starland became a stable.) The King Edward Theatre, later the Orpheum, opened in Feb. 1911 and competed with the Starland for second-rate attractions and VAUDEVILLE. The Orpheum was the first major theatre space in Saskatchewan to be destroyed by fire. (The Princess in Battleford suffered a major fire earlier in 1912 but reopened after three months.) Plans for a Saskatoon Concert Hall to replace the Orpheum failed, and the STRAND THEATRE, opening in Sept. 1913, became the city's second-rank theatre.

Stars and companies performing in Saskatchewan theatres included Robert Mantell (1908), Nellie Melba (1910), Lewis Waller (1913), Maude Adams (1913), Laurence Irving (1914), John Martin-Harvey (1914), the Stratford-Upon-Avon Players (1914), Sir Johnstone Forbes-Robertson (1915), Marie Tempest (1915), and Sophie Tucker (1915). C.P. Walker of Winnipeg, in association with Barney Groves of Regina, booked most of these attractions, along with Canadian companies. Harold Nelson SHAW toured the province repeatedly with Walker's All-Canadian Company, beginning in 1903. The first tour of the MARKS BROTHERS of Ontario in 1904-5 was marred by an accident to Tom Marks in Prince Albert, who was replaced by Jimmie Shields. An early favourite in the province was the Stultz Stock Company led by Aggie Marion Stultz. Born in Winnipeg and raised in Batoche, Mrs Stultz starred with the San Francisco Opera Company before leading her husband's company in tours of Saskatchewan in 1908 and 1909. Other Canadian touring stock companies included the Permanent Players, the Dominion Stock Company, the Majestic Stock Company, the Winnipeg Stock Company, the Eckhardt Players, and the Juvenile Bostonians. Oliver J. Eckhardt's company always performed as a first-rate attraction; the Juvenile Bostonians did so at their inception in 1906, but ten years later were reduced to touring to rural communities and second- or third-rate theatres. All the theatres housed vaudeville as well as legitimate attractions. The major touring circuits—Sullivan and Considine; Rock, Keith, and Proctor; William Morris; Alexander PANTAGES—were all represented in the province.

Amateur theatricals also thrived. The Regina Music and Dramatic Society became the Philharmonic Society in 1906, producing Gilbert and Sullivan. Reorganized as the Operatic Society in 1909, it offered popular operettas at the Regina Theatre. Formation of The Players in 1912 led to a merger of the

two groups in 1913 as the Regina Amateur Society.

In Saskatoon the Dramatic Club gave way to the Saskatoon Philharmonic Society in June 1908; their Feb. 1909 production of Gilbert and Sullivan's *H.M.S. Pinafore* toured to Regina and was revived to open the Empire Theatre in Dec. 1910. The Saskatoon Orpheus Society, formed in 1913, produced Robert Planquette's *The Chimes of Normandy* that year; active into the 1920s, the Society provided choruses for visiting touring shows.

3. *1915-45*. Theatrical activity declined with the outbreak of the First World War. Regina's Majestic closed in 1915, Saskatoon's Star in 1916, and the Strand in 1919. The Dreamland, which opened in Saskatoon in Aug. 1916 as a vaudeville house, converted to movies one month later. Summer tent shows and open-air theatre, however, continued. Billie Oswald opened the Summer Pavilion in Regina in May 1917, its success leading W.B. Sherman to re-open the Auditorium Rink as the Sherman Theatre. Notable among tent shows was the CHAUTAUQUA circuit, active across the Prairies from 1917 through the middle of the Depression, presenting lecturers, musical variety, and theatrical productions to rural communities in an educational format.

With the war's end the Empire Theatre in Saskatoon was restored at a cost of $80,000 and the new Daylight offered vaudeville and movies in the city. From 400 theatres before the war, stage activity in the 1920s diminished to the Olympia (Assiniboia); Orpheum (Estevan); Grand (Melfort); Princess (Melville); Capitol, Orpheum, and Regent (Moose Jaw); Empress (North Battleford); Strand and Orpheum (Prince Albert); Capitol and Regina (Regina); Daylight and Empire (Saskatoon); Lyric (Swift Current); and the Dominion and Princess (Yorkton).

Fewer touring attractions were available: Fred Allen (1920), Sir John Martin-Harvey (1924, 1928), Robert B. Mantell (1926), the D'Oyle Carte Opera (1927), and annual visits by the DUMBELLS with Regina native Ben Allan. The collapse of the stock market, the advent of talking pictures, and the refusal of owners to rent to live theatre reduced live theatre further to visits by the Dumbells and the English Lyric Opera Company (1931), Martin-Harvey and Sir Barry Jackson (1932), the Dumbells (1933), and Fay Baker, international fan dancer (1934). In the later years of the Depression open-air Grandstand shows toured the exhibition sites but, except for fund-raising tours, the Second World War years brought little professional entertainment to the province.

Amateur theatre had declined during the First World War, but became a major theatrical force in the 1930s. George Palmer organized the Regina Community Players, later restructured by G.R. Chetwynd and Walter Read as the Regina Little Theatre, which performed in Darke Hall on the Regina College campus after 1931. Outstanding productions included Noël Coward's *Hay Fever* in 1933, Ibsen's *A Doll's House* in 1936, Shakespeare's *As You Like It* in 1937, and Kaufman and Hart's *You Can't Take It With You* in 1941. Frances HYLAND's ability was first revealed with the Avenue Players organized by Mary Ellen Burgess.

In Saskatoon the Christ Church Dramatic Society produced nineteen plays between 1921 and 1929, toured to smaller communities during the Depression, and continued activity until 1948. The Saskatoon Little Theatre, organized by Lillian Myers, operated between 1922 and 1949 with productions such as John Drinkwater's *Bird in the Hand* in 1936, Shakespeare's *Julius Caesar* and George Kelly's *The Torchbearers* in 1939, and Joseph Kesselring's *Arsenic and Old Lace* in 1945. The Students' Dramatic Society produced Arthur Wing Pinero's *Sweet Lavender* in 1916, and began the tradition of College Nights of one-act plays in 1930. In 1945 Emrys M. Jones became Chairman of the first Drama Department in the British Commonwealth at the Univ. of Saskatchewan.

4. *1945 to the present*. Limited professional touring resumed after the Second World War, including Sidney RISK's Everyman Theatre Company in 1947, Donald Wolfit in 1948, the Winnipeg and the National Ballet companies and Charles Laughton in 1954, and the Brian Doherty New World Theatre Company in 1949 and 1950. The Univ. of Saskatchewan sponsored The Western Stage Society, a fledgeling professional company operating from 1948 to 1950. The University's Regina campus launched Theatre Saskatchewan in 1966 under Eric Salmon, which lasted three years. The GLOBE THEATRE, founded by Ken and Sue KRAMER in the same year, has developed a strong following and in 1981 finally found a permanent home in

The Globe Theatre, Regina

the renovated City Hall Theatre, which first opened in 1909.

Two professional producing companies have developed in Saskatoon. Begun as a COLLECTIVE, 25TH STREET THEATRE opened with *Gardens, Sketch #1* by director Andras Tahn in 1972. *PAPER WHEAT* in 1977 is their most memorable collective production. PERSEPHONE THEATRE, formed by Brian Richmond in 1974, operated out of various premises but now shares space with the 25th Street Theatre in the new Saskatoon Theatre Centre. Ken MITCHELL's *CRUEL TEARS*, a country-and-western musical, has been one of their most outstanding productions.

The Regina Little Theatre continued to play a vital role in the city's cultural life after the Second World War, especially with its contributions to annual productions of John COULTER's *The Trial of Louis Riel*.

Amateur theatre in Saskatoon has manifested itself in many forms. College Nights at the University continued until 1952 and the musicals staged by the Musical Directorate lasted even longer. The Drama Department opened the Greystone Theatre in 1950 and continues the university dramatic tradition. In 1947 the Quota Club began producing children's plays such as *Alice in Wonderland* and *The Emperor's New Clothes*. The concept was revived in 1962 by the Saskatoon Theatre for Children, which mounts two productions annually; a driving force recently has been Larry Fitzgerald who has acted, directed, and written for the company. The Saskatoon Community Players, formed in 1952 by Louise Olsen, continued to produce until 1959. The opening of the Castle Theatre inspired the formation of the Gateway Players, whose nearly 100 productions include William Wycherley's *The Country Wife*, Edward Albee's *Who's Afraid of Virginia Woolf?*, and Eugene Labiche's *The Italian Straw Hat*. Gateway has also co-operated with the Saskatoon Summer Players, which began producing musicals in 1964, and the francophone Unithéâtre since 1968.

See Ross Stuart, *The History of Prairie Theatre. The Development of Theatre in Alberta, Manitoba and Saskatchewan 1833-1982* (1984).

PATRICK B. O'NEILL

Saskatoon Opera House. Better known as Cairns' Hall, after its builder J.F. Cairns, who had previously managed the GRAND OPERA HOUSE in London and a theatre in Chatham, Ont., it opened on 29 Sept. 1903 with cinematograph entertainments and comic songs by the Miller Company. The National Stock Company's production of Alexandre Dumas' *The Three Musketeers*, starring Horace V. Noble, opened a month later—the theatre's first play. Other touring groups included the Crow Imperial Stock Company (1904), W. Pauline Johnson and Walter J. McRaye (1904), Walker's Comedians (1904), the Thomas MARKS Stock Company (1905), the Andrews Opera Company (1905), and Roscani's Comic Opera Company (1905). Amateur groups, such as the Saskatoon Dramatic Club with *Nellie, the Fireman's Ward* in 1905, Charles Townsend's *The Mountain Waif* in 1904, and the Saskatoon Orchestra and the Saskatoon Choral Society (both in 1905) also used the theatre.

Replacing Cairns' Hall, a larger Saskatoon Opera House opened in Nov. 1906 on the corner of 20th St and 3rd Ave. Through Winnipeg's C.P. WALKER, John Pringle (1907-8) booked primarily VAUDEVILLE and American touring companies with such shows as *We are King*, *Texas Ranger*, and Gustav Adolph Wever's *The Heart of Kentucky*. Pringle organized his own professional company in Oct. 1907 to produce three short plays, including *The Happy Pair* by Saskatoon natives, Mr and Mrs Kendall. The success of this venture and his acquisition of the Rosetown Opera House led Pringle to establish a touring stock company at the renamed Capital Opera House in Jan. 1908 with Robert Lee Forrest's *A Stranger in Town*. When this enterprise collapsed after two weeks, Pringle left and C.P. Walker took over the house for his Bread Basket Route, renaming it the Lyric Theatre and installing 550 folding opera seats. Here on 27 Oct. 1908 the Saskatoon audience received its introduction to Ibsen when Hortense Neilson appeared as Mrs Alving in *Ghosts*. Both Tom Marks and the Stanford Dodge Shakespeare Company appeared that same year. The opening of the 800-seat EMPIRE THEATRE in 1910 diverted Walker's attractions and the former Saskatoon Opera House was sold again, for $18,000, becoming in 1910 the Starland (and replacing an earlier Starland closed at this time). Nellie Melba appeared here in 1910, and the William Morris Agency of New York provided regular fare as part of the Western Canada Vaudeville Circuit. In Sept. 1911 a new electric sign in front of the theatre announced another name change to the Star. William B. Sherman, who had arrived on the Prairie vaudeville circuits around 1900 with an educated goat, purchased and renovated the theatre in 1913, renaming it the Sherman-Star under the management of M. McNaughton. The Sherman-Star became a small-time vaudeville and movie house later that year when Sherman acquired the Strand Theatre to house his better attractions. As the Gaiety in Dec. 1915, the theatre briefly housed Sid Cox and his Gaiety Girls before beginning its final transformation as the Eckhardt Theatre between 30 Mar. and 27 May 1916. Finding the old theatre inadequate as a home for Saskatchewan's most popular touring stock company, Oliver Eckhardt moved his troupe to the Empire and the one time Saskatoon Opera House closed its doors permanently. In 1918 the site was occupied by the Star Rooming House.

PATRICK B. O'NEILL

Sauvageau, Yves (1946-70). Born Yves Hébert in Waterloo, Que., where he founded a theatre company, La Lanterne, in 1962, he studied and worked as an actor and author in Sherbrooke, and was a student at the NATIONAL THEATRE SCHOOL from 1965 to 1968, where he adopted the pseudonym Sauvageau. He was a member of the Jeunes Comédiens du THÉÂTRE DU NOUVEAU MONDE on their 1968-9 Canadian tour.

As Yves Hébert he won both the first and

Yves Sauvageau's Wouf wouf!, *Nouvelle Compagnie Théâtrale, Montreal, 1974, with Gilles Renaud (standing) and Jacques Lavallie*

the third prizes in a 1966 Radio-Canada contest for young authors for his plays *Les Enfants* (1966), on the problems of ageing, and *Le Rôle* (1966), in which Mr Common is stripped of his well-being by three women—Love, Loneliness, and Despair—of his personality by Mr Complex, and of his life by Mr Fate. His next three plays—*Jean et Marie*, *Papa*, and *Les Mûres de Pierre* (all published in 1977)—use black humour to portray problems of identity and expression, although psychology is less important to Sauvageau than dreams and play.

Wouf wouf! (1970), produced in 1971 at the Univ. of Montreal by Gilbert David, and in an abbreviated version by André Montmorency at the Salle du GESÙ in 1974, is Sauvageau's most important work. Spectacle—parodic, psychedelic, hysterical—abounds: in history, literature, the city, the mass media, but above all in the mind of Daniel, the young hero—poet and knight of peace, desire, and 'glittering anarchy'. After satisfying his physical needs, Daniel lives out his fantasies, obsessions, and regressions by

means of sport, recitation, vaudeville, police comedy, melodrama, and zany ballet. Despite some occasional self-indulgence, *Wouf wouf!* constitutes a powerful anti-establishment adventure that is both exceptional and representative of its era.

Prior to his suicide, Sauvageau planned an opera, *De Jésus la Pop Ublique Vie*, about alcoholism in Quebec. Several of his unpublished works are in the library of the Université de Montréal.

See Jean-Cléo Godin and Laurent Mailhot, *Théâtre Québécois II. Nouveaux auteurs, autres spectacles* (1980).   LAURENT MAILHOT

Savage God. Named from Yeats's reaction to *Ubu Roi*: 'After us, the Savage God?', this was an ongoing series of exploratory projects in theatre and other media under avant-garde director John JULIANI. In 1966 Juliani, while teaching and directing at Simon Fraser University, Vancouver, named his first production venture—plays by Fernando Arrabal and Michel de Ghelderode—as *Savage God #1*. Further Savage God projects—whether productions of plays by Strindberg, Chekhov, or Beckett, or the 'staging' of his own wedding ceremony in the Vancouver Art Gallery—remained provocative, demonstrating his quest for new forms in the mixing of the processes of art, life, and therapy.

In 1971 Juliani staged probably his most notable work, a three-week long PACET project ('pilot alternative complement to existing theatre') in Vancouver—a search for a mobile, highly creative and inexpensive range of productions that would be free to the public and a viable alternative to the established regional and commercial theatres. About fifty theatre events—from *gestalt* sessions to Beckett's *Happy Days* (performed in a tree trunk in Stanley Park)—were held over three weeks to demonstrate that a stimulating range of inexpensive and free alternative theatre could be realized.

Juliani places much of his subsequent work under the general title 'Savage God', whether theatre (*Picasso* in Edmonton, 1977), film (*Latitude 55*, 1982), or radio (as a CBC producer).   JAMES HOFFMAN

Scarfe, Alan (b. 1946). Born in Harpenden, Eng., he immigrated with his parents to Canada and was raised in Winnipeg and Vancouver, where he appeared as Mark Antony in *Julius Caesar* in 1964 at the VANCOUVER PLAYHOUSE. He returned to England to train as an actor at the London Academy of Music and Dramatic Art, graduating in 1966. From 1966 to 1968 he worked as an actor and director in British repertory theatres before returning permanently to Canada. In the late 1960s he acted regularly at the Vancouver Playhouse, and in 1969 he appeared in the inaugural production at the NATIONAL ARTS CENTRE as the Magistrate in George RYGA's *The ECSTASY OF RITA JOE* and in the world première of Beverley SIMONS' *CRABDANCE* at Seattle's Conservatory Theatre. He began a long association with the STRATFORD FESTIVAL in 1972, playing Tony Lumpkin in Oliver Goldsmith's *She Stoops to Conquer* and Lear; he was an associate director of the Festival, 1976-7. A bravura actor with a commanding stage presence and powerful voice, Scarfe has acted and directed at most of the country's major theatres and has also performed extensively on radio and television and in films, including *Deserters*, *The Wars*, *The Bay Boy*, and *Joshua Then and Now*.

L. W. CONOLLY

Schafer, Lawrence (b. 1940). Born in Kitchener, Ont., he studied architecture and art history at the Univ. of Toronto while working in the properties department of the STRATFORD FESTIVAL from 1960 to 1964. These two formative experiences led him to a general design style that combines space and symbolic structural elements embellished with carefully chosen and often lavish decorative detail, frequently including oversized graphics.

Schafer has designed more than 150 productions for most of Canada's major theatres as well as for the Canadian Opera Company (*Deirdre*, 1966, *The Luck of Ginger Coffey*, 1967, *The Glove*, 1975) and the National Ballet Company (*La Prima Ballerina*, 1967). For Edmonton's CITADEL THEATRE he designed such works as Colin Higgins's *Harold and Maude* (1978), Cliff Jones's *Hey Marilyn* (1980), and Charles Strouse's *Flowers for Algernon* (1978), which also played at the Queen's Theatre, London, in 1979. He made his Stratford Festival début in 1977 when he designed sets for Noël Coward's *Hay Fever*, his seventy-fifth commission.

Schafer is widely known for his collaborations with Alan LUND, both on established musicals at the BANFF CENTRE and on original works at the CHARLOTTETOWN FESTIVAL (*Private Turvey's War*, 1970, *Singin' and Dancin' Tonight*, 1982, and *Babies*, 1986).

MARTHA MANN

Schellenberg, August (b. 1932). Born in Montreal and trained at the NATIONAL THEATRE SCHOOL, his acting début at the STRATFORD FESTIVAL earned him the Tyrone GUTHRIE Award for further study in 1967. His Indian heritage led him to roles such as Jaimie Paul in George RYGA's *The ECSTASY OF RITA JOE* at the VANCOUVER PLAYHOUSE in 1967, but he has urged young ethnic actors to 'beat the stereotype', and he has himself portrayed a wide diversity of characters in over one hundred stage performances, including the title role in Ryga's *Paracelsus* in Vancouver in 1986. Now devoting most of his time to television and film, Schellenberg has created over seventy-five roles on television and has appeared in over fifty films since his first cinema lead, in *The Coffin Affair*, brought him to national and North American attention. He has been nominated for numerous awards: a Canadian Film (1977); two Genies (1981, 1983); two ACTRAs (1984,

492

1985, both for radio work); and two Earle GREYs (1985, 1986).   REID GILBERT

Schull, Joseph (1910–80). Born in Watertown, South Dakota, and raised in Moose Jaw, Sask., he attended Queen's Univ. and the Univ. of Saskatchewan. His two earliest plays, *The Ladies* and *Pardon*, were published in 1928. In 1935 he settled in Montreal, returning there after wartime Navy service.

Schull wrote about eighty-five original radio plays and some fifty adaptations. The original plays are of four distinct types: dramatic documentaries on maritime or biographical subjects, such as *The Left-Handed Admiral*, on Lord Nelson, produced in 1954; entertaining comedies, often with a social commentary—*Davy Jones*, produced in 1947; allegories and satires—*The Land of Ephranor*, produced in 1945, and *Heat Wave*, produced in 1949; and serious, even tragic, dramas— *The Sound of the Weeds*, produced in 1945, and a magnificent epic, *The Jinker*, about the blood-ritual of the seal-hunt off Newfoundland, produced in 1955 and published in 1987.

Schull wrote five plays for the stage, two of which were produced: *Shadow of the Tree* at the London Little Theatre in 1952 and *Counterpoint* at Greystone Theatre, Univ. of Sask., in 1967. *The Jinker*, a novel based on his radio play, was publishd in 1968.

See also RADIO DRAMA IN ENGLISH.   HOWARD FINK

Shatner, William (b. 1931). Born and raised in Montreal, he studied business at McGill University, where he also wrote, directed, and acted in annual revues. After graduation in 1952 he became assistant business manager for Ottawa's CANADIAN REPERTORY THEATRE, but was soon playing juvenile leads. He acted at the MOUNTAIN PLAYHOUSE, Montreal, in the summer of 1953, and from 1954 to 1956 appeared at the STRATFORD FESTIVAL—in 1956 understudying and once replacing Christopher PLUMMER in *Henry V*. He won the Tyrone GUTHRIE award for 1956, and in that year travelled with the company to the Edinburgh Festival, and appeared in Guthrie's production of Christopher Marlowe's *Tamburlaine the Great* in Toronto and New York. Between Stratford seasons Shatner acted (and occasionally wrote and directed) in live television and for the National Film Board. He moved to New York in 1956, making his Broadway début as

the lead in Paul Osborn's *The World of Suzie Wong* in 1958. His film début was as Alexei in Richard Brooks' *The Brothers Karamazov* in 1958. He starred as Captain James T. Kirk in the cult television series 'Star Trek' (1966-9), a role well suited to his energetic, physical acting style. He has since completed four motion pictures as Kirk, while continuing to pursue other film and television projects.   STEPHEN JOHNSON

Shaw Festival, The. From modest amateur beginnings in 1962 it has grown to a major theatrical organization in Niagara-on-the-Lake, Ont. Grossing some $6 million in box office (1988) and with an annual budget of over $10 million (1988), it employs an ensemble of some sixty to seventy actors in three theatres for a season of more than 500 performances.

Founder Brian Doherty had twenty-five years' experience, both as a producer and a playwright, when he joined with Calvin Rand, John Couillard, and others in 1962 to organize a 'Salute to Shaw': Maynard Burgess directed eight performances of Shaw's *Candida* and the 'Don Juan in Hell' sequence from *Man and Superman*, spread over four weekends in the town's 115-year-old courthouse. The success of this first season led to the establishment of the Court House Theatre in July 1963 to conduct an annual Shaw Festival, to stimulate interest in Shaw and his period, and to advance the development of theatre arts in Canada.

The Festival continues to rent the second floor of the courthouse from the town; improvements have included the installation of elevated seating (including a small balcony), which now accommodates 360 on three sides of an 18' by 20' acting area; behind a 24' proscenium arch, a further 16' by 24' inner-stage is available. The Festival Theatre, built at a cost of $3 million, opened on 12 June 1973 with a production of Shaw's *You Never Can Tell*. Toronto architect Ronald J. Thom's low-profile building is of rose brick with a cedar-shake roof. Seating 847 in a cedar-lined intimate auditorium, the theatre has a large proscenium stage (52'6" deep with a 40' wide proscenium arch) with an apron (5'9") and orchestra pit, but little storage space for multi-set shows; other facilities include workshops, administration offices, and a rehearsal hall. In 1980 the Royal George Theatre, seating 240, was acquired from the Canadian Mime Theatre for $172,854 with the aid of a provincial government grant of $127,000. Originally built in 1913 as a VAUDEVILLE venue for troops stationed at Niagara-on-the-Lake, the theatre's 22' by 20' proscenium stage, with an 8' apron, is adequate for small-scale shows, including musicals; expansion projects in 1984, 1986, and 1988 improved stage and workshop facilities, restored the auditorium, and added a concealed orchestra pit.

The Festival's mandate has been differently interpreted by successive artistic directors. From 1963 to 1965 Andrew ALLAN's literal interpretation and ensemble approach provided for steady though unspectacular growth. In 1966 Barry Morse attracted top-rate actors, tripled ticket sales, expanded the season from six to nine weeks, and gave the Festival a national reputation. From 1967 to 1977 Paxton WHITEHEAD offered entertaining productions with wide appeal, but largely ignored the provocative and iconoclastic elements of Shaw's plays. He introduced tours across North America, expanded the season to twenty-one weeks, and added plays by other writers deemed stylistically compatible with Shaw—such as *Forty Years On* by Alan Bennett in 1970 (the first Festival production by a living playwright), *The Royal Family* by George S. Kaufman and Edna Ferber in 1972 (the first play by an American playwright), and *G.K.C.* by Tony VAN BRIDGE in 1970 (the first play by a Canadian playwright). Outstanding Shaw productions under Whitehead were *Heartbreak House* in 1968, *The Philanderer* (1971), *Misalliance* (1972), *The Devil's Disciple* (1974), and *Man and Superman* (1977). Ben Travers' farce *Thark* in 1977 crystallized complaints from the critics that the Festival was settling for popular success at the expense of dramatic worth, but the public flocked to see it.

During Whitehead's sabbatical in 1975, Tony van Bridge enlivened a relatively poor season with his *G.K.C.* After Whitehead's resignation, Richard Kirschner became both artistic director and general manager for the 1978 season, in which attendance fell for a program that included *Heartbreak House*, *Major Barbara*, and Ibsen's *John Gabriel Borkman*. More popular was Leslie Yeo's 1979 selection: three plays by Shaw and four by other playwrights—Jerome Kilty, Michael Voysey, Emlyn Williams, and Noël Coward. The Festival's current artistic director,

Christopher NEWTON, determined to build a strong ensemble company around established Festival actors and such new blood as Nora McLellan and Susan Cox; other key newcomers included designer Cameron PORTEOUS, and producer/director Paul Reynolds. Newton has presented a more adventurous repertoire than any of his predecessors. He shocked conservative audience members in his 1980 opening season with Brecht's *A Respectable Wedding*, in which Derek GOLDBY staged a controversial wine-bottle rape; nudity followed in 1981 in Robert MacDonald's *Camille*; and in 1981 Newton provocatively proposed cutting the epilogue to *Saint Joan*—this was vetoed by the Shaw Estate's literary adviser Dan H. Laurence, who subsequently became literary adviser to the Festival.

Although Newton's commitment to Shaw remains strong, the playwright has become less central to the Festival: often only three of ten or eleven plays are by Shaw, while other productions conflict openly with Shaw's aesthetics and convictions, causing critics to question the validity of the Shaw Festival's mandate. A typical season now features one Shaw play at each theatre—a major production at the Festival Theatre, a less-familiar play at the Court House, and a one-act play at the Royal George lunchtime series. Since 1982's superb production of Edmond Rostand's *Cyrano de Bergerac* (designed by Porteous, directed by Goldby, and starring Heath LAMBERTS), the Festival Theatre has annually staged a lavish spectacle—such as the North American première of Coward's *Cavalcade* in 1985, remounted in 1986. Another regular feature has been farce, such as Feydeau's *A Flea in her Ear* in 1980. The Royal George is the venue for popular entertainment—American musicals such as George Gershwin's *Girl Crazy* in 1986, and murder mysteries such as Agatha Christie's *Murder on the Nile* in 1985.

Recognizing the danger of becoming a museum theatre for plays of the 1850-1950 period, Newton initiated the 'Toronto Project' in 1982 to explore contemporary scripts before a younger, more cosmopolitan audience. Toronto productions have included co-productions with TORONTO FREE THEATRE, such as François-Louis Tilly's *Delicatessen* in 1984. *B-Movie, the Play* is a measure of the success of this exploration: written by Festival actor Tom Wood and workshopped at the Shaw Academy (the Festival's academic,

Noël Coward's Cavalcade, *Shaw Festival, 1985*

literary, and training body), *B-Movie* later played to capacity audiences in Toronto in 1987 and 1988. Plans for a permanent Toronto space to perform new work appear justified. Popular shows from the summer season have transferred profitably to Toronto in winter—*The Women* by Clare Booth Luce, in 1987, is one example.

Another new venture by Newton was the 'Risks' program, established in 1983 to mount low-budget productions of historically important plays with limited appeal. Plays by Romanian playwright Ion Luca Caragiole and Polish Stanislaw Witkiewicz were adventurous choices, but those by Coward, Pirandello, Strindberg, and Wilde have also been classed as 'risky', indicating the restrictions imposed by a conservative audience.

Since 1967, when *Major Barbara* made a profitable post-season tour to the MANITOBA THEATRE CENTRE and Expo 67 in Montreal, tours have regularly extended the season and publicized the Festival throughout Canada and the U.S. In 1988 *You Never Can Tell* played at the Calgary Winter Olympics prior to the Festival's summer production. The Festival also presents popular and classical music; and a winter program of concerts, films, and plays maintains local interest in the Festival. The Shaw Seminars—begun by Doherty and co-sponsored by Brock (1965-72), McMaster (1973-7), and York (1978-88) Universities—offer three days of lectures, music, and plays.

Despite relatively low levels of government funding (1988 federal and provincial grants respectively of $465,000 and $660,000 amount to only 13.5% of total revenue), the Festival's policy of taking risks mainly on small-scale shows, reviving previous hits, and providing popular entertainment alongside more serious drama has given it a measure of financial stability unusual among arts organizations.

The archives of the Shaw Festival are housed at the Univ. of Guelph. See Brian Doherty, *Not Bloody Likely, The Shaw Festival 1962-73* (1974). LISBIE RAE

Shaw, Harold Nelson (c.*1865-1937*). A native of Nova Scotia, he left home in his teens to go on stage, appearing eventually with the companies of Edwin Booth and Dion Boucicault. After graduating from Acadia Univ. in 1891, he became principal of the School of Elocution at Toronto's Conservatory of Music.

In 1902 the 'Harold Nelson' company began a series of ambitious theatrical tours of western Canada, appearing in almost every town hall and opera house accessible by rail between Rat Portage (now Kenora) and the Rockies. Although he presented a wide-ranging repertoire, he was most noted for his productions of Shakespearean and Romantic tragedy. Among his best parts were Hamlet, Mephistopheles in Lewis Morrison's version of Goethe's *Faust*, and the title role in Bulwer-Lytton's *Richelieu*. The lofty tone of his productions and the crusading zeal of his lectures on Shakespeare helped make theatre-going more widely accepted in western Canada.

Shaw often advertised his companies as 'All-Canadian' and in his interviews and curtain speeches spoke of his goal of creating 'a national school of dramatic art with traditions and ideals of our own—and of the best.'

Although Shaw toured until 1910, his greatest successes came during the three seasons in which he was managed by C.P. WALKER (1903-6). From 1912 to 1922 he taught in Vancouver; in the late 1920s he moved to Hollywood, where he appeared in small roles in films and taught elocution to actors facing the new demands of the 'talkies'. DOUGLAS ARRELL

Sherman Grand Theatre. The oldest surviving theatre in Calgary, it opened on 5 Feb. 1912 as part of the seven-storey Lougheed Building, an office complex constructed by McNeil and Trainer of Calgary for Senator James Lougheed at an estimated cost of $500,000. Designed by L.R. Wardrop, and named after local entrepreneur W.B. Sherman, the Sherman Grand was among the largest theatres in the country, with a stage measuring 42' deep by 80' wide and having a proscenium opening of 39' and a height of 86'. With one large balcony and six private boxes, it had a seating capacity of 1,509. The interior was decorated throughout with elaborate ornamentation in wood and plaster, complemented by brass railings, rich tapestries, and carpets.

As part of the U.S.-Canadian Orpheum Circuit the theatre offered drama, musical comedies, operas, religious spectacles, symphony concerts, and circuses. Touring companies and stars appearing at the Grand included the San Carlo Grand Opera Co., the British Guild Players, the Royal Collins Players, Margaret ANGLIN, Tom MARKS, the DUMBELLS, Bransby Williams, Sophie Tucker, Ethel Barrymore, Sir John Martin-Harvey, the Marx Brothers, George Burns and Gracie Allen, Fred and Adele Astaire, George Jessel, Jack Benny, Aimee Semple McPherson, and Sarah Bernhardt (in 1913 and 1918). For a limited time in the early twenties the theatre had its own repertory company, the Grand Players.

In 1937 it was sold to J.B. Barron, who converted it into a moviehouse. In 1965 the stage and the boxes were removed. Four years later the Odeon Corporation bought the theatre and in 1972 the house was divided into two twin cinemas with a sound-proof wall. During the summer of 1985 the Grand Theatre was renovated. The centre wall dividing the theatre was removed, the main floor was restored as one cinema, and the old balcony as another. It reopened as the Showcase Grand. JEFFREY GOFFIN

Silver, Phillip. (b. 1943). Born in Edmonton, Alta, he studied English at the Univ. of Alberta and theatrical design at the NATIONAL THEATRE SCHOOL in Montreal, leaving in 1966 to design for Douglas Seale at Center Stage in Baltimore, Maryland. Returning to Edmonton in 1967, he worked briefly as a designer for the Edmonton Opera and then for eleven years at the old and new CITADEL THEATRES. For artistic director John NEVILLE he designed—among other notable productions—Shakespeare's *Much Ado About Nothing* (1973), Cole Porter's *Anything Goes* (1974), and Tennessee Williams' *The Night of the Iguana* (1978)—as well as helping to design Shakespeare's *Romeo and Juliet*, the inaugural production at the new Citadel in Nov. 1976.

In 1978 Silver settled in Stratford, where he designed and lighted *The Merry Wives of Windsor*, subsequently becoming Robin PHILLIPS' resident designer in 1983-4. Responsible for many productions at the STRATFORD FESTIVAL, he has made a distinctive impression with his sparse, clean, skeletal, and yet stylized settings, particularly at the Avon Theatre. Perhaps best remembered is his design for Edna O'Brien's *Virginia* in 1980, starring Maggie Smith, which later transferred to London's Theatre Royal, Haymarket. Here, as in his other work, Silver's guiding principle was to achieve a design shaped to embody the spirit and intention of the text, a design that was sculptural—as opposed to pictorial—in feel and inspiration.

For some years Silver has been teaching design at York Univ., though he maintains an active career designing for Halifax's NEPTUNE THEATRE, THEATRE NEW BRUNSWICK, Toronto's THEATRE PLUS, YOUNG PEOPLE'S THEATRE, Gemstone Productions, and other companies. MARTHA MANN

Simons, Beverley Rosen (b. 1938). Born in Flin Flon, Man., she moved with her family in 1950 to Edmonton, where she studied music with a view to a career as a concert pianist and composer. Her one-act verse-drama *Twisted Roots* (1956) won her a writing scholarship to the Banff School of Fine Arts (see BANFF CENTRE), and as a student at McGill Univ. (1956-8) she chaired the Players Club Experimental Theatre and directed and produced plays. She transferred to the Univ. of British Columbia in 1958, completing her BA in English and Theatre in 1959. She also attended UBC's summer school, where she was taught by Robert GILL and the British director and educator Brian Way. Between 1959 and 1961 she travelled, worked, and studied in Europe before settling in Vancouver. Visits to the Orient in 1967-8 and 1986 enabled her to find new inspiration in formal and ritualistic theatrical traditions.

Simons' overriding concern as a playwright has been the struggle for authentic self-expression in a fragmented and alienating world, as in *The Elephant and the Jewish Question* (first produced by the Vancouver Little Theatre in 1968), in which a young Jew leaves home in search of his identity. *CRAB-DANCE* (1969), Simons' best and most frequently produced and studied play, presents a middle-aged woman's fruitless search for identity, while *Green Lawn Rest Home* (1973), first produced by SAVAGE GOD in Vancouver in 1969, is a despairing analysis of old age. In *Preparing* (1974), a monologue first produced by TAMAHNOUS THEATRE in 1973, a woman constantly prepares for important stages in her life, including death. *Preparing* was published again in 1975 as the title play in a quartet of short plays that also includes *Prologue*, *Triangle*, and *The Crusader*. *Triangle* and *The Crusader* powerfully confront death—of an actor and soldier/murderer respectively; *The Crusader* was produced at Seymour College in 1978. Simons' last play, *Leela Means to Play* (1976, unproduced), most clearly reveals an Oriental influence; episodic and symbolic in form, it features characters who explore new ways to play the game of life. Characteristic stylistic elements of Simons' plays include disjointed time sequences, multiple protagonists, lyricism, and sudden reversal at the end of a play; thematic concerns include minority groups, power, madness, and the Jocasta complex.

Simons has also written scripts for film, television, and radio, but since 1976 she has turned her attention primarily to fiction. In 1984 she was artist-in-residence at the Univ. of Lethbridge.   ROTA HERZBERG LISTER

Simple Soldat, Un. One of Marcel DUBÉ's most successful plays, it was televised in 1957 and produced at La COMÉDIE-CANADIENNE on 31 May 1958. A revised version was mounted at the same theatre in 1967. The two versions were published in 1958 and 1967 respectively by the Institut littéraire du Québec and Les Éditions de l'Homme. The action of the play stretches from May 1945 until the summer of 1952 and concerns Joseph Latour, an unskilled school dropout who returns from non-combat service during the Second World War to the home of his father Edouard, his half-sister Fleurette, and stepmother Bertha and her two children, Marguerite and Armand. An impetuous rebel who hates exploitation, fraudulence, and lies, Latour wanders from job to job and from one part of Canada to another before returning to Montreal and betraying his father's faith in him, thereby causing the old man's death. He disappears once again, turning up as a soldier in the Korean War, where he is killed.

The title of the play applies not only to Joseph, but also to Edouard; they are both 'combatants' who die in absurd battles. In both cases the epithet 'simple' is ironic. There is also a possible allusion in the name 'Joseph Latour' to the hero of Antoine GÉRIN-LAJOIE's play Le *JEUNE LATOUR* (1844), in which the father betrays the French cause in the struggle with the British for Acadia, while the son Joseph Latour heroically upholds his heritage. Dubé's Joseph, the rebel without a (clear-cut) cause, strikes out blindly and alone against the system, his inability to pinpoint the sources of his alienation going hand in hand with his ideological confusion. *Un simple soldat* has been seen as a kind of sequel to Gratien GÉLINAS's *TIT-COQ*, which Dubé saw five times when still a student. Both protagonists, products of the Depression, seem crushed by a form of socio-economic 'original sin'.

Although the social aspects of the play—developed through references to the Asbestos strike, the nuclear threat, the Conscription crisis, Dieppe—are less reflections of the characters' perceptions than authorial discourse artificially attributed to them, and although the play sometimes lacks focus, the emotional impact of the key scenes is unforgettable.

BEN-Z. SHEK

Sinclair, Lister (b. 1921). Born in Bombay, India, he received his early schooling in England. In 1941 he entered the Univ. of British Columbia to study science but instead became an actor and writer with Andrew ALLAN, director of drama at CBC Vancouver. Sinclair was prominent among a team that joined Allan in Toronto after he was appointed CBC national radio drama supervisor in 1944, helping to create the radio-drama 'Stage' series.

Sinclair took leading roles in many CBC plays while writing successful dramas and adaptations. His adaptations include a wide variety of plays and novels, and he has also written many historical and documentary plays. Sinclair created two types of plays that bear his unmistakable stamp. The first is the serious and ambitious verse-drama on a universal theme, such as *Socrates* (produced in 1947, published in 1952), *Encounter by Moonlight* (produced in 1947), and *Return to Colonus* (produced in 1954, published in 1955). The other type is the witty and ironic satire-fantasy, such as *All About Emily* (produced in 1945, published in 1948). In all, he wrote about 150 plays up to 1962, some eighty of them original.

Sinclair continued to write plays for radio through the 1960s and 1970s while branching into other forms of radio, including intellectual documentaries, especially in CBC's 'Ideas' series. He has also written a number of television plays. Some of his plays have been produced on stage, including *Socrates* and *The Blood is Strong* (1948), which has received many television and stage productions. A selection of his plays has been published in two collections: *A Play on Words and Other Radio Plays* (1948) and *Ways of Mankind* (1954). His *The Art of Norval Morrisseau* was published in 1979. Among his honours are the Ohio State Radio Drama Award and the John Drainie Award for Contributions to Broadcasting.

See also RADIO DRAMA IN ENGLISH.

HOWARD FINK

Skerrett, George (1810-55) and **Emma** (1817-87). After immigrating to the U.S. from England in 1844, the Skerretts played winter seasons in American stock companies, George specializing in eccentric character parts such as Tony Lumpkin in Oliver Goldsmith's *She Stoops to Conquer*, and Emma, a charming and popular actress, excelling in such roles as Lady Teazle in R.B. Sheridan's *The School for Scandal*. In summer he managed companies in Canada, beginning at Montreal's Olympic Theatre in 1845 and 1846. In 1846 Skerrett's company also performed in Toronto and Kingston, and in 1847 Hamilton as well. The 1848 Montreal season, which featured touring opera and dance companies in the large new THEATRE ROYAL, was financially disastrous for Skerrett, and he did not return to Canada until 1851, when he played his final season at Skerrett's Bandbox in Montreal, a theatre too small to be profitable. Nonetheless the Skerretts helped keep professional theatre alive in Montreal between 1845 and 1851, 'elevating dramatic entertainments from their previous degradation', according to the *Montreal Gazette*, and making theatregoing not only respectable but fashionable.

MARY SHORTT

Slade, Bernard (b. 1930). Born in St Catharines, Ont., he moved with his family to England when he was five, returning to Canada when he was eighteen. He acted in Ontario's SUMMER STOCK at the Red Barn Theatre, and in 1954 he and his wife, the Toronto actress Jill Foster, with American actor Warren Hart, managed Prudhomme's Theatre in Vineland, Ont., for a twenty-five week season. Slade also wrote scripts for such CBC variety shows as 'Hit Parade', 'Live a Borrowed Life', and 'Flashback', and had his first comedy, *Simon Says Get Married*, produced in 1961 by Toronto's CREST THEATRE. A second comedy, *A Very Close Family*, was produced by the MANITOBA THEATRE CENTRE in 1962. In 1964 Slade went to Hollywood where he created seven TV sitcoms (including 'The Partridge Family' and 'The Flying Nun'), writing more than 100 episodes. His international success, *Same Time, Next Year*, opened on Broadway in 1975 starring Ellen Burstyn (who won an Emmy award). A domestic comedy with strong characterization, witty dialogue and situations, it has drawn comparison with the best work of Neil Simon. Other Broadway plays include *Tribute* (1978), *Romantic Comedy* (1979)—a Valentine to the stylish comedies of Philip Barry, Slade says—and *Special Occa-*

sions (1982), a flop that opened and closed on the same day. *Fatal Attraction*, a psychological thriller, premièred at Toronto's ST LAW-RENCE CENTRE in 1984 but received poor notices. His most recent play, *Return Engagements*, opened in 1986 on Broadway.

EUGENE BENSON

Small, Ambrose Joseph (1866-1919?). Born in Bradford, Ont., he moved in 1876 with his family to Toronto, where his father ran a public house near, and a bar room in, the GRAND OPERA HOUSE. While a student at St Michael's College, he worked as an usher at the Grand, subsequently becoming a regular employee. In 1886, after a quarrel with manager O.B. Sheppard, Small left the Grand and walked fifty yards to the Toronto Opera House, a VAUDEVILLE and melodrama theatre, where he soon became treasurer. By 1892 he held mortgages on the Toronto Opera House and the Regent Theatre. The example of New York theatrical syndicate magnates taught him to orchestrate bookings in Ontario, and between 1893 and 1919, on his own and through association with C.J. Whitney of Detroit—who controlled a circuit of twenty-two theatres in eighteen cities in Ontario, Ohio, and Michigan—he came close to his goal of monopolizing bookings in Ontario. At one point he had control—as owner, lessee, or booking agent—of thirty-four theatres, half in Ontario. In conjunction with his wife Theresa, an astute and wealthy business partner whom he had married in 1902, he accumulated theatre properties that fetched $1.75 million when—facing increasing production costs and realizing that theatrical touring was a declining business—he sold them to Trans-Canada Theatres in 1919. Included in the sale were the Grand Opera Houses in Toronto, Hamilton, London, Peterborough, Kingston, and Ottawa, as well as booking contracts in Orillia, Barrie, Galt, Stratford, Midland, Lindsay, Pembroke, Renfrew, Brockville, North Bay, Sudbury, Sarnia, St Catharines, and Brantford.

After depositing in a Toronto bank a cheque for one million dollars from the sale, Small promptly disappeared without a trace. Rewards were offered—as late as 1974—for information on his whereabouts. *Mail and Empire* critic Hector Charlesworth wrote: 'His end was the culmination of a life successfully devoted to the acquisition of money, and came swiftly and mysteriously on the very day when his dreams of the irresponsible possession of a vast fortune had at last been completely realized.' Unfortunately the sensation surrounding his disappearance, his enemies, and his penchant for women and horse-races have obscured Small's very serious and valuable contribution to Canadian theatre. Although his motive was profit, his business acumen brought the best of North American touring theatre to a generation of Canadians.

See Mary Brown, 'Ambrose Small: A Ghost in Spite of Himself', in *Theatrical Touring and Founding in North America* (1982), ed. L. W. Conolly. KATHLEEN FRASER

Somerset, Dorothy Maud (b. 1900). Born in Perth, Australia, she moved with her family to Vancouver in 1913. She obtained her AB at Radcliffe College, where a stage role with the Harvard Dramatic Club began a distinguished, mainly educational, role in the theatre. In Vancouver she acted, then directed in the early seasons of the Vancouver Little Theatre. In 1930 she attended the Central School of Speech Training in London and worked as assistant to Cedric Hardwicke. At the Univ. of British Columbia she founded a theatre summer school (1939), and taught the first credit courses in theatre (1946). In 1952 she opened—in a converted snack bar—the Frederic Wood Theatre and presented an annual series of plays, beginning with Earle BIRNEY's *Trial of a City*. In 1958 she became head of the new UBC theatre department, established largely through her efforts. She retired in 1965. A studio theatre on campus was named for her, and the university awarded her an honorary D. Litt.

JAMES HOFFMAN

Spackman, John Rudolph (1829?-85). In 1867 American-born 'Spack' joined the HOL-MAN Co., in which he and his first wife, Ella Palmer, acted at Toronto's ROYAL LYCEUM. For many succeeding summers he organized companies to play short seasons at the Royal Lyceum or to tour nearby towns. In 1874, with T.J. HERNDON, he launched the Queen's Theatre, Toronto, enjoying a highly successful summer. He was a member of Charlotte MORRISON's company from 1875 to 1876, and later managed the Royal Star Combination, touring many Western Ontario towns. A long-time favourite in Hamilton, he was the first manager of its GRAND OPERA HOUSE, which he opened in

1880. His versatile comic talent won him applause in such varied roles as Polonius, Squeers in the stage adaptation of Dickens' *Nicholas Nickleby*, and Cuffee, a fugitive slave in George Almar's *Seven Sisters*.

MARY SHORTT

Springford, Norma (b. 1916). Born Norma Linton and raised in St John, N.B., she graduated from the Univ. of New Brunswick and studied theatre with Elizabeth Sterling HAYNES. She was a director in community theatre from 1935 until 1942, when she moved to Montreal with her husband William Springford. She quickly became involved with the MONTREAL REPERTORY THEATRE, where she was general manager from 1944 to 1961, and with other Montreal theatres. She was production manager for Montreal's Open-Air Playhouse (1946-9), director-instructor for the Canadian Art Theatre (1945-8), and producer and owner of the MOUNTAIN PLAYHOUSE (1951-61). Springford directed the Players Club at McGill University from 1950 to 1959, and during the 1960s she was active as an adjudicator for amateur theatre competitions across Canada and in the U.S. On the drama faculty at Concordia University from 1958 to 1982, she acted as design consultant for Concordia's Douglas Burns Theatre, which opened in 1962, and was its manager until 1982.   HERBERT WHITTAKER

Spring Thaw. When Hugh Kemp's adaptation of Hugh MacLennan's novel *Two Solitudes* could not be prepared in time for a 1948 opening for Toronto's NEW PLAY SOCIETY, the cast decided to substitute a revue—of the kind that had annually been produced by the ARTS AND LETTERS CLUB. Andrew ALLAN suggested the name 'Spring Thaw'; prepared within two weeks, the show was built around the plot line of a Toronto store's being unionized, and featured a recognized revue star, Jane MALLETT, well known for her 'Town Tonic' shows. Supporting actors included New Play Society regulars Donald HARRON, Peter Mews, Robert CHRISTIE, Pegi Brown, and Mavor MOORE. Moore directed the revue in the tiny basement Museum Theatre of the Royal Ontario Museum. The production was a collective creation, many of the actors contributing ideas and sketches. The opening song, 'We All Hate Toronto', however, had words by

Lister SINCLAIR and music by Lucio Agostini. Other writers included Pierre Berton, Robert Fulford, Harron, and Moore, who also wrote much of the music. The show ran for three nights and its success initiated an annual series. Memorable items from early 'Thaws' were cantatas by Godfrey Ridout celebrating the rivalry between Eaton's and Simpsons, a campaign to save Toronto's ravines, ballet on snowshoes, and satires on Toronto critics and CBC personalities.

Spring Thaw ran from 1948 to 1971 and from 1980 to 1986; it played at a variety of Toronto locations besides the Museum Theatre, including the CREST THEATRE, the ROYAL ALEXANDRA, the Avenue Theatre, and the Bayview Playhouse. The show regularly toured Ontario and in 1967 appeared at the Vancouver Festival. In 1964 it toured Canada.

In its long history *Spring Thaw* served as a showcase for many Canadian artists. Choreographers included Brian MACDONALD and Alan LUND; writers included Timothy Porteous and James Domville (who had helped create McGill's MY FUR LADY), Ben Wicks, Eric NICOL, Dennis Lee, Johnny Wayne and Frank Shuster, Rick SALUTIN, Jim Betts, and Hart Pomerantz and Lorne Michaels (of 'Saturday Night Live'); music was written by composers as different in approach as Ridout, Gordon Lightfoot, Joni Mitchell, and Ben McPeek. *Spring Thaw*'s performers represent a *Who's Who* of Canadian theatre: Robert Goulet, Barbara HAMILTON, Dave Broadfoot, Anna Russell (who parlayed her 1953 routines into her internationally acclaimed solo act), Dinah Christie, Salomé Bey, Toby ROBINS, Paul Kligman, Lou Jacobi, Hugh Webster, David GARDNER, Ted Follows, Douglas Chamberlain, Jack CRELEY, Rich Little, Don Francks, Norman Jewison, Catherine McKinnon, Tom Kneebone, Pat GALLOWAY, Joan Stuart, Rosemary Radcliffe, and Mary Trainor. From 1967 to 1971 Mavor Moore (who had purchased the title from the New Play Society in 1962) leased *Spring Thaw* to various managements, who changed the character from an intimate satiric revue to a format relying more on song-and-dance routines. When revived in the 1980s under producer Alan Gordon, it seemed dated and irrelevant; its demise was formally acknowledged on 20 Apr. 1986 when Araby LOCKHART organized 'An Evening of Spring Thaw' as a benefit for the re-naming of a ST

LAWRENCE CENTRE auditorium after Jane Mallett, the star of the 1947 *Spring Thaw*.

HERBERT WHITTAKER

Sprung, Guy (b. 1947). Born in Ottawa and educated at McGill University (BA, 1970), he was assistant director at the Schiller Theatre, West Berlin, in 1970, and in 1971 co-founded the Half Moon Theatre in London, Eng., serving as artistic director until 1975. In Canada he gained a national reputation for productions that included several premières: W.O. MITCHELL's *Back to Beulah* (THEATRE CALGARY, 1976) and *The Black Bonspiel of Wullie MacCrimmon* (FESTIVAL LENNOXVILLE, 1980); David FENNARIO's *Nothing to Lose* (CENTAUR THEATRE, 1976) and *BALCONVILLE* (Centaur Theatre, 1979); Rick SALUTIN's *Les CANADIENS* (Centaur, 1977); Anne CHISLETT's *Quiet in the Land* (BLYTH FESTIVAL, 1982); and both the 1979 national tour and the TORONTO FREE THEATRE production of *PAPER WHEAT*.

Sprung's career gained a new impetus in 1981 when his production of *Balconville* toured to London and Belfast, and in 1982 when he directed the Canadian première of Brian Friel's *Translations* at the STRATFORD FESTIVAL and was appointed artistic director of Toronto Free Theatre, where his work has received wide and positive attention. His chosen repertoire has comprised a mix of provocative, contemporary international fare (including more premières, such as Paul Gross's *Dead of Winter* and Lazlo Barna's *Prisoners of Time*) and classical plays (including such bold choices as Thomas Middleton's and William Rowley's *The Changeling*). These productions revealed Sprung's interests and directorial qualities: a theatre of vigorous intellectual and social inquiry mirrored by an equally serious inquiry into theatrical style; a taste for both the classical and the contemporary, ranging through farce, comedy, social drama, and tragedy; a gift for visual composition and naturalistic precision juxtaposed against a spirit of theatrical experiment, the latter notably revealed in his collaborations with the composer/performer John Mills-Cockell on musical underscoring.

In 1986-7 Sprung had a one-year interim appointment as artistic director of the VANCOUVER PLAYHOUSE and in 1986 he laid the groundwork for Toronto Free Theatre's merger with Toronto's CENTRESTAGE—which culminated in 1988 with the founding of the CANADIAN STAGE COMPANY of which he is co-artistic-director with Bill GLASSCO.

BRIAN SMITH

Stahl, Rose (1870-1955). An expatriate actress of German and French-Canadian descent, born and educated in Montreal, she was known for her capacity to mix comedy and pathos. With tangled blonde hair and hazel eyes she began acting as a teenager with the Girard Ave. Co. in Philadelphia, and in her twenties she worked with stock companies in Boston, Philadelphia, Columbus (Ohio), and New York City, playing such roles as Juliet, Trilby, and Camille. She also toured with the American tragedian Daniel Bandmann in 1888-9. In 1902-3 she starred in the short-lived Broadway production, Paul Ford's and Edward Rose's *Janice Meredith*, and gained enduring recognition in 1904 with *The Chorus Girl*, a music-hall sketch by fellow-Canadian James Forbes that was turned into a full-length comedy, *The Chorus Lady*, in 1906. Stahl's role as a tough, slangy showgirl protecting a younger sister signalled an end to Victorian values, and the show broke records in America and England for five seasons. Later hits were Charles Klein's *Maggie Pepper*, which toured in Canada in 1911; Channing Pollock's and Rennold Wolf's *A Perfect Lady*, 1914; George V. Hobart's *Moonlight Mary* and Hobart's and Edna Ferber's *Our Mrs. McChesney*, 1916; and *Pack Up Your Troubles*, 1918. She retired from the stage in 1918.

DAVID GARDNER

Steiner, Eric (b. 1946). Born and raised in Toronto and educated at Emerson College, Boston, he joined Toronto's FACTORY THEATRE in 1971 and became its most important director. He staged the original productions of Sheldon ROSEN's *The Love Mouse* in 1971; Larry FINEBERG's *Stonehenge Trilogy*, 1972; Louis Del Grande's *Maybe We Could Get Some Bach*, 1972; George F. WALKER's *Bagdad Saloon*, 1973, and *Beyond Mozambique*, 1974; and Bryan WADE's *Underground*, 1975, and *This Side of the Rockies*, 1977. Steiner also directed revivals of Herschel HARDIN's *Esker Mike and His Wife, Agiluk* in 1972, 1973, and 1986. For TORONTO FREE THEATRE he staged the first productions of Tom HENDRY's *Gravediggers of 1942* in 1973 and Fineberg's *Life on Mars* in 1979. At TARRAGON THEATRE he directed the premières of Wade's *Blitzkrieg* in 1974 and Carol BOLT's *One*

Night Stand, 1977, and the Toronto première of John MURRELL's *WAITING FOR THE PARADE*, 1979. Many of Steiner's productions are notable for their suspense, dark humour, and strong visual style. Steiner has also directed for the STRATFORD FESTIVAL and remains a sought-after free-lance director across Canada.   DENIS W. JOHNSTON

Still Stands the House. This one-act 'drama of the Canadian frontier' (as it is subtitled) is one of five plays Gwen Pharis RINGWOOD wrote while earning her MA in drama at the Univ. of North Carolina. First produced by the Carolina Playmakers on 3 Mar. 1938, and first published in 1938 in the *Carolina Play-Book*, vol. II, it is one of the most popular plays in the Canadian dramatic repertory.

The cast consists of only four characters, and the action, which takes place in the Warrens' prairie farmhouse during a blizzard, is stark and simple. A real-estate salesman offers Ruth a vision of a new future near a city. Opposed to her is Hester, her sister-in-law, whose allegiance is to a house and farm as sterile as her own life. Caught between them is Hester's brother Bruce Warren, who is married to Ruth. Bruce is lost in the blizzard, and Ruth is murdered by Hester, who lapses into madness.

With its claustrophobic setting in the living-room of the isolated farmhouse, presenting a powerful metaphor of Canadian life during the Depression, and its winter blizzards, offering an image of a disorder in nature that is reflected in the disorder of the Warren household, the play is a folk tragedy. Its key symbols—the broken hyacinth, the lamp not filled, the mare about to foal—reinforce Ringwood's theme of disorder and madness.

Still Stands the House—perhaps the most frequently anthologized Canadian play—has been described by Edmonton playwright Elsie Park GOWAN as 'the best one-act play ever written in Canada'.

See Judith Hinchcliffe, '*Still Stands the House*: the Failure of the Pastoral Dream', *Canadian Drama*, 2 (1977).
          ROTA HERZBERG LISTER

St Lawrence Centre for the Performing Arts. Conceived as a community centre for Toronto in celebration of Canada's Centennial, it contained the first theatre in the city built expressly for a resident company. Mavor

MOORE was the main artistic force behind the building, which was designed by the Toronto firm of Adamson Associates as a two-theatre, multi-purpose facility. Its undisguised concrete construction was deemed drab, and its final cost of $5.2 million (far less than other centennial projects of comparable stature) was achieved only by eliminating the secondary spaces originally planned for community groups and for on-site technical facilities. Town Hall—the smaller space, seating about 500—opened on 2 Feb. 1970 with a series of debates on current issues. Other non-theatrical events have continued to take place there, along with many musical series, and THEATRE PLUS has occupied the space each summer since 1973.

The 830-seat main theatre opened on 26 Feb. 1970. Its steeply raked auditorium, 87' deep, promoted a sense of separation between audience and actor, though the stage could be altered from thrust to proscenium to a triptych that enveloped the audience—but in each case part of the audience experienced sightline problems. The theatre has been occupied since its opening by a resident company—first Toronto Arts Productions, then CENTRESTAGE, and now the CANADIAN STAGE COMPANY. In 1981 it closed for renovations (at a cost of $5.8 million), and reopened on 19 Mar. 1983. The depth and rake of the auditorium were greatly decreased and a balcony and boxes were installed, increasing the seating to 890, and the proscenium stage was made more versatile by a retractable arch and a forestage that can sink beneath the auditorium to create an orchestra pit. In 1983 the theatre was renamed the Bluma Appel Theatre, and the Town Hall became the Jane MALLETT Theatre in 1985.
          STEPHEN JOHNSON

St Louis Theatre. In 1844 the officers of the Coldstream Guards garrisoned at Quebec City created a theatre on the second floor of a riding-house belonging to the Château Saint-Louis, near Dufferin Terrace. Constructed of stone, the building was 80' long and 40' wide. Since only two entrance doors were provided at ground level, two more were added in the course of renovations; but only a single wooden staircase connected the lobby area with the auditorium above.

Opened in Jan. 1845, with accommodation for 300, the St Louis Theatre quickly became the city's most stylish playhouse. In its seventeen months of existence some fifty performances of English melodramas, comedies, and farces were staged there by the garrison amateurs (see GARRISON THEATRE) and by the City Amateur Theatrical Association, as well as productions by French-Canadian troupes of works by Victor Hugo, Jean-Jacques Rousseau, and Eugène Scribe. Vocal and instrumental concerts and dioramas were also frequently presented.

On 12 June 1846 a capacity audience attended an exhibition of 'illuminated Chemical Dioramas (in the style of Daguerre)' given by M.R. Harrison of Hamilton. About 10:15 p.m., just as spectators were preparing to leave, a camphine lamp was upset on stage, setting the scenery alight. The crowd panicked and jammed the single stairway leading to the exterior. Forty-six people were burned or trampled to death and the theatre was gutted. JOHN RIPLEY

Strand Theatre. This 750-seat theatre on Saskatoon's 20th Street east of 3rd Avenue opened on 2 October 1912, managed by G. Potsby and owned by R.E. Hagerty. Following a disastrous first season, it was renamed the Provincial in 1913 and booked a month of VAUDEVILLE through the short-lived Canadian Provincial Theatre Circuit. Purchased by William B. Sherman and reopened on 25 Dec. 1913 as the Sherman, the theatre continued to offer vaudeville attractions until becoming home, for six months in 1914, for the Streeter Bryan Stock Company, which played popular comedies and melodramas. Refurbished and restored to its original name in Jan. 1916, the Strand presented the Famous Bostonians (formerly the Juvenile Bostonians) in *Iroma* and continued to offer vaudeville booked through the Chicago-based Western Vaudeville Managers' Association, who also booked for the EMPIRE, the most popular Saskatoon vaudeville house in its time.

Wartime demand for wheat and livestock made money plentiful but manpower scarce, leading to a proliferation of all-female productions, represented in 1917 by musical-comedy companies such as Smith's Musical Girls or Harris and Proy's U.S.A. Girls, and modern morality plays such as *Her Unborn Child*, to which ladies only (and no one under sixteen) were admitted. Charles W. Wirth's Londonian Belles appeared in 1918, as did Fred Carmelo's Musical Comedy Company,

with a jazz trio that played Saskatoon for two months. Some returning soldiers assumed the management on 26 May 1919 and renamed it the Thelus Theatre in honour of the third Canadian objective on Vimy Ridge; but the theatre reverted to its old name, the Strand, later that year. The Strand closed with *In Judgement Of*, 27-9 Oct. 1919.
PATRICK B. O'NEILL

Stratford Festival, The. Widely regarded as Canada's foremost theatre company, it has attracted many of the country's most talented theatre artists who have performed for audiences and critics throughout North America and beyond, its productions having been seen from coast to coast on television, and having toured to the U.S. and as far afield as Australia and the Soviet Union. Yet the Stratford Festival is an anomaly: a classical theatre in a country without a strong classical tradition— a defiantly international institution in an increasingly nationalistic age. Although Stratford helped create contemporary Canadian theatre, it was then spurned by the new generation of ALTERNATE THEATRES in the 1960s and 1970s, in part because the Festival has been unable to train directors to fulfil its unstated mandate of interpreting the classical repertoire within a uniquely Canadian context.

The Stratford Festival was the brainchild of local journalist Tom Patterson, who had been profoundly moved by wartime productions he had seen in Europe. Patterson thought a Shakespearean festival might rejuvenate the small Ontario town of Stratford but never anticipated that his festival would one day become its major employer. With a modest grant from the town council, he was able to pursue his dream. After an unsuccessful trip to New York to meet Laurence Olivier, Patterson (on the advice of Robertson DAVIES and Dora Mavor MOORE) contacted Tyrone GUTHRIE at the Old Vic in England. Guthrie agreed to come to Stratford to give advice, primarily because he wanted to see how Canada had changed since the 1930s when he had directed 'The Romance of Canada' radio series. Once in Stratford he quickly accepted the irresistible challenge of creating a festival in his own image.

To lend his infant adventure credibility and to attract audiences, he recruited Alec Guinness as his star attraction for the first season in 1953 and supported him with three other

Stratford Festival

actors from England, Irene Worth, Douglas CAMPBELL, and Michael Bates. With his long-time collaborator Tanya MOISEIWITSCH as designer and a trio of experienced English personnel in charge of production management, wardrobe, and properties, high standards were ensured. Because there was no other suitable facility available, Guthrie decided to use a large canvas tent for his theatre. The tent also encouraged the holiday atmosphere that Guthrie considered appropriate for a truly 'festive' experience, and that led to the picnics by the Avon River that have become an accepted part of Stratford theatregoing.

The novel thrust stage that Guthrie and Moiseiwitsch designed tried to recreate the original style of Shakespearean performance. It rescued the actor from painted scenery and restored the primacy of the spoken word. With the general shape and features of the Elizabethan platform stage, surrounded on three sides by an auditorium reminiscent of classical Greece, the stage also encouraged spectacle and movement, characteristics Guthrie exploited to the full as one colourful scene flowed smoothly into the next with a constant swirl of lavish costumes, eye-catching properties, and waving banners. It has been remodelled several times, but most of the changes have been minor adjustments, such as those in the height and number of steps, although Michael LANGHAM and Tanya Moiseiwitsch made substantial changes between the 1961 and 1962 seasons. They

The original tent stage, Stratford Festival, 1953

enlarged the side entrances to permit sweeping processionals and reduced the number of balcony pillars to open up the inner-stage area. The only other significant change occurred in 1976 during Robin PHILLIPS' tenure, when the balcony was made portable so that it could be removed when it was not required.

When Alec Guinness stepped onstage as Richard III on 13 July 1953, the success of the Stratford Festival, with its predominantly Canadian company, was assured—and confirmed by glowing reports from New York theatre critics. The first season, which also included *All's Well That Ends Well*, had to be extended by a week. During those six weeks attendance reached sixty-eight thousand. Thirty-four years later, in 1987, over 443,000 attended fourteen productions in three theatres over a season that lasted six months. The theatre's phenomenal growth is a living tribute to the foresight of its two founders.

Stratford's ancillary activities, however, have produced mixed results. Although lectures and art exhibits in conjunction with the local gallery are a continuing part of each season, an international film festival was abandoned. Guthrie believed that music should play a large part in the festival. Sixteen afternoon concerts, featuring Glenn Gould among others, were presented in the first season, under the direction of Louis Applebaum, and celebrated musicians performed in the seasons immediately following. Concerts by celebrities or by members of the festival orchestras have continued, but attempts to supplement and highlight musical activities have been curtailed—though Stratford's emphasis on theatre has allowed other summer music festivals—in Elora and Parry Sound, for example—to flourish.

Guthrie enjoyed launching brave new ventures—but not running them. Wanting to concentrate on directing in 1954, he relegated the duties and title of artistic director to his former production manager Cecil Clarke; but because Clarke could not command the love and loyalty of the company, Guthrie had to resume full control. The highlight of the second season of three plays was Stratford's staging of its first non-Shakespearean work, Guthrie's production of *Oedipus Rex* performed with masks and exploiting all the opportunities for movement available on the open stage. Guthrie reluctantly returned for a third season, fully aware that the Stratford Festival had to begin to stand on its own or risk forever being nothing more than Tyrone Guthrie's theatre, and this time he was successful in planning an orderly leadership transition. His chosen successor was Michael Langham, a protegé from England who had made his Festival début directing *Julius Caesar* in 1955. An inspired production of *Henry V* in 1956, starring the young Montreal actor Christopher PLUMMER, confirmed Langham's reputation. He conceived *Henry V* in a distinctively Canadian manner, using Anglo-Canadians in the English parts and Quebec actors in the French. This turned the final act into a celebration of Canadian unity. During Langham's long tenure at Stratford, 1956–67, he provided careful guidance that allowed the Festival to mature.

After the 1956 season the tent was dismantled and cut into pieces for souvenirs. Construction started on a new building that was designed by Toronto architect Robert Fairfield to retain the ambience of the tent while providing every necessary modern theatrical amenity. The new building was the physical embodiment of many of Tyrone Guthrie's cherished principles, and the stage was its physical and psychological centre. One part of the circle contains the lobbies and other audience areas; another houses the adminstra-

tive offices; and the last—which Guthrie believed was the most important part because it was in use from morning to night—contains dressing rooms, scene and costume shops, storage areas, rehearsal halls and green room. Accordingly, Fairfield orientated the building so that the large backstage windows offered the best views of the Avon River. To accommodate over 2,200 spectators—a necessity for the theatre to generate the box-office revenue needed to support a classical repertoire—he incorporated a wide 220-degree arc in the auditorium and included a low balcony. He also retained the intimacy of the tent: no seat is further than sixty-five feet from the stage. The new building's superb acoustics eliminated the shriek of train whistles and the hammer of rain that plagued productions in the tent. Full climate control solved the problem of heat and humidity. By using a fluted roof, Fairfield even managed to retain some of the visual aspect of the tent. After less than a year of construction work the new theatre opened in 1957 with Christopher Plummer's Hamlet.

Langham mastered Guthrie's difficult thrust stage and managed to recruit and retain a strong company. He too realized the importance of stars and brought in Jason Robards Jr., Julie Harris, Tammy Grimes, Paul Scofield, Zoë CALDWELL, and Alan

The Festival Theatre, Stratford, Ontario

Bates, although he was convinced that Stratford should develop its own stars. Under Langham, Canadian actors William HUTT, Douglas RAIN, Tony VAN BRIDGE, Kate REID, Frances HYLAND, Leo CICERI, Martha HENRY, and Bruno GERUSSI rose to prominence, and George McCowan and Jean GASCON were the first Canadians to direct on the thrust stage. Brian JACKSON, originally from England, who had settled in Stratford as head of properties, and Canadian-born Marie DAY became designers.

In 1963 the Festival acquired the 1,000-seat proscenium Avon Theatre in downtown Stratford—built early in this century for touring productions and VAUDEVILLE and then turned into a cinema—which it had been using since 1956. The first notable Festival productions at the Avon were a series of Gilbert and Sullivan operettas, the first two (1960 and 1961) brilliantly staged by Guthrie. An important addition to the Festival, the Avon has facilitated the production of plays that are better suited to a proscenium stage or that appeal to a wider audience.

Finding a successor to Langham proved difficult; he remained through the 1967 season to allow the Board of Governors additional time to make a decision. When this was announced, it seemed the perfect Cana-

dian compromise: Jean Gascon from French Canada assisted by John HIRSCH from English Canada; Gascon had been associated with the Festival since 1956 when he played in Langham's *Henry V*, and Hirsch had been directing for the Festival since 1965. The two men, however, were artistically and temperamentally dissimilar and Hirsch left after the 1969 season, while Gascon—the Festival's only Canadian-born artistic director to date—remained in charge during an uneasy period of transition until 1974. He expanded the repertoire and had particular success with little-known plays such as Shakespeare's *Pericles* and Webster's *The Duchess of Malfi*. Instead of importing stars, Gascon built his company around Canadian actors—William Hutt, Douglas Rain, Martha Henry, Kenneth Welsh, and Pat Galloway. During this time Stratford found itself increasingly estranged from the burgeoning alternate-theatre movement and, partly in response to the call for Canadian plays, Gascon opened the Third Stage in a rented community hall for experimental and music theatre.

Controversy arose in 1974 with the appointment of the young English director Robin Phillips as Gascon's successor. But Phillips was an astute leader. With the help of critic Urjo KAREDA as his literary manager,

James Reaney's Colours in the Dark, *Stratford Festival, 1967*

he welcomed a new generation of talent and gave them an opportunity to play classical, modern, and new Canadian plays, all in the same week. Phillips continued to experiment by having different actors play the same role and by remounting improved versions of some of his best productions, such as *A Midsummer Night's Dream* and *Measure for Measure*. He used stars, but in unusual ways: Maggie Smith's greatest triumph was not in comedy but as the haunted Virginia Woolf in Edna O'Brien's *Virginia*; Peter Ustinov played King Lear in 1979 and again in 1980.

Exhausted by the strain of running Stratford and by lack of support for his dreams of a theatre school, a media centre, and a winter home in Toronto, Phillips resigned more than a year before the end of the 1980 season. The Board failed to act efficiently in its search for his successor, and the ensuing chaos ended only when John Hirsch agreed to serve as artistic director for a five-year term. Producer Muriel Sherrin, not Hirsch, planned the 1981 season. During his term Hirsch established contacts with the CBC that resulted in the televising of several productions, and created the Young Company at the Third Stage to provide a training ground for young actors. Although Brian MACDONALD's Gilbert and Sullivan productions were filling the Avon Theatre, the Festival as a whole was struggling with a repertoire that relied heavily on the safe comedies. Hirsch's final legacy was twofold: he left an immense deficit, but he carried through much-needed renovation to the Festival and Avon theatres, adding rehearsal space and new shops.

In 1986 John NEVILLE, an English actor/director of impeccable credentials who had served his Canadian apprenticeship as artistic director of two major theatres—the CITADEL THEATRE in Edmonton and the NEPTUNE THEATRE in Halifax—took over as artistic director. For his opening season he made some audacious choices, scheduling Shakespeare's three lesser-known late romances for the Festival theatre and enticing Robin Phillips back to direct *Cymbeline*. Lest this repertoire should hurt attendance, Neville moved the annual musical from the Avon to the Festival theatre and presented Rodgers and Hart's *Boys from Syracuse* instead of Gilbert and Sullivan. Neville has managed to reduce the Festival's deficit and contain falling attendance, and under his direction Stratford has begun the process of renewal. It will

never again be the centrepiece of Canadian theatre, but it will remain important to the Canadian theatrical mosaic.

It was announced in Aug. 1988 that Neville will be succeeded by British director David William, who has directed regularly at Stratford since 1966. Now a Canadian landed immigrant living in London, Ont., William will begin a three-year term as artistic director on 1 Nov. 1989.

See John Pettigrew and Jamie Portman, *Stratford: The First Thirty Years* (1985).

ROSS STUART

Stratton, Allan (b. 1951). Born in Stratford, Ont., and educated in Switzerland and at the Univ. of Toronto, he began his involvement with theatre working in James REANEY's Alpha Centre, Stratford, Ont., and acting in a number of theatres across the country. Reaney produced and published Stratton's first play, *The Rusting Heart*, in 1968; it was broadcast on CBC radio in 1974. In 1977 the VANCOUVER PLAYHOUSE produced Stratton's second play, *72 Under the O* (1977). Although its energy is somewhat unfocused, it points to the pacing and surprise that characterize Stratton's later work and that keep audiences fully involved. In his next play, *Nurse Jane Goes to Hawaii* (1980), Stratton demonstrates just how effectively he can control complex action within the conventions of farce. *Nurse Jane* develops a series of overlapping comic situations, and a clever subplot that is the play's chief success. The central character is a writer of pulp romance novels who dictates her next book into a tape recorder even as she participates in the main action; by superimposing the delightfully bad story of Nurse Jane and her adventures in Hawaii on to the more predictable plot-turns of the farce, Stratton is able to make the 'real' characters into 'fictional' ones and to comment on the action. The clichés of pulp fiction not only complement the farce, but identify the educated urban audience for whom the humour is intended. Aiming his satire at this audience occasionally leads Stratton to use overly sarcastic one-liners, or overly academic dialogue, but these errors in tone are soon masked by sharp rejoinders and quick turns of events. First produced at Toronto's PHOENIX THEATRE in 1980, *Nurse Jane* has enjoyed enormous success in over a hundred productions.

Rexy! (1981), produced at Phoenix Theatre in Feb. 1981, is a more challenging piece that incorporates humour, fantasy, historical reportage, and greater character development. Based on the wartime conscription crisis of 1944 and on details of the personal life of Prime Minister Mackenzie King as revealed in his diaries, *Rexy!* portrays the contradictions of King's public and private *personae*. Dream interludes expand the characterization and shift attention from the outer documentary to the inner man, showing King as vain and star-struck, compulsive and guilt-ridden, shrewd and opportunistic. *Rexy!* won the CHALMERS (1981), Dora Mavor MOORE (1980-1), and *Canadian Authors Association* (1982) awards.

Stratton returned to farce in *Friends of a Feather* (1985)—his adaptation of Eugène Labiche's *Célimare*—produced by the SHAW FESTIVAL in 1984. *Joggers* (1983), first produced at TORONTO FREE THEATRE in Dec. 1982, maintains Stratton's characteristic pace, but shifts style to explore psychological terror. Not uniformly well received, *Joggers* suffers from underdeveloped comic-book characters and predictable sexual business, but it creates a chilling atmosphere and compels audience empathy with the protagonist's fear.

Papers—first performed at TARRAGON THEATRE, Toronto, in Nov. 1985—explores people's difficulty in expressing emotion. Here, as in his earlier works, Stratton combines moods and tones: romance, naturalistic characterization, and (as always) humour. Stratton's sure sense of the comedic, and his excellent control of the stage, account for the marked commercial and critical success of his plays. *The 101 Miracles of Hope Chance*—a satire on television evangelism—opened in Winnipeg in 1988 and was also produced at Hamilton's THEATRE AQUARIUS in Jan. 1989.

Words in Play, Three Comedies (1988) contains *Nurse Jane Goes to Hawaii*, *The 101 Miracles of Hope Chance*, and *Joggers*.

REID GILBERT

Stuart, Eleanor (1901-77). Born Eleanor Stuart Nichol in Montreal, she gained her early theatrical experience with the Comédie Française in Paris and with the Ben Greet company in England. In 1926 she replaced Fay Compton when the Haymarket production of Ashley Dukes' comedy *The Man With a Load of Mischief* went on tour. Her success led to Broadway roles in Gregorio and Maria Martinez-Sierra's *The Kingdom of God* and Alberto Casella's *Death Takes A Holiday* in 1929. She toured the U.S. with George Arliss in Winthrop Ames's production of *The Merchant of Venice* in 1928, understudying Peggy Wood's Portia. When she returned to Montreal in the mid-1930s Martha ALLAN invited her to join the MONTREAL REPERTORY THEATRE as a leading player and acting coach. MRT revived *The Man With a Load of Mischief* for her in the 1934-5 season. Stuart also acted for the Lakeshore Summer Theatre and for the CBC. Her only classic role during this period was in Theodore Komisarjevsky's modern-dress, open-air production of Shakespeare's *Cymbeline* at Montreal's Open-Air Playhouse in 1950.

In 1953 Stuart appeared in the STRATFORD FESTIVAL's inaugural season, playing the Countess of Rossillion in *All's Well That Ends Well* and the Duchess of York in *Richard III*. She played Jocasta opposite James Mason in 1954 and opposite Douglas CAMPBELL in 1955 in *Oedipus Rex*, and in 1961 Volumnia to Paul Scofield's Coriolanus.

A beautiful voice being one of her strongest assets, Eleanor Stuart appropriately ended her career as a teacher at the NATIONAL THEATRE SCHOOL, specializing in voice.

HERBERT WHITTAKER

Studio Lab Theatre. Among the earliest ALTERNATE THEATRES in Toronto, it was founded as the Studio Children's Theatre in 1965 by Ernest Schwarz, who had emigrated from the U.S. in 1959 after studies at the Yale School of Drama. Its repertoire consisted of traditional pieces, such as *Pinocchio* and *Jack and the Beanstalk*, performed in a lively, improvisational manner.

In 1968 Schwarz introduced an adult program, which catapulted the company into the vanguard of Toronto's experimental theatre with such plays as Megan Terry's *Comings and Goings* and Paul Ableman's *Tests*. In 1969 the company was renamed Studio Lab Theatre to reflect its new orientation, and initiated what would become an annual tour of Northern Ontario.

In Dec. 1969 Studio Lab became the first group outside of New York to produce Richard Schechner's environmental *Dionysus in '69*. It caught the imagination of young audiences in Toronto and generated a cult following. In 1970 Schwarz remounted the play as *Dionysus in '70*; by the time it closed in Jan.

1971 it had played 168 performances (chiefly on weekends) to a total audience of 45,000.

By 1971, when it was invited to the Venice Biennale, Studio Lab was the second-largest theatre company in Toronto. Nathan COHEN called it 'one of the most enterprising and serious artistic companies in Canada.' But its next major venture, *The Brothers*, an adaptation by Rex DEVERELL of Plautus's *Menaechmi*, failed to recapture the audiences of the previous year.

Overshadowed by the newly emerging alternate theatres, with their commitment to indigenous drama, Studio Lab continued its children's program until it ceased operations in 1976. Schwarz went on to a successful career as an independent producer in Toronto. In 1983 the company made a brief return at Toronto's Harbourfront, reviving its popular *Just So Stories*.   ALAN FILEWOD

Sudbury Theatre Centre. Incorporated as a professional theatre company in 1971, its first production—Bertolt Brecht's and Kurt Weill's *Threepenny Opera*, co-produced at Laurentian Univ. with Toronto's STUDIO LAB THEATRE in Apr. 1972—was not well received. The appointment of Tony Lloyd shortly afterwards as the company's first artistic director, however, helped to establish STC's credibility. Lloyd—who had emigrated from England in 1953 and began his theatrical career in Canada with the CANADIAN PLAYERS—offered a standard regional theatre repertory of British and American musicals, comedies, and thrillers, but also introduced modern classics by Eugene O'Neill, Sean O'Casey, Joe Orton, and Edward Albee, and gradually increased the theatre's commitment to Canadian drama: David FREEMAN, Joanna GLASS, Allan STRATTON, Rex DEVERELL, and John MURRELL.

With substantial assistance from the International Nickel Company in 1972 STC renovated the old INCO Club into an intimate 270-seat theatre. In 1977 the company moved its rehearsal space, administrative offices, and workshop to King St, and performed in university facilities while it lobbied for a new building. Despite economic hardship in the region, in Sept. 1982 a fully equipped $2.1 million theatre opened, with a fan-shaped auditorium seating 297 and office, workshop, and rehearsal facilities. It opened with Lionel Bart's *Oliver!* (with fifty local children in the cast).

STC attracts about 4,000 subscribers, some from as far away as North Bay, Elliot Lake, and Espanola. In addition to its regular fall-winter season, it mounts two DINNER THEATRE productions a year and operates a summer Youth Theatre, a drama program for children, and (since 1985) the Sudbury Theatre Centre Touring Company, which travels annually to more than 250 schools and community centres across the province—but particularly in the north, where its productions have included Chekhov's *A Marriage Proposal*, Carol BOLT's *Cyclone Jack*, and adaptations by Irene Watts of Tolstoy's folk tales.

In Dec. 1988 Tony Lloyd announced his resignation; he was succeeded on 1 July 1989 by Mark Schoenberg, associate director of Edmonton's CITADEL THEATRE. Lloyd became artistic director of the Huron Country Playhouse, Grand Bend, Ont.
                    STEPHEN JOHNSON

Sullivan, Sean (1923-85). Born and educated in Toronto, he began acting with local amateur companies (including the Belmont Theatre Group) and the NEW PLAY SOCIETY. In the 1950s he acted extensively on British TV, and by 1959 had also made some 300 appearances on Canadian TV. He is best known, however, for creating the role of the father in David FRENCH's plays *Leaving Home* and *Of the Fields, Lately*, in their 1972 and 1973 premières at Toronto's TARRAGON THEATRE. This role suited Sullivan's ability to convey introspection, integrity, and controlled intensity—characteristics that were finely developed when he played Willy Loman in Arthur Miller's *Death of a Salesman* in a 1976 production of Theatre London (see GRAND OPERA HOUSE). He won an ACTRA Award in 1977 for best actor in the CBC-TV version of *Of the Fields, Lately*. Sullivan's film work included roles in *2001: A Space Odyssey* and *Atlantic City*.   EUGENE BENSON

Summers, George H. (1865-1941). Born Horatio George in Newmarket, Ont., this genial character comedian made his professional début at sixteen, in Toronto with the HOLMAN company, becoming their leading comic actor within a year. In 1890 he joined Charles J. Stevenson's Ottawa-based troupe, and in 1892 married Isabella 'Belle' Stevenson (1869-1947); they toured with various American comedy companies during the 1890s. In 1901-3 Summers starred in road company tours of *The House That Jack Built* and *Hot Scotch Major*. For the summer of 1903 the Summers Stock Co. was engaged in Hamilton by William B. Sherman at his Sherman Park Theatre, and for ten seasons (1905-14) they ran pioneer professional summer theatre on the Hamilton mountain ('always a breeze'), with access by the East End Incline Railway. The roofed, wood-and-stucco Mountain Park Playhouse had a fully equipped stage and an auditorium open on one side to a view of the city and Lake Ontario. Melodrama and comedy were popular fare and in 1910 attendance reached 73,000; Walter HUSTON was an early member of the troupe. An original comedy, *The Man from Ottawa*—adapted by Summers from M. Quad's Bowser Stories in the *Detroit Free Press* and set in Toronto's Rosedale district—opened the 1911 season. On 21 Dec. 1914 the theatre was gutted by fire; plans for a new 2,000-seat, theatre/cinema/restaurant complex were blocked by a residents' protest group. Summers kept his stock company alive until 1916, playing the fall and winter seasons in southern Ont. and frequently on the prairie circuit. In 1916-17, Summers won rave reviews as 'Canada's Foremost Comedian' in a cross-Canada tour of Minnie Jaffa's *In Walked Jimmy*; between 1917 and 1918 he played musical comedy on the PANTAGES West-coast circuit and for six months at Camp Lewis in Tacoma, Wash. After flirting briefly with motion pictures, he returned to the New York area in 1919 to appear in *The Girl He Left Behind*, and opened an office on Broadway as a director and script doctor before returning to Toronto in the mid-1920s. In his later years he wrote poetry, song lyrics, and film scenarios, and comedy sketches for the CBC and, in 1920, a series of seven articles on Toronto theatre history for *The Star Weekly*.　　DAVID GARDNER

Summer Stock. Summer stock refers to the offering—by a more-or-less permanent dramatic company under one management—of a series of plays during the summer season in resort areas or, infrequently, in cities. To a great extent Canadian summer stock, modelled on similar ventures in New England and Michigan, has been concentrated in Ontario, Quebec (see SUMMER STOCK, Quebec), and British Columbia. Although it began in Canada as early as the 1880s, it assumed significant status only after the First

World War with the decline of touring from the U.S. and England and the growth of summer-vacation areas and resorts made possible by the automobile and a radically improved road system. Vacationers—used to theatre in the cities—provided a new summer audience, but the advent of air-conditioning in the 1920s allowed summer stock, once primarily associated with the countryside, to be mounted in Canadian cities as well. In Ontario in the late 1940s commercial theatres opened in resorts from the Thousand Islands in the east to Crystal Beach in the west, from Jackson's Point, Peterborough, and Port Carling in the north to Niagara Falls in the south. They performed light comedies, thrillers, and sentimental dramas from Broadway and London. During the 1950s, however, the founding of the STRATFORD FESTIVAL led to a reduction in the number of these theatres or transformed them during the 1960s and 1970s into community-oriented, non-profit companies, performing in parks, barns, second-storey opera houses, and modern theatres.

Indicative of the original need for entertainment in summer resorts is the example of playwright Merrill DENISON who, starting in 1918, staged outdoor performances for guests at his mother's hotel in Bon Echo (now a Provincial Park) near Ottawa. The skits, enacted by members of the hotel's staff, had an impromptu *commedia dell'arte* flavour and poked fun at the lodge and its guests.

John HOLDEN's Actors' Colony launched summer stock in the Muskoka Lakes region in 1934. An experienced actor-director, Holden established his model for Canadian 'straw-hat' theatres in the tiny community of Bala, about equidistant from Port Carling and Gravenhurst, Ont. He turned the town hall into a makeshift theatre and presented a different play each week every summer for eight years. Holden gave up his theatre after the 1941 season, many of his players having left to join productions presented by the Armed Services.

Summer stock never prospered in Toronto, although it first appeared in places like the amusement park at Hanlan's Point on the Toronto Islands, where comic opera, drama, and BURLESQUE were performed in the 1880s. Ernest Rawley, manager of the ROYAL ALEXANDRA THEATRE, produced summer seasons from 1940 to 1948 presenting everything from lavish musicals to Shakespeare. Often

The Straw Hat Players, 1953. Back row (l. to r.): Deborah Cass, David Gardner, John Blatchley, Pierre Lefèvre, Murray Davis. Seated (l. to r.): Norma Renault, Norman Ettlinger, Ruth Springford, Aileen Seaton, Louise Nichols. Front row (l. to r.): Richard Lamb, Ivan Thornley Hall, John Rutherford

these shows were package tours from the U.S. or Britain, but many others featured a predominantly Canadian company supporting a handful of well-known American stage and screen stars. The best seasons were in 1944-6 when Robert Henderson, formerly of the Hollywood Playhouse, served as director. Toronto's Melody Fair, which opened in 1951 in a 1,600-seat tent at the Dufferin Park raceway and closed four years later, was housed indoors in the Mutual Street Arena. Although Canadian-owned, Melody Fair was modelled on the American chain of summer musical theatres and employed Americans as directors and leading performers, with Canadians in supporting roles. A similar endeavour, Music Fair, performed during 1958-60 in a 2,000-seat tent in Toronto's suburban Dixie Plaza.

Ontario's best-known summer theatre, the Straw Hat Players, was born in cottage country, after the war, in the Memorial Hall in Port Carling near Bala, Ont. Its roots were in Toronto's HART HOUSE THEATRE, where students Donald DAVIS and Murray DAVIS and their sister Barbara CHILCOTT, with the help of producer Brian Doherty, launched the company in 1948 with a production of the melodrama *The Drunkard* that featured classmates Araby LOCKHART, Eric HOUSE, Char-

mion KING, and Ted Follows. When the Davises went on to found the CREST THEATRE in Toronto in 1953, they increasingly left the running of the summer company to others, such as Peter Potter, Russell Graves, Pierre Lefèvre, John Blatchley, Henry Kaplan, George McCowan, Leon MAJOR, and Bruce Maller.

The Davises finally relinquished control of the Straw Hat Players after the 1955 season. Two of the Crest's backstage staff, William Bennett and Wilf Pegg, then put together a company like the first one, using many students. The following year, L.C. (Toby) Tobias and James Hozack took over in Port Carling. In 1958 William Davis, a cousin of Donald and Murray, and his friend Karl Jaffray, both Univ. of Toronto students, recreated the Straw Hat Players and ran the company until 1961. For the next three years it was operated by a team of university students headed by Peter Wylde. Alan Hughes took over as producer for the 1965 and 1966 seasons, hiring Nicholas Ayre to direct young professionals and students. Next came a company called Theatre 21, which kept theatre alive in Port Carling for three more years, primarily under the direction of Edwin Stephenson. In 1969 Stephenson recruited Michael Ayoub, a young actor-director from

Timmins who had been trained in New York, and his actress-wife Mary Bellows. Ayoub presented his first summer season in 1972 and has established a model that he continues to follow: two separate companies, one doing two musicals, the other two plays, both emphasizing Canadian writing and each performing half a week at the Gravenhurst Opera House and the rest of the time at the Port Carling Memorial Hall.

The success of the original Straw Hat Players quickly spawned imitators, similar in purpose and repertoire, and featuring many of the same actors and directors. Arthur Sutherland's and Drew Thompson's INTERNATIONAL PLAYERS produced seasons in Kingston, 1948-55, and the Peterborough Summer Theatre opened in 1949 with Robertson DAVIES' Fortune, My Foe. Michael Sadler, an Irish-born Canadian producer and director, ran the Peterborough Summer Theatre for its nine seasons (until 1958), with Robert GILL serving a season as resident director (and upon occasion as an actor).

After two seasons of running the Midland Players, Toronto drama teacher Jack Blacklock moved his company in 1950 to the more populous Niagara peninsula, where it became the Niagara Barn Theatre. That first season in an old barn lasted seventeen weeks, the longest season in Canada at the time. In 1952 Blacklock moved his company to Vineland, where the Prudhomme brothers built Blacklock a 450-seat playhouse adjoining their motel and garden centre. After two seasons there, the company moved for the last time to Stoney Creek on the outskirts of Hamilton. But the strain of producing long seasons of weekly stock had taken its toll and Jack Blacklock gave up after the 1954 season.

Prudhomme's theatre in Vineland lasted much longer. Bernard SLADE and his wife Jill Foster assumed control in 1954 with American actor Warren Hart as their partner, and christened their new venture the Garden Centre Theatre. But after only one draining twenty-five week season, Slade and Foster had had enough. After two more unsuccessful years, John Prudhomme finally decided to bring in experienced Americans, producer Nat Godwin and director Robert Herrman. Herrman stayed until the theatre finally closed in 1966. He served as producer, directed frequently, and even acted on occasion, while his actress-wife Terry Clemes was a featured performer and assisted her husband

in running the theatre. Under the Herrmans the Garden Centre Theatre hosted a large number of package tours from the U.S. and also imported television and film personalities to star in Canadian productions.

The Niagara Falls Summer Theatre opened in 1950 in a school auditorium with a production of Mary Chase's Harvey. For the first two seasons the producers included Bruce Yorke, Michael Sadler (from the Peterborough Summer Theatre), and, most importantly, Maud Franchot, an American. In 1952 Franchot took over sole management and began to import stars to work with a resident company of Canadians and Americans. She gave up after the 1953 season, which set attendance records but still lost money. In 1954-5 a new Niagara Falls Summer Theatre featured the LONDON THEATRE COMPANY, led by Leslie Yeo, who presented seasons of summer stock between winter tours and regular engagements in Newfoundland.

The Red Barn Theatre in Jackson's Point on Lake Simcoe, which opened in 1949 in a converted nineteenth-century barn, never seemed to thrive, no matter who was in charge or what was being presented. The original producer, Archie Mulock, lasted one year. Then Brian Doherty assumed control, trying first a season of musicals followed by a season of traditional summer stock. After two years of neglect, the Red Barn reopened in 1954 with producers Marvyn Rosenzveig and Stanley Jacobson in charge and Leon Major as director. The sole high point of the Red Barn's history occurred under the management of Marigold CHARLESWORTH and Jean ROBERTS, from 1959 to 1964. Patricia Carroll Brown and her Harlequin Players then managed to keep the theatre open until 1966. The Red Barn struggled on into the seventies and eighties from season to season, with almost annual changes of management—many people, from director Bill GLASSCO to talent-agent Karen Hazzard tried to make a success of it. It is still in existence.

By the mid-1950s summer stock had begun to decline, a victim of Stratford's success on the one hand and the arrival of television on the other. Yet theatres continued to open. The Scarborough Summer Theatre came and went in 1952, despite the talents of many stock veterans such as Lorne GREENE, Bud Knapp, and Jane MALLETT, and director Robert CHRISTIE. In the summer of 1956 other veterans converted a 700-seat cinema on

Toronto's Centre Island into the Centre Island Playhouse. Andrew ALLAN directed several productions, including the season opener, André Roussin's *The Little Hut*, starring Toby ROBINS, Jack CRELEY, and George McCowan. Kate REID, Austin Willis, and Bernard Slade appeared in F. Hugh Herbert's *The Moon is Blue*. Actress Martha HENRY made her professional Canadian début at the Sun Parlour Playhouse in Leamington, which opened in 1956 and lasted three seasons. London's Grand Theatre also hosted two seasons of summer stock in the 1950s.

The opening of the SHAW FESTIVAL in 1962 gave summer stock further competition; companies that had opened in the sixties and seventies as non-profit operations were obliged to offer alternatives. The oldest of these, the Kawartha Summer Theatre—which uses Lindsay's Academy Theatre, built in 1893—is the only remaining theatre in Canada that produces a different play each week. The first Kawartha Summer Festival was held in 1965, with actor Norman Welsh in charge. Dennis Sweeting, a veteran administrator of Actors' Equity and the CANADIAN PLAYERS, began his long association with the Kawartha Summer Theatre in 1966. As artistic director, Sweeting emphasized Canadian plays by writers such as Allan STRATTON, David FRENCH, Aviva RAVEL, Jack Northmore, Munroe Scott, Alden NOWLAN, Walter LEARNING, and Peter Colley. Anne CHISLETT's *The Tomorrow Box* premièred in Lindsay.

The Huron Country Playhouse concentrates on proven hits and musicals. Founding director James Murphy, then a Univ. of Guelph professor, and William Heinsohn, who became executive producer, opened their summer theatre in 1972 in a tent just outside the resort town of Grand Bend on Lake Huron. After two profitable seasons the Playhouse moved into a new theatre, designed by architect Peter Smith and constructed of barnboard. Although the Playhouse does not have an adventurous repertoire, it has developed a loyal audience under successive artistic directors Aileen Taylor-Smith, Ronald Ulrich, Steven Schipper, and Sandy MacDonald.

The Gryphon Theatre in Barrie is a regional theatre that has been unable to break the bounds of summer operation. Brian Rintoul, formerly a stage manager at the Stratford Festival, headed a group that launched the Gryphon's first season in July 1970 in a church hall. In 1973 the Gryphon Theatre moved into a new theatre at Georgian College, where it has remained. Under a succession of artistic directors—including Sean MULCAHY, Ted Follows, Vernon Chapman, and Virginia Rey—the Gryphon fought to avoid collapse, but it was veteran actor James B. Douglas who finally managed to bring the deficit under control and restore stability after he took charge in 1984.

The St Lawrence Summer Playhouse, a theatre-in-the-round, opened in 1967 in a tent in Gananoque, near Kingston. Created by Lee Tammarello, an American director, and Kingston broadcaster Gerry Tinlin, it featured amateurs instructed by professionals from the U.S. and Canada, performing popular musicals and comedies. The theatre moved to a Kingston park in 1969, where it lasted until 1976, when it was succeeded by the amateur Kingston Summer Theatre. Greg Wanless, an actor-director and veteran of the Stratford Festival, resurrected summer theatre in Gananoque in 1982 with his Thousand Islands Playhouse. It was initially semi-professional, relying heavily on student help from the Queen's Univ. Drama Department.

Links between post-secondary educational institutions and summer theatres began with the Straw Hat Players' association with the Univ. of Toronto. In addition to the Queen's/Thousand Island Playhouse link, York Univ. and Wilfrid Laurier Univ. have sponsored seasons in Orillia. The Laughing Water Festival in Meaford was associated with Ryerson Polytechnical Institute. Moonlight Melodrama in Thunder Bay, which specializes in melodramas, was founded by Confederation College theatre instructor William Pendergast in 1972. At the Univ. of Alberta in the 1960s the outdoor Torches Theatre provided theatre students with practical summer experience in a professional situation.

Toronto's THEATRE PLUS, founded in 1973, is unlike traditional summer stock in presenting an often challenging, yet still entertaining, season of plays. It remains one of Ontario's most distinctive and important summer theatres.

Until the BLYTH FESTIVAL, founded in 1975, no summer theatre devoted to Canadian plays had prospered. Keith TURNBULL worked closely with playwright James REANEY in a London, Ont., summer theatre for only one season, 1965-6. ALTERNATE

Summer Stock

THEATRES in Stratford run by John PALMER and Martin KINCH also failed. From 1974 to 1977 Joseph E. McLeod, a teacher of theatre and English, ran the second Peterborough Summer Theatre, producing only Canadian plays. From 1972 to 1982 FESTIVAL LENNOXVILLE tried to build an audience for English-Canadian plays in the Eastern Townships of Quebec.

There is now a new generation of summer theatres in Ontario. The Port Stanley Summer Theatre on Lake Erie, near London, started in 1978. Peterborough's Arbor Theatre, under John Plank, became fully professional in 1979. The Lighthouse Festival in Port Dover, near Simcoe, opened in 1980, using a renovated town hall as a theatre. The Town Hall Theatre in Cobourg's historic Victoria Hall chose as its inaugural production, in 1983, a play called *Tracks*, by bp nichol and Mary Barton, and directed by a veteran of the Red Barn, Burton Lancaster. Skylight Theatre in North York (metropolitan Toronto), modelled after Joseph Papp's Shakespeare in the Park in New York, opened in Aug. 1980 with a free professional open-air production of Antoine de Saint-Exupéry's *The Little Prince*. In 1983 TORONTO FREE THEATRE launched its extremely popular 'The Dream in High Park', an annual free outdoor summer production, usually of one of Shakespeare's plays.

Summer theatres outside Ontario include, in Quebec, the BRAE MANOR Playhouse, founded by Filmore Sadler and Marjorie Sadler in Knowlton, Quebec, which offered summer theatre between 1936 and 1954; Montreal's English-language MOUNTAIN PLAYHOUSE, which flourished from 1950 to 1961; Théâtre de Sun Valley, founded in 1953; THÉÂTRE DE LA FENIÈRE, founded in 1958; and THÉÂTRE DE MARJOLAINE, founded in 1960, which specializes in Canadian musicals. Vancouver's outdoor THEATRE UNDER THE STARS, a showcase for musicals and operettas, lasted from 1940 to 1963 until bad weather, among other factors, forced it to close. But Rainbow Stage in Winnipeg, also an outdoor theatre dedicated to the production of non-Canadian musicals since it was reorganized in 1966, has prospered. The CHARLOTTETOWN FESTIVAL opened in 1964 and became a home for Canadian musicals under artistic director Alan LUND. In that same year the Piggery Theatre in North Hatley, Quebec, began as a primarily amateur operation.

It became fully professional in 1972, offering a popular summer-stock alternative to nearby Festival Lennoxville's all-Canadian repertoire.

Although summer stock has recently been seen at the King's Playhouse in Prince Edward Island and at Winnipeg Beach in Manitoba, it has been more successful in British Columbia. The White Rock Summer Theatre, founded in 1976, and the Sunshine Theatre in Kelowna, which started a year later, both offer popular seasons of summer stock. In Barkerville the Theatre Royal performs in an authentic reconstruction of a nineteenth-century theatre. The most unusual summer company in B.C. is the Caravan Stage, founded by Nick Hutchinson in 1970, which tours the province in horse-drawn wagons, performing socially relevant plays usually written by members of the company. Canada's newest summer festival, the Stephenville Festival in Newfoundland, was launched in 1979 by artistic director Maxim Mazumdar and administrator Cheryl Stagg.

ROSS STUART

Summer Stock (Quebec). The first record of summer stock in the province of Quebec shows that English plays were performed in Quebec City from June to Aug. 1852 at the THÉÂTRE CHAMPLAIN at 70 Champlain Street. A small summer theatre festival was held in Montreal in 1904 when the THÉÂTRE NATIONAL presented L.-N. Sénécal's *Une Volupté nouvelle* on 23 June and Ernest Trouille's *La Justice des hommes* a week later. On 24 June, Germain Beaulieu's *Diplomatie conjugale* appeared at the MONUMENT NATIONAL and C.-J. Gauthier's *Un Abonné de la campagne* at the Salle Poire on 24 July. There was a production of *Le Coeur n'a pas d'âge* (by a Mlle Casgrain) created at the Château Bel-Air on the Île d'Orléans on 30 July 1907.

The first companies to become involved in summer theatre were Pierre DAGENAIS's L'ÉQUIPE, which presented *Le Songe d'une nuit d'été* (*A Midsummer Night's Dream*) in the gardens of L'ERMITAGE in Aug. 1945 (with Marjolaine Hébert); Mario Duliani of the MONTREAL REPERTORY THEATRE offered the same show at Laval-sur-le-lac in Aug. 1947, the same month in which Les COMPAGNONS DE SAINT-LAURENT presented Molière's *Les Précieuses ridicules* and *Le Médecin malgré lui* at the Chalet on Mount Royal. The Chalet subsequently became the scene of several summer performances, notably *King Lear* in 1953, presented by the Shakespeare Society under the direction of Pierre Dagenais, with sets designed by Herbert WHITTAKER. In the summer of 1952 La Jeune Scène presented *De l'autre côté du mur* by Marcel DUBÉ at the St Adele Lodge in the Laurentians, and in 1953 the Théâtre de Sun Valley, directed for many years by Henri Norbert, was founded in a nearby inn. In 1957 Paul HÉBERT, recently returned from London's Old Vic, opened a theatre in the Chantecler Hotel at Sainte-Adèle and staged Pirandello's *Six Personnages en quête d'auteur* (*Six Characters in Search of an Author*), with Gilles PELLETIER and Dyne Mousso, among others.

Other summer theatres include the THÉÂTRE DE LA FENIÈRE, founded at Loretteville in 1958 and located today at l'Ancienne Lorette; the THÉÂTRE DE MARJOLAINE at Eastman, Que., founded in 1960 in—like La Fenière—a converted barn; and The Piggery, established in North Hatley in 1964. All of these theatres, except for the Sun Valley, are still active; they are the oldest of some eighty summer theatres scattered throughout the Quebec countryside. Other interesting, but ultimately unsuccessful, summer theatrical ventures undertaken towards the end of the 1960s include, among others, the Centre d'art de Percé, directed in turn by Charlotte Boisjoli, Jacques LANGUIRAND, and Françoise Graton; the Théâtre des Prairies, founded at Joliette by Jean DUCEPPE; the Théâtre de l'Egrégore at Sainte-Marguerite-du-Lac-Masson; La Grenouille, housed in the marina of a hotel at Lac Beauport; and the THÉÂTRE DU NOUVEAU MONDE at Repentigny.

Whether or not such companies last, summer theatre in Quebec clearly survives as part of the province's culture. It is also a worthwhile enterprise, considering, for example, that the Théâtre de Marjolaine alone, during its first twenty years, created fifteen new Quebec works, gave employment to five composers, eight directors, eleven set designers, and 117 actors—in some 1,200 performances before approximately 355,000 spectators. And although the summer-theatre repertoire is usually light fare, which suits the average vacationer, it can still occasionally offer the avant-garde, as was the case in the first presentations at Sainte-Adèle, at Percé, and at Sainte-Marguerite-du-Lac-Masson.

ANDRÉ-G. BOURASSA

Sutherland, Donald (b. 1934). Born in New Brunswick and educated in Nova Scotia, he auditioned for his first play on a bet while attending the Univ. of Toronto. After experience at HART HOUSE THEATRE under Robert GILL and with Muskoka's Straw Hat Players, he went to England in 1958 to study at the London Academy of Music and Dramatic Art. He appeared in several London stage productions, but following his 1964 screen début in an Italian horror movie, *Il Castello dei Morti Vivi*, he became increasingly attracted to film. Supporting roles in a number of British and American films, including *The Dirty Dozen* (1967), followed before he established an international reputation in *M*A*S*H* (1970). He has remained primarily a screen actor ever since. In addition to numerous European and American films, Sutherland has appeared in several Canadian (or jointly produced) films, of which *Act of the Heart* (1970) and *Murder by Decree* (1979) are perhaps the best known. A continuing interest in Dr Norman Bethune was reflected in his portrayal of the Canadian medical pioneer on CBC television and in Ted ALLAN's film *Bethune: the Making of a Hero* (1989).

Sutherland's return to the stage in the 1981 Broadway production of Edward Albee's adaptation of Vladimir Nabokov's *Lolita* was regrettably brief. While savaging the play, reviewers reported that Sutherland's power and versatility as a performer were not confined to the screen. His extraordinary skill as a film actor, together with the great success of films such as *Ordinary People* (1980), however, probably ensure that his stage appearances will continue to be infrequent.

Sutherland is the subject of the National Film Board documentary *Give Me Your Answer True* (1987).   NEIL CARSON

T

Talking Dirty. Vancouver playwright Sherman Snukal's comedy opened at the ARTS CLUB Theatre, Vancouver, in Oct. 1981 and played almost continuously for three years, with over 1,000 performances, including a B.C. tour and ten weeks in Toronto. Bearing all the elements of a stock bedroom farce, the play's success may be attributed to its local and contemporary setting (the action takes place in a Vancouver apartment) and allusions. Michael, a Philosophy professor, after living three years with Beth, has reached an 'agreement' with her, freeing him to sleep with others. He is visited by Karen, an easy-going English professor, and Dave, a Toronto lawyer, eight years married and seeking a fling. Dave—concealing his marriage—sleeps with Karen, then finds that she was merely seeking revenge for a failed relationship with Michael, who in turn realizes too late that he truly loves Beth. Jackie, the would-be sophisticated 'space cadet from Burnaby', drifts in from a nearby party. *Talking Dirty* was published by Playwrights Canada in 1981.

Snukal's second full-length play, *Family Matters*, was staged at the Arts in 1985.

MALCOLM PAGE

Tamahnous Theatre. Founded in Vancouver in the summer of 1971 by Univ. of British Columbia graduates led by John GRAY and Larry Lillo, Tamahnous (from the Chilcotin Indian word meaning 'magic') was known in its first year as Theatre Workshop. Rooted in the idealism of its time, the group was a COLLECTIVE, practising equality and favouring the unstructured and experimental.

The early years were a struggle, and Tamahnous did not emerge as the city's leading ALTERNATE THEATRE until 1977, when it became resident company at the VANCOUVER EAST CULTURAL CENTRE on Venables St, offering four shows annually. The company also took over the house next door as its rehearsal and administrative space. Although personnel changed frequently after 1978, Tamahnous flourished, its budget reaching $300,000 in 1981. Tamahnous enjoyed touring, whether in try-outs at Brackendale Art Gallery, Squamish, in prisons and schools, or on longer tours.

By the end of 1985 Tamahnous had produced some fifty shows. Many of the best were ensemble works using such texts as *Dracula* and *The Bacchae* (both produced in 1971, revived in 1974) as starting points, or unusual and demanding pieces totally developed by the company, like *Vertical Dreams*, 1979, which was based on the members' dreams, and *Foolproof*, 1980, based on forms of clowning. Other shows commented directly on provincial politics: Jeremy Long's *84 Acres* and the collective creations *Deep Thought* (both produced in 1976), and *A State of Grace* (produced in 1982). The theatre's political thrust was represented also in plays by Bertolt Brecht, Dario Fo, and David Hare (*Fanshen*). Successful new Canadian scripts included Long's *The Final Performance of Vaslav Nijinsky* (produced in 1972, revived in 1976); John Gray's musical *18 Wheels*, produced in 1977; Glen Thompson's play about rum-running on the B.C. coast in the 1920s, *Liquid Gold*, produced in 1978; and the 'post-nuclear cabaret', *Last Call*, by Morris Panych and Ken MacDonald, 1982.

The collective principle was abandoned early in 1984 when Morris Panych became artistic director. He wrote and produced two musicals (*Contagious* and *Cheap Sentiment*), but like other shows (such as a feminist treatment of Kafka's *The Trial*), they found only small audiences. In 1986 Kathleen Weiss became artistic director and continued the experimental mandate of the company with such creations as *The Haunted House Hamlet* (produced in Aug. 1986), adapted from Shakespeare by Peter Eliot Weiss in the environmental manner of John KRIZANC's *TAMARA*, and *Neverland* (Dec. 1986), adapted by Patricia Ludwick from J.M. Barrie's *Peter Pan*, which used experimental dance for its flying sequences.

MALCOLM PAGE

Tamara. John KRIZANC's environmental theatre epic was first produced during the 1981 Toronto Theatre Festival by the Necessary Angel Theatre Company, directed by Richard ROSE, in Toronto's historic Strachan House. A surprise hit, *Tamara* swept the Dora Mavor MOORE Awards including the award for best new play. It has since opened in Los Angeles, 1984, Mexico City, 1986, and New York, 1987. The Los Angeles production, again under the direction of Rose, won a number of Los Angeles Drama Critics' Circle Awards.

Tamara is written for performance before a limited audience in a large house, in which audience members follow characters of their choice from room to room, piecing together the action themselves. Set in 1927 fascist Italy, in the house of the Italian nationalist poet Gabriele d'Annunzio, who allows his poetry to be exploited by the fascists in exchange for sensual pleasures, it deals with the failure of d'Annunzio and the rest of the play's artists to take a political stand, and also with the failure of poetic language to respond to the demands of *Realpolitik*. It employs the self-reflexive techniques of metadrama to probe the evasions associated with an aesthetic of art for art's sake. *Tamara*'s most innovative and notable feature, however, is its form. Through its environmental staging Krizanc attempts to 'give choices back to the audience', and thereby to reinforce the play's thematic concerns by undermining what he sees as the fascism of the theatre itself. RICHARD PAUL KNOWLES

Tara Hall. Located at 119-123 rue Sainte-Anne in Quebec City, it was built in 1816 as a Wesleyan chapel, and served the congregation until 1848 when a new chapel opened on rue Saint-Stanislas. The original chapel, known as the Lecture Hall, functioned for the next quarter-century as a venue for temperance lectures, music concerts, and touring attractions, including, in Oct. 1863, General Tom Thumb and his company.

In Jan. 1874 the building was renamed Victoria Hall. Two years later it was bought by the St Patrick's Literary Institute for $5,500 and renamed Tara Hall. Throughout the rest of the century the Hall was primarily a cultural centre for Irish immigrants. The Young Irishmen's Literary and Dramatic Club and similar amateur cultural groups gave performances there, and the building was rented from time to time to touring companies. In Dec. 1887 it was partially destroyed by fire, but was immediately reconstructed. In the first decade of the twentieth century Tara Hall was a popular auditorium for musical concerts, and later became the Nickel Cinema. It was destroyed by fire in 1917. JOHN RIPLEY

Tarragon Theatre. Founded in Toronto in the fall of 1971 by Bill GLASSCO and his wife Jane Gordon, Tarragon has been extraordinarily successful in discovering and producing new Canadian plays. Among the major Canadian playwrights whose works have premièred at Tarragon are Carol BOLT, David FREEMAN, David FRENCH, Joanna GLASS, Margaret HOLLINGSWORTH, Steve PETCH, Sharon POLLOCK, James REANEY, Erika RITTER, Allan STRATTON, Judith THOMPSON, Michel TREMBLAY (in English translation), George F. WALKER, and Tom WALMSLEY.

From its inception the theatre has been located in a converted factory on the northwest fringe of Toronto's scattered theatre district. For the first four years the auditorium seated 180. A renovation in 1976 increased seating to 200; the theatre now can hold 210. It is a flexible space, one of the few in Toronto that can be radically altered to suit specific productions.

Tarragon has a large and faithful audience (in 1987, half were subscribers) that accepts a wide range of theatre, from the conventional naturalism of David French's *Salt-Water Moon* to the bizarre expressionism of Judith Thompson's *White Biting Dog*, both produced in 1984, and that strongly supports Tarragon's policy of producing new work.

The theatre's original manifesto announced ambitious goals: to nurture Canadian playwrights, especially through the collaborative efforts of playwright, director, and actors; to maintain a high standard of production; and 'to act as a testing ground for new plays, to provide a source from which other Canadian theatres can draw'—in sum, to 'make a contribution to this country's culture'. Unlike many manifestos, this one has governed Tarragon's development to a remarkable degree. David Freeman's CREEPS, which began the 1971-2 season, and David French's *Leaving Home*, which ended it, demonstrated Tarragon's objective to be a writer's theatre with high professional standards.

In the 1972-3 season revivals of plays produced elsewhere in Canada were added, thus opening up to Toronto audiences the riches of French-Canadian theatre. Beginning with *Forever Yours, Marie-Lou (À TOI, POUR TOUJOURS, TA MARIE-LOU)* in 1972, Tarragon has regularly premièred the plays of Michel Tremblay in translation—is indeed responsible for his fame in English Canada—as well as many plays by other Québécois play-

Tarragon Theatre

wrights (including, for example, Roland LEPAGE and René-Daniel DUBOIS).

In 1974 a playwright-in-residence program was begun under the direction of Bena Shuster, which continues to the present; and in 1982 Urjo KAREDA, who that year succeeded Bill Glassco as artistic director, instituted the Six Playwrights Unit, an intensive year-long program for promising writers. In addition, over 450 unsolicited playscripts are read and assessed annually without charge. Tarragon has benefited from the special gifts of Glassco and Kareda: Glassco's for directing exemplary productions of new plays, Kareda's as a dramaturge.

In 1976, following a year's 'sabbatical' for Glassco, during which Tarragon did not mount a season, the mandate was widened to include classic and contemporary foreign plays, with an emphasis on new Canadian translations such as French's of Chekhov's *The Seagull*, produced in 1977, and John Murrell's of Racine's *Bajazet*, in 1979, and Ibsen's *Master Builder*, produced in 1983. In 1978 Glassco announced that henceforth seasons would be chosen to nurture not only playwrights but actors; perhaps the most visible sign of this policy is Clare COULTER's growth in stature over nearly a decade of association with Tarragon. In 1980 Tarragon opened the Maggie Bassett Studio to provide a professional-development program for actors. Finally, in a move benefiting both actor and playwright, The Extra Space, seating 100, was opened in 1983, widening the scope of Tarragon's own programming, and providing a low-cost rental space for numerous small-scale independent productions. In Dec. 1986 Tarragon received a grant of $645,000 from the government of Ontario towards the $1.3 million cost of purchasing and renovating the building it had rented since 1971.

Tarragon's mandate has always placed the playwright at the centre. Although play-development at Tarragon engages director and actors as collaborators, the emerging script is very much the playwright's own. There has thus been virtually no attention to collective creation nor to work in which gesture and image, not language, constitute the commanding centre. A passion for language and a dedication to the playwright define Tarragon's identity and represent its greatest strength.

The archives of Tarragon Theatre are housed at the Univ. of Guelph.

ROBERT C. NUNN

Tavernier, Albert (1854-1929). Born in Boston and raised in Hamilton, Ont., the son of actor-elocutionist W.J. Taverner, he began his stage career in John A. Ellsler's stock company in Cleveland, where he was influenced by the veteran character-actor C.W. Couldock. In the late 1870s he toured Canada with the McDOWELL and NANNARY troupes. After marrying Ida VAN CORTLAND in 1881 and touring the U.S. with her in various companies, Tavernier (the slight change in spelling has never been explained)

Albert Tavernier in Two Nights in Rome

518

and his wife formed their own company, touring Canada and the northern U.S. from 1882 to 1896. Although the repertoire focused on Ida's emotional acting, Albert established a reputation for comic and character acting; in W.J. Florence's *The Mighty Dollar* he played Bardwell Slote with great success. As manager of the company, Tavernier fought an uphill battle against escalating costs in rents, transport, board, costumes, salaries, and royalties. In an attempt to bolster the family's income, he unsuccessfully managed opera houses in Jackson, Mich. (1888-9) and in Guelph, Ont. (1894-6). After separating from Ida, he played supporting and leading roles in New York and on tour in *Don't Tell My Wife*, T.E. Pemberton's *Money Bags*, and other plays. Tavernier died in Boston following a tour, starring Katharine Cornell, of *The Age of Innocence* (adapted from the novel of the same name by Edith Wharton).   KATHLEEN FRASER

Television Drama in English. The history of television drama in English Canada is inextricably linked to that of the Canadian Broadcasting Corporation and falls into three distinct phases: an expanding, adventurous, outward-looking period between 1952 and 1968, when live studio drama eventually yielded to tape and film; a period of sagging morale, the exodus of talented people, and declining quality between 1968 and 1973; and a renewal of creativity during 1974-87, along with an increase in nationalistic and topical concerns in the context of rapidly changing broadcast technology.

From 1952 to 1968 CBC television served the cause of Canadian theatre well. Canadians with little access to live theatre could see new drama by Harold Pinter, Samuel Beckett, Bertolt Brecht, James Saunders, Eugène Ionesco, Jean Anouilh, and Arnold Wesker, as well as classics by Oscar Wilde, Bernard Shaw, Molière, Luigi Pirandello, and John Webster. Live television drama familiarized viewers with area lighting, unit sets, impressionist design, and, most notably, brilliant performances by a new generation of Canadian actors who worked at the STRATFORD FESTIVAL in the summer and with the CBC in the winter: Leo CICERI, Tony VAN BRIDGE, Douglas RAIN, Martha HENRY, John COLICOS, Lloyd Bochner, Frances HYLAND, William SHATNER, Lorne GREENE,

and Bruno GERUSSI, among others. Producers and directors—such as Henry Kaplan, David Greene, Silvio Narrizano, Eric Till, David GARDNER, Paul Almond, Harvey Hart, and Mario Prizek, and designers Nicolai Soloviov and Rudi Dorn—extensively explored the new medium under difficult working conditions.

Emulating CBC RADIO DRAMA, notably Andrew ALLAN's 'Stage' series, television drama continued to expand the boundaries of acceptable content with plays about the aftermath of the Korean war, single motherhood, censorship, and corruption in politics. Topical subjects also appeared in Sydney Newman's sponsored anthology series, notably 'General Motors Presents' (a one-hour show) and 'On Camera' (thirty minutes), which were the major outlets for Canadian scripts. 'Folio' and 'Festival'—prestige full-length anthologies—were showcases for opera, ballet, music, and classical and contemporary drama, very little of which was Canadian. In the early 1960s 'Q for Quest' and 'Eyeopener' presented short, experimental, and often highly controversial plays in 10 p.m. or 10:30 p.m. time-slots.

With the increasing sophistication of video-recording and the decision to use film (against considerable resistance from the CBC establishment), two parallel production streams developed in the late 1960s—studio drama under Robert Allen and drama shot on tape or film under Ronald Weyman. As series drama on location swiftly displaced the anthologies in the United States, CBC-TV drama responded with the first serials in North America, including an unconventional 'western' called 'Cariboo Country' (1960-7, written by Paul St Pierre, produced and directed by Philip Keatley). 'Wojeck', a smash-hit, was the first television series to blend documentary and direct cinema conventions with the detective show (1966-8, written by Philip Hersch, produced and directed by Ron Weyman). 'Hatch's Mill' (1967-8) was a stereotyped family comedy series that offered serious social comment and dollops of reasonably accurate historical writing. Other series that modified the usual formula to produce fine one-act plays disguised as 'episodes' were 'The Manipulators', 'Sidestreet', 'A Gift to Last', 'Home Fires', and 'Seeing Things'.

The period 1968-73—with a few exceptions, such as Munroe Scott's *Reddick* and Grahame Woods' *12 and ½ Cents* and *Vicky*—was a bad time for CBC-TV drama. *Jalna*, unsuccessfully adapted from Mazo de la Roche's novels, represented its nadir. But when John HIRSCH took over the drama department for four brief years of upheaval and change, he introduced many of the performers and playwrights of the vigorous nationalist theatre of the 1970s: Michel TREMBLAY's *Les BELLES-SOEURS*; the collectives *1837*, *The FARM SHOW*, and *TEN LOST YEARS*; Carol BOLT's *Red Emma*; CODCO's *Festering Forefathers*; and David FRENCH's *Leaving Home*, among others. Some were truncated or badly served by the medium or the director; others were both good theatre and good television. Hirsch also presided over Canadian television's first successful 'sitcom'—'King of Kensington'—and a scattering of theatrical dramas ranging from Carl Zuckmayer's *The Captain from Kopenick* to a superbly imaginative *Freedom of the City* by Brian Friel.

The period 1974-87 was one of shrinking dollars and available broadcast hours, of indifference on the part of the Canadian Radiotelevision and Telecommunications Commission (CRTC), and continuing resistance to spending on Canadian television drama from the privately owned, though publicly licensed, CTV network. The CBC has increasingly been plagued with crisis management, favouring expediency over policy, from both Liberal and Conservative governments, and contradictory government Commissions. In 1983 the Applebaum-Hébert Federal Cultural Policy Review Committee recommended that the CBC produce nothing but news and current affairs. In 1986 the Report of the Task Force on Broadcasting by Gerald Caplan and Florian Sauvageau—a realistic, thorough, and sensible document—recommended extending Canadian content and suggested practical ways to finance it. Telefilm, the government initiative to encourage more independent production of television drama, is supported by the CBC's provision of on-air scheduling and financing. Some of the programs—*Loyalties* in 1987, and *Anne of Green Gables* in 1986, for example, were first class. But they were commercial ventures; 'in-house' CBC production provides more adventurous and controversial television drama, such as Judith THOMPSON's *Turning to Stone*, directed by Eric Till and produced by John Kastner, broadcast in 1986.

International drama adapted for television has now disappeared, although the head of television drama, John Kennedy (1978-87), resisted both internal and external pressure to play the ratings game and secured a tenuous survival of anthology drama on Canadian TV—and thus international sales to many other national broadcasting systems. Nevertheless for millions of viewers abroad the face of Canada is that of Bruno Gerussi in 'The Beachcombers'. Kennedy's tenure coincided with a serious erosion in CBC funding, the loss of five prime-time hours to 'The National', and a progressive failure of political will to maintain a distinctive Canadian television service. Kennedy responded by concentrating his resources on original Canadian scripts. The topical drama anthology 'For the Record' (1975-86) produced many excellent dramas: *Dreamspeaker*, *Ada*, *Don't Forget 'Je Me Souviens'*, *A Question of the Sixth*, *Cementhead*, *Ready for Slaughter*, *I Love a Man in Uniform*. Other major drama specials in the last decade include *Gentle Sinners*, *Charlie Grant's War*, *You've come a Long Way, Katie*, *War Brides*, and *Chautauqua Girl*.

Canadian Playwrights. In English Canada television playwrights have never had the recognition accorded to them in Britain. Yet excellent scripts have been written throughout most of the CBC's history. Initially live TV drama depended on two sources for scripts: CBC radio dramatists and plays written for the few theatres then in existence. Lister SINCLAIR, Harry Boyle, Tommy TWEED, Mavor MOORE, Joseph SCHULL, Stanley Mann, Len PETERSON, Charles Israel, Eric NICOL, and W.O. MITCHELL wrote for radio, television, and sometimes for the theatre in the 1950s and 1960s. Scripts might appear in all three media—for example, Peterson's *BURLAP BAGS*, Mitchell's *The Black Bonspiel of Wullie MacCrimmon*, Mavor Moore's *Come Away, Come Away*, and Patricia JOUDRY's *Teach Me How to Cry*. Other television plays—such as Gordon PINSENT's *A Gift to Last*, Mitchell's *The Devil's Instrument*, and the Donald HARRON/Mavor Moore musical *ANNE OF GREEN GABLES*—have been adapted and produced on stage right into the 1980s.

George RYGA honed his craft and his strongly visual yet abstract sense of theatrical action in George McCowan's studio production of *Indian* in 1962, an economical and

George Ryga's Indian, *CBC-TV, 1962*

powerful precursor of *The* ECSTASY OF RITA JOE. A new kind of realism in TV drama appeared with his *Two Soldiers*, the first on-location taping of a play. Ryga's *The Tulip Garden* has been produced for television three times, most recently in the 1980s Atlantis films anthology of Canadian short stories. *The Ecstasy of Rita Joe* has never been broadcast, but Don S. Williams' Winnipeg production of the ballet version, brilliantly adapted for television, was seen nationally. Rick SALUTIN wrote the script for one of the most effective social dramas broadcast in the 1970s, *Maria*, directed by Alan King. Carol Bolt, David French, Sharon POLLOCK, Ken GASS, Allan STRATTON, and Judith Thompson have all written television scripts in the last decade.

Both W.O. Mitchell and Paul St Pierre have turned their plays into short stories or their short stories into TV scripts. Novelists Morley CALLAGHAN, Mordecai Richler, Margaret Atwood, and Timothy FINDLEY (who wrote the CBC's first full-length colour film, *The Paper People*, the dramatized segments of 'The National Dream', and two scripts for 'The Newcomers'—*1832: The Scots* and *1911: The Danes*) have also written plays for television. Arthur Hailey began as a writer with *Flight into Danger*, the CBC's first orig-inal popular hit, and Bernard SLADE learned his craft in the 1950s on CBC TV.

Adaptations of theatre productions for television. The CBC broadcast a 1959 CREST THE-ATRE production of John Osborne's *The Entertainer*, and in 1967 'Festival' televised the THÉÂTRE DU NOUVEAU MONDE produc-tion of Gratien GÉLINAS's *Yesterday the Chil-dren Were Dancing* (HIER, LES ENFANTS DANSAIENT). Other than a joint production of Henrik Ibsen's *Peer Gynt* in 1957 and a version of Dumas's *The Three Musketeers* in 1969, the CBC did not broadcast or adapt directly any other Stratford or SHAW FESTI-VAL productions until the early 1980s, when executive producer Sam Levene found a way to tape live Stratford productions that avoided the static look of a filmed stage pro-duction. He taped Shakespeare's *The Tempest* and *The Taming of the Shrew*, Molière's *Tar-tuffe*, and Gilbert and Sullivan operettas directed by Brian MACDONALD and produced by the CBC specialist in musicals and ballet, Norman Campbell. Shaw Festival produc-tions of Edmond Rostand's *Cyrano de Ber-gerac* and Ray Cooney's and Tony Hilton's *One for the Pot* were taped. Successful TV adaptations of Canadian plays include Linda GRIFFITHS' and Paul THOMPSON's *Maggie and Pierre*, John GRAY's BILLY BISHOP GOES TO

WAR, and Gray's musical *Rock and Roll* (called *King of Friday Night*)—all three made in collaboration with various independent or foreign state-owned broadcasters, such as BBC Scotland.

Nevertheless scripts from Canadian theatre appear irregularly and often in odd timeslots with little publicity. A few emerged in prime time (8-10 p.m. week nights), but many were condensed for 'experimental anthology slots' like 'Q for Quest', 'Programme X', or 'Peepshow'. There have been a few adaptations from Canadian theatre since Hirsch's departure, notably Eric Nicol's *Ma!* and Allan Stratton's *Rexy!* TAMAHNOUS THEATRE's brilliant satirical cabaret *Last Call* was produced in Vancouver and shown through regional CBC exchanges in every region but Ontario. Its revue format and subject (it is performed by the last two survivors of a nuclear war) were not considered appropriate for prime time. Ironically, David FENNARIO's *BALCONVILLE* appeared in prime time on many small and medium-sized CBC affiliates—but not until 11:30 p.m. in the huge Toronto market.

The Regions. By the late 1950s regional centres for drama production had found their own voices with anthologies like Montreal's 'Shoestring Theatre' and 'Teleplay' and Vancouver's 'Studio Pacific'. A few regional plays recorded on kinescope were telecast nationally every summer. Occasional drama specials continue to come from the regions. 'Up at Ours' and 'Wonderful Grand Band', two comedy series from Newfoundland, found regular slots for a season or two in the late 1970s and Codco returned in 1988-9. The successful 1980s mini-series 'Empire Inc.' originated in Montreal. Surprisingly, Ontario has never had a regional presence in television drama, even though indigenous Ontario plays and theatre companies developed in the 1970s. The other regions have always been the counter-balancing, occasionally subversive, and often very creative element in the CBC-TV drama mix, but cutbacks in funding in the 1980s hurt regional productions of all kinds.

Regional playwrights had their first chance to write for local television in the 1950s to the mid '60s, before the contraction and centralization of CBC operations. After a hiatus of many years, an attempt to redress the imbalance resulted in a half-hour regionally based anthology, 'The Way We Are' (1985-

8). In Winnipeg television writer/director Alan Kroeker has produced a body of consistently enjoyable, sometimes striking, work for independent stations in the West. Other primarily regional television playwrights who have appeared regularly on the national network but who have concentrated on the flavour and the stories of their particular places are Merv Campone, Dennis Donovan, and Kay Hill.

Although it is rarely acknowledged by anglophone academics or critics, a large body of work exists by fine writers working mainly for television—Grahame Woods, Anna Sandor, Bill Gough, Douglas Bowie, and Cam Hubert (see Anne CAMERON), for example. But there is little informed analysis of anglophone television drama in Canada. With scripts now more accessible—particularly through the collection at York University, the extensive holdings at the National Archives of Canada, and provincial-archives collections of kinescopes and tapes, and with bibliographies, VCRs, and perhaps video sales of the best of CBC television drama—that should change.

1987 marked the end of a CBC drama department organized around one central figure. New government policy and departmental reorganization into 'series', 'movies and mini-series', and 'comedy/sitcom' divisions will likely produce a different kind of television drama for the 1990s.

See Mary Jane Miller, *Turn Up the Contrast* (1987).   MARY JANE MILLER

Television Drama in Quebec. Production of television drama in Quebec was prolific in the 1950s: between 1953 and 1961 at least ten plays were produced annually—a figure greatly exceeded in 1956 and 1957 when nineteen and twenty-nine plays were produced respectively. Even in 1972 and 1976—following a period of significant decline—ten plays were produced, but the average in the 1970s and 1980s has been limited to five or six a year. Despite the decline (caused by Radio-Canada's perception of audience interests and budget restrictions), the interest of Quebec playwrights in television drama has remained strong over a thirty-year period.

During the early years of television, plays were generally produced in a particular series: 'D'Iberville' and 'La Feuille d'érable' (which offered ongoing historical narratives), 'Trio', 'Quatuor', Théâtre Populaire', 'Scénario',

'Théâtre du dimanche', 'Théâtre d'été', and 'Les Beaux Dimanches'—landmark shows that formed the tastes of the viewing public with original plays, translations of foreign plays, and adaptations of novels. Important revues included 'Bye Bye', which ran for over ten years and was notable for its keen irony, its humour, and its socio-political criticism—extremely rare in fictional works for television. 'Samedi de rire' was similar in character, but its quality was not always as high. Among the most important situation-comedy series were 'Moi et l'autre', 'Du tac au tac', 'La Petite semaine', 'Y'a pas de problème', 'Jamais deux sans toi', and 'Vaut mieux en rire'. Serialized drama—in episodic form with a continuous narrative and characters—has become the most popular type of television drama in Quebec. Among the best of these serials were 'La Famille Plouffe' by Roger Lemelin (1953-6), 'Cap-aux-sorciers' (1955-8) and 'Les Forges de Saint-Maurice' (1972-5) by Guy DUFRESNE, 'Le Colombier' by Eugène Cloutier (1957), 'La Pension Velder' by Robert Choquette (1957-61), 'Sous le signe du lion' by Françoise LORANGER (1961) and—in the 1980s—'Le Temps d'une paix' by Pierre Gauvreau (1980-6), 'Le Parc des Braves' by Fernand Dansereau (1983-7), 'La Vie promise' by Marcel DUBÉ (1984-5), and 'L'Héritage' by Victor-Lévy Beaulieu (1987-9). Initially broadcast live, television drama has increasingly become technologically more sophisticated, incorporating, for example, the use of documentary dramas, as in 'Johanne et ses vieux' (24 Oct. 1976). Similarly the form and content of the plays have developed from the standard conventions of the 1960s—in which form was dominated by the classical unities and content by psychological or sociological analysis—towards the avant-garde and experimental.

A number of individual works in the literature of Quebec television drama deserve recognition. Marcel Dubé's *Zone* (16 May 1953) set the standard for dramatic excellence, followed by his *Chambre à louer* (21 Nov. 1954). In the same period Yves THÉRIAULT went from radio to television and provided *Tant va la cruche* (28 July 1954), *La Marque dans la peau* (11 Mar. 1955), and *Le Marcheur* (15 Jan. 1956). André Laurendeau presented *La Vertu des chattes* (30 June 1957), and Jacques LANGUIRAND *Les Grands départs* (1 Oct. 1957). Pierre Perrault's *Au coeur de la rose* was produced on 30 Nov. 1958 and

in 1961 there were many significant productions: Guy DUFRESNE's *Les Traitants* (15 Jan.); Maurice Gagnon's *La Porte close* (2 Apr.); *Comme je vous aimais* by Eloi de GRANDMONT (23 Aug.); and *Isabelle* by Pierre DAGENAIS (12 Nov). Important in 1963 were *Sous le règne d'Augusta* by Robert Choquette (7 Feb.) and *Les Mains vides* by Claude JASMIN (29 Sept.), who a few months later also offered *Blues pour un homme averti* (12 Nov. 1964). Three works from 1965 are worthy of mention: *Tuez le veau gras* by Jasmin (17 Jan.), *Le Marin d'Athènes* by Réal Benoit (14 Mar.), and *Un Cri qui vient de loin* by Françoise Loranger (28 Nov.). In 1968 there was *La Morte Saison* by Jacques Brault (31 Mar.), *Table tournante* by Hubert Aquin (22 Sept.), and *La Neige en octobre* by André Langevin (20 Oct.). 1969 featured Aquin's *Vingt-quatre heures de trop* (6 Mar.) and Michel TREMBLAY's *Trois petits tours* (21 Dec.). The outstanding work of 1970 was *Une maison . . . un jour* by Loranger (4 Oct.), while 1971 proved to be a particularly rich season: *Voyage de noces* by Pierre DAGENAIS (3 Jan.), AU RETOUR DES OIES BLANCHES by Dubé (7 Feb.), *En Pièces détachées* by Tremblay (7 Mar.), and *Encore cinq minutes* by Loranger (4 Apr.). Worthy of mention in 1972 are *Double-Sens* by Aquin (30 Jan.) and *Les Semelles de vent* by André Langevin (5 Nov.).

In 1973 viewers saw *Le Bon monde: n'écrivez jamais au facteur* by Michel Faure, *Drôle de couple, ou du tac au tac* by Robert Choquette (13 Mar.), and *L'Homme aux faux diamants de braise* by Jean-Robert Rémillard (7 Oct.); in 1974, *Goglu* by Jean BARBEAU (3 Mar.), *Aujourd'hui peut-être* by Serge Sirois (17 Mar.), and *Il est une saison* by Marcel Dubé and Louis-Georges Carrier (29 Sept.); in 1975, *Un Arbre chargé d'oiseaux* by Louise Maheux-Forcier (30 May) and *C'était le fil de la vie* by Dubé (30 Nov.); in 1976, another rich season, *Octobre* by Dubé (8 Feb.), *L'Océan* by Marie-Claire BLAIS (28 May), and *Le Temps devant soi* by Gilles Archambault (17 Dec.); in 1977, *Plus ça change moins c'est pareil* by Ronald Prégent (17 Jan.), *Vendredi 16h45* by Pierre Gauvreau (30 Jan.), and *Procès devant juge seul* by Claude Jasmin (13 Mar.). Notable in 1979 were *Loto-nomie* by Jean-Pierre Plante (25 Feb.) and *Un aller simple* by Monique Proulx, (25 Mar.). During the 1980s, despite program cutbacks, several works by new authors appeared: between 1981 and 1986 there was *Entre soleil et l'eau* by Sylvie Sicotte-Gélinas,

Television Drama in Quebec

Fermer l'oeil de la nuit by Francine Ruel, *L'Été* by Nicole France, *Antoine et Sébastien* by Françoise Tessier-Dumoulin, *Api* by Robert GURIK, *À voix basse* by Gilles Archambault, *Les Grandes marées* by Jacques Poulin, *Encore un peu* by Serge Mercier, *La Chose la plus douce au monde* by Pierre Morency, *Appelez-moi Stéphane* by Louis Saia and Claude Meunier, *Arioso* and *Le Piano rouge* by Louise Maheux-Forcier, *Noces de juin* by Marcel Beaulieu, *Bonne fête, maman* by Elizabeth Bourget, *Les Hauts et les bas d'une diva* by Jean-Claude Germain, and *Terre des jeux* by Jean-Marie Lelièvre.

All of these works are marked by an assured style and originality of content. Some authors, such as Pierre Dagenais, are expert with complex plots or suspense; others, such as Guy Dufresne, have a talent for bringing history to life; while Robert Choquette, Françoise Loranger, and Yves Thériault successfully create authentic human characters. In addition, certain works—apart from being well written and well crafted—have made innovations in the use of the medium and the language of television itself, particularly the plays of Hubert Aquin, most of which were directed by Louis-Georges Carrier. Similar innovation is apparent in Françoise Loranger's *Un Cri qui vient de loin*, *Une Maison...un jour*, and *Encore cinq minutes*, and in Pierre Dagenais's *Voyage de noces* and *Au prochain crime j'espère*, both directed by Jean Faucher. Another television landmark was Jacques Languirand's absurdist *Les Grands départs*, directed by Georges Carrier. And Michel Tremblay brought new life and energy to television drama with his *En Pièces détachées* and *Trois petits tours*, both directed by Paul BLOUIN.

Other key television directors include L.-P. Beaudoin, Guy BEAULNE, Louis Bédard, Jean Boisvert, André Bousquet, Pierre DAGENAIS, Claude Désorcy, Fernand Doré, Charles Dumas, Jean Dumas, Jean Faucher, Florent FORGET, Jean-Paul Fugère, Jacques Gauthier, Georges Groulx, Jean-Paul Ladouceur, Jean-Yves Laforce, Paul Leduc, Paul Legault, Jean Léonard, Maurice Leroux, J. Martin, Bruno Paradis, Guy Parent, Pierre Pétel, Fernand Quirion, Roger Racine, Gérard Robert, Jean-Pierre Sénécal, Jean Valade, and René Verne.

See Renée Legris and Pierre Pagé, *Répertoire des dramatiques québécoises à la télévision 1952-1977* (1977), and Société Radio-Canada, *Vingt-cinq ans de dramatiques à la télévision de Radio-Canada, 1952-1977* (1978).

RENÉE LEGRIS

Ten Lost Years. Created in 1974 by TORONTO WORKSHOP PRODUCTIONS, it became one of the most successful plays in Canadian theatre history. The original production played for three months in Toronto, followed by a three-month national tour; it was revived for one month in 1975, and again in 1981 for another three. The group-theatre techniques that George LUSCOMBE had practised at TWP for fifteen years found their ideal subject in Barry Broadfoot's best-selling anthology (1973) of oral history about the Great Depression.

Working collectively (see COLLECTIVE CREATION) with dramaturge Jack Winter and a cast that featured Jackie BURROUGHS and musician Cedric Smith (whose idea the show was), Luscombe turned the book into a complex visual collage of memories. Dressed in 1930s costumes, the six men and four women of the cast each assumed a typical character, dividing the material by class and occupation. The juxtaposition of time, in which present prosperity recalls bygone adversity, is paralleled in the structure of the scenes. Typically, a monologue from the book is interrupted by music and improvised dialogue; the speeches create a present-tense framework for the past-tense stage action. The material is arranged to express an anti-capitalist critique of the Depression, blaming it on social greed as much as on natural disaster.

In the unanimously positive reviews, critics pointed to the play's brilliant theatricality (in which actor-created sound effects and a rectangle of light conjured the image of a moving freight train crowded with hobos) and the natural poetry of ordinary Canadian speech. The script was published in *Canadian Theatre Review* 38 (Fall 1983).

A second dramatization of Broadfoot's book, under the same title, was compiled and directed by Scott Swann at NORTHERN LIGHT THEATRE, Edmonton, in 1977. Although he used many of the same incidents as Luscombe, Swann's production was less theatrical, and placed greater stress on direct monologue.

ALAN FILEWOD

Theatre Aquarius. Located in Hamilton, Ont., since 1973, it was founded in Ottawa

Ten Lost Years, *St Lawrence Centre, Toronto, 1975*

by Peter Mandia and opened at the NATIONAL ARTS CENTRE Studio in May 1970 with a production of English playwright Ann Jellicoe's *The Knack*. In 1972, under Mandia and co-artistic director Nanci Rossov, Theatre Aquarius produced five new Canadian plays, including John PALMER's *The Great Beaver Conspiracy* and Elinore Siminovitch's *Tomorrow and Tomorrow*. Frustrated by a lack of popular and critical recognition in Ottawa, Mandia and Rossov moved their company to Hamilton in Jan. 1973 to become the main tenants of the 327-seat Studio Theatre in the new Hamilton Place arts complex. Because of construction delays, however, their first productions in Hamilton were performed elsewhere: Peter Luke's *Hadrian VII* (directed by Rossov) at Mohawk College, and a revue, *Crumpets and Tea*, outdoors at Dundurn Castle. Their first production at Hamilton Place (Oct. 1973) was Neil Simon's *The Gingerbread Lady*, directed by Mandia and starring Kate REID.

Theatre Aquarius built a large subscription audience (from 300 in 1973 to 7,000 in 1987)

by offering mainly proven successes from New York, London, and Toronto. It also produced two premières, in 1977 and 1986 respectively, of Canadian plays: Frank McEnaney's *To Covet Honour*, about the assassination of John F. Kennedy, and Munroe Scott's *McClure*, about the career of the Canadian missionary and churchman Robert McClure, which was given a national tour in 1987-8. In addition Theatre Aquarius has provided a wide range of theatrical services for its region, including original plays for young audiences and community educational programs.

The small capacity of the Studio Theatre has contributed to Theatre Aquarius's financial problems: in 1978 only a $50,000 loan from the city of Hamilton kept the company from folding. Beginning in 1981 the company proposed several heritage buildings as potential sites for a new theatre. Finally, in 1987, the city's gift of a vacant downtown lot initiated planning for a new theatre, scheduled to open in 1990. Despite earlier difficulties, the management of Theatre Aquarius has remained remarkably stable. Although Rossov left the company in 1975, she still returns occasionally to perform or to direct; the production manager, Stephen Newman, has been with the company since 1973; and Mandia is still artistic director.

DENIS W. JOHNSTON

Theatre Arts Guild. In Mar. 1931 Hugh Mills, J. Frank Willis, and Captain G.R. Chetwynd merged the Halifax Dramatic and Musical Club and the Garrison Dramatic Club to form Halifax's Theatre Arts Guild. In May the Guild produced its first play, A.A. Milne's *The Dover Road*, at the Garrick Theatre (now the NEPTUNE THEATRE) with Chetwynd directing. The group subsequently converted St Andrew's Hall on Coburg Road into a theatre.

H. Leslie Pigot, a former professional actor, directed A.E.W. Mason's *Green Stockings* in Feb. 1932 and most Guild productions during the next thirty years. In 1936 the Guild moved to the Navy League Building at South and Barrington Streets. The building was soon taken over by the Royal Canadian Air Force, and on the outbreak of the Second World War members of the Guild, led by Hugh Mills, organized the Halifax Concert Parties Guild to entertain armed forces personnel in the Atlantic region. In 1945 the group toured England, Holland, Germany, and Belgium.

TAG reformed in 1950 with its production of Samson Raphaelson's *Accent on Youth*, and opened a new home in the old College Street School with Daphne du Maurier's *Rebecca* on 13 Oct. 1952. On 25 Jan. 1959, during a rehearsal of Bernard Shaw's *Candida*, fire destroyed the building and $25,000 of props, costumes, and other equipment. For the next seven years TAG held rehearsals in a house on Victoria Road and performed in the St Patrick's High School gymnasium. In 1966 they renovated a former church hall in Jollimore as the Pond Playhouse, where they continue to produce an annual season of plays.

TAG has been the training gound for many successful Canadian performers, including J. Frank Willis, Austin Willis, John Fisher, Max Ferguson, Claude Bede, Florence Paterson, Joan Gregson, Joan Orenstein, and John Dunsworth. PATRICK B. O'NEILL

Theatre Calgary. The oldest professional theatre in Calgary, Alberta, had its roots in fecund postwar amateur theatre activity. When Christopher NEWTON became the first artistic director in 1968 he moved into the 497-seat Betty MITCHELL Theatre, former home of the Arts Centre Theatre Company (1963-6). But the inspiration for the new organization came from the old Isis movie house, where the MAC 14—a merger of Don Boyes' Musicians and Actors Club and Betty Mitchell's Workshop 14—had been doing a lively business for five seasons. Newton's commitment to produce at least one Canadian script annually has been generally honoured by subsequent artistic directors, giving Theatre Calgary an enviable list of important premières. Harold Baldridge (1972-8) produced Sharon POLLOCK's *Walsh* (in 1973) and W.O. MITCHELL's *Back to Beulah* (in 1976). Rick McNair (1978-84) commissioned and produced (in 1981) an adaptation of Robert Kroetsch's novel *The Words of My Roaring*, stage versions of Mitchell's *The Black Bonspiel of Wullie MacCrimmon* and *The Kite* (produced in 1979 and 1981 respectively), John MURRELL's *Farther West* (in 1982), and Sharon Pollock's *Whiskey Six Cadenza* (in 1983) and *Doc* (in 1984).

Locally based designers who contributed significantly to the success of these openings include Richard Roberts (*Walsh* and *Beulah*), Pat Flood (*Wullie MacCrimmon*), Gavin Semple (*Words of My Roaring*), and Terry Gunvordahl (*Doc* and, with Sheila Lee, costumes, *Whiskey Six*). Daphne Dare's design for Robin PHILLIPS' production of *Farther West* was favourably reviewed by national critics; the excellence of local designers is seldom similarly acknowledged.

The tenures of other artistic directors were brief. Clarke Rogers served one season, 1971-2, after Newton and before Baldridge; Joseph Green first accepted, then mysteriously declined, the job in 1972; and Sharon Pollock spent a stormy three months as head in 1984 following McNair's resignation 'to pursue his interests in freelance directing and writing.' Martin KINCH, appointed in 1985, introduced George WALKER's plays to Calgary and retained Gordon Pengilly as playwright-in-residence, but no substantial new works have appeared since McNair's resignation.

Professionals whose careers began in Calgary include performers Michael Ball, Robert Haley, and Sheila Moore, all regulars in MAC 14 and early Theatre Calgary seasons, and Kenneth Dyba, playwright and novelist, who

The Max Bell Theatre in Calgary's Centre for the Performing Arts, home of Theatre Calgary

was artistic director at MAC 14 in its final year. A strong tradition of support for young people's theatre—Joyce Doolittle's work for both the Arts Centre and MAC 14, Douglas RISKE's Arts Centre Children's Company, Youth Theatre leaders David Lander and Don Shipley and McNair, who came originally to Calgary to direct for children—declined under Pollock and Kinch.

The 1985 move to the Max Bell Theatre in Calgary's Centre for the Performing Arts was one of the most important events in the company's history. The new 750-seat house is a conventional end-stage theatre but has an adjustable proscenium arch, an optional thrust stage, and hinged box seats that can be adjusted to conform to the width of the proscenium. Although no seat is further than sixty feet from the stage, patrons complain about poor acoustics and a feeling of distance from the performers. The first season, budgeted to lose $121,000, ended with a $33,000 surplus, but by 1988 the theatre had a deficit of $424,000, despite a windfall of $628,000 for rental fees during the 1988 Olympic Arts Festival.

Two separate companies—ALBERTA THEA-TRE PROJECTS and Theatre Calgary—share the same facility: they have a common box office, cheek-by-jowl administrative offices, and share the services of the Joint Venture production company. How well this arrangement will work out in the long run is an open question. There are even similarities in the repertoire and style of the two companies.

Theatre Calgary received more than one third of its three-million-dollar budget for 1985-6 from the Canada Council, Alberta Culture, The Alberta Foundation for the Performing Arts, and the Calgary Regional Arts Foundation. Private and corporate donations fluctuate wildly in the boom-and-bust economy that Calgary's reliance on oil, wheat, and cattle has traditionally engendered. However, in two decades it has grown from a modest grass-roots operation to a multi-million dollar business with high artistic standards and a respectable record of Canadian premières.   JOYCE DOOLITTLE

Théâtre Canadien, Le. At the beginning of 1907 Damas Larose, manager of Le Parc

Théâtre Canadien

Sohmer in Montreal, and Georges Gauvreau, who had just sold his THÉÂTRE NATIONAL, purchased a lot at 472 and 474 St Catherine St East, near Saint-André, and built the Nationoscope, a 1,100-seat cinema, about 82' long, 40' wide, and 43' high. Seriously damaged by a fire in 1909, the hall was turned into a theatre in the same year by its new owners, Blaise Montesano and Alphonse Demers.

In Mar. 1912 Julien DAOUST's company, cramped for space on their tiny stage at the Parisiana, moved into the building and changed its name on 7 July 1913 to Le Théâtre Canadien; it later became known as Le Théâtre Canadien-français. But Daoust's French-Canadian company met with difficulties, and in Sept. 1914 the theatre came under the direction of Fernand Dhavrol with a primarily French company. This was quickly replaced by Armand Robi's operetta company and from then on, with two brief interludes (under Gustave Scheler in 1917 and Paul CAZENEUVE in 1918), Le Théâtre Canadien was used for operettas and revues, such as those of Paul Gury—his Envoye! Envoye! had more than 100 performances in Mar. 1919, a record for Montreal.

In 1925 Albert DUQUESNE became manager, with Antoine Godeau as director. Along with actors Marthe THIÉRY and Fred BARRY, they gave the Canadien a brief renewal of popularity. But owner Alex Silvio, heavily in debt, closed the theatre in Nov. 1926.

Although it never had the same historic importance as the Théâtre National, between the wars Le Théâtre Canadien was Montreal's melting-pot, where most of the city's dramatic artists could be seen.

JEAN-MARC LARRUE

Théâtre Champlain. Situated on Champlain St, near the Queen's Wharf, Quebec City, and opened on 21 June 1852, it was built by the P.T. Barnum organization in order to present its panorama of the 1851 exhibition at London's Crystal Palace. The representations of the huge panorama (measuring 15' high by many thousands of feet long) filled the hall for two shows daily, at three and eight p.m. until 2 July. Left with a small but well-laid-out theatre with a gallery and four safety exits, its owner (John Jones) hired Charlotte MORRISON and a few actors who had just finished performing in the Upper Town with the John NICKINSON

touring company. They put on some twenty plays from 19 July to 17 Aug., including J.B. Buckstone's Good for Nothing, Douglas Jerrold's Black-Eyed Susan, J.R. Planché's Faint Heart Never Won Fair Lady, Shakespeare's The Merchant of Venice, David Garrick's The Irish Widow, and J. Maddison Morton's Box and Cox. During the week of 27 Aug. 1852 Adrien, 'king of the magicians' performed.

Because the theatre was located in a part of town with an unsavoury reputation, audiences were small, and when the MUSIC HALL opened on Saint-Louis St early in 1853 the Champlain folded. The building was turned into an apartment house and was finally torn down in 1914.   JOHN E. HARE

Théâtre Club, Le. In 1953, during a formative period in the development of contemporary theatre in Montreal, Monique LEPAGE and Jacques Létourneau founded Le Théâtre Club with a mandate to provide high-quality but popular productions from the classical and modern repertoires. The company played in the D'Arcy McGee auditorium, La Salle du GESÙ, the COMÉDIE-CANADIENNE, and, from 1957 on, in a rented 200-seat studio on rue St-Luc. It presented an average of four productions a year, introducing authors new to Quebec (J.B. Priestley, Valentine Petrovich Kataev, Luigi Pirandello, Jacques Audiberti), successfully revitalizing the classics (Shakespeare's La Nuit des Rois [Twelfth Night], Dumas's Les Trois Mousquetaires, Corneille's Cinna), and premièring seven plays by promising Canadian authors (including Marcel DUBÉ, Jacques FERRON, and Jacques LANGUIRAND). Le Théâtre Club also offered student matinées and professionally produced plays for children, including Luan Asslani's Les Trois Désirs de Coquelicot. Jacques Létourneau directed most of the plays and invited guest directors Jean Doat, Marcel Sabourin, and Florent FORGET to work with such gifted comedy actors as Gilles PELLETIER, Monique Lepage, and Paul HÉBERT, and designers Robert PRÉVOST and Jean-Claude RINFRET. Clermont Pépin composed original scores for La Nuit des Rois and Audiberti's Le Mal court.

At first entirely self-supporting, the company received government grants from 1957 ($10,000) to 1964 ($35,000). Subsidies were then discontinued and the company closed in 1965.

See Pierre Lavoie, Le Théâtre Club (1953-

1964), Centre d'Études québécoises, Université de Montréal (1976).

HÉLÈNE BEAUCHAMP

Theatre Compact. Although this company was active only from April 1976 to April 1978, it presented some of the most distinctive productions seen in Toronto. Led by James Edmond and Alan Richardson, it was a 'compact' of sixty of Toronto's most experienced actors and directors, who agreed to accept minimal salaries to work in Toronto on significant plays. Founding members included Kate REID, Amelia HALL, Charmion KING, Frances HYLAND, Jane MALLETT, Barbara CHILCOTT, Donald DAVIS, Barry Morse, Ron Hartmann, Gordon PINSENT, and George LUSCOMBE.

There were just six productions: Hugh Leonard's *Da* in 1976; the English-language première of Nikolai Erdman's *The Suicide* (1976); August Strindberg's *Easter* (1977); the triple bill *Orators* (1977)—*Swan Song* by Chekhov, *Hands* by Yuli Daniel, and *Rounders* by Michael Brodribb; Georg Büchner's *Woyzeck* (1977); and Joseph Kesselring's *Arsenic and Old Lace* (1978). All but the last were directed by Alan Richardson; designers included Astrid JANSON and Maurice Strike. Lacking its own space, Compact played at TORONTO WORKSHOP PRODUCTIONS, the Bathurst Street Theatre, and other locations. Response to its adventurous repertoire and high standards was positive, but the company was finally crippled by chronic financial problems and, despite an announced 1979 season at the Music Hall on Danforth Ave (including a play by Margaret Atwood called *Grace Marks*) under Burton Lancaster and Edmond, no further productions were mounted.

HARRY LANE

Théâtre d'Aujourd'hui, Le. In 1968 three small Quebec theatre companies—Le Mouvement contemporain (directed by André BRASSARD), Les SALTIMBANQUES (directed by Rodrig Mathieu), and Les APPRENTIS-SORCIERS (then under the direction of Jean-Pierre Saulnier)—amalgamated to found in an old garage, fitted out as a 100-seat theatre that had been used by the Apprentis-Sorciers since 1965—Le Centre du Théâtre d'Aujourd'hui. The founders believed that this site, located approximately in mid-Montreal, could become a genuine *centre* that would attract any and all companies that were producing non-traditional theatre. Le Centre d'essai des auteurs dramatiques (CEAD) had its offices there until 1972.

In the first season productions were mounted separately by the founding companies, while CEAD organized public readings—one of which was of Michel TREMBLAY's *Les BELLES-SOEURS* in Mar. 1968. In the following season Les Saltimbanques and Le Mouvement contemporain ceased their activities, and under the direction of Pierre Bégin Théâtre d'Aujourd'hui henceforth devoted itself entirely to the production of Québécois drama.

The first show of the 1969-70 season—a production by Le Théâtre de Même Nom called *Les Enfants de Chénier dans un autre grand spectacle d'adieu*—set the tone, striking a blow against the perceived dominance of foreign theatre on the Quebec stage and offering parodies of works from the classical repertoire. Subsequent TMN shows at the Centre—*Diguidi, diguidi, ha! ha! ha!* in 1969 and *Si Aurore m'était contée deux fois* in 1970, for example—built the company's reputation for irreverent satire of Quebec's cultural and political élite. In 1972 Jean-Claude GERMAIN, formerly executive director of CEAD, became artistic director of Le Théâtre d'Aujourd'hui, soon setting on it the stamp of his strong personality and writing, and directing over half the plays presented there until his resignation in 1983. During these years Le Théâtre d'Aujourd'hui became a Mecca for Québécois drama, questioning—often harshly—the province's political and cultural heritage in plays such as Michel GARNEAU's *Strauss et Pesant* (produced in 1974); Germain's *Les Hauts et les bas dla vie d'une diva: Sarah Ménard par eux-mêmes*, 1975, and *Un Pays dont la devise est je m'oublie*, 1976; Roland LEPAGE's *Le Temps d'une vie*, 1975; Michelle Lalonde's *Dernier recours de Baptiste à Catherine*, 1977; and Victor-Lévy Beaulieu's *La Tête de Monsieur Ferron*, 1979.

This was not only a theatre of writing but a theatre of acting, and the productions of the Aujourd'hui called repeatedly on the same actors to perform: Roger Blay, Normand Chouinard, Murielle Dutil, Nicole Leblanc, Guy L'ÉCUYER, Denise Morelle, Guy Nadon, and Jean Perraud. From 1978 to 1983 each production was accompanied by a program, *Le Pays théâtral*, in which Germain provided an overview of current theatrical and paratheatrical activities, and reiterated the need

529

Théâtre d'Aujourd'hui

Victor Lévy-Beaulieu's Ma Corriveau, *Théâtre d'Aujourd'hui, 1976, with (l. to r.) Evelyne Regimbald, Diane Ricard*

for a drama dealing with contemporary issues.

In the 1980s a new generation of writers emerged at Aujourd'hui—Suzanne Aubry (*J'te l'parle mieux quand j'te l'écris*, 1981); Élizabeth Bourget (*Bernadette et Juliette*, 1979); Maryse Pelletier (*Du poil aux pattes comme les CWACS*, 1982, and *Duo pour voix obstinées*, 1985); and Gilbert Turp (*La Saint-Jean du p'tit monde*, 1980)—and in 1983 Gilbert Lepage became artistic director. Among the subsequent notable plays were Michel-Marc Bouchard's *La Contre-nature de Chrysippe Tanguay, écologiste*, 1983; René Gingras's *Le Facteur réalité*, 1985; Jean-Raymond Marcoux's *Bienvenue aux dames, ladies welcome!*, 1983; and *Camille C.*, by Jocelyne Beaulieu and René Richard Cyr in 1984. Lepage also gave opportunities to a new generation of directors, such as Alain Fournier, Geneviève Notebaert, Lorraine Pintal, Michelle Rossignol, as well as François BARBEAU and Michèle Magny, who made their débuts as professional directors at Aujourd'hui. In May 1987

Lepage resigned and was replaced by the actor and author Robert Lalonde.

PIERRE MACDUFF

Théâtre de la Fenière, Le. Quebec's first professional summer theatre, it was founded by Georges Delisle in Ancienne Lorette, west of Quebec City, in 1958. He remained its director until Oct. 1986, when he handed over the 400-seat theatre (once a barn) to a new administration composed of Marielle Kirouac, Yvon Sanche, and Carl Jessop. Kirouac, who combines the functions of general director and artistic director, has acted regularly at La Fenière since 1968, and Sanche has designed and built the sets there for over twenty years. Jessop, a lawyer, acts as secretary and legal counsel for the company, a non-profit organization without subsidies.

The theatre's mandate, established by Delisle, is to present light comedy performed by Quebec actors. Performers have included Paule Bayard, Dorothée Berryman, Marie-Hélène Gagnon, Gisèle Gallichan, Diane Jules, René Arthur, Camille Ducharme, Michel Daigle, and Paul HÉBERT. During the early years of La Fenière the repertoire was drawn from French comic playwrights such as André Roussin, Jean de Letraz, Maurice Hennequin, and Marcel Achard. The first Quebec play was Yves THÉRIAULT's *Bérangère ou la chair en feu*, produced in 1965. René Massicotte's *Octobre en famille* was produced in 1971, and to mark the theatre's thirtieth anniversary in 1988 two further Quebec plays were selected: Jean Daigle's *Un Cheveu sur la soupe* and André Jean's *A frais virés*. Given the scarcity of light comedies by Quebec playwrights, however, it is inevitable that the theatre will remain dependent on the French *boulevard* repertoire so long as it retains its current mandate.

See also SUMMER STOCK (Quebec).

CHANTAL HÉBERT

Théâtre de la Marmaille, Le. This Montreal children's theatre company was founded in 1973, and is still operated by, Monique Rioux, Daniel Meilleur, and France Mercille. From its beginnings La Marmaille ('marmaille' means 'kids' or 'brats') defined itself as a research group exploring theatre in its relationship to young spectators through writing workshops and creativity sessions with both young and adult audiences and with groups from different social and ethnic

Théâtre de la Marmaille

L'Âge de Pierre, *Théâtre de la Marmaille, 1978, with (l. to r.) Jocelyne France, Benoit Ranger, Monique Rioux, André Gosselin*

backgrounds. Its research has been published in book form, on records, and in television and film series. The company's productions have toured widely in Canada, Europe, and the U.S.

Théâtre de la Marmaille's mandate was influenced by Monique Rioux's refusal to accept fairy tales as the sole content of children's theatre and her rejection of the prevalent compulsory participation by children. Instead in 1973-4 she organized workshops where writers and actors entered into creative co-operation with children. Characters, themes, and story-lines that emerged were shaped by author Marie-Francine Hébert into the company's first scripts: *Le Tour du chapeau* in 1973, and *Tu viendras pas patiner dans ma cour* and *C't'assez plate* in 1974. These workshops acknowledged the fact that children could be creative partners; they showed clearly how participants of varied social and ethnic backgrounds invent characters and dramatic situations reflecting their experience of life; and they proved that theatrical form and content could be made directly relevant to young audiences.

While continuing to emphasize workshops, La Marmaille gradually expanded the scope of its productions. *A quoi qu'on joue?*, produced in 1976, was a theatre game for 100 players that was meant to stimulate the imagination and heighten social awareness.

In *Pourquoi tu dis ça?*, first performed in 1976, past, present, and future are examined from the viewpoint of the adolescent. *La Vie à trois étages*, published in 1980, is a play for adults created through interviews and workshops. It was commissioned by the NOUVELLE COMPAGNIE THÉÂTRALE for the 1977 opening of Théâtre Denise PELLETIER in the Hochelaga-Maisonneuve quarter. The play celebrated the history of the people of this area.

La Marmaille has often mounted COLLECTIVE productions such as its 1978 *L'Âge de Pierre*, a musical comedy in sketch form on the fears assailing children between ten and twelve. The company has also attracted distinguished dramatists who have provided plays—*Une Ligne blanche au jambon* (1974) and *Cé tellement 'cute' des enfants* (1975) by Marie-Francine Hébert; *On n'est pas des enfants d'école* (1984) by Gilles Gauthier in collaboration with the company; and *Pleurer pour rire* (1984) by Marcel Sabourin. Realistic in dialogue and characterization, these plays present recognizable situations and ask blunt questions: what happens when children say 'No'? Should emotions be hidden? Is school also for children? Such thematic realism contrasts sharply with set and costume design (by Daniel Castonguay since 1980), which, complemented by music, emphasizes the surreal and subconscious dream world of the characters. Michel Robidoux's music also

Théâtre de la Marmaille

enhances the personal character of the emotions in contrast to the clown-like or expressionistic work of the actors.

See Monique Rioux, Diane Bilz, Jean-Marie Boisvert, *L'Enfant et l'expression dramatique* (1976). The company's playscripts are available at the Centre d'essai des auteurs dramatiques, Montreal.

See also CHILDREN'S DRAMA AND THEATRE IN FRENCH.   HÉLÈNE BEAUCHAMP

Théâtre de la Place Jacques-Cartier, Le. A 2,000-seat hall on the second floor of a market building constructed in 1855 (extended in 1866) at Notre-Dame des Anges and Jacques Cartier Sts in the Lower Town of Quebec City, it was opened on 17 Aug. 1871 by Alfred Maugard and his 'Compagnie lyrique et dramatique française des Antilles'. It underwent extensive renovations at various times that added 300 seats, loges, and ground-floor boxes. This early attempt at professional theatre was not, however, initially a success: the élite did not like to venture out from the Upper Town, and the clergy opposed the project.

Maugard presented twenty-five shows in 1871—comedies, tragedies, operettas, and VAUDEVILLE—and other companies, amateur and professional, used the theatre sporadically in subsequent years. Productions were a mix of French, Quebec, and European works. In 1881, for example, Offenbach's *Jobin et Nanette*, Félix-Gabriel MARCHAND's *Une double méprise*, and Louis FRÉCHETTE's *Dimanche à l'hôtel du Canada* were presented. French plays at the Jacques-Cartier included Adolphe d'Ennery's *La Grâce de Dieu* in 1873, his popular melodrama *Marie-Jeanne; ou La femme du peuple* in 1891 (produced by Blanche de la SABLONNIÈRE's Compagnie franco-canadienne), and Jules Verne's *Michel Strogoff* in 1897.

From 1902 to 1911 there were resident professional companies: from 1902 to 1907 under the direction of Louis Bertin and from 1907 to 1911 of Julien DAOUST, under whom the Jacques-Cartier became the centre for French-language theatre in Quebec City. Daoust chose popular French plays such as Paul Féval's *Le Bossu* and Edmond Rostand's *Cyrano de Bergerac*, but did not hesitate to produce unknown French-Canadian works—Mathilde Casgrain's *Les Surprises du coeur*, Germain Beaulieu's *Diplomatie conjugale*, and Daoust's own *La Nativité de Jésus*, for exam-

ple. Known at various times as the Théâtre Royal (around 1883), the Théâtre Français (1895), the Théâtre de la Gaîté (1898), the Théâtre Populaire, and the Théâtre National (from Aug. 1910), and advertised frequently as the Salle Jacques Cartier, it was destroyed by fire on 26 Nov. 1911.

See André Duval, *Place Jacques-Cartier; ou Quarante ans de théâtre français à Québec, 1871-1911* (1984).

JOHN E. HARE, RAMON HATHORN

Théâtre de Marjolaine, Le. Founded in 1960 as Théâtre la Marjolaine in a barn in Eastman, Que., it was named after actress Marjolaine Hébert who—with Gilbert Comtois, Hubert Loiselle, and Louise Rémy—was a member of the first artistic directorate. The present name and the actual incorporation of the company date from 1962, when Hébert joined forces with Louis-Georges Carrier to develop this tiny summer theatre (272 seats). They began by offering Quebec plays. The first—Marcel DUBÉ's *Zone*—was followed by new works such as *Pour cinq sous d'amour* by Dubé and Carrier. Plays by Hubert Aquin, Jean Besré, François Cousineau, Eloi de GRANDMONT, Sylvain Lelièvre, and Albert Millaire have also been produced. In 1964 they presented the first French-Canadian musical comedy, *Doux temps des amour*, with libretto by Carrier and de Grandmont and music by Claude Léveillé. For several seasons thereafter musical comedy became the company's specialty. In 1967 the company purchased and renovated its theatre, which in 1971 became the property of Les Entreprises Hebcar Inc.

Théâtre de Marjolaine has successfully survived some years of financial difficulty while producing Quebec plays at a time when there were few such opportunities for Quebec playwrights, and enhancing the careers not only of major actors such as Georges Groulx and Denise PELLETIER, but also of young unknowns who subsequently achieved wide recognition—notably Robert Charlebois, Louise Forestier, and Louise Marleau.

ANDRÉ-G. BOURASSA

Théâtre de Neptune en la Nouvelle-France, Le. The first play composed and performed in North America, it was presented on 14 Nov. 1606 on the water at the mouth of the Annapolis River and on the shores surrounding the little *Habitation* of

Port Royal (the name given to the modern town of Port Royal, N.S., where a reproduction of the *Habitation* stands in Port Royal National Historic Park). Written by French lawyer Marc LESCARBOT, it was first published in his *Histoire de la Nouvelle-France* (Paris, 1609) and comprises only ten pages of text.

Composed in verse, *Neptune* is primarily a *réception* or short dramatic piece performed or recited to mark the visit of a religious or civil dignitary. On this occasion the ship carrying the colony's leader, Jean de Biencourt de Poutrincourt, had just reappeared in the harbour after a prolonged exploration southward, and Lescarbot's lively text is a heartfelt expression of joy at his patron's return. The central focus is Neptune, god of the sea and patron of mariners. With long beard and flowing hair, he sits, trident in hand, in a small boat decorated to resemble a chariot. This boat-chariot is drawn by six Tritons, half-fish, half-men; as it meets Poutrincourt's landing-craft, Neptune, perhaps played by the author, addresses the colony's leader. There is a peal of trumpets, then Poutrincourt draws and presents his sword for the second tableau, wherein the Tritons address him in turn, sprinkling in a few words of Micmac. In the next sequence another boat arrives with four 'Indians' (Frenchmen in costume) who bring presents and offer submission. The fourth movement comprises an improvised speech (not recorded) by Poutrincourt, thanking Neptune and all present, inviting them to break bread with him at the *Habitation*. Then the cannons speak and the brass trumpets sound again, and all set out on foot for Port Royal. At its gates they are greeted by a 'companion in a merry mood' who summons them to a magnificent feast.

Neo-classical in inspiration and form, full of Latin and Greek mythological allusions, *réceptions* like *Neptune* were firmly rooted in French cultural history. Lescarbot's text belongs to another tradition as well: that of the public masques, triumphal entries, and nautical extravaganzas so integral to French and English courtly life. The function his little play served on this occasion was faithful also to the most ancient origins of drama: a communal celebration, an act of participation, a sort of 'total theatre' with cannons, trumpets, and costumes—with fifty or so Frenchmen and a couple of dozen Micmacs assembled in what splendour they could mus-

ter; all this in the spectacular natural setting of the Annapolis basin in autumn.

Lescarbot's text, in a translation by Harriette T. Richardson, was re-enacted at the original site on 15 Aug. 1956 to mark the 350th anniversary of its première. It has been translated several times since, most recently by Eugene Benson and Renate Benson in *Canadian Drama*, vol. 8 (1982).

See L.E. Doucette, *Theatre in French Canada, 1606-1867* (1984).   L.E. DOUCETTE

Théâtre de Quat'Sous, Le. Founded in Montreal in 1955 by Paul Buissonneau, it mounted ten productions—most of them directed by Buissonneau—over its first ten years, mainly at the GESÙ, the COMÉDIE-CAN-ADIENNE, the ORPHEUM, and La POUD-RIÈRE. Its repertoire of comedy and spectacle—*Orion le tueur*, *La Tour Eiffel qui tue*, *La Bande à Bonnot*, for example—was performed by actors such as Yvon DES-CHAMPS, Mirielle Lachance, Claude Leveillée, Jean-Louis Millette, and François Tassé. In 1963 the company was incorporated as a non-profit organization, and in 1965 it moved into its own theatre, a 160-seat converted synagogue on Est, ave des Pins.

Buissonneau's objective was to challenge both the prevailing aesthetics of theatre and dominant social values through provocative, innovative productions. He offered generous opportunities to talented young artists, who often made their début at the Quat'Sous, notably in directing. In May 1968 Buissonneau directed *L'Osstidcho*, which introduced Robert Charlebois, Yvon Deschamps, Louise Forestier, Mouffe, and the Quebec Free Jazz Quartet. The uncommon musical and dramatic vitality of this 'happening' made a memorable contribution to the changing cultural values in Quebec in the late 1960s.

Quat'Sous was closely involved in the development of Quebec drama, both in COL-LECTIVE CREATIONs and in new plays such as Jean Morin's *Vive l'empereur* (produced in 1969), Robert GURIK's *À coeur ouvert* (1969), Marie Savard's *Bien à moi marquise* (1970), and Serge Sirois's *Aujourd'hui peut-être* (1972). The 'Belles-Soeurs' cycle of plays by Michel TREMBLAY—with the exception of *Les BELLES-SOEURS* itself—was produced at Quat'Sous, directed by André BRASSARD, who was also responsible for an outstanding production of Racine's *Andromaque* in 1974

Théâtre de Quat'Sous

and for the première of Michel GARNEAU's *Quatre à quatre*, also in 1974.

The Quat'Sous also collaborated in co-productions with ALTERNATE THEATRES such as Le GRAND CIRQUE ORDINAIRE (*T'es pas tannée, Jeanne d'Arc?*, 1970; *La Tragédie américaine de l'enfant prodigue*, 1975; *Mandrake chez lui*, 1976) and Omnibus (*Zizi & Co*, 1978, *Casse-tête*, 1980). Buissonneau continued to direct established works (*Théâtre de chambre* by Jean Tardieu, 1977, *Exercice de diction et de conversation française pour étudiants américains* by Eugène Ionesco, 1978, *La Résistible ascencion d'Arturo Ui* (*The Resistible Rise of Arturo Ui*) by Bertolt Brecht, 1983) and to introduce a new generation of playwrights (Marc Drouin, Normand CHAURETTE, René-Daniel DUBOIS), but his course as artistic director seemed increasingly erratic. A second very tiny stage was opened—Le Quat'Sous Bar—where Alexandre HAUSVATER directed, before graduating to the main stage with *Metamorphosis*, adapted from Kafka, 1980; *Le Decameron*, adapted from Boccaccio, 1982; and Shakespeare's *Hamlet*, 1982. Musical performers André Gagnon, Diane Juster, Renée Claude, and Claude Léveillée also appeared on the main stage, as did experimental works by Le Théâtre Ubu and its director Denis Marleau (*Le Coeur à gaz et autres textes dada*, 1982, and *Portrait de Dora* by Hélène Cixous, 1983).

In 1984 Buissonneau was succeeded as artistic director by the actress Louise Latraverse, who managed during her brief tenure to re-establish the Quat'Sous as a theatre of daring and excellence. She obtained grants for the updating of stage equipment and theatre furnishings and commissioned a new version of *AURORE L'ENFANT MARTYRE* by Léon Petitjean and Henri Rollin, directed by René Richard Cyr in 1984. Latraverse presented Quebec City's Théâtre Repère (*Circulations*, 1984, and *Vinci*, 1986, performed by Robert Lepage), and Jovette MARCHESSAULT's *Anaïs dans la queue de la comète* directed by Michèle Magny and *Being at Home with Claude* by René-Daniel Dubois, directed by Daniel Roussel, both in 1985. In April 1986 she joined with Le Grande Cirque Ordinaire in producing *Avec Lorenzo à mes côtés*. Latraverse left the Quat'Sous following a disagreement with the board about programming; she was succeeded as artistic director by Louison Danis (1986-8) and Pierre Bernard (1988-). PIERRE MACDUFF

Théâtre des Variétés, Le. Opened in 1913 as the Dominion Theatre (later known as Le Figaro), this 726-seat east-end Montreal BURLESQUE house—synonymous with working-class entertainment and vulgar shows of dubious artistic merit—gained a new lease on life on 23 Sept. 1967 when Gilles Latulippe officially opened it as Le Théâtre des Variétés.

Many famous burlesque artists have appeared there: Rose Ouellette ('La Poune'), Manda Parent, Juliette Petrie, Pic-Pic, Swifty, Pizzy-Wizzy, Olivier GUIMOND, Tizoune, and others. In its heyday a new show—usually improvised from a basic traditional structure—was given every week, but after the decline of burlesque the theatre relied more on scripted shows. Since 1972 director Gilles Latulippe has presented standardized variety programs of threadbare comic routines and stereotyped jokes laced with sexual innuendo. In addition to Latulippe, popular performers today (all well known from television) include Suzanne Langlois, Muriel Berger, Roger Giguère, and Jacques Salvail. The theatre receives no government subsidies and draws up to eighty per cent of its audience from outside Montreal—often bus-loads of shoppers who complete their outing by seeing a show. CHANTAL HÉBERT

Théâtre du Nouveau Monde, Le. Founded in Montreal in 1951 by Eloi de GRANDMONT, Guy HOFFMANN, Georges Groulx, and two former members of Les COMPAGNONS DE SAINT-LAURENT—Jean-Louis ROUX and Jean GASCON (who ran it until 1966)—the company opened on 9 Oct. 1951 with Molière's *L'Avare*, which ran for twenty-six performances (attracting 15,000 spectators—a record for the time) at the Salle de GESÙ. The company leased the Gesù for six seasons before moving in 1957 to the ORPHEUM. For one season only, 1966-7, the company returned to the Gesù before moving into the Port-Royal theatre at the PLACE DES ARTS. They remained there until 1972, when they took possession of one of the best-equipped theatres in the country, the COMÉDIE-CANA-DIENNE, renamed Le Théâtre du Nouveau Monde.

Despite the eclectic selection of plays—*L'Avare*, J. B. Priestley's *Un Inspecteur vous demande* (*An Inspector Calls*), Eugène Labiche's *Célimare le Bien-Aimé*, and Jan de Hartog's *Maître après Dieu*—the first season was a success, particularily *L'Avare*.

534

Georges Feydeau's La Main passe, *Théâtre du Nouveau Monde, Montreal, 1974, with (l. to r.) Jean-Marie Moncelet, Germaine Giroux, Jean-Besré, Jean Perraud, Lise Lasalle, Gaëtan Labrèche, Jean-Louis Roux*

Although critics were divided on Gascon's interpretation of the role of Harpagon, they were unanimous in their praise of the young company's high standards and professionalism. By the end of its second season the TNM had a relatively stable team that changed only slowly over the years: the manager, Gascon, and Jean-Louis Roux, who succeeded him in 1966, were the principal directors; Robert PRÉVOST was in charge of costumes and sets, and Gabriel CHARPENTIER of music; the same actors, many of them former members of Les Compagnons de Saint-Laurent, appeared in one production after another.

In 1952 TNM opened a theatre school. Apart from the company's founding members, teachers included actor Jean Dalmain, set designer Jacques Pelletier, and voice coach Lucie de Vienne-Blanc. Several of the students became well-known actors—Jacques GODIN and Marc Favreau (who created the clown character 'Sol'), among others. In 1954 an English branch of the company opened, but it closed in 1959 after playing William Inge, Kafka, Tennessee Williams, and Eugene O'Neill to half-empty houses. A competition for new Canadian works, begun in 1956, was abandoned in 1961 after plays such as André Langevin's *L'Oeil du Peuple*

(produced in 1957) and André Laurendeau's *Deux Femmes terribles* (1961) were poorly received.

Other innovations were more successful. In 1963 the company opened a summer theatre at Repentigny near Montreal, and in the same year 'Les Jeunes Comédiens du TNM' toured across Canada and into the U.S. In 1968—in conjunction with the Université de Montréal—the theatre organized lectures on current productions, and in 1969 they launched a newsletter, *L'Envers du décor*. 'Lundis du TNM', begun in 1968, allowed young artists to use the theatre's facilities, and at 'Mardis du TNM', begun in 1971, theatre people met to discuss various productions. 'Théâtre-Midi', a LUNCH THEATRE that gave Montrealers a chance to see works by little-known dramatists, was established.

Early in its history TNM found itself torn between a need to fill seats and its responsibility to serious drama. The result was a great diversity in repertoire and a surprising juxtaposition of plays—Aeschylus next to Feydeau, or a play by Paul Claudel beside a musical comedy. However, after a few seasons weighted towards serious drama, TNM found in the late 1960s a formula that it has maintained: a famous international play; a

Théâtre du Nouveau Monde

Quebec work; a significant contemporary play; a major modern piece; and a classic—frequently Molière.

TNM has a successful history of international touring. In 1955 they were invited to perform three farces by Molière at the Paris International Festival, making TNM the first Canadian company to play in France and the first foreign company to perform there in French. Parisian audiences and critics welcomed the company's 'rejuvenated' interpretation of Molière. The same production was presented with equal success at Ontario's STRATFORD FESTIVAL in 1956, and in 1958 TNM toured New York, Paris, and Brussels with three farces and *Le Malade imaginaire* by Molière, and a French-Canadian play, *Le Temps des lilas*, by Marcel DUBÉ. In 1965 the company took part in the Commonwealth Festival of the Arts in London, offering Molière's *L'École des femmes* and *Klondyke*, a COLLECTIVE CREATION written with Jacques LANGUIRAND with music by Gabriel Charpentier. This first appearance by a French-Canadian company at the Old Vic was appreciated more by the audiences than by the critics. A 1971 tour of over a dozen European cities, including Moscow, presented Molière's *Tartuffe* (with Albert Millaire) and Roch CARRIER's *La GUERRE, YES SIR!*.

In addition to Molière, major TNM successes have included Brecht's *La Mère courage* (*Mother Courage*)—directed by John HIRSCH, with Denise PELLETIER in the title role (1966)—and *L'Opéra de quat'sous* (*The Threepenny Opera*), directed by Jean Gascon (1961); Eloi de Grandmont's adaptation of Shaw's *Pygmalion* (1967), which used Montreal as the setting and translated the cockney passages into *joual*; Aristophanes' *Lysistrata*, adapted by André BRASSARD and Michel TREMBLAY (1969); and V. Lanoux's *Ouvre-boîte*, starring the well-known monologuist Yvon DESCHAMPS (1974).

Despite some initial failures, the company's productions of Quebec drama have been considerable. Apart from Languirand, Dubé, Carrier, and the experiments of 'Théâtre-Midi', TNM has produced plays by Anne HÉBERT, Guy DUFRESNE, Jacques FERRON, and Jovette MARCHESSAULT, to name only the most prominent. Several premières have been among the company's greatest successes—notably *Les Oranges sont vertes* by Claude GAUVREAU, directed by Jean-Pierre RONFARD (1972), and *Les FÉES ONT SOIF* by Denise BOUCHER, directed by Jean-Luc BASTIEN (1978). In the 1975-6 season *La Nef des sorcières*, a work written by a group of Quebec women authors, and directed by Luce GUILBEAULT, had a success comparable to TNM's outstanding production in French of Peter Shaffer's *Equus*, staged by its present artistic director, Olivier Reichenbach.

In the past few years TNM has faced serious problems: conflict with its union members; criticism from Quebec's ALTERNATE THEATRES about the size of its grants and the rising costs of production; and a burdensome accumulated deficit. The crisis reached such proportions that the company had to cancel the 1984-5 season and sell its theatre, where TNM is now only a tenant.

NORMAND LEROUX

Théâtre du Rideau Vert, Le. Founded in 1948 by the actress Yvette BRIND'AMOUR, it began at Le Théâtre des Compagnons on Montreal's Sherbrooke St. During its first three seasons the company produced only five plays beginning with Lillian Hellman's *Les Innocents* (*The Children's Hour*) in Feb. 1949, followed by a Parisian success, *K.M.X. Labrador*, by Jacques Deval, which helped to enlarge both the audience and the reputation of the young company. In 1952 it attempted more challenging fare—Jean Giraudoux's *Ondine*, performed at the GESÙ—but despite meticulous direction and an outstanding performance by Brind'Amour in the title role, it was a failure. Michel Durant's light comedy *Sincèrement* also played to empty houses in 1952, causing the company to cease operations. It resumed in 1956 with its first French-Canadian play, Félix LECLERC's *Sonnez les matines*, which—despite bad reviews—attracted an audience of over 15,000 at the Gesù. That year the Rideau Vert moved to the Anjou on Drummond St, the foremost 'théâtre de poche' in Montreal, accommodating only ninety people. The first production there, *La Boutique aux Anges*, by Canadian playwright Roger Sinclair, was a critical success only. Its next play, however, *Guillaume le confident* by the French playwright Gabriel Arout, was successful both critically and at the box office. Other hits—after several failures—included the French plays *La Petite Hutte* by André Roussin and *Le Complexe de Philémon* by Jean Bernard-Luc, but the 1958 production of Jean-Paul Sartre's *Huis-Clos*, with Brind'Amour as

Antonine Maillet's Évangéline Deusse, *Théâtre du Rideau Vert, Montreal, 1976, with (l. to r.) Paul Guèvremont, André Cailloux, Guy Provost, Viola Léger*

Inès, disappointed critics and audiences. An unexpected success in 1958 was Henry de Montherlant's contemporary classic *Reine Morte*, produced at the Gesù, designed by Robert PRÉVOST; it is still considered one of the finest productions in the history of the company. Critics were extremely harsh the following year, however, with *Dialogues des Carmelites* by George Bernanos. Following this failure the Rideau Vert decided to devote the 1959-60 season entirely to French-Canadian drama; but the first production, Maurice Gagnon's *Edwige*, was a flop and the season ended abruptly.

For the 1960-1 season Rideau Vert moved to the THÉÂTRE STELLA, opening with *Adorable Julia* by Somerset Maugham. Maugham was followed by such popular French playwrights as Jean de Letraz, Jacques Deval, and Barillet Gredy. Quebec plays were also becoming more prominent in the repertoire and in an unprecedented move the company toured a Quebec play abroad in 1965. *Une maison . . . un jour* by Françoise LORANGER was presented at the Mossoviet Theatre in Moscow and at the Palace of Culture in Leningrad. At the Odéon in Paris it alternated with a production of Shakespeare's *Le Songe d'une nuit d'été (A Midsummer Night's Dream)*, which captivated the French critics. Its production of Michel TREMBLAY's *Les BELLES-SOEURS* in 1968 was highly successful, and

in 1973 the company picked another winner with Antonine MAILLET's *La SAGOUINE*. Both became international successes, an inducement to produce more Canadian plays: *ENCORE CINQ MINUTES* by Françoise Loranger in 1967 and *L'Exécution* by Marie-Claire BLAIS in 1968; *Les Posters* by Louis-Georges Carrier, *Le Coup de l'étrier* and *Avant de t'en aller* by Marcel DUBÉ in 1969; *Moi, je n'étais qu'un espoir* by Claire Martin in 1972; *Émile et une nuit* by Jean BARBEAU and *La Débâcle* by Jean Daigle in 1979; and *Albertine, en cinq temps* by Tremblay in 1984. Antonine Maillet became the company's star dramatist. With the exception of *Les Crasseux*, all her plays have premièred at Rideau Vert.

Despite the highs and lows and false starts of a heterogeneous repertoire, Le Théâtre du Rideau Vert has endured for forty years; by virtue of this fact alone it occupies a special place in the world of Quebec theatre.

NORMAND LEROUX

Théâtre du Trident, Le. Since opening in Jan. 1971, this Quebec City theatre has presented some eighty different productions in 2,000 performances to about a million spectators, in the Octave Crémazie theatre of the GRAND THÉÂTRE DE QUÉBEC. Each season offers a mixed program of Québécois works and foreign classics. Canadian productions have included works by Gratien GÉLINAS,

Théâtre du Trident

Michel TREMBLAY, Réjean DUCHARME, Antonine MAILLET, Roland LEPAGE, and Marie LABERGE; from the foreign repertoire Molière, Brecht, Chekhov, Pirandello, and Tennessee Williams have proved popular. Plays for young audiences have also been included, particularly under the leadership of author and director François Depatie in the early 1970s. On the whole, however, Trident programming has been conservative, with little experimentation with scripts or production styles.

Approximately seventy-five per cent of Trident actors and stage personnel have been residents of Quebec City—a reflection of the unusually close relationship the city's artistic community has with the theatre. Trident's twenty-eight-member board is composed of equal numbers from the general public and the artistic community, while the company's administrative council consists of four representatives from the public and four from artists, together with artistic director Guillaume de Andréa and administrative director Rémi Brousseau.   ANNE BÉDARD

Théâtre Engagé. 'L'engagement' or 'commitment' is one of the constant features of French-Canadian and Québécois theatre, although it is possible to isolate two major periods when this commitment was strongest: 1890-1935 and 1958-76.

At the end of the nineteenth century French-Canadian theatre was committed, as were other cultural activities, to building a national identity. A good many authors, companies, and shows promoted patriotism by dramatizing the great moments of national history (the origins of New France, the Conquest, the 1837 Rebellion) and celebrating the great national heroes (Maisonneuve, Dollard des Ormeaux, Montcalm) for sympathetic audiences in colleges, dramatic and literary societies, and, at the start of the twentieth century, in holiday camps and parish halls. Commitment later became propaganda as amateur theatre groups staged works whose themes restated those of the great campaigns of Catholic social action, preaching the benefits of colonization, abstinence, accepted standards of electoral behaviour, French survival in North America, and the value of Catholic art, closed retreats, and missionary work. Father Laurent Tremblay carried this campaign into comedy with some thirty plays

for the amateur companies of the Bon Théâtre that were performed in Quebec, Acadia, the U.S., and the Canadian West until the 1950s.

Professional theatrical propaganda appeared in politically important periods. During both world wars several plays advocated enlistment by portraying the atrocities committed by the enemy. The emergence of the modern trade union movement, the economic crisis of the 1930s, revolutions, and civil wars became pretexts for anti-communist propaganda. *Les Mains rouges* by Louis-Philippe Hébert, which took a position in favour of Franco against the Spanish Republic, was first produced on Radio-Canada in Jan. 1938, but only after cuts insisted upon by the Spanish Consul had been made. (The uncensored version was presented at the MONUMENT NATIONAL in Apr. 1938.) The ultimate form of this conservative commitment was the religious drama of Father Gustave LAMARCHE and others, which revived medieval dramatic conventions in the 1930s and 1940s in order to promote the Catholic religion in pageants and celebrations that brought together as many as 20,000 spectators. Father Émile LEGAULT's Les Jongleurs de la Montagne prolonged the life of this theatrical form until the 1960s.

A new route to commitment—political, secular, and progressive—was set with Jacques FERRON's plays *Les Grands Soleils* (1958) and *La Tête du roi* (1963), which initiated reinterpretations of painful moments of national history: the 1837 Rebellion and the Métis rebellions of 1870 and 1885. Quebec theatre of the 1960s also fiercely criticized Canadian federalism in the form, for example, of parodies of the two founding cultures as seen in plays such as *Hamlet, Prince du Québec* (1968) by Robert GURIK, and *Le Cid maghané* (produced in 1968) by Réjean DUCHARME. The new Quebec nationalism also gave prominence to *joual*, seeking to reappropriate French-Canadian culture, and criticizing traditional institutions such as the family. This theatre became increasingly populist, especially in the works of dramatists such as Jean BARBEAU, Jean-Claude GERMAIN, Michel TREMBLAY, and the monologuist Yvon DESCHAMPS. Prior to the 1960s radical plays were seldom produced by the major theatres and were rarely published. A sexually frank 'happening', *Double Jeu* (produced in 1969) by Françoise LORANGER, was a courageous venture.

Apart from the work of these important

Théâtre Français de Toronto

dramatists, an alternate theatre began to develop, signalling its nationalist commitment in 1972 by founding—on the dissolution of L'Association canadienne du théâtre amateur—L'Association québécoise du jeune théâtre (AQJT), and showing its social commitment in 1975 when ten companies left AQJT, denouncing it as an association that had 'become servile to bourgeois ideology' ('Manifeste', *Jeune Théâtre*, 1975). This alternate theatre, a product of the sixties counterculture movement, gained credibility with the founding of the GRAND CIRQUE ORDINAIRE, which toured collectively written plays such as *T'es pas tannée, Jeanne d'Arc*, produced in 1969, and *T'en rappelles-tu Pibrac?*, produced in 1971. This was resolutely popular theatre, decentralized—regional even—and critical not only of bourgeois society but of the conventions of theatre itself. It challenged the hierarchy of production, professionalism, and the primacy of the text by creating co-operatives (Le Parminou), by making a profession of amateurism (Le Théâtre des Cuisines), and by writing collective creations—the type of writing most used by these groups. They even called into question the autonomy of the theatre by bringing in political groups (Le Théâtre Euh!), or by associating themselves with unions, with popular groups, with the feminist movement, and by writing—to order—a drama of intervention meant to institute social or economic change. Such practices have gone beyond the Quebec borders to include Acadia (see ACADIAN THEATRE) and Le Théâtre du Nouvel-Ontario (Sudbury), where they have been developed by companies preoccupied with the political and cultural survival of francophones outside Quebec.

In Quebec the assumption of power by the Parti Québécois in 1976, and the weakening of federalism, had the effect of slowing down considerably the commitment of groups that had invested in promoting national autonomy in Quebec. The economic crisis of the 1980s put several companies out of business and drove others to compromise themselves by becoming professional. The only theatre that now retains its political commitment is that linked to movements such as ecology, feminism, or pacifism.

See also ALTERNATE THEATRE, COLLECTIVE CREATION, FEMINIST THEATRE, POLITICAL AND POPULAR THEATRE.

LUCIE ROBERT

Théâtre Français de Toronto, Le. The largest Canadian French-language theatre outside Quebec, and among the six largest theatres in Toronto, it opened in 1967 with a production of Félix LECLERC's *Le P'tit Bonheur*, naming itself Le Théâtre du P'tit Bonheur until adopting its present name in 1987. The small amateur group performed in various church halls until 1971, when John Van Burek, the company's bilingual artistic director, found a third floor office on Danforth Ave to convert into a flexible performing space seating about sixty-five. The group turned professional in 1973, and in 1978 moved to Adelaide Court, where it shared two theatres (seating 200 and 100) with OPEN CIRCLE THEATRE and NEW THEATRE. After the closing of Adelaide Court in 1987 Le Théâtre français moved to Harbourfront, where it rents the du Maurier Theatre Centre. The company plans to build its own facility at Harbourfront.

Québécois plays have featured prominently in the repertoire. In Van Burek's first tenure (1971 to 1974), nine of fifteen plays were Québécois; European playwrights such as Jean Genet, Peter Weiss, Stanislaw Witkiewicz, and Molière were also represented. An emphasis on Franco-Ontarian plays during a short-lived alliance with Sudbury's Le Théâtre du Nouvel Ontario and Ottawa's L'Atelier in the mid-1970s proved less popular in Toronto than in Sudbury and Ottawa. Between 1974 and 1976 the theatre was run by volunteer artistic directors Claire Pageau and Carmelle Brodeur. Moncton-born Eugène Gallant (artistic director, 1976-80) produced Antonine MAILLET's *La SAGOUINE*, played unforgettably by Viola Léger in French in 1979 and in English in 1980 to 93 per-cent-capacity houses, and was revived in 1988. Since his return as artistic director in 1980 Van Burek has staged a Michel TREMBLAY play most years, sometimes while the English version (translated by himself and Bill GLASSCO) played at TARRAGON THEATRE, as in the 1985 back-to-back productions of *Albertine, en cinq temps*. In 1988 Van Burek received the Toronto Drama Bench Award for his contribution to Canadian theatre.

Despite the popularity of Tremblay, European classics draw the largest audiences—Molière's *Le Malade imaginaire* (1981), *L'École des femmes* (1982), *L'Avare* (1984), and *Le Misanthrope* (1988); Carlo Goldoni's *La Locandiera* (1983); Pierre Marivaux's *Le Jeu de*

Théâtre Français de Toronto

l'amour et du hazard (1986); and Georges Fey-deau's *Le Système ribadier* (1987). Surveys indicate that forty per cent of the theatre's audience is anglophone, mostly fluent in French, while the francophones come from backgrounds as diverse as France, Africa, Quebec, Acadia, and Ontario. Toronto's French-speaking population of 300,000 provides a strong audience base, while school matinées and a flourishing children's series help build future audiences.

Designers such as Michael EAGAN, John PENNOYER, Sue LePAGE, and Louise Guinand frequently work at Le Théâtre français, and a core of strong actors such as Dennis O'Connor (outstanding in Tremblay), René Lemieux, Francine Vézina, Carmelle Le Gal, and Marie-Elaine Berthiaume are generally well received by the critics, as is Van Burek's directing.

Of the company's 1988 budget of $1 million, sixty-one per cent came from grants, thirty-two per cent from box office, and seven per cent from fund-raising. Federal contributions to the operating budget totalled $135,000, provincial $107,000, and municipal $70,000, with extra French-language funding of $55,000 from the Secretary of State. A prime concern is the 1987 deficit of $99,000, caused in part by relocation expenses; a successful 1988 season reduced this to $74,000, but such financial liabilities limit the group's ability to take risks in programming.

The archives of Le Théâtre français de Toronto are housed at the Univ. of Guelph.
LISBIE RAE

Théâtre National, Le. With the help of architect Albert Sincennes and photographer A. Racette, Julien DAOUST prepared the plans for the Théâtre National, which opened on 12 Aug. 1900 at the corner of St Catherine and Beaudry Streets in Montreal. Daoust's ambition was to promote French-language theatre, but he quickly ran into financial difficulty and was obliged to put the National into the hands of businessman Georges Gauvreau on 9 Sept. 1900. Gauvreau appointed Paul CAZENEUVE—a French actor who had become a star in the U.S.—artistic director, and under him the National began to thrive.

From 1900 to 1913—the golden age of the National—the theatre employed an array of artists from France, but from 1915 on (the war disrupting tours from France) French-

Canadian actors increasingly took the place of their French colleagues playing melodramas, dramas, comedies, and even some Canadian plays. The many difficulties of the theatrical business during war dealt a severe blow to the National. In 1918 the Spanish influenza epidemic forced the theatre to close, although Paul Gury brought new life and a new style to it between 1919 and 1921.

Following two poor seasons the National began to offer BURLESQUE shows with the Pizzy-Wizzy troupe in 1923. The success of this new approach was consolidated after 1936 under the brilliant direction of Rose Ouellette and her company. Several important comedians emerged from the National at this time (Manda Parent, Pizzy-Wizzy, Caroline, Olivier GUIMOND—father and son—and Swifty).

The arrival of television in 1952, together with the new vogue for CABARET, brought an end to more than fifty years of theatre at the National. Today it operates as the 'Cinéma du Village', showing pornographic films to a homosexual clientele.   DENIS CARRIER

Theatre Network. Edmonton's Theatre Network, like Saskatoon's 25TH STREET THEATRE, was founded 'specifically to mirror prairie life through drama,' thus creating 'a network of common awareness among people who share a cultural heritage.'

Although they premièred George RYGA's *Seven Hours to Sundown* in 1976, the company (composed of Jonathan C. Barker, Jeurgen Beerwald, Shay Garner, Dennis Robinson, Tanya Ryga, and artistic director Mark Manson) functioned largely as a collective between 1975 and 1980, working from project to project rather than on a seasonal basis, and in various locations. They opened in Sept. 1975 with *Two Miles Off*, a COLLECTIVE CREATION about the small town of Elnora, Alta. Theatre Network scored its first major success in 1977 with *Hard Hats and Stolen Hearts: A Tar Sand Myth*. Written by the company with the help of dramaturges Gordon Pengilly and Leslie Saunders, the play toured Alberta, eastern Canada, and New York over the 1977-8 season. Both productions also appeared at 25th Street Theatre, with which Theatre Network has maintained a close association. The following two years (1978-80) were marked more by revivals and workshop projects than by new collective work.

Following Mark Manson's resignation in 1980, the company re-organized from a collective into a community theatre offering a regular season, although the original mandate remained. Retaining Andras Tahn of 25th Street Theatre as a consulting artistic director for the early part of the 1980-1 season, Network acquired the former dance studio Espace Tournesol, Edmonton, as a home and mounted three productions (including a co-production of *Rumpelstiltskin Busts Out* by E.H. Carefoot with 25th Street Theatre), held public readings of the Clifford E. Lee playwriting competition winners, and hosted a weekly Twilight Series, featuring a potpourri of offerings by local artists.

With the 1981 appointment of Stephen Heatley as artistic director, the theatre entered a new period of consolidation and growth. Interpreting the company's mandate as a commitment to broaden the base of local dramatic activity and to stage new work by prairie and particularly Albertan playwrights, the new administration expanded Network's activities in both directions. In co-operation with other groups, or independently, the theatre has premièred work by several prairie playwrights—including Paul Gross, Kelly Rebar, Lyle Victor Albert, and Kenneth Brown—and has particularly helped foster the careers of Raymond Storey (*Country Chorale*, 1982, *Angel of Death*, 1984, and *Something in the Wind*, 1986) and Governor General Award nominees Frank Moher (*Odd Jobs*, 1985, *The Third Ascent*, 1987) and Michael McKinlay (*Walt and Roy*, 1985, *Penguins*, 1987). The theatre has also mounted its own collective musicals: *The Other Side of the Pole* in 1982 and *Working Title* in 1984. Many Network plays have toured, or been produced elsewhere, and both Lyle Albert and Raymond Storey have occupied the playwright-in-residence position begun in 1983-4. Since 1983 the theatre has run a drama-training program for teenagers (Youtheatre Network). Beginning in 1981-2 it introduced the improvisational game THEATRESPORTS to the city on a weekly basis, making Edmonton an active centre in the national Theatresports network. MOIRA DAY

Theatre New Brunswick. Theatre New Brunswick had its beginnings in Lord Beaverbrook's gift of a playhouse, in Fredericton, to the people of New Brunswick. The Beaverbrook Auditorium Act (1961) established the 'Beaverbrook Auditorium', with its Board of Governors appointed by the province and by the Beaverbrook Foundation. The 1,000-seat PLAYHOUSE, the only professional theatre building in New Brunswick at that time, opened in 1964 with Alexander Gray as its director. Gray and his successor, Brian Swarbrick (1966-8), ran the Playhouse more as a civic than a provincial theatre. Gray founded an amateur drama group, The Company of Ten, which provided Fredericton with light entertainment. Under its first two directors, however, the Playhouse functioned largely as a rental hall for touring orchestras, ballet, and theatre companies. Professional summer theatre seasons were mounted in 1966 and 1967 with the financial assistance of the Beaverbrook Foundation.

With the appointment in May 1968 of Walter LEARNING as the Playhouse's artistic director, TNB began to take shape. Funding a summer season on box office receipts alone, Learning mounted professional productions of light fare: André Roussin's *The Little Hut*, Muriel Resnik's *Any Wednesday*, Benn Levy's *Springtime for Henry*, and Neil Simon's *Barefoot in the Park*. With a budget of $20,000, the venture ended with a deficit of only $100. Having thus proved himself to his Board, Learning moved to fulfil Beaverbrook's mandate that the Playhouse serve the whole province. With a small grant from the Foundation ($15,000), Learning established TNB as a touring company with close administrative links to the Playhouse. During the winter of 1969 TNB travelled to provincial centres with Leslie Stevens' *The Marriage-Go-Round*, John Osborne's *Inadmissible Evidence* (cast largely with Univ. of New Brunswick students), Marc Camoletti's *Boeing Boeing*, and Tennessee Williams' *The Glass Menagerie*. The circuit was 650 miles long, and New Brunswick became the country's only province with its own provincial touring company. During the next few years TNB's main focus was on the development of a theatre audience. Beginning with seasons composed mostly of British and American comedies, Learning gradually widened both his touring circuit and the appeal of his offerings. By 1971 TNB's home base of Fredericton was selling 3,500 season subscriptions in a population centre of 35,000. On the basis of TNB's provincial achievement the Beaverbrook Foundation agreed to fund major renovations to the Playhouse. Structural

Theatre New Brunswick

changes, including the addition of a fly gallery, were completed in 1972. TNB then had a 763-seat home base, a two-week touring circuit of 1,300 miles, and a production budget of a quarter-of-a-million dollars.

Much of Learning's time during his ten years in Fredericton was spent travelling throughout the province in a successful effort to strengthen TNB's foundations. In 1974 he began the TNB Young Company, a small group (eventually bilingual) of young professionals who carried theatre to provincial schools. As well, Learning began a collaboration with poet/playwright Alden NOWLAN that provided TNB with successful original scripts.

In 1978 Learning was succeeded by Malcolm BLACK, who brought twenty years of wide-ranging experience in Canadian and American theatre. During his six years (1978–84) as TNB's artistic director, subscriptions doubled to over 10,000, the renewal rate was over ninety per cent, and box-office revenue continued to rise. Black expanded the tradition of working with local playwrights, introduced provincial audiences to operas by Mozart, Humperdinck, and Britten, and challenged subscribers with demanding productions of Shaw, Beckett, and Shakespeare cast with some of Canada's leading professionals.

With the arrival from Ontario's BLYTH FESTIVAL of Janet AMOS in 1984, TNB went in new directions. Instead of a balance between established international playwrights and new Canadian works, Amos leaned heavily on recent Canadian scripts. She also experimented with a second stage, offering to the Fredericton audience productions of scripts from the international repertoire that would be impossible to mount within the touring framework of TNB. In the 1985-6 season TNB's budget rose to $1.3 million and its audience averaged around 11,000 per production. In 1988 Amos was succeeded as artistic director by Sharon POLLOCK.

While its base remains in Fredericton, TNB now tours all of its mainstage productions to nine provincial centres, and travels occasionally to other provinces. Its bilingual Young Company performs over 300 times a year in schools throughout the Maritimes.

EDWARD MULLALY

Kenneth Wickes and Barbara Stephen in The Dollar Woman *by Walter Learning and Alden Nowlan, Theatre New Brunswick, 1977*

Theatre Newfoundland and Labrador. Founded in 1979 in Stephenville, Nfld, by actor/playwright Maxim Mazumdar (1953-88), it was the first Newfoundland professional theatre company outside St John's. An offshoot of the Provincial Drama Academy—founded at Stephenville (also in 1979) to provide professional training to students throughout Newfoundland and Labrador—TNL produces a wide range of works from the classical and modern repertoire: David FRENCH's *Salt-Water Moon*, John GRAY's *BILLY BISHOP GOES TO WAR*, Bernard SLADE's *Same Time, Next Year*, Arthur Miller's *Death of a Salesman*, Tennessee Williams' *The Glass Menagerie* and *A Streetcar Named Desire*, as well as such musicals as *My Fair Lady*, *Oliver*, *Fiddler on the Roof*, and *Cabaret*. Under artistic director Edmund McLean the company also complements and enhances the secondary-school curriculum with a touring program of plays from a broad range of historical periods and genres. The company is supported by federal and provincial government grants and individual and corporate donations. Now based in Corner Brook, it operates out of the ARTS AND CULTURE CENTRE, maintains a close relationship with the Stephenville Festival, and its actors continue to take courses at the Provincial Drama Academy.   C.J. SKINNER

Theatre Passe Muraille. It was founded in 1968 by Jim GARRARD at Rochdale College, an experimental educational facility near the Univ. of Toronto. Its mandate calls for 'an exploration of the theatre in society,' and proclaims (in Antonin Artaud's words) that 'theatre is event, not architecture.' To this end Theatre Passe Muraille ('Theatre without Walls') has developed a style of performance and play development that is not reliant on the physical reality of a theatre building.

Since its inception, TPM's goal has been to delete artificial boundaries between actors and audience. Theatre as event is meant to link the spectator to the performer, joining their experience of the theatrical moment and uniting them. Thus the concept of 'theatre without walls' refers in part to theatre that reaches past the imaginary fourth wall of the stage. In keeping with the commitment to community involvement, the original mandate of the theatre stated its intention to keep ticket prices accessible: no more than $1.50 per ticket.

Over its subsequent history, the aims and goals of TPM have remained essentially the same. While it is no longer feasible to charge so little for a ticket, the theatre has a low-cost subscription series and maintains (as do other theatres in the country) a Sunday Pay-What-You-Can matinée.

The theatre's most controversial early production (at the Central Library Theatre) was Rochelle Owens' *Futz*. Obscenity charges were laid against the producer, director, and actors, but were subsequently quashed (see CENSORSHIP). Partially as a result of the furore, and in order to build a more professional company, Garrard reorganized the group and moved it to a church hall at 11 Trinity Square. He hoped to work towards the socially committed ensemble theatre he had envisioned, producing plays such as Genet's *The Maids* and John PALMER's *Memories for My Brother. Part I—Before the Guns*.

Garrard resigned in 1969 to teach theatre at Simon Fraser University in British Columbia, and the artistic leadership of the ensemble fell first to Martin KINCH (1969-71) and then to Paul THOMPSON in 1972. Despite these changes, the collective artistic policy-making

continued, with each member of the group tending towards different themes and different styles of performance.

A COLLECTIVE CREATION, *Doukhobors*, produced in Apr. 1971, was a DOCUMENTARY DRAMA built from the contribution of the entire ensemble and shaped by Thompson. Carol BOLT's *Buffalo Jump* followed in 1972, and the nationally acclaimed *The FARM SHOW*—which premièred at Clinton, Ont., in 1972—popularized the method and product of the collective process and brought TPM to the attention of the general public. Other early collective plays include *1837: The Farmers' Revolt*, written with Rick SALUTIN and produced in Jan. 1973; *Under the Grey-wacke*, produced in Aug. 1973; and *I Love You, Baby Blue*, produced in Jan. 1975. *I Love You, Baby Blue*, which examined the morals and mores of modern Toronto society, created a furore (because of its many nude scenes) equal to that caused by *Futz* six years before. The popularity and financial success of the show allowed TPM to buy its present building at 16 Ryerson Ave, in a sense ending the era of wholly movable theatre, but also giving the spirit of TPM a space to take root and grow. The building had been, among other things, a candy factory, bakery, and stable, but it was a space flexible enough to accommodate various styles of production with seating ranging from 200 to 400. Renovations (designed by Jim PLAXTON) took place in 1984 to increase seating capacity, improve sight-lines, and provide improved facilities for audiences, staff, and actors.

One of the most successful productions at Ryerson Ave was *Maggie and Pierre*, written by Linda GRIFFITHS with Paul Thompson and produced in Nov. 1979. This one-person show depicting Prime Minister Pierre Trudeau's relationship with his wife, and offering the additional perspective of an Ottawa reporter, played across Canada, was produced off-Broadway by Phoenix Theatre, and has been filmed for television. This production epitomized Thompson's ability to encourage Canadian artists (and audiences) to see how the lives and events of the present day can be the stuff of a distinct Canadian mythology.

Thompson retired as artistic director of TPM in 1982 and was succeeded by the then associate director Clarke Rogers. Rogers' commitment to new Canadian play development led to a continuing growth in TPM's Seed Show Program (playwrights are funded

Theatre Passe Muraille

in the research, developmental, and workshop stages of their projects) and an ongoing emphasis on producing new Canadian plays. Thompson continued his involvement in the theatre (he has called himself 'resident idealogue'). Although Rogers worked more with scripted material, Thompson's collective methods are still very much in evidence. The honesty of the plays, the immediate relationship of the actor to the play and to the audiences, and in turn the audience's recognition of the universality in the portrayal of recognizable personalities and events all prove that the goals of Theatre Passe Muraille have been achieved and sustained. In 1988 Brian Richmond and Jane Buss were appointed to succeed Rogers, who resigned in Nov. 1987.

The archives of Theatre Passe Muraille are housed at the Univ. of Guelph.

JUDITH RUDAKOFF

Théâtre Patagon, Le. Opened in a large home on the Côte de la Canoterie, near the Hope Gate in Quebec City, by a Mr Ormsby (manager of the Albany Theatre, N.Y.) on 15 Oct. 1804, with John O'Keeffe's comic opera *The Castle of Andalusia* and Isaac Bickerstaffe's farce *The Absent Man*, it accommodated some 200 people. After a short and unprofitable season Ormsby moved his company to Montreal, and a group of French-Canadian amateurs performed plays by Molière and Philippe Destouches at the Patagon, as well as two performances of Joseph QUESNEL'S *COLAS ET COLINETTE*. During the summer of 1805 the building and its theatrical accessories were unsuccessfully offered for sale for £800, and Ormsby opened another season in Oct. In Nov., however, he appears to have returned to Albany and there is no further record of the theatre.

JOHN E. HARE

Theatre Plus. Founded in Toronto in 1973 by Marion ANDRE, who remained artistic director until 1985, Theatre Plus has disproved two common misconceptions about summer theatre: that audiences will not attend theatre in the city during hot weather, and that performances they *do* attend must be frivolous. Adopting a mandate to produce unfamiliar works—frequently Canadian premières—by internationally renowned playwrights (especially plays addressing important moral and political issues), Andre opened at the 500-seat Town Hall (renamed

the Jane MALLETT Theatre in 1985) in the ST LAWRENCE CENTRE with a season of three serious comedies: Joe Orton's *Loot*, Keith Waterhouse's and Willis Hall's *Say Who You Are*, and John Guare's *The House of Blue Leaves*. The ten-week season attracted some 15,000 spectators, leading to an expanded second season of four productions: Christopher Hampton's *The Philanthropist*, Lillian Hellman's *The Little Foxes*, Hugh Leonard's *The Au Pair Man*, and Jean Anouilh's *The Rehearsal*. In subsequent seasons plays by Friedrich Dürrenmatt (whose *Physicists* was a success of the 1975 season), Trevor Griffiths, Luigi Pirandello, Frank Wedekind, Brendan Behan, David Rabe, Tennessee Williams, Arthur Miller, Eugene O'Neill, Anton Chekhov, and Henrik Ibsen have sustained Theatre Plus's mandate. The first Canadian play produced at Theatre Plus was Michel TREMBLAY'S *Forever Yours, Marie-Lou* (*À TOI, POUR TOUJOURS, TA MARIE-LOU*) in 1976; in 1977 Andre made a commitment to produce one Canadian play each season. In 1981 an annual January production was introduced.

Major actors—among them Douglas RAIN, Frances HYLAND, Alan SCARFE, Donald DAVIS, Jennifer PHIPPS, Richard MONETTE, and Brenda DONOHUE—have appeared at Theatre Plus, and guest directors have included Tom KERR, Kurt REIS, R.H. THOMSON, Jackie Maxwell, and Robert Rooney. Malcolm BLACK—a frequent guest director—succeeded Andre as artistic director in 1986 and has consolidated Theatre Plus's position as a distinct summer alternative to the STRATFORD, SHAW, and other Ontario seasonal theatre festivals.

The archives of Theatre Plus are housed at the Univ. of Guelph.   STEPHEN JOHNSON

Théâtre Populaire du Québec, Le. Founded in 1963 by Jean Valcourt, with the support of the Ministry of Cultural Affairs and a mandate to 'take the theatre to places where it doesn't exist', TPQ has now toured over seventy productions to more than forty towns in Quebec as well as to New Brunswick, Ontario, and New England. Under Valcourt the company presented a traditional repertoire that included Corneille, Racine, Molière, Musset, Feydeau, Anouilh, and Pirandello—much the same kind of repertoire that dominated the programs of all Quebec theatres during the mid-1960s.

Albert Millaire—who succeeded Valcourt

in 1969—wagered, however, that within three years the company would have a program in which eight out of ten plays would be by Quebec authors. He quickly integrated productions of Le GRAND CIRQUE ORDINAIRE into TPQ's touring schedule, providing that intractable, helter-skelter company with wide exposure: the first TPQ/GCO tour, the COLLECTIVE *T'es pas tannée, Jeanne d'Arc?*, played to 100,000 people. The 1971 *T'en rappelles-tu Pibrac?*—about cultural and political repression in Quebec—was suppressed by the government and Millaire was dismissed.

Jean-Guy SABOURIN, artistic director from 1972 to 1976, reaffirmed TPQ's commitment to Québécois works. Nine of his fourteen productions were by Quebec playwrights—including Marcel DUBÉ, Jean BARBEAU, Roch CARRIER, and André Major. The company's fourth director, Jean-Yves Gaudreault (1976-9), established a seasonal three-production formula: one Quebec work, one classical, and one modern play. He abandoned the policy of commissioning texts, preferring to produce those that had already gained success elsewhere—for example, *Bousille et les justes* by Gratien GÉLINAS, and *Le Temps d'une vie* by Roland LEPAGE, which toured Canada before appearing at France's Avignon Festival in the summer of 1979.

Nicole Filion, who became artistic director in 1979, continued the policy of her predecessor while improving the company's administration. Her productions have included *Bernadette et Juliette* by Elizabeth Bourget, *La Famille Toucourt en solo ce soir* by Eric Anderson, *Un Pays dont la devise est je m'oublie* by Jean-Claude GERMAIN, *À TOI, POUR TOUJOURS, TA MARIE-LOU* and *Albertine, en cinq temps* by Michel TREMBLAY, *Les Enfants de silence* (*Children of a Lesser God*) by Mark Medoff, and *Camille C.* by Jocelyne Beaulieu and René-Richard Cyr.

ADRIEN GRUSLIN

Theatre Royal (Halifax). Known also as the Garrison Amateur Theatre and Spring Gardens Theatre, the Theatre Royal was constructed from a large hay barn at Spring Gardens by the Garrison Amateurs, who opened on 2 Dec. 1846 with J. Maddison Morton's *The Sentinel* and Thomas Bayly's *You Can't Marry Your Grandmother*, afterwards offering subscription series annually into the 1850s. Beginning on 19 June 1856,

Isherwood and Stewart's New York Company presented two months of legitimate drama. On 22 June 1857 E.A. Sothern opened with W. Bayle Bernard's *The Mummy* and Dion Boucicault's *The Willow Copse*, remaining for a winter season so financially disastrous that benefit performances were necessary to enable the company to return home. Nevertheless Sothern returned for the summers of 1858 and 1859. His scene painter, a Mr Selwyn, designed renovations to the building—which was renamed Sothern's Lyceum—removing private boxes, adding a gallery, and transforming what had recently been termed 'our miserable apology for a theatre' into 'a little gem'. *Hopkins City Atlas of Halifax* (1878) shows the building fronting on Queen St, though it had originally stood back, its front displaying three evenly spaced entrance doors, three shuttered windows on the second floor, and a low-pitched gable roof. Originally the Theatre Royal contained a 'small' pit of undetermined size, boxes to seat 'over 160 people' on red baize-covered benches that were insufficiently inclined, and a private box hung with glazed cotton curtains, large enough for six. Walls were pink, drop curtains green, and the scene painting done 'by the Lady of an officer'. Lighted by gas, and with only one stove in the pit, the theatre was 'literally as cold as a Barn' in winter. In the 1860s amateurs were the chief occupants, though Moses W. Fiske, complaining of the lack of a proper theatre in Halifax, managed summer seasons in 1865-7. After 1868 companies used the Temperance Hall. An exception was a performance given by the Amateurs of the 60th Rifles in Feb. 1874. The Theatre Royal was torn down in 1885.

MARY ELIZABETH SMITH

Theatre Royal, Haymarket. Quebec City's first theatre was housed on the second storey of a building at the corner of Queen Anne and Garden Streets, near the hay market. The hall opened in 1790 with a season of amateur French theatricals, and was used irregularly for the next several years. In 1805 a new theatre was built on the same site, eventually becoming known as the Haymarket, or Theatre Royal Hay-Market. Although very small, seating perhaps 200 spectators, the theatre was equipped with front and back boxes, gallery, and pit. The first manager was a Mr Ormsby, who led a small professional company. Performances were also given by officers of the garrison and other amateur groups, both French and English. In the summer of 1818 a professional company from Montreal presented a series of classical and contemporary plays, after which the hall reverted to amateur use until 1824, when it ceased to function as a theatre after the opening of the more spacious Royal Circus (see THEATRE ROYAL, Quebec City). From 1824 to 1831 it was used as a meeting-house and Masonic Hall and for occasional concerts and lectures. After extensive renovation, it reopened as a theatre on 25 July 1831, and from Aug. to mid-Sept. was engaged by a largely American company headed by Vincent DeCamp. This company also included William Forrest, brother of Edwin, and Frederick BROWN. The high point of the season was the appearance of Charles Kean for four performances in mid-Aug. The Haymarket rapidly fell into disuse after the 1832 reopening of the renovated Royal Circus. It became an auction-room and, in 1835, a gymnasium, although it was still used occasionally for exhibitions until at least 1836.   SUSAN M. WILLIAMS

Theatre Royal (Montreal). In the later months of 1824 and early 1825 a group of interested citizens, predominantly English merchants led by John Molson, agreed to establish the first permanent theatre building in Montreal. Ninety joint stock subscribers, with Molson as the major shareholder, financed the building, which opened on 21 Nov. 1825. Located on the southwest corner of St Paul and Victor Streets, the theatre was 50′ wide, 110′ deep, and 32′ in height from the level of St Paul Street. The main entrance opened onto a salon that led to two tiers of boxes with a gallery above the boxes. Along the sides of the upper house were slips and in front of the stage the pit benches. The theatre held approximately 1,000 spectators. The stage had a full proscenium arch, windows above the two proscenium doors, and the overhead angled to act as a sound board. The orchestra was below and in front of the forestage, divided from the pit by a low wooden partition. The basement storey below the stage held two dressing rooms and a green room; two flights of stairs led to the stage.

Frederick BROWN, first manager of the Theatre Royal, gathered a company of some fifty actors, technicians, and musicians who carried out an extensive first season of 100 nights, including guest appearances by R.C. Maywood, Eliza Riddle, Thomas S. Hamblin, Mrs Gilfert, and Edmund Kean. Kean's appearances in late July and August were the highlight of the season, which comprised 111 different full-length plays and after-pieces. This, however, was not sufficient to prevent an overall loss for the season and Brown was forced to give up his lease on 31 Oct. 1826.

Following two years of housing amateur performances, the theatre was leased by Vincent DeCamp, who was to occupy the position of manager longer than anyone else. DeCamp presented three summer seasons between 1829 and 1833. There was no theatre in 1830 and a cholera epidemic prevented public entertainments in 1832. DeCamp brought Clara Fisher, Mr and Mrs Edward Knight, James Hackett, Edwin Forrest, Charles Kean, Charles Kemble, and Fanny Kemble to play in Montreal at different times during his management.

After DeCamp, the theatre was leased on a yearly basis to a succession of managers from England and the U.S., none of whom were financially successful. Over the years the frequency of performances fell rapidly and civic disorders in 1837 limited all public performances. Companies of actors from Boston, New York, or Philadelphia spent one or two months each summer in Montreal and Quebec City. On occasion leading personalities—such as Charles Dickens, William Macready, William Dowton, Ellen Tree, and Miss Jean Davenport—made brief appearances at the Theatre Royal.

In 1844 the theatre, then owned solely by

Theatre Royal, Montreal

Frederick Brown and Eliza Riddle in James Sheridan Knowles's Virginius, Theatre Royal, Montreal, 1825

the Molson family, was sold and razed to make way for the Bonsecours Market.

A. OWEN KLEIN

A second Theatre Royal opened on 10 July 1847. Popularly known as the Hays House, it was located at the corner of Notre Dame St and Dalhousie Square in the posterior hall of a new four-and-a-half storey building built by John Wells for Moses Hays. The auditorium seated 2,400, the stage measured 110' by 76', and the proscenium featured four large fluted columns. The first season—under the management of George SKERRETT—was remarkable for a flurry of well-received Shakespeare performances. In July, James Wallack appeared as Benedick in *Much Ado About Nothing*, Shylock, and Hamlet, and in August James Anderson played Hamlet, Macbeth, and Othello. Neither as intimate nor as acoustically pleasing as its predecessor, this Theatre Royal was soon considered inadequate for drama. By June—after a season managed by Henry Preston—the interior fittings had been sold to Jesse Joseph and stored for use in a playhouse not yet built, also to

be named Theatre Royal. The Hays building was destroyed on 9 July 1852 in a Montreal fire that left thousands of people homeless.

Joseph's Theatre Royal, again designed by John Wells, was built two storeys high at Côté and Craig Sts. Innovative safety features included doors that swung either in or out, windows placed within seven feet of the floor, and access lanes nine feet wide on both sides of the building, extending to a back lane eighteen feet wide. The exterior featured a large carriage entrance and an Anglo-Italian style portico. Overlooking the pit benches, which extended from the stage to the back of the house, were two tiers of boxes linked by a staircase. There was no gallery to restrict the rise of the box seats, all of which afforded an excellent view of the stage. The drop-curtain, a likeness of Windsor Castle, came from the Hays Theatre. The auditorium seated 1,500, and was so constructed that a prefabricated floor, kept in storage, could be laid over the pit from stage to boxes to make a hall suitable for promenade concerts or public meetings.

The theatre opened on 31 May 1852 under

Theatre Royal (Montreal)

the management of John Wellington BUCKLAND, who remained until the end of the 1868 season and returned briefly during the early part of 1870 and again in 1872. After Buckland—following short tenures by several others—the manager most continuously associated with the theatre was J.B. Sparrow (1879–1913), who for some years (1884–8) was in partnership with H.R. Jacobs. The long list of leading actors who appeared at the theatre includes Clara Fisher (1852, 1854), Agnes Robertson (1853, 1860), Charles Mathews (1858), Barry Sullivan (1859), Charles Dillon (1861, 1866), Charles Kean and Ellen Tree (Mrs Charles Kean) (1865), Dominick Murray (1871), Thomas C. King (1874), Adelaide Neilson (1877, 1880), Sarah Bernhardt (1880, 1891, 1896), Tomasso Salvini (1881), Lily Langtry (1883), and Sir Henry Irving (1884, 1894–5). John Wilkes Booth was a member of Buckland's stock company for a few months prior to his assassination of President Lincoln in Apr. 1865.

The main centre for dramatic and musical performance in Montreal until 1875, the Theatre Royal's advancing age and increased competition from other theatres and concert halls made its existence precarious in the last decades of the century. Extensive remodelling to the interior of the theatre before the 1900–1 season extended the theatre's life, but it was finally condemned and torn down in 1913.   GORDON TWEEDIE

Theatre Royal (Quebec City). Constructed in 1824 by the American promoters William West and C.W. Blanchard and originally named the Royal Circus it was located behind a hotel on the rue Saint-Jean, with access by a passage off rue Saint-Stanislas. The building was designed as an equestrian theatre with facilities for animal and acrobatic spectacles on the parterre and legitimate drama on the stage. Some 1,000 spectators could be accommodated.

In its first two years the house featured equestrian melodrama, horsemanship exhibitions, pantomimes, ballets, and the occasional play. The apogee of the West-Blanchard management came with the appearance of Edmund Kean in Sept. 1826. Other distinguished visitors included the touring stars Robert Campbell Maywood, Thomas Hamblin, and Mrs Jack Barnes. West and Blanchard gave up the management in the autumn of 1826; for the next five years local ama

teurs, garrison performers (see GARRISON THEATRE), and brief appearances by Clara Fisher (1829), Céline Céleste (1829), and Charles Kean (1831) were the principal attractions. In 1831 the building was sold to Chief Justice Henry Sewall, who remodelled it and leased it to a Mr Logan. Renamed Theatre Royal, it reopened on 15 Feb. 1832 with a renovated auditorium that was circular in shape and had two tiers of boxes around the greater part of its circumference and a large gallery. The shallow stage was flanked on either side by heavy white proscenium doors, each of which was surmounted by a box. Since most performances were given by garrison players and other local amateurs, visits by Charles and Fanny Kemble (1833), Vincent DeCamp's company (1833), and Céline Céleste (1835) were particularly welcomed.

Thomas Ward became manager in June 1836 and operated the theatre until late in 1839, when Sewall died and his family closed the building. Highlights of Ward's management were appearances by Ellen Tree in Sept. 1838 and, a year later, by the English actor-manager Thomas Donald Davenport and his ten-year-old daughter Jean, a prodigy who played Richard III and similarly inappropriate roles. Also worthy of note was a political skirmish in Oct. 1839 when a pro-Patriotes revival of Voltaire's *La Mort de César* roused the ire of English civil authorities.

The Sewall heirs permitted the theatre to reopen late in 1840, and for the next six years it featured equilibrists, illusionists, amateur theatricals, and, in July 1844, a concert by the Norwegian violinist Ole Bull. St Patrick's Church purchased the building in Sept. 1846 and promptly demolished it to construct a hall for the St Patrick's Catholic Institute.

See Pierre-Georges Roy, 'Le Cirque Royal ou Théâtre Royal', *Le Bulletin des recherches historiques*, 42 (1936).   JOHN RIPLEY

Theatre Royal (Victoria, B.C.). Originally known as the Victoria, this 600-seat theatre opened on 3 Jan. 1861 with the Robinson family in John Tobin's *The Honeymoon*. By 22 Jan. the Robinsons were replaced by the combined companies of John S. Potter and James Stark, a Canadian-born actor, who appeared intermittently for the rest of the year while the theatre was enlarged to accommodate over 700 in a 129′ × 48′ room. Beginning in Dec. 1861 a reorganized Potter company played for a month, returning as

548

the Bell-Potter troupe from 16 Aug. to 20 Dec. 1862, and again, as the Potter Company from 22 Dec. 1862 to 5 May 1863. During these years Victorians saw such plays as *Hamlet* (5 performances); E. Bulwer-Lytton's *Richelieu* (6) and *The Lady of Lyons* (4); *The Lady of Lions* (4), a burlesque by O.E. Durivage; *The Brigands* by James Planché; *Ten Nights in a Bar Room* by William Pratt; and several plays by Dion Boucicault, including *London Assurance* (3), *The Corsican Brothers* (2), and *Jessie Brown; or The Relief of Lucknow*.

The next important company at the Victoria was that of Thomas Ward, an Englishman, playing from 26 Oct. 1863 to 19 Feb. 1864, 5 Oct. 1864 to 18 Feb. 1865, and from 13 Oct. to 11 Dec. 1865 (a major Australian-American actress, Mrs Fanny Morgan Phelps, appeared in the latter engagement). In the ten months of Ward's tenancy, the company offered popular plays, relying heavily on twelve dramas by Boucicault, including *Jessie Brown* (12), *The Colleen Bawn* (8), and *The Octoroon* (8), and three plays by Bulwer-Lytton: *The Lady of Lyons* (3), *Money* (2), and *Richelieu* (2). August Kotzebue's *The Stranger* (4) was popular, as were George L. Aiken's *Uncle Tom's Cabin* (4), and Douglas Jerrold's *Nell Gwynne* (6) and *Black-Eyed Susan* (5).

For nine nights, 12-21 Dec. 1864, the theatre was packed when Charles and Ellen (Tree) Kean visited, *en route* home to England from Australia via San Francisco. Supported by the Ward company, the Keans' most popular productions were *Louis XI* (Boucicault), *Macbeth*, *Hamlet*, and *King Lear*.

R.G. Marsh, who had performed with his juvenile company at the Victoria in 1863, took it over in July 1865, but used it only sixteen times before renovating and renaming it the Theatre Royal in mid-1867. Until its demolition in 1882, it was the only regular playhouse in Victoria. (Alhambra Hall offered plays briefly in 1874.) Even so, it was closed for extended periods: ten months in 1876; seven months on five other occasions. It housed only 538 performances in fifteen years.

A few visiting American companies had long runs: J.W. Carter (six weeks); F.M. Bates (twelve weeks); Fanny Morgan Phelps (nine visits, forty-one weeks). J.B. Robinson returned after a twelve-year absence, when his company remounted five former productions: Charles Dance's *Naval Engagements*,

Lawrence Hanray's *Betsy Baker*, T.H. Bayly's *The Barrack Room*, *Black-Eyed Susan*, and J.B. Buckstone's *A Kiss in the Dark*. Boucicault's plays remained in the repertoire of visiting companies, the most popular being *The Colleen Bawn* (8), *The Streets of New York* (7), *Dot, or The Cricket on the Hearth* (5), and *Jessie Brown* (4). Of Bulwer-Lytton's plays, only *The Lady of Lyons* (12) had a continuing popularity. Other plays frequently presented were *Uncle Tom's Cabin* (13), Mrs Henry Wood's *East Lynne* (11), and Augustin Daly's *Under the Gaslight*.

Other performance venues in Victoria attempted to fill the void left by the 1882 demolition of the Theatre Royal. From 22 Feb. to 21 Apr. 1883 American touring manager Alf Wyman ran the St Charles Music Hall—part of the St Charles Hotel—which he had renovated from a seating capacity of 200 to 400 and renamed the New Theatre Royal. Subsequently run by Amos Arnold and C. Farleman as the London Theatre, Oct.-Dec. 1883, and by Henry Graham from Sept. to Nov. 1884, it was apparently not a successful theatrical venue. On 1 Jan. 1894 the Philharmonic Hall (built in 1873, renovated and renamed the Imperial in 1891)

The Alf Wyman Stock Co. production of Little Eva and Uncle Tom, *New Theatre Royal, Victoria, 1883*

Theatre Royal (Victoria)

reopened as another Theatre Royal, but closed on 7 Feb. 1894, reverting to the Philharmonic Hall.   ROBERT G. LAWRENCE

Theatresports. Founded in 1977 by Keith Johnstone at Calgary's Loose Moose Theatre Company, Theatresports is an improvisational game performed by teams of actors before a live audience and a panel of judges. It is now played in organized leagues in several Canadian and U.S. cities and in Europe and Australia. (The LIGUE NATIONALE D'IM-PROVISATION is a comparable development in Quebec.) In addition to its performance value, Theatresports is an important means of actor training (in theatre companies, schools, and universities) and audience development.

The rules of Theatresports vary in minor details from place to place, but the basic components remain the same: two teams of actors compete in improvisation before a panel of judges; a coin flip determines who will begin, and that team holds the stage until it loses it either to a challenge from the other team or for boring the audience or judges. Penalties (sitting with one's head in a paper bag) are incurred for obscenity or harassment. Points are awarded by the judges not only for the quality of each improvisation, but for duration, in order to discourage brief and undeveloped scenes ending in one-liners. Audience members are encouraged to respond to the action vocally or by throwing foam bricks, or even custard pies, at the participants or judges.

Although Theatresports has been criticized for cultivating cheap tricks and clowning, the value of the form when practised properly lies in freeing actors to respond more openly in all types of rehearsal situations, and in encouraging more active participation and response than is usual among theatre audiences. See Keith Johnstone, *Impro: Improvisation and the Theatre* (1981).

RICHARD PAUL KNOWLES

Théâtre Stella, Le. This 443-seat theatre on Montreal's rue Saint-Denis opened in 1912 as the Chantecler. The Bella Ouellette company appeared there in 1924 and the Barry-Duquesne company in 1927. Briefly a cinema in 1929, the Chantecler became the Théâtre Stella in 1930, again occupied by Fred BARRY and Albert DUQUESNE with a company that included director Antoine Godeau and actors

Bella Ouellette, Antoinette GIROUX, Marthe THIÉRY, Mimi d'Estée, Jeanne Demons, Jeanne Deslauriers, Gaston Dauriac, Henry DEYGLUN, and Pierre Durand (who put up the $5,000 to start the theatre). On 11 Aug. 1930 the Stella opened with *La Lettre* by Somerset Maugham. An instant hit, it heralded two successful seasons (with a new show each week) of VAUDEVILLE, light comedy, and Parisian hits. For the first time in the history of Quebec theatre a French-Canadian company offered a viable alternative to visiting companies from abroad. In the third season, however, there were signs of flagging that coincided with the arrival of a new artistic director, Henri Letondal, whose revue *Stelle-ci Stella* played for four weeks, but under whom box-office receipts declined. Even Paul Gury's well-known play about venereal disease—*Le mortel baiser*—drew poor crowds. In addition, a fire interrupted the run of Marcel Pagnol's *Marius*, a potential hit.

Letondal's company returned, however, in Sept. 1933 as the Académie canadienne d'art dramatique, with new members Germaine GIROUX, Ferdinand Biondi, André Laurent, Liliane Dorsenn, Germaine Geranne, Guy Maufette, and Jacques Auger—the first French-Canadian to have played the Odéon in Paris. The Académie organized lectures on theatre, music, and literature, set up a theatre school—directed by Laurette Larocque-Auger, better known by the pseudonym Jean Desprez—and produced a string of successes, mainly comedies interspersed with melodramas and social dramas, such as an adaptation by Le Gouriadec of Louis Hémon's novel *Maria Chapdelaine*. The Académie, however, disbanded in May 1934, ending the fourth season in some uncertainty.

In Sept. 1934 Antoinette Giroux became artistic director, renaming the company L'Union artistique canadienne. Her first production, Michel Duran's *Liberté provisoire*, contained too many allusions to European politics to interest a Montreal audience. Succeeding shows, however, were more favourably received. Local actors were often singled out for special praise, while the actors Giroux brought from France did not impress the critics, some of whom also judged Giroux's productions harshly. The Stella suspended operations from Jan. to Mar. 1935, when Henri Letondal again took over. After five shows, including *Cocktail* and *Marie-Claire* by

Yvette MERCIER-GOUIN, the season—for lack of an audience—ended abruptly.

In Sept. 1935 a new company, La Comédie franco-canadienne, made up mainly of French actors, attempted unsuccessfully to breathe life into the old theatre, but on 15 Dec. 1935 it again became a movie house. It did not regain its original status until 1960 when Le THÉÂTRE DU RIDEAU VERT became the resident company. In 1968, completely renovated, the Stella became known as Le Théâtre du Rideau Vert.   NORMAND LEROUX

Theatre 3. It was founded in 1970 in Edmonton by actress Anne Green (general manager) and university professor Mark Schoenberg (artistic director). Concerned about the lack of job opportunities for local professionals and the 'boulevard fare' of the existing CITADEL and Walterdale theatres, the founders felt the city could support an intimate, professional art theatre dedicated to 'presenting important plays of a non-commercial nature from the classic and modern repertoire, and, whenever possible, plays that reflect contemporary Canadian life.'

Opening on 20 Jan. 1971 with Edward Albee's *The Zoo Story* and Strindberg's *Miss Julie*, the theatre quickly gained a reputation for innovative stagings of seldom-seen foreign classics and original plays or adaptations by local writers. During its three-year tenure in the flexible 90-seat 'Theatre Beside' in Victoria Composite High School, Theatre 3 staged plays by Pinter, Racine, Calderón, Beckett, Sartre, and Genet as well as offering a season of all-Canadian work in 1972-3.

Theatre 3 entered a new era of growth in its fourth season. Continuing to offer a mixed repertoire of classical and Canadian work, it relocated in the 250-seat Centennial Library Theatre for the next three years. While disliking the larger downtown theatre's restrictive proscenium form, the company more than doubled its subscriptions, expanded its season from four to six plays, and hired Schoenberg full-time. Over the 1974-5 season, Theatre 3 purchased, and began renovating, an old welding shop, and on 15 Feb. 1977, opened its seventh season with Brendan Behan's *The Hostage* in its own 250-seat theatre.

Some concessions to popular taste had been made earlier with the addition of an annual family Christmas show and the staging of such popular classics as Tennessee Williams'

The Glass Menagerie. Under the tenure of Keith Digby, who replaced Schoenberg in the spring of 1978, the work of such contemporary British and American playwrights as Simon Gray, Christopher Hampton, David Rabe, and Heathcote Williams came strongly to the fore. Nonetheless, neither Schoenberg nor Digby forgot the theatre's commitment to Canadian work or to recreating the classics. Many audiences saw the work of Friedrich Dürrenmatt, Ferenc Molnár, Euripides, Machiavelli, Arthur Schnitzler, and Ibsen for the first time on a professional stage. Theatre 3 also featured, or hosted, touring productions of work by Canadians Joanna GLASS, Michael COOK, and Michel TREMBLAY. It also premièred Sharon POLLOCK's *BLOOD RELATIONS* in 1980, THEATRE PASSE MURAILLE's production of Rudy Wiebe's *Far As The Eye Can See* (in 1977), Gaetan Charlebois's *Aleola* (in 1979), and plays by local writers Warren Graves (*The Last Real Summer*, 1981) and Frank Moher (*The Broken Globe*, 1976).

Attendance increased from 24,500 to 32,000 over Theatre 3's final three years. But it had gone dangerously into debt to acquire its own theatre space, and ambitious seasons, combined with poor fundraising and financial mismanagement, brought about its bankruptcy and demise in June 1981. Its mandate was continued by PHOENIX THEATRE.   MOIRA DAY

Theatre Toronto. Theatre Toronto flourished briefly in 1968-9 when it was created by the amalgamation of the CREST THEATRE and the CANADIAN PLAYERS. Clifford Williams (an associate director of the Royal Shakespeare Company) was hired as artistic director, and the season opened at the ROYAL ALEXANDRA THEATRE with a successful production of Rolf Hochhuth's controversial play *The Soldiers*, starring John COLICOS.

After this propitious beginning, however, two Canadian plays, Jean Basile's *The Drummer Boy* and John Hearn's *A Festival of Carol's*, were undistinguished, and Jules Feiffer's *Little Murders* puzzled Toronto audiences. The first season's attendance totalled a disappointing fifty-four per cent of capacity.

A second season opened in Jan. 1969 with considerably less fanfare. There was no world première, and the plays (works by Marlowe, Shaw, Günter Grass, and Carlo Goldoni) seemed indistinguishable from earlier

Theatre Toronto

Toronto repertory seasons. The theatre's efforts to educate a Toronto audience through a workshop series produced few tangible results at the box-office. Furthermore, growing dissatisfaction with Williams' absentee style of management and with his $40,000 annual salary (three or four times what other artistic directors were earning at the time) damaged the theatre's public image. In the midst of growing criticism and dwindling support Williams resigned after the second production, leaving the artistic direction in the hands of Richard Digby Day. The company completed its second season, but the accumulated deficit of $80,000 caused the theatre to amalgamate with the newly formed ST LAWRENCE CENTRE.   NEIL CARSON

Theatre Under the Stars. Established in 1940 by Basil Horsfall, a conductor, A.S. Wootten, Parks Board superintendent, and actor E.V. Young, it presents musicals outdoors in summer in the Malkin Bowl, Stanley Park, Vancouver. The Bowl's band-shelter was redeveloped for large-scale musicals in 1945. In the late 1940s and early 1950s as many as seven shows were presented in consecutive weeks, to audiences as large as 3,500. Operetta dominated: *Song of Norway*, Franz Lehar's *The Count of Luxembourg* and *The Merry Widow*, Oscar Straus's *The Chocolate Soldier, Timber!* staged in 1952, 'was the first musical written and composed in Canada and by Canadians ever to hit the professional boards.' Book and lyrics were by David Savage and Doug Nixon, music by Dolores Claman. In 1952 Theatre Under the Stars became fully professional, but bad weather led to bankruptcy in 1963.

A small-scale resumption was made in 1969 with a new name, Theatre in the Park. Musicals previously done in winter by such local groups as the Dunbar Musical Society were repeated. In the 1970s and 1980s two musicals were presented each season for about six weeks in July and August. The repertoire was almost entirely from post-Second-World War Broadway, perhaps to appeal to American tourists. The original name was re-adopted in 1980.

Theatre Under the Stars aims to offer inexpensive family entertainment—though admission rose to $11 in 1987—and to involve the community. Four or five cast members may be professional, but volunteers provide the large choruses and backstage workers. The

Bowl was damaged by fire early in 1982 and only fully restored for the 1985 season, during which Alan Jay Lerner's and Frederick Loewe's *Brigadoon* and Richard Alder's and Jerry Ross's *Damn Yankees* were presented. Howard Ashman's and Alan Merken's *Little Shop of Horrors* and Arthur Laurents', Stephen Sondheim's, and Leonard Bernstein's *West Side Story* were produced in 1988.

See also MUSICAL THEATRE.

MALCOLM PAGE

Thériault, Yves (1915-83). Born in Quebec City and raised in Montreal, he left school at fifteen and, after a variety of jobs, worked as a script-writer for the National Film Board from 1942 and for Radio-Canada from 1945 to 1950. A writer of enormous creative output, Thériault published his first short story in 1941 and his first novel in 1950; he has written more than 1,000 short stories (many remain unpublished), and published more than forty volumes of collections and novels, including the internationally known *Agaguk* (1958), a story of Inuit life. Despite a debilitating stroke in 1970, he continued to work until his death at his home in the Laurentians. He received numerous awards, including the Prix de la Province de Québec, the Molson Prize, and the Prix French-Canada. In 1959 he was named to the Royal Society of Canada.

Although Thériault is often overlooked as a dramatist, he wrote more than 1,300 radio and television scripts. *Samaritain* (1958) is the only radio script to be published; it was broadcast on Radio-Canada in 1952. Thériault also wrote four stage plays, *Frédange* and *Les Terres neuves* (two full-length plays published together in 1970, but not produced); *Le Marcheur* (1968), a three-act play first produced in 1950 by Montreal's Salle du GESÙ, and *Bérengère; ou la chair en feu* (unpublished), first performed by the amateur company of the THÉÂTRE DE LA FENIÈRE (Lorettville, Quebec) in 1965.

Thériault's plays are dominated by a dialectical tension between rootedness and departure, and its effect on the family and community. In *Le Marcheur* an intransigent, tyrannical father awaits death offstage, pacing the floor while the family settles accounts. The father—whose monotonous footsteps can be heard throughout the play—may be said to symbolize Quebec before the Quiet Revolution, an inflexible guardian of traditions incapable of adapting to change. In similar fashion the mother in *Frédange* maintains almost complete silence while refusing to allow herself to die, much to the despair of her son (Frédange), who has returned home in hopes of an inheritance. In *Les Terres neuves* a community leaves its barren village in search of more fertile land; their long march gives rise to profound questioning of the individuals who organized it.

Thériault's plays are traditional in form, but the dialogue has not worn well. The political symbolism, however, especially in *Le Marcheur*, gives a certain thematic depth.

JEAN-FRANÇOIS CHASSAY

Thiéry, Marthe (1902-79). Born Marthe Godeau in Montreal, the daughter of director and stage manager Antoine Godeau, she played several child and adolescent roles in the companies and theatres in which her father worked before she left for France to study medicine. She eventually abandoned these studies and returned to Montreal, where she joined the Barry-Duquesne company. There she met Albert Simard, known as Albert DUQUESNE, whom she married.

A self-taught actress, Thiéry played roles in new plays, notably that of Maria Chapdelaine in Paul Gury's adaptation of Louis Hémon's novel at the THÉÂTRE NATIONAL in 1923 and on tour in Eastern Canada and the U.S. In 1928 she helped found the THÉÂTRE STELLA in Montreal.

One of the best-known actresses of her generation, Thiéry pursued an active career in radio, television, film, and theatre, playing over a hundred parts. For health reasons she was obliged to end her career soon after the release of her last film, *Une Saison dans la vie d'Emmanuel* (1973).   LUCIE ROBERT

Thomas, Powys (1926-77). The son of a Welsh preacher, he worked as a coal miner during the Second World War and from 1948 to 1950 studied acting at the Old Vic School under Michel SAINT-DENIS, before joining the Young Vic (1950-2) and Royal Shakespeare (1952-4) companies. After he immigrated to Canada in 1956 his roles at the STRATFORD FESTIVAL between 1957 and 1974 included Glendower in *Henry IV, Part I*, Athos in *The Three Musketeers*, Vladimir in Samuel Beckett's *Waiting for Godot*, and Filippo in Alfred de Musset's *Lorenzaccio*. He played Captain Shotover in Shaw's *Heartbreak House* at the CREST THEATRE in 1960, and at the MANITOBA THEATRE CENTRE he played Marcus Lycus in Stephen Sondheim's *A Funny Thing Happened on the Way to the Forum* and Vershinin in Chekhov's *Three Sisters*. At the VANCOUVER PLAYHOUSE he appeared as Jacob in David FRENCH's *Of the Fields, Lately* and as King Lear. Thomas also appeared on Broadway in Dylan Thomas's *Under Milk Wood* (after directing a 1959 Crest Theatre production of the same play), and he acted in French for Le THÉÂTRE DU NOUVEAU MONDE. He appeared in the film *The Luck of Ginger Coffey* and in numerous radio and television productions.

Thomas made a major contribution to the teaching of acting in Canada, serving as founding artistic director of the English section of the NATIONAL THEATRE SCHOOL (1960-5), first director of Stratford's Actors' Workshops (1968-9), and the founding artistic director of the Vancouver Playhouse Acting School (1975-7). His teaching—emphasizing commitment and selflessness—combined profound emotional release with a rigorous sense of structure; he believed that only by realizing their full human potential could people become good actors.

DAVID BARNET

Thompson, Henry Denman (1833-1911). Born in Pennsylvania, he spent his adolescence in Swanzey, N.H., and in 1854 joined John NICKINSON's company at Toronto's ROYAL LYCEUM where, except for brief intervals, he remained under successive managers until 1867 and became the city's favourite comedian. With his shock of red hair and round good-natured face, Thompson was a natural comic. He specialized in Irish roles and also excelled in black parts, but achieved his greatest Toronto success as the Yankee Salem Scudder in Dion Boucicault's *The Octoroon*. Charged in 1868 with complicity in American express-train robberies, he hid in Toronto, where an offered reward found no takers, and where, on his return to the stage in 1871, enthusiastic crowds greeted him with undiminished affection. Thompson (based once more in the U.S.), drew packed houses in 1879, 1880, and 1884 when touring Canadian cities in his play *Joshua Whitcomb*, about a quaint and kindly New Hampshire farmer. His last, triumphant, appearance in Toronto was in Nov. 1886 when he presented—after its Boston première, but before its historic opening in New York—his classic rural drama *The Old Homestead* (written with George W. Ryer). Thompson spent virtually the rest of his career playing the role of Joshua Whitcomb—'Uncle Josh'—in this play. MARY SHORTT

Thompson, Judith (b. 1954). Born in Montreal, she graduated from Queen's Univ. in 1976 and the NATIONAL THEATRE SCHOOL in 1979. She worked as an actress before turning to playwriting full time after the success of her first play, *The Crackwalker* (1981), which premièred at THEATRE PASSE MURAILLE, 26 Nov. 1980, directed by Clarke Rogers. Her second play, *White Biting Dog* (1984), premièred at TARRAGON THEATRE, 12 Jan. 1984, directed by Bill GLASSCO, and won the 1984 Governor General's Award for Drama. *I am Yours* premièred at Tarragon, 17 Nov. 1987, under director Derek GOLDBY.

These plays, which combine poetically rendered speech patterns of various Ontario regions with characters who are conceived in an essentially naturalistic manner, are punctuated by monologues that serve as structural pivots. In *The Crackwalker* a brutally realistic depiction of the seamier side of Kingston, Ont., is enriched by a central image of the madonna and child. *White Biting Dog*, set in Toronto's Rosedale district, involves naturalistic characters in a sustained anti-realistic plot about sacrificial love. Heightened symbolism moves the play into a realm perhaps best described as 'magic naturalism'. *I am Yours* contains the most explicitly religious symbolism of Thompson's plays, as its tortured characters' search for love culminates in a redemptive birth.

Thompson has also written two radio plays, *Quickening* and *A Kissing Way* (broadcast on the CBC in 1984 and 1986 respectively), and *Turning to Stone* for CBC-TV, broadcast in 1986.

See George Toles, ' "Cause You're the Only One I Want": The Anatomy of Love in the Plays of Judith Thompson', *Canadian Literature*, 118 (1988).

RICHARD PAUL KNOWLES

Thompson, Paul (b. 1940). Born in Charlottetown, PEI, raised in southwestern Ont., and educated at the Universities of Western Ont., Paris, and Toronto, he is a primary force in the development of COLLECTIVE CREATION in Canada. He returned to France in 1965 to apprentice with director Roger Planchon and his Théâtre de la Cité at Villeurbanne. Planchon nurtured Thompson's love of dialectic and open communication, both of which have become integral to his creative process and trademarks of his productions.

Thompson worked briefly in amateur theatre in Sault Ste Marie and then spent two seasons as an assistant director at the STRATFORD FESTIVAL. Stratford, however, was ideologically foreign to Thompson, whose interest lay in investigating the ethos of Canadians. Moving to Toronto in 1969, he found a congenial ideological and artistic environment at THEATRE PASSE MURAILLE, and eventually, in 1972, became its artistic director. Intent on creating new work with Canadian subject-matter and themes, he developed a collective play-making process: the actors, who had been given the general topic of the play, came to rehearsals having done their own research and formulated their own opinions. Thompson then allowed them to improvise while he observed for hours (sometimes even days), rarely commenting. At this point the play had no set characters, no plot, no structure: the shaping came in the next phase of play-making. Thompson has an instinctive dramaturgical sense of structure and dialogue. His own term for his role in this collaboration is 'glue-pot'. Early products of this collective process are *The FARM SHOW*, produced in 1972, and *1837: The Farmers' Revolt*, 1973 (written with Rick SALUTIN). A later example is *Maggie and Pierre*, created with actress Linda GRIFFITHS and produced in 1979. The episodic structure of these plays, their presentational style, and the naturalistic language are features now associated with collective theatre in Canada. (See COLLECTIVE CREATION.)

In 1982 Thompson resigned as artistic director of TPM. Free of the responsibilities of running what had become one of Toronto's larger ALTERNATE THEATRES, he undertook a number of freelance assignments, including a return to TPM in 1987 to direct *Young Art*, a science fiction comedy by Brad Fraser, and creating *The Games of Winter*, a play about the Olympic Games that toured Canada en route to the 1988 Calgary Olympics. In 1987 Thompson was appointed director-general of the NATIONAL THEATRE SCHOOL. JUDITH RUDAKOFF

Thomson, R.H. (b. 1947). Educated at the Univ. of Toronto and trained at the NATIONAL THEATRE SCHOOL and the London Academy of Music and Dramatic Art, he toured England with Tina Packer's Shakespeare & Co. before returning to Canada in 1972 to begin an impressive acting career in theatre, film, and television. His stage career has been defined by a series of roles impressive both in range and depth, including Tom in Tennessee Williams' *The Glass Menagerie* (NEPTUNE THEATRE, 1976); Mark Antony in *Julius Caesar* (STRATFORD FESTIVAL, 1982); farcical roles in Georges Feydeau's *Hand to Hand* (TORONTO FREE THEATRE, 1983) and Caryl Churchill's *Cloud 9* (Bayview Playhouse, Toronto, 1984); the title role in David Edgar's adaptation of *The Jail Diary of Albee Sachs* (TORONTO WORKSHOP PRODUCTIONS, 1984); De Flores in Thomas Middleton's and William Rowley's *The Changeling* in 1985 and Hamlet in 1986, both for Toronto Free Theatre; and Tesman in Ibsen's *Hedda Gabler* for Toronto's CENTRESTAGE in 1985. Thomson's work is characterized by a skilful fusion of internal and external perception that at its best combines finely observed details of voice and physicality with deeply felt moral passion. An accomplished film and television actor, he won national acclaim for his portrayal of Charlie in CBC-TV's *Charlie Grant's War* in Jan. 1985.   BRIAN SMITH

Tit-Coq. Gratien GÉLINAS's first full-length drama is widely regarded as the harbinger of contemporary Québécois theatre, and to a considerable degree its role-model. For the first time the Québécois working-class saw itself onstage in authentic urban and rural settings; colloquial Quebec French was spoken without apology; Quebec's traditional social and moral values, and the stresses placed on them by urbanization and war, were recognized, if not confronted; and the province's deep-seated obsession with cultural alienation and marginality—a key concern of later dramatists such as Marcel DUBÉ and Michel TREMBLAY—found symbolic incarnation in the play's illegitimate and dispossessed hero, Tit-Coq.

Based on two sketches from Gélinas's *FRIDOLINONS* revues—*Le Départ du conscrit* (*The Conscript's Departure*) and *Le Retour du conscrit* (*The Conscript's Return*)—*Tit-Coq* (Little Rooster) treats a two-year period in the life of a rambunctious young army private,

Arthur Saint-Jean (nicknamed Tit-Coq). Deeply scarred emotionally by his illegitimacy and orphanage-upbringing, Tit-Coq falls in love with the warmhearted family of his army chum, Jean-Paul Desilets, during a Christmas celebration at the Desilets's rural home. He woos Jean-Paul's youngest sister, Marie-Ange, and dreams of becoming part of a large family at last. No sooner has he become engaged, however, than he is shipped overseas, proudly clutching Marie-Ange's family photograph album, his passport to belonging.

During his absence, Marie-Ange pines for entertainment and is pressured by her family to go dancing with a family friend, Léopold Vermette. Within six months the pair are married, and almost immediately Marie-Ange regrets her rashness. On his return at war's end, Tit-Coq learns of the betrayal and angrily confronts his errant lover. Disarmed at once by Marie-Ange's remorse, he persuades her to go off with him despite the social stigma attached to adulterous relationships in a conservative Catholic milieu. At the last moment, thanks to the intervention of an army padré, Tit-Coq realizes his love for Marie-Ange is inseparable from his urge to belong to her family, a privilege that will be denied him by his illicit union. Worse still, children born of the liaison will be, like himself, illegitimate and obliged to bear the same anguish he has experienced. Unwilling to penalize his offspring, he leaves Marie-Ange to her husband, and resumes the life of an outsider.

Directed jointly by Gélinas and Fred BARRY, and with Gélinas in the title role, *Tit-Coq* opened at Montreal's MONUMENT NATIONAL theatre on 22 May 1948. Its popular and critical reception was ecstatic, and the play enjoyed a total run of some 300 performances over a two-year period. The French text of the drama was published in 1950 by Beauchemin (Montreal). In the same year the play reopened in Montreal in an English translation by Gélinas and Keith Johnstone, and subsequently enjoyed a national tour that accounted for another 200 performances. The English translation was published in 1967 by Clarke, Irwin & Co. (Toronto). In 1952 the play was filmed, directed by René Delacroix, with Gélinas in the lead role.

In spite of the fact that *Tit-Coq* is remembered for the profound effect it had on its

Tit-Coq

Gratien Gélinas (Tit-Coq) and Muriel Guilbault (Marie-Ange) in Gélinas's Tit-Coq, *La Comédie-Canadienne, Montreal, 1958*

audiences, there is little doubt that it was overpraised when it first appeared: comparisons with Molière, Chaplin, and Pagnol were overblown, to say the least. Four decades later the play reveals itself to be both flawed and dated. Apart from Tit-Coq himself and Marie-Ange, the characters—gentle padré, jolly father, domestic mother—are stereotypical, and the structure (three acts and thirteen scenes; two acts in the English version) is fragmented and disjointed. The play's sombre Catholicism and repressive sexuality have scant relevance for contemporary theatregoers. Its flattened characterization, its soft-focus wartime settings, and its uncomplicated, even naïve, portrait of love and marriage suggest a faded snapshot rather than a living reality. Nevertheless the play was an important pioneering attempt to convey local authenticity in setting, language, character, and theme.

See Jean-Cléo Godin, 'Orphelins ou bâtards: Fridolin, Tit-Coq, Bousille', in Jean-Cléo Godin et Laurent Mailhot, *Le Théâtre québécois* (1970); Arthur Laurendeau, 'Pour la 150ième de Tit-Coq', *Action Nationale* (March-April, 1949); Edouard Laurent, 'Tit-Coq, un conscrit que passera à l'histoire',

Culture (Dec. 1948); Renate Usmiani, *Gratien Gélinas* (1977).   JOHN RIPLEY

Toronto Free Theatre. The original mandate (1971) of the Toronto Free Theatre was formulated by the founding members of its board of directors: Adrienne Clarkson, Judith Hendry, Thomas B. HENDRY, Martin KINCH, John PALMER, K. Gray Perkins, and Richard Schouten. The theatre would be free both in its admission policy and in the sense of experimentation with, and ideological exploration of, all avenues of theatrical expression, especially those followed by Canadian theatre artists. The name of the company was inspired by the Théâtre Libre of André Antoine in France and the German Freie Bühne. Its first production was Tom Hendry's *How Are Things with the Walking Wounded?* in June 1972.

The theatre—at 26 Berkeley St, Toronto—has two flexible performance spaces: the Theatre Upstairs (a 28' × 20' stage and seating for up to 180) and the Theatre Downstairs (a 50' × 21' stage and seating for up to 280). Built in the late 1880s, the building was a functioning Gas Works until 1955. Renovations in 1972, 1976-7, 1982, and 1988-9 have cumulatively upgraded the theatre's facilities.

The free admission policy lasted only until 1973, though since July 1982 the company has produced free outdoor summer productions of mainly Shakespeare plays in Toronto's High Park. Initiated by artistic director Guy SPRUNG, and known under the umbrella term of 'The Dream in High Park', this annual event has been attended by up to 60,000 patrons each year. The Free has also retained its Sunday Pay-What-You-Can matinées.

The original commitment to nurturing new Canadian theatre artists, particularly playwrights, has endured. In a 1977 policy statement the Free reaffirmed its priorities while re-assessing its role in the development and production of new work by Canadian dramatists. To this end a policy of commissioning new Canadian plays was introduced in tandem with a workshop program. Carol BOLT, Anne CHISLETT, David FENNARIO, Paul Gross, Erika RITTER, and George F. WALKER are among the playwrights whose work it has developed.

The 1977 statement also identified the need to develop a subscription audience to attend an entire season of plays: in 1986 the Free's subscription list stood at over 8,500. The 1977 statement also said that 'the creation of a national theatre, in the spiritual rather than the physical sense, must be our ultimate goal. Toronto Free Theatre has something to give the country: the plays, and our techniques for developing the plays. For it is only the plays, and the recreation of Canadian plays across the country, that will ultimately tie us together.' In the light of these sentiments it was not altogether surprising that the Free and Toronto's CENTRESTAGE Company merged in 1988 to achieve just this goal as the CANADIAN STAGE COMPANY. This amalgamation will not mean the end of the Free Theatre; productions will continue to be mounted in premises on Berkeley St, which will now be known as the Canadian Stage Company, Free Theatres Upstairs and Downstairs.   JUDITH RUDAKOFF

Toronto Truck Theatre. Founded in 1971 by Peter Peroff as a touring company (transporting its free outdoor shows in a six-ton truck), it moved in 1973 to Toronto's 200-seat Colonnade Theatre, where Peroff produced mainly popular comedies. In 1975 Peroff also leased (and later purchased) a former church on Belmont St seating 170; and in 1978 he purchased the Bayview Playhouse, a former art deco cinema seating 520, for an expanding subscription audience and later for rentals. A non-Equity company, Toronto Truck Theatre receives no government funding and has won scant critical approval, although it flourished in the late 1970s when local commercial theatre dominated ALTERNATE THEATRE in Toronto. Its most noteworthy production has been Agatha Christie's *The Mousetrap*, which in 1987 celebrated a continuous run of ten years on Belmont St.   DENIS W. JOHNSTON

Toronto Workshop Productions. The oldest theatre company in Toronto and the most consistent in style and vision, TWP's founding in 1959 marked the beginning of Canada's ALTERNATE THEATRE movement. For its first twenty-seven years TWP expressed the ideas and styles of its artistic director George LUSCOMBE. In 1986 Luscombe stepped down to be succeeded by Robert Rooney. Leon Pownall was named artistic director in July 1988.

When Luscombe founded Workshop Productions (the 'Toronto' was added in 1963 when the theatre received its charter from the city) in donated space at 47 Fraser Ave, he planned to train a highly skilled ensemble based on Joan Littlewood's Theatre Workshop. In 1963, following two summers under a tent at Stratford and a southern Ontario tour of one-act plays as Theatre 35, TWP merged with the remnants of the Arts Club Theatre and made the leap to professional status. Having outgrown the 100-seat theatre on Fraser Ave, TWP moved to its present 300-seat home at 12 Alexander St in 1967. The theatre was seriously damaged by fire in 1974, one day before the opening of Jack Winter's controversial *You Can't Get Here From There* (about the 1973 Chilean coup), but was immediately restored. In 1977, and again in 1980, the theatre's lease was terminated, but a major public-relations drive won government funding to purchase the land and it was rezoned for exclusive use as a theatre. At that time a board of directors was installed, the first in the company's history.

TWP's work is characterized by polished ensemble acting, spectacular but minimal theatricality, and a commitment to left-wing politics. Although its reputation has wavered with the critics, it has won recognition abroad: at the Venice Biennale in 1969 with *Mr. Bones* (by Luscombe and Jan Carew) and Mario Fratti's *Che*, in New York in 1970 with *Chicago '70*, and with a 1976 European tour of its greatest hit, *TEN LOST YEARS*.

The theatre has experienced severe financial problems in recent years; both the 1985-6 and the 1987-8 seasons were curtailed because of reduced funding and poor box office returns. In 1988, in a controversial move to eliminate a growing deficit, TWP announced a plan to redevelop its site as a new theatre and retirement home in a joint venture with Performing Arts Lodges of Canada.

ALAN FILEWOD

Toupin, Paul (b. 1918). Born and educated in Montreal, he later studied in France, receiving his doctorate from the Université d'Aix-Marseille. In Paris he became acquainted with the contemporary French theatre. On his return to Montreal he helped promote French drama. His play *Le Choix* (1950), performed in 1951, presents the dilemma of a mother during the Second World War forced to choose which of her sons is to be taken as a hostage. *Brutus*, performed and published in 1952, is a historical tragedy; the main theme is twice stated in the Prologue: 'Do we love as much as we should those who love us?' Brutus rejects the friendship of Caesar and the love of his wife Portia to pursue a political dream. This betrayal of friendship and love becomes the dominant theme of Toupin's trilogy *Théâtre* (1961), which contains a second version of *Brutus*, a medieval tragedy *Le Mensonge*, and a contemporary drama *Chacun son amour*. The revised *Brutus* puts greater emphasis on the friendship of Caesar for Brutus, while significantly reducing the role of Portia. Set against a background of unrest in 1480, *Le Mensonge* (originally published in 1960) recalls the love and marriage of Robert d'Arcourt with a châtelaine of Brittany whose family motto is 'La Vérité'. Banished by the châtelaine for lying, d'Arcourt seeks revenge; when the châtelaine is mortally wounded by accident, husband and wife reaffirm their love. The principal character of *Chacun son amour* is Stéphane, an aging, verbose, and cynical Don Juan; weary of his present love, Hélène, he is drawn to Céleste, engaged to his secretary Fernand. Eventually, however, Stéphane wishes the couple a happy marriage. Later, while dictating the story of his love affairs,

he suffers a fatal seizure. *Son dernier rôle* (1979) evokes the last day of a great actor who collapses while rehearsing Racine's *Phèdre*. Hospitalized, he talks of his life and career with a journalist and a chaplain.

Toupin's plays are rarely performed. *Le Choix* and *Brutus* were staged at the GESÙ theatre. *Chacun son amour* and *Son dernier rôle* were broadcast on television, *Le Mensonge* on radio. Audiences preferred drama with Canadian themes and characters to Toupin's plays, which reflected Toupin's concept of himself as the author of 'un théâtre dans un fauteuil'. Other published works include *Souvenirs pour demain* (1960), a personal memoir, and *L'Écrivain et son théâtre* (1964), a defence of his plays and a critique of other Canadian playwrights. *Le Coeur a ses raisons* (1971) presents charming portraits of two women Toupin admired: Didi, the devoted family maid, and Madame de Courcy, who made him welcome in Paris. A third portrait depicts the nightmare marriage of a lawyer's wife, a marriage in many ways similar to that of Marie-Lou and Léopold in Michel TREMBLAY's *À TOI, POUR TOUJOURS, TA MARIE-LOU*.

Toupin's writing conforms to the traditions of the Académie française. His literary style, praised by critics, remains a distinctive trait of his work.   ODETTE CONDEMINE

Touring Stars and Companies (American). American actors and troupes routinely included Canadian cities as part of a continental tour. After the completion of the Canadian Pacific Railway across Canada in 1885, tour routes began to develop exclusively in Canadian territory, and increased in number and prestige after the turn of the century.

The earliest American company to penetrate territory north of the border was the American Company of Comedians, which performed John Home's *Douglas* and David Garrick's *Miss in Her Teens* in Halifax on 26 Aug. 1768 and stayed for a fall season. Other eighteenth-century American theatrical visitors included John B. Ricketts' circus from New York, which performed in Montreal in 1797. The early nineteenth century brought John Bernard from Boston's Federal Street Theatre to Montreal and Quebec City in 1809, and 'Noble' Luke Usher to Montreal in the 1810s. Addison B. Price's company organized seasons in Halifax in 1817 and 1818. Companies of performers, however, rarely toured in the early years of the century (largely because of harsh travelling conditions) and the travelling star, unaccompanied by other actors, remained the norm until the 1870s. Montreal was frequently on the tour route of such performers as Jean Davenport, Edwin Forrest, Charlotte Cushman, and Louisa Lane (later Mrs John Drew).

Touring became a continent-wide phenomenon in the last thirty years of the nineteenth century. Frequently the northern terminus of a tour was in Canada: companies and actors performing in Seattle normally continued north to Victoria and Vancouver; Winnipeg was reached via Minneapolis; Calgary from Spokane; cities in Ontario from Detroit, Buffalo, or upstate New York; while Nova Scotia, New Brunswick, and Prince Edward Island were visited by companies touring from New York or from Maine. Railway connections within Canada made tour routes still easier; certainly touring conditions in the latter part of the century were vastly improved over the horrendous accounts left by Fanny Kemble following her 1834 tour (see *The Life and Correspondence of Charles Mathews the Elder, Comedian*, 1860), or Mrs Sam Cowell's record of tribulations suffered by her comedian husband in 1860 and 1861 (published in *The Cowells in America*, 1934).

American stars who toured Canada in the late years of the nineteenth century constitute a roster of the major figures of English-language theatre in the period: Edwin Booth, Joseph Jefferson, Minnie Maddern Fiske, Clara MORRIS, Lawrence Barrett, Madame Modjeska, Lotta Crabtree, Robert B. Mantell, Maude Adams, James O'Neill, and many others who routinely included Canadian cities as part of their annual tours. Lesser lights also appeared; many stages in the nineteenth century were frequently occupied by provincial stars unknown in metropolitan centres. Thus, Phosa McAllister was hailed in Winnipeg in 1880, as was Katie Putnam; Thomas W. Keene toured throughout Canada in the 1880s and 1890s, playing his last engagement before his sudden death in 1896 in Hamilton; Mlle Rhea, Belgian-born but based in North America, was popular in Montreal in the 1890s; Denman THOMPSON brought *The Old Homestead* regularly to London and Ottawa; and Salisbury's Troubadours included Toronto on their schedules. Walker Whiteside was particularly popular in Winnipeg in the 1890s, while Louis James and Frederick Warde took Shakespearean repertory across

Saskatchewan and Alberta into Vancouver in 1892.

Popular entertainments also toured regularly: *Uncle Tom's Cabin* companies, perhaps understandably, found Canadian audiences supportive, while American minstrels, variety artists, and VAUDEVILLE performers were also well received. European stars—Ernesto Rossi, Tommaso Salvini, Charles Fechter, and Sarah Bernhardt among them—who toured the U.S. also appeared in Canada. Bernhardt was particularly successful—and often controversial—performing in Canada on her many tours between 1880 and 1918.

At the end of the nineteenth century Canadian theatres fell under the control of business interests, repeating a pattern developed in the United States, where the Theatrical Syndicate's organization in 1896 represented the establishment of a theatrical monopoly controlling all aspects of production and performance. The Canadian Theatrical Managers' Association came into existence shortly thereafter and, under contract to Klaw and Erlanger—Theatrical Syndicate partners—controlled major theatres and tour routes in eastern Canada. In western Canada Winnipeg's C.P. WALKER became a major force, owning or controlling a circuit of theatres stretching through Manitoba south to Minnesota and North Dakota.

The centralized control of theatrical business in the hands of the Theatrical Syndicate provoked reactions from Anglo-Canadian interests, leading to the establishment of the British-Canadian Theatrical Organization in 1912 and the Anglo-Canadian Booking Office in 1913, with the objective of breaking the Syndicate's monopoly by bringing large numbers of stars and companies from England. Sir John Martin-Harvey toured under the Office's auspices, but the scheme was stopped by the outbreak of the First World War.

Post-war tours by American companies established certain patterns: most frequently, major companies played regularly in Montreal and Toronto as part of the standard North American tour. Companies that played in Seattle often also performed in Vancouver—productions of R.C. Sherriff's *Journey's End* and Ben Hecht's and Charles MacArthur's *The Front Page* in 1929, and the musical *Good News!* in 1930, for example. The Depression ended tours to most cities and towns outside of a handful of major centres. By 1938 major companies generally visited only Montreal and Toronto. Audiences there regularly saw stars such as Katharine Cornell, Helen Hayes, Tallulah Bankhead, and Maurice Evans. The main Toronto venue was the ROYAL ALEXANDRA THEATRE, which hosted many Broadway touring shows, often with the original stars. It continues to host such touring shows, as does the O'KEEFE CENTRE. Outside Toronto and Montreal, however, audiences had to be content with minor figures, or with the constant tours of Jack Kirkland's *Tobacco Road* in the 1930s or *Oklahoma!* in the 1940s and early 1950s. The Shubert production of Sigmund Romberg's operetta *Blossom Time* was as constant a visitor to Canadian theatres in the 1930s and 1940s, as it was elsewhere in North America.

Little changed in the years following the Second World War, although post-war prosperity gave rise to larger numbers of touring productions. Increased efficiency of transportation encouraged productions to move greater distances, reducing the chances of occasional stops in smaller towns, and in many instances Toronto became the only stop. During and immediately after the war many Broadway productions generally played in both Montreal and Toronto—as Ruth Gordon did in her own comedy, *Over 21*, in 1945—but Edward Everett Horton in Noël Coward's *Present Laughter* played only Toronto before moving to Chicago in 1949, and Martyn Green's only Canadian appearance in Bernard Shaw's *Misalliance* in 1954 was in Toronto.

Major touring companies continued to appear in Toronto throughout the 1950s: Bette Davis in *The World of Carl Sandburg* in 1959, and the post-Broadway tour of Paul Osborn's *The World of Suzie Wong* in 1960, for example. Alan Jay Lerner's and Frederick Loewe's *My Fair Lady* was one of the few touring productions in the late 1950s to play other cities, reverting to earlier touring patterns in 1959, when it played Vancouver after a run in Seattle, then travelled east to Edmonton and Calgary. The 1959 North American tour of Katharine Cornell in Jerome Kilty's *Dear Liar* (with Brian Aherne)—which appeared in Toronto at Massey Hall—was her last, and marked the end of an era in which actors routinely toured the continent after a run in New York.

The 1960s saw not only the end of the triumphant star tour, but the virtual disappearance of extended tours prior to Broadway

engagements (with only the occasional exception to prove the rule, such as the Carol Channing tour in *Lorelei* in 1973 or Yul Brynner in 1975 in *The Odyssey*, both of which played Toronto). Although there were periodic bus and truck tours, such as the 1968 tour of James Goldman's *The Lion In Winter*—which resembled much earlier tours by playing one- or two-night stands in Peterborough, Kingston, and London—most pre-Broadway productions emulated Dorothy Fields' and Cy Coleman's musical comedy *Sweet Charity*—also in 1968—which played its only Canadian engagement in Toronto.

In more recent years only major successes have travelled to Canada; again usually only to Toronto. (But *Camelot*, starring Richard Burton, previewed at the O'Keefe Centre in 1960 before going on to Broadway.) Edward Kleban's and Marvin Hamlisch's *A Chorus Line*, the major musical of the 1970s, however, reaffirmed the pattern set by earlier blockbusters such as *My Fair Lady* and *Oklahoma!* by playing all across Canada. As had been the case with earlier successes *A Chorus Line* had several companies touring simultaneously for several years, so that smaller locations eventually were covered. Companies organized specifically to play Canadian cities occasionally appeared, as with the 'Fats' Waller revue *Ain't Misbehavin'* in 1979 or Andrew Lloyd Webber's *Cats* in 1985 (although the latter, a Canadian production of a New York success adapted from a British musical hit, defies exact classification as to national origin), but remained the exception.

As the theatrical road shrank in the United States after the Second World War, so it also shrank in Canada. As in the U.S., the slack has been taken up by productions of American successes by numerous Canadian regional theatres, along with academic and amateur theatres. Although there have been several attempts to create uniquely Canadian touring companies (for example, SPRING THAW tours), the touring commercial theatre in Canada remains essentially a product of the commercial theatre in the United States, subject to the vagaries of that country's ailing theatrical business.   ALAN WOODS

Touring Stars and Companies (British). North America attracted actors from England, and a few from Scotland and Ireland, from about 1820, until the Depression and then the Second World War broke the long

Edmund Kean as a Huron chief

performed in Montreal and Quebec City to uncrowded houses, offering five plays by Shakespeare, Philip Massinger's *A New Way to Pay Old Debts*, John Tobin's *The Honeymoon*, and *The Iron Chest*. During 1863-5 Charles and Ellen (Tree) Kean toured Australia and the U.S., and visited Victoria, B.C. (12-21 Dec. 1864) and Montreal (14-18 Aug. 1865), performing (among other plays) *Hamlet*, *Macbeth*, *Henry VIII*, and *Othello*.

Before Ellen Tree married Charles Kean in 1842, she too toured North America, briefly calling at Montreal (15-30 Aug. 1838) and Quebec City (4-14 Sept. 1838), offering plays like *The Stranger*, Edward Bulwer-Lytton's *The Lady of Lyons*, James Sheridan Knowles' *The Hunchback*, and Thomas Noon Talfourd's *Ion*. Charles Kemble and his daughter Fanny also came from the U.S. to Montreal and Quebec City in July-Aug. 1833, performing Thomas Otway's *Venice Preserv'd*, H.H. Milman's *Fazio*, R.B. Sheridan's *The School for Scandal*, *Romeo and Juliet*, *The Stranger*, and *The Hunchback*.

Until the 1880s only a few actors from Great Britain came to Canada—transportation was primitive, and the theatres (outside of Montreal and Toronto) were small and often makeshift. The gradual linking of regional railway lines and the building of new theatres prepared the way for later artists.

A few English actors, such as Sir Henry Irving, began some of their tours in Canada, either for convenience or to test their plays on theatregoers in Quebec City, Montreal, Ottawa, Kingston, and Toronto, where they could find audiences with largely English forebears, before travelling on to large U.S. cities. Irving's eight visits to North America were hugely profitable (in excess of £100,000); he came to Canada on six of them (Feb. 1884, Sept.- Oct. 1884, Feb. 1894, Sept. 1895, Mar. 1900, Jan.-Feb. 1904), accompanied by Ellen Terry on all but the last. Offered repeatedly to sold-out houses were standbys such as *The Merchant of Venice*, *Hamlet*, Leopold Lewis's *The Bells*, Dion Boucicault's *Louis XI*, and Conan Doyle's *Waterloo*. Irving's two sons later toured in Canada, H.B. in 1906 and Laurence in 1910 and 1914 (when he drowned in the sinking of the *Empress of Ireland* in the St Lawrence River).

Lillie Langtry came twelve times between 1883 and 1916, touring through Ontario and Quebec, and to Halifax and Winnipeg.

tradition of transatlantic journeys. The earliest performers were enticed by the possibility of new audiences and large profits in New York, and by an awareness of other potential profits in Boston, Philadelphia, Montreal, Toronto, and many growing cities along the eastern seaboard.

Edmund Kean was the first important English actor to visit Canada. After a controversial stay in the U.S., he performed in Montreal (31 July-28 Aug., 19-30 Oct. 1826) and Quebec City (4 Sept.-4 Oct. 1826). Like many of his successors, he depended on companies in both cities to support him in his repertoire, which included—among other plays—eight by Shakespeare, George Colman the Younger's *The Iron Chest*, and August Kotzebue's *The Stranger*. He had to endure illness, drunken and incompetent supporting actors, barking dogs, and unruly audiences. On a more positive note, Kean was made an honorary chief by the Huron Indians.

Edmund's son, Charles Kean, journeyed four times to North America and once to Australia. Between Aug. and Oct. 1831 he

Touring Stars and Companies (British)

Famous in North America for her friendship with the Prince of Wales, she performed profitably in Oliver Goldsmith's *She Stoops to Conquer*, in *As You Like It*, *The School for Scandal*, Bulwer-Lytton's *The Lady of Lyons*, Sydney Grundy's *The Degenerates*, and Percy Fendall's *Mrs. Deering's Divorce*, among other plays.

Other major English performers to come to Canada between 1890 and 1910 were Mr and Mrs William Kendal, Wilson Barrett, Olga Nethersole, and Ben Greet, who toured fifteen times with *Everyman* and (later) Shakespeare out-of-doors. Mrs Patrick Campbell came eight times, 1908-16, in controversial plays such as Arthur Wing Pinero's *The Second Mrs. Tanqueray*, Ibsen's *Hedda Gabler*, and Shaw's *Pygmalion*. Martin Harvey, later Sir John Martin-Harvey, once a junior member of Henry Irving's organization, returned with his own company to make eight almost exclusively Canadian tours, 1903-32. Sympathetic to conservative Canadian tastes, he drew very large audiences to old-fashioned romantic plays such as Freeman Wills's and Canon Langbridge's *The Only Way* (offered during four tours approximately 190 times), Lewis's *The Bells*, John Rutherford's *The Breed of the Treshams*, and Boucicault's *The Corsican Brothers*.

Diminishing Puritan suspicion of theatre and the westward expansion of the Canadian Pacific Railway encouraged the trickle of British performers to become a flood by 1914. Many artists, having discovered that British immigrants were eager to see them, devoted their tours wholly to Canada. Shakespeare, Goldsmith, Wilde, Boucicault, T.W. Robertson, and adaptations of Dickens's novels were popular; modern comedies such as Charles Hawtrey's *The Private Secretary*, W.H. Risque's *Dear Old Billy*, Graham Moffatt's *Bunty Pulls the Strings*, Arnold Bennett's and Edward Knoblock's *Milestones*, and Richard Ganthony's *A Message from Mars* were performed thousands of times between Halifax and Victoria; English-Canada delighted in music-hall stars such as Marie Lloyd, Albert Chevalier, Vesta Victoria, Cissie Loftus, Harry Lauder, Laddie Cliff, and Fred Karno (with Charles Chaplin in his vaudeville troupe in 1911-13).

British players touring Canada usually began in September in Montreal (sometimes in Halifax in winter) or Toronto, performed in smaller Ontario cities, moved westward to Winnipeg (always a profitable pause), and on to Regina, Saskatoon, Calgary, Edmonton, Vancouver, and Victoria. They played these and other towns on the return journey, during tours that lasted for six or seven months. Some centres had only one-night stands by minor troupes. By the Second World War British performers had visited seventy-four Canadian cities and towns.

Early in the new century these performers included older artists (Wilson Barrett, Edward Terry, and John Hare) on the verge of retirement, well-established ambitious actors (such as Martin Harvey, who got extra years and profits from plays that had had their day in London and were threadbare in the English provinces), and, most important, the young and impecunious. The last often purchased cheaply foreign rights to recent London successes, bringing to Canada dramas such as José G. Levy's *The Glad Eye*, Henry Seton Merriman's *With Edged Tools*, C.M.S. McLellan's *Leah Kleschna*, and Cosmo Hamilton's *The Blindness of Virtue*. Other young actors later to be famous—Matheson LANG, Gordon McLeod, George Arliss, Basil Rathbone, Laurier Lister, Donald Wolfit—gained valuable touring experience within established companies.

By 1915 almost every important star of the British music halls and the legitimate stage had played in Canada. Canadian audiences saw the Abbey Players, the Stratford-upon-Avon Company, Marie Tempest, Harry Tate, Cyril Maude, Tom Terriss, Josie Heather, Chris Richards, Alice Lloyd, Johnston Forbes-Robertson, and Constance Collier. The wartime hazards of Atlantic voyages curtailed their visits between 1914 and 1918, although a few—like Tempest, Lauder, and Forbes-Robertson—returned, and some remained in Canada or the U.S. during and after the war. English performers found much work in London and the provinces after the war; few—apart from Lauder, Martin-Harvey, Lang, Heather, Marie Lohr, H.V. Esmond, Cyril Maude, and Percy Hutchison—made Canadian tours until about 1925. British visits, however, climaxed in the prosperous years of 1928-9. Then on tour were previous visitors such as Arliss, Lauder, Martin-Harvey, the Abbey Players, and the Stratford-upon-Avon Company, and Hetty King. Performers venturing for the first time on major tours were George Robey, Gordon McLeod, Beatrice LILLIE, Evelyn Laye, Bransby Williams, Maurice Colbourne, Barry Jones (who brought Shaw to resisting Canadian play-goers), Seymour Hicks, Ellaline Terriss, the Brandon Thomas Company (with light comedies, including the perennial favourite by Thomas, *Charley's Aunt*), Philip Rodway (with the extravagant pantomimes *Humpty Dumpty* and *Mother Goose*), and companies that presented *When Crummles Played*, J.B. Fagan's *And So to Bed*, R.C. Sherriff's *Journey's End*, and John Drinkwater's *Bird in Hand*. But fewer British music-hall stars came to Canada because the VAUDEVILLE houses were dominated by American artists and full-length movies. Despite the great popularity in Canada of British performers, there was strong competition from the U.S. Throughout Canada during the first forty years of this century approximately one play in ten came from Britain; the remainder were American.

Growing sentiment against attempts by New York's Theatrical Syndicate and the rival Shubert Organization to establish American control over Canadian theatres led to the formation in 1912 of the British-Canadian Theatrical Organization (BCTO) to organize coast-to-coast tours of British stars and companies. In the 1913-14 season it brought over Eva Moore and Henry V. Esmond in Esmond's *Eliza Comes to Stay*, Laurence Irving in repertory, and, most successfully, John Martin-Harvey—but the outbreak of the First World War put an end to the venture.

After the war the disarray in the American touring system, compounded by the expanding movie industry, convinced a group of entrepreneurs, led by Lord Shaugnessy, that the objectives of the BCTO could be revived. Using the CPR's transportation and accommodation system as a touring framework, in 1919 the newly formed Trans-Canada Theatre Society bought Ambrose SMALL's chain of Ontario and Quebec theatres, secured leasing rights to the C.P. WALKER chain of theatres in the Prairies, and also bought Walker's United Producing Company. For eight months, beginning in Dec. 1919, the organization toured an English company headed by Percy Hutchison, after which the TCTS had complete control over a national chain of eighty theatres (at its peak 125), with a mandate to present British imports. To the summer of 1921 Hutchison's productions, Martin-Harvey's company, Oscar Asche's lavish London spectacles—*Chu-Chin-Chow* and *Mecca*, among other productions—toured

this circuit. But TCTS could not import enough good British productions to keep their theatres filled and had to rely on the Shubert Organization to support the season. Nor was it lucrative for British productions to tour Canada without touring the Shuberts' U.S. circuit. TCTS was thus at the mercy of its relationship with the Shuberts. Its alternative was to import lesser British productions, which did not sit well with Canadians in general—they had emerged from the war more nationalistic and sophisticated—and in particular with enthusiastic supporters of the LITTLE THEATRE movement, whose fare was very different from that of TCTS. By mid-1922 the organization had dissolved. Some British players continued to tour and prosper in Canada, but under individually organized, or American, booking arrangements.

During the 1920s British performers could count on a growing number of immigrants from the mother country to provide enthusiastic theatre audiences indulging in nostalgia. By 1930 almost three million people from the British Isles had settled in Canada (of a total population of about ten million). Eighty per cent of the population of Victoria, B.C., was of British stock. The stock-market crash of October 1929 swiftly affected theatre attendance in Canada, which had already been reduced by competing attractions—the automobile, bridge, tennis, radio, and movies. Tickets for major plays then cost 50¢ to $2.00; a movie cost 10-25 cents. During the 1930s and early 1940s few British touring companies and music-hall artists made the long and still expensive journey to Canada. The Barry Jackson Company, heavily subsidized by its patron, did a transcontinental tour, as did Colbourne and Jones, and Martin-Harvey. A few Canadian theatregoers saw Edith Evans, John Gielgud, Maurice Evans, and Gladys Cooper.

The Second World War disrupted theatrical travel across the Atlantic even more seriously than the Great War had done. After 1945 the airplane made the journey faster and easier and also more expensive for theatre companies and their impedimenta. When Canada Council subsidies for Canadian playwrights, producers, and actors took effect after 1957, there was less need and demand for British touring actors in Canada. John Gielgud, Donald Wolfit, Flora Robson, the Old Vic Company, and a few others played in several cities, but the great days of the touring performers from the British Isles ended in 1930.

For over a century several thousand British performers—many of them very conscious of their contributions to reinforcing the ties of Empire—brought pleasure to Canadian audiences and reminders of their native land to thousands of expatriates.

See L.W. Conolly, ed., *Theatrical Touring and Founding in North America* (1982).

ROBERT G. LAWRENCE

Town Theatre, The. Founded in 1967 by the Theatre Foundation of Ottawa, it was an immediate popular and artistic success when, under artistic director Frank Daley, it produced three plays in its first season, attracting over 3,000 subscribers. It brought to Ottawa audiences some of the finest actors in Canada in a variety of plays from the modern international repertoire—Murray Schisgal's *Luv*, Jean Anouilh's *Antigone*, and Brian Friel's *Philadelphia, Here I Come!*—first at La Salle Academy (former home of the CANADIAN REPERTORY THEATRE) and, in its last year, at three local high schools. In its 1968-9 season it offered five plays and expanded its plans to include studio presentations of music, films, readings, plays, and workshops, as well as puppet theatre, televised plays, and an Ontario tour.

When the company ran into financial difficulties in 1968, the Theatre Foundation used its building fund of $24,000 to liquidate the debt, hoping the group would not need its own theatre but would become the resident company when the NATIONAL ARTS CENTRE opened in 1969. Neither this proposal nor an offer to become a summer-comedy troupe at the NAC was accepted by the Centre, and the Town Theatre ceased operations in 1969. Its last show was Neil Simon's *The Odd Couple*, starring Ken James and Hugh Webster. In grant money it had received only $6,000—from the Ontario Arts Council—during its short life.

Had it not been rebuffed by the NAC, it had the potential to become an alternate company there, with involvement of the local community, an ingredient often lacking at the NAC.

See Léa V. Usin, 'Creon's City: A History of Ottawa's Town Theatre', *Canadian Drama*, 12 (1986).

JAMES NOONAN

Townsend, John (1819-92). Born in Deptford, Eng., he went on the stage early, but left it in 1852 for business and politics. In 1857 he was elected Liberal MP for Greenwich, an office he soon lost through bankruptcy, but often cited on playbills. On immigrating to Canada he settled in Kingston, where he resumed acting, first in leading roles with the Garrison Amateurs, and then as manager of the Theatre Royal, City Hall, for the 1864-5 season. In June 1865 he became manager of HER MAJESTY'S THEATRE, Ottawa, but left in Sept. 1867, to tour small towns in Ontario and the border states from a base in Hamilton. In Kingston and Ottawa, Townsend's wife, daughters (Florence and Constance), and son (Harry) played most of the leading roles under the stage name of Grosvenor. On tour the Townsend Family Company also included a third daughter, Sarah, and sons Burnet, Thomas, Ernest, and George, as well as Mrs Harry Townsend, a popular vocalist. A stout defender of the stage as an intellectual entertainment, Townsend made Shakespeare the core of his repertoire, Richard III being his favourite role. After retiring from touring in 1877, he coached aspiring Hamilton actors, including Ida Lewis, who later achieved stardom as Julia ARTHUR. Harry succeeded his father as company manager for a few years, and was the only family member still on the stage when John Townsend died.

MARY SHORTT

Translations, English to French. The rarity of translations of Canadian plays from English to French is but another indication of the absence of creative and collaborative dialogue between the country's two language groups. Even in recent years, when translations in other literary genres have served to make important English texts available in French, few original plays from English Canada have been translated, published, or performed in French Canada. The reasons for this are complex: political divisions and separate cultural traditions; the domination (until the 1970s) of both groups by American commercial theatre; and the relative youth of professional theatre in Canada, which has meant that few plays that merit translation have been created in either language. But perhaps the most important reason is that, although Quebec dramatists in the last thirty years have been more innovative than their English counterparts—drawing heavily on

European and American theatrical experimen-tations—their best plays are regional in the sense that they present striking portraits of Quebec society and act as social commentary in their strong statement of opposition to Quebec's minority situation.

Although English-language plays from England and the U.S. have quite often been translated and performed in Quebec, the first play from English Canada to be performed in French was George RYGA's *The ECSTASY OF RITA JOE*, produced during the 1969–70 season by Gratien GÉLINAS at the COMÉDIE-CANADIENNE. The translation was not pub-lished. In their *Bibliography of Canadian Books in Translation/Bibliographie de livres canadiens traduits* (1975), Maureen Newman and Philip Stratford list only three play titles, the earliest dating from 1971: John HERBERT's *FORTUNE AND MEN'S EYES* (*Aux yeux des hommes*, tr. René Dionne, 1971); John T. MCDONOUGH's *CHARBONNEAU & LE CHEF* (*Charbonneau et le chef*, tr. & adapted by Paul HÉBERT and Pierre Morency, 1974); and Mordecai Richler's *The Bells of Hell Ring Ting-a-ling* (TV-script, *Les Cloches d'enfer*, tr. Gilles Rochette, 1974). All three translations were published by Leméac. The only translation to be published to date by another publishing house, in this case Édi-tions Héritage, is David FENNARIO's *On the Job* (*A l'ouvrage*, tr. Robert Guy Scully, 1979).

These four translations do not, however, adequately represent the current situation, since unpublished translations and adaptations for workshop and production purposes are an increasing fact of Quebec theatre, as in the case of Gélinas's production of *The Ecstasy of Rita Joe*. A second example is W.O. MITCH-ELL's *Back to Beulah* (*Aux Hirondelles*, tr. Arlette Francière, adapted by Albert Mil-laire), staged with great success by La COM-PAGNIE JEAN DUCEPPE in 1978. This was followed by Gaëtan Charlebois's *Aléola* (*Aléola*, adaptation by Jean Daigle, at Le THÉ-ÂTRE DU RIDEAU VERT in 1980). A sign of a new sense of the theatre community that transcended linguistic and cultural barriers was the invitation from Le THÉÂTRE D'AU-JOURD'HUI in 1978 to members of Paul THOMPSON's THEATRE PASSE MURAILLE com-pany to work with Claude Roussin on an adaptation and production of Rick SALUTIN's *Les CANADIENS* for a French-speaking Mon-treal audience.

Two productions in particular point to increasing contact between English- and French-language cultures in the theatre. The collective creation *BROUE* was first produced in French by Le Théâtre de Voyagements in 1979; it has, however, toured so extensively in English and been adapted so frequently to each fresh social context that few would con-sider it to be a translation in either language. Similarly, David Fennario's bilingual *BAL-CONVILLE*, first produced at Montreal's Eng-lish-language CENTAUR THEATRE in 1979, is unique in calling simultaneously upon the rich resources of both French and English, while holding up a mirror to a shared social reality.

Le Théâtre d'Aujourd'hui has continued to favour dialogue and collaboration, as has Le Centre d'essai des auteurs dramatiques (CEAD). In 1984 artistic director Gilbert Lepage included in the Théâtre d'Au-jourd'hui season a successful production of David FREEMAN's *Battering Ram* (*Le Bélier*, adapted by Louison Danis). New trends in the work of Quebec experimental companies led CEAD to collaborate in the organization of translation workshop exchanges with the publishing venture, New Dramatists, in New York in 1985 and 1986. At the same time the program 'Transmissions' was established jointly with Playwrights' Workshop Mon-treal in which English- and French-language playwrights work in close collaboration with translators and teams of professional actors and directors to prepare showcase produc-tions in each language. This led, for example, to the 1985 French production in Montreal of George WALKER's *ZASTROZZI* (tr. René Gingras). A similar collaboration began in 1984 in Quebec City, with productions by a variety of companies of John GRAY's *Rock and Roll*, Sharon POLLOCK's *BLOOD RELA-TIONS*, Tom WALMSLEY's *Something Red*, and Dennis Foon's *New Canadian Kid*, as well as two other productions by GREEN THUMB THEATRE of Vancouver, *Feeling Yes, Feeling No* and *Not So Dumb*. The Theatre Festival of the Americas, held in Montreal in 1985, offered many opportunities for theatre prac-titioners in French and English to collaborate in productions and discussions. In 1987 Jean-Louis ROUX's translation of Ralph Burd-man's *Eye to Eye* (*Tête à Tête*) was presented at the Café de la Place in Montreal.

It is clear that francophone and anglophone playwrights, directors, actors, and audiences have found common ground for the first time

Translations, English to French

in Canada's theatrical history, which may help them transcend the barriers imposed by language difference.

See A. Brisset, 'Institution théâtrale au Québec et problèmes théoriques de la traduction', *L'Institution littéraire* (1986).

LOUISE H. FORSYTH

Translations, French to English. Although drama related to Canada appeared in print in French as early as the 1609 publication in Paris of Marc LESCARBOT's *Le THÉÂTRE DE NEPTUNE EN LA NOUVELLE-FRANCE*, this text was not available in English translation until 1926. By contrast, Michel TREMBLAY's *Albertine, en cinq temps* was published in English in 1986, only two years after it appeared in French. This greatly reduced hiatus between French and English publications of a play is a very recent and somewhat misleading phenomenon, as a brief survey of the history of French-Canadian drama in English translation makes clear.

While it is known that British soldiers performed plays in French after the Conquest, these were invariably imported plays. Between 1800 and 1950 approximately 1,000 French-Canadian plays were written, the work of more than 250 playwrights. Only two of these, however, had been translated by 1950—Lescarbot's play and Louvigny de Montigny's *Je vous aime* (as *I Love You*, in 1937). In fact many of the original plays remained unpublished in either French or English, and few have attracted as much interest as modern works. The most significant of these plays prior to 1900 have appeared in translation in Anton Wagner's edition of *Canada's Lost Plays. Volume 4, Colonial Quebec: French-Canadian Drama, 1606 to 1966* (1982). This anthology contains plays by Marc Lescarbot, Joseph QUESNEL, Antoine GÉRIN-LAJOIE, Louis FRÉCHETTE, and Elzéar PAQUIN; they cover a range of historical issues, from earliest settlement to the Riel uprising. (Oddly, the Wagner anthology also includes Gratien GÉLINAS's *Yesterday the Children Were Dancing*, a 1967 translation by Mavor MOORE of *HIER, LES ENFANTS DAN-SAIENT*, which was not published in French until 1968.)

Wagner's historical range takes us from the beginnings of French drama in Canada to the beginnings of modern drama in French in Quebec. The inclusion of Gélinas suggests his pivotal role in the turn towards a more engaging and creditable drama in Quebec, dating from the appearance of *TIT-COQ* in 1950, which was not translated into English until 1967. In the 1960s English-Canadian playwrights showed a growing interest in French-Canadian subjects (John COULTER's *RIEL* plays, John Thomas McDONOUGH's *CHARBONNEAU & LE CHEF*), and anglophone audiences developed a deeper interest in Quebec drama, partly in response to evolving political realities there. As a result there was a marked increase in translation activity after the 1970 October Crisis. By the end of 1988 a total of fifty-three French-Canadian plays—thirty-nine of them first published in French since 1969—had been translated into English. Of these, twenty-seven translations appeared before 1977—one in the 1920s, one in the 1930s, four in the 1960s, and twenty-one in the period from 1970 to 1976—the work of eleven playwrights and fifteen translators. Michel Tremblay's work, rendered into English primarily by John Van Burek and Bill GLASSCO, accounted for almost half of the total. In the subsequent decade (1977-88) translations of twenty-six plays by eighteen playwrights have appeared, with the collaboration of Tremblay, Van Burek, and Glassco still the most prominent. It is clear that the pace of translation activity of the early 1970s has abated considerably in the past decade, despite the attention paid to the work of Michel Tremblay, the only Quebec dramatist whose *oeuvre* is almost entirely available in English and widely known internationally.

Tremblay's fellow playwrights have not been so well served in English, even though many of them have received critical acclaim. Of the six Quebec dramatists who won Governor General's Awards in the poetry and theatre category from 1960 to 1980—Paul TOUPIN, Jacques LANGUIRAND, Françoise LORANGER, Jacques Brault, Michel GARNEAU, and Réjean DUCHARME—only Ducharme's 1966 *L'Avalée des avalés* has been translated into English (in 1968 as *The Swallower Swallowed*). In 1981 the Canada Council created a specific Governor General's category for drama in French. Of the six winners—Marie LABERGE, Réjean Ducharme, René Gingras, René-Daniel DUBOIS, Maryse Pelletier, and Anne Legault—only three have been translated: Ducharme's *HA! ha!...* as *HA! HA!*, Gingras's *Syncope* as *Breaks*, and Dubois's *Ne blâmez jamais les bédouins* as *Don't Blame the Bedouins*, all published in

1986. Thus the recent prize-winning work of several of Quebec's female dramatists remains unavailable to anglophone readers. To these regrettable oversights must be added many other dramatic texts still unavailable in English, especially plays of the 1950s and 1960s (by Paul Toupin and Marcel DUBÉ, for example), the works of innovative and experimental dramatists (Claude GAUVREAU, Yves SAUVAGEAU), and the works of other important female dramatists (Françoise Loranger, Elizabeth Bourget, Jovette MARCHESSAULT). All the more inexcusable is the absence of published translations in cases where English translations have been prepared for productions of plays—by Jean Basile, Roch CARRIER, Roland LEPAGE, Michel Garneau, and René Gingras, for example.

In a few odd cases (Renald Tremblay and Serge Sirois), English translations make available to us works unpublished in French; but inaccessibility by unilingual anglophones to many important Quebec plays is more usual. Typical is the case of Claude JASMIN's *Le Veau dort*, which won the best-play award at the DOMINION DRAMA FESTIVAL in 1963 and was published in French in 1979, but has yet to appear in English translation. Moreover, at a time when many modern French-Canadian plays are less rigidly tied to particular social/political issues in Quebec, we might reasonably expect them to find a wider audience through translation.

A partial redress of such oversights seems to be under way, according to *The Canada Council 28th Annual Report 1984/85—Supplement* (1986). It lists seven projects to translate Quebec plays for production in English, including Michel Garneau's *Les Célébrations*, but there is no indication of publication plans for most of these works. Too little of the excellent work by translators such as Linda Gaboriau is made accessible to the anglophone reading public. Despite a June 1985 workshop in Montreal on translations-in-progress, very few publishers in Canada seem interested in drama in translation. Notable exceptions are Simon & Pierre of Toronto and Talonbooks of Vancouver, who have provided exemplary leadership in bringing Quebec drama to anglophone readers. Simon & Pierre's support was vindicated in 1979, when Allan Van Meer won the Canada Council Translation Prize for three plays published in the anthology *A Collection of Canadian Plays, volume V, Seven Authors from*

Quebec (1978). In 1981 Ray Ellenwood also won this prize for *Entrails* (Coach House), his translation of Gauvreau's *Les Entrailles*.

Reviews of these and other translations of Quebec drama published since 1976 can be found in the 'Letters in Canada' summer issue of the *University of Toronto Quarterly*, beginning in 1977 and, as of 1986, in the fall issue. A partial bibliography of Quebec drama in translation can be found in Philip Stratford's *Bibliography of Canadian Books in Translation* (1977), which will be updated in the forthcoming third edition.

While it may not now take three centuries for some translations to appear, it regularly takes many months and sometimes several years. Even the exceptionally popular *BROUE* did not appear in an English production for three years, which demonstrates the great need for a more active translation of new works, especially since theatre often reflects contemporary issues more fully and directly than other literary genres. Too many important French-Canadian plays remain inaccessible to unilingual anglophone readers, and too much of what is available has not been accorded adequate editorial scrutiny. What is needed for the future is more rigorous vetting of manuscripts, as well as greater interest in this genre both by the country's best translators and by a wider range of publishing houses, large as well as small.

JOHN J. O'CONNOR

Tremayne, William A. (1864-1939). Born in Portland, Maine, he was acting in local stock companies and writing film scripts for the Vitagraph Motion Picture Company by the 1890s. Eventually he turned his attention wholly to the stage. In collaboration with Logan Fuller he wrote *Lost, 24 Hours*, produced in 1895 at Hoyt's Theatre, New York, by Robert Hilliard. On 17 Jan. 1898 the play was produced at the Criterion Independent Theatre as *A New Yorker*.

During the late 1890s Tremayne formed an association with the actor Robert Bruce Mantell, who appeared in Tremayne's *The Secret Warrant* (1897), and, in Toronto, during March 1900, in an adaptation (unpublished) of Joseph Hatton's novel *The Dagger and the Cross*. Other Tremayne plays produced in this early period include *The Rogue's Daughter*, written in 1898, and *A Free Lance*, a great success in England in 1901. *The Triumph of Betty* played the RUSSELL THEATRE in Ottawa

Tremayne

in 1906, with Adelaide Thurston in the lead. *The Black Feather*, which had a Canadian setting, premièred at the Toronto GRAND OPERA HOUSE on 8 Sept. 1916, produced by actor-manager Albert Brown, and was later presented in Montreal with Basil Donn in the lead role of Dick Kent. It was published in Boston as *The Man Who Went* (1918). Tremayne's plays were for the most part romantic and melodramatic star vehicles; but they were widely popular, and refreshingly stage-worthy when compared to the poetic dramas of his Canadian contemporaries.

During his years as a professional playwright Tremayne began to make his mark as a director with various amateur groups in Montreal. He was appointed stage director of the Trinity Players in 1911, and also directed for The Weredale Players of St Stephen's Church, the Emmanuel Church Players, the Xmas Tree League Players of St Lambert, the Court Players, the Dickens Fellowship, the Community Players, and the Little Theatre Players.

Tremayne died in Montreal in Dec. 1939. He remains one of our most prolific early playwrights and his work as a director in Montreal must inevitably prove important to that city's theatrical history.

MURRAY D. EDWARDS

Michel Tremblay

Tremblay, Michel (b. 1942). An innovator in language and technique, Michel Tremblay, beginning with the landmark production of *Les BELLES-SOEURS* in Aug. 1968, has been instrumental in effecting the transition from 'French Canadian' to 'québécois' theatre.

Born on 25 June 1942—son of Armand Tremblay, a linotype operator, and Rhéauna Tremblay—on rue Fabre, in the Plateau Royal district of East Montreal, he won a scholarship to attend a collège classique in 1955 as 'best-in-French' student in the province. The academic setting proving too snobbish for his taste, he soon returned to public school—continuing, however, to read the classics independently. Another major love was television; as he began to write, at the age of twelve, his characters were modelled on the popular 'Famille Plouffe' series.

In 1959, after finishing high school, he became a linotype operator; but with the success of *Les Belles-Soeurs* he dedicated himself entirely to writing. His developmental years were strongly influenced by the cultural ferment created by Quebec's Quiet Revolu-

tion, reflected in theatre by the dominant modes of psychological realism, structural experimentation, and forthright political expression. The work of Tremblay achieves a happy synthesis of all three. He was greatly assisted in finding his way as a dramatist by André BRASSARD; the two first met in 1964, became close friends and, later, collaborators.

Tremblay's early work, written in classical French, deals mainly with the fantastic; he now refers to it as 'foreign subliterature'. It includes two short plays, *Les Socles* (published in French and English in *Canadian Theatre Review*, 24) and *Les Paons* (performed in 1971 by L'Atelier d'Ottawa); a collection of short stories, *Contes pour buveurs attardés* (1966), translated by Michael Bullock as *Stories for Late-Night Drinkers* (1977); and a novel, *La Cité dans l'oeuf* (1969). A decisive change of direction occurred in 1965 when Tremblay, having seen (with Brassard) yet another unsatisfactory French-Canadian movie, recognized the source of the problem: the artificiality of the language—'foreign' classical

French. In three weeks Tremblay wrote *Les Belles-Soeurs*, using *joual* as his dramatic idiom. All his major works are written in *joual* or—a subsequent modification—in *québécois*. Two settings only are used: rue Fabre with its monstrous domestic life, and The Main, a dubious escape into marginality, transvestism, and illusion.

The rue Fabre plays include *Les Belles-Soeurs*, *En Pièces détachées*, *À TOI, POUR TOU-JOURS, TA MARIE-LOU*, and *Bonjour, là, bonjour*; the Main plays are *Trois petits tours*, *La Duchesse de Langeais*, and *Hosanna*; the two areas come together in *Sainte Carmen de la Main* and *Damnée Manon, Sacrée Sandra*, which concludes the *Belles-Soeurs* cycle. The cycle constitutes a complete universe, which Tremblay subsequently complemented with the 'Chroniques du Plateau Royal' novels: *La grosse femme d'à coté est enceinte* (1978), *Thérèse et Pierrette à l'école des Saints-Anges* (1980), and *La Duchesse et le roturier* (1982); the first two have been translated by Sheila Fischman as *The Fat Woman Next Door is Pregnant* (1981) and *Thérèse and Pierrette at the École des Saintes Anges* (1982). The novels provide the background of the characters of the plays; *Les Belles-Soeurs* begins where the last 'Chronicle' leaves off.

Tremblay's drama shows the influence of his favourite writers: the Greeks, especially the choral tragedies of Aeschylus; Shakespeare's soliloquies; the absurdism of Beckett; American playwrights, especially Tennessee Williams. Tremblay's plays are highly complex and theatrical, yet early criticism tended to concentrate on the political aspect of his plays, much to the author's disappointment. *Les Belles-Soeurs* (1968), for example, was originally interpreted mainly as a political statement (the use of *joual*, the focus on women, symbols of oppression and exploitation). For some the play presented too sordid an image of French Canada, while radical critics (e.g. Michel Bélair) acclaimed it as the first manifestation of a genuine québécois theatre. In 1973 it received rave reviews in Paris (the language issue did not seem a problem): 'Les Belles-Soeurs sont en joual comme Andromaque est en alexandrins' (Jacques Cellars, *Le Monde*).

En Pièces détachées (1970), next in the family cycle, exists both in stage and television versions (1969, THÉÂTRE DE QUAT'SOUS; 1971, French-language CBC-TV). Translated by Allan Van Meer (published as *Like Death Warmed Over* in 1973 and as *Montreal Smoked Meat* in 1975), the play returns to an earlier sketch, which had a late-night production in 1966 by Brassard's Mouvement Contemporain as *Cinq*. Like the 'maudite vie plate' refrain in *Les Belles-Soeurs*, a reiterated 'chus pas capable' ('I just can't') sums up the underlying attrition motif. It centres on old Robertine, whose long monologue ('j'ai jamais rien eu'/'I've never had anything') Tremblay considers the best thing he has ever done. Of her two children, one, Hélène/Thérèse, lives out a life of frustration and alcoholism; the other, Marcel/Claude, has been committed to an insane asylum. On his visit home the madman's sense of omnipotence contrasts starkly with the impotence of the other characters.

The next play in the cycle, *À toi, pour toujours, ta Marie-Lou* (1973)—translated by John Van Burek and Bill GLASSCO as *Forever Yours, Marie-Lou* (1973)—is Tremblay's starkest indictment of Quebec family life. A powerful examination of human relations, it is also a political parable, the parents representing a hopeless past, Manon an ineffectual present, and Carmen a possible liberation.

Largely autobiographical, and dedicated to Tremblay's father, *Bonjour, là, Bonjour* (1974) (translated into English, with the same title, by Van Burek and Glassco, 1975), explores a father-son relationship against a setting of sexual frustration and poor communication (hampered by the father's deafness). Serge, the only son in a family of three older sisters and two spinster aunts, is the victim of sexual and emotional turmoil. Only when he and his father fully accept Serge's incestuous love for his sister Nicole does the possibility for love present itself—an unusual affirmation in Tremblay. The play is structured along musical lines in a sequence of scenes from 'solo' to 'octuor'.

The Main cycle of plays presents characters who have escaped the rue Fabre only to find disillusionment and frustration in the cheap showbiz and prostitution scene of the Main. It is aptly introduced by *Trois petits tours* (1969, French-language CBC-TV), made up of three sketches of alienation in showbusiness life: *Berthe*, *Johnny Mangano and his Astonishing Dogs*, and *Gloria Star*. *La Duchesse de Langeais* (1970), first performed by Les Insolents de Val d'Or, Quebec, 1969, translated by Van Burek with the same title (1976), is a two-act play, carried entirely by

Tremblay

one character who, as in Beckett's *Krapp's Last Tape*, reconstructs her life in a single monologue. The play is set on a café terrace in a southern resort where Tremblay's aging drag queen battles a broken heart. A psychological drama on the tragedy of aging and on alienation, *La Duchesse de Langeais* exploits language to indicate shifting levels of reality. Fabricating a glamorous past she never had, La Duchesse (one of Tremblay's most memorable characters) speaks in somewhat pretentious classical French, only to revert to *joual*, crudeness, and scatology when she returns to the real facts of her life as a transvestite prostitute rejected by the young lover she adores.

Hosanna (1973)—first performed at Théâtre de Quat'Sous and translated with the same title by Van Burek and Glassco (1974)—is the most ambitious and political of Tremblay's transvestite plays. The identity crisis undergone—and eventually overcome—by Hosanna reflects the identity crisis of the Quebec people. 'We have been transvestites for 300 years, that's no joke,' says Tremblay. This two-act play also examines a crisis in the relationship between two lovers. Hosanna has spent endless effort to dress up as Elizabeth Taylor-as-Cleopatra for a Halloween party. When her scheme fails, and even her lover Cuirette joins in the ridicule, she is deeply humiliated. Each act can be seen as an emotional boxing match; each ends in an affirmation of love—the first tentative; the second, a final acceptance of Hosanna as he turns his nude body towards Cuirette.

In other plays Tremblay relates his two worlds: the sisters of *À toi, pour toujours, ta Marie-Lou* make another, and final, appearance. Tremblay's mystical tendencies, often hidden under surface realism, come to the fore in *Sainte Carmen de la Main* (1976, PLACE DES ARTS, Montreal), translated as *Sainte Carmen of the Main* (1976) by Van Burek, and *Damnée Manon, Sacrée Sandra* (1977, Théâtre de Quat'Sous), also translated, with the same title (1981), by Van Burek.

Described by Tremblay as an 'opéra parlé', *Sainte Carmen* follows the structural pattern of Greek tragedy (episodes separated by choruses), with the choral parts composed in the form of musical scores. This classical structure is combined with a tawdry setting (the Main) and even more tawdry characters: the heroine is a yodelling queen in a cheap cabaret, the choruses are whores and transvestites. It was a bold experiment that backfired

when the play was first produced with a stylized all-white set and costumes emphasizing the element of Greek tragedy. A 1978 version at the THÉÂTRE DU NOUVEAU MONDE stressed realism in set and characters. The evolution of Carmen from tentative liberation in the first play to martyrdom in the second is existentialist: from awareness to freedom to responsibility to action. When Carmen changes her program to songs written by herself, in the language of her audience and about their own concerns and problems, the effect is electrifying. But Carmen becomes a victim of her 'boss', who is intolerant of change. Her death serves as a parable of the artist's freedom and mission, and of the archetypal Saviour figure's inevitable destruction at the hands of an uncomprehending society. A 'pop song fantasia' musical version of *Sainte Carmen* (music by Sydney Hodkinson, libretto by Lee Devin) was produced at the 1988 Guelph Spring Festival.

The worlds of rue Fabre, of the Main, and of The Great Beyond finally come together in *Damnée Manon, Sacrée Sandra*, which closes the cycle (1977, Théâtre de Quat'Sous, translated, with the same title, 1981, by Van Burek). Two disparate but complementary characters, 'born on the same day and in the same house' on rue Fabre, pursue their separate search for ecstasy: one through sensuality, the other through mysticism, until the two become one in their quest—which, we discover, has taken place in the mind of the author. In this play—which reflects the tension between surface puritanism and repressed sexuality typical of Quebec—Tremblay set out 'to prove that religion and sex take their source in one and the same need for an absolute' (*La Presse*, 26 Feb. 1977). The theme is expressed through an elaborate system of complementary images (Sandra in white, in a room painted black; Manon in black, in a room painted white; red rosary v. green lipstick; sensual use of a religious object v. religious use of a sexual object). Manon, daughter of Marie-Lou and still living in her mother's room, relentlessly pursues the delights of mystical union; Sandra, having returned to her birthplace after a lifetime of transvestite debauchery, follows Manon's activities from her window across the street as he/she tries to create her own perverted ecstasies. In the finale both characters, aware they have been 'created by Michel', return to the crucible of their author's mind, opposites finally reconciled.

Following the completion of the *Belles-Soeurs* cycle, Tremblay dedicated his energies mainly to the 'Chroniques du Plateau Royal'. He has, however, written other plays. *L'Impromptu d'Outremont* (1980, Théâtre du Nouveau Monde), translated by Van Burek as *The Impromptu of Outremont* (1981), is a satire on the cultural values of the bourgeoisie and their 'auto-colonisation'. *Les anciennes odeurs* (1981, Théâtre de Quat'Sous), translated by John Stowe as *Remember Me* (1984), is another psychological study of the homosexual couple, dealing, says Tremblay, with 'the complicity and the tenderness which remain after a couple has broken up' (*Lettres québécoises*, 23, p. 55). *Albertine, en cinq temps* (1984, NATIONAL ARTS CENTRE, Ottawa; translated by Van Burek and Glassco as *Albertine, in Five Times*) is another technical *tour de force*, with one character, Albertine, in dialogue with her various selves at ages 30, 40, 50, 60, and 70, her sister Madeleine functioning as a kind of chorus. Tremblay's most recent play, *Le vrai monde?* (1987, National Arts Centre, translated by Van Burek and Glassco as *The Real World?*), explores the writer's responsibility to the people and events from which he draws his material, analysing familiar themes such as lack of communication within the family and father/son tensions.

Tremblay's other dramatic works include *Le train*, written in 1960, which won first prize in Radio-Canada's Young Author's Competition, and *Surprise! Surprise!* (1977; translated by Van Burek, 1976), which was first performed at Théâtre du Nouveau Monde in 1977. He has written two musical comedies: *Demain matin, Montréal m'attend* (1972), with music by François Dompierre, produced in 1970 at the Jardin des Étoiles, La Ronde, Montreal; and *Les Héros de mon enfance* (1976), with music by Sylvain Lelièvre, produced at THÉÂTRE DE MARJOLAINE, Eastman, Quebec, in 1976. His translations include Aristophanes' *Lysistrata* (1969), which opened the National Arts Centre, Ottawa, in 1969; Paul Zindel's *The Effect of Gamma Rays on Man-in-the-Moon Marigolds* (1970) and *And Miss Reardon Drinks a Little* (1971); *I'm Getting My Act Together and Taking It On The Road* by Gretchen Cryer and Nancy Ford (performed in 1975); *Mystero Buffo* by Dario Fo (performed at the Théâtre du Nouveau Monde in 1973); and

Chekhov's *Uncle Vanya* (an adaptation with Kim Taroshevskaya, performed at the National Arts Centre in 1984).

Tremblay has written a number of film scenarios, including three directed by Brassard, and a 1977 television adaptation of Gabrielle Roy's novel, *Bonheur d'occasion*. *Backyard Theatre* (1972) is a National Film Board documentary about Tremblay and Brassard, featuring characters from the plays.

Tremblay's plays in English translation have been successsfully premièred in various parts of Canada: *Forever Yours, Marie-Lou* in 1972, *Hosanna* in 1974, *Bonjour, là, Bonjour* in 1975, *Sainte Carmen of the Main* in 1978, *Albertine, in Five Times* in 1985, and *The Real World?* in 1988, all at TARRAGON THEATRE, Toronto; *Damnée Manon, Sacrée Sandra*, at Mount St Vincent Univ., Halifax, in 1978 (and at Tarragon in 1979); *Les Belles-Soeurs* in 1973 at the ST. LAWRENCE CENTRE; *La Duchesse de Langeais* in 1978 at New College, University of Toronto; *Like Death Warmed Over* in 1973, at the MANITOBA THEATRE CENTRE; and *The Impromptu of Outremont* in 1980, at the Vancouver Arts Centre. The plays have also been performed internationally, especially in the U.S. and France.

See Michel Bélair, *Michel Tremblay* (1972); Renate Usmiani, *Michel Tremblay* (1982); *Voix et Images* (Winter 1982), a special Tremblay issue; and Donald Smith, 'Interview avec Michel Tremblay', *Lettres québécoises* 23 (automne 1982).   RENATE USMIANI

Turnbull, Keith (b. 1944). Born in Lindsay, Ont., he attended the Univ. of Western Ontario (BA, 1965) and became interested in new plays when co-directing the première of James REANEY's *The Sun and The Moon* for London's Campus Players in 1965. At the MANITOBA THEATRE CENTRE he directed classical, contemporary, and experimental works as director of the Second Stage (1968–70) and as artistic director (1971-2). From 1968 to 1970 he also assisted Jean GASCON and John HIRSCH at the STRATFORD FESTIVAL and directed the 1970 Stratford production of Jean-Claude van Itallie's *America Hurrah!* at Ottawa's NATIONAL ARTS CENTRE. In 1973 he led summer workshops in Halifax on *Sticks and Stones*, the first part of Reaney's *The DONNELLYS* trilogy, which opened at TARRAGON THEATRE in Toronto on 24 Nov., followed by *The St Nicholas Hotel* (16 Nov. 1974), and *Handcuffs* (29 Mar. 1975). Influenced by Northrop Frye and Shakespeare, and representing one of the finest achievements of the ALTERNATE THEATRE movement, the productions used emblematic staging techniques to communicate a mythic story shaped by romance conventions. Under Turnbull's direction the newly formed NDWT company then took the trilogy on a daunting cross-Canada tour (Sept.-Dec. 1975), vividly described in Reaney's *Fourteen Barrels From Sea To Sea* (1977). Based in Toronto and furthering its commitment to new work and new audiences, NDWT presented four more Reaney premières (1976-81), together with experimental plays by young writers (Gordon Pengilly, Bryan WADE), and in 1979 toured the revue *Northern Delights* to northern communities in Ontario, Manitoba, and the Northwest Territories. In 1982 administrative, financial, and artistic problems forced the company to disband. Turnbull has been Vice-President (1978) and President (1979-80) of the Toronto Theatre Alliance, and has taught at the NATIONAL THEATRE SCHOOL (1972-4 and 1980) and at the Univ. of Calgary (1982-6), where he directed the première of Reaney's *The Canadian Brothers* in Nov. 1983. DENIS SALTER

Tweed, Tommy (1908-71). Born Thomas William in Medicine Hat, Alta, he attended the Univ. of Manitoba from 1928 to 1932 and acted with the University Players. From 1932 he acted with the Winnipeg Little Theatre and on radio with Esse LJUNGH, while writing scripts and continuity for radio station CKY. In 1941 Tweed moved to Toronto, where he free-lanced as a script-writer for radio and as an actor for radio, film, and on stage for the NEW PLAY SOCIETY.

Tweed played a major role as actor and playwright during the golden years of CBC radio drama from the early 1940s, particularly in the prestigious 'Stage' and 'Wednesday Night' series, working with Esse Ljungh, Frank Willis, Hector MacFadyen, and Andrew ALLAN.

His plays for radio include wry historical documentaries such as *The Honorable Member for Kingston* (produced by Andrew Allan, Toronto, 1953), about Sir John A. Macdonald, and *The Brass Pounder from Illinois* (produced by Allan, Toronto, 1960) on Van Horne and the CPR, and many adaptations of famous novels. But it was his puckish satires, informed by his prairie populism and

often directed at Canadian history, that made his reputation. These satires include *Ti' Jean and the Devil's Playing Cards* (produced by Esse Ljungh, Toronto, 1947); *Secret Treaty* (produced by Andrew Allan, Toronto, 1946), on Canada as seen by native Indians; and his hilarious satire about a prairie river-battle during the Riel Rebellion, *Full Speed Sideways* (produced by Allan, Toronto, 1961, published in 1987). Tweed wrote some 130 plays for CBC (of which about sixty are originals) and fourteen complete serials, including nine originals. He also acted and wrote for CBC-TV from 1964.

Tweed's stage plays include *Sir John A. Beats the Devil*, at the CONFEDERATION CENTRE, Charlottetown, PEI, and NEPTUNE THEATRE, Halifax, both in 1964, and *The Dream Play* produced by Jane MALLETT on a western tour in 1966. Tweed's *The Dream*, first produced in 1965, was published by the Ottawa Centennial Commission in 1965. Tweed won Ohio State Radio Drama awards in 1944 and 1945.

See also RADIO DRAMA IN ENGLISH.

HOWARD FINK

25th Street Theatre. One of a handful of Canadian theatres dedicated almost solely to the production of new Canadian plays, it was founded in Saskatoon in 1971 by Andras Tahn and other Univ. of Saskatchewan graduates as an art centre and theatre but soon came to focus entirely on theatre. Its first major production was Tahn's *Covent Garden* in 1973, and its first success was Tahn's and the company's collective, *The Ballad of Billy the Kid* in 1975. During the summer of 1975—while Paul THOMPSON and THEATRE PASSE MURAILLE were in Saskatchewan to research and produce *The West Show*—Thompson taught the company his methods of COLLECTIVE CREATION. The first result of that process was *If You're So Good Why Are You In Saskatoon?* in 1975; the most successful product was *PAPER WHEAT* in 1977.

Other collective productions included *Heartbreak Hotel* by Layne Coleman and the company in 1976; *Generation and ½*, a sequel to *Paper Wheat*, in 1978; two summer productions—*Prairie Psalms* in 1977 and *Don'tcha Know the North Wind and You in My Hair* in 1978; *Rodeo* by Don Wise, Layne Coleman, and the cast in 1981; and *Jessica* by Maria Campbell, Linda GRIFFITHS, and Paul Thompson in 1982.

While Tahn, artistic director until 1980, has been the most important figure in the theatre's history, actors Layne Coleman and Linda Griffiths—who began their careers with the company—have become important authors and directors in their own right. Coleman was artistic director for the 1980-1 season, and Tahn, Coleman, and Griffiths shared this post from 1981 to 1983; Gordon McCall was artistic director for the 1983-4 season; and Tom Bentley-Fisher from 1985 to the present.

In addition to collective creations, the theatre has also premièred authored texts: E.H. Carefoot's *Matonabbee* in 1980; Brad Fraser's *Wolfboy* in 1981; Alun Hibbert's *Playing the Fool* in 1981; Paul Quarrington's *The Second* in 1982; Ken MITCHELL's and Michael Taylor's *Laffin Jack Rivers' Show* in 1983; Thelma Oliver's *Diefenbaker* in 1983; Ken Mitchell's *The Plainsmen* in 1985; and Don Kerr's *The*

Great War in 1985. The artistic directors also contributed original scripts: Andy Tahn, *Jacob Keep* in 1979 and *In Search of a Sin* in 1983; Layne Coleman (with William Hominuke), *The Queen's Cowboy* in 1979; and Linda Griffiths (with Patrick Brymer), *O. D. on Paradise* in 1982.

The theatre has never had a permanent home for more than two seasons and has almost always been on the brink of economic disaster, particularly in the fall of 1982 when the board of directors resigned, and in the fall of 1984 when McCall resigned as artistic director. But it continues by sheer will-power and commitment. Because its audiences vary from show to show, it has never developed a large permanent local following.

The theatre's archives are deposited in the Short Collection, University of Saskatchewan Archives.

DON KERR

U

University Alumnae Dramatic Club. Founded by women graduates in 1918 as the Dramatic Club of the University College Alumnae Association, Univ. of Toronto, it mounted plays throughout the 1920s and 1930s in the Women's Union (now the Union) of University College, the Toronto Conservatory of Music, and HART HOUSE THEATRE. Members were joined in performance by men from the ARTS AND LETTERS CLUB, local theatre companies, and radio. Plays were chosen from the current British and American repertoire, with the addition of some English classics. The Club continued to meet through 1939-45, although a number of its members were actively involved in troop shows. At the end of the war the Club's membership was broadened to include women graduates of other post-secondary institutions, and its name was changed to the present form. In 1947 the Club returned to its pre-war pattern of activity, concentrating on its regular entry to the DOMINION DRAMA FESTIVAL (where, in 1937, it had won first

place with an act of Martinez Sierra's *The Cradlesong*) as well as on performances in Hart House.

This pattern proved unsuitable in the 1950s, when Canadian semi-professional and professional theatre began to provide competition in Toronto. New sights for the Club were set by critic, director, and designer Herbert WHITTAKER. He chose challenging plays for the UADC Festival entries and attracted actors who were then trying to make their way professionally. Successes included Bernard Shaw's *In Good King Charles's Golden Days* in 1951 with John COLICOS (who won the best actor award at the DDF finals), Ted Follows, William NEEDLES, and Ron Hartmann in the cast; and T.S. Eliot's *Family Reunion* in 1953 (with Richard EASTON and David GARDNER). Both won DDF awards as the best productions in English. Henry Kaplan, E.G. Sterndale Bennett, William Needles, and Robert GILL also directed for UADC in the 1950s and early 1960s.

In 1956 Leon MAJOR's production of Patri-

University Alumnae Dramatic Club

Ruth Norris, John Colicos, Christopher Taylor, and Sheila Craig in Toronto's University Alumnae Dramatic Club's 1957 production of Bernard Shaw's In Good King Charles's Golden Days

cia JOUDRY's *Teach Me How to Cry* won the DDF finals. The prize money ($1,000) enabled the UADC to modify its programming and operation by renting premises to produce plays from outside the standard repertoire, cutting down production expenses, and mounting longer runs. The new repertoire included the first presentation of Samuel Beckett to Toronto audiences (*Waiting for Godot* in 1957, directed by Pamela Terry, with Fred Euringer, Kenneth Wickes, Ivor Jackson, and Powell Jones) and the first Ionesco production (*The Lesson* in 1959, directed by Gordon Johnson). The première production of James REANEY's *The Killdeer* (1960, directed by Pamela Terry) went to the DDF finals. The repertoire of the UADC has continued to be an eclectic mix of classical and contemporary plays, supplemented by staged readings from scripts prepared by members: these have included Anne Tait's scripts from Brecht, W. B. Yeats, and D.H. Lawrence; Francess Halpenny's from Emily Carr and

Alice Munro; and Juliana Saxton's *Women of Margaret Laurence*, which Norma Edwards tours nationally and internationally.

Since 1972 the UADC has been housed in the Alumnae Theatre at 70 Berkeley St, a 154-seat theatre designed by Ron Thom, with backstage workshops and storage and the 75-seat Elizabeth Mascall studio. Previous UADC premises (known as Coach House Theatres) have been on Huntley St (a 7′ × 14′ stage and thirty-five seats), Bedford Rd, Huron St (a converted synagogue), and Maplewood Ave.

UADC has never been eligible for arts grants, but with the aid of fees, rentals, box office, and immense volunteer assistance, it has remained solvent. Its aim has always been to provide opportunities for its casts, directors, and crews to learn and to experiment, and, in the ambience of a small theatre, to offer its audiences plays they might not see elsewhere.

FRANCESS G. HALPENNY

V

Van Bridge, Tony (b. 1917). Born in London, Eng., Valentine Anthony Neil Bridge trained at the Royal Academy of Dramatic Art in 1938. He acted with the Young Vic and Old Vic companies before coming to Canada in 1954, working first in radio, then with the STRATFORD FESTIVAL Company from 1955. He soon made his mark as a comic actor notable for a delightful combination of style and humanity as Bardolphe in *Henry V* in 1956, the Gravedigger in *Hamlet* in 1957, Dogberry in *Much Ado about Nothing* in 1958, and Bottom in *A Midsummer Night's Dream* in 1960. His Falstaff in both parts of *Henry IV* in 1965 won universal acclaim as a 'Fat Jack with a mind', both 'engaging and repulsive'.

While with the CANADIAN PLAYERS (1954-9) van Bridge began to direct and, as an actor, to develop a Shaw repertoire as significant as his Shakespeare. In 1968 he played Cauchon in *Saint Joan* at New York's Lincoln Centre and Shotover in the SHAW FESTIVAL's *Heartbreak House*. In 1970 the Shaw Festival premièred *G.K.C.*, van Bridge's popular one-man show about G.K. Chesterton. In 1974-5 van Bridge was acting artistic director of the Shaw Festival. His most notable directing achievement to date (he has directed about a dozen plays in the U.S. and Canada) was his full-length *Man and Superman* at the Shaw Festival in 1977, a five-and-a-half hour production in which he also played Mendoza and the Devil. One critic called this feat 'theatre worth flying across an ocean to experience'.

In the 1980s van Bridge has continued occasional stage work, but spends most of his time in television, including the title role in 'Judge', a 1982 half-hour CBC series.

SUSAN STONE-BLACKBURN

Van Cortland, Ida (1854-1924). Born Ellen Buckley in Manchester, Eng., she grew up in Chicago and was the only member of her family to survive the Chicago fire of 1871. She taught in Chicago and Guelph before beginning her acting career in 1877 as a member of Charlotte MORRISON's stock company at Toronto's GRAND OPERA HOUSE, adopting the stage name of Ida Van Cortland. While touring the Maritimes with William NANNARY in 1881 she met Albert TAVERNIER;

Ida Van Cortland in Joaquin Miller's The Danites

they married in New York in 1881 and had a daughter in 1887. After a few seasons of touring with U.S. companies, they formed their own company and toured Ontario and the northern U.S. until 1896. Ida was the artistic centre of the Tavernier Company, playing heavy emotional roles in the manner of Clara MORRIS and Fanny Davenport. Favourite parts included the title role in Alexandre Dumas *fils's Camille*, Cora in Augustin Daly's adaptation of Adolph Belot's *Article 47*, and Stéphanie de Mohrivart in Philip Merivale's *Forget-Me-Not*. Separated from her husband in 1896, she retired from acting in 1898 and died on Big Island, Blue Sea Lake, Quebec.

KATHLEEN FRASER

Vancouver East Cultural Centre. Situated on Venables St, Vancouver, in the former Grandview United Church (built in 1909 and closed in 1970), it needed to be only slightly adapted to become a performing arts venue. Recognizing the building's potential, Chris Wootten secured a $32,000 Local Initiatives Program grant for the conversion, and $16,000 from the city for equipment. The Centre—seating 350, and with Wootten as director—opened in Oct. 1973 with performances by the Anna Wyman Dance Theatre. The auditorium is approximately 60' wide by 40' deep, with a small open stage. A balcony

Vancouver East Cultural Centre

The Vancouver East Cultural Centre's touring production of John Gray's Rock and Roll, *National Arts Centre, 1983, with (l. to r.) Babs Chula, Jay Brazeau, Alec Willows, Frank Mackay, Andrew Rhodes*

extends around three sides, and there is a large lounge. The theatre's initial mandate included multi-cultural activity, community service (a function later taken over by the nearby Britannia Community Centre), and local theatre-group activity, by troupes such as the GREEN THUMB THEATRE FOR YOUNG PEOPLE and West Coast Actors. Other uses have included Masterpiece and New Music series, Sunday-night folk and jazz concerts, childrens' films, and an annual Christmas craft fair. Wootten has claimed that the Centre draws a larger working-class audience than any other theatre in the city.

Vancouver East evolved in three directions from the mid-1970s. Wootten sought visiting companies, among them Newfoundland's CODCO; Toronto's THEATRE PASSE MURAILLE with *1837* and *The FARM SHOW*; Toronto's TARRAGON with Michel TREMBLAY's *Hosanna*; Saskatoon's 25TH STREET THEATRE with *PAPER WHEAT*; and Newfoundland's Rising Tide with *Joey*. The Centre has also sponsored several co-productions: Ken MITCHELL's *CRUEL TEARS* with the ARTS CLUB; Richard MONETTE in Barry Collins' *Judgement* with the STRATFORD FESTIVAL; John GRAY's *Rock and Roll* with the NATIONAL ARTS CENTRE; and Felix MIRBT's puppet productions of August Strindberg's

A Dream Play and Brecht's *Happy End*. The biggest and most profitable venture was Gray's BILLY BISHOP GOES TO WAR in 1978. From 1977 to 1985 TAMAHNOUS was the Centre's resident company, offering four shows annually.

Jeremy Long replaced Wootten as director from 1982 to 1984, followed by Wendy Newman (1984-9), who reduced the commitment to theatre, emphasizing instead children's entertainment, ethnic programs, music, and especially dance. MALCOLM PAGE

Vancouver Opera House. From 1891 to 1912 it served as Vancouver's principal theatre for touring companies and major individual performers. It was built adjacent to the first Hotel Vancouver at Georgia and Granville Streets at a cost of over $100,000 by the Canadian Pacific Railway Company, and owned by them until 1909. The seating capacity (including orchestra, gallery, and boxes) was 1,211, increasing to over 1,600 after substantial renovations in 1907. The original stage measured 33' x 70' and the proscenium opening 32' wide and 20' high. The theatre opened on 9 Feb. 1891 with a performance of Wagner's *Lohengrin* by the Emma Juch English Grand Opera Co. In the following September Sarah Bernhardt appeared in Victorien Sardou's *Fédora* and *La Tosca*. During the depression of the 1890s the Opera House was not fully utilized, but its fortunes improved, along with the economy, after the turn of the century and it shared in the heyday of touring road companies. (See TOURING STARS AND COMPANIES.) It was managed during this period by Englishman Ernest Ramsay Ricketts, under whom the number of annual performances regularly averaged between 150 and 200, and the Opera House benefited from formal links with impresarios in New York, notably John Cort. The official receipt books for 1906-7 and 1910-2 (kept in the Vancouver Public Library) chart the theatre's economic fortunes in detail. In 1911, for example, the gross receipts were almost $200,000.

In 1912 the theatre was acquired by the Sullivan-Considine VAUDEVILLE chain, and the following year a remodelled version of the building became the 'New Orpheum', linked with the Chicago-based Orpheum vaudeville circuit. Occasionally, however, it still served as a civic theatre. Performances by opera singers, classical instrumentalists, and Anna Pavlova shared the building with the vaudeville acts. The most frequently recalled performance at the New Orpheum is that of Sarah Bernhardt on her 1917 farewell tour when she was confined to a wheelchair.

Primarily a Famous Players movie theatre after that, it was known variously as the Vancouver Theatre (1927-35), the Lyric Theatre (1935-47), the International Cinema (1947-60), and (again) the Lyric Theatre (1960-9). It was demolished in 1969 to make way for Eaton's department store.

See R.B. Todd, 'The Organization of Professional Theatre in Vancouver, 1886-1914', *B.C. Studies*, 44 (1979-80), and 'Ernest Ramsay Ricketts and Theatre in Early Vancouver', *Vancouver History*, 19 (1980).

R.B. TODD

Vancouver Playhouse. This 670-seat theatre was completed in 1962 as the Queen Elizabeth Playhouse, but with few backstage facilities since it was intended for small touring companies and local community groups. In 1963, however, the Playhouse Theatre Company was formed, opening on 31 Oct. with Brendan Behan's *The Hostage*, directed by Malcolm BLACK. Like other regional theatres, it offers winter seasons of about six productions of recent London and New York hits, a few classics, and an occasional Canadian play.

In the first season Michael Johnston served as manager, producer, and designer. Malcolm Black followed as artistic director, 1964-7. He featured the first new Canadian play, Eric

Vancouver Opera House

Vancouver Playhouse

NICOL's *Like Father, Like Fun*, in 1966, following this with new works by James Clavell and Paul St Pierre. The first major season-ticket campaign, 1966-7, drew 6,000 subscribers. The budget in the first year was only $47,000; in the next twenty years the budget increased to almost three million dollars.

Joy COGHILL, artistic director 1967-9, had a triumph with George RYGA's *The ECSTASY OF RITA JOE* (which had been commissioned by Black), and again the following season with his musical about hippies, *Grass and Wild Strawberries*, produced in 1969. These years were difficult, nevertheless, with constant money problems and a board that preferred light entertainment. Coghill initiated a second stage, Stage 2, which presented low-budget productions in other locations: James REANEY's *Listen to the Wind* was particularly admired.

David GARDNER (1969-71) also had to cope with an unsympathetic board and inadequate finances, which forced him to close down Stage 2 in the spring of 1970. Gardner's productions of Peter Shaffer's *The Royal Hunt of the Sun* and of Tom Stoppard's *Rosencrantz and Guildenstern Are Dead* reached new heights of success, and Gardner also added theatre for young people to the Playhouse's functions in 1969, when it amalgamated with HOLIDAY THEATRE, which was a Theatre-in-Education wing of the Playhouse until 1977. When the board refused to allow Gardner to produce Ryga's controversial new play, *Captives of the Faceless Drummer*—about the 1970 FLQ crisis in Quebec—Gardner resigned.

His successor Paxton WHITEHEAD (1971-3), combined his Vancouver duties with directing the SHAW FESTIVAL. While his flair for such authors as Georges Feydeau and Alan Ayckbourn ensured success, he also presented the Canadian première of Beverley SIMONS' challenging *CRABDANCE* and new plays by Eric Nicol and Merv Campone.

Christopher NEWTON's six-year term, 1973-9, was marked by consistently high standards. Recognizing the inexperience of local directors, he brought in foreign directors such as Alan Dossor, Derek GOLDBY, and Philip Hedley from Britain. Liviu Cielei from Roumania directed a brilliant treatment of Georg Büchner's *Leonce and Lena*. Newton established a theatre school in 1975, headed first by Powys THOMAS, followed by Roger Hodgman and David Latham. He also

revived the second stage in 1975, which has survived under several names, such as the New Company, New Stage, and the New Series. To promote ensemble work, a permanent company on 36-week contracts was established in 1975-6. Successes included several plays by Shakespeare, Molière's *Tartuffe*, Bernard Shaw's *Pygmalion*, Peter Shaffer's *Equus*, Tom Stoppard's *Travesties*, and David FRENCH's *Leaving Home* and *Of the Fields, Lately*. Stephen Katz and Mary Kerr were responsible for turning Machiavelli's *Mandragola* and Bertolt Brecht's *The Caucasian Chalk Circle* into colorful extravaganzas. Despite the quality of Newton's work, playwright John GRAY notes of these years that 'when they did the same old stuff, only the subscribers came and they lost money; when they did adventurous work, the subscribers walked out and they *really* lost money.'

Roger Hodgman (1979-82) was Newton's obvious successor because of fine productions of David Storey's *The Contractor* and Odon Von Horvath's *Tales from the Vienna Woods*. Administrative demands defeated him, however, and quality and audiences declined. His play selection was something-for-everyone: a dirty-wig and worn-clothes production of William Congreve's *Love for Love*, Arthur Kopit's *Wings*, Noël Coward's *Blithe Spirit*, and George Kaufman's and Moss Hart's *The*

Robert Clothier and Laura Press in Seneca's Oedipus, *Vancouver Playhouse, 1978*

Man Who Came to Dinner. Unfortunately, Hodgman wasted time and money on Tennessee Williams' *The Red Devil Battery Sign* and on Williams' appalling re-write of Chekhov's *The Seagull*, called *The Notebook of Trigorin*.

Walter LEARNING (1982-7) took over a demoralized institution and set a tone of flair and showmanship. He spoke of plays of 'celebration' and presented a record twelve plays in his first season (including a summer season, and some productions at the VANCOUVER EAST CULTURAL CENTRE). While Newton had brought Heath LAMBERTS to the company and Hodgman Diane D'Aquila, Learning was the first to use stars regularly: William HUTT and Robin PHILLIPS unforgettably in Ronald Harwood's *The Dresser*, Gordon PINSENT as Prospero in *The Tempest*, Hutt in the lead in Robert Bolt's *A Man for All Seasons*, and others. Creditable productions included Michael Meyer's *K-2*, Caryl Churchill's *Cloud 9*, Peter Shaffer's *Amadeus*, Arthur Miller's *Death of a Salesman*, and Claire Luckham's *Trafford Tanzi*, with Learning playing the referee. *Godspell* was the best of several musicals and David French's *Salt-Water Moon* and Jean BARBEAU's *The Guys* were among the few Canadian works. The second stage continued to have low priority, offering only two plays in 1985-6, then none: the twelve plays of Learning's first season on the main stage had dwindled to only six. Audiences responded disappointingly even to such fine achievements as *The Dresser*. Guy SPRUNG took over as artistic director on an interim basis for the 1987-8 season, succeeded by Larry Lillo, starting with the 1988-9 season.

All directors have complained about their dependence on rented office and rehearsal space—at first two blocks away from the theatre, and subsequently on West 7th, two kilometres away. Directors have hoped in vain for a new building; Learning wanted a floating theatre in False Creek.

In the 1960s the Playhouse had begun to forge an identity with the plays of local writers Eric Nicol, George Ryga, Paul St Pierre, Beverley Simons, and Merv Campone. Newton gave it an identity of artifice and theatricality. Since his tenure it has floundered, overshadowed by its more commercial rival, the ARTS CLUB. A report released in 1987, however, announced ambitious plans for a year-round operation, more Canadian plays, a new second theatre for alternate drama, and a plan to eliminate a substantial accumulated deficit.   MALCOLM PAGE

Vaudeville. A mélange of comic, musical, magical, acrobatic, animal, and dance acts, it was often accompanied by short films or audience-participation sing-alongs illustrated with slide projections. First-class vaudeville normally consisted of eight star acts, each approximately twenty minutes long and performed twice daily; in small-time vaudeville there were as many as four or five shows a day, with only one star. Vaudeville flourished throughout North America between 1871 and 1940, reaching its peak in the first quarter of the twentieth century when, as a mass family entertainment, it competed directly with the legitimate theatre through syndicated chains and circuits of about 2,000 theatres. Roughly synonymous with the British Music Hall, it is considered the successor of 'variety', an earlier (less savoury) American equivalent presented in taverns and honky-tonk 'free and easies' catering to all-male drinking audiences and prostitutes. 'Clean' vaudeville resulted when the risqué routines and 'girlie' elements were siphoned off into BURLESQUE. As early as 1871 Toronto's famed minstrel Colin 'Cool' BURGESS had called one of his troupes in Ottawa the Gaiete Vaudeville Co., and in the same year an American company, Sargent's Great Vaudeville, opened in Louisville, Kentucky. These are possibly the earliest recorded uses of the term in North America. Another early example was the attempt by T.J. HERNDON in 1874 to turn Toronto's Queen's Theatre into a respectable 'vaudeville and novelty' house. The American entrepreneur Tony Pastor visited Toronto's GRAND OPERA HOUSE on 20 July 1875 with his cleaned-up variety show and by 24 Oct. 1881, when he opened his celebrated 14th Street family theatre in New York, 'vaudeville' was becoming identified with polite variety.

Benjamin Franklin Keith (1846-1914), who managed the Gaiety Musée in Boston, aided by Edward Franklin Albee (1857-1930), a former circus man, quickly turned polite vaudeville into a syndicated business. Whereas Pastor ran only one theatre, Keith and Albee built spacious new playhouses, bought out the F.F. Proctor and B.S. Moss chains, and eventually pioneered control over an eastern circuit of approximately 1,500 theatres in the

Vaudeville

U.S. and Canada. The twin IMPERIAL THE-ATREs in Montreal and Saint John; Halifax's Strand (today's NEPTUNE THEATRE); and Toronto's Shea's Yonge, Shea's Victoria, and Shea's Hippodrome were part of their chain. Because Keith-Albee houses banned drinking, smoking, whistling, and spitting, as well as off-colour stage routines, they earned the nickname 'Sunday School Circuit'. But in business the team was ruthless. Movies were unwelcome and Keith artists were forbidden to appear on radio. At the turn-of-the-century they had established the United Booking Office, which effectively controlled the hiring and firing of most performers. In 1911 they also paid legitimate-theatre syndicates—such as the Shuberts, and Marc Klaw and Abe Erlanger—to stay out of vaudeville for ten years. The Keith-Albee monopoly, however, was challenged by the independent agent William Morris and, later, by the Shuberts and Marcus Loew. Ottawa's Capitol and Toronto's ELGIN/WINTER GARDEN complex and Uptown were Loew's theatres. In the West the San Francisco-based Orpheum circuit was pre-eminent until it eventually merged with Keith-Albee. Major ORPHEUM theatres existed in Winnipeg and Vancouver. (In 1928-9 Joseph P. Kennedy—J.F.K's father—engineered the merger of a small film company with Keith-Albee-Orpheum to create a new motion-picture chain, Radio Keith Orpheum: RKO. Albee's name was pointedly omitted.)

The largest independent vaudeville circuit was developed by the Greek-born Alexander PANTAGES, who began his training by managing Dawson City's Orpheum Theatre in 1900-1 with 'Klondike Kate' Rockwell, the Queen of the Yukon. Illustrious Pantages houses in Canada included the McPherson Theatre in Victoria, the Playhouse in Winnipeg, Edmonton's Strand, and Toronto's Imperial/Pantages (the largest in the country, seating 3,626). There were also smaller Canadian vaudeville-cum-film circuits, most of which were founded in 1906. In the West the management of W.B. Sherman stands out, as does C.W. Willis's and W. Cosgrove's Western Canadian Theatrical Circuit; in the east C.W. Bennett of London, Ont., was affiliated with Keith-Albee from 1906 to 1910, while the Allen Family (Bernard and his sons Jule and Jay) began in Brantford, Ont., and eventually controlled forty-five theatres, which they sold to Famous Players

in 1922. Another eastern vaudeville entrepreneur was Hamilton-based John Griffin, who sometimes worked with Ambrose SMALL.

In its heyday vaudeville attracted audiences that outnumbered those for legitimate plays by a ratio of ten to one. Competition led even Toronto's esteemed ROYAL ALEXANDRA THEATRE and PRINCESS THEATRE to become vaudeville houses briefly in 1921 and 1922. Established stage stars—such as Sarah Bernhardt, and Canadian expatriates Marie Dressler, James K. Hackett, May IRWIN, and Clara MORRIS, softshoe dancer George PRIMROSE, McKee RANKIN, and Rose STAHL—appeared on vaudeville bills performing scenes, songs, monologues, or specialty acts for huge salaries of $600 to $3,000 a week. Many so-called legitimate comedies were also vaudeville shows in disguise—a series of acts held together by the flimsiest of plot-lines. Vaudeville charged only twenty-five cents for the best seat, whereas a ticket for a play cost two or three dollars.

At the turn of the century vaudeville also embraced the new medium of film, but once the novelty had worn off the early silent one-reelers were used as 'chasers' to empty the theatres for the next show. As the movies evolved into feature-length entertainments the situation was reversed and short vaudeville programs ('tab shows') were sandwiched between the features. With the advent of the 'talkies' in 1927 and the high costs of converting to sound, movie managers discovered that the vaudeville acts were no longer economical or necessary to draw an audience. The sometimes exorbitant salaries, high freight rates, and free radio programs combined with the stock-market crash of 1929 to sound the death-knell for most touring attractions. Vaudeville survived a little longer, but its days were numbered. The demise was signalled when Broadway's Palace Theatre (the flagship of the Keith-Albee chain) dropped its high-class two-a-day policy and succumbed to the five-a-day grind. In 1932 it became a movie house. Subsequent revivals, especially on Ed Sullivan's television show (1948-74) and in the skilled acrobatics of the 1980s' 'new vaudeville' and hardrock's clowning have kept the spirit of vaudeville alive.

Many film luminaries, such as Charlie Chaplin and Fred Astaire, began in vaudeville as unknowns, as did Canadians Walter HUSTON and Gene Lockhart. But Canada's greatest contribution to vaudeville was the blonde singing and dancing comedienne Eva Tanguay (1878-1947). Born in Marbleton, Que., of a Parisien physician and a French-Canadian mother, the 'I Don't Care Girl' was billed as 'The Girl Who Made Vaudeville Famous' and 'Vaudeville's Greatest Box Office Attraction'. Swathed in feathers, she topped the bill for over thirty years earning $2,500 to $3,500 a week by flouting Keith's puritanical dicta. Her most provocative act, 'Salome', was introduced in 1908. Tanguay lost two million dollars in the 1929 crash and died, practically blind, in relative obscurity. Other Canadian headliners were Ontario's versatile Brown Brothers who are credited with making the saxophone famous, and Toronto's singing O'Connor Sisters. The Brown Brothers' comedy saxophone quintette and sextet moved from minstrel shows in the late 1880s and 1890s to ragtime recordings, appearances in at least four Broadway musicals, and continuous exposure on the vaudeville circuits until 1925. The six O'Connor Sisters were real sisters and proudly sang without a microphone. In 1929 they played for twenty-two weeks in Detroit's huge Fox Theatre, virtually selling out the 6,000 seats nightly. They flourished as a sextet in vaudeville between 1910 and 1937, and then entertained the troops during the Second World War as a smaller unit. Another popular vaudeville troupe that toured widely was the Winnipeg Kiddies, a juvenile concert party of up to forty children, aged three to eighteen, who sang and danced between 1915 and 1934. The Glasgow-born but Toronto-raised Jack Arthur (1889-1971), later the musical director of countless Toronto entertainments—he produced the Canadian ARMY SHOW and the CNE Grandstand Extravaganzas (1952-67)—began as a child prodigy on the violin and toured in vaudeville with Sir Harry Lauder. Some lesser-known Canadians who also brightened the vaudeville stages were Fifi D'Orsay (née Yvonne Lussier) (1904-), who worked with Will Rogers and ended up in films; the musical comedy star Mabel Barrison; Edna Phillips, leading lady with Chauncey Olcott; the singer Minnie Allen; comedienne Amelia Summerville; actor-playwright Willard Mack, and William Courtleigh of Guelph, who wrote vaudeville sketches; and Hamilton-born Dick Wilson, remembered for his comical drunk act. Canadian playwrights George V. Hobart (1867-1926) and James Forbes (1871-1938) also wrote skits for vaudeville. (Forbes' hit play *The Chorus Lady*, 1906, was derived from one.)

See also BURLESQUE.   DAVID GARDNER

Victoria Theatre. It opened in Victoria, B.C., on 16 Oct. 1885 with an amateur pro-

Victoria Theatre, Victoria, B.C.

Victoria Theatre

duction of Gilbert and Sullivan's *The Pirates of Penzance*. Originally seating 800, the theatre was renovated in 1892 to a new capacity of 1,000. Used only occasionally after the opening of the Royal Victoria in Dec. 1913, it was incorporated into Spencer's store, now Eaton's, in 1918.

The theatre was frequently dark in its early years. In 1897 only twenty-one plays were presented. In some thirty years the total number of performances did not exceed 1,700. The best year was 1912, with 149 performances. Major American touring attractions at the Victoria included the Madison Square Theatre Company, Katie Putnam, J.H. Haverly, McKee RANKIN, Augustin Daly, James O'Neill, Frederick Warde, Blanche Walsh, Harry Beresford, Paul Gilmore, and Margaret ANGLIN. British visitors included the Wood-St John Company, Brown-Potter and Kyrle Bellew, Olga Nethersole, Mrs Patrick Campbell, J. Forbes-Robertson, Edward Terry, and Alice Lloyd.

Before 1900 patrons at the Victoria repeatedly saw *East Lynne* (4 times), adapted from the novel by Mrs Henry Wood; *Camille* (5), by Alexandre Dumas *fils*; *Alvin Joslin* (5) by Charles L. Davis; *David Garrick* (6) by T.W. Robertson; and *Charley's Aunt* (4) by Brandon Thomas. Some of these plays occasionally reappeared. There was, however, some change in the repertoire after 1900, with productions of *The Private Secretary* (5) by Charles Hawtrey; *Human Hearts* (5) by Gus Knittle; *The Bonnie Brier Bush* (4) by Ian MacLaren; *In Old Kentucky* (5) by C.T. Dazey; *Arizona* (6) by Augustus Thomas; *The Squaw Man* (5) by Edwin M. Royle. The theatre was also used by opera troupes, lecturers, magicians, and wrestlers, as well as for movies before it closed in 1918.

ROBERT G. LAWRENCE

***Vie et mort du Roi Boiteux*.** This cycle of seven plays by Jean-Pierre RONFARD is widely recognized as one of the outstanding works of contemporary Quebec dramaturgy. Consisting of *La Naissance* (first produced on 20 July 1981 at Montreal's NOUVEAU THÉÂTRE EXPERIMENTAL), *L'Enfance* (21 July 1981), *Le Printemps* (22 July 1981), *La Jeunesse* (26 November 1981), *Les Voyages* and *La Cité* (8 June 1982), and *Épilogue* (9 June 1982), the complete cycle was presented on 24 and 26 June 1982 at the Expo Theatre in Montreal, on 3 July at FESTIVAL LENNOXVILLE, and on

11 July at the NATIONAL ARTS CENTRE in Ottawa. A Nouveau Théâtre Expérimental project originally titled 'Shakespeare Follies', this unorthodox work of huge proportions breaks theatrical conventions, probes human passions, and examines the political foundations of society.

The misshapen and avaricious young Richard, born near the Montreal Arsenal, dreams of succeeding his mother, the fiery Catherine Ragone, and reigning over a kingdom that stretches from Mount Ararat to the Empire State Building and passes through Abitibi, Azerbaijan, and the North Pole. In the manner of the historical epic, this grotesque and bloody saga recounts the fate of King Richard, of the rival Roberge and Ragone families, and of a horde of characters both contemporary and historical (Golda Meir, Albert Einstein, Mona Lisa, the Ayatollah Khomeiny, Mata Hari, Einstein, Joan of Arc, and others).

Insisting on 'chaotic, incoherent, anarchic' drama, Ronfard has created a carnival-like work whose extraordinary length (the seven plays are supposed to be presented in one day, constituting a theatrical marathon of fifteen hours), use of outdoor settings (hangars, roofs of buildings, waterways), and 'primitive' style (celebrating the body) revives—in a deeply moving manner—the concept of theatre as a festive event in which the actor is central (twenty-five actors play 150 roles). The play was published in two volumes in 1981.

See Paul Lefebvre, 'Notes sur *Vie et mort du Roi Boiteux* de Jean-Pierre Ronfard', *Jeu*, 21 (1981); Collectif, '*Vie et mort du Roi Boiteux*. Nouveau théâtre expérimental. Un cycle de chair et de sang', *Jeu*, 27 (1982); and Collectif, '*Vie et mort du Roi Boiteux*', *Pratiques théâtrales*, 13 (1981).

GILLES LAPOINTE

Voaden, Herman (b. 1903). Born in London, Ont., he was the most significant English-Canadian playwright and cultural *animateur* from 1930 until Robertson DAVIES began writing for the theatre in the late 1940s. He graduated from Queen's University (BA, 1923, MA, 1926, with a thesis on Eugene O'Neill). He also studied playwriting and production at Yale University under George Pierce Baker (1930-1).

Voaden's theatrical career began in Nov. 1927 when he became the founding artistic director of the Drama Club of Sarnia, an art theatre, and its successor, the Sarnia Drama League. In 1928 he was appointed head of English at the Central High School of Commerce in Toronto, where he established an adult play-production group that quickly became the leading Canadian experimental theatre company of the 1930s. Renamed the Play Workshop in 1934, this group produced nearly all of Voaden's stage experiments and his own non-realistic dramas until 1942. From 1945 to 1948 Voaden served as founding president of the Canadian Arts Council, and in 1949-50 he assisted with the writing and presentation of the CAC submission to the Massey-Lévesque Royal Commission on National Development in the Arts, Letters and Sciences. Following his retirement from Central High in 1964, he served as national director of the Canadian Conference of the Arts in 1967.

Active in acting and directing in Toronto (including HART HOUSE THEATRE), Sarnia, and Detroit, Voaden applied his multi-media 'symphonic expressionist' staging style to productions such as the Canadian première of T.S. Eliot's Murder in the Cathedral in 1936 and adaptations of Louis Hémon's Maria Chapdelaine (1938), Maurice Maeterlinck's Sister Beatrice (1939), and Edgar Allan Poe's The Masque of the Red Death (1943). His own early playwriting between 1927 and 1930 is marked by a search for a dramatic style that would express his romantic idealism and belief in the invigorating vitality of Canadian nature. These unpublished one-act plays include the symbolist fantasy The White Kingdom; the realistic Northern Storm; the partly expressionistic Northern Song; and the folk drama Western Wolfe. The expressionist Symphony: A Drama of Motion and Light For a New Theatre (1982), was co-authored with the painter Lowrie Warrener in 1930. His most successful realistic drama, Wilderness: A Play of the North (1978), was produced at Yale in May 1931. Against Baker's advice, Voaden henceforth abandoned realistic playwriting, formulating in 1932 his 'symphonic expressionist' theory, which he has described as a synthesis of 'musical themes, rhythmic light, sound and colour, dancing, formalized movement, and lyrical speech', and with which he continued to experiment for the next decade.

These symphonic expressionist dramas— Rocks (a revised version of Wilderness), performed in 1932; Earth Song: A Drama in Rhythmic Prose and Light (1976), first produced in Sarnia in 1932; Hill-Land (1984), produced in 1934; Murder Pattern (1975), produced in 1936; and Ascend as the Sun, pro-

Herman Voaden's Ascend as the Sun, Hart House Theatre, Toronto, 1942

duced in 1942—express Voaden's idealistic 'new faith' in Canada, his conviction in man's ability to perfect himself and society, and his belief in the transcendence of death through love and union with nature.

Toronto critics were generally more impressed with Voaden's technical skills as a director than with his playwriting, which they never fully comprehended though Lawrence Mason championed his work in the *Globe*. The regional adjudicators of the DOMINION DRAMA FESTIVAL also criticized the dramatic effectiveness of Voaden's plays in the 1933, 1935, 1936, 1938, and 1939 competitions. While audiences and critics were frequently moved by his 'theatre of beauty', few perceived that symphonic expressionism, with its aim to 'open wide the doors of beauty and imagination', was fundamentally a religious aesthetic ritual. For Voaden, the multi-media language of symphonic expressionism was—like Lawren Harris's use of light in his semi-abstract paintings—a means of attaining a greater spiritual reality.

Voaden concluded his symphonic expressionist period with the as yet unproduced and unpublished *Decision: A Poem for Chorus and Orchestra*, begun on 7 Aug. 1945 following

the atomic bombing of Japan. His last major dramatic work (unpublished) was the realistic *Emily Carr: A Stage Biography with Pictures*, which was produced at Queen's University in 1960 with Amelia HALL in the title role.

Voaden's playwriting and theatre experimentation of the 1930s were rediscovered in the mid-1970s. A number of his dramas were published for the first time in theatre journals and were included in Canadian play anthologies. Heinar Piller's sensitive revival of *Murder Pattern* at Toronto's George Brown College in Mar. 1987—with projections of Group of Seven paintings and nature photography and an electronic music score by David Walden—successfully captured the dramatic impact and lyric beauty of the play.

Voaden is the editor of several anthologies of plays, including *Six Canadian Plays* (1930). An anthology of his own plays, *A Vision of Canada: Herman Voaden—Dramatic Works 1928-1960*, edited by Anton Wagner, is scheduled for publication in 1990. A member of the Order of Canada and a Fellow of the Royal Society of Canada, Voaden has deposited his papers at York University.

ANTON WAGNER

Wade, Bryan (b. 1950). Born in Sarnia, Ont., he studied creative writing at the Univ. of Victoria (BFA, 1974) and film and television at the Univ. of California, Los Angeles (MFA, 1979). He gained prominence as a playwright with a number of highly original works, including the one-act plays *Lifeguard* (1973), *Electric Gunfighters* (1976), and *Alias* (1974), and the full-length *Blitzkrieg* (1974) and *Underground* (1975). The first three plays were produced, respectively, by Vancouver's NEW PLAY CENTRE in 1973, by Toronto's TARRAGON THEATRE in 1973, and by the Univ. of Guelph's Drama Dept. in 1975. *Blitzkrieg*, first produced at Tarragon in 1974, is a series of sado-masochistic rituals conducted by Adolf Hitler and his mistress Eva

Braun. Derived from a mélange of popular culture (Hollywood romantic film), propaganda (the mass-produced imagery of Nazism), and nightmare, the play explores the link between power and sexuality, a gun and a shaft of light from a film projector serving as symbols of perverted eroticism. *Underground*, produced at Toronto's FACTORY THEATRE Lab in 1975, carries the substitution of ritual for plot even further. In its three scenes a young man and a woman, the woman and an older man, and finally the two men, play out three variations on the theme of pursuit and evasion of certainty, a cruel game that corrodes notions of stability of personality, relationships, and time itself. The one-act *Tanned* (1976), about three women and the men in their lives, was produced by Factory Theatre Lab in 1976. A three-act version was published in 1979.

This Side of the Rockies (1977), produced at Factory Theatre Lab in 1977, and *Breakthrough* (unpublished), produced by NDWT in 1978, have as their theme the power of the Canadian wilderness to both inspire and destroy. In *This Side of the Rockies* three young men find the dead body of a young woman in the wilderness. The corpse disappears, then reappears very much alive, dropping hints that she is a nature spirit, and seduces the most lost and desperate of the three, leaving him with a silver star on his cheek as a sign of some kind of spiritual transformation. Juxtaposed against these happenings is the repeated appearance of mysterious, violent hunters, who perhaps symbolize the dark side of the wilderness. This aspect of the wilderness is more prominent in *Breakthrough*, a peculiar allegory about Canadian art in which the artist Tom Thomson loves a high-strung Englishwoman who is strangled by a brutal backwoodsman from Algonquin Park.

Polderland, produced at the BLYTH FESTIVAL in 1985, exemplifies the themes that pervade Wade's work, including the extent to which ritual and routine determine, and pervert, personality. The setting is a Dutch farm on New Year's Eve, 1944. Wade uses the rural ambience to powerful effect in a play that concerns Canadian soldiers and their young German prisoner who share an understanding of the rituals of farming life. This common understanding is shattered when the youngest, and seemingly most innocent, of the Canadians kills the prisoner.

Wade has also worked on collaborative projects, including *Orders from Bergdorf*, a musical (with Kerry and Kelly Knickle), produced by NDWT in 1979, and *Wild Child* (with Felix MIRBT) for the Quinzaine Internationale du Théâtre, Quebec, in 1986. He has also written for television, notably 'A Brief History of the Subject' for CBC-TV in 1975, and numerous radio plays.

ROBERT C. NUNN

Waiting for the Parade. In one of the most frequently produced plays in the modern Canadian theatre, John MURRELL portrays the lives of a group of women in Calgary during the Second World War. The disruption of war variously creates tension, bore-

dom, and excitement as the five women characters cope, individually and collectively, with the changes forced upon them. For Janet, the bossy organizer of volunteer groups, war offers the chance to take on a 'man's role' and to cover her own emotional emptiness; the musical scene with which the play begins, repeated at the end, has her lead the other women onto the dance floor in a determined attempt to prove that life goes on as usual. Catherine, losing the memory of her soldier husband 'one piece at a time', movingly allows herself to succumb to the attentions of another man. The play consists of a series of twenty-four scenes, most of them quite short, shifting place freely in an unlocalized setting. While not a simple 'slice of life', the play succeeds as an unpretentious portrayal of ordinary existence in unusual circumstances: Murrell began by interviewing people who had lived through the war in Calgary.

Waiting for the Parade has received many outstanding productions, starring several leading Canadian actresses. It was first performed by ALBERTA THEATRE PROJECTS, Calgary, on 4 Feb. 1977; it has since been produced in Edmonton, Toronto, Victoria, Montreal, and Vancouver. In 1979 a production by the NATIONAL ARTS CENTRE toured the country, visiting communities from British Columbia to New Brunswick, and, after playing in Ottawa, also in the Yukon and the Northwest Territories. Outside Canada the play was presented in London, England, in 1979, and in New York in 1981. It was broadcast on CBC radio in 1981; in 1984 a shortened version appeared on CBC television based on a 1983 stage production by Robin PHILLIPS at Theatre London. It was published by Talonbooks in 1980.

JOHN H. ASTINGTON

Walker, Corliss Powers (1853-1942). Born in Poultney, Vermont, he moved to the midwest and, with his brothers, set up a printing business in Fargo, North Dakota. In the 1890s he acquired the Fargo Opera House and shifted his interest to theatre management. In 1897 Walker leased the Winnipeg Theatre at Notre Dame and Adelaide Streets, Winnipeg, and moved there to manage it personally. This completed for Walker a chain of theatres along the Northern Pacific railway route from Fargo to Winnipeg. This Red River Valley (or 'Breadbasket') Circuit

Walker

C.P. Walker, c. 1913

included theatres in Grand Forks and Grafton, North Dakota, and Fergus Falls, Minnesota, as well as the Winnipeg and Fargo houses. Booking his season directly from New York's Theatrical Syndicate, Walker drove his competition out of business, and by 1900 established a theatre monopoly in Winnipeg. In the panic following Chicago's disastrous Iroquois Theatre fire (Dec. 1903), attempts were made to close the Winnipeg Theatre for alleged fire-safety violations. Walker staved off these efforts, but in 1907 he opened a fire-proof modern theatre, the WALKER THEATRE.

From his arrival in Canada to the end of the 1920s, Walker held effective control of booking and theatre management in the Canadian West. Allying himself with operators of other regional chains in the northwest and south-west United States, he became an important figure in the North American theatre business. With the collapse of touring in the early 1930s, Walker attempted to establish a repertory stock company to keep the Walker Theatre in operation. The venture failed, and Walker, then eighty years old, closed his theatre and retired

from active theatre management. The city seized the building for taxes in 1936.

See Ruth Harvey, *Curtain Time* (1949), a memoir by Walker's daughter.   REG SKENE

Walker, George F. (b. 1947). Born and raised in Toronto's working-class East End, he was a cabbie when he saw a FACTORY THEATRE Lab handbill inviting script submissions; the result was *The Prince of Naples* (1972), a one-act piece in which Walker reverses the usual power structure of student and teacher: a young pseudo-prophet of the 'liberated' sixties seeks to overturn the conventional thinking of an older man. With this play Walker established a close association with FTL, which produced his first seven plays and four later ones. He also served as its playwright-in-residence from 1971 to 1974. Walker's early work at Factory Theatre Lab was usually either ignored by critics, or subjected to virulent attack. Critical wariness stemmed from several sources. Rare in Canadian drama until recently, comedy is often suspect, especially from a playwright as obsessively serious about comedy as Walker—he has written eighteen disturbing comedies in sixteen years. At the beginning of his career, Walker's sensibility was urban and influenced by electronic media, when the

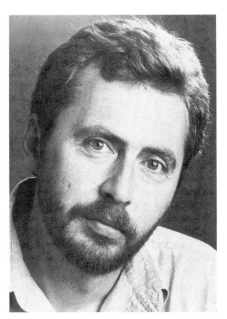

George F. Walker

rural and the naturalistic were fashionable. His early plays—*The Prince of Naples* (1972), *Ambush at Tether's End* (1972), *Sacktown Rag* (1972), *Bagdad Saloon* (1973) and the unpublished *Demerit* (all produced between 1971 and 1974)—exhibit the vigour and anxious speed characteristic of his style: a quirky sense of humour that juxtaposes elements of high and low comedy, and a non-linear structure that employs the association of images and ideas, reflecting Walker's preoccupation with the rapid disintegration of the world, against which the only defences are laughter and a chaotic depiction of chaos. Walker has also been preoccupied with defining the nature of evil; hence his plays feature a proliferation of sometimes engaging villains (mad scientists, Nazis, gangsters, politicians, fallen women) and those obsessed with detecting evil (detectives, priests, poets, visionaries, mothers, all flawed in Walker's world). He is also preoccupied with obsession.

In *Beyond Mozambique* (1975), first produced by FTL in 1974, Walker uses the B-movie as a frame: in a crumbling jungle outpost, Rocco, the mad scientist, and his wildly disparate fellow exiles play out their obsessions, oblivious to each other and to the drumming that threatens to overwhelm them. This and subsequent plays that draw on B-movie conventions—stock characters resembling those in melodrama, stock situations, a simplified view of life—are not simple parodies but ironic commentaries within a political context.

Walker returned to the B-movie mode, this time with the detective genre, in *Ramona and the White Slaves* (1978), first produced by FTL in 1976. Set in what is apparently a brothel in turn-of-the-century Hong Kong, it portrays Ramona the Madame/Mother and her convoluted relationship with her daughters, their lovers, her crippled son, and a man who may be her pimp, her missing husband, or both. The dream-within-a-dream structure is extremely intricate, and the comment on the devouring mother/whore is even more unpalatable than the disintegration of society suggested in *Beyond Mozambique*. *Ramona* left many critics and audience-members bewildered.

In an attempt to be 'more generous', Walker wrote *Gossip* (1984), first produced by TORONTO FREE THEATRE in 1977. The familiar detective figure of the B-film moves centre-stage when a political reporter, Tyrone

Power, is assigned to solve a high-society murder; his subsequent investigation, so comically complex that the original question is often forgotten, leads through layers of deception to an exposé of corruption pervading all aspects of that society. *Gossip* has reached a broader audience largely through its many American productions. Its popularity is matched only by that of his next play, *ZASTROZZI* (1977), premièred by Toronto Free Theatre in 1977, a swashbuckling confrontation of good and evil in a neo-Gothic setting.

The reporter Power returns in *Filthy Rich* (1984), another Toronto Free Theatre première (1979), and acquires the stock sidekick, Jamie, a young would-be private eye who conspires with circumstances to compel the now-reclusive novelist *manqué* (Power) to undertake another investigation, again into the murky world of wealth and politics. *Filthy Rich* makes more efficient use of its B-movie model to reinforce the disillusionment of the now Bogart-like Power.

With *The Art of War* (1984), produced by FTL in 1983, Walker completes the substantial 'Power Plays' trilogy. This time Power's investigation leads him into international politics. His by-now alcohol-sodden liberal idealism is confronted with the machinations of the neo-fascist bureaucrat and arms dealer Hackman. In this conflict neither side is attractive: Jamie, the clear-eyed pragmatist, emerges as the 'hero'. Power's disintegration may be seen as a model of the collapse of the ideals of Walker's generation, from the activism of the 1960s to dropping-out in the 1970s, to vengeful and 'ridiculous' neo- activism in the 1980s.

The first of the plays written between *Gossip* and *Filthy Rich*, *Rumours of Our Death* (1980), premièred by FTL in 1980, is a parable about the political manipulation of language; the dialogue is so spare that the published play has generated little enthusiasm, although it had a great success as a punk-rock musical under Walker's direction. The script, which is unusually open to the actor's improvisational inventiveness, reflects Walker's growing respect for, and accommodation of, the art of acting. *Theatre of the Film Noir* (1981), first produced by FTL at the Toronto Theatre Festival in 1981, is on the other hand vintage Walker: the B-movie is acknowledged and moral values are comically and chillingly obliterated in post-war

Paris, where a murder that occurred during the liberation of the city is investigated. The comedy *Science and Madness* (1982), a reworking of the Frankenstein legend that was first produced by TARRAGON THEATRE in 1982, is competent, although in the context of Walker's work, it seems repetitive.

The next play seen by Canadian audiences, *Criminals in Love* (1984), first produced by FTL in 1984, marks a return to Walker's roots in Toronto's East End, which he had not exploited since *Sacktown Rag*. Gail and Junior, self-described 'young lovers doomed', are pulled down the slippery path to crime—from stealing food from the Salvation Army to blowing up a bank—by Junior's father, a habitual but hopelessly inept criminal, and Wineva, a bourgeois revolutionary. William, a philosophical bum, tries unsuccessfully to save them, denying the 'hanging shadow' that obsesses him and the force of 'destiny' that obsesses Junior. Whether the young lovers are 'doomed' by Fate, socio-economic factors, heredity, their preoccupation with their own romantic legend—or a combination thereof—is never made clear, but the 'nature/nurture' and 'destiny/free-will' debates have seldom been expounded in such a highly successful farce. The play won a Governor General's Award in 1984.

Better Living, produced in 1986 by CENTRESTAGE, portrays Gail's mother and two sisters before and after the possible reappearance of her father, who has been presumed dead for ten years. The play mixes the politics of family and society when the women first resist, then succumb to, the patriarch's regime of 'Consumer Socialism'. Reaction to *Better Living* was at best luke-warm. Walker too seemed dissatisfied with the play. An earlier, much different version was given a semi-workshop production at Cornell University in 1982. The so-called East End plays became a trilogy in the fall of 1987 with the Factory Theatre's production of *Beautiful City*, a confrontation between east enders and real-estate developers.

Walker's adaptation of Turgenev's *Father and Sons*, called *Nothing Sacred* (1988), was directed by Bill GLASSCO and produced at Toronto's CentreStage in Jan. 1988. It won four Dora Awards and has subsequently been produced throughout Canada and the U.S.

Walker himself directed the premières of *Ramona and the White Slaves*, *Rumours of Our Death*, *The Theatre of the Film Noir*, *The Art of War*, and *Criminals in Love*, as well as a production of *Zastrozzi* by the Nimrod Theatre in Sydney, Australia.

Walker's plays have been produced widely in Canada, the U.S., England, and Australia. In fact his work achieved much of its initial success outside Canada. In 1981 Walker was playwright-in-residence with Joseph Papp's Public Theatre in New York, where *Zastrozzi* was directed by Andrei Serban. He lives in Toronto's East End with his wife, actress Susan Purdy.

Bagdad Saloon, *Beyond Mozambique*, and *Ramona and the White Slaves* were collected in *Three Plays by George Walker* (1978); *Gossip*, *Filthy Rich*, and *The Art of War* were collected in *The Power Plays* (1984). *The East End Plays* (1988) includes *Beautiful City*, *Better Living*, and *Criminals in Love*.

See Chris Johnson, 'George F. Walker: B-Movies Beyond the Absurd', *Canadian Literature*, 85 (1980); Denis W. Johnston, 'George F. Walker: Liberal Idealism and the "Power Plays"', *Canadian Drama*, 10 (1984); and Robert Wallace, 'Looking for the Light: A Conversation with George F. Walker', *Canadian Drama*, 14 (1988).   CHRIS JOHNSON

Walker Theatre. Located on Smith St at Notre Dame Ave in Winnipeg, this theatre was the city's major touring house from its opening in 1907 until the collapse of the Canadian theatrical touring system in the early 1930s. It was built by theatre entrepreneur C.P. WALKER to be the leading theatre in his Red River Valley Theatre Circuit, a regional chain affiliated with New York's Theatre Syndicate. Planned at a time of intense public concern for theatre safety after Chicago's 1903 Iroquois Theatre fire, the Walker was of steel-cage construction and 'fully fireproof'. It was equipped with a modern ventilating system and its own electrical plant, with power for two thousand lights. The stage area measured 40' deep, 80' wide, and 70' high. Seating capacity at the time of the opening was 1,798, including boxes, orchestra, balcony, and gallery. The combined stage and auditorium of the theatre is almost 150' long. The Walker Theatre was originally designed to be part of a hotel/office building/theatre complex, but the non-theatrical aspects of the project were abandoned. Edwardian in style and décor, its interior finished in marble and weathered oak, with red carpeting, green and gold drapery, and

Walker Theatre, Winnipeg, 1907

tapestried walls, the Walker was one of the most impressive theatres ever built in Western Canada. Architects were Howard Stone of Montreal and L.T. Bristow of Winnipeg. Steel work was by Dominion Bridge Company and general construction by Canadian White Company of Montreal.

The theatre opened on 18 Feb. 1907 with Henry Savage's production of Puccini's *Madama Butterfly*. Until the outbreak of the First World War, programs at the Walker Theatre were virtually identical to those of major Syndicate theatres in Chicago or New York. During the regular winter season two to three New York shows a week could be seen, with occasional extended runs of major Shakespearean, Grand Opera, and Light Opera repertory companies. The Walker operated year-round; the summer season was booked to stock and repertory companies and other independent touring organizations. In this period the Walker presented such stars as the blackface team of McIntyre and Heath, Dustin Farnum, Lillian Russell, Henrietta Crossman, Mrs Leslie Carter, Otis Skinner, Viola Allen, Olga Nethersole, Mrs Patrick Campbell, May Robson, Chauncey Olcott, Victor Moore, Robert Mantell, Billie Burke, David Warfield, and Blanche Bates. For a brief time in 1910 it became a VAUDEVILLE house, hosting William Morris's 'Transcontinental Vaudeville'; but after a few months it returned to a program of 'high class' legitimate touring attractions. In Jan. 1914 the

Walker hosted the Winnipeg Political Equality League's satirical presentation *How The Vote Was Won/A Women's Parliament*, a highly successful agit-prop women's suffrage piece by Mrs C.P. Walker, Nellie McClung, Francis Beynon, Mrs A.V. Thomas, and others.

Between 1919 and 1922 C.P. Walker leased his theatre to Trans-Canada Theatres Limited, a Canadian corporation that attempted to set up an all-Canadian touring system, using British attractions. In 1922 Walker resumed control of the theatre and operated as an independent for the rest of the decade, booking major British repertory companies for runs of several weeks at a time, together with local amateur productions, and whatever American touring shows were still available. In this period the Walker hosted the companies of Sir John Martin-Harvey, Maurice Colbourne, and Sir Barry Jackson, the D'Oyly Carte Opera Company, the Stratford-Upon-Avon Company, and the Abbey Players. In 1930 Famous Players Canada Limited, a subsidiary of Paramount Pictures, moved to protect its investment in talking pictures by banning live productions from the stages of all Famous Players theatres. Since this corporation controlled all theatres in many Canadian cities, its ban on live shows effectively destroyed the economic base for touring. Independent managers like Walker could not import attractions without sharing expenses with a circuit of theatres across Canada. He attempted to establish a stock company, failed, and in the spring of 1933 ceased regular operation of the Walker Theatre. In 1936 the city seized the theatre for taxes, then sold it in 1945 to Odeon Theatres. It still exists, but as a movie house under the name Odeon Theatre, with a false ceiling to decrease the height of the auditorium and to seal off the gallery.

See Ruth Harvey, *Curtain Time* (1949), a memoir by Walker's daughter.   REG SKENE

Walmsley, Tom (b. 1948). Born in Liverpool, Eng., and raised in Oshawa, Ont., he dropped out of grade ten in 1965. He continued his education in the streets of Toronto and Vancouver, counting welfare fraud, robbery, and a six-year heroin habit among his experiences before turning to writing. In 1975 Vancouver's NEW PLAY CENTRE produced his first play, *The Workingman* (1976); in 1977 TORONTO FREE THEATRE presented this play in a double bill with *The Jones Boy* (1978). Two books of poetry, *Rabies* (1975) and *Lexington Hero* (1976), and a novel, *Dr. Tin* (1979), occupy the same bleak territory as his early plays, which also included *Something Red* (1980), produced in 1978 at the New Play Centre, and *White Boys*, produced in 1982 by TARRAGON THEATRE. Walmsley has lived in Toronto since 1982.

Walmsley's plays depict a brutally naturalistic world of junkies, boozers, and failed rip-off artists engaged in often violent tests of honour and manhood. Walmsley deromanticizes his 'outlaws', revealing the weakness and pain that neither sex, drugs, nor alcohol can alleviate. His young males' bravado only thinly masks their fear and self-disgust. They tend to run in pairs and take out their personal frustrations on their women. Relationships for Walmsley's characters are as much a dependency as heroin or liquor.

Something Red, Walmsley's most powerful work to date, is a drama of the lower depths, both sociological and emotional—a study in paranoia and the chilling symbiosis between sex and violence. His more recent plays have tried different approaches to similar kinds of characters and situations. *White Boys*, a CHALMERS Award runner-up, deals comically with the subject matter of the earlier plays; *Getting Wrecked* (Gas Station Theatre, Winnipeg, 1985) is a musical treatment of teenage alcohol abuse aimed at high school students;

Mr. Nice Guy (Toronto Free Theatre, 1986), written with Dolly Reisman, examines wife-battering in a middle-class milieu. All these plays are marked by the same authentic voice that has made Walmsley Canadian theatre's chief chronicler of the dark underside of Canadian urban life.   JERRY WASSERMAN

Wasserman, Dora (b. 1920). Born in Zhitomir, Ukraine, she trained at the Yiddish Art Theatre in Moscow and performed with the Kiev State Theatre during the Second World War, immigrating to Montreal in 1950. In 1956 she formed the Yiddish Drama Group with a nucleus of graduates from the Jewish People's and Peretz Schools. The group was offered a permanent home at the SAIDYE BRONFMAN CENTRE in 1973. Accomplished presentations of classical and modern Yiddish plays draw large and appreciative audiences not only in Canada, but on tour in the U.S. and Israel. Productions have included *It's Hard To Be a Jew* (Sholem Aleichem), *Kiddush Hashem* (Sholem Asch), *The Unseen* (Isaac Bashevis Singer), *Green Fields* (Peretz Hirschbein), *Hotsmakh* (Itsik Manger), and *The Duke* (Alter Kacyzne). Among the most popular presentations were *A Bintel Brief* ('A Bundle Of Letters'), based on immigrants' letters to the editor of *The Forward*, a New York-based Yiddish daily, and *Papineau*, derived from a hand-scripted journal kept by Y. Herman, the Beadle of a synagogue in the Papineau distinct of Montreal from 1904 to 1956. Both plays were created by Abraham Shulman.

Dora Wasserman has received many awards for her outstanding contribution to Quebec life.   AVIVA RAVEL

Watmough, David (b. 1926). Born in London, Eng., he was brought up in Cornwall. After studying in London and France, he lived in the U.S. and then settled in Kitsilano (Vancouver) in 1959. Early work included theatre reviewing for the *Vancouver Sun*, 1966-7, and three allegorical plays, *Names for the Numbered Years*, published by the Bau-xi Gallery, Vancouver, 1967.

In 1969 Watmough began writing monodramas, stories designed for him to perform. He wrote over sixty and gave more than 600 performances in Canada, the U.S., and Europe. They are essentially oral works, acted with inflections and gestures. All concern Davey Bryant, a Cornishman whose experiences resemble Watmough's own. A record, *Pictures from a Dying Landscape* (Kanata, 1972), contains three monodramas; a number are also included in *Ashes for Easter and Other Monodramas* (1972) and *Love and the Waiting Game* (1975). In the late 1970s Watmough abandoned writing and performing monodramas while continuing Bryant's story in novels.

See Geoff Hancock, 'Interview with David Watmough', *Canadian Fiction Magazine*, 20 (1976), and George Woodcock, *The World of Canadian Writing* (1980).   MALCOLM PAGE

Watson, Wilfred (b. 1911). Born in Rochester, Eng., he immigrated to Canada in 1926, studying at the Universities of British Columbia and Toronto (Ph.D. in 1951). He taught English at the Univ. of Alberta until his retirement in 1976, and won a Governor General's Award for his poetry collection *Friday's Child* (1955). Most of his plays were written in the 1960s. An admirer of Wyndham Lewis, he collaborated with Marshall McLuhan on the 1970 book *From Cliché to Archetype*, and in his plays he strove to find a vocabulary and method of presentation to complement the mood of the new technological age. His first venture, *Cockrow and the Gulls* (unpublished), produced at the Univ. of Alberta in 1962, borrows from absurdist themes to depict a visit to the realm of death. Allegorical and episodic in structure, it exhibits the strong sense of ritual and the parade of characters in a limbo-like setting that became trademarks of Watson's plays. Similar is the action in *The Trial of Corporal Adam*—produced at Coach House Theatre, Toronto, in 1964—which begins in a realistic realm, with the characters being subsequently reassembled in a non-realistic setting for a trial conducted by allegorical figures.

Two of Watson's plays were produced at Edmonton's Yardbird Suite, a former jazz club that presented poetry readings and small-scale productions of plays in the 1960s. The first, *Wail for Two Pedestals* (1965), produced in 1964, confronts potential devastation by the atomic bomb and the youth-oriented, sexually permissive society of the 1960s. The second, *Chez Vous, Comfortable Pew* (unpublished), produced in 1965, is a light-hearted satire on Edmonton as a prime example of Canada's complacent affluent society.

Three further plays, all produced at the Univ. of Alberta, experimented with theatrical form. *O holy ghost, DIP YOUR FINGER IN THE BLOOD OF CANADA AND WRITE, I love you* (unpublished), produced in 1967, dispensed with the conventional proscenium and with auditorium seats, which were replaced by mattresses and backrests. The 1969 *Let's Murder Clytemnestra According to the Principles of Marshall McLuhan* (unpublished) incorporated technology into the action in the form of ten television cameras that monitored the action on stage.

Gramsci X 3 (1983) was first performed in 1986. Based on the life of the Italian Communist Nino Gramsci, it is written in Number-Grid Poetry: numbers on the page direct the actor how to deliver the lines. Two other plays—*Over Prairie Trails* (1973), a satire, and *The Woman Taken in Adultery* (1980), a modern-day Mystery play—have not been produced.

Watson's use of multi-media, his rejection of the narrative form as unrepresentative of a media-deluged technological age, and his unconventional use of space, departed from the prevailing realism of Edmonton's contemporary theatre. Watson now lives in Nanaimo, B.C., where he continues to write plays and poetry.   DOREEN WATT

Webber, H. Price (1845-1927). Born in Brixham, Eng., he escaped to Halifax from a printer to whom he was apprenticed. He found employment on the *Nova Scotian* under Joseph Howe, and six months later, when he was still only thirteen, he was with the *Globe* in Saint John. He was later compositor for the *New Dominion and True Humorist*. Until 1870 he was an actor, cornet player, and stage manager with various amateur dramatic and minstrel troupes, including the Home Circle Minstrels, the Scribner Bros. Minstrel Troupe, and the Provincial Dramatic Society. He began his professional career in 1871 as agent for the Flora Myers Company, was agent for Marietta Ravel and John Murray and in 1880 became manager of the Boston Comedy Company after the death of E.M. Leslie. He toured in the Maritimes, Quebec, and New England until 1915 with his old-fashioned repertoire, including Tom Taylor's *Hidden Hand*, Augustin Daly's *Leah* and *Under the Gaslight*, and Edward Bulwer-Lytton's *Lady of Lyons*, endeavouring to give people 'clean entertainment'. He is said to have appeared as an actor in 514 different plays in a total of 11,000 performances, and

H. Price Webber as Rip Van Winkle

never to have missed an engagement because of ill health. Contributing to Webber's popularity were reasonable prices (15¢, 25¢, 35¢); local hits; a lack of histrionic pretence; publicly expressed appreciation of his audience, orchestra, and the press at the end of each engagement; determination that enabled him to continue even when he lost all uninsured equipment in a Truro fire in 1893; flexibility that allowed him to change a bill at short notice; and reliable standards of production (even if the critics sometimes demurred). His leading lady was his wife, Edwina Grey (Marcella Moore).   MARY ELIZABETH SMITH

Whitehead, Paxton (b. 1937). Born in East Malling, Kent, Eng., he trained at the Webber-Douglas School, London, and made his professional acting début in Eastbourne in 1956 as Alphonse in Harold Brooke's and Kay

Bannerman's *All For Mary*. After a season with the Royal Shakespeare Company in 1958 and roles with British touring companies, he went to New York in 1960, making his Broadway début in Sept. 1962 in Ronald Millar's *The Affair*. In 1965 he appeared at the MANITOBA THEATRE CENTRE, Winnipeg, in Oscar Wilde's *The Importance of Being Earnest*, Bernard Shaw's *Heartbreak House*, and Peter Shaffer's *The Public Eye*. Whitehead's long association with the SHAW FESTIVAL began in 1966, when he played Lord Summerhays in *Misalliance* and Magnus in *The Apple Cart*. He was appointed artistic director of the Festival in 1967, a position he held until 1977 (with a sabbatical in 1975). His policies at the Shaw (where he acted more than he directed) were artistically and financially conservative. He initiated tours in Canada and the U.S. and expanded the company's repertoire beyond the plays of Shaw, while stressing popular appeal and eschewing controversy. From 1971 to 1973 Whitehead was also artistic director of the VANCOUVER PLAYHOUSE, where he premièred new Canadian plays. Since leaving the Shaw he has acted in New York and in U.S. and Canadian regional theatres—playing, for example, Henry Carr in Tom Stoppard's *Travesties* at the MTC and Oscar Wilde in the Canadian première of Peter Coe's *The Trials of Oscar Wilde* at Edmonton's CITADEL THEATRE (both in 1979). On Broadway he appeared in the successful run (1983-5) of Michael Frayne's *Noises Off*. As skilled in farce as in the classical repertoire, Whitehead has also adapted (with Suzanne Grossman) two Feydeau plays: *La Main Passe* (produced at the Shaw Festival in 1968 as *The Chemmy Circle*) and *Le Dindon* (produced at the STRATFORD FESTIVAL in 1971 as *There's One in Every Marriage*).

L.W. CONOLLY

Whitehead, Robert (b. 1916). Born and raised in Montreal, and educated at Lower Canada College, he attended the New York School of the Theatre and appeared in the 1936 New York production of Emlyn Williams' *Night Must Fall*. After service in the Second World War he produced a number of notable Broadway successes in partnership with Oliver Rea, including *Medea* with Judith Anderson and John Gielgud, *Crime and Punishment* with Gielgud and Lillian Gish (both in 1947), and Carson McCullers' *Member of the Wedding* with Julie Harris and Ethel

Waters in 1950. Whitehead's major productions of the 1950s included Mary Chase's *Mrs. McThing* (with Helen Hayes, 1952); Arthur Laurents' *Time of the Cuckoo* (with Shirley Booth, 1952); Jean Anouilh's *Waltz of the Toreadors* (with Ralph Richardson, 1957); Friedrich Dürrenmatt's *The Visit* (with Alfred Lunt and Lynn Fontanne, 1958); and Robert Bolt's *A Man for All Seasons* (with Paul Scofield, 1961). From 1960 to 1964 he was joint producer-director of the Lincoln Center for the Performing Arts. After the death of his first wife, Virginia Bolen, Whitehead married the Australian actress Zoë CALDWELL, who had become well-known at the STRATFORD FESTIVAL; she starred in his 1968 and 1982 productions of Jay Allen's adaptation of Muriel Sparks' novel *The Prime of Miss Jean Brodie* and *Medea*.

HERBERT WHITTAKER

Whitfield, Michael J. (b. 1944). Born in Victoria, B.C., he studied theatre at the Univ. of Victoria and pursued graduate studies at Villanova Univ. and the Univ. of Illinois. He then taught at the Univ. of Windsor from 1973 to 1974, the Univ. of Toronto from 1974 to 1978, and subsequently at York Univ. for three years.

In 1974 Whitfield began his association with the STRATFORD FESTIVAL, as assistant lighting designer to Gil Wechsler, at the Third Stage. He has since developed into the Festival's principal lighting designer, having done some seventy-five productions between 1974 and 1988, notably the 1979 Peter Ustinov *King Lear*, the 1980 Maggie Smith *Virginia* (which went on to the Haymarket in London), and the highly successful 1982 *Mikado*, which was also presented in New York. From 1974 to 1980 he designed for Halifax's NEPTUNE THEATRE plays that included Shaw's *Misalliance*, Shakespeare's *King Lear*, and Peter Shaffer's *Equus*, and he was principal designer for Robin PHILLIPS' prestigious 1983-4 season at London's Grand Theatre (see GRAND OPERA HOUSE). He has also designed for the BANFF CENTRE, the MANITOBA THEATRE CENTRE, the NATIONAL ARTS CENTRE, and the Canadian Opera Company. Whitfield's guiding principle as a lighting designer has consistently been that the lighting should serve the director's interpretation without becoming obtrusive.

MARTHA MANN

Whittaker, Herbert (b. 1910). Born in Montreal, he studied design at the École des Beaux-Arts and began designing for amateur theatre productions in 1933. He learned the craft of newspaper criticism by reviewing films, ballet, and theatre for the *Montreal Gazette* from 1935 to 1949, when he joined the staff of the Toronto *Globe and Mail*. Writing reviews for the *Globe*, he was an important critical voice for theatre, particularly Canadian theatre, until his retirement in 1975. Whittaker avoided the simple yea or nay of newspaper reviewing, perfecting a descriptive and contextually evaluative style of criticism. Impressionistic, and coloured by his own involvement in the theatre, his reviews made him an influential presence for forty years. From the most successful days of the LITTLE THEATRE movement, through the rise of professionalism at the STRATFORD FESTIVAL, the CREST, and in regional theatres, to the explosion of theatre activity that began in 1967, Whittaker was a faithful recorder and celebrator of the awakening and flourishing of professional theatre in Canada.

He has also distinguished himself as a theatre artist. In the thirties and forties, as a designer for such lively Montreal amateur groups as the MONTREAL REPERTORY THEATRE, the 16-30 Club, the Shakespeare Society, and the Everyman Players, he produced colourful, whimsical work that earned him a local reputation. In Toronto, Whittaker also worked as a director, mainly for groups affiliated with the University (HART HOUSE THEATRE, the UNIVERSITY ALUMNAE DRAMATIC CLUB, Trinity College). He was also a designer for such notable professional productions as the JUPITER THEATRE's *Galileo* in 1951, and the CANADIAN PLAYERS' Inuit-inspired *King Lear* in 1961.

Among Whittaker's many distinctions is the Order of Canada, which was awarded in 1976 not only for his work as a critic, but also for the time and energy he has devoted to such organizations as the DOMINION DRAMA FESTIVAL, the Toronto Drama Bench, and the NATIONAL ARTS CENTRE. Still active as a writer and as a supporter of various theatrical causes since his retirement, Whittaker has lately been lobbying for the establishment of a Canadian Theatre Museum.

See *Whittaker's Theatre. A Critic Looks at Stages in Canada and Thereabouts 1944-1975* (1985), ed. Ronald Bryden with Boyd Neil, and Whittaker's memoirs in *Canadian Drama*, 12 (1987). JONATHAN RITTENHOUSE

Wood, John (b. 1938). Born in Montreal and educated at Bishop's University, Lennoxville, Que., where he directed student productions, he worked for a year in British theatre before moving to Toronto. From 1963 to 1968 he worked frequently for the CBC while also pursuing a career as a stage director. After assisting artistic director Barry Morse at the 1966 SHAW FESTIVAL, Wood directed primarily at the MANITOBA THEATRE CENTRE until 1972, specializing in young people's theatre, before a period of successful free-lancing across Canada, including the STRATFORD FESTIVAL, THEATRE CALGARY, and FESTIVAL LENNOXVILLE. In 1974 Wood became artistic director of NEPTUNE THEATRE, Halifax, where from the start his ambitious programming and uncompromising artistic policies brought him into conflict with a cautious and budget-conscious board of directors. He resigned in 1977 and was immediately appointed artistic director of English Theatre at the NATIONAL ARTS CENTRE, where he began the difficult task of attempting to build a national company. In the view of some critics, however, the uneven and at times inadequate quality of the acting company he assembled (exacerbated by shrinking budgets) limited Wood's achievements at the NAC. While some large-scale productions—such as his 1978 *Troilus and Cressida*, 1980 *Mother Courage*, and 1983 *Oresteia*—drew nationwide attention, much of the company's work remained primarily of local interest. Wood left the NAC in 1984 to begin a period of free-lance work that included productions in Britain, Australia, and New Zealand. Since 1972 he has frequently directed productions at the Stratford Festival—where he is an associate director—including a widely praised *Cherry Orchard* in 1987.
HARRY LANE

Workshop West. Founded in Edmonton in 1978 by Univ. of Alberta graduate Gerry Potter, and loosely modelled on TORONTO WORKSHOP PRODUCTIONS, TARRAGON THEATRE, and THEATRE PASSE MURAILLE, it was dedicated to the production of Canadian plays and the development of playwriting talent in Alberta. The first season opened on 14 Mar. 1979 with a double bill of new works: *Punch and Polly* by Rick McNair and *Some-body Waves Goodbye* by Howard Dallin. These were followed by Carol BOLT's *One Night Stand* and David FENNARIO's *On the Job*. A ten-week playwriting course was also offered.

Between 1979 and 1985 the seasons continued to alternate between new work—often developed through Playwrights' Circle courses and workshops—and the plays of major writers such as David FRENCH, Sharon POLLOCK, Michel TREMBLAY, David FREEMAN, and John GRAY. During the 1983-4 season Workshop West established a playwright-in-residence position (filled first by Gordon Pengilly), and found a permanent home in the Kaasa Theatre in the Northern Alberta Jubilee Auditorium. Since 1985 the company has focused more on the production of new plays written for or with a specific ensemble of actors, designers, and musicians, and on creating a 'company style' in COLLECTIVE CREATIONs (*Sweatlodge Tales*, 1985, *It's Your Turn to Get Up*, 1985), new scripts (Frank Moher's *Sliding for Home*, 1987), and adaptations of novels (Henry Kreisel's *The Rich Man*, adapted by Joanne Osborne and Gerry Potter, 1987) that stress storytelling, symbolism, choral work, and 'popular theatre' skills.
MOIRA DAY

Wuethrich, Hugo (b. 1927). Born in Switzerland, he studied in London before immigrating to Canada in 1951. He took up residence in Toronto, married, and worked as an assistant designer for the CBC. In 1961 he moved to Montreal, where he was hired as a set designer for CBC television. Pursuing two careers, he had a showing of his paintings at Le Salon du Printemps, and was involved in the Quebec theatre boom of the 1960s, working both for stage and television. Among his many achievements are set designs for television productions of *Un Cri qui vient de loin* by Françoise LORANGER, R. Murray Schafer's opera *Toi*, and Rossini's *Barber of Seville*, which won an Emmy Award in 1965.

Wuethrich has designed at least fifteen shows for Le THÉÂTRE DE QUAT'SOUS, from J. Canole's *Florentine* (in 1965) to Michel GARNEAU's *Quatre à quatre* (in 1974). Among his more than twenty designs for Le THÉÂTRE DU RIDEAU VERT from 1966 to 1974 some are especially significant: those for Calderón's *La Vie est un songe*, Maeterlinck's *L'Oiseau Bleu*, Claudel's *Partage de midi*, and Antonine MAILLET's *Le Mariaagélas*.

Wuethrich has also worked for La COMÉ-DIE-CANADIENNE, Le THÉÂTRE DE MARJO-LAINE, Le THÉÂTRE POPULAIRE DU QUÉBEC, La NOUVELLE COMPAGNIE THÉÂTRALE, and La COMPAGNIE JEAN DUCEPPE—in association most often with directors Paul Buissoneault, Louis-Georges Carrier, Yvette BRIND'AMOUR, and André BRASSARD. Wuethrich has become known for the introduction into his sets of strong, solid architecture, influenced by constructivism.

RENÉE NOISEAUX-GURIK

Wyatt, Rachel (b. 1929). Born in Bradford, Eng., she immigrated to Canada in 1957. She published four novels between 1970 and 1985 in addition to two stage plays, while over fifty of her radio plays (see RADIO DRAMA) have been broadcast in Canada, Britain, Australia, and New Zealand.

Wyatt's fine ear for dialogue and her often humorous manipulation of contrapuntal speech effects are well illustrated by her radio plays, whether they use Canadian voices, as in *Point of Departure*, or the accents of her native Yorkshire, as in *One Man Killed*. A character's inner monologue is frequently interwoven with external dialogue to create depth and irony. Her characters often reveal a witty self-consciousness about words and a sharp awareness of metaphor.

One of Wyatt's main concerns is with the disturbing of established relationships by one or more outsiders, usually friends or family members. *Geometry* (1983), first performed at Toronto's TARRAGON THEATRE in 1983, is a drawing-room comedy of manners with dark undertones. A teacher's uneasy marriage is both disrupted by, and destructive of, the lives of two younger unmarried colleagues. There is a mathematical inevitability about the rituals of their married life, with its exploitation of the emotional needs of others. Faintly reminiscent of Edward Albee's *Who's Afraid of Virginia Woolf?*, it sets up emotional triangles that always have at their base the egotism and manipulativeness of husband and wife. In *Chairs and Tables* (1984), first performed at Tarragon Theatre in 1984, an intense girlhood friendship maintains its hold on a woman's emotions; the friend's presence, whether real or imaginary, threatens the harmony of the woman's marriage. This further study of the invasion of fragile personal space uses chairs and tables as visual metaphors; at the end of the play the couple

makes a barricade of them in order to protect their relationship.   JOAN COLDWELL

Wylie, Betty Jane (b. 1931). Born and educated in Winnipeg, Betty Jane McKenty studied French and English at the Univ. of Manitoba for BA and MA degrees. In 1953 she married William Wylie, an accountant, and they had two sons and two daughters. Wylie's first plays were adaptations of classics and works for children. Ibsen's *Enemy of the People* (1985) and Molière's *George Dandin*, both reset on the Prairies, and *Kingsayer* (1978), a children's play about playground peer pressures and growing up, were produced at the MANITOBA THEATRE CENTRE in 1962, 1964, and 1967 respectively. Her early PUPPET plays led to an appointment as script adviser to the Puppeteers of America (1967-73); to a book, *Don't Just Stand There, Jiggle* (1980); and to the creation of an important hand-puppet character in her adult script, *A Place On Earth* (produced by TORONTO WORKSHOP PRODUCTIONS in 1982, and published the same year). It was through his wife's playwriting that William Wylie entered the theatre, first as business manager for the Manitoba Theatre Centre, and later for the STRATFORD FESTIVAL. The slow, lingering death of her father inspired *Mark* (1979), produced at Stratford in 1972; and her husband's sudden death in 1973 accelerated her career as a freelance writer. 'If you break eggs, make an omelet' was a Wylie family saying; its pragmatic philosophy led to *Beginnings: A Book for Widows* (1977), a best-seller in Canada, the United States, and England. It also launched her speaking career as 'a professional widow and portable resource of the insurance industry.' The children's play, *The Old Woman and the Pedlar* (1978), based on the nursery rhyme 'Lawk 'O Mercy' and produced at the YOUNG PEOPLE'S THEATRE in 1977, was a further response to her widowhood: an old woman rediscovers her identity after confrontations with vaudevillian stereotypes—doctors, bureaucrats, and well-meaning optimists.

Wylie's writing includes thirteen books and numerous works for radio, film, magazines, and newspapers, but her first love is theatre. She tries to make her journalism feed her playwriting. For example, *A Place On Earth*—inspired by a series Wylie wrote for the *Toronto Star* following a stint living in a rooming house in the guise of a pensioner—

Wylie

is an ingenious and moving one-woman show (with puppet *alter ego*) about a widow, eking out a living on an Old Age Pension, who survives a sexual assault and the derision of police to whom she reports the rape. A second *Star* assignment, this time to masquerade as an ex-mental patient, gave Wylie material for *Time Bomb*, produced by the Waterloo Community Playhouse, Waterloo, Iowa, in 1986. It explores the tragic circumstances of people released from institutions without adequate income or support systems. Wylie's profusion of professional activities—in addition to her journalism she has appeared on

television and radio, notably with the radio program *Betty Jane's Diary* (broadcast 1977-81, published 1982), and she has taught drama to handicapped children—helps to explain the wide-ranging topics of her twenty plays. They are well-crafted and enlivened by a wry wit and love of language. Her lyric gifts are most evident in words for songs in musicals with composers Victor Davis (*Beowulf*, performed in New York, 1975) and Quenten Doolittle (*The Second Shepherds' Play*, produced by Storybook Theatre, Calgary, 1981).

JOYCE DOOLITTLE

Y

Young People's Theatre. Founded in Toronto in 1966 by Susan Douglas RUBES, it is the only theatre centre in English Canada devoted exclusively to programs for young people. In its first decade a reputation for professionalism in family holiday shows and school tours was firmly established and rewarded with international recognition. The 1967 production of Eric NICOL's *The Clam Made a Face* was invited to the 1972 Fifth General Assembly of ASSITEJ (Association Internationale de Théâtre pour Les Enfants et La Jeunesse) in Montreal; the Montreal Cultural Olympics included Larry Zacharko's *Maximilian Beetle* (produced in 1976); and the company successfully toured to London,

Eng., in 1975, with its 1973 production of Henry BEISSEL's poetic drama, *Inook and the Sun*. Several new plays were also commissioned and produced by Rubes in the early years: *The Dandy Lion* (in 1966), *Little Red Riding Hood* (in 1968), and *The Popcorn Man* (in 1969), all musicals by Pat Patterson and Dodi Robb; *Almighty Voice* (in 1970) and *Billy Bishop and the Red Baron* (in 1975) by Len PETERSON; and four plays by Carol BOLT—*Cyclone Jack* (in 1972), *My Best Friend is Twelve Feet High* (in 1972), *Tangleflags* (in 1973), and *Maurice* (in 1973). Many young theatre workers had their first professional job with Young People's Theatre, and Rubes often employed influential directors, includ-

Henry Beissel's Inook and the Sun, *Young People's Theatre, Toronto, 1975*

ing Marigold CHARLESWORTH, Paul THOMP-
SON, Timothy Bond, Jane Heyman, John
PALMER, Keith TURNBULL, Ken GASS, Mar-
tin KINCH, Des McANUFF, Carl Hare, and
Ron Singer, who acted as artistic adviser for
several seasons.

A permanent home was established when
the company leased a historic building at 165
Front St, Toronto, and renovated it to contain a 350-seat proscenium house and a more
informal space (the Nathan COHEN Theatre)
seating up to 175. (Built by the Toronto
Street Railway Company in 1881 to house
580 horses, and used briefly as a generating
station, the building sat empty from 1909
until Dec. 1977.) The first YPT production
there was an adaptation by Jan Rubes of the
Czechoslovakian Lanterna Magica creation,
The Lost Fairy Tale, designed by Josef Svoboda. This was followed by Frances Goodrich's and Albert Hackett's *The Diary of Anne
Frank*, starring the well-known American
actors Eli Wallach and Anne Jackson and
featuring Canadians Paul Soles and Kate
REID. YPT received the Toronto Historical
Board Award of Merit for its imaginative and
sympathetic treatment of the old stable.

After Susan Rubes left in 1979 to head
CBC Radio Drama, the artistic directorship
was held briefly by Richard OUZOUNIAN,
who was succeeded in 1980 by Peter Moss.
He has reduced debts, expanded the larger of
the two theatre spaces—it now seats 468—
and continued the Rubes tradition of big
names for little people. Directors John
HIRSCH, Robin PHILLIPS, and Christopher
NEWTON, and players Eric PETERSON, Jennifer PHIPPS, Michael Hogan, Sheila
McCarthy, Eric DONKIN, and David FOX are
a few of the many talented Canadians who
have been featured in productions.

A main-stage season normally includes a
classic, often Shakespeare; a play designed to
attract teenagers—John Osborne's *Look Back
in Anger*, John Steinbeck's *Of Mice and Men*,
and John and Joe Lazarus's *Dreaming and
Duelling* (produced in 1981) have filled this
slot; two family shows, one at Christmas;
and two plays for six-to-twelve-year-olds, of
sufficient complexity and stature to sustain
the attention of the parents who buy the
tickets and accompany their children. Jim
Betts's romantic adventure plays have been
particular successes for six-to-twelve-year-

Joseph and the Amazing Technicolour Dreamcoat, *by
Tim Rice and Andrew Lloyd Webber, Young People's
Theatre, 1978, with (l. to r.) Elizabeth Richardson, Robyn
Lee, David Nairn*

olds: *The Mystery of Oak Island* won the
CHALMERS Award for Best Children's Play
in 1983. It was followed by *The Last Voyage
of the Devil's Wheel* (in 1984), *The Treehouse
at the Edge of the World* (in 1986), and *The
Haunting of Elijah Bones* (also 1986).

Sensitive, controversial issues are treated in
scripts written for school tours. Young People's Theatre's commitment to produce
works relevant to contemporary children has
been strengthened by the 'Green Thumb
Connection'—with Dennis Foon from Vancouver's GREEN THUMB THEATRE FOR
YOUNG PEOPLE serving as playwright-in-residence in 1983–4 and contributing scripts
from time to time. Divorce, racial discrimination, nuclear power, and pollution are
examples of topics recently covered in school
shows.

A thriving theatre school, run by Peter
Gallagher since 1983, and a concert series,
'Musical Mondays', featuring music by living
composers, offer additional exposure to the
lively arts.

The archives of Young People's Theatre
are housed at the Univ. of Guelph.

See Joyce Doolittle and Zina Barnieh, *A
Mirror of Our Dreams: Children and the Theatre
in Canada* (1979). JOYCE DOOLITTLE

Z

Zastrozzi: The Master of Discipline. Since its première at TORONTO FREE THEATRE on 2 Nov. 1977, directed by William LANE and starring Stephen Markle in the title role, George F. WALKER's play has been produced across Canada and in the U.S., England, Australia, New Zealand, and Germany. Together with *Gossip*, also produced in 1977, it changed Walker's reputation from that of an abstruse and difficult playwright with a cult following only to recognition as one of the country's leading playwrights—a unique if sometimes quirky theatrical voice.

Zastrozzi originated, it is said, with Walker's reading of an encyclopaedia description of the teen-aged Shelley's novelette of the same title. Zastrozzi, the 'master criminal', hunts Verezzi the *artiste* through 1890s Europe, ostensibly for revenge, but really because Zastrozzi dislikes Verezzi's smile and what it stands for: amateurism, vagueness, beauty, the dawn of small 'l' liberalism. Zastrozzi is aided by Bernardo, a thug who aspires to take Zastrozzi's place, and Matilda, 'the most accomplished seductress in Europe'. Verezzi is defended by Victor, a failed priest who honours a promise to Ver-

ezzi's father to look after the holy fool (who believes he is an upwardly mobile saint). Victor is an Everyman who pits common sense, common decency, and a sense of humour against Zastrozzi's absolute discipline and Verezzi's absolute aspiration. Matters are complicated by the fortuitous appearance of Julia, who wins the love of both Verezzi and Zastrozzi, as well as the implacable hatred of Matilda.

The action proceeds through plot and deliciously perverse counter-plot in a prologue and ten scenes—mostly of the one-on-one, close-range confrontational sort Walker favours—to a *grand guignol* climax in a deserted prison in which characters kill each other off one by one until only Zastrozzi and Verezzi survive to play out their one scene on stage alone together. Zastrozzi first forces Verezzi to recognize the imminence of death, then releases him, giving him a head start before resuming the pursuit: the ultimate villain needs the 'preoccupation' of the chase—each needs the other to justify his existence.

Zastrozzi, like most Walker plays, is a peculiar mixture: the primary ingredients are gothic melodrama and Walker's well-known

George F. Walker's Zastrozzi, *Toronto Free Theatre, 1977, with (l. to r.) Stephen Markle, George Buza, Diane D'Aquila*

brand of black comedy (with a dash of Errol Flynn B-movie thrown in for good measure). The play is not entirely melodramatic because the hero is not entirely heroic, and, more importantly, the villain is not entirely villainous. Walker manipulates empathy and engineers a sequence of theatrical and moral ambushes by making Zastrozzi surprisingly attractive and engaging at one moment, but graphically brutal and cruel in the next. Walker says, 'If you laugh at his jokes, you cannot disassociate yourself from his actions', and—ever suspicious of over-simplifying moral and political issues—Walker does not want his audience to exonerate itself by sitting in judgement on this apparently quintessential villain.

Zastrozzi was published by Playwrights Co-op, Toronto, in 1977 with an introduction by William Lane. It is reprinted in *Modern Canadian Plays* (1985), ed. Jerry Wasserman. See Chris Johnson, 'George F. Walker: B-Movies Beyond the Absurd', *Canadian Literature*, 85 (1980), and 'George F. Walker Directs George F. Walker' [*Zastrozzi*], *Theatre History in Canada*, 9 (1988).

CHRIS JOHNSON

Index

Bold-face type indicates an entry.

Index

'Another Point of View' 319
Another Season's Promise 99
Another Story 353
Another Theatre Company 394
Anouilh, Jean 23, 55, 92, 101, 103, 108,
   110, 120, 132, 283, 297, 327, 328, 368,
   380, 415, 427, 474, 476, 519, 544,
   564, 593
Ansky, Solomon 133, 269, 329
Ansley, John 182
Answer to a Question 283
Anthologie de la littérature québécoise 182
Anthologie du théâtre québécois, 1606-1970
   182
Anthologie thématique du théâtre québécois
   au XIXe siècle 182
Anthony's Villa 70, 360
Anti-féministe, L' 116
Antigone (Anouilh) 92, 110, 120, 132,
   564
Antigone (Sophocles) 24, 171, 269, 302
Antigone 310
Antler River 461
Antoine, André 141, 303, 556
Antoine et Sébastien 524
Antony and Cleopatra 8, 73, 92, 119, 291,
   300, 416
Antoons, Jacques 457
Any Wednesday 33, 541
Anything Goes 228, 496
APA Repertory Theatre 190
Api 2967 178, 250, 293
Apollo Theatre 471
Apollon de Bellac, L' 110
Appelez-moi Stéphane 524
Appia, Adolphe 8, 141, 303
Apple Cart, The 73, 369, 592
Apple in the Eve, The 167, 272
Applebaum-Hébert Federal Cultural
   Policy Review Committee 139, 364,
   474, 520
Applebaum, Louis 111, 246, 504
Apprenticeship of Duddy Kravitz, The 102
Apprentis-Sorciers, Les 25, 96, 177,
   482, 485, 486, 529
April, Gilbert 3
Aquin, Hubert 457, 523, 524, 532
Arbor Theatre 403, 514
Arbre chargé d'oiseaux, Un 523
Arbuzov, Aleksei 422
Arcade, L' 138, 338
Arcand, Adrien 138
Arcand, Denys 249, 310, 474
Arcand, Jeannette 87
Archambault, Gilles 523, 524
Archambault, Jean 41, 59, 180
Archambault, Joseph-Sergius
   ('Palmieri') 25-6
Arche de Midi, L' 260
Archibald Cameron of Locheill 26,
   172
Architect and the Emperor of Assyria, The
   225
Architecture 26-9, 39, 262, 451
Archives and Collections 29-30
Archives des lettres canadiennes 48, 411
Archives nationales du Québec 30
Arcop Associates 420
Ardal, Maja 408
Arden, John 114

Arden Theatre 29
Are You a Mason? 234
Are You Lonesome Tonight? 89, 90
Area Belle, The 465
Arena 358
Arena Theatre 52
Arete Mime Company 12
Arété Physical Comedy Company 340
Argosy Weekly 104
Arioso 524
Aristophanes 110, 536, 571
Arizona 582
Arlequin, serviteur de deux maîtres 225
Arlésienne, L' 86
Arlie Marks Players 194
Arliss, George 432, 508, 562
Armani, Giorgio 411
Arms and the Man 78, 128, 133, 154, 192,
   198, 278, 280, 291, 335, 380, 459
Armstrong, Gillian 213
Army Show, The 31, 224, 279, 359,
   366, 476, 581
Arnason, David 427
Arngrim, Thor 62
Arnold, Amos 549
Around The World in Eighty Days 2, 432
Arout, Gabriel 536
Arrabal, Fernando 59, 225, 237, 474,
   485, 491
Arrivée du Père Lefebvre en Acadie, L' 3
Arsenault, Guy 3
Arsenic and Old Lace 254, 489, 529
Art Gallery Theatre (Edmonton) 383
Art Institute of Chicago 103
Art of Norval Morrisseau, The 498
Art of War, The 168, 201, 213, 431, 587,
   588
Artaud, Antonin 78, 227, 230, 343, 543
Arthur, Jack 581
Arthur, Julia 5, 31, 241, 242, 318, 399,
   433, 564
Arthur, René 530
Artichoke 32, 46, 161, 235, 329
Article 58 322
Article, L' 47 349, 575
Artisan, L' 146
Artisans, Les 481
Arts Against Apartheid Festival 356
Arts and Culture Centre (St John's)
   29, 32, 115, 258, 348, 361, 377, 378,
   542
Arts and Letters Club (Toronto) 32-3,
   70, 117, 135, 139, 154, 304, 343, 359,
   500, 573
Arts and Letters Players (Toronto) 33
Arts Centre Children's Company
   (Calgary) 527
Arts Centre Company (Calgary) 74,
   526
Arts Club (Vancouver) 29, 33, 38, 63,
   79, 82, 103, 111, 342, 412, 418, 516,
   576, 579
Arts Club Revue Theatre (Vancouver)
   33
Arts Theatre (London, Eng.) 15
Arts Theatre (Toronto) 413
Arts Theatre Club (London, Eng.) 274
Arts Theatre Club (Toronto) 85
'Arts This Week, The' 104
Artsboard 434

As Thousands Cheer 476
As-tu vu? Les Maisons s'emportent 205
As You Desire Me 188
As You Like It 24, 31, 56, 60, 73, 190,
   269, 277, 329, 367, 411, 415, 463, 489,
   562
As You Were 188
Ascend as the Sun 583
Asch, Sholem 590
Asche, Oscar 325, 563
Ashcroft, Peggy 101
Ashes 417, 463
Ashes for Easter and Other Monodramas
   591
Ashman, Howard 552
Asmodée 60, 127
Assaly, Ed 362
Asselin, Émile 36
Asselin, Jean 141, 340
ASSITEJ Canada 435
Asslani, Luan 96, 457, 528
Associated Designers of Canada 433, 434
Association canadienne du théâtre
   d'amateurs 7, 19, 47
Association canadienne du théâtre
   amateur 177, 309, 539
Association d'histoire du théâtre au
   Canada 435
Association des auteurs Canadiens 275
Association des critiques de théâtre du
   Canada 433
Association des professeurs d'expression,
   L' 193
Association for Canadian Theatre
   History 30, 435
Association internationale du théâtre
   pour l'enfance 271
Association of British Columbia Drama
   Educators 450
Association of Community Theatres 330
Association of Mime 340
Association of Producing Artists 190
Association québécoise de jeune théâtre
   7, 16, 19, 45, 309, 424, 448, 539
Association québécoise des critiques de
   théâtre 125
Astaire, Adele 496
Astaire, Fred 313, 428, 496, 580
At My Heart's Core 33-4, 59, 130,
   131, 158, 279
At the Gates of the Righteous 130
'At the King Edward Hotel' 235
Atarel et les Pakmaniens 3
Atelier Continu 387
Atelier de la Nouvelle Compagnie
   Théâtrale 44
Atelier, L' (Ottawa) 363, 539, 568
Atelier, L' (Sherbrooke) 176, 237
Athalie 110, 232
Atienza, Edward 378
Atkinson, Brooks 248
Atlan, Liliane 80
Atlantic City 463, 509
Atrium, L' 99
Attenborough, Richard 15
Atthis 206
Atwood, Margaret 521, 529
Au Coeur de la rose 25, 177, 523
Au Pair Man, The 544
Au pied de la lettre 99

602

Index

Index

Index

Index

Index

Index

Index

Index

Index

Index

Index

Index

626

Index

Index

Index

630

Index

Index

Index

Index

Index

Index

Index

Index

Index

Index

Index

Index

Index

Index

Index

Index

Index